SEXUALITY, THE FAMILY, AND F...

Abortion Information Service
(800) 321-0575
(800) 362-1205 (Ohio)

American Adoption Congress
P.O. Box 23641
Washington, D.C. 20024

American College of Nurses and Midwives
1522 K Street, N.W., Suite 1120
Washington, D.C. 20005
(212) 347-5445

American College of Obstetricians and Gynecologists
(800) INTENDS

The American Fertility Society
1608 13th Avenue, South
Birmingham, AL 35256

American Foundation for Maternal and Child Health
30 Beekman Place
New York, NY 10022

Association for Voluntary Surgical Contraception
122 East 42nd Street
New York, NY 10017
(212) 351-2500

Battered Women's Shelter
(800) 333-SAFE

Batterers Anonymous
(714) 383-2972

Birth Control Information Hotline
(800) 468-3637

Birthright
(800) 848-5683

Child Abuse Hotline
(800) 422-4453

Childwatch
National Child Safety Council
4065 Page Avenue
P.O. Box 1368
Jackson, MI 49204
(800) 222-1464
(800) 248-1464 (Canada)

Committee...
P.O. Box 15084
Chevy Chase, MD 20015

Committee on Population
National Research Council
2101 Constitution Avenue
Washington, D.C. 20418
(202) 334-3167

Emerge (for battered women)
25 Huntington Avenue, Room 324
Boston, MA 02116

Family Service Association of America
11700 West Lake Park Place
Milwaukee, WI 53224
(414) 359-2111

Federation of Parents and Friends of Lesbians and Gays
P.O. Box 24565
Los Angeles, CA 90024

Information Service of the Kinsey Institute for Sex Research
416 Morrison Hall
Indiana University
Bloomington, IN 47401

La Leche League International
9616 Minneapolis
Franklin, IL 60613
(312) 455-7730

March of Dimes Birth Defects Foundation
1275 Mamaroneck Avenue
White Plains, NY 10605
(914) 428-7100

National Abortion Federation Consumer Hotline
(800) 772-9100
(202) 546-9060

National Abortion Rights Action League (NARAL)
1101 14th Street N.W., Suite 500
Washington, D.C. 20005

Continued on back endsheet

HUMAN
SEXUALITY

HUMAN SEXUALITY

SECOND EDITION

NANCY W. DENNEY, Ph.D.

Professor, Psychology Department
University of Wisconsin
Madison, Wisconsin

DAVID QUADAGNO, Ph.D.

Professor, Department of Biological Sciences
Florida State University
Tallahassee, Florida

with 314 illustrations
including 45 in full color and 33 in two colors

Illustrations program by
DAVID MASCARO, M.S., A.M.I.

with additional illustrations by
Medical and Scientific Illustration:

WILLIAM C. OBER, M.D.

CLAIRE GARRISON

MARGARET B. OBER

Mosby
Year Book

St. Louis Baltimore Boston Chicago London Philadelphia Sydney Toronto

**Mosby
Year Book**
Dedicated to Publishing Excellence

Acquisitions Editor Vicki Van Ry-Malinee
Editorial Assistant Francine Trtanj
Project Manager Patricia Tannian
Designer Elizabeth Fett
Illustrators David Mascaro, M.S., A.M.I., Medical Illustration
   Services, 105 Lakemont Dr., Augusta, Georgia 30904; and
   Medical and Scientific Illustration: William C. Ober, Clare Garrison,
   and Margaret B. Ober, P.O. Box 487, Crozet, Virginia 22932
Cover Art: "Everlasting Love." Copyright © 1991, by Ty Wilson.

Credits for all materials used by permission appear after index.

Printed in the United States of America
11830 Westline Industrial Drive
St. Louis, Missouri 63146

Library of Congress Cataloging in Publication Data
Denney, Nancy W.
    Human Sexuality / Nancy W. Denney, David Quadagno ; illustrations
  program by David Mascaro, with additional illustrations by   William
C. Ober, Claire Garrison, Margaret B. Ober.—2nd ed.
      p.   cm.
    Includes bibliographical references and index.
    ISBN 0-8016-6374-1
    1. Sex. 2. Sexual ethics. 3. Hygiene, Sexual. 4. Sex
(Psychology)   I. Quadagno, David. II. Title.
    [DNLM: 1. Sex. 2. Sex Behavior. HQ 21 D399h]
HQ21.D394 1992
306.7—dc20
DNLM/DLC
for Library of Congress
                                                91-29929
                                                CIP

92 93 94 95 96 GW/CD/VH 9 8 7 6 5 4 3 2

To Our Children
Stephanie Erin
Jennifer
Bryan

About the Authors

Nancy W. Denney received a Ph.D. in psychology from the University of Washington in Seattle in 1970. She spent two years in the Psychology Department at the State University of New York College at Buffalo and twelve years at the University of Kansas. In 1984, she moved to the University of Wisconsin–Madison.

Dr. Denney has done extensive research in the area of developmental psychology, and her work frequently appears in the leading psychological journals such as *Developmental Psychology, Psychology and Aging, Child Development,* and the *Journal of Gerontology.* In addition, she has published a number of articles in the area of human sexuality, including research on postpartum moods, sex differences in sexual needs and desires, and the treatment of dysmenorrhea.

Dr. Denney was honored with the Outstanding Woman Teacher Award by the University of Kansas in 1983.

David Quadagno received his Ph.D. in biology from the University of Illinois in 1969. After completing his doctoral work, he spent one year at the University of California–Los Angeles Brain Research Institute doing research in the area of reproductive neuroendocrinology. He was a professor at the University of Kansas from 1971 to 1987 in the Department of Physiology and Cell Biology. Dr. Quadagno is currently a professor at Florida State University in the Department of Biological Sciences and he also teaches in the Program in Medical Sciences. Among his teaching duties is a course for medical students in the medical aspects of human sexuality. Dr. Quadagno has taught a human sexuality course for eighteen years.

Dr. Quadagno has published many articles in the field of reproductive physiology, with an emphasis on the influence of hormones on behavior, as well as articles in the area of human sexuality and acquired immunodeficiency syndrome. His work has been supported by numerous research grants from various funding agencies. In 1975 he was the first recipient of the Chancellor's Distinguished Teaching Award at the University of Kansas and in 1988 he received the President's Teaching Award at Florida State University.

Preface

RECENT DEVELOPMENTS

The eighties were an eventful decade for the field of human sexuality.

We've watched Louise Brown, the first child conceived by in vitro fertilization, grow into a young lady, and in the meantime we have seen the process of uniting egg and sperm outside the body become a commonly practiced procedure. Techniques have become more and more sophisticated; the ability to freeze zygotes produced by in vitro fertilization, for example, has raised many ethical questions. What should be done with the unused zygotes? Do they have any legal rights?

In 1981 a fatal disease, acquired immunodeficiency syndrome (AIDS), was identified. Because it can be transmitted through intimate sexual contact and has no known cure, AIDS has changed our sexual behavior. Public awareness of AIDS has caused the inclusion of more sex education in our schools and an increased use of condoms to facilitate "safer sex." At the same time we have seen much debate on the topic of AIDS research. Should traditional testing methods be put aside to speed up research? Can we guarantee the safety of vaccines if those methods are bypassed? Are we making a great enough effort to fund AIDS research? Although drugs now on the market such as AZT slow the progression of AIDS, moving into the new decade we are still no closer to a cure.

High research and development costs combined with legal liability costs have caused delays in the testing of contraceptive methods. As a result, we have actually seen a *decline* in the number of contraceptive methods available to the North American public. Norplant, a time-released hormone implant, is the first new contraceptive technology to come along in more than a decade and is the only exception to the decline.

In 1973, after much debate, the U.S. Supreme Court made the landmark decision in *Roe v. Wade*, which guaranteed women the right to choose an abortion and recognized that choice is a decision to be made between the woman and her physician. In the late 1980s and into the 1990s the issue of abortion has polarized the United States. Legislation of the past decade has gradually restricted women's ability to obtain abortions; in 1991 the Supreme Court ruled that agencies receiving federal Title X funds for family planning services may not provide information about abortions to their clients (*Rust v. Sullivan*). If this ruling stands, it will have far-reaching implications for many women and for health care providers who provide abortion services.

These issues illustrate the complexity of human sexuality today. How do we as educators present these various and complex dimensions of sexuality—the sociological, psychological, biological, and legal—to our students?

Balance is the key. In *Human Sexuality* we strive to present *factual, balanced,* and *unbiased* information, allowing students to examine each issue from many perspectives and to form their own ideas and make their own decisions about their sexuality. Wherever possible we provide the most current research available on the topics we cover. We, as authors, contribute our own special perspectives—as psychologist and biologist, as a woman and a man—to offer the student a special balance that covers the wide spectrum of sexuality. Lastly, we try to present each topic from a neutral, unbiased position and to explore issues from a variety of viewpoints.

AUDIENCE

This text is written so that the student does not need prior courses in psychology or biology to understand the ideas and concepts presented. We recognize that students come to a human sexuality course from many areas of study. Because of such a varied audience, the text is written to engage the reader in the learning process. All material is presented in a concise, factual manner, but in all sections of the book we point out controversies, alternative theories, and shortcomings in methodological designs of studies presented. We seek to show readers the dynamic nature of the field, while keeping the text useful and understandable to the widest number of students.

OVERVIEW OF THE TEXT

We begin with a historical perspective, illustrating where many ideas and attitudes about sexuality originated. The second chapter deals with sex research, explaining how we learn about sexual behaviors and attitudes in our society. It allows us to compare present-day sexual behaviors to those of 20 to 30 years ago and to see which behaviors have changed and which have remained the same. This chapter is important because it presents the methodologies used by modern-day sex researchers and also illustrates for the student potential problems in surveys of sexual behaviors and attitudes.

We present sexual anatomy and physiology in Chapters 3 and 4, providing the student with the basic knowledge needed to understand how men and women respond to sexual stimulation (Chapter 5) and the intricacies of conception and pregnancy (Chapter 6). In Chapter 7 we cover the biological and psychological aspects of childbirth, as well as a unique and realistic perspective of parenthood. Chapter 8 is concerned with contraception, a topic of great interest for today's college-age student. This chapter presents a detailed coverage of contraception, including the advantages and disadvantages of each available method, providing the reader with the information needed to make informed decisions about contraceptive use.

The topic of sexual behavior is presented in Chapter 9. This chapter discusses various sexual behaviors including kissing, masturbation, sexual intercourse, and oral and anal sex. Chapter 10 focuses on gender roles and gender role socialization. Gender differences in sexual behavior are also covered here.

Chapter 11 presents a sensitive and unbiased discussion of both homosexuality and bisexuality.

Chapters 12 and 13 examine developmental changes in sexual functioning that take place from infancy through old age. The important topics of love, attraction, and intimacy are found in Chapter 14. The scientific research and theories of love and attraction are presented along with a discussion of the development of intimate relationships. In addition, the relationship between love and sex is discussed.

Chapter 15 offers a unique look at sexual life-styles and includes discussions of marriage, remarriage, singlehood, and cohabitation. Most other textbooks do not provide a detailed discussion of the various sexual life-styles that are common today. This is followed by another unique chapter (16), which explores sexuality and disabilities.

Sexual dysfunctions, their treatment, and sexual health are addressed in Chapter 17. A chapter of great interest to students is Chapter 18, which deals with sexually transmitted diseases (STDs). The material in this chapter is relevant to all readers whether they are already sexually active or will be in the future. The appearance of widespread cases of genital herpes, genital warts, and chlamydia in the 1980s has made everyone aware of the risks of indiscriminate sex. This chapter offers students the facts they need to make informed decisions that will reduce their chances of contracting an STD. A new chapter, Chapter 19, has been added to this edition and deals with the clinical and social aspects of AIDS. This chapter presents the most current information available and contains many studies specific to college-age individuals.

Sexual variations are addressed in Chapter 20. Chapter 21, Sexual Assault and Coercion, deals with incest, child sexual abuse, and rape. The important topic of date or acquaintance rape, an increasingly common occurrence on college campuses, is discussed in detail in this chapter.

Chapter 22 deals with sex and the law and includes such topics as prostitution, pornography, rape, and sexual harassment. Chapter 23 examines sex education in the home and school, as well as the effects of sex education on sexual behavior. Current controversies regarding sex education that have been raised by problems such as the fear of AIDS and the high teenage pregnancy rate are also discussed.

Chapter 24 addresses the religious and ethical concerns related to sexuality. The views of Judaism, Catholicism, and Protestantism are explored in addition to other determinants of sexual attitudes and behaviors. Controversial issues such as abortion, extramarital sex, in vitro fertilization, and surrogate parenthood are also covered in this chapter.

FEATURES
Content Highlights

CURRENCY Topics such as acquired immunodeficiency syndrome (AIDS), sexually transmitted disorders including chlamydia and genital warts, surrogate parenthood, date rape, sexual harassment, abortion, and contraception have generated a great deal of discussion, concern, and controversy in recent months. These topics and other relevant issues are presented with the most up-to-date detail and are supported by the most current references available.

WRITING STYLE Throughout the text, topics are presented in a clear, concise, and unbiased manner and reflect contemporary male and female perspectives. Sensitive treatment of topics like those in Chapter 11 (Homosexuality and Bisexuality), for example, is found throughout the text.

CONCEPTION TO PARENTHOOD Recognizing that it is important to consider the results of having children as well as the process, we devote two chapters to the process of conception and parenthood. Chapter 6 (Conception and Pregnancy) includes comprehensive coverage of conception and pregnancy, and Chapter 7 (Childbirth and Parenthood) offers a detailed discussion of parenthood. The text examines the positive and negative aspects of parenthood, as well as the effect of having children on the couple's sexual relationship.

SEXUAL LIFE-STYLES In Chapter 15 (Sexual Life-Styles) is a more thorough discussion of the advantages and disadvantages of various life-styles—marriage, cohabitation, and singlehood—than can be found in other books. We feel it is important to consider the relationship in which sexual behavior takes place, as well as the behavior itself.

SEXUALITY AND DISABILITIES Unlike many texts, we devote an entire chapter to sexuality and disabilities. Chapter 16 dispels some of the myths and misconceptions some people have about the effects of disability on sexual function and emphasizes that disabilities influence, but do not negate, sexual expression. In addition to addressing the special situations of persons with spinal cord injury, mental retardation, visual impairment, hearing impairment, cardiovascular disease, and diabetes, we include new coverage of stroke, arthritis, multiple sclerosis, cerebral palsy, and cancer.

RELATIONSHIPS For a complete understanding of human sexual functioning, the interpersonal context of sexual relationships is thoroughly explored. This text considers the interpersonal aspects of sexual relationships, including heterosexual, homosexual, and bisexual relationships, as well as parent-child relationships. Heterosexual relationships are discussed in Chapter 15 (Sexual Life-Styles). Homosexual and bisexual relationships are addressed in Chapter 11 (Homosexuality and Bisexuality) and Chapter 15. Parent-child relationships are covered in Chapter 7 (Childbirth and Parenthood), Chapter 12 (Childhood and Adolescence), and Chapter 23 (Sex Education).

SEXUALLY TRANSMITTED DISEASES For the past decade the public's attention has been focused on the deadly AIDS virus to the point where other sexually transmitted diseases have been all but ignored. However, incidences of chlamydia, genital herpes, and gonorrhea have continued to grow at alarming rates. Chapter 18 (Sexually Transmitted Diseases) presents the most up-to-date information about these and a wide range of other STDs, along with useful information on preventive measures.

ACQUIRED IMMUNODEFICIENCY SYNDROME The disease AIDS, which is spread in several ways, including sexual contact, has profoundly affected many aspects of life in the United States. This disease has no cure and at the present time is fatal. Unlike most human sexuality textbooks, we have devoted a complete chapter (Chapter 19, Acquired Immunodeficiency Syndrome) to AIDS and to the clinical and social aspects of this disease.

SEX EDUCATION Since sex education may hold the solutions to current problems such as teenage pregnancy and the spread of sexually transmitted diseases, much attention is given to this topic in Chapter 23 (Sex Education). Controversies in sex education that have recently developed as a result of the threat of AIDS are thoroughly explored in this chapter.

RELIGIOUS AND ETHICAL VIEWS OF SEXUALITY   Many ethical issues are raised concerning recent technological advances. Comprehensive discussions of artificial insemination, in vitro fertilization, surrogate parenthood, and prenatal screening are all included in light of the ethical questions that they raise.

CROSS-CULTURAL VIEWS   Because culture shapes sexuality, references to cross-cultural aspects of sexuality are presented throughout the text. For example, in Chapter 3 (Sexual Anatomy) we examine the practice of female circumcision in various cultures.

Design

This edition of *Human Sexuality* incorporates a bold, contemporary design, making it exciting and approachable for the student. Boxed essays (*A Personal Glimpse, Across Cultures, FYI,* and *News in the 90s*) have easily identifiable icons. Elements such as tables and *Questions for Thought* are designed to stand out boldly from the page and capture the student's attention.

Many illustrations have been added or reworked to look more three dimensional. All of the sexual position illustrations have been redrawn to give them a more realistic, yet softer and more tasteful, appearance.

Chapters 3 (Sexual Anatomy) and 6 (Conception and Pregnancy) include full-color illustrations to help students understand important concepts. Chapter 6 also contains a spectacular photo essay on the journey of the fetus from conception to birth and features recent photos by the internationally acclaimed photographer Lennart Nilsson. A second color is used extensively throughout the text to enhance the visual appeal and reinforce important concepts.

Pedagogy

Each chapter in this book contains effective learning aids and interest-generating materials.

CHAPTER-OPENING QUOTATION   Each quotation provides the reader with a flavor of what is to follow in the chapter.

FACT OR FICTION   Every chapter begins with a unique *Fact or Fiction* section. Before reading the chapter the student is presented with several statements and asked to decide whether the statements are true or false. The answers are found at the end of each chapter. This feature is an excellent learning device because it gives the student an opportunity to think about several important concepts that will be presented in the chapter and evaluate his or her knowledge before and after reading the chapter. The *Fact or Fiction* section is an enjoyable and educational way of testing one's knowledge and reinforcing important concepts.

BOXED SECTIONS   Four new types of boxes appear in this edition. *Across Cultures* explores sexuality as it is experienced in other cultures around the world. *A Personal Glimpse* presents personal experiences of sexuality such as the powerful passage in Chapter 21 dealing with incest. *FYI* boxes are full of interesting facts and the newest research in the field of sexuality. Many have been prepared by expert researchers in their field of study. *News in the 90s* covers current topics of interest to the student.

QUOTATIONS FROM AUTHORS' FILES   Interspersed throughout the text are quotations that have been taken from the authors' own files and that relate specifically to the chapter topic. These quotations offer a realistic perspective that enhances readers' interest in and understanding of the material.

MARGINAL MATERIALS   Key terms are boldfaced in the narrative and defined in the margins, with pronunciation guides provided when necessary. These terms are defined again in the glossary at the end of the text. Cross-references to related material in other chapters have also been placed in the margins. These aids were designed to increase students' interest in comprehension of the material.

CHAPTER SUMMARIES   Each chapter ends with an enumerated summary that reinforces the key points of the chapter for the student.

QUESTIONS FOR THOUGHT   Questions at the end of each chapter provide students with an opportunity to synthesize and personalize the chapter content by making the students think about their own beliefs and values in relation to the topics covered in the chapter.

REFERENCES   Each chapter has a thorough reference list (located at the back of the text) with current sources, including the most up-to-date research from the 1980s and 1990s.

SUGGESTED READINGS   Each chapter is followed by a brief annotated list of timely resources to which the student can refer for additional information on the chapter topic.

COMPREHENSIVE GLOSSARY   Key terms have been defined at the end of the text, including those that appear in the margins throughout and additional relevant terms to which the student can refer.

SUPPLEMENTARY MATERIAL
Instructor's Manual

Prepared by John P. Elia, M.A., of San Francisco State University, the *Instructor's Manual* provides text adopters with substantial support in preparing to teach human sexuality with this text. The manual is perforated and three hole punched for convenience.

- Unique *Conversion Notes* indicate how the coverage of each chapter in *Human Sexuality* differs from other leading human sexuality texts. These conversion notes enable the instructor to make a convenient transition to *Human Sexuality* from other texts.
- *Learning Objectives* identify key concepts in each chapter.
- A detailed *Chapter Outline* of each chapter is included, along with notes, teaching suggestions, and suggested transparency masters related to specific topics.
- Several student *Self-Assessment Exercises*, designed to encourage interest

in the textual material as well as promote value clarification, are provided in each chapter. These can be photocopied by the instructor and used as handouts.

- Each chapter contains individual and group *Class Activities* that encourage student participation and involvement.
- Each chapter includes current *Related Issues* to stimulate class discussion of topics related to the chapter.
- A comprehensive list of *Media Resources* suggests lecture supplements.
- Fifty key illustrations and charts appearing in the text are reproduced as full-page *Transparency Masters* at the back of the manual. Masters are also provided for supplemental material not appearing in the textbook.
- An extensive *Test Bank*, including more than 2,000 multiple-choice, completion, true/false, and essay questions, is contained in the manual. The test questions have been carefully evaluated by reviewers of the text for clarity, accuracy, and level of difficulty.

Transparency Acetates

A set of 54 overhead transparency acetates in two and four colors is available free to qualified adopters of the text. These include the most important illustrations from the text, as well as illustrations that have been developed to supplement the text.

Computerized Test Bank

A computerized version of the test bank (Diploma II) is available to instructors on disks for IBM and Apple personal computers and compatibles. Diploma II provides instructors with the opportunity to add questions of their own, as well as to modify or rearrange existing questions.

Human Sexuality Self-Assessment Software

A unique interactive disk enables students to assess their knowledge, attitudes, and values. Both IBM and Apple versions are available free to qualified adopters of the text.

Sexuality Student Manual

Healthy Sexuality: A Self-Assessment Manual, prepared by M. Patricia Fetter, Ph.D., of Northeastern University, is a comprehensive manual offering invaluable help to students by reinforcing concepts presented in the text and integrating these with innovative activities. The guide provides the following:

- Learning objectives
- Terminology review
- A variety of questions to help students prepare for tests
- Abundant activities and exercises to encourage students to apply what they have learned from the text to their daily lives

ACKNOWLEDGMENTS

Special gratitude goes to those instructors who contributed a number of helpful suggestions throughout the revision process. They will find their fingerprints throughout the text, because their valuable reviews shaped its outcome:

Wayne Anderson
University of Missouri–Columbia

Martha Bristor
Michigan State University

Gerald P. Carlson
University of Southern Louisiana

Raymond Eastman
Stephen F. Austin University

John P. Elia
San Francisco State University and
Center for Education and Research in Sexuality

James G. Erickson
Fort Lewis College

Randy Fisher
University of Central Florida

Kenneth George
University of Pennsylvania

Molly Laflin
Bowling Green State University

Charles Lyons
Eastern Oregon University

Beth Meyerowitz
Vanderbilt University

Herbert P. Samuals
LaGuardia Community College

David Schlundt
Vanderbilt University

Sherman Sowby
California State University–Fresno

We would also like to thank our students, friends, and colleagues who contributed ideas and suggestions to our text, in particular Wendy M. LaBine, Dr. Jill Quadagno, and Lisa Pfenninger. Our thanks also to the International Planned Parenthood Federation for their timely publications, *Research in Reproduction* and *Medical Bulletin*.

In addition, we thank the staff at Mosby–Year Book, Inc.: Edward Murphy, Vice-President and Publisher; Vicki Van Ry-Malinee, Acquisitions Editor; and Patricia Tannian, Project Manager. All have been a pleasure to work with and have contributed much of their valuable experience. In particular we would like to thank Francine Trtanj, Editorial Assistant, who provided numerous suggestions and thoughtful insights from the beginning of this project to the end.

Nancy W. Denney
David Quadagno

Contents in Brief

CONTENTS IN BRIEF

Contents

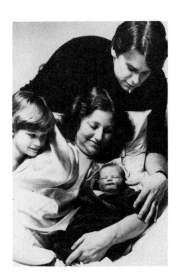

13 Adulthood and Aging, 380

14 Love, Attraction, and Intimacy, 402

HUMAN
SEXUALITY

1

The History of Human Sexuality

FACT
OR
FICTION

1
In Mesopotamia and Egypt in earliest recorded history, both male and female prostitutes worked in the temples.

2
During early Greek civilization, homosexuality, usually between middle-aged men and adolescent boys, was not only common, but condoned.

3
During the Middle Ages women of all social classes gained more rights and respect as a result of the rules of courtly love, which put women on a pedestal.

To begin at the beginning. Life on earth has been going on for three thousand million years or more. For two-thirds of that time organisms reproduced themselves by cell division. Division produces identical offspring as a rule, and new forms appear only rarely, by mutation. For all that time, therefore, evolution was very slow. The first organisms to reproduce sexually were, it now seems, related to the green algae. That was less than a thousand million years ago. Sexual reproduction begins there, first in plants, then in animals. Since then its success has made it the biological norm.

J. BRONOWSKI
The Ascent of Man, p. 388

ew topics generate as much interest in people of all ages and all walks of life as human sexuality. Not only is sexuality a subject of great appeal, but it is also a topic that pervades every aspect of our lives. Today sexual issues are dealt with openly in books, magazines, newspapers, films, and television programs. Furthermore, many individuals in our culture freely discuss their sexual attitudes and experiences with their friends. The purpose of this book is to investigate this highly intriguing topic from a scientific perspective. In the chapters that follow we will explore the biological, psychological, and sociological aspects of human sexuality. But we will begin with an attempt to define sexuality, followed by a historical overview of how sexual attitudes and behaviors have changed with time.

WHAT IS SEXUALITY?

Sexuality is a difficult term to define because it encompasses so many aspects of our lives. We express our sexuality through a variety of behaviors. These include actions that quickly come to mind when we think about sexuality, such as touching, caressing, kissing, hugging, and sexual intercourse. However, they also include a variety of more subtle behaviors, such as the way we walk, talk, and dress. Although physical sexual acts may be thought of first when we consider sexuality, our sexuality involves many other biological, psychological, and sociological dimensions as well.

The biological dimension comprises both sexual anatomy and sexual physiology. Our sexual anatomy determines whether we are male or female and, at least in part, our sexual appearance and attractiveness. Our sexual physiology is important not only in determining our sexual anatomy and reproductive functions, but also in influencing our sexual thoughts, feelings, and behaviors.

In addition to the overt sexual behaviors described previously, the psychological dimension encompasses our thoughts, beliefs, and values regarding sexuality, as well as our sexual feelings. Our sexual thoughts include any thought about any aspect of sexuality. One example would be the thought that the person sitting next to you in class is sexually attractive. Our sexual beliefs also include a wide range of beliefs about any aspect of sexuality. An example is the belief that sexual satisfaction is an important component of a good marriage. Our sexual values include all our views about what is right and wrong, good and bad, in the sexual sphere. An example is the view that abortion is always immoral. Our sexual feelings include a variety of emotional responses, such as feelings of attraction or arousal.

Our relationships with other people and with cultural institutions make up the sociological dimension. Clearly our interactions with others are a vital component of our sexuality. We may have sexual intercourse with our lovers, discuss our sexual beliefs and values with our friends, and experience sexual feelings toward people we do not even know. These are only a few ways our sexuality causes us to interact with other people. Our sexuality has an important influence on our relationships just as our relationships have an important influence on our sexuality.

Cultural institutions are important in determining our sexual attitudes, feelings, and behaviors. All societies have developed rules and institutions to regulate sexual behavior. Our religious institutions have historically been the most important determinant of what we consider right and wrong in terms of sexual behavior, as well as defining appropriate attitudes, feelings, and behavior for males and females in general.

Not only does sexuality involve many aspects of our lives, but also these various dimensions affect one another. For instance, if a college student notices an attractive person sitting next to her in class, she may respond with thoughts, feelings, and behaviors. She might have thoughts about how attractive the person is, she might respond with feelings of sexual arousal, and she might initiate a conversation with the person. This example illustrates how an individual's thoughts and feelings can affect behavior and how an individual's thoughts, feelings, and behaviors can affect the social relationship between two individuals. An individual's thoughts, feelings, and behaviors influence and are influenced by biological factors as well. The attraction the college student feels to the person sitting next to her stems at least in part from her hormonal state; in turn, the sexual thoughts and feelings the student has in response to that person can affect her hormonal state.

All of these elements of sexuality are covered in this book. We will discuss the biological aspects of sexuality first, followed by the psychological, and finally by the sociological. The purpose of this text is to give the reader a greater understanding of all aspects of human sexuality. Before we begin our study of the biological aspects of human sexuality, however, we want to present some examples of how the culture and time in which a person lives influence that person's sexual attitudes, feelings, and behaviors, as well as sexual interactions with others. Our purpose in this chapter is to (1) give the reader a greater understanding of how culture and historical time influence sexuality and (2) demonstrate how increased knowledge about human sexuality has changed attitudes about sexuality and sexual practices.

OUR HISTORICAL HERITAGE

In this section we present a brief history of human sexuality to illustrate that the sexual attitudes and behaviors considered appropriate change with time and across cultures. Individuals in any given culture and era tend to think that their sexual attitudes and practices are more natural and normal than those of other groups and periods. The following historical overview demonstrates that what is considered natural and normal depends on the time and place.

An ancient Indian temple.

Earliest Civilizations

Although written records from Mesopotamia and Egypt have been found that date back 5,000 years, we do not completely understand sexuality during that time. However, early records do indicate that people of these cultures associated their gods with sex and **fertility. Religious rites** were instituted to ensure the blessings of the gods. Sexual symbolism played an important role in these rituals. The sacred nature of sexual intercourse is evidenced by the fact that **copulation** was at times regarded as an act of worship. Special importance was attached to the first occurrence of sexual intercourse of a woman. Women were expected to be ritually deflowered by an artificial **phallus,** a priest, or a stranger (Sussman, 1976).

Sacred prostitution at the temples was another indication of the relationship between religion and sexuality. Both male and female prostitutes worked in the temples, performing a wide variety of sexual acts for payment. The payment of the temple prostitutes was apparently responsible for most of the temples' revenue.

Although most societies in the Near East at this time were relatively free of sexual prohibitions and fairly matter of fact and permissive about their own sexuality, there were prohibitions against both **incest** (Tannahill, 1980) and extramarital intercourse (Sussman, 1976).

fertility
The ability to sexually reproduce.

religious rites
Religious ceremonies.

copulation
(KOP yuh lay shuhn) Sexual intercourse.

phallus
(FAL uhs) Penis; or representation of the penis.

incest
(IN sest') Sexual activity between close relatives.

Jewish Tradition

Although the Jews were probably similar to their Near Eastern neighbors in their early history, they eventually rejected the more permissive sexuality and the connection between religion and sexuality. They no longer accepted the fertility rites and temple prostitution. For the Jews the ultimate justification for sexual intercourse was **procreation** (Gregersen, 1983). Their God had instructed them to "be fruitful and multiply." As a result, **masturbation, celibacy,** homosexuality, and **bestiality** were considered sinful because they did not result in offspring (Sussman, 1976).

Although procreation was the most important function of sexuality, the pleasurable aspect of sexuality was not denied. As long as people did not commit any of the forbidden acts, it was acceptable for them to thoroughly enjoy sexual intercourse.

Women were clearly considered inferior to men in the early Jewish culture. They were treated as property, first by their fathers until marriage and then by their husbands. Although the punishment for women who had extramarital sexual relations was to be stoned to death, men were allowed to have secondary wives and **concubines.** In fact, Solomon is reputed to have had 700 wives and 300 concubines (Tannahill, 1980). The inferior status of women is also exemplified by the higher value placed on male children than on female children. This view is expressed in Psalms 127:4-5: "Like arrows in the hand of a warrior are the sons of one's youth. Happy is the man who has his quiver full of them!"

Greek Tradition

Whereas the early Jews were somewhat restrictive with respect to sexuality, prohibiting masturbation, homosexuality, incest, and adultery, the early Greeks were sexually permissive and uninhibited. Their permissiveness is reflected in the behavior of their gods. The gods were portrayed as engaging in very human endeavors—being flirtatious, seducing any number of other gods and goddesses, and marrying numerous times. Zeus, for example, supposedly married at least seven times and had many other sexual affairs with both mortal and immortal men and women (Sussman, 1976).

The Greeks also considered women to be inferior to men. Women were given no more legal or political rights than were slaves. They received no formal education and were subject to the absolute authority of their male kin. They were typically confined to the women's quarters of the house and were seldom allowed to go out. They were rarely even permitted to eat dinner with their husbands (Tannahill, 1980). Women were regarded as useful for little other than having children and taking care of household affairs.

Greek men married women to have children. However, men received their most important intellectual, social, emotional, and **erotic** companionship from other males, particularly adolescent boys. Once an adolescent boy had completed his formal education, he was taken under the wing of a more mature man who became responsible for his moral and intellectual education. These relationships between adolescent boys and their mentors tended to be emotionally supportive and sexual as well as intellectual. Thus in early Greek culture homosexuality was not only permitted, but condoned.

procreation
(proh′ kree AY shuhn) Production of offspring.

masturbation
(mas tuhr BAY shuhn) Stimulation of one's own genitals to produce sexual pleasure.

celibacy
Abstention from sexual behavior.

bestiality
(bes′ chee AL i tee, bees′-) Sexual activity between a human being and an animal.

concubine
(KONG kyuh byn′) Woman who lives with a man without being married to him.

An erotic engraving of the Greek mythical hero Hercules and his wife Deianira.

erotic
(i ROT ik) Causing sexual feelings or desires.

The Greeks were tolerant of masturbation, prostitution, and other sexual outlets. By current standards, Greek culture was fairly permissive and accepting of sexuality.

Roman Tradition

The Romans appear to have been even more permissive and positive with respect to sexuality than the Greeks. The Romans had few regulations regarding sexual conduct; they were for the most part frank and uninhibited in terms of sexuality. Homosexuality, however, was less pervasive than in the Greek culture. Many of the prominent Romans were bisexual. For example, Julius Caesar was called "every woman's man and every man's woman" by his contemporaries (Sussman, 1976).

Prostitution flourished during early Roman culture, and Romans were open about their sexual activities. Romans commonly had sexual interactions in public places such as temples, circuses, and arenas.

Although Roman women were considered the property of men just as the Greek women were, they were afforded more freedom and treated with more importance. Women were expected not only to take care of the household and children, but also to have an active role in the wider business of the family (Tannahill, 1980). Thus women were allowed more independence and interaction with the world outside the family.

Christian Tradition

The decline of the Roman Empire about 300 AD was accompanied by a rise in Christianity. Christianity was much less accepting of sexual activity of any kind than previous cultural traditions. Prostitution, homosexuality, masturbation, **polygyny** and **polyandry,** bestiality, and premarital intercourse were prohibited. The only sexual relationship permitted was in a **monogamous** marriage when reproduction was the intention. Even within the context of marriage, sexuality was not something to be enjoyed for its own sake.

Given that procreation was the only justifiable reason for sexual intercourse, both contraception and abortion were considered sinful. If a couple were engaging in sexual intercourse for procreative purposes, there would be no need for either contraception or abortion.

Although sexual intercourse was permitted in marriage when reproduction was the purpose, celibacy was considered a better way of life. A person who remained celibate could devote himself or herself more completely to religious activities. This early belief that celibacy was a religiously superior way of life helps to explain why Roman Catholic clergy are celibate today.

Marriage was considered a concession to those who were too weak to live without it. Even the reproductive aspect of sexuality was thought to be of questionable value. Early Christians were not sure that the prescription in the Old Testament to "be fruitful and multiply" was still valid (Tannahill, 1980). Its original purpose had been to provide a line of people from whom the Messiah would descend. However, after the Messiah had been born, it was not clear that procreation was any longer necessary.

polygyny
(puh LIJ uh nee) Marriage of one man to two or more women.

polyandry
(POL ee an' dree) Marriage of one woman to two or more men.

monogamy
(muh NOG uh mee) Marriage of one man to one woman.

An Ancient Polygynous Society: China

The following is a description of the polygynous traditions of Chinese culture before the Middle Ages:

While the Fathers of the early Christian church advocated sexual abstinence as the only sure route to heaven, other equally devout men in another part of the world took precisely the opposite view. "The more women with whom a man has intercourse, the greater will be the benefit he derives from the act," said one, and another added, "If one night he can have intercourse with more than ten women it is best." This is one of the doctrines of Tao, "the Way," "the Supreme Path of Nature," a philosophy that permeated the whole structure of Chinese thought and society for more than 2,000 years (p. 164).

Polygamy on the generous Chinese scale differed from polygamy in most other societies and, as a system, lasted much longer. Though Solomon, for example, had a great number of wives and concubines, the vast majority of his subjects probably considered themselves lucky to have one each. As far as is known, this was equally true for the Chinese peasantry. But between peasantry and royalty in China there was an unusually substantial middle class, a class that was very much family conscious. The ordinary middle-class householder had between three and a dozen wives and concubines, the lesser nobility thirty or more—which made the handbooks' insistence on intercourse with ten different women in one night not only practicable but strategically necessary.

The rights of every wife and concubine had to be respected, for it was the husband's absolute duty to provide for his women not only economically, but emotionally and sexually. The Li-chi, the Confucian "Book of Rites," stated categorically that "even if a concubine is growing older, as long as she has not yet reached 50, the husband shall have intercourse with her once every five days." Favoritism in the hothouse atmosphere of the women's quarters was calculated to result in the ruin of domestic peace, which in turn could damage a man's career. One who was unable to keep his own household in order was unlikely to be trusted in a position of official responsibility (p. 184).

The Chinese gentleman, practical in all things, took care not to cause emotional crises in the women's quarters when he introduced a new concubine. There was a "correct" way to do this, as everything else. In about 1550, a wealthy landowner or merchant (whose identity is unknown) left to his sons a piece of sound advice on how to deal with the situation. "The right method," he said, "is for the man to control his desire, and for the time being not to approach the newcomer, but to concentrate his attention on the others. Every time he has sexual intercourse with his other women, he should make the newcomer stand at attention by the side of the ivory couch. Then, after four or five nights of this, he may have intercourse with the newcomer, but only with his principal wife and other concubines present. This is the fundamental principle of harmony and happiness in one's women's quarters" (p. 195).

From Tannahill, 1980.

Christian women were encouraged to be quiet and submit to the instruction and guidance of men. Women were considered to have been created for the benefit of men, and they were therefore expected to defer to men. In addition, women were forbidden to teach in the church, a prohibition reflected today in some Christian denominations that refuse to allow women to join the clergy.

While other early societies condemned some sexual practices, such as adultery, contraception, homosexuality, masturbation, abortion, and bestiality, the Christian church forbade them all. Whereas other societies suggested suitable frequencies for sexual intercourse, the Christian church maintained that it should not occur at all except for procreative purposes. While other societies considered sexuality to be pleasurable, the Christian church considered it sinful except for procreation and even then it was not to be enjoyed. As a result men and women of normal sexual needs and desires became obsessed by guilt. Christianity was one of the traditions that was least accepting of and most negative about sexuality.

Romeo and Juliet: an example of courtly love.

Middle Ages

The period from the fall of the Roman Empire to the beginning of the Renaissance is called the Middle Ages. During this time the relationship between men and women in the upper classes changed dramatically. Until then women had been treated as inferior to men and not useful except for producing children and taking care of household responsibilities. During the Middle Ages upper-class women were put on a pedestal and treated with admiration and respect (Tannahill, 1980).

It is not clear what factors were responsible for the development of the set of rules by which the game of courtly love was played. They may have originated in the ballads sung by the **troubadours** who traveled from castle to castle when the lords were away from home during the Crusades. In these ballads a nobleman falls in love with a lady. The nobleman has to work hard to demonstrate his worthiness for her love. After he has proved his worthiness by chivalrous acts, the lady eventually falls in love with him. Courtly love was based on the ideal of "pure love." Pure love was defined as the sharing of emotional and

troubadours
Poets and poet-musicians who lived in Europe in the eleventh, twelfth, and thirteenth centuries and wrote about love and chivalry.

spiritual love but not sexual love. Sexual abstinence was regarded as the greatest virtue.

Apparently ladies and courtly lovers began to live out the plots of the ballads (Tannahill, 1980). These lovers were never the ladies' husbands. Pure love or courtly love was assumed to be incompatible with a contractual marriage. Instead the courtly love relationships were extramarital. Whether most relationships involved sexual intercourse or lived up to the ideal of sexual abstinence is difficult to know. There are many stories, however, of lovers who would lie in bed together naked but show their virtue by not consummating their relationship. It is impossible to know what really took place.

As a result of this turn of events, women were considered almost perfect—in some ways superhuman individuals. They were believed more worthy than their aspiring lovers. The lovers had to prove themselves deserving by heroic deeds and chivalrous behavior. Thus upper-class ladies were given higher status in relation to men than any of their predecessors. Never before had women been so admired and respected.

However, it is clear that the elevation of the status of women occurred only with upper-class women. Women of lower social standing were treated no better than they had been in previous times. The nobility was free to use the women of the lower classes in any way they wanted. These women were not protected by either law or moral opinion (Sussman, 1976). The nobility could use them sexually, brutalize them, or even kill them with impunity.

The negative view of women during the Middle Ages can be illustrated by the persecution of "witches." Diseases, illness, and disasters of all sorts were considered the work of the devil. Witches were individuals who supposedly were assistants to the devil and thus had supernatural powers. The so-called witches were accused of being responsible for much of the evil in the world. People believed to be witches were tortured and killed. Virtually all individuals accused of being witches were women because of the view that women were more likely to be evil.

The chastity belt is also an indication of the place of women in the Middle Ages. The chastity belt was a metal belt with a metal piece that went between the woman's legs. Holes in the metal piece allowed elimination, but the metal piece prohibited sexual intercourse. Husbands locked such belts on their wives and kept the keys. Clearly husbands treated their wives as property.

The chastity belt is an indication of the place of women in the Middle Ages.

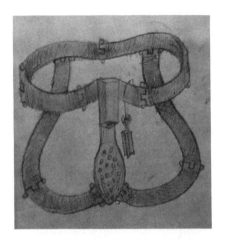

　　　　HUMAN SEXUALITY

Prostitution was prevalent. Temple prostitution was even introduced to Europe during this time. In a church **brothel** in Avignon the women spent part of their time in prayer and religious activities. Pope Julius II was said to have been so impressed with the Avignon church brothel that at the beginning of the sixteenth century he founded one just like it in Rome (Tannahill, 1980). As well as ordinary brothels, there were bath houses where prostitutes could meet their customers. The Crusaders apparently brought the idea of bath houses back from the Muslim world.

With the Renaissance of the sixteenth and seventeenth centuries came a loosening of restrictions on sexual behavior. The Protestant Reformation, led by Martin Luther, resulted in somewhat less negative views of sexuality than those advocated by the Catholic Church. The Protestants did not view sexuality as inherently sinful and did not regard celibacy as a virtue. These changes gave people more freedom to enjoy their sexuality. Furthermore, there was a relaxation of constraints on sexual expression in art, literature, and everyday life (Sussman, 1976). As a result of the weakening strictures on sexual behavior, many types of sexual behavior became more prevalent. However, at this time severe restrictions were placed on prostitution as a result of an outbreak of **syphilis.** Some speculate that sailors returning from their voyages to the New World brought syphilis to Europe (Tannahill, 1980).

Puritan Tradition

During the Renaissance another religious movement emerged from the Protestant Reformation in reaction to the liberalism of the time. The followers of this movement were called Puritans. They seceded from the Church of England, and many emigrated to America and settled along the coast of New England.

The Puritans were family oriented, and they approved of sex only in the context of marriage. They put few restrictions on what kinds of sexual relations were acceptable between married people. However, any sexual behavior outside of marriage was forbidden and severely punished if detected. For example, individuals who had premarital sexual relations were flogged and made to confess their sin publicly in church. Individuals who had extramarital sexual relations were treated in a similar fashion and were sometimes branded as well. At times in New England the laws even called for the death penalty for **sodomy,** bestiality, rape, and adultery (Bullough, 1976). Despite the severe sanctions against violating the sexual laws, however, Bullough (1976) concludes that "colonial America had at least its share of sexual adventures. Though the only proper sex was within marriage, the colonials no more observed this provision as a group than their predecessors or successors" (p. 525).

One of the unique customs of colonial times is the courtship pattern called **bundling.** Families had to work on the farm during the daylight hours, and shortly after dark they generally went to bed. If a young man wanted to court a young woman, he often had to travel some distance to get to her farm. Usually he did not have time to make the trip and return in the same evening; as a result, he would often spend the night at the young woman's house. Since most families did not have large enough houses to give the young man a room of his own, he was allowed to spend the night in the same bed as the young woman. A variety of techniques were used to ensure that the young couple did not have sexual contact. In some instances a board was placed between

---

brothel
House where prostitutes meet customers for sexual activity.

syphilis
(SIF uh lis) A sexually transmitted disease caused by a spirochete.

sodomy
(SOD uh mee) Sometimes refers to sex with animals, sometimes to oral and anal sex, and sometimes to sex between same-sexed individuals.

bundling
Courting custom that was formerly used in New England in which a courting couple would sleep in the same bed with all their clothes on. The couple was typically separated by some barrier.

them in the bed. In other cases a large bag similar to a laundry bag was pulled up over the woman's body to her armpits, or the woman's clothes were sewn in strategic places to prevent sexual contact. Both the young man and woman always slept fully clothed. Bundling allowed a young man and woman to get to know each other in spite of the distance that needed to be traveled and the lack of space. Eventually the custom of bundling disappeared as more people began to settle in communities, time for leisure activities increased, and homes were constructed with more room, including parlors for entertaining (Murstein, 1974).

Victorian Era

In the mid-1800s the trend toward more liberal sexual attitudes and behaviors in Europe began to reverse itself. During the Victorian era sexual repression, modesty, and prudery again became pervasive. Views about the nature of men and women also changed. In the Middle Ages women were considered more evil and lustful than men, evidenced by the fact that women were more often convicted and burned as witches. In the Victorian era, however, women were regarded as delicate, refined, and virtually asexual. Rather than being considered lustful, women were thought to need protection from the lust of men.

During the Victorian era sexual repression, modesty, and prudery became pervasive.

Henry Havelock Ellis and Sexuality in Victorian England

An important early contribution was made to the scientific study of sexuality by Henry Havelock Ellis. Ellis was a physician in Victorian England who took a particular interest in human sexuality. To better understand his subject, he studied a variety of types of material, from anthropological studies to medical findings to case studies. Ellis published his views regarding sexuality in a series of six volumes titled *Studies in the Psychology of Sex*, published between 1897 and 1910.

Ellis' views were remarkably tolerant and forward looking for his time. Much of his work was aimed at fostering a more accepting attitude toward a variety of sexual practices that were considered deviant in Victorian England. For example, he argued that homosexuality was congenital (present at birth) and therefore not a matter of individual choice. As such, he reasoned, it should not be considered a vice. Ellis argued that masturbation should not be thought of as abnormal behavior but rather as a common occurrence in both sexes. Furthermore, Ellis believed that normal, respectable women, like men, had sexual desires.

Henry Havelock Ellis was an important contributor to the scientific study of sexuality.

To protect the virtue of women and children, efforts were made to suppress sexual references throughout the entire culture. Sussman describes the extremes to which the men and women of this era went to avoid making sexual allusions:

> In some Victorian homes, piano legs were draped. . . . In much of the literature, Victorian women had no legs—they had limbs. . . . Women also lacked breasts—they had bosoms, instead. At the dinner table, one spoke of a chicken's neck, instead of its breast. Some persons even suggested that works by authors of the two sexes should not be kept side by side on the bookshelf, unless the authors happened to be married.
>
> Sussman, 1976, p. 57

In addition to trying to eliminate sexual references, individuals were terribly concerned about the effects of various sexual practices on physical health. During the 1800s Sylvester Graham, a physician, suggested that many of the health problems from which men suffered, such as skin disease, lung disease, headaches, nervousness, and "weakness of the brain," were a result of sexual excesses in marriage. Like other individuals at the time, Graham believed that 1 ounce of **semen** equaled nearly 40 ounces of blood. If too much semen were lost, the man's resistance to disease and death would be lowered. Graham recommended, and most physicians concurred, that men should limit their sexual encounters to 12 times a year. Such abstinence, he said, would replenish their nervous energy. Graham believed that diet, particularly the use of whole-grain flours, was also important for good health. In fact, the Graham cracker was named after him.

semen
(SEE muhn) Mucous secretion containing sperm that is discharged from the urethra of a male at the time of ejaculation.

At the same time other physicians were writing about female sexuality. In 1857 William Acton reported that based on his medical practice women had little sexual feeling and remained indifferent to sexuality in marriage. He went on to say that women submitted to their husbands only out of fear of desertion. Acton added that since sexual intercourse put such an enormous strain on the male's nervous system, the man should complete intercourse in as short a time as possible, preferably in a few minutes. Authors advised women

> to remain cold, passive, and indifferent to the husband's sexual impulses. Careless and amative acts destroyed the "innate dignity" of the wifely role and led to the misuse of sexual function in immodest responses in the male. . . . Purity authors agreed that the experience of "any spasmodic convulsions" in coition would interfere with conception—the primary function of the marriage act.
>
> Haller and Haller, 1974, p. 101

In the Victorian era the consequences of masturbation were considered especially severe. Sex manuals of the time warned girls that masturbation had the following consequences:

> The young girl who practiced the solitary vice would never escape the consequences of her indiscretion. She would become subject to a multitude of disorders such as backaches, tenderness of the spine, nervousness, indolence, pale cheeks, hollow eyes, and a generally "languid manner." Her attitude, once pure and innocent, would turn peevish, irritable, morose, and disobedient; furthermore, she would suffer loss of memory, appear "bold in her manner instead of being modest," and manifest unnatural appetites for mustard, pepper, cloves, clay, salt, chalk and charcoal.
>
> Haller and Haller, 1974, pp. 105-106

Male masturbation also had supposed consequences:

> By his shy and retiring mannerisms, his display of "unusual sadness," and his suspicions of those around him, the polluter publicly admitted his guilt. Confused by defective memory and hearing, he soon became negligent in his personal habits and acted dull and stupid before other people. In conversation, the masturbator

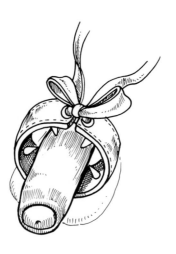 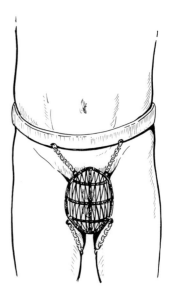

Nineteenth-century anti-masturbation devices.

could never look a person in the face, but averted his eyes. He avoided the glances of women, yet stole every opportunity to look at them. He was known for his pallid, bloodless countenance, hollow, and "half-ghastly eyes." When the habit continued for any length of time, however, his eyes acquired black and blue semi-circles popularly known as "plague-spots." Eventually his memory failed, he lost his power to concentrate, ceased to be self-reliant, succumbed slowly to the poisonous venom of pollution. This changed the color of his skin and made his muscles flabby, he avoided work as distasteful, and complained of backaches, dizziness, and indigestion. Soon the stooping hollow-chested skeleton of the former man wasted away, succumbing after long illness to consumption, diabetes, jaundice, or general blood diseases.

Haller and Haller, 1974, pp. 203-205

Victorian Treatment for Masturbation

Treatment for masturbation reflected a potpourri of medical folklore, mechanical gadgetry, and medieval torture, all designed to simultaneously control the vice and punish the sinner. Although some practitioners merely recommended pure thoughts, early rising, a brisk walk before breakfast, and marriage, most looked to more ingenious cures such as ice or cold cataplasms to the sexual parts at bedtime, electromagnetism, and hydrotherapeutic techniques. One water cure, the so-called "sweating process," consisted of encouraging perspiration and then alternating with cold air or baths; in another method, a wet sheet was wrapped around the person and as soon as he became warm, the sheet was replaced with another. More mechanically inclined doctors constructed special beds to prevent the sleeper from turning over, and sold "hand bags" which were tied to the side of the bed at night, and designed a chemise which reached below the feet and was drawn together at the bottom to prevent the careless ex-

ploring of hands. In Sylvanus Stall's *What a Young Boy Ought To Know*, the author suggested straight-jackets for masturbators to sleep in; he also recommended tying the hands to the posts of the bed, or to rings in the wall. These procedures were originally suggested in the 1840s by Deslandes, who not only prescribed the "straight waistcoat fastened behind, which may force the arms to rest on the chest," but also, in the event that the measure was not quite sufficient, ordered parents to tie the feet so that the thighs would remain separated. In some instances, he contrived "cork cushions" which he placed on the inside of the thighs to keep them apart. In addition, he fashioned a metal truss of silver (or tin) in which the penis and scrotum were placed and held by springs, and to add to the security of the truss, he prescribed clothes which opened from behind.

These so-called "genital cages" were a nineteenth-century derivative of the chastity belts of the Middle Ages, and could be purchased from

a variety of suppliers who advertised in popular journals and newspapers. R.J. Culverwell advertised in his *Professional Records* (1846) a special chair designed to serve as a douche bidet for the masturbator. The contraption consisted of an arm chair with an open seat, beneath which was a zinc pan filled with cold water or a "medicated refrigerant fluid." By means of a pump, the masturbator could direct the fluid to his genitals, thereby "cooling" his sexual ardor during those moments when he was most susceptible to the acts of unnatural venery. Other doctors treated the habit by blood-letting, or applying leeches and cups around the sexual parts to remove "congestion." Still others perforated the foreskin of the penis and inserted a ring, or cut the foreskin with jagged scissors. Drugs included applications of red iron, tartar emetic ointment, or a Spanish fly-blister to make the genitals tender to the touch. "It is better to go to any amount of trouble and to endure any physical discomfort," wrote Henry Guernsey, M.D., in his *Plain Talks on Avoided Subjects*, "than to sacrifice one's chastity, the loss of which can never be replaced."

From Haller and Haller, 1974.

Although the Victorian culture was prudish, evidence suggests that many Victorian women enjoyed their sexuality.

Even though the social norms were prudish and repressive, we should not assume that everyone behaved strictly according to the dictates of the culture. Although pornography was banned in many countries, many read underground pornography. Prostitution flourished in Europe. Social pressures compelled men to delay marriage until they had saved money and secured a home. Thus, faced with many years without a wife, followed by marriage to a sheltered bride, Victorian men sought prostitutes for both companionship and sexual contact.

Furthermore, there is evidence opposing the Victorian stereotype of the passionless female. Most of the 45 Victorian women in a study done by Clelia Mosher expressed a desire for sexual intercourse and denied feeling distaste or reluctance toward engaging in sex. The diaries of Victorian women suggest that at least some of them enjoyed their sexuality.

Twentieth Century

Early in the twentieth century Susan B. Anthony and Elizabeth Cady Stanton pressed hard for women's rights: for the right to obtain custody of their children in a divorce, the right to attend college and enter professional careers, the right to own property in their own names after marriage, and the right to vote. As a result of such women's efforts, women came much closer to gaining equality with men.

Sexual attitudes and behavior became somewhat more permissive. Sigmund Freud's theories of sexuality were in part responsible for the change. Freud rejected the Victorian notion that women and children were sexually innocent. Instead, he suggested that sexuality is a major force in human development from the time of infancy onward. He further set forth the idea that repressive attitudes toward sexuality are the primary cause of all neuroses. Freud's views were not well received when first proposed. In time, however, they clearly had a liberalizing impact on sexual attitudes and beliefs, as well as on sexual behavior. Freud made it possible to talk about sexual issues in intellectual arenas, and he made it difficult to deny the importance of sexuality to the physical and mental well-being of individuals of all ages.

In the early 1900s a nurse named Margaret Sanger also had an effect on attitudes about sexuality. She tried to do something about the large number of unwanted pregnancies, infant deaths, and maternal deaths in the crowded New York City slums. She believed that every woman had a right to birth control. As a result she tried to provide the poor residents of New York with contraceptive information and devices. Margaret Sanger encountered great difficulty achieving her goals because of opposition from police and religious leaders. However, in New York City in 1916 she opened the first birth control clinic in the United States.

The 1920s were a time of exuberance caused in part by the end of World War I. This excitement was reflected in both the dance of the time—the Charleston—and the fashions: women wore very short skirts for the first time in American history. Attitudes toward sexuality were correspondingly permissive. The incidence of both premarital and extramarital sex rose. Widespread

Margaret Sanger believed that every woman has a right to birth control.

Kinsey's research is
discussed in Chapter 2.

A description of various
contraceptive techniques is
found in Chapter 8.

ownership of automobiles may have increased sexual behavior among the young. Teenagers who had access to automobiles could be assured of a degree of privacy for courtship that was unavailable to previous generations.

The age of the **flapper** ended with the Great Depression in the 1930s. The 1930s saw a strong reaction against the permissiveness of the 1920s. Skirt lengths dropped again, music became more sedate, and attitudes toward sexuality became stricter. This relatively conservative period lasted almost three decades.

In the 1940s and 1950s Alfred Kinsey and his colleagues published their studies of male and female sexual behavior. Kinsey's work was one of the first scientific studies of human sexuality. His work was based on detailed sexual histories of thousands of Americans of both sexes, all ages, all areas of the country, and all socioeconomic classes. The results of Kinsey's studies were shocking at the time. They revealed that American men and women were much more sexually active than had been thought. The reception of Kinsey's work, especially his study on female sexuality, was not positive. The public did not strongly object to finding out that American men were more sexually active than had been believed. However, they were less willing to accept the findings on women's sexual activities. Kinsey reported that 30% of single women were not virgins by the age of 23, one in four girls had some sexual contact by the age of 12, and women were more likely to have orgasms as a result of masturbation than during sexual intercourse. The public was not ready for some of these surprising findings. In fact, some newspaper editors refused to publish reports on Kinsey's work because they thought it would be too offensive.

Kinsey's work set the stage for further study of sexuality. Since his reports were published, more and more investigators have begun to study sexual behavior in a scientific fashion. The scientific study of sexuality has made sexuality a more acceptable topic for public discussion. It has made society aware of the kinds of sexual behavior in which individuals engage and thus has decreased the discrepancy between the public's view of prevailing sexual conduct and the actual sexual behaviors of both men and women.

In the mid-1950s the birth control pill was developed. Because of "the pill" and other effective contraceptive devices that were made available in the latter part of the twentieth century, the reproductive function of sexuality could be separated from its other aspects. People could engage in sexual intercourse simply for the pleasure of it. They no longer had to fear an unwanted pregnancy. Certainly the introduction of the pill along with the development of other simple-to-use and effective contraceptive techniques contributed to the sexual revolution that took place in the 1960s (Tannahill, 1980).

The sexual revolution of the 1960s occurred as a part of the larger cultural change that began in that decade. The young people in the United States renounced the values of previous generations. The rebellion was probably brought about by a number of factors, including the war in Vietnam, the assassinations of John F. Kennedy, Martin Luther King, and Robert F. Kennedy, and the civil rights movement. These events prompted young people to both question and rebel against their parents' values. They expressed their views in such statements as "Make love, not war."

In addition to questioning other values, the youth rebelled against the older generation's sexual attitudes and behavior. Thus the 1960s, like the 1920s,

The 1960s, like the 1920s, was a time of more daring, permissive sexuality.

became a time of more daring, permissive sexuality. Hemlines rose again, hippies, or flower children, lived in communes, some of the youth advocated free love, others advocated open marriage, living together without getting married was common, and nudity at public gatherings such as rock concerts was not unusual.

The 1960s was clearly a time, at least for the youth, of extreme sexual permissiveness. Although many in the older generation did not agree with most of the sexual attitudes and beliefs young people espoused, they were not untouched by the sexual revolution. Some of the changes pervaded the entire culture. For example, the divorce rate and the incidence of premarital and extramarital sexual relations increased sharply, sexuality in books, television, and movies was more widely accepted, and open discussions of sexual issues became commonplace.

In the 1970s the trend toward liberalization of sexual attitudes and behaviors continued in some spheres. In 1973, for instance, the U.S. Supreme Court ruled that state laws prohibiting abortion are unconstitutional. The Court decided that the decision of a woman to have an abortion falls under the constitutional right to privacy. Gay rights groups became more active and visible. Women's groups such as the National Organization for Women (NOW) continued to press for women's equality.

The legal aspects of abortion are presented in Chapter 21.

The mood of the 1980s, however, took a more conservative turn. Evidence of the new conservatism can be seen by the success of the New Right and the Moral Majority in elections in 1980, 1984, and 1988. The Moral Majority and other conservative groups have tried to prohibit sex education in the schools for fear that sex-related information would promote promiscuity.

A Modern-Day Polygynous Society

The following is a description of a polygynous society in a remote corner of Botswana on the northern edge of the Kalahari Desert. The !Kung San people are one of the last remaining hunter-gatherer societies.

Equality between the sexes is probably greater among gatherers and hunters, including the !Kung, than in most other societies around the world. Despite the prominence of !Kung women, however, men generally have the edge. One reflection of their dominance is the pressure they can exert on their wives to accept other women as co-wives in marriage. Polygynous marriage is something many men want and about 5 percent have at any one time. The advantages for the man are obvious: he gains a new sexual partner, he is likely to have additional children, and he adds a substantial new provider of food to his family. The usual advantages of obtaining a first wife also apply: he gains recognition and status in the community, and he extends his social and political influence to include his new in-laws, their village, and their foraging grounds. Therefore, if a man has proved himself to be a good hunter and if life has treated him and his first family well, he may seriously think about taking a second wife. If his first wife has a younger, unmarried sister, she will be a likely choice. The wife of a deceased brother is another logical candidate.

Most women, however, do not want to become involved in such relationships. Many become furious when their husbands suggest it. They claim that sexual jealousy, rivalry, subtle (and not so subtle) favoritism, and disputes over chores and other responsibilities make the polygynous life a very unpleasant one. Co-wives either share the same hut or have separate huts only a few feet apart; either way, each woman's life with the husband is carried on in full view of the other. If the second wife is neither a close relative nor a friend, this enforced intimacy is even harder to tolerate.

Sisters are more likely to remain at peace with each other, so the !Kung say, because they are already used to living in close contact and cooperation. For co-wives who get along, the arrangement does offer benefits: constant companionship, someone to share chores and child care, someone to take over in the event of illness or disability, and a possible ally in struggles with the husband. The outcome of such marriages is largely dependent not only on the strong consent but on the personalities of the women involved. If they are compatible and work well together, they may even form intensely loyal bonds (pp. 169-170).

And how did the wives feel about co-wives? The following is a 50-year-old !Kung woman's description of what is likely to occur when a husband takes a second wife:

When a man marries one woman, then marries another and sets her down beside the first so there are three of them together, at night, the husband changes from one wife to another. First he has sex with the older wife, then with the younger. But when he goes to the younger wife, the older one is jealous and grabs him and bites him. The two women start to fight and bite each other. The older woman goes to the fire and throws burning wood at them, yelling, "What told you that when I, your first wife, am lying here that you should go and sleep with another woman? Don't I have a vagina? So why do you just leave it and go without having sex with me? Instead you go and have sex with that young girl!" Sometimes, they fight like that all night, until dawn breaks.

A co-wife is truly a terrible thing! (p. 172)

From Shostak, 1983.

The Right to Life movement with cooperation from both the Reagan and Bush administrations has tried to limit a woman's freedom to have an abortion if she chooses. Both Reagan and Bush oppose the 1973 Supreme Court ruling in *Roe v. Wade* and feel that some form of constitutional amendment is needed to overturn the decision (Bush, 1987; Wead, 1988). In the summer of 1989 came the first crack in the legal foundation of *Roe v. Wade*. In *Webster v. Reproductive Health Services*, the Supreme Court's conservative majority upheld the constitutionality of a Missouri law that sharply restricted the availability of publicly funded abortion services and required doctors to test for the viability of a fetus at 20 weeks. Their ruling has essentially given state legislators the opportunity to regulate abortion. Their ruling has essentially given state legislators the opportunity to regulate abortion. Since the Webster decision, the Supreme Court has also upheld state legislation requiring unwed teenagers to notify both parents (or obtain a judicial bypass) before having an abortion in the case *Hodgson v. Minnesota*. In addition, the Supreme Court's 1991 decision in the case *Rust v. Sullivan* upholds federal regulation prohibiting family planning clinics that receive federal funding from giving any information about abortion. Pro-choice advocates fear that this decision may prevent many pregnant women who rely on low-cost clinics from understanding their full range of options, which includes legal abortion.

In addition to supporting the limitation of women's freedom to have an abortion, the Bush administration supports legislation that would require parental consent for teenagers to obtain contraceptives (Wead, 1988). As evidenced by his policies, Bush places great emphasis on reinforcing the family structure:

> We have engaged in a lot of social experimentation over the last 25 years, but the fact is that much of it, from permissiveness to promiscuity, from open classrooms to open marriages, just hasn't worked. Much of it has been destructive to our family structure.
>
> Family is not a neutral word for me; it's a powerful word full of emotional resonance. . . .

Wead, 1988, p. 114

Will the conservative political trends result in a return to more restrictive views of sexuality in the 1990s? Or will the more permissive attitudes of sexuality be maintained despite the current conservative political trends?

Another factor that may result in more conservative sexual behavior is the threat of **acquired immunodeficiency syndrome** (AIDS). Indeed, if the birth control pill was a symbol of sexual freedom that helped launch the sexual

acquired immunodeficiency syndrome
Sexually transmitted disease in which the immune system fails to protect the individual from other diseases.

Will the permissive standards regarding sexuality continue, or will our views become more conservative?

Old Rites Bring New Hopes to Zambian Marriages

Among the Bemba people, who farm on a high rugged plateau in northern Zambia, sacred clay emblems were traditionally used in initiation ceremonies for women about to be married.

After generations of being largely discarded, these emblems—shapes of animals and mythical objects—and their attendant ceremonies have now come back into fashion as a way of fighting promiscuity and thus, it is thought, AIDS.

In January, a traditional initiation ceremony involving the emblems, known as Mbusa, was acted out every night throughout the month as a dozen women, married and with children, learned anew how, according to Bemba custom, to keep their husbands faithful.

In the privacy of one of their huts they showed a visitor the rhythmic dances they were taught by the initiator and now perform for their husbands. Accompanying each dance was a song, often to do with not being lazy and working hard for the sake of the husband. And with each performance, there was an accompanying clay emblem, a lion, a monkey, a special kind of pot. They were later melted in the river or taken away.

Over the last three years AIDS has seeped, but not stormed, into Chakobe village and the three other villages scattered around this missionary outpost. In Chakobe, everybody knows someone who has returned from town to die in the hut of a relative.

An Undercurrent of Belief

It is generally understood by villagers that AIDS is spread by having many sexual partners, but at the same time there is an undercurrent of belief, gingerly expressed to an outsider, that AIDS occurs in someone who is bewitched.

And while everybody has heard there is no cure for this mysterious disease, not everyone quite believes it. Visits to folk healers for a remedy are said to be frequent.

Unlike the pattern in Western society, acquired immune deficiency syndrome is transmitted largely by heterosexual intercourse in Africa, affecting men and women in roughly equal proportions. For the most part, it has hit urban areas much harder than rural villages.

But in places like Chakobe, in the remote northeast corner of Zambia . . . there are concerns that visitors from cities may begin to spread the virus.

In January, the mother of the nine Chinyonyo sisters, all of them known as village beauties, invited a professional midwife from outside the area to perform the initiation ceremony. It was seen as a safeguard against the promiscuity of the modern era, which according to the elders in the village and anthropological literature, was never part of Bemba culture.

A Return to Ritual

"They came to me and asked permission; I thought it was a good idea," said Henry Chakobe, the 65-year-old village headman, a retired teacher. "I was called to watch the performance and the material. This initiator took a month to complete the ceremony."

But Mr. Chakobe, pleased that there had been return to a full-scale ceremony instead of the single night devoted to such matters in recent years for women about to marry, was skeptical about its effect. . . .

[Those] who took part disagreed. They were enthusiastic about the return to traditional custom, saying they vividly recalled each night of the ceremony. They were now convinced their husbands would be faithful.

This Bemba woman is one of a new generation that has turned back to traditional marriage ceremonies.

From Perlez, 1990.

revolution, AIDS can be seen as a harbinger of sexual restraint in a time that appears to have changing sexual mores (Juran, 1989). AIDS is an illness in which a virus invades the immune system and destroys its ability to fight disease. The AIDS virus has been transmitted primarily through sexual contact, needle sharing among intravenous drug abusers, or less commonly, administration of contaminated blood products. The first reported U.S. case of AIDS caused by human immunodeficiency virus type 1 (HIV-1) was diagnosed in 1981 (Centers for Disease Control, 1988). HIV-1 appears to be the most lethal member of a growing family of AIDS and AIDS-related viruses. Another AIDS virus, HIV-2, was identified in 1987.

Although AIDS was initially thought to be restricted to gay men and intravenous drug users, many experts anticipate the likelihood of an AIDS epidemic among heterosexuals (Fineberg, 1988; Masters, Johnson, and Kolodny, 1988). Therefore, regardless of one's sexual orientation and gender, anyone considering sexual relations with a new partner has yet another parameter to consider—until a cure for AIDS is found, a parameter with potentially deadly consequences. To be safe, an individual should know his or her sexual partner's history of both sexual relations and intravenous drug use before engaging in sexual activities that may lead to HIV transmission. The individual should also be aware of safe sex practices that would prevent the transmission of the HIV virus. These measures may curtail transmission of the HIV virus and thus the spread of AIDS.

> Sexually transmitted diseases are discussed in greater detail in Chapter 18.

In addition to the threat of AIDS, the increased transmission of other **sexually transmitted diseases** (STDs) in recent years may also result in more conservative sexual behavior. In the United States more than 10 million people are infected by STDs each year. Some of these STDs are easy to treat, but others, such as **herpes,** are not. The threat of contracting STDs has caused people to be more cautious about their sexual involvements (Larkin, 1985). Many single adults are getting to know their partners better before engaging in sexual relations, and many married individuals are being more careful about extramarital relationships.

> **sexually transmitted disease** Infection spread mainly by sexual contact.
>
> **genital herpes** (JEN i tuhl HUR peez) Sexually transmitted disease caused by a virus that results in painful blisters on the genitals.

Given the conservative political trends in addition to the threat of AIDS and other STDs, it is possible that the trend in sexual behavior in the 1990s will be increasingly conservative. However, as suggested by D'Emilio and Freedman (1988), the tide toward conservatism in sexuality must contend with many opposing factors. For example, the pervasiveness of sexuality throughout American culture, the extensive variety of roles available to American women, and a relatively effective contraceptive technology make unlikely a complete retrenchment of sexuality in America. Thus, just how much this most recent trend in American sexuality will rekindle conservative sexual attitudes and behaviors is difficult to predict.

WHAT DOES HISTORY TELL US?

The overview of our sexual heritage illustrates that what people consider to be natural and normal with respect to sexuality is in large part culturally determined. There have been times when very restrictive attitudes have prevailed. Other times were more permissive. These periods seem to alternate throughout history. We may believe that the permissiveness in our culture today will increase or at least remain unchanged, but that could well be what our counterparts in the 1920s thought. It is possible that we are heading toward a more conservative period once again. Women could lose some of the rights they have obtained, the U.S. Supreme Court could reverse its decision on abortion, laws against homosexual behavior could be strictly enforced, and attitudes toward premarital sex could become much more restrictive. Or the trend toward permissiveness could continue. The only thing that is certain is that in the future sexual attitudes, beliefs, and behaviors will change.

Now that we have presented a history of human sexuality in Western civilization, we can begin our study of what is currently known about sexuality. We will begin our discussion with the biological aspects of sexuality, including sexual anatomy and physiology. We will then proceed to a discussion of conception, childbirth, and parenthood, which will include consideration of both biological and psychological factors, followed by a discussion of more psychologically oriented topics such as love, marriage, and alternatives to marriage. These topics will be followed by a discussion of disabilities, dysfunctions, diseases, and variations. We will end with a discussion of the more sociologically oriented topics of the law, education, and morals as they relate to sexuality.

SUMMARY

1 In earliest recorded history people closely associated their gods with sexuality; sexual intercourse was at times considered sacred.

2 The early Jews were more sexually restrictive; masturbation, celibacy, homosexuality, and bestiality were forbidden because these acts did not result in procreation. However, the Jews saw sexuality as pleasurable as long as no prohibited acts were performed.

3 The early Greeks were sexually permissive and uninhibited. Most men thought women were good for little more than having children and taking care of household affairs. Men tended to have more intimate, sexual relationships with adolescent boys for whom they were mentors.

4 Early Romans were also permissive with respect to sexuality. Many prominent Romans were bisexual. Prostitution flourished, and sexual interactions in public were common.

5 The early Christians, on the other hand, were extremely restrictive about sexuality. All sexual behaviors that did not result in offspring were prohibited. Even procreative sexual acts were not to be enjoyed.

6 In the Middle Ages the relationship between men and women underwent a change. For the first time women were put on a pedestal. The ambivalent attitude toward women, however, is reflected by the fact that it was primarily women who were burned as witches.

7 The Renaissance brought about a loosening of sexual restrictions.

8 During the Renaissance in Europe the Puritans settled in New England. The Puritans had restrictive laws regarding sexual behavior outside of marriage and severely punished those who violated these laws.

9 The Victorian era involved a return to sexual repression, modesty, and prudery. Women were considered delicate, refined individuals who needed to be protected from the lust of men.

10 The 1920s was a sexually liberal time. Women wore short skirts, young people danced the Charleston, and the incidence of premarital and extramarital sexual intercourse increased.

11 Although the 1930s, 1940s, and 1950s were fairly conservative decades, the 1960s was a time of youthful rebellion. Hemlines rose again, hippies talked of free love, public nudity was not uncommon, and many young couples lived together without marrying. In addition, the divorce rate increased drastically, both premarital and extramarital intercourse increased, and sexuality was more openly expressed in movies and on television.

12 It is not yet clear how much political pressures and the threat of AIDS and other sexually transmitted diseases will influence sexuality in the United States in the 1990s.

ANSWERS

1 In Mesopotamia and Egypt about 5,000 years ago, sexuality and religion were closely entwined. Prostitutes worked in the temples and actually brought in most of the temples' revenue.

2 Homosexuality, often between middle-aged men and adolescent boys, was considered acceptable and was common in early Greek culture.

3 During the Middle Ages far more women than men were burned as witches because women were thought more likely to be evil and lustful. Only upper-class women were put on pedestals and gained more rights and respect.

FACT
OR
FICTION

QUESTIONS FOR THOUGHT

1 Do you think our culture will become more or less conservative with respect to sexual attitudes and behaviors in the next decade? Why?

2 Over the course of history, women have usually been accorded a lower status than men. Why do you think this may have occurred?

3 Why do you think different cultures have responded so differently to homosexuality?

SUGGESTED READINGS

D'Emilio, J., and Freedman, E.B.: Intimate matters: a history of sexuality in America, New York, 1988, Harper & Row, Publishers, Inc.
    A discussion of how the meaning of sexuality in America has changed over the last three centuries.
Haller, J.S., and Haller, R.M.: The physician and sexuality in Victorian America, New York, 1974, W.W. Norton & Co., Inc.
    An interesting book about sexual attitudes and behaviors in Victorian America.
Sussman, N.: Sex and sexuality in history. In Sadock, B.J., Kaplan, H.I., and Freedman, A.M., editors: The sexual experience, Baltimore, 1976, Williams & Wilkins.
    An informative chapter on the history of sex in various cultures.
Tannahill, R.: Sex in history, New York, 1980, Stein & Day Publishers.
    An easy-to-read history of sex in a variety of different cultures.
Trudgill, E.: Madonnas and Magdalens: the origins and development of Victorian sexual attitudes, New York, 1976, Holmes & Meier Publishers, Inc.
    An investigation of sexuality in the Victorian era.

Sex Research

FACT
OR
FICTION

1
The most difficult part of sex research is securing a representative sample to participate in the study.

2
The sexual practices of college women have changed little in response to new and serious epidemics of sexually transmitted diseases.

MASTERS & JOHNSON INSTITUTE

First of all, acknowledgement should be made to the 12,000 persons who have contributed histories, and particularly to the 5300 males who have provided data on which the present volume is based. . . . If these persons had not helped there would have been no study. It has taken considerable courage for many of them to discuss such intimate aspects of their [sexual] histories, and to risk their confidences with the scientific investigators.

A. KINSEY, W. POMEROY, AND C. MARTIN
Sexual Behavior in the Human Male, p. ix

t seems that new sex surveys and studies are appearing more frequently. Each claims to have the latest information on the sexual behaviors, acts, attitudes, and feelings of men and women in the United States. Do they really represent the sexual behaviors of the "average" man or woman? Are the studies carefully planned? How were the subjects for the studies selected? These issues are addressed in this chapter to afford a better understanding of the importance of methodological factors in sex research and in social science research in general. We hope this chapter will provide the basis for more intelligent interpretation of surveys and studies concerned with sexual behaviors.

SOME TOOLS OF THE TRADE FOR SEX RESEARCHERS
Researchers' Obligations

Sex researchers have an important moral and ethical obligation to the people in their studies. All subjects must be provided with a form to sign that indicates their informed consent. The subjects must be told what is going to happen (although the real purpose of many studies is masked so as not to bias the subjects' responses) and that they can withdraw from the study at any time. In addition, the subjects must be assured of confidentiality. No one should have easy access to the true identity of the participants. The subjects should be assigned code numbers, and the list matching the code numbers with the subjects' true identity should be kept in a safe place known only to the most senior researchers.

Before we consider some of the more important studies of human sexuality, we must define a few terms and concepts used by social science researchers and sex researchers.

Validation, validity, and reliability are important concepts used by sex researchers. **Validation** is the process of measuring the accuracy of reported behaviors in a study. If a couple is part of a study and one states that sexual intercourse occurs twice per week while the other says it occurs five to seven times per week, the researcher must question the accuracy of the data.

Validity is concerned with measuring what is claimed to be measured and not something else. For example, if we are attempting to measure the effect of a lecture about sexually transmitted diseases (STDs) and safe sex practices, we might assume that any changes in sexual behaviors reported at a time point after the lecture are due to the lecture and not to other outside influences. This may or may not be the case, since another event, such as knowing someone who recently found out he or she had an STD, may have a greater impact on sexual behavior than the lecture.

validation
Process of measuring the accuracy of reported behaviors.

validity
Process of determining that you are measuring what you claim to be measuring.

reliability
Process of using multiple or different measures to probe the same item (for example, subjects would be asked in several different ways about types of sexual behaviors they practice).

cross-sectional data
Data collected from the subjects at only one point in time.

longitudinal data
Data collected from the same subjects at several points in time.

cohort membership
(KOH hort') Factors besides age that a sample of individuals have in common; include values and mores of particular social periods.

Reliability is the degree to which multiple measures for the same attitude or behavior agree. The multiple measures may be at different points in time or at the same point in time. Reliability at the same point in time can be measured by asking the same thing in a slightly different way. For example, Denney, Field, and Quadagno (1984), using a questionnaire, asked college-age individuals what part of a sexual encounter they preferred. In one question the participants were asked to rank order (from most favorite to least favorite) the behaviors in a sexual encounter. The males tended to select the order intercourse, foreplay, and afterplay. The females tended to select foreplay, intercourse, and afterplay. In another question the subjects were asked, "Which aspect of a sexual experience do you enjoy the most?" The males tended to select intercourse, and the females tended to select foreplay. It was clear that Denney and her associates (1984) were measuring the preferences of men and women in a sexual encounter.

Another important aspect of survey research deals with **cross-sectional** versus **longitudinal data.** In almost all of the sex surveys that appear in professional periodicals and popular magazines, the researchers use cross-sectional data. Cross-sectional data are information collected at one point in time. Denney and colleagues (1984), like most other researchers, asked college-age students various questions about human sexuality at one point in time. Would the attitudes and behaviors of these individuals change with age? Would attitudes and behaviors become more conservative or more liberal? These questions cannot be answered when a cross-sectional survey design is used. To determine changes in attitudes and behavior over time, the researcher must ask the same subjects the same types of question at time intervals, that is, a longitudinal approach. Thus a longitudinal survey is one in which the same subjects are followed for several years to determine whether their behaviors and attitudes change with age. As George and Weiler (1981) point out, a cross-sectional study does not allow the researcher to separate the effects of age from the effects of **cohort membership.** The effects of the aging process cannot be distinguished from the effects of differential socialization and values and mores of particular historical periods. For example, in 1990, are differences between 50-year-old men and 20-year-old men in sexual attitudes and behaviors due to the effects of age or the effects of growing up during two different time periods in the United States?

The Sample

The first consideration of any type of research involving humans is the sample. The initial step in designing research involving humans is to define the group to be studied and then determine how to recruit a representative sample of the members of this group. The sample involved might be all men and women over 35 years of age living in the United States, or it may be a more specific group such as gay men living in large cities or divorced women over the age of 40. Obviously not all women who are over 40 and divorced can be questioned, so a way must be devised to get a good sample of this group. The sample must include individuals whose age, race, educational background, and income are *representative* of the entire group of divorced women over the age of 40 living in the United States.

In a survey researchers try to select individuals who will be representative of the general population.

Obtaining a representative sample is one of the most difficult aspects of social science research. One technique is called **probability sampling.** This simply means that all members of the group in question (divorced women over 40) have a known probability of getting into the study. Based on various personal factors, their probability of being chosen may be very high or low. Divorced women who are members of an older singles group might be receptive to such a study, whereas less social women might not want to participate.

Two types of probability samples exist. One type, a **random sample,** is a sample in which the subjects are drawn by means of a strict random procedure. In this type of sampling each person has an equal probability of being chosen to be in the study. We could use a technique called random digit dialing (RDD) to generate our sample. This technique selects a sample of people by randomly generating telephone numbers using a computer. The most common use of RDD begins with a list of three-digit exchanges in the area from which the sample will be recruited. The last four digits of the phone numbers are produced in a random manner by the computer. Returning to our example of divorced women over the age of 40, let us see how we could use RDD to collect a sample of these women. We would use RDD to call households in the geographical area of interest and ask whether there is a divorced woman over the age of 40 in the household. We would reach even unlisted numbers by using the computer to generate phone numbers, but we would not reach people who did not have a telephone. Let us assume that 5,000 phone calls are made and 500 divorced women over the age of 40 are contacted. Of this group of 500, only 100 agree to participate in the study. What about the 400 women who refused to participate? We call this the *problem of refusal* or *nonresponse.* Are these 400 women different from those who agreed to participate? The group that consented to take part may be dissimilar from the entire population being studied.

probability sampling
Method of obtaining a sample population in which all members of the population have a known probability of being recruited into the study.

random sample
Sampling in which each subject in a population has an equal chance of being recruited into the study.

This is termed *volunteer bias*. We shall discuss the problems of refusal and volunteer bias as they pertain to specific studies later in this chapter.

In our previous example of using RDD to recruit divorced women over the age of 40, we might expect a high refusal rate. Women called at home by a stranger who plans to ask them personal questions might feel uncomfortable and not volunteer. A type of probability sample that might work better in this situation is the **nonrandom sample.** A nonrandom sample is any type of non-probability sample, that is, a sample in which not all members of the population have an equal chance of being selected for the study (Suddman and Bradburn, 1985). For example, we might recruit from a singles group that we know includes divorced women. We could ask their help and guarantee their anonymity. This would be a sample of convenience, and we would get the group we wanted to study. It certainly would not be a random sample, since not all divorced 40-year-old women would join a singles club and since only certain women in the club would be willing to participate.

The size of the sample is also important. The larger the sample, assuming it was selected according to some type of probability sampling, the more confidence we can place in the results. If there were two sample groups, one with 20 divorced women over the age of 40 and the other with 200, which would give you more confidence about the findings? Obviously, the larger the sample, the better we can generalize to the total group of divorced women over the age of 40 in the United States. *We want to be able to generalize the findings from our sample to make statements about the entire group in question.*

Once the sample is gathered, major problems can still occur. Are the subjects telling the truth? Have they remembered correctly? Subjects might tell what they think the researcher wants to hear or what they think other people are doing. For example, if single men between the ages of 20 and 30 are asked how often they have sexual intercourse, they may exaggerate their response because they think men should have intercourse five times a week, although they may engage in sexual intercourse only once a month. A person who is asked how many sex partners he or she has had might not remember accurately and might give an incorrect answer.

APPROACHES TO THE STUDY OF HUMAN SEXUALITY

Information about various aspects of sexual behaviors and the biological processes that occur during sexual behavior can be gathered in several ways. We have divided the approaches to the study of human sexuality into five categories: (1) *survey research* or *sex surveys* in which subjects are asked to complete a questionnaire or be interviewed about their sexual behavior and attitudes; (2) *laboratory studies* in which subjects are observed and biological measurements are taken while the subjects are engaged in different sexual behaviors such as viewing erotic movies or having sexual intercourse; (3) *participant observation studies* in which researchers join the group they are studying and report what they observe (for example, the researchers join a club that exchanges spouses and report the behaviors observed); (4) *case studies* in which one or a few cases of a particular sexual condition or behavior are closely examined for a long period; and (5) *clinical research* in which the causes of a particular sexual problem and possible solutions are studied.

---

nonrandom sample
Sampling in which not all members in a population have an equal chance of being selected for the study.

In survey research, subjects are sometimes interviewed about their sexual behavior and attitudes.

Sex Surveys

Surveys are used when the researchers want to include large numbers of individuals in their study. The survey may employ a questionnaire that the subject completes, or the information may be gathered in a face-to-face interview. In some surveys a written questionnaire and interview are combined. Surveys are inexpensive and can generate large samples, so they are the type of instrument most commonly used to gather information about the sexual attitudes and behaviors of diverse groups of individuals. In later chapters we will refer to many findings from the surveys presented in this chapter.

Kinsey reports   The best known of all sex surveys was done by Alfred C. Kinsey and his associates. Their work appeared in two volumes, *Sexual Behavior in the Human Male* (1948) and *Sexual Behavior in the Human Female* (1953). In both studies large numbers of people (5,300 males and 5,940 females) were interviewed between 1938 to 1949. The subjects were college students and adults from moderate-sized to large cities. Trained interviewers asked the subjects questions about all aspects of their sexual activities.

The first question about any survey study is: Are the subjects representative of the total group of men and women in the target population? In other words, did Kinsey get a good cross section of men and women from the United States to interview? The answer is no. He had a sample that was overrepresented by people from Indiana, young people, college students, whites, well-educated people from upper-income families, city dwellers, and Protestants. Certain groups such as low-income individuals, people with low levels of formal education, older people, Catholics, Jews, racial minorities, and people living in rural areas were underrepresented. Thus Kinsey's information is useful if we

In the 1940s and 1950s Alfred C. Kinsey and his colleagues at Indiana University conducted the first major national sex survey.

take into consideration the sampling bias that was present. However, it would be inappropriate to project his findings to represent a low-income, older, rural, Catholic family. Obtaining a representative sample of the U.S. population is difficult in any type of survey, particularly one that involves sex research.

Certain general problems in the Kinsey studies are also of concern in other sex surveys. A major consideration is the reliability of self-reported information, since most surveys rely on individuals to tell about their sexual practices and attitudes. The subject may not remember correctly or may not tell the truth. Some people exaggerate sexual activities, whereas others purposely minimize their sexual activities. For example, a man who masturbates five times a week may think that is too much and state that he masturbates two times a week. The opposite extreme is the individual who engages in sexual intercourse once a week but thinks that four times a week sounds better. The limitations must be considered when looking at the results of sex surveys, but it is important to be aware of their significance. Although surveys have various biases, they are valuable for our understanding of the sexual habits of a population. Surveys indicate what sexual practices are being used and how sexual attitudes and behaviors vary within a population according to factors such as age. In addition, surveys conducted at different times in the same population can indicate changes in behaviors and attitudes from a historical perspective. It is important to examine each survey, evaluate its limitations, and determine how and whether its findings can be applied to the general population.

The Kinsey reports, despite their shortcomings, are classic works by which changes in sexual practices since the early 1940s can be judged. They are valuable because they reveal the sexual practices in the United States during the 1940s, given the biased sampling.

A comparison of Kinsey and Hunt findings as they relate to gender differences is presented in Chapter 10.

Hunt Report   In the early 1970s the Playboy Foundation commissioned a sex survey that was intended to produce new information on sexual practices in the United States. This information could then be compared with Kinsey's findings. In 1972 researchers gathered the information, which Morton Hunt compiled for publication, hence the name the Hunt Report (Hunt, 1974).

The subjects for the Hunt Report were obtained in the following manner. Twenty-four cities in the United States were selected based on the idea that they were typical of American urban centers. In each city names were chosen at random from the telephone book. Researchers called the people and asked them to participate. The people were told that they would be involved in small panel discussions of American sexual behavior. Their anonymity was guaranteed. Of all those contacted, 20% arrived to take part in the discussions. They were requested to fill out a questionnaire concerning their sexual acts and attitudes. All 20% who came to the discussions filled out the long questionnaire. A total of 982 males and 1,044 females participated. Hunt considered his final sample to be fairly similar to the general population of the United States in age, education, occupation, and background (urban or rural). Although people from racial groups other than whites filled out questionnaires, their responses were excluded to maintain a sample similar to Kinsey's for comparison purposes. Thus Hunt's data and Kinsey's results do not take into account responses from various minorities.

Hunt's study has been criticized for several reasons. First, the refusal rate was high. Of all of the people contacted, 80% refused to participate. The 20% who volunteered are unlikely to be representative of the U.S. population in terms of sexual behaviors and attitudes. Second, using the telephone to recruit volunteers automatically excludes the very poor who cannot afford a telephone. Therefore Hunt's sample population might be biased because of the high initial nonresponse and the use of the telephone to recruit the sample. However, Hunt's information is valuable because it contains material on modern sex practices and allows us to see changes in sexual behavior between the 1940s, when the Kinsey data were obtained, and the 1970s. We will compare the Kinsey data and Hunt information throughout this book.

Redbook surveys   The October 1974 issue of the popular magazine *Redbook* contained a questionnaire about female sexual behavior and attitudes. Questionnaires were returned by more than 100,000 women. From this number a random sample of 2,300 was drawn to obtain the data published in book form by Tavris and Sadd (1977). The results of the study were also published in the September and October 1975 issues of *Redbook*.

The women who responded to the *Redbook* survey were young, well educated, and from a high socioeconomic group. For these reasons they cannot be considered a representative sample of women in the United States. In 1977 Tavris polled 40,000 men whose wives or sexual partners read *Redbook*. The results of this study appeared in *Redbook* in 1977 and were similar to the findings obtained from *Redbook's* earlier survey.

Hite Report   In 1976 and 1981 Shere Hite published the results of surveys that examined sexual behavior and attitudes. *The Hite Report: A Nationwide*

Shere Hite published *The Hite Report: A Nationwide Study of Female Sexuality* in 1976 and followed it in 1981 with *The Hite Report on Male Sexuality*.

Study of Female Sexuality dealt with women's sexuality, and the subsequent book, *The Hite Report on Male Sexuality*, addressed male sexual attitudes and behaviors. In both studies Hite recruited her subjects through notices in magazines and through organizations such as churches and women's groups. Her response rate for the survey on women was very low (3%), and the response rate for the survey on men was only 6%.

Neither of the Hite studies can be considered representative of the general population because of the recruitment procedures. In both studies long essay answers were required, and this alone excluded large numbers of people who could not or did not want to take the time to write essay answers. The long essay questions produced personal, individualized responses, and in many cases Hite used her own interpretation of this subjective material. However, Hite's surveys do provide insights into some concerns of the women and men who participated in the surveys.

Blumstein and Schwartz: American couples study   In 1983 the book *American Couples: Money, Work and Sex* by Blumstein and Schwartz was published. This book reported an ambitious study in which more than 3,000 interviews were conducted in the homes of couples. These couples, along with others, completed a series of questionnaires as well. Several thousand of the couples were surveyed using questionnaires 2 years later. This study employed a large sample and surveyed some of the subjects over time to determine what changes, if any, had occurred in their lives.

The subjects were recruited in many ways, including seeking volunteers from various organizations; canvassing neighborhoods for volunteers; and seeking volunteers via radio, television, newspapers, and other periodicals. The majority of couples volunteered for the study after reading about the search for volunteers in a newspaper or other publication.

The couples who volunteered were varied and included married heterosexual couples (3,574), cohabiting heterosexual couples (642), gay male couples (957), and lesbian couples (772). The mean number of years the couples had been together was 13.9, 2.5, 6.0, and 3.7 for the married, cohabiting, gay male, and lesbian couples, respectively. The mean age of study subjects was 34.4 years; cohabiting women were the youngest (mean age 29.7 years) and married men the oldest (mean age 39.9 years).

The sample was essentially white (95%); most had college educations and earned a middle-class income. The majority of the subjects were employed in professional, technical, or related fields. As the authors of this valuable project state, "Thus, we need to be tentative about applying our findings to working-class or poor people, or to people with only a grade school education" (Blumstein and Schwartz, 1983, p. 548). This survey, while not representative of all people in the United States, is important. We will refer to it in later chapters and will compare it with earlier studies of the sexual behavior and attitudes of American couples of both sexual orientations.

Studies dealing with specific populations   Sorenson (1973) studied females between the ages of 13 and 19, and Zelnick and Kantner (1977, 1980) and Zelnick and Shah (1983) surveyed females between the ages of 15 and 19. Sorenson had a long questionnaire (38 pages), whereas Zelnick and coauthors had a short one. Zuckerman, Tushup, and Finner (1976) surveyed sexual attitudes and experiences of college-age students and the effect of a human sexuality course on these attitudes and behaviors. Gerrard and associates (1982, 1984) studied sexual behavior and contraceptive usage among college students. The above studies are cited in various places in this book.

Bell and Weinberg (1978) conducted a survey of sexual life-styles and behaviors of homosexuals. In this widely quoted study the researchers conducted extensive interviews with homosexual males and females. The sample was recruited in the San Francisco area through advertisements, gay bars, personal contacts, and homosexual organizations for men and women. The sample included 979 men and women of all races and a wide range of age, educational, and occupational levels. As with other surveys, the major criticism of this study is its recruitment procedure. One argument is that people who go to gay bars (30% of the sample) or belong to organizations for homosexual men and women (8% of the sample) may not be representative of all homosexuals. In addition, gay life in San Francisco may not be representative of that in the rest of the country.

In a well-designed longitudinal survey, George and Weiler (1981) examined sexuality in 278 married men and women who were 46 to 71 years of age at the start of the study. The study lasted 8 years, and the participants were given a questionnaire every 2 years. The subjects were recruited from a health insurance program, and people of lower income and educational levels were underrepresented. The sample was composed of middle-class, middle-aged and older persons who did not have financial or physical problems. To make sure marital status was not a complicating variable, the researchers included only married couples in the study. This is an excellent safeguard, because widowed individuals may desire sexual activity but not have a partner. Excluding individuals without regular sexual partners reduces the likelihood of low sexual activity rates resulting from lack of a partner.

A recently published survey examined the sexual behavior of college women in 1975, 1986, and 1989 (DeBuono et al., 1990). This study used three samples of women at three different points in time. Thus it is a cross-sectional survey looking at changes in behavior across time in a similar sample of college-age women. The authors compared the sexual practices in college women before and after the start of the current epidemic of sexually transmitted diseases (STDs), including chlamydial infection, genital herpes, and acquired immunodeficiency syndrome (AIDS). These STDs became prevelant in the 1980s.

The authors surveyed 779 college women who consulted gynecologists at the student health center of a large private university in the Northeast. The women were recruited in 1975 (486 women), 1986 (161 women), and 1989 (132 women). Each woman was invited to participate, and very few of the women approached refused to fill out a questionnaire (refusal rate of less than 5% in any given year).

A possible criticism of the DeBuono study is that women who seek gynecological care might be different in some way from women not seeking medical care from these specialists; that is, those seeking care might be more concerned about STDs or unwanted pregnancies. The authors addressed this potential problem by recruiting an additional 189 women who did not seek medical care at the health center (refusal rate was less than 3%) and found that these women were in fact less sexually experienced (a lower percentage had engaged in sexual intercourse than the groups seeking medical care). However, the sexual practices of the sexually experienced women not seeking medical care were the same as those of subjects recruited from the health center. One important finding of this study was that the sexual practices (oral sex, frequency of intercourse, and so on) of college women have not changed over the years in response to the threat of serious STDs. However, condom usage has increased. Of the sexually active women in the study, 46% in 1989 said their partners used condoms on a regular basis during sexual intercourse, compared with 12% in 1975 and 21% in 1986.

The sample of women in the DeBuono survey can best be described as young, educated, and middle class; nonwhite women were represented in each year (21%, 12%, and 11% in 1975, 1986, and 1989, respectively).

Laboratory Studies

Laboratory studies of human sexuality can be divided into two categories: *descriptive observational research* and *experimental observational research*. In descriptive observational research the researchers simply record in an objective manner what they observe in terms of biological and psychological parameters while men and women engage in sexual behavior such as masturbation and sexual intercourse. In experimental observational research certain variables are manipulated or changed and the subject's biological and psychological responses to these variables are recorded. For example, men might be shown

William Masters and Virginia Johnson were pioneers in the study of the physiological events that occur during sexual excitation.

first an erotic film depicting a man having sex with several women and then a film showing a man having sex with one woman. The men would then be asked which film was more sexually stimulating.

Descriptive observational research   The most famous study employing descriptive observational research was done by William Masters and Virginia Johnson (1966). The research population consisted of 382 women (age range 18 to 78 years) who had up to five children or were childless. Approximately 7,500 **sexual response cycles** were observed in these women. In addition, 313 men were involved (age range 21 to 89 years); approximately 2,500 orgasmic (ejaculatory) experiences of the men were observed.

Both married and unmarried men and women were in the study. There were 276 married couples, 106 single women, and 36 single men. The single individuals were usually not involved in the sexual intercourse portions of the study. All volunteers were orgasmic during intercourse and masturbation.

Observations were made with the subjects in three coital (sexual intercourse) positions: female supine (below the male), female superior (above the male), and female in the knee-chest position (knees drawn up to the chest with the female lying on her back). Observations were also made when the male or female masturbated (manual or mechanical manipulation) and when the female used artificial coital equipment. The artificial penises used were clear plastic and contained a light and a lens that allowed observation and recording of changes in the vagina during sexual excitation. The room in which the individuals were observed was windowless and contained a bed and a great deal

> The work of Masters and Johnson is discussed in detail in Chapter 5.

> **sexual response cycle**
> Series of events that occurs as a man or woman becomes sexually aroused.

Subjects' Reactions to a Sexual Experimental Situation

In a descriptive observational research study the researchers, both physicians, attempted to determine specifics of vaginal erotic sensitivity. During the course of the study the researchers, one male and one female, stimulated various areas of the vagina of 36 subjects to determine if any one area was more sensitive to touch and erotic pleasure than other areas. Immediately after the study ended, the researchers questioned the women to determine if they had any negative feelings about the nature of the study. None of the women expressed any negative feelings, and several women said it was a positive experience (Alzate and Lodono, 1984). As the authors state, the lack of anonymity at the time the women were interviewed about the experience may have influenced how they responded to the researchers. The authors also make the important point that the women who volunteered for this intrusive study are a self-selected sample that does not necessarily correspond to the average female.

Sixteen months later a subsample of the study (24 women) was contacted and given questionnaires to complete (Alzate and Lodono, 1987). All completed the questionnaires and returned them to the researchers. All respondents were guaranteed anonymity. The results of this questionnaire indicated that 79.2% of the sample found the experience "definitely positive," and 91.7% said they would participate again in the study. The authors concluded that the human subjects in this very intrusive sexual experiment experienced little or no negative experimental effect. This finding is in agreement with the results of Masters (1977), who also found that subjects did not suffer any negative effects from participating in his classic work on the human sexual response (Masters and Johnson, 1966).

of equipment used to monitor changes in the individuals during sexual excitement.

Can the results from the research done by Masters and Johnson be generalized to the general population of people in the United States? The people in the Masters and Johnson study were subjected to bright lights, probes in the vagina, numerous recording devices, and the presence of medical researchers during their sexual activities. Not all people would or could engage in sexual intercourse or masturbation under these conditions. Therefore many researchers postulate that the people who volunteered to participate are not representative of the general population of men and women in the United States. Masters and Johnson are in full agreement on this point and state: "Neither the laboratory-study subject nor the clinical-research populations are sufficiently representative of the general population to allow definitive conclusions to be supported from behavioral material drawn from these groups and reported in the text" (Masters and Johnson, 1966).

Experimental observational research   Many interesting studies cited throughout the text have used the experimental observational research approach. To illustrate this approach to sexual behavior, let us examine in some detail a study of male sexual arousal in which subjects were exposed repeatedly to erotic stimuli. The study, involving 24 men between the ages of 18 and 52 with a median age of 26, was conducted by Julien and Over (1984). The men were recruited from a university population in Australia. All men were heterosexual and sexually active with a mean of four orgasms per week. The men were exposed to erotic material in various forms, including films, slides, and spoken and written material, for 5- to 45-minute sessions separated by 24 hours or more. During each session penile **tumescence** was measured by a rubber penile strain gauge that was placed around the penis and measured the amount of erection that occurred during the session. Similar studies in females have been done in which sexual arousal, as evidenced by vaginal vasocongestion, was measured by a **vaginal photoplethysmograph.**

The researchers subjectively measured sexual arousal at the end of each session by asking the subject to indicate (on a scale provided) how excited he was during the session. They monitored the effects of exposure to erotic stimulation on sexual activities outside the laboratory by questioning the men about

tumescence
(too MES uhns) Condition of being swollen with blood. This condition causes erection of the penis.

vaginal photoplethysmograph
(VAJ uh nl foh' toh pluh THIZ moh graf) Small device shaped like a tampon that is inserted into the vagina. It measures vaginal vasocongestion, an indication of sexual arousal.

A penile strain gauge is used to record an increase in size of the penis during sexual arousal. A vaginal photoplethysmograph measures changes in vaginal vasocongestion during sexual arousal in the female.

their sexual activities before the start of the first session and at the end of the fifth session.

The results indicated that both physiological (penile tumescence) and subjective arousal increased during a session and was high across all five sessions (that is, sexual arousal as measured physiologically and subjectively did not weaken with repeated exposure to erotic material). In addition, participation in the study did not influence the sexual behaviors (frequency or type) the subjects normally engaged in with partners.

Generalization from descriptive and experimental observational research   Farkas, Sine, and Evans (1978) examined what kinds of individuals volunteer for laboratory studies of sexual behavior. Participants in the study were 108 males between the ages of 18 and 61. The men filled out a questionnaire concerned with personality and sexuality. At the end of the questionnaire was an invitation to participate in an experiment that involved watching an erotic movie with a recording device around the penis to measure erection. The people who volunteered were more sexually experienced and considerably less anxious and guilty about sex than those who did not volunteer. Wolchik, Spencer, and Lisi (1983) found a similar bias with female volunteers. These researchers collected sexual histories and personality characteristics of 296 female students in an introductory psychology course. Subjects who volunteered to view sexually explicit movies while a vaginal probe was in place (to measure sexual excitement based on vaginal blood volume) masturbated more frequently, had more exposure to erotic materials, and reported less sexual fear

Sex and Stress: A Natural Experiment

In a study that indirectly addresses the problem of sexual arousal in a private setting, Johnston and Fletcher (1979) found that in a private setting the heart rate during orgasm reached a peak level of only approximately 118 beats per minute instead of the peak of 180 beats per minute reported by Masters and Johnson. The sample included 24 men and 12 women who were 37 to 66 years of age and recovering from heart problems (heart attacks and surgery to correct blocked arteries that supply the heart). Although this sample is biased because it observed only older men and women with heart problems, it is of great interest because one man engaged in sexual intercourse twice during the same day, each time with a different partner. He had a portable electrocardiograph recorder attached to him, so that his heart rate was recorded along with other clinical measurements. When this man engaged in extramarital sex at noon, his heart rate ranged between 96 and 150 beats per minute during sexual intercourse. In the evening he had sexual intercourse with his wife and had a heart rate in the range of 72 to 92 beats per minute during intercourse. Possibly the man was more stressed during his afternoon session of sexual intercourse for reasons including the fear of being caught, quick and rushed sexual activity because of time restrictions, novelty of the partner, and whatever else pertained to his particular situation. His evening session with his wife was in a more relaxed setting and atmosphere, and he was less stressed. Of course this is speculation. Perhaps the man was more aroused in the afternoon and this was reflected by an increase in all aspects of the sexual response, including heart rate.

than nonvolunteers. Thus the results of watching the erotic movies would be biased in both the male and female studies by the fact that the volunteers were not representative of the general population. This imposes strict limits on generalizing the findings of studies involving exposure to erotic films or physiological measures of sexual arousal to the general population (Wolchik, Braver, and Jensen, 1985).

Masters and Johnson cautioned against generalizing to the general population in their work dealing with descriptive observational research. We propose that their work does represent what occurs physiologically in the privacy of people's bedrooms or other private situations because they observed the same responses under various conditions of sexual arousal with hundreds of men and women. However, the intensity and duration of each phase, as well as certain physiological changes, may not be representative of the general population because a select group of people volunteered for the study and because of the physical environment of the research laboratory.

We would argue that the men and women in the Masters and Johnson laboratory setting may have been in a stressful situation, which could have been reflected in higher heart rates, greater increases in blood pressure, and other measures associated with sympathetic nervous system stimulation. This does not present serious problems with their findings, but the reader should be aware of the possible limitations of generalizing their findings and physiological measurements to the general population.

Participant Observation Studies

In a participant observation study the researcher joins the group he or she wants to study. In this manner the behaviors and attitudes of the group are observed firsthand by the researcher, who does not usually join in the group's sexual activities. This type of research is fraught with ethical issues. Do you tell the group who you are and what you want to study, or do you remain secretive about your motives? Colleges and universities require informed consent from subjects in any research study. If you join a group and do not let the group know you are a researcher and do not receive informed consent from each subject, you will be in violation of your institution's rules of conduct for human research.

One of the best-known and most controversial participant observation studies was done by Humphreys (1970). He studied male homosexual acts in public restrooms while he acted as a lookout to warn if an intruder or a policeman was coming into the restroom. Humphreys also wrote down the license-plate numbers of the men, traced the plates, and later interviewed the men in their homes. He told the men that he was doing a general survey that included some questions on sexual activities and attitudes. In this manner Humphreys was able to determine the answers of known homosexuals to a variety of different questions. This research violated many of the ethical rules and regulations that researchers today must follow. Humphreys did not obtain informed consent from the subjects, he deceived the subjects when he interviewed them in their homes, and he invaded their privacy in many ways.

Bartell (1970) did a participant observation study of mate swapping, also called swinging, in which married couples have sex with another person or another couple. Bartell and his wife joined a swinging group and told the members they were researchers who wanted to know more about mate swapping. They attended a large number of swingers' parties and large-scale group sex activities. They made observations at these sexual events and published a research paper based on their experiences and observations.

Case Studies

Case studies involve very small sample sizes, but the subjects are studied in great detail for extended periods. Sigmund Freud (1856-1939) used case studies to propose various theories and ideas about sexuality. In many instances a sample size of one constitutes the entire study and a paper is based on a single case. Case studies are of limited value, but they do present interesting findings. For example, one study focuses on four circumcised homosexual men who are attempting to have their foreskins replaced (Mohl et al., 1981). The authors report that a distinct subgroup within the homosexual population have "an erotic attachment to and/or preoccupation with the foreskin" (Mohl et al., 1981). The authors discuss the psychological aspects of the subjects. Each subject is discussed in detail with his initials, age, and a great deal of background

Sigmund Freud had a profound effect on psychoanalytical theory. His theories emphasized that when sex drives are thwarted, symptoms of stress and inner conflict occur.

information used. The authors concluded that the subjects have a "personally motivated obsession to obtain a new foreskin, an obsession sufficiently strong that these patients are willing to undergo an experimental procedure of uncertain outcome" (Mohl et al., 1981).

Clinical Research

In clinical research the subjects are usually patients who are seeking help for a particular problem. For example, menopausal women commonly complain of symptoms such as hot flashes, sleep disturbances, depression, and pain during intercourse. These women are often given female hormone replacement therapy or various drugs to alleviate their symptoms. In some cases they are given placebos to determine whether the symptoms can be controlled without medication. The patients are followed up for several months to many years to determine how effectively the treatment controlled the symptoms. In a well-done study that compared postmenopausal women receiving estrogen (a female hormone) for 3 to 16 years (mean 8.6 years) with a similar group of women who did not receive estrogen after menopause, it was found that estrogen reduced the loss of height with age (that is, prevented spinal osteoporosis, a softening of the bone), afforded some protection against heart problems, and controlled the common symptoms of menopause such as hot flashes (Lafferty and Helmuth, 1985).

SUMMARY

1 This chapter is concerned with sex research: its problems, pitfalls, and value. Key concepts such as validation, validity, and reliability are discussed.
2 The most important consideration of social science research (which includes sex research) is to secure a representative sample. The sample selected must reflect the characteristics of the entire population in question.
3 The problems of nonresponse or refusal and volunteer bias contribute to a nonrepresentative sample.
4 The approaches to the study of human sexuality may be divided into five categories: (1) sex research or sex survey, (2) laboratory studies, (3) participant observation studies, (4) case studies, and (5) clinical research.
5 In survey research the subjects complete a questionnaire or are interviewed (or both) about various aspects of their sexual behavior and attitudes. The major sex surveys include the Kinsey reports, the Hunt Report, and studies done with specific populations, such as adolescents, college students, and homosexuals.
6 Laboratory studies involve observing the subjects engaged in different sexual behaviors and taking biological measurements. Two categories of laboratory studies can be distinguished: (1) descriptive observational research, in which the researchers simply record in an objective manner what they observe, and (2) experimental observational research, in which certain variables are changed and the subject's biological and psychological responses are recorded. The best-known example of the first type of laboratory research is the work of Masters and Johnson. However, many other studies using the experimental observational approach have been published.

7 Participant observation studies are not used often. In this approach the researchers become involved with the group they are studying and report what they observe.

8 Case studies involve extensive long-term examination of one or a few cases of a particular sexual condition or behavior.

9 Clinical research involves studying a particular problem, including the factors leading to it and the solutions.

ANSWERS

1 A truly representative sample is difficult to gather because of such factors as refusal and volunteer bias.

2 New and serious epidemics of sexually transmitted disease have produced little change in the sexual practices of college women with the exception of an increase in condom use (which still does not reach 50%).

QUESTIONS FOR THOUGHT   ?

1 Suppose you wanted to know the answer to the following question: Which gender of college students is more likely to practice safer sexual behaviors? Design a study and include how you would recruit your sample and how you would protect the identity of the subjects. List two sample questions.

2 Select several sexual surveys from popular magazines (you should have no problem here, since they appear frequently) and tell what is good about each and what flaws are in each.

3 Define the terms validation, validity, and reliability.

SUGGESTED READINGS

Blumstein, P., and Schwartz, P.: American couples: money, work and sex, New York, 1983, William Morrow & Co., Inc.
  This book examines some of the major issues all of us will face in the future. It looks at how couples, both heterosexual and homosexual, balance work and sex in their lives. A must for students interested in what to expect in the future.
Brecher, E.: The sex researchers, Boston, 1980, Little, Brown & Co., Inc.
  An easy-to-read book that examines the work of some of the classic sex researchers of the past and present.
Suddman, S., and Bradburn, N.: Asking questions, San Francisco, 1985, Jossey-Bass, Inc., Publishers.
  This book deals with all aspects of social science research, including asking questions about human sexuality. A good reference for students who will design questionnaires in the future.

3

Sexual Anatomy

FACT
OR
FICTION

1
*Routine circumcision of
newborn boys in the
United States is recom-
mended by physicians.*

2
*Wearing jockey or brief-
type underwear can
result in a type of
sterility in men during the
summer months*

3
*The absence of an intact
hymen at first intercourse
indicates that the woman
is not a virgin.*

Many couples do not know very much about sexuality and are too guilty and frightened to explore and experiment. It is still astounding to me that so many couples who seek help for the wife's lack of responsiveness or for decreasing frequency of sexual contact are basically only suffering from this sort of ignorance. Frequently neither knows where the clitoris is or recognizes its potential for transmitting erotic pleasure.

H.S. KAPLAN
The New Sex Therapy, p. 123

Many students in a human sexuality course think that they need to know only about the emotional aspects of human sexuality. Yet many of the components of human sexuality that we think of as psychological or emotional are in fact tied to biological structure and functioning. To separate fact from fallacy and to understand why we feel the way we do or why we react as we do in situations involving sexual behavior and sexuality, we must first understand the biological basis of sexual functioning.

This chapter deals with the structure, function, and development of the male and female **sexual systems.** Both the male and female sexual systems can be divided into sets of internal and external structures. The internal organs are contained within the body cavity, whereas the external organs are located outside the body. The term **genitalia** is commonly used to describe the external structures, but by definition it also refers to the structures of reproduction, both internal and external. We shall use it exclusively to describe the external structures.

MALE SEXUAL ANATOMY

The male reproductive system consists of an external and an internal set of organs. The external organs are the penis and scrotum. The internal organs include the testes, epididymis, vas deferens, seminal vesicles, ejaculatory ducts, prostate gland, and Cowper's glands.

External Structures of the Male

The penis and scrotum are the external structures. Although outside the body cavity, the testes are generally not considered part of the external genitalia.

Penis The male organ for copulation or sexual intercourse is the **penis** (Figure 3-1). The penis has taken on great significance within a cultural context. It has been an object of religious worship and a symbol of fertility. In our society the penis has become the focus of many myths.

The penis is covered by thin, hairless skin, and it contains no muscle or bone. The penis is composed of three cylinders of erectile tissue that are bound together by fibrous tissue. The two uppermost cylinders that lie side by side are called the **corpora cavernosa penis,** and the lower cylinder is the **corpus spongiosum penis.** The **urethra,** a canal for the passage of urine and semen out of the body, is contained within the corpus spongiosum penis. The **erectile tissue** of the penis consists of irregular cavities and spaces much like those of

Effect of biological chemicals that control sexual systems and influence behavior is presented in Chapter 4.

sexual systems
Anatomical structures involved in procreation, as well as mammary glands that some women use to nourish the newborn.

genitalia
(JEN uh TAY lee oh) External and internal reproductive structures.

penis
(PEE nis) Male organ for copulation.

corpora cavernosa penis
(KOR puhr uh KAV uhr NOH suh) Two side-by-side columns of erectile tissue in penis.

corpus spongiosum penis
(KOR puhs spun jee OH suhm) Erectile tissue surrounding urethra.

urethra
(yoo REE thruh) Canal for discharge of urine that extends from bladder to outside body. In male, urethra also carries ejaculate out of body.

erectile tissue
(i REK tuhl) Vascular tissue that, when filled with blood, becomes erect or rigid.

FIGURE 3-1
The penis contains three cylinders of erectile tissue that fill with blood during sexual excitation.

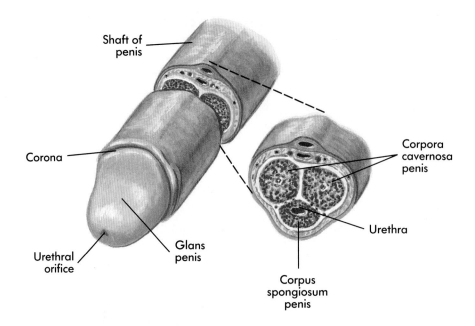

Shaft of penis

Corona

Corpora cavernosa penis

Urethra

Urethral orifice

Glans penis

Corpus spongiosum penis

flaccid
(FLAS sid) Relaxed or flabby.

glans penis
(glanz PEE nis) Bulbous tip of penis.

corona
(kuh ROH nuh) Ridge of tissue separating glans penis from shaft.

frenulum
(FREN yuh luhm) Small fold of skin that unites foreskin with glans penis.

prepuce
(PREE pyoos) Foreskin or fold of skin over glans penis.

circumcision
(sur kuhm sizh uhn) Removal of prepuce.

a dense sponge. These tissues are supplied by an extensive network of blood vessels and nerves. When the penis is not erect, that is, when it is **flaccid,** the cavities contain little blood. During sexual excitation they become filled with blood, and their constriction within the fibrous tissue causes the stiffness of the penis, or erection. The average nonerect penis is between 3 and 4 inches long, and the average erect penis is 6 inches long (Gebhard and Johnson, 1979).

At the tip of the penis is a knob called the **glans penis.** The glans has an extensive nerve supply and hence is very sensitive to physical stimulation. The ridge of tissue separating the glans penis from the shaft, the **corona,** is also sensitive to stimulation. The underside of the penis, particularly a strip of skin referred to as the **frenulum,** is usually more sensitive to stimulation than the topside of the penis, and the body or shaft is far less sensitive to physical stimulation than the glans. The base or root of the penis attaches to the body near the pubic bones.

Along the base of the glans penis the skin forms a fold termed the **prepuce,** commonly called the foreskin, which covers the glans to a variable degree. Removal of the prepuce, **circumcision,** is a rite of certain religions and is also done for hygienic reasons. Circumcision has had a long history (see the accompanying box), but this procedure has caused controversy among the medical community and the general public.

In 1971 the American Academy of Pediatrics (AAP) stated that circumcision—the surgical removal of the foreskin of the penis—was an unnecessary medical procedure. Physicians and parents began questioning the validity of what had become one of the most commonly performed surgeries in the United States. In 1988, however, the AAP decided to reconsider its position in light of new medical findings and stated that circumcision does have some medical advantages but that it also carries some risks (American Academy of Pediatrics, 1989). The recent findings that urinary tract infections are much more common in uncircumcised infants persuaded the AAP to take a neutral position. These urinary tract infections can move up to the kidneys and cause serious medical

Historical Account of Male Circumcision

The practice of circumcision can be traced back to at least 6000 BC. Egyptian mummies from this period show evidence of circumcision. The first written account of circumcision appears in the Bible when Abraham made a covenant with God to have all of his male descendants circumcised. From this time forward, circumcision took on a religious as well as a cultural significance for some groups. Why was circumcision done before Abraham's covenant with God, and where did the prac-

tice originate? No one knows. It is thought that circumcision was practiced by people of Semitic origin (a group now represented by Jews and Arabs but originally including the ancient Egyptians, Hebrews, Babylonians, Assyrians, and Moslems), as well as by various non-Semitic groups in Africa, Australia, and North and South America.

There are many speculations as to why people began to circumcise their males. They include hygiene, more attractive appearance of the

circumcised penis, circumcision as a rite of passage into adulthood, circumcision as a means of reducing sex drive, circumcision as a means of increasing sex drive, circumcision as a means of increasing fertility, and circumcision as a mark of purity. In the United States almost all circumcisions of newborns are done for religious reasons (especially among Jews and Moslems), hygienic reasons, or cosmetic reasons.

Groups that circumcise their males have always been in the minority. It is estimated that only 15% of the world's population practices circumcision at the present time.

---

problems. Circumcised males are 10 to 39 times less likely than uncircumcised males to have urinary tract infections during infancy, and while uncircumcised males made up 20% of a population of male infants in one study, they accounted for 70% of urinary tract infections (Wiswell, Smith, and Bass, 1985; Wiswell, 1990).

Critics of routine newborn circumcision point to its medical disadvantages, which include pain to the infant, possible irritation of the penis, and the risk of complications and surgical errors. In addition, critics argue that the removal of the foreskin subjects the sensitive glans penis to rubbing and friction that could cause decreased sensitivity of the glans (Figure 3-1). However, the noted sex researchers Masters and Johnson (1966) found no effect of circumcision on the sensitivity of the glans penis in adult males.

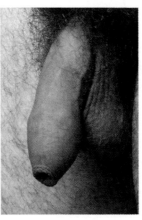

The external genitalia of the male can show variation. One male is circumcised; the other is uncircumcised.

FIGURE 3-2
Glands beneath the fore-
skin secrete a cheeselike
substance called smegma.

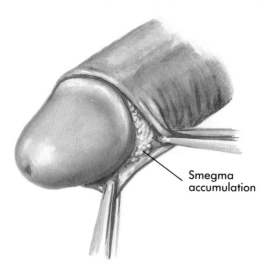

Smegma
accumulation

smegma
(SMEG muh) Secretions produced by sebaceous glands
(produce sebum) located beneath prepuce.

Yeast infections are dis-
cussed in Chapter 18.

Proponents advocate circumcision for several reasons, the most notable of
which is cleanliness. Bacteria and secretions termed **smegma** (such as oil from
glands located on the glans penis and dead skin sloughed off from the glans)
can be trapped under the foreskin and can cause problems unless uncircumcised
boys are taught hygiene practices to prevent the accumulation of materials
under the foreskin (Figure 3-2).

In parts of the world where circumcision is not practiced and hygiene is
poor, the penile cancer rate is higher than in countries where routine newborn
circumcision is practiced. It was previously thought that the female partners
of uncircumcised men had a higher risk of cervical cancer, but new findings
indicate that the incidence of cervical cancer depends on many factors (Wallenstein, 1980; Rombert, 1985).

Almost all sexually transmitted diseases occur more frequently among uncircumcised men than among circumcised men (Parker et al., 1983; Fink,
1987). Some recent data suggest that circumcision may reduce the spread of
sexually transmitted diseases, including acquired immunodeficiency syndrome
(AIDS), syphilis, gonorrhea, and genital warts (Marx, 1989; Wiswell, 1990).

At present in the United States more than 80% of newborn boys are circumcised, usually before they leave the hospital. The circumcision rate fell
from a high of 85% to 87% in the late 1970s to 71% in 1984 (Wiswell, 1990).

As illustrated in Figure 3-3, *A*, an infant circumcision involves cutting of
the foreskin that covers the glans penis. Various techniques are used, but all
involve freeing the foreskin from the glans penis so that a bell-shaped device
can be placed over the glans to protect it. Tissue connections, called adhesions,
between the glans and the foreskin must be broken before a circumcision. The
foreskin is then pulled up over the bell-shaped protector and cut completely
around the bell.

No type of anesthesia is used during an infant circumcision. The person
doing the surgery would have to inject an anesthetic into the foreskin all around
the site of the cut, and this would hurt as much as the cut itself. The use of
a topical anesthetic (one that could be applied to the skin) would not be effective
because reactions of babies indicate that the most painful part of the procedure
is the separation of the foreskin from the glans penis, and there is no way to

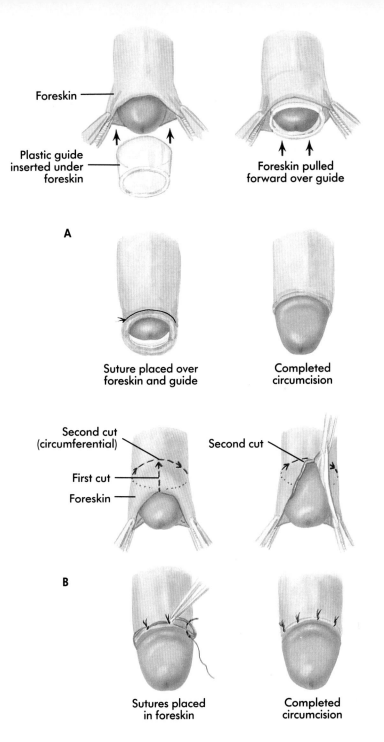

Foreskin

Plastic guide inserted under foreskin

Foreskin pulled forward over guide

A

Suture placed over foreskin and guide

Completed circumcision

Second cut (circumferential)

First cut

Foreskin

Second cut

B

Sutures placed in foreskin

Completed circumcision

apply a topical anesthetic under the foreskin as it is being separated from the glans.

Research is constantly adding to the pool of information about the benefits and disadvantages of circumcision. Ultimately, each family is unique and makes its decision based on what it feels are the most compelling arguments—on what is best for the child.

scrotum
(SKROH tuhm) Pouch consisting of muscles and skin that contains testes.

Scrotum The **scrotum** is a pouch that contains the testes, blood vessels, nerves, and other portions of the male reproductive tract. The scrotum maintains the testes, also called testicles, at a temperature of about 5° F below the core body temperature, which is approximately 98.6° F. The layers of the scrotum are skin and a smooth muscle layer. When the scrotal muscle contracts, the scrotum is wrinkled and the testes are held close to the body, where they receive warmth. When the fibers of the scrotal muscle are relaxed, the scrotum is pendulous and hangs free away from the body. Thus in warm environments the scrotum is pendulous, and the large skin area allows heat to be lost from the scrotum and the area surrounding the testicles. In a cold environment the scrotum is small, contracted, and close to the body. In this situation heat is gained from the body to increase the temperature of the area surrounding the testicles.

The sperm-producing cells of the testicles are extremely sensitive to elevated temperatures. These cells cease normal sperm production when they are exposed to temperatures equal to or greater than body temperature. Males of many species, including humans, have been noted in some instances to become sterile during the summer months (Nalbandov, 1976). In many cases men wore jockey or brief-type underwear or shorts that held the testicles close to the body. Even though the scrotal muscle layer was relaxed, the testicles could not move away from the core of the body and as a result were exposed to elevated temperatures. These males produced abnormal-looking sperm cells that were incapable of fertilization (Hafez, 1980). Furthermore, men with prolonged fevers may become temporarily infertile because of the elevated temperature of the blood supplying the testicles. Infertility caused by elevated testicular temperatures is temporary and should not be relied on as a method to prevent pregnancies.

Internal Structures of the Male

testes
(TES teez) Paired structures located in scrotum that produce sperm and male hormones.

The internal structures of the male include the testes, epididymis, prostate gland, Cowper's glands, vas deferens, seminal vesicles, and ejaculatory ducts (Figure 3-4). The prostate gland and seminal vesicles contribute their secretions to the male ejaculate. The male ejaculate, semen, is a mixture of sperm from the testes and fluids contributed by the various structures associated with the male reproductive system. The semen contains carbohydrates, proteins, salts, and about 100 million sperm cells (spermatozoa) per milliliter. With each ejaculation approximately 3.5 milliliters of semen is discharged, which would equal about 1 to 2 teaspoons of fluid and contain 200 to 500 million sperm cells (Hafez, 1980).

hormones
(HOHR mohnz) Chemical substances produced in specialized structure. Chemicals are carried via blood to influence specific tissues within the body.

seminiferous tubules
(sem′ uh NIF uhr uhs TOO byoolz) Specialized tubular structures that produce sperm cells.

Testes Located in the scrotum, the **testes** (Figures 3-5 and 3-6) are paired oval structures that produce the male gametes, called sperm, and male hormones. **Hormones** are powerful chemicals that travel via the blood to affect many parts of the body. The testes contain two specialized tissues: the **seminiferous tubules** for sperm production and the **Leydig cells** for the production of the male hormones. Each testis is made up of numerous seminiferous tubules surrounded by connective tissue that contains the Leydig cells. The tubules constitute approximately 90% of the testicular mass. The tubules would be miles long if straightened out. The tissue that lines the tubules contains two

Leydig cells
(LY dig) Hormone-producing cells of testes.

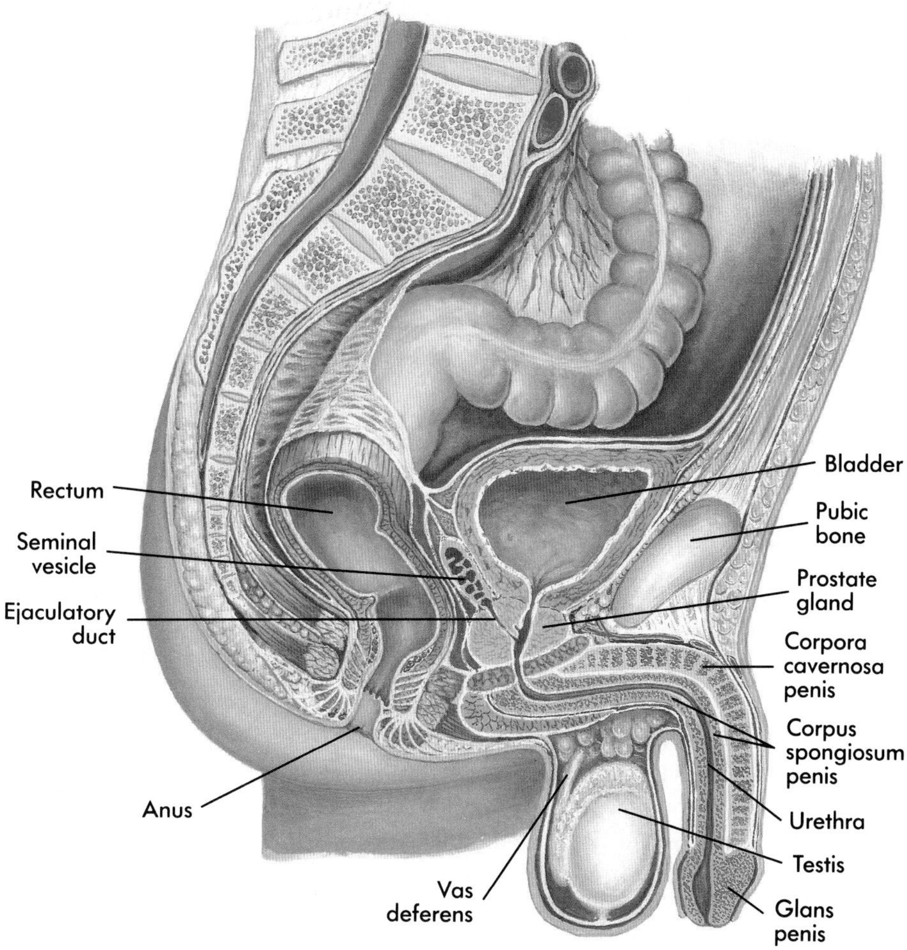

FIGURE 3-4
Section through the pelvis
of the male.

Rectum

Seminal
vesicle

Ejaculatory
duct

Anus

Vas
deferens

Bladder

Pubic
bone

Prostate
gland

Corpora
cavernosa
penis

Corpus
spongiosum
penis

Urethra

Testis

Glans
penis

types of cells: spermatogenic (sperm-producing) cells and Sertoli cells, which provide nourishment for the developing sperm cells. When the sperm cells become mature, they move from the seminiferous tubules into the head of the epididymis.

Epididymis   A comma-shaped structure, the **epididymis** (Figures 3-4 and 3-5) curves over the upper end of each testis. It is an irregularly twisted tube or duct having an uncoiled length of approximately 15 to 20 feet with a diameter about the size of a pencil lead. The head of the "comma" is the head of the epididymis, and the "tail" is called the tail of the epididymis. In the tail portion the duct increases in diameter and joins the vas deferens. The developed sperm cells move from the testes into the epididymis. Here the sperm further mature, develop their motility (swimming ability), and then move into the vas deferens.

Vas deferens   About 45 centimeters (17 inches) long, each **vas deferens** (Figures 3-4, 3-5, and 3-6) runs a path from the tail of the epididymis, through the inguinal canal (the opening into the abdomen), and then behind the bladder (the organ for urine storage). In the region of the bladder the vas deferens

epididymis
(ep′ i DID uh mis) Comma-shaped structure that receives sperm cells from testes.

vas deferens
(VAS DEF uh renz′) Long tubular structure that receives sperm cells from epididymis and conveys sperm cells to urethra.

FIGURE 3-5
Schematic section through testicle showing seminiferous tubules.

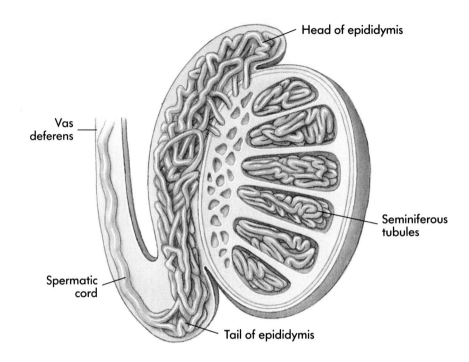

Head of epididymis

Vas deferens

Seminiferous tubules

Spermatic cord

Tail of epididymis

ampulla
(am POOL uh, -PUL uh)
Widened portion of vas deferens that acts as prime storage area for sperm cells.

Discussion of vasectomy as a contraceptive method is provided in Chapter 8.

seminal vesicles
(SEM uh nuhl ves uh kuhlz)
Saclike structures connected to vasa deferentia at ejaculatory ducts. Produce thick fluid that forms part of semen.

enlarges to form the **ampulla.** The ampulla then becomes narrow and joins the duct of the seminal vesicle to form the ejaculatory duct. In the vas deferens, particularly the ampulla, the sperm are stored before ejaculation. While in the vas deferens the sperm are relatively dormant and show little motility.

In the method of contraception called vasectomy the scrotal portion of the vas deferens is cut. The individual with a vasectomy produces an ejaculate that is missing sperm cells but contains all the other constituents of the semen. A man with a vasectomy produces the same volume of ejaculate as a man who has not had a vasectomy. Sperm cells make up a minute portion of the ejaculate, and their absence is of no consequence to ejaculate volume.

Seminal vesicles   About the size of a small finger, the **seminal vesicles** (Figures 3-4 and 3-6) are pouches that lie along the posterior portion of the bladder. Each vas deferens runs along the side of a seminal vesicle. Above the base of the prostate gland each seminal vesicle forms a narrow duct. The duct of the seminal vesicle joins the final portion of the vas deferens, and the junction of these two ducts is called the ejaculatory duct. It was once thought that the seminal vesicles stored sperm. This is not the case. They are secretory glands, not sperm storage areas. The seminal vesicles produce and secrete a fluid that resembles thin mucus. This fluid contains fructose (a sugar) and protein that is sticky and yellow. At ejaculation the seminal vesicles empty their contents into the ejaculatory duct shortly after the vas deferens empties sperm into the ejaculatory duct. These secretions add to the volume of the ejaculated semen. The fructose and other substances in the seminal fluid provide important nutrients for the ejaculated sperm cells, function as a medium or vehicle for the transport of the sperm cells to the female reproductive tract, and increase sperm motility and survival.

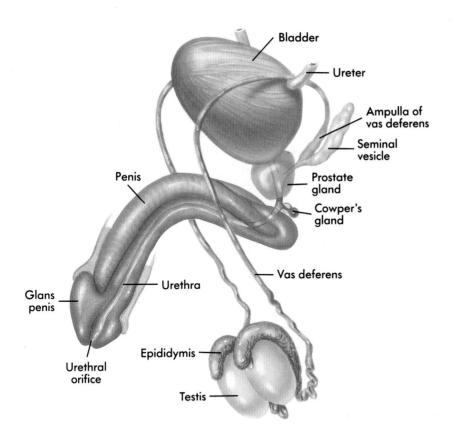

FIGURE 3-6
Internal reproductive structures of the male.

Bladder

Ureter

Ampulla of
vas deferens

Seminal
vesicle

Prostate
gland

Cowper's
gland

Penis

Vas deferens

Glans
penis

Urethra

Urethral
orifice

Epididymis

Testis

Ejaculatory ducts Formed by the junction of the ducts of the seminal
vesicles and vas deferens, the **ejaculatory ducts** (Figures 3-4 and 3-6) are about
2 centimeters (1 inch) long and open into the portion of the urethra that passes
through the prostate gland. The urethra carries sperm from the ejaculatory
ducts to the tip of the penis and urine from the bladder to the tip of the penis.
The ejaculatory ducts empty their contents at the time of ejaculation.

Prostate gland The **prostate gland,** a blunted cone about the size of a
golfball, lies beneath the bladder (Figures 3-4 and 3-6). The prostate gland
becomes enlarged in many men over the age of 60. Because the urethra enters
and passes through the prostate gland, the enlarged gland constricts the urethra
to cause varying degrees of pain and discomfort, especially during urination.
The rectum is just behind the prostate gland (Figure 3-4). This anatomical
relationship allows a physician to place a finger into the rectum and feel the
prostate gland to determine whether it is enlarged or to squeeze the gland to
force out the contents for examination. As men age, the prostate gland should
be examined routinely during physical examinations.

The prostate gland secretes a thin, milky fluid that contains high concentrations of citric acid and acid phosphatase (Hafez, 1976). During ejaculation
the prostate gland constricts simultaneously with the contractions of the vas
deferens and seminal vesicles. Most researchers believe that the prostatic secretions increase sperm motility and protect the sperm against the acidic environment of the vagina (Hafez, 1980).

ejaculatory ducts
(i JAK yuh luh tuh ree duhkts)
Narrowed portions of male
reproductive tract where vasa
deferentia join ducts of seminal vesicles.

prostate gland
(PROS tayt) Gland that surrounds outlet of bladder and
secretes thin fluid into urethra at ejaculation.

Clinical conditions of the
prostate gland are discussed
in Chapter 17.

Cowper's glands   Two small glands about the size of peas, the **Cowper's glands** (Figure 3-6) are located on both sides of the urethra below the level of the prostate gland. The Cowper's glands empty their secretions directly into the urethra before ejaculation. The secretion adds lubricating and protective mucus to the semen as it passes through the urethra, removes urine from the urethra, and helps neutralize any acidity in the urethra. Secretions from the Cowper's glands occur before ejaculation (preejaculatory emission). A small amount of clear fluid from these glands flows from the urethral orifice. It is remotely possible that a small number of sperm that have leaked through the ejaculatory ducts will appear in the preejaculatory emission (see accompanying box). The numbers of sperm would be extremely small compared with the amount in the ejaculate.

Urethra   Beginning at the outlet of the bladder and ending at the tip of the penis, the urethra (Figures 3-4 and 3-6) conducts urine from the bladder to the tip of the penis and also receives secretions from the ejaculatory ducts and prostate gland.

At the time of ejaculation the male releases a fluid called semen. The various components of semen (spermatozoa, epididymis fluid, and the fluids from the seminal vesicles and prostate gland) are ejaculated at slightly different times, resulting in their varying distribution in the ejaculate. Sperm cells, fluid from the epididymis, and prostate gland fluids appear in the early portions of the ejaculate, whereas secretions from the seminal vesicles appear in the final portion of the ejaculate. When ejaculation is frequent, a decrease occurs in volume but not in the relative concentrations of the different factors. The average volume of ejaculate per emission has been calculated at 3.5 milliliters with a range of 2 to 6 milliliters.

Do Preejaculatory Emissions Really Contain Sperm?

Many textbooks state that the preejaculatory emission occurring during sexual excitation before ejaculation contains sperm. We found only two studies that actually examined preejaculatory emissions for the presence of sperm. In one study no sperm cells were found in the pre-ejaculatory emission fluid from the Cowper's glands of 10 men (Hafez, 1976). On the other hand, Masters and Johnson (1966) state, "Frequently, active motile spermatozoa have been demonstrated in microscopic examination of preejaculatory fluids." However, Masters and Johnson do not reveal how many men were in the study or what percentage of the men studied had sperm cells in the preejaculatory emission. Evaluating Masters and Johnson's findings or comparing the two studies is therefore difficult. It is probably safe to say that coitus interruptus (withdrawal of the penis from the vagina before ejaculation) is a risky form of contraception and should not be used. It is certainly possible that preejaculatory emissions could contain sperm, particularly after a recent ejaculation. Thus urination should occur between acts of intercourse to flush sperm from the urethra if couples are using coitus interruptus as a method of contraception. When coitus interruptus fails to prevent conception, it is usually because the male failed to withdraw the penis from the vagina before ejaculation or because the male ejaculated on the female close to the entrance to the vagina.

FEMALE SEXUAL ANATOMY

The female reproductive system also consists of external and internal organs. The external genitalia are collectively known as the **vulva** and contain the labia majora, labia minora, clitoris, vestibule of the vagina, hymen, bulbs of the vestibule, Bartholin's glands, and mons pubis (Figure 3-7). The internal organs include the ovaries, fallopian tubes (oviducts), uterus, and vagina.

External Structures of the Female

Labia majora   Two prominent folds, the **labia majora** (also called the outer lips) are the boundaries of the vestibule of the vagina (Figure 3-7). These folds taper and decrease in size as they approach the anus, but anteriorly they blend into one another to form a rounded fatty structure called the mons pubis. The skin on the outer surface of each labium is pigmented and has hair. The inner surfaces are smooth and contain numerous glands.

Labia minora   Two small folds located between the labia majora are the **labia minora,** also called the inner lips (Figure 3-7). Their hairless skin is smooth and moist like the inner surfaces of the labia majora. The labia minora extend backward toward the anus and then disappear. In the region of the clitoris each labium divides to form the **prepuce or hood of the clitoris.** The structure of the labia minora varies from woman to woman as illustrated in Figure 3-8.

Clitoris   The **clitoris** contains two cylinders of erectile tissue rather than three as in the penis. These cylinders, called **corpora cavernosa clitoridis,** are enclosed in a thick fibrous membrane and become filled with blood during sexual excitation. The erectile tissue can be considered analogous to a sponge.

vulva
(VUHL vuh) External genitalia of female.

labia majora
(LAY bee uh muh JOR uh) Two folds of tissue lying on either side of vaginal orifice to form outermost borders of vulva.

labia minora
(LAY bee uh muh NOR uh) Two thin folds of tissue that lie within boundaries of labia majora and enclose vestibule of vagina.

prepuce or hood of clitoris
(PREE pyoos/KLIT uhr is) Fold of labia minora that covers clitoris.

clitoris
(KLIT uhr is) Small erectile structure located beneath prepuce that is very sensitive to sexual stimulation.

corpora cavernosa clitoridis
Two columns of erectile tissue within clitoris.

FIGURE 3-7
Vulva of the female.

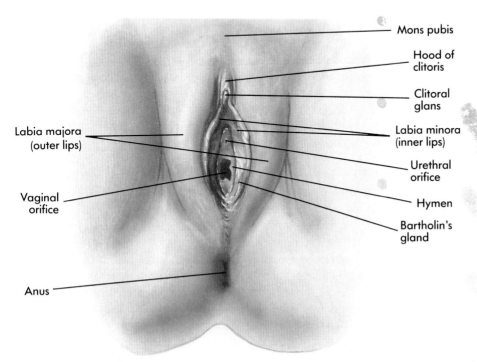

Mons pubis

Hood of clitoris

Clitoral glans

Labia minora (inner lips)

Urethral orifice

Hymen

Bartholin's gland

Labia majora (outer lips)

Vaginal orifice

Anus

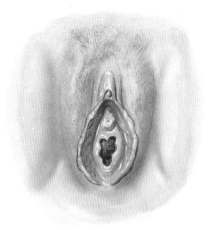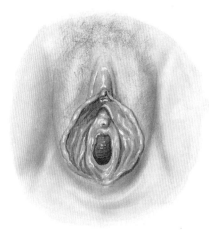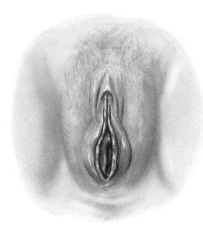

FIGURE 3-8
In the female, as in the male, there are variations in the appearance of external genitalia.

A network of blood vessels allows the tissue to fill with blood. Because the corpora cavernosa clitoridis are constricted by a fibrous membrane, the entire clitoris becomes swollen and hard when the erectile tissue fills with blood, the same mechanism that causes erection of the penis. The body or shaft of the clitoris is approximately 2.5 centimeters long, and the free end has a small rounded tip called the glans (Figure 3-7). Like the glans of the penis it is covered by an extensive network of nerves and is extremely sensitive. For many women the clitoris is the primary subjective focus of arousal (Masters and Johnson, 1966). In some societies the clitoris, sometimes with a portion of the labia minora, is removed around the time of puberty. This is discussed in the box on pp. 56 and 57.

Vestibule of the vagina   The opening between the labia minora is the **vestibule of the vagina.** When the labia minora are spread apart, the openings of the urethra, vagina, and ducts of the Bartholin's glands can be seen (Figure 3-7). The opening of the urethra is called the **urethral orifice** and is the outlet for urine. The vaginal opening is the **vaginal orifice** or vaginal introitus. **Bartholin's glands** are pea-size glands located on either side of the vaginal orifice. The glands were once thought to produce important amounts of lubrication for sexual intercourse, but the work of Masters and Johnson (1966) indicates that they do not produce enough fluid to be significant. The exact function of these glands is not known.

Hymen   A structure that was of great importance in the past as a sign of virginity is the **hymen** or **maidenhead** (Figures 3-7 and 3-9). The hymen is a thin membrane that covers the vaginal opening to various degrees in different women (Figure 3-7). If it completely covers the opening, the hymen usually has holes in it to allow the menstrual flow to pass out of the vagina. In rare cases it completely covers the vaginal opening and must be cut by a physician to allow the escape of menstrual flow. Some hymens allow sexual intercourse without tearing or discomfort. In other cases the hymen may be torn accidentally in nonsexual activities, such as horseback riding and bicycle riding. The presence of an intact hymen at first intercourse does not necessarily indicate virginity, nor does a lack of bleeding signify nonvirginity.

vestibule of the vagina
(ves tuh byool/vuh JY nuh)
Structure located between labia minora that houses urethral orifice and vaginal orifice.

urethral orifice
(yoo REE thruhl OR uh fis)
Outlet of urethra located in vestibule of vagina.

vaginal orifice
(VAJ uh nl OR uh fis)
Entrance to vagina located in vestibule of vagina.

Bartholin's glands
(BAR tl inz) Two small mucus-producing glands located on each side of vaginal orifice.

hymen or maidenhead
(HY muhn) Membrane that can cover vaginal orifice to various degrees.

 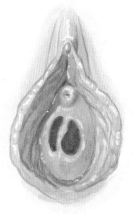  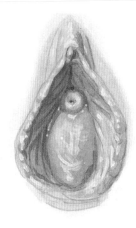

FIGURE 3-9
The hymen can cover the vaginal orifice to a various extent in different women.

Bulbs of the vestibule Elongated masses of erectile tissue that fit on either side of the vagina, the **bulbs of the vestibule** become filled with blood during sexual excitation (Figure 3-7). Muscles covering the bulbs of the vestibule can press the bulbs around the vaginal orifice. In this manner some women can constrict the vaginal orifice.

Mons pubis Also called the mons veneris or mound of Venus (after Venus, the Roman goddess of love), the **mons pubis** is a fatty cushion that rests on the anterior surface of the pubis (Figure 3-7).

Structures beneath the vulva If the skin and related structures of the vulva were removed, the bulbs of the vestibule and the **pubococcygeal muscles** would be visible (Figure 3-7). This muscle group, along with other pelvic muscles, supports all of the pelvic contents such as the bladder, rectum, and uterus in the female. In addition, the muscles act as sphincters to constrict or close the vaginal orifice, urethral orifice, and anus (O'Rahilly, 1983). The pubococcygeal muscles have received attention because Kegel stated that "sexual feeling within the vagina is closely related to muscle tone, and can be improved through muscle education and resistive exercise" (Kegel, 1952).

The Kegel exercises have been proposed for women after childbirth when the vagina loses some elasticity or for women who leak urine when they sneeze, cough, or have an orgasm. The woman identifies the muscles involved by deliberately stopping the flow of urine. After she has identified the muscles, she can begin to contract these muscles on a regular schedule. Some studies have suggested that continued exercise of these muscles increases the woman's sexual pleasure and allows her to exert muscular pressure on the penis of her partner (Barbach, 1975; Messe and Geer, 1985). However, Chambless and her colleagues (1982) found that the strength of the pubococcygeal muscles was not positively related to frequency of self-reported intensity of orgasm. In addition, women with higher pubococcygeal strength did not report that vaginal stimulation contributed more to attainment of orgasm or did not rate vaginal sensations during intercourse as more pleasurable (Chambless et al., 1982).

bulbs of the vestibule
(VES tuh byool') Masses of erectile tissue located on either side of vaginal orifice.

mons pubis
(monz pyoo bis) Pad of fatty tissue in pubic region.

pubococcygeal muscle
(pyoo boh kok SIJ ee uhl) Muscle that acts to constrict vaginal orifice, urethral orifice, and anus.

Female Circumcision or Clitoridectomy

Females in certain parts of the world undergo a type of circumcision before puberty. The term *circumcision* in this case is misleading. The prepuce or hood of the clitoris is not removed as the prepuce is removed in the male; instead, the entire clitoris and other closely related anatomical structures are removed. The practice of clitoridectomy (removal of the clitoris) has disappeared with the exception of some countries in Africa and to a lesser extent some cultures in the southern part of the Arabian Peninsula, Malaysia, and Indonesia (Mahran, 1978). Each country or culture uses its own technique of clitoridectomy according to religious, cultural, or folklore background. In the most conservative operation it is similar to a male circumcision. The prepuce or hood is removed along with a portion of the labia minora. This procedure saves the clitoris and has the fewest associated medical complications. Another type consists of removing the glans of the clitoris along with the adjacent parts of the labia minora. This is the most common type in Egypt. The most extreme form of clitoridectomy involves the removal of the entire clitoris, all of the labia minora, and part of the labia majora. The remaining outer edges of the labia majora are then brought together so that when the wound has healed, they are fused so as to leave a very small opening. This results in an artificially created "chastity belt" of thick fibrous tissue (Lightfoot-Klein, 1989). As a final step the vaginal opening is closed with sutures except for an opening about the size of a pinhole to allow the escape of menstrual flow and urine. The vagina is opened at the time of marriage and childbirth. This type of procedure is called a pharaonic circumcision (Mahran, 1978). Who carries out these circumcisions? Physicians sometimes do it, but most often it is done by nonmedical women who carry on the procedure as a family tradition. Some women are experienced, whereas others have limited skills. This is a traumatic experience; Mahran (1978) reports that the young girl often suffers shock, severe pain, bleeding, infection, and accidental damage to adjacent structures.

Female circumcision has psychosexual complications that affect the female and male. Mahran (1978) did an extensive study of 2,000 circumcised women in Egypt who had the glans and adjacent parts of the labia minora removed. Ten percent of the women had a feeling of "reduced femininity." They believed they were deprived of important parts of their reproductive structures and felt inferior psychologically and physically to women who were not circumcised. One third of the women had a less frequent desire for and decreased frequency of sexual intercourse. This percentage of women was significantly higher than women in the noncircumcised control group. The women reported painful intercourse, vaginismus (muscular spasms at the entrance to the vagina), and lack of orgasms compared with noncircumcised women. The circumcised women had a divorce rate of 6% compared with 1% in noncircumcised women. Mahran (1981) concluded that the psychological and physical complications for the women in the study can be an important cause of divorce.

Many husbands of the circumcised women had sexual dysfunctions including different grades of erectile dysfunction or sexual impotence and premature ejaculation. This was not found in the control groups. Mahran thought that this was caused by painful intercourse and vaginismus in their wives. The husbands had a higher rate of extramarital sex, which probably contributes to the high divorce rate for couples in which the wife has had a circumcision.

The truly drastic long-term consequences of pharaonic circumcision are discussed by Lightfoot-Klein (1989). She interviewed 300 Sudanese women and 100 Sudanese men over a 5-year period. This procedure is performed on girls between the ages of 4 and 8. In rural areas the procedure is done without the aid of anesthesia or antiseptic conditions, but in urban areas it is done in a cliniclike setting by medical personnel.

Lightfoot-Klein states that urination is usually difficult and often takes a long time to accomplish because of the pinhole-sized opening. Urine may accumulate behind the opening and cause recurrent urinary tract infections. Menstruation is difficult, painful, and greatly prolonged and produces odors because of the retention of menstrual blood behind the opening. Infections are frequent following menstruation.

At the time of marriage the husband opens the infibulation (closing or fastening) with a little knife. He enlarges the tear with his penis over a period of days, weeks, or months until the hole is large enough to allow intercourse (Lightfoot-Klein, 1989). At the time of birth the opening of the infibulation must be made larger to allow passage of the baby. After birth the woman is infibulated again and the process of reopening by the husband for intercourse must be repeated. The cycle is repeated each time a child is born.

We see the process of pharaonic circumcision as repulsive and damaging to the health and well-being of the women in Sudan. However, the people in Sudan, both men and women, see it as an important part of their culture. The Sudanese believe that this ritual purifies and ennobles women. As Lightfoot-Klein states, "Its staunchest defenders are its survivors, self-assured, respected old women, who choose to inflict the most extreme mutilations on their granddaughters, in order to optimally enhance their value [the granddaughters] as a family commodity and to insure a favorable marriage for them" (1989, p. 89).

The pharaonic circumcision has been practiced for centuries, and as Lightfoot-Klein states, it "distinguished 'decent' and respectable women from unprotected prostitutes and slaves, and it carries with it the only honorable, dignified and protected status that is possible for a woman in the society. Without circumcision a girl cannot marry. . . . [An] unmarried woman has virtually no rights and practically does not exist as a social entity" (1989, p. 81). Chastity and sexual purity are the major motives for circumcision. It ensures that the woman will remain a virgin until marriage.

Many organizations, including the World Health Organization (WHO) and the United Nations International Children's Emergency Fund (UNICEF), oppose female circumcision. Both of these organizations, in collaboration with the heads of state of various countries, have developed programs against this and other harmful practices that affect the health and well-being of women and children (Ladjali and Toubia, 1990). In the past, laws against the practice of female circumcision were passed but were of little value, since they were both ignored and not enforced. As Ladjali and Toubia state, "Among the many lessons learned, the most important are that people cannot be forced into social change by passing laws" (1990, p. 2). The means for correcting practices harmful to women and children appears to lie in education and improving the status of women in countries where female circumcision is practiced.

Internal Structures of the Female

The internal organs of the female are the ovaries, fallopian tubes (oviducts), uterus, and vagina (Figures 3-10 and 3-11). The ovaries are the female gonads, which produce ova or eggs and the female hormones estrogen and progesterone. The oviducts conduct the ova from the ovaries to the uterus. The site of fertilization, if it occurs, is the oviduct. The fertilized egg usually implants in the uterus, where development of the embryo and fetus takes place. The vagina is the connection of the uterus to the exterior of the body.

Ovaries Paired structures that lie against the lateral pelvic walls, the **ovaries** are about the size of a walnut in a woman of childbearing age and become smaller later in life (Figures 3-10 and 3-11). The ovary is attached to the uterus by various ligaments, and other ligaments and tissues attach the ovary to the wall of the pelvis. The ovaries produce the female gametes and the female hormones estrogen and progesterone.

Fallopian tubes The **fallopian tubes**, also called the oviducts, extend from the ovaries to the uterus and are approximately 4 inches long (Figures

The topic of egg production by ovaries is presented in Chapter 4.

ovaries
(OH vuh reez) Paired structures located in pelvis that produce eggs and female hormones.

fallopian tubes
(fuh LOH pee uhn) Short tubes, also called oviducts, that connect ovaries with uterus.

FIGURE 3-10
Section through the pelvis
of the female.

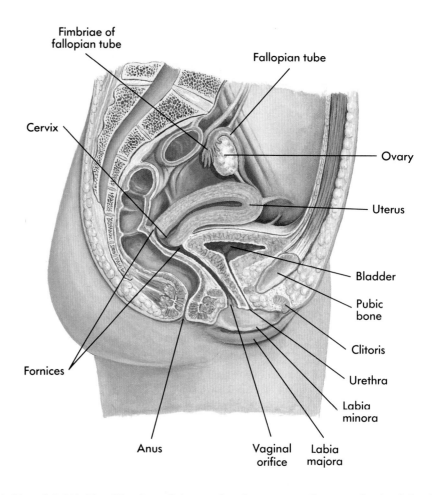

Fimbriae of
fallopian tube

Fallopian tube

Cervix

Ovary

Uterus

Bladder

Pubic
bone

Clitoris

Urethra

Labia
minora

Fornices

Anus

Vaginal
orifice

Labia
majora

fimbriae
(FIM bree ee′) Fingerlike
projections that form fringe
around entrance to fallopian
tubes.

cilia
(SIL ee uh) Hairlike pro-
cesses found in various parts
of the body.

**Discussion of pregnancies
"outside" the reproductive
tract is in Chapter 6.**

**Discussion of tubal ligation
as a contraceptive method
is provided in Chapter 8.**

uterus
(yoo tuhr uhs) Hollow, muscular, pear-shaped structure
that is organ for containing
and nourishing developing
embryo and fetus.

3-10 and 3-11). Fertilization of the egg by the sperm cell occurs in the fallopian tubes. Each tube runs over the top of the ovary, where it becomes a funnel-like structure formed by many irregular fringed and branched portions called **fimbriae**. This structure covers most of the surface of the ovary, and one large process clings to or covers the top of the ovary. Within the funnel is the opening of the fallopian tube. The ova or eggs released from the surface of the ovary are swept or drawn into this opening by **cilia** that line the surface of the oviduct (Page et al., 1981). The ova must travel through an open space between the surface of the ovary and the opening of the tube, and thus it is possible for an ovum not to reach the opening of the tube. In some cases a fertilized egg moves back toward the ovary and "falls" into the pelvic area out of the reproductive tract. In a method of contraception called a tubal ligation the oviducts are blocked or cut so that the ova are prevented from meeting the sperm.

Uterus Commonly called the womb, the **uterus** is a muscular, pear-shaped organ that projects into the vagina at the cervix (Figures 3-10 and 3-11). The fertilized egg normally implants in the uterus, and the development of the embryo and fetus takes place in this organ. The uterus can be displaced or moved upward by the upper surface of a full bladder, and the converse is also true. During pregnancy the uterus, as a result of the growing fetus, exerts pressure on the bladder. This causes frequent urination in many women during

58   **HUMAN SEXUALITY**

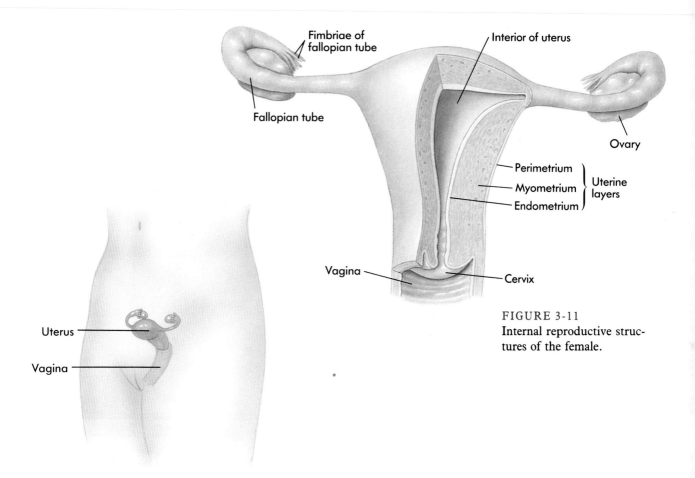

Fimbriae of
fallopian tube

Interior of uterus

Fallopian tube

Ovary

Perimetrium
Myometrium   } Uterine layers
Endometrium

Uterus

Vagina

Vagina

Cervix

FIGURE 3-11
Internal reproductive structures of the female.

different stages of pregnancy. More frequent urination in early pregnancy is caused by increased pressure on the bladder from the expanding uterus. This symptom tends to disappear as the uterus increases in size and rises upward toward the abdomen and away from the bladder. Frequent urination occurs again toward the end of pregnancy when the head of the fetus drops downward into the region of the pelvis. Figure 3-10 illustrates the anatomical relationship between the uterus and bladder.

The uterus is divided into three distinct layers: **perimetrium** (outer layer), **myometrium** (muscular layer), and **endometrium** (inner layer). The myometrium is arranged in a circular fashion so that contractions of the uterus cause a downward movement to bear on any contents of the uterus. The endometrium is a thin glandular tissue lining the cavity of the uterus. It consists of numerous glands and an extensive network of blood vessels. A portion of endometrium is shed during the menstrual flow.

Vagina   A tube composed of muscle and membranes, the **vagina** extends from the vaginal orifice to the cervix. Its upper end surrounds the vaginal portion of the cervix in such a way that small pouches called **fornices** exist between the wall of the vagina and the cerivx. The fornices allow the internal pelvic and abdominal organs to be indirectly felt during a medical examination (Figure 3-11). The vagina has a mucous coat continuous with that of the uterus.

perimetrium
(per' uh MEE tree uhm)
Outer covering of uterus.

myometrium
(my uh MEE tree uhm)
Muscular layer of uterus.

endometrium
(en doh MEE tree uhm) Mucous membrane lining of inner surface of uterus.

vagina
(vuh JY nuh) Muscular membranous tube that connects cervix of uterus with vulva.

fornices
(FOR ni seez) Structures with vaultlike or arched shape.

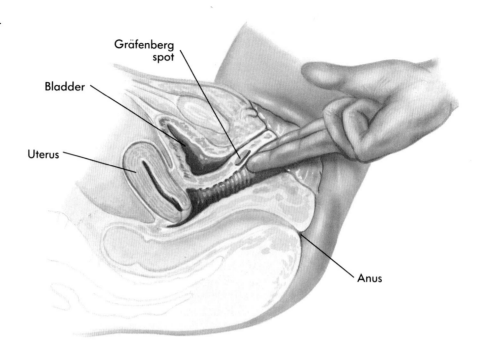

FIGURE 3-12
According the some sexologists, the Gräfenberg spot (G spot) is located on the upper surface of the front of the vagina.

Gräfenberg spot

Bladder

Uterus

Anus

menses
(MEN seez) Monthly blood flow from uterus.

A thin layer of erectile tissue separates the mucous and muscle coats. Unless something is introduced into the vagina, the walls touch each other and only a *potential cavity* exists. The vagina is the female organ of copulation and recipient of semen. Menstrual products pass through the vagina from the uterus at the time of **menses,** and the baby passes through the vagina at the time of birth. Urine does not pass through the vagina. The walls of the vagina are rather insensitive, but the entrance of the vagina is highly sensitive to stimulation. One supposed area of sensitivity within the vagina is called the Gräfenberg spot (see the accompanying box and Figure 3-12).

Female Ejaculation and the G Spot: Fact or Fiction?

When her loins begin to shake, and when there is "trembling between her anus and cunnus," the girl is about to have her orgasm. Lifting of the loins . . . is the signal of ecstatic crisis and "complete happiness" followed by a violent throbbing of the vagina and a torrential burst of fluid (Edwards and Masters, 1963, p. 118). The description of a flood of fluid at orgasm in the female such as that above may be found in past literary works as well as present-day popular magazines dealing with sexual behaviors and activities. The implication is that the female is expelling or ejaculating a fluid at the time of orgasm. Is this just literary imagination? Or did the writer personally experience the phenomenon or observe it during sexual activities?

Gräfenberg's G Spot

In 1950 Ernst Gräfenberg stated that some women expelled large quantities of a clear fluid from the urethra during orgasm. He noted an area on the anterior wall of the vagina (at the front and upward in the vagina) that was sensitive to the touch. Stimulation of this area, he believed, caused fluid release at orgasm. This area is now called the Gräfenberg spot or G spot (Figure 3-12). Our present knowledge indicates that this general area contains the paraurethral glands or Skene's glands. They are located close to the urethral orifice where it opens into the vestibule of the vagina. These small vestigial (remnant of something formerly present or more fully developed) glands are derived from the same tissue in the embryo that gives rise to a portion of the male prostate gland. In fact, some researchers call the Skene's glands the "female prostate gland." If in some women fluid is expelled at orgasm through the urethra, does the fluid come from these glands? Probably not.

Other Research

In 1981 the topic of female ejaculation, or orgasmic expulsion, was again being discussed in talk shows, popular magazines, and books. Research papers concerned with female ejaculation were published in the *Journal of Sex Research* in 1981 (Addiego et al., 1981; Perry and Whipple, 1981). They in fact appeared in the same issue, and Perry and Whipple were authors or coauthors of both of them as well as a book (Ladas, Whipple, and Perry, 1982). In *The G Spot and Other Recent Discoveries About Human Sexuality*, Ladas, Whipple, and Perry claim that all 400 women examined in the sample had a G spot. According to the authors the fluid was not urine but contained glucose and an enzyme called prostatic acid phosphatase, which is found in the prostatic component of semen. Substances such as urea and creatinine, which are found in urine, were also found in the fluid produced at orgasm. These papers, however, have been severely criticized for their poor methodology and small sample sizes, including one paper with a sample of one woman. A more recent study of five women determined that the composition of the fluid expelled during heightened sexual arousal (it was not stated whether orgasm occurred, and the sites of stimulation varied from the G spot, the clitoris, and the "neck of the urinary bladder and posterior urethra") resembled prostatic secretions (Zaviacic et al., 1988b). The authors state that the "higher fructose level in the ejaculate than in urine [of the same women] suggests that the female ejaculate cannot simply be regarded as urine, although urine is a regular component of urethral expulsion" (Zaviacic et al., 1988b). Fructose is the largest component of the male ejaculate.

While some studies have failed to provide evidence supporting the idea of a discrete area of heightened sensitivity on the anterior wall of the vagina (Goldberg et al., 1983; Alzate and Londono, 1984), one study did claim to find that 27 women out of 27 had a sensitive site on the anterior wall of the vagina, that is, the site of the G spot (Zaviacic et al., 1988a). When the researchers exerted some pressure on the anterior wall of the vagina with one or two fingers or used a vibrator, a detectable swelling developed at the site of stimulation. When stimulation was continued, 37% of the women produced a urethral expulsion of fluid with or without orgasm. This is the first report that expulsion of fluid can occur without orgasm.

Conclusion

What can we conclude from the available data on orgasmic expulsion? Masters and Johnson (1966) in their work on the sexual response cycle reported that at orgasm "a small number of women who had given birth one or more times expressed some concept of having an actual fluid emission or of expending in some concrete fashion." Masters and Johnson further state: "Previous male interpretation of these subjective reports may have resulted in the erroneous but widespread concept that female ejaculation is an integral part of the female orgasmic expression." We must assume that Masters and Johnson did not objectively note, record, or photograph this phenomenon in the 382 women in their study. This does not mean orgasmic expulsion does not exist; instead we must await further objective empirical evidence from different laboratories and clinics for the existence of this phenomenon. It is probably safe to say that some women experience expulsion of some type of fluid during heightened sexual arousal or at orgasm, just as some women experience multiple orgasms on a regular basis. Individual differences in anatomical and psychological variables contribute to the wide range and diversity of the human sexual response.

MAMMARY GLANDS

The mammary glands are not involved in the procreation process; however, they are important for the maintenance of offspring because they secrete milk for the nourishment of the infant. The mammary glands are modified sweat glands that lie in the fatty tissue under the skin (Figure 3-13). The breasts have a circular pigmented area called the areola, which surrounds the nipple. The mature female breast consists of glandular tissue embedded in fibrous and connective tissue infiltrated with fat. Each breast is divided into 15 to 20 lobes. Every lobe is drained via a milk duct, and each duct passes to the nipple. The surface of the nipple has 15 to 20 pinpoint openings for milk release. The left breast is usually bigger than the right breast. Some hair may be present around the nipple. The nipple contains erectile tissue and becomes erect if the woman is sexually stimulated or is exposed to cool temperature. Because breasts are composed of glandular tissue infiltrated with fat, they *cannot* be enlarged through exercise. However, the muscles beneath the breasts can be developed through exercise, and this promotes firm-looking breasts. Advertisements that promise increases in breast size through exercises or creams should be viewed with skepticism. Most women are happy with their breast size.

The mammary glands change in size and shape during both the life cycle

FIGURE 3-13
Internal anatomy of the breast.

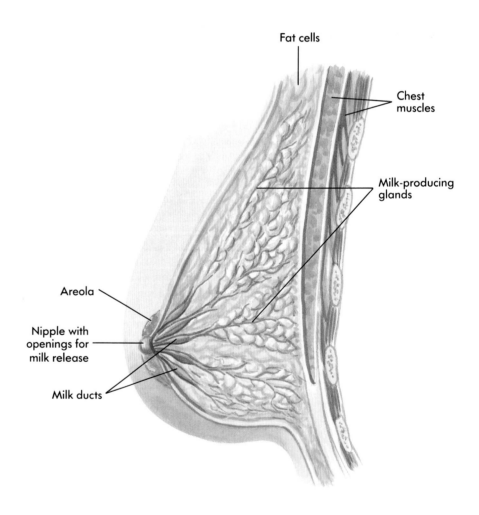

Fat cells

Chest muscles

Milk-producing glands

Areola

Nipple with openings for milk release

Milk ducts

and the menstrual cycle. At puberty marked growth occurs, and during each menstrual cycle the gland fluctuates in size as a result of cyclical hormonal changes. During pregnancy the breasts greatly enlarge with the formation of new glandular tissue. After menopause the glands atrophy because of the lack of hormonal stimulation.

The lymphatic drainage (the drainage of fluids from among cells) of the mammary glands has important implications because of the relatively high incidence of cancer of the mammary glands as compared with other sites in the female. The lymphatic network located throughout the body can spread the cancer cells to other parts of the body through **metastasis**. The need for monthly breast self-examinations is important to detect any changes in breast configuration, which can be indicative of cancer.

metastasis
(muh TAS tuh sis) Movement of cells from one part of the body to another.

PRENATAL DEVELOPMENT OF THE MALE AND FEMALE REPRODUCTIVE SYSTEMS

The genetic sex of each individual is established at **fertilization** when the sperm and egg unite. Half of all sperm cells carry an X **chromosome**, and the other half carry a Y chromosome. At fertilization the sex-determining chromosomes (X and Y) start the "program" that will determine the development of a male or female (Figure 3-14). Two X chromosomes (XX) in the fertilized egg (one contributed by the sperm cell and one by the egg) begin the differentiation of a female. One X chromosome and one Y chromosome (XY) in the fertilized egg (the X contributed by the egg and the Y by the sperm) start the development of a male. In most cases the process of growth and differentiation goes according to plan: a genetic female (XX) is born with the appropriate internal and external reproductive structures, and a genetic male (XY) is born with male reproductive organs. Even though genetic sex is established at fertilization, the influence of

The method for monthly breast self-examination as suggested by the American Cancer Society is presented in Chapter 17.

fertilization
(fir tuhl uh ZAY shuhn) Union of egg and sperm cell, which usually takes place in fallopian tubes.

chromosome
(KROH muh sohm') A structure in the nucleus of a cell containing genetic information.

Sex Chromosomes: Too Many and Too Few

The abnormalities of the sex chromosomes, X and Y, in humans involve either the loss of one chromosome or the addition of extra chromosomes. It is possible to have only one sex chromosome, but it must be the X chromosome as in Turner's syndrome, indicated by the expression 45,XO. The 45 indicates that each cell has only 45 total chromosomes instead of the normal 46 and that there is only one sex chromosome, an X. The O indicates the absence of a second sex chromosome. The loss of an X chromosome from an XY combination is lethal, and no human being has ever been found with a 45,OY combination.

Individuals with Turner's syndrome look like females with short stature, lack ovaries (hence are sterile), and may have some impairment of intelligence. Individuals with 47,XXX, 47,XXY, and 47,XYY have been identified. The 47,XXX individual looks like a female, and the 47,XXY and 47,XYY look like males. Males with 47,XXY genetic information in each cell are said to have Klinefelter's syndrome. An individual with this often-studied condition looks like a male with some breast development, small testes, and impaired intelligence.

We can state that the absence of a Y sex chromosome in humans produces an individual with a female body type and that the presence of a Y sex chromosome leads to the development of a male body type.

FIGURE 3-14
External genital differentiation in the human.

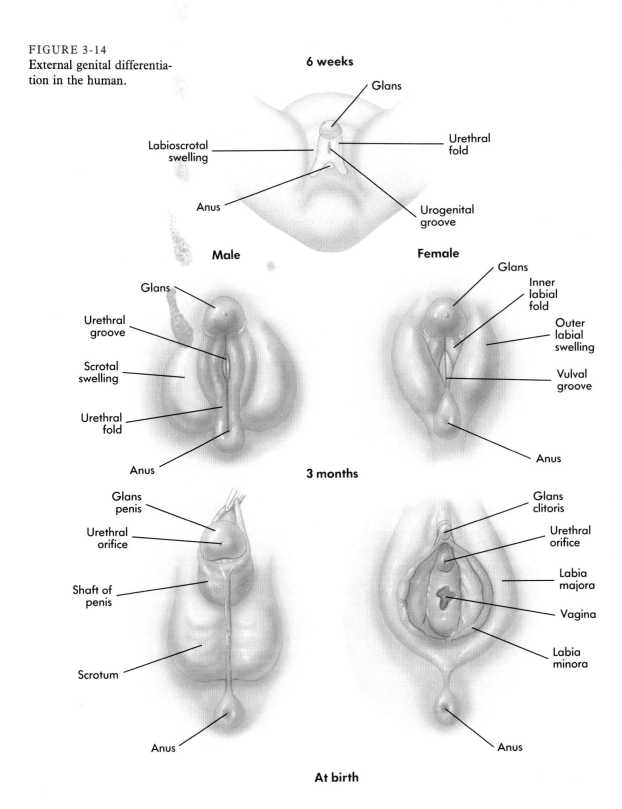

6 weeks

Glans

Labioscrotal
swelling

Urethral
fold

Anus

Urogenital
groove

Male

Female

Glans

Urethral
groove

Scrotal
swelling

Urethral
fold

Anus

Glans

Inner
labial
fold

Outer
labial
swelling

Vulval
groove

Anus

3 months

Glans
penis

Urethral
orifice

Shaft of
penis

Scrotum

Anus

Glans
clitoris

Urethral
orifice

Labia
majora

Vagina

Labia
minora

Anus

At birth

the sex-determining chromosomes is not evident until approximately the seventh week of embryonic development. Until this time the genetic male and the genetic female look the same (Figure 3-14). Sexual differentiation begins with the gonads (testes or ovaries), followed by changes in the internal structures and finally development of the external male or female genitals.

The gonads, whether ovaries in the female or testes in the male, have a common beginning. Therefore they are said to be **homologous structures**. They develop from exactly the same common embryonic tissue. This undifferentiated gonad has two parts: an inner portion called the medulla and an outer portion named the cortex. If the genetic sex is male, the medullary portion of the primitive gonad develops and the cortical portion degenerates and almost disappears. This pattern is reversed in the female; the cortical portion develops and the medullary portion degenerates. The process of differentiation in the male begins about 7 weeks after conception and is thought to be directed by the presence of the Y chromosome (Oppenheimer and LeFevre, 1984).

In addition to the gonads developing as ovaries or testes, other reproductive organs begin to change from an undifferentiated state into a male or female condition. Both the male and female have two paired duct systems present between the fifth and sixth weeks of pregnancy. These are the *müllerian duct system* and the *wolffian duct system*. By the eighth week after fertilization a chemical known as müllerian duct–inhibiting substance begins circulating in the blood of the male, causing the müllerian ducts to shrink and almost disappear. Simultaneously, male hormones from the embryo's testes activate the development of the wolffian ducts to give rise to the epididymis, vas deferens, seminal vesicles, prostate gland, and ejaculatory ducts. Male hormones also stimulate the development of the penis and scrotum. In the female fetus, sexual differentiation is thought not to depend on hormones. The female gonads usually develop about the twelfth week after fertilization, and the müllerian duct system gives rise to the uterus, oviducts, and inner third of the vagina (Figure 3-15 and Table 3-1).

Before the fourteenth week of development the embryo (or fetus) has one pair of gonads, two sets of ducts, and undeveloped external genitalia. Without any hormonal stimulation the embryo and then the fetus will develop as a female. Thus the inborn program of sexual differentiation is female unless the fetus has testes secreting hormones that program "malelike" differentiation of the original bisexual or inherently female embryo or fetus (Money and Ehrhardt, 1973).

Money and Ehrhardt state:

> In the total absence of fetal gonadal hormones, the fetus always continues to differentiate the reproductive anatomy of a female. Ovarian hormones are, according to present evidence, irrelevant at this early stage. Testicular hormones are imperative for the continuing differentiation of the reproductive structures of a male.
> Money and Ehrhardt, 1973, p. 2

The growth of the female müllerian duct system is suppressed in the male when müllerian duct–inhibiting substance is present, and the male wolffian duct system under the influence of androgens becomes the internal male reproductive system. Subsequently, fetal male hormones induce the rest of the internal and external reproductive structures into the male pattern. Highest levels of fetal male hormones occur during the first 3 months of pregnancy

homologous structures (hoh MOL uh guhs) Structures that are similar in developmental origin.

In terms of prenatal development, it is customary to call the product of conception an embryo from the second to the eighth weeks of development. From the eighth week until birth it is referred to as a fetus.

FIGURE 3-15
Differentiation of internal
reproductive structures in
the human.

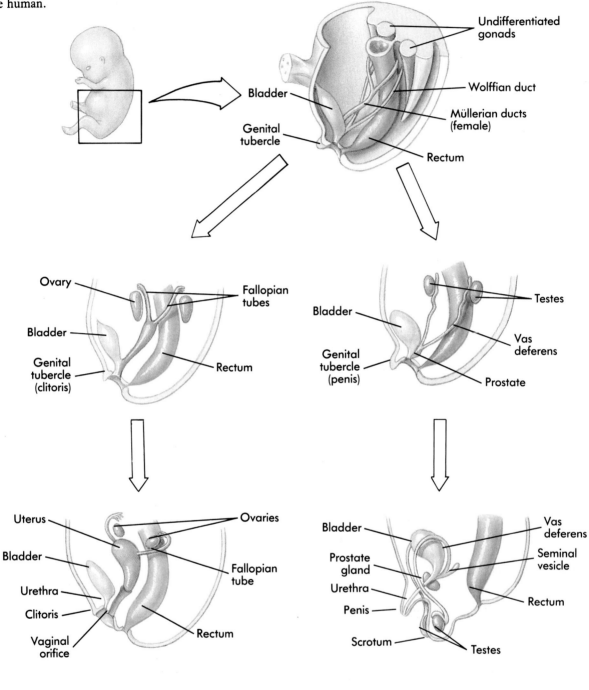

Undifferentiated
gonads

Wolffian duct

Müllerian ducts
(female)

Bladder

Genital
tubercle

Rectum

Ovary

Fallopian
tubes

Bladder

Genital
tubercle
(clitoris)

Rectum

Testes

Bladder

Vas
deferens

Genital
tubercle
(penis)

Prostate

Uterus

Ovaries

Bladder

Fallopian
tube

Urethra

Clitoris

Rectum

Vaginal
orifice

Bladder

Vas
deferens

Prostate
gland

Seminal
vesicle

Urethra

Penis

Rectum

Scrotum

Testes

Female

Male

TABLE 3-1 Undifferentiated Tissues and Development of Male and Female Reproductive Systems

Undifferentiated tissue	Female structure	Male structure
INTERNAL STRUCTURES		
Gonad	Ovary	Testis
Wolffian duct system	Undeveloped or rudimentary structures	Epididymis Vas deferens Ejaculatory ducts Seminal vesicles
Müllerian duct system	Oviducts Uterus Portion of vagina	Undeveloped or rudimentary structures
Urogenital sinus	Urethra Vestibule of vagina Portion of vagina Bartholin's glands	Urethra Cowper's glands Prostate gland
EXTERNAL GENITALIA		
Genital tubercle	Glans clitoris Corpus (body or shaft) clitoris	Glans penis Corpus (body) penis
Urethral folds	Labia minora	Raphe (midline fusion) of scrotum and penis
Labioscrotal swellings	Labia majora	Scrotum

Modified from Nalbandov, 1976.

(Wilson, 1981). This appears to be the critical period for differentiation of reproductive structures.

In summary, if the genetic sex is female, the cortical portion of the gonad develops and the medullary portion regresses. This process occurs between the tenth and twelfth weeks of pregnancy. The male wolffian duct system regresses, and the female müllerian duct system differentiates into the internal female reproductive system. Subsequently, the rest of the internal and external reproductive structures develop into the female pattern. Female hormones are produced by the gonads; however, they are not necessary for the female structures to differentiate. Although males and females are anatomically different at birth, their reproductive structures develop from the same tissues during embryonic and fetal life. The presence of male hormones before birth causes the fetus to develop male anatomical structures, and the absence of male hormones allows the fetus to develop female anatomical structures.

HUMANS AND PRENATAL HORMONES

Numerous studies with rats, mice, and monkeys have shown that a female who is exposed to male hormones before birth (prenatal period) will look like a male in terms of external genitalia at the time of birth. Female animals subjected to male hormones prenatally act more like males in adult sexual behavior, aggressive behavior, maternal behavior, and play behavior (Quadagno, Briscoe, and Quadagno, 1977).

What about human females exposed to male hormones during the prenatal period? Do such females exist? In fact, two situations occur in which human female fetuses are exposed to prenatal male hormones and have malelike (virilized) genitalia at birth. In all cases they are genetic females with two X chromosomes and have the internal structures of a female (ovaries, oviducts, uterus, and vagina). Their external genitalia consists of an enlarged clitoris and a fusion of the labia majora and labia minora so that there is no opening to the vagina. In rare cases the virilization is so great that the clitoris becomes a penis and the labia fuse to form a normal but empty scrotum.

One condition in which females are exposed prenatally to male hormones is the **adrenogenital syndrome** (the male hormones called androgens are produced in large quantities from the fetus' overactive adrenal glands). Another situation of excess male hormones before birth occurs in females whose mothers received progesterone injections during pregnancy. The synthetic hormone progesterone (once thought to be needed to maintain pregnancies in women who have had or threaten to have miscarriages) had a virilizing effect on the fetus because it was chemically changed to androgen in the mother's body. Actually there has been no documentation that treatment with synthetic progestins prevents miscarriages (Wentz, 1977), and progesterone is no longer used in women who may have miscarriages. Thus the adrenogenital syndrome and the **progesterone-induced hermaphroditism** syndrome produce genetic females with female internal reproductive organs and virilized external reproductive structures. The photographs on the following page represent two children who are genetic females with adrenogenital syndrome. At birth the children had ambiguous external genitalia (enlarged clitoris and some fusion of the labia, which concealed the vagina). Despite the fact that both females had the same genetic (female), gonadal (female), and fetal hormonal (male) components, one child was raised as a female and one was raised as a male because of different medical opinions.

Numerous papers report that females exposed prenatally to male hormones are more like males in their social behaviors, including play behaviors, lack of interest in taking care of infants, clothes preferences, and even sexual orientation (prenatally exposed children have some homosexual preferences). This finding has been reported by researchers in the United States, Germany, and Russia (Money and Ehrhardt, 1972; Dittmann, Kappes, and Kappes, 1991). In an often quoted paper Quadagno, Briscoe, and Quadagno (1977) point out that the influence of prenatal hormonal exposure cannot be separated from

Mild virilization of female genitalia.

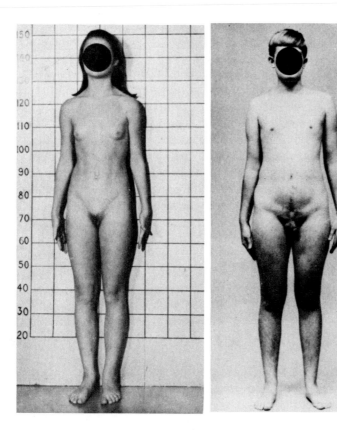

Two females with adreno-
genital syndrome. Both are
genetic females; however,
one was raised as a male
and the other as a female.

psychosocial influences. The children exposed to excess prenatal hormones also had ambiguous genitalia. It is quite likely that girls with undeveloped penises were treated differently by their parents than normal girls. Thus, although the later behaviors of the girls were more masculine, it is impossible to tell whether this masculinization was by the hormonal exposure or by parental response to daughters they perceived as tomboys. Dittmann, Kappes, and Kappes (1991) acknowledge the possibility of social factors influencing the change in behaviors seen in females exposed to prenatal androgens.

Many authors still quote this research on prenatal exposure and later be- haviors—which implies that the brain undergoes some type of virilization like the genitalia—without questioning whether the findings are truly accurate. Asserting that the brain can become masculinized is making a big assumption that has yet to be proved.

The cases of the adrenogenital syndrome and progestin-induced hermaph- roditism illustrate three important concepts. First, sexual differentiation of the reproductive structures is under hormonal control. Second, female external reproductive tissues exposed to male hormones during prenatal development differentiate into malelike structures. Third, because of timing the male hor- mones were not present in the early portion of the pregnancy to influence the development of the internal reproductive organs in either the females with the adrenogenital syndrome or those with the progestin-induced hermaphroditism syndrome. The question as to whether the brain undergoes a differentiation like the reproductive structures remains unanswered.

SUMMARY

1 The external male reproductive structures consist of the penis and scrotum. The penis is the organ of copulation and has an extensive nerve supply, which makes it sensitive to stimulation. The penis contains erectile tissue that becomes filled with blood to create an erection. The testes are within the scrotum, which keeps them at a temperature of about 5° F below the core body temperature to facilitate sperm production.

2 The internal male reproductive structures are the testes, epididymis, vas deferens, seminal vesicles, ejaculatory ducts, prostate gland, and Cowper's glands. Sperm are produced in the testes and travel through the epididymis to the vas deferens where they mature. At the time of ejaculation, sperm from the vas deferens are mixed with secretions from the seminal vesicles and prostate gland to compose semen. The testes also produce male hormones.

3 The external female reproductive structures are collectively known as the vulva. The vulva comprises the labia majora, labia minora, clitoris, vestibule of the vagina, hymen, bulbs of the vestibule, Bartholin's glands, and mons pubis. The clitoris is richly endowed with nerves and is sensitive to stimulation. The clitoris contains erectile tissue, which fills with blood during sexual excitation. The opening of the vagina is partially covered by the hymen.

4 The internal female reproductive structures consist of the ovaries, oviducts, uterus, and vagina. The ovaries produce eggs and female hormones. The oviducts conduct the eggs to the uterus, a hollow muscular organ, part of which protrudes into the vagina. The vagina has a rich nerve supply at its opening but not in its walls.

5 The breasts are modified sweat glands that produce milk.

6 Under normal conditions, differentiation of the male and female reproductive systems in the fetus before birth depends on the presence or absence of male hormones from the testes. If these hormones are present, the fetus develops internal and external male reproductive structures. If they are absent, the fetus develops as a female.

F A C T
OR
F I C T I O N

ANSWERS

1. The American Academy of Pediatrics has a neutral position on circumcision of newborn boys. The academy feels that circumcision has some medical advantages but that the procedure also carries some risks to the newborn.

2. It has been proved that wearing tight-fitting underwear in hot weather causes summer sterility in some men. Tight-fitting underwear prevents the testes from moving away from the core of the body, thus causing testicular temperatures to rise. Sperm cells are extremely sensitive and undergo abnormal changes incompatible with fertilization when subjected to temperatures equal to or greater than body temperature.

3. The absence of an intact hymen at first sexual intercourse does not indicate that the woman is not a virgin; the hymen can be ruptured by many kinds of nonsexual activities.

1. If you had a male child, or if friends asked you if they should have their child circumcised, what would you say about having your child or your friends' child circumcised? Explain your answer.

2. What does the term *homologous structures* mean? Name four structures in the male and female that are homologous.

3. Design an experiment to determine whether preejaculatory emissions contain sperm cells.

SUGGESTED READINGS

Boston Women's Health Book Collective: Our bodies, ourselves, New York, 1984, Simon & Schuster, Inc.
   A very readable book concerned with all aspects of female sexuality and health. A good section on female anatomy is included.
Romberg, R. Circumcision: the painful dilemma, South Hadley, Mass., 1985, Bergin & Garvey Publishers, Inc.
   A well-written book that opposes routine circumcision but presents both sides of the argument.
Thibodeau, G., and Patton, K.: Structure and function of the body, ed. 9, St. Louis, 1991, Mosby–Year Book, Inc.
   A beautifully illustrated anatomy and physiology textbook appropriate for the nonscience major. The section on reproduction is excellent.

4

Sexual Physiology and Behavior

FACT
OR
FICTION

1
Some women synchronize menstrual cycles with other women.

2
Castration of a male does not always reduce his sex drive.

3
The menstrual cycle has a negative effect on athletic performance.

4
Engaging in sexual activities before a sporting event will hurt athletic performance in men.

Memory and anticipation are as peculiarly human attributes as humor, guilt, generosity and pride, and they confuse the simple cause and effect relationship of the senses (hearing, touch, sound, sight and smell) on . . . physiologic processes.

S. STURGIS
"Psychophysiologic Disorders and Ovulatory Failure," p. 40

The opening quotation points out that basic physiological functioning, including reproductive processes, is governed by brain areas involved in the highest levels of learning and associations. The two studies that follow illustrate the brain's profound influence on reproductive physiology.

Twenty men who had difficulty maintaining an erection were treated with either a hormone that indirectly causes the testicles to produce male hormones or a placebo (sterile water). Both groups of men reported an improvement in their sexual activity. Their reports of erection difficulties were less, and both the hormone group and the placebo group reported that their performance during sexual intercourse showed significant improvement (Benkert et al., 1975).

Ovulation is the release of an egg from the ovary each month. Ovulation is taken for granted, yet some women do not ovulate, even though all medical tests indicate the women are normal in terms of hormone production and reproductive structures. These women are often treated with Clomid, a drug that has been effective in inducing ovulation. Sixty-two women who were judged to be good candidates for Clomid were divided into groups. One group of 31 received Clomid, while the other group of 31 received a placebo (sugar pills). Both groups were told that they were receiving a very effective drug to induce ovulation. The results showed that 48% of the women receiving Clomid ovulated and 42% of the women receiving the placebo ovulated. Both groups responded in the same manner (Connaughton et al., 1974).

The previous two clinical studies show that reproductive functioning is governed by both the brain and the reproductive system. In both cases some individuals responded to the placebo as if they had received medication. Obviously the brain and associated thought processes were important in mediating the body's responses to the placebo.

To understand the examples just discussed and to learn about the normal functioning of the reproductive systems in the male and female, we need to look at the relationship between the brain and the reproductive system. To do this we must briefly discuss the sciences of endocrinology and neuroendocrinology.

BRAIN CONTROL OF THE REPRODUCTIVE SYSTEM
Endocrinology

Endocrinology is the study of the endocrine glands and their products. Endocrine glands do not have **ducts.** They empty their products directly into the bloodstream. In contrast, sweat glands have ducts and empty their products, sweat, onto the skin surface. Hormones, the chemical messages produced by

endocrinology
(en doh kri NOL uh jee)
Study of endocrine glands of body and the hormones they produce.

duct
(duhkt) A tube for the passage of secretions.

TABLE 4-1 Gonadotropin and Sex Hormone Effects

Hormone	Origin	Principal effects
FSH	Anterior pituitary gland	*In female:* Growth of ovarian follicles; estrogen and progesterone production *In male:* Initiates sperm production
LH	Anterior pituitary gland	*In female:* Causes ovulation; progesterone and estrogen production *In male:* Stimulates androgen production; maintains spermatogenesis
Estrogen	Ovary (follicle)	Thickens endometrium of the uterus; inhibits FSH production and stimulates LH production at ovulation; initiates and maintains female secondary sex characteristics
Progesterone	Ovary (corpus luteum)	Thickens estrogen-primed endometrium of uterus; maintains pregnancy; inhibits LH production
Testosterone	Testes	Maintains sperm production; initiates and maintains male secondary sex characteristics

posterior pituitary gland
(pi TOO i ter′ ee) Portion of pituitary gland that develops from nervous tissue and is connected to brain by nerves. Storage area for neurohormones produced in hypothalamus.

anterior pituitary gland
(pi TOO i ter′ ee) Portion of the pituitary gland that develops from nonnervous tissue and is connected to the brain by blood vessels.

trophic hormones
(TROF ik HOHR mohnz) Hormones that stimulate the secretion of other hormones.

gonadotropins
(goh nad′ uh TROH pinz) Hormones, produced by anterior pituitary gland, that stimulate gonads.

neuroendocrinology
(noo′ roh en′ doh kri NOL uh jee) Study of how central nervous system and endocrine system interact to promote normal body functioning.

endocrine glands, travel throughout the body and have specific effects on many tissues and organs. Endocrine glands include the pituitary gland, thyroid glands, adrenal glands, pancreas, ovaries, and testes. The pituitary gland and its relationship to the sex glands, the ovaries and testes, will be our major focus as we discuss the endocrine system. The adrenal glands, located on the top of the kidneys and a source of male and female hormones, will also be mentioned here and in later chapters.

The pituitary gland is a pea-sized structure at the base of the brain. The pituitary gland is divided into the **posterior pituitary gland,** which is attached to the brain by nerves, and the **anterior pituitary gland,** which is attached to the brain by blood vessels. The anterior pituitary gland controls the functioning of the ovaries and testes through hormones it produces called **trophic** (from the Latin "to nourish") hormones, which stimulate the ovaries and testes to produce their own hormones. The anterior pituitary hormones that stimulate the gonads are called **gonadotropins** (because they nourish or stimulate the gonads) (Table 4-1). The gonadotropins in the female are *follicle-stimulating hormone* (FSH) and *luteinizing hormone* (LH). A third hormone, *prolactin,* induces milk production in the breast of a pregnant woman. In the female, FSH stimulates follicles in the ovary to "ripen" and to produce the sex hormones estrogen and progesterone. LH causes the follicle to rupture and release its egg at ovulation. LH also causes the ovary to produce estrogen and progesterone. In the male, FSH stimulates the testes to produce sperm and LH causes the testes to produce the male sex hormones called *androgens.*

Neuroendocrinology

The science of **neuroendocrinology** is concerned with the relationship between the central nervous system (brain and spinal cord) and the endocrine system.

HUMAN SEXUALITY

The pituitary gland, which is attached to the brain, controls most of the other endocrine glands and in turn is controlled by the brain. The portion of the brain that is connected to and controls the pituitary gland is the **hypothalamus,** which receives information from many different brain areas, such as those involved with emotion, learning, and memory. The hypothalamus produces chemical substances that travel to the pituitary gland and control the output of chemical messages from it (Figure 4-1).

How does the hypothalamus-pituitary system work? What controls the system so that the proper amounts of pituitary hormones are released? The answers to these questions are important to our understanding of the psychological influences on reproduction. The control of the posterior pituitary gland by the hypothalamus is relatively simple. Specific areas of the hypothalamus produce chemical messages called **neurohormones.** Neurohormones, also called releasing hormones or releasing factors, travel down the nerves that connect the hypothalamus and the posterior pituitary gland (Figure 4-1). They are then stored in the posterior pituitary gland until a nervous stimulus such as suckling on the nipple activates their release into the bloodstream.

Oxytocin is an example of a posterior pituitary hormone that is made in the hypothalamus and stored in the posterior pituitary gland. It travels throughout the body via the bloodstream and causes the contraction of the smooth

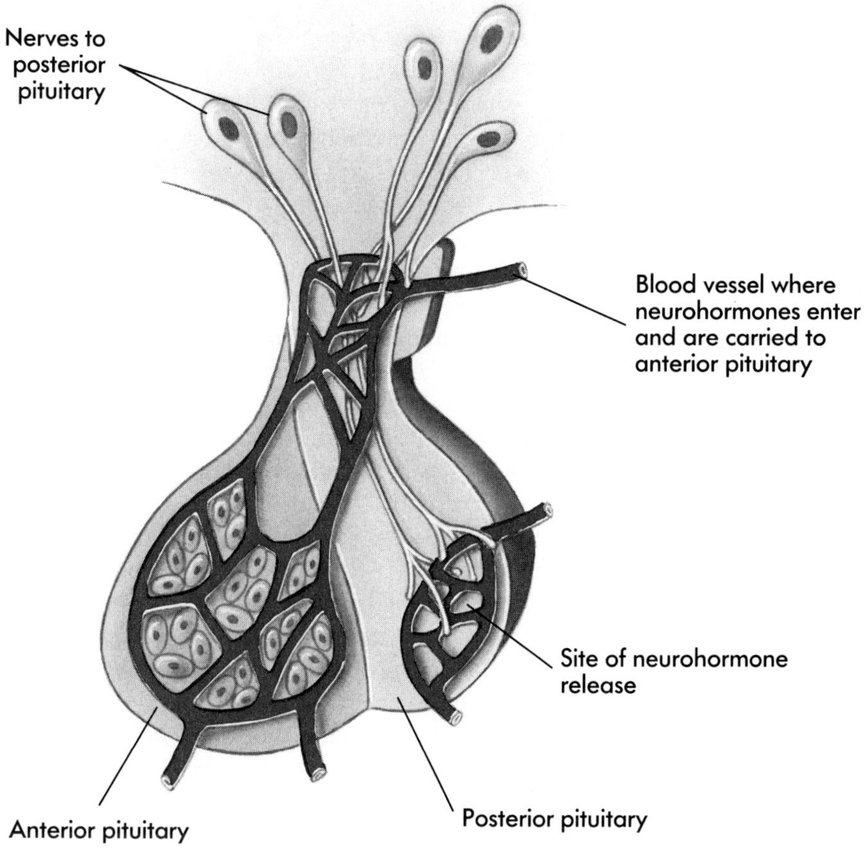

hypothalamus
(hy puh THAL uh muhs) Portion of brain that is in direct contact with pituitary gland. Secretions from hypothalamus control pituitary gland.

neurohormones
(noo′ roh HOR mohnz) Hormones produced in hypothalamus.

oxytocin
(ok si TOH sin) Posterior pituitary hormone involved in "milk-letdown" in lactating women.

FIGURE 4-1
The hypothalamus is connected to the anterior pituitary gland by blood vessels and to the posterior pituitary gland by nerve cells.

Nerves to posterior pituitary

Blood vessel where neurohormones enter and are carried to anterior pituitary

Site of neurohormone release

Anterior pituitary

Posterior pituitary

The release of oxytocin during breast-feeding is illustrated in Figure 7-4.

neuroendocrine reflex
(noo′ roh EN doh krin) A reflex involving input to the nervous system and output by an endocrine gland.

negative feedback system
A feedback system in which stability is maintained by opposing change.

muscle system in the breast. Oxytocin is released in a breast-feeding woman when an infant sucks on the nipple. The suckling is the stimulus, and oxytocin release and "milk-letdown" are the response. In many women just the sound of an infant crying will cause the release of oxytocin from the posterior pituitary gland, and hence milk will move into the milk duct system to the nipple. The discharge of oxytocin occurs as a quick response called a **neuroendocrine reflex,** taking place 10 to 30 seconds from the start of suckling.

The control of the anterior pituitary gland by the hypothalamus is more complicated. The hypothalamus is attached to the anterior pituitary gland by blood vessels rather than by nervous tissue connections (Figure 4-1). Neurohormones produced in the hypothalamus are released into the blood vessels and travel down to the anterior pituitary gland, where they come in contact with the anterior pituitary cells. In most cases the anterior pituitary gland responds by producing and releasing hormones into the blood. An example of a neurohormone transmitted from the hypothalamus to the anterior pituitary gland is *gonadotropin-releasing hormone* (GRH). As previously mentioned, the anterior pituitary gland produces the gonadotropins FSH and LH. GRH causes the release of these hormones from the anterior pituitary gland.

We now know how the hypothalamus causes the release of hormones from the anterior pituitary gland. What directs the hypothalamus to convey neurohormones to the pituitary gland? The answer is simple. The hypothalamus–anterior pituitary–gonad system can be compared to a thermostat and furnace. The hypothalamus can be likened to the thermostat and the gonads to the furnace. If the thermostat is set at 68° F and the temperature drops to 65° F, the thermostat will signal the furnace to turn on and produce heat. When the room temperature rises above 68° F, the thermostat monitors this increase and signals the furnace to shut down. This is a classic **negative feedback system** because as the temperature rises, the furnace is activated. The thermostat monitors the changes in temperature. In the same manner the hypothalamus monitors the levels of gonadal hormones in the blood. When the hormone levels are low, the hypothalamus responds by sending neurohormones to the anterior pituitary gland. The anterior pituitary gland responds by releasing FSH or LH, which stimulates the production of hormones in the gonads. When hormone levels from the gonads are high, the hypothalamus stops stimulating the anterior pituitary gland. The anterior pituitary gland then stops releasing FSH and LH. This results in the gonads not being stimulated, and they decrease their production of hormones (Figure 4-2).

An instance of negative feedback between the brain, pituitary gland, and gonads involves women using oral contraceptives. Oral contraceptives add additional amounts of estrogen and progesterone to the normal levels produced by the ovaries. The elevated levels of hormones are monitored by the hypothalamus, which responds by reducing the amount of releasing factor (GRH) sent to the anterior pituitary gland (Casper and Yen, 1983). The anterior pituitary gland then reduces its output of gonadotropins. The estrogen and progesterone from the oral contraceptives prevent the cyclical release of gonadotropins, which thereby prevents ovulation and pregnancy.

Another example of the negative feedback system that exists between the hypothalamus, pituitary gland, and gonads can be seen in postmenopausal women. Women past the age of menopause have high levels of gonadotropins

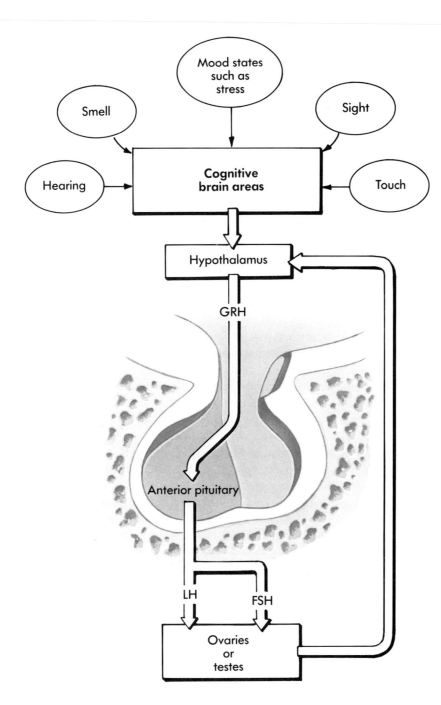

FIGURE 4-2
Higher brain centers in-
volved in processing sen-
sory information as well as
mood states influence control of the hypothalamus.
The hypothalamus in turn
controls the anterior pituitary gland, which stimu-
lates output of the gonads.

from the anterior pituitary gland. Their ovaries no longer function to produce the hormones estrogen and progesterone. Thus the hypothalamus is attempting to induce production of the hormones from the ovaries by stimulating the anterior pituitary gland with GRH to release FSH and LH. The anterior pituitary gland responds by releasing FSH and LH, but to no avail because the ovaries are no longer capable of producing estrogen and progesterone. These elevated levels of FSH and LH are usually maintained for the rest of the woman's life. Men who are castrated (testicles removed) also have high levels of gonadotropins because of their negative feedback system. In the absence of testes no male hormones are produced and the anterior pituitary responds by releasing gonadotropins in an attempt to stimulate the nonexistent testes to produce male hormones.

We can conclude that the levels of gonadal hormones control the output of the hypothalamus and consequently the anterior pituitary gland. This involves a negative feedback relationship. We can liken the hypothalamus–anterior pituitary–gonad system to a three-messenger system. The hypothalamus produces the first chemical message (GRH), which stimulates the anterior pituitary gland to produce FSH and LH (second message). The second message travels through the body to stimulate the gonads to release estrogen, progesterone, and testosterone (third message). The third message, hormones from the gonads, stimulates many tissues in the body. It is the gonadal hormones that regulate the output of GRH from the hypothalamus. When the levels of gonadal hormones are high, the hypothalamus slows down its production of GRH. Conversely, when the levels of gonadal hormones are low, the hypothalamus speeds up its production of GRH.

In summary, the brain exerts an important influence on reproductive functioning in men and women. The hypothalamus, which controls the endocrine system, receives information from numerous brain areas involved in learning, memory, and emotion. These inputs from other brain areas can affect reproduction. The exact way this occurs is unknown, but it certainly involves changes in chemical communication between different brain areas. These alterations in the transmission of information are probably the cause of upsets in reproductive functioning resulting from stress, sudden changes in the environment, anxiety, or new situations. In the two examples in which placebos were used, the men and women thought they were receiving a medication to help them. They may have felt, "Now that I have help, I will ovulate" or "I now can maintain an erection." The *idea* of the medication may have helped to reduce tension and stress, which was the real cause of dysfunction.

MALE SEXUAL PHYSIOLOGY

The male reproductive system produces sperm constantly, in contrast to the female system, which produces eggs on a cyclical basis. The male produces sperm at a relatively constant rate from puberty until well into old age (Bremner et al., 1983). Male hormones do show cycles; however, sperm production is relatively constant. Men do not have a fertility cycle as women do; the normal healthy male is fertile at any given time of the month or the year.

As previously mentioned, sperm and hormone production occurs in the testes. The seminiferous tubules of the testes contain the sperm-producing cells, and the process of sperm production is illustrated in Figure 4-3. The spermatozoon, or mature sperm cell, has a head, body, and tail. The head contains all of the genetic material (hereditary information) that will be passed on to the offspring should an egg be fertilized. The body of the spermatozoon contains energy-producing structures that provide the energy necessary to move the tail in a whiplike fashion. This tail movement gives sperm cells the motility to move like tadpoles.

Egg production

Sperm production

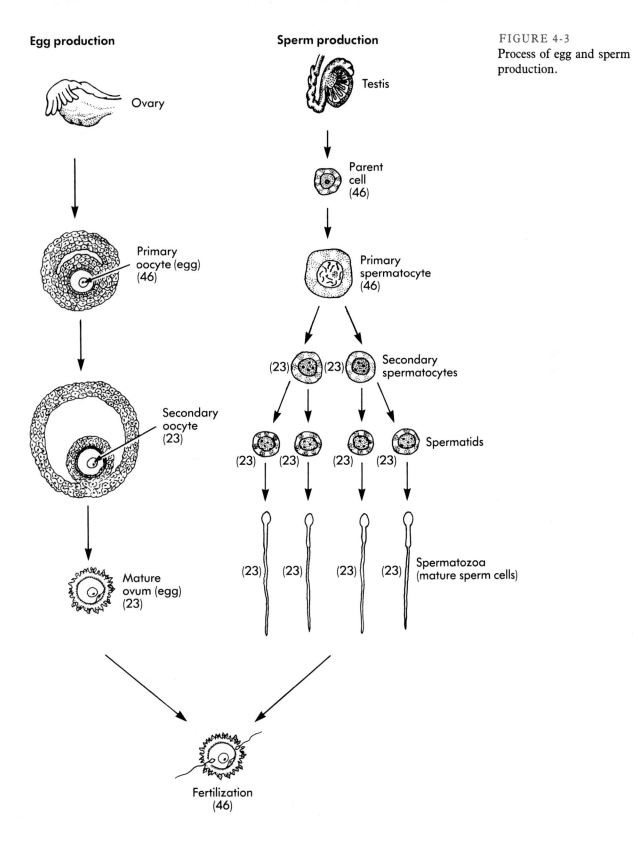

FIGURE 4-3
Process of egg and sperm
production.

Ovary

Primary
oocyte (egg)
(46)

Secondary
oocyte
(23)

Mature
ovum (egg)
(23)

Testis

Parent
cell
(46)

Primary
spermatocyte
(46)

(23) (23) Secondary
spermatocytes

(23) (23) (23) (23) Spermatids

(23) (23) (23) (23) Spermatozoa
(mature sperm cells)

Fertilization
(46)

Sexual Activity and Athletic Performance: Is There a Relationship?

One major league baseball manager, when asked if he thought that having sex before a big game would hurt his players' performance, replied that it wasn't the sex that hurt them, it was the staying out all night trying to find a woman that knocked them out. Most researchers agree that having sex before an athletic competition does not hurt athletic performance. Thornton interviewed many researchers and athletes and concludes that, "In view of the lack of scientific evidence on the subject, most athletes these days probably wouldn't give a second thought to having sex the night before an athletic contest. Indeed, depending on the athlete's frame of mind, it couldn't hurt—and it might help" (1990, p. 154).

One study cited by Thornton attempted to determine whether sex the night before an athletic event has a negative effect on performance. In this unpublished study (done by Loren Cordain, a professor at Colorado State University, and Wendy Newton, a graduate student at the same university), having sexual intercourse the night before testing had no effect on athletic performance as measured by physiological measures, strength, and coordination. The subjects were 10 married men in the age range of 18 to 45 years who exercised regularly. The subjects were randomly assigned to two groups. One group was tested on the morning following sexual intercourse and then again after 5 days of abstaining from any type of

sexual activity. The other group was tested in the reverse order. The tests included grip strength with the hand, balancing tests, lateral movement reaction times, stair-climbing exercise, and a test to measure maximal oxygen consumption (this is a measure of fitness and determines the maximal amount of oxygen that can be consumed per minute during maximal exercise—the greater the amount of oxygen, the more fit the individual). The researchers found no differences in test performances after a night of sexual activity as compared with nights when no sexual activity occurred.

We can conclude that sexual activities the night before an athletic competition are not detrimental to performance. Some researchers have suggested that the anxiety before a major competition can prevent sleep and that sex in a relaxed setting promotes relaxation and hence sleep.

---

testosterone
(tes TOS tuh rohn) Potent male hormone belonging to androgen class of hormones.

inhibin
(in HIB in) Chemical secreted by the testes that inhibits FSH output by the anterior pituitary gland.

FSH initiates the process of sperm production within the seminiferous tubules, and LH is responsible for maintaining sperm production (Table 4-1). LH also stimulates the Leydig cells to produce **testosterone,** a potent male hormone. Testosterone is thought to act directly on the seminiferous tubules to maintain sperm production. A negative feedback relationship exists between LH production and testosterone. As testosterone levels rise, LH levels fall, and when testosterone levels drop, LH levels rise to stimulate testosterone output by the testes. The substance **inhibin,** produced in the testes, is thought to be involved in the control of FSH. High levels of this substance inhibit FSH production and output by the anterior pituitary gland (Ramasharma et al., 1984).

FEMALE SEXUAL PHYSIOLOGY

There are major differences between the male and female reproductive systems. Probably the most important involves the steady, constant production of gametes, or sperm, in the male compared with the cyclical production of gametes, or eggs, in the female. Approximately every month from puberty until menopause an egg is released from the ovary. The hormones estrogen and proges-

80   HUMAN SEXUALITY

terone are also released from the ovary in a similar cyclical pattern. The human female thus has definite fertile periods, unlike the male, who is theoretically fertile all the time. The process of egg production, however, is similar to that of sperm production (Figure 4-3).

Menstrual Cycle

The **menstrual cycle,** with its flow of blood and tissue approximately once a month, is a normal biological process. Despite this fact the menstrual cycle and the blood flow associated with the cycle have taken on surprising connotations. Some negative associations between the menstrual flow and "curses" and "supernatural powers" can be found in the Bible. In Leviticus 15:19 we find: "And if a woman shall have an issue, and her issue in her flesh be blood, she shall be separated seven days; and whosoever touches her shall be unclean."

Many cultures ascribe magical powers to menstruating women. In an attempt to control this "power," the women are isolated from men. In several cultures the women spend the time during the menstrual flow in small huts removed from other individuals. Men are warned not to approach menstruating women (Paige, 1977). Pliny, a Roman historian, states in *Natural History* that a menstruating woman destroys crops, dries gardens, kills plants, makes fruit fall from the trees, kills bees, sours milk, and causes miscarriages in mares. If a menstruating woman touches wine, it turns to vinegar.

Remnants of negative attitudes toward menstruation are still found in our culture. Many couples abstain from sexual intercourse during the menstrual flow for religious reasons, because of anxiety over menstrual blood, and also for the more pragmatic concern that it can be messy. Advertisements for tampons and feminine napkins promise that when using their product, women can conceal the fact that they are having their menstrual flow. A more insidious or subtle form of negativism toward the menstrual cycle occurs when individuals who are ignorant of biological and psychological facts argue that a woman cannot control her emotions and cannot perform intellectual tasks before and during the menstrual flow. This is not true, as will be discussed.

Biological Aspects of Menstrual Cycle

Menstruation has often been defined as the failure of pregnancy to take place, because the events occurring before the onset of menstruation in each monthly menstrual cycle are preparations for pregnancy. Menstruation, or cyclical uterine bleeding approximately every 28 days, happens only if the woman does not become pregnant. In the normal female menstruation begins at puberty and continues at regular intervals for approximately 30 to 35 years. The first menstrual flow that takes place during puberty is called **menarche.** Menstrual cycles cease during **menopause.** The menstrual cycle is under the control of the hypothalamus, pituitary gland, and ovaries.

By convention the first day of the menstrual cycle is considered the day of the onset of bleeding, which is the shedding of the uterine endometrium. All other references to the cycle assume day 1 is the first day of the menstrual flow. Thus day 15 of the cycle is 15 days after the onset of vaginal bleeding. For the following description it will be assumed that the woman has a 28-day

menstrual cycle (MEN stroo uhl) Cyclical recurrent series of changes occurring in the female reproductive tract associated with menstruation.

menstruation (men stroo AY shuhn) Cyclical uterine bleeding.

menarche (muh NAR kee) Onset of menstruation.

menopause Time that marks permanent cessation of menstrual activity.

Puberty and menopause are presented in Chapters 12 and 13, respectively.

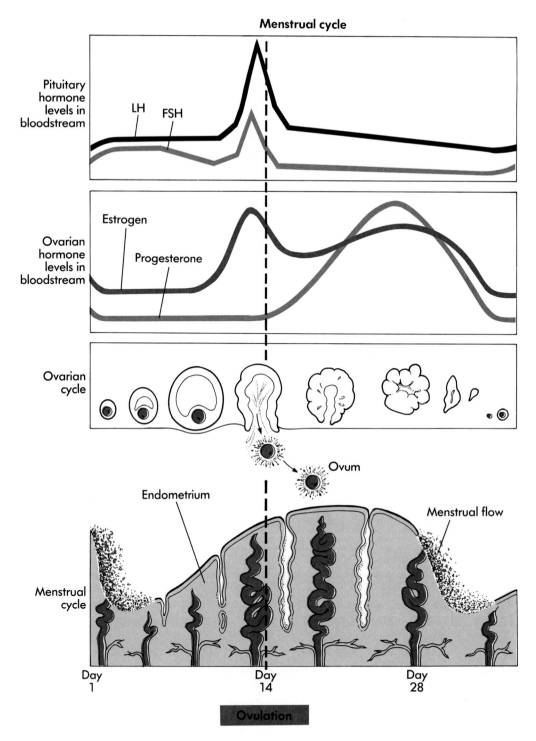

FIGURE 4-4
The biological events of the menstrual cycle: pituitary hormone levels, ovarian hormone levels, ovarian follicle, corpus luteum, and endometrium.

HUMAN SEXUALITY

menstrual cycle. A 28-day cycle is often used for purposes of discussion, but normal cycles do not have to be 28 days. Each woman has her own cycle length that is normal for her. It will be helpful to refer to Figure 4-4 for this part of the discussion.

The menstrual cycle can be divided into four phases: (1) menses, (2) estrogenic phase, (3) ovulation, and (4) progestational phase (Table 4-2). During the menstrual flow or menses (usually days 1 to 5) the ovaries are relatively inactive and the two major hormones produced by the ovaries, estrogen and progesterone, are not being released in high amounts. As discussed earlier, when levels of estrogen are low, the hypothalamus–anterior pituitary–gonad system responds by releasing gonadotropin-releasing hormone (GRH) from the hypothalamus. This causes the release of follicle-stimulating hormone (FSH) and luteinizing hormone (LH) from the anterior pituitary gland. FSH causes the developing ovarian follicles to release estrogen, which has numerous effects that are discussed below and summarized in Table 4-1. The **ovarian follicles** are blisterlike structures near the surface of the ovary that produce eggs, estrogen, and progesterone.

The estrogenic phase of the menstrual cycle usually includes days 6 to 14 of the cycle. When a woman has cycles of differing length, it is usually this phase that varies. During the estrogenic phase the reproductive system undergoes many changes. The increased amounts of FSH stimulate ovarian follicles to start growing. The follicles are filled with fluid and contain the maturing eggs, or ova. In the human female one follicle grows faster than the others, and for reasons that are unknown, 99% of the time only one follicle per cycle finally matures to produce an ovum. The obvious exception is the case of fraternal twins, which can occur when two follicles mature and yield two eggs.

ovarian follicles (oh VAR ee uhn FOL i kuhlz) Structures in the ovaries that produce female gametes—eggs.

TABLE 4-2 Summary of Hormonal and Biological Changes During Menstrual Cycle*

Phase	Length (days)	Cycle days	Hormonal/biological events
Menses	5	1-5	Low levels of estrogen and progesterone; varying amounts of menstrual flow; possible backache, headache, cramps; loss of water retention; FSH and smaller amounts of LH from anterior pituitary gland
Estrogenic phase	8	6-12	Estrogen levels rise; low levels of progesterone; FSH levels rise; LH levels are low
Ovulation	1	13-14	Estrogen levels peak; progesterone levels begin to rise; dramatic peak in LH with lesser peaks in FSH
Progestational phase	14	15-28	Progesterone and estrogen levels high; FSH and LH levels drop; toward end of cycle progesterone and estrogen levels drop dramatically and FSH begins to rise; possible water retention, breast swelling, and weight gain

*A 28-day cycle with 5 days of menstrual flow is used as an example.

As the follicle grows, it manufactures estrogen in increasing amounts. The follicle also produces a small amount of progesterone.

In addition to the production of estrogen and progesterone by the ovaries, androgen levels also rise during the estrogenic phase of the cycle. Half of the androgens are derived from the ovaries, and the other half come from the adrenal cortex (Berne and Levy, 1992).

During the estrogenic phase the elevated estrogen levels from the follicle stimulate the growth of the endometrium. The uterus demonstrates growth in its arterial blood supply and glandular growth (mucus-producing glands) under the influence of estrogen. As estrogen levels continue to rise, FSH levels fall (negative feedback). At the end of the estrogenic phase the follicle is mature and ready to release its ova. The process of ovulation is dependent on a "spike" or rapid surge of LH from the anterior pituitary gland, which in turn is controlled by a release of GRH from the hypothalamus. The LH surge usually occurs on day 13, and ovulation on day 14.

The rising estrogen levels, which usually reach a peak on day 12 or 13, and the smaller increases in progesterone levels trigger the LH surge by a positive feedback mechanism. Just before ovulation, estrogen exerts a positive feedback effect on LH and FSH as distinct from its negative feedback effect at other times in the cycle (Page, Villee, and Villee, 1981). Rising estrogen levels from the follicle are thought to prime the hypothalamus to respond by releasing GRH, which leads to FSH and LH release from the anterior pituitary gland. The LH surge is the critical event in the ovulatory process. Without the LH surge, ovulation would not occur. The androgens produced by the ovaries and adrenal cortex reach their peak at about the time of ovulation and then decline.

At ovulation the follicle ruptures and the ovum and fluid in the follicle are released to the surface of the ovary. When the follicular wall ruptures, it may produce some bleeding. Some of the blood and follicular fluid may escape into

At the time of ovulation the egg ruptures the follicle and is drawn into the fallopian tubes.

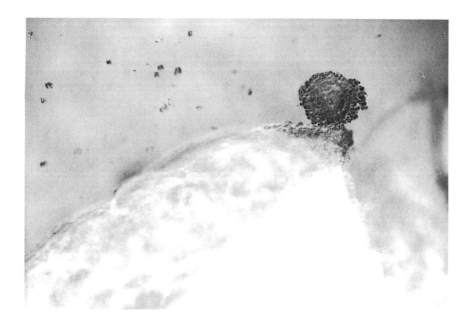

the abdominal cavity. This material irritates the lining of the pelvis and abdomen and can cause abdominal pain. This phenomenon is known as **mittelschmerz,** a German word that means *midpain.* The pain may be minimal, or it may be severe enough to mimic acute appendicitis. For many women mittelschmerz allows them to know when they are ovulating; they become sensitive to or aware of a normal body function. Once ovulation has occurred, the ovum is usually drawn up into the fallopian tubes. At this time certain cells within the ruptured follicle divide rapidly, filling it to form a yellowish structure, the **corpus luteum.** The corpus luteum continues to produce small quantities of estrogen but produces greater and greater amounts of progesterone.

When ovulation has occurred and progesterone levels are high, the cycle is in its progestational phase. During this phase, body temperature increases. An increase of 0.4° F (0.2° C) above the average body temperature occurs on the days preceding ovulation (Figure 4-4). The high progesterone levels cause the rise in body temperature. The increasing levels of progesterone act on the estrogen-primed endometrium of the uterus to cause cellular growth, production of mucus, production of glycogen (a nutrient for the potential fertilized egg), fluid retention, greater arterial blood supply, and increased glandular development. This phase usually takes place during days 14 to 28 of the cycle. *In 90% of women the length of the progestational phase of the cycle is between 13 and 15 days.* This phase is the least variable portion of the menstrual cycle and is the interval between ovulation and the onset of the next flow. *To calculate the probable day of ovulation, count back 13 to 15 days from the day of the onset of the menstrual flow. This means that the probable day of ovulation can be calculated, but only after ovulation has occurred and a new cycle has begun.*

During the progestational phase the endometrium is thick and spongy because of the influence of estrogen and progesterone and contains numerous mucus-producing glands. The rising levels of progesterone suppress LH secretion from the anterior pituitary gland (the negative feedback mechanism is in effect). If pregnancy occurs, the corpus luteum survives and continues to produce high levels of progesterone for approximately 3 months into the pregnancy. Through a mechanism yet unknown the fertilized egg sends a neural or hormonal signal to the hypothalamus to prevent the onset of the next menstrual cycle (Page, Villee, and Villee, 1981). If pregnancy does not occur, the corpus luteum decreases in activity, which results in lowered production of estrogen and progesterone. The corpus luteum degenerates, and the endometrium is sloughed off from the walls of the uterus. There is a discharge from the uterus, which consists of cells, mucus, and blood. This material passes through the vagina on its way outside the body. The amount of an average monthly discharge varies depending on the day of the cycle and between individual women. As the corpus luteum degenerates, the very low estrogen levels stimulate an increase in FSH release from the anterior pituitary gland. A new set of follicles begins to grow, and a new menstrual cycle starts.

In summary, the process of ovulation involves a dynamic and finely tuned system that includes the hypothalamus, anterior pituitary gland, and ovaries. The ratios of hormones at specified times in the cycle are critical for proper functioning of the system. The ratios of estrogen to progesterone and of FSH to LH are constantly changing throughout the cycle. The hypothalamus and

mittelschmerz
(mit TIL shmertz) Abdominal pain occurring at time of ovulation.

corpus luteum
(KOR puhs LOO te uhm) Small structure that develops within ruptured ovarian follicle and secretes progesterone.

The fertile time in a woman's cycle is discussed in Chapter 6.

the anterior pituitary gland are continually monitoring changes in the absolute and relative amounts of estrogen and progesterone. It is these two hormones that control the output from the hypothalamus and anterior pituitary gland through negative and positive feedback actions. If any part of the system is disrupted, the system will cease functioning. Disruption may result from various causes, including (1) oral contraceptives; (2) disorders such as insufficient levels of hormones from the anterior pituitary gland, ovaries, or other endocrine glands; or (3) emotional, social, or nutritional factors.

Changes in Mammary Glands During Menstrual Cycle

Because estrogen and progesterone affect the mammary glands, the breasts would be expected to show cyclical changes during the menstrual cycle. The breasts enlarge to a variable degree, depending on the woman, during the week just before a menstrual flow, or the premenstrual stage (approximately day 21 of the cycle). At this time progesterone levels are very elevated and estrogen levels are moderately elevated (Figure 4-4). The enlargement is caused by **edema** and **hyperemia** of the **alveoli.** There is swelling and tenderness, and many women experience pain in the breasts during the premenstrual stage of the cycle.

Common Problems During Menstrual Cycle

Three common problems related to the menstrual cycle are premenstrual tension, painful menstruation (dysmenorrhea), and the abnormal absence of menstrual cycles in a female of reproductive age (amenorrhea). Premenstrual tension refers to the negative mood changes and physical symptoms occurring in some women before the menstrual flow and is discussed later in this chapter. A more serious condition, premenstrual syndrome (PMS), is experienced by a smaller number of women before the menstrual flow. PMS can be considered a more severe form of premenstrual tension (Norris, 1983) and is discussed following premenstrual tension.

Dysmenorrhea Painful menstrual flow, or **dysmenorrhea,** affects a large number of women. Some women experience abdominal cramps, leg aches, headaches, backaches, nausea, and general discomfort during the flow, yet other women have few or no symptoms. Usually the first 2 days of the flow are the most troublesome because of lower abdominal cramps and cramping in the back. The cramps can be moderate to severe in intensity. One possible cause of the cramps is the uterine contractions associated with premenstrual and menstrual times (Lein, 1979). Biological compounds called **prostaglandins** are manufactured throughout the body in both men and women. Prostaglandins were first identified in semen. Women produce them in several organs, including the ovaries, and they are found in menstrual fluids. Prostaglandins are thought to have a significant role in causing the uterus to contract during menstruation. These compounds are similar to hormones in their actions, and they can travel through the blood to influence specific structures and tissues. Strong and continued contractions of the uterine muscles initiated by the pros-

edema
(i DEE muh) Accumulation of fluid within tissues of body.

hyperemia
(hy′ puh REE mee uh) Increased amount of blood that expands or distends blood vessels.

alveoli
(al VEE uh lee′) Small sacs within mammary glands that contain milk-producing cells.

dysmenorrhea
(dis men′ uh REE uh) Painful or difficult menstruation.

prostaglandins
(pros′ tuh GLAN dinz) Group of chemical compounds produced by many tissues of the body. These compounds mimic actions of hormones; they can act at a distance from where they are produced.

taglandins reduce the blood supply to the muscles because the contractions squeeze down the blood vessels supplying the muscles. An analogy presented by Lein (1979), in a very readable account of the menstrual cycle, likens these contractions to the pain of a muscle spasm or leg cramp. Pain results when any muscle is overexerted and receives an inadequate supply of oxygen (ischemia). Menstrual cramps can be considered an example of ischemic pain. As long as uterine contractions continue with an inadequate blood supply, pain results. Other causes of menstrual cramping have been proposed, including a failure of the endometrium of the uterus to break down completely (Masters and Johnson, 1966).

Scientists generally believe that the severity of the symptoms of dysmenorrhea has both biological and psychological foundations. In a study that examined whether awareness that the effect of the menstrual cycle on menstrual symptoms was being monitored would influence reporting of symptoms, women who knew the purpose of the study reported greater cyclical changes in negative moods than women who did not know the purpose of the study (Gallant et al., 1990).

What can we conclude from the study by Gallant and associates? Preconceived ideas and notions can greatly affect perceptions of pain and discomfort during the menstrual flow in *some* women. We emphasize "some" because many women have minor or no discomfort during menstruation and many experience pain as a result of organic causes associated with the onset of menstruation. If a young girl is told that the menstrual cycle and menstrual flow are normal, naturally occurring events in her life, she will probably experience less menstrual difficulty than a girl who constantly hears adults describe the flow in negative terms (such as "the curse") and feels she is in for discomfort once a month for 30 to 35 years of her life (Paige, 1973). The relative contributions of the biological and psychological causes of dysmenorrhea are difficult to determine for each woman. As is the case for most other reproductive events, a combination of biological and psychological factors is probably at work. In some cases organic factors, acting without any psychological influences, can be isolated as the sole cause of menstrual cycle symptoms.

What can be done to alleviate the symptoms of dysmenorrhea? Usually aspirin is sufficient, and the nonprescription drug ibuprofen (marketed under such names as Advil and Nuprin) is a powerful prostaglandin inhibitor. Aspirin and ibuprofen inhibit prostaglandin production, which explains their effectiveness in controlling dysmenorrhea symptoms. Antiprostaglandin drugs also relieve menstrual cramping. Some women rest more during the first day or two of the flow. Masters and Johnson (1966) report that some women experience relief through orgasm. The contractions of the uterus during orgasm increase the rate of the menstrual flow and provide relief from the cramping. Masters and Johnson propose that the endometrium of the uterus is sloughed off faster during orgasmic contractions.

Amenorrhea **Amenorrhea** is the abnormal absence of menstruation in a female of reproductive age. There have been many accounts of disturbances in the menstrual cycle caused by emotional and stressful situations, exercise, prolonged dieting, and **anorexia nervosa.** Psychological factors mediated by

amenorrhea
(ay men' uh REE uh) Abnormal absence or suppression of menstruation in woman of reproductive age.

anorexia nervosa
(an uh REK see uh ner voh suh) An abnormal psychological condition in which a person loses his or her appetite, eats very little, and loses weight.

FYI

Delayed Menarche and Amenorrhea in Ballet Dancers

One study has shown that female ballet dancers have delayed menarche (onset of the first menstrual flow associated with puberty) and amenorrhea (Frisch, Wyshak, and Vincent, 1980). The study included 89 dancers who were studying in professional schools or dancing in professional companies. The women were classified in three groups: (1) those who reported that menarche had not begun were considered as having primary amenorrhea, (2) those who did not have a menstrual cycle for longer than 3 consecutive months were classified as having secondary amenorrhea, and (3) those with intervals between cycles of between 38 days and 3 months were considered to have irregular cycles.

Ten percent of the 89 women reported primary amenorrhea at 18.5 years of age, and 12% noted no onset of the menstrual flow at 14 years. Thirty-three percent reported irregular cycles, and 15% noted secondary amenorrhea.

The researchers concluded that the dancers had disordered reproductive cycles because of lack of body fat. Dancers with amenorrhea and irregular cycles were significantly leaner than those reporting regular cycles. Weight relative to height was used to calculate thinness. The ratio between weight and height was less than the critical ratio to maintain cycles. Thus this study

Many ballet dancers exhibit amenorrhea caused by low body weight relative to their height.

supports the idea that strenuous athletic training and consequent low weight for height ratio (leanness) contribute to delayed menarche and amenorrhea (Sanborn, 1986). Factors other than a critical percentage of body fat have been implicated in athletic amenorrhea. These factors include intensity of athletic training, psychological stress from intensive training and competition, diet, and hormonal changes (Sanborn, 1986; Shangold, 1988).

brain areas other than the hypothalamus, such as the cerebrum (that part of the brain involved in awareness, thinking, and memory), influence the control of releasing factors from the hypothalamus in a way that is not fully understood.

In a controlled study a group of researchers withdrew blood from two hospitalized, healthy volunteers for a period of 7 to 10 days around the suspected time of ovulation in an attempt to monitor the LH surge at midcycle. Blood samples were obtained at 4-hour intervals through an indwelling cannula (a needle left in the vein and attached to flexible tubing). LH and adrenal hormones were measured. Both women (23 and 28 years of age) had a history of regular menstrual cycles, which was confirmed by basal body temperature patterns from the three cycles before hospitalization. A single blood sample was taken daily at 8 AM beginning on the first day of the fourth cycle. The volunteers were then hospitalized before the suspected time of ovulation based on their previous three cycles and blood that was taken. In both women the preovulatory surge of LH was delayed and did not occur until 48 hours after the women were discharged from the hospital. *This was 1 week after its expected occurrence*. The levels of adrenal hormones associated with stress were elevated during the hospital stay. The authors concluded that the emotional stress of the hospital stay caused the delay of ovulation. They suggested that the elevated hormone levels from the adrenal glands provided circumstantial evidence that stress had occurred because certain adrenal hormones have been found to increase during times of stress in humans (Peyser et al., 1973).

Irregular cycles or complete amenorrhea has been found among women athletes who participate in strenuous sports activities (Dale et al., 1979). When women reduce their training, they revert to normal cycles. Quadagno and colleagues (1981) have shown that casual exercise (defined as swimming, tennis, or jogging) increases cycle length; however, it does not cause irregular cycles. College students who exercised regularly (6 to 7 days per week, 1 hour or more per day) had longer cycles than women who did not exercise or who exercised for shorter periods. Researchers have proposed the existence of a critical ratio between body fat and muscle mass (often expressed as weight to height); when this ratio falls because of the loss fat, the cycle is disrupted (Frisch and McArthur, 1974). Women athletes often show disrupted hormone levels and altered ratios of estrogen and testosterone (Dale et al., 1979). Some women athletes become infertile during strenuous training sessions, but this infertility is reversible when training is reduced or stopped (see accompanying box).

INFLUENCE OF HORMONES

Now that we have dealt with the basic physiology and hormones of the human sexual systems, we can examine the way hormonal cycles affect the behavior of men and women. Do men have hormonal cycles? Do men or women show heightened periods of sexual activity during different times of the month or year? Are women negatively affected by cyclical changes in hormones during the menstrual cycle? Are men negatively affected by hormonal changes? Can humans send chemical messages to each other to influence another's behavior or biology? Can interpersonal relationships between women influence their menstrual cycles? We shall answer these fascinating questions in this section.

Certain hormones from the outer portion of the adrenal gland (called the cortex) reach elevated levels in the blood during stressful times.

Psychological Aspects of Male Sex Hormones

Male sex hormones and male sex behavior   Males whose testes do not produce enough of the male sex hormone, testosterone, sometimes show a decreased sexual interest and level of sexual activity (Davidson, 1984). This condition is known as hypogonadism. When these men are given testosterone, their self-reported levels of sexual interest and activity increase (Kwan et al., 1983; Carey et al., 1988). Drugs, such as cyproterone acetate, that interfere with the action of testosterone appear to reduce sexual interest and sexual activity (Cooper et al., 1972).

The testes of some sex offenders are surgically removed in some European countries.

When males are castrated (testicles removed), the frequency of sexual intercourse, masturbation, and sexual thought is believed to be reduced. This was the reason for putting a eunuch (a male castrated before puberty) in charge of harems and castrating male sex offenders. If hypogonadism occurs before the onset of puberty, the male is slow to show the normal physical changes of puberty and may never develop an active sex life (Bancroft, 1984). If hypogonadism occurs in adulthood, the outcomes are not as predictable. For example, in a study of 39 released sex offenders who had agreed to castration while imprisoned in West Germany, many of the men had reductions in all aspects of sexual behavior, including sexual desire and sexual arousability (Heim, 1981). The information was gathered through mailed questionnaires concerning the men's sexual activities before and after castration. Self-reported data on sexual behavior are always open to question. The subjects may not be telling the truth or may be telling the researcher what they think the researcher wants to hear. However, in Heim's group some men (31%) did continue to engage in sexual intercourse for years after castration. The average age of men at the time of the study was 49. The average age when they were castrated was 42. The men had been out of prison for an average of 4 years.

Heim concluded from his study and many earlier studies that it may be a myth that males stop engaging in sexual activity after castration. Sexual behavior is influenced by both hormones and past experience. The effects of castration may depend on the man's psychological attitude toward castration. Another possibility is that androgens produced by the adrenal glands help maintain sexual behavior (Davidson et al., 1983). If this is the case, suppression of the adrenal glands should reduce sexual behavior. This area requires more study before definite conclusions can be made about castration and later sexual behavior.

In a study of 20 normal men (Kraemer et al., 1976), the subjects had higher testosterone levels in the blood when engaging in sexual activity to orgasm (intercourse, masturbation, or any other activity that led to orgasm) than during periods of no sexual activity. The men had blood taken every other day for 2 months, and they kept a simple record of sexual activity during the two 24-hour periods preceding blood collection. The authors concluded that the elevation in testosterone was a consequence of sexual activity and not a precursor to sexual activity. Thus testosterone levels rose in response to sexual activity and not in anticipation of sexual activity. Other researchers, however, have found no relationship between sexual activity and testosterone levels (Lee, Jaffe, and Midgley, 1974; Brown, Monti, and Coniveau, 1978). In view of the complexity of the variables that influence sexual behavior in men, it is not surprising that circulating levels of testosterone explain little of the great differences in sexual behavior between individuals.

Humans are much less dependent on gonadal hormones for sexual expression than are other animals. Ford and Beach state this clearly:

> The progressive reduction in hormonal control of sexual behavior is best understood in its relationship to another series of evolutionary changes. These are changes in the size and complexity of certain parts of the brain. The most recently evolved part of the nervous system is the cerebral cortex. . . . Ninety percent of the adult human brain consists of cortical substance. . . . As the cortex has grown in size and complexity its control over behavior has increased. . . . Sexual impulses and responses are no exception. . . . It is to be expected, therefore, that a high degree of cortical development will be associated with more variable behavior and with more easily modified inherited behavioral tendencies. . . . This explains why, in human beings more than in any other species, sexuality is structured and patterned by learning.
>
> Ford and Beach, 1951, pp. 254-255

Do men show cycles in hormone production from the testes? Are peaks of sexual activity evident during certain times of the month or year? Is fertility higher during specific seasons of the year? To answer some of these questions, Reinberg and Lagoguey (1978) studied the sexual activity and blood levels of hormones of five healthy men (21 to 32 years old) for 14 months. The subjects were medical students and biochemists living in Paris. Only one was married at the start of the study; we do not know whether any of the others married during the course of the study. The men recorded their sexual activities (sexual intercourse and masturbation) each day for 14 months. Every 2 months for 14 months they had blood taken at 4-hour intervals for 28 straight hours. Men in this study showed peaks in sexual activity in the late evening and early morning. Testosterone levels showed peaks during the course of a day (24-hour period) that demonstrated a shift or change during the year. The peak of testosterone production found in the blood was in the early morning in May (8 AM), and this gradually shifted to the early afternoon in November (2 PM). Thus testosterone peaks during 24-hour periods varied with the time of the year.

Yearly rhythms or cycles for sexual activity and hormones were also discovered. A peak in sexual activity occurred in October, and testosterone levels peaked during the same month. The authors suggested that the yearly peak in testosterone levels in the autumn may have favored the autumn rise in sexual activity. Another possible explanation is that the sexual activity caused the rise in testosterone as seen in Reinberg and Lagoguey's study (1978). Their study indicates that the human male has 24-hour and yearly cycles in hormone production and secretion. Whether rises in testosterone levels cause increases in sexual activity or affect other behaviors is a much more complicated issue.

In terms of the life cycle men also show a definite pattern in testosterone production (Ewing, Davis, and Zirkin, 1980). Peaks occur before birth at between 12 and 18 weeks of gestation and then at 2 months of age. The peak at 2 months may be required for further differentiation of tissues in the male (Ewing, Davis, and Zirkin, 1980). Testosterone levels then decline to very low levels until puberty. The pubertal increase occurs between 12 and 17 years of

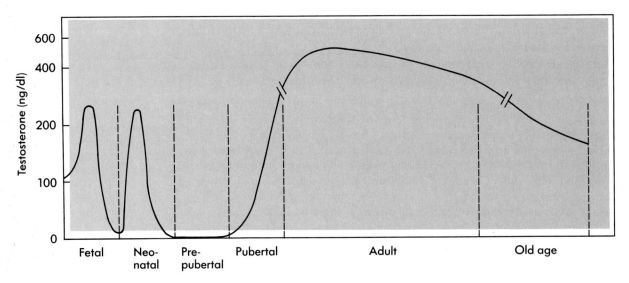

FIGURE 4-5
Testosterone levels over the
life cycle.

age. Testosterone production reaches its maximum levels between the ages of
20 and 30 years and then slowly declines throughout life. Figure 4-5 shows
the levels of testosterone over the life cycle.

Male sex hormones: mood and aggression As will be discussed later,
a large amount of information indicates that women undergo mood changes
during the menstrual cycle. These changes have been correlated with alterations
in hormone levels from the ovaries. Do males show cycles of mood changes
and related behaviors such as hostility, anxiety, and depression? Are elevated
levels of testosterone found in more aggressive individuals? It is commonly
believed that hormones play a role in human male aggression, dominance, and
competition. If a relationship does exist between hormones and these behaviors,
it is a complex one (for review see Gladue, Boechler, and McCaul, 1989).

Some evidence has linked hormones with aggression (intent to inflict injury)
or dominance (intent to achieve or maintain a higher status than others). Mazor
and Lamb (1980) found greater elevations in testosterone in men who won a
tennis match than in losers of the match, and Elias (1981) found that winners
of a wrestling match had testosterone levels that were higher than losers.
Because testosterone levels are elevated in response to exercise, regardless of
winning or losing a competitive event (Cumming et al., 1987), these studies
recorded a rise in testosterone produced by exercise and then an additional
rise in the winners when compared to the losers. In a well-done study, Christiansen and Knussmann (1987) found that blood levels of testosterone were
higher in men (mean age of 24.1 years and a sample size of 117) who rated
themselves as spontaneously aggressive than in men who did not see themselves
as initiating an aggressive verbal or physical act against a nonthreatening person
or animal.

In a clever series of studies, Gladue, Boechler, and McCaul (1989) showed
that winners in a competitive event that did not require energy expenditure
also had a rise in testosterone relative to the losers of the event. Gladue and
colleagues had 40 men "compete" in a computer-driven reaction-time task.

Each competitor was told to press a button when he saw the word "GO" appear on the computer screen. Two competitors were separated from each other by a wood panel, and each subject was told that he was competing against the male on the other side of the panel. At the end of the competition a winner was declared, but this "winner" was selected by the experimenter. Winning and losing had nothing to do with how fast or slow the button was pressed. During the competition, testosterone was monitored via saliva sampling. In this technique the saliva, rather than blood, was assayed for testosterone. Saliva levels of testosterone correlate closely with plasma levels and do not require puncture of a vein for measurement. The subjects spit before, during, and after the competition.

Gladue, Boechler, and McCaul found that the men who were told that they had a decisive victory (won 80% of the 50 button-pressing trials) or close contest (won the majority of trials) showed elevated testosterone levels when compared with the losers. This study shows a causal relationship between behavior and hormones. It also shows that testosterone levels can be elevated after a change in status (in this case either beating a competitor or being told that you beat a competitor). As Gladue and associates state, "Only the perception or knowledge of being victorious (or not) appears sufficient to trigger differential hormone responses. Simply stated, from a hormonal point of view, winning or losing is it" (1989, p. 419).

In a study concerned with mood, 20 healthy men between the ages of 20 and 30 were examined to see whether an association exists between mood and blood levels of testosterone. Every other day for 2 months the males had blood taken and at the same time completed a questionnaire concerned with changes in mood, such as hostility, anxiety, and depression. No consistent relationship between mood and blood levels of testosterone was found (Doering et al., 1975). This type of study should be repeated with large sample sizes to determine whether mood changes exist in males and whether they are related to circulating hormone levels. Often small sample sizes do not detect differences or changes that might be detected in studies with larger sample sizes.

Psychological Aspects of Female Sex Hormones

Menstrual cycle and sexual arousal Does the human female have certain times during her menstrual cycle when she is more sexually aroused and more likely to engage in sexual activity? In almost all other mammals the female becomes sexually receptive only at the time of ovulation ("heat" or estrus). She will not permit the male to mate with her except when she is in estrus. Mating at ovulation greatly increases the chances for fertilization. The human female does not restrict her sexual activities to a specific part of the cycle, but early studies using daily questionnaires to determine whether sexual intercourse had taken place during the past 24 hours indicated a slight peak in reported sexual intercourse at the time of midcycle or ovulation. None of the women were using oral contraceptives. In these early studies, however, it was not determined whether the male or female initiated the sexual activity. In a study by Adams, Gold, and Burt (1978) this problem was eliminated. Both the husband and wife filled out a daily questionnaire in which they recorded all sexual experiences (intercourse, masturbation, and sexual fantasies) in the past 24 hours, who initiated sexual activity (mutual, self, or partner), and whether the participant rejected an invitation by the partner or vice versa. Twelve of the 35 couples were using oral contraceptives, and the rest used other contraceptive methods, including vasectomies. The researchers found a pronounced peak for both females' autosexual experiences (masturbation and sexual fantasies) and female-initiated heterosexual activities (sexual intercourse) on the days closest to ovulation in women not using oral contraceptives. The researchers calculated the suspected day of ovulation by counting backward 14 days from the next menstrual onset. The women using oral contraceptives did not show peaks in autosexual or heterosexual activities at midcycle. Because of the effect of the oral contraceptives on the hypothalamus and anterior pituitary gland, these women do not have a cyclical release of hormones from the ovaries.

The midcycle peak in sexual activities among women not using oral contraceptives and its absence in women using oral contraceptives may be caused by changes in hormone levels around the time of ovulation. Adams, Gold, and Burt (1978) concluded that the midcycle peak in women's initiation of sexual activity (and in other sexual experiences) is probably related to estrogen because this hormone peaks strongly in the ovulatory phase and because both the midcycle peak and overall levels of estrogen are greatly reduced in women taking oral contraceptives. As stated earlier, androgen levels do peak at midcycle but are not decreased by oral contraceptive use. Thus it appears that estrogen is a critical hormone in sexual activities in the ovulatory phase. The autosexual activity pattern of unmarried college women is similar to that of married women, with a peak at midcycle. The college students studied had no midcycle peak for female-initiated heterosexual behavior (Adams, 1980), perhaps because of the lack of a steady partner or for personal reasons.

A major criticism of the Adams, Gold, and Burt study was that the method used to calculate the time of ovulation was unreliable (Sanders and Bancroft, 1982). When Sanders and Bancroft repeated the study using 55 women and determining ovulation by hormone assays, the results were different. The peak in sexual activity involving a partner occurred just after menstruation (days 6 to 10 of a 28-day cycle) and not around the time of ovulation. Initiation by the woman or by both partners was also more likely to occur shortly after menstruation. Sanders and Bancroft proposed that a hormonal explanation involving a delayed reaction of testosterone may explain this peak in sexual activity after menstruation. There is a rise in ovarian testosterone and other androgens during the normal menstrual cycle. These hormones are at their highest levels during the late estrogenic phase (days 11 to 14 of a 28-day cycle) and the early progestational phase (days 15 to 18 of a 28-day cycle) (Figure 4-6). According to Sanders and Bancroft, based on evidence that testosterone has a delayed effect in men (maximum effect is delayed 2 weeks), testosterone released in the early progestational phase of the cycle may influence behavior during the next menstrual cycle.

Feder (1984) sums up the situation of hormones and sexual behavior in women in a clear and concise way: "Overall, evidence tends to suggest subtle facilitative effects of estrogen . . . on female sexuality, but this generalization must be hedged with so many qualifications as to make its force negligible; certainly no deterministic role of steroids (estrogens or androgens) in human

The possible role of androgens in female sex drive can be found in Chapter 13.

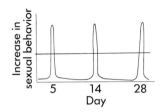

—Not taking oral contraceptives

—Taking oral contraceptives

FIGURE 4-6
Peaks in sexual activity among women not using oral contraceptives versus women using oral contraceptives.

HUMAN SEXUALITY

Menstrual Synchrony and Pheromones

On August 28 the new semester began, and Jill, Ann, and Sara became college roommates. The onset of their menstrual flows was randomly distributed over a 3-week time span. Jill's began on August 15, Ann's began on August 1, and Sara's began on August 21. Unknown to each other, the onset of their cycles began to get closer and closer to each other's. When they left for Christmas vacation, the women found that their menstrual cycles were synchronized to each other's. The onsets of their flows were only 4 days apart. They continued to have their menstrual flows at approximately the same time each month.

AUTHORS' FILES

The occurrence of menstrual synchrony, a decrease in the time differences between the beginning of the menstrual flow for women who live together or spend time together, has been reported by several research groups (McClintock, 1971; Quadagno et al., 1981). What is the cause of menstrual synchrony? It is thought that a pheromone might be involved. A pheromone is a chemical agent, released into the environment by one member of the species, that has an effect on the biology or behavior of another member of the same species. Preti and associates (1986) did an interesting study to test the idea that a pheromone is involved in menstrual synchrony. Researchers employed "sensory donors" who wore sweat pads under their arms during their menstrual cycle. The sweat pads from all donors were grouped in 3-day segments; that is, all pads from cycle days 1 to 3 were combined and termed "combined donor day 2" (first day of menstruation always equals day 1 of a cycle), all pads from days 4 to 6 were combined and termed "combined donor day 5," and so forth. In this manner "donor cycles" of combined donor days 2, 5, 8, 11, 14, 17, 20, 23, 26, and 29 were formed. The sweat pads from the donor cycle were rubbed on the upper lip just under the nose in one group of women (experimental subjects), and plain unused pads were used on a second group of women (control subjects). This procedure was done for three times each week for 10 to 13 weeks. The "donors" did not use any type of underarm deodorant during the odor collection period. At the end of the experiment the difference in the onset dates of the menstrual flow had been reduced to 3.4 days from 9.3 days in the experimental group (synchronization had occurred). The difference in the onset dates of the menstrual flow for the control subjects was not reduced. Before the experiment the control subjects' cycle onsets were 6.7 days (average for the groups) from the donors', and at the end of the experiment they were 7.9 days apart. No synchronization was evident. Preti and associates' results indicate that odors (pheromones) from one woman may influence the menstrual cycle of another woman.

Can people purchase pheromones that would attract the opposite sex? The popular press and the manufacturers of various perfumes and scents would have us believe that they do; however, there is no evidence that pheromones are sex attractants in humans (Quadagno, 1987).

female sexual behavior is supported." Svare and Kinsley make an even stronger statement: "First and foremost, it is acknowledged by most behavioral endocrinologists that social learning, culture, and other environmental factors are infinitely more important than are hormonal influences in human sex-related behaviors. . . ." (1987, p. 33). Feder states that all studies dealing with cyclical variations in ovarian steroid secretions and changes in female sexual behavior have many methodological problems, including (1) failure to analyze hormones, (2) failure to define and adequately measure sex drive and arousability, (3) failure to separate sexual feeling from feelings of well-being, (4) failure to use rigorous statistical tests, and (5) failure to distinguish between female- and male-initiated sexual activity. Some studies adequately deal with some of these concerns but not with all of them.

The reader should be cautioned about absolute relationships between circulating hormone levels and sexual behavior in the female. Like men, women show great variations in hormone production over the cycle. Whalen (1975) cautions that women who have the same cycle length do not necessarily have similar patterns of hormone production during the cycle. Many researchers, including Adams, Gold, and Burt (1978) and Sanders and Bancroft (1982), have found peaks of heterosexual sexual activity in the female just before and just after menstruation. Possibly the peak in sexual activity at midcycle is a result of circulating hormone levels. Morris and associates (1987) found a relationship between testosterone levels and intercourse frequencies in married women who were not using oral contraceptives or any type of fertility awareness methods of contraception. The authors concluded that the midcycle hormonal events with its peak of testosterone influences the female to engage in sexual activities. The peak in sexual activity observed during the postmenstrual time may be motivated by the fact that this is a "safe" time in terms of not becoming pregnant. This is in fact the time of the cycle when unprotected sexual intercourse is least likely to produce a pregnancy, but if a pregnancy is not desired, some form of contraception should always be used during intercourse. The postmenstrual peak might also occur as a result of sexual deprivation during the menstrual cycle for couples who abstain from sexual relations during menstruation. Finally, peaks may be caused by the nonspecific effects of feeling good during certain phases of the cycle (Sanders and Bancroft, 1982). In all of these cases hormones might not be involved. Thus the midcycle peak could be a result of hormonal fluctuations, and the premenstrual and postmenstrual peaks could be a result of nonhormonal influences. There is a complex interaction between the hormonal system and psychological and social factors in the patterning of sexual behavior during the menstrual cycle.

Menstrual cycle, moods, and premenstrual tension It has long been assumed that women experience mood fluctuations with the different phases of the menstrual cycle. Research on the relationship between mood and menstrual cycle phase supports this notion. Negative feelings, such as irritability, anxiety, hostility, and depression, tend to increase 2 to 4 days before the start of the menstrual flow and continue until the end of the menstrual flow. These negative mood changes are often called premenstrual tension. Furthermore, self-confidence and self-esteem tend to be high at ovulation. These conclusions are based on a variety of research. Generally speaking, studies in this area have

Women with premenstrual tension may exhibit such symptoms as irritability, anxiety, hostility, and depression around the time of their menstrual flow.

employed retrospective and prospective research design. Retrospective designs are more likely than prospective studies to be associated with reports of cyclical changes in symptoms. In addition, symptoms reported retrospectively are often consistent with negative stereotypic beliefs concerning menstrual symptoms even though prospective ratings of symptoms for the same cycle *do not* show such symptoms (Parlee, 1982).

Some research is based on women's self-reports. For example, women were asked to rate on a questionnaire how they experienced various moods during the premenstrual, menstrual, and intermenstrual (phase between menstrual and premenstrual phases) phases of their last menstrual cycle. Such research typically indicates that women believe that they experience more negative feelings during the premenstrual and menstrual phases of their cycles than during the intermenstrual phase (Moos, 1968).

Researchers have developed other measures to monitor moods and the menstrual cycle. Gottschalk and associates (1962), for example, asked women to speak freely on any topic they wanted for 15 minutes; the tape recordings of these 5-minute talks were then scored according to the negative feelings exhibited. Using this technique Gottschalk and his associates found that more negative feelings were apparent in the talks given in the premenstrual phase than in those given at other times during the menstrual cycle; fewer negative feelings were reported at ovulation than at any other time.

Are hormonal fluctuations during the menstrual cycle responsible for mood changes during different phases of the cycle? Paige (1971) looked at the effects of hormones and moods by investigating the effects of different types of oral contraceptives. Paige compared three groups of women: women not taking oral contraceptives, women taking sequential pills (15 days of estrogen followed by 5 days of estrogen and progesterone; these pills are no longer used for contraception), and women taking combination pills (estrogen plus progesterone in a steady, unvarying dose throughout the cycle). Comparing the effects of sequential and combination pills allowed Paige to determine the effects of hormones because the two kinds of oral contraceptives provide different types of hormones because the two kinds of oral contraceptives provide different types of hormones at different times during the cycle. Paige found that the women taking the sequential pills showed the same mood fluctuations during their cycles as the women who were not using oral contraceptives. However, the women taking the combination pills did not show any mood fluctuations over the course of their cycles. These results indicate that hormones did affect the moods of the women in the study.

Similar findings were obtained by Rossi and Rossi (1977). They monitored 67 women and 15 men for mood changes over a span of at least 40 days. The individuals were between 17 and 21 years of age. Each day they filled out rating slips to record their moods of the preceding 24 hours. Of the women 24% were using oral contraceptives. The researchers looked at daily mood measures based on the day of the week (for example, Monday, Tuesday) for males and females and day of the menstrual cycle for females. Thus for men mood changes were studied over the course of 7-day periods, and for women mood changes were studied over the course of 7-day periods and for the day of the menstrual cycle. The researchers knew what day of the week each woman's flow began and what day of the week she ovulated. Using sophisticated statistical analysis techniques, the researchers concluded the following for women: (1) the ovulatory phase or midcycle was characterized by an increase in positive moods and fewer negative moods, (2) only days 1 and 2 of the cycle (the onset of the menses) showed a significant increase in negative moods, (3) the progestational phase of the cycle was characterized by an increase in negative moods and fewer positive moods, and (4) there was no significant increase in negative moods in the premenstrual phase, which contradicts other studies. The only change exhibited by women taking oral contraceptives was an increase in negative feelings on the first day of the flow.

Rossi and Rossi (1977) also looked at social week and mood patterns and concluded that positive moods peak on Fridays and the low point is reached on Tuesdays. Their data suggest that men's moods are more strongly structured by the social week than women's, perhaps because women's moods are also affected by the menstrual cycle phase. However, the researchers did not find that either menstruation or ovulation taking place on a weekend produced a significant change in mood when compared with the occurrence of these events on the weekdays. In a more recent study, Gallant and associates (in press) found that for both women and men, negative moods were higher on Wednesday and feelings of well-being were lower on Tuesday, Wednesday, and Thursday and highest on Friday and Saturday. Negative physical symptoms tended to be higher on Monday for both men and women. Gallant and colleagues found that the phase of the menstrual cycle was more important than the day of the week for variations in physical symptoms and depression, but not for dysphoric moods (dissatisfaction, anxiousness, and restlessness), suggesting that the cycle more strongly influences depression than dysphoric moods.

In a recent study, cyclical changes in moods and symptoms were monitored in 34 women with normal cycles and 23 men (Gallant et al., in press). The women in the study were divided into two groups. One group (the awareness group) was told that the specific purpose of the study was to investigate changes in mood, behavior, and physical symptoms during the menstrual cycle. The other group of women (the unaware group) and the men were told that the study's purpose was to investigate the effects of daily experiences on physical and emotional health. No mention of the menstrual cycle as a variable was made to these subjects. The women were monitored for two menstrual cycles, and the men were followed for a two-month period that coincided with the two menstrual cycles of the females. An artificial 28-day cycle was created for the men by randomly selecting one of their daily reporting days as day 1 and constructing two 28-day cycles from this day. Each subject, including the men, completed daily rating of moods and symptoms. All female subjects had hormone measurements, basal body temperature data, and self-reports of the menses to determine cycle phase.

Gallant and associates (in press) found that daily ratings revealed five factors, including dysphoric moods (defined by the authors as dissatisfaction, anxiety, and restlessness), well-being, physical symptoms, personal space (a desire to spend time alone), and depression. Women in the awareness group showed cyclical changes on all of these measures over the course of the menstrual cycle, while women in the unaware group reported cyclical changes in physical symptoms, well-being, and depression, but not personal space and dysphoric moods, during the cycle. Thus the pattern of cyclical variation in the measures differed in the two groups, but the two groups did not differ in absolute ratings of the measures at any cycle phase. For example, although both grops did show more depression during the menses, the amount of depression was not greater in the aware group than in the unaware group. For dysphoric moods, the aware group showed an effect based on cycle phase, but the severity of the negative moods was not different from the unaware group, who did not show an effect of cycle phase on this measure. The unaware group of women was not different from the men in degree of negative or positive ratings of any measures, and the aware group differed from men only in reporting more severe physical symptoms premenstrually than the men reported at any time during the 2 months of the study. Women in the aware group tended to show in the course of their cycles (1) greater dysphoric moods during the menses, (2) greater physical symptoms during the premenstrual and menstrual phases, (3) greater feelings of well-being around the time of ovulation, (4) a desire for personal space during the menstrual and premenstrual phases, and (5) greater depression during the menses. The women in the unaware group also reported cyclical changes in physical symptoms, well-being, and depression that were similar to those in the aware group. Gallant and associates concluded that being aware of the nature of the study did yield cyclical fluctuations in the measures studied, but that the degree and intensity of cyclical changes were not as great as expected.

In a study that measured hormones and moods during phases of the menstrual cycle, no significant fluctuations in mood as a function of the menstrual phase were found (Lahmeyer, Miller, and DeLeon-Jones, 1982). This study confirms a similar study that also attempted to correlate moods with hormone fluctuations during the menstrual cycle (Abplanalp et al., 1977). We can conclude that most studies do find variations in mood as a function of the menstrual cycle. It is more difficult to correlate these mood changes with absolute hormone levels during the menstrual cycle.

PREMENSTRUAL SYNDROME   The term *premenstrual syndrome* (PMS) refers to a wide variety of symptoms that always occur before the onset of the menstrual flow (Rolker-Dolinsky, 1987). The type and severity of PMS symptoms vary from woman to woman. The most common symptoms are tension, irritability, anger, depression, tiredness, anxiety, headaches, backaches, breast swelling and tenderness, bloating, sleep disorders, a craving for sweet (chocolate) or salty (potato chips) foods, and a sense of not being in control. In more severe PMS, women have motor function impairment, including decreased coordination and clumsiness.

The cause of PMS is not understood, but hormones are thought to play a major role (see accompanying box), with psychosociocultural aspects contributing to the symptoms (Rolker-Dolinsky, 1987). Depending on the study and the definition used to describe PMS, estimates of the incidence of PMS among women in the United States vary from 15% to 95% (Rolker-Dolinsky, 1987). A competent physician or a women's self-help group can refer a woman with suspected PMS to a PMS support group.

The American Psychiatric Association (APA) does not include PMS on its official list of recognized mental disorders that appears in the revised third edition of the *Diagnostic and Statistical Manual of Mental Disorders* (1987). The APA proposed a narrow definition of PMS, which they termed *periluteal* (around the time of the luteal part of the cycle when progesterone predominates) *phase dysphoric* (feeling of depression without apparent cause) *disorder* (PPDD). The criteria used to diagnose PPDD are stated in the APA text; the patient must have certain symptoms, including irritability, anger, anxiety, depression, and at least one other listed in the text, for the diagnosis of PPDD to be confirmed.

A recent article by practicing physicians reviewed the various treatments for PMS and suggested the best approaches to achieve successful management of this disorder (Chuong and Gibbons, 1990). The use of placebos to treat PMS has produced positive results 40% to 95% of the time (Chuong and Gibbons, 1990). Because placebos give such highly positive results, drug therapy does not seem to be the first course of action for most women with PMS. Chuong and Gibbons recommend that education, diet, and exercise should be the first order of business in women with PMS. If after 1 or 2 months the patient does not report some relief, drug therapy should be added to the treatment.

Education for a patient with PMS involves reassuring her that PMS is a problem common to many women. It means listening to her and encouraging her to keep a diary of her moods, feelings, activities, and symptoms during the premenstrual time. This, according to Chuong and Gibbons (1990), allows

Premenstrual Syndrome

In the past 15 to 20 years there has been considerable interest in premenstrual symptoms. Probably as much has been written about premenstrual syndrome (PMS) in the lay literature as in the medical literature. Despite the recent popularity of the subject and interest in the condition, PMS remains loosely defined and without an understanding of its cause or therapy. There is no single definition of the syndrome, and no agreement in the medical community as to how many symptoms should be included in PMS. As of 1990, numerous hypotheses had been advanced to explain PMS, but a cohesive formula to explain the physiological and pathological aspects of PMS has yet to be established. PMS has been attributed to estrogen excess; progesterone deficiency; insufficient vitamin B, vitamin B_6, or vitamin A; hypoglycemia; allergy to the female hormones; psychosomatic causes; fluid retention; prolactin excess; thyroid hormone imbalance; and abnormalities within the neurotransmitter system of the brain. One of the more popular theories to explain PMS is an imbalance of estrogen-progesterone levels during the latter part of the menstrual cycle. Dr. Kathryn Dalton, a British physician and one of the champions of PMS, has postulated that women with severe PMS have a deficiency of progesterone; however, measurement of the blood levels of progesterone in women with PMS has failed to show a consistent reduction in the level of progesterone. Other investigators have suggested that although women with PMS may not have an absolute deficiency of progesterone, they may have a relative imbalance in the estrogen/progesterone ratio during the latter part of the menstrual cycle. PMS symptoms have also been attributed to fluid retention in various organs. It has been suggested that the major symptoms in an individual patient are determined by the particular tissue or organ with fluid retention: fluid retention in the brain will produce headache; in the intestinal tract, nausea and bloating; in the breast, swelling, tenderness, and pain. Although many women with PMS feel bloated and note swelling of the abdomen or extremities, few have actual weight gain. This failure to show weight gain has raised the possibility that the symptoms of PMS are related to redistribution of fluid rather than abnormal retention. It has also been suggested that the weight gain in some patients with PMS is not a result of the PMS process itself, but of the excessive carbohydrate and salt some women ingest during the latter part of their cycle. Most recently there has been interest in the influence or regulation of the menstrual cycle by endorphins of the central nervous system (the brain and spinal cord). *Endorphins* are proteins that are widely distributed throughout the body and that may function as transmitters of neurological information within the brain. It is conceivable that excessive release and sudden withdrawal of endorphins in the body over the cycle could cause many of the symptoms of PMS. Although the basic cause of PMS—if there is a single basic cause—is unknown, a number of therapies have been used to treat PMS: progesterone administration, lithium carbonate, vitamin B_6, testosterone, estrogen, oral contraceptives, tranquilizers, regular breakfast, aspirin, orgasm, bromocriptine, scientific information and emotional support, potassium, calcium, magnesium, low-sodium diet, high-protein diet, high-fiber diet, amphetamines, and diuretics. Few of these therapies have been studied in an appropriate double-blind controlled investigation, that is, one in which the patients and researchers are not aware of which treatment group each subject is in. None of the treatments has been shown to be superior to a placebo (sugar pills, sterile water) for treatment of premenstrual symptoms, and many have provided only temporary improvement, on the order of a few months, in symptoms of PMS. The lack of objective findings in patients with PMS has made the condition difficult to study. Usually, a beneficial therapeutic effect is viewed as an improvement in the patient's sense of well-being—a relatively vague and intangible marker. This lack of tangible or objective findings complicates evaluation of different therapeutic trials.

In the absence of any well-established therapy that does not have serious adverse effects, many physicians are reluctant to treat premenstrual symptoms with drugs. Physicians who do treat PMS will often initially try to assure the patient that many of her perceptions are not imagined, that indeed her symptoms are real. Patients are encouraged to follow a high-protein diet with frequent feeding and to initiate or continue regular exercise throughout the latter part of the menstrual cycle.

From Ann McBride, M.D., University of Kansas.

the physician to determine whether the problem is in fact PMS and allows the patient to be conscious of the specific changes that are happening to her and then to decide, with her physician, how she can cope with them. Once the physician has decided that the patient has PMS, the patient and physician agree on a course of treatment.

The first thing that Chuong and Gibbons (1990) and others (Abraham and Rumley, 1987) recommend is a change in life-style that involves diet and exercise. The PMS prevention diet (Lark, 1985; Abraham and Rumley, 1987) includes whole grains, legumes, seeds, nuts, vegetables, and fruits and promotes avoidance of foods high in sugar and fat. Reducing the intake of caffeine and salt is also recommended.

In addition to dietary changes, many researchers recommend regular exercise (Chuong and Gibbons, 1990). A study in Finland found that PMS symptoms were milder in women who participated in sports than in women who did not exercise regularly (Timonen and Procope, 1971).

If significant relief is not found through life-style changes, Chuong and Gibbons (1990) recommend that patients with mild to moderate symptoms be given vitamins and minerals or progesterone. Some research suggests that PMS symptoms may be related to vitamin and mineral deficiencies (Abraham and

Regular exercise can help to relieve some symptoms of premenstrual syndrome.

HUMAN SEXUALITY

Rumley, 1987), but other studies have found no differences in vitamin or mineral concentrations in the blood of PMS patients and control subjects (Chuong and Dawson, 1987; Mira et al., 1988). As Chuong and Gibbons (1990) point out, blood levels of the vitamins and minerals might not differ between these groups, but whether blood levels reflect levels in the brain is not known and requires further study. In any case, vitamin and mineral supplementation has been found to relieve PMS symptoms (Abraham and Rumley, 1987; Kendall and Schnurr, 1987; London, Murphy, and Kittowski, 1987). Only the study by London and associates employed a double-blind research design (neither the patients nor the researchers knew who was receiving the supplementation and who was receiving the placebo), so the positive effects in the other two studies could have been due to a placebo effect.

If no improvement is seen after 2 to 3 months of vitamin and mineral supplementation, the patient is given naltrexone. Naltrexone is an opioid antagonist (antagonizes the opioid compounds naturally produced by the body). The rationale for giving this drug is that naltrexone helps to maintain levels of beta endorphin (a chemical in the brain). Beta endorphin levels decrease in PMS patients just before menses, and perhaps this decrease is responsible for some PMS symptoms. Patients with severe PMS symptoms receive naltrexone at the beginning of treatment. If naltrexone does not provide relief in 2 to 3 months, Chuong and Gibbons (1990) consider the use of a gonadotropin hormone–releasing hormone (GnRH) agonist (an agonist mimics the drug or naturally occurring compound and produces its effects). The GnRH agonist acts on the anterior pituitary gland to release FSH and LH, which stimulate the ovaries to produce estrogen and progesterone. The rationale for using the GnRH agonist is to provide extra estrogen and progesterone to the patient. As previously stated, some researchers have implicated deficiencies of estrogen and progesterone as causing some PMS symptoms. In addition, extra estrogen and progesterone might be given to the patient. *In conclusion, every treatment works for someone, but no single treatment works for everyone.*

A number of investigators, such as Dalton (1961), report that the number of women prisoners who had committed their crimes during either the premenstrual or menstrual phase of their cycles was much greater than would be expected by chance. Likewise, studies of women admitted to hospitals because of accidents indicate that a much higher proportion of these women than would be expected by chance were in either the premenstrual or menstrual phase of their cycles (Dalton, 1960). Admissions to psychiatric hospitals also appear to occur more frequently during the menstrual phase of the cycle than during the nonmenstrual phase (Dalton, 1959). Further, it is reported that women are more likely to commit suicide (Ribeiro, 1962) or call a suicide prevention center for help (Mandell and Mandell, 1967) during the menstrual and premenstrual phases of their cycles.

All of the previously cited studies (which are referenced in many human sexuality textbooks without any cautionary notes about interpretation) were done before 1970, and all are flawed methodologically. Dalton's work tends to be cursory, and Mandell and Mandell rely on self-reported data. *It is important to remember that the same stressful situation that caused the severe psychological problems could have caused the onset of an early flow. A serious accident could have the same effect. We cannot be sure that these problems occurred in response to*

Menstrual Cycle and Athletic Performance

Although many women athletes (and their coaches) are convinced that menstruation and the time just before menstruation negatively affect their athletic performance, few studies have explored this important topic. In some studies women have been asked when in their cycle they think their athletic performance is worst. Studies of this type are called retrospective studies because the woman is asked to remember something in the past. In the retrospective studies women claim to have had performance decrements during the premenstrual and menstrual phases of the cycle.

The correct way to determine whether the menstrual cycle influences athletic performance is to use a prospective research design. In this research design the women keep a daily log of their menstrual cycle phases and a person such as a coach keeps track of how they perform in their particular athletic event. Performance measures may be monitored during practice or during actual competitions. Quadagno and associates (1991) recently completed a prospective study to determine whether the phase of the menstrual cycle influenced athletic performance as measured by weight lifting and swimming. All subjects had regular menstrual cycles and did not use oral contraceptives.

The subjects in the weight-lifting study were 12 recreational weight lifters (mean age 24.3 years) who lifted weights at least three times per week. The strength tests were done during the premenstrual (3 to 4 days before menses), menstrual (day 1 or 2 of the flow), and postmenstrual (usually 1 to 12 days after onset of menses) phases of the cycle. The strength tests consisted of the bench press and leg press. In the bench press the subject lies flat on her back and moves the weight upward with the arms. In the leg press the subject sits upright and moves the weight outward with the legs. The maximum weight each subject could lift was determined for each phase of the cycle, and also each subject was tested to determine the maximum number of times 70% of the maximum weight could be lifted. The results (see the table below) indicated that the phase of the menstrual cycle had no significant effect on strength as measured by the bench press and leg press.

Weight-Lifting Performance by Cycle Phase for the Mean Number of Times the Subject Could Lift 70% of Her Maximum Weight (Numbers in parentheses are maximum weight subject could lift in pounds)

Phase	Bench press	Leg press
Premenstrual	13.8 (87.7)	25.8 (185.9)
Menstrual	13.9 (87.6)	24.1 (185.8)
Postmenstrual	12.5 (87.5)	24.4 (182.9)

The subjects in the swimming performance study were women who swam for the Florida State University varsity swim team (mean age 19.2 years). The subjects performed repeated time trials for the 100-meter and 200-meter free-style events during the same three phases of the menstrual cycle as described for the weight lifters. No significant differences were found in swim times during any of the cycle phases (see the table below), although times tended to be a little slower in the 200-meter event during the menses.

Swimming Performance Times (in Seconds) in 100- and 200-Meter Events by Cycle Phase

Phase	100 meters	200 meters
Premenstrual	68.4	144.1
Menstrual	70.7	151.3
Postmenstrual	69.1	147.2

Although many women athletes feel that their performance is impaired during the premenstrual and menstrual phases of the menstrual cycle, the phase of the menstrual cycle does not affect athletic performance as measured by strength and swimming speed in short-distance events. Perhaps the cycle would influence athletic events of longer duration, but no studies have explored this question.

menstrual cycle changes. It may be that the menstrual cycle changed in response to the problems. This important area needs more study.

Dalton, of London's Premenstrual Syndrome Clinic, claims that she has studied certain women who have violent outbursts just before the onset of the menstrual flow. She attributes these episodes of violence to the drop in progesterone level that occurs just before the menses. Using the theory that hormones influence the behavior of women beyond their ability to control their actions, Dalton has testified at various legal trials in Great Britain and has succeeded in having legal charges reduced. In one case a woman killed someone with a knife, and the charge was reduced from murder to manslaughter on the grounds that she committed the crime when she was experiencing PMS (Laws, 1983). Whether this controversial defense tactic will become widespread in the legal system of other countries, including the United States, remains to be seen (Rolker-Dolinsky, 1987). Many women's groups worry that such a defense would reinforce the negative myths about the menstrual cycle that already exist. The decision by the APA not to include PMS as a mental disorder will help to reduce myths about mental health and the menstrual cycle.

Menstrual cycle and intellectual performance Since mood varies as a function of the menstrual cycle, we might suspect that the menstrual cycle could affect intellectual performance as well. It seems reasonable that the way we feel will affect how we perform. However, studies have found little if any relationship between intellectual performance and the phase of the menstrual cycle. Sommer (1973) found no correlation between perceptual-motor performance and the phase of the menstrual cycle in college students. Wickham (1958) found no significant differences in women's scores on intelligence tests during the 4 days before and 4 days after the onset of the menstrual cycle. Sommer also did not find any menstrual cycle–related performance differences either in class examination performance or on a test of critical thinking. These findings were confirmed by Bernstein (1977), who studied the academic performance of 126 undergraduate women during their menstrual cycles.

We can conclude that no clear relationship exists between phases of the menstrual cycle and intellectual performance, even though some women believe that they perform less well during the premenstrual and menstrual phases of their cycles. Perhaps these reports are more related to negative moods than to an accurate self-assessment of performance.

SUMMARY

1 Endocrinology is the study of the endocrine glands of the body. These glands produce hormones that travel via the bloodstream to affect various tissues.
2 Neuroendocrinology is the study of how the central nervous system, in particular the brain, controls the endocrine system.
3 The anterior pituitary gland is controlled by hormones produced in the hypothalamic portion of the brain. These hormones govern what hormones are released from the anterior pituitary gland through a negative-feedback system that involves other endocrine glands affected by anterior pituitary hormones.

4 The posterior pituitary gland stores hormones produced in the hypothalamic portion of the brain until a nervous stimulus activates their release.

5 The healthy male produces sperm in the testes at a relatively constant rate well into old age.

6 The healthy female produces eggs in a cyclical manner and has definite fertility periods when compared with the male, who theoretically is fertile all of the time.

7 Biologically menstruation has been defined as the failure of pregnancy to occur because the events that take place before the onset of menstruation in each monthly cycle are preparations for pregancy. The first day of the menstrual cycle is considered to be the day of the onset of bleeding. If a 28-day cycle is assumed, the menstrual cycle may be divided into four phases: menses, estrogenic phase, ovulation, and progestational phase.

8 Three common problems that occur during the menstrual cycle are premenstrual tension, dysmenorrhea or painful menstruation, and amenorrhea or abnormal absence of a menstrual flow.

9 Testosterone is not essential for the display of male sexual behavior in humans because sexual behavior is influenced by both hormones and past experiences.

10 There is little evidence that males undergo hormone-related changes in mood.

11 Some evidence indicates that human females may be more sexually aroused during the days closest to ovulation.

12 Many women experience some mood fluctuations during the course of the menstrual cycle.

13 Intellectual performance appears to have little if any relationship to the menstrual cycle.

FACT
OR
FICTION

ANSWERS

1 Several studies have indicated that women who live together or who spend a great deal of time together become synchronized in the onset of their menstrual flows.

2 Castration of a male does not always lead to a reduction or loss of sex drive.

3 Although many women think their athletic performance is poorer during the premenstrual and menstrual phases of the cycle, evidence indicates that this is not true.

4 No evidence indicates that athletic performance is hindered by engaging in sexual intercourse before the event.

1. Discuss the structural relationship between the hypothalamus and the anterior and pituitary glands. What relationship exists between the anterior pituitary gland and the ovaries and testes in terms of the anterior pituitary gland release of hormones?

2. Discuss the hormonal events that occur during each of the four phases of the menstrual cycle and the events occurring in the uterus during each phase.

3. Pretend that you had to teach your son or daughter about the menstrual cycle, both biological and psychological factors. Write out what you would try to impart to the child.

SUGGESTED READINGS

Kelley, K., editor: Females, males, and sexuality, Albany, 1987, State University of New York Press.
Chapters by contributing authors deal with PMS, hormones, and sex-related behavior. The discussion of PMS is excellent.

Maddux, H.: Menstruation, Wayne, Penn., 1981, Banbury Books, Inc.
An easy-to-follow book that deals with female anatomy, menstruation, menstrual problems, menopause, and ways to prevent menstrual difficulties.

Tortora, G., and Anagnostakos, N.: Principles of anatomy and physiology, ed. 5, New York, 1989, Harper & Row, Publishers, Inc.
This biology book for the non–biology major contains easily understandable sections on endocrinology and neuroendocrinology.

Human Sexual Response

FACT
OR
FICTION

1
Heterosexual individuals respond differently to sexual stimulation than homosexuals do.

2
Women respond to sexual stimulation differently from men.

3
Erections in men are controlled by two separate areas of the spinal cord.

When people talk about sexual arousal, they frequently say they are "turned on," "revved up," or "hot." Each phase likens sexual arousal to an energy system, and as a starting point, this comparison is useful. From a scientific perspective, sexual arousal can be defined as a state of activation of a complex system of reflexes involving the sex organs and the nervous system.

W. MASTERS, V. JOHNSON, AND R. KOLODNY
Masters and Johnson on Sex and Loving, p. 56

How do men and women respond to sexual stimulation? What changes occur in the body when a person is sexually stimulated by another person? Do these same changes occur in the body if the person is having a sexual fantasy, masturbating, or looking at erotic magazines or films? Thanks to the work of Masters and Johnson (1966) and others we can answer these interesting and important questions. This chapter deals mainly with the physiological responses that occur during sexual excitation. Sexual response has many aspects, including social and cultural factors, personal feelings and beliefs, the physical environment, gender, age, the relationship between the sexual partners, and the degree of communication between the individuals engaging in the sexual experience. We discuss some of these variables that contribute to the sexual response in Chapters 9 and 14.

Masters and Johnson (1966) make it clear that "there is wide individual variation in the duration and intensity of every specific physiologic response to sexual stimulation." A variety exists in types of sexual activity, including sex acts with others and masturbation. Individuals subjectively feel that at some times sex acts are more exciting and pleasurable than at other times. Some orgasms feel more intense and satisfying when compared with previous orgasms. Thus there is variation in sexual response within the individual. There are also tremendous differences among individuals.

Masters and Johnson have studied the biological responses that occur during sexual excitation. All the information in this chapter is applicable to men and women regardless of their sexual orientation. In 1979 Masters and Johnson studied homosexual men and women and found no differences in physiological functioning related to sexual arousal and orgasm.

HUMAN SEXUAL RESPONSE CYCLE

Masters and Johnson describe the human sexual response cycle in their classic study *Human Sexual Response* (1966), which involved approximately 11 years of work. To illustrate and describe the physical changes that occur during sexual excitation, Masters and Johnson divided the human cycle of sexual response into four phases. The entire cycle is called the sexual response cycle. The four phases are (1) the excitement phase, (2) the plateau phase, (3) the orgasmic phase, and (4) the resolution phase (Table 5-1). Two basic physiological responses occur during sexual excitation. The first and primary response is **vasocongestion,** a generalized congestion of blood in the internal and external reproductive structures. Vasocongestion causes erection of the penis and swelling of the clitoris, vagina, labia majora, and labia minora, as well as other reproductive structures in the male and female. The secondary response is a

vasocongestion
(vas' oh kuhn JES chuhn)
Increased amount of blood concentrated in body tissues.

TABLE 5-1 Sexual Response Cycle of the Human Male and Female—Extragenital Reactions

	Excitement phase	Plateau phase	Orgasmic phase	Resolution phase
Breasts	Nipple erection; increase in breast size in females only	Nipple becomes hard; further increase in breast size; areolar engorgement	No changes	Blood leaves areolae; erection of nipple disappears; decrease in breast size
Sex flush	Appearance of rash in late phase; first appears on upper part of abdomen, then on breasts	Well-developed; may have widespread body distribution	Reaches peak of color	Rapid disappearance of rash
Myotonia	Voluntary muscles of arms and legs tense; involuntary muscles become tense	Further increase in voluntary and involuntary muscle tension; may be grimaces of facial muscles, tension in neck muscles, and involuntary contractions in hands and feet	Loss of voluntary control; involuntary contractions or spasms of muscle groups	Muscles return to relaxed state within 5 minutes after orgasm
Rectum	No change	No change	Involuntary contractions of rectal sphincter occurring at same time as contractions of orgasmic platform and of ejaculation	Return to normal
Hyperventilation (faster and deeper breathing)	None	Occurs late in this phase	Respiratory rates as high as 40 breaths/minute	Return to normal
Tachycardia	Heart rate increase begins	Recorded rates average from 100-175 beats/minute	Recorded rates range from 100-180 + beats/minute	Return to normal
Blood pressure	Increase begins	Increased elevation	Greater increases	Return to normal
Perspiration	No change	No change	No change	Appearance of widespread film of perspiration

Modified from Masters and Johnson, 1966.

The first phase of the human sexual response cycle, called the excitement phase, begins with physical or psychological sexual stimulation.

generalized increase in muscle contractions termed **myotonia.** This muscle tension develops in both voluntary and involuntary muscles.

myotonia
(my′ uh TOH nee uh) Involuntary muscle tension.

Excitement Phase

The first phase of the sexual response cycle is the **excitement phase.** It can develop from either physical stimulation, such as manual touching of the genitals or other erogenous areas of the body, or psychological stimulation, such as erotic fantasies or remembering past sexual activities. If the stimulation continues, the intensity of the response of the male or female will increase rapidly. The excitement phase can be short or prolonged depending on the stimuli and the individual. If the stimuli become objectionable or an interruption occurs, the excitement phase may be prolonged or it may end. For instance, if one partner touches the other in a manner that is not pleasurable (for example, rubbing the clitoris too hard or squeezing the testicles with too much pressure), the excitement phase will be longer because of the interruption in pleasurable stimulation. If the stimuli are really objectionable, the excitement phase could end and the couple could cease their sexual activities. It is during the excitement phase that sexual arousal first occurs. Sexual arousal can be defined as a drive state based on the need to relieve sexual tensions (Kelley and Byrne, 1983). Sexual arousal consists of both physiological and psychological changes from an unaroused state to an aroused state.

excitement phase
First phase of human sexual response cycle, which results from physical or psychological sexual stimulation. Vasocongestion and myotonia begin at this time.

Changes in female The major changes occurring in the female are that the nipples become erect (Figure 5-1), the breasts swell (20% to 25% increase in size as a result of vasocongestion), the clitoris becomes engorged or filled with blood and increases in diameter, and the vagina begins to exude a clear

FIGURE 5-1
Changes in the breasts during the female sexual response cycle.

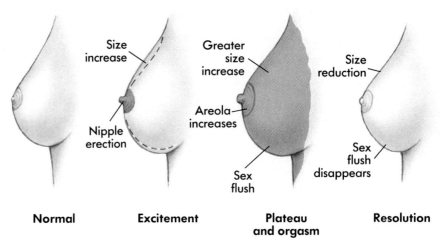

Normal   Excitement   Plateau and orgasm   Resolution

fluid and lubricate itself 10 to 30 seconds after stimulation begins (Figure 5-2, *A*, and Table 5-2). This vaginal lubrication is caused by vasocongestion in the vaginal walls. Individual droplets of mucuslike material appear on the inside of the vagina like perspiration. As excitement increases, the droplets run together to form a smooth, glistening coating for the entire vagina. The upper two thirds of the vagina opens or expands, and the vagina increases in length. In the unexcited state the vagina is only a potential cavity, with its walls touching each other; now it opens up like a balloon being blown up. This ballooning action helps the vagina accommodate the penis if intercourse is to

---

TABLE 5-2 Sexual Response Cycle of the Human Female—Genital Reactions

Genital structure	Excitement phase	Plateau phase	Orgasmic phase	Resolution phase
Clitoris	Vasocongestive increase in diameter, and to lesser degree, shaft elongation	Clitoral body (shaft and glans) retracts from normal position to position against the anterior border of pubic symphysis beneath prepuce	No change	Return to normal size and position
Vagina	Appearance of vaginal lubrication within 10-30 seconds after stimulation begins; expansion and distension of vaginal barrel	Development of orgasmic platform (vasocongestion of outer one third of vagina)	Contractions of orgasmic platform occur 3-15 times	Return to normal
Labia majora	Flatten and move away from vaginal opening because of vasocongestive increase in size	No change	No change	Return to normal
Labia minora	Increase to two to three times usual because of vasocongestion	No change except in color	No change	Return to normal
Uterus	Elevates and increases in size because of vasocongestion	Uterus is fully elevated	Contractions of uterus	Return to normal

Modified from Masters and Johnson, 1966.

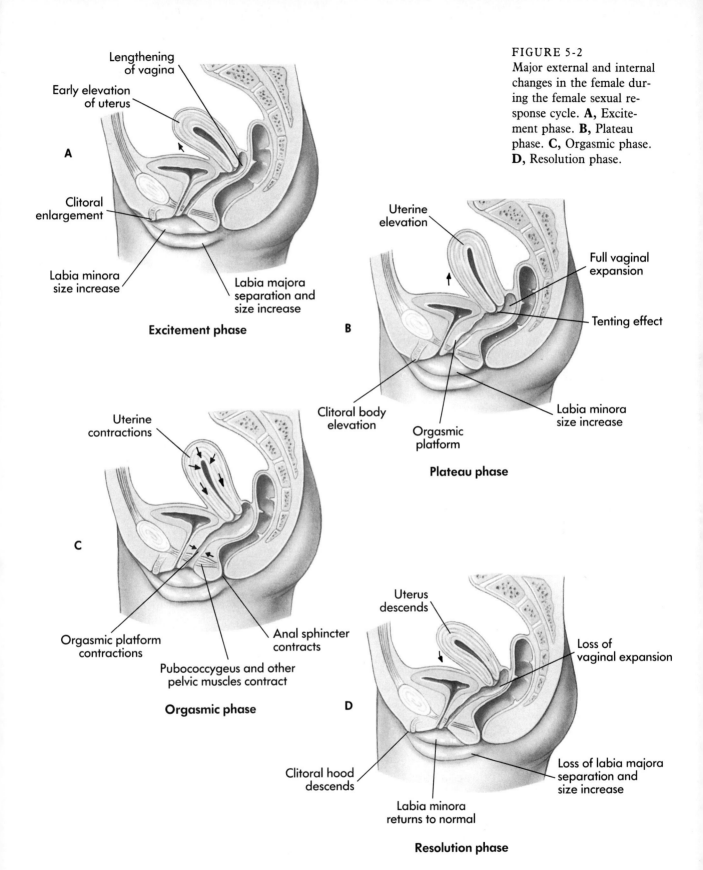

FIGURE 5-2
Major external and internal changes in the female during the female sexual response cycle. **A,** Excitement phase. **B,** Plateau phase. **C,** Orgasmic phase. **D,** Resolution phase.

A

Lengthening of vagina

Early elevation of uterus

Clitoral enlargement

Labia minora size increase

Labia majora separation and size increase

Excitement phase

B

Uterine elevation

Full vaginal expansion

Tenting effect

Labia minora size increase

Clitoral body elevation

Orgasmic platform

Plateau phase

C

Uterine contractions

Orgasmic platform contractions

Pubococcygeus and other pelvic muscles contract

Anal sphincter contracts

Orgasmic phase

D

Uterus descends

Loss of vaginal expansion

Clitoral hood descends

Labia minora returns to normal

Loss of labia majora separation and size increase

Resolution phase

TABLE 5-3 Sexual Response Cycle of the Human Male—Genital Reactions

Genital structure	Excitement phase	Plateau phase	Orgasmic phase	Resolution phase
Penis	Becomes erect	Increase in penile circumference at coronal ridge	Expulsive contractions of entire penile urethra; contractions start at 0.8-second intervals and after the first three or four they are reduced in frequency and force	Return to normal
Scrotum	Elevates and skin thickens because of vasocongestive response	No change	No change	Return to normal
Testes	Increase in size and pulled toward body	Enlargement of testes and elevation against the perineum	No change	Return to normal
Cowper's glands	No change	2-3 drops of fluid "leak" out—preejaculatory emission	No change	No change
Secondary organs (seminal vesicles, prostate gland)	No change	No change	Contractions of organs	No change

Modified from Masters and Johnson, 1966.

occur. The uterus elevates from its normal position and moves upward. The labia minora enlarge as a result of vasocongestion, and the labia majora flatten, swell, and move apart for partial exposure of the vestibule of the vagina.

Changes in male   The major changes that occur in the male are erection of the penis (3 to 5 seconds after stimulation in young men and longer with age), elevation of the testes closer to the body, swelling of the testes, thickening of the scrotal skin, and nipple erection (Figure 5-3, *A*, and Table 5-3).

Changes common to female and male   Changes that may occur in both males and females include a **sex flush,** an increase in muscle tension, and an increase in heart rate and blood pressure. The sex flush is easily detected in fair-skinned individuals but difficult or impossible to detect in dark-skinned men and women.

Plateau Phase

If effective sexual stimulation continues, the individual moves from the excitement phase to the **plateau phase.** In this phase sexual excitement and sexual tensions are greatly increased, and the individual may move from this phase to the orgasmic phase. The duration of the plateau phase depends on the stimuli

sex flush
Red rash resembling blush caused by dilation of blood vessels just below skin in region of face, neck, and chest.

plateau phase
(pla TOH) Second phase of human sexual response cycle. Sexual tensions reach fairly steady level.

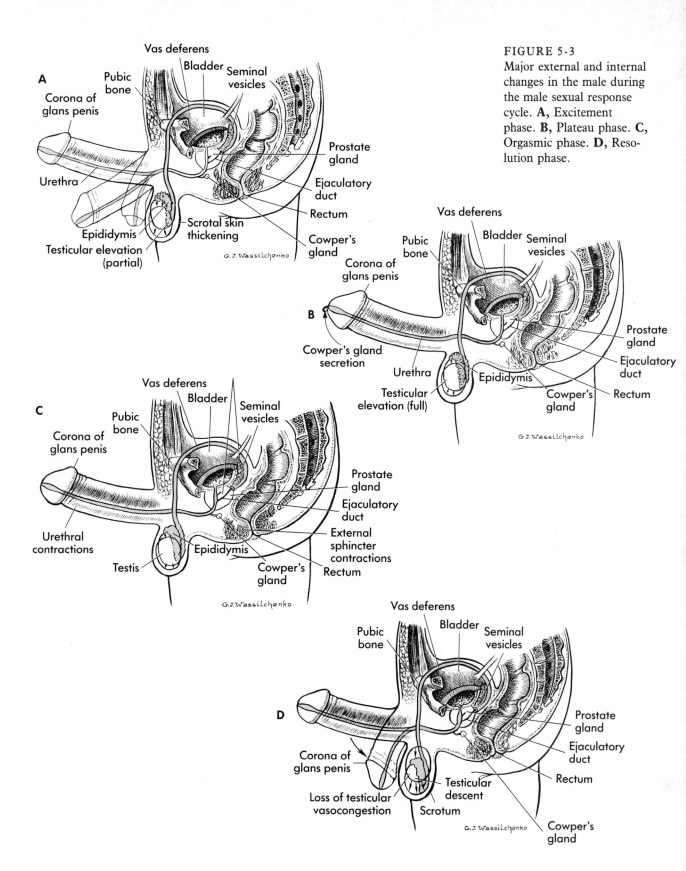

FIGURE 5-3
Major external and internal changes in the male during the male sexual response cycle. **A,** Excitement phase. **B,** Plateau phase. **C,** Orgasmic phase. **D,** Resolution phase.

A
Vas deferens
Pubic bone
Bladder
Seminal vesicles
Corona of glans penis
Prostate gland
Ejaculatory duct
Rectum
Cowper's gland
Urethra
Epididymis
Testicular elevation (partial)
Scrotal skin thickening
G.J.Wassilchenko

B
Vas deferens
Pubic bone
Bladder
Seminal vesicles
Corona of glans penis
Prostate gland
Ejaculatory duct
Cowper's gland secretion
Urethra
Epididymis
Cowper's gland
Rectum
Testicular elevation (full)
G.J.Wassilchenko

C
Vas deferens
Pubic bone
Bladder
Seminal vesicles
Corona of glans penis
Prostate gland
Ejaculatory duct
External sphincter contractions
Urethral contractions
Testis
Epididymis
Cowper's gland
Rectum
G.J.Wassilchenko

D
Vas deferens
Pubic bone
Bladder
Seminal vesicles
Corona of glans penis
Prostate gland
Ejaculatory duct
Rectum
Cowper's gland
Loss of testicular vasocongestion
Testicular descent
Scrotum
G.J.Wassilchenko

and the individual's drive to end sexual tension. For example, if the partners have been apart and have not engaged in sexual intercourse or other sexual activities for an extended period, the plateau phase may be short because of the mutual desire to relieve sexual tensions. On the other hand, if the partners agree to pleasure each other a great deal before orgasm, the plateau phase could last for 30 minutes or longer. If the stimuli or sexual interests are inadequate, the individual will not achieve orgasmic release and will go from the plateau phase into a prolonged resolution phase (phase four).

Changes in female   The major change that occurs in the female is greater vasocongestion, which causes more swelling of the breasts, labia majora, labia minora, and vagina (Figure 5-2, *B*, and Table 5-2). The Bartholin's glands secrete several drops of mucus in the region of the opening of the vagina. Before the work of Masters and Johnson, the lubrication seen during sexual arousal was thought to be from the Bartholin's glands. However, this is not the case; the Bartholin's glands produce only a few drops of mucus and do not account for the large quantity of lubricant in the vagina during sexual arousal. The clitoris elevates or retracts beneath the clitoral hood (prepuce). Thus penile thrusting or manual contact stimulates the clitoris indirectly through the clitoral hood. Clitoral retraction may be a mechanism to protect this sensitive structure from overstimulation during advanced sexual excitation (Masters and Johnson, 1966). The walls of the outer third of the vagina and labia minora, collectively called the orgasmic platform, become further congested with blood. The orgasmic platform narrows the outer third of the vagina as a result of vasocongestion. The upper two thirds of the vagina expands, and the uterus elevates. This causes a tenting effect to occur between the uterus and the inner portion of the vagina.

A complete discussion of preejaculatory emission is presented in Chapter 3.

Changes in male   The major change that takes place in the male is continued vasocongestion, which causes the penis, in particular the glans, to become larger and the testicles to swell 50% beyond their normal size and be pulled closer to the body (Figure 5-3, *B*, and Table 5-3). The preejaculatory emission from the Cowper's glands appears as a few drops of fluid at the tip of the penis.

Changes common to female and male   Changes that occur in both males and females include an increase in the sex flush in some women and its appearance in some men; greater voluntary and involuntary muscle tension in the legs, arms, abdomen, neck, and face; hyperventilation; further increases in heart rate (100 to 175 beats per minute as compared with approximately 75 beats per minute in the unexcited state); and an elevation in blood pressure.

orgasm
(OR gaz uhm) Release of sexual tensions. This phase of human sexual response cycle is reached when maximum sexual (physical or psychological or both) stimulation occurs.

Orgasmic Phase

What is the stimulus that causes **orgasm** in the male and female? In almost all cases it is genital stimulation. Some women can reach orgasm through breast or anal stimulation or fantasy, and some males can also reach orgasm during anal stimulation. Physical stimulation causes the orgasm, but we really do not know much about the neurological (nervous system) and biochemical events that trigger the orgasm. We express orgasm in terms such as a release from muscle tension and blood vessel engorgement and talk about the subjective experience of orgasm, but we do not know exactly what causes orgasm.

The orgasmic phase is limited to those few seconds when sexual tension is released. When it occurs, this involuntary climax is reached at the level that represents the maximal physical and psychological sexual stimulation for the particular occasion. In addition to the pleasurable sensations in the genital area, orgasm in both males and females is a cerebral cortex phenomenon. That is to say, orgasm is a subjective and personal experience. The cortex receives information and sensations from the reproductive structures, and this information is integrated with psychological information to produce the subjective experience and feeling of orgasm. Subjective awareness of the orgasm is pelvic in focus.

Both the male and female show a reduction in voluntary muscle control, which is evidenced by muscle spasms throughout the body. During orgasm both sexes have increases in blood pressure, heart rate (up to 180 beats per minute has been recorded), and breathing.

Female orgasm   The female's subjective awareness of orgasm seems to be concentrated in the clitoris, vagina, and uterus (Figure 5-2, C, and Table 5-2). In the female the onset of orgasm is accompanied by powerful involuntary contractions of the muscles of the uterus, perineum, anal sphincter, and lower abdomen. In addition, contractions of the orgasmic platform start at 0.8-second intervals and recur five to twelve times. After the first three to six contractions the intervals lengthen and the strength of contractions decreases. The first five or six contractions are the most pleasurable in subjective terms for the majority of women. Orgasmic platform and anal contractions occur simultaneously, and the contraction patterns vary among women (Bohlen et al., 1982).

The woman senses the orgasmic response subjectively from 2 to 4 seconds before to 1.5 seconds after she has the first regular contraction (Masters and Johnson, 1966; Bohlen et al., 1982). Thus the pleasurable sensation usually precedes the physiological response or begins shortly thereafter. Masters and Johnson (1966) state that female orgasm is an intricate mixture of psychological, physiological, and social influences. These factors all enter into the subjective aspect of the orgasmic experience. Masters and Johnson compiled a description of subjective responses of orgasm from 487 women in their clinic. They describe three distinct stages of a woman's subjective progression through orgasm.

> [Stage I] Orgasm has its onset with a sensation of suspension or stoppage. Lasting only an instant, the sensation is accompanied or followed by an isolated thrust of intense sexual awareness, clitorally oriented, but radiating upward into the pelvis. A simultaneous loss of overall sensory acuity (a reduction in sensation from all senses) has been described as paralleling in degree the intensity and duration of the particular orgasmic episode.
>
> [Stage II] A sensation of suffusion of warmth specifically pervading the pelvic area first and then spreading progressively throughout the body. [This feeling of warmth during an orgasmic experience was described by almost every woman in the study.]
>
> [Stage III] A feeling of involuntary contraction with specific focus in the vagina or lower pelvis, pelvic throbbing.
>
> Masters and Johnson, 1966, pp. 134-135

Thus the subjective feeling of orgasm for the women in the Masters and Johnson study, and presumably for most women, can be described as follows: At the onset of the orgasm the woman feels as if everything within her and around her has stopped. She feels suspended in time. This sensation lasts for only an instant, and then she experiences an intensely pleasurable feeling in the region of the clitoris and the pelvis. She has a reduction or loss of sensation of her surroundings and environment. A feeling of warmth spreads over the body, and then a feeling of pelvic throbbing occurs.

CONTROVERSIES ABOUT FEMALE ORGASMS The dispute about the nature of female orgasm began with Sigmund Freud (1856-1939), the famous Viennese psychoanalyst who showed the importance of sexuality to human life. Freud thought that women have two types of orgasm: clitoral and vaginal. He believed that clitoral orgasms are evidence of psychological immaturity and that a woman must progress to vaginal orgasms induced by coitus. According to Freud, clitoral stimulation must be eliminated for a woman to progress to a mature level of sexual responding. This view is not in vogue at the present time; however, it caused many problems for women when Freud's thinking dominated psychoanalytical theory.

Masters and Johnson (1966) stated that all female orgasms show the basic physiological response patterns regardless of how the orgasm is induced or stimulated. Orgasm always consists of contractions of the orgasmic platform and of the muscles surrounding the vagina. A woman who stimulates her own clitoris or has it stimulated by a partner shows the same physiological responses at orgasm as does a woman who has an orgasm in response to vaginal intercourse or breast stimulation. In addition, based on their intensive observations, Masters and Johnson believe that clitoral stimulation is almost always involved in producing an orgasm. Even if the clitoris is not directly stimulated, it is indirectly stimulated because of its relationship with the clitoral hood and labia minora. Penile thrusting exerts pressure on the labia minora, which in turn moves the clitoral hood back and forth over the clitoris. Therefore vaginal stimulation also involves some clitoral stimulation.

The subjective experience of orgasm, that is, how good it feels, is an entirely different matter and varies from one woman to the next depending on many factors, such as the type of stimulation, partner, physical environment, and time since the last sexual encounter.

Not all researchers agree with Masters and Johnson that orgasm requires clitoral stimulation. Other researchers believe that a woman can also experience vaginal and uterine orgasms. For example, Singer and Singer (1978) and Perry and Whipple (1981) have proposed that *vulval* (clitoral) orgasms are different from *uterine* orgasms. Vulval orgasms show physiological patterns as described by Masters and Johnson, but uterine orgasms are characterized by contractions of "deeper" muscles, which they believe are focused in the uterus. Women describe these orgasms as being deeper inside of them as opposed to sensations in the clitoral area. Singer and Singer classified female orgasms into three categories: (1) *vulval orgasm*, induced by coital or noncoital stimulation and characterized by involuntary and rhythmical contractions of orgasmic platform; (2) *uterine orgasm*, induced by deep coital stimulation of cervix and characterized by gasping breathing and breath holding, with the breath being exhaled at orgasm; and (3) *blended orgasm,* which is a combination of a vulval orgasm and a uterine orgasm. Other researchers have concurred that some women state they experienced their orgasms in the clitoris, others were convinced that the site was the vagina, and still others experienced orgasms at both sites. Although the physiological response pattern may be the same for all women, each woman's experience of orgasm is different and the pleasure sites are subjective.

Male orgasm   The male's subjective awareness of orgasm seems concentrated in the penis, prostate gland, and seminal vesicles (Figure 5-3, *C,* and Table 5-3). In the male the onset of orgasm is accompanied by rhythmical contractions of the vas deferens, seminal vesicles, ejaculatory ducts, and prostate gland. The contraction of these structures moves semen into the urethra and lets the male know that ejaculation is about to happen. After the semen is in the urethra, expulsive contractions of the entire length of the urethra occur. The contractions start at 0.8-second intervals, and after three or four powerful contractions they are followed by less powerful contractions at irregular intervals for several more seconds. Muscles in the pelvis and perineum contract vigorously to force the semen through the urethra. The anus contracts rhythmically at 0.8-second intervals along with the muscles in the pelvis and perineum.

In the male the first three or four expulsive contractions feel the most pleasurable. As in the female, orgasm in the male involves both psychological and physiological factors. Masters and Johnson (1966) questioned approximately 500 men about their subjective feelings at orgasm. They concluded that the subjective experience of orgasm can be divided into two stages. In stage I there is a sensation of ejaculatory inevitability followed by a brief interval of 2 to 3 seconds during which the male feels the ejaculation coming and can no longer contain, delay, or in any way control the process. This is caused by the semen collecting in the urethra before ejaculation. The distension of the urethra by the semen probably contributes to the sensation of ejaculatory inevitability.

During stage II of the ejaculatory process (propulsion of semen through the urethra) the male has two different sensations. First he feels regularly recurring contractions of the urethra, and second he can sense fluid volume in the urethra as the fluid is forced out under pressure. The subjective experience of male orgasm can be described as follows: Sexual excitement increases until the male feels that the ejaculation is imminent. The male senses semen moving into the urethra from the prostate gland, seminal vesicles, and ejaculatory ducts. This, in addition to the swelling of the urethra, probably contributes to the feeling that he is about to ejaculate. Like women, many men feel suspended in time. An intensely pleasurable feeling in the penis and pelvis during the powerful contractions of the urethra follows. It is interesting to note that unlike women, who report after multiorgasmic experiences that the second or third orgasmic episode usually is "more satisfying or more sensually pleasurable than the first orgasmic episode," male study subjects who have had several orgasms in the laboratory inevitably report that the first is the most satisfying experience (Masters and Johnson, 1966).

Orgasmic phase changes common to female and male   Both the male and the female show a reduction in voluntary muscle control, which is evidenced

Subjective Experience of Orgasm

Are there differences in what an orgasm feels like for a male as compared to a female? To answer this question, Vance and Wagner (1976) asked students in an introductory psychology of sexual behavior course each to write a description of orgasm. The researchers selected 48 written descriptions of orgasm (24 male and 24 female) and changed words that could identify the sex of the individual. For example, *partner* was substituted for *wife, husband,* and *boyfriend; genitals* was substituted for *penis* and *vagina.* The written descriptions were then given to groups of medical students, obstetrician-gynecologists, and clinical psychologists of both sexes. The judges were simply instructed to read each description and indicate whether it was written by a male or female. The results demonstrated that the judges could not distinguish the sex of the person who wrote the description of orgasm. Also, in terms of the judges, neither sex was better at guessing the sex of the person who wrote the description. Un-

til there is empirical evidence to the contrary, it is reasonable to assume that the experience of orgasm for males and females is essentially the same (Vance and Wagner, 1976). Unfortunately, the authors did not indicate in their paper which descriptions were written by males and which were written by females. The reader should be cautioned that the descriptions were written by college-age students and hence may not be applicable to the entire population. Perhaps with age and experience males do subjectively experience orgasm differently from females. The males and females in Masters and Johnson's study (1966) did in fact describe the experience of orgasm in different subjective terms that were related to the physiology of the orgasmic response. In addition, college-age individuals could share a more common vocabulary and more similar experiences than does the general population and this may account for some of the findings. Many students in their descriptions employ terms used by

Masters and Johnson (1966), which seems to indicate that the subjects all had common information on the topic of orgasm and this could account for the similarities in descriptions of orgasm. The following are four random written descriptions of orgasm taken from Vance and Wagner:

Feels like tension building up until you think it can't build up any more, then release. The orgasm is both the highest point of tension and the release almost at the same time. Also feeling contractions in the genitals. Tingling all over.

There is a great release of tensions that have built up in the prior stages of sexual activity. This release is extremely pleasurable and exciting. . . . It is extremely intense and exhilarating. There is a loss of muscular control as the pleasure mounts. . . . This is followed by the climax and refractory states.

Orgasm amounts to a buildup of muscle tension accompanied by an increase in respiration rate. . . . All in all, a highly pleasurable physical sensation.

A feeling where nothing much else enters the mind other than that which relates to the present, oh sooo enjoyable and fulfilling sensation. . . .

Vance and Wagner, 1976, pp. 94 and 97

---

by muscular spasms throughout the body. At the end of the orgasmic phase the man or woman progressively moves into an unexcited state, which is the last phase of the sexual response cycle.

Resolution Phase

resolution phase
(rez′ uh LOO shun) Last phase of human sexual response cycle when man or woman returns to unexcited state.

The final phase of the sexual response cycle is called the **resolution phase.** This is a period of involuntary relaxation, which returns the individual to a sexually unexcited condition. The extra blood that has filled the sexual tissues now drains away.

Changes in female In the female the blood that had filled genital tissues rapidly leaves (Figure 5-2, *D,* and Table 5-2). The inner two thirds of the vaginal barrel shrinks to its unexpanded condition. The uterus returns to its normal position. The labia minora empty of the additional blood that they contain and decrease in size. The extra blood in the labia majora also drains, and these structures close over the vestibule of the vagina. The clitoris returns to its normal position. The nipples and breast decrease in size. The sex flush also disappears.

Changes in male The major events that occur in the male during the resolution phase are a decrease in muscle tension and a draining of the extra blood from the sexual tissues (Figure 5-3, *D*, and Table 5-3). The penis reverts to its unexcited state, and the scrotum drains of blood, allowing the testes to descend and return to normal size. The nipple erection and sex flush disappear.

Changes common to female and male During the resolution phase both men and women return to normal heart rate, blood pressure, and breathing. There may be a film of perspiration on the body.

Refractory Periods and Other Sex Differences

The human body's response to sexual stimulation is basically the same for men and women: vasocongestion and myotonia. However, one of the most important differences between the male and female sexual response occurs during the time just after orgasm. According to Masters and Johnson (1966), the male has a **refractory period** as the last contractions of the urethra occur. In this period, regardless of the stimulation, the nerves and muscles are incapable of responding to produce another orgasm (Figure 5-4). A refractory period, in the biological sense, refers to the inability of a tissue to respond to further stimulation for some period of time. The idea of a refractory period in men has been challenged because Masters and Johnson did not clearly separate orgasm and ejaculation. Robbins and Jensen (1978) interviewed 13 males (ages 22 to 56) who had reported that they experienced multiple orgasms (described as pleasurable sensations) before the ejaculation of semen.

In a more recent study, and only the second one on this topic, Dunn and Trost (1989) interviewed 21 men who reported having multiple orgasms. Dunn and Trost defined multiple orgasms in men as follows: "Male multiple orgasms are two or more orgasms with or without ejaculation and without, or with only very limited detumescence [loss of erection] during one and the same sexual encounter" (1989, p. 379). Dunn and Trost consider orgasm and ejaculation to be two distinct events and believe that orgasm (pleasurable sensations) can occur without an ejaculation. The men in this study were not observed having multiple orgasms but described their experiences. Dunn and Trost are the first to propose a good working definition of multiple orgasms in men. What is needed now are some descriptive observational research studies that describe and confirm the phenomenon of multiple orgasms in physiological terms under the laboratory conditions used by Masters and Johnson (1966).

The topic of some men having multiple orgasms before ejaculation warrants further study. Perhaps the refractory period in men should refer to the time required for a male to ejaculate a second or third time in the same uninterrupted sexual encounter.

In most men studied, the refractory period varied with age. In a young

refractory period
(ri FRAK tuhr ee) Time period immediately after orgasm when a man cannot be sexually restimulated.

FIGURE 5-4
Graphic representation of the male sexual response cycle.

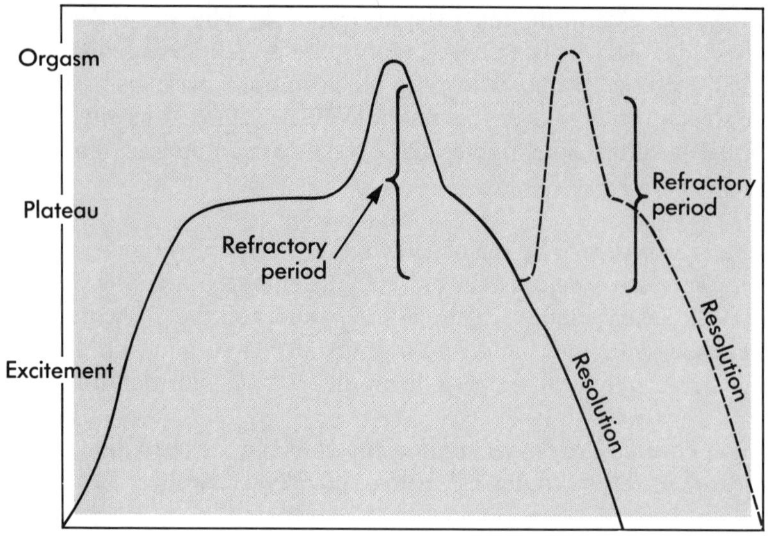

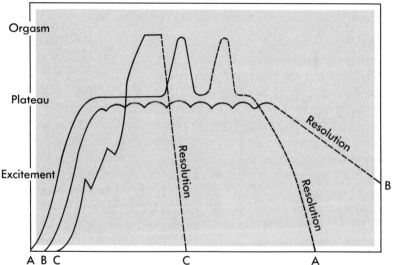

FIGURE 5-5
Graphic representation of three basic patterns of the female sexual response cycle (A, B, C). See explanation in text.

teenage male this refractory period is often 1 or 2 minutes, whereas in a male past 30 it may be 1 or 2 hours. In the Masters and Johnson laboratory one young male subject was observed to ejaculate three times in 10 minutes (the amount of semen was reduced in the second and third ejaculations). The refractory period involves psychological influences as well. For example, a couple who has been married for many years may have a pattern of sexual intercourse that involves one ejaculation by the male, followed by sleep by both partners. Their sexual activities are generally confined to the evening. When they go on vacation and are free to engage in sexual intercourse at different times during the day, the male may have two or three ejaculations in a relatively short time. This is because the freedom to engage in intercourse at different times of the day and being in a new setting under conditions of privacy contribute to increased sexual activity. A certain novelty of the situation is also involved. Another example is a male who has a new partner and is extremely excited about having sexual intercourse with her. Under these conditions he might have a much shorter refractory period than his refractory period with a habitual partner. The concept of refractory periods is a relative one and difficult to quantify because of the psychological factors involved. Therefore this particular measurement should not cause undue concern.

The human male shows a more stereotyped sexual response cycle than the female. Figure 5-4 shows the "classic" male pattern. There are variations, but they are usually related to the length of each of the phases (Masters and Johnson, 1966). These variations can be exhibited by one person at different times and among assorted people.

Females have no refractory period after orgasm. Women have the ability to have multiple orgasms with adequate stimulation; they can move from orgasm to the plateau level of sexual stimulation and then back to orgasm, repeating this pattern several times.

The female shows more diversity in responses to sexual stimulation than the male (Figure 5-5). Masters and Johnson (1966) have graphed three basic patterns that are simplifications of those most frequently observed in their laboratory. In the first pattern (A) the female goes through the excitement and plateau phases and then reaches orgasm. She may have a second or third orgasm (only two are illustrated) before she enters the resolution phase. In this pattern the orgasms are distinct and spaced in time so the female subjectively experiences each one separately. In pattern two (B) the woman reaches the plateau level without going on to orgasm, followed by a prolonged resolution phase. In the third pattern (C) the woman experiences sudden, steady rises in levels of excitement as she achieves a single orgasm that is followed by a rapid resolution phase.

If orgasm does not occur, some males and fewer females may feel uncomfortable for a time because the pelvic area is congested with blood. Masturbation may provide relief from this feeling of heaviness in the pelvic region.

The four phases of the sexual response cycle are not discrete phases but a continuum of physiological response to sexual stimulation. Psychological factors are also involved in the human sexual response. For example, the novelty

Engaging in sexual activities in a new environment may increase sexual arousal in some couples.

of a new partner could shorten the plateau phase and bring the person to orgasm sooner. The opposite could also occur, and a new sexual partner could produce anxiety, which might lengthen the cycle. A couple engaging in sexual activity in a new environment, for example, by the side of a pool or in an open field, could have a shortened plateau phase because of the novelty of the situation; the level of sexual excitement would build quickly to orgasm. Negative influences such as an interruption during the excitement or early plateau phase could prolong the entire cycle.

Alternatives to Masters and Johnson's Human Sexual Response Model

Not all sex researchers agree that Masters and Johnson's conceptional framework of the human sexual response is the best approach. Kaplan (1979) has proposed a triphasic model of the sexual response cycle. This model has a desire phase, a phase of vasocongestion of the genitalia (roughly equivalent to the excitement and plateau phases of Masters and Johnson), and the involuntary muscular contractions of the orgasmic phase. Kaplan believes that these phases are relatively independent of one another and are not successive stages as Masters and Johnson (1966) postulate. In Kaplan's model emphasis is placed on the desire phase and the resolution phase is eliminated, since this phase is really a lack of sexual response or a phase in which the individual returns to the unexcited sexual state. The desire phase of the sexual response cycle, which would precede the excitement phase of the model proposed by Masters and Johnson, is critical; without it the sexual response cycle would never begin. Sexual desire or sexual motivation is difficult to define, but when a person experiences sexual desire, he or she is moved to relieve sexual tensions by seeking out and being receptive to sexual stimulation (Rosen and Leiblum, 1987).

Zilbergeld and Ellison (1980) propose a five-component model of the human sexual response that takes into account the psychological or subjective factors of the response. Masters and Johnson (1966) dealt with the psychological aspects of the human sexual response in a superficial manner because they were more interested in the physiological responses. Zilbergeld and Ellison propose five phases that are related but also independent. They are (1) interest or desire; (2) arousal; (3) physiological readiness, such as vaginal lubrication and vasocongestion of the male and female reproductive structures; (4) orgasm; and (5) satisfaction, the subjective feeling of the sexual experience.

It is evident that there are several ways to analyze the sexual response cycle. Regardless of what model is used, Masters and Johnson's work on the anatomical and physiological changes is incorporated.

MECHANISMS OF ERECTION AND EJACULATION IN THE MALE
Erection

A vascular phenomenon, **erection** is an enlargement and hardening of the penis controlled by blood flow into the penis. The activity of nerves produces an opening or relaxation of the penile arteries and a closing of the penile veins. These two events cause enlargement as a result of increased blood flow into

The topic of disorders of sexual desire is presented in Chapter 17.

A quotation from Kaplan concerned with sexual desire is found on p. 490 in Chapter 17.

erection
(i REK shuhn) Vascular phenomenon that produces enlargement and hardening of penis.

the three erectile cylinders of the penis. Erection is a nervous reflex much like the knee-jerk reflex or removing your hand from a hot stove; nervous reflexes are involuntary and do not require any thought on the part of the individual. Nervous reflexes have three components: receptors, reflex centers, and effectors. The receptors receive information or stimuli. This information is then conveyed to specific reflex centers in the brain or spinal cord where it is processed. The processed information is then transmitted to the effectors, which may be a muscle or gland.

When the penis or other **erogenous** areas are touched, the stimulus is received by receptors in the skin. This information is conveyed by nerves to the erection centers in the spinal cord (Figure 5-6). This area is located in the region of the sacrum, in particular sacral segments S-2 to S-4 (Weiss, 1973).

erogenous
(i ROJ uh nuhs) Sexually sensitive areas that produce sexual arousal when touched.

FIGURE 5-6
The spinal cord, showing erection and ejaculation centers.

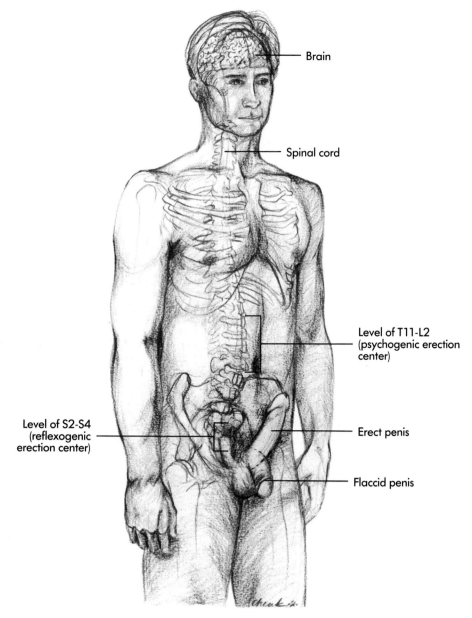

CHAPTER 5   HUMAN SEXUAL RESPONSE   125

parasympathetic nervous system
That part of the autonomic nervous system that tends to relax the various organ systems (e.g., decrease heart rate) in the individual as when a person is at rest or after a large meal.

The fact that the spinal cord has two erection centers has important implications for men who have spinal cord injuries. This is discussed in Chapter 16.

sympathetic nervous system
That part of the autonomic nervous system that tends to stimulate or excite the various organ systems in the individual as in preparation for an emergency (e.g., increase heart rate).

ejaculation
(i JAK yuh lay shuhn) Expulsion of semen from penis caused by muscular reaction.

Erection mediated by the center located in the region of the sacrum is controlled by the **parasympathetic nervous system** (part of the autonomic nervous system). The erection center responds by transmitting information by nerves to the arteries supplying blood to the erectile tissues of the penis. The arteries open, and blood fills the erectile tissues of the penis. The veins of the penis become filled with blood, but because of the compression of their walls by the enlarged and blood-swollen erectile tissue of the penis, the veins cannot drain. Thus erection occurs because blood is trapped in the penis. This type of erection caused by physical stimulation is called a reflexogenic erection.

What about erections caused by erotic thoughts or sexual fantasies, or those produced by sights (such as viewing erotic material), sounds, smell, and the sense of touch (such as touching another person)? How do these erections occur? They are thought to be mediated by a center higher in the spinal cord (Figure 5-5), in the thoracic and lumbar regions (segments T-11, T-12, and L-1, and L-2). This erection center is under the control of the **sympathetic nervous system,** which is also part of the autonomic nervous system (Weiss, 1973). This type of erection produced by thoughts is called a psychogenic erection. During sexual excitement and activity both the sacral segments and the thoracic and lumbar segments are involved in producing an erection as a result of the physical and psychological inputs to erection. Erections may also occur during erotic dreams and during certain sleep phases.

Ejaculation

The expulsion of semen from the penis, **ejaculation** is a muscular phenomenon. It involves three distinct processes: (1) seminal emission, (2) ejaculation, and (3) closing of the urinary bladder. The three processes are dependent on reflexes. In this reflex incoming stimuli are relayed from the genitalia by nerves to the cerebral cortex of the brain. Outgoing information from the cortex travels down the spinal cord by parasympathetic nerves and leaves the spinal cord in the region of the thoracic and lumbar vertebrae. The activity of these nerves produces important events in the following order:

1. Contraction of the smooth muscles of the reproductive tract, moving sperm from the epididymis and vas deferens to the ampulla of the vas deferens
2. Contraction of the smooth muscle of the ampulla of the vas deferens, prostate gland, and seminal vesicles
3. Partial closure of the outlet of the bladder
4. Semen propelled into the urethra (called seminal emission)

Activity of the sympathetic system causes alternating contraction and relaxation of muscles in the perineum and other pelvic, leg, and trunk muscles. These responses together with complete closing of the bladder result in rhythmical expulsion or ejaculation of semen through the urethra. When it is closed, the urinary bladder prevents seminal fluids from entering the bladder and also does not allow urine from the bladder to mix with seminal fluid. If the outlet of the bladder does not close, the ejaculation is said to be **retrograde ejaculation.** The semen, instead of being forced out of the urethra through the tip of the penis, is pushed or forced in the opposite direction and empties into the urinary bladder.

retrograde ejaculation
(RET ruh grayd i JAK yuh lay shuhn) Abnormal condition in which semen is emptied into urinary bladder because outlet of bladder does not close before ejaculation.

SUMMARY

1 Masters and Johnson divide the sexual response cycle in both sexes into four phases: excitement, plateau, orgasmic, and resolution.
2 The biological changes that occur during sexual excitation are generalized congestion of blood (vasocongestion) in the internal and external reproductive structures and increase in muscle tension (myotonia).
3 During the excitement phase the female experiences vaginal lubrication and the male has an erection.
4 During the plateau phase sexual arousal has increased above excitement phase levels and vasocongestion and myotonia increase.
5 Orgasm is limited to a few seconds of sexual tension release. This highly pleasurable sensation represents the maximal physical and psychological stimulation for the particular occasion. In both sexes a series of muscular contractions occurs. Masters and Johnson state that orgasm is a whole body response and that clitoral and vaginal orgasms are not separate biological entities.
6 The resolution phase of the sexual response cycle is a time when the individual returns to the sexually unexcited state.
7 Although men and women respond to sexual stimulation in the same manner, some women are able to have multiple orgasms whereas most men have a single orgasm followed by a refractory period of variable length.
8 Erection in the male is a vascular phenomenon controlled by blood flow to the penis. Erections may be caused when the penis or other erogenous areas are touched, or they may be caused by erotic fantasies. The erection centers are located in different areas of the spinal cord.
9 Ejaculation is a muscular phenomenon that involves seminal emission, ejaculation or expulsion of semen from the penis, and closing of the urinary bladder.

FACT
OR
FICTION

QUESTIONS FOR THOUGHT

1. List the four phases of the human sexual response cycle as defined by Masters and Johnson. For each phase list the major biological changes that occur in women and men.

2. Describe Kaplan's and Zilbergeld and Ellison's alternative conceptualizations of the human sexual response as described by Masters and Johnson.

3. Describe the events of erection and ejaculation in the male.

SUGGESTED READINGS

Brecher, R., and Brecher, E.: An analysis of human sexual response, New York, 1966, New American Library.

A very readable account of Masters and Johnson's work on the human sexual response.

Griffitt, W.: Females, males and sexual responses. In Kelley, K., editor: Females, males and sexuality: theories and research, Albany, 1987, State University of New York Press.

An excellent chapter dealing with all aspects of the human sexual response, including arousal and affective, cognitive, and behavioral responses to sexual stimuli. Some of these topics are discussed in other chapters of this book, but the chapter by Griffitt is a must for the student who will continue in psychology and human sexuality studies.

Levin, R., and Wagner, G.: Orgasm in women in the laboratory—quantitative studies on duration, intensity, latency, and vaginal blood flow, Arch. Sex. Behav. 14:439-450, 1985.

An article that is critical of the classic work of Masters and Johnson on human sexual response. In particular, Levin and Wagner point out that previous studies did not examine the duration of orgasm in women, and they describe how they conducted their study on orgasm duration in women.

Conception and Pregnancy

FACT
OR
FICTION

1
Some fetuses suck their thumbs and are born with calluses on one thumb.

2
Accurate, easy to use home kits are available to determine the time of ovulation and to determine whether a woman is pregnant.

3
Between 10% and 15% of couples in the United States have difficulty conceiving a child.

Women questioned about the impending birth of their child echo a common theme: "as long as it's healthy." This concern overshadows all other considerations such as sex [of child], familial characteristics, and labor anxieties.

R. CEFALO AND M. MOOS
Preconceptional Health Promotion: A Practical Guide, p. 3

This chapter concentrates on the biological processes of conception and pregnancy. New and exciting changes have occurred in these areas, and research continues to yield advances that were beyond our expectations several years ago.

As stated in the chapter's opening quotation, most women are more concerned about delivering a healthy baby than about the sex of the baby or which parent the child looks like. Concerns about labor and the birth process also take a back seat to the health and well-being of the newborn. Although most women change many of their habits during pregnancy, that is, stop smoking, reduce their alcohol intake, and modify their eating habits, most do not realize the critical significance of the weeks that precede the confirmation of their pregnancy. Many sources advocate measures that would improve health during the time that conception is being attempted and not after pregnancy has been confirmed (Institute of Medicine, 1985; Cefalo and Moos, 1988). The newly conceived offspring will depend on the mother for its nutrition and well-being weeks before the mother knows she is pregnant. If the potential mother is a smoker and is abusing alcohol and illegal drugs during this early critical period of development, the offspring is at a decided disadvantage. We shall promote preconceptional health throughout this chapter. If you are planning a pregnancy, you and your partner should begin to plan a healthy life-style for yourselves and possible offspring.

Psychological aspects dealing with decision to have children, childbirth experience using alternative birth methods, and effect of children on marital relationship are discussed in Chapter 7.

SPERM CELLS AND THEIR PREPARATION FOR CONCEPTION

Conception, technically called fertilization, is the union of the male sperm cell and the female egg cell (Figure 6-1). Before conception is possible, certain changes must occur in the sperm cells. The sperm cells must mature in the male reproductive tract before ejaculation and undergo still more biological changes in the female reproductive tract before they can fertilize an egg.

The human sperm cell is one of the smallest cells in the body. Mature sperm cells swim like miniature tadpoles with an undulating movement of the threadlike tail. The sperm cell is made up of a head, body, and tail. Within the head is the nucleus, which houses all genetic material necessary to pass the father's traits to the offspring. The body of the sperm cell contains mitochondria, which supply energy through chemical reactions. The mitochondria supply the energy for the swimming motions of the sperm cells.

conception
Union of male sperm and egg of female; also called fertilization.

Sperm Transport in the Female Reproductive Tract

During the process of ejaculation the sperm cells are combined with secretions from the male reproductive tract to form semen. If the male ejaculates into or

Semen production is presented in Chapter 3.

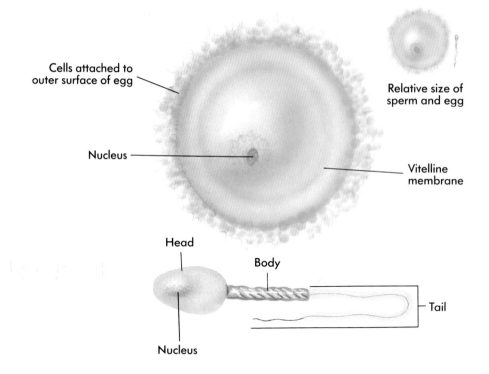

Cells attached to outer surface of egg

Relative size of sperm and egg

Nucleus

Vitelline membrane

Head

Body

Tail

Nucleus

around the entrance of the vagina, the sperm have a chance to cause fertilization. In the human it is estimated that approximately 200 to 500 million sperm are deposited in the vagina at ejaculation, and of this number fewer than 100 are thought to reach the oviducts (Odell and Moyer, 1971). Almost 99.99% of the sperm are lost in various ways. Many leak out of the vagina, and others are killed because of the acidic environment of the female reproductive tract. The semen coagulates after it is deposited in the vagina and becomes gelatinous as a result of the interaction of prostate and seminal vesicle secretions. This jellylike mass or plug is thought to prevent the semen from running out of the vagina (Johnson and Everitt, 1980). If the woman is in the early or middle portion of her menstrual cycle, the cervical mucus is of a consistency to allow the sperm to pass into the uterus. Sperm cells have been found in the oviducts as early as 30 minutes following coitus during ovulation (Rubenstein et al., 1951). If progesterone is the dominant hormone, as in the late part of the cycle, the cervical mucus inhibits sperm penetration past the cervix.

How do the sperm cells travel from the vagina to the oviducts where fertilization occurs? There are several theories. Some authorities believe that muscular contractions of the female reproductive tract (caused by prostaglandins from the sperm) and the swimming ability of the sperm move the sperm to the oviducts. Others think that the spermatozoa move in currents of fluid set up by the action of uterine cilia (Johnson and Everitt, 1980; Berne and Levy, 1988).

Capacitation of Sperm Cells

Capacitation, which occurs in the female reproductive tract, is a physiological process by which sperm cells acquire the ability to penetrate the **zona pellucida**

Cycle of cervical mucus as it influences fertility is discussed in Chapter 8.

capacitation
Process of biochemical changes in sperm cell that allows sperm to penetrate egg.

zona pellucida
(ZOH nuh puh LOO sid uh) Thick, jellylike membrane envelope surrounding egg.

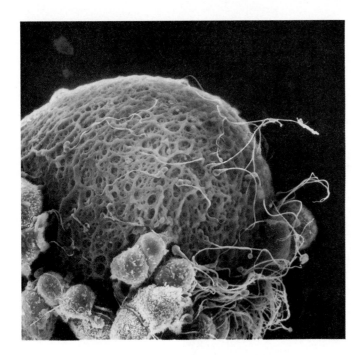

During capacitation the cap of the sperm gradually disappears, releasing enzymes that help the sperm to penetrate the zona pellucida of the egg.

of the egg (Page, Villee, and Villee, 1981). During capacitation certain proteinlike molecules are stripped from the surface of the sperm cells. If sperm cells are placed in an artificial laboratory setting (that is, in vitro, commonly called test-tube), fertilization will not take place or a long delay will occur before fertilization is observed. Sperm cells taken from the uterus or oviducts a few hours after ejaculation are capable of immediate fertilization of an egg under artificial circumstances because the sperm cells have undergone capacitation. Once capacitated, the sperm must be activated before fertilization.

Activation of Sperm Cells

Activation of the sperm cells is a complex process that occurs in the vicinity of the egg in the oviducts (Guyton, 1986). Most scientists think that the egg induces activation, but others believe that activation occurs via chemical processes produced in the sperm cell independent of stimulation by the egg. Only if the sperm are activated can they fertilize the egg. During the activated state the sperm change their mode of movement from regular undulating movements of the tail to more powerful movements that propel them forward in a lurching fashion. In addition, the sperm cell membrane alters so that it can fuse with the zona pellucida (surface covering) of the egg. After both capacitation and activation, the sperm and egg are capable of conception.

activation
Series of biochemical changes in sperm cell that affect its swimming motion and membrane to allow it to fuse with egg.

CONCEPTION

The capacitated and activated sperm cells and the egg cell meet in the fallopian tube (that portion closest to the ovary) (Figure 6-2). It is here that conception, or fertilization, usually takes place. Changes in the sperm cells that occurred

FIGURE 6-2

Sperm cells deposited into the vagina during sexual intercourse travel to the fallopian tube to meet the egg produced in the ovary. Fertilization, if it occurs, will take place in the fallopian tube.

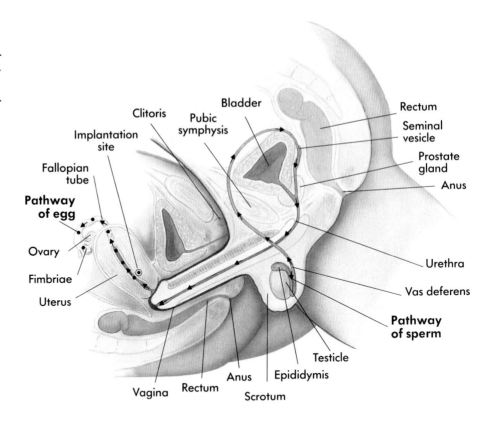

during activation allow the release of an enzyme called hyaluronidase from the sperm cells. This compound works to dissolve the zona pellucida and other cells making up the outer layer of the egg cell and allows the sperm cell to advance toward the center of the egg to join with its nucleus. At fertilization the 23 chromosomes from the sperm combine with the 23 chromosomes of the egg to form the zygote. The **zygote** is the fertilized egg and contains the full complement of 46 chromosomes (Figure 6-3). The genetic information from the male combines with that of the female to produce a unique set of chromosomes. This genetic information determines hair color, eye color, height, and all of the other physical and mental traits that are passed from parents to offspring. One pair of chromosomes is the sex chromosomes. Genetic males have one X and one Y chromosome, and genetic females have two X chromosomes.

Only one sperm cell penetrates the egg and combines its genetic material with the egg (Figure 6-4). The egg cell is the largest cell in the body, and the mature egg, as previously mentioned, is surrounded by a jellylike capsule called the zona pellucida. Beneath the zona pellucida is the **vitelline membrane.** Many sperm cells penetrate the zona pellucida and attach themselves to the surface of the vitelline membrane. However, once one sperm cell has penetrated the vitelline membrane, a biochemical process occurs that transforms the vitelline membrane into a protective fertilization membrane. No other sperm cells can then penetrate the egg.

Division of the egg into two cells occurs about 36 hours later. Cell division continues as the dividing cell mass is moved by the cilia in the oviducts toward the uterus (Figure 6-4). The cell mass takes approximately 3 to 5 days to reach

zygote
(ZY goht′) Fertilized ovum before cell division.

vitelline membrane
(vi TEL in) Membrane forming surface layer of egg.

HUMAN SEXUALITY

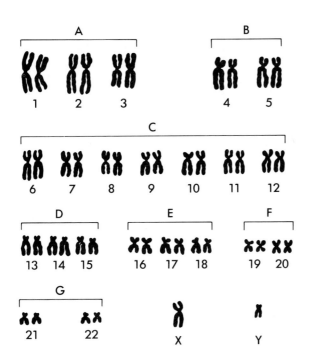

FIGURE 6-3
Chromosome pairs.

the uterus and is now called a **blastocyst.** The blastocyst usually floats freely in the uterus for 1 to 2 days before it "burrows" or implants into the lining of the uterus. According to some authorities, implantation marks the beginning of pregnancy (also called gestation). Medical terminology calls the product of conception the conceptus. For the first 8 weeks of gestation it is called an embryo, and from then until birth it is called a fetus (Wilson et al., 1991).

blastocyst
(BLAS tuh sist) Mass of cells that results from repeated divisions of zygote.

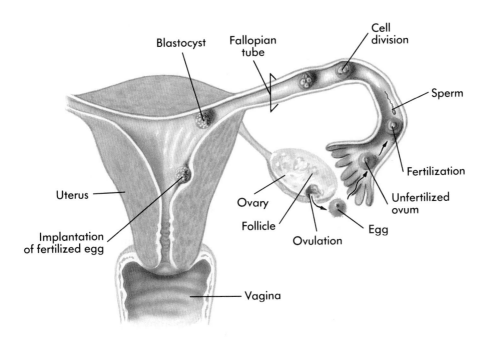

FIGURE 6-4
Fertilization occurs in the fallopian tube, and the blastocyst (cell mass produced by union of sperm and egg) moves out of the tube and implants in the uterus.

Throughout history people have been interested in what factors determine whether an offspring is male or female. Attempts to predetermine the sex of offspring have taken place since antiquity. The ancient Greeks thought that having intercourse in a north wind would produce a boy and intercourse in a south wind would produce a female child. Other ideas involved the phase of the moon, on what side the male lay during coitus, and if the male had his shoes on or off during coitus.

At the present time two approaches can be used to choose the sex of an infant. One is selective termination of pregnancy; that is, the woman could have an abortion if the fetus is not the desired sex. This approach is fraught with legal, moral, medical, and religious considerations. The other method is to influence the probability that an X-bearing or a Y-bearing sperm cell will do the fertilization, which determines the sex of the child.

Since the male ejaculate contains approximately equal numbers of X- and Y-bearing sperm, normally the probability of a boy or girl is 50%. Any consistent change in this proportion would mean success. Two techniques are used to alter the X and Y chromosomal balance. The first involves separating the ejaculate into two portions before insemination. One portion contains the X-bearing sperm and the other the Y-bearing sperm. A method using columns made of cattle albumin (one of a group of protein substances) of increasing densities indicates that human Y-bearing sperm swim and diffuse downward into the densest albumin portion. When these Y-enriched sperm were used to artificially inseminate a small number of women, it was found that 72% of the offspring were male. However, the yield of Y-bearing sperm portions was very low. This loss of sperm count led to low conception rates, and even the fractions of sperm with 80% Y-bearing sperm produced female offspring. At the present time this technique cannot be used on a large scale.

A second technique to influence the probability that an X-bearing or Y-bearing sperm will do the fertilization involves altering the vaginal environment to favor either X- or Y-bearing sperm. Early work on humans and other species indicated that more males were conceived when intercourse took place before or at the time of ovulation. Other researchers have shown that for both natural and artificial insemination, the human sex ratio changed significantly during the menstrual cycle (Guerrero, 1975; Harlap, 1979). A high proportion of male infants was observed among couples in whom intercourse with ejaculation occurred several days before ovulation. The proportion of males then dropped to a minimum on the day of ovulation, and then the proportion of females rose steeply for infants conceived 2 to 3 days after ovulation. Researchers believe that changes in the vaginal pH (whether acidic or alkaline) are responsible for the alterations in the sex ratio over the menstrual cycle. In 1970 Shettles and Rorvik published a book instructing couples on how to produce male or female offspring. They argued that human sperm could be divided into androsperm (Y-bearing) or gynosperm (X-bearing) based on the form and speed of movement of the sperm. These characteristics would influence survival of the sperm in the vagina. The ideas proposed by Shettles and Rorvik have not been replicated by other researchers and clinicians.

ProCare Industries markets a product called Gender Choice, which the company claims can increase the chances of having a boy or a girl. Many ideas

Multiple Births

At seven weeks an ultrasound was taken and detected twins. I couldn't believe it! My husband, George, held my hand tightly as I laughed, cried and laid on the table in shock.

George is having anxiety over financial planning for two at the same time. Even though he is elated, finances are a real part of it all. I keep reassuring him that everything will work out.

Gavalas, 1990

Not all pregnancies result in the birth of a single child. About 1% of pregnancies produce twins. There are two types of twins. The first kind, dizygotic or fraternal twins, result from the fertilization of two separate ova (dizygotic meaning *two zygotes*) by two separate sperm cells. About 70% of twins are dizygotic.

Fraternal twins have a different genetic makeup from each other, just like any other pair of siblings. They are no more similar in appearance than any brother or sister and may be of the opposite sex. The second type of twins is called monozygotic or identical twins, and they result from the fertilization of one egg by one sperm cell, hence the term *monozygotic* meaning *one zygote*. About 30% of twins are monozygotic. Very early in development the conceptus splits in half, and each half develops into an individual embryo. The twins look alike, are the same sex, and have the same tissue types. In some cases identical twins are conjoined, or born connected to each other. This condition is commonly referred to as Siamese twins because a very famous pair had a Siamese mother. Studies have not shown the existence of a genetic or hereditary pattern to the production of monozygotic twins. Such twins are caused by anomalies during very early development. However, the incidence of dizygotic twins does run higher in certain families, and thus there is a hereditary component to fraternal twins. It is thought that certain genetic information controlling hormones that cause the ovulation of two eggs is passed from one generation to the next. Obviously this trait could only manifest itself in a woman; however, a man could pass the trait on to his daughter. In addition to twins, multiple births can also involve three, four, and five children. The more children born, the rarer the probability.

In 1934 were born five girls, the Dionne quintuplets, who were monozygotic; that is, they all came from the same egg. This is an extremely rare event. These children were the object of great publicity throughout their young lives, and even today stories appear about their present lives. Births of triplets and quadruplets often occur after women use fertility drugs to stimulate ovulation. Quintuplets and sextuplets are also produced because the fertility drug causes the ovulation of three, four, five, and six eggs, all of which may be fertilized by individual sperm cells. In these cases the children would be comparable to dizygotic twins and share the same genetic relationship as siblings. Many times multiple births occur prematurely, and usually survival is not possible for all of the infants because of low birth weight and other developmental problems.

Nancy and George Gavalas with their new twins.

used in the development and method of the Gender Choice kit are similar to the theories of Shettles and Rorvik. As previously mentioned, the theories proposed by Shettles and Rorvik have not been proved and some have been disproved (Harlap, 1979).

PREGNANCY

Pregnancy lasts an average of 266 days from the time of fertilization or 280 days from the first day of the last menstrual period if the menses are regular at 28 days. The gestation period is divided into trimesters or three phases of approximately 3 calendar months each. Because many women do not have regular 28-day cycles, it is often difficult to pinpoint when fertilization occurred. Physicians usually date pregnancies in weeks, and since all times are dated from the first day of the last menstrual period, this method yields due dates that are about 2 weeks later than embryological or actual developmental due dates. Remember, the physician is assuming the woman became pregnant on day 14 of a 28-day cycle. This may or may not be the case. Thus 280 less 14 equals 266 days. We commonly say that the gestation period is 9 calendar months, which is midway between 266 and 280 days. To calculate the expected due date using the formula that is used by physicians, add 1 week to the first day of the last menstrual flow, subtract 3 months, and add 1 year. For example, the last menstrual flow was January 8, 1990. Add 1 week (which is January 15,1990), subtract 3 months (which makes it October 15, 1989), and add 1 year. This equals October 15, 1990, as the due date. Sixty percent of births occur within 5 days of the dates predicted in this manner.

Hormonal Changes During Pregnancy

The mother's system undergoes tremendous changes in levels of estrogen and progesterone during pregnancy (Figure 6-5). In addition, two hormones found only in pregnant women, human chorionic gonadotropin (HCG) and human placental lactogen (HPL), appear in the blood. Secretion of follicle-stimulating hormone and luteinizing hormone by the anterior pituitary gland is suppressed throughout pregnancy.

You will recall from Chapter 4 that in nonpregnant women the corpus luteum regresses and menstrual flow starts.

Specific cells in the outer portion of the developing embryo start to secrete HCG shortly after implantation. It is the presence of this hormone in the woman's system that produces a positive pregnancy test. HCG can be detected in the mother's blood and urine. This hormone prevents the corpus luteum from degenerating. Large amounts of HCG are produced during the first trimester and stimulate the corpus luteum to secrete estrogen and progesterone. The corpus luteum is essential for the maintenance of early pregnancy, and if it regresses, a **spontaneous abortion** (miscarriage) results.

miscarriage or spontaneous abortion
Abortion that occurs without cause or is medically un-aided.

The fetus and placenta increase in size and contribute increasing quantities of estrogen and progesterone to the maternal blood system. After the first 3 months of pregnancy the corpus luteum is no longer essential to maintain the pregnancy because the placenta is producing large amounts of estrogen and progesterone. Progesterone suppresses uterine contractions during pregnancy and stimulates the alveoli of the breasts. Levels of HCG fall to low levels after

HUMAN SEXUALITY

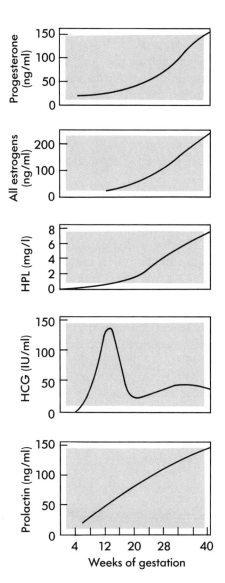

FIGURE 6-5
The maternal system un-
dergoes dramatic changes
in hormone levels during
pregnancy.

the first 3 months (Figure 6-5). The fetus' adrenal glands produce a precursor hormone during the first 3 months of pregnancy that is converted to estrogen in the placenta; thus the fetus plays a role in maintaining the pregnancy. Estrogen levels rise throughout the pregnancy (Figure 6-5) and then rapidly fall off at birth.

Progesterone production and secretion by the placenta increase continuously during pregnancy and rapidly decline at birth. HPL levels rise throughout the pregnancy, and as birth approaches, the levels become reduced. Low levels of HPL, however, can be detected after birth. HPL is thought to stimulate breast growth during pregnancy and to prepare the breasts for lactation (Guyton, 1986). HPL also has growth-promoting properties and may be responsible for the physical changes that occur in the maternal system to accommodate the growing fetus.

Diagnosis of Pregnancy

The first sign that a woman might be pregnant is the absence of an expected menstrual flow. She may also experience nausea with occasional vomiting at the early stage of pregnancy. The nausea and vomiting are thought to be caused by HCG from the conceptus and estrogen from the placenta. These two hormones act on the digestive system to cause irritation, which produces nausea and vomiting. Breast engorgement may also be noticed. This swelling is caused by increasing levels of estrogen and progesterone and is an extension of what most women notice during the second half of their menstrual cycle before menses.

A woman who is pregnant and has missed a period for 2 weeks shows several possible signs of pregnancy: uterine enlargement, softening of the cervix, and color change of the vagina and cervix to bluish or purple. A urine test for HCG is positive at this time. HCG can be detected with great accuracy 9 days after conception in the blood and urine of the mother (Berne and Levy, 1988).

Within the past few years reliable, accurate, and easy-to-use home pregnancy testing kits have come on the market and can be purchased in pharmacies. These kits depend on the presence of HCG in the urine to detect pregnancy and are accurate on the first day of a missed menstrual flow, which in a 28-day cycle would be the 15th day after conception. The urine tests for HCG are immunological analyses. One pregnancy detection kit (Clearblue Easy) simply involves placing the absorbent tip in the first morning urine and then looking at the tip 3 minutes later for a color change. As stated previously, HCG in the blood can be detected as early as 9 days after conception using a test called the beta-subunit HCG radioimmunoassay. In the future this new test, performed in professional laboratories, will probably replace the urine test for HCG that is done in professional laboratories.

Pregnancy testing kits such as Clearblue Easy, readily available at the pharmacy, have made pregnancy detection a simple process.

BLASTOCYST, EMBRYO, AND FETUS
First Trimester

A large portion of the blastocyst will become the embryo, and a smaller portion eventually develops into the membranes that surround the embryo. For about 6 or 7 days after fertilization the blastocyst draws its food from self-contained nutrients that were part of the egg cell. When the blastocyst embeds itself in the uterine lining, cells in the uterine lining are damaged and nutrients in the blood from the damaged tissues surround the blastocyst. The blastocyst then derives nourishment by absorption of this material.

Certain cells that surround the embryonic cell mass will become the protective membranes that enclose the embryo during the prenatal period. The outer membrane is called the **chorion,** and the inner membrane is the **amnion.** The chorion and the **allantois membrane** form the fetal part of the **placenta,** which becomes rooted in the endometrium through growths called **chorionic villi.** These branching extensions eventually carry the fetal blood vessels close to the maternal blood system. The placenta is also formed by tissues produced by the mother. As development progresses, the embryo is connected to the placenta by the umbilical cord, which carries two arteries and one vein. The placenta serves as the kidney, digestive tract, and lungs for the embryo and fetus. The placenta, as previously mentioned, also secretes hormones that are essential for a successful pregnancy.

The placenta continues to grow throughout pregnancy. The structure and function of the placenta are such that the maternal circulation is completely separate from the developing offspring's circulation. However, certain substances can pass through the placental membrane that separates the two blood systems. A great deal remains to be learned about the placental barrier, but it is known that such substances as carbon dioxide, oxygen, glucose (a nutrient), and certain drugs readily cross the barrier.

The amnion forms a sac around the embryo, and the sac becomes filled with a clear fluid called amniotic fluid. The embryo floats protected in this "bag of water" attached to the mother through the umbilical cord, which is its life support system.

In summary: (1) The placenta has a fetal component formed from the chorion and allantois membrane and a maternal component formed from a layer of cells in the endometrium. (2) Attached to the fetal component of the placenta is the umbilical cord, which runs to the embryo or fetus. (3) Material, including gases, nutrients, and wastes, passes from the maternal system to the embryonic system and vice versa.

Germ layers The embryo contains three layers of discrete cells that are genetically programmed. Each layer, called a germ layer, produces a certain kind of cells, tissues, and organs. The three layers are called ectoderm, mesoderm, and endoderm: the **ectoderm** gives rise to the nervous system and the skin; the **mesoderm** produces the supporting system of the body, such as the bones and muscles, in addition to the urogenital and circulatory systems; the **endoderm** develops into the digestive tract and associated glands.

During the first trimester of pregnancy the conceptus goes through the embryonic stage and into the fetal stage. The major features of the body are established by the eighth week of intrauterine development, or the end of the

chorion
(KOR ee on') Outer membrane that forms outer wall of blastocyst.

amnion
(AM nee uhn) Inner membrane that holds fetus suspended in amniotic fluid.

allantois membrane
(uh LAN toh is) Tissues that contribute to development of placenta.

placenta
(pluh SEN tuh) Structure through which fetus derives its nourishment and rids itself of waste products.

chorionic villi
(KOR ee on ic vil ee') Fetal part of placenta; branching extensions that carry fetal blood vessels close to maternal blood vessels.

ectoderm
(EK tuh duhrm') Outer layer of cells in embryo that will develop into skin structures and nervous system.

mesoderm
(MEZ uh duhrm') Middle layer of cells in embryo between ectoderm and endoderm that will give rise to muscular, skeletal, circulatory, and urogenital (structures common to urinary and genital) systems.

endoderm
(EN duh duhrm') Innermost layer of cells in embryo that will develop into digestive tract.

embryonic period. The ectodermal germ layer of the conceptus gives rise to those organs and structures that make and maintain contact with the outside environment: brain and spinal cord; nerves that supply muscles and sense organs; sensory tissue of the ear, nose, and eye; and skin, hair, and nails. The mesodermal germ layer produces the supporting tissues of the body, including muscles, cartilage, and bone. In addition, the mesoderm develops into the heart, blood vessels, lymph vessels, blood and lymph cells, and urogenital system, including the gonads and their duct systems. The heart begins to beat by the 24th day of gestation. The endodermal germ layer provides the lining of the digestive tract and respiratory tract. At the end of the embryonic period the conceptus has tail folds and a huge head. There are arms, legs, fingers, and toes. The large head contains a nose, ears, lidless eyes, and a mouth.

Sexual differentiation of reproductive structures is discussed in Chapter 3.

In the first trimester organ formation occurs. Because of this, the developing organism is very susceptible to environmental influences that may induce abnormalities in development. During this period drugs, alcohol, viruses such as the rubella virus, and x-ray irradiation are particularly dangerous to the developing embryo and fetus.

At the end of the first trimester the fetus looks much like a tiny human infant with a large head. The sex of the fetus is evident. In summary, the first 3 months of life in the uterus involves rapid, complex development of the embryo and fetus.

Second Trimester

The second trimester is characterized by maturation of the tissues and organs formed during the first trimester and rapid growth of the fetus. Few if any physical deformities occur at this time, but the death of cells in the brain or spinal cord as a result of internal or external causes could result in postnatal behavioral disturbances (Langman, 1981).

A striking change is the relative slowdown in the growth of the head. At the end of the first trimester it is about one half of the crown-rump length. Crown-rump length is the measurement from the top of the skull to the midpoint between the top of the buttocks (Figure 6-6). By the fifth month the head is about one third of the crown-rump length, and at birth the head is one fourth of the crown-rump length.

During the fifth month the mother clearly recognizes fetal movements, called quickening. Fetal movements may now be recognized as kicking or turning.

> Sometimes an elbow, a foot, a head, or the buttocks may be identified through the abdominal wall. Occasionally the fetus will hiccup, causing rhythmic jarring of the mother's abdomen every 2 to 4 seconds. . . . Periods of drowsiness and sleep alternate with periods of activity, much as in the newborn infant. Sleeping habits begin to appear. The mother can sometimes detect and anticipate them, and even determine when the fetus awakens and stretches.
>
> Rugh and Shettles, 1971, p. 68

vernix caseosa
(VUHR niks KAY see oh sa)
Covering produced by fetus to protect skin.

The fetus is covered with small, fine-textured hairs, and the skin is covered with a cheeselike paste called the **vernix caseosa.** This coating protects the delicate skin of the fetus from the fluids that constantly bathe the fetus in the amniotic sac.

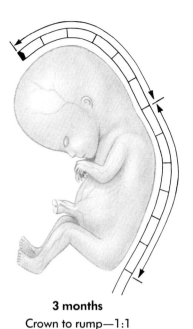

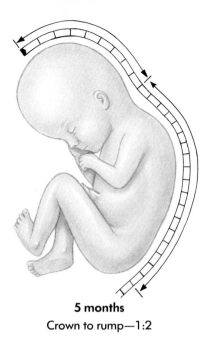

3 months
Crown to rump—1:1

5 months
Crown to rump—1:2

9 months
Crown to rump—1:3

FIGURE 6-6
The crown-rump length is used to measure the size of the fetus throughout the pregnancy. Note the relative size of the head compared with the crown-rump length at the different stages of development.

A fetus born during the sixth month or in the first half of the seventh month has difficulty in surviving. Although many organ systems are functioning, the respiratory system and central nervous system are still not completely developed and coordination between the two systems is not well established (Langman, 1981).

The fetus opens its eyes for the first time toward the end of the second trimester, and studies have shown that the fetus is now sensitive to sounds and light. For example, the fetus can be made to move about when stimulated by sounds in the range of human hearing.

Third Trimester

During the last trimester the fetus gains about 5 pounds and finds it difficult to move about in the now small amniotic sac. The fetus has a well-rounded body shape because of fat deposits beneath the skin. The fetus may suck its thumb, and some infants are born with calluses on one thumb as a result of fetal thumbsucking (Rugh and Shettles, 1971).

During the ninth month the fetus appears to be less active than in previous months, possibly because it fills most of the available space inside the mother. Just before birth almost all fetuses assume a position with the head pointing down into the pelvic region of the mother. The vernix caseosa is lost over most of the body except for the back.

From its mother the fetus acquires antibodies against various diseases, including measles, mumps, whooping cough, and even colds and influenza. These antibodies were formed by the mother before or during her pregnancy. Some antibodies are also passed to the infant through breast-feeding. The infant is usually protected for about the first 6 months from various diseases for which the mother had produced antibodies.

Text continued on p. 148.

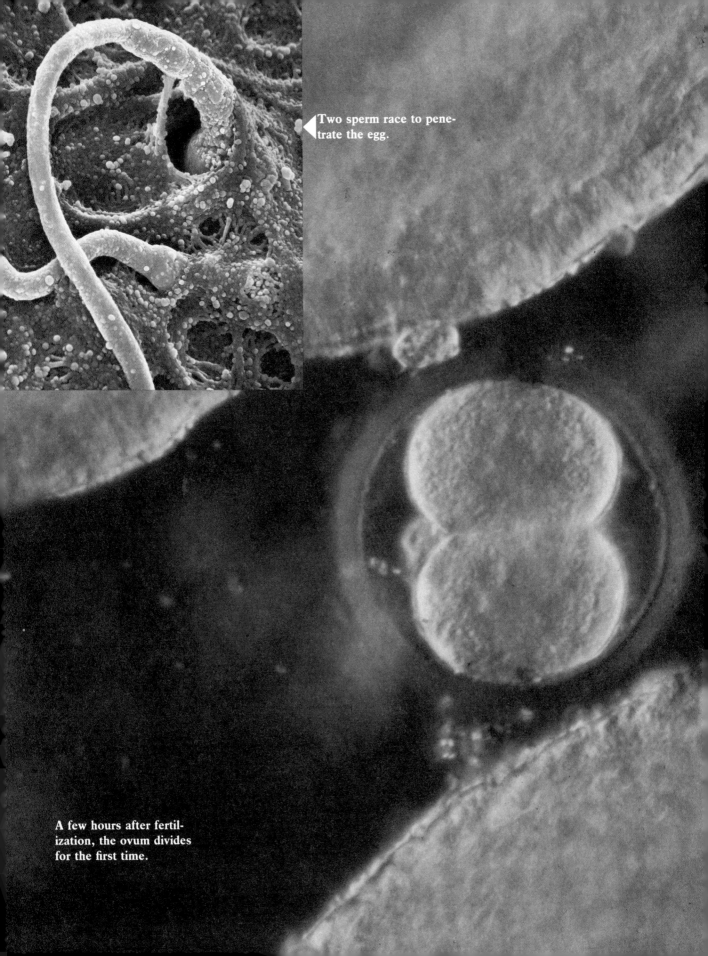

Two sperm race to penetrate the egg.

A few hours after fertilization, the ovum divides for the first time.

The blastocyst has implanted on the endometrium of the uterus.

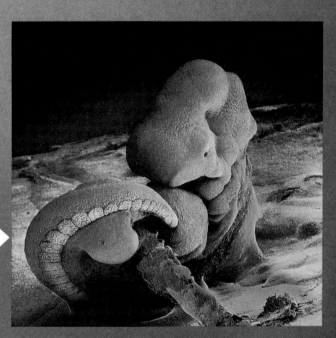

At 4½ weeks the embryo looks more like a prehistoric dinosaur than a human. The vertebrae, along with arm and leg buds, are just beginning to form.

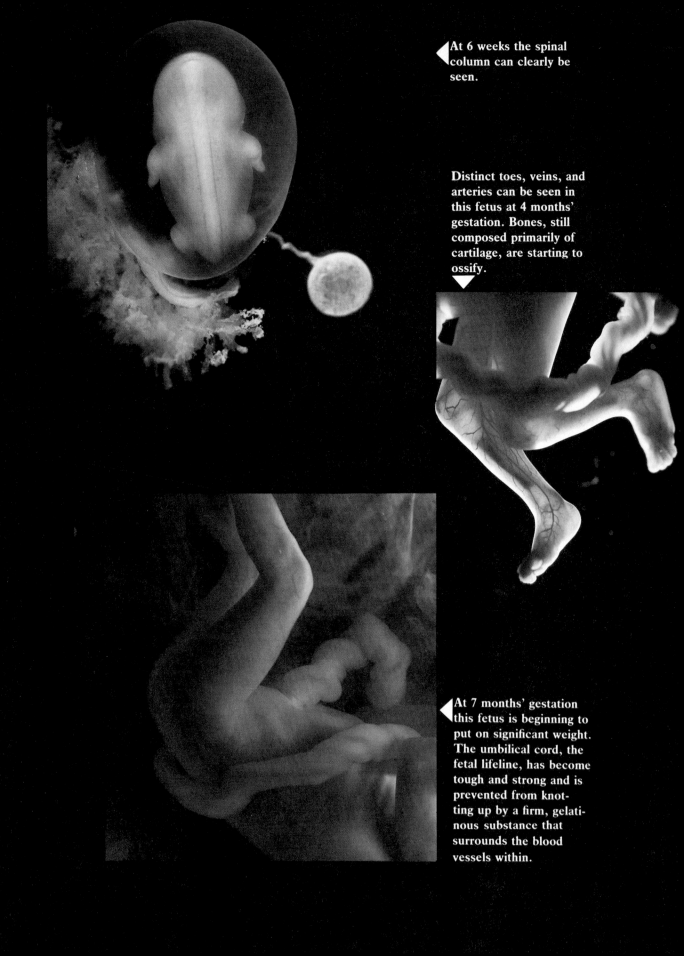

At 6 weeks the spinal column can clearly be seen.

Distinct toes, veins, and arteries can be seen in this fetus at 4 months' gestation. Bones, still composed primarily of cartilage, are starting to ossify.

At 7 months' gestation this fetus is beginning to put on significant weight. The umbilical cord, the fetal lifeline, has become tough and strong and is prevented from knotting up by a firm, gelatinous substance that surrounds the blood vessels within.

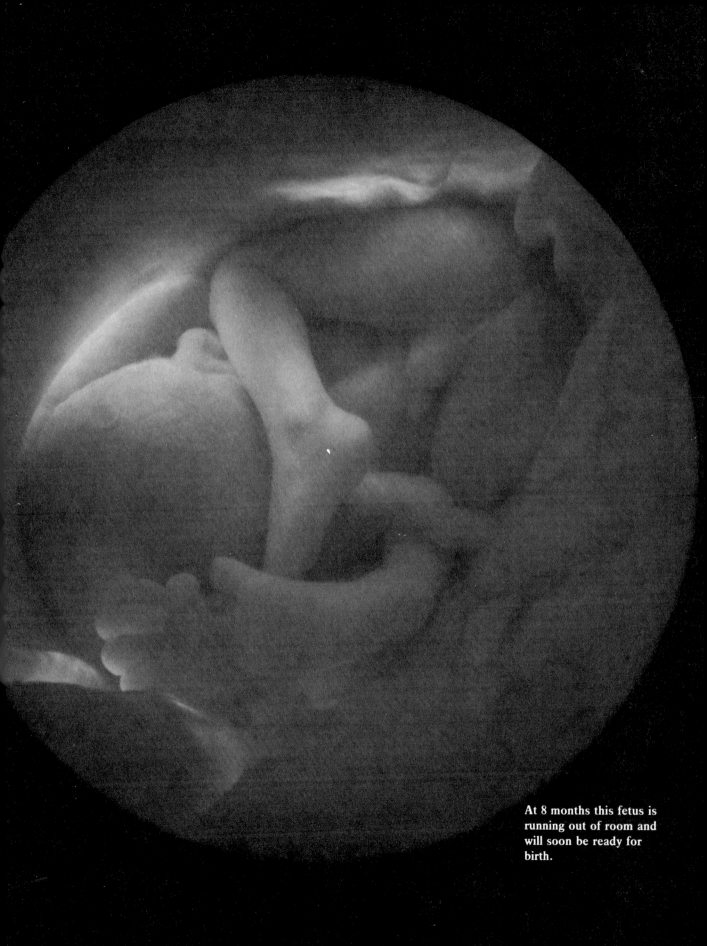

At 8 months this fetus is
running out of room and
will soon be ready for
birth.

In fetuses of both sexes the breasts are developed as a result of the hormones that have been acting on the mother's breasts to prepare her for the possibility of breast-feeding her child.

Eyes are usually blue, regardless of their future color. The eye pigmentation has not fully formed and will not for several weeks after birth. The eyes must be exposed to light for the pigmentation to develop.

The sexual characteristics are obvious, and the testes have usually descended into the scrotum. At 28 weeks of age the fetus is capable of survival outside the uterus but only with medical intervention. At the time of birth the skull has the largest circumference of all body parts and is the most difficult to get through the birth canal.

THE MOTHER AND FATHER
First Trimester

During the first few weeks of pregnancy the prospective parents show a variety of emotions depending on their feelings about the pregnancy. Was the pregnancy planned or unplanned? And if planned, do both parents really want the pregnancy? Let us assume for the rest of this discussion that the couple wanted a child and that the pregnancy was planned. Quotations of pregnant women in Marzollo's book *9 Months, 1 Day, 1 Year* (1976) as well as quotations from the diary of Nancy Gavalas (1990), a friend of the authors who was pregnant with twins at the time we were writing this edition, are used to illustrate some physical and psychological aspects of pregnancy.

Motivations and social pressures to have children are presented in detail in Chapter 7.

The early physical symptoms of pregnancy include a tenderness of the breasts, which makes them very sensitive, and a tingling sensation in the breasts. Nausea and vomiting, known as morning sickness even though they can occur at any time of the day, are early signs of pregnancy and the most common complaints during the first trimester. Approximately 33% of pregnant American women are affected with vomiting or digestive disturbances (Hotchner, 1979). This usually stops by the end of the first trimester. As mentioned earlier, rising levels of estrogen are thought to irritate the stomach and cause nausea and vomiting in some women (Johnson and Everitt, 1980). Frequent urination, tiredness, and the urge to sleep are some other early signs of pregnancy.

> I'm preoccupied. I think I'm pregnant. Beyond the faint nausea and the ache in my breasts, I'm delighted.
>
> Marzollo, 1976, p. 18

The physical changes and the symptoms produced during the first trimester are largely a result of the increasing levels of hormones. The breasts swell, and the areolae and nipples often darken. Urination becomes more frequent because of hormonal changes that affect the adrenal glands, which are involved in water balance, and the growing uterus presses against the bladder, which results in the need to urinate. Bowel movements may become irregular as a result of hormone changes and lack of exercise.

> Fortunately I have been feeling great. My only symptom is feeling tired early in the afternoon and I have developed an intolerance for milk.
>
> Gavalas, 1990

If your bathroom is close to your bedroom, try to get there and back without opening your eyes. It will be easier to fall back asleep.

Marzollo, 1976, p. 42

I never understood why pregnant women constantly talked only about babies, being pregnant, and the changes taking place until now. I find myself totally consumed with my two precious babies growing inside of me.

Gavalas, 1990

While the prospective mother's body is undergoing all of the changes just described, she and the father are also experiencing emotional changes. The father worries about his partner's health, the health of the infant, and his own adequacies as a father. In addition, there are joy and excitement about the prospect of being a parent. However, many fathers and mothers worry about the financial considerations of a child and how the addition of the child to the family will affect the family's interactions.

I had lots of questions about whether I was ready to have a baby. I was scared about responsibilities and abnormalities in the baby.

Marzollo, 1976, p. 46

I want to start getting the nursery ready, but a part of me keeps holding me back. I hope the fear of miscarriage will pass once I reach 12 weeks.

Gavalas, 1990

Second Trimester

As the pregnancy progresses, the woman experiences a growing awareness of the movements of the fetus. The woman's abdomen expands, and it becomes obvious that she is pregnant. Most women find that the unpleasant physical symptoms of the first trimester disappear. Other physical problems may occur during the next 2 to 3 months. These include constipation, hemorrhoids (the result of increased pressure on the veins of the anus), and nosebleeds (because of increased blood volume, which puts pressure on the tiny blood vessels in the nose). Water retention and swelling (edema) may occur in the face, hands, wrists, ankles, and feet.

I feel absolutely marvelous physically. There is no nausea at all any more, I sleep like a top.

Marzollo, 1976, p. 19

I am not sleeping very well. I have so many questions about the future: Will I be a good mother? Are the twins going to be healthy? What will it be like giving up my career for the immediate future? Will George and my relationship change?

Gavalas, 1990

We had another ultrasound which was unbelievable. The most amazing thing was seeing the interaction between the two at this early point in their lives. Baby A was jumping, stretching and hitting the sac Baby B was in. Baby B was less active. We could see Baby A head up and Baby B head down. You could see their legs and fingers. The technician knows the sex of both babies, but we want it to be a surprise! I can't believe I have two precious babies inside me.

Gavalas, 1990

During the second trimester many expectant fathers enjoy the newfound energy of their mates. The couple does more things together, and the father

During the second trimester of pregnancy the woman begins to show obvious physical signs of pregnancy.

really knows that an infant will be arriving in a short time because he can feel the fetus kicking and see the physical changes taking place in his partner.

Third Trimester

The fetus and consequently the uterus are rapidly increasing in size. The expanding uterus and its contents create a new set of problems in the later stages of pregnancy because the uterus exerts pressure on other organs of the mother. She may have shortness of breath as a result of the uterus crowding the thoracic cavity and lungs, and indigestion is common because the stomach is being compressed. The large amount of weight the woman is carrying makes her feel off balance (Figure 6-7). Many women compensate for this by changing their normal walking pattern to a waddling gait. The uterus undergoes contractions called Braxton Hicks contractions. These intermittent, painless contractions, which can occur every 10 to 20 minutes, are not the contractions of labor but are thought to strengthen the uterine musculature.

As birth approaches, the fetus changes its position so that the head drops down toward the pelvis. This is called lightening or engagement and usually takes place 2 to 3 weeks before the onset of labor in women who are having their first infant. Women who have already had children may not experience lightening until early in labor. When lightening occurs, breathing may become easier because the fetus has settled lower down and the pressure on the thoracic cavity is reduced. Walking may become more difficult, however, because of the increased pressure on the hip joints.

The last trimester is psychologically stressful for many women. They have become impatient and are ready for the infant to be born and the pregnancy to end. Many worry that their infant will be deformed and are anxious about

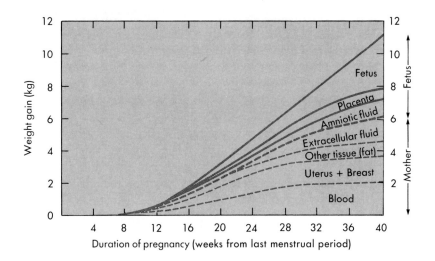

FIGURE 6-7
Maternal weight during a
normal pregnancy.

labor and delivery. They are also concerned about their ability to be good mothers. Fathers often have anxieties about the safety of their mate during the birth process and about the possibility of a deformed child. Some typical reactions were collected by Marzollo:

> If you have a nightmare about the birth of the baby, don't conclude it's a bad omen. Fears about unsuccessful births and abnormal babies are normal. Practically every woman has them. . . . After a nightmare, wake yourself up thoroughly and wake your husband too. Share it with him and let him reassure you. Another time you will reassure him.
>
> Marzollo, 1976, p. 43

> Pregnancy is like a political campaign, two months too long.
>
> Marzollo, 1976, p. 43

> I had a dream that someone was coming to take away my babies.
>
> Gavalas, 1990

In summary, pregnancy is a time for both elation and depression. The physical discomforts and anxieties are balanced by the fact that a new life has been created and is being nurtured within the body. Expectant couples are concerned about the well-being of the developing fetus, as well as with their own anxieties about pregnancy, the birth process, and parenthood. It is an emotional time, and the following quotations sum up three women's feelings:

> A tumultuous nine months. I experienced joy, profound ups and downs, many fears, and intense wonder.
> Pregnancy provided an in-depth, full force, no screens-up experience of myself. It was ecstatic, primal, scary, rough, revealing. No wonder our Victorian forebearers were put off. It was real. More real than anything before it. Everything since happens at a deeper level.
>
> Marzollo, 1976, p. 17

> Although every pregnancy has some difficulties, it has to be the most magnificent miracle to ever take place and pain is easily forgotten.
>
> Gavalas, 1990

Many couples experience a closeness and sense of accomplishment by attending childbirth classes before the birth of their child.

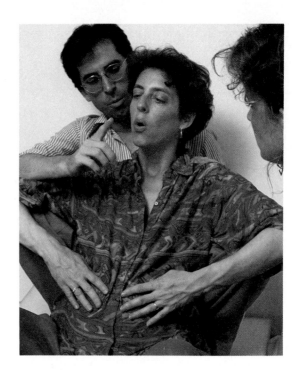

As the birth date gets closer, some men find that they are not attracted sexually to their mates because of the changed physical appearance. In certain instances some intimacy is temporarily lost. Conversely, many men feel a special bond toward their partners during the last trimester of pregnancy, and they feel protective and loving toward them. To maintain closeness and to feel part of the pregnancy experience, a man can (1) listen to the baby's heartbeat, which will make the pregnancy a reality; (2) attend childbirth classes; and (3) compliment his partner as much as possible on her looks because some women feel unattractive in the later stages of pregnancy (White and Reamy, 1982). However, many women feel a great sense of well-being and beauty at this time.

MATERNAL BEHAVIOR AND HABITS

We shall review some important areas of concern and interest to the prospective mother and father. These topics should be discussed with a physician if there is any concern about the expectant mother's health or the well-being of the fetus. A healthy life-style during the preconceptional period is just as important as a healthy life-style during pregnancy.

Nutrition

An adequate diet during pregnancy is essential for both maternal and fetal health. Many researchers have shown that when nutritional standards for the mother are not met, the fetus has deficiencies in weight, length, and condition at birth (Cefalo and Moos, 1988). In addition, the fetus demonstrates the organ weights and cellular changes of starvation.

TABLE 6-1 Recommended Daily Allowances of Proteins, Carbohydrates, Vitamins, and Minerals for Pregnant Women and Nonpregnant Adults

Nutrient	RDA		Dietary sources
	Nonpregnant	Pregnant	
Protein	45 g	75 g	Meats, fish, poultry, grains, dairy products
Carbohydrates	100 g	200 g	Grain products, fruits
Vitamin A (retinol)	4,500 IU	5,000 IU	Fortified milk, deep yellow or orange fruits and vegetables, green vegetables
Vitamin D	200 IU	400-600 IU	Fortified milk, liver, eggs, codfish, exposure of skin to sunlight
Vitamin E (tocopherol)	30 IU	30 IU	Vegetables, oils, milk, eggs, nuts, grains
Vitamin B_1 (thiamine)	1 mg	1.4 mg	Enriched grains
Vitamin B_6	2.0 mg	2.6 mg	Liver, chicken, potatoes, bananas, wheat germ, beef, egg yolk
Vitamin C (ascorbic acid)	60 mg	80 mg	Citrus fruits, tomatoes, green pepper, cantaloupe
Folic acid	400 g	800 g	Liver, spinach, asparagus, broccoli, grains, leafy vegetables
Vitamin B_1 (cyanocobalamin)	3 g	4 g	Animal proteins
Vitamin B_2	1.2 mg	1.5 mg	Liver, milk and dairy products, enriched cereals, eggs
Niacin (pantothenic acid)	13 mg	15 mg	Fish, liver, meat, poultry, eggs, enriched grains, milk
Iron	18 mg	60 mg	Meats, eggs, grains
Calcium	800 mg	1,200 mg	Dairy products
Phosphorus	800 mg	1,200 mg	Dairy products, grains, eggs, dried beans
Iodine	175 mg	175 mg	Iodized salt, seafood
Zinc	15 mg	20 mg	Oysters, meat, potatoes

From Cefalo and Moos, 1988.

Nutritional standards have been established for the intake of calories, protein, vitamins, and minerals during the course of pregnancy (Table 6-1). Many clinicians suggest that the pregnant woman take a supplement containing folic acid, iron, and pyridoxine (vitamin B_6) because the typical diet does not supply the amounts a pregnant woman needs. Clinicians commonly prescribe a daily supplement containing the total minimum requirements of all vitamins and minerals. Assuming that an adequate diet is being maintained, the mother should increase her protein intake during the second and third trimesters because protein is essential for building fetal tissues.

Good nutrition is essential to good health for both mother and child.

Any woman considering becoming pregnant should evaluate her diet. Is she consuming too many calories? Is she meeting the recommended daily allowance (RDA) of proteins, carbohydrates, vitamins, and minerals proposed by the Food and Nutrition Board, National Academy of Sciences, National Research Council?

Changing a poor diet to a sound one during pregnancy is critical, but the early product of conception has nutritional needs that must be met. Often a woman is pregnant for 2 to 3 weeks before she suspects that she is pregnant. During this early part of the pregnancy the conceptus draws on nutrients from its mother in two ways. Before implantation in the uterus the blastocyst absorbs nutrients directly from fluids in the oviducts and uterus (Page, Villee, and Villee, 1981). During implantation, and before the establishment of the placenta, the blastocyst absorbs nutrients directly from the maternal blood. If the prospective mother has an inadequate diet in terms of RDA of proteins, carbohydrates, vitamins, and minerals, is abusing alcohol, and smokes a great deal, her child will be at a disadvantage before the woman even knows she is pregnant.

Cigarette Smoking

Maternal smoking has clearly been identified as the single most important determinant of low birth weight and **perinatal** death in the United States (Longo, 1982). Low birth weight (5½ pounds or less) has been associated with many infant problems, including both physical and mental problems (Cefalo and Moos, 1988; Wilson et al., 1991). Links have been reported between maternal smoking and (1) infertility; (2) spontaneous abortions (miscarriages); (3) ectopic pregnancies; (4) low birth weight; (5) placental irregularities; (6) infant deaths; and (7) long-term effects on the physical, emotional, and intellectual development of the child (Cefalo and Moos, 1988).

Any woman who smokes does not have her own best health interests in mind, and a woman who smokes while she is pregnant clearly does not have the health interests of her child in mind. A women who is trying to conceive a child should get help to quit smoking. Her husband (or partner) should also stop smoking. If both of the prospective parents are trying to quit together, this will enhance success (Cefalo and Moos, 1988). In addition, if the mother stops and the father continues to smoke during the pregnancy, the fetus will be exposed to the hazards of secondary smoke (Cefalo and Moos, 1988). Various studies have shown an increased incidence of birth defects and low birth weights in infants of women who did not smoke but whose partners smoked during the pregnancy (Longo, 1982; Martin and Bracken, 1986).

The evidence of the negative impact of smoking on fetal and child well-being is overwhelming. A few statistics will illustrate the point. Smoking during pregnancy results in an estimated 50,000 spontaneous abortions and between 4,000 and 14,000 infant deaths per year (Feldman, 1985; Lincoln, 1986). Compared with the nonsmoker, a woman who smokes has twice the risk of giving birth to a child that weighs less than 2,500 grams (5½ pounds), and the more cigarettes the mother smokes, the lighter the infant will be at birth (Cefalo and Moos, 1988). If an expectant mother smokes less than one package per day, her risk of having a low birth weight baby increases by 53%; smoking more than one package per day increases the risk by 130% (Kline et al., 1980).

Cigarette smoke contains many chemicals and gases, including nicotine (the addictive substance and the chemical that inhibits blood flow to the fetus), carbon monoxide (interferes with the oxygen-carrying capacity of the red blood cells so less oxygen reaches the fetus), thiocyanide, plutonium, resins, tars, polycyclic aromatic hydrocarbons, cadmium, and vinyl chloride (Cefalo and Moos, 1988). Many of the chemicals and gases in smoke easily pass from the mother to the fetus via the placenta. The exact mechanism by which cigarette smoke causes such negative consequences to the fetus and later to the developing child are not known, but the cause-and-effect relationship leaves no doubt about the harmful effects of smoking.

Cigarette smoke has many harmful chemicals that pass easily through the placenta to the fetus. A woman who smokes during pregnancy has twice the risk of giving birth to a low-birth-weight baby.

Alcohol

Alcohol in modest quantities is not thought to harm the fetus, but excessive amounts can have very negative effects on the fetus (Rosett, 1979). In fact, alcohol abuse in pregnancy is the third leading cause of mental retardation in the United States (Cefalo and Moos, 1988) and the leading cause of developmental disabilities and birth defects (Centers for Disease Control, 1984).

How much alcohol is a modest amount? Will the same amount of alcohol have the same effect on all women? We do not know the answers. However, in 1981 the Food and Drug Administration advised all pregnant women to abstain from alcohol during pregnancy. There is no doubt that excessive alcohol consumption by the mother can lead to fetal alcohol syndrome (FAS). This syndrome may include growth deficiencies before and after birth, mental retardation, facial abnormalities, spontaneous abortions, and low birth weight. FAS is one of the most common causes of mental deficiency in the United States, ranking close to Down's syndrome (Page, Villee, and Villee, 1981). Alcohol-related causes of mental retardation can be prevented by abstaining from alcohol during pregnancy. Ethanol (the active portion of the alcohol or a by-product of this substance) appears to be the causative factor in FAS. Ethanol easily passes from mother to fetus. In a study of the infants of 42 women who were classified as heavy drinkers (5 to 6 drinks per day on some occasions and an average of at least 45 drinks per month), Rosett (1979) found that the frequency of congenital abnormalities, growth retardation, and functional abnormalities was more than double that found in a control group that did not drink alcohol or drank only moderate amounts.

Alcohol has also been linked to spontaneous abortions. Women who reported drinking at least one alcoholic drink per day were two to three times more likely than nondrinkers to have spontaneous abortions (Harlap and Shiono, 1980).

Many researchers have observed the association between excessive drinking and smoking. The combination of these two factors seriously affects the health of the fetus. It is sometimes difficult to separate the effects of these two maternal habits on the outcome of the fetus (Rosett, 1979; Harlap and Shiono, 1980). The type of alcoholic beverage (beer, wine, or liquor) is not important; the amount consumed is the critical factor.

These three children have fetal alcohol syndrome.

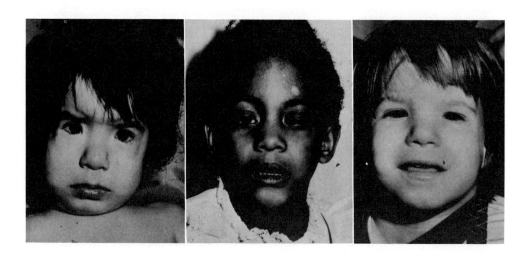

HUMAN SEXUALITY

Caffeine

Caffeine is found in coffee, tea, cocoa, chocolate, soft drinks, and various nonprescription drugs, such as stimulants, pain relievers, cold remedies, and weight-control aids. Caffeine consumption and its effects on the human fetus have been inferred from animal studies. Pregnant rats that received high levels of caffeine produced offspring that showed abnormalities of the digits (toes), and rats that received low levels of caffeine gave birth to offspring that showed delayed skeletal development. The Food and Drug Administration, based on animal data, advises pregnant women to eliminate or limit their consumption of caffeine. Human studies are sparse. One often cited study indicated that coffee drinking during pregnancy had no detectable negative effects on the infants of more than 12,000 women (Linn et al., 1982). Linn and associates concluded that coffee drinking was not related to low birth weight, premature births, or birth defects. The Linn study has been criticized. The Food and Drug Administration stated that the sample size of 12,000 was too small to detect the rare abnormalities that may be caused by caffeine, and it still suggests that caffeine intake be eliminated or reduced during pregnancy. The study of Linn and associates has also been questioned by several other research groups (Bracker et al., 1982; Luke, 1982; Steinmann, 1982). The criticisms concern the facts that only caffeine ingestion from coffee was studied and that the effects, if any, of caffeine on fertility or early pregnancy outcomes, such as ectopic pregnancies or miscarriages, were not studied. However, other human studies have also failed to show a relationship between caffeine ingestion and low birth weight, premature births, or birth defects (Rosenberg et al., 1982; Kruppa et al., 1983).

Medications and Chemicals

Many medications, both prescription and nonprescription, can have a negative effect on the developing fetus. Addictive drugs such as heroin or morphine can cause addiction in the fetus. The fetus must be gradually weaned from the drug just as adult addicts are helped to reduce their dependence. Some tranquilizers have been implicated in **congenital** birth defects. Various antibiotics have been implicated in tooth and bone problems and deafness. The list of agents that can cause fetal defects and malformations is long. One of the most commonly used medications is aspirin, which has been implicated in prolonging pregnancy and the birth process itself. Aspirin is a potent antiprostaglandin agent, and prostaglandins are involved in uterine contractions, which are essential at the time of birth. Chemical agents may act as mutagens, teratogens, or carcinogens. **Mutagens** can cause permanent changes in the genetic information in the sperm and egg cells. These changes can lead to serious developmental problems or death of the offspring. **Teratogens** influence the developing product of conception via maternal exposure. The drug thalidomide, a tranquilizer, received worldwide attention in the early 1960s when it caused serious birth defects in the offspring of women who used it early in pregnancy (Miller, 1981). **Carcinogens** are substances capable of increasing the incidence of cancer. The synthetic estrogen called diethylstilbestrol (DES) was once used to prevent spontaneous abortions in pregnant women and to prevent implantation in women who had recently had unprotected intercourse. It was found that the prenatal exposure of the conceptus to DES increased the risk for

congenital
Present at birth.

mutagen
(myoo tuh juhnz) Agent that causes permanent changes in the genetic information of cells.

teratogen
(TER uh tuh juhnz) Causing fetal defects and malformations.

carcinogen
(kar SIN uh jen) Cancer-producing substance.

cervical and vaginal cancers in daughters born to these women and that the sons showed abnormalities of the reproductive tract.

Probably the ingestion of all but the most essential medication should be avoided during pregnancy. Any substance that enters the mother's body can potentially act on the fetus in a negative way. A list of many agents and their effects on the embryo and fetus can be found in Table 6-2.

Irradiation

Irradiation (the exposure to a radiation source) of all kinds, in particular x-ray irradiation, should be avoided during pregnancy unless absolutely essential. Irradiation can cause birth defects in the fetus (Miller, 1981; Page, Villee, and Villee, 1981).

Exercise

Exercise should be discussed with the woman's physician, but most researchers in the field of exercise physiology and obstetrics believe that exercise is beneficial during pregnancy and should be encouraged. If a woman has been an active tennis player, jogger, or swimmer, she may continue her exercise program throughout most of the pregnancy. A woman should not initiate a new vigorous exercise program during pregnancy if she had not been exercising before the pregnancy. Activities such as skiing and skating, in which physical danger from falling is possible, should be avoided in late pregnancy. Common sense is the key to exercise during pregnancy.

A sensible exercise program can provide both physical and psychological benefits to the pregnant woman.

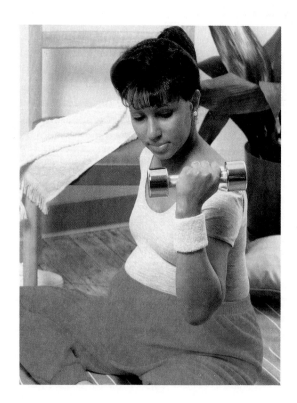

HUMAN SEXUALITY

TABLE 6-2 Environmental Agents That Can Affect Embryo or Fetus

Influence	Effect on embryo or fetus
INFECTIOUS AGENTS	
Bacteria, including those causing syphilis and gonorrhea	Spontaneous abortion, neonatal death, mental retardation, physical malformations, deafness, and blindness
Rubella virus (German measles)	Spontaneous abortion, heart defects, blindness, deafness, mental retardation, cleft palate, harelip, and spina bifida (exposed spinal cord); the earlier in pregnancy the woman is exposed to rubella, the greater the probability that she will have a child with a birth defect
Smallpox virus, chickenpox virus, mumps virus, herpes simplex virus type 2 (genital herpes), cytomegalovirus, and rarely herpes simplex virus type 1 (oral herpes)	Spontaneous abortion, neonatal (newborn) death, mental retardation, growth retardation, hearing loss, and neuromuscular disorders
Toxoplasmosis (caused by the one-celled organism *Toxoplasma gondii*)—contact with cat feces and eating poorly cooked meats containing the organism are two routes of transmission to mother and fetus	Eye disorders or blindness, mental retardation, and other neurological problems
RADIATION	
Irradiation, including x-rays	Physical malformations, cancer, and the potential to pass on harmful genetic information to subsequent generations
MEDICATIONS AND CHEMICALS	
Antibiotics	
Streptomycin	Deafness
Tetracycline	Brownish stain or physical malformations of the teeth, cataracts of the eyes (rarely)
Anticancer drugs including aminopterin, busulfan, chlorambucil, and methotrexate	Spontaneous abortion, physical malformations
Anticonvulsant drugs (to treat epilepsy)	
Phenytoin (Dilantin)	Physical malformations and heart defects
Trimethadione	Physical malformations
Aspirin, indomethacin, and ibuprofen (Motrin, Nuprin, and Advil)—all are prostaglandin inhibitors used for pain relief and arthritis	Heart defects

Data from Page et al., 1981; Jones, 1984; Cefalo and Moos, 1988.
See Chapter 18 for discussion of how various sexually transmitted diseases can negatively affect fetus.
See Chapter 2 for discussion of male hormones and their influence on developing embryo.

Continued.

TABLE 6-2 Environmental Agents That Can Affect Embryo or Fetus

Influence	Effect on embryo or fetus
MEDICATIONS AND CHEMICALS—cont'd.	
Bendectin (used for morning sickness)	Heart defects, physical malformations, and defects in the structure of the stomach
Tranquilizers (Librium, Valium, and Equanil)	Physical malformations
HORMONES	
Diethylstilbestrol (DES)—used to induce early spontaneous abortion ("morning after pill") and prevent spontaneous abortions later in pregnancy	Vaginal cancer in adolescent and young women; defects in reproductive structures of male fetus
Estrogens	Defects in reproductive structures of male fetus
Oral contraceptives (taken during pregnancy)	Physical malformations
Progestins and certain androgens—testosterone most potent	Virilization (male characteristics) of female fetus
ILLICIT AND RECREATIONAL DRUGS	
Alcohol	Fetal alcohol syndrome
Caffeine	Low birth weight
Heroin	Low birth weight, fetal addiction, respiratory depression
LSD (lysergic acid diethylamide)	Spontaneous abortion, stillbirth
Morphine	Fetal addiction, low birth weight
Nicotine and carbon monoxide from smoking	Low birth weight, spontaneous abortion, stillbirth
METALS	
Lead: solder, lead pipes, batteries, paints, ceramics, smelter emissions	Abnormal sperm, menstrual disorders, spontaneous abortions, stillbirths, mental retardation
Mercury: thermometers, mirror coating, dyes, inks, pesticides, dental fillings (for those who prepare the filling material)	Impaired fetal motor and mental development
SOLVENTS	

Dry cleaning fluids, paint strippers, drug and electronics industry
   Trichloroethylene
   Chloroform
   Benzene
   Toluene
	Birth defects

Carbon disulfide: textile industry	Decreased fertility, increased spontaneous abortion rate

Influence	Effect on embryo or fetus
VINYL MONOMERS	
Vinyl chloride: plastic manufacturing	Decreased fertility, chromosomal aberrations, spontaneous abortions, stillbirths, birth defects
POLLUTANTS	

Rubber, chemical and electronics industries
  Polychlorinated biphenyl (PCB)
  Polybrominated biphenyl (PBB)
	Infertility, stillbirths

PESTICIDES	

Farm, home and garden insect sprays
  2,4,5-T
  2,4-D organophosphates (e.g., malathion)
	Birth defects, spontaneous abortions, low birth weight

GASES	
Automobile exhausts, furnaces, cigarette smoke Carbon monoxide	Low birth weight, stillbirths
Anesthetic gases: dental offices, operating rooms, chemicals industries	Decreased fertility, spontaneous abortions, birth defects

Sexual Intercourse

Studies of sexual intercourse during pregnancy have had conflicting findings. Should the couple continue to have intercourse until birth? Should they cease intercourse during the last trimester? The answers to these questions must be decided by the prospective mother and father and the physician.

Positions used during sexual intercourse are discussed in Chapter 9.

Masters and Johnson (1966) state that if the pregnancy is normal in all respects, intercourse can continue safely at least until 4 weeks before the infant is born. The important word here is *normal*. Many women have problems during pregnancy, and they would not fit this category. A study of almost 30,000 pregnancies during the years 1959 to 1966 indicated that infections of the amniotic fluid and deaths of premature infants occurred more often in women who had intercourse at least once a week during the month before giving birth (Naeye, 1979). However, in a study involving almost 11,000 women, Mills, Harlay, and Harley (1981) concluded that women who engaged in intercourse during the seventh, eighth, and ninth months of pregnancy showed no increased risk of premature rupture of membranes, low birth weight, and amniotic fluid infections. Some clinicians think that female orgasm promotes uterine contractions and may lead to premature delivery, but this finding was also challenged by Mills, Harlay, and Harley.

Page and coauthors in their widely used medical textbook suggest that intercourse is an option well into the third trimester of pregnancy: "Coitus certainly should be prohibited in the presence of any uterine bleeding or painful uterine contractions and possibly after the thirty-sixth week of pregnancy;

FIGURE 6-8
The side-by-side position of sexual intercourse is frequently used during late pregnancy because it does not put any weight on the abdomen of the pregnant woman.

beyond that, the evidence of harm is not sufficiently firm to draw conclusions" (Page, Villee, and Villee, 1981).

When couples perform intercourse during late pregnancy, certain positions are easier. The side-to-side position is probably the most comfortable (Figure 6-8). White and Reamy (1982) report that for most of the pregnancy the majority of women continue to have intercourse at frequencies that are essentially the same as before pregnancy. It is during the last trimester, in the seventh and eighth months, that a decline becomes evident. During the last month of pregnancy the frequency of intercourse greatly diminishes (White and Reamy, 1982). In one study approximately 40% of women reported reduced amounts of intercourse and 60% reported no intercourse during the last month of pregnancy (Wagner and Solberg, 1974).

In summary, sexual activity during pregnancy is a personal matter that must be decided by the couple and the physician. Sexual intercourse is just one way to achieve sexual gratification. Numerous other sexual techniques may be used by the couple during the later stages of pregnancy.

Noncoital types of sexual behaviors are presented in Chapter 9.

PROBLEMS DURING PREGNANCY

Not all pregnancies proceed perfectly. Some are interrupted early when the egg implants outside the uterus, others end in miscarriage and an aborted embryo, and still others end in a premature birth. In addition, problems such as toxemia of pregnancy may occur during the pregnancy and other disorders such as Rh incompatibility may develop after the birth. We shall briefly discuss the more common problems that happen during pregnancy and shortly after birth. Most of the basic facts in this section were taken from Page, Villee, and Villee's text on reproductive and perinatal medicine (1981).

Ectopic Pregnancy

ectopic pregnancy
(ek TOP ik) Result of implantation of fertilized egg outside uterus.

Ectopic pregnancy occurs when the fertilized egg implants someplace other than the uterus (Figure 6-9). The most common site of an ectopic pregnancy is the oviducts; more than 95% are located here. Other sites are the ovaries, abdominal cavity, and cervix. The incidence of ectopic pregnancies varies from 1 in 80 to 1 in 250 pregnancies, depending on the sample population. If a

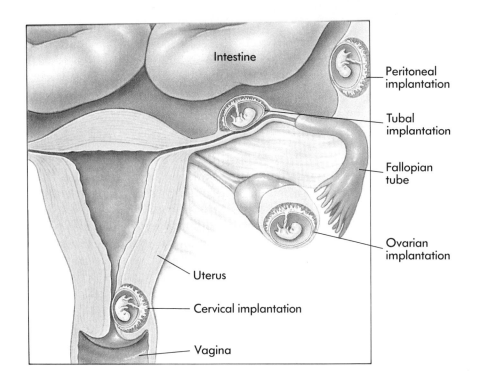

FIGURE 6-9
Ectopic pregnancies are the result of the fertilized egg becoming implanted at the site outside of the uterus.

woman has an ectopic pregnancy in the oviduct, her chances of having another in the oviduct on the opposite side are increased. The causes of ectopic pregnancy include all factors that impede or delay the normal transport of the fertilized egg from the oviduct to the uterus. One of the chief causes is previous infection in the oviducts.

What happens during an ectopic pregnancy? Does the fetus grow? Can a live birth occur? The answers depend on the location of the ectopic pregnancy. Pregnancies in the oviducts usually rupture or spontaneously abort. A ruptured oviduct requires immediate medical attention. Abdominal pregnancies have been known to go to term, with a live child delivered through an abdominal incision.

Spontanous Abortion

A spontaneous abortion or miscarriage is the termination of a pregnancy as a result of natural causes before the conceptus is capable of surviving on its own. Miscarriages occur in about 15% of all pregnancies between 4 and 22 weeks after the last menstrual period. Before the fourth week the percentage is much higher, but the rate is unknown because most women do not even know they are pregnant. A woman may notice vaginal bleeding or spotting but think it is connected with a menstrual flow.

Page, Villee, and Villee (1981) state that "well over 50 per cent of spontaneous abortions involve defective embryos. Gross chromosomal defects have been found in as high as 60 per cent in one series and as low as 22 per cent in another. . . . Falls, automobile accidents and pyschic trauma rarely are responsible." Spontaneous abortions seem to be caused by the presence of a defective fetus, a serious maternal disease, or an abnormality of the uterus. Endocrine disorders have been proposed as another cause but are not always at fault.

Prematurity

Premature labor may be defined as occurring before the 37th week of gestation, but this assumes that 40 weeks represents the length of time before a fully developed infant would be born and that determining when the 37th week has been reached is possible. A premature infant has been defined as one weighing less than 5½ pounds and born 4 weeks or more before its expected delivery date. The premature infant has less chance of survival and an increased risk of various other disorders. The final 2 to 4 weeks of gestation is very important to complete the maturation of the various organ systems. The incomplete maturation of the organ systems is one cause of fetal disorders and deaths.

The possible causes of premature labor and birth are numerous, but the exact cause of many premature births may go unexplained. Certain habits and characteristics of the mother or the pregnancy may contribute to premature labor. These include poor nutrition, smoking, multiple pregnancy (for example, twins), mother's age (teenage mothers tend to experience premature labor and deliver premature infants), and weight of mother (women under 100 pounds tend to have premature labor and deliver premature infants).

Toxemia of Pregnancy

toxemia of pregnancy
(tok see mee uh) Condition of preeclampsia and eclampsia.

preeclampsia
(pree' i KLAMP see uh) Condition of high blood pressure, protein in urine, water retention, and swelling of legs during second half of pregnancy.

eclampsia
(i KLAMP see uh) Coma and convulsive seizures during second half of pregnancy in a woman with preeclampsia.

Toxemia of pregnancy is a term used to describe the conditions preeclampsia and eclampsia. These are both hypertensive (high blood pressure and its effects) disorders. **Preeclampsia** is a combination of high blood pressure, severe water retention, swelling of the legs, and protein in the urine during the second half of pregnancy. **Eclampsia** includes the problems of preeclampsia and convulsions.

With preeclampsia the usual sequence of events is a rapid weight gain because of severe water retention and a rise in blood pressure, followed by the appearance of protein in the urine. As preeclampsia progresses to eclampsia, the woman may have a blurring of vision and a severe headache caused by fluids exerting pressure on the brain. Convulsions may follow. What is the cause of preeclampsia-eclampsia? There is no definite answer. Some women are more prone to this disorder than others. Factors implicated include giving birth for the first time, diabetes mellitus, a family history of toxemia, carrying multiple fetuses, extremes of mother's age, and preexisting chronic hypertension or hypertensive kidney disease.

Preeclampsia-eclampsia cannot be prevented in all women, but several studies indicate that the avoidance of excessive salt in addition to a high-protein diet supplemented by vitamins may reduce the incidence (Page, Villee, and Villee, 1981). If detected in its early stages, the disorder can be treated before it becomes more serious. Treatment includes bed rest, drugs to reduce high blood pressure, salt restriction, and drugs to control convulsions if the disease

HUMAN SEXUALITY

has progressed. If a woman is under the care of a competent physician, pre-eclampsia-eclampsia should be detected easily and not pose a threat to the mother or fetus.

Disorders of Development

During the nineteenth century it was believed that an infant could be physically marked by maternal activities. Page, Villee, and Villee (1981) describe a case reported in an 1881 medical journal of a woman who developed a craving for oysters when she was pregnant. Fearing that this food craving might mark her child, she clapped her hand on her buttock and proposed that if the child had a mark, it should be on the buttock. At birth the child was born with a mark of a well-formed oyster on his buttock!

Today we have scientific evidence showing that the developing embryo or fetus may be negatively affected by various factors. These include genetic anomalies caused by chromosomal abnormalities such as **Down's syndrome,** previously known as mongoloidism, in which there are abnormalities of the face, eyelids, and tongue and various degrees of mental retardation, and gene abnormalities, which have been termed inborn errors of metabolism. Gene abnormalities include such conditions as **phenylketonuria** (PKU), which, left untreated, causes mental and physical retardation. In PKU the amino acid phenylalanine is not broken down and the elevated levels of the amino acid cause problems in the development of the brain and other organs. The artificial sweeteners Nutrasweet and Equal (technical name is aspartame) are used in many products, and the American Medical Association has determined that this food additive does not appear to be teratogenic (Cefalo and Moos, 1988). However, this additive does contain the amino acid phenylalanine, which crosses the placenta. Fetal safety has not been determined in pregnant patients who have elevated levels of phenylalanine or carry the gene for PKU (Cefalo and Moos, 1988). PKU is one of the most common inborn errors of metabolism, occurring in approximately 1 in 10,000 live births. This disorder is treated with dietary therapy that restricts ingestion of phenylalanine.

In addition to genetic disorders that negatively affect normal embryonic or fetal development, unfavorable environmental influences may have an adverse effect on the developing conceptus. Exposure of a pregnant woman to the rubella virus that causes German measles can have disastrous effects on the developing embryo. This virus causes serious birth defects in approximately half of the embryos exposed during the first month of pregnancy; the number of children born with defects then decreases with exposure during the second and third months of gestation. After the third month of gestation the rubella virus is much less of a threat. Children prenatally exposed to rubella often are deaf and have heart defects, mental retardation, and slowed growth.

A technique known as **amniocentesis** can be used to detect some disorders of development, determine the sex of the child, and examine how well developed certain biological systems are before birth (Figure 6-10). Amniocentesis may be defined as puncture of the intrauterine amniotic sac through the abdominal wall with a special needlelike instrument to obtain a sample of amniotic fluid. Various components of the amniotic fluid are analyzed. For example,

Down's syndrome
Congenital condition of various degrees of mental retardation and abnormal development caused by extra chromosome, usually number 21 or 22 (i.e., there are three instead of two chromosomes).

phenylketonuria
(fen′ uhl keet n OOR ee uh) Recessive hereditary disease caused by body's inability to convert phenylalanine (an amino acid) to tyrosine because of defective enzyme.

amniocentesis
(am′ nee oh sen TEE suhs) Procedure to detect fetal abnormalities in which the amniotic sac is punctured with needle and syringe and amniotic fluid is obtained for analysis.

FIGURE 6-10
Amniocentesis. Amniotic
fluid (containing fetal cells)
is withdrawn and analyzed
for indications of the fetus'
age, sex, and chromosomal
abnormalities.

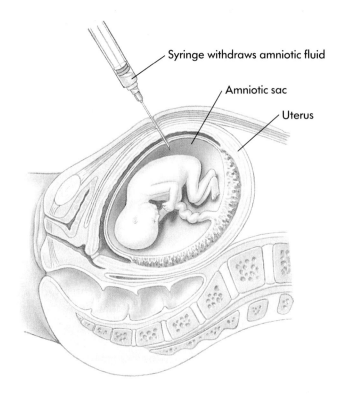

Syringe withdraws amniotic fluid

Amniotic sac

Uterus

skin cells that are sloughed off by the fetus accumulate in the fluid. From these cells the sex and age of the fetus can be determined. The total number of chromosomes and their structure can also be discovered. The chromosome count is important because any deviation from the normal number of 23 pairs, or 46 chromosomes, potentially means that the developing fetus, if it is not spontaneously aborted, will be born with various physical deformities and mental retardation. In Down's syndrome, for example, there are usually three number 21 chromosomes (in some cases three number 22 chromosomes), making the chromosome count 47 instead of the normal 46. In some cases the extra number 21 or 22 chromosome is attached to another chromosome, but this can be detected. In Turner's syndrome a chromosome is missing and the infant is born with only one sex chromosome, which is an X chromosome. Amniocentesis would reveal 45 chromosomes. The child has short stature, no ovaries, juvenile female genitalia, and poorly developed breasts. Many other chromosomal abnormalities can be detected through amniocentesis.

In addition to sloughed-off skin cells in the amniotic fluid, the fluid contains dissolved gases that can be measured to determine the amount of oxygen the fetus is receiving. The acidity of the fluid is also an indicator of oxygen flow to the fetus. The chemical composition of the fluid can reveal metabolic disorders caused by missing or defective enzymes indicative of inborn errors of metabolism. These abnormalities can result in metabolic disturbances in the newborn, as well as mental retardation and physical malformations, depending on the disorder.

Amniocentesis is usually done 14 to 16 weeks after the last missed menstrual flow. If a defect is noted in the fetus, the mother may consider an abortion at this early date. Amniocentesis is used for women who are over the age of 35, which places them at risk for a child with chromosomal abnormalities (especially Down's syndrome), women who have had a previous child born with an inherited inborn error of metabolism, and women who are thought to be carriers of a genetic defect (Wilson et al., 1991). The incidence of children born with Down's syndrome increases dramatically with age. For example, 25-year-old women give birth to 0.7 to 0.9 Down's syndrome babies per 1000 live births, while 36-year-old women give birth to 3.2 to 5.0 Down's syndrome babies per 1000 live births (Cefalo and Moos, 1988). Amniocentesis is routinely done to detect Tay-Sachs disease in the fetus. This inherited disorder is fatal to the infant and sometimes occurs in individuals with Eastern European ancestry.

Amniocentesis poses risks to the mother and fetus, but these hazards may be reduced when sonography (a technique for detecting objects by recording sound waves reflected by them) is also used to locate the placenta. Amniocentesis has been associated with spontaneous abortion, and some are concerned about the possible effects of sonography on the fetus (Hotchner, 1979). This problem is now being studied in the United States. The routine use of amniocentesis and sonography as diagnostic tools is a controversial topic. Before these methods are used, the parents should carefully discuss their necessity with several physicians.

As stated, amniocentesis cannot usually be done until 14 to 16 weeks of pregnancy. Another technique, called **chorionic villi sampling** (CVS), may be used as early as 5 weeks of pregnancy. To perform CVS, the physician inserts a long thin tube into the uterus via the cervix or through the maternal abdominal wall (Brambati, 1987). Using ultrasound recorders to avoid puncturing the fetus, membranes surrounding the fetus, and the placenta, the physician places the tube between the lining of the uterus and the chorion. Some of the chorionic

chorionic villi sampling (KOR ee on ic vil ee') Procedure to detect fetal abnormalities in which the chorionic villi are examined.

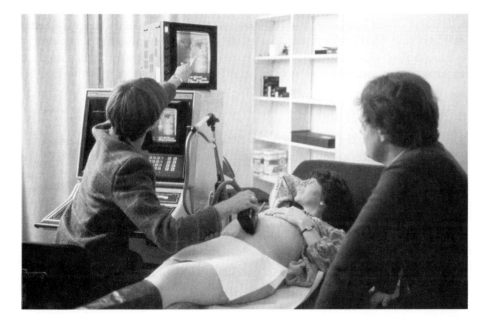

Sonography produces a picture of the fetus through the use of sound waves.

FIGURE 6-11
Chorionic villi sampling involves taking chorionic tissue for analysis of fetal problems.

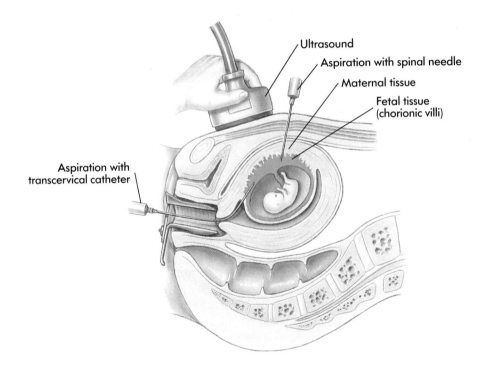

Ultrasound

Aspiration with spinal needle

Maternal tissue

Fetal tissue
(chorionic villi)

Aspiration with
transcervical catheter

villi are sucked into the tube. As mentioned, the chorionic villi are part of the embryo and hence have the same cells. Any genetic defects noted in the villi are also present in the embryo.

Until 1941 all fetal abnormalities were considered to be genetic in origin and the idea of environmental influences on fetal development was denied. During the 1940s great strides were made in research on birth defects and it was shown that they could be produced by the rubella virus or by dietary deficiencies. We now know that certain viruses (rubella virus and cytomegalovirus) cause birth defects and that other viruses (smallpox, herpes, mumps, and hepatitis) are suspect. Toxoplasmosis, which is usually transmitted to humans by raw meat or by cat feces, can cause serious defects in the fetus.

Rh Blood Incompatibility

Red blood cells in the body carry on their surfaces proteins called antigens. These antigens are genetically determined and are passed from parents to offspring. We are all familiar with the ABO blood system, and we often hear people say that they are A positive or B negative. The positive or negative term concerns the Rh system. Individuals with the Rh factor are said to be Rh positive, and those without the Rh factor are Rh negative. The ABO and Rh systems are inherited independent of each other. Thus a person whose red blood cells carry both the A antigen and the Rh factor has an A-positive blood type. If a person with Rh-negative blood is given a blood transfusion from an Rh-positive person, he or she will develop antibodies against the Rh antigens. If the same person then receives a second Rh-positive transfusion, the results

Approximately 85% of whites and 88% of blacks in the United States are Rh positive; thus 15% of whites and 12% of blacks are Rh negative.

could be fatal. The body will attack the red blood cells with the antibodies it has made.

Rh blood incompatibility can occur between a mother and fetus. If the mother is Rh negative and the father is Rh positive, the fetus may be Rh positive (depending on the exact genetic components of the father for the Rh factor). This may lead to a serious problem. Some of the Rh antigens from the fetus may leak into the maternal blood system. This usually occurs at the time that the placenta is being delivered. It is thought that cuts or breaks where the placenta breaks loose from the uterine wall allow fetal blood to mix with maternal blood (Page, Villee, and Villee, 1981). The Rh antigens get into the mother's bloodstream, and her immune system begins to produce antibodies against the Rh factor. The woman with Rh-negative blood now has antibodies against the Rh factor. If the woman becomes pregnant again, her second Rh-positive baby will be at risk because the maternal antibodies against the Rh factor may cross the placenta and begin to destroy the fetal red blood cells. This condition is known as **erythroblastosis** or Rh disease. It can be fatal or cause disorders in the newborn such as anemia, heart failure, jaundice, and mental retardation.

erythroblastosis (i rith′ roh bla STOH sis) Disease of newborn caused by transmission of maternal antibody that involves maternal and fetal blood group incompatibility.

Fortunately, Rh disease poses little danger since the discovery of drugs that desensitize the blood of an Rh-negative mother after the birth of an Rh-positive baby. These drugs, RhoGAM and RhoImmune, stop the maternal system from producing the anti-Rh antibodies. They are given at 28 weeks of gestation and again within 72 hours of birth if necessary. The drugs prevent the mother from producing anti-Rh antibodies, and a second Rh-positive fetus can be carried without fear that Rh disease will develop.

INFERTILITY IN MEN AND WOMEN

Up to this point in your life, making love has been an experience prompted by romantic urges. Any couple has its own patterns of sexual communication that develop as the relationship develops. Making love according to the dictates of the woman's monthly cycle, something infertile couples often must do to conceive, can come as a shock. It can damage spontaneity, changing sexual intercourse from an expression of love and passion to an exercise in self-consciousness. In the extreme, it can make a couple dread going into their bedroom. When ovulation seems imminent, the pressure to perform intensifies.

Schwan, 1988, p. 22

Most of us take for granted that sexual intercourse will result in conception. In fact, if 100 couples do not use any form of contraception for a year, a pregnancy will result for 90% of them (see Table 8-4). What about the other 10%? Why will the women not become pregnant? It is estimated that 10% to 15% of married couples in the United States are affected by **infertility**. This means that they have difficulty producing offspring. If there is no chance that conception can occur, the condition is referred to as **sterility**. According to one source, if 100 couples who have tried unsuccessfully to produce a pregnancy for 6 months seek medical help, the following statistics are usually noted: in 33% of the couples the cause of infertility is found in the woman alone, in 33% in the man alone, in about 20% in both partners, and in 14% the cause of infertility is unknown (Schwan, 1988). A slightly different breakdown of causes

infertility Diminished ability to produce offspring.

sterility Inability to produce offspring.

FIGURE 6-12
Causes of infertility.

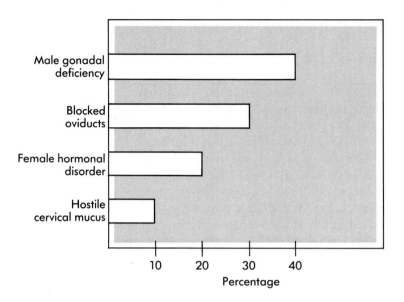

FIGURE 6-12
Causes of infertility.

using more specific causative factors has been proposed. For about 40% of the couples infertility is related to male gonadal deficiency, for 20% a female hormonal disorder affects ovulation, for 30% the oviducts are the cause (usually blockage), and for 10% the cervical mucus is "hostile" to the sperm, a shared problem (Figure 6-12) (Berkow, 1988). Most physicians concur that if a couple tries to conceive for 6 months without success, they should seek medical assistance.

Male Infertility

The man should have his ejaculate evaluated before the woman undergoes the many complicated and expensive tests for infertility. The ejaculate is checked for numerous things, including total volume of semen, sperm count, motility (Table 6-3), and presence or absence of abnormal-appearing sperm. If the man's sperm production and motility are less than the norm, medication may be prescribed. Abnormal sperm may be due to an infection of the reproductive

TABLE 6-3 Some Factors of Importance When a Semen Sample Is Examined for Signs of Infertility

Factor	Normal limits or amounts
Volume	The amount of seminal fluid from seminal vesicles should be 2-5 cubic centimeters.
Motility	At least 60% of sperm cells should be at average to good speed. Speed is measured by forward motion.
Sperm count	Count is expressed by number of sperm cells per cubic centimeter of semen. Normal range is 40 million to 60 million.
Sperm cell appearance	At least 60% should be normal in appearance.

TABLE 6-4 Tests and Procedures for the Man in a Couple Experiencing Problems Conceiving a Child

Test or procedure	What test is looking for	When test is performed
Medical history	Past clues to infertility and life-style factors in infertility	Office visit
Physical examination	General health; clues to infertility-related conditions	First appointment or at visit to specialist
Semen analysis	Sperm count, sperm quality, seminal fluid, infections	As directed by specialist

tract or exposure of the testes to excessive heat. Table 6-4 lists the medical tests performed on the male and the purpose of each test. These tests and the physical examination are usually done by a urologist.

Several specific factors have been identified in male infertility. These include **varicoceles,** undescended testes, and damage to reproductive organs or duct systems caused by infections, drug usage, and exposure to various environmental agents and toxins (Table 6-2). Varicoceles (varicose veins in the testes) are enlargement and twisting of the veins that drain the testes and related ducts in the testes. This poor drainage contributes to lowered levels of sperm production and poor motility of the sperm, perhaps as a result of the extra heat this condition causes in the testes. Many men with varicoceles do not have impaired fertility, but 40% of infertile men have varicoceles and correction via surgery has been shown to elevate the sperm count (Schwan, 1988).

Undescended testes can cause infertility because sperm-producing cells are extremely sensitive to heat. Obviously, if the testes are in the abdominal cavity, they will be at body temperature, which is too high for sperm production. Undescended testes are rarely a cause of infertility because this situation is usually corrected surgically before puberty.

Hormonal problems in men can account for a low sperm count. If all other causes of male infertility can be ruled out, medications are used in an attempt to boost the sperm count. The medications, clomiphene citrate (Clomid) and human chorionic gonadotropin (HCG), increase spermatogenesis by increasing testosterone production by the testes. The increase in testosterone, which is essential for sperm production, may be enough to elevate the sperm count to within normal limits.

The very fine seminiferous tubules, or vasa deferentia, can be damaged by scar tissue when these structures are subjected to diseases such as mumps or a sexually transmitted disease such as gonorrhea. Mumps, which can infect the testes and damage the seminiferous tubules, is rarely a cause of infertility, but gonorrhea and other sexually transmitted diseases such as *Chlamydia* infection have been implicated in blocking the vasa deferentia to cause infertility (Hatcher et al., 1990). In some cases microsurgical techniques can be used to repair a vas deferens damaged by infection.

The use of various drugs has also been implicated in male infertility. Weight

varicoceles
(VAR i koh seelz') Twisting and enlargement of veins that drain the testes.

Role of scrotum in maintaining testicular temperature is discussed in Chapter 3.

Negative feedback systems are discussed in Chapter 4.

lifters who take male steroids to increase strength may not produce enough sperm because of the negative feedback system that exists among the hypothalamus, the anterior pituitary gland, and the testes. Heavy marijuana users have been reported to have low sperm counts as well, and the use of cocaine has been shown to lower sperm counts, lower motility, and produce abnormal sperm cells (Bracken et al., 1990). Table 6-2 lists the effects of numerous environmental substances including drugs and workplace hazards on male and female reproductive functioning and fetal development.

The widespread use of cocaine and "crack" cocaine (cocaine that has been heated and allowed to harden into small pieces) has serious implications for both male and female infertility and fetal development. In a national study 30% of men aged 26 to 34 reported cocaine use at some point in their lives, 17% reported use in the past year, and 8.6% reported use in the past month. High levels of cocaine inhibit luteinizing hormone release, which would lead to a reduction in testosterone from the testes; testosterone is essential for sperm production (Bracken et al., 1990). Also, cocaine may act directly on sperm development, and because cocaine causes constriction of arteries, it may cause a problem in sperm production when blood flow to the testes is reduced (Bracken et al., 1990). The effect of cocaine on the developing fetus is presented in Table 6-2.

Female Infertility

If the male's sperm count and sperm motility are in the normal range, the female should undergo a series of tests to determine whether she has a hormonal disorder and is not ovulating, whether her oviducts are blocked, or whether she has cervical mucus that is "hostile" to her partner's sperm (Table 6-5). In some cases a woman's system builds antibodies to her partner's sperm and the sperm are "attacked" as if they were a foreign protein. In these cases the man is instructed to use a condom for varying periods in the hope that the woman's immune system will stop producing antibodies to his sperm.

Basal body temperature as a predictor of ovulation is discussed in Chapter 8.

Normal ovarian function, and hence cyclical ovulation, is usually established using such means as monitoring basal body temperature and examining the uterine endometrium at selected times in the menstrual cycle. Accurate home testing kits such as Clearplan Easy can now be used to predict and determine ovulation. Some common causes of ovulation failure include hormonal problems (hormones from the ovaries, anterior pituitary gland, and hypothalamus are not in correct ratios or timing is incorrect), anemia, malnutrition including anorexia from excessive dieting or exercise, physical or psychological stress, and drug abuse (Schwan, 1988).

If the woman is ovulating, tests must be done to determine whether her oviducts are open to permit the union of the sperm and egg or whether her cervical mucus is "hostile" to the sperm because of erosions and infections. If the oviducts are not open, surgery may correct the problem.

If the woman is not ovulating, certain drugs such as clomiphene and human menopausal gonadotropin (HMG) can be used to induce ovulation. These have been very successful compared with treatment of the male for low sperm count and low sperm motility. Clomiphene has side effects that include sleep disturbances, hot flashes, fatigue, breast tenderness, nausea, and blurred vision

TABLE 6-5 Overview of Possible Tests and Procedures for the Woman in a Couple Experiencing Problems Conceiving a Child

Name of test or procedure	What test is looking for	When test can be performed (in average 28-day cycle)
Medical history	Past clues to infertility problem	First appointment
Physical examination	General health and signs of fertility problems	At first appointment or at a subsequent appointment
Pelvic examination	Shape, position of reproductive organs, condition of cervix and mucus, general reproductive health	Not during menstrual period
Blood tests	Assay hormone and general health	When needed
Urine test	General health	At physical examination
Temperature charts for basal body temperature	Length of cycles, signs of ovulation, record of sexual activity	Take temperature at home in mornings
Postcoital or Sims-Huhner test	Quality of cervical mucus, ability of sperm to penetrate it, approximate sperm count, signs of sexually transmitted diseases or bacteria	Near time of ovulation, days 12 to 14
Endometrial biopsy	Check uterine lining	After day 21 when it has been established that the woman is not pregnant
Hysterosalpingography	To determine whether fallopian tubes are open, shape of inner uterus	Early in cycle, days 7 to 10
Diagnostic laparoscopy	Abdominal adhesions, signs of endometriosis, scar tissue, damage of fallopian tubes	After ovulation in most cases

and occasionally multiple pregnancies (Schwan, 1988). This drug has been very successful in stimulating ovulation. When used on patients in whom all other factors are normal, clomiphene stimulates ovulation for about 75% of patients and pregnancies occur in 65% of these women (Schwan, 1988).

If the woman is ovulating but her oviducts are blocked, the outlook is poor. In a few women with blocked oviducts, in vitro fertilization may be the answer. Cervical mucus problems are treated in various ways with mixed results. Bypassing the "hostile" mucus by inserting sperm into the uterus has been done with some success. Conditions such as endometriosis and pelvic inflammatory disease may lead to infertility or sterility.

Several technological advances have aided infertile couples. One of these is in vitro fertilization (IVF). *In vitro* literally means *in glass* (hence the name "test-tube fertilization"). This technique is also known as extracorporeal fertilization or out of the body fertilization. Different combinations of hormones and drugs are used to induce multiple ovulation. While the prospective mother

Various clinical conditions that can lead to infertility are discussed in Chapters 17 and 18.

LOOK, LADY— YOU'RE THE ONE WHO ASKED FOR A FAMOUS MOVIE STAR WITH DARK HAIR, STRONG NOSE AND DEEP SET EYES...

is under general anesthesia, a laparoscope is used to find the mature eggs in their follicles. Using a vacuum-controlled aspirator, the physician sucks the eggs out of the follicles and places them in a bottle. The eggs are then taken to another room in the hospital where they are placed in a culture dish that contains a special culture medium (nourishments, follicular fluid, and other materials necessary to sustain the eggs and induce capacitation in the sperm). Sperm cells from the prospective father are then placed in the dish with the eggs, and fertilization takes place.

When the eggs have divided into the eight-cell stage or blastocyst, about 2 days after fertilization, several are placed in the tip of a needlelike instrument. This instrument is carefully placed in the prospective mother's uterus through the cervix, and the blastocysts are released in the top of the uterus (the area where the uterine tubes enter the uterus). With good luck and skill on the part of the physician, at least one blastocyst implants and develops into a viable embryo and then a fetus.

The standard procedure used in IVF involves placing one to three (occasionally four) embryos in the uterus (Edwards and Steptoe, 1985). This procedure is completed in less than a minute and usually does not require general anesthesia. The process of IVF has been refined and will continue to be made safer and more effective in the years ahead. The rate of pregnancies reported in the most successful IVF clinics in the United States ranges between 15% and 25% per egg retrieval cycle (Edwards, 1984; Andrews, 1987; Seibel, 1988). The more times the couple tries, the higher the success rate becomes; after six egg retrieval cycles the pregnancy rate may be as high as 60% (Seibel, 1988). Typical costs approach $5,000 per egg retrieval attempt. A new development, freezing the blastocyst, allows physicians to save frozen embryos for future attempts. This reduces risks to the woman, since she does not have to go through the process of egg retrieval, which requires general anesthesia, and also costs less over the course of several implantation attempts.

A method called gamete intrafallopian transfer (GIFT) is now being used to treat infertile women. This technique differs from IVF in that IVF fertilization occurs outside the body and then the fertilized egg is placed into the uterus. In GIFT the egg and sperm cells are placed together in a healthy fallopian tube and fertilization takes place in the tube rather than outside the body. The GIFT procedure can be used only on a woman with a healthy fallopian tube. (The most common cause of infertility is blocked fallopian tubes.) The GIFT procedure is limited to women with medical conditions such as endometriosis (growth of the endometrium outside the uterus, causing infertility for reasons other than a blockage of fallopian tubes) and to cases in which no known cause of infertility in the woman can be identified. The same methods of ovarian stimulation, egg collection, and sperm preparation are used in both IVF and GIFT procedures. The only difference is that fertilization occurs in the fallopian tubes in the GIFT procedure and in a glass dish in the IVF method. The GIFT procedure has a slightly higher rate of successful pregnancies (30%) than does IVF (IVF, Gift, 1987) and is less expensive (Seibel, 1988).

In a new and experimental procedure sperm are simply injected into the abdominal cavity. Specifically, the sperm cells are placed in the pouch of Douglas (located behind the uterus) after ovulation has been stimulated in the woman. As previously stated, the ends of the fallopian tubes communicate with the abdominal cavity and the sperm cells can make their way to the tubes to fertilize the egg in the tubes. A pregnancy rate of 20% has been recorded with this method (IVF, Gift, 1987). Most of the patients treated with this procedure had cervical mucus problems that prevented sperm cells from passing through the cervix into the uterus and to the fallopian tubes.

In vitro fertilization is not the only high-technology method for treating infertility in couples desiring an infant. In vitro fertilization is used when the woman's oviducts are blocked, but 40% of couples using this technique fail to

Adoption is an alternative for infertile couples who want to have children.

A Personal Glimpse

Infertility, Intimacy, and Sexual Satisfaction

At first it was a real challenge to be diligent enough to remember every morning. Then you were taking your temperature and didn't even realize it—it became instinct. And how about the mornings you forgot? Did you cheat a little and put down a temperature anyway? Of course you did. Or have you awakened, put the thermometer into your mouth, then fallen back to sleep?

Schwan, 1988, p. 43

A year and a half ago, my husband and I went to our infertility specialist for a postcoital test. . . . The nurse instructed me . . . to have intercourse two-three hours beforehand, to lie flat for an hour afterward and not to douche.

Since our appointment was for 8:15 AM we were supposed to have intercourse at about 5:30 that morning—something we certainly had not done before. After lying down for the requisite time and enjoying an extra hour of sleep, I showered and we drove to the clinic.

Schwan, 1988, p. 77

I remember having to go to the urologist to leave a semen sample. My appointment was for 9:00 AM and when I entered the office the nurse handed me a small glass jar and told me to "deposit a semen sample." She pointed toward a men's room and off I went. It was very difficult to ejaculate under the circumstances, but I finally did so. It was also embarrassing to hand the jar back to the nurse.

AUTHORS' FILES

The three stories above illustrate some of the situations that occur during treatments for infertility. In a study examining sexual activity and intimacy among 22 infertile couples, most of the couples reported unsatisfactory sex lives (Greil, Porter, and Leitko, 1989). Sex was negatively affected for four reasons: (1) because couples had to schedule sexual intercourse; (2) because intercourse became a means to an end; (3) because privacy was invaded when physicians and others required information about lovemaking; and (4) because the act of intercourse itself was a reminder of the couples' infertility. On the positive side, half of the individuals in the study reported that their marriages had become better because of the shared experience of infertility.

---

produce children because the man's sperm count is too low or the sperm lack motility. Medical procedures and medications can help overcome low sperm counts and lack of motility, but if these fail, the only other answer at this time is to use donated sperm, a process called artificial insemination by a donor (AID). The couple chooses sperm of a donor who resembles the male partner in physical traits such as height, hair color, and complexion. The sperm has been mixed with a preservative, divided into small portions, frozen, and stored at low temperatures. When the woman has ovulated, as evidenced by hormone tests or basal body temperature records, a single portion of the donor's ejaculate is placed deep in the vagina near the cervix. A glass pipette is sometimes used to insert the semen. A plug, similar to a cervical cap, is then placed in the vagina to prevent the semen from leaking out. With frozen semen the conception rate is higher than during natural reproduction, most likely because the time of ovulation has been determined and the probability of fertilization is higher than with intercourse at various times during the cycle. Because a "fresh" egg is available in artificial insemination whereas older eggs are fertilized in natural reproduction, the number of birth defects and the spontaneous abortion rate are lower with artificial insemination (Edwards, 1984). For example, if an egg that is 60 hours old and close to dying is fertilized, the probability of its developing normally is less than if the egg is only a few hours old. Spontaneous abortions are more likely when an older egg is fertilized. The age of the sperm is also a factor, but not much research has been done in this area.

The controversial topic of surrogate motherhood is discussed in Chapter 21. A surrogate mother can be used in various ways. She can supply the egg and be artificially inseminated with the sperm of a man whose wife is sterile. The surrogate mother then carries the infant to term and legally gives the child to the sperm donor father and his wife. Other possibilities for the use of a surrogate mother are shown in Figure 6-13.

New Approaches to Infertility

Figure 6-13 illustrates the many new ways to create a child using the techniques of artificial insemination and in vitro fertilization. The eggs may be supplied by the mother of the child or by a donor who only supplies eggs and does not have any contact with the child after birth. The sperm may be supplied by the father or by a donor who only supplies the sperm and does not have any contact with the child after birth. In addition to the possibilities illustrated in Figure 6-13, the blastocyst can be frozen until needed. To simplify the legal and ethical problems associated with some of the situations shown in Figure

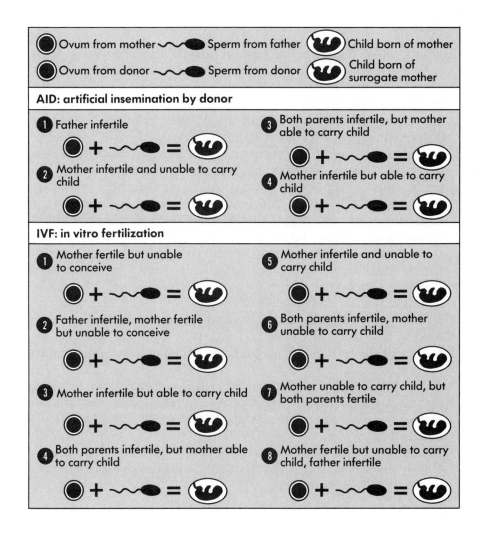

FIGURE 6-13
A sperm and egg can be united in many ways to produce a child.

6-13, we are calling the person the "father" or the "mother" if he or she will be rearing the child after birth.

Infertility can have detrimental psychological effects because of a perceived sense of failure on the part of the individual, pressure from parents, spouses, and friends to have children, and the necessity to have sexual intercourse on a schedule. Many couples show signs of stress, anxiety, and depression while they are being treated for infertility and trying to conceive a child (Domar, Seibel, and Benson, 1990). In an interesting study Domar and colleagues recruited 54 women to complete a 10-week behavioral treatment program based on the relaxation response (deep muscle relaxation and various stress reduction techniques). Women undergoing this novel treatment indicated a significant decrease in anxiety, depression, and fatigue and an increase in vigor compared with pretreatment levels. The authors concluded that stress reduction has a place in the long-term treatment of infertility (Domar, Seibel, and Benson, 1990). Unfortunately, no control group was employed, but this does represent a good preliminary study that should be repeated with control subjects.

SUMMARY

1 Fertilization, also called conception, is the union of the sperm cell and egg cell.
2 At fertilization the genetic information from the father combines with that of the mother to produce a unique set of chromosomes.
3 The product of conception is called the conceptus; for the first 8 weeks of development, it is an embryo; from then until birth it is called a fetus.
4 Pregnancy, also called the gestation period, lasts 266 days from conception. The gestation period is divided into three equal periods, or trimesters.
5 The mother's system undergoes tremendous hormonal changes during pregnancy. The placenta is the source of most of these hormones. A woman can be tested for the hormones to determine whether she is pregnant.
6 During the first trimester of pregnancy the conceptus develops from a fertilized egg into a fetus that looks much like a small human infant with a large head. During the second trimester there is a maturation of the tissues and organs formed during the first trimester and growth of the fetus. During the third and final trimester the fetus completely fills the uterus.
7 During the three trimesters of pregnancy the mother and father undergo several emotional and psychological changes. During pregnancy many women report discomfort such as constipation, hemorrhoids, and some swelling of various body parts.
8 Maternal behaviors and habits can be beneficial or detrimental to the developing fetus.
9 Not all pregnancies proceed perfectly. Some common problems are ectopic pregnancies, miscarriage or spontaneous abortions, premature births, toxemia of pregnancy, disorders in the development of the fetus, and Rh blood incompatibility.
10 Infertility is estimated to affect 10% to 15% of the married couples in the United States. Treatment involves medication to enhance sperm count and motility or to induce ovulation.
11 Infertility can take an emotional toll on a couple.

ANSWERS

1 Many children have been born with calluses on one thumb because of thumb-sucking in the uterus.
2 Accurate, easy-to-use home pregnancy and ovulation detector kits are now available in pharmacies.
3 Approximately 10% to 15% of couples in the United States will have difficulty conceiving a child. In some cases the problem is easily treated, but in other situations more complicated approaches may be tried.

QUESTIONS FOR THOUGHT ?

1 Please complete this statement: "If I found out I was infertile. . . . "
2 Compare the three trimesters of pregnancy in terms of embryonic and fetal development and parenteral reactions and feelings.
3 Make a list of all of the potentially harmful elements in your environment (both voluntary, such as smoking and diet, and involuntary, such as toxins). Tell how you would attempt to change them if you were planning a pregnancy or were pregnant. For males, indicate how you would change your behaviors under the same circumstances described above.

SUGGESTED READINGS

Cefalo, R., and Moos, M.: Preconceptional health promotion: a practical guide, Rockville, Md., 1988, Aspen Publishing Co., Inc.
    An excellent source book for health measures people should take before conception and pregnancy. (The recommendations are for general health and well-being and apply to everyone, whether trying to conceive or not.) This book presents preconceptional health concerns of prospective parents. For example, instead of waiting for pregnancy to stop smoking, this book promotes the idea that smoking should cease before conception.
Gauthier, M.: Guidelines for exercise during pregnancy: too little or too much, Physician Sportsmed. 14:162-169, 1986.
    A practical article that provides guidelines about the type and amount of exercise appropriate during pregnancy.
Schwan, K.: The infertility maze, Chicago, 1988, Contemporary Books.
    An easy to understand book that deals with all aspects of infertility. A must if you are faced with infertility in the near future.

CHAPTER

7

Childbirth and Parenthood

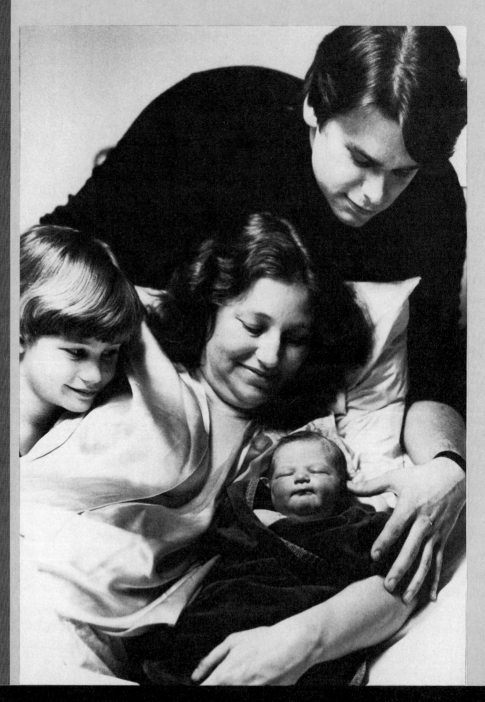

Last year I talked about black humor and the impact of the common market
  on the European economy and
Threw clever little cocktail parties in our discerningly eclectic living room
With the Spanish rug and the hand-carved Chinese chest and the lucite chairs
  and
Was occasionally hungered after by highly placed men in communications,
  but
This year we have a nice baby
And pablum drying on our Spanish rug,
And I talk about nursing versus sterilization
While the men in communications
Hunger elsewhere.

Last year I studied flamenco and had my ears pierced and
Served an authentic fondue on the Belgian marble table of our discerningly
  eclectic dining area, but
This year we have a nice baby
And Spock on the second shelf of our Chinese chest,
And instead of finding myself I am doing my best
To find a sitter
For the nice baby banging the Belgian marble with his cup
While I heat the oven up
For the TV dinners.

Last year I had a shampoo and set every week and
Slept an unbroken sleep beneath the Venetian chandelier of our discerningly
  eclectic bedroom, but
This year we have a nice baby,
And Gerber's strained bananas in my hair,
And gleaming beneath the Venetian chandelier,
A diaper pail, a portacrib, and him,
A nice baby, drooling on our antique satin spread
While I smile and say how nice. It is often said
That motherhood is very maturing.

JUDITH VIORST
"Nice Baby"

In an evolutionary sense the purpose of our sexuality is to reproduce—to have children. A full understanding of sexuality requires consideration of the consequences of sexual interaction when it is used for reproductive purposes. In this chapter we discuss both the process of childbirth and the factors that should be taken into account in the decision to have or not have children.

STAGES OF LABOR

On the average, birth occurs about 266 days after conception. The birth process is called **labor.** Exactly what causes labor to begin is still not known. However, the most recent evidence suggests that labor may be initiated by hormones secreted by the infant's adrenal glands into the blood and then into the placenta and uterus (Pritchard and MacDonald, 1980). These hormones supposedly

labor
Series of processes involved
in giving birth.

FIGURE 7-1
Movement of the baby during the birth process.

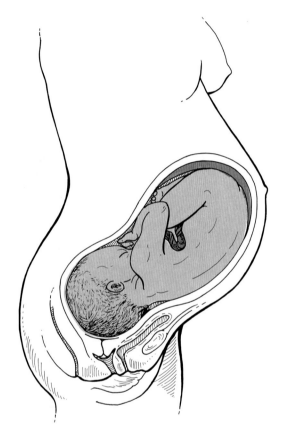

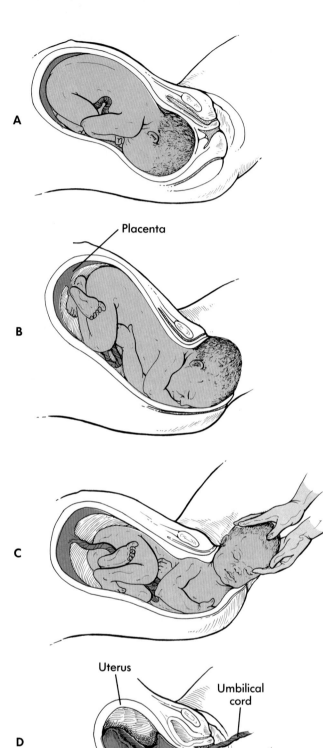

A

Placenta

B

C

Uterus

Umbilical cord

D

Placenta

HUMAN SEXUALITY

stimulate the release of prostaglandins in the mother, which then cause the uterus to begin contracting.

The first sign of the onset of labor may be the onset of uterine contractions; the appearance of a small amount of bloody discharge from the vagina, which is the mucous plug from the cervix (often called the bloody show); or the release of **amniotic fluid** from the vagina, which results from the rupture of the **amniotic sac.** For a woman having her first child, labor often lasts from 13 to 15 hours after the onset of labor. However, the amount of time women spend in labor, for both firstborn and later-born children, varies a great deal from woman to woman.

Labor is divided into three stages (Figure 7-1). The first stage is by far the longest. For the average woman having her first child, it lasts about 12 hours. For a woman who has had previous children, it lasts about 7 hours. The first stage begins with mild contractions of the uterus, which are 15 to 30 minutes apart. As the first stage progresses, the contractions become stronger and more frequent. During the contractions the muscles in the upper portion of the uterus are constricting, pushing the fetus downward. As the fetus is pushed toward the **cervix,** the cervix begins to dilate (Figure 7-1, *A* and *B*). The first stage lasts until the cervix is completely dilated and the contractions are strong and only 1 or 2 minutes apart.

A woman usually enters the hospital during the first stage of labor. Most women are instructed to wait until the contractions are approximately 5 minutes apart before calling the physician or going to the hospital.

amniotic fluid
Watery fluid that surrounds a developing embryo and fetus in the uterus.

amniotic sac
Sac containing the amniotic fluid and the developing embryo and fetus in the uterus.

cervix
The lower part of the uterus that extends into the vagina.

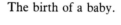
The birth of a baby.

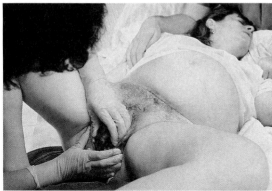

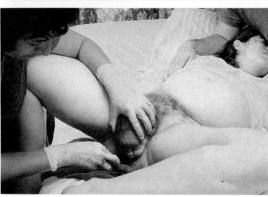

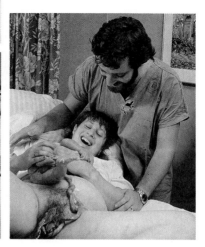

The second stage of labor begins when the cervix is fully dilated to about 10 centimeters. The fetus is pushed by the uterine contractions through the dilated cervix and down the **birth canal** (Figure 7-1, *C*). During this stage the woman often has an urge to bear down during the contractions. The woman can help in the delivery process by pushing because her abdominal muscles aid the uterus in sending the fetus down the birth canal. The second stage of labor ends when the fetus is born. For the majority of women the second stage of labor does not last long. The average duration is about 50 minutes when giving birth to firstborn children and 20 minutes when giving birth to successive children.

During the second stage of labor the physician may perform an **episiotomy** (Figure 7-2). An episiotomy is a surgical cut from the bottom of the entrance to the vagina down toward the anus. The purpose of the episiotomy is to decrease the likelihood of vaginal tearing when the infant's head and shoulders pass through the vagina. After the infant is delivered, the physician stitches up the incision. For a time episiotomies were routine. Today, however, they are more controversial because they cause some discomfort when they are healing and many believe that they are not necessary unless a woman is giving birth to an exceptionally large infant or has a small vagina.

birth canal
Passage through which the fetus travels during childbirth.

episiotomy
(i pee′ zee OT uh mee) Incision in the mother's perineum that provides more room for the infant during delivery and helps prevent tearing of the vaginal tissues.

FIGURE 7-2
How two types of episiotomies are performed. The cut may be made in the midline of the body (median) or off to one side of the midline (mediolateral).

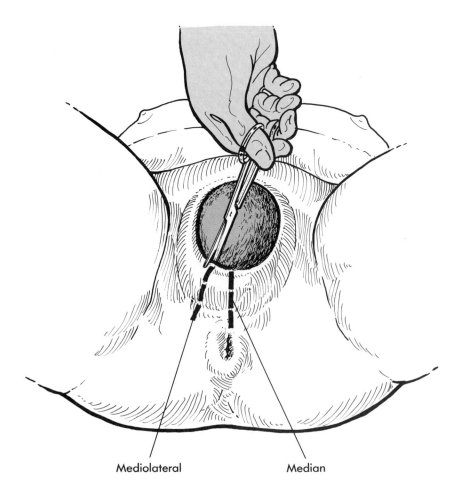

Mediolateral   Median

During labor many hospitals routinely use **electronic fetal monitoring** (EFM) to follow the progress of how the fetus is responding to the stress of labor. EFM measures uterine contractions and fetal heart rate patterns. What does EFM tell us? It can indicate when the fetus is being deprived of oxygen, a condition known as fetal distress.

The routine use of EFM is not without controversy. Barta and Thacker, in a 1979 report prepared under government auspices, state that EFM (1) is often inaccurate, indicating stress when it is not occurring or failing to indicate stress when it is actually occurring, (2) increases maternal mortality and disease and causes unnecessary cesarean sections, and (3) costs the consumer millions of dollars each year.

Technological improvements will probably refine EFM techniques in the future. More important, guidelines for the use of EFM must be established because EFM is an excellent example of double-edged technological advances. EFM may help to deliver more healthy infants, but at the risk of endangering the mother as a result of the use of cesarean section.

The third stage of labor begins immediately after the baby's birth. During this stage the uterine contractions continue until the placenta separates from the wall of the uterus and the **afterbirth** is expelled (Figure 7-1, *D*). This process lasts from 5 to 20 minutes. If the woman has had an episiotomy, the physician stitches it closed at this time. The third stage of labor ends with the expulsion of the placenta.

Immediately following birth the infant's mouth and throat are cleared of fluid, the **umbilical cord** is tied and cut, and silver nitrate drops are put in the eyes to prevent blindness in case the infant acquires **gonococcus bacteria** from the mother's cervix or vagina during the birth process. The newborn's heart rate, reflexes, activity, muscle tone, respiration, and color are assessed to determine whether further medical care is needed. A bluish or yellowish tinge to the skin indicates that one of the infant's systems is not functioning properly and that he or she needs medical help. Frequently the Apgar scoring system is used to rate the infant's condition based on this assessment. The Apgar score ranges from 0 to a highest score of 10. A low score 5 minutes after birth indicates the need for expert medical intervention. In addition, the newborn is bathed and has his or her footprints taken for identification. As with fingerprints, no two footprints are identical.

CHILDBIRTH PROCEDURES
Traditional Methods

The procedures used during childbirth today are very different from those in the past. Before the Middle Ages women gave birth in their homes without help from anyone other than friends and relatives. During the Middle Ages women in Europe still gave birth in their homes, but they were assisted by **midwives.** Women assumed a sitting, squatting, or kneeling position so the pull of gravity would help the infant move down the birth canal. They gave birth without the help of medical personnel, medical equipment, or medication.

By the 1600s physicians in Europe had assumed the role of delivering infants. Some women began to go to hospitals to have their children. The procedure of having women lie on their backs (**supine position**) during child-

electronic fetal monitoring
Observation of fetal heart rate and maternal uterine contractions through an internal or external monitoring device.

afterbirth
The placenta and amniotic sac that are expelled after the infant is delivered.

umbilical cord
(uhm BIL i kuhl) Tubelike structure that connects the embryo and fetus with the placenta through which nutrients and wastes are passed.

gonococcus bacteria
(gon' uh KOK uhs) Bacteria that cause gonorrhea.

midwives
Individuals other than a physician who have been trained to assist a woman during childbirth.

supine position
(soo PYN) Lying on one's back.

birth was reportedly instituted by Louis XIV (Arms, 1975). According to historical accounts, he enjoyed secretly watching from behind a screen while his mistresses gave birth. He convinced the court physician to have the women lie on their backs during childbirth so he could get a better view than he could if they were sitting or squatting. Since that time the popularity of this position for childbirth has become so widespread that it is almost the only position used in "civilized" societies. However, when a woman lies on her back, the force of gravity no longer helps the infant descend the birth canal. In fact, this loss of gravity during delivery is one reason that physicians began to use forceps in some instances to pull the infant out of the birth canal.

Liu (1988) compared the length of labor in women who were in an upright position during the first and second stages with the length of labor of women who had to remain lying in bed. Liu found that the duration of labor was significantly shorter in women who assumed an upright position. In Liu's study the mean duration of the first stage of labor for women using an upright position was 196.02 minutes and the mean duration of labor for women using a horizontal position was 262.50 minutes. In the second stage of labor the mean duration was 54.87 minutes for the upright position and 90.41 minutes for the horizontal position. Thus labor was 66.48 minutes shorter in the first stage and 35.54 minutes shorter in the second stage for women in an upright position than for women in a horizontal position. As a result of findings demonstrating the advantage of upright positions during labor, many hospitals have begun to use adjustable delivery tables so that a woman can sit upright, lie on her back, or assume a position somewhere in between these extremes to shorten labor and hasten delivery.

By the 1900s hospitalization, the supine position, the use of forceps, and

Birthing chair.

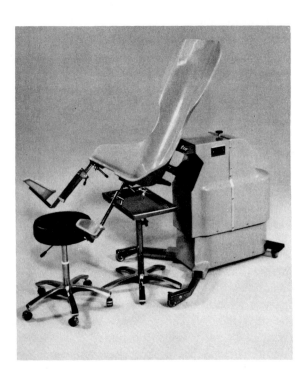

Birthing bed.

the administration of painkilling drugs were standard childbirth procedures. The woman was admitted to the hospital, treated like a patient, and separated from family and friends. Her pubic hair was shaved to reduce the possibility of infection, and she was often given an enema to empty the bowels and thus provide more space in the lower pelvis. Sometimes intravenous solutions were administered to supply the woman with the necessary fluids. When the physician decided that the labor was not progressing rapidly enough, labor was occasionally induced through the administration of drugs.

Today 97% to 99% of all births in the United States take place in hospitals (Taffel, 1984; Wegman, 1987). Americans view childbirth as a medical event, requiring both professional help and relocation to a specially equipped environment. The hospital setting for most births includes both a delivery room and a central nursery. The delivery room is a sterile environment that is brightly lit and maintained at 77° F (25° C). During a normal delivery the mother often lies on her back with legs spread apart, knees raised, and feet supported by stirrups. A sheet is draped over her knees to keep the area around the vaginal opening as clean as possible. In this position the mother cannot see the infant being born. However, in some hospitals mirrors are arranged so the mother is able to view the birth.

In some hospitals, after delivery the infant is separated from the mother for 12 to 24 hours and is returned to the mother for feeding at 4-hour intervals during the day. When not with the mother, the infant remains in a central nursery. The primary concerns in a newborn nursery are protecting the newborn from infection and observing changes in respiration, circulation, temperature, and neurological and gastrointestinal functioning during the first days of life. To minimize the spread of infection, nursing care emphasizes cleanliness, minimal contact between visitors and newborns, and no contact between one infant and another. Traditionally the father has even been denied contact with his infant. Infants who are delivered outside a hospital environment are not admitted to the newborn nursery. If the development of an infectious condition is suspected, the infant is isolated in a separate nursery.

Recent Developments

In recent years research has confirmed what many have suspected all along—that impersonal, sterile hospital procedures are not the optimal conditions in which to give birth. Adrienne Rich (1977) refers to the experience of childbirth with the traditional hospital protocol as "alienated labor." She says that "the experience of lying half awake in a barred crib, in a labor room with other women moaning in a drugged condition, where 'no one comes' except to do a pelvic examination or give an injection, is a classic experience of alienated childbirth." The feeling of estrangement many women experience when giving birth according to traditional hospital procedures increases because they are separated from their family and friends, drugged, and confined to an impersonal hospital setting. However, in recent years a number of these practices have been changing.

rooming-in program
Program in which the mother is allowed to keep her newborn in her hospital room most of the day rather than in a hospital nursery.

Many hospitals now provide a **rooming-in program** that allows the mother to keep her infant in her room most of the day. The infant is returned to a central nursery at night or at the mother's request if she becomes overtired. Rooming-in programs allow the mother to practice caring for her infant before she has to take him or her home from the hospital and be totally responsible for care. Thus the mother can gain some confidence in her child care abilities before she is required to care for the infant by herself. With rooming-in the mother and the infant get to know each other from the beginning. In a study

Mother-Infant Bonding: Are Those First Few Hours Important?

Klaus and Kennell (1976) reported the first study of mother-infant bonding. They compared two groups of mothers: one group spent the first hour after birth with their babies and also had extended contact with their babies in the first few days after the birth, and the other group followed normal hospital procedures and were therefore separated from the babies more often. Klaus and Kennell reported that the mothers who spent more time with their infants immediately following birth showed evidence of stronger maternal-infant bonds than the other mothers up to a year after birth. As a result, they proposed that mother-infant bonding would not develop optimally if mothers were separated from their babies in the first few hours after birth.

Since publication of Klaus and Kennell's work in the mid-1970s, a number of other researchers have conducted studies of maternal-infant bonding. Most of these researchers (e.g., Chess and Thomas, 1982; Lamb, 1982) have not found a relationship between time spent together immediately following birth and the strength of the maternal-infant bond. Rather than being greatly affected by contact during the first few hours after birth, the mother-infant bond apparently is determined by the nature of their interactions over much more extended periods.

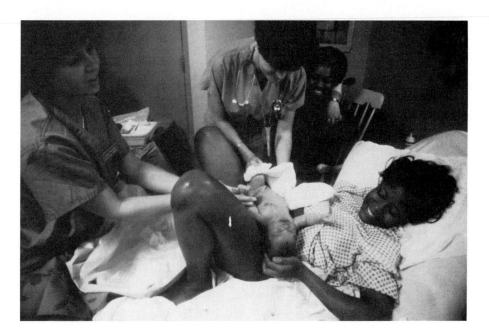

This woman has just given birth in the comfortable surroundings of a birthing center.

in which rooming-in mothers were compared with mothers who were not involved in rooming-in programs the rooming-in mothers felt more competent and confident as mothers when they left the hospital (Greenberg, Rosenberg, and Lind, 1973). Furthermore, the father is allowed to interact with the infant in the rooming-in situation. As a result, he becomes involved with the infant earlier than has traditionally been the case.

A number of hospitals now offer **birthing rooms.** In such alternative birth arrangements the surroundings are made to look as much like a home and as little like a hospital as possible. The rooms are often furnished with double beds, easy chairs, carpets, and plants. The mother may have anyone she wishes visit her, including her other children. Delivery takes place in the same room in which the mother will stay after the birth. The infant is left with the mother and father rather than being removed to a nursery. Drugs are used only if complications arise. When complications do occur, the mother is usually transferred to the regular hospital ward. Usually within 6 to 12 hours after a normal delivery, the mother and infant are allowed to go home. Birthing centers are similar to birthing rooms in hospitals, but they are not located in hospitals. The personal experiences of women who delivered children in birthing centers and their homes are presented in boxes on pp. 190 and 195.

In 1984, only 3% of all American births took place outside of hospitals (Taffel, 1984), while during the same year 30% of Dutch births were home deliveries (Torres and Reich, 1989). The Netherlands has a long-standing tradition of home births and midwifery. A woman in the Netherlands may elect to give birth in a hospital, in a maternity center, or at home with either a midwife or a physician in attendance. If a woman is considered to be at high risk for complications, she receives hospital care from an obstetrician of her choosing. Since hospitals are within easy reach of all homes, a woman or her

birthing rooms
Rooms for childbirth that are made to be as much like home and as little like a hospital as possible.

infant can be admitted quickly to a nearby hospital if complications occur in a home delivery. Traditionally, obstetricians in the Netherlands attend only births with complications.

After giving birth the mother may choose either hospital confinement for up to 10 days or "maternity home help." The home help is an unusual combination of paramedic and housekeeper who supplements the care given by the midwife or family physician at home births (or hospital births in which the mother chooses an early discharge). The home help supplies daily care for the mother and newborn for 10 days after the birth.

Such a wide range of choices for childbirth is unparalleled in any other country. The reader might wonder what the results of the Netherlands' childbirth system are. In 1986 a study of 21 industrialized countries indicated that the Netherlands had an infant mortality rate of 8 per 1,000 births at a time when the United States had a corresponding rate of 10 (Statistical Bulletin, 1988). Thus it appears that in the Netherlands the option of giving birth at home is a safe one. Furthermore, a woman given choices in her pregnancy would likely fare better psychologically and emotionally than a woman treated as a patient and given little control in one of the most significant events in her life (Livingston, 1987).

Medication Effects

The administration of medication during childbirth has also changed. The use of painkilling medication supposedly began when Queen Victoria accepted an anesthetic to relieve the pain of childbirth (Arms, 1975). The administration of anesthetics increased greatly thereafter to the point where such drugs were used routinely during labor and delivery. However, research indicates that anesthetics can cross the placenta and have a negative effect on the fetus. For example, some researchers have reported that the babies of mothers who receive painkilling drugs during labor and delivery are less attentive and more irritable, have poorer muscle tone, and are weaker than those whose mothers do not receive such drugs (Brackbill, 1979; Sepkowski, 1985). As much as 1 year after delivery, infants whose mothers received medication during delivery are not as behaviorally advanced as infants whose mothers did not (Brackbill, 1978). The extent of these drug effects varies with the kind of drug administered, the dose given, and the stage of labor when it is administered (Lester, Als, and Brazelton, 1982; Brackbill, McManus, and Woodward, 1985). Brackbill and colleagues even argue that high levels of painkilling drugs may be responsible, at least in part, for the high incidence of learning disabilities in the United States. As a result of such research findings, a number of changes have been made in standard delivery procedures.

Natural or Prepared Childbirth

The "natural childbirth" movement has been an important factor in changing the delivery procedures. **Natural childbirth** refers to techniques and procedures for teaching women about the childbirth process to alleviate fear and pain, involve the women and often their husbands (or family member or friend) in the childbirth process, and ensure that minimal medication is used.

natural childbirth Childbirth in which minimal medication is used and the mother is educated about the birth process and taught breathing techniques to reduce fear and increase relaxation.

The natural childbirth movement was started by an English physician, Grantley Dick-Read (1932). During his travel in Africa, Dick-Read witnessed births in which the women were not hospitalized and were not given any painkilling drugs. Many of the women he observed showed no evidence of pain. Dick-Read concluded that the pain experienced in childbirth is often exaggerated by tension and fear. He developed a method that he called natural childbirth. This method was an attempt to eliminate fear by giving the woman an understanding of the birth process, teaching her breathing exercises to help her relax, and having the husband present to provide support. Although Dick-Read considered painkilling drugs valuable and justified in unusual circumstances, he believed that most women do not need them.

Fernand Lamaze, a French physician, was another important influence in the natural childbirth movement. Lamaze had women spend the months before the childbirth practicing breathing techniques they were to employ during the delivery. The idea of the breathing techniques is to keep the woman focused on her breathing rather than on pain. As labor progresses, the breathing tech-

Lamaze method
(luh MAZ) Method of childbirth that emphasizes relaxation, controlled breathing, and knowledge of the birth process.

niques become more complicated to keep the woman totally involved with the breathing process. In addition, the **Lamaze method** involves the use of a coach to encourage the woman to keep using the breathing techniques and to provide emotional support. When possible, the woman's husband serves as the coach. In addition to the breathing exercises and coaching, the Lamaze method includes education in relevant anatomy and physiology and relaxation techniques. Because the method involves concentration and hard work, proponents suggest that it should not be called "natural" childbirth but rather "prepared" childbirth.

A Personal Glimpse

A Father's View of Childbirth

When Jeff and Liz were born eleven and nine years ago, I really acted as an outsider. Also, no other fathers seemed to be involved with pregnancy and birth that many years ago. We really weren't expected to participate, so why would we even think of being in the delivery room?

Actually, I never saw Jeff for 1 to 1½ hours after he was born, and then it was through glass nursery walls in an incubator. It was the same way with our second child, except that lack of sleep due to a bout of false labor made us very tired at the second birth so that we just wanted it to be over.

By the time we were expecting Rebecca, five years ago, I wanted a different experience—one that would involve me and let me experience this birth. A couple in our church had their baby using Lamaze techniques with the husband present and told us what a terrific experience it was for them. So Karen and I talked it over and decided to attend Lamaze classes to prepare for a shared birth.

The total experience was tremendous. Preparation was the key thing for me, and without all the preliminaries and involvement ahead of time, I probably wouldn't have gone through the birth experience because to me, the preliminary preparation for birth was part of the birth experience. All the learning and sharing we did made me part of the experience—not just an observer.

This time when we went to the hospital, we were excited and ready to go as a team. What made the experience so fantastic was knowing quite a bit about what takes place during labor, and thus being able to help my wife and the doc-

tor. I remember saying, "Push, push, now hold it," and seeing the baby's black hair appear, and then ten minutes later, holding her, all wrapped up and warm.

Karen and I were crying because we were so happy. I remember counting all the baby's fingers and toes and asking, "Does she have them all?" As soon as I knew she was alright, I relaxed. The aura of newness, awakening, and joy was so strong that I don't remember all the little details about the experience; however, I do remember the feeling of completeness that I experienced. I felt complete as a father. Because I was there at the birth and was active in preparing for it, there was a sense of fulfillment for me as a father and a husband. The experience gave me great joy. The neat thing about Rebecca's birth was that I saw her so closely, from only a few feet away, for her birth and aftercare. Then when I came back to see her the next day, I recognized her, which was a different experience than I had with the first two babies. To get acquainted with them, I had to look them over closely on the day after they were born. With Rebecca I felt that I knew her.

Several years after Rebecca's birth we shared a similar feeling after we had worked very hard planting, tending, and then harvesting grapes. On our way home from unloading a gondola of grapes, we experienced a fantastic sunset together, and felt elation and joy. After all the work we had done together, it was like an applause, a final acknowledgement, a "well done." We compared our feelings to that unique experience we had when Rebecca was born. It was valuable, rewarding, everlasting joy.

From Phillips and Anzalone, 1982.

Research suggests that Lamaze childbirth preparation has a positive effect on maternal attitudes toward childbirth and reduces anxiety and pain during childbirth (Wideman and Singer, 1984). A few problems also exist, however. Some women who go through such childbirth training find that they need more medication than expected, possibly because they have lower pain thresholds or because they have been unable to overcome their fear. They often feel disappointed with themselves when they cannot go through the delivery without asking for pain medication. Recently, most "natural" or "prepared" childbirth training programs have tried to respond to this problem by informing women ahead of time that circumstances might make some pain medication necessary; in this way they will not believe that needing pain medication indicates failure.

In addition to alterations in the amount of medication given to women during labor and delivery, changes have occurred in the degree to which women are isolated from their families at the time of childbirth. In the United States fathers traditionally had no involvement in the pregnancy and simply remained in the waiting room during the delivery. After the delivery they often had little or no interaction with their infants because they visited during hospital visiting hours when the infants were in the nursery. Now, however, many fathers go through childbirth preparation programs with their partners for months before the delivery. These men thus feel involved in the pregnancy. Furthermore, in many hospitals fathers are allowed to be with their partners throughout labor and delivery even if the mothers are not involved in a childbirth preparation program.

Research suggests that the father's involvement in his partner's pregnancy and delivery may have beneficial effects. Manion (1977) compared couples who participated in childbirth preparation classes with couples who did not. The couples who participated in the classes were found to have more positive attitudes toward pregnancy. In addition, the wives whose husbands were with them during labor and delivery reported the birth to be a much more positive emotional experience than wives whose husbands were not present. Similarly, fathers present at the delivery had heightened emotional reactions to birth (Entwisle and Doering, 1981) and were more likely to view the event as a "peak emotional experience" (May and Perrin, 1985). Thus it appears that the father's involvement in his partner's pregnancy, labor, and childbirth has a positive effect on both parents' attitudes and experiences regarding the pregnancy and birth (see accompanying box).

Leboyer Method

In the traditional hospital delivery the infant emerges from the birth canal into the hands of the physician, who holds the infant upside down and slaps its bottom. The infant starts to cry. The infant is cleaned, weighed, and measured. When this procedure has been completed, the infant is removed from the mother and taken to the hospital nursery.

In his book *Birth Without Violence* (1975), Frederick Leboyer, a French physician, suggests that the traditional birth process is probably a traumatic experience for the infant. Before birth the fetus is contained in a dark, quiet, warm, soft, fluid environment. At birth the infant is suddenly forced out of this environment into a world that is cold, bright, noisy, and hard.

A father giving a newborn a Leboyer bath.

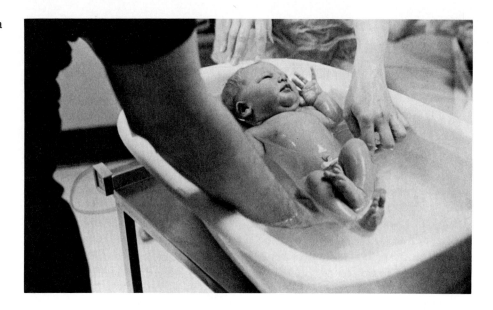

Leboyer developed a method of delivery, the **Leboyer method,** to make the birth process less traumatic for the infant. The lights in the delivery room are kept relatively dim and the personnel speak quietly. Instead of holding the infant upside down and slapping it to get it to breathe, the physician places the infant on the mother's stomach immediately after the delivery. The umbilical cord is left intact for about 4 or 5 minutes to ensure an adequate oxygen supply for the infant until it begins to breathe independently. After the umbilical cord is cut, the infant is washed in a bath at body temperature before being wrapped in warm, soft blankets. The infant is kept with the mother as much as possible throughout the delivery procedure.

Leboyer claims that his method of delivery should result in healthier and better-adjusted infants. To test this claim, Nelson and associates (1980) compared infants born by the Leboyer method with those delivered by more traditional methods. Measures of health and behavior performed immediately after birth, several days after birth, and 8 months after birth showed no differences between the two groups of infants.

• • •

In summary, the changes that have taken place in hospital childbirth procedures, such as educating the husband and wife about the childbirth process, allowing the husband to be present during labor and delivery, and decreasing the amount of painkilling medication administered, can have positive effects on the infant's physical health and well-being and on the marital and parent-child relationships (see accompanying box).

Cesarean Section

Approximately 25% of the infants born in the United States are delivered via **cesarean section** rather than through the vagina. In this procedure the woman

A Personal Glimpse

Recollection of a Home Birth

My first two children were born when there were no alternatives available to the local hospital routines. During labor and delivery I was given unnecessary drugs and strapped by wrists and ankles to the delivery table while trying to push the baby out uphill. The membranes were broken, and hormones administered to speed labor. I was given large episiotomies that required a lengthy healing time. I was not allowed to hold my babies for hours after birth—and then only on the 3-hour hospital schedule. This was normal at the time— no worse and, in fact, better than many other hospital birth experiences. But the procedures so disturbed me that I knew I had to find a better way to have our next child.

I met other women who felt, as I did, that childbirth should be less technical and more humane to both mother and child. We read all the information we could find and talked to doctors and midwives about birth alternatives. When I became pregnant with our third child, I decided to give birth at home.

My husband was somewhat nervous about the idea but was supportive of my wishes. This was especially important during the pregnancy because our families were appalled by our plans. Until right before I went into labor, they tried to talk us into going to the hospital to have the baby. Of course, when they visited and held the baby a few hours after birth, they were not so upset. I had chosen a different doctor for this pregnancy. He agreed to do my prenatal care and to meet us at the hospital if we experienced complications at the birth. I was fortunate in having a doctor who was this agreeable. Others simply refused to accept women planning home births as patients.

Our daughter was born on a winter evening in a room full of friends. Unfortunately we had to go to the hospital after her birth because I needed some stitches. We encountered hostility from the doctor who did the repair (our doctor was out of town that weekend). However, even his attitude didn't ruin the wonderful experience we'd shared.

Our fourth child was also born at home. Her father was the first to hold her, and he rocked her and talked to her while the placenta was delivered. We had no complications. Rebecca and I spent most of the first week in bed getting to know each other. Our older children enjoyed staying with Grandma nearby, and I enjoyed having my husband home to take care of us. From the beginning, Rebecca "belonged" to all of us.

We found many advantages of having a baby at home. There was such a difference between our home births and hospital births that the only similarity was in having a new baby afterward. The babies probably benefitted the most from being born at home. They were eased into the world in a warm, loving environment rather than pulled into an icy delivery room. They were held and nursed and warmed by their mother's body—not put under a glaring "warming light" in an Isolette. Instead of being scrubbed, weighed, and left in the nursery to cry alone, they stayed in my arms and gazed at the faces around them. They nursed when their squirming indicated they were hungry—not when the hospital schedule said they should eat. Far from routine, their births were unique and magical for all who attended. The bonding we experienced in the hours and days after birth enveloped our other children too. We were drawn closer as a family through sharing the new babies.

AUTHORS' FILES

---

is under general or local anesthesia. The surgeon then makes an incision in the mother's abdomen through to the uterus, suctions out the amniotic fluid, and removes the fetus from the uterus. Cesarean sections have traditionally been performed when complications occur that would make a vaginal delivery threatening to either the mother or the infant. Cesarean sections are done, for example, when the infant or the infant's head is too large to pass through the mother's pelvic area, when the infant is not in a good position (i.e., not in a

FIGURE 7-3
Most babies are born head
first in what is called ce-
phalic presentation (**A**).
However, some are born
buttocks first in what is
called breech presentation
(**B**). Sometimes babies are
in the transverse presentation position (**C**) at the
time of birth; in this case
an attempt must be made
to change the baby's position before birth.

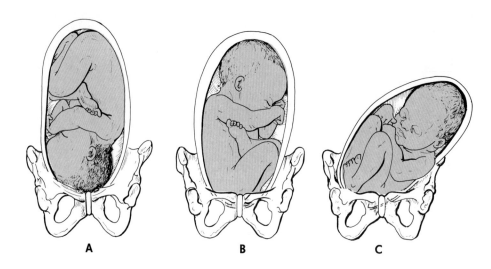

head-down position) for delivery through the vagina (Figure 7-3), when no
progress seems to be occurring during a long and difficult labor, when the
fetus is not receiving enough oxygen, and when other such medical emergencies
occur.

The use of cesarean section has undoubtedly saved the lives of many mothers
and infants. There is some concern, however, that unnecessary cesarean sections are being performed. Over the last two decades the reliance on the surgical
method of delivery has risen dramatically. From 4.5% in 1965, the cesarean
section rate has escalated to as much as 24.1% in 1986 (Kazandjian and Summer, 1989). This rate is much higher than that in most other industrialized
countries (Norton, Placek, and Taffel, 1987). In fact, the cesarean rate has
continued to increase despite efforts to publicize the overuse of the operation
and the increased risks of postpartum infection and other medical complications
for the mother, often without benefit to the child (Brody, 1989; Kazandjian,
Dans, and Scherlis, 1989). If the national trend continues, a rate of 40.3% is
expected by the year 2000 (Kazandjian, Dans, and Scherlis, 1989).

Why has the percentage of cesarean deliveries continued to rise so drastically? Research findings have suggested several reasons for the increasing cesarean rates, including (1) the older age at which mothers give birth, which
may increase their risk of complication; (2) the belief of physicians that cesarean
sections reduce the risk of malpractice suits; and (3) improved technology,
which has increased physicians' ability to detect fetal problems. Furthermore,
many physicians automatically perform cesarean sections on women who have
had previous cesarean sections. However, evidence that many women who have
had previous cesarean sections can give birth vaginally in subsequent births
has led hospitals to attempt vaginal deliveries in such women (Kolata, 1980;
Kazandjian and Summer, 1989).

Given that cesarean sections entail greater risks for the mother and that
more cesarean sections are performed than need be, perhaps the trend toward
increasing use of cesarean sections will be reversed in the future.

POSTPARTUM PERIOD

The first few weeks following the delivery are called the **postpartum period.** During this time the mother, father, and other children in the family, if there are any, must adjust to the addition of a new infant. This can be stressful for the entire family. The new mother must adjust both to physiological changes as her body readjusts to the nonpregnancy state and to psychological differences that result from her new status as the mother of an infant. Both types of change can have definite effects on the mother's emotional state.

After the birth of a child the levels of estrogen and progesterone in the mother's body decrease sharply. In addition, reductions and other changes occur in metabolism. Some women report negative changes such as increased sweating, constipation, and loss of appetite. These alterations in physical functioning may contribute to the negative emotional reactions sometimes observed in the postpartum period (Hamburg, Moos, and Yalom, 1968).

postpartum period (pohst PAR tuhm) The time period following birth.

The hormonal changes that take place in the mother following childbirth are discussed in Chapter 6.

Postpartum Depression

The negative emotional reactions that some women report following the birth of a child have been called **postpartum depression.** A woman with postpartum depression often feels fearful and sad and frequently breaks into tears. Leifer (1977) studied emotional reactions of 20 first-time mothers. Immediately after the birth, many of the mothers felt elated and satisfied with the birth process. In a short time, however, they began to feel anxious and depressed. Two thirds of the women in the study experienced the postpartum period as negative; the women reported feelings of isolation, depression, and irritability. Two months after the birth of the child, most women reported being bored rather than anxious and depressed. Seven months after the birth, the women still reported predominantly negative moods.

postpartum depression (pohst PAR tuhm) Mild to moderate depression that occurs in some mothers following the birth of their infants.

However, in a more recent study Quadagno and associates (1986) found that the postpartum period is not necessarily marked by depression. The researchers asked married couples to rate the extent to which 20 different moods represented how they felt before the birth of their child, during the postpartum period, and 6 months after the birth. In these couples the postpartum period was not marked by an increase in depression. Rather, the moods that increased in *both* women *and* men in the days immediately following childbirth were those reflecting anxiety and concern for their ability to cope, such as "nervous," "worried," "helpless," and "anxious," and positive emotions, such as "enthusiastic" and "happy." The results of this study clearly show that not all women experience depression in the postpartum period.

For women who do experience the postpartum period as emotionally stressful, it is important to understand that depression at this time is normal and that it will pass. If women are not aware that such depression is common, they may feel something is terribly wrong with themselves or their situation. Such an interpretation of the circumstances will make them even more anxious and depressed. If, however, they know that such feelings are normal and temporary, they will be less inclined to believe that something is seriously wrong and they will be better able to keep their feelings in perspective.

One to two in every thousand women in the postpartum period experience a more serious depressive episode, postpartum depressive psychosis (Kendell, 1985). Postpartum depressive psychosis is characterized by thought disorder, hallucinations, and delusions, as well as the confusion and anxiety present in the less severe and more common postpartum depression (Hamilton, 1989). Women with postpartum depressive psychosis frequently require professional psychiatric treatment (Romito, 1989).

It is important to realize that not all women undergo postpartum depression. Some women experience feelings of elation that decrease very gradually until they return to their normal emotional state.

The fact that some women encounter feelings of anxiety and depression following childbirth while other women experience elation has led some investigators to propose that postpartum depression may be more a result of psychological aspects than the consequence of the physiological changes that accompany childbirth. Some of the psychological factors that have been proposed as contributing to feelings of anxiety and depression in the new mother are:

1. She suddenly becomes almost solely responsible for an infant who is totally dependent.
2. She has fears regarding her ability to take care of an infant.
3. She suddenly loses her freedom and ability to control her own life.
4. She often loses sleep as a result of her infant's nighttime waking.
5. Her marital relationship is often altered as a result of the arrival of a new infant.

These changes require drastic readjustments in the women's life, and not surprisingly, many women respond with anxiety and depression.

A Personal Glimpse

One Mother's Postpartum Experience

I've read a lot about postpartum depression. I guess a lot of women get depressed after the birth of a child, but I sure didn't. When I went into the hospital I remember thinking that the baby would be red and wrinkly and would cry a lot in the beginning but that after about 6 months it would become cute and much more fun. That's how I felt immediately after the baby was born. I thought, "Yes, this baby is red and wrinkly and kind of funny looking." I felt very matter-of-fact about the baby—not any different from how I felt when I went into the hospital. But within an hour or so I began to feel absolutely elated. I felt so happy and so excited it was as if I had been given some kind of drug. I was so happy I just wanted to smile all the time; I had to work to stop myself from smiling when I was around other people. Several times

I woke up in the night and realized I had even been smiling in my sleep. Along with this feeling of elation I suddenly developed a very strong attachment to my baby. The baby was no longer red and wrinkly in my mind; she was absolutely beautiful. She was all I could think about and, when I was in the hospital, I just lived for the times when the nurses would bring her to me. I couldn't think about anything else; I couldn't watch T.V. or read. I just wanted to think about the baby. This degree of attachment really surprised me because I had always assumed that I would come to love my baby much more gradually.

My elation decreased only very gradually until I returned to my normal mood state. I never felt depressed at all during the postpartum period. In fact, I remember that time as the most exciting and satisfying time in my life.

AUTHORS' FILES

The birth of a child can be emotionally stressful for new fathers as well. Fathers often find that they have much less freedom than they did before the birth of the infant, their wives pay less attention to them, their sex lives are much more restricted, and their wives are often irritable, depressed, and tired. Both the husband and the wife may need more emotional support at this time, yet each has less to give to the other. As a result, many marital relationships are strained by the arrival of a new infant. Couples need to understand that these stresses will occur but will be only temporary. They should not interpret the stress as necessarily indicating that something is seriously wrong with their relationship.

In summary, the postpartum period is one in which both physiological and psychological changes occur in the mother. It is a time when many women report experiencing anxiety and depression. The time is stressful for the father as well. Because all of the family members have to make adjustments as a result of the arrival of a new infant in the home, they all need more emotional support than usual. However, since all family members have the same needs, they sometimes find it difficult to provide the extra emotional support required by the others. If each family member is aware that these stresses are normal and that they will soon pass, and if each tries to be as supportive as possible of the others, the family should survive this period without much difficulty. Not all families experience the postpartum period as stressful; some report it to be a rewarding and satisfying time.

Breast Changes

As mentioned in Chapter 6, during pregnancy the hormone **human placental lactogen** stimulates breast growth and prepares the breasts for milk production, or **lactation** (Figure 7-4). During pregnancy the breasts also begin to produce

human placental lactogen (HYOO muhn pluh SEN tuh LAK tuh jen) Hormone that stimulates breast growth during pregnancy.

lactation Production of milk in the female breasts.

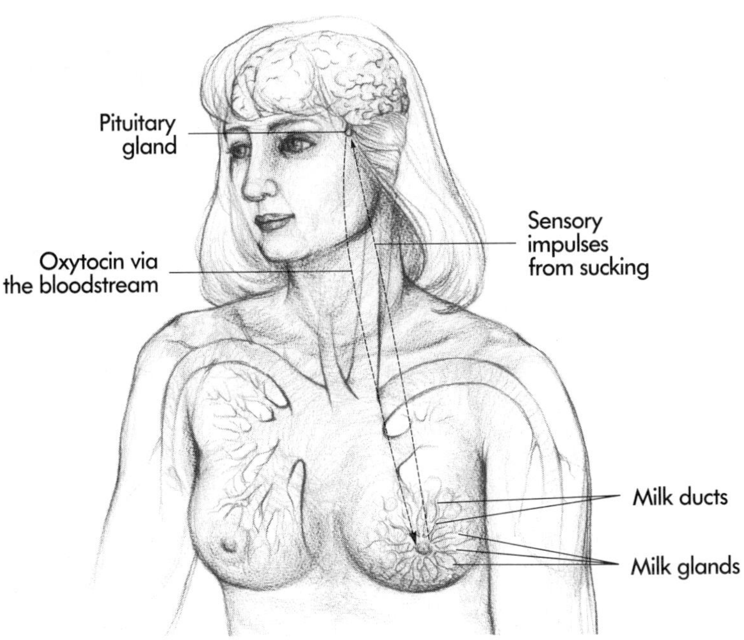

FIGURE 7-4
The stimulus of suckling by the breast-feeding infant triggers the release of oxytocin from the posterior pituitary gland. Oxytocin travels via the blood to cause the contraction of the smooth muscles surrounding the milk glands, forcing the milk into the milk ducts.

Pituitary gland

Oxytocin via the bloodstream

Sensory impulses from sucking

Milk ducts

Milk glands

colostrum
(kuh LOS truhm) Thin yellowish fluid secreted from the nipples at the end of pregnancy and during the first few days after birth.

The effect of human placental lactogen on breast growth during pregnancy is also presented in Chapter 6.

prolactin
(proh LAK tin) Hormone, secreted by the anterior pituitary gland, that is involved in lactation.

A discussion of prolactin appears in Chapter 4.

Oxytocin is also discussed in Chapter 4.

and secrete **colostrum,** a thin, yellowish fluid that is rich in proteins and antibodies. The mother's breasts continue to secrete colostrum for 2 or 3 days after the birth of her infant. If she nurses her infant, the colostrum will be the infant's first nourishment. The antibodies in the colostrum are thought to protect the infant from a number of infectious diseases to which the mother has built up immunity. Within a couple of days after the birth, however, colostrum production ends and milk begins to be secreted instead.

What causes milk production? During pregnancy the placenta yields high levels of estrogen and progesterone. After the placenta is expelled during the third stage of labor, both estrogen and progesterone levels decrease markedly. The sudden reduction in estrogen causes the anterior pituitary gland to secrete **prolactin,** which stimulates milk production in the milk glands of the mother's breasts. Prolactin continues to be manufactured as long as the mother breast-feeds her infant. Although prolactin is responsible for the production of milk, it is oxytocin, a posterior pituitary hormone, that causes the milk to move from the milk glands into the milk ducts, where it becomes available to the infant. Oxytocin secretion is a reflexive response to the infant's sucking. When the infant sucks the mother's breasts, a message is transmitted to the brain, which causes oxytocin to be released from the posterior pituitary gland. The oxytocin stimulates contractions in the smooth muscles surrounding the milk glands in the breasts, which cause the milk to move into the milk ducts. Once the milk is in the ducts, the infant can extract it by sucking.

In the past few decades an increasing number of American mothers have been choosing to breast-feed their infants (Grossman et al., 1989). In 1970 only about 25% of the women who gave birth chose to breast-feed their infants while in the hospital; that figure increased to 61% by 1984 (Martinez and Krieger, 1985). Furthermore, in 1970 only 5.5% of new mothers were breast-

Newborn breast-feeding a few minutes after birth.

HUMAN SEXUALITY

feeding their 5- and 6-month-old infants; by 1984 that figure had increased to 27.5% (Martinez and Krieger, 1985). The increase in breast-feeding has probably occurred because many women believe that their own milk is better for their infants than commercially prepared milk. Indeed, research has demonstrated that breast-fed children tend to have fewer colds and infections and are generally healthier than bottle-fed infants.

Breast-feeding has definite advantages. The mother's milk is easily available, does not require bottle preparation, sterilization, or heating, contains antibodies that protect the infant from a number of diseases, and is inexpensive. Just as the oxytocin that is released as a result of the infant's sucking causes contractions in the breasts, it also causes contractions in the uterus, which help it to return to its normal, nonpregnant shape more quickly. Some women report that they find the sensations that occur during nursing to be sexually arousing.

Breast-feeding also has some definite disadvantages. Sometimes the mother's milk is not adequate to feed her infant. In such cases the mother can supplement her milk with commercially produced milk or can rely on bottle-feeding completely. Mothers must be careful about taking medications because drugs taken by the mother can be transmitted to the infant via her milk. Bottle-feeding may be necessary for mothers who work outside the home or who for other reasons cannot be with their infants on a full-time basis.

In summary, breast-feeding has both advantages and disadvantages. Each woman has to make her own decision regarding how she will feed her infant based on her own needs and life-style.

Sexual Relations

Most physicians ask women to refrain from sexual intercourse for the first 3 to 6 weeks after childbirth to allow the episiotomy to heal and the vagina and uterus to return to normal. During the first couple of weeks most women are not interested in having sexual intercourse because of tenderness in the vaginal area, general fatigue, and decreased sexual desire, presumably resulting from hormonal changes associated with childbirth (Reamy and White, 1987). Most couples resume sexual intercourse within 4 to 8 weeks after childbirth when the woman's sexual desire returns and she finds she can engage in sexual intercourse comfortably. Some research suggests that sexual desire may return more quickly in women who breast-feed (Lawrence, 1989).

Women should always use some form of contraception when they resume having sexual intercourse following childbirth if they do not want to become pregnant. Menstruation takes time to resume after childbirth; the interval between childbirth and the first menstrual period varies from woman to woman. However, breast-feeding delays the resumption of menstruation. Women who do not breast-feed often resume menstruating in the first 2 months, whereas women who breast-feed may take several months longer (Lawrence, 1989). In any case, even before they have resumed menstruation, women should use some form of contraception because ovulation after childbirth can occur *before* the first menstrual period. Thus women who do not use contraception until their first period has occurred might be unprotected during ovulation and could therefore become pregnant.

COSTS AND BENEFITS OF HAVING CHILDREN

Traditionally couples did not "decide" to have children; they were expected to have children. Married couples did not ordinarily practice contraception. Not until recently have social and technological changes provided men and women with some degree of control over such decisions as how many children to have, how long to wait before having a child, how many years should elapse between the births of siblings, and whether to have children at all. These changes have had a substantial effect on the makeup of the American family. In recent decades the birth rate in the United States has dropped steadily. The current fertility rate is 1.8 births per woman, 50% below the baby boom peak of 3.6 reached in 1957 (Rubenstein, 1989).

Despite the changes in their options, most individuals assume that they will have children after they marry. Over 95% of adults in the United States who are in a position to choose whether to have children decide to have them (Worthington & Buston, 1986). In most cases this decision is not based on a detailed assessment of the pros and cons of raising a family. Instead, it tends to be based on the assumption that having children is "the thing to do" once a couple gets married. Many pressures in our society reinforce this notion. Few people ask young married couples *if* they plan to have children; rather people ask them *when* they plan to have children. The parents of young married couples often put pressure on them by expressing an interest in having grandchildren. Advertisements for diapers, baby bottles, and baby food often sell motherhood, as well as the baby products; they portray mothers as happy, content women and motherhood as easy and satisfying. After all, the mother can simply throw soiled diapers and used bottles away. Magazines and television programs aimed at a female audience also depict motherhood as a profoundly fulfilling occupation and portray the lives of women without children as empty and sad. These subtle and not so subtle pressures reinforce the idea that married couples should have children.

There were good reasons in the past for encouraging parenthood. Traditional demands for parenthood were in large part based on the need for farm labor. In agricultural economies with little machinery, the more family members to help with the crops the better. Thus the more children a family had, the more successful it could be. However, with the advent of mechanized agriculture and urbanization, the farm labor value of children has declined. No longer is there a need to encourage couples to have large families. However, some of the cultural pressures that were established when large families were beneficial have continued to be influential.

Since many of the attitudes and pressures toward parenthood are based on a social reality that no longer exists, prospective parents must consider both the costs and benefits of parenthood today rather than allowing themselves to be influenced by societal pressures from the past. A number of the costs and benefits of parenthood will be presented. These are factors that prospective parents should take into account when deciding whether to have children.

Benefits of Parenthood

Most adults who have been parents feel that the benefits outweigh the costs. Research consistently indicates that if they had the decision to make over again,

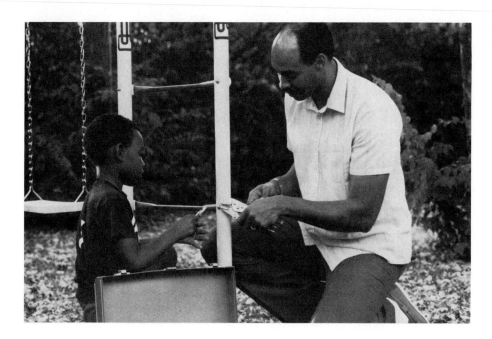

Children are often very rewarding.

the majority would still choose to become parents (Goetting, 1986). Further, in Goetting's study (1986), 87% of parents reported that parenthood provided them with either a great deal or a lot of fulfillment and only 4% reported little or very little satisfaction. In a large study of parents who had had their first child, Russell (1974) found that both fathers and mothers were much more likely to report feelings of enjoyment associated with having children than they were to indicate problems.

Veroff, Douvan, and Kulka (1981) report that when parents were asked what the "nicest thing" about having children is, 44% mentioned personal pleasure such as "they make you happy" or "they are fulfilling." Another 37% cited the parent-child relationship with such statements as "there is someone to love" or "you have good times together." Fewer parents mentioned being able to influence the child (6%), a sense of achievement (5%), and improvement in their relationship with their spouse (2%).

In a study of 200 parents, Lamanna (1977) asked them what they perceived to be the costs and the benefits of childrearing. The satisfaction most often reported by parents was the excitement of having children around. Children often bring fresh and novel responses to a household. They are active and are constantly changing. As a result, they add spontaneity and energy to what might otherwise be a routine existence. In addition, many of the parents stated that their children gave their lives meaning, purpose, and a sense of destiny. Other parents reported that their satisfaction came from belonging to a close family unit that included children rather than just a spouse:

> I think it brings the husband and wife a lot closer. You can't just go your separate ways; there has to be some kind of unity. . . . I think life is more or less having a family, children, having a relationship with your wife and togetherness and it brings you a lot closer.
>
> Lamanna and Riedmann, 1981, pp. 254-255

Related to this sense of satisfaction is the statement by some parents that having children gave them more to do and talk about together.

Many parents studied by Lamanna reported that they enjoyed nurturing the emotional and physical growth of their children. They felt that these aspects of childrearing helped to fill needs for creativity, achievement, and competence.

> What I like best of being a parent is that my wife and I have an opportunity to share our lives with someone other than ourselves and to be able to do something for someone directly associated with us other than the two of us. . . . I think that is the best part, the sharing. I think we all have our own ideas on how children should be raised. It's interesting to see our children reacting to us and our ideas and their response to the way we treat them; it's a challenge.
>
> Lamanna and Riedmann, 1981, p. 255

Costs of Parenthood

The potential benefits of having children are well known in our culture. However, most young couples know little about the problems associated with parenthood. One of the least anticipated costs of parenthood is the effect on the marital relationship. In our culture people often assume that having a child brings the two parents closer together and increases marital satisfaction. However, evidence indicates that this is not the case. Many couples report that the happiest times in their marriages are *before* the arrival of the first child and *after* the departure of the last child. Research on family happiness and stability shows that often children detract from, rather than add to, marital happiness (Spanier and Lewis, 1980; Glenn and McLanahan, 1982; Worthington and Buston, 1986).

Parenthood has costs as well as benefits.

A number of factors increase marital stress during parenthood. First, less time is available for the married couple to spend together (LaRossa, 1983; Ventura, 1987). Furthermore, the couple often finds that their sex life changes after the birth of a child (LaRossa, 1983; Ventura, 1987). Many couples report being too tired to have the same kind of sexual relationship they once enjoyed. They do not have the quiet time together that they need for sexual intimacy. After a child is born, the roles of husbands and wives become more separate and distinct (Cowan and Cowan, 1988). Fathers tend to focus more of their time and attention on occupational and outside interests, while mothers concentrate on the children and home. This separation of roles occurs in most couples with young children regardless of the husband's and wife's employment.

The husband and wife involved in parenting also experience personal costs. Wives frequently mention the problems of time pressure, juggling home and work responsibilities, physical tiredness, interrupted sleep, emotional upset, and worry (LaRossa, 1983; Ventura, 1987). Husbands most often report interrupted sleep, increased money problems, and additional amount of work required (LaRossa, 1983; Ventura, 1987). Although not all of the parents experience severe problems, a majority admit to being bothered somewhat in a number of areas.

One of the greatest personal problems associated with the addition of a new child to the family is the lack of time for parents to pursue their own interests. A household that includes children takes much more time to run. In a study of the time devoted to housework, Walker and Woods (1976) confirmed the impact that children can have on their parents' home responsibilities. As family size increases, so does the time spent on housework. The wife contributes most of the increased time and energy, whether she is employed or not. An employed wife with no children spends less than 4 hours per day on household work, compared with more than 6 hours per day after the first child is added to the family. Many husbands not only spend less time on these tasks than their wives but also are less inclined to increase their time contribution as children come into the family. Thus many mothers find that they have virtually no time to relax and do what they want.

Financial costs are also associated with parenthood. In 1984 the Urban Institute set out to determine the cost of raising a child up to age 18. Included in their estimate were the direct costs of food, clothing, housing, medical care, education, and transportation. They came up with figures ranging from approximately $52,000 for a child in a poor family to $143,000 for a child in a well-off family (Calhoun & Espenshade, 1985). As this wide range shows, a child costs what parents want to spend or can afford to spend. Furthermore, in addition to the virtually immeasurable direct costs, indirect costs are involved (DeParle, 1988). If one parent stays home to raise the child, the couple loses that parent's income. If both parents choose to work, they may have to pay a great deal for child care. Furthermore, if the couple had not had the child, they would have been able to invest and earn interest on the money that goes into childrearing.

Other Considerations

In addition to the costs and benefits of parenthood, several other considerations should be taken into account in the decision to have children. One or the other of the parents may have to spend at least some time raising the child by himself or herself. Divorce is creating nearly 600,000 new single-parent families each year. If present trends continue, more than one third of all children in the United States will spend part of their childhood in a single-parent home as a

Many parents today are single.

HUMAN SEXUALITY

result of marital disruption (Clarke-Stewart, 1982). Marital separation and divorce are now the most common causes of single parenthood. Nine of ten single-parent homes are headed by women.

As pointed out earlier, parenthood tends to be stressful even when two parents are involved. However, when one parent has to assume the role of sole parent and homemaker, parenthood becomes exceptionally stressful. The average amount of money awarded by the court for child support is less than half of what it costs to maintain a child at poverty level (Lamanna and Riedmann, 1981). Furthermore, a large proportion of the child support awarded by the court is never paid. Thus the parent who receives custody of the child or children following a divorce usually must seek full-time employment to support the family. Full-time jobs are demanding even for someone without other responsibilities. The single parent must return from his or her full-time job and then begin doing the cooking, cleaning, laundry, shopping, yard work, and child care. There is not enough time in the day for one parent to do the work that two parents typically find demanding. Thus some of the demands frequently go unmet.

Social isolation is an additional problem for many single parents. The demands of running their homes are so great that they do not have time to enjoy themselves and be involved in social activities. Furthermore, single parents often cannot afford baby-sitters and as a consequence are unable to socialize outside their homes. In addition, many single parents have problems fitting in well socially with married couples or with single adults who do not have children. As a result of their isolation, single parents have difficulty meeting potential mates.

In addition to the problems of work overload and social isolation, many single parents feel the strain of not having anyone with whom to share the problems and pleasures associated with childrearing. For example, the single parent may not have anyone who can take care of the children when he or she is sick. The single parent also does not have anyone with whom to share the decisions involved in childrearing and may feel overburdened by having total responsibility.

In spite of all the hardships involved in single parenthood, some individuals manage to make it a rewarding experience:

> There's always someone here for me to love and who loves me. And it's a deeper feeling than any relationship I've ever had in my life. It's brought more dimensions to living than I ever dreamed possible.
>
> Klein, 1973, p. 163

Since such a large number of marriages currently end in divorce, it seems reasonable that couples consider the possibility of raising children alone when they make the decision to have children. If either feels that he or she would be totally unwilling or unable to raise a child alone, the couple should be hesitant to have children.

Another consideration that couples should weigh is parental age. Evidence suggests that having children is biologically safer during the mother's twenties than at either an earlier or a later age. Teenage pregnancy is riskier both for the mother and for her child than it is for women in their twenties. The children of teenage mothers are at high risk for premature delivery, low birth weight, and birth defects (Monkus and Bancalari, 1981). Infants born to adolescent mothers are twice as likely to die during infancy as infants born to older women (Graham, 1981).

Risks are also associated with parenthood when the mother is beyond the age of 30. Women in their thirties have a slightly higher chance of dying during pregnancy and delivery than women in their twenties (Buehler et al., 1986; Resnik, 1986). The chances that women will be infertile or will have medical difficulties that interfere with normal growth and delivery of an infant increase with age (Bongaarts, 1982; Resnik, 1986). The chance of Down's syndrome jumps from 1 in 2,400 for women under age 20 to 1 in 32 for women over 45 (Kuchner and Porcino, 1988). In spite of these risks, however, some health care professionals take a liberal, optimistic view of pregnancy in older women. They point out that only 1 in 10 middle-aged mothers actually runs a high risk and that the problems can be minimized through excellent nutrition, rest and exercise, training for birth, and a positive attitude (McCauley, 1976).

Despite the chance of increased medical problems, many white, middle-class, urban women have begun to delay pregnancy and childbirth until they are in their thirties (Kuchner and Porcino, 1988). Some postpone childbearing because they choose not to get married until their late twenties or thirties. Others delay because they want to take advantage of personal freedom before having children. Others want to begin careers and establish themselves professionally before taking on the additional burden of children. Some want to become financially secure before starting a family.

Because of the development of amniocentesis, the increase in age at which women are choosing to have children is less a problem today than it would have been one or two decades ago. With the use of amniocentesis, medical personnel can detect some of the abnormalities in the fetus that tend to increase in frequency in correlation with the age of the mother, such as Down's syndrome (Powledge, 1983). When such abnormalities are detected early, the parents have the option of choosing abortion rather than allowing the pregnancy to continue. Thus older women who would be willing to choose abortion if a serious abnormality were detected may feel that they are taking less of a risk in having a child at a later age than older women might have 20 or 30 years ago.

REMAINING CHILD FREE

Some couples today are choosing to remain child free. Although many people consider it unusual for a couple not to have children, childlessness can have definite advantages. In many of the couples who choose not to have children, both the husband and wife have a strong commitment to their careers. In the past, when a husband was highly involved in his career, his wife was often willing to do most of the child care. Today, however, many women are also heavily invested in professional careers. Some couples decide that the time and energy involved in raising children would not allow them to devote as much to their careers as they would like.

Not having children also affords some couples the opportunity to have more time to themselves. If a couple does not have children, they have more time and energy to devote to themselves, to each other, and to their relationship. Furthermore, they have more time to devote to hobbies, travel, and other

Down's syndrome is discussed in Chapter 6.

The procedure of amniocentesis is presented in greater detail in Chapter 6.

leisure-time activities. In addition, these couples have more money to spend on their houses, cars, and leisure activities. Thus for some couples remaining child free is desirable because of the additional freedom and flexibility it allows.

SUMMARY

1 Labor has three stages. The first stage lasts the longest and ends when the cervix is fully dilated. The second stage is over when the infant is born. The third stage is finished when the placenta is expelled.

2 Before the Middle Ages women gave birth in their homes without help from anyone other than friends and relatives. By the 1600s in Europe physicians began to assume the role of delivering the infant. Today 97% of all births in the United States take place in hospitals.

3 Research has indicated that impersonal, sterile hospital rooms are not the optimal places in which to give birth. Many hospitals now provide a rooming-in program that allows a mother to keep her infant in her room most of the day, and a number of hospitals also offer birthing rooms that are as much like home as possible.

4 Evidence suggests that most painkilling drugs used during childbirth can have negative effects on the infant. As a result, the extent to which medication is used during childbirth has decreased.

5 In the United States the father traditionally had no involvement in the pregnancy or delivery. Now, however, many fathers go through natural childbirth training programs with their wives and learn to help their wives during labor and delivery.

6 Today cesarean sections are performed in about 25% of all births in the United States. In a cesarean section the fetus is removed through an abdominal incision that opens the uterus.

7 The first few weeks following the delivery of an infant are called the postpartum period. This time can be stressful for the entire family. However, not all families find the postpartum period stressful.

8 Recent social and technological changes provide men and women with some degree of control over the reproductive process. As a result, the birth rate in the United States has been dropping steadily.

9 More than 95% of all adults in the United States who are in a position to have children do so.

10 The responsibilities of parenthood can influence marital relationships in both positive and negative ways.

11 Single parents tend to be isolated socially. Many feel that they cannot become involved in social activities because the demands in maintaining their families are so great. Others cannot afford baby-sitters to enable them to spend time away from their homes. Furthermore, single parents are often isolated because of their special social status.

12 Evidence suggests that having children is biologically safer during a woman's twenties than at either an earlier or a later age. Beyond the age of 30 the chances that a woman will be infertile or will experience medical difficulties during pregnancy increase.

13 Many couples today are choosing to remain child free. One of the advantages of not having children is that individuals have more time for themselves and their careers.

FACT
OR
FICTION

ANSWERS

1 The number of cesarean sections has tripled over the last decade.
2 The husband's involvement in his wife's labor and delivery has a positive effect on both the wife's and the husband's attitudes regarding their childbirth experience.
3 Studies indicate that children often detract from, rather than add to, marital happiness.

QUESTIONS FOR THOUGHT ?

1 Why do you think some women experience postpartum depression?
2 What, in your opinion, would be the advantages and disadvantages of having children?

3 If you were a man whose wife was about to give birth to a baby, how would you feel about being in the delivery room?

SUGGESTED READINGS

Ashford, J: The whole birth catalog: a sourcebook for choices in childbirth, Trumansburg, N.Y., 1983, The Crossing Press.

A collection of readings about different types of childbirth procedures available today.

Genevie, L., and Margolies, E.: The motherhood report: how women feel about being mothers, New York, 1987, Macmillan, Inc.

In this book a study that includes virtually every aspect of motherhood is reported. This book is rich in personal comments from the various mothers who took part in the study.

Grossman, F., Eichler, L., and Winickoff, S.: Pregnancy, birth and parenthood, San Francisco, 1980, Jossey-Bass, Inc., Publishers.

A report of a study of both mothers and fathers during pregnancy, childbirth, and the first year of parenthood.

Messenger, M.: The breastfeeding book, New York, 1982, Von Nostrand Reinhold Co., Inc.

An excellent book on breast-feeding.

Michaels, G.Y., and Goldberg, W.A., editors: The transition to parenthood: current theory and research, Cambridge, Eng., 1988, Cambridge University Press.

This book includes an excellent collection of professional level readings on the transition to parenthood, including parenthood under condition of risk and intervention strategies.

Contraception and Abortion

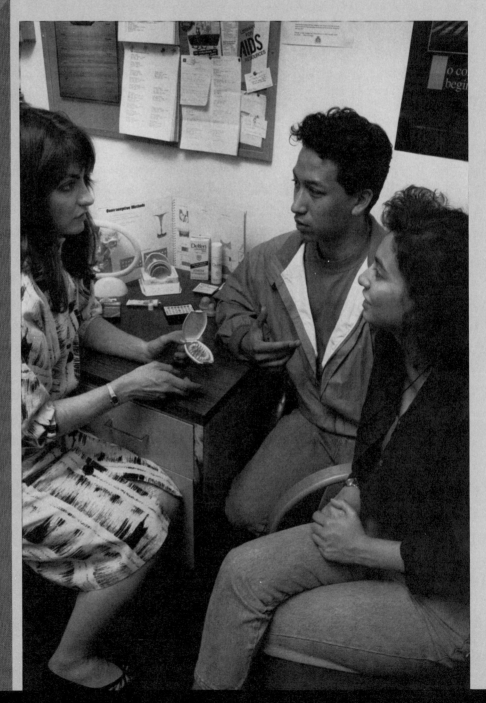

"Is the condom really effective?"

"Which will be the most effective contraceptive method for me?"

"Why did one magazine say diaphragms are 98% effective and another say they're 80% effective?"

"Can you still get pregnant if you take your birth control pills every day on schedule?"

"Can certain contraceptive methods help protect me against sexually transmitted diseases?"

MODIFIED FROM R. HATCHER ET AL.
Contraceptive Technology

The topic of contraception is important to many individuals, and this chapter will help to answer the questions raised in the introductory quotations. Before the 1960s many couples limited their family size by using condoms, withdrawal of the penis before ejaculation (coitus interruptus), diaphragms, or fertility awareness techniques such as the rhythm method. In the last 20 years many new contraceptive methods have become available in the United States. We now have at our disposal numerous methods of contraception that include the old mainstays, such as the condom and diaphragm, and also oral contraceptives, intrauterine devices (IUDs), vaginal spermicides, vaginal contraceptive sponges, cervical caps, long-lasting injections of hormones, more sophisticated fertility awareness methods, and relatively uncomplicated sterilization procedures for men and women. Some of these methods have become very popular, while others such as the IUD have lost favor because of many serious problems encountered by American women using this device (Hatcher et al., 1990b). The most popular methods of contraception in America are listed in Table 8-1.

A brief look at Table 8-1 indicates that 7% of women of childbearing age do not use any type of contraception. Of the noncontraceptors, 3% are married and 13% are single. Ninety-three percent of all women of childbearing age use contraceptives, and 97% of all married women use contraception, in contrast to 87% of single women. As an example of how to read Table 8-1, we see that 32% of all women in the survey used oral contraceptives (the pill), with 22% of the married women and 48% of the single women using this method. Thus a higher proportion of single women than of married women use the pill.

Forrest and Fordyce (1988) found that contraceptive choices changed between 1982 and 1987. The information in Table 8-1 is from their 1987 study. The use of condoms increased from 9% to 16% (in response to concerns about sexually transmitted diseases), and pill use among all women increased from 27% to 32% (in response to fewer fears about side effects). In contrast, IUD users dropped from 7% to 3% (Forrest and Fordyce, 1988), and Hatcher and associates (1990b) estimate that only 1% of contraceptors use an IUD.

SEX BEHAVIORS THAT ELIMINATE THE NEED FOR CONTRACEPTION

Before discussing contraceptive measures, we should mention two behaviors that remove the need for any type of contraception. They are abstinence from sexual activities and sex without intercourse. Not all couples engage in sexual

Sexual behaviors, including those that do not involve intercourse, are discussed in Chapter 9.

TABLE 8-1 Percentages of Women and Men Using the Various Contraceptive Methods Available in the United States

Method	Total*	Married†	Single‡
Nonusers of any method	7	3	13
Users of some method	93	97	87
Sterilization	36	51	13
Female	22	28	12
Male	16	24	1
Pill	32	22	48
Condom	16	15	16
Intrauterine device	3	3	3
Diaphragm	4	4	4
Spermicidal foam	1	3	1
Spermicidal suppositories	1	1	1
Sponge	3	1	4
Withdrawal	5	5	6
Douche	1	1	1

From Forrest and Fordyce, 1988.
*This column indicates total of both married and single individuals in the study.
†This column is only married individuals.
‡This column is only single individuals.

intercourse during each session of sexual activity. Many of our students make the important point that "having sex" and sexual intercourse are not the same thing. Sexual gratification and excitement may come from holding hands, hugging, kissing, petting, mutual masturbation, oral-genital sex, and the other behaviors. We stress that ejaculation on or next to the vaginal orifice can produce a pregnancy. Sex without intercourse is satisfactory for many couples. In one study of 400 married couples, 84% of the men and 80% of the women regularly achieved orgasm without intercourse (Fliegelman, 1986).

EFFECTIVE CONTRACEPTION: PROS AND CONS

The increase in contraceptive methods has had both positive and negative aspects. Women now have at their disposal effective methods of contraception that they control. However, some women feel that because most methods are for the female, they have total responsibility for contraceptive decisions with little or no shared obligation from men. Another aspect involves control of one's body. In addition, many women and men feel that although certain methods of contraception such as oral contraceptives and IUDs are very effective, "they are examples of technologies that exceed our grasp, that interfere too powerfully with basic life processes in ways we do not fully comprehend, and that consequently have a capacity to cause us harm in ways we can only partially predict and rarely prevent" (Bruce and Schearer, 1979). As we shall see later in this chapter, concern about future harm was borne out by many American women using certain IUDs.

Sexually active people are faced with a choice between highly effective methods of contraception that have some degree of risk and other methods

Noncontraceptive Benefits of Contraception

In addition to preventing pregnancies, certain contraceptive measures have other benefits to the user. The noncontraceptive benefits are summed up below:

Method	Noncontraceptive benefits
Oral contraceptives containing estrogen and progesterone	Protection against pelvic inflammatory disease (PID) due to certain pathogens,* protection against cancers (endometrial and ovarian), and benign tumors, decreases menstrual bleeding, reduces anemia, minimizes menstrual cramping
Latex condoms	Protection against many sexually transmitted diseases (STDs) including acquired immunodeficiency syndrome (AIDS); delays premature ejaculation
Progesterone-only pills, injections, and implants	May protect against PID, may decrease cramping and blood loss, and may protect against certain cancers (endometrial and ovarian)
Diaphragm, cervical caps, sponges, spermicidal foams and jellies	Protection against certain STDs, including AIDS; used with a condom they provide excellent contraception and STD protection

*Pills decrease the loss of menstrual blood and blood acts as growth medium facilitating development of PID. Pills also thicken cervical mucus, making it difficult for pathogens to get into uterus. Although numerous articles have noted that pills discourage PID resulting from certain pathogens, the pills do not seem to protect against PID caused by *Chlamydia;* in fact, they may enhance PID from this pathogen (Hatcher et al., 1990b). The pill does not protect against STDs but in many cases does prevent the STD from causing PID.

---

that have few side effects but may detract from sexual enjoyment and that have a higher failure rate.

Many couples use fertility awareness methods as a form of contraception, either alone or in combination with other methods. Couples selecting fertility awareness methods are motivated by religious beliefs (many religions forbid the use of any types of artificial methods to prevent conception) and other personal concerns such as worry about side effects associated with many contraceptive methods. The fertility awareness methods are discussed separately in this chapter because they do not involve the use of physical devices, anatomical alterations, or medications to prevent fertilization. Other contraceptive methods can be placed into four basic categories: (1) barrier methods that prevent the union of the egg and the sperm, (2) methods that prevent implantation of the egg (the IUD), (3) methods that prevent ovulation (oral contraceptives), and (4) sterilization.

Fertility Awareness

A thorough presentation of the structure and function of the male and female reproductive systems appears in Chapters 3 and 4. We need this information to understand the menstrual cycle. In particular, we should know when in the

Biological changes that occur in the female during the menstrual cycle are presented in Chapter 4.

Contraceptive Effectiveness

When the effectiveness of a contraceptive method in preventing pregnancies is discussed, two terms are often used: theoretical effectiveness and actual-use effectiveness. Theoretical effectiveness of the method refers to the maximal effectiveness of that method when used exactly according to instructions, with no user error (Hatcher et al., 1990b). Actual-use effectiveness of a method takes into account all users of the method whether they use the method correctly or not. It is obvious that the actual-use effectiveness rate will be lower than the theoretical effectiveness rate; that is, the method will "fail" more often and more women will become pregnant. For example, the theoretical failure rate of spermicidal vaginal foam is 3%, or it is 97% effective, but the actual-use failure rate for all women using it, including those

who use it incorrectly, varies from 1.5% to 29% depending on the population of women studied (Hatcher et al., 1990b).

Theoretical failure rates, often referred to as *lowest failure rates*, and *actual-use failure rates*, also referred to as *typical failure rates*, are expressed as the number of pregnancies that occur per 100 women years. This simply means that if 100 fertile women use a particular method for 1 year, a certain number will become pregnant. This percentage is the failure rate of the method. This way of calculating the failure rate of contraceptive methods has its problems because the longer a researcher studies a group using a particular contraceptive measure, the lower the failure rate will be. A better way to express failure rate is to control for the length of use and ask the question, "Of 100 women

who start to use a method and *continue* to use it unless it fails, how many will become pregnant in the first year, second year, third year, etc.?" (Hatcher et al., 1990b). For example, theoretically 3 out of 100 women using spermicidal foam would become pregnant each year. However, in actual use 1.5 to 29 women out of 100 using the foam become pregnant each year. Why should there be such a difference between theoretical and actual-use failure rates? Incorrect use of the method is the major cause. Users make such mistakes as using too little foam, failing to shake the container, not realizing the foam bottle is empty, failing to use the foam on every occasion of intercourse, and douching too soon after intercourse. Correct and consistent use of the method of choice is essential for maximal protection.

The lowest expected failure rates and typical failure rates for the contraceptive methods available in the United States are shown in Table 8-2.

---

cycle a woman is fertile; this is known as fertility awareness. Both the male and the female should be knowledgeable in fertility awareness so that they can make important decisions about what contraceptive method is best for them and so that they realize why they need maximal contraceptive protection during certain times of the cycle. Fertility awareness also aids the couple in bringing about the desired conception of a child. In addition, a woman who knows her body well will more readily recognize any abnormal changes.

One of the most important changes during the menstrual cycle is the fluctuation of various hormones from the anterior pituitary gland and the ovaries. The cyclical variations in these hormones are reflected in numerous biological, and to some extent psychological, alterations over the cycle. Some of the changes that occur as a result of cyclical hormones are fluctuations in basal body temperature patterns and variations in the type of cervical mucus produced. Many woman are able to relate these outward signs to their fertility cycles.

Methods of fertility awareness include the calendar method, basal body

TABLE 8-2 **Lowest Expected (Theoretical) and Typical (Actual-Use) Failure Rates During the First Year of Use of Various Contraceptive Methods Available in the United States**

Method	Percent of women experiencing accidental pregnancy in first year of use	
	Lowest expected (theoretical)	Typical (actual-use)
Chance	85	85
Douching	40	40
Vaginal spermicides	3	21
Fertility awareness		
Calendar	9	19-23
Ovulation (mucus)	3	15
Basal body temperature	7	21
Withdrawal	4	18
Cervical cap	6	18
Sponge		
Parous	9	28
Nulliparous	6	13
Diaphragm	6	2-18
Condom	2	12
Condom with vaginal spermicide	<1	5
Intrauterine device		
Progestasert	2	3
Copper T	0.8	3
Pill		
Combined	0.1	3
Progesterone only	0.5	1.1-9.6
Injectable progesterone	0.4	0.4
Implants (Norplant)	0.04	0.04
Female sterilization	0.2	0.4
Male sterilization	0.1	0.15

From Hatcher et al., 1990b.

temperature method, and cervical mucus or ovulation method. Some couples use the fertility awareness methods as contraceptive techniques, and others use them to time intercourse if a pregnancy is desired. In their earlier editions of *Contraceptive Technology* (1986, 1987, etc.), Hatcher and associates discussed fertility awareness and considered in detail failure rates and other aspects of the methods. In their most recent edition (1990b), very little space is devoted to fertility awareness techniques. Does this mean that Hatcher and associates do not think the fertility awareness methods are of value as a contraceptive method? In contrast, Carl Djerassi, one of the discoverers of oral contraceptives, believes that we should take another look at fertility awareness techniques, since U.S. companies are making little effort to develop new contraceptive methods because of costs, federal regulations to get permission to sell products in the United States, and possible liabilities with finished products (Research in Reproduction, 1990). Djerassi states that we should try to improve the low efficiency of the fertility awareness techniques now available. Only time will indicate whether research will be directed at improving these techniques.

Calendar Method

The least difficult method that can be used for fertility awareness is the **calendar method,** sometimes called the rhythm method. In using this system the woman records the length of her menstrual cycles over a 6- to 8-month span. As pointed out in Chapter 4, the first day of vaginal bleeding is always considered day 1 of the cycle. Thus day 14 of a woman's cycle is the fourteenth day after the onset of the menstrual flow.

To use the calendar method to increase fertility awareness, as a contraceptive method, or to enhance conception, the woman must record the length of six to eight menstrual cycles. When the cycle lengths have been recorded, the following calculations are made. The earliest day on which the woman is likely to be fertile is computed by subtracting 18 days from the length of her shortest cycle. By subtracting 11 days from the length of her longest cycle, the woman determines the latest day on which she is likely to be fertile. Thus the numbers indicate the beginning and end of her fertile time. The calculations are summed up in Table 8-3.

Calculation of the fertile period, or the time when the probability of conception is the greatest, is based on three assumptions: (1) ovulation occurs on day 12 to 16 of the menstrual cycle; (2) sperm can live for 48 to 72 hours in the female reproductive tract; and (3) the egg can live for 48 to 72 hours after it has been released from the ovary. It is immediately apparent that there is some leeway in the assumptions. This uncertainty makes the calendar method a very marginal one if the intent is to avoid pregnancy. We would not recommend the calendar method as a contraceptive method by itself, but it is a good way to learn about fertility awareness and to enhance the probability of conception. A failure rate with perfect use and abstinence both before and after ovulation would yield a failure rate of about 9% and an actual-use failure rate of approximately 20% (Hatcher et al., 1990b).

TABLE 8-3 Calculation of Fertile Days Using Calendar Method

If shortest cycle has been (no. of days)	First fertile (unsafe) day is	If longest cycle has been (no. of days)	Last fertile (unsafe) day is
21	3rd day*	21	10th day*
22	4th	22	11th
23	5th	23	12th
24	6th	24	13th
25	7th	25	14th
26	8th	26	15th
27	9th	27	16th
28	10th	28	17th
29	11th	29	18th
30	12th	30	19th
31	13th	31	20th
32	14th	32	21st
33	15th	33	22nd
34	16th	34	23rd
35	17th	35	24th

From Hatcher et al., 1986.
*Day 1 = first day of menstrual bleeding.

HUMAN SEXUALITY

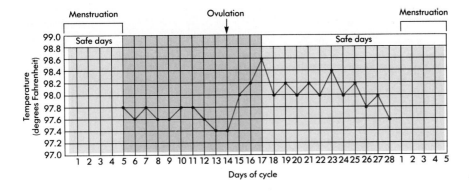

FIGURE 8-1
Daily charting of a woman's basal body temperature indicates a slight drop at the time of ovulation and then a rise in temperature that persists until the next menstrual flow.

Basal Body Temperature Method

The **basal body temperature** (BBT) **method** of fertility awareness is also used by some couples to avoid pregnancy and by others to aid in conception. It is based on the observation that from 24 to 72 hours after ovulation a noticeable rise in the resting body temperature occurs. The great increase in progesterone after ovulation is generally assumed to cause this body temperature increase.

Figure 8-1 illustrates the variations in body temperature during a hypothetical menstrual cycle of 28 days. The BBT drops at about the time of ovulation and increases 24 to 72 hours after ovulation. The BBT remains elevated until the approach of the next menstrual flow. Thus, if a woman abstains from intercourse or does not engage in unprotected intercourse until the BBT has risen and has remained elevated for 3 full days, she has an extremely low probability of becoming pregnant because the egg should no longer be capable of fertilization, assuming that an egg or ovum can live for only 48 to 72 hours after it has been released from the ovarian follicle. This would be using the BBT method with intercourse only after ovulation has occurred as evidenced by a temperature rise. Some couples who use the BBT method have intercourse both before and after the suspected time of ovulation, and this increases the risk of pregnancy. If BBT is used perfectly and intercourse only occurs no sooner than 3 days after the rise in body temperature, the failure rate is approximately 7% (Hatcher et al., 1990b).

basal body temperature method
Fertility awareness method that involves charting body temperature daily until a rise in temperature, associated with ovulation, is noted.

Cervical Mucus Method

The **cervical mucus method** of fertility awareness is also known as the ovulation method or the Billings method (Billings, Billings, and Catarinch, 1974). Just as the basal body temperature varies during the menstrual cycle, the characteristics of cervical mucus change as a result of changes in ovarian hormones during the cycle. The amount, viscosity (consistency), and color of the mucus change during the cycle, and these variations can be correlated with ovulation.

The effectiveness of the cervical mucus method varies depending on whether intercourse occurs only after ovulation or both before and after ovulation. If this method is used correctly and intercourse occurs only after ovulation, a failure rate of 3% has been reported (Hatcher et al., 1990b). Combining the BBT method with the cervical mucus and calendar methods greatly improves fertility awareness; the mucus and calendar methods indicate when ovulation can be expected, and the BBT indicates that ovulation has occurred.

cervical mucus method
Method in which the fertile period is calculated by examining changes in types of cervical mucus produced, which are correlated with fertile and nonfertile portions of cycle.

Clearplan Easy is one product now available that detects ovulation 24 to 36 hours before it occurs. However, such products should not be relied as the sole means of contraception, since sperm cells can survive from 48 to 72 hours in the female reproductive tract.

We can conclude that fertility awareness methods will become more effective in the near future as new products are marketed to help pinpoint the time of ovulation. For example, devices that monitor hormonal changes in saliva and vaginal fluids will be able to predict ovulation up to 1 week in advance. At present tests (e.g., Clearplan Easy) can be used at home to detect luteinizing hormone (a sign that ovulation will occur in the next 24 to 36 hours). Unfortunately, intercourse before ovulation could still cause a pregnancy because sperm cells can survive from 48 to 72 hours in the female reproductive tract. The most recent failure rates for fertility awareness techniques are shown in Table 8-2.

Barrier Methods of Contraception

Barrier methods of contraception physically block the passage of the sperm into the vagina or uterus or chemically inactivate the sperm in the vagina. This group of contraceptive methods, particularly the condom and diaphragm, has been in use for decades. Newer methods such as spermicidal vaginal agents and contraceptive sponges are becoming increasingly popular because of their low incidence of side effects and the protection they provide against sexually transmitted diseases. Approximately 25% of all couples in the United States use a barrier method or a combination of barrier methods for contraception (Forrest and Fordyce, 1988).

Sexually transmitted diseases are discussed in Chapter 18.

diaphragm
(DY uh fram′) Dome-shaped rubber cup that blocks cervix so sperm cannot reach egg in fallopian tubes (oviducts). Must be used with spermicide to be effective.

Diaphragm First developed in Germany in the 1880s, the **diaphragm** was the first effective, easy-to-use contraceptive totally controlled by the woman. It enjoyed great popularity in the United States until the introduction of oral contraceptives in the 1960s.

The diaphragm is a dome-shaped cup, usually made of latex rubber, that has a spring in the flexible rim. The diaphragm is inserted before intercourse so that it completely covers the cervix (Figure 8-2). *For maximal effectiveness, a spermicidal jelly or cream is placed in the dome before insertion.* In addition to killing sperm cells, the jelly or cream (nonoxynol-9) offers protection against certain sexually transmitted diseases such as human immunodeficiency virus (HIV; the AIDS virus), gonorrhea, chlamydia, and trichomoniasis (Hatcher et al., 1990b). The diaphragm may be inserted just before intercourse or up to 6 hours before intercourse and *must* be left in place for at least 6 to 8 hours after intercourse. The diaphragm works as a contraceptive device both by providing a physical barrier that helps to prevent the sperm from entering the cervix and by holding a spermicide. Any sperm that do get past the diaphragm will in all likelihood be killed by the spermicidal jelly. The diaphragm is available in different rim sizes and rim styles to accommodate the depth of the vagina and muscle tone of its walls. When fitted properly, it covers the cervix.

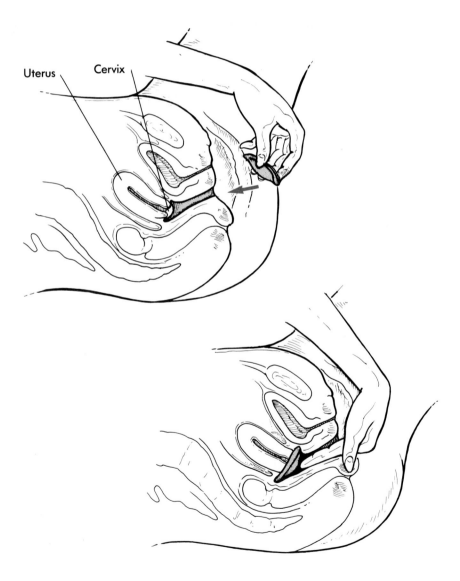

FIGURE 8-2
After spermicidal jelly is placed in the diaphragm, the diaphragm is folded lengthwise, inserted into the vagina, and placed against the cervix so that the cup portion with the spermicide is facing the cervix. The outline of the cervix should be felt through the central part of the diaphragm.

The popularity of the diaphragm as a contraceptive method has increased in recent years because of its great effectiveness and lack of associated serious side effects.

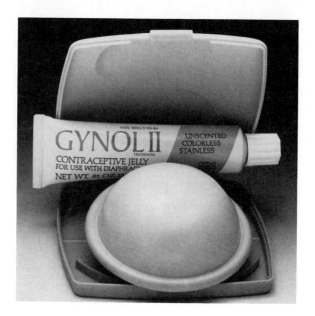

The actual-use effectiveness of the diaphragm as a contraceptive method varies a great deal depending on the study. Actual failure rates from different studies range from 2 to 18 pregnancies per 100 women during the first year of use. The lowest expected failure rate for the diaphragm is 6% (Hatcher et al., 1990b).

The diaphragm has few risks or side effects. Occasionally one partner finds the spermicidal jelly or the rubber of the diaphragm irritating. Changing to a different brand of jelly or diaphragm often ends the problem. Some women experience pelvic pain, cramps, urine retention, and aggravation of recurrent bladder or urinary tract infections. If refitting the diaphragm does not alleviate the symptoms, the woman may not be able to continue its use.

The diaphragm has other disadvantages. Some women do not like the fact that the diaphragm must be inserted before intercourse. They believe it takes away from the "spontaneity" of intercourse. Some do not like to touch their genitals or put their fingers into the vagina to insert or remove the diaphragm (Bruce and Schearer, 1979). Some couples do not like the smell, taste (if put in before oral sex), and messiness of the jelly. In addition, the diaphragm can become dislodged during vigorous intercourse (Johnson and Masters, 1962), and some men claim they can feel the diaphragm during intercourse.

cervical cap
Tight-fitting cap, made of rubber or plastic, that fits over the cervix so sperm cannot reach the egg in the fallopian tubes.

Cervical cap   Like a small diaphragm with a higher dome, the **cervical cap** fits over the cervix as the diaphragm does, but it is held in place by suction between its firm, flexible rim and the cervix-vaginal junction (Figure 8-3). Spermicide is placed inside the cup. The cervical cap is most commonly made of plastic or soft rubber.

The cervical cap may be a good choice for women who are unsuccessful in being fitted for a diaphragm. Women who feel discomfort when the diaphragm is in place and those who find the cap less messy (since it does not require as much spermicide) are also candidates for the cap. The cap may be inserted up

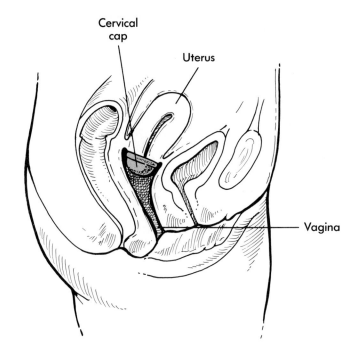

Cervical cap

Uterus

Vagina

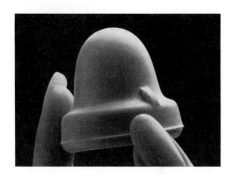

FIGURE 8-3
After the spermicidal cream or jelly is placed in the cervical cap, the cap is inserted into the vagina and placed against the cervix.

to 6 hours before intercourse and left in place at least 6 to 8 hours after intercourse. The cap is equal in effectiveness to the diaphragm (Table 8-2) and it is similar to the diaphragm in terms of use (Hatcher et al., 1990b).

Contraceptive sponges The **contraceptive sponge,** introduced into the United States in 1983, is a sponge impregnated with the spermicide nonoxynol-9. It is placed in the vagina before sexual intercourse. The spermicide in the sponge kills sperm within the vagina, and the sponge also acts as a mechanical barrier to prevent sperm from passing through the cervix. In addition, the spermicide nonoxynol-9 in the sponge has been shown to afford protection against HIV, gonorrhea, chlamydia, pelvic inflammatory disease, cervical neoplasia, and trichomoniasis (Rosenberg et al., 1987; Hatcher et al., 1990b).

The sponge is used only once and can be purchased in most food and drug stores. A small retrieval loop is attached to the sponge so it can easily be removed. Before insertion into the vagina, the sponge must be moistened with tap water to activate the spermicide.

The sponge may be inserted up to 24 hours before intercourse and should be left in place for at least 6 hours following intercourse. In terms of effectiveness, the sponge is comparable to the diaphragm and cervical cap in women who never have had children (nulliparous women) and slightly less effective in women who have had children (parous women) in clinical trials in the United States (Table 8-2). It is proposed that a better fit occurs between the cervix and sponge if a woman has not had children. In worldwide clinical trials with much larger samples of women, there were no differences in effectiveness between nulliparous and parous women.

In worldwide studies the sponge has had a theoretical failure rate of 6% to

contraceptive sponge
Small, spermicide-impregnated sponge that is inserted into vagina before intercourse.

The contraceptive sponge contains a powerful spermicide and also acts as a mechanical barrier to prevent sperm from passing through the cervix.

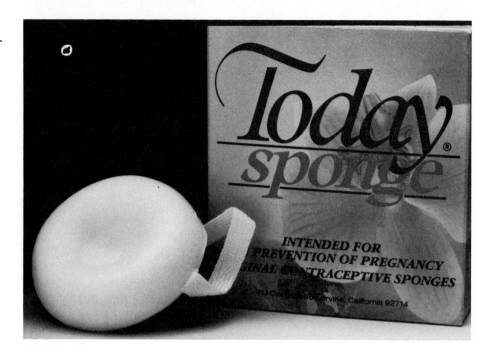

9% and an actual-use failure rate of 13% to 28%. The advantages of the sponge are that (1) it can be purchased without a prescription; (2) it is easy and not messy to use; and (3) sexual spontaneity is enhanced because the sponge can be inserted up to 24 hours before intercourse. The major disadvantage at this time is the price. Depending on where sponges are purchased, they can cost between $1.00 and $1.30 each.

The topic of toxic shock syndrome is presented in Chapter 17.

Few cases of toxic shock syndrome (TSS) have been reported in clinical trials of contraceptive sponges. In the latest report in 1985, 13 cases of TSS were reported in 25 million sponges sold for a rate of 1 per 100,000 sponge users (North and Vorhauer, 1985). The Food and Drug Administration suggests that the sponge not be left in place for more than 24 hours.

condom
Rubber or natural skin sheath that fits over the penis and catches sperm in its end at ejaculation.

Condom The earliest **condoms** were made of animal skin formed into sheaths. They were used initially in the early eighteenth century as protection against sexually transmitted diseases and only later as a form of contraception. The latex condom has recently become more popular as a contraceptive and as a form of protection against the fatal sexually transmissible disease AIDS. The latex condom provides considerable protection to both partners from the transmission of the virus that causes AIDS. The latex condom is more effective than natural skin condoms against disease transmission. The most effective defense against sexually transmitted diseases is a latex condom lubricated with the spermicide nonoxynol-9.

Sexually transmitted diseases are discussed in Chapter 18.

A condom is a sheath that fits over the penis to prevent ejaculated semen from entering the vagina during sexual intercourse. Condoms are usually made of latex rubber, but a small percentage of condoms used in the United States are made from the intestines of lambs. Besides being a contraceptive device, the condom provides some protection against sexually transmitted diseases such as AIDS, gonorrhea, syphilis, trichomoniasis, and genital herpes (Hatcher et al., 1990b).

The effectiveness of the condom as a contraceptive method varies depending on the population being studied. The actual-use failure rate of latex condoms is about 12% (Table 8-2). User error contributes to the failure rate more than does failure of the condom to hold the sperm.

To prevent some of the common errors that contribute to the failure of condoms, the user must be sure that the rim of the condom is rolled all the way down to the base of the penis. If the condom does not have a reservoir tip, about ½ inch of empty space should be left at the tip to hold the ejaculated semen. After intercourse the condom should be held near the base of the penis. This prevents semen from seeping out around the base of the condom. The penis should be withdrawn from the vagina before the erection is lost or the condom may slip off and permit semen to enter the vagina (Figure 8-4).

Condoms should not be stored in a hot place and should not be carried in a wallet for extended periods, since body heat and wear and tear in the wallet could cause deterioration of the latex. Another method of contraception should

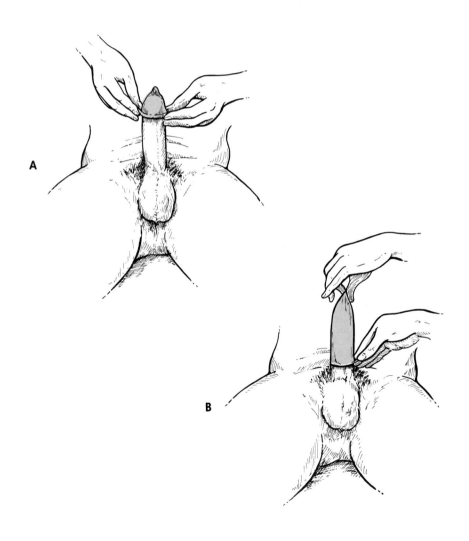

FIGURE 8-4

A, The rim of the condom must be rolled all the way to the base of the penis before the penis is inserted into the vagina. **B,** A reservoir should be left at the tip of the condom to accommodate ejaculated sperm. After ejaculation the condom should be held near the base of the penis to prevent seepage of semen out around the base of the condom.

Condoms are designed to prevent semen from entering the vagina, and they vary in texture and color. Condoms also provide protection against several sexually transmitted diseases.

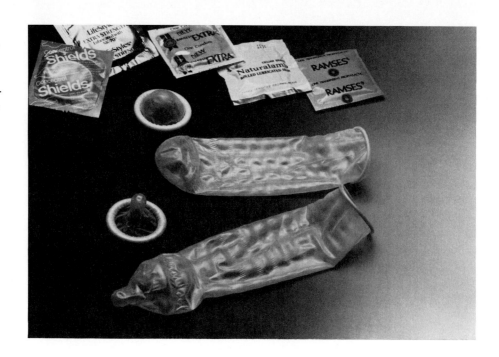

Condom Use Strategies

An excellent article by Grieco (1987) tells how to talk about condoms with a resistant, defensive, or manipulative partner. A few of his suggestions and some of our own are given below. Latex condoms lubricated with the spermicide nonoxynol-9 are the recommended condoms.

If your partner says:	You can say:
"I'm on the pill, you don't need a condom."	"I'd like to use it anyway. We'll both be protected from infections we may not realize we have."
"I'm a virgin."	"I'm not. This way we'll both be protected."
"I can't feel a thing when I wear a condom; it's like wearing a raincoat in the shower."	"Even if you lose some sensation, you'll still have plenty left when you make love to me."
"I love you! Would I give you an infection?"	"Not intentionally. But many people don't know they're infected. That's why this is best for both of us right now."
"Just this once."	"Once is all it takes."
"I don't have a condom with me."	"I do." or "Then let's satisfy each other without intercourse."
"You carry a condom around with you? You were planning to seduce me!"	"I always carry one with me because I care about myself. I have one with me tonight because I care about both of us."
"It will break the mood to put one on."	"Not the way that I am going to put it on you."

be used in conjunction with a condom. Spermicidal foam plus a condom greatly increases the effectiveness. The condom plus a spermicidal agent has a theoretical failure rate of less than 1% and an actual-use failure rate of 5%. If used correctly, the condom plus a spermicidal agent can be almost as effective as oral contraceptives in preventing pregnancies.

What are the known side effects and drawbacks to using a condom as a means of contraception? In rare cases a man cannot maintain an erection with a condom on, and some men and women are allergic to the rubber in condoms. In the latter case a natural skin condom may be used. The most common drawback to condoms is probably that a high percentage of men and a small percentage of women feel that the condom reduces sensitivity of the reproductive structures. Men in particular are reluctant to use condoms. *Regardless of whether the condoms are being used for contraception or protection against sexually transmitted diseases, several strategies exist to convince your partner to use a condom* (see accompanying box). Another reported drawback to condom use is that the condom must be put on the penis before insertion of the penis into the vagina. Many people believe this is disruptive, although a smaller number find it sexually exciting to put a condom on the erect penis.

Female condoms A new development involves the testing of female condoms. Two types are being tested. The first is a latex rubber G-string that contains a condom pouch located in the crotch. When the penis enters the vagina, it pushes the latex pouch into the vagina. The second type is placed in the vagina with an inner circular rim going deep into the vagina and an outer rim that is outside the vagina. Both types of female condoms work by preventing the penis and semen from making physical contact with the walls of the vagina.

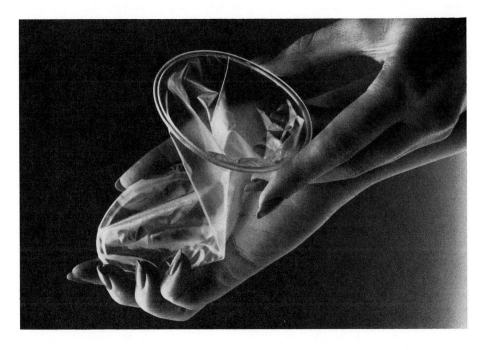

The newest barrier method of contraception, the female condom, fits into the vagina, preventing the penis and semen from physical contact with the vagina.

In addition to condoms lubricated with spermicides, several different types of spermicide are available. **A,** Spermicidal suppositories. **B,** Vaginal contraceptive film. **C,** Foam and applicator.

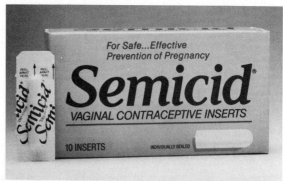

A

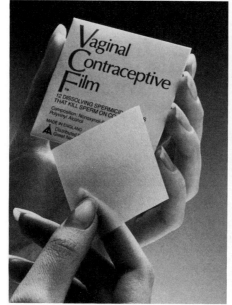

B

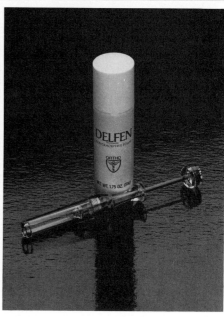

C

vaginal spermicide
(SPER muh syd') Chemical preparation that is placed in vagina and has sperm-killing properties.

Vaginal spermicides **Vaginal spermicides** have been in use for thousands of years. Lemons were once hollowed out much like a cervical cap and placed over the cervix. The acidic lemon juice acted as a spermicide, and the lemon was a physical barrier of sorts. Sponges and lint were soaked with various substances such as honey and tannic acid in an attempt to kill sperm.

The four basic types of vaginal spermicidal preparations are (1) creams, jellies, and foams; (2) spermicidal suppositories; (3) vaginal contraceptive film (a paper-thin sheet containing spermicide); and (4) condoms lubricated with a spermicide.

In the case of the creams, jellies, foams, suppositories, and film, the spermicidal preparations have two parts: an inert base or medium, which holds the spermicidal agent in the vagina against the cervix, and the spermicidal agent itself, which kills the sperm. The most widely used spermicidal agents are nonoxynol-9 and to a lesser extent octoxynol.

Spermicidal creams and jellies are recommended for use with a diaphragm only and not by themselves. Spermicidal foams, which are in preloaded applicators or in containers from which applicators are filled, are placed deep in the vagina in the vicinity of the cervix. The foams mechanically block the entrance to the cervix so that sperm cannot enter the uterus, and the chemical effect of the spermicidal agent immobilizes and kills the sperm cells. The foams are propelled by chlorofluorocarbons. Contraceptive suppositories and films contain the same spermicide as the foams. They effervesce to the proper consistency and stability within the vagina in the case of suppositories or melt in the moisture and warmth of the vagina in the case of film. If a foam, suppository, or film is used and the woman wants to douche, she should wait at least 8 hours after the last intercourse.

How effective are spermicidal foams? As with diaphragms the actual-use failure rates vary depending on the study and the population of women in the sample. The theoretical failure rate is 3 pregnancies per 100 women in the first year of use, and the actual-use failure rate is approximately 21 (Table 8-2). The method must be used according to the directions from health care clinicians or according to the instructions on the package and container (Figure 8-5). Many couples have used foam as their sole means of contraception with excellent

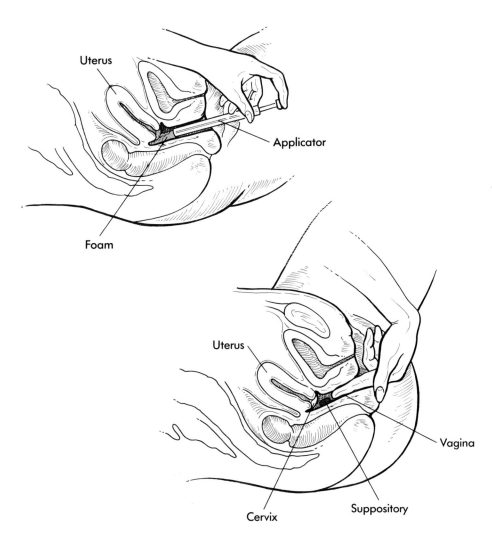

FIGURE 8-5
Spermicidal foams and suppositories are placed deep in the vagina in the region of the cervix no longer than 30 minutes before intercourse.

results; others have used a condom plus foam for extremely high levels of effectiveness. We cannot stress enough that the woman must use the product correctly each time intercourse occurs.

Use of a condom with the foam has a theoretical effectiveness rating almost equal to that of oral contraceptives (Table 8-2). In addition, foam decreases the transmission of certain sexually transmitted diseases, such as gonorrhea and trichomoniasis, and provides vaginal lubrication (Hatcher et al., 1990b).

Vaginal spermicides, including those used with diaphragms, do have some drawbacks. Some people are allergic to the foam, cream, or jelly. Foam has an unpleasant taste, which almost precludes oral sex once the foam is inserted. Vaginal spermicides have also been tentatively implicated in birth defects. The prevalence of certain major birth defects was 2.2% of infants of women who had used a vaginal spermicide in the 10 months before conception, whereas the occurrence of such congenital anomalies in infants born to women who did not use vaginal spermicides was 1% (Jick et al., 1981). There are many problems with the study by Jick and associates, and a more recent study failed to confirm their findings (Shapiro et al., 1982). Two recent well-conducted studies using large samples have found no link between spermicides and birth defects (Louik, et al., 1987; Warburton et al., 1987). A study by Scholl and associates (1983) indicated that women who use spermicides before they realize they are pregnant have a higher rate of spontaneous abortions than other women.

Interference with Fertilization and Egg Implantation: The Intrauterine Device

intrauterine device
(in' truh YOO tuhr in) Small object placed in uterus to prevent implantation of fertilized egg.

An **intrauterine device** (IUD) is an object placed in the uterus through the cervix. The IUD is left in place for an indefinite period and prevents pregnancies from the time it is placed in the uterus until it is removed.

The TC-380A is one of two intrauterine devices (IUDs) currently available in the United States. Other versions of the IUD, including the Dalkon Shield, have been alleged to cause pelvic inflammatory disease, infertility, sterility, and even death. These versions have been discontinued, but the IUD continues to decline in popularity.

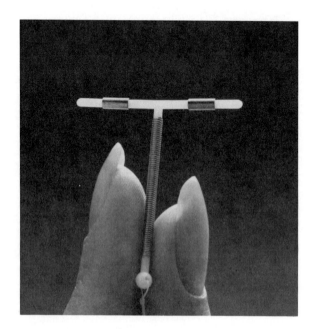

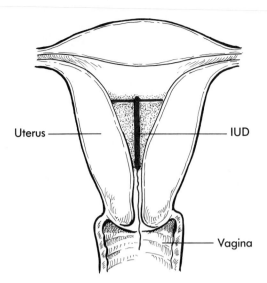

Uterus —————— ———— IUD

————— Vagina

FIGURE 8-6
New studies indicate that
the intrauterine device may
interfere with fertilization
rather than implantation as
was once thought.

IUDs must be inserted by a clinician, and an anesthetic may be injected into the cervix before the IUD inserter is passed into the uterus. The IUD has an attached string that passes through the cervix and into the vagina. The woman can feel for the string to assure herself that the IUD is in place in the uterus. IUDs once came in various shapes and styles, but in the wake of lawsuits charging that IUDs caused pelvic inflammatory disease, infertility, sterility, and perhaps death, only two IUDs (Figure 8-6) are available in the United States, the TCu-380A (Para Gard) containing copper and the progesterone T device (Progestasert).

IUDs reduce the number of sperm cells that reach the oviducts and decrease the viability of those sperm cells that do get to the oviducts. It was once proposed that the primary mode of action of IUDs was to prevent implantation and therefore that they induced abortion (Hatcher et al., 1990b). Numerous studies of the mode of action of IUDs have not found frequent evidence of fertility (as evidenced by biochemical markers of early pregnancy in blood and urine). Thus it is proposed that IUDs interfere with fertilization and not implantation (Sivin, 1989; Hatcher et al., 1990b). Most likely the IUD acts on both fertilization and implantation, with the major action on fertilization. More research will clarify this question. The theoretical failure rate of the IUD is between 0.8% and 2% for first year of use, and the actual-use failure rate is 3% (Table 8-2).

Because of the past problems with IUDs their popularity has declined, and in the future IUDs probably will not be widely available in the United States. Most pharmaceutical companies do not want the liability that has been associated with the IUD.

Some women should not have IUDs inserted. Anyone with an active pelvic infection, including gonorrhea, or a pregnant woman should never have an IUD placed in her uterus. Insertion of an IUD is strongly contraindicated if a woman has recent or recurrent pelvic infections, inflammation of cervix or vagina, history of ectopic pregnancies (outside the uterus), valvular heart dis-

Contraceptive Usage in Other Countries

The contraceptive methods most commonly used in the United States are listed in Table 8-1. Sterilization, either of the male or female, is the most popular method of contraception (36% of couples), followed by oral contraceptives (32%) and condoms (16%). The intrauterine device (IUD) is not a popular method in the United States (3% of couples).

Other countries show different patterns of contraceptive usage. Examining married couples from 15 to 44 years of age around the world, we see that sterilization is popular in China (39% of couples), IUDs are used by 32% of couples, but oral contraceptives are not widely used (5% of couples). Oral contraceptives are very popular in the Netherlands (40% of couples). In Japan oral contraceptives are used by only 1% of couples and condoms are used by 43%. The ineffective method of coitus interruptus (withdrawal) is used by only 5% of couples in the United States, but this method is used widely in Turkey and Poland (30% of married couples in each country), Italy (29%), and France (17%).

Data from Hatcher et al., 1990a.

ease, and abnormal Papanicolaou (Pap) smears. Other, less serious conditions may argue against the IUD as the contraceptive method, and a competent clinician should discuss these with the woman before a choice is made. Puncturing of the uterine wall is a serious risk with IUD use and usually occurs at the time of insertion. Common side effects include bleeding and cramping, and many women have spotting between periods. Women who use IUDs are also at an increased risk for pelvic inflammatory disease, which can lead to infertility (Cramer et al., 1985; Daling et al., 1985).

Ovulation Prevention: Oral and Hormonal Contraceptives

oral contraceptive
Commonly called "the pill," this drug preparation, taken by mouth, suppresses ovulation and makes cervical mucus "hostile" to sperm cells so that sperm cannot penetrate mucus.

See Figure 4-4 for a review of hormone levels during menstrual cycle.

The normal process of ovulation is described in Chapter 4.

As the name implies, **oral contraceptives** are taken by mouth. Two types of oral contraceptives, or birth control pills, are widely used in the United States. One type, the combined oral contraceptive, contains varying amounts of the female hormones estrogen and progesterone. The second type contains only progesterone and is commonly called the mini-pill or progestin-only pill.

There are two basic types of combined oral contraceptives. In the first type the levels of estrogen and progesterone are the same in each pill. In a newer type of combination pill, called triphasic oral contraceptives, the levels of estrogen and progesterone vary. In two widely used triphasics the amount of progesterone is steadily increased throughout the cycle. Drug companies promote these pills as "more natural," since they mimic the menstrual cycle. However, as Hatcher and associates (1990b) ask, "Is more natural synonymous with better?" (p. 258). Hatcher and associates conclude that "all oral contraceptives are designed to produce an unnatural state: anovulation [no ovulation] in a woman who is not pregnant or lactating." Hence, "more natural" is not necessarily better than the same-dose estrogen and progesterone combination pill. Same-level estrogen and progesterone pills and triphasic pills work in the same manner to prevent pregnancies and are discussed together in this section.

Many brands of oral contraceptives are marketed today, and they all exert their main action by suppressing ovulation.

Combined oral contraceptives Combined oral contraceptives either are taken each day for 21 days followed by 7 days with no pills or are taken for 28 straight days with placebo pills for 7 days. The pills are taken independent of sexual intercourse.

Researchers developed oral contraceptives in the late 1950s using newly discovered synthetic hormones that interfered with the normal process of ovulation. These synthetic hormones act on the hypothalamus and probably on the anterior pituitary gland to suppress the hormones necessary for ovulation. Combined oral contraceptives interfere with the feedback system involving the hypothalamus, the anterior pituitary gland, and the ovaries. When oral contraceptives are given, the hypothalamus–anterior pituitary–gonad system becomes disrupted, and the hormones from the anterior pituitary gland are not released in a "spurt" or "surge" large enough to cause the egg to leave the follicle in the ovary. Women taking oral contraceptives do not show preovulatory peaks of estrogen from the ovaries or follicle-stimulating hormone (FSH) and luteinizing hormone (LH) from the anterior pituitary gland or the postovulatory rise in progesterone.

In addition to inhibiting ovulation, the progesterone agents in combined oral contraceptives have other effects that contribute to contraception. The presence of progesterone causes the cervical mucus to be hostile to sperm transport and decreases the sperm's ability to penetrate the thick hostile mucus surrounding the cervix.

With most oral contraceptives the woman starts taking the pills on approximately day 5 of her cycle. This is about when menstruation ceases. At this time the reproductive system is resting and all hormone levels are low. The combined oral contraceptive greatly increases the level of estrogen, which inhibits FSH output by the anterior pituitary gland. Follicles on the ovaries do not grow or mature without FSH. Oral contraceptives also prevent the great surge of LH from the anterior pituitary gland from triggering ovulation. If a woman is following a regimen of 21 days on oral contraceptives and 7 days off, she will have a menstrual flow during the 7 days she is not taking pills. For those women whose oral contraceptives are taken for 28 straight days, bleeding usually starts after 21 days. The last seven pills taken during each cycle are inert; they do not contain any hormones. They are included simply to keep the woman on a regular pill-taking schedule.

The theoretical effectiveness of combined oral contraceptives approaches 100%, and the actual-use failure rate of oral contraceptives for the first year of use is approximately 3%. Thus, even though oral contraceptives are theoretically extremely effective, they must be taken every single day according to instructions.

Women with the following medical problems or situations should never take combined oral contraceptives:
1. Blood clots within the heart or blood vessels
2. History of stroke
3. Disease of the arteries that supply the heart
4. Impaired liver function
5. Benign tumor of the liver
6. Cancer of the breast or reproductive tract
7. Pregnant state

In addition, women with severe migraine headaches, high blood pressure, diabetes, mononucleosis, and various other health problems should carefully discuss these conditions and the risks of taking birth control pills with a health care worker.

Once a woman decides to use oral contraceptives, she should be aware that some oral contraceptive users have side effects (Hatcher et al., 1990b). These effects may be divided into three basic groups: minor, serious, and possibly life threatening. The minor side effects include nausea, weight gain, mild headaches, spotting between periods, missed menstrual flow, yeast infections, vaginal itching or discharge, and mood changes. The serious side effects include gallbladder disease and high blood pressure or hypertension. The possibly life-threatening side effects involve blood clots in various body areas, including the legs, pelvis, lungs, and heart, and rupture of the capsule of the liver as a result of the growth of benign tumors on the liver. Women who smoke and are over 35 are at the greatest risk of heart attacks. In most cases women have aches and complaints that indicate the presence of a problem. *Severe pain in the abdomen, chest, or legs and severe headaches and eye problems should be reported to a physician immediately.*

The most serious complications of oral contraceptives may be minimized or avoided by following two simple rules:
1. Be aware of all contraindications so that use of oral contraceptives may be avoided if necessary.
2. Learn the early danger signals.

Mini-pills The mini-pill contains no estrogen, only small doses of the same progestins found in combined oral contraceptives. The mini-pill exerts its contraceptive action by creating hostile cervical mucus, inhibiting ovulation by elevating progesterone levels, and disrupting the feedback system of the hypothalamus, anterior pituitary gland, and ovaries. Women who should use the mini-pill as their oral contraceptive are those over 35 and those with a history of severe headaches, high blood pressure, or severe varicose veins. Mini-pills are often recommended for young girls who are sexually active and for women who have experienced one of the estrogen-related side effects caused by the combination oral contraceptives, such as headaches, high blood pressure, leg pain, weight gain, and nausea. Mini-pills are not recommended for all women because they are less effective than combined oral contraceptives.

Who should not use progestin-only pills? Any woman who should not use combined oral contraceptives because of medical problems should also not use mini-pills.

The mini-pill has fewer side effects than do combined oral contraceptives. Side effects of mini-pills include irregular menses, decreased duration and amount of menstrual flow (not necessarily an adverse effect), spotting, and amenorrhea. An increased risk of blood clotting in users of the mini-pill has not been established.

The theoretical effectiveness of the mini-pill is slightly less than that of combination pills (Table 8-2). Actual-use failure rates are approximately 1.1 to 9.6 pregnancies per 100 women in the first year of use (Hatcher et al., 1990b).

The noncontraceptive advantages of combined and progesterone-only pills are contained in the box on p. 215. Numerous studies have shown that combined oral contraceptives minimize menstrual cramps, decrease the number of days of bleeding and the amount of blood loss, produce regular menstrual periods, eliminate the pain of mittelschmerz, and reduce premenstrual tension, anxiety, and depression for many women (Report of the Royal College of General Practitioners, 1974). In addition, studies show a decreased incidence of ovarian cysts, fibrocystic breast conditions, and fibroadenomas of the breasts in women who use oral contraceptives. Acne may also be improved. Women taking oral contraceptives have not been found to be in more danger from cancer than non–pill takers. In fact, oral contraceptive users appear to have enhanced protection against ovarian cancer and certain uterine cancers, and oral contraceptives have been found to suppress pelvic inflammatory disease (Kaufman et al., 1980; Kowal et al., 1982; Cancer and Steroid Hormone Study Group, 1987; Statement on steroidal oral contraception, 1987).

See Chapter 17 for a presentation of fibrocystic breast conditions and fibroadenomas.

A major disadvantage of oral contraceptives is that they do not provide protection against sexually transmitted diseases. An oral contraceptive user who has multiple sexual partners or a new partner should use condoms to protect against such diseases, including AIDS.

Progesterone-only injections and implants   In addition to progesterone-only oral contraceptives and IUDs containing progesterone, there are three other progesterone (progestin)-only approaches to contraception:
1. Progestin injections that provide from 3 to 18 months of contraception
2. Progestin implants that provide from 18 months to 5 years of contraception
3. Vaginal rings that contain progesterone and provide 1 to 6 months of contraception

All of the methods listed, including the progestin-only pill and the IUD containing progesterone, release progesterone into the body. The progesterone prevents pregnancy in various ways, including (1) inhibition of ovulation, (2) thickening of cervical mucus so that sperm cannot pass into the uterus, (3) inhibition of proper uterine endometrium, and (4) premature degeneration of corpus luteum (Hatcher et al., 1990b).

PROGESTERONE INJECTIONS Long-acting progestin injections, sometimes called "the shot," are used in many countries but have not been approved for use in the United States as of this writing. Medroxyprogesterone (Depo-Provera) is the most common of the injectable progestins. The long-acting progestin injections, which are usually given as an intramuscular injection every 3 to 4 months, have a theoretical and actual-use effectiveness of almost 100%.

Depo-Provera has not been approved for contraceptive use in the United States for several reasons, including the fact that beagle dogs and rhesus monkeys developed cancers after being administered Depo-Provera and a concern that the drug might cause deformities in the fetus if the method failed (Hatcher et al., 1990b). Although the Food and Drug Administration has not approved use of Depo-Provera as a contraceptive in the United States, some U.S. women have been able to obtain it. Women interested in this form of contraception should consider that it has basically the same benefits and risks as the mini-pill. One additional side effect is that Depo-Provera causes irregular bleeding patterns and can cause amenorrhea in some women. These two conditions could mask disorders of the reproductive tract or prevent the woman from realizing that she is pregnant.

PROGESTERONE IMPLANTS The newest contraceptive method to be approved for use in the United States is an implant containing progesterone. In December 1990 the Population Council of the United States introduced Norplant, which they financed and developed. Norplant implants contain progesterone, specifically the progestin levonorgestrel. The implants, which are slender flexible tubes inserted under the skin on the inside of the upper arm, are effective for 5 years in preventing pregnancies. If the woman wants to become pregnant, she has the tubes removed.

Based on studies in countries other than the United States, the Norplant implants are almost 100% effective in both theoretical and actual use (Table 8-2) for the first 5 years after implantation but must be replaced at the end of 5 years (Hatcher et al., 1990b). The advantages of Norplant implants are that they are long lasting, highly effective, unrelated to sexual intercourse, easily removed to restore fertility, and lacking in estrogens so that they do not produce estrogen-related negative side effects (Hatcher et al., 1990b). The most common side effects of Norplants are menstrual cycle irregularities and to a lesser extent insertion or removal problems.

Norplant is recommended for women who want long-term protection from pregnancies or have had side effects from combined oral contraceptives.

The Norplant implant is a nonbiodegradable capsule that contains progesterone, and the capsule must be removed if the contraceptive effect is to be reversed. Other implants are also available in biodegradable capsules. The capsule or pellet is placed under the skin and releases progesterone in the same

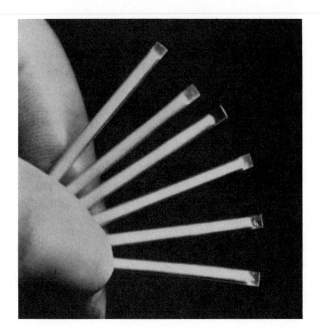

Norplant tubes are inserted under the skin on the inside upper arm. They prevent pregnancy by secreting progesterone slowly into the body over a period of 5 years. At the end of the fifth year the implants are surgically removed and replaced with new ones.

manner as the Norplant. The capsule itself is absorbed by the body and does not have to be removed. However, once implanted the capsule cannot be removed; it must be absorbed by the body and all of the progesterone must be released. The contraceptive effect lasts for 12 to 18 months depending on the type of capsule or pellet implanted. The risks and benefits of the biodegradable implants and pellets are the same as for Norplant implants, but these products have not been approved for use in the United States as of this writing. It is predicted that the biodegradable implants may be available by the mid-1990s.

Vaginal rings   Vaginal rings containing progesterone are effective for 1 to 6 months and are being tested in various countries around the world. The rings may be removed during intercourse if they cause a problem.

Marginal or Ineffective Contraceptive Methods

Douching   Flushing the vagina with a liquid, or **douching,** after intercourse has been called by some an exercise in futility, and by others an exercise in fertility. In other words, douching after sperm has been deposited in the vagina has little effect on preventing fertilization and as a contraceptive method has a failure rate of 40% or greater (Table 8-2). In addition, frequent douching can upset the balance of the normal microorganisms in the vagina and cause vaginal irritation.

douching
(DOOSH ing) Flushing of vagina with liquid.

Withdrawal   Also called coitus interruptus (interrupted intercourse), **withdrawal** involves a couple having intercourse until ejaculation is inevitable, at which point the male withdraws his penis from the vagina. Ejaculation should occur completely away from the vagina and vulva to prevent sperm from

withdrawal
Known as coitus interruptus, this involves withdrawing the penis from the vagina just before the male ejaculates.

As pointed out in Chapter 3, Cowper's glands produce a preejaculatory emission that may contain sperm. Thus removal of penis before ejaculation may not prevent pregnancy.

Anxiety can contribute to sexual dysfunctions, which are discussed in Chapter 17.

reaching the entrance of the vagina. Great self-control is demanded of the male partner in this method. Coitus interruptus may be used at any time and is always available if no other method is convenient. In developing countries such as Turkey and Poland, 30% of all married couples use this method (Hatcher et al., 1990b). Unfortunately, it has a failure rate of approximately 18% (Table 8-2). Both the man and the woman can become anxious while using this method. The man must try to always be in control, and the woman may be concerned that her partner might not withdraw in time.

Table 8-4 summarizes the approximate costs and the advantages and disadvantages of all the common contraceptive methods discussed in this chapter.

Postcoital Contraception

As long as condoms break, inclination and opportunity unexpectedly converge [to produce unprotected sex], men rape women, diaphragms and cervical caps are dislodged, [and] pills are lost or forgotten, we will need morning-after [postcoital] birth control. Our birth control technology is imperfect, and human behavior is imperfect. . . .

Hatcher et al., 1990b, p. 423

In the cases stated above, unprotected intercourse carries a probability of pregnancy. A woman in any of these situations has several options. Medications containing synthetic estrogens or progestins (or both) may be taken within 72 hours of unprotected intercourse to prevent implantation, but they are considered emergency methods and should never be used as a regular form of contraception. These medications, such as Ovral (high estrogen and progesterone levels) and high-dose progesterone-only pills carry the same risks as oral contraceptives. The synthetic estrogen diethylstilbestrol (DES) is no longer approved for use in the United States as a postcoital contraceptive.

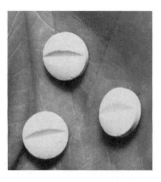

RU 486 is a progesterone antagonist that induces menstruation, thus preventing implantation, or if implantation has occurred, causes the zygote to be sloughed off with the uterine endometrium. RU 486 is currently unavailable in the United States.

The drug RU 486 antagonizes the actions of progesterone and has been used extensively in Europe to induce early abortions. Even if available in the United States RU 486 would not be the drug of choice as a postcoital contraceptive; Ovral is preferred immediately following unprotected intercourse (Hatcher et al., 1990b).

In limited cases the insertion of a copper-containing IUD within 5 to 7 days of unprotected intercourse prevents pregnancy, most likely by preventing implantation, although the actual mechanism of action is in doubt (see the preceding discussion of IUDs). IUDs should not be used for nulliparous women, women with previous multiple sexual partners, women who have been raped, or women who have a recent history of pelvic inflammatory disease (Hatcher et al., 1990b).

RISK OF CONTRACEPTION VERSUS PREGNANCY

What about health risks from the various contraceptive methods? Many physicians believe that a comparison of the relative safety of different contraceptives must include a consideration of the risk of illness or death associated with any unplanned pregnancies that occur when a contraceptive method fails. Mishell (1981) takes this medical approach and states, "Unwanted pregnancy is a disease and should be treated as such. Treatment of this disease—as of any disorder—

TABLE 8-4 Theoretical and Actual-Use Failure Rates* and Costs of Contraceptive Methods

Method	Approximate cost (yearly)	Advantages	Disadvantages
Tubal ligation	$500-1,000†	Permanent and effective	Some risk in procedure; permanent
Vasectomy	$150-300†	Permanent and effective	Permanent
Combined oral contraceptives	$150	Highly effective; no loss of spontaneity; protection against pelvic inflammatory disease	Cost; possible side effects
Mini-pill	$150	Highly effective; no loss of spontaneity	Cost; possible side effects
Condom (with vaginal spermicide)	$130-150	Easy to purchase and use; protection from STDs	Loss of spontaneity; loss of sensations
Condom	$100	Easy to purchase and use; protection from STDs	Loss of spontaneity; loss of sensations
Intrauterine device	$30-100†	Effective; no loss of spontaneity	Possible side effects including infections and sterility
Diaphragm (with vaginal spermicide)	$50	Easy to use; no side effects, STD protection	Must be inserted before intercourse
Vaginal spermicidal foam	$30-50	Easy to purchase and use, STD protection	Messy; loss of spontaneity
Vaginal spermicidal suppositories	$40-50	Easy to purchase and use, STD protection	Messy; loss of spontaneity
Contraceptive sponges	$160	Easy to purchase and use, some STD protection	Cost; some loss of spontaneity
Fertility awareness methods (natural family planning)			
Calendar method only	None	No cost; accepted by religions that prohibit contraceptives	Poor effectiveness; prolonged abstinence
Basal body temperature method	$15	Little cost; accepted by religions that prohibit contraceptives	Prolonged abstinence; time consuming
Cervical mucus method	$15	Little cost; accepted by religions that prohibit contraceptives	Prolonged abstinence; time consuming
Coitus interruptus	None	No cost	Poor effectiveness; can lead to anxiety
Douching after intercourse	None-$25	None	Ineffective
Chance—no protection and sexually active	None	None	Ineffective
Norplant implant	$300-600	No loss of spontaneity	Irregular cycles, problems with removal

Data from Hilgers, Prebil, and Daly, 1980; Kleinman, 1985; Hatcher et al., 1990b.
STD, Sexually transmitted disease.
*Presented as number of pregnancies during first year of use per 100 fertile women.
†One-time costs.

TABLE 8-5   Annual Deaths in U.S. Women Not Using or Using Contraceptive Methods

Method or condition	Number of deaths					
	15-19 yr	20-24 yr	25-29 yr	30-34 yr	35-39 yr	40-44 yr
Barrier/abortion	<1	<1	<1	<1	<1	<1
Intrauterine device	<1	<1	1.2	1.5	1.8	2
Pill—nonsmoker	1.5	1.5	1.3	1.9	5	6.5
Pill—smoker	1.6	1.6	1.6	10.8	13	58.9
No contraception (pregnancy and birth complications)	5.5	5.9	7.5	14	20.5	22

Modified from Tietze, 1977.

Deaths in women not using contraception are deaths caused by pregnancy and birth complications. Deaths for other women are related to the particular method of contraception used. All abortions were done during the first 3 months of pregnancy when the risks are lowest and when barrier method (condom or diaphragm) failed. Numbers are total deaths per 100,000 women in 1 year. All social classes and races are included in the data.

carries with it both benefits and risks. In 1976 the death rate among women of all ages, social classes, and races during childbirth in the United States was 77 deaths per 100,000 women (Tietze, 1977), and later studies report a similar death rate (Hatcher et al., 1990b). Table 8-5 shows that at all ages deaths from complications of pregnancy and childbirth exceed deaths from the use of contraceptive methods. The only exception is for women over the age of 40 who smoke. Many believe that the risk of death from contraceptive methods should be compared with the death rate of childbirth. This is what Mishell means by "benefits and risks." The major benefit of effective contraception is the prevention of pregnancy and medical problems associated with childbirth. The risks are the side effects, both minor and serious, caused by the contraceptive method.

One additional point concerning Table 8-5 involves access to high-quality medical care. Good prenatal care and competent care at birth reduce maternal mortality. The converse is also true. Poor or no prenatal care and poor health facilities contribute to maternal mortality.

PSYCHOLOGICAL AND SOCIAL ASPECTS OF CONTRACEPTIVE USE

There are over 11 million teenagers in America today who have sexual intercourse from time to time. No more than 20 percent of them use contraceptives regularly. The result is 700,000 unwanted pregnancies a year, followed soon after by 300,000 abortions, 200,000 out-of-wedlock births, 100,000 hasty and often short-lived marriages and nearly 100,000 miscarriages.

Byrne, 1980

More recent figures indicate that teenagers had 350,000 abortions in 1984, 345,428 in 1985 (Centers for Disease Control, 1989), and approximately 382,000 in 1990 (Hatcher et al., 1990b).

When numerous contraceptive methods are available and sex education is taught in many schools, why do so many unplanned pregnancies occur? The answer to this question goes beyond simple knowledge of contraception and sex education. It involves attitudes and feelings about certain aspects of sexual behavior. As we grow, we acquire both positive and negative feelings about sexual matters. We learn that sexual behaviors such as masturbation are pleasurable, but at the same time negative beliefs surface about subjects such as sexual pleasure, nudity, and masturbation. This mixture of positive and negative attitudes produces individual patterns of sexual attitudes and behaviors that have been labeled **erotophobia** and **erotophilia** (Byrne, 1980). These two words describe attitudes of individuals at either extreme of the sexual continuum. Erotophobes disapprove of premarital sex, think sex is unimportant, believe it should always be linked to love, consider erotica potentially harmful, dislike oral-genital sex, disapprove of birth control clinics and abortion, do not discuss sex at home, and rate themselves as sexually conservative. Erotophiles hold beliefs at the opposite extreme. Of course, most individuals fit somewhere between these two extremes (Fisher et al., 1988).

Byrne and his colleagues have found that a person's sexual attitudes affect contraceptive practices. Byrne (1983) has listed five conscious steps employed in effective contraception:

1. Accumulation of accurate information about contraception
2. Admission that there is a good probability that sexual intercourse is possible; that is, if we do not admit this, we will not be prepared
3. Obtainment of the contraceptive device or medication or information about contraceptive methods
4. Communication with sexual partners about contraception so someone will be responsible
5. Correct use of the chosen contraceptive measure

erotophilia
(i ro' tuh PHIL ee uh) Set of attitudes and behaviors that characterize a sexually liberal individual.

erotophobia
(i ro' tuh FOH bee uh) Set of attitudes and behaviors that characterize a sexually conservative individual.

Contraception should be a decision shared between partners.

Teenagers are not the only group that does not always use contraceptives for the preceding reasons. Many unmarried women in college avoid the use of contraceptives for exactly the same reasons (Byrne, 1980; Gerrard, 1982). Byrne found that of a sample of 91 undergraduate college women who stated that they were "sexually active, less than one third said they always used contraceptives, and more than one third never did. This was true even though half of them, contraceptive users and nonusers alike, had undergone the frightening experience of believing they were pregnant" (Byrne, 1980).

How can the number of unwanted pregnancies be reduced? Sex education courses, both formal and informal, family discussions about sexuality and contraception, and positive attitudes about sexual behaviors to lessen guilt and anxiety about natural sexual functions seem to be the answer (Milan and Kilmann, 1987). Sex education information in the schools and at home should be accurate and should include a discussion of the consequences of unwanted pregnancies and explicit details about obtaining and correctly using each type of contraceptive method.

STERILIZATION

sterilization
Process by which the male or female reproductive tract is altered so the individual cannot produce offspring.

Sterilization is considered a permanent form of contraception for men and women. An estimated 12 to 15 million people in the United States use this method to prevent unwanted pregnancies (King and Zabin, 1981). Sterilization is now the most popular form of contraception, used by 51% of married couples in the United States (Hatcher et al., 1990b). It surpasses oral contraceptives, which formerly were the most widely used method of married couples in the United States. The change probably reflects reactions to the inconvenience and fear of side effects linked to IUDs and oral contraceptives (Fliegelman, 1986). Birth control pills still rank as the most popular method among unmarried women, with 48% of single contraceptors using this method (Bachrach and Mosher, 1984; Hatcher et al., 1990b).

Sterilization is an effective method of contraception: theoretical failure rates are 0.1% to 0.2% or 1 to 2 pregnancies per 1,000 women per year, and actual-use rates range from 0.15% to 0.4% (Table 8-2). As with any surgical procedure, certain risks are involved. Depending on the procedure, the mortality from female sterilization procedures (also known as tubal ligations) is approximately 3 deaths per 100,000 women, a rate greater than that associated with vasectomies (King and Zabin, 1981; Hatcher et al., 1990b). Major complications of female sterilization procedures include damage to the intestines, bleeding, and infections; in vasectomies they are bleeding and infection.

Female Sterilization

tubal ligation
(TOO buhl ly GAY shuhn) Female sterilization procedure that involves blocking or cutting the fallopian tubes.

Female sterilization involves blocking or cutting the oviducts so that eggs produced in the ovaries are prevented from meeting sperm deposited in the vagina. This procedure is commonly called **tubal ligation** or "tying the tubes," even though the tubes are usually sealed rather than tied (Figure 8-7). The earliest method of female sterilization, which is still used, involves making an incision through the abdomen, or in rare cases through the back wall of the vagina, to locate the oviducts. Both oviducts are either cut and tied or cauterized

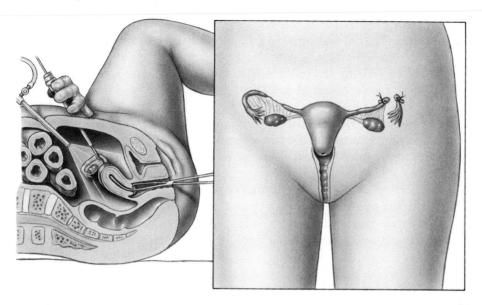

FIGURE 8-7
Tubal ligation involves a
procedure that prevents the
egg from traversing the fallopian tubes. This can be
done by either cutting or
cauterizing the tubes. The
most common way is
through the endoscope with
electrocautery equipment.

shut. In cauterization, tissue is coagulated or destroyed by a chemical or heat. This surgical procedure requires hospitalization and the use of general anesthesia.

At the present time **laparoscopic surgery** is the most common procedure of female sterilization. A general anesthetic is administered, and a small incision is made through the navel. A gas such as carbon dioxide is introduced through the incision. This expands the abdominal cavity and makes more space for the physician to work. The physician then inserts an endoscope, an instrument with its own light source that allows the physician to view the abdominal cavity. A second incision is usually made at the pubic hairline, and the physician introduces the cauterizing instrument through this incision. While looking through the laparoscope, the physician locates the oviducts and cauterizes them shut. This procedure is also known as "band-aid" sterilization because the incisions are covered with adhesive bandages. The woman may return home the same day. The cauterizing instrument can also be introduced with the light source and viewer, in which case only one incision is made. When the procedure is done through the back wall of the vagina, it is called a vaginal tubal ligation. Rarely, this procedure is done through an abdominal approach, which carries less risk of infection (Hatcher et al., 1986).

New procedures for female sterilization have been developed recently. They are called hysteroscopic procedures and involve surgery that can be done in the physician's office. With the woman under local anesthesia, the physician passes an instrument (a hysteroscope) similar to an endoscope through the vagina, cervix, and uterus up to where the oviducts enter the uterus. A cauterizing instrument is passed through the hysteroscope, and the oviducts are sealed shut with the cauterizing instrument where they join the uterus. No incisions are used in this procedure. Since hysteroscopic techniques are difficult and expensive and have low success rates in terms of producing sterility, they are not commonly used in the United States (Hatcher et al., 1990b).

laparoscopic surgery
(LAP uhr uh skop′ ik) Surgical procedure in which an endoscope, a small tubelike instrument that contains a light and optical system, is inserted through incision in abdomen and allows physician to view the oviducts and other structures.

Another recent advance in female sterilization is the sealing of the oviducts with a latex material (called a tubal plug). The physician approaches the oviducts through the cervix and uterus as in a hysteroscopic sterilization, but instead of cauterizing the tubes shut, the physician forces latex material into the tubes to block or seal them. This experimental method has the potential to be a reversible form of sterilization.

A major side effect of laparoscopic cautery procedures is an increased incidence of ectopic pregnancies, that is, implantation of the fertilized egg outside the uterus. The reason for this is not known. Implantation of the fertilized egg often occurs in the oviducts and represents "true" method failure (King and Zabin, 1981). Thus laparoscopic surgery is easy to perform but carries a risk not associated with other female sterilization methods. Tubal pregnancy must be terminated with surgical intervention, and this carries additional risks that must be taken into account when sterilization methods are being considered.

Male Sterilization

Male sterilization involves the interruption or cutting of the vasa deferentia so that sperm cells from the testes cannot reach the urethra and be expelled during ejaculation. This procedure of cutting the vasa deferentia is known as a **vasectomy** (Figure 8-8). A vasectomy is described in the box on the following page.

A relationship between vasectomy and atherosclerosis (hardening of the arteries) has been suggested in research on monkeys, but a study of human subjects did not find any relationship between vasectomies and blood vessel disease (Walker et al., 1981). Vasectomy procedures should be considered permanent, although reversal is possible in some cases.

vasectomy
(va SEK tuh mee) Male sterilization procedure that involves cutting and/or blocking the vas deferens.

FIGURE 8-8
A vasectomy is a simple procedure in which the vasa deferentia are cut or cauterized shut to prevent sperm cells from being ejaculated. It is done in a physician's office with the patient under local anesthesia.

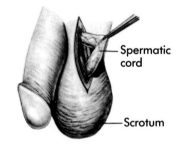

Spermatic cord

Scrotum

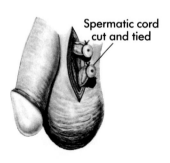

Spermatic cord cut and tied

Vasectomy Procedure as Described by a Physician

The surgical procedure termed vasectomy or bilateral vasectomy (done on both vasa deferentia) is intended to render a male free of sperm in his semen by blocking the vasa deferentia. It is not a technically difficult operation, but since it is in some cases an irreversible step, it should not be done without previous thought and discussion. The operation is usually done in my office using a local anesthetic such as Xylocaine, which deadens the nerves in the area where it is applied. This makes the procedure essentially painless.

I discuss with the patient and his wife (if he is married) before the vasectomy what the procedure involves and its consequences. I tell them it is not an easy procedure to reverse once it is done and answer questions about what a vasectomy will mean for both of them in terms of contraception. I try to make sure they are absolutely convinced this is what they want to do before I perform a vasectomy.

Usually a few days after my discussion with the husband and wife the male arrives for his vasectomy.

He has shaved his scrotum the night before the procedure. I carefully clean the scrotal skin with an antiseptic and inject a small amount of Xylocaine into the scrotal skin near the midline of the scrotum. I palpate (feel) the scrotum until I can identify one of the vasa deferentia. It feels like a partially cooked piece of spaghetti. When I find it, I move it over to the area where I have anesthetized the skin. I hold it there and make a small incision and remove a small segment. I either tie off the two cut ends with suture material and coagulate (seal up) with an electric needle, or I clip the two ends shut with metal clips and coagulate the ends shut. Most of the time both vasa deferentia can be operated on through the one small skin incision. I usually do not use skin sutures on the scrotal incision. An adhesive bandage is applied to the incision, and some type of scrotal support (jock-strap) is worn during the recovery period. The procedure usually takes me 15 to 30 minutes to perform.

After the operation I spend some time explaining to the patient what

he should and should not do for the next few days. He should take it easy when he goes home and use an ice pack on the scrotum for 4 to 6 hours. He can expect a slight amount of bleeding, some swelling, and mild discomfort. He should keep the scrotum dry for 24 to 48 hours after the surgery. He usually can resume his sexual activities in 3 to 5 days, but he is warned that even though the vasa deferentia have been cut, he still has fertile sperm in the distal portions of the vas deferens. The sperm located "downstream" from where the vasa deferentia were cut must be ejaculated out of the body. It will take between 5 to 15 ejaculations before the male has ejaculated all fertile sperm out of his body and has become sterile. There is no way that the patient will know when sterility has occurred, since his ejaculate will look and feel the same to him as it always has. Thus the patient is instructed to bring a sample of semen in a condom to the office after 12 ejaculations. We use the microscope to look for the presence or absence of sperm. I prefer to view at least two consecutive ejaculations without sperm before I assure the patient that he is sterile.

From Michael A. Well, M.D.

CONTRACEPTION AND THE FUTURE

What will birth control be like in the year 2001? In my opinion, the specific birth control methods used in 2001 will most likely be partially indistinguishable from those we have today.

Djerassi, 1981, p. xiii

Djerassi's long-range prediction made in 1981 has turned out to be basically true. However, some novel approaches to contraception might be in use by the year 2001. A list follows.

1. Researchers are experimenting with the use of vaginal rings, the size of a small diaphragm, impregnated with progestins. The rings will be placed high in the vagina and left for 3 days. They are not supposed to interfere with sexual intercourse, and they work by altering the cervical mucus so that sperm cannot pass through the cervix. This product is being tested now and has an actual-use failure rate of 3% (Progestagen-releasing vaginal rings—an update, 1985; Hatcher et al., 1990b).

2. The use of immunological approaches to the control of fertility is being examined. Research is being done on immunizations against placental hormones to interfere with the implantation process. Attempts are being made to develop vaccines that would interfere with the production of anterior pituitary hormones. These could be used in men to control sperm production because the testes are dependent on anterior pituitary hormones to produce sperm cells. In addition, through research in which proteins produced in the testes and located on the sperm surface have been injected into female baboons, it was found that the female produced antibodies against all male baboon sperm for up to 6 months. This approach will be tried on humans next.

3. Drugs that reversibly affect anterior pituitary hormones are being tested. These would interfere with anterior pituitary hormones and gonadal functioning and would thus disrupt sperm production. They are administered by nosedrops or nasal sprays.

4. Research is continuing to learn whether the time of ovulation can be determined based on breath or saliva. Certain sulfur-containing chemicals vary with the reproductive cycle and manifest themselves in the breath and saliva. Levels of some of these substances are 10 times higher at ovulation than at other times in the cycle (Tonzetich, Preti, and Huggins, 1978).

5. Oral contraceptives for men may become a reality. Gossypol, an oil isolated from cotton plants in China, decreases the percentage of motile sperm, increases abnormal sperm, and gradually decreases the sperm count until no sperm cells are produced by the testes. This effect is reversible, and sperm production returns to normal about 3 months after the man stops taking gossypol (Gossypol, a new contraceptive for men, 1979).

6. Scientists are researching the use of drugs that would inhibit the sperm from penetrating the egg and hence prevent fertilization.

ABORTION

abortion
Termination of pregnancy before embryo or fetus is viable. Abortions are classified as spontaneous (natural causes) or induced (brought on by deliberate intervention).

Abortion may be defined as the spontaneous or induced expulsion of an embryo or fetus before it is viable or can survive on its own. A spontaneous abortion is commonly called a miscarriage. This section is concerned with artificially induced abortions to terminate a pregnancy.

Although we can define what an abortion is and describe objectively how it is performed, we can scarcely begin to present the variety of subjective attitudes or beliefs about abortion. The topic of abortion has polarized the U.S. population, although many people hold a position somewhere between the two extremes. One group, usually termed the pro-choice group, firmly believes that each woman should be able to decide for herself whether she

The issue of abortion is one that deeply divides the nation.

wants an abortion. This group feels that no one should control another person's body and that each woman has the legal right to make decisions about her own body. They believe that abortions should be easy to obtain, legal, and safe and available to anyone regardless of economic and social status. The other group, usually called pro-life, takes the position that abortions should never be performed because the fetus is a living being that must be protected and represented. They feel that abortions should not be allowed because abortion is the taking of a human life. They state that from the moment of fertilization a new person has been created and has the right to life.

Religious and ethical views of abortion are discussed in Chapter 24.

On January 22, 1973, The U.S. Supreme Court recognized the right of a woman to choose an abortion as a constitutionally guaranteed right and ruled that the decision should be one between a woman and her physician. Two landmark decisions, *Roe v. Wade* and *Doe v. Bolton*, provided that an abortion decision during the first trimester of pregnancy can be determined by a woman and her physician. An abortion during the second trimester requires input from the state, which regulates the abortion decision in ways that relate to the woman's health. The state may prohibit an abortion beyond the second trimester unless it is essential to the life or health of the pregnant woman.

The legal aspects of abortion are presented in Chapter 22.

In 1976 the Supreme Court further ruled that the right to choose or reject abortion belongs solely to the pregnant woman, and this decision does not need the consent of a parent, spouse, or sex partner. However, even though abortions are now legal, this has not been followed by parallel changes in the moral definitions of abortion. Many people continue to view abortion as an immoral act. "For many women, the guilt feelings which result from the discrepancy between what is legally permissible and moral belief is the price which they must pay" (Zimmerman, 1977).

On July 3, 1989, the 1976 Supreme Court decision was weakened when the Supreme Court upheld state laws prohibiting teen-age girls from having an abortion without first notifying their parents or in some states receiving permission from a judge (judicial bypass). In addition the Supreme Court ruled that states could restrict the provision of abortion services by such measures as requiring waiting periods, mandating specific informed consent, and refusing to pay for abortions for poor women (Hatcher et al., 1990b). This 1989 decision is known as *Webster v. Reproductive Health Services.*

Abortion is such a powerful issue that it is interfering with the unity of East and West Germany (Protzman, 1990). Along with other issues, abortion is a focal point of the unification treaty. At this writing, abortion is illegal in West Germany except under special circumstances and then only during the first 12 weeks of pregnancy. Exceptions are made in the case of rape or when medical or social factors such as poverty prevail. In East Germany abortion is legal in the first 12 weeks of pregnancy and illegal after 12 weeks with the same exceptions as in West Germany.

In the United States various means are used to terminate an unwanted pregnancy. The surgical methods are the most common and include vacuum curettage, dilatation and curettage (D & C), and dilatation and evacuation (D & E). Abortions may also be performed using medications that induce abortion without surgical intervention: prostaglandins, hypertonic saline, and urea.

The death rate from legal abortions is extremely low. Most deaths are due to complications from general anesthesia (Hatcher et al., 1990b). The earlier the abortion, the less the likelihood of complications. Hatcher and associates (1990b) report that for the period 1972 to 1982 the death rate for women whose abortions were performed before or during the eighth week of pregnancy was 0.5 per 100,000 procedures. The death rate was 1.8 per 100,000 at 11 to 12 weeks, 4.3 per 100,000 at 13 to 15 weeks, and 11.8 per 100,000 during or after the twenty-first week. Six deaths were reported in 1985 from all legal abortions performed in the United States (CDC, 1989). The CDC (1989) reports that in 1984 and 1985 approximately 89% of reported legal abortions were performed at or before 12 weeks of gestation, with the rest done at 13 weeks or more of gestation.

Surgical and Nonsurgical Methods Used During Abortions

Vacuum curettage   The most widely used abortion technique in the United States is the **vacuum curettage.** This fairly simple procedure is done while the woman is under local anesthesia (Figure 8-9), and 96% of all legal abortions are done with this technique (CDC, 1989). The cervix is dilated, and a vacuum curette (an instrument consisting of a tube with a scoop attached for scraping away tissue) is inserted into the uterus. The other end of the tube is fastened to a suction-producing apparatus, and the contents of the uterus are aspirated or sucked out.

Vacuum curettage is usually performed during the first trimester of pregnancy, or until 13 weeks of gestation, but may be done up to 20 weeks. The length of the pregnancy is determined from the onset of the last menstrual

vacuum curettage
(kyoor' i TAZH) Method of abortion employing a scraping instrument (curette) and vacuum or suction apparatus.

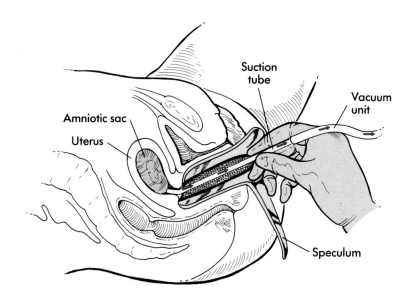

FIGURE 8-9
During vacuum curettage the cervix is dilated and the contents of the uterus are scraped and then aspirated out. This procedure is used to perform abortions up to 20 weeks of gestation.

flow or last missed period. Through 13 weeks of pregnancy this procedure can be done in an office setting with appropriate backup facilities for unexpected medical problems.

Dilatation and curettage   The **dilatation and curettage** (D & C) technique is used in many gynecological procedures, but rarely in abortions (CDC, 1989; Hatcher et al., 1990b). A sharp curette is used to scrape out the contents of the uterus. This technique requires that the woman be under general anesthesia and is used during the first 8 to 20 weeks of pregnancy. The reasons that it is rarely used in abortions in the United States are that it is more painful than the vacuum curettage method, causes more blood loss, and requires larger dilatation (Hatcher et al., 1990b).

Dilatation and evacuation   Dilatation and evacuation (D & E) is a procedure that combines the D & C and vacuum curettage approaches. It is usually done between 13 and 16 weeks of gestation. At this time the cervix needs to be dilated to a greater extent because the products of conception are larger.

Nonsurgical methods   The use of prostaglandins, which are potent biochemical compounds produced by the male and female, to terminate pregnancies has increased in recent years. The prostaglandin compounds may be used intraamniotically (injected into the sac that surrounds the fetus) or inserted into the vagina as suppositories. Prostaglandins are used in second-trimester pregnancies (14 to 24 weeks of gestation). Prostaglandins cause the uterus to expel the fetus.

Hypertonic saline may be used in second-trimester abortions. In such instances the saline is infused slowly into the amniotic cavity to cause fetal death and expulsion of the fetus from the uterus. A hypertonic solution of urea is also employed to induce abortions. The hypertonic solution is infused into the

dilatation and curettage (DY lay tay shuhn/kyoor′ i TAZH) Widely used gynecological procedure in which the contents of uterus are scraped out after cervix is dilated.

dilatation and evacuation (DY lay tay shuhn/i vak′ yoo AY shuhn) Gynecological procedure that combines dilatation and curettage and vacuum curettage.

amniotic cavity and works like the saline solution; it is often used with prostaglandins to ensure fetal death before expulsion from the uterus.

In some abortions, laminaria, a type of seaweed, is used to dilate the cervix. In approximately 6 hours a stick of laminaria inserted into the cervix dilates the cervix sufficiently for an abortion. Oxytocin, a product produced in the posterior pituitary gland and also commercially manufactured, is often used to facilitate uterine contractions. It is commonly used with the D & C method and with hypertonic saline during second-trimester abortions.

RU 486 is a progesterone antagonist that has been used as an agent to induce early abortions. When RU 486 is given orally within 3 weeks of the expected onset of the missed menstrual flow, abortion occurs in 85% of the women (Hatcher et al., 1990b). RU 486 is also used in conjunction with drugs similar to prostaglandins to induce abortions. RU 486 has not been approved for use in the United States, and almost all information about this drug comes from studies in Europe.

As with all medical procedures, health risks are associated with the various abortion techniques. Abortion-related health risks are greatly reduced if the pregnancy is terminated as early as possible, if the patient is healthy, if the clinician is skilled and uses sterile technique, and if the woman is confident in her decision to have the abortion (Hatcher et al., 1990b). The risk of death or serious complications increases dramatically as the gestation period increases. The most common postabortion problems include infection, retained products of conception in the uterus, continuing pregnancy, cervical or uterine trauma, and bleeding.

Long-Term Medical Consequences of Abortion

Long-term postabortion complications are rare when the vacuum curettage method is used. A lengthy review of studies dealing with long-term postabortion complications indicates that an early first-trimester abortion has little if any effect on later fertility, spontaneous abortions, premature delivery, and low birth weight babies (Hogue et al., 1982). Hatcher and associates (1990b) state that any long-term effects that do occur are due to prior abortion technique or age of gestation at which the abortion was performed. Hogue and associates (1982) conclude that postabortion problems are more likely for women who have had one or more previous induced abortions.

Social and Psychological Aspects of Abortion

Who has an abortion? People having abortions vary in age, race, socioeconomic status, and marital status. The one thing they have in common is an unwanted pregnancy. Some situations that lead to unwanted pregnancies occur when contraception fails, when a teenager becomes pregnant and does not want to marry, when genetic defects in the fetus are detected through amniocentesis, and when the woman's health is threatened by the pregnancy. The CDC compiled the characteristics of women receiving legal abortions in 1985, and this information is shown in Table 8-6.

What are the psychological effects of abortion on a woman? Because of the social, medical, and personal aspects of abortions, the psychological response

TABLE 8-6 **Characteristics of Women Obtaining Legal Abortions in the United States in 1985**

Characteristic	Percentage
Age (years)	
≤19	26.3
20-24	34.7
≥25	39.0
Race	
White	66.6
Other (black, Hispanic, etc.)	33.4
Marital status	
Married	19.3
Single	80.7
Number of live births before abortion	
0	56.3
1	21.6
2	14.5
3	5.1
≥4	2.5

From Centers for Disease Control, 1988.

to abortion varies greatly among women. Men are also sometimes affected psychologically by abortion, and in our discussion the implications of abortion for men will be mentioned whenever possible. The first difficult period is the decision-making time when the woman finds out she is pregnant and must deal with the issue of wanting or not wanting an infant.

Although it was published in 1977, Mary Zimmerman's book *Passage Through Abortion: The Personal and Social Reality of Women's Experiences* examined many aspects of the abortion experience that are relevant today (Howe, 1984; Shostak and McLouth, 1984; Kenny, 1986). Zimmerman conducted long interviews with 40 women aged 14 to 39 to create this important book. The typical woman interviewed was single, childless, and between the ages of 18 and 22. Two thirds of the women Zimmerman interviewed were displeased on learning they were pregnant. However, this did not mean that all of them did not want to have an infant. One third of her sample did not want the child; 12 women, or approximately 30% of the total sample, said that they had wanted to have the infant; and the remaining women did not express any feeling about wanting the infant.

> He [male partner] was kind of sad about it [abortion], I think. (Do you mean that he wanted a baby? [question from interviewer]) Yeah, but I did, too. I had to keep telling myself, "This is the right way." I always had to keep telling myself that so I would go through with it.
>
> Zimmerman, 1977, p. 110

A 40-year-old woman sums up her abortion experience as follows:

> I had a 6-year-old daughter at the time that I learned I was pregnant. I was 27 years old. I was using a diaphragm, but diaphragms aren't foolproof. The pregnancy

was unplanned, but I wanted to have the baby, and thought it would be nice to give my daughter a sibling, too. I do not believe in abortion. I really did not think I could go through with it, but I felt I had no choice. My husband did not want any more children, and he absolutely insisted that I have the abortion. He said that if I did not have the abortion, he would divorce me and refuse to pay child support for the baby. I kept the whole thing secret from my daughter until she was a teenager. My aunt, who happens to be in town, accompanied me when I went to have the abortion. I felt sad and empty afterward, and I still carry around a great deal of guilt.

AUTHORS' FILES

After reaching the decision to have an abortion, a decision that almost always involved others, the women had abortions. Zimmerman (1977) found in 33% of the cases a parent or parents went with their daughter when she was to have the abortion. Forty-three percent of the time the male partner in the pregnancy went, and 22% of the time a friend or a sister went to the abortion with the woman. In only one case did the woman go by herself. Nearly half of the women in Zimmerman's study had an abortion experience that could be termed "positive" (easy and stigma free), and slightly less than 25% had what could be termed a "negative" experience (difficult, uncomfortable, and medically questionable). The remainder of the women were categorized somewhere in between. The women in Zimmerman's study had their abortions in a hospital (4 women), in one of two clinics operated by physicians (35 women), or in a doctor's office (1 woman). One clinic was a very modern facility, and the other was an old building in an older section of the city. The women going to the clinic in the old building were more likely to question the legitimacy of the clinic, and they tended to have more negative experiences than the other women in the study.

A Personal Glimpse

Men and Abortions

In their book, *Men and Abortion: Lessons, Losses and Love,* Schostak and McLouth (1984) gave out questionnaires to 1,000 men whose partners had a recent abortion in a clinic in the United States. Some of their written comments from the questionnaire appear below:

I have two small, great and beautiful children, but we really can't handle a third right now—it would really hurt us. (married, 29, Catholic, white)

I can now understand the importance of birth control. I now have a deeper respect for being able to have sex with a woman. (single, 20, college student, white)

I wish it wouldn't seem like we're doing something dirty. (married, 30, Protestant, white)

Killing the fetus may be a crime, but child abuse and neglect is a bigger crime, I feel. (single, 26, Protestant, black)

My strongest concern is for my relationship with my fiancee—emotionally and mentally I believe she will never feel the same about me, herself, children, and life in general. I have already experienced some neglectfulness and deep-seated guilt on the part of my fiancee. (living together, 27, Protestant, white)

It has opened my eyes to life and love. (single, 26, Protestant, white)

When the abortion was completed, how did the women in Zimmerman's study feel psychologically? When she interviewed them a few hours and again a few days after the abortion, slightly more than half (21 women) reported that they were untroubled by the experience:

> Oh, I felt great. . . . It didn't bother me at all. [My husband] said, "My God, you act like you've never been through it." No, I felt super, I didn't have any trouble at all.
>
> Zimmerman, 1977, p. 181

A 20-year-old woman relates her abortion experience at the age of 16:

> I had an abortion when I was 16. I was in this clinic, where you had to wait with all these other girls. They were really upset, crying and hysterical except for me. It didn't bother me at all. I came out happy and smiling and all these girls around me were an emotional disaster. I wasn't in love with the guy who got me pregnant. I told him I missed my period and I never heard from him again, but that did not surprise me. I think if it happened with someone I loved, I wouldn't be able to handle it [the abortion]. Then I'd be an emotional wreck. I don't think I'd be able to go through with an abortion under those circumstances, especially if I was done with college and in a position, financially, to care for a child.
>
> AUTHORS' FILES

The remaining 19 women reported some troubled times following their abortions:

> It's not very pleasant, really . . . it's kind of something I'd just as soon forget. I mean, I'll always remember it, but I'd just as soon forget. (How was that week right after? [question from interviewer]) I had some, I don't know—I was thinking—some nights, you know how you just sit and think? You shouldn't do that sometimes, but I'd just sit and think about it and it would upset me. . . . I don't know, it was just like, "Why did I do it?"
>
> Zimmerman, 1977, p. 183

Feelings about the abortion had diminished somewhat by the time of the interview, 6 to 10 weeks after the abortion. The feelings had not disappeared completely, but most women thought about it less frequently and with less intense feeling.

The reactions of men to the abortion of their child vary from a sense of relief to a feeling of loss. This is, of course, the same continuum of emotions experienced by a woman having an abortion. Some abortion clinics allow the man to hold his partner's hand during an abortion; hence the man and woman are together during this time of potential crisis. Many men feel guilt because they caused the pregnancy and now the partner must bear the physical discomforts and possible pain of an abortion. Some quotations from men who have had a personal experience with abortion appear in the accompanying box.

The abortion experience is an individual one that is influenced by situational and personal factors. The type of medical facility, the attitudes of the clinical staff, and the emotional support from significant people such as parents, male partner, and close friends all have an important effect on the woman having an abortion. These factors influence the medical and psychological outcome of the abortion experience.

SUMMARY

1 There has been a great deal of research and development in the field of contraception in the last 20 years.

2 The topic of contraception is controversial for many individuals. Some feel that they do not always understand and have control over how the method influences their bodies, and hence they do not have control of their bodies. In addition, some methods carry health risks that are of concern to many contraceptive users. Some women feel that they have the total responsibility for contraceptives and that their sexual partners do not share in the decision-making process about contraception.

3 The fertility awareness methods (calendar or rhythm method, basal body temperature method, and cervical mucus method) are used to monitor fertility. They may also be used to avoid intercourse during fertile times in the cycle.

4 Certain behaviors such as abstinence or sex without intercourse remove the need for any types of contraception.

5 Barrier methods of contraception physically block the passage of sperm into the vagina or uterus or chemically inactivate the sperm in the vagina. The barrier methods include the diaphragm, condom, spermicidal vaginal agents, and cervical caps. With almost all barrier methods the device must be inserted or applied at the time of intercourse, and for some individuals this takes away spontaneity. These methods all provide some protection against sexually transmitted diseases.

6 The intrauterine device (IUD) is an object inserted into the uterus through the cervix and is thought to prevent pregnancy by preventing fertilization. It can be left in place for extended periods but has lost popularity in the United States because of past negative side effects.

7 Oral contraceptives are taken by mouth and are very effective in preventing pregnancies by inhibiting ovulation and creating "hostile" cervical mucus, which prevents the sperm from entering the uterus. They have been associated with various minor and major side effects and health risks and do not provide any protection against sexually transmitted diseases.

8 The newest contraceptive device to be approved for use in the United States is the Norplant progesterone implant. It has a low failure rate and needs to be replaced once every 5 years. It is easily removed to restore fertility.

9 Sterilization is a permanent form of contraception for men (cutting the vasa deferentia—vasectomy) and women (blocking or cutting the oviducts—tubal ligation).

10 Artificially induced abortions have legal, biological, and psychological consequences. The abortion experience is an individual one that is influenced by situational and personal factors.

11 The psychological aspects of contraceptive usage vary. If a person feels guilty about his or her sexual activities, he or she is less likely to use an effective method of contraception.

ANSWERS

F A C T
OR
F I C T I O N

1 The most popular form of contraception for married couples is sterilization and for single couples is oral contraceptives.
2 A condom combined with a vaginal spermicide is very effective in preventing pregnancies, with an actual-use failure rate equal to that of oral contraceptives, and provides excellent protection against many sexually transmitted diseases, including AIDS.
3 Being pregnant and carrying a baby to term carries a greater risk than any form of contraceptive.

QUESTIONS FOR THOUGHT ?

1 Define induced abortion, describe the most common medical technique used to perform an abortion, and discuss the controversy that surrounds abortion.

2 Discuss the positive and negative aspects of all of the contraceptive methods discussed in this chapter.
3 Write a letter that only you will see explaining your feelings and beliefs about abortion.

SUGGESTED READINGS

Hatcher, R.A., et al.: Contraceptive technology, ed. 15, New York, 1990, Irvington Publishers, Inc. This is the definitive reference on contraception. It is updated each year and explains, in a technical manner, all you could ever want to know about contraception. It is for the person who really wants to study the options before making a decision about contraception.

Shostak, A., and McLouth, G.: Men and abortion: lessons, losses and love, New York, 1984, Praeger. Although the name implies that the book deals only with men, it includes both male and female perspectives on abortion as a personal experience. The men tell how they interacted with their partners to reach the decision and describe their feelings before, during, and after the abortion.

Howe, L.: Moments on Maple Avenue: the reality of abortion, New York, 1984, Macmillan, Inc. Maple Avenue was the address of a clinic that performed abortions, and the author tells us what happened there. This is an excellent book, written in a style that grips the reader.

CHAPTER 9

Sexual Behaviors

What is the most sensitive, most erotic and most powerful sex organ in the human body? Now think for a moment before you answer. No, it's even more sensual than the genitals or the skin. It's the mind, of course. The mind is the most erotic part of the body. The mind is amazingly powerful. The mind can make fair sex good and good sex great. The mind can enhance physical sensations, create relaxed environments and can visualize images of techniques and modes of sexual expression that people might like to try.

J.E. STEINHART
Sexology Today, p. 50

So far we have focused primarily on the biological aspects of human sexuality. As was mentioned in Chapter 1, human sexuality includes a behavioral dimension as well. We will turn our attention in this chapter to that dimension—actual sexual behavior. We broadly define sexual behavior as all of those activities and behaviors that produce sexual excitation. According to this definition, solitary activities, such as sexual fantasies and masturbation, and interpersonal activities, such as kissing, touching, sexual intercourse, and oral-genital stimulation, are all sexual behaviors.

In recent years a great deal of attention has been paid to sexual behavior in our culture. Magazine articles, books, and television and radio programs have been devoted to topics such as how to increase one's sexual pleasure, how to satisfy one's partner, and how to keep a long-term sexual relationship from becoming dull and routine. This trend in media coverage suggests that there is a great deal of interest and concern about sexual behavior. In this chapter we will be discussing many of the most common solitary and interpersonal sexual behaviors.

SOLITARY SEXUAL EXPRESSION

When we think of sexual behavior, we tend to think of interpersonal sexual activity. However, if we define sexual behavior as activities that produce sexual excitation, we also have to include solitary sexual activity. Solitary sexual activity includes sexual thoughts, fantasies, and masturbation. These behaviors are often referred to as self-stimulation or autoeroticism.

Sexual Fantasies

As was mentioned, sexual fantasies are a form of **autoeroticism.** In sexual fantasies the individual either recalls erotic, sexually stimulating episodes that occurred in the past or imagines sexually arousing situations. Erotic or sexual fantasies are common. Kinsey and his associates found that 84% of men and 67% of the women in their studies reported having sexual fantasies (Kinsey, Pomeroy, and Martin, 1948; Kinsey et al., 1953). Some individuals have fantasies while engaged in other sexual activity; for example, many individuals report having sexual fantasies when they are masturbating or engaged in sexual intercourse. Others have fantasies in the absence of additional sexual activity; for instance, a person might fantasize while driving to work or while sitting through a boring lecture.

autoeroticism
(au toh i ROT i siz′ uhm)
Sexual self-pleasuring.

Dr. Ruth: Sexuality in the Media

This sexual advice column written by Dr. Ruth Westheimer, a psychosexual therapist, is an example of our culture's concern with sexual behavior.

Q. I don't mind giving oral gratification to my lover, but I don't like him giving it to me. This may sound funny, because I know you hear more from women who don't want to give it to men, and you tell them to do nothing they don't want to when it comes to sex.

But I don't like him doing it, and the trouble is that he is insistent on it. I think he has the idea that I ask him to forget it because he isn't doing it well, which is not the case. I don't want him to do it at all. I am happy with everything else in our sex life, and I have orgasms during intercourse just like the heroines of paperback romances. How do I get my hero to give up on this?

A. Flattery may not get you everything you want, but it usually makes it easier. Tell him—and this is the truth, so you don't have to cross your fingers—that he is a terrific lover and you have a great and rare thing with him because only 30% of American women have orgasms during intercourse.

It is common for the woman to have an orgasm before or after intercourse, and that is a great pleasure and perfectly healthful, permissible and so on. But he makes it possible for you to have orgasms during intercourse, and that is what you like best at present—you aren't really interested in his giving you oral stimulation.

I would leave it open about the future so far as this activity is concerned, because it won't be a final rejection of what he wants to do for you. By the way, I do hear more often from women who don't want to give oral gratification, but I know that many, many women feel as you do. And nowhere is it written in stone that lovers have to do anything to keep up with the style of the times.

The sample used in Hunt's sexual survey is presented in Chapter 2.

Hunt (1974) found that some themes in sexual fantasies tend to be reported by both men and women. The most common fantasy was that of having sexual intercourse with a loved one. As can be seen in Table 9-1, 75% of the men and 80% of the women interviewed by Hunt reported having had such a fantasy. The second most common fantasy was that of having sexual intercourse with a stranger. Somewhat less common fantasies were having sex with more than one person of the opposite sex at a time, being forced to have intercourse, forcing someone else to have intercourse, and having sex with someone of the same sex. The frequencies with which each of these fantasies were mentioned by males and females are presented in Table 9-1. Hunt's results indicate that men and women tend to have the same types of fantasies.

TABLE 9-1 Common Themes in Sexual Fantasies

Fantasy	Males (%)	Females (%)
Having intercourse with a loved person	75	80
Having intercourse with strangers	47	21
Sexual interaction with more than one person of opposite sex at the same time	33	18
Doing things you would never do in reality	19	28
Being forced to have sex	10	19
Forcing someone else to have sex	13	3
Having sex with someone of the same sex	7	11

Data from Hunt, 1974.

A more recent publication on sexual fantasies did not find the same results as those of Hunt (1974). Arndt, Foehl, and Good (1985) found that the most common fantasy involves somebody paying a great deal of sexual attention to the person having the fantasy. Women tend to have romance involved in their sexual fantasies, while men have more physical pleasure in their fantasies. One fantasy reported commonly in both Hunt's and Arndt and associates' studies was that of having sex with a stranger. This is one of the most common fantasies for individuals in ongoing relationships. In addition to being a more recent study, the study by Arndt and associates used male and female college students whereas Hunt's subjects were older. The most common fantasies of men and women from the study by Arndt and associates are presented in Tables 9-2 and 9-3.

What purpose do sexual fantasies serve? It is proposed that we have fantasies for several reasons, including feeling more wanted by someone and for sexual stimulation. Our fantasies do not always reflect what we would like to happen in reality. For example, Klinger (1990) cites the case of a woman who likes having various lovers but is afraid of contracting a sexually transmitted disease. She has limited her lovers to a select few, but one of her favorite fantasies involves being with many couples at a large party. Couples are dancing and

TABLE 9-2 Sexual Fantasies in Men

Fantasy	Men (%)
Being excited by a woman's shapely legs	96
Kissing a woman's large breasts	91
A woman forcing her attentions on him	87
Getting a woman so excited that she screams with pleasure	87
A woman telling him she wants his body	86
Two women admiring his nude body	65
Being at a party where everyone is having sex with everyone else	62
Watching a man and woman have sex	60

TABLE 9-3 Sexual Fantasies in Women

Fantasy	Women (%)
A man kissing her breasts	92
A man gently removing her clothes and having sex in a secluded place	90
Being glamorous and having sex with a handsome man	71
Having sex with a man where they risk being caught	65
Being at a party where famous men admire her	64
Wearing skin-tight clothes with men staring at her	51
Having sex with two men at the same time	40
Being at a party and summoning the desirable men, one by one, to have sex with her	33

having sex all over the place. A handsome man approaches her and gives her a deep kiss. Soon they are making love. A short time later a different man repeats the same scenario. This happens over and over again, each time with a different man, in her fantasy. The woman knows her behavior would be dangerous in the real world, but acquired immunodeficiency syndrome and other sexually transmitted diseases do not exist in her fantasy world. As Klinger states, she enjoys the sex and avoids the consequences in her fantasy. It is also of interest that many of the fantasies noted by Hunt (1974) and Arndt and associates (1985) contain taboo people, places, and activities (Dickson, 1989). We imagine sex with a stranger, on a train, in a dentist's chair, or in other places where sex does not usually occur.

Masturbation

The frequencies of masturbation among men and
women at different ages are
presented in Chapter 13.

Gender differences in
the frequency of masturbation are discussed in Chapter 10.

Masturbation may be defined as self-stimulation of the genitals to produce sexual excitement and pleasure. Masturbation is common in both males and females, although it is more frequent in males. Hunt (1974) concluded that masturbation "is utilized regularly and frequently by nearly all single males and a majority of single females, and, though less frequently, by substantial percentages of married men and women."

Hunt (1974) asked individuals why they engaged in masturbation. The most commonly stated reason was to relieve sexual tension. However, other reasons were to comfort themselves, to relieve feelings of loneliness, and to ease other nonsexual tension such as that caused by personal or career problems.

Although masturbation is a common sexual outlet and source of sexual gratification, Hunt (1974) found that it still carries negative connotations for most individuals:

> Yet, aside from pubescent boys (who are often proud of their new accomplishment), most persons who masturbate remain more or less guilt-ridden about it, and nearly all of them are extremely secretive about their masturbating and would be horribly embarrassed to have anyone know the truth. In speaking of the act, practically everyone is jocular, condescending or scornful, thus tacitly implying that it is something he or she could never stoop to. Even though any reasonably well-informed single young man or woman knows that nearly every other single man or woman masturbates at least occasionally, almost no one will admit, even to an intimate friend, that he or she does so. It is far easier to admit that one does not believe in God, or was once a Communist, than that one sometimes fondles a part of his own body to the point of orgastic release.
>
> Hunt, 1974, pp. 66-67

Female masturbation techniques Females tend to masturbate in a variety of ways. However, the object of almost all female masturbation techniques is to stimulate the clitoris (Figure 9-1). This may be done by stimulating the shaft of the clitoris, the glans of the clitoris, the mons pubis, or the vaginal lips (labia minora and labia majora) with the hand or an object. Masters and Johnson (1966) reported that most women avoid direct stimulation of the glans of the clitoris because of its extreme sensitivity.

The clitoris can be stimulated by a number of methods. Many women rub up and down on the clitoral shaft in a circular motion or pull on the vaginal lips, causing the skin that covers the glans to slide back and forth. Some rub

FIGURE 9-1
Female masturbation.

or squeeze their thighs together or massage the entire mons pubis area. Other women use a combination of these methods. Masters and Johnson (1966) found that most women stimulate the entire mons pubis area rather than restricting their stimulation to the clitoris.

Hite (1976) reported that the majority of women (73%) lie on their backs while stimulating the clitoral-vulval area with their hands. Some women (5.5%) indicated stimulating the clitoral-vulval area with their hands while lying on their stomachs, 4% preferred pressing the clitoral-vulval area against a soft object, 3% reported pressing their thighs together rhythmically, 2% indicated using a water massage on the clitoral-vulval area, 1.5% reported inserting objects into their vaginas, and 11% reported using a combination of these methods.

Contrary to what is commonly assumed, these figures indicate that few women insert objects into their vaginas during masturbation; however, a few women are able to reach orgasm in this way. Furthermore, some women can reach orgasm with only breast stimulation (Masters and Johnson, 1966), and a few women (2%) in Kinsey and associates' sample (1953) indicated that they could reach orgasm with fantasy alone.

Some women report using vibrators or other instruments during masturbation (Hite, 1976). Women typically hold the vibrators where they will stimulate the clitoral or mons pubis area, although some women may insert them into the vagina (many vibrators are penis shaped). Some women use dildos (artificial penises) that can be inserted into the vagina when they masturbate. However, as mentioned previously, not many women actually insert objects into their vaginas during masturbation.

Kinsey and associates (1953) found that the average woman reported having an orgasm in a little less than 4 minutes after beginning to masturbate and some have an orgasm in less than 30 seconds. Thus women do not take much more time than men to reach orgasm during masturbation. Men report experiencing orgasm within about 2 or 3 minutes of masturbation (Kinsey, Pomeroy, and Martin, 1948). Although women have been commonly thought to need more stimulation than men to reach orgasm, this appears not to be the case if women are properly stimulated. Masters and Johnson's findings (1966) concur that women who are properly stimulated reach orgasm as quickly as men.

FIGURE 9-2
Male masturbation.

Male masturbation techniques   There is less variety in the masturbation techniques used by men. Masters and Johnson (1966) found that the most common technique is to encircle the shaft of the penis with the hand and move the hand up and down to stimulate the shaft and sometimes the glans of the penis (Figure 9-2). A slow up-and-down motion is often used at the beginning, and as arousal increases the man often moves the hand faster and faster. The tightness with which the penis is held and the speed of hand movement vary from man to man. During ejaculation some men hold the penis very tightly, others slow the hand movement, and others discontinue all penile stimulation. Many men report that continued stimulation of the glans after ejaculation is unpleasant (Masters and Johnson, 1966).

Although the majority of men masturbate with their hand, some men use other methods. A few men report lying on a pillow and thrusting the penis into the pillow. Others indicate using water pressure or thigh pressure to reach orgasm. Some use vagina-like objects into which the penis is inserted. Common household objects may be used to substitute for a vagina, and vagina-like objects are sold specifically for the purpose of masturbating. These vary from artificial vaginas made of various soft materials to life-sized dolls that come equipped with vaginas, anuses, breasts, mouths, and hair.

COMMUNICATION REGARDING SEX

So far we have discussed solitary sexual expression. Now we will turn our attention to interpersonal sexual expression. However, before discussing sexual behaviors that individuals may engage in together, we need to discuss interpersonal communication because it is such an important component of a sexual relationship.

Communication is a vital part of a good sexual relationship. As indicated in the discussion of sexual fantasies and masturbation techniques, different people find different types of stimulation arousing. Not all people respond in the same way to the same kind of stimulation. Communicating one's likes and dislikes to one's sexual partner can greatly increase the likelihood that both partners will receive the kind of stimulation they want and need to be sexually satisfied. Each partner will be able to discover what is pleasurable and exciting or objectionable for the other.

Some common sexual problems could be reduced or eliminated if sexual partners freely discussed their likes and dislikes with each other. For example, many heterosexual women report that they seldom have orgasms during sexual intercourse. Many others indicate that they need a long period of stimulation to have orgasms during intercourse. However, as pointed out in our discussion of female masturbation, the majority of women are able to have orgasms with only a few minutes of sexual stimulation if it is done properly. Therefore if women who have a difficult time having an orgasm during sexual intercourse would tell their partners what kind of stimulation they need to achieve an orgasm, they might begin to be able to have orgasms with their partners.

Many people are uneasy about discussing sexual issues with their partners because people in our culture tend to be shy and inhibited about sexuality and find it difficult to talk openly and freely about sex (Dickson, 1989). Even if they feel free to talk about some aspects of sex, they find it hard to tell their sexual partners what they most enjoy and what they dislike. If such inhibitions were overcome, sexual interactions would inevitably become more satisfying.

Communication can take many forms. Talking directly to one another about sexual preferences is one way. This can be done during a lovemaking session ("That really feels good"), before a lovemaking session ("Do you know what I would really like to try?"), or after a lovemaking session ("Do you know

Good communication between partners is an important part of any sexual relationship.

A Personal Glimpse

Communication During Sex

"It's very important that you be able to communicate your needs to a man in bed. Here's an example that happens somewhat frequently: Your partner has been at it for quite a while, and you're beginning to think he's never going to come. Meanwhile, you're getting dry and swollen and you're in pain. Instead of enduring the pain, I just say, 'I need a break,' or I say, 'This is getting uncomfortable,' and I offer to go down on him instead. If the position we're in isn't comfortable, I say, 'Move over to the left a little' or 'Let's try it this way.' I don't want to make him think that I'm dissatisfied with his lovemaking, which I'm not, so sometimes it helps to make comments that are humorous, but not sarcastic, and still get the point across; that way I don't sound critical. After we have sex, my partner and I talk about new things that we'd like to try sometime." (24-year-old woman, college graduate, accountant)

"I am a lot more open and expressive in bed now than I used to be. I used to feel very uncomfortable talking to a guy (or having him talk to me) about sexual preferences while we were having sex. Of course, there are other ways of communicating. For example, if a guy is on top and he wants his partner to be on top, he just rolls himself and his partner over. If a woman prefers to be on top she can initiate sex by climbing on top of her partner, undressing him, and kissing/fondling his frontal body parts, such that she is on top even before penetration occurs. If a guy is doing something I don't like, I usually just move his hand or move my body into a different position. A critical aspect of sexual communication, in my opinion, is saying or doing things in such a way that your partner feels enlightened rather than criticized or put down. The whole point of communicating your preferences is to make sex more relaxing and more gratifying; if you make your partner feel inadequate, sex is likely to become tense and unsatisfying instead. One other thing I'd like to add is that nothing is more stimulating than to be told when you're driving your partner crazy with excitement, so I always try to let my partner know when he makes *me* feel that way too!" (22-year-old woman, college graduate, management trainee)

"I like to be the aggressor; I'll initiate whatever I want to do in bed, and if he doesn't like it, then he can change it. We find out what each other likes by trying new positions and saying 'Do you like this? Does this feel good?' If he's been on top for awhile and he's getting tired, he either just rolls us over or he says 'O.K., baby, it's your turn.' If he's doing something that's not comfortable for me, I either roll over and get on top to stop him from doing whatever he's doing, or I just tell him that hurts or I don't like that. I definitely think, in any case, that you can feel a lot more at ease and have more fun with someone in bed if you can feel free to talk to each other about what you like and don't like." (20-year-old woman, college student)

"My girlfriend used to not talk to me when we were messing around. When I was going down on her, if she liked the way I was doing it, she'd breathe heavily and move her pelvis along with what I was doing. But when she squirmed a certain way, I thought it was because she felt good, when in fact she did that when I was hurting her or her clitoris got overly sensitive." (19-year-old man, college student)

"When a girl is doing something I like, I make sure I tell her how good that feels. As far as pleasing her is concerned, I try things and I ask her if that feels good, or I just judge from the way she responds." (24-year-old man, no college education, shoe store manager)

"I try different things and pay attention to the way she responds, like the look on her face and her moans. If I don't like something she's doing or if she's hurting me, I tell her. If I want her to roll over or put her leg up towards the ceiling, I say so. After we've had sex, we throw around new ideas and talk about different things that we can try in the future. I definitely think that after a sexual encounter with a person, if you decide you're going to continue having a sexual relationship, then discussing your sexual preferences would improve the quality of that relationship." (18-year-old man, college student) what I liked the most?"). Talking directly about the activities that one finds unpleasant can also be helpful but should be done tactfully (for example, "After I ejaculate, my penis becomes very sensitive, so I don't like to continue thrusting at that time"). Information must be conveyed in a supportive and nonjudgmental manner. Since most people are sensitive about their sexuality, they may feel less comfortable with a partner they perceive as critical of their performance. Such inhibitions can negatively affect the sexual relationship between two people.

Another way in which partners can share information about their sexuality is to share sexual fantasies. Shared sexual fantasies can heighten the arousal of both partners. Sometimes the couple might want to act out their sexual fantasies. This sharing will add variety to the couple's sexual interactions and allow the partners to get to know each other's sexual likes and dislikes better.

One method some couples use to initiate discussions of sexual preferences is to read erotic books, look at erotic photographs, or view erotic videos. Reading or viewing such erotic material together often facilitates conversation about sexual issues, increases sexual arousal, and introduces new sexual behaviors the couple may want to try.

Sexual communication does not have to be verbal. Partners can indicate to their partners what they like and dislike nonverbally. Moving a partner's hand is an excellent way to show what one would like him or her to do. It is also easy to show a partner what is enjoyable by the way one moves, moans, or sighs. Moving a partner's hand away if the partner is rubbing an area that is too sensitive or irritated is a way to indicate to the partner what one dislikes. Again, this should be done tactfully so as not to inhibit or discourage one's partner, which could negatively affect the sexual relationship.

The ability to communicate one's sexual preferences in an open, positive, and supportive manner greatly increases the enjoyment one can get from sexual interactions with another person. Without such communication a sexual relationship is unlikely to be as enjoyable.

Foreplay or Shared Touching

As indicated earlier, the term *foreplay* can be misleading. Perhaps shared or mutual touching might be more accurate. Foreplay implies that it always precedes something, usually sexual intercourse, whereas many couples end their sexual activities with mutual stimulation of the genitals either manually or orally. Thus foreplay might comprise the entire sexual encounter. For couples who are not ready in their relationships to engage in sexual intercourse, foreplay might be the ultimate in sexual stimulation and mutual affection.

The behaviors usually considered in a discussion of foreplay or share touching are kissing or mouth-mouth stimulation, touching, and oral-genital sex.

Kissing

Kissing is one of the most common sexual behaviors. Of course many individuals kiss to show affection in settings we would not necessarily call sexual. When intended to be affectionate but not sexual, kisses are placed on the lips, cheek, or forehead.

Kissing is a widely practiced sexual behavior.

Kisses can also be sexually arousing. Kisses that are intended to be arousing may be placed on the lips, and the lips may be left closed or may be opened. In kisses in which the lips are open the partners may nibble on each other's lips, explore each other's mouths with their tongues, and suck on each other's tongues. Kisses may also be placed anywhere on the body: ears, neck, hands, feet, breasts, navel, and genitals.

Within a sexual encounter many people consider kissing to be one of the most intimate acts. Blumstein and Schwartz (1983) found that couples kiss somewhat less when they feel emotionally removed and when they are feeling a lot of tension over matters that have nothing to do with sex or affection.

Touching

The skin has been called our major extragenital sex organ by many authors (e.g., Comfort, 1972; Masters and Johnson, 1980). The term *erogenous zones* usually refers to areas of the skin that are very sensitive and may lead to sexual excitation when stimulated. The genitals in the male and female and the breasts, particularly the nipples, in the female and some males are the most obvious examples, but erogenous zones can be found all over the body, depending on the individual and the particular circumstances of the sexual situation. For many people, the lips, neck, and inner thighs are erogenous zones; however, the inner surface of the forearm, ears, armpit, arch of the foot, and many other skin surfaces can also be erogenous zones. Each individual has his or her own response to touching. Communication between partners can establish which skin areas produce the greatest amount of sexual excitement when touched.

Tactile stimulation of the skin is part of all sexual contacts between individuals; however, as Masters and Johnson point out, it is not solely a means to an end:

> But for the man and woman who value each other as individuals and who want the satisfaction of a sustained relationship, it is important to avoid the fundamental error of believing that touch is a means to an end. It is not. *Touch is an end in itself.* It is a primary form of communication, a silent voice that avoids the pitfall of words while expressing the feelings of the moment. It bridges the physical separateness from which no human being is spared, literally establishing a sense of solidarity between two individuals. Touching is sensual pleasure, exploring the texture of skin, the suppleness of muscle, the contours of the body, with no further goal than enjoyment of tactile perceptions.
>
> Masters and Johnson, 1980, p. 253

Hence touching, which includes hugging and caressing, is a form of sensual pleasure for both partners. The person being touched and the person doing the touching are in harmony with each other. There is a simultaneous combination of pleasant feelings and sensual pleasure.

Manual Stimulation of the Male Genitals

Thus far we have considered touch as a sexual stimulant in a general sense. Now we will turn to a discussion of manual stimulation of the male genitals. A good technique to begin with is to do the same thing that men typically do when they masturbate. Since most men masturbate in essentially the same way, such stimulation will be arousing for many men.

Many techniques can be used to produce an erection if a man does not already have one. One way is to roll the penis between the palms of the hands. Another method involves applying firm pressure with one finger at the midpoint between the base of the penis and the anus. The penis or penis and testicles can also be stroked or rubbed.

Once an erection is obtained, hand stimulation usually consists of using the thumb and forefinger or the entire hand to encircle the penis. The hand or fingers can then be moved up and down on the shaft and glans. Many men do not like direct stimulation of the glans because of its sensitivity.

Although the stimulation techniques mentioned are sexually stimulating for most men, it is important that partners communicate about their individual likes and dislikes. With communication, partners can tailor their stimulation to make it maximally arousing for their partner and satisfying for themselves.

Manual Stimulation of the Female Genitals

There are many ways to stimulate a woman's genitals. Since women masturbate in a variety of ways, it appears that there is less consistency in what is arousing to women than in what stimulates men. Thus we cannot describe a way of stimulating a woman's genitals that will be arousing for all women. However, there are some general types of stimulating with which one might begin. By paying attention to the type of stimulation to which the woman is most responsive, the partner can change the technique to better satisfy the woman's particular preferences.

Comfort (1972) provided the following description of manual stimulation of the female genitals:

> For preparation as well as orgasm, the flat of the hand on the vulva with the middle finger between the lips, and its tip moving in and out of the vagina, while the ball of the palm presses hard just above the pubis, is probably the best method. Steady rhythm is the most important thing, taking it from her hip movements, and alternating with gentle lip stretching—then [touching] . . . clitoris and its hood with the forefinger or little finger, thumb deeply in the vagina.
>
> Comfort, 1972, pp. 118-119

Although this technique is good to begin with, it is important to pay attention to what appears to be most arousing for the individual partner and to modify the technique of the basis of such feedback. Just as the glans of the penis is sensitive, the area around the clitoris is also sensitive. It can be irritated if it is rubbed in the wrong way, too hard, or without lubrication.

A woman's partner might also ask how she masturbates and then try to stimulate her in the same way she stimulates herself. In this way the partner can find out how to better stimulate the woman. The sharing of such information typically happens as intimacy develops. In the first sexual interactions the woman's sexual partner will have to try to find out what the woman finds arousing by the trial-and-error method. It is important to remain sensitive to the feedback that is given in terms of verbal statements, moans and groans, and movements.

In addition to manual stimulation of the genitals, most women find stimulation of the breasts arousing. The breasts can be massaged, kissed, or sucked. Many women find the nipple and area around the nipple to be particularly sensitive. Again, different women are aroused by different stimulation. Paying attention to the verbal and nonverbal feedback given during breast stimulation will allow one to determine what is particularly arousing to an individual woman.

Other Sexual Stimulants

In addition to kissing, touching, and manual stimulation of the genitals, other factors can add to sexual arousal. For example, what one wears before and during a lovemaking session can be very stimulating. Many women wear sexy lingerie to enhance arousal. Men also can wear underwear that is sexually stimulating. Some individuals respond to scents such as perfume and after-shave lotion. Others are more likely to be aroused by the natural odors of the body than by artificial scents. Partners need to instruct each other in the odors and scents they find most arousing.

What is said during lovemaking can also be stimulating. Some people like to have their partners talk explicitly about sexual activities—for example, about what they want their partners to do to them or about what they are going to do to their partners. Some like to tell and be told sexual fantasies while making love. Others like it best when their partners talk about how they are feeling during sexual interaction. Some find it most arousing when their partners talk about love and affection rather than talking in a more sexually explicit manner. Partners need to learn about each other's likes and dislikes through verbal and nonverbal communication.

Smells, clothing, and verbalization are all aspects that can be sexually stimulating. Environmental factors can also enhance a sexual encounter. For example, some people find that candlelight and music enrich a sexual setting. Others find it exciting to watch their own sexual interactions in a mirror. As was mentioned previously, some individuals read erotic stories, look at erotic pictures, or view erotic tapes before a sexual interaction.

ORAL-GENITAL SEXUAL ACTS
Cunnilingus

Cunnilingus translated from Latin literally means "to lick the vulva"; it refers to oral stimulation of a woman's genitals. Blumstein and Schwartz (1983) found that of the married and cohabiting couples they studied, 93% reported that they had engaged in cunnilingus. This rate is higher than that found in Kinsey's studies of sexual behavior in the 1940s and 1950s. Thus it appears that cunnilingus is becoming much more common in our culture, although possibly people are just more willing to report engaging in cunnilingus today.

Cunnilingus may be performed in a variety of ways. The following is a description of how cunnilingus might be performed between a man and a woman, but the same techniques may be used by two women:

> The man generally begins by kissing and fondling the inner thighs or the mons veneris, then kissing on the outside of the vaginal lips, arriving at the point where he puts his tongue inside the minor vaginal lips and moves it in various ways. He may begin by locating the clitoris and moving his tongue from side to side across it, slowly at first, then moving at a more rapid speed. He may move his tongue

cunnilingus
(kun' uh LING guhs) Sexual stimulation of the female genitals using the mouth and tongue.

upwards from the entrance of the vagina to the clitoris and then across the clitoris. He may explore the clitoral shaft. . . . The man may then stiffen and harden his tongue and insert it into the vaginal opening itself in imitation of the penis, or he may use the same licking motions at the opening of the vagina. The insertion of one or two fingers into the vagina while he is licking or sucking the clitoris produces high stimulation for the woman.

Sadock and Sadock, 1976, p. 213

As with all sexual acts, there are individual differences in what is enjoyable and a woman's partner may discover what is best by way of verbal and nonverbal communication. Not all women enjoy cunnilingus. Blumstein and Schwartz concluded:

We feel that vestiges of former sexual taboos may also inhibit women from enjoying cunnilingus. Some women have learned to be self-conscious about their genitals and are embarrassed to allow a man the kind of intimacy oral sex entails. Even a woman who escapes negative feelings about her own body may still be uneasy receiving oral sex. . . .

If her partner performs cunnilingus, a woman may view it as submissive on his part and feel it is unseemly for him. Some women who do perceive that their partners have no other motive than to give them pleasure are still uncomfortable with the practice.

Blumstein and Schwartz, 1983, pp. 234-235

However, many women enjoy cunnilingus as illustrated in the following statements from one woman interviewed by Blumstein and Schwartz:

I encourage him to go down on me. . . . I think it is the best thing in the world. For me it is the most erotic act. I'm surprised at how much I enjoy it. I can say to him that I'm not interested in sex tonight, but that's the way to change my mind. It feels warm, so good, and he's so good at it and he enjoys it so much. Which is why I enjoy it.

Blumstein and Schwartz, 1983, p. 236

Fellatio

fellatio
(fuh LAY shee oh) Sexual stimulation of the male genitals using the mouth and tongue.

Fellatio translated from Latin literally means "to suck"; the term is commonly used to refer to oral stimulation of the male genitals. Fellatio, like cunnilingus, is a common sexual practice. Blumstein and Schwartz (1983) reported that only 10% of their sample of married and cohabiting couples said that they never engaged in fellatio. Comparison with Kinsey's figures (1948; 1953) suggests that fellatio is a much more common practice today than it was in the 1940s and 1950s. Perhaps more people admit to performing fellatio today.

Fellatio may be performed in a number of different ways. The following is a description of how fellatio might be performed between a man and a woman, but the same techniques may be used by two men during fellatio:

This oral-genital activity has many variations. The woman kneels at the side of the man, who lies on his back, or she kneels between his legs and, perhaps after a short manual caressing, licks the glans of the penis, the shaft of the penis itself, and sometimes the testicles, gently taking them partly into her mouth. . . . She may then move her mouth, being careful that the penis is not scratched by her teeth, down to the base of the penis or part way down. She may move gently at first and then more rapidly. Or she may change from the in-and-out motion that imitates the thrusting of the penis in the vagina and move her tongue in a circular fashion around the top of the penis or flick her tongue horizontally across the corona. . . .

To bring a man to orgasm through fellatio, the woman then proceeds to encourage a deeper penetration of the penis into her mouth and returns to the familiar in-and-out motion. She may keep her hand loosely encircling the base of the penis and move the penis up and down rhythmically in a motion involving hand and mouth, the hand acting in a sort of milking fashion as it tightens around the penis. Thrusts deepen, bringing the penis well back into the mouth.

Sadock and Sadock, 1976, pp. 213-214

During fellatio, some men ejaculate into their partner's mouth, but this is considered a high-risk behavior in terms of the transmission of the virus responsible for the transmission of AIDS. Some partners may catch the semen in their mouth and then spit it out; others swallow it. Many men like the sensation and find the idea of ejaculating into their partner's mouth exciting. However, some individuals do not like to have their partners ejaculate in their mouth; many perform fellatio to stimulate their partner, but when the partner is about to ejaculate, they turn to intercourse or manual stimulation to bring their partner to orgasm. Some couples use a very thin condom during fellatio so the man can ejaculate into the condom while his penis is in his partner's mouth. The use of a condom is a good safeguard against the possible transmission of the virus that causes AIDS.

There is some indication that oral sex is more important to the sexual satisfaction of men than it is to the sexual satisfaction of women. Blumstein and Schwartz (1983) found that heterosexual men who perform cunnilingus on their partners and who receive fellatio are more satisfied with their sex lives and their relationships than are men who do not. The same was not true for women; those who engaged in oral sex were not more satisfied with their sex lives than those who did not. Furthermore, homosexual men are more likely to engage in fellatio than homosexual women are to engage in cunnilingus. Blumstein and Schwartz reported that men also have fewer ambivalent or negative reactions to oral sex than women:

> It is easy to understand why men like to receive oral sex. They learn very early in life that their genitals are a source of great pleasure. And post-Freudian society accepts the idea that a penis is valued by both men and women. Men often think their genitals should be the main focus of the couple's sex life.
>
> Blumstein and Schwartz, 1983, p. 231

One of the men in the Blumstein and Schwartz sample expressed his feelings about oral sex in the following way:

> Oral sex is very important to me. I enjoy the sensation so much. I've never liked dealing with female inhibitions against it. . . . I like a combination of intercourse and oral sex. But for pure physical pleasure, oral sex is better. . . . I think oral sex is a bit less intimate because you're not face-to-face, kissing. But it is more exciting in a peak physical sense.
>
> Blumstein and Schwartz, 1983, p. 231

The ingestion of semen has been implicated in the transmission of the virus causing AIDS. See Chapter 19.

Simultaneous Mutual Oral Sex

Some couples like to take turns performing oral sex on each other. Such turn-taking allows a partner to concentrate on either providing or receiving pleasure. However, other couples like to perform oral sex on each other at the same

FIGURE 9-3
Mutual oral-genital stimulation.

time. This can be accomplished by either lying side-by-side or having one partner over the other with each partner's mouth opposite the genitals of the other. This position (Figure 9-3) is known as *soixante-neuf* (69) because of its likeness to the position of the 6 and the 9 in the number 69.

ANAL SEXUAL ACTS

A variety of sexual behaviors involve the anus. These acts are often engaged in by homosexuals but are used by many heterosexual couples as well. Anal intercourse refers to the penetration of the anus by the penis. Since the entrance to the anus is richly endowed with nerves, this area can be very sensitive and sexually arousing. However, a couple needs to be careful in performing anal intercourse for many reasons. The anal sphincter muscle tends to be tight and when stimulated tightens even more. As a result, when the penis is inserted, it can be painful if care is not taken. Furthermore, the anus has no natural lubrication of its own, which increases the possibility of pain. If the penis is forced into the anus without lubrication, it can sometimes cause injury and the tearing of tissue. Usually anal intercourse can be accomplished without discomfort if precautions are taken. A lubricant such as K-Y Jelly (but never petroleum-based lubricants such as Vaseline, since they weaken condoms) should be used around the opening of the anus and on the penis. The anal sphincter muscle should be relaxed with manual stimulation before the penis is inserted. The penis should be inserted slowly and carefully. The partner whose anus is being penetrated should be as relaxed as possible. The thrusting of the penis should be controlled and gentle. Once the penis has been in the anus, it should not then be put in the vagina unless it is washed first. Bacteria that are normally found in the anus and rectum can cause infections when introduced to the vagina.

In addition to anal intercourse, other sexual activities involving the anus are fairly common. Some couples insert a finger into the anus; this can be done alone or while performing some other sexual activity such as oral sex or stimulation of the clitoris or penis. Objects such as slender vibrators can also be inserted into the anus. **Anilingus,** in which the tongue is used to stimulate the anus area, is also used by couples. Of course, couples can use just their hands and fingers to stimulate the area around the anus. Again, objects or fingers that have been in the anus should not be inserted into the vagina without being washed first.

anilingus
(ay' nuh LING guhs) Erotic stimulation of the anus with the tongue.

HUMAN SEXUALITY

Anal intercourse for both heterosexual and homosexual individuals carries many risks (Hearst and Hulley, 1988). Anal intercourse has been associated with the transmission of the virus responsible for AIDS and hepatitis B, and for this reason the occurrence of anal intercourse will probably decline during the next several years. Anyone engaging in anal intercourse should use a latex condom and never use a petroleum-based lubricant. In addition, after anal sex has occurred, the genitals should be washed thoroughly before vaginal or oral sex begins.

Anal intercourse is one of the highest-risk sexual behaviors implicated in the transmission of the virus causing AIDS. See Chapter 19.

SEXUAL INTERCOURSE

Sexual intercourse, or coitus, refers to the insertion of the penis into the vagina. The term *coitus* is derived from the Latin word *coitio,* which means "a coming together or a joining together." Although the term *intercourse* is usually used to refer to the insertion of the penis into the vagina, it is also used to refer to oral intercourse or anal intercourse in which the penis is inserted into the mouth or the anus, respectively.

sexual intercourse
Coitus; the insertion of the penis into the vagina.

Numerous love manuals, such as the famous *Kama Sutra* and *The Perfumed Garden,* have described and illustrated many positions that can be used for sexual intercourse. Most of these are variations on four basic positions.

Face-to-Face Positions

Man-on-top position The man-on-top position (Figure 9-4) is the one most commonly used in our culture (Masters, Johnson, and Kolodny, 1986). It is often called the missionary position. Polynesians who preferred a squatting position coined this term because it was the position used by the missionaries

FIGURE 9-4
Couple in man-on-top, face-to-face position during sexual intercourse.

in their villages (Comfort, 1972). In this position the woman lies on her back with her legs spread apart. The man lies on top of the woman and usually supports his weight with his arms. The penis may be placed manually into the vagina by the man or the woman, or the man can guide the penis into the vagina by moving his body so that the penis enters the vagina by itself. Once the penis is in the vagina, the male usually makes thrusting movements while the female moves her pelvis away from and toward the erect penis as it thrusts in and out of her. Many couples use this pattern, but there are infinite variations. Sometimes the woman moves her body in a circular motion beneath the man, or the man makes subtle thrusting motions instead of vigorous thrusting with the penis.

One advantage of the man-on-top position is that the man and woman can look at each other, kiss each other, and hug each other while making love. It is a position that allows the man freedom of movement so he can easily achieve the type of stimulation he wants. The man can touch and kiss the female's breasts. The woman can reach down with her hands and fondle the testicles of the male or touch his back, neck, and other body areas. This position is not the best one when either the male or woman is obese or when the woman is in the advanced stages of pregnancy. Both of these conditions would prevent insertion of the penis into the vagina or make it difficult.

Woman-on-top position The woman-on-top position is used less frequently than the man-on-top position (Masters, Johnson, and Kolodny, 1983), probably because it has traditionally been assumed that the man should be the more active partner. When the man is on top, he tends to be the one in control of how the lovemaking proceeds. In recent years women have begun to take a more active role in lovemaking and as a result are more likely to assume the woman-on-top position in which the woman is in greater control.

In the woman-on-top position the man lies on his back with his legs straight and the woman kneels over his body so that her vagina is placed in the region of the penis (Figure 9-5). The penis is guided into the vagina by the male or the female. The female then lowers herself onto the erect penis. After the penis

FIGURE 9-5
Couple in face-to-face position during sexual intercourse with the woman on top.

HUMAN SEXUALITY

is within the vagina, some women move themselves up and down on the erect penis while they are still in a kneeling position above the male. Other women slowly stretch out so that their legs are between those of the male; the woman then supports her weight with her arms in a position exactly the reverse of the man-on-top position (Sadock and Sadock, 1976). Many couples start out in the man-on-top position and carefully roll over to the female-on-top position, keeping the penis in the vagina.

When the woman is on top, she can control the movement of the couple and the depth of penetration of the penis within the vagina. The female can move up and down, in a circular motion, or sideways on the penis. If she moves forward, she will exert pressure on her clitoris. The woman can also remain still while kneeling above the man and allow the man to move his pelvis up and down to achieve thrusting of the penis within the vagina.

The woman-on-top position probably provides the greatest degree of clitoral stimulation for a woman (Sadock and Sadock, 1976). The female has more control, and more clitoral stimulation is possible. The man has his hands free to touch the woman's breasts, clitoris, buttocks, and face.

Side-to-side position Another of the four basic positions is the side-to-side position. In this position the man and woman lie on their sides, facing each other (Figure 9-6). The man and woman are free to kiss and look at each other. One of the advantages of this position is that neither partner puts his or her weight on the other; thus both partners have freedom of movement. This allows both the man and woman to get the kind of stimulation they want to a greater extent than either the man-on-top or woman-on-top position. This position, however, does not allow deep penile penetration. It is often used when a woman is in an advanced state of pregnancy (Sadock and Sadock, 1976).

FIGURE 9-6
Couple in side-to-side position during sexual intercourse.

FIGURE 9-7
Couple in rear-entry position during sexual inter-
course.

Rear-Entry Positions

In rear-entry positions the man faces the woman's back. The man then puts his penis in the woman's vagina from this position (Figure 9-7). This can be done with the man and woman lying on their sides, with the woman lying face down and the man lying on top of her, or with the woman on her hands and knees and the man kneeling behind her.

With rear-entry positions the man's hands are free to touch almost all parts of the woman's body. The woman can also reach backward and touch the man's testicles. Rear-entry positions provide psychological and physical stimulation that is different from the stimulation provided in face-to-face positions (Sadock and Sadock, 1976).

Variety of Intercourse Positions

Couples who use only one position are most likely to use the man-on-top position. However, many couples tend to use more than one position. A comparison of Kinsey and associates' data (1948, 1953) on sexual behavior in the 1940s and 1950s with Hunt's data (1974) on sexual behavior in the 1970s suggests that the use of varied sexual positions has increased in recent decades. Their data indicate that younger couples use a greater variety of positions than older couples. The fact that couples have become more experimental suggests that the variety difference according to age may be a result of cultural change. Because people in our culture seem to be becoming more experimental, younger people are more likely to be experimental than older individuals who have more well-established ways of behaving. Thus it is not clear that there is an actual change according to age in the use of varied sexual positions. There is no reason to expect that as couples get older, they will tend to reduce the variety of sexual positions they use.

ORGASM

Many of the sexual behaviors that we have described may result in orgasm for either or both of the partners. Orgasms vary for men and women. When a man has an orgasm, it is usually accompanied by an ejaculation of semen, although these two events do not necessarily occur together. Men generally have only one orgasm at the time of ejaculation, which is followed by a refractory period in which they cannot be sexually aroused. In contrast, some women are capable of having multiple orgasms within a relatively short period.

Men are more likely to have an orgasm in the typical sexual encounter. In part this is because women often do not get the most effective stimulation in sexual interaction with a partner. In many cases this is not a problem for the woman. She can enjoy a sexual encounter even if she does not have an orgasm. If her partner seems upset that she has not had an orgasm, she will feel that she has to work at having an orgasm, even though she may be content not to have one. Each partner should be able to interact sexually without feeling that he or she has to have an orgasm. Sexual behaviors can be pleasurable and rewarding for their own sake, not just because they result in orgasm.

Given our awareness that women are capable of multiple orgasms, some individuals have come to expect that they should give their partners multiple orgasms or have multiple orgasms themselves. This kind of thinking leads to the view that the woman should "work" at having multiple orgasms and that her partner should "work" at giving them to her. The belief that sex is work can detract from the couple's enjoyment of their sexual interactions. Sex should be relaxing and pleasurable and not something about which couples need to feel anxious and worried.

This does not mean that couples should not try to please each other. It is desirable for men and women to try to find out what their partners might enjoy by learning as much as they can about sexuality and by talking to their partners about their likes and dislikes. Of course, they should try to please their partners as best they can. If what they do does not result in multiple orgasms or orgasms in each and every sexual interaction, they do not need to become anxious about their sexual performance.

Some couples work to have simultaneous orgasms. This is often difficult to achieve and is certainly not necessary for both partners to have satisfying sexual interaction. Couples might consider it pleasant when it happens but not something that marks the success of their sexual interaction. If they think they need to achieve simultaneous orgasms, sex will become work and therefore be less enjoyable. Since a man usually loses his erection after having an orgasm, one strategy that couples who want to achieve orgasms through sexual intercourse might use is to allow the woman to have an orgasm or multiple orgasms first, and then the man might have his orgasm. Of course, if the man has his orgasm first, he can try to stimulate his partner to have an orgasm in some other manner.

AFTERPLAY

Afterplay can be defined as whatever a couple does immediately following a sexual interaction (Halpern and Sherman, 1981). In a short questionnaire Halpern and Sherman asked 234 married and unmarried couples between the ages

A description of the biological events that occur at orgasm and a discussion of differences in orgasmic capacities between males and females are presented in Chapter 4.

Gender differences in orgasm are described in Chapter 10.

Gender differences in afterplay preferences are presented in Chapter 10.

Afterplay is a peaceful time for many couples.

of 17 and 63 what they did after a sexual encounter. The subjects were from a variety of geographical and socioeconomic backgrounds.

Halpern and Sherman found that the three behaviors occurring most frequently following sexual intercourse were sleeping, maintaining physical contact, and talking. Other behaviors that were mentioned somewhat less frequently were getting clean, dry, and comfortable; listening to music; having more sex; eating and drinking; smoking; watching television; reading; and working.

The following are statements—one by a man and one by a woman—about what they do, or like to do, after making love:

> If I stay in bed, I usually hold or stroke my partner and we talk for a while—about our lovemaking or other shared experiences. I feel that talking about intercourse has rewards that are at least as great as the act itself, with tangible benefits to both partners. The difficulty is breaking the taboo that exists; we don't talk about sex often enough. Talking about sex is like the act itself—once you start doing it, you don't want to stop. (man, 25)

> When my husband and I share good moments after sex, be it hugging each other, laughing together or talking and enjoying a favorite food, I go to sleep feeling good and wake up feeling good. The feeling of well-being that lingers after sex continues on into the next morning. Frequently I wake up feeling relaxed and warm and, at first, not even quite sure what's causing the sensation. (woman, 32)
>
> Halpern and Sherman, 1981, pp. 43-44

CROSS-CULTURAL ASPECTS OF SEXUAL PRACTICES

As we conclude this chapter, a brief look at the sexual practices and attitudes of other cultures is helpful to place our own attitudes in perspective. We are products of our culture, and our sexuality reflects social and cultural influences.

Because sexual behaviors are shaped by social and cultural influences, observing other cultures is of interest to understand how their behaviors differ from our own. In this section we shall see that behaviors we consider common in our society are nonexistent in others and behaviors that we usually consider unacceptable are commonplace in many cultures.

> There are cultures, such as the Manus in Papua, New Guinea and Inis Beag [a small island off the coast of Ireland that was given the pseudonym Inis Beag] in which all aspects of sex are considered ugly and shameful; even marital intercourse is so degrading and sinful that it is justifiable only in the service of procreation. At the opposite extreme, there are other cultures in which sex and everything related to it is beautiful, and beauty, in general, is erotically associated with sex.
>
> The emotions usually associated with sexual arousal and gratification are not the same in all societies, and correlations that are considered aberrant in our culture may represent the norm for other peoples. For instance, among the Gusii of Kenya, sexual arousal occurs only in combination with hostility and antagonism. . . . Normal intercourse has to take the form of ritualized rape if it is to provide mutual gratification.
>
> Behavior patterns condemned and punished in one society are encouraged and rewarded in another. Premarital intercourse is virtually enforced by some peoples and heavily penalized by others. All adolescent males in one South Pacific society are urged to be exclusively homosexual before marriage, whereas such behavior is considered shameful and punished in other cultures.
>
> Beach, 1978, pp. 115-116

Sexual acts and sexuality vary tremendously from culture to culture. The act of sexual intercourse reflects cultural conditioning. In the United States the most common position for sexual intercourse is the man-on-top position. Intercourse usually occurs in the privacy of a room within a house during the evening or early morning hours. Coitus in the man-on-top position is the usual pattern in most societies studied (Ford and Beach, 1951). Another common position in some countries starts with the man squatting or kneeling in front of a woman who is lying on her back. The man draws the woman toward him so that her legs straddle his thighs. Penetration occurs in this position. Lying side by side is the preferred position for sexual intercourse in several cultures such as the Masai (Africa) and Kwakiutl (North American native), and intercourse in the sitting position with the woman squatting over the man is the dominant pattern in only two of the 190 societies studied by Ford and Beach (1951). Coitus with the male entering the female from the rear did not occur as the dominant practice in any of the societies Ford and Beach studied.

The cross-cultural information on masturbation is less clear than the material on sexual intercourse. However, some generalizations can be made. Many societies do not approve of male masturbation because they attribute weakness and debility to loss of semen (Davenport, 1978). Other societies, especially African cultures, disapprove of masturbation because it is thought to cause weakness of spirit and body and increased proneness to personal disaster. In spite of this, 40% of all males in these societies have practiced masturbation and 20% practice it regularly (Davenport, 1978). It is interesting that these ideas are similar to those prevalent in the United States 100 years ago. The Bala of the Congo are tolerant of both male and female masturbation and mutual manual stimulation among boys.

Many societies consider masturbation a juvenile practice or habit. When it is continued after marriage, it is thought to be a childish practice and is discouraged.

The information on female masturbation is sparse. One society, the Kgtala-Tswana of Africa, strongly disapproves of masturbation for males of all ages but is more tolerant of masturbation by females and even condones it for married women who are neglected by their husbands (Davenport, 1978).

SUMMARY

1 Solitary sexual expression refers to sexual behaviors that occur with oneself. These behaviors include sexual thoughts, fantasies, and masturbation.
2 Masturbation, or self-stimulation of the genitals to produce sexual excitement and pleasure, is a widespread practice. In spite of this, many individuals, because of personal and religious convictions, feel guilty about the use of masturbation as a sexual outlet and source of sexual gratification.
3 Females use a variety of masturbatory techniques; males use fewer methods of masturbation.
4 Interpersonal communication, verbal and nonverbal, is an important component of a good sexual relationship. By discussing likes and dislikes partners can discover what each finds pleasurable or objectionable.
5 Foreplay, or shared touching, can involve kissing, touching, manual stimulation of the genitals, or oral-genital sex.
6 Common erogenous zones are the lips, neck, and inner thighs; areas such as the inner surface of the forearm, ears, armpit, and arch of the foot can also be erogenous zones.
7 Cunnilingus, or the oral stimulation of a woman's genitals, and fellatio, the oral stimulation of a man's genitals, are common sexual practices.
8 There are four basic positions for sexual intercourse: man on top, woman on top, side to side, and rear entry.
9 Younger couples use a greater variety of positions than older couples.
10 A pleasurable and satisfying sexual interaction does not have to involve orgasm.
11 The three most common afterplay behaviors are sleeping, maintaining physical contact, and talking.

F A C T
OR
F I C T I O N

ANSWERS

1 The percentage of married and cohabiting couples engaging in oral-genital sex has been steadily increasing over the past 30 years.
2 If properly stimulated, women can reach orgasm during masturbation as quickly as men.
3 In many cases we do not want to act our fantasies. We often have fantasies about situations that would be dangerous in reality, such as multiple sex partners at the same time. Many of us would be too concerned about sexually transmitted diseases to engage in sex with total strangers, but in a fantasy the diseases do not exist.

HUMAN SEXUALITY

1 What purpose do you think sexual fantasies serve for you? For others of the opposite sex?
2 Discuss sexual communication using specific techniques from this chapter and your own experiences if applicable.
3 Why is the term *foreplay* a poor term for many sexual encounters?
4 Discuss the advantages and disadvantages of each of the sexual intercourse positions presented in this chapter.

SUGGESTED READINGS

Anand, M.: The art of sexual ecstasy, Los Angeles, 1989, Jeremy P. Tarcher, Inc.
   An illustrated book about sexual techniques that may be of interest to both the sexually experienced and the inexperienced.
Friday, N.: Men in love: sexual fantasies, New York, 1980, Dell Books.
   This is a book of men's fantasies as told to the author. The fantasies in this book may be familiar to many men.
Dickson, A.: The mirror within: a new look at sexuality, New York, 1989, Quartet Books.
   An interesting book that looks at human sexuality, particularly women's sexuality. It discusses women's fantasies, sexual behaviors, and relationships to men and other women. There is also an excellent section on sexual communication.
McKay, M., Davis, M., and Ganning, P.: Messages: the communication book, Oakland, Calif., 1983, New Harbinger Publishers.
   This book deals with all aspects of communication, including sexual communication. It is well written and easy to read.

Gender Differences in Behavior

FACT
OR
FICTION

1
There are no behavioral differences between male and female infants during the newborn period.

2
If properly stimulated, women are able to be aroused and reach orgasm as quickly as men.

3
Men tend to be more satisfied with the typical sexual interaction than women.

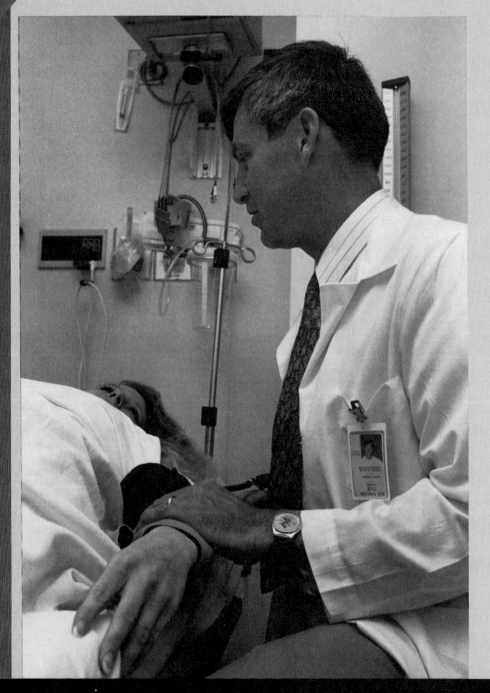

A growing number of men are entering nursing, a profession in which women predominated in the past.

Woman wants monogamy;
Man delights in novelty,
Love is woman's moon and sun;
Man has other forms of fun.
Woman lives but in her lord;
Count to ten, and man is bored.
With this the gist and sum of it,
What earthly good can come of it?

DOROTHY PARKER
"General Review of the Sex Situation"

The preceding chapter was concerned with sexual behavior. This chapter deals with behavioral differences between men and women in both sexual and nonsexual behavior. Many commonalities in the behavior of men and women exist. In fact, there are probably more similarities than differences. However, the commonalities are not emphasized here. Rather, we focus on how the behavior of males and females differs.

Some of the differences may result directly from biological variations between males and females, whereas others may be purely a result of the ways in which males and females are socialized. Still others may be caused by an interaction between biological factors and environmental influences. These biological and environmental influences affect both gender roles and gender identity. Gender roles are culturally determined prescriptions for how males and females are supposed to behave. Gender identity refers to the individual's identification as either male or female. This chapter begins with a discussion of gender roles, followed by a discussion of gender identity and then a discussion of gender differences in sexual behavior.

GENDER ROLES

As was mentioned previously, **gender roles** are the culturally prescribed behaviors for males and females. In all cultures the prescribed behaviors for males and females, or gender roles, differ. In our own culture it has traditionally been assumed that women are supposed to be more passive, emotional, dependent, and concerned about others, and men are expected to be more assertive, rational, independent, and competitive.

It has been suggested that gender roles are based in part on biological differences between the genders. For example, there is evidence that prenatal exposure to male sex hormones increases aggressiveness in both males and females (Reinisch, 1981). On the other hand, there is also research evidence that to some extent gender roles are arbitrarily determined. Gender roles differ considerably from culture to culture. Such variation would not be expected if gender roles were determined by biological factors alone. For example, Margaret Mead (1963) reported that the gender roles of the Tchambuli, a tribe in New Guinea, were almost opposite of those of our culture. The women were in charge of fishing, manufacturing, and commerce, and the men were primarily artists—musicians, dancers, and wood carvers. The women shaved their heads and dressed plainly, and the men wore elaborate hairdos and were particular

gender roles
Societal expectations about how males and females should behave.

about their dress. The women were the ones concerned with wealth and power; the men were more concerned with social relations and the details of daily living.

The example of the Tchambuli tribe demonstrates that culture has a definite effect on gender roles. The Tchambuli tribe is the exception; gender roles in most cultures tend to be more similar to those in our own. The most reasonable conclusion, based on the available evidence, is that gender roles are determined in part by biological differences between the genders and by arbitrary cultural influences. Although males and females may be biologically predisposed to behave in certain ways, cultural influences are also important in determining behavior.

CHANGING GENDER ROLES

In our own culture, gender roles have been changing somewhat in recent years. Today most women are employed, and more and more women are beginning to work in fields that were traditionally reserved for men. Women are becoming physicians, attorneys, scientists, police officers, and mechanics. It is also now more acceptable for men to participate in activities that have customarily been considered appropriate only for women. Today men are more likely to participate in cooking, housecleaning, and child care. Some men take pride in being gourmet cooks and others in being the primary caretaker of their children. An increasing number of men receive either full custody or joint custody of their children after a divorce. More men are realizing that they are capable of nurturing and caring for children, a role traditionally reserved for women.

Today more and more women are working in fields that were traditionally reserved for men.

HUMAN SEXUALITY

U.S. military women find Saudi customs perplexing

Cox News Service

AT AN AIR BASE IN SAUDI ARABIA—To launch an F-15, the U.S. Air Force uses "expediters" who rush around the flight line in pickup trucks making sure all the gear is ready. Pilots say Master Sgt. Rhonda, 33, of Florida, is one of the best.

But for the first four days Rhonda was stationed here, she was blocked from doing her job by centuries of desert customs. Because she is a woman, she was not allowed to drive.

Now Rhonda is back behind the wheel. It is a glimpse of how one of the most sex-segregated nations in the world has had to accommodate the U.S. women in the military.

"I went through that for three or four days before they finally let me drive," she said. "I still can't drive over on the other side of the base (where the Saudi pilots are). And when the Saudis come over here, I don't drive."

It is part of the Saudi culture that Americans have found most perplexing since the oil workers and their wives began appearing in the kingdom half a century ago.

One U.S. government handbook on Saudi Arabia said in 1976:

"Saudis assume, often explicitly that men and women are different kinds of creatures. Women are thought to be weaker than men in mind, body and spirit, more sensual, less disciplined, and in need of protection both from their own impulses and from the excesses of strange men. . . .

"The honor of the men of a family, which is easily damaged and nearly irreparable, depends on the conduct of their women, particularly sisters and daughters; consequently, women are expected to be circumspect, modest and decorous and their virtue to be above reproach."

Rhonda's job is helping to make sure the Saudis are still around to enjoy their honor.

It ranges from ordering up jet fuel to fill the F-15 tanks, to making sure there is oxygen for the pilots' air-breathing systems. The Pentagon may not call that a combat job, but the place she works is more likely to be targeted by Saddam Hussein than any of the desert foxholes occupied by the all-male infantry units.

"It's hot and stuffy over here, but I really believe in helping these people," Rhonda said. "They've treated us well, and I'd like to help them too. And we all need gas. It's the only way we can stabilize the economy."

From Wisconsin State Journal, 1990.

It is now more acceptable for men to participate in activities that were once considered appropriate only for women.

In addition to cultural changes in the activities deemed suitable for men and women, alterations have occurred in the kinds of dress and behavior considered appropriate for men and women. It is now acceptable for women to wear pants and for men to wear gold chains. Women can cut their hair short, and men can grow their hair long. In addition, some women are trying to learn to be more assertive, and many men are trying to learn better ways to express their feelings. Thus today it is more acceptable for women to behave in ways that were formerly approved only for men and for men to behave in ways that were reserved for women. As a result, both males and females have more freedom of choice in virtually all spheres of life than was traditionally the case.

At the same time that the culture has been granting a new flexibility in gender roles, psychologists have developed a new system for categorizing individuals with respect to their gender role behavior. Traditionally in our culture we view "masculinity" and "femininity" as two ends of the same continuum; that is, we tend to believe that the more masculine a person is, the less feminine that person is and vice versa. However, Sandra Bem (1981) has suggested that masculinity and femininity should be considered two independent dimensions. According to this view, an individual could be high in both masculinity and femity, low in both, or high in one and low in the other. For example, an individual who is high in both masculine and feminine traits could be a highly competitive professional football player who is also a sensitive, expressive, and supportive husband and father, or a successful neurosurgeon who is also a fantastic cook and nurturant mother.

HUMAN SEXUALITY

ANDROGYNY

Bem proposed that individuals who are high in both masculinity and femininity be called **androgynous.** She suggested that androgynous individuals are marked by a healthy flexibility in their behavior. When the situation calls for it, they act in ways that have traditionally been considered masculine, but at other times they are able to behave in ways that have been regarded as feminine. Such an individual, for example, might act in an assertive fashion when confronted with an unreasonable demand by a boss or co-worker but behave in a tender fashion with a lover or child.

Bem has conducted research to test her hypotheses about androgynous individuals. To carry out her study, she developed a paper-and-pencil test to measure the extent to which individuals are identified with masculine and feminine traits. Her test is called the Bem Sex Role Inventory (BSRI). When an individual takes the BSRI, he or she is asked to rate on a scale from 1 ("Never or almost never true") to 7 ("Always or almost always true") the extent to which a number of traits are characteristic of himself or herself. Some are traits that have usually been considered masculine, others are characteristics that have traditionally been regarded as feminine, and still others are neither masculine nor feminine. Examples of the masculine traits are "aggressive," "assertive," and "ambitious." Examples of the feminine characteristics are "affectionate," "compassionate," and "yielding." Examples of the neutral traits are "happy," "jealous," and "truthful." Individuals who endorse more masculine items than feminine items are said to have a masculine gender role. Individuals who endorse more feminine traits than masculine traits are said to have a feminine gender role. Individuals who endorse approximately equal numbers of male and female traits are said to be androgynous.

Research with the BSRI tends to support the hypothesis that in at least some situations androgynous individuals exhibit greater flexibility than gender-typed individuals. Bem (1975) found that androgynous individuals of both genders were more likely to display both independence under pressure to conform (a stereotypically masculine type of behavior) and playfulness with a kitten (a stereotypically feminine type of behavior) than more sex-typed or gender-typed individuals of either gender. Likewise, Kelly, O'Brien, and Hosford (1981) investigated individuals' ability to use complimentary behavior when the situation warranted it (a behavior thought of as more feminine) and to use refusal when presented with an unreasonable request (a behavior categorized as more masculine). They found that androgynous individuals were indeed able to perform more competently in both situations than were gender-typed individuals. In particular, androgynous males were better able to be

androgynous
Having both masculine and feminine characteristics.

CHAPTER 10   GENDER DIFFERENCES IN BEHAVIOR

287

warmly complimentary than gender-typed males, and androgynous females were more effective in refusing an unreasonable request. Both of these studies suggest that androgynous individuals may in fact exhibit more flexible behavior than gender-typed ones. However, other studies suggest that while androgyny may be beneficial for women, it is less clearly beneficial for men (Taylor and Hall, 1982).

Does the greater flexibility generally found in androgynous individuals have an effect on their sexuality? It may. Results from a number of studies indicate that androgyny is related to positive sexual attitudes and behavior. For example, in one study androgynous individuals of both sexes were found to be more "comfortable" in their attitudes toward sexuality than more traditionally gender-typed individuals; however, the difference between androgynous and gender-typed women was greater than between androgynous and gender-typed men (Walfish and Myerson, 1980). In another study androgynous women reported experiencing orgasms more frequently than more gender-typed women (Radlove, 1983). In a third study androgynous women reported experiencing more sexual satisfaction than more gender-typed women (Kimlicka, Cross, and Tarnai, 1983). While androgynous women appear to be more comfortable with their sexuality, research indicates that masculine males are even more comfortable with sex than are androgynous females (Walfish and Myerson, 1980). Hence, while gender role is an important determinant of positive sexuality, sex is also important. Furthermore, the beneficial effect of androgyny on sexual behavior may be greater for women than for men (Radlove, 1983; Howells, 1986).

Why would androgynous individuals, particularly androgynous women, have more positive sexual experiences than more gender-typed individuals? Presumably their increased flexibility allows them to engage in both the traditionally masculine and the traditionally feminine sexual behaviors. For example, androgynous individuals might be expected to exhibit traditionally masculine behaviors, such as initiating sex and taking an active role in sexual encounters, at the same time that they are able to exhibit more traditionally feminine behaviors, such as being tender and gentle. Such flexibility might be expected to increase sexual satisfaction because androgynous individuals obtain the satisfaction associated with both masculine and feminine types of behavior. For example, women who can be more assertive during sexual encounters (a traditionally masculine trait) may be more likely to experience sexual satisfaction and to have more orgasms because they are able to tell or show their partners what type of stimulation they prefer and to initiate sexual relations when they are in the mood. And men who can be tender and nurturing (a traditionally feminine trait) may be more likely to experience emotional satisfaction, as well as physical satisfaction, in their sexual encounters.

In summary, androgynous individuals are those who exhibit both masculine and feminine characteristics. Androgynous individuals have been shown to be more flexible in at least some situations than more gender-typed individuals. They are able to adopt traditionally masculine behaviors when the situation warrants and traditionally feminine behaviors when the situation warrants. Such flexibility appears to have a beneficial effect on individuals' sexual attitudes and behaviors. Androgynous individuals have more positive attitudes toward sexuality and report experiencing more sexual satisfaction.

GENDER ROLE SOCIALIZATION

How do males and females learn to behave in culturally prescribed ways? From an early age children are taught how they are expected to behave in all areas of life. They are instructed how to dress, eat, read, and interact with others. This process is called **socialization.** The child is "socialized" to live in his or her particular culture. Part of socialization involves teaching males how males are supposed to behave and females how females are expected to act. This process is called **gender role socialization.**

Gender Identity

The child must first learn whether he or she is a boy or a girl; that is, the child must develop a **gender identity.** Most children begin to use gender labels shortly after they begin to talk, at about 18 months. However, they do not have a firm sense of their own gender identity until they are about 2½ years old, and they do not realize that gender remains constant until about 5 to 7 years of age. Before a child realizes that gender does not change, he or she might make such statements as, "When Johnny grows up and becomes a mommy, will he wear dresses just like you?"

Parental Influences

Parents have the first significant influence on their children, and research suggests that parents may begin to treat boys and girls differently at birth (Sedney, 1987). They tend to dress them in different clothing, decorate their rooms differently, and respond to them differently. They are less responsive

socialization
Process by which one learns to behave according to the expectations of one's culture.

gender role socialization
Process by which one learns the cultural expectations for the two genders.

gender identity
Feeling or belief that one is either male or female.

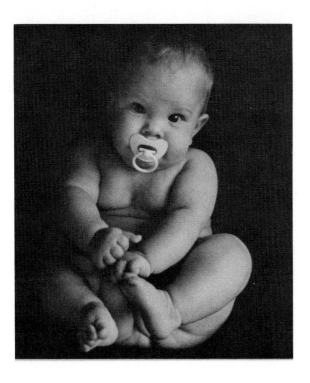

Research indicates that parents treat boys and girls differently from early infancy.

and attentive to girl babies and tend to allow girls less freedom to explore (Block, 1983). Parents also describe their infants differently within the first 24 hours after birth. Rubin, Provenzano, and Luria (1985) interviewed parents of newborn boys and girls. Although the babies did not differ in size, the parents of boy babies described their infants as "big" significantly more often than the parents of girl babies and the parents of girls described their infants as "little," "beautiful," "pretty," and "cute" more often than the parents of boys.

Not only do parents treat their own infants differently depending on their sex, but they also treat other babies differently. For example, Smith and Lloyd (1978) had women who were mothers themselves interact with 6-month-old infants. The infants were randomly assigned gender labels. When the women were told that the infant was a male, the women encouraged the infant to exhibit vigorous motor activity. Frisch (1977) conducted a similar study with 14-month-old infants. When the infants were identified as boys, the adults tended to encourage gross motor activity, such as tricycle riding or playing with blocks. When the infants were identified as girls, the adults were inclined to talk to them or provide them with dolls.

Are there gender differences in the behavior of infants? Yes, it appears that there are even some behavioral differences in newborns. For example, Phillips, King, and DuBois (1978) observed newborns whose sex they did not know for 2 days and recorded their findings. Significant gender differences were noted.

Changes that are occurring in adult gender roles and expectations are evident in children's behavior.

HUMAN SEXUALITY

Boys were awake more often, grimaced more, and showed more low-intensity
activity. There was, however, no gender difference in crying.

By the time children reach the age of about 2 years, the gender differences
in behavior become much more obvious. Clear gender differences in toy and
play preferences appear. Girls prefer to dress up, to play with dolls, and to
act out domestic roles (Giddings and Halverson, 1981; Davie et al., 1984).
Boys, on the other hand, are inclined to be much more active and rough, to
play with toys like cars and trucks, and to play with balls (Giddings and
Halverson, 1981; Davie et al., 1984).

Do parents promote such gender differences? The research suggests that
they do. Parents encourage and reward boys for exploring and being independent, yet they do not encourage, and may actually discourage, such behaviors
in girls. Fagot (1978), for example, observed 2-year-old children with their
parents. She found that girls were encouraged to be "helpers" and to ask for
assistance, and boys were prompted to manipulate objects and explore the
environment. Thus, even though they were not aware that they were doing
so, the parents were teaching the boys to be independent and the girls to be
dependent. Furthermore, Langlois and Downs (1980) found that both mothers
and fathers tend to reinforce sex-typed play in both their preschool sons and
daughters.

In summary, parents treat boys and girls differently from early infancy.
Probably such variations in treatment are responsible for some of the gender
differences in behavior that have been observed in very young children. However, since at least some gender differences have been found in the behavior
of newborns who have not spent much time with their parents, it is also possible
that some gender differences are biologically determined.

Peer Influences

As children get older, their peers begin to have a significant influence on their behavior. Peers, like parents, tend to reward children for gender-typed behavior and punish children for cross-gender behavior. For example, Lamb, Easterbrooks, and Holden (1980) found that preschool and kindergarten children are inclined to punish peers for cross-gender behavior by criticizing them, asking them to stop engaging in such behavior, refusing to play with them, diverting their attention, or physically intervening to stop the behavior. They discovered that such punishments were effective; the children who were treated in these ways by their peers tended to stop their cross-gender behavior almost immediately. These results suggest that peers as well as parents are involved in gender role socialization.

Teacher Influences

Teachers are also responsible for gender role socialization. Serbin and associates (1973) reported that preschool teachers often encouraged boys to do things on their own by giving them verbal instructions when the boys had difficulty completing a task. When girls had difficulty, however, the teachers were more likely to complete the task for them. This type of response does not support independence and competence but rather encourages dependence. Furthermore, preschool teachers tended to encourage gender-typed play and discourage cross-gender-typed play, just as parents and peers do.

Preschool teachers are not the only ones who treat males and females differently. In a study, Sadker and Sadker (1985) found that teachers also treated elementary school boys and girls dissimilarly. They discovered that the boys talked in the classroom three times as often as girls. Girls tended to raise their

Research indicates that teachers encourage sex-type behaviors in boys and girls.

hands and wait to be called on by the teacher, while boys usually called out their answers. These behavioral differences may be a result of the teachers' discriminative treatment of boys and girls. When boys called out their answers without raising their hands, teachers tended to accept their answers. However, when girls called out their answers, the teachers told them that such behavior was inappropriate. Sadker and Sadker concluded that "The message was subtle but powerful: Boys should be academically assertive. . .; girls should act like ladies and keep quiet."

In summary, teachers, as well as parents and peers, play a part in gender role socialization in our culture.

Media Influences

Parents, peers, and teachers are not the only forces that push children toward gender role conformity. In our culture television, books, magazines, and movies contribute to gender role socialization. The discussion in this chapter is limited to television; however, all of the media tend to portray women and men in similar stereotypical gender roles.

Television is an important socialization medium for children. The average school-age child watches television between 3 and 4 hours a day (Liebert and Sprafkin, 1988). Given the amount of time children spend watching television, the material presented has great potential to influence children's attitudes, values, and behavior. How might television affect children's views about sex roles?

Portrayals of men and women on television are often consistent with traditional sex role stereotypes (Atkin, 1982). Television programs have three times as many male characters as female characters; this is true even for children's public television programs such as *Sesame Street* and *The Electric Company*. When males and females interact in television programs, the male is depicted as dominant, giving advice and orders to females. Furthermore, the characteristics of the women who are portrayed on television are not representative of women in general. The women portrayed on television are younger, more homebound, and in lower-status occupations than is true of women in general. Kalisch and Kalisch (1984) also found evidence that television portrayals of the proportion of males and females in occupations are more extreme than is representative of the distribution that occurs in our society. They found that 99% of all nurses on prime-time television are female and 95% of all doctors are male.

Tavris and Wade (1984) made the following observations about the gender roles conveyed by television:

> Not only do male central characters outnumber females, but they get to have most of the fun (McArthur, 1982). Males solve problems, exercise creativity and imagination, give orders, and help to save others, and they are likely to be rewarded for their actions. Females are more deferential, passive, and compliant; instead of issuing orders, they obey them. They are far less likely than males to express an intention to do something and to then follow through. Not all images of males are positive; most villains are male. And not all images of females are negative; female characters often hug and kiss, cooperate with others, and share. But both as heroes and villains, it is the males who have an impact on the course of events.

On adventure shows aimed at children and adults, men portray freewheeling cops, private eyes, and secret agents; women in these shows tend to be interested mainly in romance, their families, or the boss's welfare. Women are also victims— but they are less likely to risk victimization if they are married, which may imply that if women want to be safe and secure, there's no place like home. . . . To land the job of TV heroine, a woman must still be slender, attractive and young. Male adventurers during the past decade, while often attractive (Magnum), have also been fat (Cannon), bald (Kojak), old (Barnaby Jones), or plain (Quincy).

Tavris and Wade, 1984, p. 231

Similar gender role stereotypes are perpetuated by the way men and women are depicted in television commercials. In the early 1980s Mamay and Simpson (1981) reported that women were typically presented in maternal and house-keeping roles or as "glamorous creatures interested mainly in being clean and physically attractive." Men, on the other hand, were often depicted as experts, showing women how to use the products being advertised, while women were rarely shown explaining anything to men. In a more recent investigation Bretl and Cantor (1988) found that many of these stereotypes are still present in commercials but the gap between depicted male and female roles has decreased. While in 1988 it was still true that fewer women than men were portrayed as employed, men were more often presented as spouses and parents with no apparent occupation. Women were still more likely to be presented in domestic settings, using domestic products, although the difference was not as great as it had been earlier. One area in which the gap between male and female roles has not changed in recent years is the percentage of male and female narrators. Consistently over the last 10 years males have been the narrators or "voice of authority" in approximately 90% of all commercials.

Do the gender stereotypes portrayed on television actually affect viewers' behavior or attitudes? A study by Morgan (1982) suggests that they might. In 1975 and again in 1977, Morgan gave teenagers a questionnaire intended to assess sexism. He found that the more the teenagers watched television between the two administrations of the questionnaires, the more likely they were to exhibit an increase in sexist views from the first to the second administration. By viewing more television, the teenagers may have been exposed to more gender stereotypes and, as a result, may have become more gender typed themselves. Since there may have been many other differences between the teenagers who watched television a great deal and those who did not, the finding does not prove that more television viewing increases gender-typed attitudes; however, it is suggestive.

A study conducted by Kimball (1986) suggests a similar relationship between television viewing and gender role stereotypes. Kimball studied children in three different communities. One community received no television, one received only one channel, and one received four channels. The children in the communities that had television exhibited more stereotyped gender roles than children in the community without television. Further, after television was introduced to the community that previously had no television, the attitudes of the children in that community became more stereotyped. Again, these results suggest that watching television may increase gender-role stereotyped attitudes in children.

TRANSSEXUALISM: WHEN GENDER IDENTITY AND BIOLOGICAL SEX ARE DIFFERENT

Most individuals have a gender identity that matches their biological sex. Most males identify psychologically with being a male and most females identify with being a female. For some individuals, however, their psychological gender identity does not match their biological sex. These individuals identify psychologically with the opposite sex. A biological male, for example, may feel that he is a female "trapped in the body" of a male. **Transsexualism** is the term used to refer to this condition. Transsexuals experience gender dysphoria. **Gender dysphoria** refers to (1) discontent with one's biological sex, (2) the desire to possess the body of the opposite sex, and (3) the desire to be regarded by others as a member of the opposite sex (Blanchard, Clemmensen, and Steiner, 1987). Transsexualism is often defined as extreme gender dysphoria that persists for at least 1 year.

The prevalence of transsexualism is unknown, but various surveys of treated individuals in the United States and Europe indicate ranges from 1 of 40,000 to 1 of 100,000 men and from 1 of 103,000 to 1 of 400,000 women (Roberto, 1983). The ratio of men to women treated for transsexualism was 3:1 in the early 1970s, but more recent reports from gender identity clinics in the United States and Europe show an almost equal sex ratio (Roberto, 1983).

Desire for Sex Reassignment Surgery

Since transsexuals do not feel comfortable with their biological sex, many attempt to change their original biological sex to fit their psychological gender identity. In the 1960s and early 1970s physicians began performing sex change operations on such individuals.

When an individual decides to undergo a sex change operation, he or she must go through a long and difficult transition process. The transition involves psychological counseling, hormonal treatment, and major surgical procedures. Shore (1984) describes the procedure in most gender identity clinics as follows. The candidate for sex reassignment (called the client) may be recommended for sex reassignment by a physician, or the client may initiate the process. All requests are evaluated by a "gender identity team," which usually consists of a psychologist, psychiatrist, obstetrician-gynecologist, and various consultants such as endocrinologists, urologists, and surgeons. The team usually follows guidelines used worldwide for the evaluation of transsexuals. The client is given numerous interviews, clinical and sexual histories are taken, and the client completes a series of psychological tests.

Before the surgery clients are expected to live in their new gender role as completely as possible for 1 to 2 years to allow them to develop all of the behaviors of the new sex. This long trial period also gives the clients time to think about the irreversible decision they are making before sex reassignment surgery is begun. The clients are not guaranteed that they will receive surgical sex change procedures, but if they are accepted for sex reassignment, they will be referred to facilities that will carry out the sex change operation. During the time that the client is living in his or her new gender role, various procedures are begun. Male-to-female transsexuals have facial and body hair removed via

transsexualism
(tran SEK shoo uhl izm)
Condition in which individuals feel uncomfortable with their anatomical sex and want to change their sexual anatomy and live as a member of the opposite sex.

gender dysphoria
Situation in which an individual is not content with his or her biological sex, desires to possess the body of the opposite sex, and desires to be regarded by others as a member of the opposite sex.

Transsexuals are discussed at greater length in Chapter 20.

electrolysis and are given female hormones (estrogen or, less often, estrogen plus progesterone) to stimulate breast growth, soften skin, and decrease muscle mass to create a more female appearance to the hips and buttocks. Other physical transformations such as voice pitch and length of hair are accomplished without medical assistance. The female-to-male transsexual is given testosterone (male hormone) to promote the growth of body hair, lower the pitch of the voice, and suppress menstruation.

If the client is accepted for the final stage of sex reassignment, he or she undergoes surgery. This final stage occurs only if the gender identity team feels confident that the person is psychologically stable and can adjust to his or her new gender identity and gender role. The male-to-female transsexual has the penis and testes removed. The sensitive skin of the penis with its nerve endings is used to create a functional artificial vagina sensitive to sexual stimulation. In fact, many male-to-female transsexuals report experiencing sexual arousal and orgasm postsurgically (Blanchard, Legault, and Lindsay, 1987). The female-to-male transsexual has her breasts and internal reproductive organs (ovaries, oviducts, and uterus) removed. An artificial penis is constructed and takes the place of the vagina. This procedure is a difficult one compared with the surgical process of creating an artificial vagina. The penis is constructed from a tube of skin that is usually taken from the abdomen. This artificial penis is not functional in that it cannot become erect or feel tactile sensations; however, sexual arousal and orgasm are still possible if the clitoris is left embedded at the base of the constructed penis. In addition, inflatable implants help some individuals to achieve an erection.

The cause or causes of transsexualism are unknown, but three theories have been proposed. One theory proposes that fetal exposure to excessive sex hormones of the opposite sex influences adult behaviors, including transsexual behavior. No real proof exists for this theory, and much of the work dealing with prenatal hormones and adult behaviors has been criticized because of

A, Genitals of male-to-female transsexual. **B,** Genitals of female-to-male transsexual.

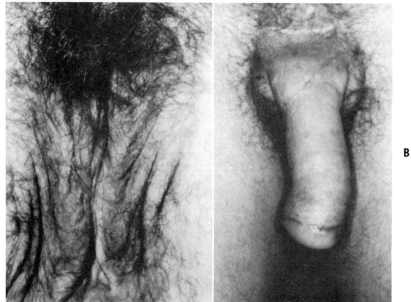

HUMAN SEXUALITY

In the mid-1970s transsexual Renee Richards, formerly Richard Raskind, made headlines when she attempted to enter a women's professional tennis tournament. The question that was raised at the tournament was, should she be allowed to play against women when she is a biological man?

methodological problems and alternative explanations (Quadagno, Briscoe, and Quadagno, 1977; Ehrhardt et al., 1985). A second theory to explain transsexualism states that adult levels of sex hormones are different in transsexuals than in heterosexual males and females and that this hormone difference influences transsexual behaviors. However, many research studies have shown that adult sex hormone levels are the same in transsexuals as in control subjects (Meyer et al., 1986). A final theory to explain transsexualism involves social learning in childhood (Green, 1975). For example, a male-to-female transsexual may have been rewarded for acting like a girl and may have even been dressed in girls' clothing by the family. The family may have treated the child like a girl in all respects, and this behavior by the family influences the child's adult decisions about transsexualism; that is, he develops a gender identity different from his biological sex. However, many transsexual individuals do not report a childhood in which they were treated like the opposite sex, which indicates that although social learning may influence some transsexuals, it cannot be used to explain all cases of transsexualism.

GENDER ROLES IN SEXUAL BEHAVIOR

As in virtually all other areas of human behavior, gender roles exist in sexual behavior. In our culture it has traditionally been considered appropriate for men to be sexually aggressive and for women to be passive. Men are supposed to "do the asking," whether it be asking for a date, proposing marriage, or initiating sexual intercourse. Women are not supposed to take the initiative; rather, they should wait to be asked. Thus men do the choosing and women are only allowed to say yes or no. In addition, men have traditionally been expected to always be interested in, and ready for, sexual interaction. Women,

The traditional cultural expectations for males and females are covered in greater detail in the discussion of adolescent sexuality in Chapter 12.

"The big difference between men and women is
that women dance backwards."

on the other hand, are considered to be relatively uninterested in sexuality. Therefore men are expected to be continually attempting to seduce women and women are thought of as always trying to resist the sexual advances of men. Once men are able to seduce their partners, it has been assumed that they should be the active and dominant participants and women should simply go along with the activities the men initiate. As a result, men have commonly determined when a sexual interaction would occur, what behaviors would be involved, and when the sexual interaction would end.

As is the case for all other gender-typed behavior, gender roles in sexual behavior have been changing in recent years. It has become acceptable for women to be more assertive. Women may ask men for a date, pay for the date, or initiate sexual interactions. Likewise, it is much more acceptable for men to admit that they sometimes like to have women take more initiative in social and sexual interactions. Men do not have to feel that they are not "real men" if their partner is sometimes assertive and they are sometimes passive. Today individuals have more freedom to behave in less restricted ways and to act according to how they feel rather than in prescribed gender roles.

GENDER DIFFERENCES IN SEXUAL BEHAVIOR

Now that we have examined gender roles, it is time to consider differences between males and females in actual sexual behavior. The discussion begins with physiological differences and then moves to behavioral and attitudinal differences.

HUMAN SEXUALITY

Physiological Responses

The work of Masters and Johnson (1966) indicates that the physiological sexual responses of men and women are more alike than was typically assumed in the past. Some of the similarities in the sexual responses of men and women should be mentioned because they are contrary to popular opinion. Among the common characteristics that Masters and Johnson found are the following:

1. With the appropriate stimulation women can be aroused and reach orgasm as quickly as men.
2. Women, as well as men, who do not reach orgasm during a sexual encounter experience discomfort in the genital area.
3. Women have only one kind of orgasm, originating in the clitoris; there is no such thing as a "vaginal orgasm."
4. Men and women experience sexual orgasms in essentially the same way.

In spite of the similarities in the sexual responses of males and females, some differences exist. For instance, men experience a refractory phase following orgasm and ejaculation and women do not have an equivalent phase following orgasm. This means that for a certain time following ejaculation, men are physiologically unable to have another orgasm or ejaculation.

Because they have no refractory period, females have the potential to experience **multiple orgasms.** The ability to have multiple orgasms is defined as the capability to achieve repeated orgasms in a limited time (that is, within a few minutes). In surveys only a small percentage of women describe having multiple orgasms regularly. For example, about 14% of the women interviewed by Kinsey and associates (1953) reported having regular multiple orgasms, and in a survey of *Psychology Today* readers 16% of the women described having multiple orgasms regularly (Athanasiou, Shaver, and Tavris, 1970). The results of these surveys suggest that only a minority of women have multiple orgasms. However, Masters and Johnson believe that most women are capable of experiencing multiple orgasms.

> If a female who is capable of having regular orgasms is properly stimulated within a short period after her climax, she will in most instances be capable of having a second, third, fourth, and even a fifth and a sixth orgasm before she is fully satiated. As contrasted with the male's usual inability to have more than one orgasm in a short period, many females, especially when clitorally stimulated, can regularly have five or six full orgasms within a matter of minutes.
>
> Masters and Johnson, 1961, p. 792

Why does such a small percentage of women report experiencing multiple orgasms when the Masters and Johnson research indicates that most women are capable of having multiple orgasms? Probably the type of stimulation women generally receive during sexual intercourse is not conducive to the experience of multiple orgasms. This may be because the clitoris is not optimally stimulated during sexual intercourse. Furthermore, since some men do not continue with sexual intercourse after they have had an orgasm, they may finish before the female has had as many orgasms as she is capable of experiencing. The fact that women who masturbate and women who have sexual relations with other women report higher rates of multiple orgasm supports this interpretation (Masters and Johnson, 1966; Athanasiou, Shaver, and Tavris, 1970).

If having multiple orgasms is defined as having more than one orgasm within a matter of minutes, having more than one orgasm within the same sexual

The four phases of sexual response found in both men and women are presented in Chapter 5.

The refractory phase is also discussed in Chapter 5.

multiple orgasms
(OR gaz uhmz) Series of two or more orgasms that occur within a matter of minutes.

The frequency of orgasms in homosexual women is discussed in Chapter 11.

encounter but separated by more than a few minutes (for example, separated by 30 minutes or so) might be defined as having **sequential orgasms.** Although males do not have multiple orgasms because of the refractory phase, some males do have sequential orgasms. Sequential orgasms are most frequently reported by young males; the incidence drops off with increasing age. Men are probably more capable of having sequential orgasms than they realize. If they would continue their sexual interaction long enough to recover from their refractory phase, many of them might find that they are able to become aroused again and have another orgasm.

Frequency of Orgasm

There is a difference in the frequency with which males and females have orgasms during sexual intercourse. Kinsey and associates (1953) reported that only about 40% to 50% of married women regularly experience orgasm, while nearly 100% of married men do. Furthermore, these researchers found that about 30% of married women either never have orgasms or have orgasms less than 25% of the time. Two decades later Hunt (1974) found that only 10% to 15% of the women he studied said they never had orgasms or had them less than 25% of the time. Hunt also reported that 7% to 8% of men over the age of 25 failed to have orgasms during 25% or more of their sexual encounters. Thus it appears that the sex difference in ability to experience orgasms may have decreased in recent years. However, females still experience more difficulty having orgasms during sexual intercourse than males. Since the work of Masters and Johnson indicates that women can be aroused and reach orgasm as quickly as men when stimulated properly, many women may fail to reach orgasm during sexual intercourse because they are not stimulated correctly. This problem could be remedied if women were able to convey to their partners what kinds of stimulation are more arousing and if their partners were willing to use the most effective stimulation techniques.

Sexual Drive

Sexual drive refers to a person's interest in sex or feeling of need to have sex. A number of studies have shown that males are more interested in sex in general than are females. In a survey in which married middle-class adults were asked to indicate their favorite way to spend leisure time, sex was, on the average, the first choice of males but only the second choice of females. Among males sex was ranked first, watching sports second, and reading a book third. Among women reading a book was rated first and sex was rated second but barely higher than sewing, which was rated third (Mancini and Orthner, 1978).

Kinsey and associates (1953) reported that early in marriage many husbands want sexual intercourse more frequently than their wives; however, this pattern changes with increasing age. Furthermore, in a more recent survey by Hunt (1974) less than 5% of the wives said they would like to have sexual intercourse less frequently than would their husbands. These findings indicate that in terms of the amount of sexual intercourse desired, gender difference may be decreasing. This change could be a result of the recent trends toward women's equality and sexual liberation.

Men and women experience some similar physiological sexual responses.

Reasons for Engaging in Sexual Intercourse

A cultural stereotype suggests that men and women engage in sexual intercourse for different reasons. It has been said that men use love to get sex, but women use sex to get love. This saying reflects the belief that men are more interested in the physical aspects of sex and women are more concerned with love and romance. DeLamater (1987) suggests that men and women have different "sexual scenarios." Sexual scenarios define the kinds of sexual behaviors and the types of partners that are appropriate, as well as the times and places in which sexual encounters are expected to occur. DeLamater suggests that gender differences in sexual scenarios result in different orientations to sexual relationships. He further suggests that the goal of women tends to be to express affection in a committed relationship, whereas men tend to have a more recreational orientation, with the goal being physical gratification.

Bardwick (1971) presented some evidence that women do, in fact, engage in sex in order to get love. She asked women, "Why do you make love?" Most of her responses suggested that for women sex is not important in its own right. Rather, most women indicated that sex was a way of communicating love that they hoped was mutual in a relationship. Some also implied that they engaged in sex because they felt that the relationship might end if they did not. The following are some of the responses that Bardwick received:

Because it's a means of getting closer to him.

I guess because I love him. I enjoyed it to a certain extent. If I like the person, I have a desire to please; desire to please rather than be pleased.

Right now, to please him.

Because it's a natural expression of what I feel for him and it's mutual.

I think it's really necessary as a symbol of involvement.

Bardwick, 1971, p. 55

Bardwick suggests that this difference in the meaning of sex may have several origins. She proposes that women view sex as something that is not extremely pleasurable in its own right because (1) women do not have as high a sex drive as men, (2) the female sexual organs are not as easily stimulated as the male sexual organs (they are less exposed), and (3) women have fears associated with penetration and pregnancy. The sexual development of males, she suggests, is much simpler. Males have an extremely erotic penis that gives them pleasure from early childhood. Furthermore, males do not typically have strong fears associated with sexuality.

The quotations presented by Bardwick imply that women engage in sex for reasons other than physical release. However, without comparing men's reasons with women's reasons for having sex, it is not possible to say that the sexes differ in this regard. In a study of 50 married couples Brown and Auerback (1981) asked both men and women their reasons for initiating sexual intercourse. The most common reason given by women was to receive love, intimacy, and holding, while men most often stated that they initiated sex as a release of sexual tension. Carroll, Volk, and Hyde (1985) also asked male and female college students about their motives for having sexual intercourse. Again, they found that the women emphasized love and commitment while the men emphasized their physical needs and pleasure. Leigh (1989) found that this gender difference in sexual motivation holds for both heterosexuals and homosexuals.

In a recent study Sprague and Quadagno (1988) gave individuals between the ages of 22 and 57 a questionnaire dealing with motives for engaging in sexual intercourse. They found a gender difference only in the subjects between the ages of 22 to 34. In individuals over 35 no gender differences were obtained. In men and women over the age of 35, 55% of the women and 46% of the men indicated that they engaged in sex to show love for their partner. The responses of men and women over the age of 45 actually showed differences that were in the opposite direction of the younger respondents; that is, older women were more likely than older men to report physical motivations for sex and older men were more likely than older women to report emotional motivations. These results suggest that the gender differences typically obtained in motives for engaging in sex may vary as a function of age. Further research is needed to investigate this possibility.

Sexual Needs and Desires

Little systematic research has been done either on the sexual needs and desires or on the sexual dissatisfactions of males and females. Hite (1976, 1981) conducted comprehensive studies of both male and female sexuality that generated many hypotheses about gender differences in sexual needs and desires. However, because of methodological problems with her studies and the fact that she did not ask males and females the same questions, no clear-cut conclusions regarding gender differences can be drawn from Hite's studies alone.

Hite's studies suggest that males and females may in some cases have different needs and desires and in other cases simply be unaware of the needs and desires of their partners and how to satisfy their partners. For example, when Hite asked her female subjects, "How have most men had sex with you?"

Hite's studies are discussed in detail in Chapter 2.

Hite's Conclusions Regarding Women's Satisfaction with Intercourse

After questioning thousands of women between the ages of 14 and 78 about their sexual interactions with men, Shere Hite (1976) concluded that the standard sexual interaction between males and females is not very satisfactory for women. The following quotation expresses her conclusion. However, the reader should keep in mind that Hite's results are based only on the responses of women who agreed to participate; her sample may not be representative of all women.

It is very clear by now that the pattern of sexual relations predominant in our culture exploits and oppresses women. The sequence of "foreplay," "penetration" and "intercourse" (defined as thrusting), followed by male orgasm as the climax and end of the sequence, gives very little chance for female orgasm, is almost always under the control of the man, frequently teases the woman inhumanely, and in short, has institutionalized out any expression of women's sexual feeling except for those that support male sexual needs.

Many women express their frustration about this: "I don't quite understand why for men, orgasm is presumed to occur each time, but for women it must be 'worked at.' Sex as it is defined between men and women is male sex." And, "I think most of the writers I've read don't understand women at all, sexually. They regard sex as an activity engaged in by two for the satisfaction of one. The current writers are worse than the older ones, because they stress the whore-like sexual techniques used by women for men. Women's needs are less and less emphasized, except by female writers."

The reproductive model of sex insures male orgasm by giving it a standardized time and place, during which both people know what to expect and how to make it possible for the man to orgasm. The whole thing is prearranged, preagreed. But there are not really any patterns of prearranged times and places for a woman to orgasm—unless she can manage to do so during intercourse. So, women are put in a position of asking for something "special," some "extra" stimulation, or they must somehow try to subliminally send messages to a partner who often is not even aware that he should be listening. If she does get this "extra," "special" stimulation, she feels grateful that he was so unusually "sensitive." So all too often women just do without—or fake it.

Reprinted with permission of Macmillan Publishing Company from *The Hite Report: a nationwide study of female sexuality* by Shere Hite. Copyright © 1976 by Shere Hite.

---

she found a great deal of dissatisfaction, as evidenced by the following quotations:

> It is usually a short period of foreplay then male on top, female on back, with legs drawn apart, standard slam-bam-thank-you-ma'am.

> Very perfunctory. A little kiss, a little feel, a finger for arousal, a touch of breast and he is on top. Wham, it is over.

> Men are very uninformed about women's sexual desires. Most men will engage in little manual stimulation but expect women to reach orgasm during intercourse. They cannot understand that some women prefer clitoral stimulation.
>
> Hite, 1976, pp. 200-202

These comments suggest that women are dissatisfied with the amount and type of foreplay that occurs during a sexual interaction and with the fact that the sexual interaction often ends when the male has an orgasm. On the basis of Hite's study of women we might conclude that sexual interaction is arranged to fulfill men's desires and that men may desire foreplay less than women do (see boxes, above and p. 304).

When Hite (1981) asked men, "How have you usually had sex with women?" the men tended to describe in some detail what happened in a typical sexual encounter. They did not express as much clear dissatisfaction with the process

A Personal Glimpse

Sex Differences in Desire for Foreplay

From the responses of several of the women in Shere Hite's study (1976) of female sexuality, it appears that many women believe that men do not spend enough time in foreplay. Many of the women expressed the feeling that men begin actual intercourse much too quickly. The following are quotations from some of the women in response to the question, "How have most men had sex with you?":

I find that a lot of men care nothing about sex foreplay and are only interested in "getting it off." These are the kind that really burn me up. Usually, they are the type that have never had or never wanted to really love someone for the sake of love and the pleasure it brings; they are only interested in themselves.

Most men, if left to their own devices, will engage in a little foreplay of a not very imaginative kind, paying little attention to my clitoris. They then go immediately to penetration in the "missionary position," have a whale of a good time and go to sleep immediately afterwards. This is an extreme picture, but is too well defined to ignore.

Preliminaries—kissing, foreplay, clitoral-massaging— then he jumps on top and all of a sudden I don't matter anymore. Sometimes, I'm not even there to him.

They move too quickly to enter and move to their climax too fast for me to keep up. I often do, but at the expense of my feelings. It becomes a "job" to come.

Most climb on top of me. We don't even have a chance to get acquainted and love and kiss first. They are too anxious. Men differ, but most do not seem to understand a woman's body. They seem to think that vaginal penetration is the only important thing and that all else should be done only to "get you ready." They think that once you are lubricated you are immediately ready and want to be penetrated then.

Reprinted with permission of Macmillan Publishing Company from *The Hite Report: a nationwide study of female sexuality* by Shere Hite. Copyright © 1976 by Shere Hite.

as the women did. Thus in comparing the male and female responses to the same question asked in the Hite studies, it appears that males may be more satisfied with the typical sexual interaction than females.

In addition to possible gender differences in satisfaction with the usual sexual encounter and with desire for foreplay, differences between men and women may be found in the desire for afterplay. Halpern and Sherman (1979) administered a questionnaire on afterplay to 250 individuals. The questions were aimed at finding what people do after sexual intercourse and what kinds of behavior either please or displease them. Halpern and Sherman found some gender differences. First, in response to the question, "Immediately after intercourse do you prefer to be physically separated from (i.e., not touching) your partner?", a larger percentage of women (75.9%) said "never or almost never" than did men (58.1%), while a larger proportion of the men (31.2%) said "sometimes" than did women (19.9%). There were also gender differences in the kinds of after-intercourse activities that bothered men and women. First, one third of the women mentioned that they did not like it when their partners went directly to sleep after intercourse; however, only a few men referred to this as a problem. Second, more women than men complained about being ignored by their sex partner following intercourse. Third, nearly all individuals who mentioned that they felt negatively about watching TV or reading after intercourse were women. Their objection seemed to be that these activities make them feel ignored by their partner. Fourth, men stated more often than women that they did not like excessive expression of affection after intercourse. These findings suggest that women may want more afterplay or interaction with their partner after intercourse than do men.

To test some of the hypotheses generated by the Hite and the Halpern and Sherman studies, Denney, Field, and Quadagno (1984) conducted a study of gender differences in attitudes toward foreplay, sexual intercourse, and afterplay. The subjects were college students who were asked to fill out a questionnaire regarding their sexual needs and desires. The results indicated significant gender differences. Women reported that they enjoy foreplay more than intercourse, while men indicated that they enjoy intercourse most. Women wanted to spend more time in both foreplay and afterplay than did men. Furthermore, while the majority of men reported being satisfied with their sexual interactions, the majority of women indicated that they were dissatisfied with at least some aspect of their sexual interactions. The aspect of the typical sexual interaction with which women were most dissatisfied was afterplay. They reported that they wanted their partners to spend more time interacting (talking, holding, kissing) with them after intercourse was completed than their partners typically do. These findings support the earlier findings of Hite and of Halpern and Sherman that women tend to be more dissatisfied with their sexual interactions than men, that women often place more importance on foreplay and afterplay than do men, and that women are inclined to want to spend more time in both foreplay and afterplay than do men.

In a more recent study Hatfield and associates (1988) asked college students and couples who had been married for less than 2 years what they wished their partners would do more or less of during a sexual encounter. The subjects were asked to rate their preferences on a scale from 1 to 7 both on items that indicated desire for love and intimacy (e.g., "would talk lovingly much less during sex" versus "would talk much more lovingly during sex") and on items that indicated desire for partner initiation and variety (e.g., "would do much less oral-genital sex" versus "would do much more oral-genital sex"). They found that the women desired the behaviors that indicate love and intimacy more than those that indicate partner initiation and variety while the reverse was true for men. However, men and women were not much different in their desire for love and intimacy behaviors. The largest gender differences were obtained with the initiation/variety items. Men wanted their partners to be "more rough, more experimental, more willing to engage in fast, impulsive sex, initiate more sex, play the dominant role in sex more, talk more dirty during sex, be more wild and sexy, be more variable in where sex is had, give more instructions, and be more willing to do what 'I want'" (pp. 49-50). These findings are consistent with the results of research on gender differences in reasons for engaging in sexual intercourse. Both sets of results indicate that women tend to put more emphasis on the emotional than on the physical aspects of sexual encounters whereas men tend to focus on the physical aspects more than the emotional aspects.

Response to Erotic Material

It is often assumed that women are less likely to be aroused by erotic material than are men. Kinsey and associates (1948, 1953) found that women were much less likely than men to report that they had felt sexually aroused by erotic materials. Approximately half of the men interviewed by Kinsey said that they had been aroused at some time by erotic stories. Only 14% of the women interviewed by Kinsey reported such arousal, even though almost all of them admitted to having heard erotic stories. This research seemed to confirm the stereotypical view that men are more aroused by erotic material than are women.

More recent studies, however, indicate that differences between men and women in response to erotic material may not be as great as had been assumed previously. For example, Heiman (1977) had sexually experienced university students listen to tape recordings of erotic stories. In addition to obtaining the subjects' self-reports of their own arousal, Heiman obtained measures of their physiological arousal with either a penile strain gauge or a photoplethysmograph. The penile strain gauge is a flexible loop that fits around the base of the penis. When the male becomes aroused, the vasocongestion in the penis is recorded by the strain gauge. The photoplethysmograph is a small cylinder that is placed inside the entrance of the vagina. It also measures the vasocongestion that results from sexual arousal. These physiological measures gave Heiman a measure of sexual arousal that was independent of the subject's self-report.

Both the penile strain gauge and the photoplethysmograph are also discussed in Chapter 2.

Heiman had her subjects listen to one of four types of tape. One was called *erotic;* these tapes included explicit descriptions of heterosexual sex. The second type of tape was called *romantic*. On these tapes a couple was heard expressing affection and tenderness for each other. The third type of tape was called *erotic-romantic*. These tapes had descriptions of both explicit sex and romantic conversation. The fourth type of tape was used as a control. On these tapes a couple was heard engaging in a nonsexual, nonromantic conversation. Heiman found that the erotic and erotic-romantic tapes were most arousing for both men and women. The majority of both males and females responded to the erotic tapes, both physiologically and in self-reports. Neither men nor women responded, either physiologically or in self-reports, to the romantic or control tapes. Thus males and females may not respond differently to erotic and romantic material. This finding was confirmed by the work of Rubinsky and associates (1987), who used an erotic film as a stimulus.

Heiman obtained another interesting finding. She found that women were sometimes unaware of their own physiological arousal. When the physiological instruments indicated vasocongestion, all of the men reported that they were sexually aroused, yet only half of the women with vasocongestion reported arousal in their self-ratings. If women are less aware of their physiological arousal than men, the gender differences in arousal to erotic material that have been obtained in earlier studies may have been incorrect because the studies were based on self-report. When only self-report is used to measure arousal, the arousal of women will probably be underestimated.

Additional research indicates that males and females may not differ much in what they find arousing. Both males and females appear to be aroused by scenes of the opposite sex engaging in sexual activity but are turned off by watching their own sex doing the same thing. Hatfield, Sprecher, and Traupmann (1978) showed college students films of males and females masturbating. They found that when the film showed males masturbating, a number of men left the room, and when it showed females masturbating, some of the women left the room. They also noted that both males and females reported being

HUMAN SEXUALITY

moderately aroused by watching someone of the opposite sex masturbate and being moderately turned off by watching someone of their own sex masturbate. In another experiment in which students were exposed to scenes of heterosexual and homosexual interactions, the males reported finding female homosexuality extremely arousing and male homosexuality extremely unarousing. To a lesser extent, the females found male homosexuality to be arousing and female homosexuality to be unarousing. Hatfield, Sprecher, and Traupmann suggested that their subjects may have been identifying with the members of their own gender in the sexual film and feeling upset about activities that were disapproved of for their own gender. When the other gender was involved in the films, they did not identify with the individual and thus did not feel embarrassed or upset.

In summary, males and females seem to respond similarly to erotic material. Since the gender difference reported by Kinsey was greater, the sexual revolution may have lessened these gender differences as women have become more open about their own sexuality. However, it may just be that women's willingness to report arousal has increased in recent years. Whether the similarity of male and female reactions is a result of a change in a willingness to report arousal or of an actual change in arousal is not known.

Masturbation

Men and women seem to differ widely in their experience with masturbation. Kinsey and associates (1948, 1953) reported that 92% of the males they interviewed had masturbated to orgasm at least once in their lives and only 50% of the females had. Almost all the males said they had masturbated before the age of 20; most began to masturbate between the ages of 13 and 15. A fairly large percentage of the women, on the other hand, reported masturbating for the first time between the ages of 25 and 35. Several decades later Hunt (1974) reported that gender differences in terms of masturbation still existed. He found that 94% of the males and 63% of the females he interviewed had masturbated to orgasm at least once. In addition, although he found that both males and females began masturbating at an earlier age than those in Kinsey's studies, males still began at an earlier age than did females. Thus it appears that in the decades between the Kinsey and the Hunt studies there has not been much of a change in the percentage of males and females who report masturbating to orgasm. These results suggest that males masturbate more than females. However, these data are based on self-report, and it is possible that women are simply less likely to report masturbating.

Homosexuality

Males are both more likely to have homosexual experiences and more likely to be exclusively homosexual than are females (Kinsey, Pomeroy, and Martin, 1948; Kinsey et al., 1953; Hunt, 1974; Centers for Disease Control, 1988). Sexual attraction between individuals of the same sex is common. By the age of 45 approximately one third of all men and one fifth of all women have had at least one homosexual experience (Kinsey, Pomeroy, and Martin, 1948; Kinsey et al., 1953; Hunt, 1974). The number of individuals who are exclusively homosexual is much smaller. As reported in the classic studies of Kinsey and associates and Hunt, estimates of the number of males who are exclusively homosexual range from 3% to 5%, while estimates of the number of females who are exclusively homosexual range from 1% to 2% (Kinsey, Pomeroy, and Martin, 1948; Kinsey et al., 1953; Hunt, 1974). In a more recent survey of homosexual experiences the Centers for Disease Control (1988) estimated that 2.8% of males and 0.2% of females are exclusively homosexual. In all of these studies a clear gender difference emerges.

The gender differences in the sexual behavior of heterosexuals mentioned previously have also been found in homosexuals. Male homosexuals often become involved in sexual relationships at earlier ages than do female homosexuals (Riddle and Morin, 1977). In addition, female homosexuals are more likely than male homosexuals to place importance on emotional attachment rather than on sexual behavior (de Monteflores and Schultz, 1978; Blumenfeld and Raymond, 1988). Furthermore, male homosexuals tend to have sex more frequently, with more partners, and in the context of more short-term relationships than do female homosexuals (Kinsey et al., 1948, 1953; Bell and Weinberg, 1978). However, largely because of the acquired immunodeficiency syndrome (AIDS) epidemic, homosexual men have made significant modifications in their sexual behavior, including a reduction in the number of sexual partners (Martin et al., 1989; Siegel and Glassman, 1989). Because AIDS is virtually nonexistent among lesbians (Monzon and Capellan, 1987), AIDS has probably not affected their sexual behavior (Leigh, 1989). Therefore, although no study has directly investigated this area, gender differences in the number of sexual partners of male and female homosexuals have probably diminished but not disappeared. Thus it appears that the gender differences in sexual behavior that have been found among heterosexuals hold for homosexual individuals as well.

To summarize, the research on gender differences in sexual behavior indicates that (1) females have the capability for multiple orgasms and men do not; (2) males are more likely to have an orgasm during sexual intercourse than women; (3) men tend to be more interested in sex for the sake of sex, and women are inclined to be more interested in the emotional aspects of sex; (4) women tend to be more dissatisfied with their sexual interactions than men; (5) women often place more importance on foreplay and afterplay than men; and (6) males start masturbating at an earlier age than females and continue to masturbate more frequently throughout life.

CAUSES OF GENDER DIFFERENCES IN SEXUAL BEHAVIOR

Both biological and environmental factors have been proposed as possible causes of gender differences in sexual behavior. This discussion begins with the biological explanations, which include hormonal, anatomical, and evolutionary factors.

Hormones

For a complete discussion of gender differences in sex hormones, see Chapter 4.

Some of the gender differences in sexual behavior have been thought to result from hormone differences. Since males and females have different concentrations of different sex hormones, and since the various sex hormones appear to have different effects on sexual behavior (Feder, 1984), some of these hormonal differences might be responsible for at least some of the gender differences in sexual behavior mentioned previously.

Anatomy

Differences in sexual behavior between males and females may result in part from the significant differences in their sexual anatomy. The male's penis is much more visible and accessible than the female's genitals. Because the boy handles the penis when urinating, and because the penis is often stimulated by clothing and other environmental objects, the boy is more likely than the girl to learn that stimulation of his genitals is pleasurable. This may be one reason that boys are more likely to masturbate and that they start at younger ages than girls.

When boys become aroused, the fact is obvious—they have erections. Girls have no obvious external cues to tell them when they are aroused. Because the female genitals are more hidden and the female arousal response is less obvious, females may be less aware of the sexual aspects of themselves and therefore less likely to respond to and develop those aspects.

Evolution

Sociobiologists have proposed that female and male sexual behavior may differ because of evolutionary pressures (Fisher, 1982). If we look at behavior from a sociobiological perspective, we need to see the "purpose" of life as the perpetuation of life. The "purpose" of an individual is to ensure that his or her genes will be passed on to future generations. The sex cells, or cells that carry genes on to future generations, differ for males and females. The female gamete, or egg, is substantially larger than the male gamete, or sperm. According to sociobiologists, this difference in size has important implications for sexual behavior. Because the female produces significantly fewer and larger sex cells, she has invested much more energy in each egg than the male has invested in each of his much more plentiful, smaller sperm cells. Furthermore, during her pregnancy, the female has a greater commitment to each of her offspring.

Since females have more invested in their individual offspring than do males, sociobiologists suggest that the best reproductive strategy for females, that is, the strategy most likely to result in the females transmitting their genes to future generations, is for females to concentrate their energy on raising their children and trying to keep their children's father around to help. This is, of course, a monogamous strategy. However, the male's best strategy for conveying as many of his genes as possible to future generations is to be less monogamous. Once a male has impregnated one female, he cannot impregnate that same female again until she is no longer pregnant. He can increase the probability of having other offspring, however, by mating with other females. Since the male has an investment, albeit small, in making sure that the offspring of his first mate are raised to maturity so that they can reproduce, the male's best reproductive strategy is to stay with the mother of his offspring (at least until she is capable of raising the children on her own) but at the same time to be somewhat more promiscuous, that is, to mate with other females.

Some have suggested that the preceding sociobiological hypotheses explain

Do Males Prefer Sexual Variety?

In at least some species males appear to get renewed sexual interest when they are exposed to a novel female. In the laboratory, males of many mammalian species typically copulate several times with an estrous female, but after several ejaculations they seem to lose interest. It was first assumed that the males were fatigued after several ejaculations. However, if a male who has stopped copulating with one female is then exposed to a new estrous female, the male will immediately begin to copulate with her. This phenomenon is called the Coolidge effect. It got its name because of a story told by Dr. Frank Beach, a noted psychologist. The story involves an indirect exchange between President and Mrs. Coolidge when they were visiting a government farm. According to the story, President and Mrs. Coolidge were taken on different tours. When Mrs. Coolidge was taken past the chicken pens, she asked her guide if the rooster copulates more than once a day. "Dozens of times" was the reply. "Please tell that to the President," Mrs. Coolidge requested. When the President was taken by the chicken pens and told of Mrs. Coolidge's request that he be told about the rooster's sexual behavior, he asked, "Same hen every time?" "Oh no, Mr. President, a different one each time," was the answer. Mr. Coolidge nodded slowly and replied, "Tell that to Mrs. Coolidge."

---

certain gender differences in sexual behavior such as the lower sex drive in females and the stronger emphasis on relationships and commitment by females. A stronger sex drive in males say ensure that they are more likely to use their best reproductive strategy, that is, that they are highly motivated to mate with other females and therefore less likely to remain monogamous. If females had extremely high sex drives, they might be more "promiscuous" and thus less likely to devote all of their energy to raising their offspring. Also, since the best reproductive strategy for females is to try to get the fathers to stay around and help them raise their offspring, the females should be more concerned about relationships and commitment than about actual sexual behavior. Since males' best reproductive strategy is to mate with as many females as possible, they should be more concerned with sexual behavior than with commitment to relationships. Thus sociobiological principles are not inconsistent with some of the gender differences that have been found in sexual behavior. However, since the hypotheses derived from sociobiology cannot be experimentally tested, we cannot determine whether they are correct or incorrect. Sociobiological theory must be judged according to how well it fits the facts it attempts to explain. It cannot be experimentally tested or "proved."

Environmental Explanations

In addition to biological explanations for the gender differences that have been found in sexual behavior, environmental explanations have been proposed. Some have suggested that the differences in gender roles in our culture contribute to differences in sexual behavior. For example, in our culture men are supposed to be active and aggressive and women are expected to be passive and dependent. These roles carry over into sexual behavior and other aspects of life. With respect to sexual behavior, men are supposed to be aggressive and women are supposed to be passive.

It has also traditionally been assumed that men are supposed to seek out and enjoy sex; in fact, success in sexual encounters is viewed as a sign of masculinity. Women, on the other hand, are not expected to seem too interested in sex and are not supposed to initiate sex. Having sexual experience before marriage tends to detract from, rather than add to, a woman's worth. Women with a lot of sexual experience may be labeled as "cheap." Even if there were no biological differences that resulted in differences in sexual behavior, these gender role differences would probably affect behavior. If masculinity is, at least in part, judged according to how much sexual experience a man has had, men will be more likely to behave as if they have high sex drives. If sexual experience is considered to cheapen a woman, women will be less likely to behave as if they have high sex drives.

Evidence suggests that gender role differences were responsible for at least some of the gender differences in sexual behavior observed in the past. For example, Kinsey and associates' data (1948, 1953) indicate that although 71% of the males reported engaging in premarital sex, only 33% of the females reported doing so. More recently, however, Hunt (1974) stated that 95% of the men and 81% of the women he interviewed reported engaging in premarital sex. These results suggest that even though both men and women have become more likely to engage in premarital sex since the 1940s, the difference between the percentages of men and women engaging in premarital sex has decreased substantially. This decrease is probably a result of the changes in the gender roles that occurred between the 1940s and 1970s. At the time of Kinsey's studies, when the double standard for sexual behavior was much stronger than it is today, there were great differences in premarital sexual behavior. However, today, when the double standard seems to be weaker, the difference is smaller. While this change is probably a result of environmental factors rather than a result of alterations in biological factors, males and females still differ with respect to premarital sex; the recent change in gender roles has clearly not eliminated gender differences in this type of sexual behavior. Although environmental factors may be responsible for some of the differences, biological factors might also be important.

Another aspect that may influence gender differences in sexual behavior is the fact that women get pregnant and men do not. Young girls are often advised of the dangers associated with sexual intercourse. They are warned of the possibility of pregnancy and of the terrible consequences that might result from becoming pregnant. Thus they often learn to fear and and avoid sex. Boys, on the other hand, are seldom discouraged from participating in sexual activities; they are more likely to be encouraged. The fact that girls are taught to be fearful of sex and boys are encouraged to enjoy sex could certainly be responsible for some of the gender differences in sexual behavior.

Another environmental reason for some of the gender differences in sexual behavior may be that women do not receive as much gratification from sexual intercourse as do men. Although Masters and Johnson found that women can reach orgasm during masturbation as quickly as men can, women have much more difficulty achieving orgasm during sexual intercourse. Sexual intercourse almost always provides men with the type of stimulation they need to achieve orgasm, whereas sexual intercourse often does not stimulate women to achieve orgasm. As a result, women are much less likely than men to obtain physical release in sexual intercourse and are therefore much less likely than men to show great interest in sexual intercourse.

There are a number of potential explanations, both biological and environmental, for the gender differences observed in sexual behavior. Which causal factors are most important is unknown. However, it is likely that both biological and environmental factors contribute to the observed sex differences.

SUMMARY

1 Gender roles are the prescriptions for how males and females are supposed to behave. Gender roles vary from culture to culture, and individuals within a culture vary in the extent to which they can take on traditional masculine and feminine characteristics.

2 In our culture gender roles have become more flexible in recent years. It is more acceptable for males and females to participate in activities that were once reserved for the opposite gender.

3 Bem applied the term *androgynous* to individuals who were high in both masculine and feminine characteristics. At least some research suggests that androgynous individuals are more flexible in responding to social situations, using more masculine types of behaviors when they are called for and more feminine types of behaviors when they are appropriate. As a result, androgynous individuals may be more socially competent.

4 Some research indicates that androgynous individuals are more comfortable in their attitudes toward sexuality than gender-typed individuals and that androgynous women experience orgasms more frequently and report more sexual satisfaction than gender-typed women.

5 From an early age children learn the culturally prescribed gender roles; this process is called gender role socialization.

6 Children do not have a firm sense of their gender identity—that is, whether they are a boy or a girl—until they are about 2½ years of age.

7 Research indicates that parents begin to treat boys and girls differently from early infancy. It appears that some gender differences in boys and girls begin at this time.

8 Research shows that peers and teachers reinforce gender-typed behaviors in children.

9 Books, magazines, movies, and television also reinforce gender-typed behavior by portraying the vast majority of male and female behavior as strongly gender typed. On television programs and commercials more characters are male, women are portrayed in low-level occupations, and when males and females interact, the male is typically presented as dominant, often giving the female instructions.

10 At least some research suggests that the more television children watch, the more sex typed they are. This suggests that the gender-typed roles presented on television may increase gender-typed attitudes and behavior.

11 Sometimes people do not develop a gender identity that matches their biological sex. Rather, they develop a gender identity that corresponds with the opposite sex. These individuals are called transsexuals.

12 There are gender roles in sexual behavior, as well as in other types of behavior. Men have traditionally been expected to be initiators, active, dominant, and always interested in sexual encounters. Women, on the other hand, have traditionally been expected to be passive and relatively uninterested in sexual interactions.

13 Research on gender differences in sexual behavior indicates that (1) females have the capability for multiple orgasms and men do not; (2) males are more likely to have an orgasm during sexual intercourse than are women; (3) men tend to be more interested in sex for the sake of sex, and women are often more interested in the emotional aspects of sex; (4) women tend to be more dissatisfied with their sexual interactions than men; (5) women are inclined to place more importance on foreplay and afterplay than men; and (6) males begin masturbating at earlier ages than females and masturbate more frequently throughout life.

14 Homosexual individuals show the same gender differences as heterosexual individuals; that is, male homosexuals tend to engage in sex more frequently, with more partners, and at earlier ages than female homosexuals. It appears that gender differences in sexual behavior usually apply despite differences in sexual orientation.

15 Both biological and environmental factors have been proposed as causes of gender differences in sexual behavior. The biological factors are hormones, anatomy of the male and female genitals, and evolution. The environmental factors are gender roles, female pregnancy as an outcome of sexual intercourse, and differences in the pleasure obtained from sexual intercourse.

ANSWERS

1 In one study of newborns, boys tended to be awake more often, grimaced more, and showed more low-intensity activity than girls.

2 With the appropriate stimulation women can be aroused and reach orgasm as quickly as men.

3 Interview studies indicate that males may be more satisfied than women with the typical sexual encounter.

F A C T
OR
F I C T I O N

QUESTIONS FOR THOUGHT   ?

1. In what ways did your parents encourage traditional gender role behavior in you?
2. Why do you think gay and lesbian couples differ in sexual behavior?
3. Why do you think there are gender differences in sex drive?

SUGGESTED READINGS

Hite, S.: The Hite Report: a nationwide survey of female sexuality, New York, 1976, Macmillan Publishing Co., Inc.
    A detailed report of the results of an interview study of female sexuality.
Hite, S.: The Hite Report on male sexuality, New York, 1981, Alfred A. Knopf, Inc.
    A detailed report of the results of an interview study of male sexuality.
Intons-Peterson, MJ: Children's concept of gender, Norwood, N.J., 1988, Ablex Publishing Corp.
    A book about how children acquire knowledge about gender and the factors that determine gender stereotyped behavior.
Reinisch, J.M., Rosenblum, L.A., and Sanders, S.A., editors: Masculinity/femininity: basic perspectives, New York, 1987, Oxford University Press.
    Readings about the meaning, development, and implications of masculinity and femininity.
Tavris, C., and Wade, C.: The longest war: sex differences in perspective, New York, 1984, Harcourt Brace Jovanovich, Inc.
    A readable account of sex role socialization and its consequences.

Homosexuality and Bisexuality

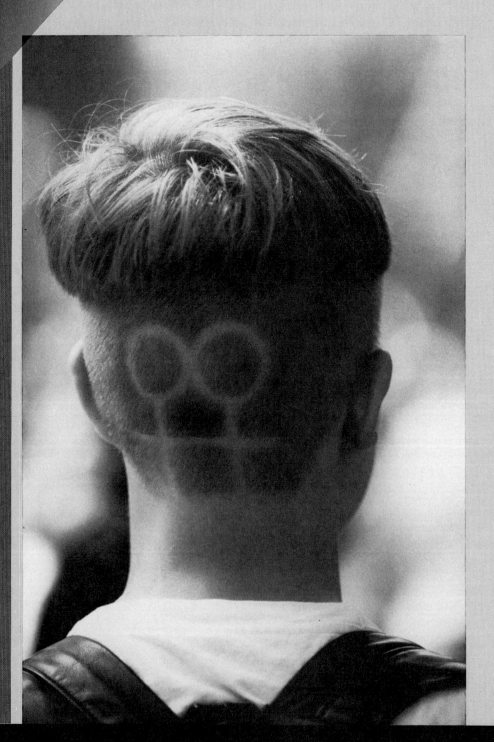

FACT OR FICTION

1
By the time boys and girls reach adolescence, their sexual preference is likely to be already determined.

2
Gay males tend to prefer the activities of the opposite gender during childhood.

3
Lesbians appear to have orgasms in their sexual interactions more frequently than do heterosexual females.

We two boys together clinging,
One the other never leaving,
Up and down the roads going—North and South excursions making,
Power enjoying—elbows stretching—fingers clutching,
Armed and fearless—eating, drinking, sleeping, loving.

WALT WHITMAN
"We Two Boys Together Clinging"

n our discussion of gender differences in the previous chapter, we focused primarily on **heterosexual** behavior because it is the most common in our society. In this chapter we explore two alternatives to heterosexual behavior: **homosexuality** and **bisexuality.** An individual's sexual attraction to members of the opposite sex (heterosexuality), members of the same sex (homosexuality), or members of both sexes (bisexuality) is referred to as that person's **sexual orientation** or *sexual preference.* Although we will use the terms *homosexuality* to refer to males and females who are attracted to members of the same sex and *bisexuality* to define males and females who are attracted to members of both sexes, other terms are also commonly used. Many homosexuals prefer to be called **gay** because of the negative connotations that are often associated with the term *homosexual.* Although the term *gay* is sometimes used to refer to both male and female homosexuals, others use it only to refer to male homosexuals. Female homosexuals are often called **lesbians.**

Sexual orientation or preference can be defined by a number of criteria. The first criterion is *sexual behavior.* Does the individual in question engage in sexual behavior with someone of the opposite gender, someone of the same gender, or members of both genders? The second criterion is *erotic orientation.* Does the individual become sexually aroused by individuals of the same gender, the opposite gender, or both genders? The third criterion is *self-definition.* Does the individual regard himself or herself as homosexual, heterosexual, or bisexual? These three factors should be taken into account when determining sexual orientation.

If only one criterion is used to assign sexual orientation, mistakes can be made. For example, if only sexual behavior were used to determine sexual orientation, a male who had engaged in sexual behavior with another male during time spent in prison might be classified as homosexual. However, the same male may, when released from prison, return to exclusively heterosexual relationships. Furthermore, his erotic orientation and self-definition may always have been heterosexual. In such a case the individual would be predominantly heterosexual, even though an observer who looked only at the sexual behavior during the imprisonment might label him homosexual. Thus all three criteria must be considered together.

It is important to keep in mind that an individual is not necessarily exclusively homosexual, heterosexual, or bisexual throughout his or her entire life. After intensive interviews with thousands of men and women, Kinsey and his colleagues (1953) devised a scale to represent sexual orientation as a continuum from exclusively heterosexual to exclusively homosexual behavior. The percentages of males and females falling into each of the seven categories on Kinsey's scale are presented in Table 11-1. A range of percentages is given

heterosexual
Person who is sexually attracted to members of the opposite sex.

homosexual
Person who is sexually attracted to members of the same sex.

bisexual
Person who is sexually attracted to members of both sexes.

sexual orientation
Sexual preferences—whether one is attracted to members of the same sex, opposite sex, or both sexes.

gay
Homosexual; usually refers to male homosexual.

lesbian
(LEZ bee uhn) Female homosexual.

TABLE 11-1 Individuals in Kinsey's Studies with Homosexual and Heterosexual Experience

Rating	Description	Females (%)★	Males (%)★
0	Entirely heterosexual experience		
	Single	61-72	53-78
	Married	89-90	90-92
	Previously married	75-80	—
1-6	At least some homosexual experience	11-20	18-42
2-6	More than incidental homosexual experience	6-14	13-38
3-6	Homosexual as much as heterosexual experience	4-11	9-32
4-6	Mostly homosexual experience	3-8	7-26
5-6	Almost exclusively homosexual experience	2-6	5-22
6	Exclusively homosexual experience	1-3	3-16

From Kinsey, A.C., et al.: Sexual behavior in the human female, Philadelphia, 1953, W.B. Saunders Co. Reprinted with permission of the Kinsey Institute for Research in Sex, Gender, and Reproduction, Inc.
★The ranges of percentages were obtained from different groups of people that differed in such factors as age and marital status.

because the percentage differs depending on the person's age, marital status, and other factors.

As can be seen from Table 11-1, a majority of men and women report being exclusively heterosexual and only a small percentage of either men or women report being exclusively homosexual. However, between 18% and 42% of the males and between 11% and 20% of the females admit having at least one homosexual experience. These percentages suggest that there is a continuum of sexual orientation rather than a clear-cut dichotomy. Fairly substantial percentages of males and females have had both homosexual and heterosexual experiences. Kinsey estimated that 37% of the males and 13% of the females he interviewed had homosexual experiences at some time in their lives and that even more had experienced erotic responses to individuals of the same gender.

Although a moderate percentage of individuals have had sexual experiences with both genders, it would not be appropriate to call all such people *bisexual*. For example, if a woman had been heterosexual all her life with the exception of one incident of sex play with a female friend during adolescence, she should not be considered bisexual. Furthermore, individuals who say they are exclusively heterosexual and respond erotically only to individuals of the opposite gender should not be labeled as bisexual just because they report that they were involved in sex play with individuals of the same gender while attending sex-segregated schools.

Although people tend to base labels of sexual orientation on sexual behavior alone, fewer mistakes will be made if sexual behavior, erotic orientation, and self-definition are all taken into account. Although a fairly substantial percentage of the population reports having had sexual experiences with both genders, a much smaller percentage of individuals would actually be classified as bisexual if all three criteria were included.

CHILDHOOD EXPERIENCES

An awareness of sexual orientation typically develops gradually during childhood and particularly during adolescence. Children become aware of their attraction to members of the same gender, the opposite gender, or both genders. At the same time they may begin to have sexual experiences with members of the same gender, the opposite gender, or both genders. Finally, individuals begin to define themselves as homosexuals, heterosexuals, bisexuals, or **asexuals.** When individuals find themselves feeling attracted to members of the opposite gender, having sexual experiences with members of the opposite gender, and defining themselves as heterosexual, the development of sexual orientation is relatively smooth because heterosexuality is considered normal in our society. However, when individuals find themselves feeling attracted to and having sexual experiences with members of the same gender, the development of self-definition may be much more complicated and conflictual. This process is considered in detail here; the development of heterosexual behavior is covered in more detail in Chapter 12.

asexual
Person who does not have sexual desires.

The development of heterosexual behavior is covered in more detail in Chapter 12.

Much of the research presented in this chapter was conducted with self-report studies in which the subjects were asked to divulge information about their present and past lives. Self-report data are subject to many biases; participants may distort what they tell. Retrospective data are subject to the same distortion as self-report data, and in addition individuals may have lapses and changes of memory. The reader should remember that the findings of these self-report and retrospective studies are suggestive but not definitive.

A study of lesbians indicates that their awareness of their homosexuality develops gradually over a number of years (Wolf, 1979). Many reported having felt some attraction to a childhood playmate of the same gender, having had a crush on an older female such as a teacher, having had a romantic relationship during the teenage years with a partner of the same gender, feeling boredom or reluctance about dating boys, and finally beginning to realize that they might be homosexuals (Wolf, 1979). Thus the development of homosexual behavior seemed to occur after the women realized as young girls that they were attracted to members of the same sex.

A study of gay males indicates that they may exhibit different nonsexual behavior during childhood than heterosexual males (Whitam, 1977). Whitam found that males who eventually became homosexuals tended to play with toys considered more appropriate for girls, dressed in female clothing, joined girls in their activities, and were regarded as "sissies" more often than males who did not become homosexuals. Although gay males were more likely to have these experiences than heterosexual males, fewer than half of the gay males studied by Whitam reported such experiences. However, in another study up to two thirds of adult homosexuals recalled preferring the activities of the opposite gender during childhood (Gadpaille, 1981).

In addition to finding a tendency among gay males to be more involved in traditionally feminine behaviors as children, Whitam (1977) found that gay males were much more likely than male heterosexuals to be interested during childhood in sex play with boys than with girls. Although 82% of the adult male heterosexuals said that they were not more interested in sex play with boys than with girls, 78% of the adult male homosexuals said they were more interested in sex play with boys than with girls during childhood (see accompanying box). Whitam reports that although some adult male homosexuals said they became aware of their homosexuality in early childhood or as late as 35, most reported becoming aware of their sexual orientation between the ages of 10 and 13.

Silverstein (1981) conducted an interview study of gay males. He concluded that homosexual males begin to differ from heterosexual males during childhood and adolescence. He summarized some of these differences in the following way:

What is the difference then between gay and straight boys? Gay boys differ from their playmates, but not in their sexual behavior. In general, gay boys are serious about the business of physical contact in a way straight boys are not. They feel different from their friends. The claim made by some gay men that they were aware of their homosexuality at an early age appears to be true. Listening carefully to their stories, one realizes that a deep sense of love and commitment often accompanied sexual interest in another boy. There are many references to tender feelings toward older boys and young men, and here, too, there is a desire for closeness that is qualitatively different from what one would expect from straight boys. Straight boys can play sexually for awhile and then give it up; it is merely play to them, merely "getting it off." Gay boys also seem to see and study the male body more closely than their straight counterparts. They are not only genitally aroused; if they could (and lots of them try while others learn very early not to), they would admire the entire body as a source of pleasure. But many of them appear to recognize just how different their motivations are from those of their straight friends, and one of two things invariably occurs. One type of gay boy will become an initiator, leading the other into game playing more deeply. . . . The other type of boy is more circumspect. He, too, knows how different he is from his straight friends, but instead of being excited by them, he is reluctant to exhibit his interest in their bodies. He shies away from them, while never forgetting how much he wants them. This boy always feels that something is not right, although frequently he doesn't exactly know what.

Silverstein, 1981, pp. 102-103

Bell, Weinberg, and Hammersmith (1981) conducted an interview study of homosexual and heterosexual males and females to gain a better understanding of the development of sexual preference. On the basis of their research, they came to the following conclusions about such development:

1. By the time boys and girls reach adolescence, their sexual preference is likely to be already determined, even though they may not yet have become sexually very active.
2. Among our respondents homosexuality was indicated or reinforced by sexual feelings that typically occurred three years or so before their first "advanced" homosexual activity, and it was these feelings, more than homosexual activities, that appear to have been crucial in the development of adult homosexuality.
3. The homosexual men and women in our study were not particularly lacking in heterosexual experiences during their childhood and adolescent years. They are distinguished from their heterosexual counterparts, however, in finding such experiences ungratifying.
4. Among both the men and the women in our study, there is a powerful link between gender nonconformity and the development of homosexuality.
5. Respondents' identification with their opposite-sex parents while they were growing up appears to have had no significant impact on whether they turned out to be homosexual or heterosexual.
6. For both male and female respondents, identification with the parent of the same sex appears to have had a relatively weak connection to the development of their sexual orientation.
7. For both men and the women in our study, poor relationships with the fathers seemed more important than whatever relationships they may have had with their mothers.
8. Insofar as we can identify differences between male and female psychosexual development, gender nonconformity appears somewhat more salient for males than for females, and family relationships are more salient for females than for males.

Bell, Weinberg, and Hammersmith, 1981, pp. 186-190

Although homosexual individuals may become aware of their homosexual tendencies during childhood and adolescence, actually taking on the self-definition is a much more gradual process. Self-definition as a homosexual takes longer than self-definition as a heterosexual because of the negative valuation of homosexuality in our culture. Children often learn about homosexuality in the context of hearing derogatory comments about homosexuals and homosexuality. Thus they get the impression that there is something terribly wrong with homosexuality. When they become aware of their own homosexual tendencies, they must come to terms with the fact that they have inclinations that are judged to be "abnormal," "filthy," and "disgusting" by the rest of society. Therefore it is no surprise that individuals with homosexual tendencies might

These teenagers are proud of their homosexuality. However, most teens who discover themselves to be gay or lesbian cannot fully accept their homosexuality until they are in their twenties.

not immediately acknowledge those tendencies and admit them publicly. Rather, it appears that a number of years may intervene between recognizing one's homosexual inclinations, labeling oneself as a homosexual, and publicly acknowledging one's homosexuality. For example, Troiden and Goode (1980) studied 150 gay males and found that the average age at which these men first thought they might be homosexual was 17. However, it was almost 7 years, on the average, before these men experienced their first homosexual love relationship. Blumstein and Schwartz (1977) suggest that it is much more difficult for males to accept a homosexual identity than it is for females. The researchers think this may be because in our culture masculinity is a major criterion for a male's feeling of self-worth. Because homosexuality is seen as unmasculine or feminine, many males believe that others will look down on them and they will lose their self-esteem if they accept a homosexual identity.

For females there tends to be about 1½ years between the time they recognize that they may have homosexual inclinations and the time they have sex with another woman. Lesbians on the average have their first homosexual affair when they are 20 or 21. Often these lesbian women have tried heterosexual relationships before having a homosexual relationship or taking on a homosexual identity. Typically they find heterosexual relationships to be unsatisfying.

Once an individual has accepted a homosexual identity, there remains the problem of revealing his or her sexual orientation to others. Since our culture has such a negative view of homosexuality, some homosexuals are unwilling to let others know about their sexual orientation. These individuals are referred to as **closet homosexuals.** Others are blatantly open about their homosexuality. Still others, probably the majority, are somewhere between these extremes. When homosexuals decide to let others know about their homosexuality, they are said to have "come out of the closet" or simply to have "come out."

closet homosexual
Homosexual who is not open about his or her homosexuality.

320   **HUMAN SEXUALITY**

THE COMING OUT PROCESS

Coming out may be defined as letting other individuals know about one's homosexuality. There are many degrees of "coming out." Some individuals reveal their sexual orientation only to other homosexuals. Some also tell close friends and family. Others may inform virtually everyone with whom they come in contact. It used to be that few individuals told other people about their homosexuality. Now, however, as a result of the "gay liberation" movement, more homosexual individuals are being open about their sexual orientation. Even today, though, most homosexual men and women are not completely open about their sexual orientation. Bell and Weinberg (1978) report that homosexuals of lower social status are somewhat more likely to be open about their sexual orientation than individuals with higher education and income levels.

The coming out process may extend over a period of years (see box below). Some individuals may, for example, tell close friends long before they try to tell their families and co-workers about their sexual orientation. However, others decide suddenly that they are going to be public about their sexual orientation. Deciding to "come out of the closet" can be difficult because such a negative view of homosexuality exists in our society. Many homosexuals are afraid that their friends and family will not be able to accept such a disclosure.

coming out
"Coming out of the closet"; becoming open about one's homosexuality.

A Personal Glimpse

One Example of the Difficulty of Coming Out

When I was in my senior year in high school I couldn't stand to be around other people. So a week after I graduated I moved into the canyon, two and a half miles inside the canyon, with no people around. At the time I didn't know why, I just had to, and I didn't want to know why. I just knew I had to get away from everybody. I always knew that there was something going on with me. The fact is, I was getting away because I was a homosexual, because I wasn't feeling good about myself.

The time in the canyon was like trying to say, "OK, well you've got to get yourself excited about women," because all of my fantasies when I jacked off were about men. Once in a blue moon I could somehow fit a woman in there.

Then there was a flood in town, and a lot of loose people moved into the canyon. They were young people my age, so I became friends with them. There were women who took off their clothes in front of me and did everything for me, and I didn't get it. As I looked back on the situation a few months later, I got beet-red in the face and thought, "My God, how obvious can it be?"

Last year I came back for Christmas, and one night my older brother and I were alone in the room, and he went down to get himself a six-pack of beer, downed it real fast, and said, "What would you think if I were to tell you that I'm gay?" And it was like a rush went through my body, and I just sat there for a while. Then I said, "I'm gay, too. I think I'm gay, too." I cried all the way back to the canyon. I had been fighting the fact of being a homosexual for years. I had become a recluse. I went out to the very end of the canyon and lived there and never came into town for anything. I'd fought it for years. But when my brother told me that he was gay, then I thought that I can be, too, because I had always looked up to him, and I saw him as an example in the family.

From Silverstein, 1981.

The "gay liberation" movement has brought many people into full awareness and appreciation of their homosexuality.

Rather than risk losing their friends and the support of their family, they often prefer to hide their sexual orientation. In fact, many families and friends have difficulty accepting that someone closely associated with them is homosexual. Weinberg and Williams (1974) state that "difficulties with parents are among the most significant problems in the lives of many homosexuals."

Even with all of the problems involved in telling one's parents about one's homosexuality, it appears that homosexuals are more likely to tell their families than they are to tell other members of society (Bell and Weinberg, 1978). Furthermore, mothers are more likely to be told than fathers. Of course, many practical risks are involved in being open about one's homosexuality. A sizable number of families have disowned homosexual children, and other institutions in society have also rejected homosexuals. One needs to balance these risks against the benefits of being able to be open about one's life-style.

HOMOPHOBIA

The difficulty that many homosexuals have in admitting to themselves and others that they are attracted to individuals of the same sex is not surprising, given the extent to which homophobia pervades our culture. **Homophobia** is a persistent and irrational fear of homosexuals, as well as a negative attitude and hostility toward homosexuals.

Despite efforts by the gay liberation movement, negative public attitudes toward homosexuality have not dissipated. Polls have consistently found that approximately three fourths of the American public feel that homosexuality is morally wrong (Davis and Smith, 1987). Unfortunately, such attitudes are the foundation for behavioral manifestations of homophobia. Kirk and Madsen (1989) have identified three broad classes of homophobic behavior: (1) actions that prevent homosexual behavior per se, (2) actions that deny gays their fundamental civil rights, and (3) actions that unleash public disapproval against homosexuals.

homophobia
(hoh' muh FOH bee uh)
Persistent and irrational fear of homosexuals; negative attitude and hostility toward homosexuals.

Actions That Prevent Homosexual Behavior Per Se

Homophobia may be expressed through local, state, or federal laws that criminalize the sexual acts identified with homosexuality (most commonly sodomy), as well as court decisions that uphold such legislation. Twenty-four states still have laws against sodomy. Manifestations of homophobic actions against homosexual behavior can be found even in the U.S. Supreme Court. In 1986, a five to four ruling in *Bowers v. Hardwick* found that the Constitution does not protect homosexual relations between consenting adults, even in the privacy of their bedrooms. In a footnote the court observed that the constitutional right to privacy might protect heterosexuals engaged in sodomy (that question was left undecided). Although many such laws go unenforced, in the books they continue to brand homosexuality with the state's disapproval. Therefore the ruling of the Supreme Court and the widespread sodomy laws reinforce and legitimize the nation's homophobia, providing grounds for discrimination against homosexuals (Kirk and Madsen, 1989).

Actions That Deny Homosexuals Their Fundamental Civil Rights

Another class of homophobic behaviors includes, among other things, efforts to keep gays from marrying, parenting children, and working in particular occupations. No state legally recognizes gay marriages (Kirk and Madsen, 1989). Such recognition would appear to condone homosexuality. Unfortunately, this lack of recognition both debases homosexuality and sabotages the durability of gay relationships. In addition, it undermines any evolution of mutual property and inheritance rights between homosexual partners, rights that married couples are automatically afforded.

In addition to not recognizing homosexual marriages, the state does not act favorably toward homosexual parenting (Risman and Schwartz, 1988; Kirk and Madsen, 1989). Homosexual parents are often accused of being unfit parents and are placed in jeopardy of losing custody of their children. These accusations are based on the homophobic belief that homosexual parents would exert an "unwholesome" influence that would steer the children toward homosexuality. Such fears are unfounded. Studies comparing children raised by homosexual parents with children raised by heterosexual parents have found no unusual gender identity development, no greater inclination toward homosexuality, and no serious social or emotional difficulties among the children raised by homosexual parents (Risman and Schwarz, 1988; Kirk and Madsen, 1989). Despite such findings, some states as recently as 1987 have passed laws specifically outlawing adoptions by homosexuals (Kirk and Madsen, 1989).

In addition to preventing homosexuals from marrying and parenting, homophobic attitudes lead to job discrimination. According to a 1987 Gallup Poll, two thirds of the public believe gays should never be hired as elementary school teachers (Gallup, 1987). Such opinions are based on fears that homosexual teachers would seduce their pupils or at the very least exert an influence that would turn previously straight students toward homosexuality. Neither fear is empirically founded (Ruse, 1988). A majority of the public also believe that homosexuals should not be allowed to become clergy, and at least 40% believe that homosexuals should not be hired as doctors or be allowed into the Armed Forces (Gallup, 1987). Although measures outlawing employment discrimi-

Advertising promoting gay
and lesbian rights.

nation against homosexuals in the public and private sectors have been adopted in some places, the machinery of hiring and promotion often evades the regulating grasp of the law (Kirk and Madsen, 1989).

Actions That Unleash Public Disapproval Against Homosexuals

A third class of homophobic behavior entails the harassment, brutalization, and public rejection of homosexual individuals. Homosexual men and women in the United States are targets of a wide range of assaultive behaviors ranging from verbal expressions of dislike to violent attacks. Assaults appear to be on the rise. The National Gay and Lesbian Task Force reported 7,031 complaints of antigay violence and harassment in 1989, compared with 2,042 reports in 1985. Statistics, however, do not convey the horror of these homophobic assaults:

> In Maine, three high school students attack an effeminate young man and throw him off a bridge to his death. . . .
> In San Francisco, while witnesses look on, a young man is stabbed to death by four youths shouting "Faggot! Faggot!" In the same city, a lesbian is beaten in the face, knocked to the ground and kicked repeatedly while attackers scream "dyke" and "bitch."
> In New Jersey, three college-aged men entrap a twenty-year-old gay at midnight in a shopping mall; after working him over and burning cigarettes in his face, they tie him by the ankles to their truck and drag him down the road.
> In New York City, a gay couple steps out of a taxi and, before reaching the front door of their Greenwich Village apartment, they have received broken ribs, concussions, and severe internal injuries.
>
> Kirk and Madsen, 1989

Not all cases are as inhumane as those above. However, homosexuals must live with the knowledge that they may be harassed, beaten, or even killed merely because of their sexual orientation. In addition, and in many ways as painful, "coming out" carries with it a risk of rejection by family, friends, and colleagues (Moses and Hawkins, 1982) at a time when the individual is in dire need of emotional support.

Causes of Homophobia

The perpetrators of homophobic violence are most frequently teen and young adult males (Greer, 1986; Herek, 1988); however, as Kirk and Madsen (1989) point out, "The real perpetrators are those who taught them to hate." Television advertisements, movies, comedians, talk show hosts, religious leaders, and politicians all broadcast their homophobic attitudes. The lesson learned: homosexuals should be harassed and brutalized.

Researchers have identified characteristics of individuals who tend to have strong homophobic attitudes (Herek, 1987, 1988; Whitley, 1987). Individuals with negative attitudes are (1) more likely to espouse traditional, restrictive attitudes about gender roles, (2) more likely to believe that their peers hold negative attitudes toward homosexuals, (3) less likely to have had personal contact with homosexuals, and (4) more likely to subscribe to a conservative religious ideology. Finally, many have suggested that persons with hostile attitudes toward homosexuality are themselves insecure about their gender identity or sexual orientation (Kirk and Madsen, 1989). However, this is difficult to prove empirically (Herek, 1988).

Strategies to Extinguish Homophobia

Targeting those who most typically carry homophobic attitudes and understanding the process involved in the transformation of hostile attitudes into homophobic behaviors may result in more effective strategies for changing their attitudes and behaviors. Kirk and Madsen (1989) suggest several approaches, one of which is referred to as desensitization. Desensitization makes homosexuals responsible for changing the attitudes of heterosexuals. Kirk and Madsen contend that if homosexuals present themselves as overwhelmingly different and threatening, heterosexuals will be driven to overt acts of political persecution and physical violence. If, however, homosexuals live alongside heterosexuals "visibly but as inoffensively as possible," the fear heterosexuals feel may eventually diminish and tolerance may ensue. Desensitization is designed to provide individuals with positive experiences with homosexual persons. Stevenson (1988) reports that such an approach does in fact appear to be effective in reducing homophobic attitudes held by heterosexual individuals.

While the behaviors suggested by Kirk and Madsen may result in less homophobia, homosexuals should not be solely responsible for changing the homophobic attitudes and behaviors of heterosexuals. Heterosexuals need to accept some responsibility for their beliefs and actions. One approach to effecting change is through education. It has already been demonstrated that homophobic attitudes can be changed through education, especially courses on human sexuality (Stevenson, 1988). Such efforts should be increased.

Effect of AIDS on Homophobia

Polls have shown no significant change in attitudes toward homosexuality since the beginning of the AIDS epidemic. In both 1973 and 1987 approximately three fourths of those surveyed believed that sexual relations between two adults of the same sex are "always wrong" (Davis and Smith, 1987). It appears that AIDS is giving people who *already* have homophobic views justification for

Homophobic behavior such as housing discrimination has increased because of the AIDS epidemic.

their beliefs (Schneider, 1987). According to Jerry Falwell, the founder of the Moral Majority, AIDS is a "definite form of judgment of God upon society" (Moral Majority report, 1985). Likewise, Patrick Buchanan (1983), a conservative political columnist, attests, "The poor homosexuals—they have declared war upon Nature, and now Nature is exacting an awful retribution." Such statements manifest classic "blame the victim" mentality. Unfortunately, blaming the victim has led to further oppression and persecution of homosexuals. AIDS has become "a convenient vehicle for expressing hostility toward homosexual persons" (Herek and Glunt, 1988). Had the AIDS epidemic not been so strongly identified with gay men, perhaps legislation outlawing homosexuality and limiting homosexuals' civil rights would be less widespread today. And, perhaps, instead of an increasing number of incidents of harassment and violent attacks against homosexuals, feelings approaching tolerance toward homosexuals would have evolved among those who view homosexuality as immoral. Instead, many homosexuals must face not only the threat of AIDS but also the perils of a homophobic society.

LIFE-STYLES

The sexual life-styles of heterosexuals and homosexuals are also discussed in Chapter 15.

As with heterosexuals, there is great diversity among the life-styles of homosexuals. Some homosexuals try to pass as heterosexuals by fitting into a heterosexual life-style. They may even marry and have children. Although they have homosexual feelings and desires, they may not act on them. Others lead

HUMAN SEXUALITY

overtly heterosexual lives while being covertly involved in homosexual activity. For example, some homosexuals are married and have children but secretly have homosexual relationships. At the other extreme, some homosexuals have life-styles that are very different from those of most heterosexuals. For example, some homosexuals spend a good deal of time **cruising** in gay bars, gay baths, and public restrooms (see box, p. 334). Thus there is no more consistency in homosexual life-styles than in heterosexual life-styles.

cruising
Looking for a sexual partner.

Attempts have been made to classify different homosexual life-styles. Bell and Weinberg (1978) proposed five types. Individuals in the "close coupled" category look to one partner for most of their sexual satisfaction and emotional closeness. These individuals are less likely than other homosexuals to have sexual relationships outside of their primary relationship and are less likely to frequent gay baths and gay bars. The "open coupled" category is composed of individuals who, although they live with their partners, are less committed to them than individuals in "close coupled" relationships. Because these individuals tend to be less satisfied with their relationships, they usually rely on a larger circle of friends and look for other sexual partners in gay bars and baths. Individuals in the "functional" category do not have one special sexual partner. They tend to have a large number of sexual partners and to organize their lives around their sexual activity. They often frequent gay bars and baths. The "dysfunctionals" are inclined to regret their sexual orientation and report having sexual problems and worries. They seem to have difficulty finding a permanent sexual partner, although they apparently try. The "asexual" category is made up of individuals who indicate that they have low levels of sexual activity and few partners. They feel that they are not attractive and report having a number of sexual problems. They also describe themselves as lonely and unhappy.

Silverstein (1981) has suggested that gay males can be divided into two types: excitement seekers and home builders. Silverstein defines an excitement seeker as "one who emphasizes novelty and change, rather than stability and longevity in a relationship." A home builder is "one who looks for permanence in a relationship, who wants to plan for the future with another man. He judges a relationship more by the degree of intimacy achieved than by the level of sexual excitement." Silverstein says that excitement seekers enjoy sexually catching someone in what they call "the hunt," "the chase," or "the seduction." Without the thrill of competition these men may even view sex as dull. Silverstein also says that excitement seekers value sex as a physical experience but tend to avoid intimacy. Excitement seekers seem to place importance on masculine symbols such as penis size, and they find it extremely difficult to form a sexual attachment to any man who does not "measure up" physically. Excitement seekers value the masculine trait of independence. They resist any attempt by a lover to interfere with their freedom. In addition, excitement seekers are not very domestic. They tend not to be interested in finding and taking care of a home and cooking meals.

Home builders, on the other hand, are homosexuals who are most likely to form long-lasting relationships (see box, p. 328). They seem to want to be part of a family-like unit. They tend to want the stability and comfort of a well-furnished and decorated home. Home builders are also more likely to want to keep their ties with their parents and siblings. Home builders value conti-

A Personal Glimpse

Troy and Ed

Troy is in his mid-fifties; Ed, in his early sixties. Both are practicing psychologists. After interviewing them, I am convinced they are the forefathers of "open marriage." Not only were they "in" before it was "in," but they will be "in" after open marriage is "out."

Their open marriage began twenty-five years ago. Talking with me in his plant- and clutter-filled office, Troy explains: "I was twenty-nine and Ed was thirty-seven when we met. After four years of struggling with sexual incompatibility—call it what you will—I decided I didn't need the tension. I mean, we didn't chart it out or anything like that. But I knew I could get plenty of good sex with regulars I'd known for years. Quite simply, there was something neurotic going on in me with this monogamy thing: so I gave it up."

Ed stretches out comfortably on the living room couch. His feet are happily resting on top of a magazine-laden coffee table. "Understand," he says, "the first few years we did try to be true to each other, you know, monogamy and all that. But after a few years, we started finding other people. Certainly, at first, we were both very secretive about it. But I think we both understood and accepted the idea that there *would be* other people. In fact, when we became honest with each other about 'other people,' we had a couple of threesomes. However, we never got too far with that. Troy never liked threesomes—that is, not with me as a third."

"You're young"—Troy smiles at me—"but when you've lived with someone twenty-five years, little roots intertwine in a way that hurts if you try to pull them apart. Someone might say to you, 'Get rid of that old pair of slippers.' But you look at them and you think to yourself, "They might be old, but they're mine. They're comfortable. They're an important part of me and my life. I'm simply not going to give them to you.' When you love someone you can live comfortably with that person—you're not going to give him up. There are always plenty of people around to sleep with. Why"—he laughs—"I've had somewhat of a stable of men with whom I've been sleeping, some for twenty-five or thirty years. Not all at the same time, of course. But with Ed, he's the person I *live* with. It's all the things you know the other person would like to be interested in. It's the joke you wait to tell him or the question you wait to ask him. It's knowing that somebody is going to come home between five-thirty and six. That person is there—sorting out the mail, messing up the living room. You even get involved with his laundry. I mean, after twenty-five years you can instinctively recognize *his* laundry."

I ask Ed how he explains his twenty-five-year relationship with Troy. He sits there staring out the window and swinging the microphone around by the wire. The silence is deafening. I can hear buses and taxi cabs blasting their horns on the street below. Finally: "Sexual attraction seems to fade quickly"—he sighs—"so the 'staying power,' certainly between Troy and me, had to be in terms of other things. Troy saw me through the death of my mother very early in our relationship. And I saw him through the death of his mother in 1972. We've seen each other through many major disappointments. These things all count. They make a fabric of experience with a great many threads going through it, and I can't say any one of these threads in particular has held us together. It's a whole lot of threads. We love and trust each other. We look to each other for comfort and guidance."

From Mendola, 1980.

nuity and are concerned about planning for the future. Because of their concern for intimacy and continuity, home builders are much more likely to be involved in dependent relationships with other individuals. Furthermore, they are more likely to be monogamous than are excitement seekers.

The sexual relationships between lovers are very different for excitement seekers and home builders. Excitement seekers are looking for sexual competence in a lover. Their life-styles are likely to include cruising in gay bars, gay baths, and public restrooms. For home builders sex is not as important as intimacy, trust, and a feeling of "home." Home builders are much less likely than excitement seekers to spend time cruising.

Contrary to stereotypes, the majority of gay males would probably be classified as home builders. Bell and Weinberg (1978) estimate that 52% to 58% of male homosexuals have lived with a male partner for at least 3 months and many relationships have lasted more than 5 years. This percentage has probably increased because of the threat of AIDS (Risman and Schwartz, 1988).

Another major contribution to research concerning homosexuality focuses on the developmental characteristics of long-term male homosexual relationships. McWhirter and Mattison (1984) interviewed 156 male couples whose relationships lasted from 1 to 37 years with an average of 8.9 years. Through their extensive interviews with these gay couples, they were able to identify six developmental stages through which the partners in the couple progressed in a relationship.

Stage one, *blending*, occurs in the first year the couple is together. Blending is characterized by merging, limerence, equalizing of partnership, and high sexual activity. Merging refers to the two individuals joining together and in a sense becoming one person. Merging includes both taking on the other's

Like heterosexuals, homosexuals have life-styles that vary from close, caring relationships to casual encounters.

qualities and focusing on the couple's similarities. In this stage differences tend to be downplayed or overlooked. Limerence refers to the feelings of falling in love. As one participant explains, "I loved everything about him, from the way he walked to the way he parted his hair. I thought his interest in country music was scholarly! He could do no wrong" (McWhirter and Mattison, 1984, p. 27). During this stage, homosexual couples are confronted with the opportunity and challenge of developing equality in their relationship without the gender-based sex roles of heterosexual relationships, which although compatible are noted for their pervasive inequality.

Stage two, *nesting*, occurs in the second and third years of the relationship. Nesting is a time of homemaking and finding compatibility and is also characterized by feelings of ambivalence and a decline of limerence. Homemaking in stage two symbolizes the male couple's commitment to the relationship and gives them the opportunity to display their union to their friends and family. One participant in this stage explained his feelings, "After a while I really wanted 'our' home. You know, a place we were proud of, where we could have friends and family. We had a lot of fun fixing it up together" (McWhirter and Mattison, 1984, p. 41). Despite the couple's involvement in homemaking, however, limerence tends to decline in the second stage. The illusions of stage one, including the blurring of differences, vanish; instead differences become highlighted. To find harmony, the couple must balance or resolve these differences. Finding compatibility refers to the male couple's need to discover ways to live together harmoniously. As a result of the conflicts of homemaking, difficulties in finding compatibility, and decline of limerence, ambivalence toward the relationship develops. Individuals in the couple feel a concurrent attraction and aversion toward their relationship. As one participant in this stage confessed, "One day I'd be gung-ho about us, and then the next I'd be wishing I was alone again. My thoughts about us were on a seesaw. I was confused . . . ." (McWhirter and Mattison, 1984, p. 56).

Stage three, *maintaining*, occurs in the fourth and fifth years of the relationship. One predominant characteristic of stage three is the reappearance of one's individuality. In the maintaining stage, male couples learn to deal with conflict, begin taking risks, and establish traditions. According to McWhirter and Mattison, out of the struggle with ambivalence of stage two evolves a need for the reappearance of the self and the need to develop methods of dealing with conflict. The couple comes to realize that too much togetherness may result in stagnation of the relationship. They feel the relationship is by this time strong enough to support the emergence of individuality. This is not to say that the individuals do not experience fears of abandonment in this stage: "I went through hell when David told me he was joining a gym without me. He hadn't ever done anything like that before. I was irrational about it. It didn't make any difference that I wasn't interested in the gym; it was just the idea that he would do it without me" (McWhirter and Mattison, 1984, p. 63). Taking risks also helps prevent the threat of stagnation and promotes growth in the relationship. Risk taking not only includes expressing gripes and annoyances with one's partner, but also entails taking risks with others, including friends, fellow employees, and family. Making assertive career choices and coming out to family and friends are examples of such risks. Also, in the third stage couples develop traditions of their own—commemorating their anniversary of living together with a camping trip every year, spending every Friday night alone together, or making a special dinner to celebrate birthdays. Establishing traditions, customs, and habits not only enriches their relationship but also symbolizes the commitment they have to each other.

Stage four, *building*, which occurs in the sixth through tenth year, is a time characterized by collaborating, increasing productivity, developing a sense of dependability between the partners, and establishing independence. Collaboration refers to working together, from doing the dishes together to starting a business together. Because of their confidence in their relationship, by stage four the partners have less concern about focusing their energies on the relationship. Instead they encourage and support individual achievement, and individual productivity tends to increase. In addition, the fear of abandonment has given way to a sense of dependability on the partner and on the relationship. A person's knowledge that his partner is there for him encourages greater independence without fear of loss.

Stage five, *releasing*, occurs in years 11 through 20 of a male couple's relationship. Releasing is characterized by trusting, merging of money and possessions, constricting, and taking each other for granted. Although trust was present from the start, by the fifth stage of the relationship the trust takes on a new quality. For an individual in the fifth stage, trusting now includes the awareness that his partner knows him completely, faults and all. Despite such knowledge his partner accepts him, which creates feelings of security and contentment. Along with this trust comes the merging of the couple's money and possessions. Unlike heterosexual couples who begin sharing money and possessions legally on the wedding day, homosexual couples as yet have no such legal commitments. According to McWhirter and Mattison, the merging of the couple's money and possessions "represents the surrender of each partner's last major symbol of independence"; thus they "release" themselves to the relationship. Constriction refers to the couple's tendency to reduce their social life, including drawing away from friends and families. This may largely be due to one or both experiencing a midlife crisis and is not necessarily related to the length of their relationship. Couples at this time may take each other for granted. One participant exemplifies this attitude by saying, "I expect my heart to beat, I expect my lungs to breathe, and I expect him to be there" (McWhirter and Mattison, 1984, p. 109). The security of stage four often leads to a degree of neglect in stage five.

Stage six, *renewing*, characterizes the relationship of 20 years and beyond. Renewing is a time of restoring the partnership, achieving security, shifting perspectives, and remembering. To move from the releasing of stage five to the renewing of stage six, the couple must learn not to take each other for granted. Often a crisis provides the necessary jolt to restore their appreciation for each other. As one participant explained: "I almost lost him after his heart attack and somehow we learned. We learned to take better care of ourselves, and we remembered to take better care of each other. I say 'I love you' every night before we go to sleep now. And I mean it. We had stopped that ten years ago. It seemed like kid stuff, I suppose. But, I'll tell you, it's good medicine" (McWhirter and Mattison, 1984, p. 110). Shifting perspectives refers to the couple's shift to the present and personal concerns rather than reaching for future goals. Such a shift is due largely to their age rather than the stage of their relationship. If communication between partners is good, the shift in perspective can bring the partners closer, with each realizing he is not alone. Along with discussing their concerns of growing old, partners at this stage also spend a lot of time reminiscing. They enjoy sharing the history of their long relationship with willing audiences. McWhirter and Mattison suggest that by doing so couples in this stage hope to instill in others "the knowledge that two men can love and support each other through good and bad times for many years. They want it known that male couples have existed always, that it takes willingness and effort, and that the reward is great" (p. 123). McWhirter and Mattison's work has illustrated that homosexual and heterosexual relationships may actually be more similar than disparate.

Although no study has investigated lesbian relationships as thoroughly as McWhirter and Mattison have studied male couples' relationships, recent studies have illuminated some of the prominent characteristics of female homosexual relationships. Because lesbian couples lack the socially constructed roles of heterosexual relationships, women in homosexual relationships have the advantage and the challenge of creating a relationship without such roles. Contrary to popular stereotypes, butch-femme role-playing does not characterize female couples (Blumstein and Schwartz, 1983; Lynch and Reilly, 1985-1986). Instead, lesbians tend to create in their relationship a standard of egalitarianism favored by both women (Caldwell and Peplau, 1984; Risman and Schwartz, 1988). Blumstein and Schwarz (1983) have suggested that women in homosexual relationships tend to have greater economic independence, enjoy greater productivity, maintain greater personal autonomy, and assume greater responsibility for their own lives compared with women in heterosexual relationships. Lesbian relationships are characterized by equality in decision making (Lynch and Reilly, 1985-1986; Kurdek and Schmitt, 1986). As Risman and Schwartz (1988) noted, "It may be that after the conventions of gender are removed, power inequities are so unflattering to both that partners are intensely motivated to avoid the costs of greater power and powerlessness alike." Lesbians, with their independence from gender-based roles, may find greater equality in their relationship, which leads to greater satisfaction with the relationship (Peplau, Padesky, and Hamilton, 1982).

Gay Bars

Gay bars are bars that cater to homosexual individuals. Most large cities have a number of gay bars, and gay bars have begun to appear in smaller cities and towns. They provide an opportunity for meeting and socializing with other homosexuals.

Some gay bars are exclusively for gay males, others are for lesbians, and a few are for both males and females. There are many more bars for males than for females, and the atmosphere in male gay bars tends to be somewhat different from that in female gay bars. In male gay bars the emphasis is on finding new sexual partners, but in female gay bars more importance is placed on conversation and social interaction.

A gay bar.

Gay Baths

Another place where gay males have traditionally found sexual partners is in gay baths. Bell and Weinberg (1978), who studied the gay baths in San Francisco, conclude that "the major function of the gay bath is to provide an inexpensive place where gay men can engage in frequent, anonymous sexual activity without fear of social or legal reprisal." The baths typically consist of a large number of rooms, each with a sitting area, a single cot, a small table with an ashtray, and a clothing rack. There are also rooms for dancing, watching television, and socializing, as well as for showers and steam baths. Most of the rooms are dimly lit. When a patron arrives, he usually leaves his clothes in a room or locker and wraps a towel around his waist. Then he looks for a partner, and when he finds one, they go to one of the private rooms to engage in sex. Often there are more patrons than private rooms, so the men frequently engage in sexual activities in more public areas. Sometimes there are "orgy rooms" where patrons can engage in group sex.

Most cities have had gay baths for male clientele. Lesbian baths are rare because females are less interested in impersonal sex. In recent years many of the male gay baths have closed down because of the threat of AIDS (see the box on p. 334).

For a more complete discussion of AIDS, see Chapter 19.

Public Restrooms

Homosexuals sometimes have impersonal sex in public restrooms. Sex in public restrooms is often referred to as "tearoom trade." Members of the gay community know that they can find sexual partners in certain public restrooms. Usually these restrooms are inconspicuous and not often frequented by the public. A person approaching a known "tearoom," especially if he is seen

See Chapter 2 for a discussion of some ethical concerns that have been raised about Humphreys' research on the tearoom trade.

AIDS and the Sexual Behavior of Gay Men

Several researchers have conducted studies to determine whether the threat of acquired immunodeficiency syndrome (AIDS) has had an effect on the sexual practices of gay men. McKusick, Horstman, and Coates (1985) tracked the trends in sexual behavior of gay men in San Francisco. Men in monogamous relationships reported few changes in their sexual behaviors; they apparently felt protected by the fact that they did not have multiple partners. However, men in nonmonogamous relationships and men who were not in relationships indicated increased use of condoms and reductions in all types of sexual practice, including such high-risk practices as oral-anal contact, anal intercourse, and oral-genital contact.

Results from another study suggest there is a trend toward more monogamous relationships, less "cruising," and decreased high-risk sexual practices. Martin and associates (1989) studied changes in sexual behavior of gay men in New York. The data suggest that monogamous relationships have increased from 8% in 1981 to 19% in 1987; however, the majority of gay men reported having multiple partners in 1981 (90%) and in 1987 (75%). Martin and associates also found substantial declines in the proportion of men frequenting gay baths, public restrooms, and backroom bars for sex. For example, in 1981, 50% attended a bathhouse for sex at least once but in 1987 only 8% did so. Furthermore, concurring with the findings of McKusick, Horst-

man, and Coates, Martin and associates' data suggest significant declines in the frequency of several high-risk practices. For instance, in 1981 only approximately 26% of their participants either abstained from receptive anal intercourse or consistently used condoms; in 1987, 82.9% of the sample avoided unprotected receptive anal intercourse either by abstinence or by consistent condom use.

Despite substantial modifications in sexual practices, homosexuals have not given up many risky sexual practices. Among a sample of New York City gay men, half of the respondents (49.6%) reported no change in their sexual behavior following the advent of the AIDS epidemic (Feldman, 1986). In another study of sexual behavior changes among gay men in New York City, Siegel and associates (1988) found that although 84% of their sample had at least modified their sexual behaviors (e.g., reduced the number

of sex partners), 48% continued to engage in risky sexual behavior. Furthermore, in a study of gay men living in an area with a low incidence of AIDS, Jones and associates (1987) found that while 80% of the sample reported altering their sexual practices because of concern about AIDS, 67% reported that they had engaged in receptive anal intercourse without condoms in the preceding 12 months (Jones et al., 1987). Thus, although increasing awareness of the dangers and probable causes of AIDS has had a definite effect on the sexual behavior of gay men, high-risk behaviors continue to be practiced.

Despite the continuation of risky sexual behaviors among gay men, data suggest that the modifications they have made have reduced the number of new human immunodeficiency virus (HIV) infections (Martin et al., 1989). Nevertheless, a major risk for HIV infection remains, and without a vaccine or an effective treatment for AIDS, behavioral modification of sexual practices continues to be the only effective means of stemming the spread of the epidemic.

AIDS network march.

lingering outside it, is assumed to be looking for a sex partner. Once a partner is found, the two usually have a sexual interaction in one of the stalls. The sex act is usually completed quickly before others discover the activity. Often the two participants do not even exchange names; they simply have a quick sexual encounter and leave the restroom separately.

SEXUAL BEHAVIOR

Many heterosexuals find it difficult to imagine how homosexual individuals have sex together. However, the sexual behavior of homosexuals is not much different from what many heterosexuals do in sex play. For males the most common types of sexual interaction are fellatio, mutual masturbation, anal intercourse, and rubbing against each other's bodies (Bell and Weinberg, 1978). For lesbians the most common types of sexual behavior are mutual masturbation, cunnilingus, and body rubbing (Bell and Weinberg, 1978). Although stereotypes suggest that lesbians use **dildos** (penis-shaped objects) in their sexual activity, research indicates that this is seldom the case (Martin and Lyon, 1972).

At least for women, homosexual interactions may be more satisfying than heterosexual interactions. Coleman, Hoon, and Hoon (1983) found that, compared with heterosexual women, lesbians reported having sex more often and experiencing more frequent orgasms and more sexual satisfaction. Peplau and associates (1978) discovered that 70% of the lesbians they studied "almost always" had orgasms with their current female partner. Fourteen percent reported that they usually did, 10% reported that they occasionally did, and only 4% reported that they never did. As you may recall from Chapter 10, only about 40% to 50% of married heterosexual women report that they regularly experience orgasm. These results suggest that homosexual women are much more likely to have orgasms during their sexual encounters than heterosexual women. One reason may be that women are much more likely to understand what provides pleasure and stimulation to the female body. If they know what is satisfying for themselves, they should be able to provide satisfaction for

dildo
(DIL doh) Penis-shaped object that is used for sexual stimulation.

The difference between homosexual and heterosexual women in terms of frequency of orgasm is discussed in Chapter 10.

Lesbians report having more satisfying sexual relationships than many heterosexual women.

another woman. The following is a quotation from a woman who has experienced sexual interaction with both men and women:

> Most of the men in my heterosexual career (when I was 20 until I was 28), wanted oral stimulation from me of their penis after which they would mount me and reach their climax. After their ejaculation they would ask, "Didja come?" In general, my female lovers have taken far more creative and varied approaches to love making. All of them, however, began by being incredibly gentle and aware of my needs, as well as theirs. The women did not act as though I was a "masturbation machine" for them. Nor did they fall asleep when it was over. No woman ever asked me, "Didja come?" They knew. My love making periods with women always lasted much longer than they ever did with men. Twenty minutes for a man, at least an hour with a woman, usually more.
>
> Hite, 1976, p. 273

A similar comparison of orgasm rates for homosexual and heterosexual males would not have much meaning, since most males experience orgasm during almost every sexual encounter. Presumably, however, gay males have the same benefit as female homosexuals; that is, they are better able to please each other because they are well aware of what is pleasing to themselves.

Masters and Johnson (1979) studied the sexual interactions of homosexuals and heterosexuals. They found no difference in the physiology of the sexual response of homosexuals and heterosexuals; both homosexuals and heterosexuals went through the four stages of sexual response in the same way. However, Masters and Johnson found substantial differences in the way the couples interacted. The homosexuals took much more time for their sexual interactions; they did not seem to have the same motivation to reach a goal as the heterosexuals. Heterosexual couples appeared more performance oriented; they seemed to be working toward achieving orgasm. In the heterosexual couples the males attempted to stimulate the females by kissing and holding for approximately 30 seconds; they then moved on to genital stimulation. In the homosexual couples, however, although the females used the same techniques to stimulate their partner, they took more time. In addition to kissing and holding, the lesbians spent much more time stimulating their partner's breasts. The lesbians also tended to communicate more during sexual interactions than the heterosexual couples. There were also differences in the way heterosexual and homosexual couples tried to stimulate the male. The homosexual couples were much more likely to stimulate the nipples of the male and the area on the lower side of the penis just below the corona than were the heterosexuals. Furthermore, homosexuals were more likely to bring the male close to orgasm a number of times before actually bringing him to orgasm.

The four stages of sexual response are discussed in Chapter 5.

Homosexuals might use techniques that are more satisfying to their partners than heterosexuals because they know what will please members of their own gender. Homosexuals can do for their partners what they themselves find satisfying; heterosexuals, however, must either guess or be told what members of the opposite gender enjoy. Hite (1981) asked men who had had sex with both men and women how sex with men was different from sex with women. The following are some of their responses:

> Sex with men is different because men are more outgoing sexually. They want sex. Women will fight you off.

> It is far more relaxed, since men understand each other's bodies, feelings, reactions, and needs—we are basically the same and it is a totally *natural* thing for me.

> Men are more exciting partners; they have less inhibitions and are more willing to sexually experiment; also I find there is less of a game of coyness about getting down to sex.

Hite, 1981, p. 818

Gender Differences

There are definite differences in the sexual behavior of male and female homosexuals. For example, Peplau (1981) reports that emotional expressiveness and equality in relationships are ranked as more important by females than by males. Lesbian relationships also tend to be relatively long lasting compared with those of gay males (Peplau and Amaro, 1982). Furthermore, lesbians usually have many fewer sexual partners than do gay males. Schafer (1977)

Gender differences in the sexual behavior of homosexuals are covered in Chapter 10.

Female couples tend to have longer-lasting relationships than male couples.

asked both male and female homosexuals how many partners they had had; although the males in this study indicated having had an average of 75 different partners, the females reported an average of only 5. Moreover, Martin and Lyon (1972) report that lesbians are much less likely to have sex with other individuals when they are in a fairly stable relationship than are gay males. Bell and Weinberg (1978) found that the vast majority of gay males were involved in cruising fairly frequently; few of the females ever went cruising. Masters and Johnson (1979) found that lesbians showed greater consideration for their partners during sexual encounters than did gay males.

Some of the same gender differences in sexual behavior are evident in heterosexuals, but the differences seem to be exaggerated among homosexuals. Although heterosexual males may report more partners than heterosexual females, for example, the difference is not nearly as great as the difference in the number of partners reported by homosexual males and females. Weinberg and Williams (1974) found that gay males tend to have many more sexual partners over the course of their lives than do male heterosexuals. The homosexuals indicated having hundreds of partners; the heterosexual males reported having fewer than 10 partners. It may be that in heterosexual couples the two individuals influence each other such that the natural tendencies of the two genders are somewhat modified. However, when individuals of the same sex interact sexually, they may be likely to reinforce, or at least not attempt to modify, each other's tendencies.

HUMAN SEXUALITY

EXPLANATIONS FOR HOMOSEXUALITY
Biological Explanations

Biological theories of homosexuality have focused on either genetic or hormonal influences. Kallman (1952) studied a number of identical and fraternal twins in which one member of the twin pair was a known homosexual. He wanted to see whether the incidence of homosexuality was higher among identical twins than among fraternal twins. If it was higher among the identical twins, this would indicate a genetic component of homosexuality, since identical twins share the same genes. Fraternal twins, on the other hand, are no more alike than nontwin siblings. Kallman found that only 12% of the fraternal twins were both homosexual; however, 100% of the identical twins were both homosexual. Thus this study seemed to provide evidence for a genetic component of homosexuality. However, more recent evidence does not support Kallman's findings (Money, 1980). Another study investigated the occurrence of homosexuality in the first- and second-degree relatives of boys displaying early effeminate behavior (Zuger, 1989). The vast majority of the boys (72% to 93%) later developed homosexual orientations, but the number of homosexuals among the boys' first- and second-degree relatives about equaled the estimate for the general population. This evidence discounts the existence of a genetic influence on homosexuality. It is not clear what role, if any, genes have in sexual orientation.

More recent investigations have focused on the effects of hormones on sexual orientation. It has frequently been assumed that gay males have lower levels of androgen than male heterosexuals. However, giving female hormones to a heterosexual male does not make him homosexual; it simply decreases his sex drive. Furthermore, giving male hormones to a heterosexual female does not make her homosexual; it intensifies her interest in heterosexual activities (Bancroft, 1981). Sage (1972) administered additional androgen to male homosexuals. Rather than finding that the additional androgen caused the men to become heterosexual, he found that it increased the men's sex drive and had no effect on their sexual orientation.

A number of other investigators have tried to determine whether androgen levels are different in male homosexuals and male heterosexuals. In several studies gay men were found to have lower androgen levels than heterosexual men (Loraine et al., 1970). However, other studies have reported no differences in the hormone levels of homosexual and heterosexual males (Meyer-Bahlburg, 1980). There is some indication, on the other hand, that gay males may have higher levels of estrogen than heterosexual males (Doerr et al., 1973). On the basis of the hormone research so far, it is not possible to be certain whether hormonal differences exist between heterosexual and homosexual males. It is important to keep in mind when considering this research that androgen levels fluctuate over the course of a day, as well as from day to day. In addition, various situational factors can affect hormone levels. These fluctuations might be responsible for the conflicting research results. In many of these studies the individual males were tested only one time for hormone level. Given the variability in hormone level in one man from time to time, taking only one sample measurement is not a reliable assessment method. For a more accurate measure many more hormone samples should be taken from each individual and the average level of the hormones determined.

Recently investigators have begun to compare hormone levels in homosexual and heterosexual females. In some studies they have found that lesbians may have higher androgen and lower estrogen levels than heterosexual females (Loraine et al., 1971). However, other investigators have failed to replicate these findings (Meyer-Bahlburg, 1980; Tourney, 1980).

In summary, the research on hormonal differences between homosexual and heterosexual males and females is inconclusive. At best we can say that future studies in this area should take a more sophisticated approach to hormone assessment. Such research might provide more clear-cut results.

Another possible causative factor in homosexuality may be prenatal excesses or deficiencies of certain sex hormones (Ellis and Ames, 1987). For example, testosterone deficiency at critical times in uterine development might lead to homosexual behavior in males, and excess testosterone during prenatal development might lead to homosexual behavior in females. Animal research suggests that prenatal hormone treatments of various types (e.g., testosterone or estrogen) can result in homosexual behavior (Dorner, 1976). Furthermore, some evidence suggests that abnormal levels of prenatal sex hormones such as testosterone and estrogen may be associated with homosexuality in human beings. Studies of females who have the adrenogenital syndrome indicate that the incidence of homosexuality is higher among this group of females than among a normal group (Money and Schwartz, 1977). Females who were prenatally exposed to synthetic estrogen have been found to be more likely to be bisexual or homosexual than females who were not prenatally exposed (Ehrhardt et al., 1985).

The adrenogenital syndrome is discussed in Chapter 3.

Possibly homosexuality is influenced by genetic or hormonal factors. A recent study has shown that specific cells in the hypothalamus differ in size between heterosexual and homosexual men. This finding suggests that sexual orientation may have a biological basis (LeVay, 1991). Further studies are needed to clarify the influence of biological factors on sexual orientation.

Psychological Explanations

In addition to the biological explanations of homosexuality, a number of psychological explanations have been proposed. One of the earliest was Freud's suggestion that the infant is originally "polymorphous perverse"; in other words, the infant's sexuality can be aimed at a number of both animate and inanimate objects. Typically as a child develops, he or she becomes more and more likely to focus sexual impulses toward individuals of the opposite gender and repress other impulses. Freud theorized that overt homosexual impulses are somewhat "immature" because in normal development individuals repress such tendencies. However, he believed that all individuals have some potential for homosexual impulses that can, under unusual circumstances, become more overt.

Freud believed that homosexuality might result from an abnormal resolution of the Oedipal or Electra situation in the individual's family. Ordinarily, when a young boy reaches the Oedipal phase in development, he feels a strong love for his mother and a resentment of his father. Likewise, when a young girl reaches the Electra phase, she feels a strong love for her father and a resentment of her mother. Later in development, both boys and girls repress their love for the parent of the opposite gender and begin to identify with the parent of the same gender. However, Freud proposed that in the case of homosexuals the individual may do just the opposite: he or she may love the parent of the same gender and identify with the parent of the opposite gender.

Based on the view that particular parent-child interactions might predispose some individuals toward homosexuality, a number of empirical studies have been conducted. Bieber and associates (1962) investigated the family interactions of 106 homosexual and 100 heterosexual men who were patients of psychoanalysts. They indicated that the mothers of the homosexuals were much more likely to be dominant, overprotective, and intimate with their sons than the mothers of the heterosexuals. The fathers of the homosexuals were reported to be more detached, hostile, and rejecting. Bieber and associates suggested that men from homes with dominant, overprotective mothers and detached, hostile fathers fear heterosexual relationships because of their mothers' jealous reactions to such relationships and because of the anxiety provoked by their mothers' seductive behavior.

Wolff (1971) conducted a study with both homosexual and heterosexual women who were not psychiatric patients. She reported that the mothers of the lesbians were more likely to be perceived by their children as rejecting and indifferent than the mothers of heterosexual women, and that the fathers of lesbians were more likely to be perceived by their children as distant or absent than the fathers of heterosexual women. Wolff suggested that because the lesbians did not receive enough love and affection from their mothers during childhood, they continued throughout their lives to try to obtain such love from other women.

If Wolff's findings are correct, her explanation may apply to the results of Bieber and associates' study (1962) with gay males. Bieber and his colleagues found that gay males had distant, hostile fathers. Thus, if an individual has a parent of the same gender who is withdrawn or rejecting, that individual may look to other individuals of the same gender for the love he or she wanted but did not receive from that parent. If this is true, the parent of the same gender is more important in predisposing a child toward homosexuality than the parent of the opposite gender.

Although the types of family constellation just discussed might have some tendency to predispose children to homosexuality, such family relationships must not be construed as always resulting in homosexuality in the children. Many individuals who come from the types of family constellation just described grow up to be heterosexuals. Furthermore, many homosexuals come from families that are not of the sort just discussed (Masters and Johnson, 1979).

Another psychological theory that has been used to explain the development of homosexuality is learning theory. According to learning theory, behaviors that are rewarded or reinforced increase in frequency and behaviors that are punished decrease in frequency. In terms of this theoretical perspective, one would expect most individuals in our culture to be heterosexual because our culture reinforces heterosexuality and punishes homosexuality. Thus for most individuals heterosexual impulses, behaviors, and fantasies would be reinforced, while homosexual impulses, behaviors, and fantasies would be discouraged. However, as stated by learning theory, homosexuals should be individuals who have had either negative experiences with heterosexuality or positive experiences with homosexuality. Certainly a number of individuals have had negative experiences with heterosexuality. For example, a young girl may experience rape or incest or a young boy might undergo incest or rejection by females. Furthermore, some individuals experience very positive sexual interactions with individuals of their own gender. However, on the basis of the results of his investigation of gay males, Silverstein concluded that learning had very little to do with the development of sexual orientation:

> When asked of their first awareness of homosexuality, gay men responded with a wide range of ages from preschool (even the sandbox) to the mid-20's. It is easy to demonstrate that the awareness that came late in life was the result of sexual repression. The early memories, however, are more interesting. Quite a few men claimed that they always knew they were gay, were always interested in men: many of them recounted convincing stories of energy expended seeking out and playing with other boys and men. Most of them also remember not being fully aware of what physical acts were possible; hence, the experiences are vague and unfocused. Desire was present but planned action impossible.
>
> These reports suggest that homosexuality may have its origin outside of family communication patterns and be impervious to learning or modeling. Whether inheritance or some combination of hormonal variables during gestation is a factor is impossible to ascertain or even to suggest, given the data of this study. But neither should be discounted completely. It is possible that a complicated set of interactions is required between physiological processes and perceptual experiences to produce a predisposition towards same-sex stimuli.
>
> Silverstein, 1981, pp. 318-319

Just because individuals are frequently aware of their sexual orientation at a young age does not mean that learning factors could not be involved. Further research is needed before we will have a clear understanding of the factors that contribute to homosexuality.

Another psychological theory of the development of homosexuality has been

No satisfactory theory of homosexuality has been found.

HUMAN SEXUALITY

proposed by Storms (1981). Storms suggests that sexual orientation develops at puberty when a person first begins to have erotic feelings. He further proposes that individuals who are just beginning to have erotic feelings are most likely to focus their erotic responses on the individuals with whom they are currently interacting. If individuals mature early, they are more likely to have erotic feelings when they are still involved in interactions with same-gender peers, and thus their erotic impulses are more likely to be directed toward same-sex individuals. Persons who begin to have erotic responses at a somewhat later age, when they are beginning to interact with individuals of the opposite gender, are more likely to direct their erotic responses toward those individuals. As a result, early-maturing individuals are more likely to become homosexuals than later-developing individuals.

Some investigators' conclusions seem to contradict Storms' position. For example, as can be seen in the preceding quotation, Silverstein believes, based on his study of gay males, that sexual orientation is determined at birth or shortly thereafter. Furthermore, in an interview study of both male and female homosexuals, Bell, Weinberg, and Hammersmith found that

> by the time boys and girls reach adolescence, their sexual preference is likely to be already determined, even though they may not yet have become sexually very active. The homosexual men and women in our study were not particularly lacking in heterosexual experiences during their childhood and adolescent years. They are distinguished from their heterosexual counterparts, however, in finding such experiences ungratifying.
>
> Bell, Weinberg, and Hammersmith, 1981, p. 188

Bell, Weinberg, and Hammersmith concluded that

> homosexuality is as deeply ingrained as heterosexuality so that the differences in behaviors or social experiences of prehomosexual boys and girls and their preheterosexual counterparts reflect or express, rather than cause, their eventual homosexual preference. In short, theories that tie homosexuality to an isolated social experience cannot be expected to account well for such a basic part of one's being as sexual preference appears to be.
>
> Bell, Weinberg, and Hammersmith, 1981, pp. 190-191

The most powerful predictor of homosexuality in adulthood that Bell, Weinberg, and Hammersmith found was gender role noncomformity in childhood: "Among both the men and the women in our study, there is a powerful link between gender nonconformity and the development of homosexuality."

Other investigators have obtained similar results. Green (1987), in a long-term study of 44 males, found that two thirds of the males who were judged to be "feminine" during childhood became homosexual or bisexual adults. Further, Friedman and Stern (1980) found that gay men tended to avoid rough and tumble play during childhood.

Bell (1982) has proposed a theory to explain sexual orientation based on the finding that homosexuals tend to exhibit gender role nonconformity in childhood. Bell suggested that the extent of one's gender role conformity is determined by hormones in utero. He also proposed that gender role conformity results in children spending more of their time with children of their same gender and that gender role nonconformity results in children spending more of their time with children of the opposite gender. Finally, Bell suggested that people tend to "fall in love with" or be attracted only to individuals whom they perceive to be different from themselves and whom they can therefore idealize and find intriguing or fascinating. These assumptions lead to the prediction that children who conform to their gender role will tend to spend more time with members of the same gender during childhood and be attracted to members of the opposite gender when they reach adolescence, and children who do not conform to their gender role will spend time during childhood with members of the opposite gender and be attracted to the same gender during adolescence.

In summary, a number of biological and psychological theories have been proposed to account for homosexuality. However, at this time none of these theories seems to be strongly supported. Much more research on both the biological and psychological contributions to sexual orientation is needed before we can come to a better understanding of the determinants of homosexuality.

BISEXUALITY

As can be seen in Table 11-1, a fairly large number of individuals have had sexual interactions with both males and females. However, as was discussed earlier, it is not really appropriate to call all of these individuals bisexual. Rather, the term *bisexual* should be reserved for individuals who have been involved sexually with both males and females as well as for those who respond erotically to both males and females. If bisexuality is defined according to these criteria, many fewer individuals will fall into this category. Little research has been done on bisexuality. It has not even been determined what proportion of the population defines itself as bisexual.

Blumstein and Schwartz (1976, 1977) interviewed 156 males and females who had more than incidental sexual experience with both men and women. They found no common pattern in the sexual histories of the bisexuals they interviewed. They did find that a number had, for most of their lives, considered themselves to be either heterosexual or homosexual and then an experience with a person of the other gender had caused them to question their self-definition. Blumstein and Schwartz give the following example of such drastic changes:

> Early in the study we interviewed a young professional woman who referred to herself as "purely and simply gay," even though she had had sexual experience with men. In recounting her life history she mentioned that at the age of seven or eight she habitually initiated sexual contacts with her friends at pajama parties. Eventually one girl's mother learned about it, and our respondent was castigated by the friends' families, her friends, and her own family. If that stigmatizing experience were not enough to plant the seeds of a deviant self-definition, in adolescence she was the victim of a brutal sexual assault by a group of boys. She pointed to both of these experiences as reasons she had become a lesbian 10 years prior to the interview. We found her analysis convincing since it was so consistent with the prevailing views on the psychodevelopment of lesbianism. Then, a year later she wrote to tell us she was in love with a man and they planned to marry.
> Blumstein and Schwartz, 1977, pp. 35-36

Blumstein and Schwartz go on to say that "a very large number of both male and female respondents had made at least one full circle—an affair with a man, then one with a woman and finally back to a man, or vice versa." On the basis of such findings, Blumstein and Schwartz concluded that the "classical notions of the immutability of adult sexual preference are an overstatement and often misleading." However, it is important to keep in mind that they selected bisexual subjects for their study. Since there are few bisexual individuals in the general population, drawing conclusions about the malleability of sexual orientation based on such a select sample is probably unwise.

Blumstein and Schwartz found three types of circumstances particularly conducive to bisexuality. First, some individuals, especially women, had had sexual experimentation within the context of a very close friendship. These friends were often emotionally close for an extended period before becoming sexually involved. Second, bisexual experiences often occurred in the context of group sex. Sexual encounters with individuals of the same gender are often seen as less threatening in a group-sex situation than they are in a one-to-one situation because they are not as likely to cause the individual to question his or her heterosexual orientation. Third, some individuals became bisexual for ideological reasons. These individuals believed that a person who is really "free" and "open" should be able to love anyone regardless of gender. Some of the women studied became involved in relationships with other women because of the women's movement, which encourages women to value and care for other women. Some radical feminists even discourage sexual interaction with men.

Blumstein and Schwartz found a number of differences in the bisexual behavior of men and women. Women seemed to be able to handle initial sexual experiences with other women with less trauma than men could with other men. Women often felt that such experiences were a natural extension of affectionate behavior among women and did not necessarily have implications for their sexual orientation. Men, on the other hand, were more likely to feel that their masculinity was threatened. Blumstein and Schwartz found that many men who felt threatened by their homosexual impulses were likely to satisfy these impulses by engaging in impersonal sex in which they assumed only the masculine role. As one of the men they interviewed reported, "There are four kinds of men: men who screw women, men who screw men and women, men who screw men, and then there are the queers [i.e., the ones who get screwed]." Both the first heterosexual and first homosexual experiences of men are likely to be with strangers; however, the first experiences of women are more likely to occur with someone for whom they have a strong emotional attachment.

In a questionnaire study of 127 bisexuals Klein (1978) found three basic types of bisexuals. The *transitional bisexuals* are individuals who are in the process of changing from a heterosexual orientation to a homosexual orientation or vice versa. For these individuals bisexuality simply serves as a transitional stage. The *historical bisexuals* are individuals who have always had a mix of homosexual and heterosexual activities. The *sequential bisexuals* are individuals who alternate between homosexual and heterosexual relationships; they tend to have only one relationship at a time.

One problem that bisexuals have is the lack of a real bisexual community. Enough homosexuals are open about their sexual orientation today that homosexuals tend to have support groups and a community of their own. However, since fewer individuals define themselves as bisexuals, not enough bisexuals exist to have communities and support groups of their own. Furthermore, bisexuals are frequently rejected by both the heterosexual majority and the homosexual minority. Heterosexuals often reject anyone who is not definitely heterosexual, and homosexuals often reject bisexuals because they see them as unwilling to accept the homosexual identity and live with the consequences. Without support groups and a community, being bisexual can be especially difficult.

SUMMARY

1 It is better to determine sexual orientation by taking into account three criteria rather than the single criterion of sexual behavior. These criteria are sexual behavior, erotic orientation, and self-definition. When all three criteria are considered, fewer individuals are classified as homosexual and bisexual than when only sexual behavior is taken into account.

2 Evidence suggests that many homosexual individuals have had homosexual feelings since childhood and adolescence. Therefore homosexual orientation may not be very malleable. However, many bisexuals report changing their sexual orientation after adolescence. Thus, at least for bisexuals, sexual orientation appears to be somewhat flexible beyond the childhood years.

3 Homophobia, a persistent and irrational fear of homosexuals, affects the lives of homosexual individuals in many ways. Homophobic individuals have acted to prevent homosexual behavior itself, passed legislation denying homosexuals their fundamental civil rights, and unleashed public disapproval against homosexuals. Although AIDS appears to have had little effect on homophobic attitudes, the disease has given many of those already harboring homophobic beliefs a justification for their beliefs. Among other things, education has been proposed to change homophobic attitudes.

4 Like the life-styles of heterosexuals, the life-styles of homosexuals are diverse. Bell and Weinberg proposed five types of homosexual life-styles: close coupled, open coupled, functional, dysfunctional, and asexual.

5 McWhirter and Mattison have identified six developmental stages in male homosexual couples: blending, nesting, maintaining, building, releasing, and renewing. Their study also suggests that homosexual and heterosexual relationships may be more similar than disparate.

6 Research suggests that women in homosexual relationships find greater equality with their partners than do women in heterosexual relationships.

7 A number of theories, both biological and psychological, have been proposed to account for the development of sexual orientation. However, there is no strong evidence for any of the theories. More research is needed before the determinants of sexual orientation can be understood.

8 Evidence indicates that one of the strongest predictors of homosexuality in adulthood is gender role nonconformity in childhood. However, gender role nonconformity does not appear to be present in the backgrounds of all homosexuals. Thus one possibility that should be entertained is that sexual orientation may be determined by many factors; again, more research is needed to discover the causes.

ANSWERS

FACT
OR
FICTION

1 Research indicates that sexual preference appears to be determined by the time individuals reach adolescence.
2 A number of studies suggest that gay males tend to prefer activities of the opposite gender during childhood.
3 Statistics suggest that lesbians have orgasms more often during their sexual interactions than do female heterosexuals.

QUESTIONS FOR THOUGHT   ?

1 How do you think your parents would react if you told them that you were a homosexual?
2 How do you think you would react if you had a child who told you that he or she was a homosexual?
3 Homosexuals are currently excluded from the military. Do you think they should be? Why?
4 In what ways do you think you might be homophobic?

SUGGESTED READINGS

Bell, A.P., and Weinberg, N.S.: Homosexualities, New York, 1978, Simon & Schuster, Inc.
    The report of comprehensive study of homosexual behavior in the San Francisco area. The study focused on the life-styles, sexual behavior, and psychological adjustments of the homosexuals.
Bell, A.P., Weinberg, M.S., and Hammersmith, S.K.: Sexual preference, Bloomington, 1981, Indiana University Press.
    A comprehensive study of the antecedents of homosexuality.
Greenberg, D.F.: The construction of homosexuality, Chicago, 1988, The University of Chicago Press.
    An interesting historical and cross-cultural analysis of society's treatment of homosexuality.
Kirk, M., and Madsen, H.: After the ball: how America will conquer its fear and hatred of gays in the '90s, New York, 1989, Doubleday & Co.
    A candid account of homophobia in American society, its causes and consequences, and strategies to promote tolerance and acceptance of homosexuality.
McWhirter, D.P., and Mattison, A.M.: The male couple, Englewood Cliffs, N.J., 1984, Prentice-Hall, Inc.
    A comprehensive study of the developmental stages of gay male relationships.
Mendola, M.: The Mendola Report: a new look at gay couples, New York, 1980, Crown Publishers, Inc.
    The report of a nationwide study of the life-styles of homosexual couples.
Paul, W., et al., editors: Homosexuality: social, psychological and biological issues, Beverly Hills, Calif., 1982, Sage Publications, Inc.
    A collection of readings on diverse topics that relate to homosexuality. Topics include mental health, biology, life adaptations, and law.
Ruse, M.: Homosexuality, a philosophical inquiry, Oxford, Eng., 1988, Basil Blackwell.
    A thorough philosophical approach to theories concerning homosexuality and society's treatment of homosexuality.

Childhood and Adolescence

Throughout childhood boys and girls learn to know and experience their own bodies, each with its own unique sexual repertoire. This is the only way we can grow to understand, in later years, that sex can be a component in a mutually respectful, loving relationship. The ability to share sexual intimacy with another person and to make intelligent use of our own reproductive potential requires that you behave responsibly toward your partner as well as yourself. Full and open opportunity throughout childhood is essential for such awareness and such a capacity to be developed.

M.S. CALDERONE AND J. RAMEY
Talking with Your Child About Sex, p. 5

uman sexuality changes substantially over the life span. Many people think that sexuality originates in adolescence with the hormonal changes that occur at that time. However, recent evidence indicates that we need to consider the development of human sexuality as beginning in infancy. In this chapter we follow sexual development from infancy through adolescence.

Sigmund Freud was one of the first to recognize that an individual's sexuality does not originate at puberty but, rather, that individuals are sexual beings from birth onward. Before Freud's time children were considered to be asexual until they reached puberty. However, Freud proposed that from earliest infancy individuals are motivated by strivings toward pleasure of a sexual nature, or what he termed the **libido.** These sexual feelings and strivings are certainly not identical to those of adults but according to Freud are sexual nonetheless. Freud suggested that the focus of these sexual feelings changes in a predictable fashion with development.

In the first year of a child's life, or the **oral stage,** the mouth is the primary focus of sexual gratification. The infant tends to achieve sexual gratification from nursing and sucking in general. In the second and third years, or the **anal stage,** the child's sexual focus is on the anal region. The child gains gratification both from having bowel movements and from deliberately holding them back. In the **phallic stage,** which occurs between the ages of 4 and 5 years, the child's sexual focus becomes the genital area. During this stage the child gains pleasure primarily from stimulation of the genital region. Freud suggests it is at this stage that young boys tend to develop sexual feelings toward their mothers (the **Oedipal complex**) and young girls tend to have similar feelings toward their fathers (the **Electra complex**). Eventually children in this stage come to realize that they cannot possess their opposite-sex parent, and they then enter the fifth stage of psychosexual development. In the **latency stage,** which begins about 6 years of age, the child's sexual strivings tend to become latent for a number of years while the child pursues intellectual and social endeavors. With the onset of puberty the individual's sexuality once again becomes prominent in what Freud referred to as the **genital stage.** During this stage the individual again focuses on the genital area for sexual gratification but turns to peers of the opposite sex for gratification.

Erik Erikson extended Freud's theory of psychosexual development. He also proposed that individuals progress through a series of developmental stages similar to those proposed by Freud. In fact, there is a high degree of correspondence between the first five stages in Erikson's and Freud's theories.

libido
(li BEE doh) In Freudian theory, sexual energy or motivation.

oral stage
In Freudian theory, the first stage of psychosexual development, which occurs in the first year of life.

anal stage
In Freudian theory, the second stage of psychosexual development, which occurs in the second and third years of life.

phallic stage
(FAL ik) In Freudian theory, the third stage of psychosexual development, which occurs during the fourth and fifth years of life.

Oedipal complex
(ED uh puhl) In Freudian theory, the attraction of a young boy in the phallic stage to his mother.

Electra complex
In Freudian theory, the attraction of a young girl in the phallic stage to her father.

latency stage
(LAYT n see) In Freudian theory, the fourth stage of psychosexual development, which begins at about 6 and ends with puberty.

genital stage
In Freudian theory, the fifth and final stage of psychosexual development, which begins with puberty.

TABLE 12-1 Stages of Psychosexual Development: Freud and Erikson

Stage	Age	Freud's stage	Erikson's core conflict
1	Birth to 1 year	Oral	Basic trust vs. mistrust
2	2 to 3 years	Anal	Autonomy vs. doubt and shame
3	4 to 5 years	Phallic	Initiative vs. guilt
4	6 to 12 years	Latency	Industry vs. inferiority
5	Puberty	Genital	Identity vs. role confusion
6	Young adulthood		Intimacy vs. isolation
7	Middle adulthood		Generativity vs. stagnation
8	Later adulthood		Integrity vs. despair

However, he added three additional stages, one corresponding to early adulthood, one to middle adulthood, and one to later adulthood. Whereas Freud was concerned primarily with individual psychosexual development, Erikson focused more on the individual's interactions with family, friends, and the larger culture. For each of his stages Erikson identified what he considered to be the core developmental conflict for individuals of that age. Erikson's stages are shown along with the corresponding Freudian stages in Table 12-1. Both Erikson and Freud suggested that children are not asexual beings but rather that sexuality begins to affect behavior at a very early age. Recent research supports this view and is discussed next.

INFANCY

Recent research indicates that even infants exhibit behavior that appears to be sexual in nature. Many male infants have penile erections at the time of birth or shortly after birth (Langfeldt, 1981b). Ultrasound studies indicate that male fetuses may even have erections in the uterus (Calderone, 1983). Female infants exhibit vaginal lubrication and clitoral erection shortly after birth (Langfeldt, 1981b). Erections and vaginal lubrication continue throughout infancy, often in response to stimulation of the genital area.

Infants tend to play with their own genitals. However, it appears that in many cases such genital play is not done for sexual stimulation. Much of it does not differ from play with other body parts such as fingers and toes. However, there are exceptions. Kinsey and associates (1948, 1953) reported cases of infants who apparently deliberately tried to stimulate themselves sexually. In addition, they reported cases of both male and female infants who apparently had orgasms in response to self-stimulation. The infants' orgasms had many of the same characteristics as those of adults, including rapid pelvic thrusting, erection in the male, buildup of body tension to the point of climax, and then a period of calm and relaxation. Of course male infants do not ejaculate; males are not capable of ejaculation until they reach puberty.

In any consideration of sexuality the individual's interactions with others are as important as the individual's genital response. Although some fathers are more involved in child care now than in the past, during infancy the infant's relationship with its mother tends to be primary. The mother is the one who usually takes care of the infant's needs, including the infant's requirements for food and comfort. The major physical, and potentially erotic, encounter between the infant and the mother occurs during nursing (Martinson, 1981). Nursing infants often show alertness and rhythmical movement of hands, fingers, feet, and toes that is in association with the rhythm of sucking. Vigorous sucking by active infants is often accompanied by penile erections that may last throughout the sucking period and continue for several minutes after breast-feeding is ended (Newton and Newton, 1967). Thus infants may have sexual responses to nursing. In addition to genital reactions, the infant shows other affectionate responses to the mother in the nursing relationship. When the infant is nursing, it often puts its fingers into the mother's mouth, studies the mother's face attentively, pats the mother's breast, pats the mother's face, and hugs the mother.

In the first 18 months of life genital play may be indicative of the adequacy of the infant's affectionate interactions with others. Spitz (1949) reports that when mother-infant interactions are positive and frequent, infants occasionally engage in genital activities when by themselves. However, when the interactions between the mother and infant are problematic, genital play is much rarer, and when mother-infant interactions are absent, genital play is completely missing. Although unfortunately there is not more recent evidence on this issue, these findings suggest that during the first year of life genital activities vary with the nature of the relationship between the infant and those with whom he or she has close affectionate interactions.

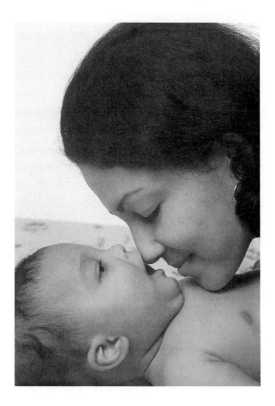

A healthy parent-child relationship early in life can positively affect the child's later development.

The association between genital activity and a close relationship with another person suggests that sexuality in infancy may be related to healthy development in general. This is contrary to what has usually been assumed in our culture. Infant sexual behavior is often considered negative, perverse, and destructive. As a consequence, some people believe that infant sexuality should be inhibited as much as possible. However, since evidence indicates that infant sexuality may be associated with positive, healthy development, these negative attitudes need to be changed. Society must recognize that sexuality does not begin in adolescence. The importance of sexuality in infancy and childhood must be acknowledged.

CHILDHOOD
Sexual Knowledge

Children have many misconceptions about sex. A significant study by Ronald and Juliette Goldman (1988) provides some intriguing information concerning children's developing understanding of sexuality. Goldman and Goldman interviewed almost a thousand children 5 to 15 years of age to learn what children at these ages think and know about sex. Since one of the more basic concepts of sexuality is sexual identity, one's own and others', one of the 63 questions the interviewers asked was, "How can you tell a newborn baby is a boy or a girl?"

According to Goldman and Goldman, children aged 5 to 7 tend to think in irrelevant physical terms. As with their thinking concerning all other aspects of their lives, children at this age make faulty generalizations about the sexual identity of babies. This is largely due to their tendency to focus on only one aspect of a problem at a time, leading inevitably to inaccurate conclusions (Goldman and Goldman, 1988). Examples of this tendency can be found in the 5- to 7-year-old children's responses:

> My brother cried like a boy. You could hear him in the next room he was so loud. (Australian boy, 5 years)

> My sister grew curly hair. It was long girl's hair. That's why they called her Kate. (English girl, 5 years)

> All big babies are boys. (Why should that be?) Cause they've got to grow up bigger 'n stronger and look after the girls. (American boy, 5 years)
>
> Goldman and Goldman, 1988, p. 6

Slightly older children generally rely on the word of authorities such as doctors, nurses and their parents.

> My mum told me it was a girl. (How did she know?) The doctor told her. (English girl, 7 years)
>
> Goldman and Goldman, 1988, p. 6

With further probing as to how the authorities know, these children once again rely on irrelevant physical details for their answers.

> Mom told me it was a boy. (How did she know?) The doctor tells her. (How does the doctor know?) He looks through a magnifying glass into their eyes and he tells by the eyebrows. (American boy, 7 years)
>
> Goldman and Goldman, 1988, p. 6

Later, between the ages of 7 and 9, most children begin to understand that babies have definite physical features that indicate their sexual identity. These physical features are not thought of as sexual but instead are seen as differences in how boys and girls urinate.

> Boys stand up to do the wee-wee and girls don't. (What do you mean?) Girls sit down. (Why should they do that?) So the pee-pee don't go over the floor. (English girl, 7 years)

> They're different down there. (How do you mean?) Well, some kind of different bottom, the shapes are different. (How are they different?) Dunno really. (Australian boy, 9 years)

> Goldman and Goldman, 1988, p. 7

Indeed, it is difficult to tell whether children genuinely do not know, are merely too embarrassed, or do not have the necessary vocabulary to describe the sex organs correctly. The Goldmans' analysis of the replies led them to the conclusion that the children's imprecise answers are probably due to a combination of all three. If any distinction is seen at all, children have a genuine confusion about what specifically is distinctive about the sex organs of babies. At the same time they recognize the clear signals they often receive from adults that this is a taboo topic, that terms referring to sex organs should not be said or at least should be disguised (e.g., "dinkle" used to refer to penis).

By the age of 11, although their information was flawed, most of the English-speaking children had more knowledge about the sex organs of babies:

> If it's got a penis or not. If it has it's a boy. Girls have a virginia (English boy, 11 years)

> Goldman and Goldman, 1988, p. 7

They found an exception to this trend in sexual knowledge in children living in Sweden. Swedish children tend to have more accurate information at earlier ages. The Goldmans attribute this to the fact that in Sweden, sex education has been required in all schools at the primary and elementary levels for more than 30 years. Thus Swedish children learn more about sex not only through the school system, but also through their parents who are probably more willing to answer the child's questions in a straightforward manner because they had sex education when they were children.

Sex Play

During the childhood years there is a marked increase in sexual interest and capacity. Kinsey, Pomeroy, and Martin (1948) reported that the percentage of individuals able to reach orgasm increases from 32% of boys in their first year of life to 57% of boys between 10 and 13 years of age. These authors did not report figures for young girls.

Masturbation is common during childhood, although not all children masturbate. In the sample studied by Kinsey and associates (1948, 1953), 45% of the males and 15% of the females reported that they had begun masturbating by 13 years of age. More recently Hunt (1974) found that 63% of the males and 33% of the females in his sample indicated that they had begun masturbating by the age of 13. Therefore in the decades between the Kinsey and the

Hunt studies the number of boys and girls who masturbated during the childhood years apparently increased. Whether this is a result of an increase in actual masturbation or an increase in willingness to report masturbation is impossible to determine. Probably today even larger percentages of individuals would report masturbating during childhood because our culture is more permissive toward masturbation now than it was in the early 1970s when Hunt collected his data. Unfortunately, more recent estimates are not available.

In addition to the gender differences in frequency of masturbation, there

A Personal Glimpse

College Students' Recollections of Early Masturbation Experiences

The following are excerpts from papers written by Michigan State University students in response to an assignment that they write an (anonymous) autobiographical paper about themselves as a sexual being. All of the comments relate to early masturbation experiences.

Female

I used to play with a girl, Julie, about three years older than I—when I was in second grade and she was in fourth grade. She once told me of a neat thing to do to make you feel really good. She explained to me how to wrap my legs around the poles of our swing set and squeeze. I used to love doing this and remember reaching states of euphoria, and losing consciousness of present reality. I remember hoping no one would see me because they would think I was crazy. I suppose I was having orgasms because I'd tense my leg muscles and the genital area. Then there would be a release of tension. Not until years later, late high school, when I reflected back, did I realize that I was masturbating. (p. 7)

Male

In eighth grade I remember getting erections when I would stare at girls' bodies. I kept *Playboy* magazines that I would fish out of our Boy Scout paper drives. I remember wishing I could someday release the desire I developed after looking at the pictures. In the tenth grade I figured out how to masturbate, and boy did I use it with the pictures. Once I masturbated six times in one afternoon. (p. 8)

Female

Like the woman in *Our Bodies, Ourselves*, I learned to masturbate with a stream of water from bathtub spout. It seems, though, that I was a slow learner because I didn't pick up this skill until I was about fourteen years old. Although I was taught nothing about this practice directly either from my parents or from books, I did feel that it was somehow harmful, and did experience guilt feelings over it. My romantic, sexual fantasy increased and came to a head during my masturbating activities which continued despite my associated guilt feelings. I also fantasized frequently about someone sleeping with me. Perhaps this replaced the withdrawal of physical affection from my parents as I got older. (pp. 8-9)

Male

In high school I was fortunate to have a progressive religion teacher who thought sexual matters were probably not sins. I admired this man, liked what he said, and finally decided to try it out. I decided to masturbate. I went down to the basement bathroom. My heart started to pound till it wanted to burst through my chest. I still had some doubts about what I was going to do. Maybe, I thought, it was a mortal sin. But I went ahead anyway. I was so nervous; my penis vacillated between being turgid and flaccid. My heart kept beating madly. I finally had an ejaculation. It was not much of an ejaculation because I was so nervous; I was only semi-hard. But it felt good. After a few times I lost my nervousness about masturbating. It became a completely enjoyable, everyday experience. (p. 10)

From Morrison et al., 1980.

are gender differences in the way children masturbate (Langfeldt, 1981a). Girls tend to masturbate in private, but boys often masturbate in groups or with one other boy. Boys usually learn to masturbate by observing other children or by being instructed by other children; girls often discover masturbation by accident (see box, p. 354).

Frequently siblings engage in sex play with each other. This is more likely to occur when siblings share a bedroom and is especially likely when they share the same bed (Martinson, 1980). Cuddling, fondling, and handling the genitals of others are common during children's play (Finkelhor, 1981). Other forms of sex play include oral-genital contact and attempted intercourse with another child (Martinson, 1980). The majority of young children become engaged in sex play with other children: brothers, sisters, or neighborhood children (see box below). This sex play typically involves children inspecting the genitals of other children.

Sex play takes place among children of both genders. During childhood sex play with members of the same gender may be even more common than with members of the opposite gender. Morrison and associates (1980) reported that 52% of the males and 37% of the females in their sample indicated experiencing sex play with members of the same gender; 34% of the males and 37% of the females reported experiencing it with members of the other gender. Although both same gender and opposite gender encounters occur in childhood, it is not clear in most of the sex play episodes what is erotic for the child and

A Personal Glimpse

College Students' Recollections of Early Sex Play

The following are excerpts from papers written by Michigan State University students in response to an assignment that they write an (anonymous) autobiographical paper about themselves as a sexual being. All of the comments relate to early sex play experiences.

Male

One of my favorite pastimes was playing doctor with my little sister who is about two years younger than I. During this doctor game we would both be nude and I would sit on her as if we were having intercourse. On one occasion, I was fondling my sister's genital area and got caught by my mother. We were sternly switched and told it was dirty and to never get caught again or we would be whipped twice as bad. So, we made sure we were never caught again. In general, I was raised with

an attitude that sex was a dirty thing that should be hidden, and certainly never mentioned, so I learned to be secretive and silent. (pp. 22-23)

Female

At an early age I played the curiosity game of doctor and nurse. That's how I found out what the major difference was between a boy and a girl. It was an educational experience, but it left a bad impression on me because my mother caught the neighbor boy and me behind the garage and spanked me and forbade the boy to come into our yard again. To this day, I think it was the hardest spanking I ever received. I can remember my mother saying, "You ought to be ashamed," and at that time I was. But now I think, "Should I have been ashamed and for what?" No, I shouldn't have been ashamed for my normal curiosities. (p. 23)

From Morrison et al., 1980.

Young siblings frequently engage in sex play with one another.

what is purely dispassionate curiosity. Sometimes the child may experience the episodes as highly erotic; at other times the child may just be curious.

A recent study by Leitenberg, Greenwald, and Tarran (1989) found no differences in the sexual adjustment of young adults who engaged in preadolescent sex play compared with those who did not. Their results suggest that young adult sexual behavior and adjustment are little affected by most sexual experiences children have with each other regardless of the age when they take place (including early adolescence). Two exceptions were noted. First, genital contact in preadolescence was associated with an earlier occurrence of premarital intercourse in young adulthood and a higher number of intercourse partners; however, it did not appear to affect sexual satisfaction, arousal, or dysfunctions in young adulthood. Furthermore, although homosexual versus heterosexual childhood sexual experiences had no effect on later sexual behavior, those subjects who reported a childhood homosexual experience with another child had a somewhat higher frequency of sexual dysfunctions in young adulthood. Leitenberg and his associates suggest that the higher frequency in sexual dysfunctions may be due to anxiety produced from the unfounded fear, often expressed by the parents, that childhood homosexual activity necessarily indicates the existence of a homosexual inclination.

As suggested by the findings of Goldman and Goldman (1988), as well as those of Leitenberg and his colleagues (1989), parents who try to curb a child's acquisition of sexual knowledge or inhibit a child's sex play may do more harm than good. It is a mixture of curiosity and natural sexual responses that leads children to engage in sex play. Sex play in many ways functions as a learning experience, especially when parents fail to give children explicit information about such basic topics as sexual anatomy (Goldman and Goldman, 1988).

If parents react to masturbation or sex play with horror, they are likely to create in the child unhealthy attitudes toward sexuality. Children whose parents make them believe that sex is something disgusting and to be avoided tend not to have healthy, happy sex lives as adults. To have a healthy attitude toward sexuality in adulthood, many of the individuals who are raised with negative attitudes toward sexuality have a great deal of unlearning to do. Some of them are able to discard these early established attitudes, but others never can.

Rather than respond with horror and disgust to a child's natural inquiries about sex or the child's sex play, parents should begin to teach the child about sexuality early. Furthermore, the parents can convey to the child that his or her sexual responses are normal and healthy. The parents should tell the child when and where sexual behavior is appropriate and when and where it is inappropriate. For example, although the parents may want to tell the child that masturbation is normal and healthy, they should also convey that the child should not masturbate in public. Moreover, even though nudity may be accepted in the child's home, the child needs to realize that he or she cannot go naked in public.

ADOLESCENCE
Biological Changes

Adolescence is marked by drastic changes in the physiological makeup of the individual. The term **puberty** is used to describe the beginning of the sexual maturation process. **Adolescence** refers to the period from the beginning of puberty to the attainment of adult status. It is a transition period between childhood and adulthood.

puberty
(PYOO buhr tee) The beginning of the sexual maturation process.

adolescence
The period from puberty to the attainment of adult growth and maturity.

As adolescence approaches, the physical development of males and female varies.

The process of puberty in both males and females is caused by a change in the output of gonadal hormones from the testes and ovaries. In the female the ovaries produce estrogen, which stimulates the growth and development of specific female organs and structures. In the male the testes begin to produce large amounts of androgens, which initiate the process of puberty and the growth of specific male organs and structures.

Girls mature about 2 years earlier than boys (Meyer-Bahlburg, 1980). The first signs of puberty in the female usually appear between 9 and 14 years of age (Figure 12-1 and Table 12-2). The most obvious change is the development of the rounded contours that distinguish the adult female figure from the adult male figure. Breast buds develop, the areolae on the breasts elevate and become darker, and fat is deposited in the hips and buttocks. Pubic and axillary hair appears. As a result of profound hormonal changes, facial acne often develops. Estrogen from the ovaries causes the growth of the external genitals, including the labia majora and labia minora, and androgens from the adrenal glands cause the clitoris to enlarge. The girl undergoes a significant growth spurt as a result of the secretion of **somatotropic hormone,** or growth hormone, from the anterior pituitary gland. This growth spurt occurs shortly before the girl's first menstrual flow.

Menarche, or the onset of the first menstrual flow, is a dramatic event in the life of a girl passing into adolescence. In the United States the average age of menarche is 12.6 years, although it often occurs in girls as young as 10 or as old as 16 years of age (Hafez, 1980). If a girl is slightly ahead of or behind schedule, there is no reason for concern. However, if the appearance of the

somatotropic hormone
(soh' muh toh TROH fik)
Growth hormone that causes the growth spurt that occurs during puberty.

menarche
(muh NAR kee) The first menstruation.

Menstruation: The Experience of Rural Greek Women

Yewoubdar Beyene (1989) conducted a cross-cultural study of menstruation. Menstruation is conceptualized differently in different cultures. The following excerpts from Beyene's work illustrate how menopause is viewed and experienced by the rural Greek women studied.

[The] Greeks also have taboos and restrictions related to menstruation and childbearing. Menstruating women, women who just gave birth, and a woman after miscarriage are all considered impure and polluted. A menstruating woman is not allowed to participate in religious activities for she is considered unclean. She should not go to church; she should not even light the candle or touch the icons in her shrine at home; should not go where the family's wine is because it would become flat; she should not bake bread because the dough would not rise; she should not touch the feta cheese because it would become contaminated and turn yellow; she should also avoid touching the oil barrels because the oil is burned at church and in the small shrine at home. (p. 106)

The above taboos also apply to a woman who just gave birth. After a woman gives birth, she should stay at home for 40 days. She should not visit anyone until the 40 days are over, because it is believed that she would bring disaster to the family she visited. After 40 days the village priest blesses the house, the mother, and the baby; they become free to move around again. (p. 107)

Rural Greeks believe that informing their daughters before onset of menarche is a sin. Thus, 50 percent of the women in the study stated that they did not know what it was and were frightened at the time of their first menses. They believed that menstruation was a curse as a result of Eve's sin and that women had to suffer. Menstrual blood was considered bad blood and women should get rid of it. Thus, heavy menstrual flow was considered good because it cleans the blood well. (p. 107)

FIGURE 12-1
Stages of development of
breasts in females.

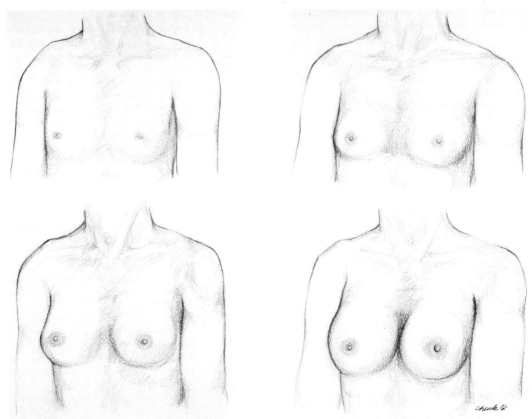

TABLE 12-2 Sequence of Puberty in Girls

Stage		Characteristics
Premenarcheal (9-11 years)	Onset:	Breast buds appear and grow
		Straight pubic hair appears
		Ovaries enlarge
		Height spurt begins
	About 1 year later:	Kinky pubic hair appears
		Height spurt at its peak
		Areolae of breasts become pigmented
	About 1 year later:	Menarche (first menstrual flow, no ovulation)
		Pelvis increases in diameter
Menarcheal (10-13 years)	One or more years later:	Full reproductive maturity with regular ovulations
		Axillary (underarm) hair
		Sweat and sebaceous glands enlarge, often resulting in the development of acne
		Growth of clitoris
		Change in body configuration—fat deposition in hips, buttocks, and breasts

The biological and psychological aspects of the menstrual cycle are covered in Chapter 4.

anovulatory
(an OV yuh luh tor' ee)
When no eggs are released from the ovaries during a menstrual cycle.

first menstrual flow occurs before the age of 9 or after the age of 17, medical attention should be sought (Hafez, 1980). Most researchers believe that a critical body weight and percentage of body fat must be attained before menarche will take place. Genetic factors can also influence the age of menarche. Most menstrual cycles for the first 12 to 18 months after menarche are **anovulatory;** that is, even though there is a monthly vaginal flow, no eggs are released from the ovaries. This phenomenon is often referred to as adolescent infertility.

In some cultures menarche is viewed as a signal of the transition from girlhood to womanhood and indicates the time at which a female is considered ready for marriage. Sometimes elaborate rituals are performed to mark this transition stage.

As was previously indicated, boys mature more slowly than girls. In males puberty usually begins between the ages of 11 and 16 (Table 12-3). Boys often produce fertile sperm by about 14 to 15 years of age. Puberty in boys is associated with changes in skin and hair (Figure 12-2). Increased activity in sebaceous glands of the scrotum, face, back, and chest results in perspiration, strong odor, and acne. Axillary and facial hair typically appears 2 years after the first growth of pubic hair. The voice of the male deepens because of the growth of the larynx. This growth, like the other changes in the male and female, is caused by hormonal stimulation.

ACROSS   CULTURES

Puberty Rituals of Males and Females

Puberty rituals vary among different cultures. In the United States religions have different ceremonies to initiate the male into full participation in the faith, signifying that the male has achieved adult status. Rituals in other cultures can be much more elaborate and complicated. In these cultures initiation for boys consists primarily of a period of seclusion during which the boy undergoes ordeals and receives instruction on sexual matters. In some cultures genital mutilations, including circumcision, subincision (slitting a section of the urethra), and, in one society, hemicastration (the removal of one testis) form a part of the initiation ceremony (Ford and Beach, 1951). In one society, the Chewa of Central Africa, the boy is put through a difficult physical ordeal. He is led blindfolded to a secluded spot where he is kept for about 1 week. He is cruelly treated: he is swung over a slow-burning fire, drawn prostrate over the hard ground, beaten with rods, and rolled in ants and itching beans. The boy is pulled about with a string tied to his penis and testes. When the ordeal is over, the boy is taken to the chief and receives his new adult name.

Menarche in a girl provides society with an obvious signal that womanhood is approaching. Ford and Beach in their classic book *Patterns of Sexual Behavior* (1951) give details regarding ceremonies that females experience at menarche in various cultures. One common ritual involves that seclusion of the girl from a few days to several months after menarche. In many cases the girl receives instructions regarding sex and marriage. In some societies the girl must undergo certain physical hardships while in seclusion. She may have her hymen ruptured with a tool made of horn or be subjected to genital mutilation such as female circumcision. Her ears may be pierced, her skin tattooed, her hair cut off, and her teeth filed or blackened. Often the ordeal ends with a feast or dance at which the girl appears in adult clothing.

TABLE 12-3 **Sequence of Puberty in Boys**

Stage		Characteristics
11-12 years	Onset:	Testicular growth spurt
		Beginning of sperm production
		Straight pubic hair
12-13 years		Androgen-producing cells develop in the testes
		Penis growth spurt
		Height growth spurt
		Kinky pubic hair appears
13-14 years		Voice deepens
		First ejaculation
		Marked increase in muscular strength
15-17 years	Later adolescence:	Sperm appear in ejaculate
		Axillary (underarm) hair
		Sweat and sebaceous glands enlarge, often resulting in the development of acne

FIGURE 12-2
Stages of development of
genitals in males.

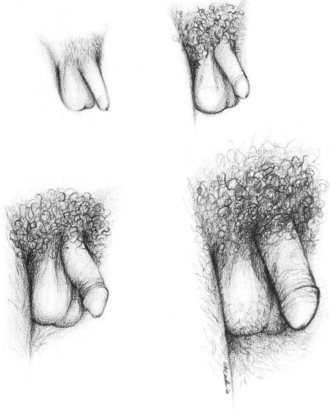

A Personal Glimpse

College Students' Recollections of Their Feelings About Bodily Changes at Puberty

The following are excerpts from papers written by Michigan State University students in response to an assignment that they write an (anonymous) autobiographical paper about themselves as a sexual being. All of the comments relate to early feelings about bodily changes at puberty.

Male

The most traumatic experience of my life came when I experienced ejaculation for the first time. Since it didn't take place during a nocturnal emission, I was able to deduce something of what had happened. A mass of emotions flooded me all at once. I felt fear, guilt, shame and worry. You see, my parents had felt that it would be in my best interest to discontinue our discussions on sexuality when I was thirteen. Instead, they suggested I read a book on the subject. The text they handed me was aimed at parents. I got only a few pages into it before it turned me off. As a result, I was totally unprepared to experience daydreams about girls, desires of masturbation, and of course, orgasm.

After all of the emotions had been penned up in me for an unknown length of time, I finally burst, and in a fit of tears and shame explained to my parents what I had experienced during my private moment. They were most understanding, giving me every reassurance that what I had done and felt was perfectly normal. They, in fact, realized the error of not discussing these things with me as a means of avoiding the difficult experience that had taken place. (p. 64)

Female

I remember becoming aware, in junior high school, that I was flat-chested. I used to be ashamed because I didn't wear a bra. Maybe if I hadn't been the oldest child my mother would have been more aware of my sensitivity about my development, but she wasn't aware and I was extremely sensitive about my body shape—so we never talked about it. Only during this very early stage of my sensitivity was I too embarrassed to talk with my mom. Other than that, I never hesitated to ask Mom anything. She was always very frank and honest with me, talking on a level I could understand. Confidences I shared with her increased as I grew older. As I grew and entered high school, I became increasingly aware of my lack of physical development, that I hadn't begun to menstruate yet and that guys didn't find me attractive. I demanded that mother buy me a bra and I got a doctor's excuse to never take gym. I couldn't stand the thought of dressing in front of other girls when I was so undeveloped. At one point I even used to "stuff" my bra with toilet paper, but I was always so self-conscious that it was lumpy, or one was bigger than the other, that I soon abandoned the practice. (p. 68)

Sexual Behavior

During adolescence, as a result of the hormonal changes that occur during puberty, the individual's sexuality changes drastically. These hormonal alterations increase both the sensitivity of the genitals and the strength of sexual urges. In the beginning, adolescents' sexual urges may be directed toward family members or friends of the same gender. The sexual urges often feel strange and frightening to adolescents. As a result, they often feel guilty about both the sexual urges and the individuals toward whom they feel these urges. The guilt frequently makes it difficult for adolescents to discuss their sexual feelings and thoughts with others; as a result, they often have to deal alone with their changing sexuality.

Although the first sexual urges of an adolescent may be directed toward family members or friends of the same sex, the adolescent's task is to learn to develop intimate, mature sexual relationships. Often this occurs as a gradual process in which the adolescent moves from having sexual urges toward family members, to having "crushes" on teachers and other older individuals of the opposite gender, and finally to same-aged members of the opposite gender.

With respect to sexual behavior, Kinsey and associates (1948, 1953) found striking differences in the sexual behavior of males and females during puberty. Boys tended to exhibit a sudden increase in sexual activity 1 year or so before the onset of puberty was noticeable. They usually reached their peak in orgasmic frequency within 1 or 2 years after the onset of puberty. For girls, on the other hand, the increase in erotic and orgasmic activities was gradual and steady; there was no drastic change around the time of puberty. Kinsey and associates reported that most females did not reach their maximum rate of orgasm until their middle twenties or thirties. Only 20% of the girls in Kinsey's sample ever experienced orgasm during puberty. Whereas boys experienced an average of 3.4 orgasms per week during adolescence, girls experienced an average of only 0.5 orgasm per week.

Gender differences in reasons for engaging in sexual intercourse are discussed in Chapter 10.

Gender differences in the frequency of orgasm are discussed in Chapter 10.

Female Orgasm

Because virtually all adolescent males experience orgasm, research has not focused on the percentage of males who have orgasms during the teenage years. However, scientists have recently begun to study the incidence of orgasm in teenage girls. Both Hass (1979) and Morrison and associates (1980) found that some teenage girls report having experienced orgasm. In fact, 42% of the girls in Hass' study indicated having had at least one orgasm. On the other hand, a fairly large number reported that they did not know whether they had ever had an orgasm or not. Although males usually ejaculate when they have an orgasm, females do not have a corresponding objective sign of orgasm. In Hass' study 33% of the girls reported not knowing whether they had ever had an orgasm and 25% indicated they had never had an orgasm. Furthermore, of the girls who had had sexual intercourse, 27% reported that they had never had an orgasm during intercourse. Hass discusses some of the reasons for their lack of orgasm:

See Chapter 5 for further discussion of the female orgasm.

> There are many obstacles to reaching orgasm during intercourse for a large percentage of women. Because of the particular movements or positions used, she may not be receiving the kind or amount of stimulation that is most arousing to her. Any anxiety, distractions, or conflict may inhibit sexual responsivity. She may not feel comfortable being assertive about her sexual preferences during intercourse. All of these factors would probably be more prevalent among teenagers than older females.
>
> Hass, 1979, p. 108

Masturbation

As was mentioned earlier, 63% of the boys and 33% of the girls in Hunt's sample (1974) reported masturbating before the age of 13. Furthermore, in both Kinsey's and Hunt's samples more than 90% of the males and more than

60% of the females reported masturbating as adults. However, because neither Kinsey and associates nor Hunt asked how many individuals began masturbating during the teenage years, their data do not tell us much about the adolescent years.

In a more recent study Hass (1979) studied sexuality in adolescents between the ages of 15 and 18. Among the 15- and 16-year-olds 75% of the males and 52% of the females reported masturbating; among the 17- and 18-year-olds 80% of the males and 59% of the females reported masturbating. The most sexually active teenagers indicated masturbating more frequently than the less sexually active. However, teenage males tended to masturbate less when they were involved in a sexual relationship and teenage females tended to masturbate more frequently when involved in a sexual relationship. Hass suggested:

> This difference may be explained by the fact that sexual encounters almost always end in orgasm for the male, while the same cannot be said for females. When she is not having regular sexual contact, a girl's sexual tension level will probably be lower than times when she is having sexual encounters which are not culminating in orgasm. This heightened tension and frustration may motivate an increasing use of self-stimulation for physical release.
>
> Hass, 1979, p. 86

Petting

petting
Sexual activity that involves touching the breasts or genitals of one's partner.

Petting is the term often used to describe sexual activity that involves touching the breasts and genitals of one's partner. Petting is most commonly used when the couple's sexual activity is limited to such contact and does not result in sexual intercourse. Hunt (1974) discusses the factors that led to the widespread phenomenon of petting in our culture:

> By 1920 or thereabouts, the changing conditions of American life brought about the spontaneous development of a new method of socializing among young unmarried people: In place of parental selection and chaperoned evenings in the family parlor, teenagers and young adults chose their partners themselves, made their own arrangements to meet and went out of the home to spend their evenings at the movies, at parties or in the back seat of parked cars. In a word, dating had been invented.
>
> Dating posed a serious problem: It afforded the young the opportunity to experiment with physical love, but gave no sanction to premarital intercourse; it liberated the young from the watchful eye of the chaperone, but not from the traditional social values implanted by their consciences. The solution to the problem was another invention, namely, petting—that whole series of acts that lies beyond mere kissing but stops short of inserting the penis in the vagina.
>
> Hunt, 1974, p. 131

Hunt also discusses the social rules involved in petting:

> Even in the "game" aspect, it was serious business: The boy tried to see how much he could get—and the girl how little she could give—by way of recompense for the time and money he had spent on her, and the better he "made out," the higher was his status among his fellows, while the less she gave in, the more desirable she was deemed. But petting was also serious business in a deeper sense; it was the acceptable middle-class means of expressing erotic and emotional feelings before marriage. The more deeply a boy and girl cared about each other, the "further"

Dating, which began in the 1920s, is a relatively new method of socialization for young single people. For this young couple from the 1950s, having a car meant having the independence to make their own dating arrangements.

they considered it all right to go. The standard enforced by the girls and grudgingly accepted by the boys held, in a general way, that kissing was all right if the two merely liked each other; "deep" or "French" kissing if they felt romantic about each other; breast touching through the clothing if they were halfway "serious" about each other, and with the bra off if they were somewhat more serious than that; and explorations "below the waist" or exposure of the naked penis to the girl's touch only if the couple considered themselves really in love.

Hunt, 1974, pp. 132-133

It appears that teenagers' attitudes toward petting have become more liberal in recent decades. Reiss (1967) reported that 67% of the males and 57% of the females he interviewed approved of petting when the relationship involves strong affection between two individuals. Hunt (1974) found that 88% of the males and 78% of the females approved of petting under the same circumstances. Hass (1979) reported even higher acceptance rates. Hass asked both males and females between the ages of 15 and 18 if it was "OK" for individuals of their age to participate in touching the breasts and genitals of members of the opposite gender. Ninety-eight percent of the males and 91% of the females reported that they thought it was acceptable for a male to touch a female's breasts. Ninety-three percent of the males indicated that they thought it was OK for males and females to touch each other's genitals. However, only about 80% of the females approved of genital touching. Hass' data clearly indicate an increase in acceptance of petting among teenagers. However, they also demonstrate that gender differences continue to exist. Males still appear to be more liberal in their attitudes toward genital touching.

Hass' results also indicate an increase in the incidence of petting among teenagers in recent decades. In 1953 Kinsey and associates reported that among unmarried individuals between the ages of 16 and 25 about 88% of the females and 89% of the males had experienced at least one incident of petting in the previous 5 years. Hass found that 90% of the males and 91% of the females in his sample had been involved in breast touching. Since Hass did not include individuals over the age of 18 and Kinsey studied individuals up to the age of 25, it is clear that petting occurs at a younger age today than it did when Kinsey's studies were conducted. Interestingly, although Hass found a gender difference in attitudes toward petting, he found no gender differences in the incidence of petting.

Oral Sex

The majority of teenagers approve of oral sex. Hass (1979) reported that approximately 90% of the males and 70% of the females in his sample of 15- to 18-year-olds believed that it is all right for individuals in their age group to engage in oral sex. However, only about 30% of the 15- and 16-year-olds and 60% of the 17- and 18-year-olds had experienced oral sex themselves. Again, it is interesting that the sexual behaviors of males and females are not very different, but males are more liberal in their attitudes.

Some teenagers engage in oral sex before they engage in sexual intercourse. Some of the females interviewed by Morrison and associates (1980) said that engaging in oral sex allowed them to retain their virginity and still be sexually active. Furthermore, oral sex does not involve the risk of pregnancy that sexual intercourse does. As a result, it may be viewed as a safer method of sexual expression than sexual intercourse.

Sexual Intercourse

Most of the survey data available on sexual development in adolescence is focused on the age at which individuals experience sexual intercourse for the first time. Kinsey and associates (1948, 1953) found that by the age of 15, 32% of the males and 10% of the females had had intercourse. Two decades later Sorenson (1973) reported that 44% of the males and 30% of the females who were 15 or younger said they had had intercourse. Even more recently Zelnik and Shah (1983) discovered that 50% of women between the ages of 15 and 19 and 70% of men between the ages of 17 and 21 reported that they had had sexual intercourse. The average age at which the females indicated having had their first sexual experience was 16.2; the average age for males was 15.7. Although these figures show an increase in sexual activity in adolescents of both genders over recent years, they indicate that the increase has been greater among females than among males. Yet males appear to be more sexually active, on the average, than females.

Attitudes Toward Premarital Sex

In addition to a change in behavior, attitudes toward premarital sex have changed. Reiss (1960) listed four standards for premarital sexual intercourse:
1. Abstinence: premarital sexual intercourse is viewed as wrong for both males and females, regardless of circumstances (e.g., degree of emotional commitment).
2. Permissiveness with affection: premarital sexual intercourse is acceptable for both males and females if the couple is engaged or the relationship is characterized by love and commitment.

3. Permissiveness without affection: premarital sexual intercourse is acceptable for both males and females, regardless of emotional commitment.
4. Double standard: premarital sexual intercourse is permissible for males but not for females. The "orthodox" double standard holds regardless of the nature of the couple's relationship; the "transitional" double standard holds for the woman unless she is in love or is engaged.

Historically in the United States attitudes toward premarital sexual intercourse resembled standards of abstinence or the double standard. However, Hunt (1974) found that the majority of people he surveyed thought that premarital sex was acceptable if the couple had a strong emotional attachment. Furthermore, although the double standard was still apparent in Hunt's data, the difference has been decreasing in recent decades.

A study by Murstein and associates (1989) investigated the trend of premarital sexual intercourse and attitudes concerning premarital sex on a New England college campus over the last 13 years. As can be seen in Tables 12-4 and 12-5, if 1986 were compared only with 1974, the change in sexual attitudes and behavior would appear slight. However, the data from 1979 suggest that

TABLE 12-4 Percentages of Men and Women Whose Last Sexual Experience Fell Within a Given Relationship Category

	Women			Men		
Relationship	1974 N = 121	1979 N = 137	1986 N = 128	1974 N = 152	1979 N = 101	1986 N = 98
Stranger	0.0	3.6	0.8	2.6	5.0	3.1
Casual acquaintance	5.0	16.1	3.2	15.1	15.8	9.3
Close but not exclusive	26.4	35.8	19.0	28.3	42.6	22.7
Steady relationship	57.0	38.7	73.8*	50.0	29.7	61.9*
Fiancé(e) or commitment to marriage	11.6	5.8	3.2	3.9	6.9	3.1

From Murstein et al., 1989.

*In 1986 questionnaire, two categories were used: "steady" and "living together." Since almost all living-together couples did not date others, these categories have been combined here for purposes of comparison.

TABLE 12-5 Percentages of Men and Women Adopting Each Sexual Philosophy as Their Primary Choice

	Women			Men		
Philosophy of sex	1974 N = 163	1979 N = 155	1986 N = 170	1974 N = 184	1979 N = 111	1986 N = 125
Primarily for procreation	0.0	1.3	0.0	1.1	0.0	0.0
Valid in marriage only	5.5	4.5	6.5	3.8	0.9	6.8
OK with fiancé(e)	6.8	14.2	7.9	5.4	0.9	8.3
As part of good relationship	66.3	42.6	72.4	57.1	31.5	63.1
As fun with consenting others	20.2	36.8	12.4	32.1	60.4	17.7
As much as possible with anyone	1.2	0.6	1.3	0.6	6.3	3.9

From Murstein et al., 1989.

in that year sexual attitudes were more permissive and sexual behavior was more promiscuous than in either 1974 or 1986. A possible reason for the trend away from promiscuity is the increase in sexually transmitted diseases such as herpes and the introduction of acquired immunodeficiency syndrome (AIDS). Murstein and his colleagues suggest that because of the prevalence of sexually transmitted diseases, individuals are more likely to limit sex to fewer and more committed partners. Because this study included only college students, the findings may not be representative of all adolescents and young adults.

Dating and Premarital Sex: Attitudes, Behavior, and Conflicts

As previously mentioned, dating is a relatively recent social invention, having become accepted in the United States around 1920 as a method of selecting a marriage partner. It has been suggested that dating has created a greater demand for premarital sex and has perhaps led to greater legitimacy for engaging in premarital sex (Bell, 1966; Hunt, 1974; Roche, 1986).

While dating, the couple progresses through a series of stages, each stage representing a difference in the quality of the relationship. Roche (1986) argues that merely investigating general attitudes toward premarital sex and sexual behaviors does not give the whole picture. Indeed, he contends, we must consider the stage of the dating relationship. By doing so, we can more clearly recognize gender differences and conflicts concerning premarital sex. Thus Roche investigated attitudes toward sexual behavior and actual sexual behavior with regard to five dating stages: stage 1, dating with no particular affection; stage 2, dating with affection but not love; stage 3, dating and being in love; stage 4, dating one person only and being in love (equivalent to "going steady"); and stage 5, becoming engaged.

Table 12-6 shows the respondents' reported attitudes toward certain sexual behaviors and actual sexual behaviors by gender and stage of dating. The most apparent change in attitudes and behavior, as illustrated in Table 12-6, is the increase in permissiveness for both males and females at each successive stage. This is no surprise; as the couple grows more emotionally involved, a more sexually intimate relationship is subjectively considered more appropriate.

Roche's results reveal a clear gender difference in the early stages of dating: males expect sexual intimacy sooner whereas females link sexual intimacy to love and commitment. In the first three stages males are less restrictive in their attitudes about what is proper sexual behavior and more permissive with regard to their actual sexual behavior in all four areas of intimacy—light petting, heavy petting, intercourse, and oral-genital contact. By stage 4 (dating one person only and being in love) the difference between males and females with regard to attitudes and behaviors virtually disappears, except with regard to oral-genital contact. For example, 10% of the males in the study believed that sexual intercourse is proper while dating without any particular affection; no females voiced this level of permissiveness. This difference in attitude toward sexual intercourse disappears only when the relationship involves love and commitment. As Roche stated, "The presence of love appears to justify sexual intimacy for females."

An individual's attitudes toward sexuality and his or her sexual behavior are not necessarily equivalent. People are generally more restrictive in what they consider to be proper sexual conduct than in their reported sexual behavior

TABLE 12-6 Percentages of Men and Women Who Believe Sexual Behaviors Proper and Their Reported Behaviors

Sex behavior	Stage 1: dating with no particular affection		Stage 2: dating with affection but not love		Stage 3: dating and being in love		Stage 4: dating one person only and being in love		Stage 5: engaged	
	Proper	Actual behavior	Proper	Actual behavior	Proper	Actual behavior	Proper	Actual behavior	Proper	Actual behavior
Light petting										
Males	17%	25%	34%	50%	79%	81%	86%	92%	93%	94%
Females	1%	8%	18%	26%	54%	59%	83%	88%	90%	94%
Heavy petting										
Males	11%	18%	23%	33%	64%	68%	76%	81%	83%	88%
Females	0%	6%	9%	19%	39%	42%	71%	82%	84%	93%
Intercourse										
Males	10%	15%	16%	18%	43%	49%	57%	63%	70%	74%
Females	0%	4%	4%	11%	28%	32%	59%	68%	74%	81%
Oral sex										
Males	16%	10%	27%	32%	54%	59%	83%	78%	86%	82%
Females	1%	2%	5%	11%	21%	24%	63%	59%	71%	66%
Number of males	84	80	84	82	84	80	84	72	84	34
Number of females	196	188	196	191	196	176	196	169	196	69

From Roche, 1986.

(Robinson and Jedlicka, 1982; Roche, 1986). In other words, their behavior is often more permissive than their attitudes. Thus trends in attitudes toward sexuality do not necessarily reflect trends in actual sexual behavior. Indeed, compared with their earlier studies in 1970 and 1975, in 1980 Robinson and Jedlicka found an increase in the percentage of students who regarded premarital sex as immoral and sinful. They did not, however, find any decline in the frequency of sexual behavior.

As illustrated in Table 12-6, Roche also found that both males and females tend to be more permissive in their reported sexual behavior than they are when specifying what is proper behavior. The gender difference found in individuals' sexual attitudes by dating stage holds for sexual behaviors as well. By stage 4, males and females reported virtually the same sexual behavior, except with respect to oral sex.

Given the gender differences in attitudes toward sexuality and the discrepancy between attitudes and actual behavior, it is not surprising that many adolescents experience both personal and interpersonal conflicts about their sexuality. The tendency for males to have more permissive views toward sexuality in the early stages of dating may lead to conflicts within the relationship. Whether such conflicts can be overcome depends largely on the male's willingness to be patient and the amount of time the female takes to perceive a high level of commitment and love in the relationship. Yet another way females may attempt to eliminate the interpersonal conflict in the relationship is to give in to sexual pressure, while actually disapproving of that behavior. This tendency may help explain the inconsistencies between attitudes toward sex and actual behavior, especially among females.

Unfortunately, when an individual engages in a sexual activity but disapproves of it, a personal conflict may occur. Because of the higher degree of inconsistency between attitudes and actual behavior among females, it would not be surprising to find a gender difference in the amount of conflict experienced after engaging in a sexual act. Sorenson (1973) studied adolescents' reactions to their first act of sexual intercourse and did find gender differences. Many girls reported that they felt guilt, sorrow, and disappointment. In addition, Sorenson found that positive reactions such as feelings of maturity and joy were about twice as common among boys as among girls. Whereas the immediate reaction of females was to feel afraid, the common immediate reaction of males was to feel excitement. The boys did not usually realize that the girls were having a negative emotional reaction.

TEENAGE PREGNANCY

In the United States each year approximately 1.1 million women under the age of 20 become pregnant (Alan Guttmacher Institute, 1982). According to Hayes (1987), 17% of the conceptions take place after marriage; 10% lead to marriage between the partners; 22% result in out of wedlock births; 38% terminate in abortions; and 13% end in miscarriage. Although the teenage pregnancy rate in the United States has leveled off in the last couple of years, it remains high. In fact, as can be seen in Table 12-7, in 1980 the teenage fertility rate in the United States was higher than that in nearly every other industrialized country, excluding only Iceland and New Zealand (Westoff, Calot, and Foster, 1983).

TABLE 12-7 Selected Measures of Teenage and Overall Fertility in 1971 and in 1979 or 1980

Population	Teenage fertility rate* 1971	Teenage fertility rate* 1979/1980	Population	Teenage fertility rate* 1971	Teenage fertility rate* 1979/1980
Australia	271	145	Italy	143	117
Austria	286	179	Japan	21	17
Belgium†	164	117	Luxembourg‡	163	82
Canada	208	140	Netherlands	112	46
Czechoslovakia	222	265	New Zealand	351	194
Denmark	145	84	Norway	232	128
East Germany	309	253	Poland	207	225
England	254	157	Portugal	162	210
Finland	149	94	Romania	321	352
France	191	125	Spain†	78	133
Greece	185	269	Sweden	170	83
Hungary	267	342	Switzerland	108	48
Iceland	372	289	United States		
Ireland†	100	113	Black	715	515
Israel			White	274	221
Arab	574	376	Total	333	266
Jewish	144	132	West Germany	228	102
Total	202	179	Yugoslavia	273	241

Modified from Westoff, Calot, and Foster, 1983.

*Per 10,000.

†Most recent data are for 1978.

‡Rates for Luxembourg estimated from reports for 5-year age categories.

A Personal Glimpse

The Story of a Teenage Pregnancy

Andrea is pretty and poised, in that teenage sort of way.

She has dark hair, dark eyes, a flashy smile and wears Calvin Klein jeans, Topsiders, pullover sweaters and turtlenecks.

She has also been pregnant.

"The test takes a minute. That was the longest minute of all my life. My head was pounding. When the nurse told me I was pregnant, I fainted."

She was 16 and more than three months pregnant before she went to the local Public Health Department for the pregnancy test. That was on a Monday. On Thursday, she went to a clinic for an abortion.

"The big thing is I'm Catholic. But my first thought was to just go and have an abortion," she said. "I never told my parents. I wanted to lots of times but I couldn't . . . I never thought about keeping the baby either. My parents would have had a heart attack. They never would have understood. I just kept thinking, 'my parents, my parents, my parents.'"

That was a year ago. Now Andrea is 17, still in high school, and eager to talk about teen-age sexual relations, pregnancy and abortion.

"I'd do anything to help another girl from getting pregnant," she said. "I want people to know it can happen to them. Everyone thinks it can never happen to them. It does. It happens to a lot of people."

She'd been dating her boyfriend for about three months. "We started having sex. He was the first one. He talked me into it one night, but still it was my decision. I could have kept saying 'no.'"

She paused and then added, "Peer pressure had a lot to do with it too. Everyone else was having sex and I said, 'Wow, I'd better too.'"

Shortly thereafter Andrea started taking birth control pills. It was too late.

"I never thought it could happen to me. I was kind of naive . . . I mean I knew I could (get pregnant) but I never used my head. I was like a dingy little girl."

But so-called "little girls" can conceive. They also have a tendency to deceive themselves.

"I missed three periods before I finally went in (to the clinic)," Andrea said. "I had a lot of friends that said, 'Aw, don't worry. That's normal.' I just kept trying to fool myself, that was the whole thing. I didn't really want to know."

Hearing the news was the first blow. There was a second.

When she told her boyfriend she was pregnant, "he didn't want to have anything to do with it," she said. "I was real surprised. He just kind of turned me off. He was laying there on his bed going 'Oh, wow.' He never once said, 'What are WE going to do?' He said, 'What are YOU going to do?'"

She continued: "Guys go along with it for a little while and then all of a sudden, they just split. Most of the girls I know who have gotten pregnant also have gotten dumped on. That's the only thing that really hurt me. I could never understand how he could do that . . . I wish I'd never dated him."

He didn't help her pay for her $275 abortion. She borrowed the money from other friends.

He didn't take her to the abortion clinic either, instead a girlfriend drove her.

Andrea talked about that experience. "I was so busy trying to get the money that I didn't even think much about it (the abortion). It never really hit me until I was in the waiting room. I was scared, really scared. I had to wait for an hour and a half. I was crying. It was hitting me all at once. The abortion took seven minutes. Then it was all over and I went home."

She added: "I just know I did the right thing. I'll never regret it."

The only thing Andrea wishes now is that she'd been a bit smarter.

"I think if my parents really sat down and explained things to me I would have found out things instead of learning them the hard way . . . I think a lot of parents think they should just leave it up to the kids to find out about sex. That's the worst thing they can do . . . My parents are great parents, they support me, they give me a car, but they just don't talk."

Andrea says she's put the experience in the past now. "I just look at it as a bad experience. I'm just sorry it happened."

From Lawrence (Kan.) Journal-World, 1981.

Pregnant Teenagers

Koenig and Zelnik (1983) found that 16% of young women between the ages of 15 and 19 had experienced a premarital pregnancy. They also reported that the risk of premarital pregnancy among sexually active teenage women was 36% within the first 2 years after the first act of sexual intercourse. The risk was highest during the first few months of sexual activity; 45% of all premarital pregnancies occurred within the first 6 months of sexual activity.

Teenage pregnancy is a severe problem for the thousands involved. An unplanned pregnancy can be extremely stressful. The young woman frequently finds herself in a situation in which she needs to make a number of important decisions in a short time. She has to decide whether she wants to have the baby or have an abortion. If she decides to give birth, she has to decide whether she wants to keep the baby or give it up for adoption. She may also have to make decisions about whether to marry the father of the baby or drop out of school to support the baby. She must deal with all of these factors while under emotional stress. Her parents may be so distressed by the situation that they are unable to give their daughter the kind of guidance and help she needs. She may find that her friends withdraw from her as well.

Teenage Mothers

In 1984 in the United States 470,000 babies were born to mothers who were 15 to 19 years old. When a teenager decides to give birth, she and her infant face greater risks, both physical as well as socioeconomic, than the risks faced by women in their twenties and their infants.

The increased risks for teenage mothers are also discussed in Chapter 7.

A teenage mother is more likely to develop medical complications during pregnancy and childbirth than a woman in her twenties (Makinson, 1985). A teenage mother is also more likely to die during childbirth. The infant of a teenage mother is more likely to be underweight and to die during infancy than the infant of a woman in her twenties (Smith and Mumford, 1980).

The problems associated with teenage mothers are not limited to the physical realm; there are socioeconomic repercussions as well. Even though pregnant teenagers are usually no longer forced to leave school, they are twice as likely to drop out before finishing high school than other teenage girls (Zellman, 1982). Dropping out of school limits their occupational opportunities and incomes and increases the likelihood that they will need to be supported by welfare (Moore and Wertheimer, 1984). In addition, marriages precipitated by teenage pregnancies have been found to be less stable than most marriages (O'Connell and Rogers, 1984; Morgan and Rindfuss, 1985).

Recently some researchers have argued that although teenage childbearing does increase the risk of social and economic handicaps, the social stereotype of the teenager mother, "an unemployed woman with many ill-cared-for children who is living on the dole," is not justified (Furstenberg, Gunn, and Morgan, 1988). Sociologist Furstenberg and his colleagues have been studying the effects of teenage pregnancy on 400 teenage mothers. The teenage mothers were initially pregnant in 1966 and 1967, and they and their children were followed up in 1984, 17 years after the initial interview.

Furstenberg and his associates concluded that many teenage mothers cope quite successfully despite the odds against them. Certainly most teenage moth-

This 16-year-old will most likely face many socioeconomic hardships as a teenage mother.

ers do not do as well as women who postpone childbearing (Furstenberg, Brooks-Gunn, and Chase-Lansdale, 1989). Five years after the pregnancy the mothers and children looked very disadvantaged. For instance, one third of them were on welfare and 49% had not graduated from high school. However, in 1984, 17 years after the pregnancy, a significant proportion of the women had made a substantial recovery. By this time, 89% had graduated from high school, with 25% having had some education beyond high school and 5% having graduated from college. Furthermore, of the 70% who had been on welfare sometime during the 17 years, by 1984 two thirds had managed to get off welfare; 67% were employed and one fourth had incomes greater than $25,000 per year, which at the time ranked them above the median income for the country.

Therefore, although teenage mothers are more likely than the general population of women to find themselves on welfare, a great diversity exists in the outcomes for adolescent mothers. Furstenberg and his colleagues suggest that perhaps the negative consequences have been exaggerated and that focusing instead on the success stories might show how some teenage mothers defeat the odds against them. They delineated several factors that lead to successful and happy lives for teenage mothers: (1) accessible resources (women whose parents are more educated and have higher incomes tend to do better because they have more resources); (2) individual differences in competence and motivation (women who had been doing well in school at the time of their pregnancy and who had more ambitious educational goals were more likely to do well after the birth of their child); and (3) intervention programs such as special schools for pregnant teenagers and hospital prevention programs. Successful employment of such programs helps the women both to complete high school and to postpone additional births, two crucial factors in the reduction of negative consequences of teenage pregnancy. Furthermore, marriage, although risky for teenage mothers, tends to be beneficial at least for those mothers who remain married, especially when further childbearing is delayed.

Children of Teenage Mothers

The children of teenage mothers are at risk in many ways. In the study by Furstenberg, Brooks-Gunn, and Morgan (1988), by the age of 17 the school records of the children born to teenage mothers displayed signs of academic failure and behavior problems. Although 92% were enrolled in school, half had had to repeat at least one grade and 44% had been suspended or expelled in the past 5 years. Furthermore, 26% of the girls reported having been pregnant. One factor that appears to help children of teenage mothers is the presence of such programs as Head Start that help prepare the children for school. In addition, marriage by the child's mother to a man with some financial resources increases the likelihood of success for both the child and the mother.

Teenage Fathers

In the United States an estimated 1 in 10 to 20 teenage boys will be responsible for a premarital pregnancy (Elster and Panzarine, 1983). The number is smaller than that for teenage girls because many girls who become pregnant have partners 2 or 3 years older than themselves (Sonenstein, 1986). In 1981 at least 129,336 newborns were fathered by teenage males (National Center for Health Statistics, 1983).

Stereotypes in our culture depict the teenage father as uncaring and interested primarily in sexual gratification (Robinson, 1988a, 1988b). In addition, the stereotype assumes the teenage father is uninvolved in the support and rearing of his child, leaving his partner and offspring to fend for themselves (Robinson, 1988a, 1988b). While this characterization may be true of some teen fathers, research has shown that teenage fathers typically remain physically and psychologically involved with their partners' pregnancy.

Indeed, young men who learn their partner is pregnant often experience the same emotional struggle and confusion as their pregnant partner. Seventy-five percent of unwed expectant teenage fathers studied by Westney, Cole, and Munford (1986) reported feeling they were not ready for fatherhood. Reactions of being scared and angry when they were told of the pregnancy were reported by 51%, and only 17% of this number said their negative reactions were mixed with feelings of happiness (Vaz, Smolen, and Miller, 1983). Other young men reported feeling sad, overwhelmed, shocked, or doubtful (Westney, Cole, and Munford, 1986). This mixture of feelings is manifested by the following statement by an adolescent father:

I kinda got the feeling that it couldn't be true—I was just scared to death, didn't know what to do. Just a million things went through my mind. I was scared on the one hand having to consult my parents about the situation and then on the other hand I was kinda excited to know that I could be a father in nine months.

Robinson, 1988a, p. 56

Also contrary to stereotypes, adolescent fathers typically intend to help the mother and child. Redmond (1985) reported that 91% of the adolescent males in his sample said they would provide financial support and 87% wanted to participate in child care. In another study 96% of unwed expectant fathers said they intended to maintain close contact with the mother and baby and to help with the baby's physical care (Westney, Cole, and Munford, 1986). Furthermore, Vaz and her associates (1983) found that 81% of the teenage fathers in their sample continued to date the mother during the pregnancy and after the birth of their child, and 75% helped her by providing money. At 18 months after the birth most of the 81 teenage fathers in the sample of Rivara, Sweeney, and Henderson (1986) remained involved in the lives of the mother and child.

Like teenage mothers, teenage fathers must face dire consequences. Research has found that unplanned and premature parenthood stifles the teenage father's education, vocational, and social experiences, which are essential to prepare him for his adult role (Marsiglio, 1986; Robinson, 1988a, 1988b). Furthermore, teenage fathers meet overwhelming odds against success in parenting and marriage.

Contrary to stereotypes, most teenage fathers want to stay involved in the lives of their children.

Despite the virtually insurmountable odds facing teenage fathers, research suggests that the father's involvement with the mother and their child does have positive effects on the child's social and cognitive development (Robinson and Barret, 1986). Perhaps to facilitate such involvement and thus children's well-being, teenage fathers should be given support and guidance rather than be subjected to the denigration that can result from negative stereotypes (Robinson, 1988a).

Considering the problems associated with teenage pregnancies for the girls involved, their sexual partners, their families, and society, more needs to be done to decrease the prevalence of unwanted teenage pregnancies. The solution lies in better sex education at home and in school. At present our society is not adequately educating children about sexual issues.

A more complete discussion of sex education is presented in Chapter 23.

HOMOSEXUAL EXPERIENCES IN CHILDHOOD AND ADOLESCENCE

Many children and adolescents have some kind of sexual interaction with individuals of the same gender. For example, in surveys by Kinsey and associates (1948, 1953) 60% of the males said that they had engaged in some form of homosexual activity before 16 years of age. Kinsey and associates further reported that 3% of adolescent females and 22% of adolescent males had had at least one homosexual experience resulting in orgasm. In Hass' more recent study (1979) 14% of the males and 11% of the females indicated having had at least one homosexual experience. Sorenson (1973) found that most adolescent homosexual experiences took place between peers. Of the teenagers in his study who reported having had homosexual experiences, 24% indicated that they had the experience with a younger person, 34% with someone their own age, 29% with an older teenager, and only 8% with an adult.

Homosexual behavior during childhood is discussed in more detail in Chapter 11.

Such homosexual activity during childhood or adolescence should not be equated with, or considered indicative of, homosexuality. In many cases the homosexual behavior is discontinued after the person has had only one or a few homosexual experiences. Homosexual behavior in childhood or adolescence is not predictive of an adult homosexual orientation.

SUMMARY

1 Freud proposed that children go through a series of stages in their sexual development: oral stage, anal stage, phallic stage, latency stage, and genital stage. It is in the phallic stage that boys experience the Oedipal complex and girls experience the Electra complex.

2 Erikson extended Freud's work by focusing on the individual's interactions with family, friends, and the larger culture. Each of Erikson's stages has a core developmental conflict with which individuals of that age must deal.

3 Contrary to what is often assumed, infants exhibit a number of behaviors that appear to be sexual in nature. Male infants have penile erections, and female infants exhibit vaginal lubrication. Infants play with their own genitals, and some are apparently capable of having orgasms.

4 Children have many misconceptions about basic concepts regarding sex. To prevent such misconceptions, parents should begin to teach their children about sexuality at an early age.

5 During childhood a marked intensification of sexual interest and capacity for erotic response occurs and masturbation, sex play, and interest in sexual topics increase.

6 Research suggests that sexual behavior and adjustment of young adults are little affected by most sexual experiences children have with each other regardless of the age when the sexual experience takes place.

7 Rather than responding with horror and disgust to the young child's natural sexual response, parents should convey to the child that his or her sexual responses are normal and healthy. The parents should tell the child when and where sexual behavior is appropriate and when and where it is inappropriate.

8 Adolescence is marked by drastic changes in the physiological makeup of the individual. These changes include the production of gonadal hormones from the testes or ovaries. In girls the hormones cause the breasts to develop, the body to take on a rounded shape, pubic hair to grow, the external genitals to grow and develop, a growth spurt to occur, and menstruation to start.

9 Boys tend to mature about 2 years later than girls. The hormonal changes that occur during adolescence in boys cause them to start producing fertile sperm, grow more body and facial hair, experience external genital growth and development, and develop a deeper voice.

10 During adolescence males show a striking and rapid increase in sexual activity. Girls, on the other hand, have a much slower and more gradual increase in sexual activity. Although males reach their peak orgasmic frequency during their adolescent years, females often do not reach their sexual peak until they are in their twenties or thirties.

11 The majority of both males and females report masturbating during adolescence. However, the incidence of masturbation is higher in males than in females.

12 Although males' attitudes are more liberal than females', there is little gender difference in actual petting behavior.

13 The age at which teenagers first have sexual intercourse has been decreasing over recent decades. Males are likely to have intercourse at a younger age than females.

14 Sexual attitudes and behavior among today's college students are more conservative than they were in 1979. The increase in sexually transmitted diseases and the introduction of AIDS may have contributed to this conservative trend.

15 Research suggests that among both males and females sexual behavior tends to be more permissive than their attitudes about what is proper premarital sex.

16 Approximately 16% of girls between the ages of 15 and 19 experience a premarital pregnancy.

17 Teenage mothers face great risks, both physical and socioeconomic. However, many teenage mothers cope successfully despite the odds against them.

18 Stereotypes in our culture depict the teenage father as uncaring, but research has shown that many teenage fathers remain involved with their partner's pregnancy and attempt to help the mother and child. Research suggests that a teenage father's involvement with the mother and their child has positive effects on the child's social and cognitive development.

19 Many children and adolescents experience some form of homosexual interaction; such homosexual activity does not appear to be predictive of an adult homosexual orientation.

FACT
OR
FICTION

ANSWERS

1 Infants are capable of erections and vaginal lubrication at, or shortly after, birth.

2 Masturbation before and during adolescence is more common in boys than it is in girls.

3 The teenage pregnancy rate has increased drastically over the last several decades; the U.S. rate is much higher than that in most other Western countries.

1 What childhood sexual experiences can you remember?

2 Did you have any homosexual experiences during childhood?

3 In 1974 Hunt said that boys try to see how much they can get from girls sexually while girls try to see how little they can give. Do you think that is still true in the 1990s?

SUGGESTED READINGS

Byrne, D., and Fisher, W., editors: Adolescents, sex, and contraception, Hillsdale, N.J., 1983, Lawrence Erlbaum Associates, Inc.
  A book about teenage attitudes and behavior regarding contraception.

Calderone, M.S., and Ramey, J.: Talking with your child about sex, New York, 1982, Random House, Inc.
  A guide for parents on how to talk with their children about sexuality.

Furstenberg, F.F., Brooks-Gunn, J., and Morgan, S.P.: Adolescent mothers in later life, New York, 1988, Cambridge University Press.
  A reassessment of teenage parenthood.

Goldman, R.J., and Goldman, J.D.: Show me yours: understanding children's sexuality, Ringwood, Aust., 1988, Penguin Books.
  An exhaustive investigation of the development of children's knowledge of sex and their sexual experiences.

Robinson, B.: Teenage fathers, Lexington, Mass., 1988, Lexington Books.
  An analysis of the experiences of teenage fathers.

13

Adulthood and Aging

1
Although men show a steady decrease in sexual activity during the adult years, women do not show such a decrease until the age of about 60.

2
Continued sexual activity throughout adulthood is the predictor of a healthy, active sex life in old age.

3
Lesbians appear to be more concerned about growing old than gay males.

Having successfully pretended for decades that we are nonsexual, my generation is now having second thoughts. We are increasingly realizing that denying our sexuality means denying an essential aspect of our common humanity. It cuts us off from communication with our children, our grandchildren, and our peers on a subject of great interest to us all—sexuality. The rejection of the aging and aged by some younger people has many roots; but surely the belief that we are no longer sexual beings, and therefore no longer fully human, is one of the roots of that rejection.

67-YEAR-OLD INDIVIDUAL
E.M. Brecher: Love, Sex, and Aging, pp. 19-20

In Chapter 11 we discussed the changes in sexual functioning that take place in childhood and adolescence. In this chapter we investigate changes that occur during the adult years. As the cartoon on the following page indicates, younger people often have difficulty imagining that individuals who are older than themselves remain sexually active. As you will see, many people remain sexually active through old age.

YOUNG ADULTHOOD

For many, adolescence is a time to explore and experiment with their newly developing sexuality. Many adolescents are not mature enough to establish a sexual relationship with another person that is marked by mutual care and concern because they are still too focused on their own developmental tasks and concerns. By the early adult years, however, most individuals are beginning to feel secure in their own identity and comfortable enough with their own sexuality to develop more mature sexual and emotional relationships.

As a result of such positive development, most individuals become ready during the early adult years to commit themselves to building a life with another person and to having children. The vast majority of men and women marry and have children during early adulthood. Since marriage and parenthood are discussed at length in Chapters 15 and 7, respectively, they are not discussed in detail in this chapter. The discussion here is limited primarily to other aspects of adult sexuality that change with age.

Frequency of Sexual Activity

During early adulthood the frequency of sexual intercourse is at its highest. Probably many factors—biological, psychological, and cultural—are responsible for this high rate of sexual intercourse. Because young adults are usually in prime physical condition, sexual motivation is probably as high during the early adult years as it is at any other time in the life cycle. In addition, usually more sexual partners are available during the early adult years. A much higher percentage of adults are single during the young adult years than during middle and late adulthood. Furthermore, many young adults attend college where they live among other single men and women. The restrictions that limit sexual expression during the adolescent years are lessened in early adulthood. For example, young adults are not as subject to their parents' control as they were

In early adulthood many young men and women begin to develop mature relationships.

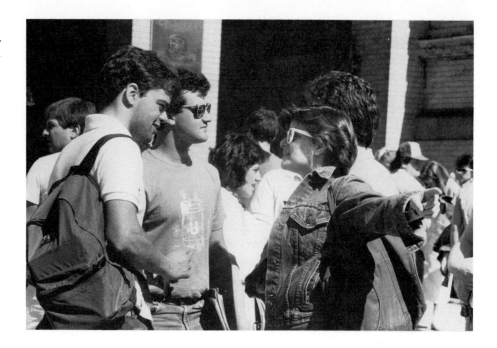

in adolescence. They often live separately from their parents, they are less financially dependent on their parents, and both they and their parents are beginning to accept the young adults' independence. For example, many young adults live in apartments or other settings that afford them the necessary privacy. It is also more acceptable in our culture for young adults to have sexual relationships. Although many individuals in our culture consider sexual relationships inappropriate for young adolescents, the vast majority accept sexual relationships among young adults.

Cohabitation is discussed in Chapter 15.

Many young adults now spend some time cohabiting before marriage. Cohabitants tend to have sex more often than married couples (Blumstein and Schwartz, 1983). Thus the fact that younger adults are more likely to cohabit than older adults may contribute to a greater frequency of sexual behavior among some younger adults.

The frequency with which a couple has sex decreases the longer the couple stays together, regardless of whether the couple is cohabiting or married (Broderick, 1982; Blumstein and Schwartz, 1983). In marriage, sexual activity is most frequent in the early months and declines precipitously in the first 3 years; average monthly frequency decreases from about thirteen to about seven during this period. Following this 3-year period, frequency declines more gradually. After 30 years of marriage the average frequency is about three times per month. Since length of marriage is closely related to age, the decrease in frequency with length of marriage means that the frequency of sex also decreases with age. However, there is a decrease in sexual activity with increasing age that is independent of the decrease associated with longevity of marriage (Blumstein and Schwartz, 1983).

In addition to age and number of years spent together, pregnancy and parenthood decrease the frequency with which a couple engages in sexual intercourse. Young adults are likely to start a family in the early years of marriage, although many couples now delay beginning a family longer than before. Sexual activity decreases over the course of the pregnancy, especially during the third trimester (White and Reamy, 1982). Children also appear to have an inhibiting effect on the frequency of sexual intercourse of the parents.

In summary, young adults tend to have a high degree of sexual interaction. Young adults have more opportunity for sexual exploration than they did during adolescence because of their increased freedom and independence and greater availability of partners. After early adulthood there are factors that tend to depress sexual frequency. These factors are discussed at greater length in the sections on middle and old age.

The effect children have on a couple's sexual relationship is discussed in greater detail in Chapter 7.

Sexual Variety

Young adults tend to include more variety in their sexual experiences. They are more likely to try different sexual activities, such as oral and anal sex, and to use a variety of positions for sexual intercourse. Possibly the desire for sexual variety decreases with increasing age. However, our culture has become more liberal with respect to sexuality as a result of the changes that took place in the 1960s and 1970s. These cultural changes are more likely to affect younger individuals than older individuals who established their behavior patterns before the cultural changes took place. Thus the age differences might not reflect actual age changes in sexual behavior but instead simply reflect cultural differences. As today's young adults age, they may not exhibit a decrease in sexual variety.

Gender Differences

Gender differences in sexual behavior are discussed at length in Chapter 10.

The effect of hormones on sexual behavior is discussed in Chapter 4.

Although sexual activity is high during the early adult years in both men and women, males tend to be more sexually active than females (George and Weiler, 1985). Although gender differences in the percentage of young adults who have experienced premarital intercourse have almost been eliminated, young men are likely to have more sex partners than young women (Mahoney, 1980; Daugherty and Burger, 1984). Young men also masturbate more often, and they have a greater number of sexual outlets of all kinds than young women (Kinsey, Pomeroy, and Martin, 1948; Kinsey et al., 1953).

It is not clear whether males are more sexually active because of the double standard in our society that condones sexual behavior to a greater extent in men than in women or whether the difference is a result of biological factors. Certainly the double standard would be expected to inhibit female sexuality. However, hormonal factors may be responsible for the greater sexual activity in males. The male hormone testosterone has long been the treatment of choice to induce or restore sexual functioning in men with hormonally based sexual problems (Schiavi et al., 1988). Androgens have also been used in the treatment of unresponsive women (Carney, Bancroft, and Mathews, 1978) and to enhance sexual desire in postmenopausal women (Greenblatt, 1987; Walling, Andersen, and Johnson, 1990). In addition, females with unusually high androgen levels caused by adrenal tumors and other abnormalities show an increased sex drive (Money and Erhardt, 1972). A number of researchers have reported a positive correlation between women's normal testosterone level and their sexual arousal (Persky et al., 1978; Bancroft, 1984). Furthermore, administration of androgens to women following hysterectomies resulted in higher levels of sexual desire and arousal than with estrogen or a placebo (Sherwin, Gelfand, and Brender, 1985; Sherwin and Gelfand, 1987). In addition to changing sexual desire, androgens have been found to be significantly related to sexual behavior. Bancroft (1984) found that the frequency of masturbation increases with the level of a woman's androgens. This research indicates that testosterone is a major determinant of sexual motivation and behavior in both males and females. Since males have higher levels of testosterone than do females, this hormonal difference may be in part responsible for the greater sexual activity of males.

Sexual activity also follows a different developmental course for males and females. As Kinsey and associates note:

> The male's capacity to be stimulated sexually shows a marked increase with the approach of adolescence. . . . The incidences of responding males, and the frequencies of response to the point of orgasm, reach their peak within three to four years after the onset of adolescence. On the other hand . . . the maximum incidences of sexually responding females are not approached until sometime in the late twenties and in the thirties.
>
> Kinsey et al., 1953, p. 714

What factor or factors are responsible for this difference is not clear. Learning may be important. Females may simply be more inhibited with respect to sexuality during their teenage and early adult years because of the double standard in our culture. They may take years to learn to enjoy their sexuality and become less inhibited. Furthermore, since sex is much more acceptable for females in the context of marriage, they may not become more sexual until they are married. Hormonal differences between males and females may also be responsible for differences in the age of peak sexual response.

MIDDLE ADULTHOOD
Frequency of Sexual Activity

The age of maximum sexuality, according to Kinsey, Pomeroy, and Martin (1948), is in the teens; sexuality decreases from the teenage years almost steadily until about 60 years of age. After the age of 60 the decline is somewhat greater. Kinsey and his associates based their conclusions on a study in which all sources of orgasm, including orgasm from sexual intercourse, masturbation, and nocturnal emissions, were considered.

Unlike males, who show a steady decrease in sexual activity during the middle adult years, females show little evidence of decreased sexual activity during middle adulthood (Kinsey et al., 1953). However, some decline may occur during the later adult years. The frequency with which women have sexual intercourse with their husbands declines, but this appears to result mainly from changes in the husbands. Kinsey and associates found that the rate with which women masturbate declines only slightly with age. Masters and Johnson (1966) did not find a decline in masturbation during the middle adult years; they reported a decrease only after the age of 60.

Gender Differences

Although the sexual decline is greater in men than in women during the middle adult years, the sexual activities of men are more frequent than those of women during this time. Kinsey and associates (1953) reported that masturbation rates for unmarried women between the teenage years and the fifties were approximately 0.3 to 0.4 per week. The comparable rates for men were 0.4 to 1.8 per week. Similarly, a comparison of data regarding all sexual outlets for men (Kinsey, Pomeroy, and Martin, 1948) and for women (Kinsey et al., 1953) shows a greater frequency of orgasm for men. Even among married individuals the frequency is greater for men.

Decreasing Sexual Responsiveness of Males

The male's sexual responsiveness decreases somewhat with age during the middle adult years. In fact Kinsey, Pomeroy, and Martin (1948) stated that "in the sexual history of the male, there is no other single factor that affects frequency of outlet as much as age. . . . Age is so important that its effects are usually evident, whatever the mental status, the educational level, the religious background or the other factors which enter the picture." However, the decrease in the sexual responsiveness of the male is very gradual.

The gradual decrease in sexual responsiveness that begins around 40 years of age may cause distress, particularly if the change is unexpected or misunderstood. "Lately I've been troubled by the fact that I seem to take longer to have a good erection. Is something wrong? Am I becoming impotent? Will sex be as pleasurable as when I was younger? Will my partner think I am inadequate?" (Butler and Lewis, 1986). Men who are unaware of normal age-related physiological changes in sexual functioning may incorrectly believe they are becoming impotent. Unfortunately, "fear of impotence can cause impotence" (Butler and Lewis, 1986).

impotence
(IM puh tuhns) Inability to get or maintain an erection.

Butler and Lewis (1986) endorse relaxation, an absence of pressure, and correct information about normal sexual functioning as reliable remedies for fear-induced impotence. The man's sexual partner should be made aware of the natural changes so that decreased responsiveness is not mistaken for lack of interest. In addition, the man's sexual partner can learn effective techniques for stimulating him to make up for the decrease in sexual responsiveness. Middle-aged men fearing inadequacy as sexual partners should keep in mind that they probably have better control over ejaculation than young men; thus they are better able to prolong sexual intercourse and may in fact be better sexual partners.

Menopause

Menopause refers to the permanent cessation of the menstrual cycle (Diczfalusy, 1987). "The manner in which menstruation ceases is variable. Occasionally it may end abruptly, but as a rule the menstrual flow becomes gradually more scanty, and the interval between periods is increased" (Hafez, 1980). Menopause results when estrogen and progesterone are no longer produced by the ovaries. It is considered complete after a women goes 1 full year without a menstrual cycle. Most women experience menopause between the ages of 45 and 55.

Since sexual activity does not appear to be strongly affected by estrogen and progesterone levels, menopause need not affect the sexual activity of women (Davidson, 1984). Some women even experience an increase in sexual interest and activity after menopause, since they no longer have to fear pregnancy (Weg, 1987). Other women, however, report a decrease in sexual interest and activity (Walling, Andersen, and Johnson, 1990).

Before menopause most women experience gradual changes in their menstrual cycles. The most common changes are occasional missed menstrual periods and longer intervals between periods. A few women experience a more abrupt cessation of menstruation.

In addition to alterations in the menstrual cycle, other symptoms are sometimes reported by menopausal women. One of the most frequently reported is the **hot flash** (Kletzky and Borenstein, 1987). The hot flash is a sensation of heat passing over the body. In most cases the sensation involves just the upper body, neck, and head; however, it sometimes includes the entire body. The sensation of heat is accompanied by a reddening of the skin. Hot flashes, which tend to last a number of minutes, vary among women in duration, frequency, and severity. They may be experienced anywhere from several months to a few years. Eventually the body adjusts to the lower levels of estrogen and the hot flashes cease (Gambrell, 1982). Although research indicates that close to 80% of women experience hot flashes at menopause, less than half of these women consider them a serious problem (Dewhurst, 1976).

Hot flashes are caused by dilation and then constriction of the small arteries. When the arteries are dilated, more blood than usual flows through the blood vessels, causing the flushing of the skin and the feeling of warmth and profuse sweating. The precise cause for the dilation and constriction of the arteries at

hot flash
Sudden sensation of warmth and blushing that commonly occurs in menopausal women.

ACROSS   CULTURES

Menopause: The Experience of Mayan Women

Yewoubdar Beyene conducted a cross-cultural study of menopause and found that it is experienced differently in different cultures. The following are some excerpts from her report of how menopause affects Mayan women from Mexico.

Menopausal and postmenopausal women in the study were asked about their own experience of menopause, the symptoms associated with menopause, and how they felt and what they believed their health status to be before and after menopause. All women in the study indicated that Mayan women did not associate menopause with physical or emotional symptomatology. None reported that they had hot flashes or cold sweats. (pp. 118-119)

Overall, the Mayan women informants themselves knew that menopause occurs, and the only major change associated in their minds with this event was the cessation of menstruation and the end of fertility. (p. 119)

The Mayan women perceived menopause as an event that occurs when a woman has used up all her blood, that is, menstrual blood. Thus, they believed that the onset of menopause occurs early for those women who have had many children because they had used up their blood by giving birth often. (p. 119)

These Mayan women perceive menopause as a life stage free of taboos and restrictions, and offering increased freedom of movement. Thus some of the women's statements (translated) were: "Finally the time has come: it's better this way." "We are happy that we do not have any more because we have time to visit." "It is not like before; I did not go out because of it." The women also said they felt relieved at the cessation of the monthly menstrual flow which was considered bothersome, and menopause represented a relief from the anxiety of accidents and staining their white garments. (pp. 120-121)

Moreover, they claimed better sexual relationships with their husbands after menopause. Because the risk of pregnancy was no longer present, they felt relaxed about sexual activities. (p. 121)

In general, Mayan women were concerned with pregnancy and childbirth but not with menopause. The information in this study indicates that Mayan village women welcome menopause, conceive of it as a natural event, and associate this stage with being young and free. They are pleased to be rid of their period, and thus premenopausal women in this study look forward to the onset of menopause. (p. 123)

Although there are some conflicting views on the psychosomatic and psychological symptoms of menopause, most Western physicians agree that hot flashes are physiological symptoms, the direct results of estrogen decline at menopause. If menopause is principally a hormonal event, one would expect that women throughout the world would experience similar symptoms. However, none of the Mayan women reported hot flashes; the only physiological change that they recognize is the cessation of menstruation. (p. 123)

From Beyene, 1989.

the time of menopause is not yet known. However, the decline in estrogen that occurs at menopause is considered to be a contributing factor (Bates, 1981; Kletzky and Borenstein, 1987).

Some symptoms of menopause are related to changes in the estrogen-responsive areas of the body such as the breasts, vagina, and uterus (Archer, 1982). As a result of the decrease in estrogen in these areas, the breasts, vagina, and uterus become smaller and the mucosal surface of the vagina becomes thinner and drier. In some women the changes in the vagina make intercourse more difficult and sometimes painful (Walling, Andersen, and Johnson, 1990).

Other symptoms that have been attributed to menopause are fatigue, dizziness, headaches, insomnia, depression, nervousness, and irritability (Weg, 1987; Spence, 1989). However, there is some controversy over whether these psychological symptoms actually result from menopause. Matthews and associates (1990) point out that a number of methodological problems are associated with the studies that have reported negative psychological effects of menopause. Many researchers either have used age as an indicator of menopausal status rather than determining actual menopausal status or have used samples of self-selected women who seek help for negative symptoms as subjects. In a longitudinal study of randomly selected women, Matthews found that when actual menopausal status is used and age is controlled, natural menopause is not associated with negative psychological outcomes.

If menopause docs have adverse psychological effects, they may be caused in part by estrogen depletion. However, they also may be caused by concurrent life changes (Steege, 1986). For example, some women may show psychological symptoms because they realize that they are aging, no longer feel attractive, or are unhappy about their children leaving home. By controlling for the effects of age, future studies may be able to determine whether psychological changes in middle age are hormonally induced or a result of other changes occurring in the women's lives.

In addition to the symptoms experienced at menopause, other changes may occur in women as a result of menopause. Postmenopausal women have in-

During menopause women often experience physical and psychological changes.

creases in **osteoporosis** (Lindsay and Tohme, 1987), cardiovascular disease (Kannel and Gordon, 1987), and musculoskeletal disorders (Diczfalusy, 1987). These changes presumably result from the decrease in estrogen levels in postmenopausal women.

Osteoporosis is a condition in which the bones become thin and brittle as a result of mineral loss. The incidence of this condition increases with age in both men and women. However, the increase is much greater in postmenopausal women. An estimated 25% of all women have evidence of osteoporosis by 60 years of age (Lindsay and Tohme, 1987). Of women who live to the age of 90, an estimated 32% suffer a hip fracture associated with osteoporosis (Diczfalusy, 1987). After such a fracture most individuals never return to normal activity and 20% die within a year. Thus osteoporosis is a significant problem.

Since menopausal symptoms appear to be caused by estrogen deficiency, physicians have sometimes used estrogen replacement therapy to help menopausal women. Estrogen replacement therapy does seem to relieve some of the menopausal symptoms. It is effective in alleviating both hot flashes (Meldrum, 1987) and the atrophy of the vagina (Hafez, 1980; Walling, Andersen, and Johnson, 1990). Furthermore, estrogen therapy significantly retards bone loss in postmenopausal women (Lindsay and Tohme, 1987). The use of estrogen therapy for the relief of other menopausal symptoms is more controversial.

Although estrogen replacement therapy seems to have some beneficial effects, physicians must be cautious in administering estrogen to menopausal women. The major concern is the relationship between estrogen and the development of cancer in estrogen-responsive tissues. There is some indication that estrogen therapy may facilitate the growth of already present breast cancer and that it may increase the risk of cancer of the uterus. Recent evidence suggests that the cyclical administration of progesterone and estrogen may reduce the risk of uterine cancer (Gambrell, 1982). However, giving postmenopausal women progestin in addition to some types of estrogen may increase the risk of breast cancer (Bergvist et al., 1989). Clearly more research is needed before strong conclusions on the safety of estrogen replacement therapy can be drawn.

Methods other than estrogen replacement have been used to treat some of the problems that arise following menopause. For example, the risk of osteoporosis can be decreased by both weight-bearing exercise (deVries, 1983) and the newly developed drug etidronate (Watts at al., 1990). Many physicians recommend that postmenopausal women take calcium supplements to reduce the extent of bone loss, although their effectiveness has been questioned. Both hormones and drugs can be used to treat hot flashes (Meldrum, 1987).

Some women do not experience any symptoms at menopause or have only slight symptoms that cause them no difficulty. Many women, in fact, are delighted to cease menstruating (Steege, 1986). They no longer need to fear unwanted pregnancies and as a result have much more sexual freedom. Many women also enjoy the freedom from maternal responsibilities that occurs around the time of menopause. As their children leave home, they have more time to pursue their own interests. In fact, in a study of attitudes toward menopause, Bowles (1986) found that "younger, premenopausal women . . . express more negative feelings than women who are of menopausal or postmenopausal age."

osteoporosis
(OS' tee oh poh ROH sis) Condition in which the bones become thin and brittle as a result of mineral loss.

Sexual Problems

Although many individuals enjoy an active sex life throughout the middle adult years, some report sexual problems. Some men experience impotence for the first time. Masters and Johnson (1970) reported that the incidence of impotence increases dramatically in men over the age of 50. Sexual problems during the middle adult years are usually not a result of physiological changes. Although physical changes in the male make sexual responses slower and of less magnitude, these gradual declines do not account for the inability of some middle-aged men to maintain an erection or achieve an orgasm. Masters and Johnson list six factors that they believe contribute to impotence in men: (1) monotony of a repetitious sexual relationship, (2) preoccupation with career or economic pursuits, (3) mental or physical fatigue, (4) overindulgence in food and drink, (5) physical and mental incapacities of the individual or his spouse, and (6) fear of inadequate performance resulting from one or more of these factors.

LATER ADULTHOOD
Frequency of Sexual Activity

As was mentioned earlier, males show a gradual decline in sexual activity from the teenage years to about 60 years of age. After 60, however, the rate of decline is greater. Kinsey, Pomeroy, and Martin (1948) found that although 90% of their 60-year-old male subjects reported being sexually active, only 70% of their 70-year-old male subjects claimed to remain sexually active. Too few men were over the age of 70 to allow a reliable judgment of the percentage of men who remain sexually active after the age of 70. However, Kinsey and associates reported that the decrease in sexual activity appears to continue with age. Brecher (1984), who focused on adults over the age of 50, found similar results: 98% of the men in their fifties reported being sexually active, 91% of the men in their sixties claimed to still be sexually active, and 79% of the men over the age of 70 reported themselves to be sexually active (Figure 13-1).

FIGURE 13-1
All types of sexual activity in men and women decrease with age, especially after the age of 60. (Data from Brecher, 1984.)

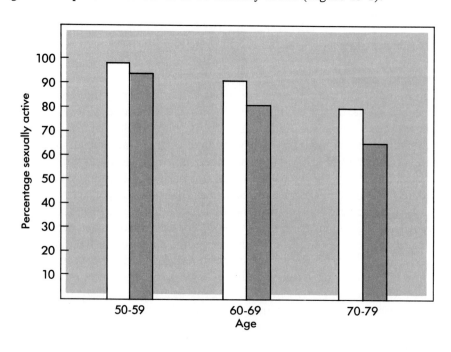

HUMAN SEXUALITY

Sexual Intercourse Frequency for Married Couples

Kinsey data (1948, 1953)		Hunt data (1974)		Sprague, Koelliker, and Quadagno data (1985)	
Age	Median frequency	Age	Median frequency	Age	Median frequency
16-25	2.45	18-24	3.25	22-31	3-4
26-35	1.95	25-34	2.55		
36-45	1.40	35-44	2.00	32-41	1-2
46-55	0.85	45-54	1.00	42-51	1-2
56-60	0.50	55 and older	1.00	52 and older	Less than once/week

The median frequency of sexual intercourse per week indicates the middle values of intercourse reported by couples of various ages. For example, for 16- to 25-year-olds in the Kinsey data, half of the sample had intercourse less than 2.45 times per week, and the other half of the sample had intercourse more than 2.45 times per week. For the Kinsey and Hunt samples, the younger the couple, the greater the frequency of intercourse per week. In Hunt's survey all couples, regardless of age, reported higher frequencies of intercourse per week than in Kinsey's surveys.

The Sprague, Koelliker, and Quadagno data were collected in 1985 from 161 married individuals who indicated the number of times per week they had intercourse when given a choice of less than once, 1 to 2, 3 to 4, 5 to 6, or 7 or more times per week.

In all of the studies younger couples had sexual intercourse more often than older couples. However, it must be remembered that when older individuals remarry or have new sexual partners, their frequency of sexual intercourse increases (see Chapter 15).

Sexual Desire and Arousal

In addition to changes in sexual activity with age, Schiavi and associates (1990) have found age-related decreases in sexual desire and arousal in men. They interviewed men between the ages of 45 and 74 who were healthy and in stable relationships. They asked a number of questions about sexual desire such as how frequently the men had sexual thoughts and how often they desired sex. They also asked a number of questions about sexual arousal such as how often the men had erections and how easily they became aroused. Gradual decreases were found in both measures with increasing age.

There is little evidence of a decrease in sexual activity in women before the age of 60. However, after the age of 60 an age-related decline takes place. Masters and Johnson (1966) found a reduction in the frequency of masturbation in women over the age of 60. However, Adams and Turner (1985) discovered that a larger percentage of women between the ages of 60 and 85 reported masturbating during their later adult years (26%) than during their twenties (10%). Thus it appears that more women may masturbate during later adult years than during early adult years. Brecher (1984) found a decline with age in the number of women who reported themselves to be sexually active: from 93% in their fifties to 81% in their sixties and 65% over the age of 70.

TABLE 13-1 Decline in Sexual Activities with Age

	All respondents		
	In their fifties	In their sixties	Age 70 and over
WOMEN			
Orgasms when asleep or while waking up	26%	24%	17%
Women who masturbate	47%	37%	33%
Frequency of masturbation among women who masturbate	0.7/week	0.6/week	0.7/week
Wives having sex with their husbands	88%	76%	65%
Frequency of sex with their husbands	1.3/week	1.0/week	0.7/week
MEN			
Orgasms when asleep or while waking up	25%	21%	17%
Men who masturbate	66%	50%	43%
Frequency of masturbation among men who masturbate	1.2/week	0.8/week	0.7/week
Husbands having sex with their wives	87%	78%	59%
Frequency of sex with their wives	1.3/week	1.0/week	0.6/week

From *Love, Sex and Aging* by Edward M. Brecher. Copyright © 1984 by Consumers Union of the United States, Inc. By permission of Little, Brown and Company.

Gender Differences

During the young adult and middle adult years males tend to be more sexually active than females. However, the decline that occurs in males during these years brings them to a level only slightly higher than that of females at the age of 60. Since males also exhibit more rapid sexual decline than females after the age of 60, presumably at some point after that age both genders are approximately the same in frequency of sexual activity. The decline in various sexual activities of men and women after the age of 50 is illustrated in Table 13-1.

Physiological Changes

In addition to a decrease in sexual activity, specific stages of the sexual cycle of the male change after the age of 60 (Masters and Johnson, 1966). These changes probably result from the gradual decrease in testosterone that occurs in men as they age. Masters and Johnson found that penile erection requires more stimulation and occurs more slowly during the later adult years. Ejaculation typically takes more time, and the refractory period (the time required after orgasm for the male to be ready for ejaculation again) increases. Masters and Johnson also found changes in the pleasure men gain from the ejaculatory process. They conclude that "The young male . . . is aware not only of the force of the explosive contractions but also of the localized sensation of fluid emissions. . . . The aging male, particularly if his erection has been long maintained, may have the experience of seepage rather than of seminal fluid explosion."

In addition to the changes in sexual response noted by Masters and Johnson, men experience other changes. Seminal fluid becomes thinner, the amount of fluid ejaculated decreases, and ejaculation pressure diminishes. The prostate gland becomes larger, and its contractions during orgasm become weaker. The testes become somewhat smaller, although most men produce viable sperm throughout their later years.

The physiological changes that begin after menopause continue in the aging female. As a result of the decrease in estrogen, the breasts, vagina, and uterus become smaller and the mucosal surfaces of the vagina become thinner and drier (Archer, 1982). Intercourse becomes more difficult for some women because of a decrease in vaginal lubricating fluids. However, this problem can be easily overcome by using an artificial lubricant such as K-Y Jelly. Estrogen replacement therapy, as discussed earlier, is also helpful. Furthermore, it appears that maintaining an active sex life throughout one's adult life reduces vaginal atrophy experienced by the older woman (Semmens and Wagner, 1982). Research by Masters and Johnson (1966) suggests that women who had maintained regular intercourse once or twice a week had no difficulties accommodating the penis, which might otherwise have been a problem because of vaginal atrophy or a decrease in vaginal lubrication.

In many older women the orgasmic phase appears to become shorter and the recovery period after orgasm longer. Some women report that their orgasms seem less intense in the later adult years (Masters and Johnson, 1966).

None of the physiological changes that take place in men or women during the later adult years typically interferes with the ability to enjoy a satisfying sex life (Woodruff-Pak, 1988). In fact, most men and women who have remained sexually active throughout their adult lives and are in reasonably good health continue to enjoy their sexuality into their later adult years (see box).

As in the middle adult years, the physiological changes caused by aging can have negative psychological effects. Some people conclude that their sexual ability is gone and arbitrarily declare themselves to be sexually incapacitated (Butler and Lewis, 1986). Once again, knowledge of the normal physiological changes of aging helps older individuals understand and cope with the changes they are encountering and thus helps preserve their sexuality.

A Personal Glimpse

A 74-Year-Old Woman's View of Sex

Sex isn't as powerful a need as when you're young, but the whole feeling is there; it's as nice as it ever was. He puts his arms around you, kisses you and it comes to you—satisfaction and orgasm—just like it always did . . . don't let anybody tell you different. Maybe it only happens once every two weeks, but as you get older, it's such a release from the tensions. I'm an old dog who's even tried a few tricks. Like oral sex, for instance; I figured it was time to find out what that's like. We weren't too crazy about it though.

He has a nice body and I don't know if I should say this, but we take baths together and he washes my body and I wash his. I know I'm getting old and my skin could use an ironing, but we love each other—so sex is beautiful.

From Wax, 1975.

Factors That Affect Sexuality in Old Age

Many people in our culture hold negative stereotypes about sexuality among the elderly. Rienzo (1985) has categorized these stereotypes or myths in the following manner:

1. Elderly people do not have sexual desires.
2. Elderly people are not able to make love, even if they wanted to.
3. Elderly people are too fragile and might hurt themselves if they attempt to engage in sexual relations.
4. Elderly people are physically unattractive and therefore sexually undesirable.
5. The whole notion of elderly people engaging in sexual activity is shameful and perverse.

Rienzo, 1985, p. 67

Contrary to such negative stereotypes about sexuality and aging, research indicates that although sexual activity decreases in the later adult years, the great majority of healthy adults maintain their sexual interest and activity well into later adulthood. Approximately 70% of healthy 70-year-olds remain sexually active and have sex once a week or more (Kaplan, 1990).

One of the most important factors in determining sexuality in old age is one's sexual history. Continued sexual activity throughout adulthood is the best predictor of a healthy, active sex life in old age (Masters and Johnson, 1966; Solnick and Corby, 1983). Those who never really enjoyed sex probably will not be sexually active older adults.

Another factor that may influence sexuality in old age is a person's self-image. If an older adult feels that he or she is no longer attractive because of some of the physical changes that have taken place with increasing age, he or she will be less likely to be sexually active. A person who feels sexually unattractive is less likely to initiate and participate in sexual activities. This may be more of a problem for women than for men, since in our culture the changes

Sexual interest and activity can be enjoyed throughout life.

HUMAN SEXUALITY

The Double Standard of Aging

The double standard about aging shows up most brutally in the conventions of sexual feeling, which presuppose a disparity between men and women that operates permanently to women's disadvantage. . . . Suppose when both husband and wife are already in their late forties or early fifties, they divorce. The husband has an excellent chance of getting married again, probably to a younger woman. His ex-wife finds it difficult to remarry. Attracting a second husband younger than herself is improbable, even to find someone her own age she has to be lucky, and she will proba-

bly have to settle for a man considerably older than herself, in his sixties or seventies. Women become sexually ineligible much earlier than men do. A man, even an ugly man, can remain eligible well into old age. He is an acceptable mate for a young, attractive woman. Women, even good-looking women, become ineligible (except as partners of very old men) at a much younger age.

Thus, for most women, aging means a humiliating process of gradual sexual disqualification. Since women are considered maximally eligible in early youth, after which their sexual value drops

steadily, even young women feel themselves in a desperate race against the calendar. They are old as soon as they are no longer very young. In late adolescence some girls are already worrying about getting married. Boys and young men have little reason to anticipate trouble because of aging. What makes men desirable to women is by no means tied to youth. On the contrary, getting older tends (for several decades) to operate in men's favor, since their value as lovers and husbands is set more by what they do than how they look. Many men have more success romantically at forty than they did at twenty or twenty-five; fame, money, and, above all, power are sexually enhancing.

From Sontag, 1972.

that take place with age are seen as more detrimental to the attractiveness of women than the attractiveness of men (see accompanying box). Women are seen as most attractive when they are in their twenties, and men are seen as being attractive from early adulthood through the middle adult years. For example, although gray hair on a woman is often considered unattractive, gray hair on a man is thought to be "distinguished." To feel totally comfortable with their sexuality, older adults need to overcome the view that age-related changes make them sexually unattractive.

Marital status may also influence sexuality in old age. Marriage provides a comfortable context within which older adults may experience their sexuality. But when one spouse dies, the survivor often has difficulty finding a new sexual partner. The importance of marital status in determining sexual behavior during the later adult years is greater for women than for men. As was reported earlier, unmarried men appear to be as sexually active as married men and unmarried women are much less active than married women. Furthermore, because men tend to die at younger ages than women, women are much more likely than men to be widowed and thus live part of their later adult years in a single state. In addition, since men tend to die younger than women, there are more older women than there are older men, making it more difficult for older women to find partners than it is for older men. Of the older men who are available, many prefer younger women, increasing the problem of finding partners for older women.

A woman widowed in her later adult years has more difficulty finding male companionship. Men tend to die at a younger age, which decreases the number of available partners.

A 67-year-old widow expressed her difficulty in finding eligible men in the following way:

> Lack of male companionship, friendship, being cherished, is the biggest blank in my life. I resolutely turn away from all advances, flirtatious or sexual, from married men. No friends ever invite me to meet an interesting man or even fill in as a dinner partner, and I am not aggressive socially. Seeing six blue-haired women competing for the attention of one overweight male on a cruise or at a gathering turns me off. I have noticed that a man my age or older, vigorous and intelligent enough to be attractive to me, is invariably going out with a 35-year-old "chick" with false eyelashes.
>
> In the ten years since I was widowed, numbers of married men have told me how attractive I was and that I should marry again—but when I once asked "Who? Where do I meet him?", the reply was a weak, "At dances and parties." (I always had to have a date to go to a dance or party as a teen-ager; I can't seem to force myself out on the town [alone] now!) Statistics, I realize, are against me. . . . I am not interested in a fireside companion or someone looking for his mother or [a] housekeeper.

Brecher, 1984, pp. 153-154

The response of the elderly individual's family and friends may also limit the possibility of remarriage. Family and friends are often opposed to the remarriage of an older adult. These individuals may feel that elderly adults do not need sex and marriage. Children and other family members may worry about what will happen to the estate if an elderly person remarries. Many elderly individuals are sensitive to this kind of pressure, and as a result may not remarry. Even if they do remarry, they might find that the opposition of family and friends has a negative effect on their marriage.

Overindulgence in alcohol can also affect sexuality. This is particularly true for men. When a man has had an excessive amount of alcohol, he may find it difficult to have an erection. When a man is traumatized by his inability to

FYI

Sexuality in Nursing Homes

Five percent of persons over 65 live in nursing homes and other long-term care institutions. As discussed in the text, sexuality, which includes the natural human needs for closeness, tenderness, and warmth, remains an important need for the elderly. Elderly in nursing homes also have this need. Unfortunately, the environment in most nursing homes denies the residents the opportunity for privacy. Residents are generally in full view of staff and roommates. Attempts to guarantee the right to privacy of nursing home residents have been largely unsuccessful. Federal regulations issued in 1978 provide limited rights to privacy for institutionalized married couples, but only in the one third of nursing homes that participate in federal Medicare and Medicaid programs. Although these nursing homes risk legal action if they fail to observe the regulations, the regulations are not consistently enforced. Furthermore, most elderly people are reluctant to complain about infringements on their rights

to privacy (Butler and Lewis, 1986).

Many nursing homes and long-term care institutions for the elderly function in a parental fashion. Instead of supporting the residents' autonomous decisions, they try to control behavior (McCartney et al., 1987). Self-stimulation among residents is often considered "seriously disturbing," and when it is detected, the resident is usually reprimanded. Furthermore, intimacies of any kind, even kissing and hugging, between unmarried residents of institutions are generally disapproved of although they are performed by consenting adults. In all fairness, a professional who observes overt sexual activities between two patients is faced with an ethical dilemma if one of the patients is suffering from dementia and may not be capable of giving consent.

The sexually repressive atmosphere in nursing homes is unfortunate, since research suggests that sexual activity can be physically, psychologically, and emotionally helpful for elders (Weg, 1983).

Physical benefits include better circulation and reduced tension. Sexual activity can enhance an elder's sense of well-being, which often suffers in institutionalized settings. Sex can offset to some extent a loss of prestige and self-confidence and can strengthen an individual's self-esteem by reaffirming his or her physical attractiveness and desirability.

Nursing homes that permit the free expression of sexual behavior have been found to have fewer problems with inappropriate behavior (Corby and Zarit, 1983). Perhaps in recognition of such benefits, some nursing homes have introduced "privacy rooms" where older people can be alone together (McCartney et al., 1987).

---

perform, he often becomes anxious about his performance. This anxiety further interferes with performance. As Masters and Johnson (1966) state:

> There is no way to overemphasize the importance that the factor "fear of failure" plays in the aging male's withdrawal from sexual performance. . . . Many males withdraw voluntarily from any coital activity rather than face the ego-shattering experience of repeated episodes of sexual inadequacy.
>
> Masters and Johnson, 1966, pp. 269-270

Although some aging males succumb to their fears, others seek out new partners to "prove" themselves. This often works because the excitement that often accompanies novelty may stimulate the lagging sex drive. Kinsey, Pomeroy, and Martin (1948) suggest that the decline in male sexuality results partly from "a loss of interest in repetition of the same sort of experience, an exhaustion of the possibilities for exploring new techniques."

In summary, a number of factors influence sexuality in the later adult years: sexual history, the availability of an acceptable partner, self-image, the reactions of family and friends to the older adult's sexuality, and overindulgence in alcohol. Although the aging adult may not have much control over some of these factors, such as the availability of a partner, he or she can influence many of them. Thus the individual can exert some control over the course of his or her sexual development during the adult years. Awareness of the factors that influence sexuality should result in more positive sexual experiences during the later adult years.

HOMOSEXUALITY ACROSS THE ADULT YEARS
Frequency of Sexual Activity

Homosexuality is covered in greater detail in Chapter 11.

The data collected by Kinsey and associates (1953) suggest that homosexual behavior increases with age during childhood and then decreases during the adult years. The percentages of males who engaged in homosexual activities at ages 13, 24, 36, and 45 were 13%, 37%, 27%, and 23%, respectively. The frequency of male homosexual contacts that resulted in orgasm followed a similar pattern over the life span. Female homosexuals reported similar frequencies. Kinsey and associates did not collect data on homosexual activity during the later adult years, but Weinberg and Williams (1974) did. In a questionnaire study of the relationship between age and frequency of homosexual activity, they compared four age groups: under 26, 26 to 35, 36 to 45, and over 45. The percentages of homosexuals who reported high frequencies of sexual activity in each of these age groups were 46%, 59%, 55%, and 41%, respectively. Thus it appears that sexual activity decreases with increasing age in homosexuals just as it does in heterosexuals. Furthermore, Blumstein and

Younger homosexuals are more likely to be involved in the social aspects of the gay life-style than older homosexuals.

Schwartz (1983) report that sexual activity decreases in homosexual couples as a function of the length of time the couple has been together and the age of the individuals.

Weinberg and Williams (1974) reported that older male homosexuals tended to be less involved than younger homosexuals in the social aspects of the gay life-style. They associated with other homosexuals less frequently and attended gay bars and clubs less often. Fifty-six percent of the males under the age of 26 went to gay bars more than once a month compared with only 23% of the males over the age of 45. Female homosexuals, on the other hand, were less likely to get involved in a gay social life-style at any age; they tended not to attend gay bars and clubs as much as men.

Gender Differences

As among heterosexuals, male homosexuals appear to be more sexually active than female homosexuals. In their sample of single homosexual women, Kinsey and associates (1953) found that 51% had had only one sexual partner, whereas only 4% had had more than ten partners. In contrast, 22% of the males had had more than ten partners. In addition to having more sexual partners than females, male homosexuals also reported more sexual interactions per week than female homosexuals (Blumstein and Schwartz, 1983). Homosexual couples tend to have more sexual interactions per week than heterosexual couples, and female homosexual couples tend to have sex less often. Somewhat surprisingly, however, Blumstein and Schwartz found that after 10 years in the same relationship male homosexual couples have sex less frequently than heterosexual couples who have been married 10 years. Blumstein and Schwartz point out that the males in long-term relationships do not just stop having sex but tend to go outside of their relationship:

> To understand gay men's sex lives we must realize that as a group they are much less monogamous than other couples. Although interest in sex with their partners declines, interest in sex in general remains high. Sex with other men balances the declining sex with the partner.
>
> Blumstein and Schwartz, 1983, p. 195

Female homosexuals have sex less frequently than either male homosexuals or heterosexual couples. When their sexual interactions decline with age and length of their relationship, they do not tend to compensate with sex outside of the relationship.

Male homosexuals seem to be more concerned than female homosexuals about growing old (Saghir and Robins, 1973) (see box, p. 400). This is surprising considering that among heterosexuals, females seem to be more concerned about growing old. Heterosexual females may be more worried about growing old because they are concerned that men will no longer find them attractive. Heterosexual males may be less concerned because they do not think that aging will greatly decrease their attractiveness to women. Male homosexuals may be more fearful of aging because they may feel that their male partners will find them less attractive; female homosexuals may not feel that their female partners will find them less attractive as a result of aging. In fact, Raphael and Robinson (1980) report that older female homosexuals prefer sexual and social partners who are members of their own age group. Thus the fear of aging may

Gender differences in homosexual behavior are discussed in Chapter 10.

A Personal Glimpse

Effects of Aging on Homosexuals

Gay males tend to see aging as a potential problem for their sex lives, as the following comment from a gay male illustrates:

Getting older for the homosexual probably means— at least it has for me—that casual partners are less available, and those that are available are less desirable. . . . The younger one keeps himself looking as he grows older, the easier it is to find casual sex partners if that is what one is interested in (as I am).

Brecher, 1984, p. 225

Aging is generally less of a problem for lesbians:

On the positive side of aging as a lesbian, I would place the fact that, as a group, lesbians place less emphasis on looks and more on character than does most of society. I don't believe there is the same premium on youth that there is in most of society.

Brecher, 1984, p. 255

result from concern about how a person's partner or potential partners might respond to his or her aging. Since men seem to be more concerned than women about physical attractiveness in their partners, individuals who want men as partners may be more worried about aging.

SUMMARY

1 Early adulthood is the time in life when the frequency of sexual intercourse is the highest.

2 Cohabitants tend to have sex more often than married couples.

3 The frequency with which a couple has sex decreases with the age of the partners and the length of the relationship.

4 During the young adult years males have, on the average, more sexual partners than females.

5 Sexual responsiveness in the male decreases gradually during the middle adult years. However, females do not appear to undergo a similar decline in sexual responsiveness.

6 Although the sexual decline is greater in men than in women, men remain more sexually active than women throughout the middle adult years.

7 Menopause refers to the permanent cessation of the menstrual cycle. Some women experience menopausal symptoms; estrogen replacement therapy alleviates some of the symptoms.

8 Most people enjoy active sex lives during the middle adult years. However, some men experience impotence for the first time during middle age.

9 Sexual activity declines in both males and females during the later adult years. However, many men and women remain sexually active into later adulthood.

10 A number of factors determine sexual activity in old age. Continued sexual activity throughout adulthood is the best predictor. Self-image is also important; an older adult who feels attractive will be more likely to be sexually active. Being married increases the likelihood of women being sexually

active during the later adult years. Overindulgence in alcohol can limit sexuality.

11 The number of homosexual contacts and the frequency with which homosexuals experience orgasm increase during the early adult years and then decrease after the age of 30 or 40.

12 Male homosexuals are more sexually active than female homosexuals.

ANSWERS

1 Research indicates that, although the sexual activity of males decreases during the adult years, little if any decrease occurs in the sexual activity of women. However, throughout most of the adult years men are more sexually active than women.

2 Studies have shown that the best predictor of a healthy, active sex life during the later adult years is continued sexual activity throughout adulthood.

3 Unlike heterosexuals, male homosexuals appear to be more concerned than female homosexuals about growing old.

F A C T
OR
F I C T I O N

QUESTIONS FOR THOUGHT ?

1 Is it difficult for you to imagine your parents having a sexual relationship? What about your grandparents? If it is difficult, why do you think it is?

2 Can you imagine a 50-year-old man being very attractive? Can you imagine a 50-year-old woman being very attractive? If you said "yes" to the first question and "no" to the second question, why do you think you find older men more attractive than older women?

3 Why do you think male homosexuals would be more concerned about growing old than female homosexuals?

SUGGESTED READINGS

Berger, R.M.: Gay and gray: the older homosexual male, Urbana, 1982, University of Illinois Press.
A report of a study of older homosexual males.

Brecher, E.M.: Love, sex, and aging: a Consumers Union report, Boston, 1984, Little, Brown & Co., Inc.
A report of a survey of the sexual behavior of more than 4,000 Americans who are 50 years of age or older.

Butler, R.N., and Lewis, M.I.: Love and sex after 40, New York, 1986, Harper & Row, Publishers, Inc.
A candid discussion of sex and stereotypes about sex in the middle and later adult years.

Mishell, D.R., editor: Menopause: physiology and pharmacology, St. Louis, 1987, Mosby–Year Book, Inc.
A collection of readings that covers the physiological, pharmacological, and psychological aspects of menopause.

Starr, B.D., and Weiner, M.B.: The Starr-Weiner report on sex and sexuality in the mature years, New York, 1981, Stein & Day Publishers.
A report of a survey of the sexual behavior of individuals over the age of 60.

Voda, A.M., Dinnerstein, M., and O'Donnell, S.R., editors: Changing perspectives on menopause, Austin, 1982, University of Texas Press.
A collection of readings that covers the biological, psychological, sociological, anthropological, and medical aspects of menopause.

Love, Attraction, and Intimacy

It's true love because
I put on eyeliner and a concerto and make pungent observations about the
    great issues of the day
Even when there's no one here but him,
And because
I do not resent watching the Green Bay Packers
Even though I am philosophically opposed to football,
And because
When he is late for dinner and I know he must be either having an affair or
    lying dead in the middle of the street,
I always hope he's dead.

JUDITH VIORST
"True Love"

Because love and sex are perceived to be closely related in our culture, love must be considered in any thorough treatment of sexuality. Defining love is no simple matter. Poets, philosophers, and social scientists have made numerous attempts over the years. Approximately 2,000 years ago the apostle Paul wrote:

> Love is very patient and kind, never jealous or envious, never boastful or proud, never haughty or selfish or rude. Love does not demand its own way. It is not irritable or touchy. It does not hold grudges and will hardly ever notice when others do it wrong.
>
> It is never glad about injustice, but rejoices when truth wins out. If you love someone you will be loyal to him no matter what the cost. You will always believe in him, always expect the best of him, and always stand your ground in defending him.
>
> 1 Cor. 13

Almost 400 years ago William Shakespeare wrote of love:

> Let me not to the marriage of true minds
> Admit impediments, love is not love
> Which alters when it alteration finds,
> Or bends with the remover to remove.
> O no, it is an ever fixed mark
> That looks on tempests and is never shaken;
> It is the star to every wand'ring bark,
> Whose worth's unknown, although his height be taken.
> Love's not Time's fool, though rosy lips and cheeks
> Within his bending sickle's compass come,
> Love alters not with his brief hours and weeks,
> But bears it out even to the edge of doom.
> If this be error and upon me proved,
> I never writ, nor no man ever loved.
>
> Sonnet CXVI

WHAT IS LOVE?

The previous passages describe an idealistic view of love. More recently social scientists have attempted to define love. For example, Erich Fromm (1956),

Erich Fromm defined erotic love as "the craving for complete fusion, for union with one other person."

a psychoanalyst, made the following suggestions about love:

> Mature *love* is *union under the condition of preserving one's integrity*, one's individuality. *Love is an active power in man;* a power that breaks through the walls that separate man from his fellow men, which unites him with others; love makes him overcome the sense of isolation and separateness, yet it permits him to be himself, to retain his integrity.
>
> Fromm, 1956

According to Fromm, "love is primarily *giving*, not receiving." In addition to giving, Fromm listed four other elements that he felt were always present in all forms of love: care, responsibility, respect, and knowledge. *Care*, according to Fromm, means an "active concern for the life and growth of that which we love." *Responsibility* refers to attending to the physical and psychic needs of the other person. *Respect* is to see a person as he or she is and to encourage that person to grow and develop in his or her own unique way. This means wanting the other person to develop in the way that is best for that person—not in the way that best meets one's own needs. *Knowledge* refers to getting to know the other person objectively in order to see his or her reality rather than to maintain one's own illusions or distorted views of the other person.

Fromm distinguished between brotherly love, motherly love, erotic love, self-love, and love of God. Most relevant to a discussion of human sexuality is erotic love. Fromm defined erotic love as "the craving for complete fusion, for union with one other person. It is by its very nature exclusive." However, Fromm went on to say that "it is also perhaps the most deceptive form of love there is" because

> it is often confused with the explosive experience of "falling" in love, with the sudden collapse of the barriers which existed until that moment between two strang-

404   HUMAN SEXUALITY

ers. But, as was pointed out before, this experience of sudden intimacy is by its very nature short-lived. After the stranger has become an intimately known person there are no more barriers to be overcome, there is no more sudden closeness to be achieved. The "loved" person becomes as well known as oneself. Or, perhaps I should better say as little known. If there were more depth in the experience of the other person, if one could experience the infiniteness of his personality, the other person would never be so familiar—and the miracle of overcoming the barriers might occur every day anew. But for most people their own person, as well as others, is soon explored and soon exhausted. For them intimacy is established primarily through sexual contact. . . .

If the desire for physical union is not stimulated by love, if erotic love is not also brotherly love, it never leads to union in more than an orgiastic, transitory sense. Sexual attraction creates, for the moment, the illusion of union, yet without love this "union" leaves strangers as far apart as they were before—sometimes it makes them ashamed of each other, or even makes them hate each other, because when the illusion is gone they feel their estrangement even more markedly than before.

Fromm, 1956, pp. 44-46

WHAT IS NOT LOVE?

We have been discussing what love is, and we have found that people define love in different ways. Although most of us believe that we know love when we feel it, we must agree that love is a difficult concept to define. Another way to come to an understanding of what love *is*, however, is to look at what love is *not*. Fromm's discussion of erotic love introduces the two feelings that are most often mistaken for love but that most people would agree are not really love: **infatuation** and **sexual attraction**.

Infatuation

Judith Viorst, when asked to distinguish between love and infatuation, said:

> Infatuation is when you think he is as sexy as Robert Redford, as smart as Henry Kissinger, as noble as Ralph Nader, as funny as Woody Allen and as athletic as Jimmy Connors. Love is when you realize that he's as sexy as Woody Allen, as smart as Jimmy Connors, as funny as Ralph Nader, as athletic as Henry Kissinger and nothing like Robert Redford in any category—but you'll take him anyway.
>
> Viorst, 1975, p. 12

This quotation illustrates several points that must be considered in a discussion of the difference between love and infatuation. In the beginning of a relationship, before we know much about the other person, we may attribute to the other person the traits that we would like him or her to have. As a result we may have an overly positive picture of the other person—a picture that may correspond very little to the actual person. At this stage in the relationship we are not really in love with the other person because we do not really know him or her. Instead, we are infatuated. The other person has enough superficial characteristics that are attractive to us that we become infatuated; we then fill in our own picture of his or her remaining characteristics, even though we have little information about him or her. Sometimes these illusions are created only when we do not have enough information on which to build a more realistic

infatuation
An attraction to another person that is based on little real knowledge of the person.

sexual attraction
Attraction to another person in which sexual satisfaction is the main goal and concern for the other person is not necessarily present.

picture. However, sometimes individuals even distort information they do have about the other person to maintain a positive picture of the object of their infatuation.

What happens with infatuation? In some cases, when we become better acquainted with the person with whom we are infatuated, we realize that we do not love that person. This often occurs because the person turns out to be different from the illusion we constructed. When we find out what the person is really like, we frequently become less interested.

Sometimes, however, as the quotation from Viorst indicates, we get to know the other person, and although the other person turns out to be somewhat different from our original illusion, we find that we can still care very deeply about him or her. This valuing, based on knowledge, can be called love. Thus infatuation can, after a period of time and increased knowledge of the other person, result in either a cooling of the romantic relationship or a growing of the relationship into a more objective love.

Sexual Attraction

Sexual attraction, love, and infatuation are interrelated. When we are in love or infatuated with someone, we are typically sexually attracted to that person. However, in some cases sexual attraction occurs without either infatuation or love. This is most likely to take place when we get to know someone who is physically attractive but who has a personality of which we are not particularly fond. Sexual attraction can be a strong motivating force, but it should not be mistaken for love. In purely sexual attraction there is little concern for the other person; sexual satisfaction is the main goal.

SCIENTIFIC STUDY OF LOVE AND ATTRACTION

Some people would undoubtedly agree with Charlie Brown in the Peanuts cartoon that not only can you not define love, but it is probably better not to even talk about it. For example, when Senator William Proxmire discovered that the National Science Foundation had awarded an $84,000 grant to psychologists who were studying love, he said:

I object to this . . . because no one—not even the National Science Foundation—can argue that romantic love lies in the realm of science; not only because I believe firmly that even if they spent $84 million, or even $84 billion, they wouldn't come up with anything the great majority of Americans would profit from. Or believe. Or even want to hear about. Some things in life should remain unprobed . . . and right at the top of the list . . . is romantic passion.

Proxmire, 1980, pp. 6-7

However, a number of social scientists have become interested in studying love and attraction. Their studies have produced some interesting results.

Rubin (1970) developed a Love Scale to measure romantic love. The following are some of the questions on Rubin's Love Scale:

1. I would do almost anything for _____ .
2. If I could never be with _____ , I would feel miserable.
3. I would forgive _____ for practically anything.
4. If I were lonely, my first thought would be to seek _____ out.
5. I feel that I can confide in _____ about virtually anything.

Rubin, 1970, p. 267

According to the instructions for the Love Scale, the individual is to rate each statement on a scale from 1 (disagree completely) to 9 (agree completely) with respect to his or her current love partner.

Using this scale with a sample of college students, Rubin found that the scores on the Love Scale were highly correlated with the individual's estimate of the likelihood that he or she would marry his or her current partner. Rubin did not find gender differences in the way the students rated the statements about their partners; thus there do not appear to be gender differences

Gender Differences in Love

It has long been assumed that women are more romantic than men. Women are assumed to be more concerned about love than men, to love their partners more than their partners love them, and to cling to their partners more than their partners cling to them. However, research indicates that this may not be the case. Rather, evidence suggests that the reverse may be true.

Hobart (1958) developed a scale to measure romanticism in order to determine whether men or women had the more romantic view of human relationships. Hobart found that men agreed with more of the romantic items than women. The following are some examples of the statements included on his questionnaire:

	Agree	Disagree
1. Lovers ought to expect a certain amount of disillusionment after marriage.	___	___
2. To be truly in love is to be in love forever.	___	___

Kanin, Davidson, and Scheck (1970) asked individuals who were involved in romantic relationships how early in the relationship they became aware that they loved their partner. These authors found that although 20% of the men indicated that they fell in love before the fourth date, only 15% of the women reported falling in love that early. In addition, 43% of the women noted not being sure that they were

in love by the twentieth date; only 30% of the men said the same. This evidence suggests that in addition to having more romantic views than women, men appear to fall in love more easily than women.

Hill, Rubin, and Peplau (1976) found that men are more likely than women to cling to dying relationships. They followed the affairs of 231 couples over a 2-year period. They discovered that it was usually the women who decided if and when an affair should end. The men tended to cling to the relationship and seemed to suffer more when it did finally end. The men reported feeling more depressed, lonelier, and unhappier than the women after a breakup. The men seemed to find it difficult to accept the fact that the relationship was over and that there was nothing they could do to make amends. The women, on the other hand, were better able to accept the fact that the relationship was over and go on. These results suggest that just as men fall in love more easily, they also cling to the failed relationship longer.

in the degree to which individuals report love for their partners (see accompanying box).

A number of other researchers have developed measures of love and attraction (Levinger, Rands, and Talaber, 1977; Lasswell and Lobsenz, 1980). Sternberg and Grajek (1984) compared individuals' responses to two of these measures (Rubin, 1970; Levinger, Rands, and Talaber, 1977) to determine the fundamental components of love. On the basis of their results, they identified the following components:

1. Deep understanding of the other
2. Sharing of ideas and information
3. Sharing of deeply personal ideas and feelings
4. Receipt and provision of emotional support to the other
5. Personal growth as a result of the relationship and helping the other grow
6. Giving help to the other
7. Making the other feel needed and needing the other
8. Giving and receiving affection

In addition to studies on the components of love, investigators have conducted research on the factors that influence love and attraction.

Physical Appearance

A number of studies have focused on what contributes to attraction between two people. When we think about what makes one person attractive to another, one of the first factors that comes to mind is physical appearance. Research shows that we usually like physically attractive people more than we like people who are not physically attractive (Adams, 1982; Berscheid, 1985). We also tend to attribute good qualities of all types to physically attractive individuals. We frequently think attractive people are more intelligent, more socially skilled, happier, more successful, more moral, more interesting, and better adjusted than less attractive individuals. Furthermore, Sternberg and Grajek (1984) found that the physical attractiveness of an individual's partner influenced his or her ratings of how satisfying, intense, and significant their relationship was. However, this occurred only in males; physical attractiveness of one's partner did not influence the ratings of females. Other research indicates that males place more emphasis on physical appearance when choosing a partner than do females (Buss and Barnes, 1986; Buss, 1989; Townsend and Levy, 1990).

Competence

Another characteristic that contributes to attraction is competence. In general, research shows that we tend to like people who are competent more than those who are less competent (Spence and Helmreich, 1972). Again, however, there appear to be gender differences. Men reported that they preferred competent women to incompetent women when they believed they would not meet the women (Spence and Helmreich, 1972), but when they believed that they would actually interact with the women, they no longer showed a preference for the more competent women (Hagen and Kahn, 1975). Research indicates that females emphasize competence more than males when selecting a partner (Buss, 1989; Townsend and Levy, 1990).

Reciprocal Liking

Reciprocal liking is another factor related to the degree of one's attraction to another person. We tend to like people who evaluate us positively and dislike those who evaluate us negatively. For example, in one experiment Backman and Secord (1959) told members of discussion groups that certain members liked them very much. Later, when smaller groups were being formed, individuals were more likely to request being in the same group with the people who supposedly liked them than with other group members. Although we tend to like people who like us, research indicates that if we see someone else's compliments as insincere and ingratiating, we usually like that individual less (Jones, 1964). Thus to be effective the reciprocal liking must be, or at least appear to be, genuine.

Similarity

Research has consistently shown that we are inclined to like individuals who are similar to us. For example, people tend to marry partners who are similar in age, education, race, social class, religion, and ethnic background (Buss, 1985; Whyte, 1990). In addition, we are often more attracted to people who share our attitudes and values (Gonzales et al., 1983). In one study students were given a questionnaire to assess their attitudes on various topics. The students were then assigned to male-female pairs for what they were told was a computer dating study. Half of the couples were paired on the basis of attitude similarity, and the other half were paired on the basis of attitude dissimilarity. Each couple met for a 30-minute "Coke date" in the student union. Afterward, couples with similar attitudes said they liked each other more and were more interested in dating each other again than were couples with dissimilar attitudes (Byrne, Ervin, and Lamberth, 1970).

Meyer and Pepper (1977) asked married couples to fill out questionnaires that measured various personality characteristics and needs and a questionnaire that measured degree of marital adjustment. The more similar the partners were in terms of personality traits and needs, the more likely they were to report being happy and well adjusted in their marriage. Thus it appears that similarity may be important in determining initial attraction but it is also significant in determining long-term satisfaction with the relationship (see accompanying box). However, Whyte (1990) found that similarity in habits, traits, values, and leisure activities is more important in predicting marital success than similarity in attributes such as race, religion, and ethnic background.

Familiarity

Research indicates that we tend to be more attracted to familiar people and things than to people or things that are totally new. Zajonc (1968) found that the more often subjects were shown a photograph of a particular person, the more favorably they responded to that person. It appears that if we do not particularly like an individual when we first meet him or her, repeated exposures tend to enhance our liking. This does not apply when we strongly dislike the other person; in such cases repeated exposure may make us dislike the individual all the more.

How to Tell When He or She Is Wrong for You

Sometimes people pretend to themselves that the fear of being alone, sexual desire, or the hope for financial and other social advantages can be turned into feelings of love. Before marrying, persons need to ask themselves the following questions about their partners.

1. *Does he or she have several close friends?* A person who has learned to enjoy and foster intimate friendships can put this talent to work in a marriage relationship. But if no one likes him or her well enough to be a close friend, shouldn't you wonder why you like him or her?

2. *Do you keep putting off introducing him or her to your friends and relatives? Does he or she put off introducing you to his or her friends and relatives? Why?* A hesitancy to show off a partner to those people who are most important to you may be a sign of uncertainty: Will the family and friends think it is a mistake?

3. *If the love relationship folded, would you still want to keep each other as friends?* For some lovers, this seems impossible. But the question here is whether the two people share enough respect and interests to want to be together even if no longer sexually intimate. Marriage involves companionship as well as sexual attraction.

4. *Do you spend most of your time trying to stay out of his or her bed?* A yes to this question can point up one of two problems: Either the "chemistry" just isn't there for you—and probably never will be—or your partner's emphasis on the importance of sex in an intimate relationship is considerably different from yours.

5. *Are you happy with the way he or she treats other people?* If he or she is condescending or rude—even physically violent—to others, you'll get the same treatment eventually. Watch how he or she deals with employees, waitresses, maids, salesclerks, parking-lot attendants, telephone operators, and so forth. Also, study his or her behavior with family members and close friends. If he or she doesn't treat them the way you want him or her to treat you, he or she is wrong for you. You may be an exception now, during courtship, but you won't be later.

6. *Do you know what he or she is like sexually?*

7. *Was your life stimulating and satisfying before you met her or him?* Never, never bind yourself to someone because you need him or her to transform your unsatisfactory life into a super one.

8. *Do you often feel apprehensive about your future happiness together?* Little panics are normal, but they should be few and far between. If you are apprehensive more often than optimistic, this should serve as a warning signal.

9. *Are there taboo topics that you can not discuss with each other?* Good relationships are built on trust, respect, spontaneity, and lack of stress. People are free to talk about almost anything. Even though they may hold very different views, not many subjects are taboo. Topics that have a bearing on the relationship are *never* taboo.

Physical Proximity

In addition to the characteristics mentioned so far, physical proximity is related to partner selection (Buss, 1985). Individuals are likely to marry someone who lives within driving distance of their home. In part this relationship may occur because people are more likely to meet those individuals who live nearby. However, it may also be that physical proximity increases familiarity, which in turn increases attraction.

• • •

In summary, we tend to be attracted to individuals who are physically attractive, competent, and effective. Similarity is also important in our attraction to other people. We seem to choose people who share our basic attitudes and values, as well as people who have similar demographic characteristics such as age, social class, ethnic background, and religion. We also like people who like us, whom we see frequently, and who are nearby.

GENDER DIFFERENCES IN PREFERENCES IN MATE SELECTION

As mentioned previously, males and females look for different characteristics in potential mates. More specifically, females place greater emphasis on the male's ambition and socioeconomic status and males place greater emphasis on the female's physical attractiveness (Buss and Barnes, 1986; Townsend and Levy, 1990). Two hypotheses have been proposed in an attempt to understand these differences in human mate preferences. One is based on evolutionary considerations (Buss and Barnes, 1986; Buss, 1989). The other is based on the differential in power between men and women in our culture (Buss and Barnes, 1986; Murstein 1986).

See Chapter 10 for further discussion of evolutionary perspective on gender differences.

According to the evolutionary hypothesis, the gender differences in mate selection have evolved so as to increase both males' and females' potential to reproduce and to raise their children successfully. Both males and females tend to select mates according to criteria that should increase their success at having and raising children.

The characteristics most closely associated with successful reproduction in women have been youth and health. Young healthy women are more likely to be able to bear and raise children. Therefore, according to this theory, males should select females on the basis of indicators of youth and health. In our culture, as in many others (Buss and Barnes, 1989), beauty is strongly associated with youth and health and therefore is a strong cue for a female's ability to reproduce.

A male's ability to reproduce is not so strongly associated with his age. Thus, selecting a male partner on the basis of his age (and thus his physical appearance) would not provide females with much of a reproductive advantage. Rather, a man's socioeconomic status can contribute to immediate and future advantages for the offspring. Therefore a woman whose mate has a higher socioeconomic status will have a selective advantage.

According to the second hypothesis, the gender differences in mate selection preferences have arisen from the tendency of females to lack independent access to socioeconomic advancement and the tendency of males to regard females as "objects of exchange" (Buss and Barnes, 1986; Murstein, 1986). Because women have had limited opportunities for individual advancement, they have had to pursue in their mates those characteristics associated with power. A higher socioeconomic status, which generally incorporates a relatively high earning capacity and possession of a college education, is such a characteristic. According to Buss and Barnes, marrying a man with a higher socioeconomic status is the primary means by which women have traditionally found upward mobility. In contrast, men place the greatest value on the "quality of exchange object" (Buss and Barnes, 1986). Thus men place greater emphasis on physical attractiveness in their selection of a mate.

According to Buss and Barnes, traditional socialization practices have preserved these differences by implanting role-appropriate values in males and females. According to this hypothesis, if traditional socialization practices changed, so would gender differences in mate selection. At this point there is no evidence supporting this prediction (Townsend and Levy, 1990).

The hypothesis would also predict that as the power imbalance between the sexes in society diminishes, the sex differences in preferences should diminish as well (Buss and Barnes, 1986). In a review of the literature, Townsend and Levy (1990) found that increases in women's socioeconomic status did not appear to reduce sex differences in partner selection criteria. In fact, according to the studies reviewed by Townsend and Levy (1990), as women's socioeconomic status increased, their economic expectations for male partners tended to increase as well. The apparent invulnerability of gender differences in mate selection to current social change should not, however, lead one to conclude that the power differential explanation is wrong. It may be too early to determine the long-range effects of women's relatively recent socioeconomic achievements on their partner selection criteria. In addition, male resistance may inhibit the changes predicted (Townsend and Levy, 1990). At this point the available evidence suggests that gender differences in mate selection are a product of both societal and evolutionary factors.

THEORIES OF LOVE

In addition to investigating the antecedents of love and attraction, social scientists have attempted to explain love and attraction. In this section we review some of their theories.

Two-Component Theory

Schachter (1964), who proposed a two-component theory of emotion, contends that an emotion consists of a physiological state of arousal plus a cognitive or mental labeling of it as a particular emotion. Based on Schachter's theory, Berscheid and Walster (1974) proposed a two-component theory of love. According to their theory, passionate love results when two conditions occur simultaneously: (1) the individual is in a state of physiological arousal, and (2) the circumstances lead the individual to apply the label "love" to the sensations. Thus, to feel one is in love, or at least attracted to another, one must have reason to attribute the symptoms of physiological arousal to the emotion of love or attraction.

Often we make appropriate connections (or attributions) between our physiological state and our emotions. For example, a person might appropriately attribute a pounding heart to attraction to someone he or she thinks is attractive. However, when finding an emotion to explain our physiological arousal, we often incorrectly identify the source of arousal. For example, upon viewing a scary movie and then seeing an attractive woman walk by, a man may attribute his state of arousal to the attractiveness of the woman instead of the scariness of the movie (certainly a more "macho" attribution!).

Dutton and Aron (1974) found evidence that fear can indeed affect a man's attraction toward a woman. In their study an attractive female interviewer approached male passersby on either a fear-arousing suspension bridge or a non-fear-arousing bridge. The fear-arousing bridge, constructed of boards, was attached to cables and had a tendency to sway and tilt; furthermore, the handrails were low, and there was a 230-foot drop to rocks and shallow rapids. The non-fear-arousing bridge was firm with only a 10-foot drop to a shallow stream below. The female interviewer asked subjects to complete questionnaires that included projective test items, which were later scored for sexual imagery.

According to Dutton and Aron's experimental design, the men on the suspension bridge would have been in a state of high physiological arousal and those on the "control" bridge would not have been. Their hypothesis predicted that the men on the suspension bridge would be more attracted to the female interviewer than would the men on the less perilous bridge. Level of attraction was measured by the amount of sexual imagery in the completed questionnaires and the amount of contact the men attempted with the interviewer after the experiment. The results did, in fact, demonstrate a link between fear and sexual arousal: fear enhanced the men's attraction toward the attractive woman.

White, Fishbein, and Rutsein (1981) also found evidence of the misattribution of arousal. In their study, male subjects engaged in vigorous exercise that created a physiological arousal response including sweaty palms and a pounding heart. Later they were asked to rate how much they liked an attractive woman they viewed on video and whom they expected to meet shortly (a confederate of the experimenters). Subjects in the exercise group reported liking the woman significantly more than the subjects in a control condition who had not exercised. Thus, according to White and his colleagues, their arousal from exercise was misattributed to their liking for the attractive woman.

Murstein (1986) has suggested that Berscheid and Walster's theory can be used to explain why otherwise unlikely situations evoke passion. For example, passion often arises during or after a quarrel between partners. Arguments often create increased tension and arousal level in the participants. According to Murstein, instead of attributing their increased arousal to anger, individuals attribute it to passionate love. For better or for worse, this phenomenon may keep many argumentative couples together.

Reinforcement Theory

According to reinforcement theory, we tend to like or love individuals who reward us and dislike individuals who punish us. When people do nice things for us or cause nice things to happen to us, we begin to associate them with good feelings. Not only do we like people who do nice things or cause nice things to happen, but we also like people who are present when we are rewarded even if they are not responsible for the reward. Similarly, we dislike people who are present when we are punished, even though they are not responsible for the punishment.

Reinforcement theory can explain a number of the research findings on attraction. Physically attractive individuals may be reinforcing because they provide us with something pleasant to look at or because other people are more likely to pay attention to us when we are with an attractive individual. Competent people may be reinforcing because they are effective and thus able to acquire rewards for themselves that we might be able to share if we are associated with them. People who have similar attitudes and values might be

reinforcing because they agree with us and therefore make us feel good about our attitudes and values. Because of their proximity, people with whom we are familiar and to whom we are physically close are much more rewarding than individuals with whom we do not come into contact.

Exchange Theory

Exchange theory represents the use by social scientists of a theory based on economics (Kelley and Thibaut, 1978). Exchange theory is not inconsistent with reinforcement theory; it simply conceptualizes relationships in a slightly different way. According to this theory, every relationship involves both benefits and costs to the individuals involved. Exchange theory is an improvement over reinforcement theory because it takes into account the fact that relationships include both costs (for example, time and energy) and benefits (for example, good company and sexual outlet). Each individual finds the relationship worthwhile to the extent that the benefits outweigh the costs. The relationship continues only if both individuals find that the benefits outweigh the costs. Of course, an individual will not necessarily stay in a relationship in which the benefits outweigh the costs. An individual will compare the cost/benefit ratios in different relationships and tend to choose the relationship that provides him or her with the best cost/benefit ratio, that is, with the greatest benefits when compared to costs.

Research conducted to test these propositions does not really support exchange theory, at least as stated above. The theory suggests that relationship success should be a function of benefits minus costs. Although some studies have found evidence that supports this prediction (e.g., Rusbult, 1980), other studies have not. Hays (1985) found that benefits *plus* costs was actually a better predictor of relationship success than was benefits *minus* costs.

Defining what is a cost and what is a benefit may not be as easy as was previously assumed. In close relationships individuals may tend to feel personally benefited or rewarded when their partner receives a benefit (Clark and Reis, 1988). In fact, Clark and her colleagues have found that people think differently about close personal relationships than they do about more distant relationships. In more distant relationships individuals generally expect that when they do something for someone else, they will be immediately compensated or repaid (Clark, 1984; Clark and Waddell, 1985). In close relationships, on the other hand, individuals not only do not expect immediate compensation but actually have negative feelings when they are immediately compensated (Clark and Reis, 1988). Thus it appears that exchange theory is too simple at present to account for the effect of the ratio of costs and benefits on attraction and commitment. Rather, the effect of costs and benefits on relationship success is undoubtedly more complex than that proposed in current theory.

Equity Theory

Equity theory states that the benefits involved in a relationship between two people should be equitable (Hatfield and Traupmann, 1981); that is, the two people in a relationship should both get as much out of the relationship as they put into it. Inequitable relationships, according to the theory, will result in psychological discomfort, which will cause one individual to attempt to change the situation by reducing the inequity. This may involve the termination of the relationship or a change in what is put into or taken from the relationship.

Evidence suggests that equitable relationships are more likely to last. For example, individuals who believe their relationships are equitable report being more confident that their relationships will last, being more content with their relationships, and experiencing more positive affect and less negative affect in their relationships than individuals who believe their relationships are less equitable (Hatfield et al., 1985; Sabatelli and Cecil-Pigo, 1985; Sprecher, 1986). However, in studies in which impressions of both equity and total number of benefits have been assessed, the total number of benefits received predicts relationship success better than perceived equity (e.g., Berg and McQuinn, 1986; Michaels, Edwards, and Acock, 1984). The fact that total number of benefits received predicts relationship success better than equity suggests that simple reinforcement theory may be better in accounting for the data than equity theory.

• • •

The reinforcement, exchange, and equity theories are not inconsistent with one another. All suggest that we like individuals who provide us with reinforcement. Exchange theory simply adds to the reinforcement theory the notion that the positive things gained from a relationship must outweigh the costs for the individual to want the relationship to continue. Equity theory contributes the idea that a relationship in which the two individuals are not giving and receiving equitably will cause discomfort (most likely for the underbenefited individual) and that this discomfort will very likely end the relationship if equity cannot be increased. All three theories are almost certainly correct to a limited degree.

Sternberg's Triangular Theory

Sternberg (1988) has proposed a somewhat different theory of love from those described previously. Rather than focusing on what causes an individual to love another person, he has developed a theory that describes the components of different types of love. Thus his theory can be used to describe different types of love rather than to explain why love occurs. Sternberg refers to his theory as the triangular theory of love. He suggests that different types of love can be understood in terms of three components of love: intimacy, passion, and decision/commitment.

Intimacy refers to close, connected and bonded feelings in loving relationships. It thus includes feelings that create the experience of warmth in a loving relationship. Sternberg and Grajek (1984) identified ten signs of intimacy in a close relationship: (1) desiring to promote the welfare of the loved one, (2) experiencing happiness with the loved one, (3) having high regard for the loved one, (4) being able to count on the loved one in times of need, (5) mutual understanding with the loved one, (6) sharing one's self and one's possessions with the loved one, (7) receiving emotional support from the loved one, (8) giving emotional support to the loved one, (9) having intimate communication with the loved one, (10) valuing the loved one in one's life.

Sternberg, 1988, p. 120

The passion component refers to the drives that lead to romance, physical attraction, sexual consummation, and the like in a loving relationship. Although sexual needs may form the main part of passion in many relationships, other needs— such as those for self-esteem, affiliation with others, dominance over others, submission to others, and self-actualization—may also contribute to the experience of passion.

Sternberg, 1988, pp. 120-121

The decision/commitment component of love consists of two aspects, one short term and one long term. The short-term one is the decision that one loves someone. The long-term aspect is the commitment to maintain that love. These two aspects of the decision/commitment component of love do not necessarily go together, for the decision to love does not necessarily imply a commitment to that love. Nor does commitment necessarily imply decision, oddly enough. Many people are committed to the love of another person without necessarily even admitting that they love or are in love with that person. Most often, however, decision will precede commitment.

Sternberg, 1988, p. 121

The three components of love can be represented in the triangle illustrated in Figure 14-1. Different types of love are made up of different combinations of these three components. The various types of love are illustrated in the

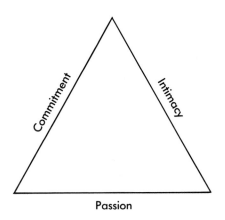

FIGURE 14-1
Sternberg's triangle: the three components of love.

FIGURE 14-2
Triangles representing the various types of love. Solid lines indicate presence of a component; dotted lines indicate absence of a component.

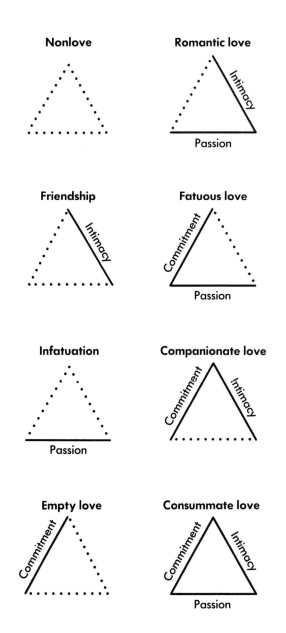

triangles in Figure 14-2. The solid lines in Figure 14-2 indicate the presence of a component, while the dotted lines indicate a component's absence.

As can be seen in Figure 14-2, intimacy alone results in friendship, passion alone results in infatuation, and commitment alone results in what Sternberg calls empty love. Friendship and infatuation probably need no explanation. But what is empty love? Imagine a couple who have been married for 30 years. Imagine also that this couple no longer feel passion for each other or share intimately with each other. The two individuals simply live in the same house but do not share friends, activities, and interests. Yet, if this couple do nothing to change their marital status, we would have to say that they have commitment in the absence of both passion and intimacy.

According to Sternberg romantic love entails a combination of intimacy and passion. Fatuous love is a result of a combination of commitment and passion. This is the kind of love we might associate with a whirlwind courtship. Imagine a couple who meet and feel a great deal of passion for each other immediately and become engaged and marry within a month. This couple made a commitment on the basis of passion. They did not even give themselves time to become intimate. Companionate love comprises both intimacy and commitment without passion. Sternberg suggests that this is the kind of love shared by many married individuals whose passion has waned. Finally, Sternberg calls the type of love that involves all three components consummate love or complete love. It is the ideal type of love for which most of us strive in romantic relationships. It can be difficult to achieve and to maintain.

In summary, Sternberg's theory differs from the other theories of love in that it does not attempt to explain why love occurs between individuals but rather describes different types of love relationships in terms of three components of love: intimacy, passion, and commitment. Thus Sternberg's theory is in competition with the other theories of love.

A Biological Theory of Love

Dr. Michael R. Liebowitz, who directed the Anxiety Disorders Clinic at the New York State Psychiatric Institute, has published a book called *The Chemistry of Love*. In this book Liebowitz makes the case that falling in love may be influenced by our brain chemistry. Liebowitz distinguishes between romantic attraction and romantic attachment because he believes them to be chemically distinct. Attraction seems to be related to surges of a brain stimulant, possibly phenethylamine (PEA). He contends that the symptoms of falling in love are much like what happens when you take amphetamines: your heart beats faster, your energy level goes up, and you feel optimistic. Certain chemicals in the brain, such as PEA, have amphetamine-like effects. Liebowitz believes that the same neurochemical changes may occur when one feels attraction as when one is under the influence of amphetamines.

Liebowitz also asserts that brain chemistry may be involved in romantic attachment. He points out that an area in the brainstem called the locus ceruleus seems to trigger feelings of panic and separation anxiety. Narcotics, such as morphine, tend to inhibit the locus ceruleus. There are also naturally occurring brain chemicals that act like narcotics; these chemicals are called endorphins. Liebowitz believes that humans may be genetically programmed to secrete endorphins when in close relationships. He also feels that when a relationship breaks up or threatens to break up, the endorphin production may be inhibited, and as a result we may feel panic or separation anxiety.

Finally, Liebowitz contends that boredom with a relationship may have a chemical basis. He states that our brains respond to increases or decreases in chemicals. He gives an example of the brain's response to change by discussing the effects of cocaine. While the quantity of cocaine in the brain increases, the effect of the cocaine is strong. However, once the amount of cocaine in the brain begins to level off, even though the absolute amount remains high, the effect of the cocaine begins to subside. Liebowitz suggests that the same thing happens with a relationship: the feelings are intense in the beginning, but soon the "high" wears off.

DEVELOPMENT OF A LOVING RELATIONSHIP

Now that we have looked at what factors tend to result in attraction between two people and at the theories that attempt to explain such attraction, it is time to examine what happens in a loving, intimate relationship once the two individuals are attracted to each other. Chelune, Robison, and Kommor (1984) have suggested that loving, intimate relationships are marked by six characteristics: (1) knowledge of the innermost being of another, (2) mutuality, (3) interdependence, (4) trust, (5) commitment, and (6) caring.

The first characteristic, *knowledge of the innermost being of another*, is usually referred to as **intimacy.** The word *intimacy* is derived from the Latin word *intimus,* which means "inner" or "innermost" (Perlman and Fehr, 1987). To be intimate with another person therefore means to share one's innermost self with the other person. This involves imparting one's most personal thoughts, feelings, and experiences to the other person and having the other person share in a similar fashion. When we first get to know someone, we tend to exchange only superficial, nonpersonal information with that person. We do not go beyond this surface level of communication unless we find that, on the basis of our experience with the other person, we can trust that person (Larzelere and Huston, 1980). Trust is based on discovering that the other person does not use the information he or she learns about us in a way that is harmful or embarrassing to us. For example, it is important that we find that the other person does not repeat confidential information to others. Furthermore, it is significant that the person not use the confidential information in an inappropriate way in his or her interactions with us. For example, we would not trust someone who uses against us in an argument information we have given him or her.

As trust increases in a relationship, self-disclosure increases; that is, the individuals share more and more personal, intimate information with each other. If this self-disclosure is mutual and if each individual finds that the other

intimacy
Sharing one's innermost thoughts, feelings, and experiences with another person.

To be intimate means to share one's innermost self with another person.

is genuinely interested in and nonjudgmental about the self-disclosures, each will feel progressively free to share his or her innermost thoughts and feelings. If such an atmosphere is maintained, intimacy will surely continue to grow and a strong, healthy relationship will result.

In addition to knowledge of the innermost being of the other person, Chelune, Robison, and Kommor (1984) have suggested that *mutuality* is important. By mutuality they mean the assumption that both partners are engaged in a joint venture that involves shared interaction. They propose that a significant aspect of mutuality is the concept of fairness. It is vital that both of the individuals involved in the relationship believe that they are receiving their fair share of the benefits in the relationship and not shouldering more than their share of the costs.

A related characteristic, *interdependence*, was also suggested by Chelune, Robison, and Kommor (1984) as a component of a healthy, intimate relationship. Interdependence refers to the way partners in intimate relationships begin to depend on each other for support, resources, understanding, and help of various sorts. Of course, the development of both mutuality and interdependence depends on the growth of trust in a relationship, just as the development of self-disclosure does.

Chelune, Robison, and Kommor (1984) point out that the increased vulnerability necessary in an intimate relationship can develop only if each individual is able to *trust* his or her partner. That means that he or she has to believe in the integrity, truthfulness, and fairness of the partner. Partners must trust each other to (1) be accepting of each other, (2) avoid purposely hurting each other, (3) have the best interests of each other and the relationship at

Self-Love Versus Love of Others

Many equate self-love with selfishness. They believe that the more an individual loves himself or herself, the less he or she will be capable of loving others. In fact, Freud held the belief that each individual had only a limited amount of libidinal energy that could be invested in oneself or in others. He believed that the more love one invested in oneself, the less that would be left to invest in others.

Most experts today, however, do not equate self-love with selfishness. They do not believe that an individual has only a limited amount of love that must be divided between self and others. Rather, they believe that the more self-love (or self-esteem) a person possesses, the more he or she will be capable of loving others. As Campbell (1984) has stated, "A healthy self-love is the

necessary condition for healthy love for others."

According to this belief, it is only the individuals who feel good about themselves (who have self-love) who are able to show genuine

concern for others. Individuals who do not feel good about themselves (who lack self-love) usually spend so much time and energy worrying about their own problems that they have little time and energy left to invest in others. Thus, individuals who love themselves or have high self-esteem will actually be less selfish than individuals who have less self-love or self-esteem.

A good parent-child relationship is an important determinant of a child's self-esteem.

heart, (4) feel warmth and care for each other, (5) respond to the needs of each other, (6) share, and (7) continue the relationship.

Commitment is also an important characteristic of a strong, intimate relationship. Commitment is the extent to which the partners accept their relationship as continuing indefinitely or try to ensure its continuation. The degree to which partners are committed to their relationship will affect all of the other characteristics of the relationship (and vice versa).

Finally, Chelune, Robison, and Kommor (1984) emphasize that *caring* is an important characteristic of an intimate, loving relationship. By caring they mean a strong affection between the partners. In the beginning of a relationship this affection may be experienced as romantic love or sexual attraction. With time it may take on the form of mutual concern and affection, and later it may evolve into a deeper form of love.

The six characteristics mentioned are those that one would expect to find in a very good relationship. Not all relationships are strong, healthy relationships. Frankel (1982) has suggested a number of criteria for judging functional (as opposed to dysfunctional) intimacy. His criteria are as follows:

1. Being able to have nondefensive, unguarded communication
2. Having empathy for each other, that is, being supportive of each other and understanding of each other's perspective
3. Being able to resolve conflicts by mutual accommodation and compromise, as well as willing to accept differences that cannot be negotiated
4. Being confirming of each other's lovability
5. Having enjoyable physical contact, from affection to sex
6. Having a "we" identity based on an aggregate of shared experiences from the joyous to the tragic
7. Being supportive of each other's individual interests, friends, hobbies, and careers
8. Being mutually available during crises
9. Being playful together

As can be seen from this list, developing a good, intimate relationship is not a simple process. Rather, it requires the effort and goodwill of two relatively mature and well-adjusted individuals (see box, p. 422).

BARRIERS TO INTIMACY

The previous discussion examined what occurs in the development of a healthy relationship. Not all relationships evolve in this way; often the intimacy does not continue to grow, and the relationship is thereby limited. Many factors may limit the development of intimacy in a relationship. Masters, Johnson, and Kolodny (1986) listed a number of these factors:

1. Shyness. Shy individuals isolate themselves socially and thereby miss out on opportunities to develop intimate relationships.
2. Aggressiveness. Aggressive individuals often scare potential partners away or cause them to be defensive for fear they would be overpowered by the aggressive person.
3. Self-centeredness. Self-centered individuals are those who want to be the center of attention, who dominate conversations, who ignore the needs of others, and who are usually unwilling to do what their partners want unless it coincides with their own needs. These individuals have difficulty maintaining long-term relationships because the one-sidedness of their relationships limits the development of real intimacy.
4. Selfishness. Selfish individuals are often manipulative and attempt to gain "a tactical advantage" over the other person in order to get their own way. Selfish people tend not to care about what is best for the other person or the relationship but only about their personal gain. Of course, such an approach to a relationship severely restricts intimacy.
5. Lack of empathy. Individuals who are unable or unwilling to understand and accept their partner's point of view and feelings will have difficulty establishing an intimate relationship because such a lack of empathy limits mutual understanding and concern.
6. Unrealistic expectations. Some individuals have such idealistic expectations about intimate relationships that no real relationship could meet their standards. These individuals are likely to continue to be disappointed in their relationships, and as a result the relationships are likely to suffer.

Jealousy in Love Relationships

Jealousy is an unpleasant emotion that is sometimes experienced in love relationships. It occurs less commonly in other types of relationships as well. What is jealousy? Buunk and Bringle (1987) defined jealousy as "an aversive emotional reaction evoked by a relationship involving one's current or former partner and a third person. This relationship may be real, imagined, or expected, or it may have occurred in the past" (p. 124). Jealous feelings occur when a person feels that his or her partner's relationship with the third person poses some threat. Buunk and Bringle (1987) suggested that the threat could be fear of the loss of (1) equality, (2) self-esteem, (3) feeling of special-

ness, or (4) the actual relationship with the partner.

Duck (1986) similarly suggested that jealousy is a result of a feeling of loss of control: "Jealousy is a response to an imagined loss of influence over a routine part of life, namely over the feelings of another person towards ourselves. When we imagine that we have lost influence over another person's feelings for us or when we are given evidence that they do not care, then we experience jealousy" (pp. 15-16).

Jealousy may well be a universal emotion. Although there are cultural differences in the way individuals exhibit and cope with jealousy, this emotion has been experienced by individuals in all cultures that have been studied (e.g., Buunk and

Hupka, 1987). This is true even in cultures in which extramarital sexual relations are accepted.

What types of people are more likely to feel jealous? Salovey and Rodin (1985) found that unmarried people were most likely to report feeling or behaving jealously. This is probably because unmarried people feel that their relationships are less committed than those of married individuals. White (1981) found that the individuals who are most likely to feel jealous are those who (1) feel inadequate as a partner, (2) place a strong value on sexual exclusivity, and (3) feel they have invested more time and effort in their relationship than their partners. Many have hypothesized that people with low self-esteem would be most likely to feel jealous. However, White did not find a relationship between self-esteem and reported feelings of jealousy.

In addition to the preceding barriers to intimacy, Hatfield (1984) has pointed out that fear of intimacy is a limiting factor in the development of a relationship. In intimate relationships people reveal their weaknesses as well as their strengths. Many people fear exposing the worst aspects of themselves because they are afraid that their partner will think less of them, or even abandon them, when he or she becomes aware of their less desirable qualities. Others fear that if they express their innermost selves to their partner, their partner may use some of the information against them later. Their partner might, for example, use sensitive, personal information later in order to gain some advantage in an argument. Yet others may fear that they will lose power and control if they share themselves with their partner. In fact, McGill (1985) has suggested that the fear of the loss of power is one of the most important reasons for avoidance of intimacy in men:

> The reason men are not more loving is that they want to retain power over themselves and attain power over others. . . . Men withhold information about themselves, they mislead and even misrepresent themselves to others. It is now apparent that they promote this mystery in order to gain mastery. This mystery-mastery behavior . . . discourages the sharing of feelings, motives, and goals with others.
>
> McGill, 1985, p. 232

Another factor that may limit the development of an intimate relationship is that one or both of the partners may not show an interest in learning about the other person. They may never have learned to listen well, they may not want to take the time to listen, or they may not have learned to show their interest in another person by asking questions and encouraging the other person to talk about himself or herself.

One or both of the partners may not be psychologically able to express their intimate thoughts and feelings to the other person. There is a tendency in our culture to try to make the best possible impression on others. Individuals, especially males, are taught to appear in control at all times and to hide many of their emotions. Sometimes individuals learn these lessons so well that they lose contact with what they really think and feel. As a result, these individuals are no longer able to share their thoughts and feelings because they no longer know what those thoughts and feelings are.

Research suggests that when intimacy is defined as the closeness and warmth of the relationship, men do not form relationships that are as intimate as those formed by women (Fisher and Narus, 1981). Women's relationships with other women tend to be the most intimate, male-female relationships tend to be the next most intimate, and men's relationships with other men tend to be the lowest in intimacy. Furthermore, research indicates that women tend to be more self-disclosing than men (Hacker, 1981; Brehm, 1985; Reis, Senchak, and Solomon, 1985). This difference is probably a result, at least in part, of the fact that males are encouraged to hide their personal thoughts and feelings in our culture and females are allowed to express their personal thoughts and emotions. Such gender roles may inhibit intimacy and the development of healthy love relationships. However, a study of self-disclosure among dating college students indicates that the traditional differences in the amount of disclosure may not be found in young, educated individuals (Rubin et at., 1980). However, even when men and women disclose to the same extent, they differ in the type of information they disclose. Men appear more likely than women to reveal their strengths and not mention their weaknesses (Hacker, 1981).

When intimacy is limited in a relationship, the relationship cannot be nearly as rewarding as it could be if the communication were honest and open. The rewards of an honest and open relationship can be great. A relationship in

Gender role socialization and gender differences in behavior are discussed in great detail in Chapter 10.

which both individuals share their innermost thoughts and feelings to a high degree is more rewarding because each individual provides the other with a more interesting partner. Furthermore, both individuals learn more about themselves through self-disclosure. In fact, Jourard (1971) has suggested that self-disclosure is both "a symptom of personality health and a means of ultimately achieving healthy personality." He goes on to say:

> When I say that self-disclosure is a means by which one achieves personality health, I mean it is not until I am my real self and I act my real self that my real self is in a position to grow. One's self grows from the consequence of being. People's selves stop growing when they repress them.
>
> Every maladjusted person is a person who has not made himself known to another human being and in consequence does not know himself. Nor can he be himself.
>
> Jourard, 1971, pp. 32-33

Furthermore, Jourard emphasizes the importance of self-disclosure to love relationships: "You cannot love your spouse or your child or your friend unless those persons have permitted you to know them and to know what they need in order to move toward greater health and well-being."

In addition to allowing us to get to know our partners and ourselves better, self-disclosure allows us to monitor the relationship. If we do not share our feelings with the other person, we do not know when problems arise in the relationship and thus are not able to make desirable modifications. As a consequence, misunderstandings and resentments begin to accumulate and the relationship inevitably deteriorates. Open communication allows us to monitor the relationship, make needed adjustments, clarify misunderstandings, and resolve conflicts; a much healthier relationship is the obvious result.

In summary, Chelune, Robison, and Kommor (1984) have suggested that intimate, loving relationships are marked by six characteristics: knowledge of the innermost being of the other person, mutuality, interdependence, trust, commitment, and caring. To be intimate with another person means to share one's innermost self with the other. Intimacy develops in a relationship as a

A relationship in which both individuals share their innermost thoughts and feelings to a high degree is rewarding because each individual provides the other with an interesting partner.

HUMAN SEXUALITY

result of mutual trust and mutual self-disclosure. However, intimacy may be limited by a number of factors, including shyness, aggressiveness, self-centeredness, selfishness, lack of empathy, unrealistic expectations, and fear of intimacy.

RELATIONSHIP BETWEEN LOVE AND SEX

As was mentioned at the beginning of this chapter, a discussion of love is included in this book because of the intimate connection between love and sex in our culture. In addition to examining the development of loving relationships, however, we must consider the association between love and sex (Przybyla and Bryne, 1981). Psychologists, psychiatrists, and other professionals who work with couples having marital or sexual problems have long realized the close connection between the quality of the interpersonal relationship and the quality of the sexual relationship. When resentments and conflicts in a relationship are not resolved, the sexual interaction of the couple almost inevitably suffers. Jourard (1971) observed this important connection:

> A healthy relationship between two loving people is characterized by mutual respect, and freedom to be and to disclose oneself in the presence of the other without contrivance. When two people are thus open, they will likewise be able to be sexually open one with the other. But let an impasse arise, say, an unexpressed resentment, an unresolved argument, something unsaid, a feeling unexpressed, some departure from spontaneous self-disclosure, and it will make sexual love-making less fulfilling. . . .
>
> Given a reasonable lack of prudery, a lusty sex life grows best out of a relationship between two persons who can disclose themselves with one another without fear of being deeply hurt when they are so unguarded. The same defenses which protect one from being hurt by one's spouse's remarks, deeds, or omissions are the very defenses which impede spontaneity in sex. Openness before a person renders one open to sights, sounds, smells in the world, and also open to the riches of one's own feelings. The person who effectively guards himself against pain from the outside just as effectively ensures virtual sexual anesthesia.
>
> Jourard, 1971, pp. 46-47

Blumstein and Schwartz (1983) studied married, cohabiting, and homosexual couples. They found that a good sexual relationship was related to a good overall relationship. Couples who indicated having frequent sexual interactions tended to report that their relationships were good in other respects as well. Couples who had infrequent sexual interactions usually had conflict in the nonsexual aspects of their relationships. It is not clear whether nonsexual problems in the relationship cause a decrease in sexual frequency or vice versa. However, Blumstein and Schwartz concluded that although it is not possible to be sure of the direction of causation, they were inclined to believe that the problems more often originate in nonsexual aspects of the relationship and then spread to the sexual relationship. They suggested that the resulting low frequency of sexual interaction then becomes a source of dissatisfaction in itself, which causes further problems in the overall relationship.

Thus the quality of a couple's interpersonal relationship appears to be closely related to the quality of their sexual relationship. When resentments and conflicts arise in a relationship and are not resolved, the sexual interaction of the couple is almost invariably affected negatively.

SUMMARY

1 Research demonstrates that we tend to be attracted to people who are physically attractive and competent. Research also indicates that we tend to like individuals who share our basic attitudes and values, as well as people who have similar demographic characteristics such as age, social class, ethnic background, and religion. We also like people who like us, whom we see frequently, and who are nearby.

2 Gender differences in mate selection preferences appear to be a product of both societal and evolutionary forces.

3 The two-component theory of love suggests that passionate love results when two conditions occur simultaneously: the individual is in a state of physiological arousal, and the circumstances lead the individual to apply the label "love" to the sensations. When finding an emotion to explain their physiological arousal, individuals often incorrectly identify the physical attractiveness of another as the source of arousal.

4 According to reinforcement theory, we tend to like or love individuals who reward us and dislike individuals who punish us.

5 Exchange theory proposes that any relationship involves both benefits and costs to both individuals involved. An individual will find a relationship worthwhile to the extent that the benefits outweigh the costs. However, an individual will not necessarily stay in any relationship in which the benefits outweigh the costs. Rather, an individual will compare the cost/benefit ratios associated with different relationships and choose the relationship that provides him or her with the best cost/benefit ratio.

6 According to equity theory, the benefits involved in a relationship between two people should be equitable; that is, two people in a relationship should both get as much out of the relationship as they put into it. Inequitable relationships supposedly produce psychological discomfort that results in attempts to reduce the inequity either by getting out of the relationship or by changing the relationship.

7 Sternberg proposed the triangular theory of love. He suggested that love relationships can involve three components: intimacy, passion, and decision/commitment. Different types of love are composed of various combinations of these components.

8 Chelune, Robison, and Kommor (1984) have suggested that loving, intimate relationships are marked by six characteristics: knowledge of the innermost being of the other person, mutuality, interdependence, trust, commitment, and caring.

9 To be intimate with another person means to share one's innermost self with the other. Intimacy develops in a relationship as a result of mutual trust and mutual self-disclosure. Increasing trust facilitates self-disclosure, and increasing self-disclosure facilitates trust. Trust and self-disclosure are fostered by partners being open and consistently accepting and supportive of each other.

10 Masters, Johnson, and Kolodny (1986) have suggested that intimate relationships are limited by at least six factors: shyness, aggressiveness, self-centeredness, selfishness, lack of empathy, and unrealistic expectations.

11 Hatfield (1984) has proposed that some people have a fear of intimacy.

12 The quality of a couple's interpersonal relationship is closely connected

with their sexual relationship. When resentments and conflicts arise in a relationship and are not resolved, the couple's sexual interaction is almost invariably affected negatively.

ANSWERS

1 Research does not indicate that familiarity breeds contempt; rather, it demonstrates that increased exposure to a particular person enhances one's attraction to that person.

2 Studies have suggested that, contrary to cultural stereotypes, men tend to fall in love more easily, cling to relationships longer, and become more upset at the termination of relationships than women.

3 Investigators have found both that women are more self-disclosing than men and that they tend to disclose different types of information. Men are more likely to reveal their strengths, and women are more likely to reveal their weaknesses.

QUESTIONS FOR THOUGHT ?

1 How important is physical attractiveness for you when you are selecting a partner? What other characteristics are important? How would you rank order these characteristics?

2 If you are currently in a relationship, what are the strengths of that relationship? What are the weaknesses?

3 What is the relationship between love and sex for you? Do you need to be in love to have sex? Does having sex tend to increase your love for a partner?

SUGGESTED READINGS

Derlega, V.J.: Communication, intimacy and close relationships, Orlando, Fla., 1984, Academic Press, Inc.
A collection of professional-level readings about theory and research on intimacy.

Fisher, M., and Stricker, G.: Intimacy, New York, 1982, Plenum Publishing Corp.
Professional-level readings about various aspects of intimacy.

Jourard, S.M.: The transparent self, New York, 1964, D. Van Nostrand Co., Inc.
A book about the importance of self-disclosure.

Kelley, H.H., et al.: Close relationships, San Francisco, 1983, W.H. Freeman & Co. Publishers.
A collection of readings about various aspects of close relationships, including chapters on topics such as emotion, power, conflict, and gender roles. It is written at a professional level.

Pope, K.S.: On love and loving, San Francisco, 1980, Jossey-Bass, Inc., Publishers.
This book contains readings about love: the development of love, psychological theory related to love, and psychotherapy and love.

Perlman, D., and Duck, S., editors: Intimate relationships: development, dynamics and deterioration, Newbury Park, Calif., 1987, Sage Publications, Inc.
A collection of professional-level articles about the development of relationships, as well as articles about the deterioration of relationships.

CHAPTER 15

Sexual Life-Styles

FACT OR FICTION

1
Almost half of all married individuals today report having at least one extra-marital sexual relation-ship.

2
Widowed and divorced men and women have sexual intercourse less frequently than their married counterparts.

3
Because women are more dependent on relationships than men, single women have more adjustment problems than single men.

I bring the children one more glass of water.
I rub the hormone night cream on my face.
Then after I complete the isometrics,
I greet my husband with a warm embrace,

A vision in my long-sleeved flannel nightgown
And socks (because my feet are always freezing),
Gulping tranquilizers for my nerve ends,
and Triaminic tablets for my wheezing.

Our blue electric blanket's set for toasty.
Our red alarm clock's set at seven-thirty.
I tell him that we owe the grocer plenty.
He tells me that his two best suits are dirty.

Last year I bought him Centaur for his birthday.
(They promised he'd become half-man, half-beast.)
Last year he bought me something black and lacy.
(They promised I'd go mad with lust, at least.)

Instead my rollers clink upon the pillow
And his big toenail scrapes against my skin.
He rises to apply a little Chap Stick.
I ask him to bring back two Bufferin.

Oh somewhere there are lovely little boudoirs
With Porthault sheets and canopies and whips.
He lion-hunts in Africa on weekends.
She measures thirty-three around the hips.

Their eyes engage across the brandy snifters.
He runs his fingers through her Kenneth hair.
The kids are in the other wing with nanny.
The sound of violins is everywhere.

In our house there's the sound of dripping water.
It's raining and he never patched the leak.
He grabs the mop and I get out the bucket.
We both agree to try again next week.

JUDITH VIORST
"Sex Is Not So Sexy Anymore"

In this chapter the three most prevalent life-styles in our culture—marriage, singlehood, and cohabitation—are discussed. The sexual behavior typical of each of these life-styles is examined. Of course, adults do not necessarily experience only one life-style. Individuals may have one, two, or even three life-styles over the course of their adult lives. In addition to the heterosexual life-styles mentioned, a variety of homosexual life-styles are discussed.

MARRIAGE

More than 90% of all individuals in our culture will get married at least once during their lives (Doherty and Jacobson, 1982; Wood, Rhodes, and Whelan,

More than 90% of all individuals in our culture get married at least once in their lives.

1989). In general, marriage seems to be beneficial; it has been found to be significantly related to self-reported happiness and to both physical and mental health (Doherty and Jacobson, 1982). However, there is evidence that marriage may be more beneficial to men than to women (Bernard, 1972).

Although most couples begin their marriages with high levels of marital satisfaction, not all couples remain satisfied with their relationship. When two individuals try to adjust to living with each other, problems inevitably arise. The romantic aspects of the relationship typically become less salient as the couple is called on to deal with family and economic responsibilities and they get to know each other very well, including each other's less desirable characteristics. Marital satisfaction tends to decline with the addition of children to the home and to increase again after children leave home (Whyte, 1990).

Given that problems exist in any marital relationship, the quality of the communication between the two partners is critical (Noller, 1987). With good communication patterns, the couple can resolve conflicts in a positive and constructive way that does not inflict permanent damage to the relationship. If, however, the problems are not resolved in a positive and constructive manner, each conflict has the potential to drive the couple further apart. A number of empirical studies support the view that open communication patterns are predictive of high marital satisfaction (Jorgensen and Gaudy, 1980; Banmen and Vogel, 1985).

Sex in Marriage

Communication patterns in marriage are significant in determining the quality of the marital relationship, which in turn is important in deciding the quality

HUMAN SEXUALITY

"Do you, Walter, promise to love and cherish, to make every effort to relate to a compatible life style, and to communicate on all meaningful levels?"

of the sexual relationship. Masters and Johnson (1970) have discussed how communication patterns influence a sexual relationship:

> Just as the willingness of a man and a woman to reveal themselves to each other and to become vulnerable brings them closer together, so their unwillingness to be vulnerable leads them not to reveal themselves and to become uncommitted. A natural sense of self-protection takes over. In learning not to be vulnerable with each other, a married couple is usually reenacting a scenario that was originally written during childhood years. When these individuals marry, they frequently find it all too easy to react to conflict by what might be described as a conditioned emotional reflex—the deadening of feelings. With their marriage partners, as they probably did with their parents, they hide behind defensive barriers. In time, their partners, too, become guarded, if not equally defensive. In such cases, the husband has not committed himself to his wife and she has not committed herself to him. Neither is willing to be emotionally vulnerable.
>
> They relate to each other much as they do the telephone company. They pay whatever price is required for service to continue—for the house to be cleaned,

meals prepared, children cared for, bills paid, possessions purchased, entertainment provided and, when either partner chooses, for sexual relations. They attend to each other's needs to the best of their ability but passion is something they must go to the movies to see.

To the extent that each fulfills his or her obligations, their marriage survives. Sexual pleasure, if it ever existed, does not survive for long. Sex becomes perfunctory at best; more often it is either dull, dormant or dead.

Masters and Johnson, 1970, pp. 263-264

The relationship between the quality of a couple's nonsexual interactions and their sexual satisfaction is also discussed in Chapter 14.

Broderick (1982) reported that emotional closeness is positively related to sexual satisfaction in marriage. Schenk, Pfrang, and Rausche (1983) found that husbands' and wives' ratings of satisfaction with their sexual interactions were significantly related to the overall quality of their marital relationship. The more appreciative, supportive, and confiding a person's spouse was, the more satisfied the person reported being with their sexual relationship.

Although the quality of a couple's sexual interactions is related to the quality of the couple's overall marital satisfaction, the cause of this association may vary between men and women. Research indicates that the quality of the sexual relationship is important in determining the man's overall marital satisfaction, whereas the woman's overall marital satisfaction is important in determining the quality of her sexual relationship (Przybyla and Byrne, 1981).

The results of the preceding studies make it clear that there are degrees of satisfaction in both marital relationships and sexual relationships. Keeping in mind that differences exist, it is useful to look at the statistics on what tends to happen to sexuality in marriage.

The results of many studies suggest that the frequency of sexual relations in marriage decreases with time (Broderick, 1982). Married couples in their first year of marriage indicate having sexual intercourse an average of about three times per week. The reported frequency drops to two times per week after about 3 years and to less than once per week after about 30 years.

In Chapter 13 the changes in sexual functioning that accompany aging are discussed in greater detail.

There are a number of possible reasons for the decline in marital intercourse. First, biological changes in the male contribute to the decline. With increasing age, men have a gradual decrease in the production of the male sex hormone testosterone, which is thought to result in a decrease in sexual responsiveness (Ewing, Davis, and Zirkin, 1980). Masters and Johnson (1966) propose that the sexual response itself changes; they found that erection and ejaculation took more time with increasing age. In females, on the other hand, there appears to be less change in sexual functioning with age during the adult years. Masters and Johnson (1966) suggest that a sexual waning also occurs in women, but after the age of 60.

In addition to biological changes that occur with increasing age, psychological factors may contribute to the decrease in marital sexual activity. Lamanna and Riedmann (1981) report three factors that contribute to less satisfying marital sex: boredom as a self-fulfilling prophecy, work before pleasure, and power politics in the bedroom.

First, Lamanna and Riedmann suggest that many couples expect sex to become less interesting and satisfying over the years of marriage. As a result of their expectation, they behave in ways that make sex dull and routine. For example, they may not try new sexual techniques or communicating about their sexuality. Couples can work to avoid sexual boredom by doing such things

HUMAN SEXUALITY

If couples want a fulfilling sexual relationship, they need to set aside time during which they can be alone together.

as going out to dinner at a romantic restaurant, having candlelight dinners at home, or going to a motel or hotel every once in a while. Furthermore, they can communicate about their sexuality by telling their partners what they like and dislike, what they would like to try and what they would not like to try, or what their sexual fantasies are. In other words, to prevent boredom, couples need to make a conscious effort to keep their sexual relationship alive.

Second, Lamanna and Riedmann (1981) mention the problem of putting work before pleasure. Many people in our culture feel that being productive is more important than leisure. As a result, couples postpone sex until everything else is done. If they are involved in their work or if they have young children, they may have little time to spend in an intimate setting. They are often too tired for sex at the end of a long and exhausting day. With children in the home it may be difficult to find time to be alone and to relax. To have a fulfilling sexual relationship, they need to set aside time to be alone together with no fear of interruption. They could, for example, set aside one night per week in which they would not bring work home, watch TV, or be with the children, but rather would be alone together. If they have young children, they could get a baby-sitter and go to a hotel or they could arrange to take vacations together without the children. If the sexual relationship is important to the couple, they must show this by devoting time to it.

Third, Lamanna and Riedmann (1981) mention the problem of using power politics in the bedroom. Sex can become an important factor in ongoing marital power struggles. For example, a wife who feels that her husband controls all other elements of their relationship may want to exert some power herself. She may find that she can easily control their sexual interactions by being "too tired" or "having a headache" when her husband is in the mood for sex. Some people are "too tired" whenever their spouse has done something they do not like. Thus they may use sex as a reward for the kind of behavior they want. When the sexual relationship is manipulated in this way, it can become a less than totally pleasurable experience for the couple.

In summary, statistics indicate that the frequency of sexual intercourse decreases gradually during the years of marriage. This decline appears to be the result of both biological and psychological factors. It is important to keep in mind that the statistics simply indicate the average trend; individual couples may find that their sexual relationship changes in very different ways across the years.

Extramarital Sex

Sexual fidelity has always been assumed to be a basic premise of marriage. Although our attitudes toward sexuality have become increasingly liberal in recent years, most people still believe that sexual fidelity is an important part of the marriage contract. For example, only 11% of the husbands and 7% of the wives studied by Blumstein and Schwartz (1983) did not think it was important that they be monogamous.

In spite of their attitudes, a large proportion of Americans do become involved in extramarital sex at some point during their marriages. Both Kinsey and associates (1953) and Hunt (1974) found that approximately one half of the married men and one fourth of the married women in their studies reported

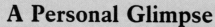

A Personal Glimpse

Extramarital Relationships Can Be Difficult

Now and again, the best laid plans and lovers get upset. Which is what happens when neighbors or friends of the married man see him with his other woman. I understand it is a common peril, especially in his home town.

An experienced woman handles this with elan. If the man is notably older than she, a woman may call him "Mr. So-and-So." One young lady did that, referring to a friendship between her father and the man in question. Another woman, without the significant age difference to aid her, merely thanked her boyfriend for the street directions he had just supposedly given her, trotted off, and met

him later at their mutual hotel. Some prefer making believe that they are not themselves. Either they break into a foreign tongue (if they have got one) or deny their identity—I'm sorry, I'm not Mrs. So-and-So's daughter.

Recognition from a man's family is more disconcerting. A stewardess drove into a gas station with her boyfriend when his daughter arrived on her bicycle. The stewardess had just gotten out of the car at that moment. She grabbed a squeegee, pretending she worked there. Her married lover tipped her generously for a topnotch job on the windshield before driving off without her. He made sure his daughter had left the area before circling back.

From Zola, 1982.

Some people become involved in an extramarital relationship because of the variety and excitement it provides.

experiencing extramarital sexual intercourse at least once. These figures are probably underestimates of the extramarital sex that actually occurred. Many individuals are reluctant to talk about their extramarital relationships, probably because attitudes toward extramarital sex are so negative. In fact, Kinsey, Pomeroy, and Martin (1948) reported that no sexual behavior caused so much evasion and dishonesty in their subjects as extramarital sex. As a result, extramarital sex may have been somewhat more frequent than the Kinsey and Hunt studies indicated.

In more recent years the incidence of extramarital sex seems to have been increasing, especially among women. Estimates of the percentage of women who become involved in sexual relationships outside of their marriages range from 38% (Atwater, 1982) to as high as 50% (Rubenstein, 1983). The apparent increase in extramarital relationships among women may be attributable, at least in part, to the fact that women are now more likely to be employed outside the home and therefore have more opportunity for such relationships. Of course, the liberalization of sexual attitudes and gender roles in our culture must also be responsible.

Why do so many adults become involved in extramarital sexual relationships when they disapprove of extramarital sex so strongly? There are a wide variety of reasons. First, a distinction must be drawn between nonconsensual and consensual extramarital sex. In **nonconsensual extramarital sex** the nonparticipating spouse does not consent to and probably does not know about the extramarital relationship. In **consensual extramarital sex** the spouse knows about and consents to the extramarital sex. Nonconsensual extramarital relationships are by far the more common form; few married couples agree that they should be free to have sexual relationships outside the marriage (Thompson, 1983).

Probably because of the threat to a marriage that is important to them and because of their relatively high sexual and emotional satisfaction, happily mar-

nonconsensual extramarital sex
Extramarital sex in which the nonparticipating spouse does not consent to and probably does not know about the affair.

consensual extramarital sex
Extramarital sex to which the nonparticipating spouse consents.

Counseling is often helpful for couples with problems.

ried individuals are less likely to become involved in risky nonconsensual extramarital relationships. They have a great deal to lose if the extramarital relationship is discovered. Walster, Traupman, and Walster (1978) reported that the more emotionally and sexually deprived individuals feel in their marriages, the more likely they are to become involved in extramarital relationships. This is especially true for men. Thompson (1983) found a stronger association between dissatisfaction with marriage and extramarital sexual relationships for males than for females. Men who are not satisfied with their marriages are more likely to engage in sex outside their marriages than are females who are not satisfied. There are, however, reasons other than marital dissatisfaction for extramarital involvements. Some individuals seek the sexual variety and excitement that extramarital sex offers. Some become involved in extramarital relationships to have more emotionally expressive communication than they have in their marriages (Atwater, 1982). Some need to prove to themselves and to others that they are still attractive. Others may be retaliating against their spouse for one reason or another. Of course, some people do not have any specific reason for becoming sexually involved with someone other than their spouse. They may have simply become acquainted with someone to whom they were particularly attracted and have become sexually involved without really planning on it.

The reasons for engagement in consensual extramarital sex tend to be somewhat different from those for involvement in nonconsensual extramarital sex. Marital dissatisfaction is less likely to be a cause. Rather the desire for sexual variety and experimentation is more likely to be the reason. In consensual extramarital sex the spouses agree with or consent to sexual relations with individuals outside the marriage. There are a number of types of agreements. The couple may have a sexually open marriage. In an open marriage the partners agree not to limit each other's relationships with other people. Although they both want the security of knowing that their relationship is primary, they agree

438 HUMAN SEXUALITY

that they are both free to establish sexual and other types of relationships with other people as long as those relationships do not threaten the marriage. Some couples have "swinging" relationships, in which couples swap mates. In such swinging arrangements the couples who swap mates try to limit outside sexual relationships to purely physical sexual encounters without emotional ties.

Evidence indicates that extramarital sex has a negative impact on marriage. For example, Blumstein and Schwartz (1983) found that the divorce rate is higher among couples in which one or both partners are engaged in extramarital relationships than among monogamous couples. Extramarital sex is one of the most frequently mentioned problems when marriages break up (Kelly, 1982). Of course, the problems are greater when nonconsensual extramarital sex is involved, but even consensual extramarital sexual relationships can cause difficulty in a marriage, especially if one of the spouses becomes emotionally involved with another person.

Although it is evident that extramarital sex can be damaging to the marital relationship, extramarital relationships are not invariably destructive (see accompanying box). In some cases the discovery of an extramarital relationship may lead the couple to realize that they have a problem in their marriage and that something must be done to correct it. In such cases the extramarital relationship might actually have a positive effect on the marriage (Atwater, 1982).

Do Extramarital Relationships Always Result in Divorce?

Zola (1982) interviewed both men and women who have been involved in extramarital relationships. Although she concluded that married women who fall in love with another man tend to leave their marriages for the man, men are much less likely to leave a marriage simply because they fall in love with another woman:

Marriage is unlikely to be the large part of a man's life that it is of a woman's. His major identity and status come from work, though this is slowly changing as women grow more career-oriented and men develop their tenderer inner selves. The relative unimportance of marriage as compared to work is especially common among high-achieving men. When they love an outside woman, this may still be peripheral to the core of their lives and doesn't, therefore, herald divorce.

Loving may be, for these husbands with girlfriends, a thing apart from marriage, not the criterion for choosing whom they live with. The biggest mistake other women seem to make is assuming that if their men love them, they will eventually leave their wives for them. What they forget is that many men have stronger demands than those of love—neurotic, practical, or cultural. These needs are potent.

Additionally, middle-, upper-middle- and upper-class men have social, financial, and familial investments they are loath to disturb. If they travel, much of their unhappiness in poor marriages is reduced. About 85 percent of the men with whom I spoke opted for the structural status quo over divorce, unless they could not stand living at home or with the hypocrisy of a double life. Those comfortable but uninspired husbands who had no new genuine love partners were least ready to consider divorce. "Why should we divorce," the husband reasons, "when we're used to each other and there's no one else I want to live with?" Even the women they love are sometimes let go in favor of property, family tradition, habit, and the need to avoid commitment to one person. As long as their marriages are satisfactory on some level, many stay put.

Zola, 1982, p. 154

Since this conclusion is not based on rigorous scientific research, one needs to view it with caution. However, it would be interesting to test the hypothesis that men are much less likely to leave a marriage because they fall in love with another person than are women.

POSTMARITAL SEX

Marriages end in two ways: through divorce or through the death of one of the spouses. Between 1950 and 1970, 35% of the marriages that terminated ended in divorce and the remaining 65% ended as a result of death (Saxton, 1977). After that time the divorce rate increased steadily up to 1980 and then leveled off or decreased slightly (Levitan, Belous, and Gallo, 1988). Approximately half of all marriages recently contracted will end in divorce (Benson-von der Ohe, 1987).

The loss of a spouse through divorce and the loss of a spouse through death are in some ways comparable. In both cases the individual has lost a person who has been significant in his or her life and he or she goes through a grieving process. There are differences, however. A person who loses a spouse through death receives a great deal of social support to help him or her get through the grieving process. The rituals associated with death help the individual deal with his or her emotional acceptance. Divorce, however, has no standard rituals to mark the dissolution of the marriage. Furthermore, much less social support is available for an individual going through a divorce. The person getting a divorce not only loses the spouse but also tends to feel guilty about the breakup of the marriage. However, the more negative aspects of divorce have some beneficial effects. The anger and resentment that often accompany divorce help the individual with emotional disengagement from the ex-spouse. The widowed individual, on the other hand, often retains a close emotional tie with the deceased mate and therefore is less likely to establish another intimate relationship.

The postmarital sexual patterns of divorced and widowed adults tend to differ. Divorced individuals often have a greater need to become sexually involved after the end of their marriage. Sometimes they attempt to build their self-esteem by engaging in sexual and other intimate relationships to demonstrate to themselves and others that they are sexually and personally attractive. Moreover, it is much more acceptable for a divorced person to become involved in postmarital sexual relationships. Widowed individuals often feel that they should be faithful to the deceased spouse. These differences are reflected in the statistics on the incidence and frequency of postmarital sex. Gebhard (1968) reported that 82% of divorced women in his study had active postmarital sex lives and only 43% of the widowed women did. Of course, part of the difference in the postmarital sex rates of divorced and widowed individuals must be attributed to the younger age of divorced individuals. However, when divorced and widowed people are matched for age, divorced individuals are still more likely to become involved in postmarital sex.

Gebhard (1968) noted that virtually all divorced and widowed men become involved in postmarital sexual relationships. In fact, Hunt (1974) reported that both widowed and divorced men have sexual intercourse slightly more frequently than their married counterparts and divorced women have intercourse with about the same frequency as their married counterparts. The frequency for widowed women is lower than that for married women. Hunt found that men have an average of about eight postmarital sex partners per year and women have only half as many. Postmarital sex also appears to be at least as satisfying as marital sex. Gebhard (1966) reported that both divorced and widowed women experience higher rates of orgasm in postmarital sex than they do in marital sex.

REMARRIAGE

Remarriage is becoming much more frequent. About four of every five adults who divorce will eventually remarry (Benson-von der Ohe, 1987). Men are somewhat more likely than women to remarry. The proportion of women who remarry declines with increasing age. Three of four women who divorce before the age of 30 remarry, three out of five who divorce between 30 and 39 remarry, and only one of four who divorce after 40 remarries (Levitan, Belous, and Gallo, 1988). Those who remarry after a divorce tend to do so quickly; half are married within 3 years following the divorce (Furstenberg, 1982). It has been estimated that one in every three marriages in the United States is a second marriage for one or both partners. Less than 3% of all marriages are third marriages.

The divorce rate among couples in second marriages is slightly higher than among those in their first marriages, especially during the early years of the marriage (Weed, 1980). The difficulties associated with stepparenting that often accompany second marriages may account for the earlier divorce pattern (White and Booth, 1985). Despite the slightly higher divorce rate, however, adults in second marriages tend to report as much marital happiness as those in their first marriages (Benson-von der Ohe, 1987). Furthermore, remarried individuals usually indicate that their second marriages are more satisfactory than their first marriages were (Furstenberg, 1982). The comparisons of first and second marriages conducted so far have focused primarily on satisfaction with the total marital relationship rather than on sexual satisfaction. Whether sexuality and sexual satisfaction differ between adults in their first marriage and those in their second marriage has not been determined.

REMAINING SINGLE

Although marriage is the most commonly chosen way to live out the majority of one's adult life, some individuals feel that traditional marriage might not meet their needs as well as other life-styles. A growing number of people in our culture are choosing to remain single. For example, in 1960, 17% of the men and 12% of the women over the age of 18 had never married (U.S. Bureau of the Census, 1960). By 1989 the percentages of men and women over 18 who had never married had increased to 26% and 19%, respectively (U.S. Bureau of the Census, 1989). Furthermore, the percentage of individuals over 18 who were divorced and had not remarried doubled during that period (U.S. Bureau of the Census, 1989).

Reasons for Remaining Single

Many factors are responsible for the increase in the percentage of single adults. People are getting married at later ages (Doherty and Jacobson, 1982). The divorce rate has increased, and divorced individuals are waiting longer before remarrying. A larger number of individuals are simply choosing not to marry. When the percentage of adults over the age of 18 who have never married (22%) is combined with the number who are divorced (8%) or widowed (8%), nearly 40% of adults in the United States are single (U.S. Bureau of the Census, 1989).

In considering the factors that contribute to the increase in the number of single individuals in our society, we must recognize that many singles see their status as temporary; the majority expect to marry sooner or later (Cargan and Melko, 1982). Furthermore, the factors that contribute to voluntary singleness must be distinguished from the factors that contribute to involuntary singleness.

One factor that contributes to voluntary singleness is the women's movement. A number of feminists have made the case that although marriage may be beneficial for men, it may not be particularly beneficial for women. For example, Bernard (1972) pointed out that the conditions and benefits of marriage differ greatly for men and women. When men marry, they acquire wives who take care of them both physically and emotionally so that they can go off to work and gain honor and prestige without having to worry about domestic affairs. Women who marry, on the other hand, find themselves waiting on and taking care of their families; they typically have no way of gaining honor and prestige on their own. The wives in this type of marriage often feel dissatisfied and unappreciated. Even when the wife works outside the home, she typically remains responsible for cooking and taking care of the house and children; in such situations the wives frequently feel overburdened. Given the differential benefits of marriage to men and women, Bernard questions whether marriage is an advantage for women.

Many individuals choose to remain single because they no longer need to get married to have a sexual relationship. In addition, many women have careers and no longer need to marry for financial support. Furthermore, many unmarried people feel that as singles they have greater freedom, more career opportunities, more possibilities to develop friendships, and more chance for personal growth (Stein, 1981).

It is important also to consider factors that might be responsible for the increasing number of individuals who are involuntarily single. Carter and Glick

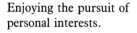

Enjoying the pursuit of personal interests.

(1970) labeled one such cause the "marriage squeeze." They pointed out that because of the increase in birth rate that began after World War II and did not subside until after 1960, a very large number of people reached the age at which people usually get married. Because women tend to marry men who are a few years older than they are, the baby boom women reached the age of marriage a few years before the baby boom men. Since more women than men were looking for marriage partners, many women who wanted to get married were unable to do so.

Another factor that may prevent some individuals from finding marriage partners is what Bernard (1972) calls the "marriage gradient." Because women tend to marry men of higher educational and occupational status, the men who have a very low educational and occupational status cannot find women with lower status to marry. At the same time, women who have a very high educational and occupational status have difficulty finding partners because they cannot find men with higher status. As a result many men with very low educational and occupational status and women with very high educational and occupational status remain single even though they may want to marry.

The "marriage squeeze" and the "marriage gradient" are two factors that may result in involuntary singleness. It is important to realize that not all singles have remained single by choice, even though an increasing number of adults are choosing not to marry.

Effects of Remaining Single

A number of studies indicate that married adults are happier and have fewer physical and mental health problems than singles (Cargan and Melko, 1982). The effects of remaining single on both physical and mental health, however, may differ for men and women. Contrary to the myth of the unhappy old maid and the swinging bachelor, it appears that single women have the advantage over single men. Kiernan (1988) found that single women have greater ability, are more highly educated, and have higher status occupations than either married women or single men. Single men, on the other hand, tend to be lower on these dimensions than either married men or single women. Campbell (1975) noted that single women of all ages report being happier and more content with their lives than single men. Stein (1981) reported that unmarried men, whether never married, divorced, or widowed, are more likely than women to experience psychological problems, including depression, neurosis, phobias, and passivity. It is not true, however, that all women are happier and healthier than men. Among married individuals, men tend to be happier and healthier than women. Thus it appears that marriage may be much more beneficial for men than for women. It is also possible that the less physically and mentally healthy men are simply more likely to remain single, whereas the women who

Wedlock May Hold Key to Longer Life

"Marriage, if one will face the truth, is an evil, but a necessary evil," said the Greek comic playwright Menander.

Indeed, for middle-aged men, it may be a lifesaver.

Men from the ages of 45 to 64 who live alone or with somebody other than a spouse are twice as likely to die within 10 years as men of the same age who live with their wives, a study has found.

Researchers at the University of California at San Francisco studied 7,651 American adults to see if there was a link between living arrangements and survival.

They found that even after accounting for differences in income and education and such other risk factors as smoking, drinking, obesity and physical activity, men who lived without a wife were twice as likely as their wedded counterparts to die within a decade.

Women who lived without a husband also had an increased chance of dying sooner, the researchers found, but that risk was more closely associated with a lower income than it was to the lack of a spouse.

"Women who had a higher income but who lived with someone other than a spouse were not at a disadvantage for survival," said Dr. Maradee Davis, associate professor of epidemiology and biostatistics, who presented the findings at a recent meeting of the American Public Health Association.

Of greatest surprise to researchers, men who lived with somebody other than a spouse, including their children, parents or non-relatives, were no better off than men who lived on their own.

"The critical factor seems to be the spouse," Davis said.

The researchers are still trying to determine why men without wives face a greater risk of early death.

Previous studies on the relationship between marriage and longevity have found men with wives express a greater sense of well-being than do non-married men, while married women did not seem especially content compared with women without husbands.

From Angier, 1990.

remain single are not as likely to be those who are less physically and mentally healthy. Bernard's "marriage gradient" suggests that this might be the case. It may not be that marriage is more beneficial for men than for women, but rather that the men who do not marry are less physically and mentally healthy than the women who do not marry.

In summary, being married may be more conducive to physical and mental health and life satisfaction than being single, particularly for men. However, single individuals probably differ greatly in their adjustment to single life. Individuals who choose to remain single might, for example, be much happier and healthier than those who remain single involuntarily. Similarly, divorced or widowed individuals may be less happy and healthy than other single individuals, at least temporarily, because they have experienced the trauma of losing their spouses. That married individuals generally appear happier and healthier does not mean that marriage is the best way for everyone to live.

Sex Among Singles

Attitudes toward sex among single individuals have changed dramatically in recent years. Although only 22% of the adults surveyed by the Roper Agency in 1959 approved of premarital sex, over half of the adults surveyed in Hunt's study in the early 1970s approved of premarital sex (Hunt, 1974).

The sexual behavior of singles, especially single women, has been changing as well. Kinsey and associates (1953) reported that only one fifth of unmarried women between the ages of 16 and 20 and one third of unmarried women between 21 and 35 indicated having had sexual intercourse. Twenty years later, Hunt (1974) found that two thirds of the unmarried women between 18 and 24 reported having had sexual intercourse. Hunt discovered that not only were a greater number of single women having sex, but they were having it more often and were enjoying it more; many more single women in the Hunt study reported having had orgasms than in the earlier Kinsey study.

Other than saying that attitudes toward sex among singles have become more permissive and that sexual activity of single women has increased, we cannot make many generalizations about the sexual behavior of single individuals. The sexual environment differs markedly for singles according to their age and life situation.

A single individual below the age of 25 has a large number of potential partners and many ways to meet them. Individuals can meet potential partners in college classes, at dances, at concerts, and at other social events. Most of the sexuality that occurs in this age group is considered "premarital"; it takes place in the context of looking for a mate.

For the person over the age of 25, however, the situation changes. There are fewer potential partners, and a structure that supports the dating and meeting of potential partners no longer exists. However, singles apartment complexes and singles bars in metropolitan areas facilitate the interaction of single adults.

Few single adults actually become involved in singles apartment living or in singles bars. Those who do so tend to be looking for either a marriage partner or recreational sex, that is, sex with no emotional involvement. The likelihood of sexual involvement among the individuals who meet in such establishments

Some singles look for partners in single bars.

is fairly high. Singles bars may be interesting places for the young and attractive to meet potential partners, but for the less attractive and the over-40 crowd (especially women) who tend to be overlooked in singles bars, such places can be depressing. Thus many singles never become involved in the "singles scene" because they feel they are too old or not attractive enough, they do not live where there are such establishments, they would be embarrassed to go to such places, they are too conservative, they do not have enough money, or they have young children whom they cannot leave alone. These individuals have to resort to the more traditional ways of finding partners—through friends and family. As they grow older, single individuals, especially women, have increasing difficulty in finding partners. Since men have traditionally dated and married younger women, men of almost any age have a relatively large number of potential partners. Women, on the other hand, usually date and marry somewhat older men; thus the older a woman becomes, the fewer potential partners are available.

In spite of the sexual focus of singles apartment complexes and singles bars, attitudes have not changed to favor recreational sex in recent years. Hunt (1974) concluded that the incidence of casual sex for men had not increased from that in the preceding generation. Although the nonmarital sexual activity of women has increased, Hunt concluded that "the overall significance of our data is that while today almost any 'nice girl' will do before marriage what only the daring girl would do a generation ago, today's 'nice girl' is still guiding herself according to romantically and historically rooted values." Thus even during the so-called sexual revolution young women tended to limit their sexual relations to men with whom they had a deep emotional attachment. Presumably this holds true now during the more conservative 1990s.

Middle-aged singles usually have more sexual partners than younger singles, and after divorce or the death of a spouse, they tend to go through a stage of experimentation in which they try a number of partners (Cargan and Melko, 1982). Most eventually settle down with one partner in marriage or in a relationship similar to marriage.

In the later adult years single women have difficulty finding sexual partners for two main reasons. First, because men tend to die younger than women, there is a shortage of men; there are three women for every man over the age of 60. Second, since physical attractiveness and youth are more important components of sexual attractiveness in women than in men, women are perceived as losing their sexual attractiveness at an earlier age than men. Men can be perceived as attractive sexual partners even into old age, especially if they have other attractive characteristics such as wealth, power, and prestige. However, since physical appearance is more important in determining who men are attracted to and since men especially value youthful attractiveness, older women are typically not considered sexually attractive.

In summary, sex among singles varies greatly depending on a number of factors such as age and gender. Thus it is difficult to make generalizations about sexuality among singles. However, it appears that society's attitudes toward sex among singles are becoming more permissive and that the sexual behavior of single women is becoming less restricted.

COHABITATION

Cohabitation refers to the situation in which two adults of the opposite gender who have a sexually intimate relationship share living quarters without being married. In 1968 Linda LeClair, a Barnard College student, made national headlines when it became known that she was living off-campus with a man in violation of college regulations. Newspapers labeled Linda LeClair "Barnard's Kiss-and-Tell Girl." The publicity that surrounded the incident indicates how uncommon cohabitation was at the time. The frequency of cohabitation has increased dramatically since then. By 1986 more than 2.2 million unmarried couples were living together in the United States (U.S. Bureau of the Census, 1986). Approximately one fourth of the college students in the United States have lived with someone of the opposite sex (Macklin, 1983). The rate is even higher among the noncollege population (Tanfer, 1987). Furthermore, the prevalence of cohabitation is predicted to increase (Knox, 1980). Although cohabitation has commonly been associated with young people, it occurs among all age groups (Macklin, 1988). For example, many elderly individuals in the United States have found that cohabitation enables them to live on the pension and Social Security money for two unmarried individuals, which is more than it would be for a married couple.

Although the prevalence of cohabitation has increased, cohabitation does not appear to be replacing marriage. Most people who cohabit intend to marry at some later time (Murstein, 1986). Moreover, the majority of cohabitation arrangements either result in marriage within a relatively short period or end; few couples cohabit indefinitely (Macklin, 1988). Kotkin (1985) reported that most married individuals who cohabited before marriage lived together no longer than 2 years before marrying. Thus cohabitation does not appear to be an alternative to marriage but rather an advanced stage in the courtship process (Tanfer, 1987).

cohabitation
Relationship in which two members of the opposite gender are sexually intimate and live together without being married.

"Yes, dear, I'll try not to be late. But, confound it, Audrey, I wish you'd marry me. We can't go on like this forever."

Characteristics of Cohabitants

Some research has focused on differences between individuals who cohabit and those who do not. Cohabitants are less likely than noncohabitants to report a religious affiliation, less likely to attend church, more likely to label themselves as liberal, and more likely to report having experienced greater sexual variety (DeMaris, 1984; Newcomb, 1986; Tanfer, 1987). Furthermore, cohabitants are more likely than married couples to have divorced parents (Tanfer, 1987) and to have been previously divorced themselves (Newcomb, 1981). Both males and females who cohabit tend to be more androgynous than those who do not (Newcomb, 1981).

Life-Styles of Cohabitants

Many more cohabiting couples than married couples believe that both partners should work and contribute to the couple's expenses (Blumstein and Schwartz, 1983). Although cohabitants subscribe to more egalitarian attitudes than noncohabitants, a number of studies have found that these couples do not actually behave in an egalitarian manner (Newcomb, 1981). Even among cohabitants the women usually do much of the housework (Blumstein and Schwartz, 1983). This is true even among couples in which the men say they are sharing the housework.

Orthner (1981) suggests that although cohabitants share the expenses for food and entertainment, few couples pool all of their resources. They tend to refer to the things that the woman brought into the relationship as "her" things and the things that the man brought into the relationship as "his" things rather than referring to them as "ours." Blumstein and Schwartz (1983) discovered that the individual who brings in more money has more power in cohabitation relationships.

Blumstein and Schwartz (1983) reported that cohabiting couples have sexual intercourse more frequently than married couples. This is true regardless of how long the couples have lived together. However, as with married couples, the frequency of sexual intercourse declines with the length of the relationship. Even though cohabiting couples have sex more often than married couples, married individuals rate the quality of their sex life slightly higher than cohabiting couples. Newcomb and Bentler (1980) found evidence that cohabiting couples may be more experimental than married couples in their sexual interactions. The main difference between married and cohabiting couples was that cohabitants report more oral sex and more female-initiated sex than married couples.

Problems of Cohabitation

One problem for cohabitants is that their parents often do not approve of their cohabitation (Jackson, 1983; Macklin, 1985). In the early 1970s when middle-class couples first began cohabiting on a large scale, the general public viewed cohabitation as immoral and couples typically tried to hide the fact that they were cohabiting from their parents. Today people tend to be much more accepting of unmarried couples living together (Macklin, 1988). However, many parents are still concerned about cohabitation, particularly for their daughters (Watson, 1983; Kotkin, 1985). Probably they are concerned that their daughters might be sexually exploited in such a relationship. Furthermore, parents are typically less accepting of their son's or daughter's partner when the couple is cohabiting than when they are married. Parental opposition is a difficult and stressful situation for the cohabiting couple (Berman and Goldberg, 1986).

Another problem in some cohabiting relationships is that the two individuals have different expectations regarding the nature of the relationship (Macklin, 1988). Men are more likely than women to mention sexual gratification as their reason for cohabiting; women are more likely than men to hope that cohabitation will lead to marriage (Arafat and Yorburg, 1973). In fact, cohabitation often does not lead to marriage; only about one third of the couples who cohabit end up marrying (Clayton and Voss, 1977). Thus it is important that the two individuals involved try to understand each other's motivations and goals for cohabiting before they begin living together. Otherwise the discrepant motivations might lead to frustration, resentment, and bitterness.

Benefits of Cohabitation

The couples Macklin (1972) interviewed reported a number of benefits that resulted from their cohabitation experience. They mentioned having gained a better understanding of relationships and of their own needs, expectations, and inadequacies. They felt that they were better able to understand and get along with others as a result of their cohabitation experience. In addition, they felt that they had gained both emotional maturity and self-confidence. Furthermore, cohabiting provided the benefit of companionship with one's partner.

Kotkin (1985) asked cohabiting couples who did not want to marry what they considered to be the advantages of cohabitation. The couples mentioned such factors as the relative ease of terminating the relationship, having a greater degree of personal autonomy, and being more likely to be treated as individuals than as a couple. In addition, some women mentioned that if they married they might lose their individuality and autonomy and become subordinated to their husbands.

Effect of Cohabitation on Subsequent Marriage

A number of researchers have tried to determine whether cohabitation might result in more stable marriages. Couples who live together should have adequate opportunity to get to know each other to make better decisions about whether they should marry. However, most of the research does not support this hypothesis. Watson (1983) found that couples who cohabited before marriage actually had poorer marital adjustment during the first year of marriage than couples who had not cohabited. However, after 4 years of marriage there was no difference in the marital satisfaction of couples who had cohabited and those who had not (Watson and DeMeo, 1987). Other investigators have also found cohabitation to be related to lower marital satisfaction (DeMaris and Leslie, 1984; Booth and Johnson, 1988). Bennett, Blanc, and Bloom (1986) found that couples who cohabited before marriage were much more likely to divorce than couples who did not cohabit and that the longer the couples had cohabited, the more likely they were to divorce. Riche (1988) reported that the divorce rate is twice as high in couples who cohabited before marriage than in those who did not.

While most research on the effects of cohabitation on marital stability indicates that cohabitation does not increase stability, Newcomb and Bentler (1980) found that for individuals who had already been divorced, cohabiting before marriage seemed to be beneficial. Hanna and Knaub (1981) conducted a study to determine why cohabitation increases the strength of a remarriage. They found that couples who had cohabited before remarriage tended to have significantly more positive communication, closeness, concern for their partner's welfare, and happiness than couples who did not cohabit. Thus if one is divorced, cohabitation before remarriage appears to be beneficial.

• • •

In summary, recent decades have seen a dramatic increase in the number of heterosexual couples who live together without being married. However, cohabitation is not replacing marriage. Rather, most cohabiting couples tend to either separate or get married within a couple of years. Although cohabiting individuals usually express more egalitarian attitudes than noncohabiting individuals, their actual behavior tends to conform to traditional sex roles. Cohabiting couples differ from married couples in that they usually keep their finances separate and they tend to engage in sexual intercourse more frequently. Cohabitation presents some couples with problems because the two individuals may have different expectations for the relationship and their families may not

Divorce Data Stir Doubt on Trial Marriage

Researchers who expected the widespread practice of "trial marriage" to usher in the era of increased marital stability have been surprised by new studies showing that those Americans who lived together before marriage separate and divorce in significantly greater numbers than couples who go directly to the altar.

Within 10 years of the wedding, 38 percent of those who had lived together before marriage had split up, as against 27 percent of those who simply married, according to a study by two University of Wisconsin researchers.

The fragility of the post-cohabitation marriages was the most surprising result of the research on American households and the fluctuating patterns of family life in what one observer last year called a "post-marital society." But Larry L. Bumpass, one of two researchers analyzing the data from a 1987-1988 Federal survey of more than 13,000 individuals, cautions against jumping to the conclusion that living together before marriage somehow causes separation or divorce.

So do other sociologists. "In a sense, the meaning of marriage may be different for people who cohabit and then marry than for those who just marry." said Frank F. Furstenberg, Jr., a sociologist at the University of Pennsylvania. "I think that people who cohabit and then marry may have higher expectations in what marriage ought to offer in the way of personal intimacy, shared experience, friendship, sex, and the like. . . ."

The findings about cohabitation and divorce, said Mr. Bumpass, "don't say that these marriages are less happy than those of the people who didn't cohabit." But he guessed that "at the same level of unhappiness they're more willing to accept divorce as a solution." Mr. Bumpass has been analyzing the data from the National Survey of Family and Households along with his colleague, James A. Sweet. . . .

The people who are cohabiting are less likely to be religious or have a lot of family pressure that's going to hold them into a marriage that is unhappy or ungratifying," said Dr. Furstenberg of the University of Pennsylvania. "There are many people who stay in marriages having as little contentment as those people who eventually divorce but simply value the stability of the relationship and are unwilling to live alone. . . ."

Other findings of Mr. Bumpass and Mr. Sweet include these:

The number of people who live together before marriage continues to climb, especially for people who marry more than once: 60 percent of those who remarried between 1980 and 1987 set up housekeeping with someone, usually the eventual spouse, beforehand.

About 40 percent of the unmarried "cohabiting unions" end within a year either because the couple marry or because they split up. Only one-third of these relationships continue two years without marriage or a split; only one in 10 lasts five years or more without marriage or a split.

One-quarter of people living together marry within the first year; half have married within three years.

High-school dropouts have always been more likely to cohabit than their more educated peers, a trend that has continued into the mid-1980s. . . .

From The New York Times, June 9, 1989.

approve of the relationship. However, cohabitation also has benefits. Some individuals report that they gained a better understanding of themselves and others from cohabiting. In addition, for divorced individuals cohabitation before remarriage seems to result in a better relationship in the second marriage. For most couples, however, cohabiting before marriage does not lead to increased stability.

HOMOSEXUAL RELATIONSHIPS

Homosexuality is discussed in greater detail in Chapter 11.

Homosexual relationships are another alternative to traditional marriage. An estimated 2% of women and 4% of men in the United States are exclusively homosexual (Bell and Weinberg, 1978). The percentage of exclusively homosexual individuals has not changed since the 1940s when Kinsey and associates (1953) obtained their data. That the percentage of individuals who have an exclusively homosexual interest has not changed suggests that the factors important in the development of sexual orientation have not changed.

Attitudes toward homosexuality have changed in recent years. The increase in acceptance of homosexuality and the additional social support provided by the gay rights movement have provided an atmosphere in which more and more homosexuals have felt free to acknowledge their sexual preference openly and even to establish marriagelike homosexual relationships.

Bell and Weinberg (1978) studied both male and female homosexuals. They found that homosexuals tended to fall into five categories depending on their sexual practices and their social and psychological adjustments. The category called *close-coupled* consists of individuals who are closely bound to their partner. The two individuals look to each other for most of their sexual satisfaction and emotional closeness. These homosexuals are less likely to have sexual relationships outside of their primary relationship, to frequent gay bars or baths, to have sexual problems, or to spend leisure time by themselves and

Some homosexual couples are closely bound and look to each other for most of their sexual satisfaction and emotional closeness.

are more likely to spend evenings at home. Although these individuals do not report the highest level of sexual activity of any homosexual group, they do report more sexual activity than most homosexuals. Furthermore, they tend to be fairly satisfied with their sexual lives and report having engaged in a wide variety of sexual techniques. Their relationships are usually satisfying in other ways as well; they report that few problems arise from communication difficulties with their partners.

The couples in the close-coupled category seem to be well adjusted. They are unlikely to regret being homosexual. They are also less tense, less paranoid, less depressed and lonely, and less likely to seek professional help for personal problems than the average homosexual. In addition, they are more self-accepting and more exuberant than the average respondent.

The category Bell and Weinberg call *open-coupled* is composed of individuals who are living with sexual partners but who are less committed to their partners than are the individuals in close-coupled relationships. Open-coupled individuals tend to be less satisfied with the relationship with their partners and as a consequence rely on a larger circle of homosexual friends. These individuals spend time looking for other sexual partners in gay bars and baths. Open-coupled individuals report more sexual activity than the average homosexual, as well as a greater variety of sexual experiences.

With respect to psychological adjustments, the open-coupled individuals tend to be less happy, self-accepting, and relaxed than the close-coupled individuals. They are, however, about average in psychological adjustment when compared with homosexuals as a whole. The only exception is that the lesbians in this group are usually less self-accepting than those in any of the other groups. Furthermore, the males tend to be more self-accepting and less lonely than the females in this group. Although more of the males fell in this category than in any other category, few females did. Thus it appears that this life-style is not very desirable for women.

Bell and Weinberg call the third category of homosexuals *functionals*. The functionals are individuals who do not have one special sexual partner and are not particularly interested in finding one. These individuals seem to organize their lives around sexual activity. They report more sexual activity with a greater number of partners than do any of the other groups. These individuals are the least likely to be concerned about being homosexuals and are the most involved with the gay community. The people in this category tend to be energetic, cheerful, optimistic, and self-reliant and to have many friends. Probably because of their open involvement with the gay community, these individuals are the most likely to have been in legal trouble involving their sexual orientation.

The fourth category is *dysfunctionals*. The dysfunctionals are the most likely to regret their sexual orientation and the most likely to report having sexual problems and sexual worries. They seem to have great difficulty finding a permanent sexual partner, although they apparently try. Other aspects of their lives also indicate a poor adjustment. This group has a higher proportion of arrests and convictions for crimes such as robbery, assault, and extortion. These individuals are more lonely, paranoid, depressed, tense, and unhappy than most of the other homosexuals. They are also the most likely to have been involved in long-term professional counseling for their emotional problems.

The fifth category is the *asexual* category. The individuals in this category report low levels of sexual activity, few partners, and little sexual experience. They feel that they are not sexually attractive and report having a number of sexual problems. These individuals spend most of their time alone and report themselves to be lonely and unhappy. Despite their lonely feelings, the individuals in this group are not likely to frequent places where they might meet other people.

Bell and Weinberg's study (1978) illustrates the fact that, like heterosexuals, homosexuals choose a variety of living and sexual arrangements. The first two categories of homosexual individuals, those who live with sexual partners, are similar to married or cohabiting heterosexuals. The functionals are like heterosexual "swinging singles." The dysfunctionals and asexuals exhibit characteristics common to the less social heterosexual singles. Since the results of the Bell and Weinberg study illustrate that homosexuals choose a variety of life-styles, they indicate that many of the stereotypes people hold about the homosexual life-style are inaccurate because they are much too narrow.

Some researchers have investigated ways in which gay and lesbian couples differ. This research suggests that compared with gay men, lesbian women report better relationships, which is defined by satisfaction with the relationship and by the degree of love and liking of one's partner (Kurdek, 1989). Lesbian couples tend to place greater importance on reciprocal expressiveness and equality of power in their relationships. Researchers have attributed this tendency to the effects of socialization. More specifically, women generally learn through socialization to define themselves in terms of relationships with others, to be caring and nurturant with others, and to subdue aggressive and competitive urges. Furthermore, many lesbians endorse feminist beliefs that stress equality. In both homosexual and heterosexual relationships egalitarian or role-free relationships appear to result in more reported satisfaction than gender role–typed relationships (Marecek, Finn, and Cardell, 1982; Peplau, Padesky, and Hamilton, 1982).

In comparison with heterosexual relationships, both gay and lesbian relationships carry a stronger tendency toward egalitarian decision making (Harry, 1988). Decision-making power in heterosexual relationships is commonly based on gender, income difference, and age difference (Blumstein and Schwartz, 1983). With respect to homosexual couples, several forces function to diminish the inequality the above factors would create. There are no gender differences to create inequality in the relationship. However, income differences do play a part, at least with male couples. If there is a significant income difference between gay partners, the one making more tends to have the greater power. However, many gay couples reduce the potential power imbalance by keeping their incomes separate.

In lesbian relationships an income difference is not likely to lead to a power difference as it would in a heterosexual or gay relationship (Blumstein and Schwartz, 1983). Researchers have explained this difference between male and female homosexuals by pointing to the different gender roles of males and females. Whether homosexual or heterosexual, men tend to evaluate themselves and other men by their income and other achievements. Women are much less likely to gauge their value or another woman's value according to the amount of money she makes. In addition, many lesbian women describe themselves as feminist or at least are sensitive to the inequalities associated with the female gender role (Harry, 1988). Therefore lesbians have a stronger tendency to use personal characteristics rather than income as evaluative criteria.

Age differences tend to lead to disparate power in decision making in homosexual relationships just as they do in heterosexual relationships (Harry, 1984). Gay males 5 years older than their partners generally have a greater influence in the relationship. (Comparable data are not available for lesbian couples.) Age and income may combine to create the unequal relationship, since partners who are older than their mates tend to make more money as well.

Sexual exclusiveness appears to be based more on gender than on an individual's sexual orientation. Blumstein and Schwartz (1983) found that 18% of the gay males in their study had been sexually exclusive or monogamous, compared with 72% of the lesbian females. Furthermore, according to available, perhaps out-of-date, research only about half of heterosexual husbands are exclusive, whereas four fifths of married women reported that they had not engaged in any extramarital relationships (Kinsey, Pomeroy, and Martin, 1948; Hunt, 1974). Nonetheless, the research suggests that gay men are generally less exclusive than lesbian women in a manner that parallels the differences in exclusiveness between married heterosexual men and women. The AIDS epidemic has probably increased the percentage of partners in relationships maintaining sexual exclusiveness, expecially among male homosexuals.

While sexual nonexclusiveness does not affect relationship quality of homosexual couples (Kurdek, 1988), nonexclusiveness plays a different role in gay than in lesbian relationships. Male couples often agree that both partners are free to have sexual contacts outside their relationship; casual sexual relations generally are not a threat to the primary relationship. However, an ongoing affair or relationship with another man would be considered a threat to the primary relationship.

Most lesbians prefer to be monogamous in their serious relationships (Clunis and Green, 1988). When lesbians involved in a serious relationship are nonexclusive, contrary to their agreed monogamy, they tend to have affairs rather than engaging in casual sex. When lesbian women engage in an outside affair, they are more likely to be unhappy with their primary relationship than are gay men who are nonmonogamous. Nonexclusiveness is therefore more likely to be a sign of trouble in a lesbian relationship.

Legal Recognition of Homosexual Relationships

Millions of couples each year marry, triggering an assortment of rights and presumptions: among other things, a married person can share in a spouse's estate even when there is no will; the spouse is typically entitled to group insurance and pension programs provided by the husband's or wife's employers; and the couple enjoys tax advantages. Marriage also creates the presumption that the couple is committed to stay together forever. Although some churches have begun to recognize homosexual marriages, no state yet permits two individuals of the same sex to marry.

Contrastingly, several European countries, including the Netherlands and Sweden, have begun to grant rights to homosexual couples. In 1989 Denmark became the first country to allow homosexual couples to enter into "registered partnerships," giving the couples many of the rights of married heterosexuals.

Denmark gives homosexual couples inheritance rights to each other's property, demands that they undertake legal divorce proceedings to dissolve a registered relationship, and may force one party to pay alimony upon divorce.

In the United States 22 states still have sodomy laws. Six of these states ban only homosexual sodomy. As mentioned previously, no state provides rights to homosexual partnerships that heterosexual married couples enjoy. Nevertheless, over the last few years several cities have passed "domestic partners" laws allowing unwed couples to register their relationship. Such ordinances exist in Seattle; Santa Cruz, California; San Francisco; and Madison, Wisconsin. Just what such ordinances include depends on the city; none comes close to providing benefits equivalent to those of heterosexual marriage, such as tax benefits, automatic inheritance, and custody rights. The San Francisco domestic partner law allows a homosexual's partner the same hospital visitation rights given to married couples (see the accompanying box). In addition, city employees in the domestic partnership have the same bereavement leave policy as married city workers. Because of the AIDS epidemic, these benefits are critical issues to San Francisco's gay community. Other domestic partner laws allow city employees health care benefits that have otherwise been limited to individuals within the traditionally defined family.

Another approach used to provide homosexual partners with rights previously limited to heterosexual couples is the expansion of the definition of "family." New York State's highest court recently decided that two gay men living together for a decade could be considered a family under New York City's rent control regulations. Proponents of expanding the definition of family to include homosexual partnerships encourage describing a family by function rather than by structure. Functions constituting a "family" would include supporting physical health and safety of members, maintaining conditions for emotional growth, helping to shape a "belief system," and establishing shared responsibility. While some argue that homosexuals will continue to hold only a subsidiary status to heterosexuals until they are able to legally marry one another, some gay rights leaders and their supporters prefer expansion of the concept of family rather than a legal recognition of homosexuals in traditionally heterosexual marital rights that many feminists find oppressive (Gutis, 1989). Others argue that domestic partnerships, to the extent that they provide equivalent rights to marriage, would give homosexual couples the legal recognition they desire without the oppression some find in the institution of marriage.

Domestic partnerships, like marriage, also include the presumption that the partners are committed to the relationship. Many gay rights activists urge legal recognition of homosexual partnerships because they believe a legal commitment may encourage partners to work through problems rather than leave a relationship when difficulties arise.

In summary, although the number of individuals who consider themselves to be exclusively homosexual has remained relatively stable in recent years, homosexuals have demonstrated a greater willingness to publicly acknowledge their sexual orientation. The increase in public acknowledgement is probably a result both of more liberal attitudes toward homosexuality and of an increase in the social support offered by the gay liberation movement. Homosexuals adopt a variety of life-styles, from those much like heterosexual singles to those similar to heterosexual marriages.

A Personal Glimpse

Woman's Hospital Visit Marks Gay Rights Fight

Karen Thompson walked into Sharon Kowalski's room at the Miller-Dwan Medical Center in Duluth, Minn., last week and said quietly: "Hi, Sharon. Do you remember me?"

Ms. Thompson said the meeting, their first in three and a half years, was "an emotionally overwhelming moment." The two women had exchanged wedding bands and shared a home in St. Cloud until Ms. Kowalski was paralyzed and suffered brain injuries in an automobile accident [in which her car was struck by a drunk driver] in November 1983. [She had lost the capacity to walk or to speak more than several words at a time and needed constant care.]

Behind the reunion was a series of bitter court battles between Ms. Thompson . . . and Ms. Kowalski's parents. . . . The dispute was over who had the right to make decisions for the 32-year-old Ms. Kowalski. . . .

Processions and Vigils

The case became a cause celebre and an important symbol around the country for groups who advocate gay rights, rights for the disabled and women's rights. Processions and vigils were organized in 21 cities on Aug. 7 to mark "National Free Sharon Kowalski Day."

The conflict over Ms. Kowalski began soon after the accident when Ms. Thompson told the Kowalskis about the nature of her relationship with their daughter. In an out-of-court agreement, Mr. Kowalski became guardian but Ms. Thompson retained broad visiting rights. In July 1985, asserting that Ms. Thompson was a detrimental and depressing influence, as he has throughout the case, Mr. Kowalski sought and received unconditional guardianship.

In 24 hours he had Ms. Thompson and other friends barred from any contact with Ms. Kowalski, including mail. In the ensuing years Ms. Thompson went to state and Federal courts on numerous occasions seeking revocation of Mr. Kowalski's guardianship, but losing at every level until last year. . . .

[In September as part of a reevaluation of Ms. Kowalski's mental competency, a judge ruled] that it was up to the hospital to decide who could visit Ms. Kowalski, to be determined according to "her reliably expressed wishes."

So Ms. Thompson and three other friends were permitted to visit Ms. Kowalski. Ms. Thompson said she arrived Thursday and stayed all day Friday, Saturday and Sunday and was asked to participate in psychological, speech and occupational therapy sessions. Psychologists at the hospital had prepared Ms. Kowalski for the encounter but Ms. Thompson said: "She seemed shocked at first. She immediately got tears in her eyes and I broke down, though I had vowed to remain calm. But for the rest of the weekend, she was all smiles and laughs.

Ms. Kowalski communicated mainly through whispering, shakes of the head, a keyboard that can be programmed to say sentences and an alphabet board.

"I told her I needed to know what she thought of me before I could pursue the fight for her, and she spelled out the word, 'lover.'" Ms. Thompson said, "It was very clear and very consistent that she thinks of me as her partner and wants to come live with me."

Donald Kowalski said yesterday, as he has many times before, that he refused to believe that his daughter was a lesbian. [He said in a telephone interview:] "I've never seen anything that would make me believe it, and I will not change my mind until Sharon is capable of telling me in her own words. . . ."

From Brozan, 1989.

SUMMARY

1 There is a positive relationship between emotional closeness in a marriage and sexual satisfaction.

2 The frequency of sexual relations in marriage decreases over time. Couples in their early twenties report having sexual intercourse an average of about three times a week. By the age of 55 the average is less than once per week. Both biological and psychological factors may be responsible for the decrease in sexual relations with time.

3 Most Americans believe that sexual fidelity is an important part of marriage, yet about half of all married individuals become involved in an extramarital sexual relationship. Research indicates that the more emotionally and sexually deprived individuals feel in their marriages, the more likely they are to become involved in extramarital relationships.

4 Divorced men are more likely to become sexually involved after the termination of their marriage than are women. Divorced women are more likely to become involved in postmarital sexual relationships than are widowed women.

5 Remarriage is becoming more frequent. Approximately four out of every five adults who divorce will eventually remarry.

6 An increasing number of individuals in our society are single because people are getting married at a later age, getting divorced more often, and choosing to remain single more often.

7 Remaining single appears to have a more negative effect on men than on women; single men tend to be in poorer physical and mental health than married men.

8 Although the incidence of cohabitation is on the rise, cohabitation does not appear to be replacing marriage. Rather, cohabiting couples tend either to separate after a short period of time or to get married.

9 Most cohabiting couples conform to traditional sex roles in their division of labor, and they tend to be monogamous. However, they are more likely than married couples to keep their finances separate and they have sexual intercourse more frequently.

10 Cohabitation presents some couples with difficulties. Two of the most prevalent problems are family disapproval and partners' dissimilar expectations of the relationship.

11 Cohabitation also seems to have a few benefits. Some individuals report that they learned more about themselves and about relationships from cohabiting. In addition, some couples prefer cohabitation because it is easier to terminate the relationship, the partners have greater personal autonomy, and they are more likely to be treated as individuals than as a couple.

12 For divorced individuals cohabitation before remarriage seems to have a beneficial effect on the second marriage. However, for the majority of couples, premarital cohabitation does not increase marital satisfaction or stability. In fact, couples who cohabit before marriage tend to be less satisfied and more likely to divorce.

13 Although the number of individuals who consider themselves to be exclusively homosexual has not increased much in recent years, there has been more public acknowledgment of their sexual orientation. This greater willingness to be open about their sexuality is probably a result of both more

liberal attitudes toward homosexuality and an increase in the social support offered by the gay liberation movement.

14 Bell and Weinberg found that homosexual relationships tend to fall into five categories: close-coupled, open-coupled, functionals, dysfunctionals, and asexuals.

15 Lesbian couples tend to report greater relationship satisfaction and more love and liking for their partners than gay couples.

16 Homosexual relationships tend to be more egalitarian than heterosexual relationships.

17 Men, whether heterosexual or homosexual, tend to be less sexually exclusive than women.

ANSWERS

1 Close to half of all married individuals report having had at least one extramarital relationship.

2 Research has indicated that widowed and divorced men have sexual intercourse more frequently than do married men, and divorced women have intercourse with about the same frequency as married women. The frequency for widowed women is lower than that for married women.

3 Single women of all ages appear to be both physically and mentally healthier than single men.

F A C T
OR
F I C T I O N

QUESTIONS FOR THOUGHT ?

1 Couples who live together before marriage are no more likely to stay married than couples who do not. Why do you think living together does not increase the likelihood of a successful marriage?

2 How do you think you would feel if your spouse had an extramarital affair? What would you do if your spouse had an extramarital affair?

3 Why do you think the frequency of sexual intercourse decreases over time in a relationship?

4 What would be the advantages for you in being single rather than married?

5 What would be the advantages for you in being married rather than single?

SUGGESTED READINGS

Atwater, L: The extramarital connection, New York, 1982, Irvington Publishers, Inc.
A study of extramarital relationships of women.

Blumstein, P., and Schwartz, P.: American couples, New York, 1983, William Morrow & Co., Inc.
A report of a study of the lives of American couples, including married, cohabiting, and homosexual couples. The study included an investigation of the effects of money, work, and sex on the lives of the couples.

Cargan, L., and Melko, M.: Singles: myths and realities, Beverly Hills, Calif., 1982, Sage Publications, Inc.
A report of a study dealing with single and married life-styles.

Englebardt, L.S.: Living together: what's the law? New York, 1981, Crown Publishers, Inc.
A book that examines the legal aspects of cohabitation.

Perlman, D., and Duck, S.: Intimate relationships: development, dynamics and deterioration, Beverly Hills, Calif., 1987, Sage Publications, Inc.
A collection of readings covering a variety of aspects of intimate relationships.

16

Sexuality and Disabilities

FACT
OR
FICTION

1
Society's attitudes often cause difficulties for the disabled.

2
Body image and self-esteem are important factors in sexual functioning in both individuals with and those without disabilities.

3
A woman with spinal cord injury cannot carry a pregnancy to term.

Dear Abby: Our daughter is 28 and a nurse. She took a job several thousand miles from home and has been gone nearly a year. We were hoping she'd come home last Christmas, but she said she'd come home this summer and bring her fiance. She has written about a young man whom she'd fallen in love with, describing his "beautiful attitudes, brilliant mind and outstanding character."

Now we know why she didn't bring him home for Christmas. He's an amputee. He lost both legs just below the knee in an accident. We learned this yesterday from a letter she wrote us.

We are heartsick. She's such a beautiful girl and could easily get a whole man. Abby, how do parents adjust to knowing their daughter will spend the rest of her life caring for an invalid?—Brokenhearted Parents.

ABIGAIL VAN BUREN
"Dear Abby"

The parents of the woman in our introductory story were greatly distressed because they believed their daughter would spend the rest of her life nursing her husband, an invalid. In their love and concern for their daughter, they did not understand that losing a body part or body function does not make someone a fraction of a person. As many as 20% of people in the United States have spinal cord injuries, cardiovascular disease, diabetes, or vision or hearing impairment. In addition, many have diseases, such as arthritis, cerebral palsy, and multiple sclerosis, that decrease mobility and reduce sexual desires and behaviors. Any illness or disease that affects mobility, well-being, self-esteem, or body image has the potential to affect sexual expression.

This chapter deals with sexuality and disabilities. The following quotation from Cole and Cole (1978) conveys the message of the chapter:

> A stiff penis does not make a solid relationship, nor does a wet vagina.
> Urinary incontinence does not mean genital incompetence.
> Absence of sensation does not mean absence of feelings.
> Inability to move does not mean inability to please.
> The presence of deformities does not mean the absence of desire.
> Inability to perform does not mean inability to enjoy.
> Loss of genitals does not mean loss of sexuality.
>
> Cole and Cole, 1978, p. 118

SPINAL CORD–INJURED ADULTS AND SEXUALITY

Glass (1977) presents an excellent account of the psychological problems confronting men and women with spinal cord damage:

> Imagine an able-bodied male athlete, strong, well muscled, with an attractive body, unquestionably a potentially desirable sex partner. Now imagine an athlete in a wheelchair. Is this also a potentially desirable sex partner, or does the wheelchair get in the way? Now imagine a pretty . . . female, again desirable and appealing. Let us look now at the . . . girl in the wheelchair, with atrophy of the muscles, the breasts, some difficulty in maintaining position—is this . . . pretty, desirable, sexually appealing? Close your eyes and recollect the last time you had sex, either intercourse, masturbation, or fantasy. Think of the room, the bed, how your skin felt, how your body parts felt, inside, your genitals, your legs, how you

moved. Now store that, and imagine yourself paralyzed from the breasts down, no sensation, no movement in your lower body and limbs, your muscles wasted away, wearing a catheter with a bag full of yellow urine. Contrast this with how you felt at the time of your last lovemaking. I think you can begin to conceive of some of the problems that the disabled have regarding their own self-concept and body image, and the difficulties professionals often have in dealing with the sexuality of people with visible deformity.

Glass, 1977, p. 181

As Anita Siler, a counselor of the disabled and disabled herself, aptly states, "We are all born sexual beings. Some of us also happen to have disabilities. If this chapter has any message it is that everyone is a person first, and some are disabled second" (Siler, personal communication, 1987).

This section is concerned both with the sexual behavior of adults with spinal cord injuries and with society's attitudes toward them. Negative attitudes toward the physically disabled are common. In 1979 Haring and Meyerson asked 100 college-age students to complete sentences regarding their attitudes about the sexuality of physically disabled women. Each completed sentence was viewed as expressing either a positive or a negative attitude toward the physically disabled. The percentages of students with negative attitudes toward various aspects of the sexuality of the handicapped are shown in Table 16-1.

Much remains to be learned about spinal cord injuries and sexual functioning. This section presents the most widely accepted current ideas, but the reader should realize that there are numerous exceptions to the generalizations proposed. A great deal of new information is available on the topic of spinal cord injury because of the large number of Vietnam veterans and accident victims with spinal injuries.

lesion
(LEE zhuhn) Injury or wound.

Many factors must be considered in studying spinal cord injury and sexuality. Determining the level of the injury or **lesion** within the spinal cord is important because the level and extent of the injury determine what functions are lost. The lesion might be located in the region of one of the "erection centers" or near the spinal area controlling ejaculation. Whether the lesion is incomplete, with the cord partially severed, or complete, with the cord totally severed, also influences which sexual functions are affected.

TABLE 16-1 Attitudes Toward Sexuality of the Physically Disabled

Aspect of sexuality	Students reporting negative reaction	
	Females (%)	Males (%)
A disabled young woman naked	100	90
A disabled young woman masturbating	54	54
Sexual intercourse between a disabled young woman and a nondisabled man	8	8
Adequacy of sexual functioning of a disabled woman	48	70
Enjoyment of sex by a disabled woman	50	51
Sex needs of a disabled woman	40	47
Amount of sex knowledge possessed by a disabled woman	28	36

Modified from Haring and Meyerson, 1979.

Sexual activity is decreased among adults with spinal cord injury, and researchers have attempted to determine whether these individuals really want to engage in sexual activity. Apparently the answer is yes. Glass (1977) did a small study of 34 men and 21 women with spinal injuries. Slightly more than half indicated that they felt uncomfortable carrying out sexual activity. One third of the men and one half of the women said that they feared sexual activity after they were disabled. The reasons for this response varied. Some found that the loss of bladder and bowel control inhibited sexual expression. Others feared that they might not be able to achieve an erection. For some the inability to move made sexual expression awkward. Sexual satisfaction, interest in sex, and frequency of sexual activity after the disability depended on sexual activity and adjustment before the disability. Changes most often noted in sexual activity after disability involved the need for change in position, the need for the spinal cord–injured person to be more passive during sex (Figure 16-1), increased use of masturbation for both the disabled and their partners, and increased use of oral sex by both partners. Heart rate, blood pressure, breath-

Many people are able to overcome their disability and have satisfying sexual relationships.

ing, and myotonia increase during sexual activity in persons with spinal cord lesions, although pelvic vasocongestion and vaginal lubrication decrease in spinal cord–injured women.

To determine the kinds of sexual activities affected most, researchers have examined the effect of spinal injury on erection and ejaculation in men and on orgasm in men and women.

Male Sexual Functioning

reflexogenic
(ri FLEK soh jen′ ik) Reflex action caused by physical stimulation.

The two types of erections, reflexogenic and psychogenic, are discussed in Chapter 5.

Some men with spinal cord injury have **reflexogenic** erections but cannot produce an erection through erotic thought (psychogenic erection). Other men can have both types of erection, but many men cannot have either. The type of erection or inability to produce a particular type is related to the level of the lesion in the spinal cord and whether it is incomplete or complete. Estimates from different studies suggest that 48% to 92% of men retain erectile capacity after spinal cord injury (Higgins, 1979). If the lesion is high in the spinal cord, men are usually able to produce a reflex erection, but lower lesions usually eliminate erectile capability.

The information on ejaculatory capability in spinal cord–injured men should be viewed as tentative in the absence of systematic studies (Higgins, 1979). In various studies ejaculatory capability ranges from none to 7% of men with complete lesions of the cord and from 27% to 32% of those with incomplete lesions. A greater percentage of men with lower lesions than of those with higher lesions are able to ejaculate. It has been estimated that the ability to ejaculate is lost by 90% of spinal cord–injured males (Kolodny, Masters, and Johnson, 1979).

Female Sexual Functioning

Women with spinal cord injury usually have transient amenorrhea, but menstrual flows resume within 6 months of the injury (Young, Katz, and Klein, 1983). Their ability to have children is the same as it was before the accident. Pregnancy is normal in most cases, and in the great majority the baby is born vaginally. Researchers have observed that many women who had previously experienced orgasms lose that ability after spinal damage. However, other women have reported having the subjective experience of orgasm even though no sensations are generated in the genital area.

Researchers questioned 24 spinal cord–injured women between the ages of 20 and 40 years about their feelings of self-esteem and attractiveness and about their sexual response before and after spinal cord injury (Fitting et al., 1978). Most of the women viewed themselves as attractive both before and after the accident, and 85% were also involved in sexual activities after the accident. However, they said they did not resume sex for a while after the accident, and the first couple of years after the accident were the hardest for them. These women enjoyed their sexual relationships, but many said they were concerned about changes in bowel and bladder function that inhibited sexual expression.

Male and Female Fertility

Fertility is impaired in most men with spinal injuries, although the exact mechanism is not known. Sperm production is reduced in some individuals, and erection and ejaculation present the greatest difficulties. Testicular atrophy or elevated testicular temperature may be a cause of infertility. When atrophy occurs, it is within several months of the injury. Some researchers suggest that ejaculated sperm be obtained and stored soon after the injury for possible later use. Women experience little reduction in fertility as a result of spinal cord injuries.

Pregnancy and Birth

Pregnancy and birth are common in spinal cord–injured women because of the increasing number of young survivors of spinal cord injury. Pregnancy and birth in these women pose such complications as anemia, bedsores, premature labor, recurrent urinary tract infection caused by indwelling catheters, and **autonomic hyperreflexia,** which is life threatening if not treated (Young, Katz, and Klein, 1983).

The most common problems during pregnancy are recurrent urinary tract infections, including **cystitis.** The risk for these infections increases during pregnancy, but they can be treated to prevent involvement of the kidneys. Another common condition during pregnancy is **anemia.** Paraplegic women are more likely to have complications of anemia because of their greater tendency for pressure sores (bedsores). They are more susceptible to infection because of decreased tissue resistance and because they are often in one position for long periods. Blood transfusions and orally administered iron therapy have been used to restore normal blood cell count. Bedsores are common in late pregnancy and can lead to infections. They are treated with physical therapy and aggressive care.

autonomic hyperreflexia
(HY per re FLEK see uh) Exaggerated response by the autonomic nervous system in response to the birth process.

cystitis
(si STY tis) Inflammation or infection of the bladder.

anemia
(uh NEE mee uh) Reduced number of circulating red blood cells.

Many women with physical disabilities can go through a normal pregnancy and birth.

The most common problems during parturition (birth) are premature labor (before the fortieth week of pregnancy) and autonomic hyperreflexia. In most cases labor proceeds rapidly and painlessly with stronger and more frequent contractions than are usually seen in labor (Young, Katz, and Klein, 1983). The syndrome of autonomic hyperreflexia is common, and the women describe extreme fear, anxiety, profuse sweating, abnormally rapid heartbeat, and high blood pressure. Less frequent symptoms are headache, nasal congestion, and abnormally slow heartbeat. The symptoms of hyperreflexia are intermittent and of variable duration. Autonomic hyperreflexia is treated with various antianxiety and sedative drugs along with drugs to treat high blood pressure and respiratory tract congestion.

Fetal heart rate monitoring shows bursts of rapid heartbeats coinciding with episodes of maternal autonomic hyperreflexia. Delivery of the baby usually occurs through the vagina, and anesthesia is unnecessary because of lack of sensation in the perineum.

Orgasmic Capability in Males and Females

Scientists can make only the most tentative generalizations about orgasm or orgasmlike phenomena in persons with spinal cord injury. Subjective sensations of orgasm may accompany ejaculation, but these are not always accompanied by the physiological reactions of orgasm, such as increased heart rate, elevated

A Counselor of the Disabled Talks About Sexuality and Disabilities

Centers for independent living have recently been opened in many communities. Most are resource centers for the severely disabled, and ideally are staffed and governed by disabled persons. Often with their help the disabled person learns to cope with everyday life, how to live in the least restrictive environment, to live as independently as possible, and to become an involved member of the community. Certainly one area of concern for each of these people has been sexuality and disability.

We are all born sexual human beings. Some of us also happen to have disabilities. But it is not abnormal to be disabled; it is simply a part of life. With this in mind, a foremost challenge to all of us is to continually fight the "myth of perfection." Every television show, every movie stresses perfection. Yet few of us—able-bodied or not—are a perfect 10, or 7, or 5.

In the area of sexuality the most frequent requests for help at our center come from those who have newly acquired disabilities or progressive disabilities such as multiple sclerosis, arthritis, or muscular dystrophy. Many times the spouse of a person with such a disability feels he or she is unable to cope with it and will ask to speak to another whose spouse is disabled. (Such is the nature of "peer helping.") Another major problem we have seen in working with the severely disabled is the difficulty of their finding a suitable partner with whom to

share feelings or sexual expressions. In this country we do not have a "touchy" society. If giving someone a big hug is often frowned on, how much more inappropriate is it thought to touch a disabled person? Consequently, so many severely disabled children and adults are starved for any form of touch and are prevented even more from any form of sexual expression. If one is the handsome, masculine actor in a wheelchair in the movie *Coming Home*, no problem. Again, there is that myth of perfection. As a counselor, what do you say to the young man who sits spastically twisted in his wheelchair, but with above average mental capability, and asks, "But why won't anyone see me as a man? All I want is a friend. All I want is someone who will see me as a nice guy. I have the same feelings and the same urges as anyone else, but no one will even let me talk about them, much less express them."

If there is any message that is conveyed, it is that everyone is a person first, and some are disabled second. We must be proud of our maleness and femaleness, and when it comes to sexuality, the disabled are no different from anyone else. We all have feelings about ourselves and feelings about others, and that is basically what sexuality is all about. The choice of how each of us expresses our sexuality is *ours* to make. The sexuality itself cannot be ignored, though the medical profession traditionally tries valiantly to do so. It is a rarity to find a physician willing to discuss sexual concerns with a severely disabled person.

Perhaps we who are reading this book can take a step in the right direction by reaching out to someone. We all need more touching. And those of us who are disabled must make an effort to reach out to others. We must become experts on our own disabilities and our own sexuality. We must become comfortable with receiving someone's touch or look of tenderness and concern. We must be in control of our own bodies. We must have privacy. We must know ourselves, and appreciate ourselves, and then at least some concerns about our sexuality may be resolved.

From Anita Siler, M.A., Counselor/Case Manager, Independence Inc., Lawrence, Kansas.

blood pressure, and increased respiration. Thus the individual subjectively experiences orgasm but does not have total body involvement. Some persons experience the subjective sensation of orgasm and the physiological reactions without ejaculation. Prior sexual experience plays a role in the subjective experience of orgasm in spinal cord–injured men and women.

In a unique situation a woman who had participated in studies of human sexual response at the Masters and Johnson Institute while she was in good health returned for studies after sustaining a spinal cord injury in an automobile accident (Kolodny, Masters, and Johnson, 1979). Her responses before injury were typical of those described in Chapter 5, although she did not derive much pleasure or excitement from breast stimulation. After the injury, a complete spinal cord lesion at the level of the lower chest, she lost all pelvic sensation and gradually found that her breasts were becoming sensitive to erotic stimulation. Six months after her injury she said that she experienced orgasm as a result of breast stimulation. When technicians monitored this woman's physiological changes in the laboratory during breast stimulation, they noted that heart rate and respirations increased in response to sexual excitation and that changes in the breast and nipples were also normal. However, there was no significant pelvic vasocongestion or vaginal lubrication. In the late portion of the plateau phase of the response cycle, which was judged by breast changes, the lips of the woman's mouth became engorged to twice their normal size. At the moment of orgasm observers noticed a pulsating wave in her lips; then the swelling dissipated rapidly. This pattern was almost identical to the pattern of dissipation of the orgasmic platform in nondisabled women. This case illustrates the ability of spinal cord–injured adults to unconsciously transfer erotic zones from one region of the body to another, in this woman the transfer of a physiological erotic reflex from its ordinary location in the vagina to a remote location in the lips of the mouth. This ability has been observed in both men and women.

Bors and Coman (1960) made some observations concerning the erotic zones of spinal cord–injured men:

> Others in this group reported feelings of sexual excitement due to stimulation of erogenous zones, especially the nipples. And two reported what they considered to be peculiar erogenous zones which had appeared since injury, in the center of the back, just above the existing sensory level (where they still had sensations). They said that stimulation of these areas caused some feelings of sexual tension and they felt pressure to continue the contact.
>
> Bors and Coman, 1960, p. 200

CARDIOVASCULAR DISEASE AND SEXUALITY

The activity of the heart and blood vessels increases dramatically during sexual activity. Men and women with high blood pressure, heart pain caused by lack of oxygen, diseases of the valves and muscles of the heart, diseases of the blood vessels such as hardening of the arteries, and **myocardial infarction** (heart attack) may experience negative changes in sexual performance and activities. These negative changes occur because of the disorder, because of psychological problems such as fear of death from exertion during sexual intercourse, because of doubting of attractiveness to the partner, or because of medicines prescribed

myocardial infarction
(my' oh KAR dee uhl in fark shuhn) Development of an infarct (area of tissue that dies because of loss of blood supply) in the heart muscle.

HUMAN SEXUALITY

With the counsel and advice of a physician, people with heart disease can continue to engage in sexual activities.

to treat cardiovascular disease. Certain medicines that control high blood pressure interfere with erection or ejaculation, and many of these drugs interfere with the autonomic nervous system, which is critical for normal functioning.

Many men and women wonder if they should stop sexual activity after a heart attack or after they are told they have a disease of the heart or blood vessels. They wonder how much energy is used during intercourse and whether that energy expenditure is enough to cause them harm. It has been estimated that sexual activity decreases or stops for 58% to 75% of all couples when the man has a heart attack (Joy of sex, 1985).

More than 14 million Americans of all ages have some sort of heart or blood vessel ailment (Wagner and Sivarajan, 1979). Physicians tell people to cut back on smoking, drinking, and eating, to keep weight under control, to reduce cholesterol levels, and to engage in moderate physical exercise on a regular basis. However, physicians and patients often do not discuss sexual activity, and many times patients reduce or eliminate sex because of their limited knowledge, fears, and superstitions (Wagner and Sivarajan, 1979).

Some information on the human sexual response cycle (see Chapter 5) has come from older people with heart disease. These data indicate that the physiological measurements of Masters and Johnson (1966) may have been biased because of the young ages of the study participants and the artificial laboratory conditions under which the measurements were taken. Masters and Johnson's subjects showed much higher increases in heart rate than did a sample of patients after heart attack (Johnston and Fletcher, 1979). Hellerstein and Friedman (1970) studied a group of middle-aged patients with heart disease and concluded that the amount of energy they expended during intercourse was modest. Other researchers have confirmed these findings in younger patients after heart attack (Wagner and Sivarajan, 1979). Physiological measurements from the Masters and Johnson Institute, then, are higher than those observed in private settings. In these studies of people who have just had heart attacks,

Masters and Johnson have recorded dramatic increases in heart rate, blood pressure, and respiratory rates during sexual intercourse and orgasm, as reported in Chapter 4.

the average maximum heart rate during sexual intercourse and orgasm was 114 to 117 beats per minute, with an absolute maximum of 140 beats per minute. Apparently, if patients can climb two flights of stairs without symptoms such as chest pain and extreme fatigue, they can resume sexual activity with their usual partners. "This is based on the belief that energy expenditure for middle-aged men during sexual activity with their usual partner is approximately equal to that of climbing two flights of stairs" (Wagner and Sivarajan, 1979).

A study of 10 couples was done to compare cardiac stress during various sexual activities with stress during walking (Joy of sex, 1985). The findings were as follows:

1. During a slow walk the average pulse for the men rose from 64 to 102 beats per minute.
2. Touching one's partner without intercourse and self-stimulation is the least stressful; in the 3 to 6 minutes before orgasm, the average pulse rate for the men rose from 64 to 102, the same as during a slow walk.
3. Sexual intercourse with the woman on top produced an average heart rate of 110 beats per minute at orgasm.
4. Sexual intercourse with the man on top produced an average heart rate of 127 beats per minute, which is less exertion than moderate walking or mowing the lawn. In most cases for the behaviors studied the peak heart rate lasted only 10 to 16 seconds.

In a study of 130 middle-aged and older women it was evident that heart attacks had a negative effect on sexual functioning and behaviors (Papadopoulos et al., 1983). Eight-four (65%) of the patients had been sexually active before the heart attack, but after the heart attack 27% did not resume sexual activity, 44% resumed with decreased frequency, 27% resumed with unchanged frequency, and one patient increased activity because she remarried.

The reasons given by the women for the decline in sexual activity were loss of sex drive, the woman's or her partner's fear of another heart attack during sexual activity, use of the heart attack as an excuse to end sexual relations (the women did not enjoy sex before the heart attack), or the husband's use of the heart attack as an excuse to stop (the men had difficulty maintaining an erection before the heart attack). In addition, couples who continued to engage in sexual activities discontinued the use of the woman-on-top position, oral sex, and masturbation.

When comparing the findings of studies of women who had had heart attacks with those of men, several similarities are noted (Papadopoulos, 1978, 1985; Papadopoulos et al., 1983): these are a decrease in sexual activity, an increase in patient fears about having chest pains or another heart attack during sexual intercourse, and the elimination of a variety of sexual techniques. More women than men expressed fears of resuming sexual activity, and only the women were worried that they might not be sexually attractive to their partners after a heart attack.

Papadopoulos (1985) concludes that all patients who have had heart attacks, and in particular middle-aged and older men and women, must receive some counseling from their physician. Such counseling should be aimed at relieving fears and anxieties and should lead to successful physical rehabilitation that will give the patients confidence about their future, including their sexual future.

Some researchers think that physicians should advise patients who have had heart attacks to resume sex only with their usual partners, because there is evidence that deaths occurring during sexual intercourse are in men who are about 20 years older than their female partners and that "the deaths frequently occurred during clandestine meeting, e.g., in hotels with a lover following the consumption of alcohol" (Kentsmith and Eaton, 1979). These deaths have been called coital coronaries.

Kentsmith and Eaton cite the work of Ueno in Japan, who "speculates that among other factors the man may feel he must be more satisfying to his younger partner and therefore more physically active. In addition, the anxiety associated with a clandestine meeting may further stress the man, precipitating a coital death." The concept of coital coronaries during extramarital relationships has been questioned by Derogatis and King (1981). These authors think that Ueno's study is deficient because the report did not give the rate of conjugal coital death in Japan. There was no comparable information for women with heart or blood vessel disease.

In summary, patients with heart or blood vessel disease can engage in sexual activities with the knowledge and advice of their physician. There is no evidence that one coital position is more energy consuming than another, so people may continue using the positions that are most enjoyable for them (Wagner and Sivarajan, 1979). Patients with cardiac disease should not eat a heavy meal or consume large amounts of alcohol before sexual intercourse. If chest pain occurs during intercourse, patients can use various medications before sexual activities (Kentsmith and Eaton, 1979).

STROKES AND SEXUALITY

Approximately 500,000 **strokes,** also termed cerebrovascular accidents (CVAs), occur annually in the United States, and it has been estimated that as many as three fourths of stroke patients experience a decrease in frequency or permanent cessation of sexual intercourse (Garden, 1990). The term *stroke* is used when a part of the brain is deprived of oxygen because of rupture of a blood vessel to the brain or blockage of a blood vessel supplying the brain. A number of factors contribute to the decline seen in sexual activity after stroke: (1) area of the brain affected by the stroke and amount of damage, which determine extent of motor and speech loss; (2) hormonal changes, including a decrease in testosterone; (3) medications taken to treat the patient, which may have a negative effect on sexual functioning (i.e., high blood pressure medication); and (4) loss of self-esteem when independence is lost and the person must depend on someone else for daily care. In addition, self-esteem suffers when the ability to speak is negatively affected or when movement is hindered. In some cases a stroke severely impairs movement, which interferes with the physical aspects of engaging in sexual activities.

Men who have had a stroke may show a decrease in the frequency in sexual intercourse, erectile dysfunction, impaired erection, and premature ejaculation, while women who have had a stroke may have a decrease in vaginal lubrication, less frequent sexual intercourse, and painful sexual intercourse (Garden, 1990). Both sexes show low sex drive and a decreased interest in sex. As Garden (1990) states, "In counseling these patients [poststroke patients], you'll need to explain that sexual activity after stroke is a normal and natural component of the recovery process for all post-stroke patients" (p. 30).

stroke
Condition in which a portion of the brain is deprived of oxygen.

ARTHRITIS AND SEXUALITY

Just as the loss of movement resulting from a stroke may negatively affect sexual functioning, so does **arthritis.** This disease involves the inflammation of joints, accompanied by pain, changes in joint structure, and frequently loss of motion at the affected joint. Many arthritic patients have only minor stiffness, but others have severe joint deformities with pain that leads to a decrease in sexual functioning. Medication may help. If stiffness and pain preclude certain sexual intercourse positions, a counselor trained in human sexuality can help the couple find other positions or other sexual activities, such as oral sex or mutual touching to orgasm (Walbroehl, 1988).

MULTIPLE SCLEROSIS AND CEREBRAL PALSY: EFFECTS ON SEXUAL FUNCTIONING

Multiple sclerosis and **cerebral palsy** are also diseases that limit movement. Multiple sclerosis (MS) is a chronic progressive disease of the brain and spinal cord. MS is characterized by the loss of the myelin sheath that covers the nerve fibers in the brain and cord. Symptoms of this disease include loss of control of voluntary movements, decreased sensations, and speech disorders. Remission and reappearance of the symptoms is common. The cause of the disease is unknown, and no cure has been found. Individuals with MS often show a loss of sexual interest, which might be due in part to a loss of sensations from the genital region that can make sexual arousal by genital stimulation difficult or impossible.

Cerebral palsy (CP) comprises a number of motor disorders resulting from damage to the brain during fetal development or at birth. The major symptom is an impairment of voluntary movement, which manifests itself by impaired speech, facial expressions, and spastic body movements. Many individuals with CP are prone to convulsive seizures (Berkow, 1987). As Berkow (1987) states, "The treatment goal is development of maximal independence within the limits of the patient's motor and associated handicaps" (p. 211). The sexuality of the person with CP should also be encouraged to the limits of the person's interests and desires. The loss of voluntary muscle control makes masturbation and sexual intercourse difficult. If the individual with CP has a sexual partner with no motor dysfunctions, the partner can help place the individual with CP in the most comfortable position for sexual intercourse, mutual touching, or oral sex.

CANCER AND SEXUALITY

The topic of cancer is presented in various chapters throughout this book. Detection and treatment of breast cancer are considered in Chapters 3 and 17, prostatic and testicular cancer is discussed in Chapter 17, and cervical cancer in relation to prenatal hormone exposure and sexually transmitted diseases is presented in Chapters 6 and 18, respectively. This section deals briefly with the sexuality of individuals with cancer. Cancer comprises a large group of malignant growths that can invade neighboring tissues, as well as distant tissues when the cancer cells travel via the blood or lymphatic system (a process known as metastasis). Cancer can negatively affect sexuality and sexual functioning in many ways. People with cancer are concerned about their future health, and this worry, concern, and anxiety can cause a loss of sexual desire and a decrease in sexual activity.

Certain treatments for cancer such as chemotherapy and irradiation therapy can cause such problems as hair loss, fatigue, and nausea. These side effects may lead to a decrease in sexual desire, which may be temporary and pass when the side effects of the treatments cease. As we have stated previously, a loss of self-esteem or a poor body image, as might result from loss of hair or chronic fatigue, can lead to a decrease in sexual interest and activity.

Surgical treatments for cancer can be devastating to self-image. The loss of a breast from breast cancer or an ostomy (a surgical procedure that creates an opening to serve as an exit for connections between the large intestine or bowel and the outside of the body) necessitated by cancer of the bowel or colon can have a very negative effect on body image. This effect is temporary in most cases, but the early stages can be difficult for some individuals. Again, the loss of self-image can cause a decrease in sexual desire and sexual activities. Some surgical procedures, such as those for cancer of the prostate gland, can cause a permanent loss of erectile capability because nerves are severed during the operation to remove the cancerous portion of the gland.

The person with cancer has many concerns and needs empathetic physicians and other health care workers to explain in easy to understand terms what is happening in terms of treatment and what will happen next. Many patients read the medical literature to learn all they can about their cancer. They find out what treatments have worked best in the past and tell their physicians what

After her mastectomy, actress Ann Jillian spoke out openly about her surgery. She continues to serve as a positive role model for women who have gone through similar traumatic operations.

they have read. They also sometimes ask the physician whether they can try a particular treatment regimen that has fewer side effects. The patient who is well informed has a feeling of some control over the illness. A caring physician should discuss all of the above information with the patient. The patient needs to know what side effects to expect. Only when the person with cancer feels that the medical situation is under control and has complete confidence in the people providing treatment can he or she get on with all the other aspects of life, including the sexual aspects.

Wise sums up the concerns of the patient with an illness such as cancer:

> The psychological reaction to medical illness, the nuances of the illness itself, and various interpersonal stresses related to the sick role may all compromise sexuality. Some patients may minimize the importance of sexuality. This may be appropriate in the face of other concerns.
>
> Wise, 1980, p. 787

> The individual, however, should not be expected to live a life without physical or interpersonal pleasure. It is the goal of treatment to provide assistance in the development of appropriate modes of physical communication.
>
> Wise, 1980, p. 801

DIABETES AND SEXUALITY

diabetes mellitus
(dy ub BEE tis muh LEE tuhs) Disorder of carbohydrate utilization characterized by a high blood glucose level and the presence of glucose in the urine.

Failure of the pancreas to secrete insulin causes **diabetes mellitus,** a disease that can be inherited. The primary abnormality is the failure to utilize adequate quantities of glucose, a product of digestion and a naturally occurring sugar. This causes blood glucose levels to be high, and large quantities of glucose are lost with the urine. If the body is unable to utilize glucose, it is deprived of a major source of energy. Patients with diabetes tend to lose weight and become weak because their bodies burn too much fat and protein. About 5% of people in the United States have diabetes (Schiavi, 1979).

Diabetic Men

A high frequency of complications in various organ systems of the body is attributable to the disease, and sexual dysfunction also occurs in a high proportion of persons with diabetes. In men the three most common sexual dysfunctions and disorders are reduced interest in sex, erectile dysfunction, and retrograde ejaculation. Erectile dysfunction, or sexual impotence, is the inability to have or maintain an erection sufficient for sexual intercourse. Erectile dysfunction eventually develops in approximately 50% of diabetic men (Pietropinto and Arora, 1989), and the probability of this dysfunction is higher in older men (Schiavi, 1979). Retrograde ejaculation occurs when the bladder outlet does not close sufficiently, allowing semen to be ejaculated into the bladder instead of being propelled out of the penis. The more severe the diabetes, the greater the possibility of sexual dysfunction.

Although many diabetic men experience erectile dysfunction, they still can achieve ejaculation and orgasm with a flaccid or semierect penis and do not always have decreased sexual interest. Retrograde ejaculation may cause some diabetic men to have little or no ejaculate during the subjective experience of orgasm and may contribute to impaired fertility.

Scientists have not yet determined how diabetes causes sexual dysfunction in men. Several theories have been advanced, but none is adequate to explain all the problems. One theory proposes that changes within the nervous system, involving peripheral and autonomic components, are responsible; another suggests that the hormonal imbalance, particularly low testosterone levels, seen in diabetes is responsible (Pietropinto and Arora, 1989). Psychosocial factors are thought to play a role in sexual dysfunction in a few men with diabetes. Some men see the illness as a chronic problem, with fear of complications, depression, and restrictions in life-style. These fears may contribute to lowered sex drive and dysfunction.

Diabetic Women

Because diabetic men have anatomical and physiological problems with reproductive structures, such as erectile dysfunction and retrograde ejaculation, they have been studied more than diabetic women. Some research has indicated that women with diabetes have higher levels of orgasmic dysfunction than women without diabetes; however, later studies (Ellenberg, 1977; Jensen, 1981) found no differences in orgasmic dysfunction between women with and those without diabetes.

VISUAL IMPAIRMENTS

People who are born blind grow up without any notion of what the opposite sex looks like. These people need special programs of sexual education. In certain Scandinavian countries live models are used to teach anatomy to blind children, but this method is not used in the United States. As with other disabilities, blindness may cause depression and low self-esteem, which may contribute to sexual dysfunction. Certain diseases, such as diabetes, that cause loss of vision can also cause sexual dysfunction.

What kind of sexual fantasies and erotic thoughts does a congenitally blind person have? One woman stated that her sexual fantasies involved the senses of touch, hearing (a sexual partner's voice can be very "sexy"), smell, and taste (personal communication from a 32-year-old woman, 1984). Blind people use the other senses to a greater extent than sighted people do.

HEARING IMPAIRMENTS

Hearing impairment is not apparent. We cannot see deafness as we can see a wheelchair or a blind person's cane or dog. And deaf people are healthy compared with patients who have had a heart attack or those with diabetes. Yet hearing impairment can have a negative effect on sexual functioning, as indicated in the box on p. 476.

SEX EDUCATION FOR THE VISION- OR HEARING-IMPAIRED CHILD

Now that many handicapped children are being "mainstreamed" (placed with nonhandicapped children) into regular classrooms, teachers must teach vision- and hearing-impaired children not only the basic subjects but also sex education when it is offered in the school curriculum. Children with sensory impairment may demonstrate a deficiency in psychosocial-sexual adjustment (Baugh, 1984), but these children have the same emotional and social needs as other children. The deficiency is usually attributable to their lack of information about their sexual needs and desires.

Baugh (1984) presents several proposals that can aid in sex education for vision- and hearing-impaired children in the regular classroom. For teachers to be successful in aiding the impaired child, they must feel comfortable with teaching any child about his or her sexuality. Teachers must recognize the educational and social restrictions that the impairment imposes on the child and be able to empathize with the child; this usually occurs as a teacher spends time with an individual child.

The goals of sex education are the same for all students. "One is still concerned with the development of sexually responsible and informed young persons who have sufficient knowledge to make appropriate decisions regarding their own sexuality" (FitzGerald and FitzGerald, 1980).

To do an effective job in teaching sex education to the vision and hearing impaired, the instructor must first evaluate what kind of sex information the child already possesses. Then a systematic teaching program can begin. How do you teach the sensory impaired about sex? The instructor must be imaginative and modify existing materials to emphasize teaching through the senses that are not impaired. Working with the hearing impaired requires visual

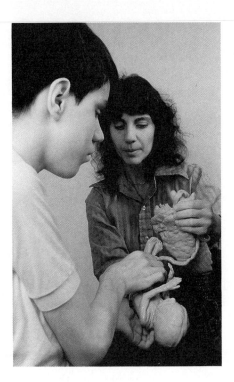

techniques, but the teacher must realize that unless the child has had enough early language exposure to establish a native language, there will be a language barrier to overcome. Sign language is the language of choice for most hearing-impaired persons (Baugh, 1984). Hence the teacher who knows sign language is best able to teach the child. Written material is also helpful but may have to be modified to accommodate the student's reading level.

The vision-impaired child depends on sound and touch for the acquisition of information, and these two senses can be used to convey sex information. The use of artificial models of the opposite sex along with verbal information is one approach, and the use of live models has been proposed for use in the United States. Tape recordings and braille can also be used to convey sexual information to the visually handicapped. In all cases of sex education for the sensory-impaired child, the parents must try to take an active role to reinforce what the child learns in school. Outside community social service agencies can also be an asset in the total development of the child, including sex education.

MENTAL RETARDATION AND SEXUALITY

People with intelligence quotients (IQs) of 70 or lower are generally classified as mentally retarded. Retarded people have limited ability to learn and can be further handicapped by emotional and physical disabilities, and approximately 3% of the population of the United States "will at some time in their life function in the mentally retarded range" (Allen and Allen, 1979).

Some causes of mental retardation include defects in the developing embryo, diseases and disorders of the nervous system, brain injury in early life, and sociocultural deprivation. Considering the variety of causes, it is foolish to

Showing affection for another is not limited by mental retardation.

assume that all mentally retarded people have the same abilities, learning capabilities, prognosis for the future, and personality traits. Everyone is unique. Most mentally retarded people are only mildly retarded, with IQs that range from 50 to 70, and can function in most aspects of day-to-day living. Eighty-nine percent of the retarded in the United States are in this category, and other people do not always realize they are retarded.

The following description is of a severely retarded woman. Her history was taken from David and Victoria Allen's book, *Ethical Issues in Mental Retardation* (1979), although we have condensed it and added a few comments of our own.

> When she was 6 years old, Martha went to live in a state institution for the mentally retarded. Now, at 32, her development age is that of a 5-year-old. She has spent most of her life in an institution; however, for the past year Martha has lived in a rehabilitation unit, where she is taught simple skills and how to cope with day-to-day activities.
>
> Although Martha shows potential in workshop training, her behavior toward men limits her community opportunities. She is easily distracted by male residents and attendants, and exhibits uncontrolled sexual curiosity.
>
> Martha has been found with men in situations that could lead to sexual intercourse and pregnancy, and thus is considered "high risk" by the staff. To prevent sexual contact with men, the staff tries to provide one-on-one supervision, and until she learns appropriate social behavior, Martha may not attend workshop training.
>
> Martha's parents are strongly against oral contraceptives for her because she has a heart condition. And if she did use birth control, they fear the staff might allow her to have random sexual relations. With the question not resolved, Martha's parents feel caught in the trend toward deinstitutionalization, which means having Martha come out into the community, with the additional freedom it would mean for their daughter. In this case the freedom could be viewed either as being more difficult for Martha or as an opportunity to be integrated into society outside of the institution.

HUMAN SEXUALITY

Martha's story raises many important questions that pertain to the sexual rights of all retarded people. The following questions are from Allen and Allen (1979).

> Do persons who are mentally retarded have sexual rights?
>
> When the person's ability to understand and to choose is limited, what are these rights? What is the state's responsibility to retarded persons living in its institutions? To prevent pregnancy? To provide sex education? To allow sexual expression?
>
> Who should decide about sterilization, birth control, or abortion for a mentally retarded person? The state? The parents? The retarded person involved? Do retarded adults have the right to marry? To bear children?
>
> What is really in the best interests of the retarded person? And who decides? And what should be done for Martha and other women and men who are physically adults, but mentally children?
>
> Allen and Allen, 1979, pp. 59-60

Martha's parents did not want her using contraceptive pills or other birth control methods because they were afraid she would engage in random sexual activities with different men in the institution. Administrators at the institution were afraid she would become pregnant, and they wanted her to use some form of contraception. Physicians used to recommend the intrauterine device (IUD) for birth control for mentally retarded women because its use does not depend on self-discipline or memory and because its effects are not permanent. A doctor can remove it at any time (Allen and Allen, 1979). Because of the problems with IUDs, the recently approved Norplant progesterone implant may be the contraceptive method of choice for the mentally retarded. However, most experts agree that parents or patients must request birth control and that any requests for contraception or sterilization must be carefully studied. "The motivation would only be valid if for the benefit of the patient, not for the benefit of the state, the parents or any other group," said Dr. Andre Hellegers, Director of the Kennedy Institute, Human Reproduction and Bioethics (Allen and Allen, 1979).

The Norplant contraceptive method is presented in Chapter 8.

Birth control for mentally retarded men is more difficult than for mentally retarded women. Vasectomies are permanent, and a condom requires advance planning and memory.

In the past the problem of birth control for the mentally retarded was often resolved by sterilization. Until the mid-1950s, physicians routinely sterilized many people before they were released from institutions, but many mildly retarded women considered sterilization a stigma. Allen and Allen (1979) quote two:

> Two or three times I could've got married, but I didn't dare tell the man I was sterilized. How could I tell a man a thing like that?
>
> I love kids. Sometimes now when I baby-sit, I hold the baby up to myself and cry and I think to myself, why was I ever sterilized?
>
> Allen and Allen, 1979, p. 75

Legal restrictions now make it more difficult to sterilize people, and the federal government has refused to pay for sterilization for retarded persons younger than 21 years of age (Hall, 1979). Such restrictions have forced the community and parents to consider alternatives to permanent sterilization (Hall, 1979).

Retarded couples must consider marriage and parenthood individually. They must think about their intellectual abilities, their emotional maturity, the number of children they will have, and what kind of support they receive from their families and the community (Allen and Allen, 1979). The possibility of marriage without the added responsibility of children is another option for the retarded couple.

To cope with their sexuality, the mentally retarded must have education. They must learn the basic facts of reproduction and contraceptive usage. In addition, to make informed choices concerning sexuality, the mentally retarded must be given information concerning interpersonal relations, dating, and marriage. Sexual and social education from the institution and the parents is essential to allow the mildly and moderately retarded to function sexually. Social and sexual education may be of limited value for the severely retarded, like Martha, but for the majority of mentally retarded individuals it is critical.

Kolodny, Masters, and Johnson (1979) state that parents of mentally retarded children or adolescents, as well as health care professionals working with the retarded, should be informed of the normalcy of masturbation. The retarded individual can usually be taught that masturbation is done privately. Institutions should allow their populations privacy and dignity in all aspects of life, including the sexual.

SUMMARY

1 Any illness or disease that affects mobility, well-being, or self-esteem has the potential to affect sexual expression.

2 The chapter stresses the idea that a stiff penis and wet vagina are not the only requirements for a relationship. Conversely, loss of genital functioning does not mean loss of sexuality. In addition to physical problems, a disabled person may have psychological problems. The person may feel unattractive to others, and self-concept and body image are negatively affected. This results in problems in expressing sexuality.

3 More than half of men with spinal cord injuries retain erectile capacity, but approximately 90% lose the ability to ejaculate. Fertility is often impaired in men with spinal cord injuries. Orgasm may occur even though ejaculation does not. Each case involves many factors, and simple generalizations may not apply to all persons with disabilities.

4 In spinal cord–injured women, menstrual flow usually resumes after the accident, and fertility is not impaired. Pregnancy and birth are common in these women. Orgasm is reported by many.

5 Many men and women with spinal cord injuries develop new erogenous zones after the accident. For example, many men find that the nipples and small of the back (areas that still have sensation) become highly sensitive, although before the accident they were not.

6 The activity of the cardiovascular system increases dramatically during sexual activity. Individuals with cardiovascular disorders such as high blood pressure, heart pain caused by lack of oxygen, diseases of the valves and muscles of the heart, and diseases of the blood vessels may experience negative changes in sexual performance and activities. These negative changes have a variety of causes, including the physical disease, psychological concerns about death from exertion after sexual intercourse, and side effects of various medications (some of which cause the loss of erectile capabilities). Frank discussions by a physician about needed limitations in

physical activities and encouragement to resume sexual activities when the patient is able are essential.

7 Multiple sclerosis, cerebral palsy, and arthritis all have a negative effect on voluntary muscular movements and have the potential to cause a decrease in sexual desire and sexual behaviors. These diseases also can have a negative effect on self-esteem and body image that compounds the muscle movement problems.

8 Diabetes can cause sexual dysfunctions and problems in men, but women seem to be less affected by this disease. Men report a loss of interest in sex, erectile dysfunction, and retrograde ejaculation (ejaculate goes into the bladder).

9 If vision or hearing impairments cause lowering of self-esteem, in addition to the physical impairment a psychological factor must be recognized.

10 The mentally retarded face unique problems in sexual expression. They must be allowed dignity in all aspects of life, including the sexual.

ANSWERS

1 It is true that men and women with spinal cord injuries must deal with society's negative attitudes toward them and that these attitudes cause many problems for the physically disabled.

2 When self-esteem falls and a person has a negative body image, sexual desire and sexual behaviors will decrease.

3 Women with spinal cord injuries do not have more difficulty than noninjured women in carrying a pregnancy to term. Certain physical conditions must be watched but do not influence the well-being of the mother or fetus if carefully monitored.

QUESTIONS FOR THOUGHT   ?

1 Discuss the negative attitudes that exist toward individuals with disabilities. How might these attitudes be overcome? Design a program that you could implement with a class to overcome these negative attitudes.

2 Discuss the physical and psychological effects of cardiovascular disease on sexuality.

3 How do you feel about mandatory sterilization for the mentally retarded? What might be some alternatives?

SUGGESTED READINGS

Comfort, A.: Sexual consequences of disability, Philadelphia, 1978, G.F. Stickley Co.
 This popular writer has edited a fine book dealing with all aspects of disability and sexuality. An excellent book for those interested in the sexuality of disabled individuals, it gives the reader insight into and understanding of various disabilities and sexual expression.
Bullard, D., and Knight, S.: Sexuality and physical disability, St. Louis, 1981, Mosby–Year Book, Inc.
 A fine collection of personal stories dealing with the sexual needs and desires of the disabled.
Rabin, B.: The sensuous wheeler: sexual adjustment for the spinal cord injured, San Francisco, 1980, Multi Media Resource Center.
 A clearly written book for the spinal cord injured, their partners, and their lovers, as well as for counselors and educators.
Sexuality and Disability, New York, Human Sciences Press.
 This journal is devoted to the study of sex in physical and mental illness. It contains clinical reports, case studies, research and survey data reports, guidelines for clinical practice, and developments in special programs for sex education and counseling for disabled persons.

Sexual Dysfunctions, Disorders, and Sexual Health

The patient was a handsome and successful 30-year-old businessman who had been divorced two years before. His partner was his fiancee who was 26 years of age. . . .

The chief complaint was impotence. The man was easily aroused and achieved an erection quickly upon commencing sex play. Almost invariably, however, his erection abated when he was about to commence coitus. His fiancee had no sexual difficulty. . . .

The history revealed that in his prior marriage, which had lasted five years and produced two children, the patient had experienced no sexual difficulty. He and his wife had coitus two to three times per week, and he invariably functioned well. His wife left him because she fell in love with and wished to marry a close friend of the family.

The divorce was very traumatic for the patient. He became depressed and was left with deep feelings of insecurity. . . .

Eight months after the separation he went to a party and met an aggressive woman who wanted to have sex with him right there. On her urging, they went to an upstairs room (which did not have a lock) and attempted to have intercourse on the floor. He became excited and erect, but for the first time in his life, lost his erection. He tried to regain his erection to no avail. He reacted with alarm to this experience. He felt depressed and extremely humiliated and embarrassed. He never saw the woman again. One month later, he tried to make love to another woman but again lost his erection when the memory of his previous failure intruded into his mind. From then on the problem escalated. He met his fiancee shortly thereafter, but initially avoided making love to her because he anticipated failure. Later, when they became more intimate, he confessed his problem to her. They attempted sex, but in most instances the patient was unable to function. Questioning revealed that he was preoccupied with thoughts about whether he would fail during lovemaking. He continued to feel humiliated and feared rejection despite his fiancee's reassurance and sensitivity.

H.S. KAPLAN
The New Sex Therapy, pp. 128-129

This chapter is concerned with **sexual dysfunctions** (such as erectile dysfunction, described in the opening quotation), which are usually of psychological origin, and **sexual disorders,** or physical conditions caused by organic (biological) problems. Both sexual dysfunctions and disorders interfere with sexual functioning. Sexual functioning depends on general physical and psychological well-being. When our physical health is impaired or we are under stress or fatigued or anxious, our sexual or reproductive functioning may also be negatively affected. In some conditions the probable cause of a sexual problem is easy to diagnose as physical or psychological; in others both biological and psychological factors seem to be involved.

This chapter begins with a discussion of the most common sexual dysfunctions. In men these specific dysfunctions include erectile dysfunction or impotence, premature ejaculation, and retarded ejaculation or ejaculatory incompetence. In women they are vaginismus (spasms of the muscles surrounding the outer portion of the vagina when intercourse is attempted) and orgasmic dysfunction (difficulty in reaching orgasm). Two problems that occur in both

sexual dysfunctions
Clinical conditions of the reproductive structures that are usually of psychological origin.

sexual disorders
Clinical conditions of the reproductive structures that are usually of biological origin.

men and women are painful intercourse and lack of sexual desire.

A discussion of some common causes of sexual dysfunction follows our discussion of specific dysfunctions, and treatment of the various dysfunctions concludes this section. The final portion of the chapter is concerned with various sexual disorders.

SEXUAL DYSFUNCTIONS IN MEN
Erectile Dysfunction

erectile dysfunction
(i REK tuhl) Inability to have or maintain an erection sufficient for sexual intercourse.

Erectile dysfunction, or impotence, is the inability to have or maintain an erection that is sufficient for penis-inside-vagina or penis-inside-anus intercourse. Since the term *impotence* has negative connotations (it literally means lacking power), we do not use it here, although it is used extensively in the medical literature. Erectile dysfunction is classified as primary or secondary. Men with primary erectile dysfunction have never been successful in any attempt at intromission (insertion of the erect penis into the vagina or anus) in either heterosexual or homosexual acts (Masters and Johnson, 1970). Primary

Alcohol and Illegal Drugs: Perceived and Actual Effects on Sexual Functioning

Most sex therapists and addiction counselors agree that sexual enhancement with psychoactive drugs occurs primarily in nonaddicted individuals and that drug-induced sexual dysfunctions predominate in addicted individuals (Smith et al., 1982). Psychoactive drugs include heroin, amphetamines, phencyclidine, alcohol, and cocaine (Smith, Wesson, and Apter-Marsh, 1984). Two widely abused drugs, alcohol and cocaine, were recently studied to determine patients' *perceptions* of how alcohol-cocaine combinations affected their sexual functioning (Smith, Wesson, and Apter-Marsh, 1984).

The subjects were 159 patients who were just beginning detoxification treatment in both outpatient and inpatient settings. Their mean age was 36.9 years. Of the men, who were primarily alcohol abusers, 60% reported that alcohol improved their sexual functioning (curtailed premature ejaculation and produced relaxation), 33% reported impaired sexual functioning (erectile dysfunction), and 3% claimed no effect. Of the women, who were previously alcohol abusers, 65% reported that alcohol improved their sexual functioning (improved ability to reach orgasm), 30% reported impaired functioning, and 5% claimed no effect.

Of the primarily cocaine users, 65% of the men reported that cocaine helped achieve orgasm, and 35% noted that the drug impaired ejaculation. In contrast, only 20% of the women thought that cocaine enhanced both sexual desire and the ability to achieve orgasm; the other 80% believed that cocaine impaired sexual functioning. The favored drug combination for sexual enhancement for both men and women was cocaine and alcohol. The patients stated that this combination increased desire and produced "staying power" so they could have sex all night long.

In a study of college-aged men (mean age 20.09 years), it was shown that alcohol can influence an objective measure of sexual responsiveness (Wilson and Niaura, 1984). The measure was penile erection in response to an erotic tape recording. The subjects were all social drinkers, and all were told that they were being given alcohol to drink. However, only half of the men received alcohol, and the others only tonic water. Intoxicated subjects showed a significantly shorter latency to the onset and peak of penile erection while listening to the tape than did their sober counterparts.

erectile dysfunction is relatively rare. Masters and Johnson (1970) report that in 245 men, erectile dysfunction was primary in only 32. Men with secondary erectile dysfunction have successfully engaged in intromission on previous occasions but now cannot have or maintain a sufficient erection. Masters and Johnson (1970) define secondary dysfunction as the presence of erection problems in 25% of sexual encounters. An estimated 4% to 9% of men in the United States have secondary erectile dysfunction, and it is the most common complaint of males seeking help for sexual dysfunction (Spector and Carey, 1990). The prevalence of erectile dysfunction increases with age, occurring in 7% of

FYI

Effects of Medically Indicated Drugs on Sexual Functioning

Some drugs or medications may affect the desire for sex; others actually negate or inhibit the physiological response of the genitals so that erection does not occur or orgasm and ejaculation are inhibited. Drugs that cause drowsiness, depression, or at the other extreme irritability are the most likely to dampen sexual desire. Drugs that interfere with the autonomic nervous system negatively affect sexual functioning. For example, patients taking medications for gastrointestinal ulcers may find that they are having erectile dysfunction. Anti-cholinergic drugs (those that block the neurotransmitter acetylcholine) used to treat ulcers are the most likely to cause erectile problems, but they are not used as extensively now. As a side effect some drugs block the nerves that control blood flow to the genitals, and because erection is a vascular phenomenon, it does not occur.

Millions of Americans take medication for high blood pressure (hypertension) and may have erectile dysfunction and ejaculation problems because the drug blocks nerves important to the reflexes involved in erection and ejaculation. Estimates of the incidence of sexual problems associated with the use of medications to control high blood pressure range from a low of 5% to more than 30% depending on the medication or combination of medications taken (Rosen, Kostis, and Jekelis, 1988).

Patients receiving therapy for psychiatric disorders often experience increased sexual desire as a result of the reduction in anxiety produced by the drug. Antidepressants that are monoamine oxidase (MOA) inhibitors have been associated with various sexual dysfunctions. Some of the more common drugs used to treat medical conditions are listed below along with their effect on sexual functioning.

Medical condition	Drug(s)	Effect on sexual functioning
Hypertension (high blood pressure)	Clonidine, propranolol (Inderal), guanethidine (Ismelin), methyldopa (Aldomet)	Men: erectile dysfunction, arousal and ejaculation problems Women: loss of orgasm and of arousal
Ulcers of stomach and small intestine	Cimetidine (Tagamet), Misoprostol (Cytotec)	Occasional reports of erectile dysfunction
Depression	MAO inhibitors: isocarboxazid (Marplan), phenelzine (Nardil)	Erectile dysfunction and ejaculation problems; women report loss of orgasm
Pain relief	Morphine, heroin, codeine	Occasional cause of erectile dysfunction and in women the inhibition of orgasm

Data from Physicians' Desk Reference, 1990.

men between 25 and 55 years of age, 27% of men 70 years of age, and 75% of men 80 years and older (Kravis and Molitch, 1990).

The man described at the beginning of this chapter had secondary erectile dysfunction. It was treated with some of the techniques described in this chapter and soon ceased.

Most cases of erectile dysfunction have a psychological cause. Some situations that can produce sexual anxiety and consequently erectile dysfunction are the fear of not being able to achieve an erection, the demand to perform immediately for a partner, and the fear of rejection by a partner if an immediate erection does not occur. These situational causes, as well as organic causes of erectile dysfunction, are explored in more detail later in this chapter.

Some men occasionally have difficulty achieving an erection because of fatigue, anxiety, drug use, stress, or overindulgence in alcohol. These isolated cases of dysfunction are transient or temporary erectile dysfunctions. Kaplan (1974) estimates that as many as half of the men in the United States experience isolated episodes of erectile dysfunction.

Premature Ejaculation

premature ejaculation
(i jak yuh LAY shuhn) Ejaculation before or just on penetration of the vagina.

Premature ejaculation is ejaculation before or just on penetration of the vagina, or the anus in the case of anal intercourse. More specific definitions state that premature ejaculation is inability to control the ejaculatory process for the first 30 seconds after penetration; others define it as inability to hold back ejaculation for 60 seconds after penetration (Masters and Johnson, 1970). Masters and Johnson consider premature ejaculation to be failure to control ejaculation for a sufficient duration during penis-inside-vagina intercourse to satisfy the partner in at least 50% of sessions of sexual intercourse. This last definition is problematic. For example, many couples engage in a great deal of mutual touching, and the woman may reach orgasm before penetration. When the man attempts penetration, he may ejaculate immediately. Thus his partner may be satisfied, but he may not be, because he wanted to have prolonged sexual intercourse. The definition also is of no value for erectile dysfunction in homosexual men. Kaplan (1974) defines premature ejaculation as absence of voluntary control over the ejaculation process. Most researchers believe that if a man thinks he ejaculates too soon or does not have enough control over the process and it concerns him, he has a dysfunction.

Premature ejaculation is the second most common sexual dysfunction in men (after erectile dysfunction). Approximately 35% of U.S. men experience this difficulty at one time or another (Spector and Carey, 1990). Premature ejaculation causes great anxiety because the man is afraid he is failing his partner. Extended foreplay before insertion often causes ejaculation because of lack of control. The problem has a negative impact on the couple's range of sexual expression and relationship.

While anxiety may be involved in premature ejaculation, during self-stimulation premature ejaculators reach orgasm in about half the time of nonpremature ejaculators (Strassberg et al., 1990). In other words, premature ejaculation may be the result of a physiologically based hypersensitivity to sexual stimulation. Strassberg and associates found in their study, which was based on a questionnaire, that anxiety during sexual intercourse was not significantly different between premature ejaculators and nonpremature ejaculators.

Dr. Helen Singer Kaplan combines psychotherapy and behavior modification in her treatment of sexual dysfunction.

As Kaplan (1974) has indicated, sexual dysfunctions may be caused by a number of interpersonal factors. Milan, Kilmann, and Borland (1988) stress the importance of a treatment approach to sexual dysfunctions that focuses on the couple, rather than on the woman or man alone, and that takes into consideration the "various sexual and nonsexual characteristics of each couple" (p. 477). For example, to understand some cases of premature ejaculation we have to take into account the actions of the female partner. Moore and Kotrla (1989) have found that certain female behaviors contribute to premature ejaculation. These authors have identified three behaviors of females that encourage and reinforce premature ejaculation in their male partners. The behaviors involved words and actions that occur during sexual intercourse and through other communications, including those that have to do with the total relationship but are not specifically related to sex (Moore and Kotrla, 1989). The behaviors include:

1. "Hurry up and finish." Some women convey this to their partner with direct and disparaging remarks expressing a lack of interest in sex or distaste for sex.
2. Enhancement of male sexual arousal. Some women stimulate their partners to high levels of sexual excitement with their mouths or hands before sexual intercourse. The male ejaculates soon after entering the female.
3. Sexual anxiety on the part of the female. A woman who is apprehensive about intercourse may convey this anxiety to her partner, who responds by ejaculating as soon as possible.

Retarded Ejaculation

Retarded ejaculation, also called ejaculatory incompetence, is the opposite of premature ejaculation. In retarded ejaculation the man can achieve an erection

retarded ejaculation
(i jak yuh LAY shuhn) Inability to ejaculate or inhibition of ejaculation.

in response to sexual stimulation but is unable to have an orgasm and ejaculate. Masters and Johnson (1970) and Spector and Carey (1990) found the problem of retarded ejaculation to be relatively rare. Some men have occasional episodes of retarded ejaculation that can be overcome by extra fantasizing or novel stimulation; however, certain men cannot ejaculate regardless of fantasies, stimulation, or partner.

Retarded ejaculation can be embarrassing and frustrating for the man. For example, the man is engaged in an exciting sexual encounter with a woman he finds sexually stimulating. He continues to thrust within the vagina but just cannot ejaculate and have an orgasm. He has two choices: fake an orgasm (by going through the muscular movements of orgasm and ejaculation) to end the session, or be honest and tell his partner that he just is unable to ejaculate. With the second choice, the woman may feel that she did not excite him enough because he did not ejaculate inside of her.

The major cause of retarded ejaculation is psychological. The male is stimulated, as evidenced by his erection, but ejaculation is slow to occur. The demand to perform, in this case to ejaculate, puts pressure on the man and he has difficulty in ejaculating. In most cases he wants to please his partner and may try too hard to ejaculate when he does experience a delay. This of course increases the problem.

SEXUAL DYSFUNCTIONS IN WOMEN
Orgasmic Dysfunction

orgasmic dysfunction (OR gaz mik) Inability to experience orgasm.

Orgasmic dysfunction, or anorgasmia, is often defined as the inability to experience orgasm. A woman who has never had an orgasm is said to have primary orgasmic dysfunction, and one who has had orgasms but stops having them is said to have secondary orgasmic dysfunction. Kaplan (1974) further delineates orgasmic dysfunction as absolute, if the patient is not able to achieve orgasm during coital or clitoral stimulation, or situational, if she can have orgasm under certain circumstances, such as self-stimulation or with one sexual partner but not another, but not during coitus. Kaplan (1974), Masters and Johnson (1970), and Spector and Carey (1990) note that orgasmic difficulties are the most common complaints of women in sex therapy. Unmarried women are more likely than married women to experience this dysfunction. An estimated 5% to 10% of U.S. females have some orgasmic dysfunction of a primary or secondary nature (Spector and Carey, 1990).

Many women report that they can easily have orgasms when they are touched either manually or orally by their partner but cannot have an orgasm during coitus. Do they have a sexual dysfunction? They do only if they are concerned about the situation. Coital stimulation is not sufficient to induce orgasm in many women. Most women require clitoral stimulation for the induction of orgasm, and intercourse does not appear to provide enough clitoral stimulation for many women. If a woman wants to experience orgasms during penis-inside-vagina intercourse but does not, she has a dysfunction by her own definition.

In most cases the cause of anorgasmia is psychological. Many individuals do not know how to engage in effective stimulation because of sexual ignorance, or they do not want to, or cannot, abandon themselves fully to the erotic experience (Kaplan, 1974). If the man does not know what is most stimulating to his partner and she does not tell him, the couple will continue to engage in unsatisfying sex.

Vaginismus

Vaginismus has been defined as painful involuntary muscular spasms of the vagina when intercourse is attempted (Stuntz, 1986). The vaginal orifice closes so tightly from the muscle contractions that intercourse is impossible (Figure 17-1). Many women with vaginismus are sexually responsive and have orgasms with clitoral stimulation. Vaginismus is often treated using penis-shaped dilators of various sizes. The woman begins with the smallest one and works her way up to the larger sizes. She does this by herself, using a lubricant. The use

vaginismus
(vaj′ uh NIZ muhs) Painful involuntary muscular spasms of the vagina when intercourse is attempted.

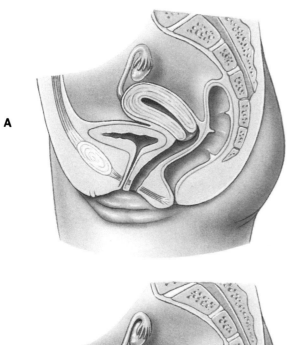

FIGURE 17-1
A, Normally the vaginal orifice permits the penetration of the penis into the vagina. **B,** In some cases the muscles surrounding the orifice contract and penile penetration is impossible. This latter condition is called vaginismus.

of the dilators allows the muscles surrounding the vaginal orifice to get used to stretching so they will not go into spasms when intercourse occurs.

Vaginismus has a strong psychological effect on a couple. The woman often feels great frustration in addition to the physical pain that occurs when penetration of the vagina is attempted, and she may avoid all sexual experiences. Or she may be afraid that her husband will leave her. The man often reacts to vaginismus with frustration, and some men have secondary erectile dysfunction in reaction to their wife's dysfunction (Kaplan, 1974). Vaginismus is not common, but no estimates of affected women in the United States are available (Spector and Carey, 1990).

Women with vaginismus have involuntary muscular spasms of muscles surrounding the vaginal orifice when intercourse or any type of penetration of the vagina is attempted. The cause of these involuntary muscular contractions is unknown. Masters and Johnson (1970) propose that vaginismus has many possible causes such as fear of intercourse, past physical or sexual assault, religious beliefs, and fear of the sexual partner.

SEXUAL DYSFUNCTIONS COMMON TO MEN AND WOMEN
Painful Intercourse

dispareunia
(dis' puh ROO nee uh) Painful or difficult sexual intercourse.

Painful intercourse, **dyspareunia,** is painful or difficult sexual intercourse. Both men and women may experience painful intercourse.

Women with dyspareunia report pain in the vaginal area during sexual intercourse. Painful intercourse may also be related to vaginismus, inadequate vaginal lubrication, abnormalities of the genital tract such as a rigid hymen, cervical disorders, and constipation (Stuntz, 1986). Depending on the sample, the percentage of women reporting dyspareunia varies from 8% to 23% (Spector and Carey, 1990).

Men report pain at various anatomical sites during sexual intercourse. The pain may be felt in external structures such as the penis or scrotum or in internal sites such as the penile urethra, prostate gland, or bladder. The pain has various causes. Uncircumcised men may have chronic irritation of the glans penis because of poor hygienic habits, and the glans hurts when it is touched or placed within the vagina or anus. **Phimosis,** or tightness of the foreskin so that it cannot be drawn back over the glans, may cause irritation, infection, and constriction of the glans, resulting in pain on erection. Infection of the prostate gland can cause pain that is felt in the region of the gland and the bladder during sexual intercourse.

phimosis
(fy MOH sis) Tightness of the foreskin so that it cannot be drawn back over the glans.

Dysfunction of Sexual Desire

Sexual desire or libido is experienced as specific sensations which move the individual to seek out, or become receptive to, sexual experiences. These sensations are produced by the physical activation of a specific neural system in the brain. When this system is active, a person is "horny," he may feel genital sensations, or he may feel vaguely sexy, interested in sex, open to sex, or even just restless. These sensations cease after sexual gratification, i.e., orgasm. When this system is inactive or under the influence of inhibitory forces, a person has no interest in erotic matters; he "loses his appetite for sex" and becomes "asexual."

Kaplan, 1979, p. 10

In the above narrative it is important to point out that the word *he* could just as easily be *she*. Certain personal and situational events, for example, illness, depression, stress, hormonal changes, intrapersonal conflicts such as the ending of a close personal or sexual relationship, and moral or religious conviction, may lead to the loss of sexual desire (Grosskopf, 1983). It is when the loss or suppression of sexual desire persists for an extended period that we can say it is a dysfunction. This definition does not include those men and women who are celibate by choice. Many people regard celibacy, including virginity, as a positive feature of their lives rather than a lack of something and consider it to be their free choice rather than indicating a lack of sexual desire.

The loss of sexual desire results from the lack of neural activity in the brain areas that regulate and control sexual behavior or the active inhibition of these sexual centers by outside influences. We do not know much about the physiological basis of this important area of sexual functioning and can only speculate about the process at this time.

The immediate causes of inhibited sexual desire are difficult to identify. Kaplan (1979) states that individuals who lack sexual desire often experience sexually related anxiety and hostility toward their partners. In such individuals "the anxiety is evoked earlier in the sexual sequence, when sex is merely anticipated or becomes a possibility, or soon as the initial sensations of erotic desire or interest are experienced" (Kaplan, 1979, p. 37). Deeper causes of inhibited sexual desire include fear of rejection and intrapsychic problems based on infant and childhood experiences.

Arousal dysfunctions are estimated to occur in approximately 34% of women and 16% of men in the United States depending on the sample (Spector and Carey, 1990).

CAUSES OF SEXUAL DYSFUNCTIONS IN MEN AND WOMEN

In each person with a sexual dysfunction a unique set of circumstances, including biological, sociological, and psychological factors, has contributed to that dysfunction. However, certain causes of sexual dysfunction appear with regularity.

Most researchers and sex therapists agree that the great majority of sexual dysfunctions are caused by psychological factors, that is, past and recent experiences that affect present and future behaviors. However, the nature of these experiential factors is controversial; many psychological causes have been proposed. There are two main schools of thought as to the cause of sexual dysfunctions. Psychoanalytical theory suggests that unconscious conflicts occurring during critical childhood experiences go unresolved and cause sexual dysfunctions in later life. The other approach is known as the behavioral model. Behaviorists think that responses detrimental to sexual functioning are learned and can be unlearned without delving into childhood experiences.

A person who goes to a psychoanalyst would talk about childhood memories in an attempt to gain insight into unconscious conflicts and resolve them. A person who goes to a behaviorist would find that the behaviorist, rather than searching for unconscious conflicts, focuses on learning the person's history (how the behavioral responses causing the problem were learned) to understand and treat the behavior(s) causing the problem.

A qualified sex therapist can help many couples overcome sexual problems.

Kaplan (1974) believes that sexual dysfunctions have both immediate and deeper causes. By immediate causes she means the here-and-now problems that interfere with sexual functioning; deeper causes refer to internal psychological conflicts acquired in childhood. According to many clinicians of the psychoanalytical school, these conflicts must be resolved before the dysfunction can be treated effectively. For example, Freud believed that great internal conflict occurs during childhood, particularly as related to the Oedipus and Electra complexes. The Oedipus complex, according to Freud, involves the male identifying with his father and repressing incestuous sexual desires for his mother. The female equivalent of the Oedipus complex is the Electra complex. The young girl, according to Freud, feels cheated that she does not have a penis and blames her mother. She wants her father in a sexual way and wants to replace her mother. Freud said that the individual must resolve these conflicts to attain adult psychological adjustment, including sexual functioning.

Some Immediate Causes of Sexual Dysfunctions

Kaplan (1974) lists four immediate causes of sexual dysfunctions that "may all result in the inability of persons to abandon themselves fully to the erotic experience and by this means produce sexual dysfunctions." These are (1) failure to engage in effective sexual behavior because of sexual ignorance or unconscious avoidance of good sex; (2) sexual anxiety related to fear of failure, the demand for performance, and excessive need to please one's partner; (3) perceptual and intellectual defenses against erotic feelings; and (4) failure to communicate with one's sexual partner.

Failure to engage in effective sexual behavior

Many couples do not know very much about sexuality and are too guilty and frightened to explore and experiment. . . . Frequently neither knows where the

HUMAN SEXUALITY

clitoris is or recognizes its potential for transmitting erotic pleasure. They have intercourse as soon as the husband has an erection and he ejaculates without considering where his partner is in the sexual response sequence. Incredibly, such couples genuinely wonder why the wife is not orgastic. . . . So, in silence, they continue their unsatisfactory sexual habits.

Kaplan, 1974, pp. 122-123

Dysfunctions resulting from sexual ignorance are easy to overcome, and the outcome of sexual therapy is usually excellent. However, some individuals have an unconscious avoidance of good or satisfactory sex.

An example of the unconscious avoidance of good sex is the man who is excited by a seductive woman but forbids his wife to behave in a similar manner. Another is the woman who is sexually excited by slow gentle touching but who pushes her partner away if he or she gently touches her breasts or buttocks. This woman does not like the feeling of erotic excitement, so she moves the sexual encounter along before she reaches high levels of sexual arousal.

Sexual anxiety Anxiety produced during sexual activities arises from three obvious sources: fear of sexual failure, demand for sexual performance, and fear of rejection by one's partner (Kaplan, 1974; Jacobs, 1986).

FEAR OF FAILURE Anticipation of being unable to perform the sexual act is perhaps the greatest immediate cause of erectile dysfunction and, to some extent, of orgastic dysfunction. "Once a man has experienced an episode of erective failure, he may on the next erotic occasion be plagued by the thought, 'Will it happen again?' Not surprisingly, the thought is often accompanied by an emotional state of fear, and by the tendency to focus his attention on the state of his erection, which insures the fulfillment of the prophecy" (Kaplan, 1974, pp. 126-127).

DEMAND FOR PERFORMANCE

Closely related to the sexual difficulties resulting from a fear of failure is the non-responsiveness which frequently follows a command or request to perform sexually. Not uncommonly the sexual history of a man with erectile dysfunction reveals that the initial episode of erective failure occurred when the man attempted coitus at a partner's demand.

Kaplan, 1974, pp. 129-130

The case described at the beginning of this chapter is a good example of erectile dysfunction caused by demand for sexual performance, with resultant erection problems and then fear of failure in later sexual encounters.

FEAR OF REJECTION BY PARTNER

The wish to give enjoyment and share pleasure with the partner is not only desirable and healthy, but it is a prerequisite for good lovemaking. However, the compulsion to please, to perform, or to serve, not to disappoint, can be a severe source of disruptive emotion. A man's thought, "I must have a rapid erection and hold it a long time or she won't be pleased," or a woman's compulsion to serve the man's sexual wishes to the point where her own needs are neglected . . .

Kaplan, 1974, pp. 130-131

Finding Help When You Need It: Selecting a Sex Therapist

Many adults have difficulty understanding why a college-age person would need the help of a sex therapist. Typically, older adults believe that students either are not or should not be sexually active or that young people could not possibly have sexual problems if they are sexually active. Clearly this is not the case. Sexual concerns are not limited by age or status.

Finding a good, competent, helping professional for sexual therapy is not easy. Most people in the helping professions do not have formal training in the treatment of sexual dysfunctions. Furthermore, the field of sex therapy is relatively new and not well regulated, and some unscrupulous persons (i.e., quacks) falsely present themselves as sex therapists. Thus the first piece of advice is to be cautious in searching for help.

Most colleges and universities have student health and mental health services. This might be a place to start, although no one with specialized training may be available. Also, most communities have mental health centers or family service agencies that might be able to help or refer. In some areas, sex therapy centers have been established in association with university medical centers, hospitals, or other human service agencies. These are the best places to seek help. Sometimes medical societies and social work and psychological associations can provide lists of qualified professionals in the area.

In seeking help the goal is to find someone who has extensive training in the treatment of sexual concerns or who is certified as a sex therapist by the American Association of Sex Educators, Counselors and Therapists. Both the Association and the Society for Sex Therapy and Research publish directories of qualified therapists.

The therapist selected should be open and receptive to questions about background and training. If he or she is not, find someone else. The therapist should hold a clinical degree in one of the helping professions and have extensive training and supervision in sex therapy. The therapist should also be willing to discuss treatment costs, estimated time involved, and plans for the treatment process.

Some cautions: If the therapist offers quick, easy guarantees or cures, suggests sexual interaction as part of "treatment," or makes you feel uncomfortable, end the process immediately.

College-age persons experience all of the sexual problems that anyone else might experience. Overwhelming feelings of guilt and shame, troubles in a relationship, and difficulties in sexual functioning such as early ejaculation and nonorgasmia are fairly common among young adults. Unless something is done, these problems will likely be carried into future relationships and primary commitments. Early help is the best help, and should be sought whenever needed.

From Dennis M. Dailey, D.S.W., Professor of Social Welfare.

Perceptual and intellectual defense against erotic feelings   A classic example of a perceptual and intellectual defense against erotic feelings is "spectatoring." Spectatoring occurs when individuals literally become spectators to their own sexual performance (Masters and Johnson, 1970). A man will observe himself and ask such questions as, "Will I become hard? Will I stay hard during the entire lovemaking session?" He becomes a spectator and cannot abandon himself to the erotic experience. He is too busy with all of his thoughts and concerns, and these are distractions.

Failure to communicate

The failure of many couples to communicate openly about their sexual feelings and experiences has been cited by authorities in the field as an important factor in the etiology of the sexual dysfunctions . . . . Open and genuine communication is a wonderful tool for correcting and remedying problems between two people. A woman with a mild degree of orgasm inhibition has the fantasy that she will be rejected if she requires lengthy foreplay to reach orgasm. She is too frightened to admit this and check it out with her husband. Her solution is to simulate orgasm. Soon she is totally unresponsive. Her husband has no idea that he is leaving her unsatisfied. So with the assumption that everything is okay, he continues in the ineffective manner he has always done . . . . It is extremely helpful to foster a system of open communication between the lovers in such situations. He might be happy to stimulate her if he only knew what she needed. If she can risk telling him what she really feels, when the rejection she anticipates does not materialize, she feels closer, more loving and perhaps relaxed enough to reach a climax.

Kaplan, 1974, pp. 133-134

Organic Causes of Sexual Dysfunctions

Organic or biological causes of sexual dysfunction account for approximately 3% to 20% of dysfunctional complaints (Kaplan, 1974). Erectile dysfunction has received a great deal of study. Its causes can be divided into five categories: (1) vascular disease that interferes with the normal dynamics of blood flow to and from the penis; (2) **neuropathy,** which is improper functioning of the nervous system because of a disease state; (3) endocrine disorders, including abnormal functioning of any one or more of the endocrine glands, especially the anterior pituitary gland, testes, and pancreas; (4) drug-related side effects; and (5) psychological causes (Kravis and Molitch, 1990). An individual may have one or more of these problems that lead to erectile dysfunction. If a male does not have early morning erections and if he does not have erections during the course of a night of sleep, his erectile dysfunction most likely has an organic cause. A simple round strain gauge is placed at the base of the nonerect penis before the man goes to sleep. If an erection occurs during the night, the erect penis will force the circle open and the patient and physician will know that the man is physiologically capable of an erection. This implies that the erectile dysfunction has a psychological cause.

In the case of erectile dysfunction related to traumatic injury to the penis, illness, or side effects of a surgical procedure, sexual functioning can be restored with the use of a **penile prosthesis.** There are two basic types of penile prosthesis, neither of which can restore sensation to the penis or ejaculation if these have been lost from biological causes (Figure 17-2). The first type involves the implanting of two semirigid silicone rods into the corpora cavernosa penis. The man is left with a semierect penis that can usually be hidden by wearing a jock strap or tight underwear. In some implants the silicone rods can be bent downward when the man is not engaged in sexual activity and straightened out when he desires an erection.

The second type of penile prosthesis is more complicated but works on the biological principle of erection. Two expandable cylinders are inserted into the corpora cavernosa penis. The cylinders are connected by a tubing system to a fluid-filled bulb implanted under the muscles of the abdomen and connected to a small pump located in the scrotum. When the man desires an erection, he squeezes the pump, and fluid moves from the bulb into the cylinders. When

As pointed out in Chapter 16, any physical illness that affects general health or self-esteem can have a negative effect on sexual functioning.

neuropathy
(noo ROP uh thee) Improper functioning of the nervous system as the result of disease.

penile prosthesis
(pee′ nyl pros THEE sis) Replacement of portions of the penis with artificial materials.

The anatomy of the penis is presented in Chapter 2.

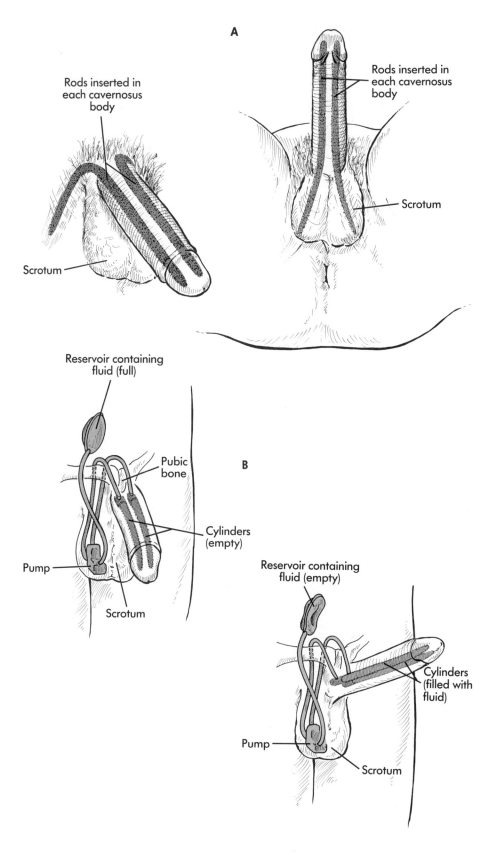

FIGURE 17-2
Penile prostheses can be of two types. **A,** In one type two semirigid silicone rods are implanted into the penis. **B,** In the second type two expandable cylinders are inserted into the penis and are connected by a tubing system to a fluid-filled bulb.

A

Rods inserted in each cavernosus body

Rods inserted in each cavernosus body

Scrotum

Scrotum

Reservoir containing fluid (full)

Pubic bone

B

Cylinders (empty)

Pump

Scrotum

Reservoir containing fluid (empty)

Cylinders (filled with fluid)

Pump

Scrotum

HUMAN SEXUALITY

he no longer desires an erection, he simply presses a release valve, which allows the fluid to leave the penis and return to the bulb.

Anatomical anomalies such as phimosis and infections in the male reproductive system can be a source of dysfunction. In women, in a condition analogous to phimosis, the clitoris adheres to the clitoral hood, causing pain when the clitoris is engorged with blood. A hymen that is rigid or imperforate (no opening), a rare condition, can also cause problems.

Interaction between organic and psychological causes of sexual dysfunction is always possible. An example is the man recovering from a heart attack. He may feel tired and ill as a result of his physical condition, and this alone could cause a decrease in sexual desire. But he is also concerned that the exertion of sexual intercourse may cause further damage to his heart or even kill him. This man may hold back from becoming excited during sexual encounters and may experience isolated episodes of erectile dysfunction that could lead to permanent erectile dysfunction because of anxiety.

TREATMENT OF SEXUAL DYSFUNCTIONS

Two major approaches are used in the treatment of sexual dysfunctions: the psychoanalytical approach and the behavioral approach. The psychoanalytical approach assumes that the sexual problems exhibited are manifestations of early childhood experiences that have created unconscious conflicts in the adult and that must be resolved through sessions with a psychoanalyst. In the behavioral approach, treatment of the problem is the major goal, with no regard as to whether the problem is caused by unconscious or intrapsychic conflicts. It is believed that most sexual dysfunctions are learned behaviors and that as such they can be unlearned or changed by behavior modification.

As in all theories and approaches to problems, there is a middle ground in which both psychoanalytical and behavioral techniques are used in the treatment of sexual dysfunctions.

Masters and Johnson have developed behavioral techniques to treat sexual dysfunctions in men and women. Their methods, as well as some developed by other sex therapists, and how they are used in specific problems are briefly discussed.

At the outset of a sex therapy program it is important to establish that both partners have basic knowledge of male and female anatomy. Simple ignorance of anatomical structures can be a source of sexual dysfunction.

Sensate Focus Exercises

Masters and Johnson pioneered the use of the **sensate focus** exercise. During sensate focus exercise, coitus and orgasm are prohibited. In essence, these exercises are designed to foster communication, both verbal and nonverbal, between the partners and to establish what "feels good" and what "does not feel good." One partner touches the other using various massage and touching techniques. The partner being touched lets the touching partner know what is most pleasurable. The couples then switch roles. Sensate focus exercise begins with two sessions during which one member of the couple touches the partner's body but is not allowed to touch the genitals or the breasts of the passive

sensate focus
(SEN sayt') Touching exercises to reduce anxiety and teach nonverbal communication.

Sensate focus.

partner. The active partner may do what he or she wishes in the way of touching, without trying to guess what the passive partner would like. The purpose of the touching is not to be erotic, but to establish an appreciation of "touch sensations" by both the touching partner and the partner being touched. During these first two sessions communication should be kept to a minimum with the exception of the person being touched. He or she must let the partner know (either verbally or nonverbally) if a particular touch is not pleasant. Thus the couple mutually explores nongenital areas that produce sexual excitation and concentrates on the sexual experience. In the second stage of sensate focus exercise the touching partner is allowed to touch the breasts and genitals of the partner, and the passive partner is instructed to move the active partner's hand to those areas that are most excited when touched. A "hand-riding" technique can be used, in which one partner places his or her hand on top of the other's hand and indicates whether more or less pressure is desired, a faster or slower pace is desired, or the hand should be moved to another place. This nonverbal communication can be important in effective lovemaking. The final phase of sensate focus exercise involves mutual touching, but intercourse and orgasm are still discouraged.

Sensate focus exercises emphasize mutual enhancement of erotic pleasure without orgasm. The stress of sexual performance is eliminated in these non-demand mutual pleasuring sessions. After several days of sensate focus exercises the couple gradually shifts to the female-on-top position, with or without intercourse. When the couple is ready and has learned the concepts of sensate

HUMAN SEXUALITY

focus exercise, intercourse is allowed. Sensate focus exercises may be used by any couple who wish to improve their lovemaking and pleasuring skills. They are certainly not limited to couples with dysfunctions.

Communication between sexual partners is critical and is an important aspect of most sex therapy programs. The behavioral techniques originated by Masters and Johnson to treat sexual dysfunctions also improve communication skills (Tullman et al., 1981). Couples were tested empirically on 10 specific skills theorized to be important in interpersonal communication, before and after undergoing sex therapy at the Masters and Johnson Institute. Both men and women became more assertive and more able to express their feelings to their partners after behavior therapy for a variety of dysfunctions.

Treatment of Sexual Dysfunctions in Men

Many therapists use the **squeeze technique** to treat premature ejaculation (Figure 17-3). Masters and Johnson (1970) have refined this technique, developed by Semans (1956) and originally called the "stop-start" method. The couple assumes a position in which the man is on his back and the woman sits in front of him and stimulates his penis with her hand. When the man feels he is getting close to ejaculation, he signals his partner. She stops stimulating him and squeezes his penis just below the corona of the glans. When done with some force, this causes the man to have a partial loss of erection, and he does not ejaculate. The force should be great enough to cause the desired effect but not sufficient to cause pain or harm. The penis may also be squeezed at its base to cause a partial loss of erection. Communication between the partners will determine the amount of force needed to cause partial loss of erection. The woman resumes stimulation until the man indicates ejaculation is imminent, then squeezes his penis again. This procedure is repeated several times

squeeze technique
Method used to reduce the tendency for rapid or premature ejaculation.

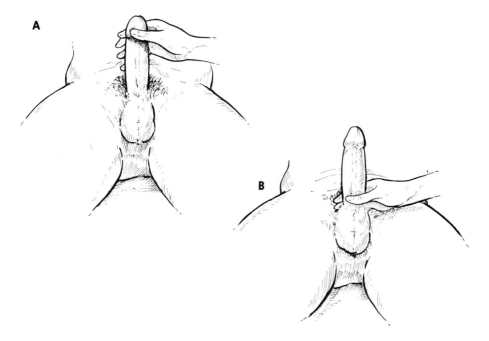

FIGURE 17-3
The squeeze technique is used to treat premature ejaculation. The sexual partner may squeeze the penis just below the corona (**A**) or at the base of the penis (**B**). Both actions produce a partial loss of erection and delay ejaculation.

before the man finally ejaculates. When the couple believes they have mastered the squeeze technique during manual stimulation, they proceed to sexual intercourse in the female-on-top position. In this position the woman can withdraw the man's penis and squeeze it when he signals that ejaculation is imminent. The squeeze technique, used correctly, has been successful in giving the man more self-control over ejaculation so that he can have intercourse without ejaculating immediately when the penis is placed in the vagina.

Kaplan (1974) uses a variation of the stop-start method devised by Semans to treat premature ejaculation. The couple is instructed to engage in limited foreplay so that the man has an erection. The man lies on his back, and the woman manually or orally stimulates his penis until he feels he is about to ejaculate. The man is told to concentrate on erotic feelings and the sensations in his penis so that he can learn to tell when ejaculation is imminent. The woman stops stimulating his penis when the man feels close to ejaculation. She then starts to stimulate him again before the erection is lost, but after he has lost the sensation that he is close to ejaculation. The process is continued, and the man is allowed to ejaculate after the fourth stop-start episode. "At no point should the patient try to exert conscious control over the orgasm, beyond signalling his wife to stop stimulation on time" (Kaplan, 1974). If the couple is successful, the stop-start technique is repeated during another session in which a water-based lubricant is used on the penis to simulate vaginal stimulation. The man is allowed to ejaculate on the fourth erection. After several extravaginal stop-start sessions the couple is instructed to engage in intercourse in the female-on-top position. The woman moves up and down on the penis until the man signals that ejaculation is imminent. The woman stops moving until the sensation to ejaculate passes, and then starts pelvic thrusting again. Coital orgasm occurs after four stop-start stimulations. The couple may move to another coital position once the male has gained ejaculatory control with the woman on top. At this point the man is instructed to thrust actively but to stop when ejaculation is imminent.

Erectile dysfunction in men without steady sexual partners has been treated in groups. In one study the men met in small groups with a male and a female sex therapist once a week for eight 2-hour treatment sessions (Price et al., 1981). The exact content of each session varied, but generally the men discussed their problems and heard presentations by the therapists on basic male and female anatomy and physiology, myths about male and female sexuality, sex role stereotypes, and the importance of communicating with partners about sexual difficulties. Sexual intercourse was banned at the beginning of the treatment program, and the men were instructed in how to become more aware of which sensations felt good. The men practiced gaining an erection, and the use of fantasy was encouraged.

Erectile dysfunction, whether of organic or psychological cause, is also treated with various medications. When an erectile problem develops over a period of months or years, the cause is most likely organic; when it develops suddenly, a psychological problem is probably the cause (Lizza and Cricco-Lissa, 1990). Endocrine disorders are a common organic cause of erectile dysfunction. It is estimated that endocrine problems cause 25% to 35% of all cases of erectile dysfunction with an organic basis (Kravis and Molitch, 1990).

The success rate with the appropriate medication is high. Common medications include testosterone when output of this hormone from the testes is low and gonadotropin hormone–releasing hormone (a preparation that stimulates the pituitary gland to stimulate the testes) when pituitary hormone output is low. Diabetic men often are good candidates for penile implants, since they often have both vascular and nerve damage that contributes to their erectile dysfunction.

A new treatment for erectile dysfunction is the use of the drug papaverine. The man injects the drug directly into the corpora cavernosa of the penis. It produces an erection that lasts long enough to have intercourse and no longer than 2 hours. The drug works by mimicking natural transmitters that allow the arteries supplying the penis and the smooth muscle in the corpora cavernosa to relax so blood can flow into the erectile tissues. Men with diabetes, nerve damage from prostatic surgery, and arterial insufficiency are often helped by papaverine. Men with erectile dysfunction of psychological origin may also be treated with papaverine, but only in conjunction with ongoing psychological counseling (Malloy and Wein, 1988).

The control of testicular functioning by the anterior pituitary gland is discussed in Chapter 4.

The role of diabetes in sexual disorders is discussed in Chapter 16.

Treatment of Sexual Dysfunctions in Women

The treatment of orgasmic dysfunction in women varies depending on the philosophy and training of the sex therapist. Kaplan (1974) aand LoPiccolo and Lobitz (1972) propose that a program of guided masturbation can be effective in teaching women who have never had an orgasm from any source of stimulation (primary orgasmic dysfunction). Both sexual partners must be told that the woman will be masturbating in an attempt to overcome orgasmic dysfunction. The program is used in the home. The woman begins by visually examining and exploring her genitals. The next step involves locating areas that produce pleasurable sensations. LoPiccolo and Lobitz, like Masters and Johnson (1966), have not found any woman who "locates the vagina as a strong source of sexual pleasure; most of our clients focus on the clitoral area as the most pleasurable" (LoPiccolo and Lobitz, 1972). Once the woman locates the pleasure-producing area(s), she is instructed to stimulate it manually. She is instructed in clitoral manipulation and the use of a lubricant to increase pleasure. The woman is encouraged to increase the intensity and duration of masturbation and to use erotic reading material, pictures, and fantasies during masturbation. If orgasm does not occur, she is instructed to purchase a vibrator and use it on the sensitive area(s). Most women reach orgasm with use of a vibrator (LoPiccolo and Lobitz, 1972).

Once the woman has achieved orgasm, the husband or other sexual partner is brought into the program. The woman now masturbates with the sexual partner present. The partner observes and learns what techniques the woman enjoys. The next step involves the partner stimulating the woman to orgasm, either manually or with a vibrator, depending on how the woman was stimulating herself. The last step in the program involves intercourse while the sexual partner manually stimulates the woman's genitals. LoPiccolo and Lobitz recommend the female-on-top, sitting, or rear-entry coital positions because they allow easy access to the woman's genitals during intercourse.

In contrast to the program of LoPiccolo and Lobitz, Masters and Johnson (1970) use the sex partner during all phases of treatment for orgasmic dysfunction. The woman is touched by her sex partner and encouraged to direct the sex partner's hand and fingers, with her hand placed over the partner's hand, to the area(s) that feels most pleasure when touched.

Milan, Kilmann, and Borman (1988) have found that the male partner's sexual functioning was of critical importance in the success of the treatment for secondary orgasmic dysfunction and conclude that "the importance of a treatment approach to secondary orgasmic dysfunction . . . focuses on the couple, rather than on the woman alone, and takes into consideration the various sexual and nonsexual characteristics of each couple" (p. 477). For treatment of secondary orgasmic dysfunction Milan and colleagues use group sessions in which the male partners are included. Their treatments vary but include a basic format in which all couples receive 4 hours of basic sex education followed by training in communication skills and sexual skills, for a total of 20 hours of instruction. Sex therapists conduct all treatments.

Formal professional help is not the only help sought for sexual dysfunctions. In a study of 503 individuals, 225 (approximately 43%) reported sexual difficulties, and of this group only 3.5% sought professional help (Catania et al., 1990). The rest turned to friends, relatives (other than spouse), and self-help solutions such as books and magazine articles.

Sex Therapy for Individuals Without Partners

One controversial area of sex therapy involves the use of surrogate partners. How do you treat a person for a sexual dysfunction who does not have a sexual partner? Men and women who have sex with men and women receiving therapy for various sexual dysfunctions are called sexual surrogates. Some consider surrogate partners to be prostitutes; others believe they provide an important means of overcoming some sexual dysfunctions. Because of the great controversy surrounding sexual surrogates as employed by Masters and Johnson, they are rarely used in sex therapy programs today (Albert et al., 1980). In fact, Kaplan never employed surrogates in her therapy program (1974).

Homosexuals and Sexual Dysfunctions

Throughout this chapter we have indicated that the sexual dysfunctions discussed may apply to any individual, regardless of sexual orientation. The treatment of sexual dysfunctions in homosexual or bisexual individuals is essentially the same as in heterosexual individuals. This topic is discussed in detail by Masters and Johnson (1979) in *Homosexuality in Perspective*.

Treatment Success for Sexual Dysfunctions

How successful are the various treatments for sexual dysfunctions in men and women? This is a difficult question to answer because some researchers inflate their success rates in various ways. How do you measure success? Is it based on a certain percentage of people who improve at the end of the treatment? What percentage of people who improve equals success? What criteria for individual improvement equal success? How long after the treatment should the "cure" last? A month, a year, 5 years? Who selects the sample of people to determine success? We could select people that respond more readily to treatment and keep them in the sample and throw out those individuals who do not respond to treatment.

In a study by Milan, Kilmann, and Borland (1988), 66 couples in which the women reported secondary orgasmic dysfunction were treated for the dysfunction. The treatments followed these therapists' basic format, described previously (p. 502). At the conclusion of treatment a greater number of the women in the treatment group compared with untreated control women had an orgasm 50% of the time or more during intercourse. Thus in this study success was measured as having an orgasm 50% of the time during intercourse. At long-term follow-up to determine how well the women were doing, women in the treatment group maintained or increased their level of orgasmic functioning during intercourse (Milan, Kilmann, and Borland, 1988). We can conclude that the treatment used by Milan and associates was a success and had a long-lasting effect. However, only 58% of the original sample responded to the mailed questionnaire. This is actually a good return rate for mailed questionnaires, but we still must ask whether the people who responded were the ones who were doing well and the other 42% who did not respond represent those who were not doing well. The authors also recognize the sampling problem and state that caution is warranted in generalizing the results of their study to the entire original sample (Milan, Kilmann, and Borland, 1988).

Masters and Johnson report their success rates in the book *Human Sexual Inadequacy* (1970). They included 790 people who were treated for various sexual dysfunctions and concluded that 648 (82%) were no longer dysfunctional at the end of the 2-week therapy program. The easiest to cure was premature ejaculation, with 97% of the men no longer having this dysfunction after treatment. At long-term follow-up, Masters and Johnson reported that after 5 years 75% of the individuals were still functioning without any problems.

The success rates of Masters and Johnson have not gone unchallenged. Zilbergeld and Evans (1980), based on the success rates achieved by other sex therapists, felt that the rates reported by Masters and Johnson (1970) were too high. Zilbergeld and Evans had many criticisms of Masters and Johnson's work, including the fact that Masters and Johnson never defined what they meant by success. As we stated earlier, what constitutes a successful treatment is critical to defining a rate of positive outcomes based on treatment. Another criticism involved the sample chosen by Masters and Johnson. They stated that certain people were rejected from therapy. Were the rejected people the difficult cases that would have lowered the success rate reported? We have no way of answering this question.

SEXUAL DISORDERS
Sexual Disorders in Men

Prostatitis **Prostatitis** is inflammation or infection of the prostate gland. The infection may be long lasting (chronic) or short in duration (acute). In some cases the seminal vesicles and bladder are also infected or inflamed.

The symptoms of prostatitis are fever, chills, pain in the perineum, frequent urination, and in some cases painful ejaculation. Some men experience only mild symptoms, such as mild discomfort in the area of the genitalia and anus.

prostatitis
(pros′ tuh TY tis) Inflammation or infection of the prostate gland.

Prostatitis is much more common in men older than 40 years. The disease is treated with antibiotics, although some difficult cases may not respond to conventional antibiotic therapy.

Prostatic cancer Cancer of the prostate gland is rare in men younger than 40 years, but it is one of the most common cancers after age 50. Approximately 75,000 new cases are diagnosed each year, and the incidence increases with age so that 1 in 100 men over the age of 70 have the disease (Vikram and Vikram, 1988). Usually it is discovered during a rectal examination while the physician is feeling the prostate gland through the wall of the rectum. Not all enlargements of the prostate gland are indicative of cancer. Localized prostate cancer is treated with radiation therapy and surgery. If the prostate must be removed (radical prostatectomy), the chance for erectile problems approaches 90% (Vikram and Vikram, 1988). Nerves from the pelvic plexus that supply the erectile tissues of the penis are disrupted in this procedure. A new procedure, nerve-sparing prostatectomy, has been developed, but its long-term effects on erectile functioning are not known. The use of radiation and localized surgical procedures to treat localized cancers does not cause the same degree of erectile dysfunction as radical surgery (Somers, 1989).

Testicular cancer Cancer of the testes is relatively rare and occurs most commonly in men in their twenties or thirties. Approximately 5,500 cases are reported each year in the United States (American Cancer Society, 1988). As with breast cancer, a testicular tumor usually does not cause great pain. A testicular tumor produces a gradual enlargement of the testis with an associated heavy sensation in the scrotum and lower abdomen. A dull ache or pain in the scrotum may occur in some cases. If detected early, testicular cancer has a high cure rate. Thus it is important for men to learn how to do self-examination for any lumps or swellings on the testicles (see box).

Testicular Self-Examination

Testicular cancer occurs most commonly in men in their twenties or thirties. Because this type of cancer does not usually cause pain, it can easily escape detection. Men should get into the habit of examining their testicles on a regular basis. The best time to check for abnormal lumps or growths is after a hot bath or shower. The hot water causes the scrotal muscles to relax, and the testicles and related structures within the scrotum are easily felt. Each testicle should be checked separately using the tips of the fingers and thumb. If any lumps are felt, a physician should check the suspected growth.

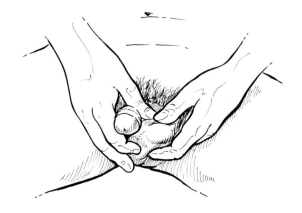

Sexual Disorders in Women

Vaginitis   Vaginitis is inflammation of the vagina. Among the causes of vaginitis are infection and irritation. Vaginitis usually causes a discharge from the vagina that may have a disagreeable odor. The woman may complain of pain during intercourse because the vagina is irritated and tender. Two conditions, trichomoniasis and yeast infections, can cause vaginitis.

Trichomoniasis and vaginal yeast infections, two common causes of vaginitis, are discussed in Chapter 18, "Sexually Transmitted Diseases," because they are spread through intimate body contact.

Gardnerella vaginitis   *Gardnerella* vaginitis, a nonspecific vaginitis, causes a thin, foul-smelling vaginal discharge. The woman may have symptoms of irritation or "rawness" in the vagina and pain with intercourse. This type of vaginitis is treated with an antibacterial medication; if the infection is well established, a cleansing vaginal cream is used. Nonspecific vaginitis is not sexually transmitted; that is, it is not spread through intimate body contact.

Endometriosis   **Endometriosis** is the presence of endometrial tissue, which is the membrane lining the uterus, in abnormal locations, including the ovaries or pelvis. Endometriosis is more common during the childbearing years. The symptoms vary, depending on the location of the endometrial tissue. Pain is the major symptom and occurs in the majority of women with endometriosis. The pain usually begins before the menstrual flow, worsens throughout menstruation, and may persist for 1 to 2 days after the flow has ceased; it recurs with each menstrual period. The pain, usually located in the lower abdomen, lower back, and pelvis, may be of the sharp cramping type and misdiagnosed as dysmenorrhea, or painful menstruation. It is important to differentiate endometriosis from dysmenorrhea. The pain from endometriosis results from misplaced uterine tissue expanding and contracting during the menstrual cycle, which causes pain in the region where the tissue is located.

endometriosis
(en doh mee tree oh sis)
Presence of endometrial tissue in locations other than the uterus.

Painful intercourse may occur during the premenstrual phase of the cycle in women with endometriosis. Fertility may be impaired in women with endometriosis, and this often brings a couple to a physician for consultation. Infertility occurs when the endometrial tissue forms patches and scars around the ovaries and within the fallopian tubes and interferes with normal ovarian and tubal functioning. It is estimated that 30% to 40% of patients with endometriosis have problems conceiving and 10% to 15% of infertility patients have endometriosis (Berkow, 1987).

Endometriosis is positively identified through surgical procedures and examination of biopsy tissue under a microscope. During surgery an attempt is made to remove all implants of the endometriotic tissue. Hormonal therapy is another treatment for confirmed endometriosis. The medication, usually an oral contraceptive, suppresses ovulation and prevents the cyclical buildup of both the uterine and extrauterine endometriotic tissue. Hormone therapy relieves the symptoms and prevents further spread of the endometrium but does not cure the disease. Pregnancy, which also prevents cyclical buildup of endometrium, causes regression of the disease and its symptoms.

Herpes simplex virus and human papillomavirus are discussed in detail in Chapter 17.

Cervical intraepithelial neoplasia and the Papanicolaou smear   Certain sexually transmitted infectious agents such as the human papillomavirus (HPV) and the herpes simplex virus (HSV) have been implicated in **cervical intraepithelial neoplasia** (CIN). The term *CIN* is used to describe early cancerous or precancerous changes of cervical epithelial cells (Hatcher et al., 1990).

cervical intraepithelial neoplasia
(in truh ep' uh THEE lee uhl NEE uh play' zhuh)
Early cancerous or precancerous changes of the cervical epithelial cells.

According to Hatcher and associates (1990), women most at risk for CIN fit into one or more of the following categories: (1) sexually active before age 20, (2) intercourse with three or more partners by age 35, and (3) intercourse with a partner who has had three or more partners.

In most cases CIN is asymptomatic, although vaginal bleeding may give a clue. Diagnosis is based on a Papanicolaou (Pap) smear in which cells are collected from the cervix. Medical treatment for CIN varies and is beyond the scope of this book. Generally speaking, surgical procedures using conventional surgery, laser surgery, and cryosurgery are employed. Hatcher and associates (1990) state that a woman at risk for CIN should have her partner use a condom and should have an annual Pap smear.

cystitis
(si STY tis) Infection or inflammation of the bladder.

Cystitis **Cystitis,** or inflammation of the urinary bladder, occurs in both men and women. The symptoms of cystitis include a painful burning sensation on urination, increased frequency of urination, cloudy or bloody urine, and lower abdominal pain.

Cystitis is more common in women than in men. The reason for this is that the female urethra is approximately 1 inch long, compared with about 6 inches in the male, and bacteria have a shorter distance to travel from the entrance of the urethra (urethral orifice) to the outlet of the bladder.

Cystitis may occur in sexually inactive or active women. A bladder infection in a woman when she first becomes sexually active or when sexual intercourse is resumed after a long period of sexual inactivity is commonly referred to as "honeymoon cystitis." Why such bladder infections occur is not known. Cystitis is treated with various antibiotics, depending on the causative organism.

• • •

The bimanual pelvic examination is used to detect the disorders that have been described. During routine pelvic examinations the Pap test or smear is used to detect early cancers of the female genital tract (Figure 17-4).

The anatomy of the mammary glands is presented in Chapter 2.

Disorders of the mammary glands The mammary glands may be affected by both benign and malignant conditions, and all women should perform a monthly self-examination to detect breast changes. In this section the most common problems and diseases of the breasts are briefly discussed.

Many women notice lumps and swellings in their breasts. Sometimes the swellings are painful and occur during the time before the menstrual flow when progesterone is the dominant hormone. Inasmuch as breast lumps may also change in size and shape over the menstrual cycle, a breast self-examination should be done at the same time each month (see the box on pp. 508 and 509). The first few days after the menstrual flow stops is a good time because the breasts are not swollen and it is easier to detect lumps.

The great majority of breast lumps are harmless. In a study of 14,328 women whose breasts were examined by a physician using techniques of palpation, 85% of solid lumps were found to be benign, or not cancerous (Mahoney and Csima, 1982).

Several conditions can produce breast lumps. Fibroadenomas are lumps or growths made up of fibrous and glandular elements and feel as if they are in a capsule. They have a firm rubbery consistency and are easily "popped" about

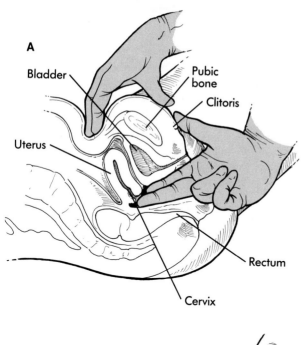

A

Bladder

Pubic
bone

Clitoris

Uterus

Rectum

Cervix

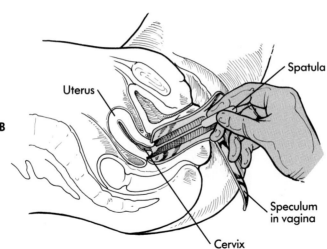

B

Uterus

Spatula

Speculum
in vagina

Cervix

FIGURE 17-4
A, The bimanual (two-handed) pelvic examination is used to check the internal reproductive structures. **B,** The Pap smear is a simple test in which cells from the cervix are examined to detect cancer.

within the breast (Berkow, 1987). They can be treated by surgical removal. Cystic mastitis or fibrocystic disease is characterized by rapid development of one or more fluid-filled cysts. About 20% of women of reproductive age have this benign condition (Berkow, 1987). These cysts may cause premenstrual breast pain. Although treatment for benign breast disease is rarely required, all breast lumps should be examined by a physician.

What contributes to the development of benign breast lumps? One theory, which we have simplified, is that the breast, like the uterus, produces a monthly buildup of fluid, glandular elements, and fibrous tissue in preparation for a potential pregnancy. Over the years the body fails to resorb some of these products, which form various types of lumps in the breast. Often cysts from

Breast Self-Examination

The following method of monthly breast self-examination (BSE) was taken from the National Cancer Institute (NCI) pamphlet *Breast Exams: What You Should Know,* published in 1985. For additional information on breast exami-

nations and breast cancer you may call the Cancer Information Service toll free at 1-800-CANCER.

The best time to do BSE is 2 or 3 days after your period ends. At this time your breasts are less likely to be tender or swollen. If you no

longer have a menstrual flow (e.g., postmenopausal women or women with a hysterectomy), the BSE should be done the first day of each month. The purpose of the BSE is to allow you to become familiar with the normal "feel" of your breasts so that if a lump or growth appears, you will detect this change quickly.

We have combined the six steps of the NCI method into five:

1. Stand in front of a mirror and inspect both breasts for any discharge from the nipples, and puckering or scaling of the skin. Gently squeeze the nipples and look for a discharge. If any of the above signs are noted, see a physician.

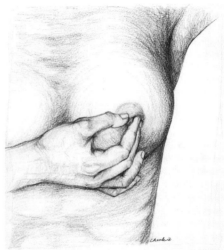

2. Steps 2 and 3 are done to note any change in breast shape or contour. Stand in front of a mirror, clasp your hands behind your head, and press hands against head.

3. Next put hands on hips and press firmly. At the same time lean your shoulders and elbows forward. Any change in the shape or contour of the breasts should be reported to a physician.

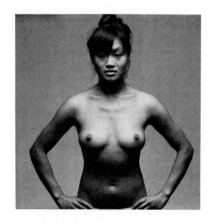

4. Raise your left arm and use the fingertips of the right hand to check the left breast. Beginning at the outer edge, press the flat part of the fingers together and move them in circles around the breast. Start at the outer margins of the breast and continue to make smaller and smaller circles until you get to the nipples. Feel for any unusual lumps or mass beneath the skin. Now raise the right arm and use the fingers of the left hand to repeat the above procedure. Carefully check the area between the breast and armpit. If you feel any lumps or thickenings, report these to your physician.

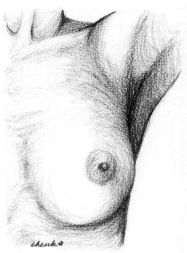

5. Repeat step 4 while you are lying down. Lie on your back, left arm over your head and a pillow under your left shoulder. In this position the breast is flattened and is easier to examine. Use the same technique with your fingers as described above to examine the breast. Repeat the procedure on the right breast.

Mammography: Another Weapon to Detect Breast Cancer

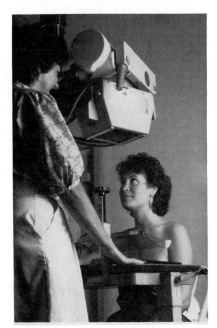

As the American Cancer Society says, "The best weapon against breast cancer is early detection." The newest preventive measure to appear on the scene in the battle against breast cancer is mammography. Mammography is a low-dose x-ray examination that helps detect the smallest of breast cancers. The earlier the detection, the greater the cure rate for this disease. The American Cancer Society offers the following mammography guidelines:

1. Women ages 35 to 39: See your doctor for a baseline mammogram. This baseline mammogram will allow early detection of changes from the normal appearance of the breast during later mammograms.
2. Women ages 40 to 49: Have a mammogram every 1 to 2 years, even if no symptoms are present.
3. Women ages 50 and over: See your doctor for a mammogram every year.
4. Mammograms may also be used when a breast lump is found in a woman of any age.

---

chronic cystic mastitis disappear during pregnancy, but fibroadenomas are less likely to regress during pregnancy.

The breast is the most common site of cancer in women. Breast cancer is rare in women younger than 30 years of age, and its incidence increases after menopause. Because cancer of the breast is usually not painful, monthly breast self-examination and prompt examination by a physician of any changes in the breast are essential. The treatment of breast cancer varies depending on the extent of the disease (that is, whether it has spread to the lymph nodes in the axillary region, or armpit) and the patient's age. Surgical treatment ranges from removal of the entire breast, the lymph nodes in the axilla adjacent to the cancerous breast, and the muscles beneath the affected breast (*radical mastectomy*) to removal of only the tumor and surrounding breast tissue.

In a study comparing the effectiveness of radical mastectomy with *partial mastectomy* (removal of the tumor and a fourth of the breast containing the tumor, axillary lymph nodes, and underlying skin and connective tissue), it was found that the less drastic procedure was equal to the more disfiguring surgery in terms of long-term survival and recurrence of disease (Veronesi, Saccozzi, and Vecchio, 1981). The researchers concluded that radical mastectomy appears to involve unnecessary mutilation in patients with early breast cancer and no involvement of the axillary nodes. Fisher and associates (1985a, 1985b) came to the same conclusion in two different studies. One study (1985b) showed that in women with no axillary node involvement, removal of only the breast (*total mastectomy*), with or without x-ray treatment, provided survival at the end of 10 years equal to that achieved with radical mastectomy. In women with axillary node involvement, radical mastectomy yielded no better survival than total mastectomy plus radiation therapy. In a second study (1985a) women with malignant tumors of 4 centimeters in diameter or smaller were studied. The sample was divided into two groups: one group underwent total mastectomies, and in the other group a limited amount of breast tissue was removed with the tumor. The survival rate at the end of 5 years was the same for both groups.

The disfigurement caused by the radical procedure is a major concern to women in addition to the fear of cancer. Many couples have difficulty dealing with the loss of a breast. The woman is worried about how the loss will affect her partner's interaction with her, and the partner may be afraid to look at the area where surgery was performed. The woman without a partner may worry about telling prospective sex partners about the surgery. Counseling or discussions with other couples or women who have undergone the same surgical treatment for breast cancer often help the woman and the couple work through the adjustment period.

SUMMARY

1 This chapter discusses sexual dysfunctions, usually of psychological origin, and sexual disorders or physical conditions caused by organic problems.
2 The most common sexual dysfunctions in men are erectile dysfunction or impotence, premature ejaculation, and retarded ejaculation or ejaculatory incompetence. The most common sexual dysfunctions in women are vaginismus and orgasmic dysfunction. Two problems common to men and women are painful intercourse and lack of sexual desire.
3 Erectile dysfunction is the inability to have or maintain an erection sufficient for intromission (penis-inside-vagina or penis-inside-anus intercourse).
4 Premature ejaculation is ejaculation before or just on penetration of the vagina or anus.
5 Retarded ejaculation occurs when the man is unable to have an orgasm and ejaculation.
6 Orgasmic dysfunction occurs when a woman has difficulty reaching orgasm.
7 Vaginismus has been defined as painful involuntary vaginal muscle spasms when intercourse is attempted.
8 Painful intercourse occurs in both men and women and is usually caused by an anatomical problem, an infection, or inadequate vaginal lubrication.
9 Dysfunction of sexual desire involves involuntary loss of interest in sex.
10 The causes of sexual dysfunctions vary, but some seem to appear with greater frequency than others, including failure to engage in effective sexual behavior, sexual anxiety, perceptual and intellectual defenses against erotic feelings, and failure to communicate with the sexual partner.
11 Sexual dysfunctions are treated with both psychoanalytical and behavioral techniques or with a combination of the two methods.
12 Orgasmic dysfunction is treated in various ways. In essence, the woman is instructed to identify those areas of her vulva that produce pleasurable sensations when touched.
13 Some sexual disorders in men include prostatitis (inflammation of the pros-

tate gland), prostatic cancer, and testicular cancer. Sexual disorders in women include vaginitis (inflammation of the vagina), endometriosis (presence of uterine tissue in abnormal locations), and cervical cancer. Cystitis, which is inflammation of the urinary bladder, may occur in both men and women.

14 The mammary glands and testes may be affected by both benign and malignant conditions, and all women and men should perform a monthly self-examination.

F A C T
OR
F I C T I O N

ANSWERS

1 The great majority of sexual dysfunctions—some estimates indicate at least 80%—are psychological in origin.

2 Alcohol and cocaine do not always have a negative effect on sexual functioning. Sexual enhancement with psychoactive drugs such as alcohol and cocaine occurs primarily in nonaddicted individuals, and drug-induced sexual dysfunctions predominate in addicted individuals.

3 Many sex therapy programs include both partners in the treatment of sexual dysfunctions.

1 In your own words describe how a monthly breast examination is done.

2 Briefly compare how the psychoanalytical approach differs from the behavioral approach in terms of the treatment of sexual dysfunctions.

3 List and define all of the male sexual dysfunctions described in this chapter.

4 List and define all of the female sexual dysfunctions described in this chapter.

SUGGESTED READINGS

Hay, L.: You can heal your life, New York, 1988, Hay House, Inc.
A self-help book designed to promote, among other things, good sexual functioning.

Heiman, J., and LoPiccolo, J.: Becoming orgasmic: a sexual and personal growth program for women, New York, 1988, Prentice-Hall.
A book that will aid women who want to experience orgasm and increase sexual pleasure by themselves or with their partner.

Kaplan, H.: The illustrated manual of sex therapy, New York, 1975, Quadrangle/Times Books.
A book illustrating many of the techniques discussed in this chapter.

Sexually Transmitted Diseases

I spend much more time in a relationship discussing my partner's sexual history. One woman I knew who was on the pill began asking her dates to use a condom and began to carry them herself. As a single guy, I might be tempted to consider her a great date, but her history says she fools around too much. I have really reduced my own sexual activities out of fear of contracting a sexually transmitted disease, especially AIDS.

28-YEAR-OLD SINGLE MAN
Authors' Files

The introductory narrative illustrates two important points. First, the man who was quoted is worried about protection against diseases that can be transmitted during sexual activities. Second is the use of the term sexually transmitted diseases. *Venereal disease* was once the term most commonly used to describe the "classic" diseases transmitted by sexual activities: gonorrhea, syphilis, chancroid, lymphogranuloma venereum, and granuloma inguinale (a disease that is rare in the United States and not discussed in this chapter). Now the term *sexually transmitted disease* (STD) has replaced it because we realize that many other diseases can be transmitted during sexual activity. Sexually transmitted disease refers to a number of diseases, infections, and infestations involving the anus, genitals, mouth, eyes, and other areas of the body. The causative agents of most of these conditions are often, but not always, passed along during intimate body contact.

Both terms, venereal disease and sexually transmitted disease, carry negative connotations. Historically, STDs were associated with sin and were thought to be the punishment for "unclean sinful acts." The truth is that venereal diseases, like other diseases, are caused by bacteria, viruses, parasitic animals, and other organisms. Their transmission through intimate sexual contact is what has given these diseases their past and present negative connotations.

Many people reading this chapter have read about and know about STDs but will not personally experience them. For other readers STDs are a personal concern. Individuals who engage in sexual encounters with many different people are more likely to contract an STD than are those who confine sexual relationships to one person over time.

Prevention, that is, avoiding infection, must be the first and most important word in any discussion of STDs (Hatcher et al., 1990). As Hatcher and associates point out:

> Persistent viral infections, including human immunodeficiency virus (the causative agent of acquired immunodeficiency syndrome [AIDS]), herpes simplex virus and human papillomavirus (the cause of genital warts); resistant strains of once easily cured gonorrhea and long term consequences of pelvic inflammatory disease . . . have all increased in number and consequence. Prevention is now the most effective way to reduce the adverse consequences of STDs for individuals and society.
>
> Hatcher et al., 1990, p. 14

As previously stated, until recently only five diseases were typically considered STDs: syphilis, gonorrhea, chancroid, lymphogranuloma venereum, and granuloma inguinale. Now the medical community realizes that many diseases have the potential to be transmitted during intimate body contact.

FIGURE 18-1
Estimates of new cases of
sexually transmitted dis-
eases per year, as projected
by the Centers for Disease
Control in 1987. Although
many new cases of sexually
transmitted diseases are reported each year, many are
also cured each year (with
the exception of genital
herpes).

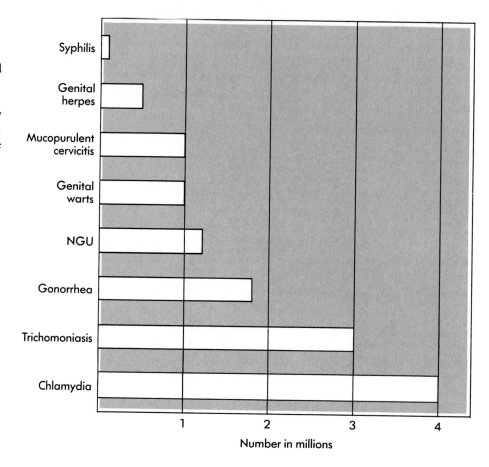

Number in millions

**The disease AIDS is dis-
cussed in detail in Chap-
ter 19.**

Each year more than 14 million persons in the United States are affected by
STDs (Figure 18-1). Some of these diseases are easily prevented from spreading; others are not. Some are easy to treat; others are difficult or impossible
to cure; and one, acquired immune deficiency syndrome (AIDS), cannot be
cured and is fatal. Many commonly asked questions about STDs are answered
in the box on pp. 518 and 519.

This chapter is concerned with various STDs, their causes, symptoms,
treatments, and prevention. In September 1989 the Division of Sexually Transmitted Diseases of the Centers for Disease Control (CDC) published new guidelines for the treatment of patients with STDs. This chapter relies on that
publication for the most up-to-date information. The diseases in this chapter
are grouped into eight categories based on a classification system used by the
CDC: (1) infections characterized by genital ulcers or swollen lymph nodes;
(2) infections of skin surfaces; (3) gonococcal infections; (4) chlamydial infections; (5) external parasitic infections; (6) miscellaneous diseases associated
with the gastrointestinal tract; (7) vaginal infections, and (8) pelvic inflammatory disease. The final portion of the chapter discusses the effect of STDs
on the fetus and newborn infant. All of the STDs presented in this chapter
are listed in Table 18-1, which summarizes causes, symptoms, and treatment
of each disease.

TABLE 18-1 Sexually Transmitted Diseases: Their Causes, Symptoms, and Treatment

Disease	Cause	Symptoms	Treatment
Genital herpes	Virus: herpes simplex virus type 2 (HSV-2)	Painful blisters that become open sores	Acyclovir to control and reduce symptoms; no cure at present
Syphilis	*Treponema pallidum* (has characteristics of bacteria and protozoa)	Hard painless sore (chancre)	Antibiotics such as penicillin
Lymphogranuloma venerum	Bacterium: *Chlamydia*	Small painless sore in genital region, swelling of lymph nodes	Same as for *Chlamydia* infections
Chancroid	Bacterium: *Haemophilus ducreyi*	Painful sores in genital region	Antibiotics such as tetracycline and erythromycin
Genital warts	Virus: human papilloma viruses	Small painless growths of various shapes	Podophyllin applied to warts; surgical removal of some
Gonorrhea	Bacterium: *Neisseria gonorrhoeae*	In men, thick discharge from urethra and painful urination; asymptomatic in most women, vaginal discharge in some	Antibiotics such as penicillin
Chlamydia infections	Bacterium: *Chlamydia* (genus includes many species)	In men, clear discharge; few symptoms in most women in early stages of infection	Antibiotics such as tetracycline and erythromycin
Nongonococcal urethritis	Bacterium: usually *Chlamydia*	In men, thin clear discharge from urethra and pain on urination	Same as for *Chlamydia* infections
Mucopurulent cervicitis	Bacterium: usually *Chlamydia* or *N. gonorrhoeae*	Discharge	Same as for *Chlamydia* infection or gonorrhea
Pubic lice and scabies	External parasites	Itching in pubic region	Insecticide shampoo
Hepatitis B	Virus: hepatitis virus	Flulike symptoms; liver is affected	Treatment of symptoms, with recovery usual
Amebiasis	Protozoa: *Entamoeba histolytica*	Ulcerlike sore in large intestine, lower abdominal pain, diarrhea	Drugs such as metronidazole
Trichomoniasis	Protozoa: *Trichomonas vaginalis*	In women, foul-smelling yellow vaginal discharge; asymptomatic in men	Metronidazole (Flagyl)
Vaginal yeast infections	Fungus: *Candida albicans*	Thick, white, cheesy vaginal discharge; asymptomatic in men	Antifungal preparations such as Monistat

Common Questions About Sexually Transmitted Diseases (STDs)

Q. What happens when a person who thinks he or she may have an STD walks into a public health clinic for help?

A. For many young people the public health clinic is an imposing place. However, many people who go to clinics do not have concerns about STDs. The majority of individuals want a pregnancy test or contraceptive information. For those concerned about an STD, the normal routine is as follows: The client walks into the reception area of the clinic and either steps up to the reception counter or is asked by the receptionist if she can help. Many clients are reluctant to say that they are concerned about an STD. Often they say, "I need to see a doctor (or nurse)." The receptionist is quite perceptive about what they really want. She often helps them by saying, "Are you concerned with VD or an STD?" The client now has only to answer yes to the question. Some male clients are flip about why they are at the clinic. Some say, "I think I got VD," or "I think I got the clap."

Once the receptionist has determined that the client is concerned about a possible infection, the client is taken to an examining room by a specially trained nurse. The nurse asks specific questions about such things as symptoms and past history of disease. At all times the nurse maintains a calm demeanor, which assures clients that they are in good hands. The nurse indicates by his or her manner that an STD, if present, is not a stigma or anything bad. The client is treated as an individual who has come in for help for a medical problem. If a blood test for syphilis is indicated, the nurse draws the blood.

After the initial interview by the nurse, the client is seen by either a physician or a nurse clinician. When I see a client, I try to put him or her at ease. I ask more specific questions after reviewing the chart, then do my examination and tests.

If a diagnosis can be made, and most times it can, I administer treatment and discuss how we will get in touch with the client's sexual contacts. Clients usually provide the names. I explain that we will not mention the client's name when we call the sexual contacts but will ask them to come in for an examination because we have reason to believe they have been exposed to an STD.

Q. Who is the typical person who comes to the clinic?

A. Virtually all of our clients are young, 15 to 25 years of age. They also tend to be sexually active and thus are at greatest risk for STDs. We rarely see married, older individuals; they usually go to their own physicians.

Q. Do most people become anxious when you get to the treatment part of the procedure?

A. For some reason most people think our needles are much bigger than other physicians' needles. I can assure you they are not! In fact, injections are not a concern because we can treat most STDs caused by bacteria with orally ingested medication. The client takes a large dose of an antibiotic, usually penicillin, by mouth while in the office.

Q. What happens when you begin to discuss the client's sexual contacts?

A. This is another area of popular misconception. Many of our clients have already called their sexual contacts and told them that they should probably see a doctor because they may have caught an STD. I am impressed by the social conscience of many of our clients. Only rarely will a client not name his or her contacts. If the contacts do not call us, we call them. In most cases the sexual contacts come in after the client calls them.

Q. How do you reassure the client that everything you do is confidential?

A. I tell all of my clients that there are three very important considerations insofar as their case is concerned. First, I want to treat and cure the disease. Second, I want to see all of their sexual contacts of the past 30 days. I must examine the contacts and give treatment if they need it. I stress that everything is confidential and that we will not use the client's name when talking to a sexual contact. Third, the

---

Answers to the questions provided by Alex Mitchell, M.D., Public Health Physician, Douglas County Public Health Office, Lawrence, Kansas, and *The STD Bulletin*, published every other month by Burroughs-Wellcome Co. *The STD Bulletin* is a publication written by health care workers for other health care professionals.

client should return in 1 week for a "test of cure." We want to be sure the disease organism has been completely eliminated by the antibiotic or other drug.

Q. How common are *Chlamydia* infections?

A. Too common. The Centers for Disease Control in Atlanta keeps us up to date on all STDs, and *Chlamydia* has shown a striking increase. In fact, according to the CDC, there are more *Chlamydia* infections than gonorrhea per year.

Q. How do you treat *Chlamydia* infections?

A. *Chlamydia* infection is insidious because it mimics the symptoms of gonorrhea in men and women. If we treat for gonorrhea by itself, the *Chlamydia* infection continues and can cause sterility and pelvic inflammatory disease in women. The man will continue to harbor the bacteria and infect his sexual partner(s). Often we find that a client with gonorrhea also has a *Chlamydia* infection. We treat the *Chlamydia* infection with either tetracycline or erythromycin for 1 week. These antibiotics usually eliminate *Chlamydia* organisms. We treat the gonorrhea with a broad-spectrum antibiotic other than penicillin.

Q. What about the future treatment for genital herpes (HSV-2)?

A. Vaccines that are under study would protect against contracting the disease and cure existing disease.

Q. Can a person contract gonorrhea during fellatio?

A. The infected male can pass the bacterium to the oral cavity of the partner performing oral sex. However, gonorrheal infections of the vulva and vagina cannot be passed to the oral cavity of the partner during cunnilingus. Also, gonorrheal infections of the oral cavity cannot be passed during mouth-to-mouth kissing.

Q. Can a person with a cold sore (HSV-1) on the lip pass the virus to the genitals of a partner during oral sex?

A. It is possible but not likely. If this did occur, the infected person would usually have the sore on a body part other than the genitals. There really has not been enough research to answer the question more specifically. HSV-1 is not as contagious as was once thought and is not always passed even during mouth-to-mouth kissing.

Q. Is HSV-2 dangerous?

A. HSV-2 is not really damaging to an adult but can cause anxiety and physical discomfort. It can be very dangerous to the fetus of an infected pregnant woman.

Q. How does gonorrhea become resistant to penicillin?

A. One common theory is that prostitutes, particularly those in developing countries and Southeast Asia, constantly use low doses of penicillin to protect themselves from gonorrheal infection. These low doses do not kill all of the bacteria, and those that survive continue to change to become more and more resistant to penicillin. Other theories involve the self-treatment of gonorrhea with regular doses of various antibiotics that can be obtained without seeing a physician and undergoing laboratory tests. Certain strains changed and became resistant to the antibiotics, and these were transmitted during sexual encounters.

Q. How common is genital herpes?

A. An estimated 5 to 20 million Americans have genital herpes, and approximately 500,000 new cases occur each year. It is most common among young, sexually active adults.

Q. How can people with herpes minimize the impact this virus might have on their sexual relationships?

A. People with herpes need to think about the best way to tell potential lovers that they have the virus. An informed discussion about how to avoid transmission is helpful. Routine use of condoms and not having intercourse when active lesions are present will help, but will not guarantee against transmission.

Q. How common is syphilis?

A. About 30,000 cases of syphilis are reported in the United States each year, making this disease the third most frequently reported infectious disease after chickenpox and gonorrhea. Certain diseases including the above three must be reported to the CDC when they are diagnosed. Other STDs including herpes and *Chlamydia* infection are much more common, but health care workers are not required by law to report them to the CDC. The disease develops in about half of the sexual partners of a person with primary or secondary syphilis.

Q. Do oral contraceptives ("the pill") protect against STDs?

A. The pill provides no protection against STDs. However, the barrier of a condom or the chemical action of a cream or jelly that kills sperm cells as well as bacteria and viruses provides some protection against STDs.

INFECTIONS CHARACTERIZED BY GENITAL ULCERS OR SWOLLEN LYMPH NODES
Genital Herpes

Herpes is the common name for several different viral infections that affect large numbers of people in the United States (Hatcher et al., 1990). Herpes simplex virus type 1 (HSV-1) infection is the medical term for the condition commonly known as cold sores or fever blisters. The infection is generally above the waist and occurs most frequently on or around the lips. In contrast, herpes simplex virus type 2 (HSV-2) infection is the medical term for genital herpes. An estimated 200,000 to 500,000 people in the United States become infected with genital herpes per year (CDC, 1987; Hatcher et al., 1990), and 5 million to 20 million Americans have the disease (Glover, 1984; Herpes relief, 1985; Hatcher et al., 1990). A genital herpes eruption consists of small painful bumps, blisters, or sores on or around the genitals. In men the most common site is the penis; in women the blisters are usually found on the cervix and vulva and sometimes on the thighs and buttocks. In a small number of cases HSV-1 is found in an area usually infected by HSV-2 or vice versa. Another difference between the two viruses is that HSV-2 is now regarded as an STD. Unfortunately, there is evidence that HSV-1 can be transferred to the genitals by the fingers or mouth and become a disease of the genitals (see box, p. 519).

The first occurrence of genital herpes after the disease is contracted is called the initial infection. It is characterized by severe blisters and pain and lasts an average of 12 days. Subsequent infections, termed recurrent infections, tend to be less painful and shorter than the initial infection. The period between recurrent infections is called the latency time.

When HSV-2 blisters or sores are evident, the disease is contagious. If these lesions make contact with the skin of a sexual partner, the noninfected partner is likely to contract the infection. Approximately 2 to 20 days after exposure the first symptoms appear and may include minor rash or itching in the genital area. As the disease progresses, one or more painful blisterlike fluid-filled sores or lesions appear; clusters of these sores are common. The sores may be accompanied by swollen lymph nodes, fever, aching muscles, and a general sickly feeling (Glover, 1984). A person with an infection of the cervix or vagina may notice only a few or no symptoms. The sores and other symptoms disappear within a week to a month, but the virus has taken up residence in nerve cells of the body, where it can remain dormant for months or years. The virus can be reactivated at any time and cause the sores and other symptoms described.

Herpes simplex virus type 1 is usually the cause of cold sores or fever blisters on and around the lips.

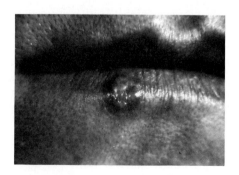

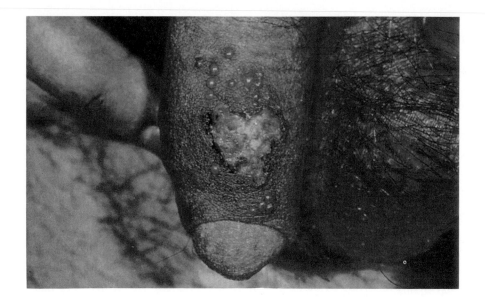

The most common site of the lesions of genital herpes in men is the penis.

Only about 30% of HSV-2 cases are new; the rest are reactivated disease. The duration and frequency of recurrences vary among individuals. Recurrences are thought to be triggered by physical and emotional stress, such as pregnancy, menstruation, poor nutrition, and anxiety.

Two studies indicate that the herpesvirus can be shed from the skin and be transmitted to a sexual partner at any time and not only when blisters or sores are present (Rooney et al., 1986; Brock et al., 1990). Just before the sores appear on the skin, the disease may be contagious (Rooney et al., 1986). This is called the prodrome phase. (*Prodrome* refers to symptoms indicative of an approaching disease state.) The prodrome phase may produce a small pimple or bump, which occurs at the site of the original infection. Herpesvirus prodromes vary among affected individuals. The most common signs that a recurrence of sores and lesions is due are tingling, itching, burning, throbbing, "pins and needles" sensation, or a prickly sensation. Intimate body contact should not occur during the prodrome. Brock and associates (1990) found that virus could also be shed during the latency time in their sample of 27 women but that this was an infrequent occurrence.

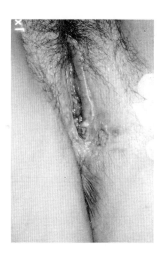

Evidence suggests a relationship between HSV-2 and cervical cancer in women. Women with HSV-2 of the cervix appear to be at more risk for cervical cancer than women who do not have HSV-2 at this site. Papanicolaou (Pap) smears every 6 months are advised for women with cervical HSV-2.

Antibiotics do not cure HSV-2 infection. Only treatment of the symptoms is available at this time. The antiviral drug acyclovir is of significant value in the treatment of genital herpes (Corey and Holmes, 1983; Hatcher et al., 1990). The drug, which is applied directly to the external genital sores or lesions, reduces the duration of viral shedding from the sores. In men and women during a first episode of genital herpes, time to complete healing or crusting of the sores was shorter with acyclovir than with a placebo. In men and women with recurrent genital herpes, acyclovir reduced the duration of viral shedding and shortened the time of healing of sores in men but not in women. Acyclovir

The most common sites of the lesions of genital herpes in women are the cervix and vulva.

does not cure the disease but only treats the symptoms. It does not stop recurrences and cannot be used for herpes involving the cervix and urethra.

Oral preparations of acyclovir (Zovirax) are now available. The oral form of the drug can reduce both the severity and the frequency of recurring attacks by inhibiting the ability of the herpesvirus to replicate. Several vaccines against this STD are being tested in animals and humans (Hatcher et al., 1990).

The man or woman with HSV-2 should not engage in intimate sexual contact while the blisters or sores are present. A condom provides some protection for a man if his partner has HSV-2 of the cervix, vagina, or anal region. If the blisters are on the vulva and the man's abdomen or thighs touch them, the virus can be spread. A condom provides some protection for a woman if the blisters are confined to her partner's penis and are not present on the scrotum. There have been isolated reports of the spread of HSV-2 from toilet seats and other environmental surfaces, but this is extremely rare.

Except for small differences in their genetic makeup, HSV-1 and HSV-2 are practically the same insofar as the sores they cause, how they are transmitted, and recurrences that can result once someone is infected. No matter where the sores are located, HSV-1 continues to be HSV-1 and HSV-2 continues to be HSV-2. Our latest information indicates that 85% of cases of oral herpes are caused by HSV-1 and 15% are caused by HSV-2. Conversely, 15% of cases of genital herpes are caused by HSV-1 and 85% by HSV-2.

A study of the effect of genital herpes on the sexual behavior of adults in the United States showed that awareness of the disease has led to changes in sexual behavior (Aral, Cates, and Jenkins, 1985). Of the 610 men and 895 women (age 18 and older) surveyed, 45% perceived themselves at risk for the disease and indicated that they had changed their sexual behavior to decrease the likelihood. Aral and associates concluded, on the basis of these findings, that people do change their behavior to reduce health risks and that education is the key.

Syphilis

Syphilis is one of the most dangerous STDs and can be fatal if untreated. An estimated 30,000 to 85,000 new cases of this disease develop each year in the United States (CDC, 1987; Hatcher et al., 1990). Syphilis occurs in four phases: primary (early), secondary, latent, and tertiary. Syphilis is caused by a unique organism, the spirochete *Treponema pallidum*. *T. pallidum* is corkscrew shaped

Syphilis is caused by the spirochete *Treponema pallidum*.

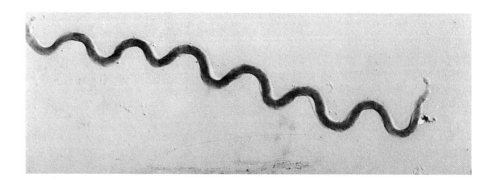

HUMAN SEXUALITY

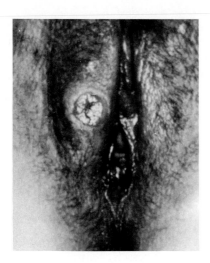

A lesion called a chancre usually appears at the site where the spirochete entered the body.

and twists and burrows its way into the body through scratches or tears in the skin or through mucous membranes such as those that line the vagina, urethra, rectum, mouth, and throat.

Primary syphilis   At the site where the spirochete enters the body, a chancre (shank′ er) usually forms. This primary lesion usually is found on the penis or vulva, although it can occur on the lips, tongue, tonsils, fingers, or thighs. The chancre is a painless hard sore that disappears without medical treatment, but this does not signal the end of the disease. The sore is usually full of the spirochetes. If it comes in contact with the broken or cut skin surface of another person, the disease is passed along. Hence the most contagious stage of syphilis is the primary stage. If an infected penis is placed in a vagina, the spirochetes invade the mucous membranes of the vagina and gain entrance to the body. In a woman infected in this way the chancre often appears on the cervix and is found during a medical examination. If a woman has a chancre in her vagina or on the labia and a penis makes contact with the lesion, the disease may be passed to the man through the mucous membrane lining of the urethra. The chancre usually develops on the penis in this case.

The chancre usually appears 15 days to 3 months after the person has become infected, then disappears after 1 to 5 weeks. Again, its disappearance in no way means the disease is cured.

Secondary syphilis   During the secondary stage of syphilis the organism has already infiltrated the body and begun to affect various systems, such as the lymph system, joints, covering of the central nervous system, eyes, liver, and kidneys. The secondary stage of syphilis usually is accompanied by headaches, loss of appetite, nausea, vomiting, constipation, and muscle or joint pain and sometimes by low-grade fever. No wonder syphilis has been called "the great imitator" of other diseases.

The major symptom of secondary syphilis is a generalized body rash that occurs 1 to 6 months after the appearance of the chancre. The chancre is usually gone by the time the rash appears. The rash is one of the few that occur on the palms and soles; it can occur on any part of the body except the face. Its color varies with the complexion of the skin, but usually in the early phase the lesions are pink or dusky rose in the center, fading in color toward the edges. Later they turn to a "raw ham" or coppery red color. In most locations on the skin the lesions are painless, but they are generally highly contagious because they contain the spirochetes. If the lesions are scraped or cut, the spirochetes can be transmitted to a partner. Thus syphilis in the secondary phase is also contagious, but not as contagious as in the primary stage.

If not treated medically, the symptoms of secondary syphilis disappear, just as did the primary lesion or chancre, and the disease progresses to the latent stage.

Latent syphilis   The latent stage of syphilis produces no symptoms, but the spirochetes are silently attacking the blood vessels, central nervous system, and bones. For most of the latent phase, except during the first part, the disease is not contagious. However, a pregnant woman with latent syphilis can pass the spirochete to the fetus.

Many people have latent syphilis for years and live out their lives unaware that they have it. However, in approximately half of those with latent syphilis the disease progresses to the tertiary stage (Schofield, 1975).

Tertiary syphilis   The three major types of tertiary syphilis are differentiated by the organ system affected. The first type, benign tertiary syphilis, usually develops between 3 and 10 years after infection. Skin, mucous membranes, bones, joints, ligaments, and muscles may be involved. In most cases benign tertiary syphilis is not fatal. The major symptom is a large gumma, or ulcerlike lesion, on the affected structure.

The second type of tertiary syphilis, cardiovascular syphilis, involves the blood vessels. The symptoms usually do not develop for at least 10 years after infection and may be delayed as long as 40 years. This disease is often fatal because of rupture of major blood vessels weakened by the spirochete.

The final type of tertiary syphilis is neurosyphilis, which occurs when the spirochetes invade the brain and the spinal cord. This disease usually appears 10 to 20 years after infection and is often fatal because of widespread destruction of the brain and spinal cord. The symptoms include blindness, psychological disorders, and paralysis. A person may have one or all forms of tertiary syphilis.

Treatment of syphilis   Syphilis is treated with penicillin unless the patient is allergic to it, in which case the antibiotic tetracycline is used. The primary and secondary stages of the disease can be successfully treated with antibiotics. During the primary stage the chancre contains spirochetes, which can be seen under a microscope. In the more common VDRL test (named for the Venereal Disease Research Laboratory of the U.S. Public Health Service, where the blood test was devised), the serum is examined for the presence of antibodies to the spirochete. This is the most useful test for syphilis to date, but not the most accurate; false-positive results are common. (A wide variety of other diseases, such as malaria, lupus erythematosus, and leprosy, yield false-positive results to the VDRL test.) A more accurate test is the fluorescent treponemal

antibody (FTA) test, which should be performed if there is any doubt about a current infection.

Latent syphilis is also treated with penicillin after the VDRL blood test indicates that syphilis is present. Successful cures occur with large doses of antibiotics. Late tertiary syphilis is treated with antibiotics and specific therapy for the various symptoms.

A condom provides some protection against syphilis. It is not effective if the chancre makes contact with broken skin not covered by the condom.

Lymphogranuloma Venereum

Lymphogranuloma venereum is caused by a member of the *Chlamydia* genus of organisms and is a disease of the lymphatic system. The lymphatic system is a system of vessels and associated organs such as lymph nodes that function in the return of tissue fluid to the bloodstream, filtration of lymph fluids, and formation of antibodies. *Chlamydia* is discussed later in this chapter.

The first early sign, a small painless sore on or around the sex organs where the organism has entered the body, occurs 1 week to 3 months after exposure. The sore is usually on the penis or on the vulva, vagina, or cervix. After the appearance of the sore the man will have swelling and pain in the lymph nodes in the groin; some women have the same swelling and pain, but others, because the deeper lymph nodes are affected, do not. Both men and women may have fever, chills, abdominal pain, loss of appetite, and a general "sickly" feeling.

Lymphogranuloma venereum is diagnosed by examining the fluid from the sore, looking for the organism in the blood, or checking for antibodies against the organism in the blood. Antibiotics such as tetracycline are used to cure the disease. A condom provides some protection against lymphogranuloma venereum.

lymphogranuloma venereum (lim′ fuh gran′ yuh LOH muh vuh NEE ree uhm) Disease of the lymphatic system caused by a member of the *Chlamydia* genus of organisms.

Chancroid

Chancroid, also called soft sore, is caused by the bacterium *Haemophilus ducreyi*. The major symptoms are painful sores or lesions on or around the genitals. The lesion looks like a syphilis chancre except that the surrounding edge is soft, not hard as in syphilis. Intimate sexual contact is the usual mode of transmission, and the sore usually appears less than a week after contact with an infected person. The lesions are more common in men than women, who may be carriers without symptoms. The bacteria are evident when material from the sore is examined under a microscope. The disease is treated with antibiotics such as tetracycline and erythromycin. Chancroid is unusual in the United States but is more common in the tropics. A condom provides some protection against chancroid.

INFECTIONS OF SKIN SURFACES
Genital Warts

Genital warts, or **venereal warts,** are caused by the human papillomavirus virus (HPV), which is usually transmitted by intimate sexual contact but may be passed along on wet underclothing or wet towels. In addition, HPV has been detected in non–sexually active young individuals, including children, without evidence of disease (Buck, 1989). The warts are caused by certain types of the HPV (most frequently types 6 and 11), and types 16, 18, and 31 have been found to be strongly associated with genital dysplasia (abnormal growth of cells, particularly in the cervical region) and cancer of the cervix (CDC, 1989). For these reasons a biopsy should be performed in all cases of atypical, pigmented, or persistent warts and an annual Pap smear should be done (CDC, 1989). The CDC (1987) estimates that 1 million new cases of genital warts occur per year in the United States. The warts appear as small growths on the skin in the genital area, on the penis, or vulva, or inside the rectum. They may also grow into the urethra and on the cervix. The warts may not appear until months after exposure to a person with genital warts. Untreated, warts can last for months or years.

The first choice for treatment of venereal warts is the use of cryotherapy with liquid nitrogen to freeze the warts (CDC, 1989). Other treatments include covering the warts with a solution of the drug podophyllin at weekly intervals, applying trichloroacetic acid at weekly intervals, and burning the warts with

Genital warts.

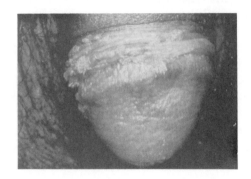

electrocautery. Laser surgery or conventional surgery is used when the warts are extensive or other treatments do not work. A condom provides some protection against venereal warts, depending on their location. All treatments are intended to reduce the numbers of viral particles present, but it is doubtful that any single treatment method consistently eliminates the virus (Buck, 1989). As Buck states, "Because persistence of the virus can lead to recurrence of lesions and transmission to sexual partners, long-term care is aimed at detecting recurrences and preventing transmission" (1989, p. 12).

GONOCOCCAL INFECTIONS
Gonorrhea

Gonorrhea, or "the clap," is caused by the bacterium *Neisseria gonorrhoeae*. It is an infectious disease involving mainly the mucous membranes of the genitourinary tract and occasionally the rectum, cervix, and throat.

Intimate sexual contact is the primary mode of transmission of this STD. Gonorrhea is one of the most communicable diseases for which records are kept in the United States. It is estimated that each year 1.8 to 2 million new cases of gonorrhea occur (CDC, 1987; Hatcher et al., 1990). *N. gonorrhoeae* cannot survive outside the body and rapidly dies if exposed to drying, heat, or soap and water.

The clinical aspects of gonorrhea are different in men and women and are discussed separately.

Gonorrhea in the male   The incubation period of gonorrhea in the male is usually about 2 to 5 days but can vary. In other words, symptoms usually appear less than 1 week after exposure to the organism. Between 5% and 15% of infected men have no symptoms. The man who does have symptoms usually waits several days to weeks before he seeks medical attention. During all of this time the infection is contagious, and it remains contagious until cured.

gonorrhea
(gon uh REE uh) A disease of the reproductive structures and mucous membranes of the throat and rectum caused by the bacterium *Neisseria gonorrhoeae*.

One of the first symptoms of gonorrhea in men is a yellowish green puslike discharge from the tip of the penis.

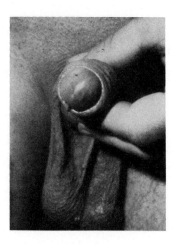

The urethra is the first structure affected, and usually painful urination is the first symptom. The burning sensation on urination is followed by a yellow or yellowish green puslike discharge from the tip of the penis that may stain the underwear and have a foul odor. If the man seeks medical attention at this point, he will be given an antibiotic. A large dose taken by mouth is usually sufficient. In rectal gonorrhea the antibiotic is injected into the buttocks, and this usually must be repeated because infections may be asymptomatic. The injection permits a prolonged release of antibiotic into the body. Gonorrhea of the throat can also be asymptomatic. Treatment is with antibiotics taken orally.

If the man does not seek medical attention for the urethral infection, it may spread upward into the deeper end of the urethra. The bladder, kidneys, prostate gland, seminal vesicles, and epididymis may become infected. Gonorrhea that is untreated or is treated late in the course of disease may result in sterility because of scar tissue that forms in the epididymis. When this occurs, the sperm cannot move from the testes through the epididymis to the vas deferens.

Gonorrhea in the female   As many as 80% of women with gonorrhea do not have symptoms, and the great majority of women with mild symptoms do not suspect that they are caused by gonorrhea (Hatcher et al., 1990). The incubation period in women is longer than in men, more than 2 weeks. Women who do suspect gonorrhea usually wait another 1 or 2 weeks before they seek medical attention. As in men, the infection is contagious from its onset. Some women receive treatment, which is the same as in men, because their infected male sexual partners who have gone for treatment have given their names to the local public health service. In many cases the infected partner tells the uninfected partner to seek medical attention because he or she has been exposed to gonorrhea.

The first symptom in women is painful urination and sometimes increased frequency of urination, followed by a slight urethral discharge that is usually not noticed or not suspected to be caused by gonorrhea. If the cervix is affected during the early phase of gonorrhea, a puslike discharge may occur. This discharge may or may not cause the woman to suspect gonorrhea.

Gonorrhea in the early stage is treated with antibiotics, as in the male. If the woman does not seek medical attention while the infection is confined to the urethra and cervix, the infection can move into the bladder, kidneys, and oviducts. Infection of the oviducts is serious because scarring of these delicate structures can lead to permanent sterility. Infection of the oviducts usually produces pelvic and lower abdominal pain, tiredness, headache, nausea, and vomiting.

If gonorrheal infection of the oviducts is not treated, the infection can spread to the ovaries. Large pus-filled abscesses may grow on the oviducts and ovaries, spreading to the entire lower abdomen and pelvis. If these abscesses rupture and pus spills into the abdomen and pelvis, peritonitis may develop and the oviducts, ovaries, and uterus may have to be removed to combat the massive infection. This complication is sometimes fatal. In some women gonorrheal infection of the ovaries, oviducts, pelvis, and abdomen can be cured with antibiotics. However, these women may be subject to recurrent pelvic inflammatory diseases (PID), including tubal and ovarian infections, pelvic pain, abnormal vaginal bleeding, and dysmenorrhea. In a small number of cases PID is caused by organisms other than those causing STDs. The topic of PID is presented later in this chapter.

Women and bisexual and homosexual men may acquire gonorrheal infection of the rectum, and rectal cultures are needed if gonorrhea is suspected. Pharyngeal (throat) gonorrheal infections can be started during fellatio when the bacteria are passed from the penis to the oral cavity. There is no evidence that gonorrheal infection of the throat can pass to the oral cavity of another during kissing. In addition, there is no evidence that gonorrheal infections of the vulva or vagina can be passed to the mouth of another person during cunnilingus.

Women taking oral contraceptives are at greater risk for contracting gonorrhea. Increased vaginal alkalinity (i.e., the environment of the vagina becomes less acidic or more basic) and increased moisture and secretions caused by the hormonal content of the oral contraceptives create a more favorable environment for the bacteria. Women using an intrauterine device (IUD) for contraception are at higher risk for spread of gonorrhea into the uterus, oviducts, ovaries, and abdomen because the string of the IUD acts as a wick to draw the infection into the uterus. In addition, the inflammation of the uterus caused by the IUD helps the infection establish itself in the uterus. Conversely, using contraceptive creams, jellies, or foam during sexual intercourse may discourage growth of the bacteria that cause gonorrhea because the spermicides create a more acidic environment. A condom provides some protection against gonorrhea.

There are no reliable blood tests for gonorrhea in the male or female. A blood test can determine whether a person has antibodies to the gonococcus, but it does not determine whether the person has current infection or had infection that has been cured. Thus detection of gonorrhea depends on identification of the bacteria in a smear from the tip of the penis, vagina, anus, or throat or by culture of the bacterium. A vaccine that could prevent gonorrhea is being tested.

Additional complications that may develop if gonorrhea is not treated include gonococcal dermatitis, with sores or lesions on the skin; gonococcal endocarditis, which is an infection of the membrane that lines the heart and the heart valves; and gonococcal arthritis.

The treatment of gonorrhea for both males and females is complicated by several factors: (1) the development of antibiotic-resistant strains of *N. gonorrhoeae*, including strains resistant to penicillin, tetracycline, and multiple antibiotics; (2) the high frequency of chlamydial infections (discussed in the next section of this chapter) in persons with gonorrhea; and (3) the recognition of the serious complications of chlamydial and gonococcal infections (CDC, 1989).

The newest treatment guidelines state that all cases of gonorrhea should be confirmed by culturing the bacteria in the laboratory and determining which antibiotic(s) will destroy the strain of gonorrhea in question. Male patients being treated for gonorrhea should also be treated for chlamydial infection if a test for *Chlamydia* is not done, since up to 45% of gonorrhea infections coexist with chlamydial infections (CDC, 1989). Rapid, inexpensive, fairly accurate enzyme immunoassay tests have recently been developed to detect *Chlamydia* in women (Ferris, 1990) and men. The drug of choice in treating gonorrhea is ceftriaxone, a broad-spectrum antibiotic (acts against a large number of bacteria). Doxycycline, a drug related to tetracycline, is given for a presumed chlamydial infection.

In summary, early and uncomplicated gonorrhea usually is easily treated with antibiotics in both men and women. If the disease progresses, the result may be sterility caused in men by scarring of the vas deferens and in women by scarring of the oviducts. Gonorrhea is usually asymptomatic in women, making them particularly vulnerable to complications. Both men and women should seek prompt medical attention if they suspect they have contracted the disease.

The effect of tetracycline on the fetus is found in Chapter 6.

CHLAMYDIAL INFECTIONS
Chlamydia

Chlamydia trachomatis
(kluh MID ee uh truh KOH muh tis) A species of microorganism that lives and reproduces within the cells of the host.

Chlamydia trachomatis is a unique bacterium that must live and reproduce within the cell of a host. This organism causes a number of diseases, such as lymphogranuloma venereum, nongonococcal urethritis, mucopurulent cervicitis (the female counterpart of nongonococcal urethritis), and pelvic inflammatory disease. A definitive diagnosis of *Chlamydia* infection is made when the organism is detected by one of several techniques, including culture, monoclonal antibody immunofluorescence, or enzyme immunoassay (Hatcher et al., 1990).

In 1985 the CDC conducted numerous surveys across the United States to estimate the prevalence of *Chlamydia* infections in men and women. The results indicated that 4.5 million new cases of *Chlamydia* infections occur each year, compared with 1.8 million new cases of gonorrhea (CDC, 1987; Washington, 1988), making *Chlamydia* infection the most common STD in the United States (Ferris, 1990). *Chlamydia* infections are easily treated with antibiotics such as tetracycline or erythromycin.

Chlamydia infections involving the genitourinary tract are sexually transmitted. In men the organism can cause nongonococcal urethritis, and in women it is often the cause of mucopurulent cervicitis. A woman should be tested for

Chlamydia infection if she has lower abdominal pain, even if other symptoms fail to suggest PID. In a study of 382 women, 40% of those found to have chlamydial infections would have gone untreated if they had not been tested for the organism (Mundy, Thomas, and Taylor-Robinson, 1986). *Chlamydia* can also be transmitted to newborns from infected mothers.

A person who has an STD caused by *Chlamydia* must refer all sexual partners for examination and treatment. Sexual intercourse should be avoided (or a condom must be used) until all infected individuals are cured. The use of a condom prevents future infections.

Nongonococcal or **nonspecific urethritis** (NGU or NSU) is often caused by *Chlamydia*. Symptoms of NGU or NSU mimic those of gonorrhea. Many public health facilities report that more than half of their male patients who come to the clinic because of a discharge or drip from the penis do not have gonorrhea but NGU. Although in many cases the cause of NGU is not known, *Chlamydia* is often responsible.

The predominant symptoms of NGU in men are a thin, usually clear discharge from the tip of the penis and inflammation of the urethra, with redness around the opening of the urethra and a tingling sensation on urination. Female partners of the infected man almost never have noticeable symptoms, although they may be infected. The disease progresses without the woman's knowledge and may lead to PID, a leading cause of sterility in women. In men, untreated disease can lead to sterility because of scarring of the epididymis. NGU does not respond to penicillin but must be treated with other antibiotics such as tetracycline or erythromycin. In many cases NGU resolves without medical treatment if the cause is not *Chlamydia*. A condom provides protection against NGU.

Mucopurulent cervicitis occurs when *Chlamydia* or *N. gonorrhoeae* settles in the cervix. The woman does not usually have symptoms, but cervical or vaginal discharge resulting from an exudate (secretions) from the cervix may occur. The infection can spread to the oviducts and lead to sterility and also cause PID. Mucopurulent cervicitis probably occurs more frequently than NGU; an estimated 3 million new cases of mucopurulent cervicitis occur each year (Hatcher et al., 1990). Mucopurulent cervicitis, if caused by *N. gonorrhoeae*, is treated in the same manner as uncomplicated gonorrhea. If *N. gonorrhoeae* is not isolated from the cervical secretion, the patient is treated as if she had a chlamydial infection.

nongonococcal or **nonspecific urethritis**
(non gon′ uh KOHK uhl/ yoor′ uh THRY tis) Urethritis (inflammation or infection of the urethra) caused by bacteria other than *Neisseria gonorrhoeae*, usually *Chlamydia*.

mucopurulent cervicitis
Infection of the cervix that produces a discharge.

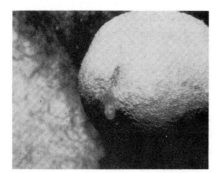

Clear mucoid discharge from nongonococcal urethritis.

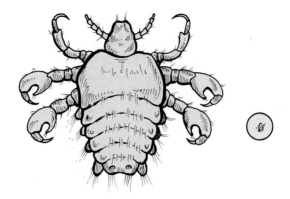

EXTERNAL PARASITIC INFECTIONS
Pubic Lice and Scabies

pubic lice and **scabies**
(PYOO bik lys/SKAY beez)
Parasites found in the pubic region that cause intense itching; can be transmitted by both sexual and nonsexual routes.

Pubic lice ("crabs") and **scabies** are skin infestations caused by parasitic organisms that are related to spiders and that feed on blood or other body fluids (Figure 18-2). The organisms are transmitted by close physical contact, through infected bedding or towels, or in rare instances on a toilet seat. Both infestations cause intense itching, particularly around the genitals and pubic hair. Pubic lice are identified by observation of the parasite or nits (white eggs) attached to the hair shafts. Scabies are identified by the burrows they make under the skin.

Both infestations are treated with an insecticide shampoo such as Kwell. The infected individual applies the shampoo at weekly intervals for 2 weeks. All bed linen and clothes that touch the skin should be washed in hot water. Condoms do not provide protection against pubic lice or scabies.

MISCELLANEOUS DISEASES
Hepatitis B

hepatitis B
(hep' uh TY tis) Disease of the liver caused by the hepatitis B virus; can be transmitted by both sexual and nonsexual routes.

Hepatitis is an inflammatory process in the liver characterized by diffuse or patchy areas of liver cell death. The three major causes of hepatitis are types A, B, and non-A, non-B (now called C) hepatitis viruses. In addition, hepatitis can be caused by drugs and alcohol. Type A is the type associated with contaminated raw shellfish such as oysters. **Hepatitis B,** formerly called serum hepatitis, is caused by a strain of the hepatitis virus. Hepatitis B may be transmitted by intimate sexual contact such as oral-genital sex following anal sex (the virus is found in semen, vaginal secretions, and saliva) and through contaminated blood transfusions, contaminated vaccines, and inadequately sterilized syringes, needles, and dental and surgical equipment. Homosexual, bisexual, and heterosexual individuals may contract this disease, and anyone who engages in oral-genital sex following anal sex is at risk. In a study of male homosexuals, 51.5% had evidence of hepatitis B in the serum, compared with 20.4% of male heterosexuals (Kolodny, Masters, and Johnson, 1979). Furthermore, a correlation was found between patterns of sexual acts and the presence of hepatitis B in the blood serum. Rates of hepatitis B were higher in men involved in primarily anal intercourse and in men who had a large number of sexual partners. These findings are probably related to the fact that oral-genital sex and anal sex are practiced more regularly by homosexual couples than by heterosexual couples.

The hepatitis B virus is spreading almost nine times faster than the virus responsible for AIDS (Kingsley et al., 1990). In anal intercourse the individual who inserts his penis into a partner is at increased risk of contracting hepatitis B, whereas an individual having the penis inserted into his anus is at increased risk for transmission of the AIDS virus (Kingsley et al., 1990). Type C hepatitis is transmitted in a manner similar to type B. For both homosexual and heterosexual individuals, the greater number of sexual partners, the higher the risk of contracting an STD.

Hepatitis B attacks the liver and may produce a variety of symptoms. Some symptoms, such as fever, loss of appetite, headache, and weakness, mimic those of influenza. Abdominal pain and jaundice (yellowness of the skin and mucous membranes caused by bile in the blood) may occur.

Treatment of hepatitis, which includes hospitalization and a variety of therapies, is beyond the scope of this chapter. A vaccine against hepatitis B is available, and persons at risk probably should be immunized.

Avoiding oral sex after anal penetration or washing the genitals after anal penetration and before oral sex helps to prevent the spread of hepatitis B.

Amebiasis

Amebiasis is caused by the protozoan or single-celled organism *Entamoeba histolytica*. This organism normally lives in the large intestine of about 2% to 5% of the people in the United States (Beeson and McDermott, 1975). Many of these people never have symptoms. The organism may be spread through oral-anal contact or anal intercourse followed by oral-genital sex, but the most common route is through local contamination of food and water.

Symptoms of amebiasis include an ulcerlike sore in the large intestine, changes in bowel movements, pain in the lower abdomen, and diarrhea. These symptoms may persist for months, and the disease may worsen or resolve without medical treatment (Beeson and McDermott, 1975). If the disease progresses and involves a greater portion of the large intestine, amebic dysentery with frequent bloody stools develops. The drug of choice to treat amebiasis is metronidazole (Flagyl).

Although anyone can contract amebiasis, homosexual men appear to be at greater risk, probably because oral-anal and oral-genital sex after anal intercourse are practiced by more male homosexual couples than heterosexual couples.

amebiasis
(am′ uh BY uh sis) Infection of the large intestine caused by the protozoan *Entamoeba histolytica;* can be transmitted by both sexual and nonsexual routes.

VAGINAL INFECTIONS
Trichomoniasis

Trichomoniasis, commonly called "tric," is a type of vaginitis, or inflammation or irritation of the vagina, caused by the single-celled organism *Trichomonas vaginalis*. It is estimated that annually 2½ to 3 million U.S. women contract trichomoniasis (McGregor, 1989).

Many infected women have a foul-smelling yellow discharge and itching and burning in the vagina. Intercourse is often painful. The organism can be seen in the discharge under microscopic examination. This parasitic infection

trichomoniasis
(trik′ uh muh NY uh sis) Vaginitis caused by the single-celled organism *Trichomonas vaginalis;* can be transmitted by both sexual and nonsexual routes.

is almost always transmitted by intimate sexual contact but can be passed by means of wet towels, washcloths, and wet underclothing. Male partners of an infected women usually have the infection but rarely have symptoms.

Trichomoniasis is treated with the drug metronidazole (Flagyl) taken orally. Both the infected woman and her sexual partners should take the drug to prevent reinfection and spread to others. Trichomoniasis may promote the growth of gonorrheal infections. Use of a condom helps to prevent the spread of trichomoniasis.

Vaginal Yeast Infections

vaginal yeast infections
Vaginitis caused by the yeast fungus *Candida albicans;* rare in men.

Vaginal yeast infections, a form of vaginitis, are caused by the yeast fungus *Candida albicans* (formerly called *Monilia*). *Candida* organisms are a normal constituent of the vagina and rectum; only when they begin to multiply out of control do they cause problems. Hence yeast infections may start on their own rather than being sexually transmitted. Any disturbance of the delicate environmental balance in the vagina can cause a favorable situation for the yeast organism to multiply. Oral contraceptives affect the pH (acidity versus alkalinity) of the vagina, and prolonged use of antibiotic drugs disturbs the natural balance of organisms in the vagina. Other conditions such as diabetes and pregnancy also alter the vaginal environment, which may encourage yeast infections.

The major symptom of a yeast infection is a thick, white, cheesy vaginal discharge. Extreme itching also occurs in many women. Yeast infections are usually treated with antifungal vaginal suppositories or creams, which are now available without a prescription. A pregnant woman with a yeast infection may transmit it to the digestive tract of her baby during birth. The infection is called thrush and is easily treated. Yeast infections in men do not usually produce symptoms and are most likely to appear under the foreskin of an uncircumcised man. The infection can be passed back and forth between partners, so both should be tested for the presence of the fungus and treated accordingly.

Antifungal vaginal suppositories and creams for the treatment of yeast infections are now easily available at the drugstore.

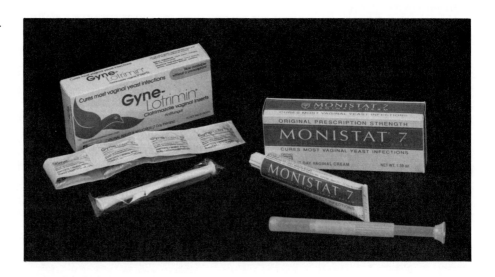

HUMAN SEXUALITY

PELVIC INFLAMMATORY DISEASE

Pelvic inflammatory disease (PID) is a serious infection of the pelvic region and is often caused by microorganisms that are transmitted during sexual activities. Specifically, PID refers to a group of pelvic infections including infections of the uterus *(parametritis)*, oviducts *(salpingitis)*, and both the oviducts and ovaries *(salpingo-oophoritis)*. Sexually transmitted organisms, especially *N. gonorrhoeae* and *Chlamydia,* are responsible for 85% to 95% of PIDs (Wolner-Hanssen, 1990). The remainder of PIDs can be traced to surgical procedures and to organisms already present in the female reproductive tract. Approximately 1 million cases of PID occur annually in the United States, and this is thought to be a conservative estimate because many cases go untreated (Wolner-Hanssen, 1990). Approximately 25% of women with PID require hospitalization (Wolner-Hanssen, 1990). A woman is also susceptible to PID during the postpartum period, after an abortion, and while using an intrauterine device.

PID can cause sterility if scar tissue closes the oviducts, preventing passage of the egg or of sperm to fertilize the egg. About 15% of women with PID become sterile after one infection, and 30% do so after two infections (Pelvic inflammatory disease, 1985). The incidence of ectopic pregnancy is also higher in women who have had PID. PID can be life threatening if the infection is not diagnosed and treated but spreads throughout the pelvis and abdomen.

PID causes pain in the abdomen, pelvis, back, or legs. The woman usually has fever or chills, vomiting, and a vaginal discharge toward the end of the menstrual flow. Many women experience pain during intercourse and menstruation and have irregular vaginal bleeding. Not all women with PID have symptoms. Many cases of infertility and sterility are traced to unrecognized PID.

PID is treated with antibiotics such as tetracycline or penicillin, bed rest, and abstinence from sexual intercourse. Prompt diagnosis and treatment lessen the chance of damage to the oviducts and subsequent infertility. The chances of getting PID are greatly reduced by the use of condoms, since they prevent the spread of gonorrhea and chlamydial infections, the cause of most cases of PID.

pelvic inflammatory disease Infection of the cervix, uterus, and ovaries, including some infections within the pelvis.

The topic of infertility is presented in Chapter 6.

PREVENTING SEXUALLY TRANSMITTED DISEASES

Use of a condom is the best way to avoid contracting an STD when engaging in sexual relations with a new partner. Condoms prevent the spread and contraction of local bacterial, viral, and fungal infections but are of no value against parasitic infections such as crabs. If the condom is used properly and exposure to the disease is limited to the body parts protected by the condom, it will provide complete protection against gonorrhea, nonspecific urethritis, and trichomoniasis and afford some protection against syphilis, genital herpes, and venereal warts (Yarber, 1980).

To be effective in preventing disease transmission, the condom must be placed over the erect penis before contact is made with the infected area. Individuals engaging in sexual relations with a new partner should consider having the male wear a condom, and perhaps supply one if the man does not have one.

Centers for Disease Control Guidelines for Condom Usage

1. Latex condoms should be used because they offer greater protection against viral sexually transmitted diseases (STDs) than natural membrane condoms.
2. Condoms should be stored in a cool, dry place out of direct sunlight.
3. Condoms in damaged packages or those that show obvious signs of age (e.g., those that are brittle, sticky, or discolored) should not be used.
4. Condoms should be handled with care to prevent puncture.
5. The condom should be put on before any genital contact to prevent exposure to fluids that may contain infectious agents. Hold the tip of the condom and unroll it onto the erect penis, leaving space at the tip to collect semen.
6. Adequate lubrication should be used. If exogenous lubrication is needed, only water-based lubricants should be used. Petroleum- or oil-based lubricants (such as petroleum jelly, cooking oils, shortening, and lotions) should not be used, since they weaken the latex.
7. Use of condoms containing spermicides may provide some additional protection against STDs. However, vaginal or anorectal use of spermicides along with condoms is likely to provide greater protection.
8. If a condom breaks, it should be replaced immediately. If ejaculation occurs after condom breakage, the immediate use of spermicide has been suggested. However, the protective value of postejaculation application of spermicide in reducing the risk of STD transmission is unknown.
9. After ejaculation, care should be taken so that the condom does not slip off the penis before withdrawal; the base of the condom should be held while withdrawing. The penis should be withdrawn while still erect.
10. Condoms should never be reused.

From Centers for Disease Control, 1988.

Contraceptive foams, creams, and jellies containing the spermicide non-oxynol-9 provide protection against gonorrhea, syphilis, genital herpes, and many other STD organisms (Judson, 1989). The spermicide not only kills sperm cells, but has been shown to destroy the microorganisms implicated in several STDs. The use of a condom and a vaginal spermicide is an excellent combination both to prevent an unwanted pregnancy and to protect against STDs.

After condom usage the rest of the methods discussed below are distant second choices in terms of efficiency in preventing STDs. Washing the genitals and hands after sexual contact can help prevent the spread of STDs. Washing should be done even if a condom is used. Washing with soap and water, particularly with an antibacterial soap, immediately after sexual contact might remove some STD organisms that have not yet penetrated the skin (Yarber, 1980). Men should soap up the genitals and work some lather into the tip of the urethra. Women should wash the area of the vulva and vestibule of the vagina.

Another measure to help prevent the spread of STD organisms is urination immediately after sexual contact. In the man urination flushes organisms out of the urethra. In the woman urination may not be as helpful because the STD organisms are usually deposited in the vagina or vestibule and not the urethra, but there is much to gain and little to lose by this practice. Douching with a soap and water solution immediately after sexual contact may kill some STD organisms but also may contribute to vaginal irritation or infection.

Showering together and having sex in the light provide opportunities for subtly inspecting a sexual partner for genital discharges and sores before sexual activity. However, casual inspection does not reveal the many subtle signs of STDs.

Finally, attitudes toward STDs are important in the control of these diseases. Honest communication between potential sex partners is essential. If you have any doubts about whether your potential partner has an STD, ask him or her. If you are afraid the potential partner will be offended by your concern and question, you must take the chance of offending him or her. A person who knows he or she has an STD should refrain from intimate contact while the disease is in the contagious phase.

In conclusion, each person should protect his or her own health and consequently the health of sexual partners by using preventive measures. When undergoing health examinations, both men and women should request an STD checkup, particularly if they have engaged in sexual relations with a new partner or partners.

In the male patient the physician or health care worker examines the skin of the trunk and thighs for spots, rashes, burrows, scratch marks, lesions, and the presence of external parasites such as crabs. If lesions are present, fluid from them is examined for the presence of *T. pallidum*, the causative agent of syphilis. Any fluid discharge from the tip of the penis is examined under a microscope for microorganisms. A urine sample is also examined for red and white blood cells and microorganisms. The anus and surrounding skin are examined for possible inflammation, discharge, lesions, and warts. The prostate gland, seminal vesicles, and Cowper's glands are examined rectally. If inflamed, these structures are gently squeezed to force their secretions out to the tip of the penis, and the material is examined for microorganisms. The individual who engages in oral-genital sex with various partners may want to request culture of throat secretions.

For many people a trip to the public health clinic because of a concern about a sexually transmitted disease causes anxiety and self-consciousness.

The health care worker carefully inspects the skin of a female patient. The vulva is examined for any discharge, inflammation, warts, or lesions. Any discharge is examined for microorganisms. The urethra is also examined, and any discharge is examined for microorganisms. The vagina and cervix are examined for inflammation, discharges, and lesions, and all material removed is examined for microorganisms. The anal region and rectum are examined as in men.

In both men and women blood is tested for syphilis. Other STD organisms such as herpesvirus and *Chlamydia* may cause the body to produce antibodies against the microorganism. The blood sample may also be checked for these antibodies if facilities are available.

SEXUALLY TRANSMITTED DISEASES IN THE FETUS AND NEWBORN INFANT

STDs are not confined to adults who contract them during intimate body contact but may also be passed by pregnant women to their children during pregnancy or the birth process. Almost all of the STDs discussed, with the exception of the external parasites, such as crab lice and scabies, and amebiasis, have the potential to be passed to the fetus or newborn. In some cases the disease organism passes from the mother to the fetus through the placenta.

In the case of congenital syphilis the spirochetes move across the capillaries that connect the maternal and fetal blood supplies, then invade the tissue of the fetus or cause a spontaneous abortion or miscarriage. About 30% of fetuses of mothers with syphilis die before birth, and of infants born alive, about 70% have active infections (Witters and Jones-Witters, 1980). Many of these children seem healthy at birth, but 2 to 6 weeks after birth lesions appear on the eyes and skin. Many are deaf or have skeletal malformations. In some children with congenital syphilis, symptoms do not appear for years. At approximately the age of 10 years, inflammation of the eyes and ears and painful swelling of the body tissues appear.

The pregnant woman may be given penicillin during the early months of the pregnancy; this cures the disease without any damage to the fetus from a syphilis infection. After the sixteenth week of pregnancy, however, the likelihood of fetal infection is high. Penicillin cures infection in both the mother and the fetus, but the damage done to the fetus by the syphilis infection may be irreversible. The newborn infant may also be given penicillin to treat syphilis; however, permanent damage to various organ systems may have occurred already.

Genital herpes, gonorrhea, and *Chlamydia* can infect the fetus in the same way. Herpes has been shown to increase greatly the rate of spontaneous abortion and premature birth in infected pregnant woman (Hatcher et al., 1990). Fetal infection with HSV-2 either in utero or at birth can lead to abnormal smallness of the head, mental retardation, and vision problems. The mortality rate for babies born with HSV-2 infections is approximately 50% (Brown, 1988). Some infections transmitted during childbirth can be prevented by cesarean delivery because the child does not have contact with the active virus in the birth canal. The physician can monitor the mother for active outbreak of the disease; if none occurs for 2 weeks before the birth, vaginal delivery is permitted. No cure has been found for genital herpes.

Gonorrhea in pregnant women can cause various problems for the newborn. *N. gonorrhoeae* has been found in 0.5% to 7% of pregnant women in the United States (Watts, 1990). As the baby passes through the cervix and vagina during birth, the gonococcus can infect the eyes, throat, respiratory tract, or anus and rectum. There is conflicting evidence on whether gonorrhea increases preterm rupture of the membranes surrounding the fetus, premature births, and neonatal deaths (Watts, 1990). The practice of putting silver nitrate or antibiotic drops into the newborn infant's eyes is a carryover from an era when gonococcal infections were common. Pregnant women with gonorrhea are treated in the same way as nonpregnant women with the disease, but they are given erythromycin (not tetracycline) for the presumed chlamydial infection that is usually found with gonorrhea.

Chlamydia infections can have serious effects on the newborn infant. *Chlamydia* has been found in 5% to 30% of pregnant women (Watts, 1990). Eye infections may develop, and there is evidence for lower birth weight and increased incidence of pneumonia in infants born to mothers with *Chlamydia* infections (Babin and Ojanlatva, 1986). *Chlamydia* infections in pregnant women cause about 10% of cases of pneumonia in infants younger than 8 weeks of age (Watts, 1990). If the mother's cervix is infected, the risk of contaminating the eyes of the infant as it passes through the cervix at birth is high.

Certain conditions such as venereal warts and some forms of vaginitis may be transmitted to the infant during the birth process. The virus that causes warts is passed to the child as it passes through the birth canal. This may be prevented with cesarean delivery. A less serious procedure, and probably the method of choice, if possible, is removal of venereal warts from the mother before delivery (Watts, 1990).

If a pregnant woman suspects that she has an STD, prompt medical attention is essential to prevent transmission of the disease to the developing fetus.

SOCIAL AND PERSONAL IMPLICATIONS OF SEXUALLY TRANSMITTED DISEASES

If you have read the first part of this chapter you realize the health hazards of STDs. Some types of the HPV have been strongly associated with cervical cancer; genital herpes, HPV, and AIDS have no cure at the present time; PID caused by STDs can cause fertility and sterility; and in the next chapter we shall see that AIDS is often fatal.

Many persons who have engaged in sexual activities with a large number of partners are becoming more cautious. A visit to a prostitute can be risky because prostitutes have many sexual partners and each partner has the potential of passing his STD to the woman. The man or woman who engages in extramarital sex is now wary of STDs.

Let us examine the psychological impact of one STD, genital herpes. Herpes, like other STDs, can be extremely stressful; it can cause depression, anger, a feeling of betrayal by the sex partner, or breakup of an ongoing

relationship or marriage, and in men it can cause impotence. Take, for example, the following true situation:

Mike, a 37-year-old professional, has lived with a woman for the past 3 years. He attended a professional meeting where he met a young woman. They had a few drinks and spent the rest of the evening in his hotel room. About 2 weeks after this sexual encounter, Mike noticed a series of blisters at the base of penis. His worst fears were realized when a dermatologist told him he had genital herpes. "I could not believe this happened to me. How could I have been so stupid as not to ask her if she had any venereal diseases? Why didn't she tell me she had herpes?" Not only will Mike suffer the physical symptoms of herpes, but also the psychological consequences of the disease. He told the woman he was living with that he had herpes and did not want to pass the disease to her. He received no sympathy for the physical pain he had, and they both knew their sexual encounters would be limited to the times when the blisters were not active. It was not long before the woman left Mike. She felt betrayed and was worried that she might get herpes from him.

AUTHORS' FILES

Consider the man or woman who contracts herpes in an extramarital affair. In many cases the disease has a destructive effect on the relationship. Unlike gonorrhea and some other STDs, which can be successfully treated, with or without the spouse's knowledge, herpes has no cure at present.

STDs have both physical and psychological effects on most people. If the individual who contracts the disease is in a relationship with another person, the problems are increased. Each person must act in the way he or she feels most comfortable, but responsibility to all concerned is important.

A Personal Glimpse

Sexually Transmitted Diseases: Some Cause for Concern

Q: Do you worry about sexually transmitted diseases? If so, how have you changed your sexual practices as a result and how do you approach the topic with your partner, particularly a new partner?

The individuals interviewed were all single and between the ages of 18 and 24. Surprisingly, the vast majority of those interviewed indicated that they did not worry about STDs, although they were sexually active and some had had an STD at some time. Those who did show concern had never discussed sexual histories with a partner unless that partner was a steady boyfriend or girlfriend with whom they had already been sexually active for quite some time. One 20-year-old female college student elaborated, "I don't worry about STDs. I know I should, especially since I've been with so many guys, but I've only used a rubber twice in my life.

A 22-year-old female schoolteacher responded to that answer, "Frankly, if you feel comfortable enough to take home a strange guy in the first place, then you should feel comfortable enough to ask him to wear a condom. If he's your boyfriend, then you should feel comfortable talking about his sexual history before you sleep with him, and if he doesn't have herpes or AIDS, then there isn't as much cause to be concerned about STDs assuming that both parties are faithful. Going back to the scenario in which you bring home a guy for the first time, all you have to say is, 'Did you bring protection?' This is a perfectly normal question to ask, especially now with this AIDS epidemic. If the encounter is unexpected or unplanned, you should still ask the guy to wear a condom, even in the heat of the moment."

Another 22-year-old female college student says the following if she's with a new partner: "I'm not protected; do you have a condom?" She asserted that a man will be less inclined to avoid using a condom if he thinks that there is a risk of his partner becoming pregnant, if he is not astute enough to be concerned about contracting or transmitting a disease. "If he does not have a condom handy," she added, "I do."

The first 21-year-old woman agreed: "Unfortunately, most young men, in my experience anyway, assume that you are on the pill, or don't care, and would gladly risk getting an STD rather than wear a condom. Nowadays, if you're going to sleep around despite all the risks involved, then you're going to have to be assertive in order to protect yourself."

Another 20-year-old female who is an office manager added, "I do worry about STDs. I just come right out and say, 'If you want to do something, we have to use a condom.' It's that simple."

Two 22-year-old, two 23-year-old, and two 24-year-old single males interviewed, none of whom has a girlfriend, and all of whom have had multiple partners, indicated that they do not use condoms and do not really ever think about STDs. The two 18-year-old male college students interviewed indicated that they do think about STDs and that they would use a condom if they didn't know the girl, but that they wouldn't be too concerned about it if it was their girlfriend. A third 20-year-old female college student responded to the question by saying, "I don't have to worry about STDs because I don't go home with strange guys, period. I would only sleep with a guy if he was my boyfriend and I'd known him long enough to ask him if he has any diseases, if he's been tested for AIDS, etc., and if I knew he'd answer me honestly."

Box prepared by Lisa Pfenninger, B.S.

SUMMARY

1 Sexually transmitted diseases (STDs) are diseases, infections, and infestations involving the anus, genitals, mouth, eyes, or other areas of the body. The causative agents are often, but not always, passed along during intimate body contact.

2 Prevention is the first and most important step in reducing the spread of STDs.

3 The Centers for Disease Control groups STDs and pelvic inflammatory disease, an outcome of many STDs, into the following categories: (1) infections identified by genital ulcers: genital herpes, syphilis, lymphogranuloma venereum, chancroid; (2) infections of skin surfaces: genital warts; (3) gonococcal infections: gonorrhea; (4) *Chlamydia* infections: nongonococcal urethritis, mucopurulent cervicitis; (5) external parasitic infections: pubic lice, scabies; (6) amebiasis; (7) vaginal infections: trichomoniasis, vaginal yeast infections; and (8) pelvic inflammatory disease.

4 Gonorrhea, *Chlamydia* infections, nongonococcal (nonspecific) urethritis, mucopurulent cervicitis, syphilis, lymphogranuloma venereum, and chancroid are caused by bacteria or bacteria-like organisms. Antibiotic medication has good to excellent results with these diseases. Vaginal yeast infections caused by a yeast fungus are easily treated with antifungal medication. Genital herpes, genital warts, hepatitis B, and AIDS are caused by viruses; genital herpes, genital warts, and AIDS cannot be cured at present, and AIDS is fatal. Trichomoniasis and amebiasis are caused by single-celled organisms called protozoans and can be cured with various medications. Pubic lice and scabies are parasitic organisms that are related to spiders and feed on blood or other body fluids; they are treated with medicated shampoos.

5 Any discharge from the penis or vagina, sores or lesions in or around the genitals, painful urination, intense itching in the genital area, and itching and burning sensations in the vagina should be reported to a health care worker so that the diagnosis of STD can be confirmed or eliminated.

6 Preventive measures against STDs include use of a condom, washing genitals and hands after sexual contact, urination immediately after sexual contact, and inspection of a sexual partner's genitals before sexual activity.

7 STDs are not confined to adults who may contract these diseases during intimate body contact. Almost all STDs, with the exception of external parasites, can be passed by a pregnant women to the fetus during pregnancy or during the birth process. STDs may cause miscarriage, stillbirth, congenital birth defects, blindness, deafness, premature deliveries, low birth weight, and infant pneumonia. Prompt medical attention is essential if a pregnant woman suspects she might have an STD. Medications and medical approaches to the problem of STDs during pregnancy greatly reduce the risk to the developing fetus and the newborn.

8 Not only do STDs cause physical symptoms, including pain and discomfort, but they can also have psychological effects, including depression, anger, a feeling of betrayal by a sex partner, and guilt. The more dangerous and severe the disease, the greater the psychological effects.

ANSWERS

1 It is true that the more sexual partners a person has, the higher the risk that he or she will contract an STD. In a monogamous relationship, the probability of contracting an STD is remote, assuming that neither partner already has an STD.
2 Genital herpes can be passed to a sexual partner even when the blisters and sores are not present, just before onset of the lesion.
3 The fetus is very susceptible to STDs of the mother during pregnancy and the birth process.

FACT
OR
FICTION

QUESTIONS FOR THOUGHT   ?

1 How would you convince a sexual partner to use a condom?
2 How has your concern about STDs influenced or not influenced your sexual activities?

3 Briefly list all of the STDs presented in this chapter and for each disease state cause, symptoms, treatment, and preventive measures.

SUGGESTED READINGS

Boston Women's Health Book Collective: Our bodies, ourselves, New York, 1984, Simon & Schuster, Inc.
An older but excellent book written by women for women. It discusses all aspects of female sexuality, including STDs. The writing style is good, and many quotations from women appear throughout the book.
Breitman, P., Knutson, K., and Reed, P.: How to persuade your lover to use a condom . . . and why you should, Rocklin, Calif., 1987, Prima Publishing and Communications.
The best defense against STDs is prevention, and the best prevention, aside from abstaining from intimate body contact, is the use of a condom. This book tells you how to communicate your desire to use a condom to a sexual partner and convinces you that it is important to use one.
Hatcher, R.A., et al.: Contraceptive technology, New York, 1990, Irvington Publishing Co., Inc.
This is the ultimate book on contraceptive devices. The most recent edition has an easy to read chapter on STDs. A practical book that states in easy-to-understand terms what STDs are, how they are transmitted, how to prevent them, and what to do if you have one.

Acquired Immunodeficiency Syndrome

It's difficult to write this without sounding alarmist or too emotional or just plain scared.

If I had written this a month ago, I would have used the figure "40." If I had written this last week, I would have needed "80." Today I must tell you that 120 gay men in the United States . . . are suffering from an often lethal form of cancer called Kaposi's sarcoma. . . . More than thirty have died.

By the time you read this, the necessary figures may be much higher.

L. KRAMER
"A Personal Appeal"

The introductory quotation was taken from a gay newspaper called the *New York Native* and was written by the AIDS activist Larry Kramer. It was written in 1981, just before the disease we know as acquired immunodeficiency syndrome (AIDS) was discovered. Based on the most recent figures from the Centers for Disease Control (CDC) (1991a), more than 120,000 gay or bisexual men have AIDS at the present time. In addition, more than 50,000 intravenous (IV) drug users have AIDS (this includes 12,000 of the 120,000 gay or bisexual men with AIDS) and more than 10,000 individuals, male and female, have acquired the disease through heterosexual contact.

The number of AIDS cases associated with IV drug use in heterosexual people, heterosexual sexual contact, and perinatal transmission (transmission of human immunodeficiency virus [HIV] to fetus or infant) has increased dramatically since Larry Kramer wrote his story in the *New York Native* (CDC, 1991a). Black and Hispanic individuals make up a disproportionate number of persons with AIDS (51% of the total number of AIDS cases in the United States), and black and Hispanic infants account for almost 80% of the total number of newborns who are infected by the virus and will eventually develop AIDS (CDC, 1991a). To put these figures in perspective, black and Hispanic individuals constitute 12% and 6% of the U.S. population, respectively (Schinke et al., 1990). Men of all races make up 86% of the adults who are known to have AIDS.

This chapter deals exclusively with AIDS. We will consider clinical, sexual, social, and psychological aspects of the disease. We will also briefly discuss some of the legal aspects of AIDS.

AIDS is a newly described disease that was first recognized in 1981. Since that time the disease has received extensive media coverage, and rational and irrational fears have surfaced.

CLINICAL ASPECTS OF AIDS

The CDC in Atlanta is the government agency responsible for keeping records on selected diseases, including AIDS. The CDC defines AIDS as follows: "AIDS is a specific group of diseases or conditions which are indicative of severe **immunosuppression** related to infection with the human immunodeficiency virus" (CDC, 1990b). In short, AIDS is characterized by a defect in natural immunity against all diseases. The person with AIDS is vulnerable to infectious organisms in the environment that would not be a threat to anyone whose immune system was functioning normally.

immunosuppression
(i MYOO noh suh PRESH uhn) Condition in which the body's immune system, which protects us from disease, is suppressed.

FIGURE 19-1
Total AIDS cases in the
United States from 1984 to
1991.

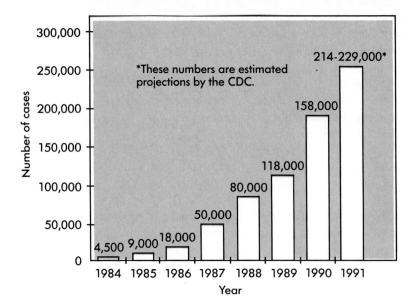

The CDC (1986) has described the following four stages of the progression of the disease from the time of infection to the terminal stage:

1. Stage I: acute HIV infection. Individuals in stage I show acute (sudden onset, short duration) infections—a mononucleosis-like syndrome with or without aseptic meningitis (usually a short-lived inflammation of membranes of the spinal cord and brain). The symptoms usually begin 2 to 8 weeks after infection and last for 10 to 14 days. Antibodies to the **human immunodeficiency virus (HIV)** usually appear in the blood 3 to 12 weeks after infection, although they may not develop until as long as 6 months after infection. In rare cases an infected person does not show antibodies to HIV.

2. Stage II: asymptomatic HIV infection. Individuals who have moved to stage II show an asymptomatic infection (no symptoms but the presence of an infection in the body). A person in stage II can transmit the virus to others. Stage II can last for years, but based on the pattern of disease seen so far, eventually symptoms will appear.

3. Stage III: persistent generalized lymphadenopathy (PGL). Individuals who have moved into stage III show PGL (disease and enlargement of the lymph nodes). This stage may last for years before any other symptoms appear. The time course for a person to go from stage II to stage III varies greatly and depends on the person's general health and well-being.

4. Stage IV: other HIV disease, including AIDS. Individuals in stage IV are said to show "full-blown AIDS." It is in this stage that the disease must be reported to the CDC. Full-blown AIDS is usually diagnosed when the infected person shows *Pneumocystis carinii* pneumonia (PCP), Kaposi's sarcoma (a rare type of cancer that occurs in young men with AIDS), and other AIDS-related opportunistic infections such as oral leukoplakia (white patches on mucous membranes of tongue and cheeks), *Salmonella* bacteremia (bacterial infection), tuberculosis, or thrush (a yeast infection of the mouth or throat). HIV may also attack the brain

human immunodeficiency virus (HIV)
The virus that causes AIDS.

and cause dementia (mental deterioration) and a wasting syndrome characterized by significant weight loss. Certain disease states are common in AIDS. PCP or Kaposi's sarcoma develops in approximately 82% of persons with AIDS (CDC, 1991a). PCP is a parasitic infection of the lungs, with symptoms similar to those of other forms of severe pneumonia. Other opportunistic infections found in patients with AIDS include severe thrush infections, cytomegalovirus infections, and herpesvirus infections.

It is in stage IV that death occurs, usually from PCP, Kaposi's sarcoma, or complications of other infections. The fatality rates increase with the duration of infection. For example, the death rate of individuals whose AIDS was diagnosed in 1981 is 92%, whereas those with AIDS diagnosed in 1987 have a death rate of 78% (CDC, 1991a).

Certain symptoms may precede the onset of AIDS. This set of symptoms has in the past been called the AIDS-related complex (ARC), although this term has lost favor with the CDC. It might be helpful to think of ARC as a progression of the disease that precedes full-blown AIDS. The symptoms include swollen lymph nodes in the neck, armpits, or groin; weight loss; fever or night sweats; chronic diarrhea; fatigue; cough; and shortness of breath. A person may die of the complications of ARC and never progress to AIDS.

The disease conditions associated with full-blown AIDS are a consequence of HIV infection in the body. In the United States, Central Africa, and other regions of the world, almost all cases of AIDS are caused by a virus termed HIV-1, but in West Africa a closely related virus called HIV-2 is responsible for most cases of AIDS (Gallo and Montagnier, 1989).

The HIV-1 and HIV-2 viruses attack white blood cells (lymphocytes) known as **T4 helper/inducer lymphocytes** (Weber and Weiss, 1989). The T4 helper cells produce substances that stimulate other lymphocytes to attack and kill pathogenic organisms, including bacteria and viruses. In addition, the T4

T4 helper/inducer lymphocyte
(LIM fuh syte) A specialized type of white blood cell that organizes the body's defenses against invading microorganisms, including HIV.

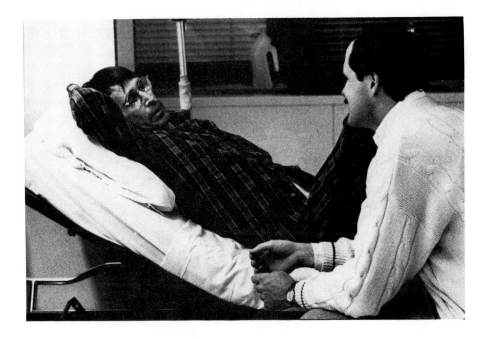

Many volunteers spend time visiting and doing errands for people with AIDS.

helper cells are critical in stimulating lymphocytes that are involved in the production of antibodies. Antibodies are chemicals produced by the immune system. These substances attack the antigen (a substance, in this case HIV, that triggers the production of antibodies). Thus we can say that the T4 helper/ inducer cells orchestrate the immune system's response to an invading virus or bacteria. Without the T4 helper/inducer cells to organize the immune system's reaction to an invading microorganism, we are at risk for many infectious diseases. Normally a person has 1,000 T4 helper cells per cubic milliliter of blood. An HIV-infected person has far fewer, under 20 cells per cubic milliliter in some cases. As of January 1992, any infected person with a count of 200 or fewer T4 helper cells per cubic milliliter will be considered to have full-blown AIDS. Taking into account the number of T4 helper cells will help to diagnose AIDS in infected women and intravenous drug users.

HIV is a type of virus known as a retrovirus. It has a protein coat that surrounds a core of ribonucleic acid. The coat of the HIV has a special protein (gp120) that has a great affinity for the T4 helper/inducer cells, and the virus binds to the cell much as a key fits into a lock (Figure 19-2). Once inside the T4 cell HIV produces new viral particles that leave the cell and move through-

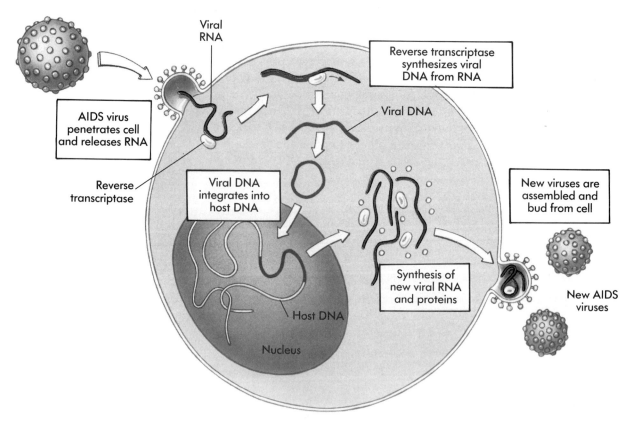

FIGURE 19-2
The human immunodeficiency virus (HIV) has a special affinity for the T4 helper/inducer cells. The protein coat of HIV contains a special protein known as gp120 that binds to the T4 cell. Once inside the cell the virus uses a special enzyme (reverse transcriptase) to translate the ribonucleic acid (RNA) core of the virus into a deoxyribonucleic acid (DNA) code. The altered DNA code then produces new viral material, and new HIV is produced. The newly synthesized HIV travels throughout the body to infect other T4 cells and other organ systems.

out the body to infect other T4 cells, as well as other organ systems.

A clear distinction must be made between being infected with the HIV and having full-blown AIDS. A person who has been infected with HIV will, with rare exceptions, show antibodies to the virus. We say that this person is **seropositive** for HIV antibodies. The person *does not* have "AIDS" (full-blown AIDS) until the appearance of the symptoms and conditions described previously for stage IV. *A person who is seropositive may show no symptoms but is infected and can pass the virus on to others during certain activities such as sexual intercourse and sharing needles during IV drug use.* A lapse of many years, up to 9.8, has been reported between infection with HIV and the onset of AIDS (Bacchetti and Moss, 1989).

seropositive
(sir′ oh POZ uh tiv) Showing antibodies to HIV.

Treatment of HIV Infection and AIDS

The specific treatments for all aspects of HIV infection and AIDS are beyond the scope of this book. Antiviral drugs that slow the progression of the disease are used routinely. The drug most widely used to treat HIV and AIDS is zidovudine (AZT). Less commonly, antiviral drugs such as dideoxyinosine (ddI) and dideoxycytidine (ddC) are used. PCP, which can be fatal in AIDS patients, is often controlled with pentamidine that is inhaled into the lungs. The AIDS symptoms are treated with drugs, irradiation, and surgery.

Tests for HIV Status

Tests for HIV infection look for the presence of antibodies to the virus and not for the virus itself. Two tests are used to determine whether a person is infected with HIV. Blood taken from a vein is assayed for HIV antibodies using a technique called the enzyme-linked immunosorbent assay (ELISA). The ELISA test costs only $2 to $3 per test and is fairly accurate (Rothstein, 1988). If a positive finding occurs with the ELISA test, confirmation is sought with a more expensive and more accurate test called the Western Blot test. This test, which costs approximately $100, helps to limit false-positive results that occur with the ELISA test. From 50% to 60% of blood samples that test positive for HIV antibodies on the ELISA test do not repeat positive in either another ELISA test or the Western Blot test (Rothstein, 1988).

Who Becomes Infected with HIV or Gets AIDS?

As C. Everett Koop, the former surgeon general of the United States, said, "Who you are has nothing to do with whether you are in danger of being infected with the AIDS virus. What matters is what you do" (Koop, 1988). We cannot emphasize enough that everyone is at risk for HIV infection and consequently AIDS. It is behaviors, not belonging to a particular group such as gay men, that place a person at risk for HIV and AIDS. However, at the present time homosexual or bisexual orientation (with or without IV drug usage) accounts for 69% of all male patients with full-blown AIDS. Among women patients, IV drug users make up 48% of the cases. The majority of other females who have AIDS are the sexual partners of men at risk for HIV infection or AIDS. *It was the behaviors practiced by the men and women patients, and not group membership, that put them at risk for the virus.* A breakdown of AIDS patients by various categories is contained in the following paragraphs.

Male patients 13 years of age or older with AIDS are identified as follows (CDC, 1991a):

1. Sexually active homosexuals and bisexuals, 66%
2. Heterosexual users of intravenously administered drugs, 19%
3. Homosexual and bisexual users of intravenously administered drugs, 7%
4. Patients with hemophilia or other disorders that prevent blood clotting who must receive blood transfusions, 1% (These disorders occur in males only and are transmitted on the X chromosome of the XY combination in the male.)
5. Heterosexual contacts of a person with AIDS or at risk for AIDS, 2%
6. Patients who received blood transfusions during surgery or because of loss of blood or tissue transplants, 2%
7. Persons who died before complete histories could be taken and patients whose mode of exposure is unknown, 3%

Female patients 13 years of age and older with AIDS are identified as follows (CDC, 1991a):

1. Users of intravenously administered drugs, 51%
2. Heterosexual contacts of persons with AIDS or at risk for AIDS, 33%
3. Patients who received blood transfusions during surgery or because of loss of blood or who received tissue transplants, 9%
4. Persons who died before complete histories could be taken and patients whose mode of exposure is unknown, 7%

More and more women are being reported among AIDS patients.

Intravenous drug users are among the growing number of people with AIDS.

Transmission of HIV

HIV has been isolated from semen, blood, vaginal and cervical secretions, breast milk, saliva, tears, urine, and feces. However, transmission of the virus has been associated only with the exchange of semen, blood, vaginal and cervical secretions, and breast milk from an infected person to a noninfected person (Cox, 1990).

The following activities are high-risk behaviors that significantly increase one's chances of being infected with the HIV:

1. Anal and vaginal intercourse, fellatio, and cunnilingus. HIV has been isolated in semen and cervical and vaginal secretions, and these fluids must not be transferred from one person to another. It is thought that tears in the anus and rectum allow the virus (in the semen) to enter the bloodstream during anal intercourse (Cox, 1990). In vaginal intercourse small breaks in the mucosa of the vaginal walls may allow the virus in the semen to enter the bloodstream. Taking semen into the mouth is dangerous because breaks in the mucosa in the mouth might allow the virus to enter the bloodstream. During cunnilingus, cervical and vaginal secretions containing the virus enter the mouth and could pass into the bloodstream if a tear exists in the mucosa of the lips or mouth.

2. Engaging in sexual activities without the use of a condom, or a latex dam in the case of cunnilingus. The dam is simply a sheet of latex that is placed over the external genitalia so that vaginal secretions are not transferred.

3. Sex with prostitutes.

4. IV drug activities in which needles are shared. The sharing of needles for intramuscular injections (e.g., of steroids for body building) also

Common Questions About AIDS

Q. What percentage of people in the United States are infected with the human immunodeficiency virus (HIV)?

A. Only cases of "full-blown AIDS" must be reported to the Centers for Disease Control (CDC), so we can only estimate the number of individuals who are infected with HIV. These infected individuals may or may not show symptoms, but they are contagious and can pass the virus to others under certain circumstances. One study done by the CDC monitored HIV in anonymous blood samples at selected hospitals in many U.S. cities. The overall rate of HIV seroprevalence (positive tests for HIV) was 1.3%, and rates ranged from 0.1% to 7.8%. A total of 89,547 blood samples from 21 cities were tested (St. Louis et al., 1990). The overall seropositive rate for the entire United States is estimated to be 0.4% (CDC, 1990a).

Q. What percentage of college students are infected with HIV?

A. As stated above, only cases of AIDS must be reported to the CDC, so we must estimate the number of students infected with the virus. The CDC did a study of anonymous blood samples from the health centers of 19 universities throughout the United States (Gayle et al., 1990). Of 16,863 blood samples, 30 (0.2%) were seropositive for HIV. Positive samples were found at 9 of the 19 schools, and all but two of the samples were from males. This is a lower rate than has been found in the general population (see answer to previous question), but the potential exists for the further spread of HIV on college and university campuses.

Q. What percentage of people who are tested for HIV antibodies are seropositive in your clinic?

A. The number has changed dramatically over the past several years. During 1989 and 1990 we had a seropositive rate of 16%. This was a self-selected group who were worried about past high-risk behaviors such as IV drug use and homosexual behaviors. During the early part of 1991 we have had a seropositive rate of only 0.9%. This is probably because we are doing a lot of HIV testing in the STD clinic and in the family planning of our health unit.

Q. Can AIDS be prevented?

A. Yes. Certain sexual practices

From Ernest Hoffman, M.D., Medical Director, Department of Health and Rehabilitative Services, Leon County Public Health Unit, Tallahassee, Florida.

increases the risk because blood can be transferred in this manner. Other high-risk behaviors include sexual interactions with anyone who has used IV drugs (drugs injected directly into the vein using a syringe or needle), had multiple sex partners, or engaged in sexual activity with a homosexual or bisexual male.

5. HIV can be transmitted through blood transfusions and other blood products, although the CDC suggests the chances of infection in this manner are only 1 in 39,000 and improving all the time (Cox, 1990).

6. Drug abuse is a serious concern because it represents a major bridge for the spread of AIDS to women and children for the following reasons:

  a. Women are infected by their heterosexual partners through sexual contact.

  b. Women are infected with HIV via needles used to inject drugs.

  c. Infected women can infect their babies through breast milk. Cox (1990) reports that the use of "crack" cocaine has a major influence on increasing the risk of AIDS because sex is often traded for crack.

should be avoided, and needles and syringes should not be shared. Specifically, the U.S. Public Health Service offers the following recommendations to prevent the spread of AIDS:

1. Do not have any intimate body contact with a person who has AIDS, a person at risk for AIDS, or a person who tests positive for HIV. If you do, use a latex condom, preferably lubricated with the spermicide nonoxynol-9, and avoid sexual practices, such as anal intercourse, that may tear the skin.
2. Do not use IV drugs. If you do, do not share needles or syringes with others.
3. If you are a woman whose sex partner is at risk (a bisexual man with many partners or a man who uses IV drugs), consider the risk to yourself and your unborn children. HIV screening should be done before or during any pregnancy.
4. Do not have sex with multiple partners, including prostitutes.

Q. Can you get HIV when you donate blood?
A. Absolutely not! The needles are sterile and are used only once.
Q. Can you get HIV when you receive a blood transfusion?
A. It is possible but not likely because all donated blood is screened for HIV as well as other disease agents.
Q. When will a vaccine against AIDS be developed?
A. Many vaccines are now being developed, and clinical testing is under way. However, a vaccine for use in the general population is not expected for another 10 years.
Q. Where can I get more specific information and the most recent news about AIDS?
A. There are many sources of information about HIV and AIDS. One of the best is your university or college health center. Student health centers usually have the most recent information from the CDC, as well as excellent pamphlets from other organizations. The materials are easy to read and are aimed at college-age individuals. Another good source of factual current information is your county public health unit. Besides providing information, the county public units in many areas perform anonymous testing for HIV status. If you desire additional information, you can call any of the following numbers for factual material:

AIDS Task Force Hot Line, 505-266-8041

National AIDS Information Clearinghouse, 1-800-458-5231

Public Health Service AIDS Hotline (available 24 hours per day and 7 days per week), 1-800-342-AIDS

HIV is not easily transferred from one person to another. No cases in which casual contact resulted in spread of the AIDS virus have been reported (Cox, 1990). Although HIV has been found in tears and saliva, it does not appear that the virus can be spread in these fluids. Health care workers caring for AIDS patients must avoid needle-stick injuries and contact with the blood of AIDS patients. The most commonly asked questions about AIDS are addressed in the box.

How HIV Is Not Transmitted

HIV is not transmitted through casual contact with a person who has AIDS. None of the parents or siblings of children infected with HIV or with AIDS have ever been infected with the virus. A study done from 1984 to 1987 followed 200 household contacts of 90 AIDS patients and found that none of the people living with the AIDS patients became HIV positive (seroconverted) (Friedland et al., 1990). As Friedland and associates point out, the individuals in their

Health Care Workers and AIDS

The concept of "universal precautions" dictates that health care providers must assume that all patients are infected with human immunodeficiency virus (HIV) and hepatitis B virus (HBV) and must use appropriate precautions. When health care workers drop their guard and fail to follow proper infection control guidelines, even once, they may be setting themselves up for an occupational accident that will put them at risk of HIV or HBV infection.

No one can simply look at a person and tell whether he or she is infected with HIV. Many people who are HIV infected do not know their antibody status. They look and feel fine and have never had any reason to be tested for HIV antibodies. Although infected and infectious, they continue their daily activities as anyone might: eating, sleeping, working, and so on. A health care worker cannot assume that a person is not infected by the way that person looks and therefore work without latex gloves or become more casual about giving an injection or drawing blood.

Health care workers are at some risk of HIV infection through occupational exposure. Many things can be done to protect workers against needle-stick injuries and exposure to patients' body fluids. The risk of exposure can be practically eliminated by wearing latex gloves when appropriate, *never* recapping contaminated needles, and hand wash-

ing constantly. Surgeons and emergency room personnel must wear protective clothing and glasses (some wear shields that cover the entire face) and surgical masks. The eyes must be protected against blood splashes, a confirmed source of HIV infection.

The primary means of infection control is hand washing. Health care workers must plan ahead and know when wearing gloves, a mask, and goggles is appropriate. They must also be aware of which body fluids are capable of transmitting HIV.

HIV lives and reproduces best in blood and semen. It also does well in vaginal secretions and breast milk. As a fragile virus, demanding proper conditions to live, HIV does not survive long outside of the body. Although HIV has been isolated in minuscule amounts in saliva, urine, and other body fluids, those fluids do not contain enough virus to be infectious.

The CDC, in a study of health care workers who were exposed to blood or body fluids from persons infected with HIV, concluded that the risk of HIV infection through occupational exposure is low (CDC, 1989). Of the 1,201 health care workers in the CDC study, 960 (80%) were exposed to HIV by needle-sticks, 8% by cuts with sharp objects, 7% by open wound contamination, and 5% by mucous membrane exposure. Of 860 workers who received needle-stick injuries or

cuts with sharp objects and whose serum was tested for HIV antibodies at least 180 days after exposure, 4 (0.47%) were positive for HIV.

Although it is known that health care workers can contract HIV from their patients, the risk that health care workers can pass the virus to their patients is less certain. In 1991 the CDC released information about a Florida dentist with AIDS who infected five patients during invasive oral surgery (CDC, 1991b). All of the patients had no other confirmed exposure to HIV, had invasive procedures performed by the dentist, and were infected with HIV strains closely related genetically to the dentist's HIV strain. The CDC concluded that inadequate infection control measures on the dentist's part may have allowed his blood to be transmitted to these patients either directly or via contaminated dental instruments. Can an infected surgeon pass the virus to a patient during surgery if the surgeon cuts himself or herself? This question is of concern to both the public and associations representing doctors and dentists. The CDC and Congress recommend (and perhaps will enact laws) that doctors and dentists be tested for HIV status.

Health care workers, using universal precautions for infection control, can reduce their risk of occupational exposure to HIV. If the health care worker is HIV positive, he or she must use all available precautions to protect the patient. As of September 1991, the only case in which transmission of HIV from an infected health care worker to patients has been "strongly suggested" was the case of the Florida dentist and his five patients (CDC, 1991b).

From Philip E. Reichert, M.P.H., Florida AIDS Program, Tallahassee.

study hugged, kissed, bathed with, shared household items with, and even slept with the AIDS patients, yet not a single one showed seroconversion at the end of the study.

Aside from sexual contact and needle sharing, HIV does not move easily from an infected person to a noninfected person. As Cox (1990) writes in *The Aids Booklet*, if AIDS were casually transmitted, it would be scattered throughout the population by now. Being near people with HIV infection or AIDS is dangerous only if you have unprotected sex with them or share needles with them. AIDS is *not* transmitted by shaking hands with, touching, or drinking from the same cup as an infected person, being sneezed on or coughed on by an infected person, or using the same toilet as an infected person. No evidence has implicated insects in the transmission of AIDS.

AIDS Prevention

No vaccine has been developed for the prevention of HIV infection, nor has a cure for AIDS been found. Thus the best way to prevent getting or spreading AIDS is to avoid risky behaviors. The following guidelines from *The Aids Booklet* will help you avoid being infected with the virus. The guidelines are based on the fact that the HIV is found in semen, blood, and cervical and vaginal secretions. Thus preventing the transfer of these fluids from one person to the next will prevent transmission of the virus.

1. Use latex condoms *and* a spermicide containing nonoxynol-9.
2. Proper lubrication (*do not* use Vaseline or other home products, which deteriorate the latex on the condom) will help prevent breakage in the condom as well as vaginal tears, both of which may allow semen into the bloodstream.

Safer Sex Options

Safe Practices
1. Massage
2. Hugging
3. Body rubbing
4. Kissing (dry)
5. Masturbation
6. Hand-to-genital touching
7. Mutual manual stimulation of the genitals

Possibly Safe Practices
1. French kissing
2. Vaginal or anal intercourse using a latex condom and nonoxynol-9 spermicide for extra safety
3. Oral sex on a man using a condom
4. Oral sex on a woman who does not have menstrual flow or vaginal infection with a discharge (a latex dam is strongly recommended)

Unsafe Practices
1. Vaginal or anal intercourse without a latex condom
2. Oral sex on a man without a condom
3. Oral sex on a woman during menstrual flow or during a vaginal infection with a discharge and without a latex dam
4. Semen in the mouth
5. Oral-anal contact
6. Blood contact of any kind, including menstrual blood, sharing needles, and any sex act that causes bleeding or tissue damage

---

3. Avoid unprotected anal and vaginal intercourse. "Unprotected" means without a condom.
4. Avoid unprotected fellatio and cunnilingus. "Unprotected" means without a condom or a latex dam.
5. Avoid sexual relations with persons who use drugs or persons who buy or sell sex.
6. Do not use alcohol or drugs to the point at which your judgment is impaired.
7. Do not share needles used for injecting drugs into veins.
8. If you are planning to have an operation, consider donating your own blood to be used if you need blood during your operation.
9. Do not think that you are "not the type of person" to get AIDS, or that a potential partner is "too nice" and "too considerate" to have AIDS. Anyone can have the virus, and any real cure remains in the distant future.
10. *Most important*, remember that safer sex requires changing behaviors with all partners, not just with partners you don't know well. Furthermore, safer sex behavior is not effective unless it is applied every time you engage in sexual activity. Inconsistency in applying AIDS prevention measures can have deadly consequences.

SOCIAL AND PSYCHOLOGICAL IMPLICATIONS OF HIV INFECTION AND AIDS

AIDS has influenced the sexual behaviors of many homosexual men (McKusick, Horstman, and Coates, 1985). Monogamous homosexual men (at less risk for AIDS than other homosexual men) have not curtailed suspected high-

Many support groups exist to help people with AIDS.

HUMAN SEXUALITY

A Personal Glimpse

Behavioral Responses to AIDS

A heterosexual man describes changes in his sexual behavior since the advent of the AIDS epidemic:

When the major sexually transmitted diseases of concern were curable, I did not question my partners very much about their sexual histories. Back then one felt that "good girls" (no prostitutes from the docks) were OK. With the discovery of herpes and the realization that the difference between herpes and true love was that herpes lasted forever, I started asking my prospective partners whether they had herpes or not. With AIDS, I want a complete history. Questions about past partners and behaviors are a necessity. In fact, women are asking me the same questions. I know that AIDS is prevalent nationwide, but the data indicate that it is safer in the Midwest. For example, on a trip to New York, I turned down an offer from a friend to hit the singles bars to pick up a date. I wouldn't even consider it.

I spend much more time in a relationship discussing my partner's sexual history. Condoms are no longer a birth control device but a necessity. One woman I knew who was on the pill began asking her dates to use a condom and began to carry them herself. As a single guy, I might be tempted to consider her a great date, but her history says she fools around too much. I have really reduced my own sexual activities out of fear of contracting AIDS. (28-year-old single male)

Many women share the same fears:

What's dating like in the post-AIDS world? Probably more difficult for older than younger people. After a certain age one's dating and sexual habits become set. For the single adult, when one goes to bed with a new partner, one goes to bed with every partner that partner has had in the past 5 years.

I recently became involved with a man who, like myself, has been single for the past 10 years. We practice "safe sex" using condoms, but find warnings about exchanging body fluids inhibiting to sexual activity. I raised the AIDS issue in this present relationship, asking, "Are you more afraid of getting AIDS from me or giving AIDS to me?" The discussion of our histories that followed was inconclusive because we don't know the sexual histories of our previous partners. It was not a major concern several years ago. To me, sex in the post-AIDS world feels a little like Russian roulette. (40-year-old single professional woman)

Homosexual men also express these fears:

I was never really too sexually active. I have had about six partners in my life and two of them lasted for about 6 months each. I never engaged in casual sex with strangers, and all of my partners were known to me or known to friends of mine. Even still I was scared about AIDS. I had an HIV test done at a health unit in my hometown. It was anonymous and it was negative. I always use condoms in anal and oral sex, and most of my friends take the necessary precautions during sex. (21-year-old male)

AUTHORS' FILES

---

risk sexual activities, including oral-anal contact, "fisting" (insertion of hand into partner's rectum), swallowing of urine or semen, and anal intercourse without a condom, because they have felt protected by their monogamy. Nonmonogamous men and those not in relationships reported reduction in oral-genital activities but not anal activities. Nonmonogamous men and men not in relationships did not show a corresponding increase in low-risk sexual behaviors such as anal intercourse with a condom, anal coitus interruptus, and mutual hand stimulation of the genitals. The frequency of sexual activity in bars, bathhouses, and public places such as park restrooms was substantially reduced. McKusick, Horstman, and Coates (1985) concluded that even though the men in their sample knew a great deal about the prescribed behavior for AIDS reduction, many continued to engage in high-risk sex practices. This

TABLE 19-1   HIV Transmission Risks Associated with Heterosexual Intercourse

	Estimated risk of infection	
	One sexual encounter	500 sexual encounters with different people
PARTNER NEVER TESTED FOR HIV		
Not in high-risk category*		
Using condoms	1 in 50,000,000	1 in 110,000
Not using condoms	1 in 5,000,000	1 in 16,000
In high-risk category		
Using condoms	1 in 100,000 to 1 in 10,000	1 in 210 to 1 in 21
Not using condoms	1 in 10,000 to 1 in 1,000	1 in 32 to 1 in 3
PARTNER TESTED NEGATIVE FOR HIV		
No history of high-risk behavior†		
Using condoms	1 in 5,000,000,000	1 in 11,000,000
Not using condoms	1 in 500,000,000	1 in 1,600,000
PARTNER TESTED POSITIVE FOR HIV		
Using condoms	1 in 5,000	1 in 11
Not using condoms	1 in 500	2 in 3

Modified from Hurst and Hulley, 1989.

*Assuming 1 chance of infection per 500 contacts with infected individual.

†The calculations are based on Centers for Disease Control–defined high-risk categories, which include homosexual or bisexual men, intravenous drug users, individuals receiving blood or blood products, female prostitutes, and heterosexuals from countries where heterosexual spread of HIV is common.

high-risk sexual behavior may be comparable to other high-risk behaviors, such as tobacco smoking and obesity, in which knowledge alone is not sufficient to change behavior.

The AIDS epidemic has spawned such clubs as Safe Adults, Peace of Mind, Inc., and The Safedate Network. These clubs require that their members be tested for HIV every 6 months, and the members carry cards to show that they were negative for HIV in their last test. The risks for engaging in heterosexual vaginal intercourse under various conditions are given in Table 19-1.

COLLEGE STUDENTS AT RISK FOR HIV INFECTION

Because of their sexual practices and drug use, sexually active adolescents and young adults are at risk for contracting HIV. According to Friedland and Klein (1987), the student population is characterized by high levels of the behaviors that lead to HIV transmission (Platt, 1987). The past 30 years have been marked by increasing engagement in premarital sex and a continual decrease in the

average age at which individuals begin having sexual relations (Clayton and Bokmeier, 1980). In addition, the average marrying age is increasing. Thus the average number of partners young people today have before marriage is much higher than it used to be, increasing the opportunity for HIV transmission (Denning, 1987). All of these factors make young adults a vehicle for the spread of AIDS into the heterosexual population.

Baldwin and Baldwin (1988) surveyed 513 unmarried college students in southern California who had engaged in sexual intercourse within the past 3 months. The average age of the participants was 20, 51% were female, and 88% were white. Their average number of sexual partners in the preceding 3 months was 1.5. Twenty percent had had sex with a stranger or casual acquaintance in the past 3 months. Although knowledgeable about how AIDS is transmitted, the students believed they had little risk of contracting AIDS; almost half did not worry about contracting AIDS from their sexual activity, and another 39% worried about it only "a little bit." Sixty-six percent reported never using condoms. Condom use was more frequent, however, in students whose parents had higher incomes and education and in students who began having sex at a later age. The students' knowledge about AIDS did not affect condom use, but concern about the possibility of contracting AIDS did promote condom use. Casual sex was *less* common among those who knew more about AIDS transmission, among older students, and among students who had their first sexual experience at a later age. A sex education course that focused on transmitting knowledge did not lead to greater caution, nor did higher levels of religious commitment.

According to many studies, most college students know how AIDS is transmitted and about proper preventive measures, but few students are practicing safe sex as a result (Edgar et al., 1988; Kegeles et al., 1988; Manning et al., 1989).

Much attention is being given to AIDS-related education for adolescents and college students. Schuster and associates (1986) emphasize the need to educate students of all ages. They recommend modifying the program content to suit the age group of the students and the degree of risk in the students' neighborhood (i.e., IV drug use in the area increases the risk).

The testing of patients' blood for HIV would allow health care workers to

AIDS protestors are being arrested in many demonstrations. Demonstrators want more funds for AIDS research and easier access to new drugs to fight AIDS.

know a patient's status, which would help safeguard the health of the health care worker. Proponents of involuntary testing argue that health care workers who know that a patient is HIV positive and are exposed to this patient's blood will be more likely to undergo periodic HIV testing and to practice safe sex if seroconversion does occur. Opponents of mandatory testing say that the test has limited value and that forced testing could be a dangerous precedent. Opponents say that health care workers should treat all patients as if they had an infectious disease and should follow universal precautions with all patients. Many opponents of involuntary testing feel that if it is proved that a drug treatment can prevent infection after an exposure to HIV, then involuntary testing of certain patients will be warranted. At present, certain drugs such as AZT have been shown to slow the progression of the disease but do not prevent HIV infection from continuing on to AIDS.

ADOLESCENTS AT RISK FOR HIV INFECTION

Adolescents, because of their naiveté, their lack of concern over and lack of perceived personal vulnerability to the AIDS epidemic, their sexual promiscuity and drug use, and the absence of safe sexual practices in their population, need intervention programs designed to prevent the further spread of AIDS into the heterosexual population. Adults in their twenties (who in most cases acquired the virus as teenagers) make up 20% of all reported AIDS cases (Brooks-Gunn, Boyer, and Hein, 1988). Furthermore, 15- to 19-year-olds have a higher prevalence of sexually transmitted diseases than any other age group. Most adolescents do not use contraceptives until 1 year after their first sexual experience. Even more alarming, a study by Sorenson in the 1970s revealed that about 41% of the sexually experienced adolescent males in the nation had had at least 17 sexual partners by age 19, and an average of 3.2 partners in the month before the interview.

Differences in HIV transmission do exist between adolescents and adults. First, a higher percentage of teenagers with AIDS acquired the virus through heterosexual transmission. Second, a larger proportion of teenagers than adults show no symptoms, since they were infected more recently. As in adults, more teenagers with AIDS are black and Hispanic (Brooks-Gunn, Boyer, and Hein, 1988). Blacks and Hispanics constitute 56% of the reported AIDS cases in 5- to 19-year-olds and 80% of the AIDS cases in children under the age of 5 (who are usually born with HIV infection contracted from the mother) (CDC, 1991a). Results of a survey of high school students' knowledge of HIV and AIDS indicated that white students were more knowledgeable and held fewer misconceptions than black and Hispanic students (DiClemente, Boyer, and Morales, 1988). This study was done in San Francisco where AIDS awareness is high because of the incidence of the disease. A more recent study done in private schools in the Chicago area found that white and black students had similar levels of knowledge about HIV and AIDS and were more knowledgeable than Hispanic students (Crawford and Robinson, 1990).

Particular attention should be directed to potentially high-risk groups such as runaways, dropouts, drug users, and youth in prisons or detention centers. A study by Hein (1987) revealed that the average age at first intercourse among young women in a detention center was 12. Most of the female adolescents in the study (which also included females living in group homes in the Bronx) regularly had intercourse with "multiple partners with whom they had no lasting relationships and little knowledge of their partners' prior sexual or drug-related behavior." These data, according to Hein, "define a population of urban adolescents who may be at immediate risk for HIV infection."

IV drug users, according to Brookes-Gunn, Boyer, and Hein (1988) and Cox (1990) are most likely to be the link through which HIV infection enters the heterosexual population. In 1986 approximately 10% of high school seniors had used cocaine in the past year (Johnston et al., 1987). The percentage of American youth who have used drugs is undoubtedly higher because higher rates of drug use are seen in dropouts than in high school seniors. In the Bronx drug addiction is now the primary risk factor for AIDS and two thirds of all AIDS cases are due to IV drug use; half of the more than 70,000 IV drug users (primarily young adults with multiple sex partners) in the Bronx are carrying the HIV virus, making large-scale transmission of AIDS into the heterosexual population a very real prospect (Hein, 1987).

Hein also discusses physiological reasons that adolescents may be at special risk. Because of differences in the cervical mucus between adolescents and adult females, for example, sperm and other motile organisms (e.g., HIV) can more easily penetrate the cervix of an adolescent. Similarly, the adult female's vaginal pH is less conducive to the survival of many organisms associated with sexually transmitted diseases than the adolescent's. Thus teenage girls may be at even greater risk than adult women for contracting AIDS through sexual intercourse.

We have shown why young adults are particularly at risk and need to be targeted by AIDS prevention programs. Although many adolescents are vulnerable because of incomplete knowledge and misinformation, college students have demonstrated that information alone does not stimulate preventive behavior modification. To illustrate this point, we will first examine AIDS-related knowledge and attitudes among young adults, then contrast that with their sexual and drug-related behaviors.

DOES KNOWLEDGE TRANSLATE INTO SAFE SEX BEHAVIORS?

In this section we examine how adolescents and college students have responded to the AIDS epidemic. In a review of many studies, Becker and Joseph (1988) concluded that although a high level of AIDS-related knowledge seems to influence the behaviors of homosexual and bisexual men, such knowledge has little effect on the sexual behaviors of adolescents and young adults. Knowledge about HIV transmission and protection against HIV seems insufficient to impress upon many heterosexuals the need for sexual behavior changes, probably because they mistakenly perceive themselves to be at low risk for contracting the virus. This theory is supported by the finding that homosexuals in areas with a low incidence of AIDS continue to practice careless sexual behavior, whereas homosexuals in high-incidence areas such as San Francisco report taking more precautions in response to the AIDS epidemic (Calabrese et al., 1986). In sum, individuals who do not perceive themselves to be at high risk (i.e., most heterosexuals) are not modifying their sexual behaviors in response to AIDS.

A study of eleventh- and twelfth-grade students in Ohio (a relatively low-risk geographical area) by Price and associates (1985) showed that students could not correctly identify all of the AIDS risk groups or the modes of trans-

Education efforts such as AIDS mobile education units are needed to educate our youth.

mission. Disturbingly, 47% was the highest score earned on the knowledge test among all the students who took it, and only 27% of the students felt concerned about the possibility of even contracting AIDS. Most of the 1,326 14- to 18-year-olds studied in San Francisco (a high-risk area), on the other hand, could correctly identify characteristics of AIDS, and most also knew that the disease could be transmitted through sexual intercourse or by sharing a needle with another drug user; however, a fourth of these students incorrectly identified shaking hands as a method of AIDS transmission. Perhaps even more alarming is that 40% of the students did not know that correct use of a condom lowers the risk of AIDS transmission, and three quarters of them thought that a new treatment might have recently been developed to prevent or to cure AIDS. More than half, furthermore, believed that they were "not the type of person" who would contract AIDS. However, 41.8% did realize that they were at greater risk for getting AIDS by living in San Francisco.

In a 1987 survey of Massachusetts teenagers only 15% made changes in their sexual behavior out of concern about the AIDS threat, and most of the measures taken by that 15% were not very effective. Their modifications in behavior, for example, included "avoiding gays" or "being more selective" in their choice or partners. Only 3% of the teenagers interviewed altered the behaviors that actually transmit HIV (i.e., 3% began to use condoms or abstain from sex) (Strunin and Hingson, 1987).

Reuben's 1988 study of adolescents in a high-risk area (New York City, which contains one fifth of all persons with AIDS in the United States) found that "most of the adolescents engaging in the highest risk sexual behavior perceived themselves to be at low risk [for AIDS] and did not use precautionary measures during intercourse" (Brooks-Gunn, Boyer, and Hein, 1988). Chervin and Martinez (1987) found that 75% of the students surveyed at Stanford University in 1987 did not discuss their sexual health or histories before engaging in sexual activity and that a majority had not changed their behavior at all in response to the AIDS threat. Similarly, single, nonpregnant, sexually active San Francisco adolescents (aged 14 to 19) who had been exposed to both formal education about AIDS and high media coverage of the AIDS crisis, and who live in a city with a high prevalence of AIDS, reported that they knew condoms prevent sexually transmitted diseases and that avoiding such diseases was of great importance to them. Nevertheless, the females did not intend to have their partners use condoms, and the males intended to persist in not using condoms, thereby continuing to place themselves and their partners at risk for AIDS infection.

Brooks-Gunn, Boyer, and Hein (1988) report that many adolescents erroneously believe they can tell who is likely to be carrying the AIDS virus. *A person may be infected with the AIDS virus (and can therefore infect others) for 10 years or more without showing any symptoms; the person may be unaware that he or she is infected. Furthermore, tests for HIV antibodies are usually not positive until 6 weeks to 6 months after the person becomes infected, so a person who tests negative for the HIV antibody may nevertheless be infected* (Cox, 1990).

In an encouraging recent national survey of 8,098 high school students, nearly all of the students knew the two main modes of HIV transmission (IV drug use and sexual intercourse). The students who knew the most about HIV transmission were less likely to report having had two or more sexual partners and more likely to report consistent condom use (Anderson et al., 1990).

Recent studies of college-age individuals are not as encouraging. College students possess knowledge about HIV transmission and AIDS and have increased the use of condoms to lower their risk of HIV infection (DiClemente et al., 1990; Waitley et al., 1990). However, they still have misconceptions about casual contact and HIV transmission and continue to engage in high-risk sexual behaviors. For example, Waitley and associates (1990) found that the male and female college students in their study were knowledgeable about HIV transmission and AIDS (mean score on knowledge items was 9.06 for men and 8.86 for women out of a possible 10 points), yet they engaged in risky sex behaviors. Specifically, 17 of the 57 females (29.8%) ingested semen and 28 of the 50 males (56%) and 68% of the females engaged in sexual intercourse without a condom. Anal sex without a condom was practiced by 6% of the males and 3% of the females.

What, then, determines whether individuals will change their behaviors in response to the AIDS threat? Allard (1989) explored this question among adults aged 18 to 65 in Montreal, Canada; he found that, in agreement with the aforementioned research, knowledge alone is not related to behavioral change. Factors that were positively associated with carrying out practices to help prevent AIDS included (1) perceiving oneself as being at risk for contracting AIDS, (2) perceiving AIDS as a very severe illness, (3) having a strong belief in the preventability of AIDS, and (4) being health conscious overall.

With respect to condom usage, an excellent preventive measure, the San Francisco women sampled by Kegeles and associates (1988) thought that their partners would react negatively to the prospect of using condoms, when in reality the males sampled were generally quite positive about it. Some goals of AIDS education, then, might be to increase individuals' awareness of their vulnerability to AIDS; to correct males' and females' misconceptions about attitudes toward condom use; to encourage communication between partners regarding their sexual histories and participation in safer sex practices (such as asking one's partner to use a condom); to intervene in teenagers' and pregnant women's behaviors, specifically those having to do with contraceptive use and IV drug use; and to increase male condom use (through condom distribution initiatives, family planning clinic services, and school-based clinics).

CURRENT TRENDS AND THE STIGMA OF AIDS

AIDS cases associated with IV drug use, heterosexual sexual contact, and perinatal transmission continue to increase, while cases related to blood transfusions and treatment of hemophilia are decreasing (CDC, 1990a). Cases among homosexual and bisexual men continue to increase, but not as rapidly as in past (CDC, 1990a). Minority individuals are disproportionately represented among AIDS patients. Approximately 51% of adults with AIDS in the United States are black or Hispanic (CDC, 1991a). Black and Hispanic infants account for approximately 80% of the newborns infected with HIV (Rogers and Williams, 1987; CDC, 1991a). Educational programs and interventions must be aimed at the groups that are showing an increase in AIDS cases.

Children born of women with HIV infection or AIDS have a 30% to 50% chance of developing AIDS. The volunteers at this hospital are giving much-needed physical and emotional care to AIDS babies.

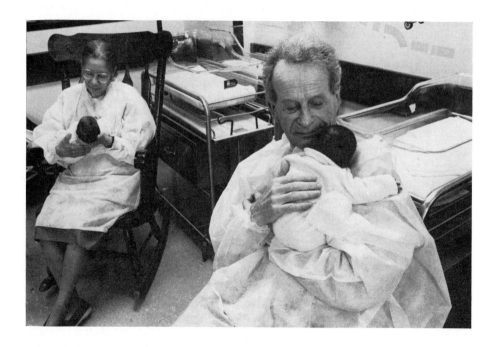

As the blood supply becomes safer, virtually all AIDS cases in children 13 years of age and younger will result from infection acquired from an HIV-positive mother (Brooks-Gunn, Boyer, and Hein, 1988). Clearly, prevention of HIV infection in children requires prevention of HIV infection in women and prevention of pregnancy in infected women (Rogers and Williams, 1987).

Women constitute approximately 14% of all persons with AIDS in the United States (CDC, 1990a, 1991a). The great majority of females with AIDS are between 13 and 39 years of age, the primary childbearing years (Guinan and Hardy, 1987; Wofsy, 1987). The major modes of transmission of HIV in women are IV drug use (51%) and heterosexual transmission (33%) (Guinan and Hardy, 1987; CDC, 1991a).

In a study of women at risk for HIV and AIDS the seropositive rate was 8.7%. Behaviors that placed the women at risk included prostitution without condom usage, use of IV drugs, use of IV drugs by a woman's main sex partner, and unprotected sex with a bisexual partner (Harrison et al., 1991; Quadagno et al., in press). Although the women in the study scored high on tests of their knowledge of HIV and AIDS, they continued to engage in high-risk behaviors. Furthermore, they did not perceive themselves to be at risk for HIV and AIDS (Quadagno et al., in press).

Dr. Jonathan Mann, director of the World Health Organization, told the Third International Conference on AIDS (held during the summer of 1987) that the AIDS stigma is on the rise. He stated that the global epidemic of AIDS has entered a third stage, in which prejudice about AIDS victims is spreading as fast as the virus. He described a rising wave of stigmatization against Westerners in Asia, against Africans in Europe, and against homosexuals, prostitutes, recipients of blood transfusions, and hemophiliacs. He told the conference that the fears of AIDS have become a direct threat to free travel between countries. Mann described the first stage of the AIDS epidemic as

AIDS TREATMENT CENTER

AIDS PHOBIA TREATMENT CENTER

don addis

the silent spread of the virus in many countries during the middle to late 1970s. The second stage was the emergence of the fatal disease in the 1980s. The present stage is the economic, social, political, and cultural reaction and response to AIDS cases.

SUMMARY

1 Acquired immunodeficiency syndrome (AIDS) is caused by the human immunodeficiency virus (HIV). AIDS is defined as a specific group of diseases or conditions that are indicative of severe immunosuppression related to infection with HIV. Only cases of "full-blown AIDS" must be reported to the Centers for Disease Control.

2 A person infected with HIV may not show any symptoms for many years. This infected individual is contagious to others under certain circumstances. A person who has been infected with HIV will, with rare exceptions, show antibodies to the HIV. This person is said to be seropositive. Tests for HIV look for antibodies to the virus, not for the virus itself.

3 Behaviors, not belonging to a particular group, place a person at risk for HIV and AIDS.

4 HIV has been isolated in semen, blood, vaginal and cervical secretions, breast milk, saliva, tears, urine, and feces. Transmission of the virus via semen, blood, vaginal and cervical secretions, and breast milk has been documented.

5 Any transfer of semen, blood, vaginal and cervical secretions, and breast milk from an infected person can transmit HIV to a noninfected person.

6 Activities and situations that significantly increase a person's chances of being infected with HIV include unprotected anal and vaginal intercourse and unprotected fellatio and cunnilingus; the sharing of needles and sy-

ringes; transfusions of blood and various blood products and tissue transplants; and pregnancy of infected women, who can infect their child during prenatal development, birth, and breast feeding.

7 HIV is not transmitted through casual contact.

8 People can protect themselves from HIV infection by abstaining from behaviors that involve the transfer of semen and cervical or vaginal secretions, or by using condoms or latex dams if they do engage in these behaviors. Maintaining a monogamous relationship greatly reduces the risk. If intravenous drugs are used, needles and syringes should never be shared.

9 The threat of HIV and AIDS has reduced risky behaviors in many individuals of all sexual orientations.

10 Adolescents and college-age individuals are often knowledgeable about HIV and AIDS but still engage in risky sexual behaviors and drug usage.

FACT
OR
FICTION

ANSWERS

1 A person who is infected with HIV does not have AIDS until specific symptoms are shown. A person may be infected for 9 years or more before any symptoms appear. Once infected, a person is contagious.

2 HIV is a difficult virus to transmit. Parents and siblings who live in close contact with a person with AIDS have never contracted the disease.

3 Risky behaviors, not membership in a particular high-risk group, put a person at risk for HIV infection and AIDS.

1 Do you think testing for HIV should be mandatory under certain circumstances? If no, why not? If yes, what circumstances?

2 List all of the modes of HIV transmission and indicate how you can protect yourself from the virus.

3 What does the statement, "It is risky behavior that places you at risk for HIV transmission and not membership in a high-risk category" mean? Be specific and give an example.

SUGGESTED READINGS

Cox, F.: The AIDS booklet, Dubuque, Ia., 1990, Wm. C. Brown Group.
    An excellent, easy-to-read booklet containing information on all aspects of HIV infection and AIDS.
Dalton, H., and Burris, S.: AIDS and the law, New Haven, Conn., 1987, Yale University Press.
    This is an excellent source of information about responses to AIDS of the government and the private sector and about AIDS in institutions. It concentrates on the legal aspects of AIDS.
Kramer, L.: Reports from the holocaust: the making of an AIDS activist, New York, 1990, Penguin Books.
    From the book jacket: "Essential documents in the history of the epidemic . . . the manifesto of AIDS activism." If you are interested in the history of AIDS activism, this is the book for you.

Sexual Variations

After years of experimenting in private, Alex finally decided to share his fantasy of cross-dressing and bondage with several women. Although his diplomatic approach convinced his partners to experiment, he felt they were merely going through the motions of tying him up or telling him to dress up like a woman, because he asked them to do so. Since the women he was attracted to were by nature submissive, they couldn't effectively perform the dominant role. They couldn't exercise real power or express the firmness, forcefulness, or meanness he wanted to experience from a woman.

J.G. SCOTT
Erotic Power: An Exploration of Dominance and Submission, p. 19

Certain sexual behaviors defy any simple classification. These behaviors have been referred to by such diverse terms as perversion, deviation, abnormal or aberrant sexual behavior, atypical sexual behavior, or unusual sexual behavior. The current trend is to use the terms *sexual variation* or *paraphilia* (abnormal liking for) to describe sexual behavior that varies from the norm, because these terms do not carry the negative connotations and moralistic tone of such words as perversion or deviation. We use the term *sexual variations* for this chapter because of its neutral tone. However, although some of the variations discussed are relatively harmless, others may have serious consequences for the nonconsenting partner or unknowing victim. Some of the activities described may be used in relatively healthy ways within the context of sexual relationships; others are exploitive and in some cases dangerous.

It is difficult to estimate how many people engage in the behaviors discussed in this chapter because only those who get into trouble with the law or have marital or personal problems attract the attention of researchers, therapists, and legal authorities (Reinisch, 1990).

> The imagery in a paraphilia, such as simulated bondage, may be playful and harmless and acted out with a mutually consenting partner. . . . In a more extreme form, paraphiliac imagery is acted out with a nonconsenting partner and is noxious and injurious to the partner as in severe sexual sadism.
>
> American Psychiatric Association, 1986, p. 267

DEFINING SEXUAL VARIATIONS

How do we decide whether a sexual behavior can be classified as a sexual variation? This is a difficult question that may be dealt with in different ways. One method is the statistical approach, which assumes that normal sexual expression is the average or statistically common expression of sexual behavior in a population. Accordingly, a sexual variation is an act or behavior that is not practiced by large numbers of people. If only a few people engage in necrophilia (sexual contact with a corpse), we can justifiably say these individuals are at variance with the normal, accepted, or average of our society. This is a simple, clear-cut example, but many sexual variances are practiced in a range from mild to severe manifestations. For example, biting, scratching, or squeezing one's sexual partner during heightened sexual arousal is not unusual, but many consider this a mild form of sadism. In rare cases a person may kill another to receive sexual gratification; this is the ultimate extreme of sadism. Further, what about the couple that experiments with sadomasochism by mutual consent? Such experimentation, considered a mild form of sadism by many, is very different from extreme acts with nonconsenting partners.

Another approach to the problem of classifying a particular behavior as a sexual variation from "normal behavior" is to take a moral stance. This approach calls on religious or moral values to decide what is "right" or "wrong" or what is "normal" or "abnormal." Some difficulties are associated with this approach. Two behaviors practiced by large numbers of people are masturbation and premarital intercourse. These behaviors are considered wrong by numerous religious groups and individuals. Should these behaviors be labeled sexual variations in the same sense as voyeurism and exhibitionism?

Robert Stoller, a widely quoted author, psychoanalyst, and professor of psychiatry, gives the following definition of sexual aberration, which we feel is also a good definition of sexual variation:

> A sexual aberration [or variation] is an erotic technique or group of techniques that a person uses as their complete sexual act and that technique(s) differs from their culture's or society's traditional, openly known definition of normality.
>
> Stoller, 1975, p. 3

Stoller states that aberrations may be of two types. The first type involves the habitual and preferred use of the sexual technique to achieve sexual gratification, and the second involves a brief experiment with certain sexual variations.

When sexual variations are motivated by curiosity, boredom, or desire for variety, they can be labeled "transitory sexual variations." In contrast, sexual variations that are a preferred, habitual, compelling method of achieving sexual gratification might be considered an "established sexual variation." Many individuals can achieve sexual gratification only through use of a particular sexual variation.

The *Diagnostic and Statistical Manual of Mental Disorders* (DSM-III), published by the American Psychiatric Association (1986), is widely used by clinicians who treat **paraphilia**. The term *paraphilia* is "preferable because it correctly emphasizes that the deviation (para) is that to which the individual is attracted (philia)" (American Psychiatric Association, 1986). For example, a pedophile (from the Greek *paidos*, meaning child) is sexually attracted to children.

The DSM-III classifies the paraphilias as psychosexual disorders and states that in general the paraphilias "are characterized by arousal (sexual) in response to sexual objects or situations that are not part of normative arousal-activity patterns and that in varying degrees may interfere with the capacity for reciprocal affectionate sexual activity."

Our discussion is limited to sexual practices in the United States and other Western countries, thus avoiding the problem of establishing universal norms for human sexual conduct in varied cultures (Beach, 1977). Heterosexual, homosexual, and bisexual individuals may engage in the variations described. They do not have to do with sexual orientation but with the expression of sexual behavior. Each variation is described, followed by a brief discussion of theories about their causes and treatment.

The sexual variations presented can be divided into two commonly accepted

paraphilia
(par' uh FIL ee uh) Sexual behavior considered to be socially undesirable.

categories (Lester, 1975; Stoller, 1977): variations that involve preferences for particular *sexual objects*, such as corpses or articles of clothing, that is, deviation from socially acceptable *ways* of seeking sexual gratification; and variations that involve *particular acts*, such as peeping into a woman's bedroom as she undresses or exhibiting the genitals to others, that is, a departure from traditional *modes* of obtaining sexual gratification.

SEXUAL VARIATIONS INVOLVING UNUSUAL OBJECTS

Variations in behavior involving a preference for unusual sex objects recognized by the American Psychiatric Association (1980) and discussed here are fetishism, transvestism, zoophilia, necrophilia, and pedophilia.

Fetishism

Fetishism is sexual arousal by an inanimate object, such as stockings, underwear, corsets, shoes or boots, materials such as velvet or silk, or a body part, such as a foot, that is not a primary (penis or vulva) or secondary (breast) sex characteristic (Gosselin and Wilson, 1980). The object used is called a fetish. More recent fetishes include "sexy underwear and a specialized range of garments in rubber, vinyl and leather" (Gosselin and Wilson, 1980). Common fetishes are feet, rubber or leather objects, shoes, and women's underwear. The fetish may have a particular smell that is associated with the owner, for example, worn shoes or undergarments. Minor fetishism involves a ritual, such as observing a female in a particular state of undress, before intercourse can occur. Fetishism is almost exclusively a male phenomenon and usually appears in adolescence. The fetish may have been associated with a particular individual, but sexual arousal is now transferred from the individual to the object. The following example is a classic case of a foot fetish.

> An unmarried man in his 20s begins to be sexually excited whenever he looks at women's feet with shoes on. He becomes more so if he sees the feet naked, and is brought to orgasm if a woman steps on his penis with her naked foot, or if in masturbation he fantasizes this action. He can only be aroused by feet.
>
> Stoller, 1975, p. 196

fetishism
Sexual arousal by nongenital body parts or inanimate objects.

Fetishism involves sexual arousal caused by an object, such as feet.

Zoophilia

Zoophilia or **bestiality** involves sexual acts or contacts with animals. Kinsey and associates (1948, 1953) found that 8% of men and 3% of women reported sexual contact with animals. Most commonly, those engaging in sexual contacts with animals were youths raised on farms. Seventeen percent had at least one orgasm through animal contact after puberty. Generally, males penetrate the anus or vagina of the animal with their penis, and females masturbate the animal. In some cases the animal licks the genitals. The following case history is an example of zoophilia:

> A single man, a farm laborer in his late 20s, has been having intercourse with animals since puberty. Being very shy, he has never gone with a woman. Although in his late teens he would have liked to, he now has no conscious desire for women. Two attempts with prostitutes found him impotent; these were his only heterosexual experiences. He has had no homosexual relations.
>
> Stoller, 1977, p. 197

Necrophilia

Necrophilia is the use of corpses for sexual intercourse. The person having intercourse with the dead body has not killed the person, but has access to the corpse. Like most variations, necrophilia has been reported only in men. Because of the difficulty in obtaining access to a corpse, those who practice this variation often resort to a simulated corpse.

A sexual encounter that incorporates some fantasy from the sexual variation of necrophilia was related by one of our students:

> I was dating this older man who was quite sexually experienced. We tried many things, such as he tying me up and me doing the same to him. One night he suggested that I take a bath in ice-cold water. He actually prepared the bath and put a bunch of ice cubes in the water. He said he wanted to pretend that I was dead and that he was going to make love to me while my body was very cold. He also wanted me to put a lot of powder on my face to take away any natural color. I did it, but it wasn't much of a turn-on for me. He seemed to like it, but I decided that this guy was too "far out" for me, and broke up with him.
>
> AUTHORS' FILES

Pedophilia

Pedophilia is a sexual variation in which children, usually younger than 13 years, are the sexual objects (Ames and Houston, 1990). The term *pedophilia* is controversial; many researchers and mental health workers prefer the terms *child sexual abuse* or *child molesting* (Finkelhor and Araji, 1986). In the past, pedophilia was defined as either (1) any sexual contact with or interest in a child, no matter how fleeting, or (2) a condition in which an adult has an enduring, often exclusive, sexual interest in children. We prefer the latter definition, as does the American Psychiatric Association (1986).

In almost all reports of pedophilia, men are the offenders (Finkelhor, 1984). What are the characteristics of pedophilia? Mohr, Turner, and Terry's classic study (1964) found heterosexual and homosexual pedophiles to have different characteristics. In heterosexual pedophilia, victims were young (6 to 12 years of age), the sexual acts usually involved touching the genitals of the child and exhibiting one's own genitals, only 6% of the men sought ejaculation, the offenses occurred primarily in the home of the adult or the child, and there was often a close relationship (including being a relative) between the pedophile and the victim. In fact, in one study 40% of the molesters of girls were their biological fathers and 15% were their nonbiological fathers (Crewsdon, 1988). However, most studies find that stepfathers are more likely than biological fathers to be serious abusers (Russell, 1982). In homosexual pedophilia the victims were of all ages; the sexual acts involved fellatio, masturbation, and anal intercourse; orgasm was sought by 50% of the men; the offenses occurred away from the home of the adult or child; and rarely were the children relatives of the adult.

A review of the behavior patterns of individuals who commit child sexual abuse showed that 70% of the victims were female and that anal contact and oral genital activities were significantly more frequent with male than female victims (Erickson, Walbek, and Seely, 1988). In a study of children taken to emergency rooms shortly after a report of abuse, vaginal contact was reported by 46% of the female victims and 17% also reported oral or anal contact, whereas 57% of the males reported anal contact (Rimza and Niggeman, 1982). Eighty-six percent of offenders against males described themselves as homosexual or bisexual. Younger children appear to serve largely as impersonal masturbatory aids for the perpetrator (i.e., fondling the victim), whereas older children are treated more like sexual partners, although unwilling ones (i.e., vaginal and anal contact and oral sex) (Erickson, Walbek, and Seely, 1988).

Groth and Birnbaum (1978) examined some of the psychosocial characteristics of child molesters in terms of the relationship between the offender's choice of victim in regard to sex and his adult sexual orientation. Their sample consisted of 175 men convicted of sexual assault against children. The adult sexual orientation and the sex of their victims were known. The sample was evenly divided into two groups: those fixated (attached or attracted) exlusively on children, and those who had regressed from peer relationships to relationships with children. All regressed offenders, whether their victims were male or female children, were heterosexual in their adult orientation. Peer-oriented homosexual men never showed any instances of regression. Groth and Birnbaum concluded that "the possibility emerges that homosexuality and homosexual pedophilia may be mutually exclusive and that the adult heterosexual male constitutes a greater risk to the underage child than does the adult homosexual male." The fears of many individuals that the homosexual poses a threat to the physical and sexual safety of underage children appear to be groundless on the basis of these findings.

Child sexual abuse may have serious immediate and long-term consequences for the victim (Rush, 1980; Becker, Skinner, and Abel, 1986). The way in which parents and other authorities deal with the situation largely determines how the child will respond. Parents and authorities should remain calm in the presence of the child so as not to upset him or her any more than necessary.

The following is the case history of a regressed sexual offender:

> The subject is a married man in his 30s. His wife was the first adult woman with whom he had sexual relations, and from the beginning to the present, these

have been joyless, with little erotic pleasure, and marred by his difficulty in getting an erection and by premature ejaculation. His wife's body never appealed to him because it is an adult female's; he avoids seeing her because to do so provokes feelings ranging from uneasiness to disgust. An extramarital experiment with another adult woman produced the same effects.

Several times a year, he has found himself suddenly, unexpectedly, intensely excited and preoccupied with wanting a prepubertal girl to fondle. He has never experienced such excitement with, or thinking about, an adult woman. When he can get close to such a little girl, he seeks only to massage her body and fondle her genitals; he has never attempted penetration. On a few occasions, he has had a cooperative child touch his penis but, because of fear, has never permitted this to advance to ejaculation. When he leaves the child, he masturbates.

When trapped into needing an erection with his wife, he fantasies fondling a little girl.

Stoller, 1977, pp. 201-202

Transvestism

transvestism
(trans VES tizm) Sexual gratification from dressing in opposite-sex clothes.

Transvestism or *fetishistic cross-dressing* is a condition in which a man becomes sexually excited by wearing women's garments (Stoller, 1977). This variation is found predominantly in men and rarely in women. Transvestism is characterized by a wish to dress in the clothes of the opposite sex. It has no particular association with homosexual behavior or with a wish to belong to the opposite gender (Gosselin and Wilson, 1980).

The topic of transsexualism is discussed in Chapter 10.

A condition often confused with transvestism is transsexualism. Transsexualism involves a person, male or female, who feels he or she is trapped in the body of the wrong gender and wants to be a member of the opposite gender. It is important to differentiate between transvestism and transsexualism; the terms are sometimes inappropriately used synonymously.

There are two types of transvestism; either only one article of women's clothing is used, such as panties or shoes, or the man dresses completely in opposite-sex clothing. The sexual orientation of the great majority of transvestites is heterosexual (Haslam, 1979; Whitam, 1987).

Prince and Butler (1972) surveyed 500 readers of a magazine for transvestites. The following personal characteristics emerged from the survey: 64% were married, 89% considered themselves heterosexual, and only 1% considered themselves homosexual. Twelve percent believed they were women "trapped" in the body of a man, which would make these individuals transsexuals.

Prince and Butler (1972) found that 69% of their sample considered themselves men with a feminine side seeking expression. Seventy-eight percent of the men felt that they had a different personality when they were dressed in women's clothes. Five percent of the men were taking female hormones, and 50% wanted to. Of the transvestites who responded to the survey, 14% wanted to undergo a sex change operation; these individuals might also be considered transsexual.

Prince and Butler's survey also indicated that 83% of the men believed they had been raised as boys and that their fathers provided a good masculine image in the home. Only 4% were treated as girls, because the mother wanted a girl; 4% were made to wear dresses as punishment. According to the men who

A male transvestite.

responded, 80% of their wives knew of their transvestite behavior, but the wives' acceptance of the behavior varied widely. A number of the men liked to wear women's clothing, most commonly a nightgown, during sexual intercourse. An estimated 18% of the men had appeared cross-dressed in public.

In an interview study of 70 male members of cross-dressing clubs, multiple comparisons between men who had and those who had not received therapy showed that the two groups were similar (Croughan et al., 1981). A man was placed in the treated group if he had on one or more occasions been seen by a physician, counselor, or other mental health professional because of problems related to cross-dressing. Major differences between the groups were that the men who had sought therapy fantasized that they were women while masturbating, engaged in sexual intercourse while dressed as a woman, currently preferred both heterosexual and homosexual encounters while dressed as a woman, and experienced more negative consequences from cross-dressing.

Croughan and associates (1981) and Gosselin and Wilson (1980) describe the typical transvestite as a heterosexual married man with children. He dresses privately at home and tends to be fairly passive and secretive about his behavior.

The following case history of a transvestite is typical:

This biologically normal man in his 20s is married, with children. He is a construction foreman.

Until he was three years old he lived with his mother and father, but his mother died, and then responsibility for his care fell upon his stepmother. When he was four years old, she dressed him in girl's clothes to punish him for getting dirty. He had not cross-dressed spontaneously. She did this several times subsequently, and within two years he had arranged with a neighbor girl to dress him up regularly during their after-school play. The dressing-up died away for several years, but at age 12, he did it once again, almost casually. On starting to put his stepmother's panties on, he suddenly became intensely sexually excited and masturbated for the first time. For several years thereafter, he would only put on his stepmother's underwear and either masturbate or spontaneously ejaculate. Then, in mid-teens, he began taking underwear from the homes of friends' sisters, and in a year or so increased this activity to stealing women's underwear wherever he could find it. Aside from the moments when he put on these garments, he was unremarkably masculine in appearance, in athletic interests, and in daydreams of what he would wish to be in the future. He was attracted to girls and went out on dates, but, being shy, he had less sexual experience than some of his friends.

He proposed to the first girl with whom he had a serious affair, confessed his fetishistic cross-dressing to her, and was surprised and relieved when she not only was not upset but assisted him by offering her underwear and by purchasing new pairs for him as he wished. Starting within a year after marriage, he found it more exciting to put on more of his wife's clothes than just her underwear, and now he prefers dressing completely in her clothes and having her assist him in putting on makeup and fixing his wig.

He feels completely male and is accepted by all who know him as a masculine man. He does not desire sex transformation. He has never had homosexual relations and is sexually attracted only by women's bodies.

Stoller, 1977, p. 210

What about the spouses or sexual partners of transvestites? How do they react to their male partner dressing in female clothing? Few studies have been done on this topic, but one study using a sample of seven female partners of male transvestites found that the women seemed to view the "secret" (cross-dressing) shared with the partner as a bonding factor in their relationship and that it served as a deterrent to infidelity (Brown and Collier, 1989). The group of women could be divided into two groups: one group, called acceptors, indicated that they helped their mates buy women's clothing and makeup, while the other group, termed rejectors, looked on their mates' cross-dressing with disdain and criticized them for dressing up as women. The couples had been married or had been cohabitating for an average of 9.9 years, and the age range of the women was 25 to 39 years.

Fetishistic cross-dressing is rare in women but has been reported (Stoller, 1982). Three cases were described in which the outstanding common feature was a "powerful masculinity present since childhood" (Stoller, 1982). Why these women use men's garments for erotic excitement is not known. Two of the three women willingly indulged in sexual intercourse, and all three had homosexual desires. The following quotation is from a thrice-divorced American woman in her forties:

I've experienced special feelings while dressed in Levis since I was very young— possibly prior to attending school. I do remember feeling definitely sexually excited around eleven years old, and being fully aware my Levis were a contributing factor. The neat part is that those same feelings are still available to me now, many years later. It was during this time that I also discovered that wearing boots intensified those feelings.

When I put on a pair of blue denim Levis—and not any other male clothing has this effect—I feel much more than just masculine. The excitement begins immediately—as I begin to pull them over my feet and up, toward my thighs. There is no sensation comparable, and that is probably because the peak of this sensation involves a large range of feelings, including impossible-to-repress sexual excitement.

Stoller, 1982, p. 105

SEXUAL VARIATIONS INVOLVING UNUSUAL MODES

The sexual variations in this section include those that diverge or depart from the society's or culture's traditional mode or manner of obtaining sexual satisfaction (Lester, 1975). Variations recognized by the American Psychiatric Association (1986) and discussed here are exhibitionism, obscene telephone calling, voyeurism, sadism, and masochism.

Exhibitionism

Exhibitionism is the exposure of the genitals to unsuspecting persons. This variation is almost exclusively performed by men. The exhibitionist may expose himself in a public or private place such as a park or street or from the window of his dwelling, but most expose themselves while sitting in a car, to a person outside the car. Some exhibitionists have an erection during the exposure. Masturbation may precede, accompany, or follow the act of exposure or may not occur at all (Lester, 1975; Langevin and Lang, 1987).

Most exposures are to unknown women, although exposure to girls also has been reported. The man does not desire sexual relations with the victim but seeks to elicit a response such as anger, fear, or surprise. Exhibitionism is one of the most common sexual variations, and acts of genital exposure account for approximately 33% of all sex offense convictions in the United States (Langevin and Lang, 1987).

The following report of exhibitionism is typical:

> This married man in his 40s has always been shy with women, and after 15 years of marriage still is passive around his wife. During their infrequent intercourse (every 6 weeks to 2 months) he has difficulty getting or maintaining an erection. While his wife constantly bullies him, he does not complain, believing that she is right to do so. In the last five years, he has succumbed to the urge to exhibit his penis to passing girls or women. This occurs on the street, in the daytime, under circumstances when he realistically runs great risk of arrest. In fact, he does this in the neighborhood where he lives, not even going to strange areas or cities.
>
> He will stand to the side of a street and show his exposed penis to women passing in cars or to women walking on the other side of the street. He has an erection at these times. If he believes he was not noticed, he will shift his position or otherwise attempt to get their attention, and when he has done so, he will not flee when he senses they are upset and might call for help.
>
> On one occasion, he exposed himself to two teenage girls, who began chuckling and advanced toward him as if interested; this is the only time he has precipitously left the scene.
>
> He has been arrested six times and has already spent time in prison. His reputation is in terrible disrepair. Nonetheless, he says he will probably repeat the act.
>
> Stoller, 1977, p. 203

Obscene Telephone Calling

Those who are involved with **obscene telephone calling** receive sexual excitement or gratification from speaking obscenely to strangers. These individuals appear to be most like exhibitionists, but they do not physically confront their victims. Obscene telephone callers are almost always men. They usually

exhibitionism
Sexual arousal from exposing the genitals to unsuspecting strangers.

obscene telephone calling
Sexual excitation from use of obscene language while speaking to a stranger on the telephone.

call total strangers and often simply pick at random a telephone number from the phone book. If a woman answers, they begin obscene talk about their masturbatory activities, their sexual anatomy, and such. Some men masturbate while calling.

Crooks and Baur (1990) propose some ways to discourage an obscene telephone caller: When you realize that you have an obscene telephone caller on the line, gently set the receiver down on the phone. Do not slam the telephone receiver down because this could cue the caller that he has upset you, which is one of the desired reactions. If the phone rings right after you hang up, ignore it. Another tactic is to pretend that you have a hearing impairment. Keep saying, "Can you speak up? I can't hear you, I have a hearing problem." Still another approach is to tell the caller to hold on while you go to another phone extension. Then just put the phone down and go about doing something else. If the caller persists, notify the phone company or the police or both.

Telephone Sex

A new and profitable form of sex for pay has appeared in recent years. This is telephone sex, also called phone sex and telephone porn. The concept is simple. The customer dials a telephone number that may have an 800, 900, or area code prefix. In some cases the customer talks with a live person on the other end of the telephone line. The caller may discuss his or her fantasies with a woman on the other end of the line, or she may ask what types of fantasies the customer would like to hear. In some cases the caller can listen to other customers as they tell their fantasies. Other telephone sex companies offer a recorded erotic message or fantasy. In this type of call, which is usually less expensive, the caller does not interact with a live person. Most telephone sex services are open 24 hours per day, 7 days per week. The prices for the different companies vary, but a typical 10- to 12-minute call costs $20 to $24. Some phone sex companies specialize in bondage and discipline fantasies or cater to cross-dressers (transvestites).

Most of the advertisements for phone sex assure the caller that he or she will be billed discreetly on a credit card account. Many of the companies have names with three initials or use the word *communications* in the company name. Many of the advertisements indicate that you must be 18 or over to place a call. The use of an 800 number or direct dial to an area code requires a credit card, but charges for 900 numbers appear directly on your phone bill. In the case of 900 number billing, both the phone company (usually a long distance company) and the phone sex company make a profit. We can say that telephone sex is a form of prostitution in which the caller pays to hear sexually explicit material.

Few obscene phone callers ever follow up with a personal appearance. To discourage obscene phone calls, women should not list their first names in the phone book, but use initials (Boston Women's Health Book Collective, 1984). Very rarely does a woman make obscene phone calls. As with most sexual variations, men are the initiators of this behavior.

Voyeurism

In **voyeurism,** sexual excitement occurs when a person secretly observes a member of the opposite sex in some stage of undress or in the sexual act (Lester, 1975). Voyeurism almost always involves men, commonly known as "peeping Toms," observing women. The woman is unaware that she is being watched and in almost all cases is a stranger to the man. Many voyeurs coincidentally masturbate, and the pleasure of looking replaces the act of intercourse for the voyeur (Langevin and Lang, 1987).

voyeurism
(vwa YER izm) Sexual gratification from secretly watching people undress or engage in sexual activities.

The following description of voyeurism is typical:

This single man, in his early 20s, drives to a different residential neighborhood each night and surveys homes to find rooms where he can observe women undressing, while he is safely hidden in the bushes outside the window. When he finds a room in which a young woman is undressing, he becomes excited and masturbates. Although he can exhaust himself sexually after a couple of such experiences a night, he never satisfies his desire to peep, which is an insatiable hunger.

He also goes out on dates and occasionally has intercourse without problems of potency. He enjoys this intercourse but less than masturbating while peeping. He is not especially aroused watching a girlfriend undress. No matter how closely her

Voyeurism.

nude body conforms to his ideal, looking at her under these permissive circumstances is fairly casual. He says, however, that if he were to watch her undressing when she did not know he was looking, her nudity would then arouse him as much as does any unknown woman's.

Stoller, 1977, pp. 202-203

Sadism

sadism
(SAY diz' uhm) Sexual arousal from inflicting pain or humiliation on others.

Sadism may be defined as sexual arousal and gratification from inflicting pain, indignity, humiliation, punishment, or torture on others. Stoller (1977) extends the definition to include animals as the objects of pain. Sadism is named for the Marquis de Sade, a French nobleman who wrote a great deal about sexual themes involving the infliction of pain and punishment. A person who receives sexual arousal and gratification from the infliction of pain is called a masochist.

Approximately 15 to 75 million American adults, depending on the study,

---

A Night at the Chateau

The following is a description of a session at a bondage and discipline (B&D) house called the Chateau. The Chateau caters to men who receive sexual gratification by receiving and giving B&D.

The Chateau resembles a social club with a waiting room like that in a doctor's office. On a typical evening, nine or ten men sit in the waiting room, silently flipping through magazines . . . gazing down at the floor, or glancing anxiously around the room. In the adjoining room women are fixing punch and dip for a party, scheduled to start at 6:30 p.m. . . . One such evening, Lorelei, a short woman with a pert elfin look, appears and asks: "Would anyone like to hit me?" She has a thin riding crop in her hand and looks around the room for takers. A few men glance about. . . . Tentatively, one man puts his maga-

zine aside, takes the whip, and whacks her lightly. . . .

A dozen or so customers follow Shara into a large unfurnished room, and they spread out in front of a large platform at one end. Then, Sir James begins the show. . . . "We've just discovered some jewelry is missing," he announces. "And I've learned that one of my slaves has taken it. But no one will talk. Well, we'll just have to make them." He calls five of the women working at the Chateau to come forward and they line up in front of him. He asks, "Who did it?" But no one will confess. He will have Shara whip them until they do. He begins with Gen, and with mock roughness pulls her from the line and pushes her toward the two cuffs dangling from the ceiling. "No, no," she protests dramatically, as he tugs off her dress reveal-

ing her frilly black underwear, and snaps her in. Shara approaches her with the whip and strikes her across the buttocks. . . .

The audience . . . watches raptly. Gen whispers to Sir James. . . and he announces . . . Shara as the thief. . . . The case is solved, it is time to party or attend sessions. Most of the men remain . . . a few disappear into one of three rooms for sessions. Victor, a Chateau regular, goes to have a session with Vickie . . . She asks him to lie across the stool and strikes him on the buttocks with the paddle . . . "Act like my school mistress," he asks—for this is his favorite fantasy. Immediately she slides into the role. "So you have been bad again. Well take this. And this. You've been a bad, bad boy. . . . "If you want to conclude the session now by masturbating to climax, go ahead" (Vickie speaking to Victor). . . . Victor masturbates to orgasm, and then thanks Vickie for an enjoyable session, saying he will see her again.

From *Erotic Power* by Jini Graham Scott. Copyright © 1983, Carol Publishing Group.

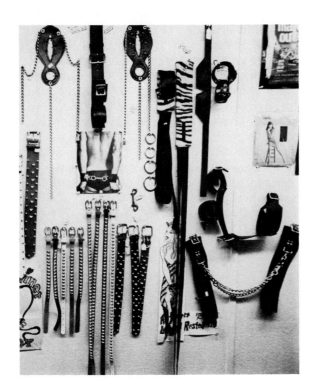

Sadomasochistic parapher-
nalia.

participate in heterosexual erotic activity that includes some form of female
dominance (Scott, 1983). In this activity the woman is dominant and the man
submissive during sexual activities. Dominance is sometimes referred to as a
form of sadism and masochism or of bondage and discipline (Scott, 1983). The
man can also be the dominant one in the erotic activities. Thus bondage and
discipline refer to a wide variety of sexual and erotic activities that involve a
consensual power exchange between willing partners.

Sadistic behaviors vary tremendously. The couple who mutually decide to
experiment with sadism may develop a ritual. For example, one partner may
blindfold and bind the hands and feet of the other, then spank with hands or
a paddle, alternately gently touching and caressing the bound partner. Other
couples may pinch, bite, or scratch each other during sexual activities. Hunt
(1974) found that more men than women enjoy inflicting pain, and more women
than men enjoy receiving pain. He also found that 5% of the men and 2% of
the women in his sample had at one time or another received sexual pleasure
from inflicting pain on a sexual partner. In a more recent report based on a
sample of 975 heterosexual men and women it was found that 25% of the
sample engaged in some form of bondage during their sexual activities (Rubin,
1990).

In the following case report, sadism has become the preferred, habitual,
and compelling method of achieving sexual gratification, and the man cannot
achieve sexual gratification in any other manner:

> This married man in his 20s requested psychiatric help because he feared he
> would soon commit murder. Since adolescence, he has been excited by fantasies
> and pornography depicting women bound and tortured. During courtship of his

wife, he introduced mild versions of his fantasy into their sex play, and in this manner only was able to proceed on to intercourse. Now, after 8 years of marriage, they invariably have intercourse by his first binding her tightly with ropes and then, with her still bound, having intercourse. She has noticed that gradually the binding has been less and less symbolic and more and more painful. On two occasions in the last year, binding around her neck choked her into unconsciousness.

It is the nature of his work to enter households of strangers to do repairs. He frequently meets housewives there, and the temptation to bind and torture them is becoming unbearable. So far, he has avoided doing so by going out to his repair truck and masturbating while looking at photographs of bound and tortured women. His fear of killing a strange woman stems not from a belief that such an act would be sexually exciting but rather that, having bound and tortured her, he would have to kill her to remove the witness.

Stoller, 1977, pp. 204-205

Masochism

masochism
(MAS uh kiz uhm) Sexual arousal from being physically or psychologically dominated by another.

Masochism, often called the mirror image of sadism, is named after Leopold von Sacher-Masoch, a nineteenth-century Austrian novelist whose writings portrayed men humiliated and tormented by beautiful women (Baumeister, 1989). While sadism involves sexual excitement from causing pain, masochism is sexual gratification from the receiving of pain. Masochism has been explained as follows:

The victim may prefer being whipped, cut, pricked, bound or spanked; but they do not seek or respond sexually to just any sort of physical pain. The areas of the body assaulted, the intensity and duration of the sadistic attack, and the person who is to inflict it are all circumscribed. The ritual must be carried out precisely or the pain will not develop its sexual character.

Stoller, 1977

Henry Havelock Ellis (1906), who lived during the time of Freud, conducted some classic studies of sadomasochism. The following excerpt is from a correspondence written to him by a woman patient. Notice the similarity to the ideas stated by Stoller.

Actual pain gives me no pleasure, yet the idea of pain does, if inflicted by way of discipline and for the ultimate good of the person suffering it. . . . I can only get pleasure in the idea of a woman submitting herself to pain and harshness from the man she loves when the following conditions are fulfilled: (1) She must be absolutely sure of the man's love. (2) She must have perfect confidence in his judgment. (3) The pain must be deliberately inflicted, not accidental. (4) It must be inflicted in kindness and for her own improvement, not in anger or with any revengeful feelings, as that would spoil one's ideal of the man. (5) The pain must not be excessive and must be what when we were children we used to call a "tidy" pain; i.e., there must be no mutilation, cutting, etc. (6) Last, one would have to feel very sure of one's own influence over the man.

Greene and Greene, 1974, p. 25

The case history that follows involves the wife of the man described earlier who enjoyed sadism:

The wife of the man described above [under "Sadism"] found, during her courtship, that their first intercourse, under cramped conditions in a car, where her husband fixed her arms and legs so that they could not move, was at first uncomfortable but soon aroused in her a feeling of "interest." In time, this progressed to mild excitement, and now, several years later, she is appalled to find herself greatly excited by being bound. She is frightened by her excitement, and she is frightened by her experiences of unconsciousness while being bound. She believes that her husband is dangerous, and at the same time she feels deeply that he loves her.

Stoller, 1977, p. 205

Other Paraphilias

Not all sexual variations fit into the two categories of unusual sex objects or unusual modes. In this section are briefly described some lesser known paraphilias and "extremes" of sexual behavior.

Frottage (from the French, rubbing) is a sexual variation in which the pressing or rubbing against someone in a crowd produces sexual excitation. Usually a man rubs his genitals against the body of a fully clothed woman in a crowded place such as a subway, bus, or elevator. He may masturbate later and use the memory of the frottage experience in his sexual fantasy.

In *klismaphilia* sexual excitation is produced from receiving of an enema.

In *troilism* the sharing of a sexual partner with a third person generates sexual excitement. The troilist is able to become sexually aroused only by watching his sexual partner and a third person engage in sexual acts.

Having sex with more than one partner is a common sexual fantasy, as mentioned in Chapter 8.

In *coprophilia* sexual excitement is generated by viewing a sexual partner defecating or by the sight and smell of feces.

In *urophilia* sexual excitement is generated by viewing a sexual partner urinating or by the sight and smell of urine.

In *coprolalia* sexual excitement occurs from using or hearing lewd or "dirty" language. Some couples use lewd language to enhance lovemaking, but this is different from coprolalia.

In *asphyxiophilia* a state of oxygen deficiency is sought to enhance sexual excitement and orgasm (Innala and Ernulf, 1989). This is a dangerous form of sexual gratification that often leads to the death of individuals engaged in the behavior. Practitioners of asphyxiophilia use ropes, chains, leather belts, or other items to apply pressure to the neck. The item is tightened around the neck to produce the desired effect and then released at the time of orgasm. Orgasm is brought on by masturbation. Asphyxiophilia is mainly a male sexual variation.

In *hypersexuality,* which has received little scientific study, sexual activities interfere with other aspects of life because (1) a great deal of time is spent searching for a partner and having sexual intercourse, (2) sex is impersonal, with no emotional attachment, and (3) despite frequent orgasms, sexual activities are usually not satisfying. (The latter two points are not unique to "hypersexual" individuals.) The terms *compulsive sexual behavior* (Weissberg and Levoy, 1986) and *hyperphilia* (Money, 1981) have been proposed for this condition.

Nymphomania is excessive sexual desire in a woman *(nymphomaniac).* In most cases nymphomania is subjective and is of little value in the study of sexual behavior. Who is to say what is excessive sexual behavior for a woman? *Satyriasis* (from the Greek for satyr, a mythical half-human, half-animal creature that spent much time at sex orgies) is excessive sexual desire in a man. Like nymphomania, the term is used subjectively, with no quantitative data to determine when it should be applied to a particular individual. Hypersexuality may be a more appropriate term and carries fewer negative connotations than either nymphomania or satyriasis. The noted sexologist John Money states, "Not very much is known in a systematic way concerning the hyperphilias and there is not even a satisfactory catalogue of them, perhaps because they are seldom experienced as a form of suffering. . . . The terminology is adequate—nymphomania in the female and satyriasis . . . in the male" (Money, 1981).

Compulsive Sexual Behavior and Sexual Addiction: Myth or Reality?

Compulsive or hypersexual behavior involves the use of compelling sexual activity for nonsexual purposes, and sexual pleasure is reduced or totally absent (Weissberg and Levoy, 1986). According to popular ideas, compulsive sex implies a man or woman being driven by sexual desire to engage in numerous sexual encounters. This is not the case according to some researchers who propose that the main motivation is distress and discomfort, not high interest in sex. As Weissberg and Levoy point out:

Compulsive behavior . . . is considered defensive—that is, it is designed primarily to avert anxiety . . . and when such a behavior is blocked the individual becomes uncomfortable. Compulsive sexual behavior is aimed primarily at avoiding unpleasant effects (feelings or emotions). Any pleasure experienced is of secondary importance.

Weisberg and Levoy, 1986, p. 129

Levine and Troiden take issue with the idea that sexual activity functions to reduce anxiety in "sexual compulsive individuals" (1988). First of all, Levine and Troiden do not believe in the concept of sexual compulsivity. According to these authors the term *sexual compulsive* is simply a value-laden definition of a person who does not fit the norm in terms of (1) frequency of sex, (2) establishment of relationships with sexual partners, or (3) appropriateness of the setting for sex. Also, a study of individuals considered "sexual compulsives" indicated that these men and women did not experience significantly higher levels of frustration or anxiety before having sex than did the matched controls with whom they were compared (Levine and Troiden, 1988).

The ideas of sexual addiction and sexual compulsion have been challenged (Levine and Troiden, 1988; Klein, 1991). The severest critics state that the criteria for these conditions are subjective and value laden. For example, in a controversial book written by Carnes (1983) dealing with the topic of sexual addiction, the signs of sexual addiction are "secrecy, abusiveness, painfulness and emptiness" (p. 158). In addition, according to Carnes, the events that trigger and fuel the addictive process are preoccupation, ritualization, compulsive sexual behavior, and despair. Levine and Troiden argue that these terms are subjective and could easily describe the intense passion of courtship or the sexual routines of "conventional couples."

Levine and Troiden (1988) conclude that the invention of sexual addiction and sexual compulsion as "diseases" threatens the civil liberties of individuals practicing unconventional erotic activities. Klein (1991) takes the argument further and states that the political implications of the concept of sexual addiction could be used to eliminate sex education programs and birth control clinics and also be used to censor certain books and magazines. The antisex forces could argue that "smut" causes sexual addiction and all erotic materials should be banned (Klein, 1991). As this chapter illustrates, deciding what constitutes normal sexual behavior is sometimes difficult. In the same manner, deciding where a healthy behavior ends and an addiction begins can also be a very difficult undertaking (Francoeur, 1991).

CAUSES OF SEXUAL VARIATION

Much is yet to be learned about the causes and treatment of the various sexual variations. Many theories make little or no distinction among the variations. According to learning theory, the individual first has a more or less accidental experience with the variation, which he finds sexually exciting. After this the individual fantasizes about the variation during masturbation, and before long this stimulus becomes more and more sexually exciting because of its association with the sexual pleasure in masturbation. Unpleasant heterosexual experiences or feelings of inadequacy may also contribute to the individual's habitual use of the variation to achieve sexual gratification. Two examples of learning theory and sexual variations follow.

In the first example, a young man has an unpleasant and uncomfortable series of dates with young women. He dreads interacting with them. One night he notices a woman undressing in her room. He watches and finds the situation highly sexually exciting. He returns home and masturbates while fantasizing about the woman he saw undressing. On other occasions he looks in her window as she undresses and sometimes masturbates while watching her. This young man soon begins to depend on "peeping" for his sexual gratification, not on interaction with young women. He has "learned" that voyeurism is sexually gratifying for him. He may date again in the future, but for the time being his preferred method of sexual gratification is voyeurism.

The second example of learning theory and the acquisition of a sexual variation involves Alex, a pediatrician, who had his first experience at cross-dressing at the age of 11. Scott describes the rest of the situation as follows:

> [Alex's] mother and sister thought it would be cute if he went to a church costume party as a girl. He found it exciting, and to recapture the experience occasionally continued to cross-dress in his mother's clothes, until she discovered him a few times. So he tried to put his interest aside, but in his teens the feelings returned, and he began to acquire magazines on cross-dressing, fantasize about being dressed up and take photographs of himself dressed. Still he felt guilty about these desires, he began to fantasize that a woman forced him to dress by tying him up and making him follow her orders. To symbolize her power, he tied himself up and soon found the bondage as exciting as the cross-dress. In a short time he was doing both.
>
> Scott, 1983, p. 17

In another theory, the psychoanalytical approach, sexual variations are determined by neurotic or psychopathic motivations. "Sexuality is seen as one area of functioning along with and as equally important as other areas. The focus is thus upon the neurotic individual rather than the neurotic sexual activity" (Lester, 1975). According to this theory a person who exhibits a preferred habitual sexual variation will also exhibit disturbances in other aspects of personality, areas of living, and relations with others. The total person is affected by neurotic motivations that affect his or her entire life, not just sexual outlets.

Still another theory involves sexual deprivation. According to this theory people turn to variant sexual acts when deprived of genital contact with other humans. Contacts with animals are an example. Stoller (1977) presents a clear summary of how some sexual variations may develop.

Sexual deviations in humans often result from the frustration of development of heterosexual interests in children by forces in the family, usually applied by parents who subtly or grossly let the growing child know that aspects of its budding sexuality are bad. If he is a boy, masculinity (as his society sees it), especially its attributes of aggressiveness and of associated pleasure in possessing females, is treated as morally bad or physically and psychologically dangerous. The reverse is done to girls and their developing femininity. The child victimized in this manner must develop compromises to preserve his or her sense of identity and capacity for sexual gratification, and at the same time comply with these parental demands. These compromises may involve new, habitual styles of behaving, and daydreams that will undo the painful, inhibiting pressures within that family. According to this theory, the specific deviation chosen is the result of the specific traumatic attitudes inflicted by the family on the developing child. The test of the theory comes only when one examines in fine detail each family member's exact modes of reacting and communicating to which the child is exposed.

Stoller, 1977, p. 193

TREATMENT OF SEXUAL VARIATIONS

How are sexual variations treated? Some variations such as pedophilia, exhibitionism, and voyeurism are violations of the law and are punishable by jail sentences. However, individuals who commit these crimes usually repeat them after they are released from prison. Thus imprisonment by itself is not the answer.

Some people who exhibit sexual variations respond well to behavior modification techniques. These techniques involve the use of conditioning and learning. In a study involving 12 persistent exhibitionists, aversion therapy decreased the probability of exposure of the genitals to others (Rooth and Marks, 1974). In the first phase of the treatment the men, aged 18 to 53 years, received mild electric shocks to the forearm when they reported thoughts of exposing themselves; in the second phase the men gave themselves shocks when they had fantasies of exposing themselves. Positive conditioning of desired behavior can also be used (Smith, 1976). For example, a voyeur was told to masturbate while looking at his favorite pornographic picture every time he had the urge to peep. The next phase involved concentrating on the centerfold of *Playboy* at the time of orgasm while masturbating. The treatment was discontinued after eight sessions, and at follow-up 9 months later the patient was free of the urge to peep. It was concluded that "by associating . . . orgasm with sexual stimuli of decreasing similarity and arousal-potential from [the voyeur's] voyeuristic fantasy, a positive attraction was created to more acceptable [sexual] objects" (Hawton, 1985).

Other behavior modification techniques involve imaginal desensitization and covert sensitization. In imaginal desensitization the patient is instructed to imagine that he does not carry out his urge to engage in the sexual variation that is causing him problems. For example, he is instructed to imagine a young woman approaching him on the street. As she gets closer he is allowed to imagine that he wants to expose himself. He is then instructed that the urge is under his control, and he is told that he walks past the woman without exposing himself. This technique is used in conjunction with muscle relaxation exercises (McConaghy et al., 1989). In covert sensitization the patient is instructed to imagine the variation for which he is being treated and to describe several aversive situations such as being verbally abused, becoming physically ill and vomiting, and being arrested for his sexual variation. The patient is then instructed to imagine that after engaging in his variation he is subjected to one of the aversive situations that he has described. Muscle relaxation is also employed with this technique (McConaghy et al., 1989).

Other therapies for sexual variations include individual psychoanalytical treatment, group therapy, hypnosis, and drug or surgical intervention.

In psychotherapy a therapist works with the person who exhibits a sexual variation. The therapist may be of the Freudian school of thought, which assumes that the variant behavior is caused by the thwarting of sex drives. Other therapists believe that variant sexual behaviors are influenced by the social, psychological, and cultural background of the offender. Successful psychotherapy depends on a competent psychotherapist and a motivated client.

Freud's psychoanalytical theories pertaining to sex are stated in Chapter 2.

Drug or surgical intervention is used to treat certain types of paraphilias. For example, the antiandrogen drug medroxyprogesterone acetate (MPA) has been used to treat certain male sex offenders, including pedophiliac sex offenders and rapists. This drug antagonizes the actions of androgens (male hormones) from the testes and has been shown to be of limited value in controlling offending sexual behavior and reducing sexual drive (Wincze, Bansal, and Malamud, 1986). The surgical procedure of castration (removal of the testes) is also used in some countries to reduce androgen levels in sex offenders, but this procedure is not always successful. Whatever the form of treatment, it should emphasize controlling impulses that lead to the unacceptable behavior and satisfying those impulses through socially acceptable means (Smith, 1976).

A discussion of castration and sex drive is presented in Chapter 4.

Adolescent sex offenders have not been studied as much as adult offenders. A study of resistance to treatment found that adolescent sexual offenders may be more resistant to treatment than adults because their sexual urges are under more direct hormonal control, whereas the sexual urges of adults are in part controlled by past experiences (McConaghy et al., 1989). McConaghy and associates studied 6 adolescent and 39 adult sex offenders and their responses to a variety of treatments, including the use of an antiandrogen. After treatment 3 of the 6 adolescents were arrested and charged with further sexual offenses, as compared with 3 of the 39 adult offenders. The adults in this study were most likely to be exhibitionists, while the adolescents included two homosexual pedophiles, one heterosexual pedophile, one exhibitionist, and two fetishists who stole women's clothing.

SUMMARY

1 Classifying a particular sexual behavior as a sexual variation is not always easy. Two common ways to classify behaviors that differ from the norm are the statistical approach and the moral approach. The statistical approach assumes that sexual variations are sex acts not practiced by large numbers of people in a particular society. The moral approach calls on religious or moral values to decide whether a behavior is normal or a variation.

2 Sexual variations may be divided into two categories: (1) sexual acts that involve preferences for particular sexual objects, such as articles of clothing, animals, corpses, or children, that deviate from socially acceptable ways of

seeking sexual gratification; and (2) sexual acts that involve a departure from traditional modes of obtaining sexual gratification, such as peeping into a woman's bedroom as she undresses, exhibiting one's genitals to unsuspecting women, and inflicting pain on others.

3 Specific examples of sexual variations include fetishism (sexual arousal by an inanimate object or a body part other than the genitals or breasts), zoophilia (bestiality; sexual acts with animals), necrophilia (sex with corpses), pedophilia (sexual acts with children by an adult), transvestism (cross-dressing), exhibitionism (displaying the sex organs to unsuspecting strangers), obscene telephone calling, voyeurism (secretly watching people undress or have sex), sadism (sexual pleasure from inflicting pain), and masochism (sexual pleasure from receiving pain).

4 The causes of sexual variations are obscure, but several theories have been proposed. Learning theory suggests that variations occur as a result of conditioning; in the psychoanalytical approach it is generally theorized that variations are determined by neurotic motivations; and according to the sexual deprivation theory, people turn to variant sexual acts when deprived of genital contact with other humans.

5 Sexual variations are treated in different ways. Illegal variations such as pedophilia, exhibitionism, and voyeurism are punishable by jail sentences. Those who commit these crimes usually repeat them after they are released from prison. Behavior modification techniques have been used with good results to treat exhibitionism and voyeurism. Other treatments include psychoanalysis, group therapy, and hypnosis.

FACT
OR
FICTION

ANSWERS

1 It is difficult to identify and define all variations of sexual behavior. Some behaviors such as necrophilia are clearly at variance with the norm; others such as bondage by mutual consent of both partners are more difficult to catalog.

2 An exhibitionist is compelled to expose himself to unsuspecting persons to obtain sexual gratification.

3 Most sexual variations are engaged in by men.

4 One of the most dangerous of all sexual variations is asphyxiophilia. In this variation oxygen deprivation is used to heighten orgasm and in many cases strangulation occurs.

QUESTIONS FOR THOUGHT ?

1 Write out your own definition for a sexual variation, and use various sexual variations from this chapter to see whether your definition will encompass them.

2 Compare the terms *transitory sexual variations* and *established sexual variations* and give an example of each type.

3 Contrast the characteristics and behaviors of heterosexual and homosexual pedophiles.

4 Discuss possible reasons that most paraphilias are reported only in men.

SUGGESTED READINGS

Baumeister, R.: Masochism and the self, Hillsdale, N.J., 1989, Lawrence Erlbaum Associates, Publishers.

An authoritative book on the topic of masochism. This book explores all aspects of masochism.

Stoller, R.J.: Sexual deviations. In Beach, F.A., editor: Human sexuality in four perspectives, Baltimore, 1977, The Johns Hopkins University Press.

An easy-to-read discussion of the sexual variations discussed in this chapter as well as other sexual variations. Case histories are presented.

Wilson, G., editor: Variant sexuality: research and theory, Baltimore, 1986, The Johns Hopkins University Press.

A comprehensive book dealing with sexual variations. The contributors to this book attempted to distinguish between sexual practices that might be seen as merely recreational and those that should be defined as pathological.

Sexual Assault and Coercion

My experience with incest began when I was 11 years old. One particular night my stepfather called me down to the basement. The other kids were in bed, my mom was gone. I went down there, and he had some men's magazines. There were pictures of various sexual acts, and he was showing me all of this. And then he made the comment, "Remember how I told you that you were going to be able to prove to me that you love me. . . . "

22-YEAR-OLD FORMER STUDENT
Authors' Files

This chapter deals with three acts—rape, child sexual abuse, and incest—that are perpetrated on unwilling or unknowing victims. In its most restricted definition, *rape* occurs if a woman chooses not to have intercourse with a specific man and the man chooses to proceed against her will. Rape involves the use of force or threatened violence to exploit another individual sexually. Many states have changed their legal definition of rape to include any forced sexual activity. Massachusetts now defines rape as sexual intercourse or unnatural sexual intercourse (oral-genital or anal-genital intercourse) by a person with another person who is compelled to submit by force or by threat of bodily injury, or sexual intercourse or unnatural sexual intercourse with a child under 16 years of age (Chapter 474, Section 7, of the Massachusetts General Laws). Rape may be forcible (i.e., the victim submits because of force or threatened force) or may occur when the victim is unable to consent to sexual relations because of age, mental retardation, mental illness, or incapacitated state caused by alcohol or drugs.

The term *child sexual abuse* is used to define a situation in which a child is exposed to sexual stimulation inappropriate for that child's age or psychosocial development (Blythe and Orr, 1985). *Incest* involves sexual contact between individuals related genetically (e.g., father, mother, brother) or legally (e.g., stepparent). In incest the victim is slowly but surely, and often unknowingly, drawn into a sexual relationship with a relative. Incest and child sexual abuse often occur together because the child being sexually abused is frequently a relative of the abuser.

RAPE

As previously stated, **rape** may be defined in many ways. An inclusive definition of rape is the "illicit carnal knowledge of a woman without her consent, effected by force, duress, intimidation, or deception as to the nature of the act" (Boston Women's Health Book Collective, 1984). Legal definitions vary from state to state and take into account the victim's age and the particular sexual act that occurred. The law in most states stipulates that rape is sexual intercourse that a nonspouse forces on an unconsenting and unwilling woman with actual force or the threat of force. The contemporary view of rape sees it as an act of violence expressing power, aggression, conquest, degradation, anger, hatred, and contempt of a male over a female (Burgess and Holmstrom, 1974b; Brownmiller, 1975). This same definition, modified to exclude the idea of a male raping a female, may be used to describe males raping males, a topic that is briefly discussed at the conclusion of this section.

rape
Oral, anal, or vaginal penetration that a person forces on an unconsenting or unwilling victim.

Sexual assault has often been depicted in art, as reflected in Bernini's *Rape of Proserpina*.

Historical Aspects

Brownmiller (1975) points out that rape has been a part of all cultures and that women have been viewed as property rather than individuals. The code of Hammurabi (Babylonian law in force about 4,000 years ago) did not recognize the female as an independent being. Either she was a betrothed virgin living with her family or she was someone's wife living in her husband's house. According to the code, if a man raped a betrothed virgin, he was killed and the woman who was raped was innocent of any guilt under the law. However, if a married woman was raped, she was accused of a crime and had to share the blame equally with the rapist. The rape of a married woman was considered a form of adultery on the woman's part as well as on the man's. The implication then, as today, was that the woman was somehow responsible for her own victimization, that she had invited the rape. In such cases both individuals were tried and if found guilty were thrown into the river to drown. However, both rapist and victim had a possible reprieve. The husband could rescue his wife, and the king could pardon the rapist.

A brief look at the possible evolution of the men's and women's roles in various societies provides some insight into the origin of the idea of women as property (Donohue, 1985). Some tribes existing today continue to live in much the same manner as prehistoric societies. The !Kung bushmen of southern Africa, for example, live in a hunting and gathering society. The women gather and bring home most of the food for the family, and the men hunt and offer only occasional wild meat. The women's contribution to the food supply is at least as highly valued as the men's in these tribes.

Farming and cultivating the land eventually occurred, and the concept of property began to extend not only to the land and the early crops but also to the family. The idea of the woman as property may have begun at this point, but she was respected property and performed work of equal value to that of men. It was not until the Late Bronze Age, about 5,000 years ago, that women began to suffer second-class citizenship. This was a time of war, famine, plague, and drastic mortality. Suddenly fertility was extremely important, and women were increasingly restricted to their homes to bear children. Women were a precious commodity and were the irreplaceable remedy for population decline. By 1,000 BC most societies had become patriarchal and the subordination of women had begun. The subordination in the Hebrew social order led to the buying and selling of virgins. The father did all he could to protect his daughter's virginity in order to maintain her property value. Men had the right to rape virgins if they subsequently claimed them for their wives. In such a social order rape was not seen as a crime against a person but as a violation of property. Brownmiller (1975) makes a case that many present-day attitudes, issues, and laws regarding rape stem from the historical status of women and rape. We can see traces of the past in our present society and its views and laws on rape. For example, it is not a crime for a man to rape his wife in most states. The law assumes that the wife is the property of the husband.

The Act of Rape

Holmstrom and Burgess (1980) studied the sexual behavior of assailants during rapes that were reported to the authorities. The females in this study were 112 rape victims between 5 and 73 years of age who were admitted to the emergency ward of a large municipal hospital during a 12-month period. Of these, 73 were assaulted by a single male and 24 were attacked by more than one male; 57% were white, 41% were black, and 3% were from other minority groups. The social class, religion, marital status, and employment of the victims varied. Most were in their teens or twenties. The information for the study was collected through in-depth interviews with the victims shortly after the rape. The two authors also interviewed police and family members and attended the court proceedings if the case went to trial.

The legal aspects of rape are discussed in Chapter 22.

Of the 112 cases of rape only 9 men were convicted for the rape of an adult or for the abuse of a female child. Holmstrom and Burgess believe that their sample may not be representative of all rapists because the rape cases they investigated were all reported to the authorities. Victims are less likely to report a rape if they know or are acquainted with the rapist (Holmstrom and Burgess, 1980; Williams, 1984). In this study 56% of the rapes were committed by strangers and 39% were committed by men the women were sure they knew.

According to Weis and Borges (1973), most people think of rape as a sudden, violent attack by a stranger in a deserted public place, after which the victim is expected to provide evidence of the attack and of her active resistance. Stereotyped notions exist about rapists, the crime of rape, and its victims. *The victims of rape also share these stereotyped notions about rape, and these preconceived ideas influence the reporting or absence of reporting of a rape* (Williams, 1984). Not all rapes conform to the "classic rape situation." For example, Holmstrom and Burgess (1980) found that a great variety of sexual, excretory, and sadistic acts occurred during the sexual assault. Some assaults were over quickly, but others lasted for hours. Victims in the Holmstrom and Burgess study were asked to describe what sex acts were performed. Vaginal intercourse was the most common act reported (96% of the cases). Forced fellatio took place in 22% of the cases, and the breasts were pulled, touched, or hit in 12%. Forced cunnilingus, touching of the victim's genitals, and forced anal intercourse occurred in 5% of the cases. Urinating on either the victim or her underclothing, forced touching of the rapist's penis, forced kissing of the victim, masturbation by the rapist, and placing semen on the victim's body occurred in 2% to 4% of the cases.

We have combined the information from assaults by one male and assaults by more than one male in the Holmstrom and Burgess study (1980). Holstrom and Burgess found rapes by more than one assailant to be similar. However, forced fellatio and touching the victim's breasts were twice as common when the female was attacked by more than one male, and forced cunnilingus was much more common in single-assailant rape than in multiple-assailant rape.

Holmstrom and Burgess (1980) concluded that "forcible rape always includes three components: 'power,' 'anger,' and 'sexuality,'" which vary in proportion. Sexuality is rarely the dominant theme. These conclusions were based on interviews with victims and rapists. Groth, Burgess, and Holmstrom (1977) state that in each case they studied, "either power or anger dominates and . . . rape, rather than being primarily an expression of sexual desire, is, in fact, the use of sexuality to express issues of power and anger."

Let us briefly examine power and anger as they are discussed by Holmstrom and Burgess (1980). In a rape in which the assailant is seeking power and control, the male wants the victim to submit and he wants to engage in sexual intercourse as proof of conquest. The following example illustrates the desire of power found in some rapes. The woman had been at home when a former boyfriend stopped by her apartment uninvited. The woman stated:

> He messed me over the street way. I'm not supposed to tell. He said he'd beat me if I tell. And he gave me a sample tonight to show me. You know, they work you over—to control you—so they can have you sexually any time they want. He hit me on the ear, pulled my hair, hit me in the back by my kidneys—very strategic. But it's not the physical part that's the thing—it's mental to control you.
>
> Burgess and Holmstrom, 1974b, p. 10

In an anger rape the rapist takes his anger, rage, and hatred out on the victim. He beats her and uses more force than necessary to get her to submit to his demands. The following case history illustrates the role of anger in rape:

> Elsa, age 31, was admitted to the emergency ward with multiple lacerations and bruises to her face, arms, chest, and pelvis. She had been invited to a party by two men she had known since high school. She later reported, "Instead of going to a party they had me in the apartment and forced me to drink two pints of wine real fast. They got me drunk and then did such terrible things to me. They beat me and were so angry and said such awful things like I deserved what I was getting and that women were no damned good."
>
> Holmstrom and Burgess, 1980, p. 436

In summary, both power and anger are involved in most rapes. Holmstrom and Burgess (1980) note that documenting the kinds of sex acts that occur during rapes helps us to understand rape more clearly. They believe that knowing what sex acts occurred is important for understanding the victim's coping strategies during the rape and her later reactions to sex in general.

Rape Reporting

Rape is one of the least reported of all violent crimes in the United States. It is estimated that only 10% to 50% of rapes are reported to the police (Williams, 1984); the number of rapes that go unreported is staggering. The number of reported rapes in 1982 was 77,763, which means that for every 100,000 women in the United States, 33 reported a rape (Uniform Crime Reports, 1983). In 1987, 91,111 cases of rape were reported in the United States, or 37.9 reported rapes per 100,000 women (Uniform Crime Reports, 1988).

The exact percentage of women reporting rape depends on the sample population. The reasons that women do not report rape include fear that the rapist will retaliate if the crime is reported; embarrassment and shame that the rape occurred; fear of rejection by husband, boyfriend, and family; a wish to protect either her own family or friends or those close to the rapist (assuming she knows the rapist and his family) from knowledge of the rape and its attendant publicity; a lack of confidence in the criminal justice system to punish the rapist; and a concern that a great deal of time will be required to participate in a criminal prosecution (Amir, 1971; MacDonald, 1971; Katz and Mazur, 1979; McDermott, 1979).

The victim's race, age, marital status, and relationship to the rapist are believed to be the factors that most strongly influence the decision to report

Today many police departments have specially trained officers who help to make the reporting of a sexual assault less traumatic for the victim.

or not report a rape (Williams, 1984). Several studies have produced conflicting results in terms of the role of marital status and age. McDermott (1979) found that the incidence of reporting increased with the age of the victim, whereas Amir (1971) and Russell (1980) found just the opposite. McDermott discovered that married or previously married women were least likely to report rape by a stranger, and Russell (1980) found that married women were least likely to report any type of rape.

If the woman knows her rapist, she is less likely to report the crime than if the rapist is a stranger. A black woman is less likely to report a rape if the rapist is white (Katz and Mazur, 1979), whereas a white woman may be more likely to report her rapist if he is nonwhite (Amir, 1971). The greater the victim's injuries, the more likely she is to report the rape (Williams, 1984).

Williams (1984) proposes that the major factor determining whether a woman will report a rape is the *circumstances* of the rape itself and in particular how the rape conforms to the classic rape situation previously discussed. According to Williams, a woman is more likely to report her rape if it corresponds to the classic rape situation. Williams states that before a woman can report a rape to the police, two conditions are necessary. First, she must identify herself as a *victim* of a crime, and second, she must be confident that others (husband, parents, friends, and police) will also identify and perceive her as a *victim*. Williams tested her hypothesis on a sample of 246 female rape victims who contacted a community organization that supports rape victims. The important variables from Williams' study are reported in Table 21-1.

Williams found that the following variables had a significant effect on the victim's decision to report the rape to police: the relationship between the victim and the offender (more reporting occurred when the rapist was a stranger or acquaintance as opposed to a friend or relative), how the rapist came in contact with the victim (more reporting occurred when rape took place in a public place or after a break-in as opposed to a social situation), threat of force (more reporting occurred when force was threatened as opposed to when force was not threatened), use of force (more reporting occurred when force was used as opposed to when force was not used), degree of injury (more reporting occurred when there was a high degree of injury as opposed to a low degree

TABLE 21-1 Summary of Williams' Study Involving 246 Rape Victims

Number reporting rape	Number not reporting rape	Age of victim	Age of rapist	Relationship of rapist to victim	Location of rape
146	100	32%—10-20 yr 48%—21-30 yr 19%—31 yr or older	10-70 yr with majority being 21-30 yr	Stranger—45% Acquaintance*—35% Friend—10%	Victim's home—35% Public place—26% Rapist's home—20%

Data from Williams, 1984.
*Someone whom the victim had just met or knew slightly.

of injury), and whether the victim obtained medical treatment (more reporting occurred when the victim received medical treatment).

Williams (1984) discovered that the following variables did not affect reporting in her sample of women: victim's race, age, employment, living situation (including married or not married), emotional support system, rapist's age and race, number of rapists, and location of assault. Williams concluded that women are more likely to report rape to the police if the circumstances of the rape correspond to the classic rape situation.

Date Rape

The **date rape,** or *acquaintance rape,* is a good example of how sex role socialization hampers a woman's ability to see herself as a victim of a violent crime. Many women are socialized to believe that it is their responsibility to control all male-female interactions, and if they were raped on a date by someone they knew and trusted in a social situation, they feel it is somehow their fault (Williams, 1984).

In the situation described in the box below the woman was a rape victim but never considered reporting the crime. The male "expected" sex and was angered when the woman had no intention of having intercourse with him. Many young women do not consider forced intercourse on a date to be rape, and many young men and women believe that submitting to unwanted sexual advances on dates may be acceptable. In a survey of 245 female and 194 male

date rape
Forced sexual intercourse by an acquaintance while on a date with the victim.

A Personal Glimpse

Date Rape

I met Dan in one of my classes. He was nice looking and he asked me out after I had known him for several weeks. He picked me up in an expensive sports car and we drove into an adjacent city. We had dinner and drinks at one of the most expensive restaurants and I was really having a good time. Dan asked me if I wanted to drive his car back to the campus because he felt he had too much to drink. I thought that this was a very responsible act and I really thought he was someone I would be dating for quite a while. When we got back to the campus it was late, approximately 1:00 AM. Dan asked me if I wanted to go back to his apartment for a while and I said "yes." I was in the mood for a little holding and kissing plus I liked him. When we got into his apartment we sat on the couch and began to kiss and touch each other. I was enjoying myself when Dan said,

"Let's go into the bedroom." I said I did not want to make love but would like to continue what we were doing. I have never seen such a quick personality change in my life! He got real mad and said I was leading him on and that he spent a fortune on me and I owed it to him. Before I knew it he was on top of me and forced himself inside of me. I did not fight him but I was extremely angry, sad, and shocked at the same time. He had intercourse with me when I did not want it. When he was done, he took me home in silence. I hated him! I know now that he raped me and I will never let it happen again. I thought rape occurred with a stranger who threatened you with a dangerous knife or gun. I blame myself in some ways and I also know that he was wrong and was guilty of forcing me to do something I did not want to do. (22-year-old female student)

AUTHORS' FILES

students at Washington State University, 5% of the women and 19% of the men in the study did not believe forced sex on a date is rape (Fischer, 1985, 1986). Fischer found that some students, both male and female, believed that forcing a date to have sex might be acceptable under certain circumstances such as if the man spent a lot of money on the woman, if she "led him on" sexually, or if she was intoxicated. In another study on date rape, Parrot (1985) surveyed 595 women at Cornell University about date rapes. She found that 19% of the Cornell women reported that they had intercourse against their will because of the use of "coercion, threats, force or violence." Only 2% of these women said that they had been raped. Parrot explains this discrepancy between the act of rape and admitting that rape occurred in the following manner. The women do not want to identify themselves as rape victims and go through all of the emotional and legal ramifications of being a rape victim. Many women feel that they did not want to have intercourse but were pushed into it, but they do not see themselves as rape victims. These ideas confirm the theory proposed by Williams (1984) that if the rape does not occur in the classic rape situation, it is not seen as a rape.

A major study was done on the scope of sexual aggression committed against women enrolled at 32 institutions of higher learning in the United States (Koss, Gidycsz, and Wisniewski, 1988). A survey was administered to a sample of 6,159 women and men enrolled at diverse colleges, technical schools, and universities across the country. Women's reports of experiencing and men's reports of perpetrating rape, attempted rape, sexual coercion, and sexual contact were obtained, including the rates of prevalence since 14 years of age and of incidence during the previous year. Koss presents her findings in the accompanying box.

Incidence of acquaintance rape   Rape occurring between acquaintances, including family members and dates, is a common and serious problem. According to many studies, about 15% of college women have been raped, and 84% to 89% of these rapes (depending on the study) were committed by someone the woman knew (Wilson and Durrenberger, 1982; Muelenhard and Linton, 1987; Koss, Gidycsz, and Wisniewski, 1988). It is estimated that only 2% of acquaintance rapes are reported (Koss, Gidycsz, and Wisniewski, 1988). In an early study conducted by Kanin (1969), 25.5% of the male undergraduates surveyed reported having forcefully attempted to have intercourse with a date against her will. Perhaps most alarming to single women is the finding that the average time that women who were date raped had known their attackers is approximately 1 year. Hence most date rapes are committed by someone the woman knows well.

Why date rape occurs   Why, and under what conditions, does acquaintance rape occur? Studies show that one primary reason for the prevalence of acquaintance rape is miscommunication between the sexes. Many common dating behaviors that women consider "friendly" are interpreted by men as indicators that a women wants sex. For example, a woman tries to look her best so that her date will find her attractive, so she wears tight jeans or a short skirt. Her date, however, is likely to interpret her clothing as an indicator that she is trying to turn him on sexually. Similarly, if a young man invites a woman

Outrageous Acts and Everyday Seduction: Sexual Aggression and Victimization Among College Students

Gender Socialization and the U.S. Dating System

Our Western culture encompasses a social structure characterized by male dominance requiring that young boys and girls be taught to play complementary roles of dominant male and submissive female. The woman is expected to appear playful and tempting while trading off the right to know her sexuality for the security of male protection and a marriage contract. The U.S. dating system is characterized by rituals and scripts that dictate the expected roles of the participants. The interaction may have a gamelike quality in which the participants are dishonest about the goals they are pursuing:

He may think that women are faced with a conflict between their desire for a pleasurable sexual experience and their moral inhibitions about engaging in sexual behavior. *He* therefore doesn't expect her ready consent but a period of foreplay in which she may make unconvincing protests. . . . *She* may have a blind faith in male protection and trust that he will not make sexual advances beyond a point that she established. She may have fantasies of seduction, but these probably do not include sexual intercourse with a mate who, in addition to not being chosen or desired, inflicts pain.

A Contemporary Picture of Sexual Relationships

I have studied the sexual experiences of college students since 1976. I have developed items to obtain from men self-reports of sexual aggressive acts toward women and items to obtain from women self-reports of sexual victimization. I have used the terms *sexual aggression* and *sexual victimization* rather than *rape* because I am interested in all forms of coerced sexuality beginning with the use of false promises and menacing verbal pressure to obtain sexual intercourse up to the use of actual physical violence to obtain sexual intercourse.

During 1984 and 1985, working in collaboration with *Ms.* magazine, I surveyed 32 college campuses and administered surveys to 6,159 students. Almost half of the women reported that they had experienced a serious victimization at least once since 14 years of age. This figure included 15.4% of the women who reported victimizations that met legal definitions of rape and 12.1% of women who reported victimizations that qualified as attempted rape. Approximately 25% of men reported that they had perpetrated an act of sexual aggression at least once since 14 years of age. Included in this figure are 7.7% who reported a behavior that met legal definitions of rape and attempted rape. Confining attention just to the school year before the survey, one woman in eight reported experiencing and one man in 23 reported perpetrating a rape or attempted rape.

Subsequent questioning of those men and women involved in rape revealed some interesting findings about the profile of rape among college students: Over three quarters of the women knew the men who raped them, and 57% of the offenders were dates; virtually 95% of the rapes involved just one man and woman. Three quarters of the perpetrators and over half of the victims were drinking at the time the incident occurred. Women believed that they had clearly communicated their lack of consent to have intercourse; men felt that the victim had been ambiguous regarding consent. The most typical force was holding down; the most typical resistance was reasoning. Women viewed both his force and her resistance as marked; men thought both were minimal.

From Mary P. Koss, Ph.D.

---

to his apartment to talk or watch a movie on his VCR, she will probably accept because she wants to talk or to watch the movie. He, on the other hand, is likely to interpret her acceptance of the invitation as her consenting to intercourse, because perhaps in his mind that is the "real reason" a man invites a woman to his place and he assumes that is mutually understood.

Still, even if the man does misinterpret his date's behavior, doesn't he realize that she does not want sex once she protests? Usually not, unfortunately!

In many instances the man thinks she is saying no merely because she feels that saying yes would make her appear promiscuous. Furthermore, society socializes men to believe that it is unmanly to stop trying just because the woman says no. Even when a woman takes precautions against letting a man think that she is interested in sexual activity, he is still likely to overestimate her desire for sex. For example, Muelenhard and Felts (1987) asked men to read a scenario in which a woman on a date engaged in behaviors that might suggest a lack of sexual interest: she drank iced tea rather than alcohol; she wore a blouse with a bow at the collar, a pleated skirt, and penny loafers; she did not kiss the man. When he made sexual advances, she said no three times and moved away. Men were asked to rate how much they thought she wanted to have sex, on a scale from 1 to 9 (1 = she did not want to have sex at all; 9 = she wanted sex very much). The average rating was 4.5, indicating that the men thought the woman was somewhat interested in having sex. In another scenario the woman wore a miniskirt, drank alcohol, and voluntarily kissed the man. In this situation the men felt the woman wanted to have sex even though she said no three times and moved away from the man. The rating was 6.72 in this second scenario. Clearly the sexes differ greatly in how sexually provocative they interpret behaviors to be, since men interpreted sexual interest even in the first scenario.

Another problem contributing to the prevalence of acquaintance rape is the attitude shared by many men that rape is justified in certain situations (i.e., if the woman is thought to be promiscuous, if she dresses provocatively, if she is intoxicated, or if she does anything that he perceives as "leading him on"). Men need to be made aware that under *no* circumstances is it all right to have intercourse with a woman without her consent. Regardless of the circumstances, having intercourse with a woman who protests is rape and is grounds for prosecution.

Profile of the acquaintance rapist Studies show that certain attitudes characterize men who are more likely to commit acquaintance rape (Rapaport and Burkhart, 1984; Muelenhard and Felts, 1987; Muelenhard and Linton, 1987). Traditional men are far more likely than nontraditional men to feel that rape is justifiable, particularly if they feel that the woman has "led them on" (e.g., did not wear a bra, smiled a lot and spoke in a low tone of voice, drank alcohol, came to the man's apartment). By "traditional" men, we mean men who believe that they are dominant over women, whereas women are passive, indirect, helpless, and submissive; that men are the entrepreneurs and the breadwinners; and that men should always take charge and be in control. Traditional men have also been found to be more likely than others to believe in rape myths (e.g., women secretly enjoy being raped; women ask for it; women who dress that way deserve what they get; sometimes the only way to get a not-so-willing woman turned on is to be forceful), making them more likely candidates for acquaintance rape than their nontraditional counterparts (Muelenhard and Linton, 1987).

In addition to having traditional gender role attitudes and believing in male dominance, sexually coercive men tend to be skilled socially; they find it easy to initiate conversations and dates with women, and they tend to be charming (Muelenhard and Falcon, 1987).

Finally, the acquaintance rapist may be more inclined to find subtle ways to establish physical contact with a date, perhaps by moving in closer to her and speaking softly, by caressing her hair, or by resting his arm on her shoulder.

Dating activities and acquaintance rape   In addition to the existence of characteristics associated with acquaintance rapists, certain other aspects of dating activities make acquaintance rapes more likely to occur (Muelenhard and Andrews, 1985; Muelenhard and Linton, 1987). Men consistently rated forcing a woman into sex as more justifiable if the woman asked the man out; the woman went to the man's apartment, to a party, or "parking"; she wore sexy clothes; she kissed him voluntarily; and she drank alcohol (Muelenhard and Andrews, 1985).

Acquaintance rapists' strategies   Men use a variety of strategies to obtain sex from unwilling women. Rapaport and Burkhart (1984) and Muelenhard and Linton (1987) both found that the most common strategy was ignoring the woman's protests, rather than using violence. Unfortunately, a woman's verbal protests are usually not enough to constitute a rape in the eyes of the law, particularly if the rapist is an acquaintance. The court requires that a woman use a reasonable amount of resistance (i.e., fighting back rather than crying and pleading). Another strategy engaged in by 42% of the men in one study was verbal coercion (Craig, Kalichman, and Follingstad, 1989). Examples include lying (falsely promising greater closeness, love, or marriage), threatening to end the relationship or find another woman to satisfy him, telling her she gave him "blue balls" (swollen testicles that hurt because of sexual stimulation), and calling her a nasty name or pushing her away. Drugs and alcohol are also commonly used to obtain sex with unwilling women; Mosher and Anderson (1986) found that 75% of college men reported using alcohol and drugs to obtain sex. Giarrusso and associates (1979) found that 39% of high school boys said it is justifiable to force a girl to have sex if she is drunk or stoned. Finally, a survey of college women revealed that 19% had engaged in unwanted intercourse because of drug or alcohol consumption (Muelenhard and Linton, 1987). Threats, force, and use of a weapon are other methods reported to have been used by acquaintance rapists.

Adjustment problems   According to McCahill, Meyer, and Gishman (1979), women who are raped by casual acquaintances have far more severe adjustment problems with women raped by strangers or friends because they come to distrust and fear all casual acquaintances, which includes most men with whom they interact. Hence, in terms of adjustment, acquaintance rape can be more damaging to the woman than stranger rape.

Preventing acquaintance rape   Before discussing specific ways to prevent acquaintance or date rape, we should consider the beliefs and attitudes that are conducive to rape, the first of which is the belief that women who say no are offering token resistance so as not to be considered "sexually loose." Muelenhard and Hollabaugh (1988) found that over one third of the 610 women surveyed had put up such token protest at some time when they really wanted to have sex. Women who thought that their dates believed in the double standard (that respectable women don't say yes, and real men don't listen to no) were most likely to offer token resistance to sex. If men are to understand that no means *no*, women must first accept responsibility for making sure that when they say no, they really mean *no*.

Another myth that encourages date rape is that paying the dating expenses entitles a man to have sex with his date. Both men and women need to realize that this is simply not true. The only situation that entitles a man to have sex with a woman is one in which she desires and consents to having sex. If a woman believes that it would be unjust to deny a man sex after he has spent money on her, she should consider paying her own way.

As previously mentioned, traditional gender role attitudes, including the conviction that men need to show women who is in charge, are positively related to rape as well. Sandy's intercultural research (1981) supports this finding. The results of this research indicate that rape-prone societies are characterized by (1) allotting little political and economic power and little influence in public decision making to women; (2) encouraging men to be tough, dominant, and aggressive and to believe that they are superior to women; (3) using violence as a primary means of solving problems; and (4) involvement in war.

Discouraging traditional gender roles and the double standard might help eliminate miscommunication between the sexes and discourage the kinds of attitudes associated with the acceptance of rape.

How can a woman avoid having unwanted sex with a man with whom she would like to begin or maintain a relationship? Telling him that she cares about him and finds him attractive but is not ready for sex is fairly effective. Men in Muelenhard and Andrews' study (1985) indicated that even if the woman wore sexy clothes, went to the man's apartment, and kissed him voluntarily, it was not justifiable for the man to engage in petting after she said no *if* she

College students in a rape prevention workshop.

Guidelines for Preventing Acquaintance Rape

Guidelines for Women
1. Be assertive, decisive, and non-apologetic about what you want (or *don't* want).
2. Communicate your intentions early on.
3. Don't say no when you mean yes.
4. Don't let a man make you feel guilty about not having sex with him; you are not responsible for satisfying a man sexually just because he became sexually aroused in your presence.
5. Beware of verbal coercion tactics, such as "You led me on"; "If you loved me, you'd want to have sex with me"; "I'll just have to find someone else to satisfy my needs"; "You're being selfish"; or "Aren't you attracted to me?"

Guidelines for Men
1. Realize that no means no.
2. Realize that a woman who refuses sex is not rejecting *you;* she is merely expressing a desire not to participate in a particular act at a particular time.
3. Sexy clothing and flirtatiousness are not invitations to have sex.
4. Respecting a woman's wishes is manly, and she will almost always respect *you* more if you do.

Box prepared by Lisa Pfenninger, B.S.

said the following before going to the man's apartment: "I hope you don't misinterpret my going to your apartment on the first date, but seriously, I don't want to do anything more than kiss or talk tonight." Not only did men rate this approach as appropriate, but most also said that they would feel positively about a woman who took such an approach. On the other hand, if she waited until he made an advance to protest, the men were more likely to feel that she was leading him on, or that her resistance was insincere, and their ratings of both how much she wanted sex and of how justifiable it would be to have sex with her against her will were considerably higher. Thus open communication early in the date is good practice, both in terms of relationship effectiveness and in terms of rape avoidance.

If a woman tries this approach and the man still disregards her refusal, the most effective methods of thwarting forced sex include screaming, kicking, punching, clawing, or slapping; claiming to have a venereal disease; or forcefully saying: "This is rape, and I'm calling the cops!"

The effectiveness of various methods was based on the responses of men surveyed who had engaged in sexual coercion and on a study comparing women who had successfully avoided rape with those whose attempts were unsuccessful (Bart and O'Brien, 1985; Beal and Muelenhard, 1987). It is important that women trying to prevent acquaintance rape (but not necessarily violent stranger rape) protest powerfully and assertively, rather than show weakness and fear.

Marital Rape

With the theory put forth by Williams (1984) it is not difficult to explain why many cases of rape by a husband go unreported. Being raped by one's husband in one's own house does not conform to the classic rape situation, and hence few women report the crime of rape when the assailants are their husbands. Other reasons are involved in the decision not to report a marital rape, including financial considerations (the woman may not be able to survive on her own) and family considerations (she does not want to break up the family). At present there are fewer than 20 states where rape against one's wife is even a crime.

Rape Aftermath

The victim of a rape often suffers from physical abuse; mental anguish caused by the shock of being sexually assaulted; terror that the assailant was going to kill her; the aftermath of reporting the crime, if it is reported; the reactions of significant others in the victim's life; the concern that the rape, if intercourse and ejaculation occurred, will cause pregnancy; and the possibility that she might have contracted a sexually transmitted disease from her assailant. With all of these traumatic events occurring without warning over a very short period it is not surprising that most rape victims suffer from short- and long-term negative psychological and physical effects.

rape trauma syndrome
Psychological adjustments that occur in the rape victim after the rape.

Burgess and Holmstrom studied the aftermath of rape in 92 victims and coined the term **rape trauma syndrome** to describe the emotional and behavioral changes that occur in the rape victim. These changes in the rape victim have also been found in other studies (for a review see Ellis, 1983). Burgess and Holmstrom divided the emotional changes that occur after a rape or attempted rape into two phases. The first phase, called the *acute phase*, begins immediately after the rape. Many victims experienced disorganization in their lives during this phase, which may last several weeks. The women studied by Burgess and Holmstrom (1974a, 1974b) exhibited a wide variety of emotions and behaviors shortly after the rape. Many women cried and expressed feelings of anger, fear, and anxiety, although other women did not show much emotion and appeared calm. There were many physical complaints as a result of bruises and cuts that occurred during the rape. Many women felt fear and self-blame, and they often thought a great deal about how they could have avoided the attack.

During the second phase of the rape trauma syndrome, called the *long-term reorganization process*, many women (approximately 47%) changed their place of residence, many changed their telephone number, and others moved in with friends or family. Many women reported upsetting dreams, and others developed fears of situations that resembled the rape situation. For example, if a woman was raped while at home, she might become afraid of remaining in her house, whereas if she was raped while away from home, she might feel safe only in her house. Many women did not want to be alone, and some experienced difficulty in resuming sexual activities with their husband or sexual partner.

Some adolescent and adult rape victims experience conflicts both within themselves and in their relationships. They may show high levels of anxiety accompanied by difficulty with normal activities such as schoolwork, housework, parenting, or employment. Many rape victims, however, cope with the aftermath of rape without excessive disruptions in their lives.

Rape Trauma Syndrome and the Court System

The American Psychiatric Association recognizes rape trauma syndrome as a psychiatric diagnosis and includes the syndrome as a posttraumatic stress disorder in its *Diagnostic and Statistical Manual of Mental Disorders* (DSM-IIIR), which states that rape trauma syndrome is diagnosed by identifying "an event outside the range of usual human experience that would be markedly distressing to almost anyone" (American Psychiatric Association, 1987). Posttraumatic stress disorder is also used as a diagnosis in many veterans of the Vietnam War who suffer from previous experiences because of the war.

As the result of the rape the victim persistently reexperiences the traumatic event, persistently avoids stimuli associated with the trauma or has a numbing of the general responsiveness to all stimuli, and has persistent symptoms of increased arousal to events associated with the rape (Block, 1990). The American Psychiatric Association states that these behaviors must persist for at least 1 month to justify a diagnosis of rape trauma syndrome (American Psychiatric Association, 1987).

Since evidence rarely exists in rape cases to substantiate the use of force or lack of consent, evidence that the victim is suffering from the rape trauma syndrome can sometimes be used to prove that force was used or that the victim did not consent (Wilk, 1984).

A number of courts have admitted expert testimony on rape trauma syndrome by psychologists and psychiatrists to prove the use of force or lack of consent (Block, 1990). In *State v. Marks*, the defendant, Marks, met the victim at a bar where he was able to persuade her to return to his home (*State v. Marks*, 1982). Once there he drugged the victim and raped her. In court Marks said that the victim consented, but a psychiatrist for the victim argued that the victim was suffering from rape trauma syndrome caused by a "frightening assault, an attack" (Block, 1990, p. 315). The court held that the testimony of the psychiatrist was admissible, since rape trauma syndrome is a reaction to rape and is relevant when the defense is arguing that the victim did not consent (Block, 1990). The logic is that if she consented, she would not be suffering from the syndrome.

Although a number of courts have admitted expert testimony on rape trauma syndrome, other courts have not admitted such testimony. These courts have ruled the testimony unreliable, prejudicial, and not of help to the jury (Block, 1990). For example, in *State v. Saldana* (1982), Saldana's defense to the charge of rape was that the woman consented. A counselor for sexual assault victims testified that the victim was suffering from rape trauma syndrome. The court ruled that even if the victim exhibits some of the symptoms of rape trauma syndrome, it does not necessarily follow that she was raped. The court also ruled that rape trauma syndrome does not constitute scientific evidence that rape has occurred (Block, 1990).

Block, an attorney, concludes that the courts are unwilling to allow expert testimony on rape trauma syndrome as evidence that the victim was raped. However, evidence of the syndrome can be helpful to corroborate the victim's assertion of lack of consent (Block, 1990).

The Rapist

Is the man who rapes different from other men in intelligence, personality, and family background? The answer appears to be no. In an article dealing with the personality characteristics of sex offenders, including rapists who were primarily strangers to their victims, it was concluded that no clear-cut personality traits distinguish rapists from other men (Levin and Stava, 1987). Brownmiller (1975) states that the "typical American perpetrator of forcible rape is little more than an aggressive, hostile youth who chooses to do violence to women." About 40% of convicted rapists are married, and about half of these men have been arrested for rape or other criminal offenses in the past. Alcohol consumption by the assailant appears to be involved in approximately 50% of rapes. The assailant controls the situation by physical force, threats of harm, or intimidation. Most rapists use a lethal weapon to threaten their victim (Abarbanel, 1979).

We must remember that most of the information that we have concerning the rapist comes from studies of convicted rapists. Rapists who were not convicted or rapists whose crimes were not reported are not included in studies dealing with rapists. We cannot generalize the findings of many of these studies because they deal with less intelligent, lower socioeconomic class individuals who are more likely to be arrested and found guilty. Hence generalizing about rapists is extremely difficult. They come from all races and social classes, they rape women they do not know, they rape women they have taken out on a date, and they even rape their own wives. In many cases they use force or the threat of force.

In a study of convicted rapists who were in prison, Scully and Marolla (1984) analyzed the excuses and justifications the rapists used to explain their actions and crimes. This study demonstrates that the rapists themselves use common stereotypes to make it seem that the victims caused the rape and also shows the rapists' own perceptions of the crime. The sample consisted of 114 men convicted of rape in Virginia. The rapists ranged in age from 18 to 60 years with 88% between 18 and 35 years of age. Twenty-six percent of these rapists had histories of emotional problems. When the rapists who volunteered for this study were compared with a statistical profile of felons in all Virginia prisons, the rapists were disproportionately white, somewhat better educated, and younger than the average inmate. The rapists were divided into two major categories: *admitters* (N = 47), who acknowledged that they had forced sexual acts on their victims and defined the behavior as rape, and *deniers*, who either denied sexual contact with the victim (N = 35) or admitted to sexual acts but did not define these acts as rape (N = 32). Deniers attempted to justify their own behavior by presenting the victim in a manner that made her appear responsible for the rape (see accompanying box). Five themes were used by the convicts to justify the rapes: (1) women provoke the rapist through seductive actions; (2) all women say no when they mean yes, but it is a societal no rather than a personal no; (3) most women eventually relax and enjoy it; (4) nice girls do not get raped, and the victims precipitated the crime through their actions such as hitchhiking, being a prostitute, or having a lot of affairs; and (5) the convict admitted the rape but stated that rape was only a minor wrongdoing. In almost all cases Scully and Marolla (1984) showed that the deniers were liars and were justifying their behavior by changing the circumstances to such

Myths About Rape

Brownmiller (1975) lists the most common myths about rape:

1. All women want to be raped.
2. No woman can be raped against her will.
3. The woman asked for it.
4. If you are going to be raped, you might as well relax and enjoy it.

Brownmiller presents powerful arguments and evidence to dispel these myths. She answers the first myth by asking the question, "Do we [women] crave humiliation, degradation and violation of our bodily integrity?" For each individual woman the answer is no, but our society has taken the rape act and transformed it into something more than a violation of a person in a physical and psychological sense. Our culture, including the mass media and novels, has given the rape act a mystique. The victim has been romanticized, quickly dismissed, or even shown to have grand passion during a rape (Brownmiller, 1975). Contrast those ideas with the following:

Rape can be the most terrifying event in a woman's life. The sexual act or acts performed are often intended to humiliate or degrade her: bottles, gun barrels and sticks may be thrust into her vagina or anus. She may be compelled to swallow urine or perform fellatio with such force that she thinks she might strangle or suffocate; her breasts may be bitten or burned with cigarettes.

National Institute of Law Enforcement and Criminal Justice, 1978, p. 15

To answer the second myth one has only to examine the incredible rape and sex murder statistics in the United States. One must multiply the number of reported rapes by a factor of 5 to 7 to include the great majority of rapes that are not reported (Brownmiller, 1975). A person is powerless at the hands of a psychotic sex murderer, and a group of men will succeed at raping a woman no matter how strong she may be. Although not all rape victims are threatened with a weapon, the great majority are threatened with death if they resist (Amir, 1971). The primary thought of almost all women during a rape is fear for their lives. Thus they let the rapist rape in exchange for their lives.

The myth that women in some way "ask for it" or precipitate the rape has been disproved by statistics from the National Commission on the Causes and Prevention of Violence. This commission describes victim-precipitated rape as occurring "when the victim agreed to sexual relations but retracted before the actual act or when she clearly invited sexual relations through language, gestures, etc." (National Commission on the Causes and Prevention of Violence, 1969). The commission concluded that only 4.4% of all of the rapes they reviewed were victim precipitated. In contrast, this commission concluded that 22% of homicides, 14% of assaults, and 10% of armed robberies were victim precipitated. Thus rape victims were responsible for less "precipitant behavior" than victims of other violent crimes.

The final myth is based on two assumptions: that all women want to be raped and that eventually the male will succeed in his attempts to rape the woman. This myth ignores the fact that physical violence is occurring and that almost all women fear for their lives during a rape. In most cases the victim feels that survival depends on compliance and submission (Abarbanel, 1979).

---

a degree that there was no truth in what was said. One example will suffice. One denier claimed he had picked up his victim while she was hitchhiking. He stated, "To be honest, we [his family] knew she was a damn whore and whether she screwed one or 50 guys didn't matter." According to police reports this victim did not know her attacker or his family and he abducted her at *knifepoint* off the street.

In contrast to the deniers, the admitters regarded their behavior as morally wrong and could not justify the rape like the deniers. The admitters blamed themselves and were quite emotional in their admissions of guilt. One rapist said, "I'm in here for rape and in my own mind, it's the most disgusting crime, sickening. When people see me and know, I get sick" (Scully and Marolla, 1984). Admitters did use excuses to explain how they were driven to rape. Three excuses were used: (1) their involvement with drugs and alcohol contributed to the crime; (2) emotional problems contributed to the rape; and (3) they described themselves as nice guys who had made a very serious mistake.

The Rape Victim

Rape victims range in age from infants to 93 years of age. No woman is immune to sexual assault. In 70% to 90% of inner-city rapes the rapist is of the same social class and race as the victim (Amir, 1971). Females between 10 and 29 years of age are in the highest risk category for rape.

Rape Prevention

Rapes involve a victim, an assailant, and a particular set of circumstances such as an unlocked door or a car that is parked in a dimly lit area. Can the chances of rape be reduced by actions on the part of women? The answer is yes, but no woman, no matter how cautious she may be, is immune from rape. The following ideas and suggestions will reduce the chance of rape:

1. Establish a signal such as a special whistle that a group of neighbors can use as a warning sign and a signal for help.
2. List only first initials in phone directories and on mailboxes. If a woman lives alone, she might add fake roommates' names to her mailbox.
3. Use dead-bolt locks on outside doors. Lock windows. Know who you are letting in the door, or the best lock is useless.
4. Keep entrances and hallways brightly lit.
5. Have your keys ready to use when you arrive at your locked car, apartment, or house door.
6. Learn self-defense techniques to gain confidence and help defend yourself against an assailant. A one- or two-semester course in karate can give a woman some basic self-defense techniques that can be used against a potential rapist.

7. If you are being attacked in an apartment, hotel, or public building, yell "fire," not "help."
8. Avoid hitchhiking because this is a high-risk activity in terms of rape.
9. Always look into the back seat of your car before you get into it (whether or not you left the car locked).

We strongly advise the interested reader to contact the nearest rape crisis center for further information on the topic of rape.

Self-defense classes teach women to defend themselves against attack.

A difficult question to answer is whether the victim of a rape should resist during the sexual attack. There is no easy answer to this question; each woman must decide what strategy is best for her depending on the circumstances of the assault (Queen's Bench Foundation, 1976). Several studies have addressed this question, and certain generalizations may be derived from their findings. The assault situation seems to be more important than variables such as the victim's prior experience with being a victim of a violent crime or demographic characteristics (race, age, marital status, and socioeconomic status) in predicting whether the woman will resist the rapist (Atkeson, Calhoun, and Morris, 1989).

The location of the rape (victim's home, parking lot) and time of day did not correlate with resisting or not resisting (Atkeson, Calhoun, and Morris, 1989). Victims who did show greater resistance were more likely to be verbally threatened, physically restrained, and injured. However, victims who showed greater resistance were forced to have vaginal intercourse but were less likely than the nonresisters to be subjected to a variety of other acts such as forced fellatio and anal intercourse (Atkeson, Calhoun, and Morris, 1989). It appears that in most cases of injury to the victim, the victim resisted because she was being injured, rather than was injured because she was resisting (Atkeson, Calhoun, and Morris, 1989). Atkeson and associates also found that when the assailant was a friend or relative, 78% of the woman resisted physically.

The findings of the study by Atkeson and associates (1989) do not support earlier findings by others. For example, in other studies the location of the rape was found to be an important variable in determining whether a woman would resist (Amir, 1971; Amick and Calhoun, 1978). If raped in her home a woman was found to resist less than if raped in a public area such as a parking lot. The findings of Atkeson and associates do support other research indicating that having a prior relationship with the rapist helps to predict whether the victim will resist (Burnett, Templer, and Baker, 1985; Amick and Calhoun, 1987). If the rapist is known to the woman, she is more likely to fight back and resist.

Males Raping Other Males

Under certain circumstances men are forced to have sexual relations with other men. The most common forced sex act between men is forced anal sex followed by forced oral sex (Groth and Burgess, 1980). A common situation is when men are confined to prisons. The males doing the raping most often consider themselves to be heterosexual and usually resume sexual relations with women when they are released. Just as in rapes involving males raping females, homosexual rapes in prisons are underreported. The male being raped is afraid of retaliation from other prisoners. Males rape other males as a way of showing power. The act is an expression of anger and aggression and not primarily a sexual release (Schwendinger and Schwendinger, 1983).

> Prison rape is generally seen today for what it is: An acting out of power roles within an all-male, authoritarian environment in which the younger, weaker inmate, usually a first offender, is forced to play the role that in the outside world is assigned to women.
>
> Brownmiller, 1975, p. 285

Rape and the Prison System

If you are a little guy and you go to prison, that's the end of it; you are going to be raped right and left. It is all a matter of power, of dominance. The inmates have a class structure of their own, based on the physical size and on seniority. The little guy or the new guy is always at the bottom of the totem pole, so he gets beaten, raped, and messed with all of the time. What you end up doing, if you are a small guy, is hooking up with one of the big guys and becoming his property and his sexual slave; in return, he protects you from being bullied, beaten up, and raped by the other inmates.

They also have their own form of prostitution. I have seen guys go up to their girlfriends and talk to them on the phones in those cubicles where they are separated by glass, and they say, "I love you," and they press their hand to the glass like they are holding hands, and they are all "lovey-dovey"; then they take the cake, cigarettes, and anything else their girlfriend gave them, and use it all as payment for sex with another inmate. If he has got a big guy that protects him, like I was talking about before, then everything he gets from his friends, relatives, and girlfriend automatically goes to the big man; it is just a built-in part of the deal.

A lot of these guys have been in for so long that they have come to prefer men, and they are not even turned on by women anymore. I spoke to one guy who was strictly heterosexual before prison. Now he says he would step over three beautiful naked women to get to a man.

I led a tour of good-looking high school females through the prison once and the guys were whistling and hollering at *me*, and telling me what a fine ass *I* had! It was a real experience! (a 26-year-old house arrest officer)

AUTHORS' FILES

Thus prison rapes serve more than just sexual functions. They are used to assert and affirm masculinity, to develop power hierarchies, and as a manifestation of violence and sadism.

Males do rape other males outside of the prison situation. Groth and Burgess (1980) categorize homosexual rape into three situations. In the first situation the assailant rapes his victim without the victim's consent; for example, the victim is drunk and does not know what is happening. An example follows:

> Mr. A was at an office party and had too much to drink. His boss offered to drive him home. . . . A short time later he [Mr. A] awoke to find himself naked in the backseat being sodomized by his boss.
>
> Groth and Burgess, 1980, p. 807

In the second and third situations, which are more common, force or the threat of force, respectively, is used to compel the victim to submit to the rapist.

Sexual Assault and Coercion of Men by Women

Men are the assailants in almost all sexual crimes against women and other men. In a small number of studies women have been reported to be the assailants in sexual assaults and coercive sexual behavior against men (Sarrel and Masters, 1982; Struckman-Johnson, 1988).

In an often cited study, Sarrel and Masters (1982) interviewed 11 men who were sexually assaulted by women. The men all had sought help at the Yale

Human Sexuality Program (part of the University Health Center) and the Masters and Johnson Institute. The men were divided into four categories: (1) forced assault in which force or threat of force was used, (2) "baby-sitter" abuse in which a young boy was seduced by an older female who was not a relative of the boy, (3) incestuous abuse of a boy by an older female relative, and (4) "dominant woman abuse" in which an adult female displayed an aggressive sexual approach to an adult male and produced great intimidation without the use of physical force.

An example of forced assault occurred when a 23-year-old medical student was bound and forced to have intercourse with a woman who threatened him with a knife. This man sought help 2 years after the incident because he was afraid of initiating contact with females (Sarrel and Masters, 1982). An example of "dominant woman abuse" is a 40-year-old man who was assaulted by his wife, from whom he was legally separated. He stated, "I felt helpless to stop her. No matter what my feelings, she was going ahead. I couldn't believe I had an erection. I was so scared. I had always equated erection with sexual excitement. And then she was sitting on me and she had a quick orgasm. And it was over. I didn't ejaculate. I felt confused and humiliated." This particular example makes an important point; men can have an erection despite experiencing negative emotions such as humiliation, anxiety, fear, or anger (Sarrel and Masters, 1982).

In 1988 Struckman-Johnson surveyed 623 undergraduate students and asked them if they had *been forced* to engage in sexual intercourse while on a date and if they *forced* someone else to engage in sexual intercourse while on a date. The results indicated that when women were forced to have sex, the force was physical, whereas the men were victims of psychological force such as verbal pressure (Struckman-Johnson, 1988). Females reported longer term negative reactions to the forced sex, while few men exhibited long-range negative effects of the experience. Another study of coercive sexual behavior in college students found that 63% of men and 46% of women reported unwanted sexual activity, that is, engaging in sexual activities when they did not want to (Muehlenhard and Cook, 1988).

The studies of Struckman-Johnson (1988) and Muehlenhard and Cook (1988) reporting the female as the aggressor in a sexual encounter are in disagreement with a large number of published studies that report that in the typical dating situation the male initiates and the woman attempts to set limits on the extent of sexual involvement (Clark and Lewis, 1977; LaPlante, McCormick, and Brannigan, 1980; Muehlenhard and Falcon, 1987; Muehlenhard and Linton, 1987; Beyers and Lewis, 1988; Koss, Gidycsz, and Wisniewski, 1988; Craig, Kalichman, and Follingstad, 1989). As Muehlenhard and Cook point out, their study and that of Struckman-Johnson used men who were relatively young (mean age 20 years). These men would be less sexually experienced and perhaps more influenced by peer pressure to have sex with a large number of partners and gain experience. These young men might have been afraid of being perceived as unmasculine or worried that their potential sexual partner would turn to others for sexual gratification if they did not have sex when she wanted sex. The topic of men being sexually assaulted and coerced sexually by women should be further investigated. Recognition of the fact that men can be sexually assaulted by women will probably lead to increased identification of male victims.

CHILD SEXUAL ABUSE

This section explores aspects of sexual contact between an adult and a child. Incest and child sexual abuse are not mutually exclusive, since a child may be sexually abused by a relative. Thus incest is a form of child sexual abuse (see box).

The legal definition of **child sexual abuse** is an act performed by an adult with a minor under 18 years of age, and it includes indecent exposure, digital manipulation of the genitals (touching and inserting the fingers), masturbation, fellatio, sodomy (anal intercourse), and coitus (Blumberg, 1984). Another definition, which is not a legal one, is exposure of a child to sexual stimulation inappropriate for his or her age, level of psychosocial development, and role in the family (Brant and Tisza, 1977).

child sexual abuse
Sexual act or acts performed by an adult with a minor under 18 years of age.

Incidence

Like incest, child sexual abuse goes unreported much of the time. Each year an estimated 200,000 to 500,000 sexual assaults occur to girls between infancy and 13 years old in the United States, whereas the number of boys of the same age who are abused is considerably lower (Sanford, 1980; Veltkamp et al., 1984). Sexual abuse of girls and boys has been identified in every socioeconomic, cultural, and intellectual level of our society (Blumberg, 1984). Blumberg summed up five studies of sexual abuse of children done after 1980 and concluded that 72% to 89% of the abused children were girls and 11% to 27% were boys. In a Canadian study of child sexual abuse involving 157 cases there were 21 boys and 136 girls with an age range of 8 months to 17 years; the majority were under 10 years of age (Grant, 1984).

The Perpetrator

The characteristics of both heterosexual and homosexual pedophiles are presented in Chapter 20.

The perpetrator of child sexual abuse seeks sexual gratification from a child. The incestuous father or stepfather or unrelated pedophile known to the child usually has a weak ego and low self-esteem and is often impotent (Blumberg, 1984). Blumberg further states that the man in question functions on an immature psychosocial level, usually expects rejection or failure in adult heterosexual acts, and therefore seduces children as sexual partners. Peters (1976) found that adults who sexually abuse children are usually of normal intelligence, are not psychotic, and do not manifest other mental disorders but that they do have passive-aggressive personality disorders with feelings of inferiority and strong dependency needs. Brant and Tisza (1977) state that child sexual abusers are often influenced by their own early sexual abuse. Generally speaking, the motivations for child sexual abuse are not hatred or violence, as in rape, so the majority of cases do not involve physical force or injury (Blumberg, 1984).

Grant (1984) analyzed the relationship of the perpetrator to the victim in 157 cases of child sexual abuse and found that a family member was responsible in 45.8% of the cases (fathers responsible in 15.9% of the cases, followed by uncles or cousins [14.0%], stepfathers or common-law relations [10.8%], and mothers or brothers [5.1%]). Nonfamily members were involved in the rest of the cases; 24.1% of the perpetrators were baby-sitters or other persons known to the child. The box contains some of the psychological and physical indicators of sexual abuse.

Indicators of Sexual Abuse

Psychological Signs

1. Fear of being alone with a specific person
2. Sleep disturbances, such as nightmares, fear of going to bed, and fear of sleeping alone
3. Irritability or short temper
4. Clinging to parent or parents
5. Unexplained fears
6. Changes in behavior and schoolwork, or in relating to friends or siblings
7. Behaving like a younger child (regression)
8. Sexual sophistication or knowledge greater than age group
9. Fear of going home or running away from home

Physical Signs (Caused by Sexual Acts)

1. Difficulty in walking or sitting
2. Pain or itching in genital areas
3. Torn, stained, or bloody underwear
4. Bruises or bleeding in external genitals, vagina, or anal areas
5. Sexually transmitted diseases
6. Pregnancy

The Victim

Not enough data have been accumulated to identify the characteristics of the victims of child sexual abuse. Approximately two thirds of the cases reported involve stepdaughters abused by stepfathers. Next in terms of frequency of reports are daughters abused by biological fathers. Third is sibling sexual abuse. Based on the data we have now, abuse typically begins between 5 and 7 years of age and continues from 1 to 5 years, although sexual abuse may continue within a family for many more years. The abuse may begin with an older child and continue with another child when the older child leaves home. At present, more reports in which a female child is the victim are made. However, some experts in the field expect that as more cases are reported, an equal number of male children will be victims. Sexual abuse may have a pronounced pattern, occurring in multiple generations of families. Those who are abused often end up abusing or marrying spouses who abuse.

Child Sexual Abuse Patterns

There are some typical and predictable patterns in the development of sexual abuse whether it occurs within or outside the family. The typical first stage is *engagement*. Somehow the abuser must entice the child into a relationship. The abuser may entrap the child, threaten to use force, or incapacitate the victim, such as tying the child up. Drugs or alcohol can also be used to gain control over the victim.

Once the child has been lured into a relationship, the next stage usually involves some type of sexual interaction. This may initially be brief, perhaps only 30 to 60 seconds. It often begins with the exposure of the genitals of either the abuser or the victim. The abuser may masturbate himself or herself and then fondle the victim. Anal or vaginal penetration and oral sex might follow the fondling.

The third stage is the *secrecy phase*. The abuser may tell the child, or somehow give the child the message, that he or she must not tell anyone. Frequently some type of strategy is employed to get the child to maintain the secret. The strategy most often used is an extension of the engagement stage, such as enticement or threat. In some sense the child will "cooperate" by going along with the strategy. The offender often instills a sense of guilt in the child that the abuser will use or exploit to continue the secrecy.

The sexual abuse is likely to continue unless the final stage, *disclosure*, occurs. Disclosure results when the victim tires of the abuse, becomes pregnant (or fears pregnancy), or wants more opportunities to be with peers, or for various other reasons. The disclosure may occur accidentally, such as someone seeing the sexual act or the child being injured in some way that draws medical attention. Disclosure can also happen if the child contracts a sexually transmitted disease. Disclosure may result if the child engages in extremes of be-

Two Mental Health Care Professionals Discuss Child Sexual Abuse

We asked two mental health care professionals to answer some of the most common questions about child sexual abuse.

Q. What is child sexual abuse?

A. Child sexual abuse is any act intended to sexually stimulate or gratify the abuser, whether or not the abuser recognizes that the act makes the child feel uncomfortable. The abuser can be an adult, an older brother, an older sister, or a neighborhood child. Some form of power differential is always present between victim and abuser. One end of the child sexual abuse continuum is simple fondling; on the other end is intercourse. Child sexual abuse is against the law whether it is fondling or intercourse, and we take the same legal steps in both cases.

Q. How many people are affected by sexual abuse?

A. The National Center for Child Abuse and Neglect in 1985 estimated that about 250,000 children are the victims of child sexual abuse each year. Stated another way, about 1 in 4 children is at risk of being the victim of some kind of sexual abuse before 18 years of age.

Q. Who commits child sexual abuse?

A. The offenders come from all social and economic levels as well as occupations. Current figures suggest that about 80% of reported child sexual abuse occurs within the family and hence also constitutes incest. The other 20% is committed by someone outside the family.

Q. Why don't children tell about sexual abuse?

A. There are many reasons that children do not inform others when they are being abused.

When a child does inform someone, it is probably the most frightening thing that child has ever done in his or her life. Once the child tells, he or she is upsetting the entire family structure and thus changing the future for everyone in the family. Many times the person abusing the child is the only person from whom the child is getting affection. The child might also know that by telling he or she is running the risk that the parents might split up or that the family might in some way be separated. Maybe it is the parent's second or third marriage, and the parent does not want to do anything to ruin it even if that means the victim still has to live with the horror that is happening in his or her life. The victim might fear going to a foster home. Victims may be afraid that no one will believe them or that they could be harmed if they tell (fears that are often directly reinforced by the abuser).

From Michaelle Hostetler Kreider, B.S.W., and Jim Kreider, M.S.W., L.S.C.S.W., Bert Nash Community Mental Health Center, Lawrence, Kansas.

havior. Sexually abused children may masturbate frequently or in public. Sexually abused teenagers often are extremely sexually active.

In a form of homosexuality known as *pederasty*, adult men seek sexual satisfaction with young boys. Another form of organized child sexual abuse involves the use of children of both sexes to produce pornographic photographs, motion pictures, and videotapes. The producer of these films is usually not a pedophile but is producing materials that appeal to pedophiles.

Long-Term Effects

The long-term effects of childhood sexual abuse have been examined in numerous studies. In adulthood, individuals sexually abused as children often show low self-esteem, guilt, depression, difficulty in trusting others, promis-

---

Q. What should a person who finds out someone is being sexually abused do?

A. Because of the complexity of problems involved with sexual abuse and also the reluctance of families to deal with the dynamics of sexual abuse, reporting to the proper authorities is essential for treatment of the problem. Reporting suspected or actual cases of sexual abuse is the law, and professionals such as doctors and teachers are often the first to note the effects of abuse. Simply confronting those involved is not likely to motivate them enough to seek help, and without help the sexual abuse will continue. Reports of child sexual abuse should be made to a state abuse prevention agency. Some professionals involved in sexual abuse treatment suggest that a simultaneous report be made to the police because sexual abuse is a crime.

Q. What is the first stage of treatment after the abuse has been disclosed?

A. Following the reporting of sexual abuse, the next step is helping everybody in the family to acknowledge that sexual abuse has occurred. Family members tend to deny that sexual abuse occurred, and this must be dealt with again and again in the course of therapy. Once those involved in sexual abuse, indirectly or directly, have acknowledged that it happened, the task becomes helping the child *recognize* and the adults *accept* that sexual abuse has occurred. The child cooperated as a victim in the sexual abuse where the child had less power than the adult. It is that misuse of power that puts the burden of responsibility on the adults' shoulders. The child faces the difficult task of learning how to trust others and realizing that he or she has been exploited for the abuser's gratification.

Q. How is child sexual abuse treated?

A. A multifaceted program is necessary to treat child sexual abuse. Treatments must include some type of legal control to accomplish several ends. The child must be protected from further sexual exploitation and abuse, and the offender must be required, as well as motivated, to have treatment that addresses his or her problems and the behavior patterns that resulted in sexual abuse. Without treatment, abusers tend to continue to abuse.

Q. Does treatment really help when sexual abuse has occurred?

A. Again we do not have enough data to comment conclusively about how treatment helps resolve patterns of sexual abuse. Even though we cannot erase the fact that sexual abuse has occurred in a person's life, we can help those involved change how they view themselves and others. It is possible that perpetrators can stop the pattern of victimizing others and develop positive and healthy ways of meeting their needs and developing satisfying lives as adults.

---

cuity or a lack of interest in sex, loneliness, inability to establish relationships with others, drug and alcohol abuse, a tendency to sexually abuse children, and a tendency toward prostitution (Blumberg, 1984; Sedney and Brooks, 1984; Veltkamp et al., 1984). Sedney and Brooks (1984) surveyed 301 college women concerning their history of childhood sexual experiences. Sixteen percent of the women reported a history of childhood sexual experiences. These women who were sexually abused as children reported significantly greater amounts and severity of depression, anxiety, and self-abuse behavior (alcohol abuse and thoughts of self-harm). Women whose experiences occurred within the family were at a greater risk for psychological disturbances than women whose experiences occurred outside the family.

The Aftermath

Once a case of child sexual abuse has been discovered, all parties (parents and authorities) must proceed in a manner that protects the child and reduces the child's feelings of guilt and anxiety. The child who has been sexually abused by someone he or she knows, such as a relative, has been victimized by a trusted person. Suddenly the child's world has been drastically changed, and the child feels that he or she somehow played a role in the situation.

Incest

Incest involves sexual contact between father and daughter, mother and son, brother and sister, father and son, or mother and daughter. The definition is also extended to include sexual relations with close relatives such as stepparents, grandparents, uncles, aunts, and cousins (Bronson, 1989). Incest is a form of child sexual abuse (Mega and Cuenca, 1984) and is predominantly a crime by males against females (Taubman, 1984). Taubman states that "incest needs to be understood as part of the pattern of male dominance and violence against women via sexual abuse."

Bixler (1983) argues convincingly that before we can diagnose and treat individual cases of incest we must draw clear distinctions among the various kinds of incest. Bixler makes the point that father-daughter incest is more common before adolescence but rare once the daughter reaches reproductive age. Incest is a situation in which distinctions about relations and ages are important. In addition, theories about incest depend on certain facts about the incestuous situation. The facts that have implications for diagnosis, treatment, and theory are as follows:

1. Specific relationship (e.g., sibling and sibling, uncle and niece, stepfather and stepdaughter)
2. Age and gender of both parties (e.g., father and prepubescent daughter, 12-year-old brother and 6-year-old sister)
3. Degree of sexual activity (e.g., father held adolescent daughter on his lap and touched her with clothes on, brother fondled sister's breast)
4. Whether both partners were willing (coercion assumed in most cases)
5. Whether the incestuous parties were associated with each other during prepubescence (e.g., lived in the same household before the child entered puberty)

Incest is condemned in most cultures (Ford and Beach, 1951). The incest taboo is thought to have evolved early in human evolution to maintain the integrity and order of the family, since sexual competition within the family disrupts the family's organization.

Gebhard and associates' survey (1965) in the United States discovered that 3.9% of the population had experienced incest, while a more recent estimate indicates that 16% of women in the United States have had an incestuous episode (Russell, 1986). Data indicate that brother-sister incest is five times as common as father-daughter incest and that mother-son incest is less common than brother-sister or father-daughter incest (Gebhard et al., 1965; Finkelhor, 1980). A survey of approximately 800 undergraduates at six New England colleges and universities found that 15% of the females and 10% of the males reported some type of sexual experience involving a brother or sister (Finkelhor, 1980). Exhibiting the genitals, fondling and touching the genitals, intercourse, and attempted intercourse were mentioned. Children below 8 years of age usually exhibited and touched the genitals. After 8 years of age, intercourse or attempted intercourse occurred in 15% to 18% of the sample. The younger children might be considered to be "playing doctor" and exploring, whereas the older children were more involved in genital stimulation (Finkelhor, 1980). The females in the sample felt more exploited and had more negative feelings about the experiences than males. Few participants of either sex had ever told anyone about the sexual activity.

The frequency of incest has been estimated to be between one case of incest per million to five cases of incest per thousand population in the United States (Mega and Cuenca, 1984). In a study in New York City in which De Francis (1969) examined sexual abuse, including incest, the average age of the victim was 11 years and the average age of the perpetrator was 31 years. There were 10 girls to every boy abused. In 13% of the cases of incestual abuse the offender was the biological parent of the victim; in 14% of the cases it was a surrogate parent such as a stepparent.

Russell (1984) analyzed interviews obtained from a random sample of 930 adult women in San Francisco. She found that 17% of the women who had a stepfather as a principal figure in their childhood years were sexually abused by him. The comparable figure for biological fathers was 2%. When a distinction was made between serious sexual abuse (experiences ranging from rape to forced fellatio, cunnilingus, and anal intercourse) and other, less serious forms (fondling and kissing), 47% of the cases of sexual abuse by stepfathers were at the very serious level, compared with 26% by biological fathers.

A very small percentage of incest crimes are reported. Sibling incest is the most common type of incest but constitutes only 15% of the reported cases, whereas father-daughter incest constitutes between 75% and 85% of the cases reported (Mega and Cuenca, 1984). The perpetrator of incest is often a man in early adulthood to middle age. There are cases of older men victimizing their granddaughters and grandsons and of teenagers victimizing their younger sisters.

A wealth of information is available on father-daughter incest (Herman, 1981) because this relationship is most often discovered and prosecuted in courts of law. What can we conclude from the available information on father-daughter incest?

1. Father-daughter incest usually occurs in an unbroken home and begins following a loss of sexual feeling between husband and wife. The in-

A Personal Glimpse

Personal Account of Incest

I am 22 years old. I work full-time and attend school on a part-time basis. My experience with incest began when I was 11 years old. Before the incestuous experience I had a fairly normal childhood. I was the oldest of four children and tended to get my way more than the other children.

I was born 1 year before my mother married my stepfather. At about 10½ or 11 years old, I was legally adopted by my stepfather. The incident started out one day when my father and I were talking, and he said that I would have a chance to prove that I really loved him or how much I loved him. I thought this comment was related to the adoption.

About 2 weeks or 1 month later, after the adoption, my mother was out during the evening. She worked evenings or went out with friends. Often my mother and father would get into fights, and my father would tell my mother to just leave. She would leave and not come back until after midnight. This happened a lot.

On this particular night my father called me down to the basement. He told me he had something to show me. The other kids were in bed, my mom was gone. I went down there, and he had some men's magazines. There were pictures of various sexual acts, and he was showing me all of this. And then he made a comment something to the effect of, "Remember how I told you that you were going to be able to prove to me that you love

me." That's how things basically started. It started very simply, just mutual touching of each other that gradually built up to intercourse.

It was very much a game for me, I think. It was like, "We'll do this, you and me. We'll have something special that no one else can have or your mom can't be involved in or anything like that." The competition built up for my father's attention between me and my mother. I fixed his lunches, I did his clothes, and I waited on him at night. At night when he wanted something, I cooked it and took it to him. My mother was tired from working, or they were fighting. I seemed to be almost placed into the role of the wife. And at that age I don't think I realized anything was really wrong or anything was really going on, except for the fact that everything seemed so secret. This went on for several years.

When I was about 14 or 15 years old, I started using it [the relationship] as a weapon against my father. For example, "If you want me to do anything with you, you're going to have to give me this or you're going to have to let me do this." He was strict about letting me go to school activities, so I would agree to do something with him. By this time in my life I started having guilty feelings about it [the relationship]. It wasn't a game anymore. I felt very ashamed about it. I felt very scared about it. I did not want anyone to find out about what was going on. So, in order for me to go to a school activity it would involve a lot of fighting and arguing or letting him have his way with me.

My mother always seemed to be against me. And so my only shelter was my dad, and my dad would always let me have my way, *if* I did what he wanted me to do. Eventually, I always did what he wanted.

Mom was never home at all. I did make a couple of attempts to tell her, but it seemed like any time I tried to tell her she would cut me off. It was like she almost knew what was coming next, but she did not want to hear it. We did not have a lot of money. My dad did not work half of the time, and my mom was very frightened of the fact that he might leave her and leave us without a father.

When I was about 18 years old, I was dating one guy that my father did not like. I came home one night from a date, and my father ran out and threatened this guy with a knife. My father was so mad. He got really violent. This was the night it really came out in the open. I was just really tired of him telling me what to do and who I could date. I lost my temper and spilled the beans right there in front of Mom, Dad, and a girlfriend who was spending the night. He denied it to the hilt, and he ended up leaving that night. Mom's initial reaction was, "Oh, you're such a liar, oh, you're rotten, you're terrible, how could you say such a thing, you slut?" Very derogatory comments and things like that. She seemed to be surprised. I kept wanting to say, "How can you stand there acting so shocked? Surely you must have known it was going on? How could you not know it was going on? You walked out on me, where were you when I needed you? How come you were never there?"

It ended up by having my father leave, and eventually they divorced. Mom was very frightened. I feel like I led her through the divorce, because she did not really want to do it, but I told her, "What if he starts doing things to my two younger sisters?" And I was really scared and concerned about them.

I remember my dad would often say it was good that I never told my mom and caused our family to break up. He would say, "You know you could never make it on your own. The family needs me." There was a lot of guilt built in if I ever told on him. I felt like I held the full responsibility for the family on my shoulders. It was a very frightening, very scary thing.

I see my father every once in a while, and I really don't hate him. My mom despises him. I don't hate him. I feel sorry for him. The effects this has had on me I just kind of wonder about. Am I dealing with it well or am I keeping it bottled up inside? One of these days is it suddenly going to explode? Is it like a stick of dynamite with a long fuse? Am I going to go to pieces like I read of other people doing? I thought that way for a couple of years. Now I have gotten to the point where I've dated a few guys steady, and I am engaged to be married. It is really like I feel I am O.K. now. It's taken a lot of thinking everything through over the past years.

AUTHORS' FILES

cestuous relationship between father and daughter occurs over an extended period and develops gradually.

2. The relationship is often made possible and later perpetuated by several family members. Father-daughter incest typically results from the mother pushing the daughter into taking on adult responsibilities. The mother is usually described as a dependent individual with low self-esteem (Herman, 1981), but a study by Groff (1987) found, using personality tests, that spouses' personality characteristics were within normal limits. A common finding was that incest frequently occurs in families in which the mother is rendered powerless through beatings by the father, physical disability, mental illness, or repeated childbearing (Herman, 1981). Herman and Hirschman (1981) believe that the powerless position of the mother, regardless of the cause, is one of the most important characteristics of families in which incest is likely to occur. Zuelzer and Reposa (1983) found that the mothers in incestuous families tend to lack a psychological investment in their children because of their own earlier emotional deprivation or lack of social skills. Such mothers have needs that are so primary and profound that they must turn to their children for physical and emotional support.

3. The incestuous fathers are often described as patriarchs (Herman, 1981). Their authority as head of the household is not questioned, and the force (directed against family members) is often used to reinforce their position of power. The incestuous father often tries to isolate his family from outside influences (Herman, 1981). The father uses his position of authority to engage his daughter in a sexual relationship (Mega and Cuenca, 1984).

4. The daughter often sees her mother as cruel and unjust. The mother may have experienced physical or sexual abuse and may not be providing an adequate sexual relationship for her husband (Mega, 1981).

5. Incest is commonly associated with alcoholism (Herman, 1981; Barnard, 1983). From 15% to 80% of incest perpetrators are chronic alcoholics or used alcohol just before the incestuous episode (Barnard, 1983).

What causes the disclosure of the incestuous relationship? The precipitating event is "often a change in the terms of the incestuous relationship which makes it impossible for the daughter to endure it any longer" (Herman, 1981). In some cases when the daughter reaches puberty the father attempts intercourse, and this frightens the daughter because of the risk of pregnancy and the new sexual act of intercourse. In other instances the father tries to restrict the daughter's social life to such a degree that the daughter discloses the incestuous relationship (see box on pp. 620 and 621). Some daughters report their fathers to protect younger sisters who are also at risk for an incestuous relationship with the father:

> My younger sisters were growing up, and I was afraid he [the father] might start on them. I couldn't see that. I could put up with it. For myself, I was willing to tolerate it, but I couldn't see him starting up with my sisters. That's when I went to the authorities.
>
> Herman, 1981, p. 132

In whom do the victims confide? Slightly over half of them (52.5%) tell a friend, relative other than their mother, baby-sitter, neighbor, or social agency, and the rest (47.5%) tell their mother (Herman, 1981). In some cases of incest the mother goes to the authorities, but it is usually the daughter who seeks help with the problem. Only 6% to 30% of incest cases are reported to the authorities (Sarles, 1980; Russell, 1983; Taubman, 1984). That means that many cases go unreported, and the incestuous relationship continues until the child leaves the house to live elsewhere.

Incest causes psychological damage because of the violation of the child's trust by the adult (Herman, 1981). Mega and Cuenca (1984) report from their clinical experiences that incest has numerous psychological effects. The victim may show pseudomaturity, especially with respect to sex, and may become promiscuous out of retaliation. There may be considerable guilt and anxiety, particularly if the family breaks up because of the disclosure of incest. Often the victim exhibits extreme masochism and a search for punishment. In some cases the victim becomes like the parents and repeats the cycle of physical or sexual abuse with his or her children. Finkelhor (1979) found that men and women who had been victims of childhood sexual abuse showed impaired sexual self-esteem. Landis (1956) studied women who had been childhood victims of incest and reported that the women complained of sexual difficulties in adult life and that some were completely disgusted with all aspects of sex. The strongest emotional reactions came from women who were abused by fathers, uncles, or brothers. Tsai and Wagner (1978) reported that women who were sexually molested as children, mostly by fathers or close relatives, complained of feelings of shame, guilt, depression, and low self-esteem. Those women also indicated problems with interpersonal relationships, feelings of isolation, mistrust of men, distorted body images, and a tendency to become involved in abusive relationships with men (Jackson et al., 1990). Jackson and associates found that the women in their study had many psychological problems because of the incest experience and also because of the general family environment in which the incest occurred. Sibling incest experiences do not seem to have as many negative long-term effects on the victim as when a girl is molested by an older male member of the family (Finkelhor, 1980).

SUMMARY

1 Historical attitudes and issues about rape have influenced many present-day issues and laws regarding rape.

2 The act of rape is motivated by power and anger and not by the sexual acts committed.

3 The relationship between the rapist and victim seems to be the most important factor influencing whether the crime will be reported. An example of this is acquaintance rape in which the woman is raped by a friend or a date. This type of rape is underreported.

4 Many rape victims suffer from rape trauma syndrome. This is a period of disorganization in the victim's personal life followed by a reorganization process during which the victim changes place of residence or moves in with family or friends. The victim develops a fear of situations that resemble the rape situation.

5 The rape trauma syndrome has been used successfully in some courts of law to argue that a woman has been raped.

6 Child sexual abuse is a sexual act or acts performed by an adult on a minor under 18 years of age.

7 Incestuous behavior involves sexual contact between a father and daughter, a mother and son, or a brother and sister. The definition may be extended to include sexual relationships between relatives.

8 The most common form of incest is brother-sister. This form is five times as common as father-daughter incest. Mother-son incest is less common.

ANSWERS

F A C T
OR
F I C T I O N

1 Incest between brothers and sisters is most common, but father-daughter cases are prosecuted more often in the courts.
2 Acquaintance rape is a common form of sexual assault and is a very underreported crime.
3 In most cases child sexual abuse is initiated by a person who knows the child.

QUESTIONS FOR THOUGHT ?

1 As a male or a female, how can you modify your behavior to reduce the incidence of acquaintance rape?
2 What are some of the consequences of rape, child sexual abuse, and incest in females?
3 Discuss the rape trauma syndrome. Do you think it is a valid legal argument to prove that rape has occurred?

SUGGESTED READINGS

Bass, E., and Thornton, L., editors: I never told anyone: a collection of writings by survivors of child sexual abuse, New York, 1985, Harper & Row, Publishers, Inc.
This is a book written by women who have been victims of child sexual abuse. A powerful and disturbing series of accounts that portray the fear and anger of the victims.
Brownmiller, S.: Against our will, New York, 1975, Simon & Schuster, Inc.
This classic account of many different perspectives of rape made the public aware of rape as a crime of violence and helped shatter the myths about rape and the rape victim.
Maltz, W., and Holman, B.: Incest and sexuality: a guide to understanding and healing, Lexington, Mass., 1987, Lexington Books.
A book for the victims of incest, as well as the significant others in their lives.
Renshaw, D.: Incest—understanding and treatment, Boston, 1983, Little, Brown & Co., Inc.
This is an account of the causes and treatments of incest. It is an excellent book for students interested in the clinical aspects of incest.

CHAPTER

22

FACT
OR
FICTION

1
Any sexual behavior between two consenting adults is legal in the United States.

2
In most states a married woman who lives with her husband can charge her husband with rape if he forces her to have sexual intercourse against her wishes.

3
Surveys of the incidence of sexual harassment indicate that the vast majority of women believe they have been subjected to such harassment.

Sex and the Law

The liberties distributed by the principles of justice typically include liberties of thought and expression (freedom of speech, press, religion, and association), civic rights (impartial administration of civil and criminal law in defense of property and person), political rights (the right to vote and participate in political affairs), and freedom of physical, economic, and social movement. The importance of these liberties rests on their relation to the primary good of self-respect, since these liberties nurture personal competencies, for example, full expression of the spirit, self-direction, security of the person, and the possibility of unhampered movement. In the United States, this has been accomplished through the constitutional guarantees of the Bill of Rights and the Fourteenth Amendment.

Contemporary understanding of the strategic importance to self-respect and personhood of sexual autonomy requires that we similarly guarantee full liberty to enjoy and express love.

DAVID A.J. RICHARDS
Sex, Drugs, Death, and the Law, p. 51

The application of the law to sexual activity dates to at least biblical times. The Old Testament dealt with almost every aspect of sexuality, including intercourse, marriage, divorce, procreation, adultery, homosexuality, bestiality, rape, and transvestism. According to the rules stated in the Old Testament, sex was limited largely to the marital state. The sex laws in our society today have come predominantly from this Judeo-Christian tradition. In our culture "proper" sex is sex that takes place between two adults of opposite genders within a marriage. In fact, until recently sex within marriage was the only form of sexual relations that was not explicitly prohibited by the law in many states.

For the most part the law in the United States has restricted legal sexual relations to people who are related by marriage, to private places, and to genital-genital heterosexual contact. Sexual activities that may be illegal because they are committed with an "inappropriate" partner include sex with a relative (incest), a member of the same gender (homosexuality), an unmarried person (fornication), a person married to someone else (adultery), oneself (masturbation), or an animal (sodomy). Sex that occurs in a public place may violate laws against public lewdness. Even when the partner and the place are not contrary to the law, the type of sexual activity may be illegal. Anal-genital sex (sodomy) and oral-genital sex (fellatio, cunnilingus) are against the law in many places.

Most laws concerning sexual behavior are state laws, which vary widely from state to state. For instance, in some states homosexual behavior is legal and in others it is not. Prostitution is legal in some counties of Nevada and illegal in other counties of Nevada and in all other states. From state to state oral-genital and anal-genital intercourse, adultery, fornication, and seduction vary from minor crimes (misdemeanors) to major crimes (felonies). The age at which one may engage in sexual activity or obtain contraceptives also varies from state to state. Although we cannot list here all the laws regarding sexual behavior in the United States, we can discuss general legal trends for a variety of behaviors.

CONSENSUAL SEXUAL BEHAVIORS

consensual sexual behaviors
Sexual behaviors that occur between adults who agree to participate.

Consensual sexual behaviors are behaviors that occur between adults who agree to participate. When considered crimes, these sexual behaviors must be considered "victimless" crimes. Such behaviors are designated illegal on the grounds of immorality; the laws are intended to protect the moral values of the society, as well as the societal structure.

As mentioned earlier, the law typically defines with whom one should have sexual relations, where one should have sexual relations, and what kind of sexual relations one should have. Our laws reflect the Judeo-Christian ethic that sexual intercourse is appropriate only within the institution of marriage. These laws reflect the society's concern with the stability of the family and property rights. Laws against nonmarital intercourse attempt to ensure that those to whom property is passed are legitimate heirs of the father. Consequently, married women often have been more harshly prosecuted than married men for engaging in extramarital intercourse. If a woman has a child, she can rest assured that it is hers; she does not have to worry about children who are not hers becoming heirs to her estate. If a man's wife has a child, however, he cannot be absolutely sure that it is his. Thus, to ensure that only a man's legitimate children become heirs to his estate, taboos against extramarital intercourse are much stricter for women than for men.

fornication
Sexual intercourse between people who are not married to each other.

adultery
Sexual intercourse between a married person and someone other than his or her spouse.

The two legal categories for nonmarital sexual intercourse are fornication and adultery. **Fornication** occurs when unmarried adults have intercourse. **Adultery** occurs when a married person has sexual intercourse with someone other than his or her spouse. In states where both fornication and adultery are crimes, fornication is usually considered the lesser crime. Laws against cohabitation also exist in some states. Many states have laws against homosexual behavior. These laws stem from biblical injunctions against sexual contact with a person of the same gender. The laws against homosexual behavior have been exceedingly punitive. People with a homosexual orientation have been tortured and put to death throughout Western history. During the Middle Ages homosexual men were tied with bundles of kindling wood called faggots (the origin of the slang term used today) and were burned at the stake. In colonial America homosexuals were put to death by drowning and burning.

Sodomy refers to a variety of sex acts, including oral and anal sex, sex between individuals of the same sex, and sex with an animal. Although sodomy laws apply to both heterosexual and homosexual behavior, they are invoked more often against homosexual people (Wing, 1986). Most arrests for sodomy between same-gender partners take place when the act occurs in a public place such as a restroom, theater, or park. In these cases sexual conduct in public may be the issue rather than, or as well as, homosexuality.

The majority of homosexual arrests are made not for sodomy but for solicitation or for loitering in public areas. Most homosexual solicitation is based on subtle gestures and comments that are not highly offensive to the public. However, the judicial system in some cities has occasionally used controversial practices to make arrests for homosexual solicitation. Plainclothes policemen attempt to entice homosexual men to make sexual propositions. If the proposition or "solicitation" occurs, another police officer standing nearby arrests the homosexual man.

The vast majority of homosexuals are never arrested for solicitation or sodomy because they limit their sexual behavior to private places. However, living under the threat of prosecution for having a sexual relationship with another consenting adult is an uncomfortable situation.

A number of sexual behaviors are illegal because of limitations on the places deemed appropriate for nudity and sexual behavior. In this category are transvestism, voyeurism, exhibitionism, and indecent exposure. Most people convicted of these crimes are men (Masters, Johnson, and Kolodny, 1986), since they are more likely than women to engage in such behaviors. Punishment for exhibitionism and voyeurism is usually relatively light. Although the offender sometimes gets several years in jail, more typically he is required to obtain psychiatric help.

Transvestism, voyeurism, and exhibitionism are also discussed in Chapter 20.

In addition to focusing on with whom one may have sexual relationships and where these sexual relationships may occur, laws are concerned with types of sexual activities. Many of the laws concerning the sexual behavior of consenting adults are derived from the Judeo-Christian ethic that views procreation as the only justification for sexual intercourse. According to this ethic, any act that does not provide the possibility of conception is sinful. In medieval Europe the Catholic Church severely restricted marital sexual behaviors. Intercourse was legal in only the man-on-top position and was illegal on Sundays, Wednesdays, and Fridays and during the days before Easter and Christmas (Taylor, 1970).

Many laws today define nonprocreative sexual behaviors as criminal. Oral-genital intercourse and anal-genital intercourse are categorized as sodomy and are classified as felonies in many states. Penalties for these crimes are often severe. Prison sentences for sodomy range from 6 months to 21 years (Dolgin and Dolgin, 1980).

Although some states have repealed their sodomy laws, such laws are still in effect in many states (Mueller, 1980). They usually pertain to all adults, whether married, unmarried, heterosexual, or homosexual. Many people oppose sodomy laws because they feel that consenting adults should be able to do whatever they want in private as long as they do not harm anyone. Opponents believe, for example, that a married couple who want to have oral sexual relations in the privacy of their home should have that privilege. Furthermore, they believe that two men who choose to have homosexual relations in private should enjoy that privilege. The right to privacy in consensual adult sexual behavior is increasing as more states repeal their sodomy laws.

PROSTITUTION

Prostitution refers to the exchange of sexual services for money. Although prostitution is legal in many countries, such as Great Britain, Germany, and Sweden, it is illegal in all states in the United States except Nevada. It is legal only in some counties of Nevada. Because prostitution is voluntary on the client's and the prostitute's part, it is often regarded as a victimless crime. Thus the laws against prostitution are designed to protect not the prostitutes or clients, but the social order, which is seen as threatened by the immorality of prostitution. Many persons believe that prostitution lowers moral standards, contributes to criminal sexual behavior, and undermines social structures such as the family.

prostitution
Exchange of sexual services for money.

Is prostitution truly a victimless crime? It has been argued that a prostitute's involvement in prostitution is far from voluntary. Prostitutes resort to prostitution to support themselves or their family when no other employment alternative appears available, to escape an oppressive family situation, or to support a drug habit (Hobson, 1986). Prostitutes are also victims because in their daily lives they face the threat of violence from their pimps, their customers, and the police.

Female Prostitutes

Most prostitutes are women who sell their sexual services to men. There are several different types of female prostitutes. Streetwalkers solicit customers on the streets or in bars. They tend to be from lower socioeconomic classes, and they usually charge less for their services than do other types of prostitutes. Because of their open solicitation, streetwalkers are more visible and thus more susceptible to arrest than other prostitutes. The majority of streetwalkers are arrested and serve a number of short jail sentences during their careers.

Most streetwalkers work for a pimp, a man who offers protection from abusive customers, competing prostitutes, and police. The pimp may provide the prostitute with a place to live and some degree of emotional security. However, he often demands a large portion of the prostitute's income. Although the pimp may take care of the prostitute when she is cooperating, he may become threatening and violent if she tries to terminate her relationship with him.

Another type of prostitute works in a brothel. A brothel is a house in which a group of prostitutes works. Brothels are common in many countries, but they are not nearly as common in the United States as they were in early American history. However, Nevada has a number of legal brothels. Brothels are usually managed by a madam, who also serves as the hostess. The madam often takes about half of a prostitute's earnings. The brothel offers a prostitute protection from offensive clients and the possibility of arrest, as well as a place to meet customers and a room for sexual activity.

Call girls are another type of prostitute. They are the least visible and best paid prostitutes. Whereas streetwalkers and brothel prostitutes tend to come from lower socioeconomic classes, call girls are typically from middle-class backgrounds. Call girls frequently accompany their customers as an escort, as well as provide sexual services; they often spend the entire evening or night with the customer. Most call girls work alone and keep all of their income. They also tend to be selective about their clients. They usually obtain clients by personal referral and have a number of regular customers. Since they tend to have little public visibility, their risk of arrest is low.

Massage Parlors

Massage parlors provide another form of prostitution. Although there are legitimate massage parlors, many parlors throughout the United States offer sexual services in addition to massages. Massage and masturbation (M & M) are often offered in massage parlors as well as oral sex and, less frequently, sexual intercourse (see accompanying box). Massage parlors generally establish

A Personal Glimpse

Working at a Massage Parlor

I am 24 years old. I used to earn 125 dollars per week as a nanny. Now I work in a massage parlor in a large midwestern city and earn 150 dollars or more per day. The other women who work with me are in their midtwenties. Most have been in the business for approximately 6 years. Only one of the seven women is married.

When I arrive at work, I put on a bathing suit. Our state law requires us to wear panty hose and shoes also. We can *not* wear transparent clothing. Some of the other women wear sexy lingerie, while others wear bathing suits. When a customer walks in the door, he can either ask for a specific person or ask to see all of the women who are working at the time he enters the massage parlor. If he doesn't care who takes care of him, we take turns and if it is your turn, you take the person. There is definitely competition for customers among the workers; if one woman has a lot of requests, the other women tend to get jealous.

Once the man has been paired with a woman, he is taken to one of the eight rooms in our building. Four of the rooms are small with low platform beds on the floor. The other four rooms vary: one room, called the mirror room, has mirrors on all walls and the ceiling; two rooms have whirlpool baths in them, and the last room has a large marble bathtub in it. The prices are explained to the customer. The man is told that he will be given a *full body* massage. As we say full body we wink and we assume he knows that we will touch his penis as well as the rest of his body. The prices are as follows: A massage given by a topless woman costs $30 and lasts 20 minutes. A massage given by a nude woman costs $100 and lasts 1

hour. The customer is told what he can touch on the woman, and this varies from woman to woman. Certain rooms cost more money. For example, the mirror room is an extra $10, and the room with the marble tub costs $25 extra. After the male indicates what he wants, we ask him to sign a form indicating that he is not a police officer, vice squad officer, or federal government employee. The man then pays, and I leave the room with his money and filled out form. I don't think anyone uses their real name on the form, and all of us [the workers] use false names at work. Almost all of our customers pay cash. Very few use charge cards. All workers are paid in cash at the end of the shift.

There are male managers or bouncers in the building to help us out in case the customer turns out to be a nut. The male workers keep a low profile and generally are not seen by the customer. All rooms are equipped with an intercom system so the male bouncers can periodically listen in to make sure we are all right.

Typically, we give a massage and then masturbate the customer to orgasm. If the guy has been drinking and can't ejaculate, we tell him his time is up, and out he goes. The customers are a mixed bunch, from blue collar workers to professionals, including doctors and lawyers. Most of the men are in their midthirties. Our busiest times are after 4 PM.

I figure I will continue this job for a while longer, accumulate cash, and then finish my last 2 years of college. As a part-time student it is taking too long to finish my degree.

AUTHORS' FILES

---

rules the women must follow to avoid arrest from undercover policemen—for example, no direct propositions and no mention of "extras" (i.e., sexual services) until the late stages of the massage, when the customer is usually sexually aroused (Prus and Irini, 1980).

Male Prostitutes

Although the great majority of prostitutes are women who sell sexual services to men, there are also many male prostitutes. Men who sell sexual services to

Male prostitutes, often called hustlers, work in a variety of settings similar to female prostitutes.

gigolo
Man who sells his sexual services to women.

hustler
Man who provides sexual services to other men in exchange for money.

women are called **gigolos.** Gigolos function more like call girls than like other types of female prostitutes. They usually are social companions as well as sexual partners for their customers, who tend to be wealthy middle-aged women who want the attention of attractive young men. Men who provide sexual services to other men in exchange for money are called **hustlers.** Male prostitution with male clients seems to be much more prevalent than male prostitution with female clients.

Male prostitutes work in a variety of settings just as female prostitutes do. Some male prostitutes work on the streets and in bars and homosexual baths; others work in establishments similar to brothels and function more like call girls. One difference between male and female prostitutes is that most male prostitutes have another source of income. One reason for this difference may be the nature of the sexual response of males and females. Women are capable of having sex as often as they choose. Men, on the other hand, can have only a limited number of erections and orgasms each day. Thus the number of clients men can service in one day is limited. This might also be the reason that most male prostitutes are very young; young men are more capable of repeated orgasms than are older men.

Prostitution and the Law

As mentioned previously, prostitution is illegal in every state of the United States except Nevada (Mueller, 1980). Over the years people have debated the usefulness of antiprostitution laws. There are two basic arguments in favor of the laws. The first is that if prostitution were not a criminal offense, many more individuals might become prostitutes and the regulation of prostitution would be much more difficult. The second is that the government is responsible for regulating public morality and that the absence of laws against prostitution might suggest government support of prostitution.

There are also arguments against defining prostitution as a criminal offense. One argument is that the enforcement of antiprostitution laws has traditionally discriminated against women. The vast majority of arrests for prostitution involve female prostitutes rather than either male prostitutes or male clients. In San Francisco in 1977, 2,101 female prostitutes were arrested but only 512 male prostitutes and 325 clients were arrested (Lynch and Neckes, 1978). Occasional efforts to arrest or at least publicize the names of male clients have met with protests because the clients are often "respectable" men whose lives would be ruined by such exposure. This protective attitude has not been extended to the female prostitutes.

Feminists, in an attempt to remedy what they view as an inequality in the legal system, have historically sought stricter laws against pimps and criminal penalties for men who procure prostitutes' services. However, even when such legislation was enacted, the laws were never enforced (Hobson, 1987). In fact, according to Hobson, such attempts resulted only in the unintended consequences of greater penalties and increased social stigma against prostitutes.

Another argument against the antiprostitution laws is that by making prostitution illegal, we are making prostitutes into criminals. Prostitutes are often sentenced to jail for short periods. During jail sentences these prostitutes may be influenced by other types of criminals. In addition, prostitutes who have police records often find it difficult to move into more legitimate types of work. Thus most prostitutes return to prostitution after getting out of jail.

Antiprostitution laws also put prostitutes in a vulnerable situation. Since their work is illegal, they can be mistreated by clients and pimps, who know that prostitutes cannot report such abuses to the police. Thus clients and pimps may beat, rape, or otherwise mistreat prostitutes. Antiprostitution laws may actually facilitate crimes against prostitutes.

Some people see antiprostitution laws as an invasion of both the client's and the prostitute's right to privacy. Many people argue that if two adults agree to participate in an activity that does not hurt anyone else, they should be allowed to do so.

Another argument against antiprostitution laws is that the laws appear to increase the prevalence of certain types of crime rather than decrease them. For example, when prostitution was legalized in Denmark, the number of reported rapes dropped by 70%. When prostitution was declared illegal in Australia, the number of rapes reported increased by 149%.

Still another argument against antiprostitution laws is that they are ineffective. Despite antiprostitution laws, prostitution flourishes in most states. In addition, enforcement of the antiprostitution laws is expensive. Court costs alone run from $500 to $1,100 for each prostitution arrest. San Francisco spends over $2 million per year on the arrest, defense, prosecution, and imprisonment of prostitutes (Lynch and Neckes, 1978). Given that attempts to enforce antiprostitution laws have not eliminated prostitution, many individuals argue that the taxpayers' money could be put to better use.

Many groups and individuals are calling for a change in antiprostitution laws. The National Organization of Women advocated the elimination of

Appeals Court Rules: Prostitution Charges Violated Women's Rights

WAUSAU (AP)—Police violated the constitutional rights of four women who were arrested for prostitution while dozens of men paying them for sexual favors were not, a state appeals court ruled Wednesday.

The women were discriminated against based on sex, violating their constitutional right to equal protection, the 3rd District Court of Appeals said in a unanimous decision upholding the dismissal of charges.

A lawyer called the ruling precedent-setting and predicted it would force police to rethink the way they investigate vice crimes.

According to court records, Michelle Davis, Sheila McCollum and Christine Hill, all of Minnesota, and Sandra Peterson, a Wisconsin resident, were arrested Oct. 8, 1989, outside Club 37 in rural Eau Claire.

Some 100 male customers, including four undercover officers, paid $7 to get into the club for what officers said was a private party featuring nude dancing by a group called "Sexy and Sweet," court records said.

A Milwaukee detective, Donald Hurrle, called in to assist the investigation, testified at a pretrial proceeding that 50 to 75 male customers fondled the woman and committed other acts of illegal sexual contact in exchange for money.

But he and another detective said no men were arrested because the focus of the investigation was on female dancers. Besides, the officers said, they couldn't identify any male patrons.

In its ruling Wednesday, the appeals court upheld Eau Claire County Circuit Judge Gregory Peterson's dismissal of prostitution charges against the women.

"The police intentionally focused their investigation on, and made their arrests of, only the female violators," the appeals court said. "There is no important governmental objective substantially related to this enforcement scheme. As such, the state selectively prosecuted the four women in violation of the equal protection clause" of the 14th Amendment.

The state argued that arresting the women served two objectives—the women represented the smallest and most manageable group of violators and the prosecution of them would result in maximum deterrence.

The court disagreed, saying deterrence would have been better served by the arrest of some local citizens involved in illicit behavior.

Robert McKinley of Chippewa Falls, Davis' lawyer, said the ruling is precedent-setting in the sense the court considered equal protection claims of women arrested for prostitution.

"The court has basically said that if you are there and observe men and women committing essentially the same crime, if you are going to arrest somebody, you have to arrest them both," McKinley said.

NEWS of the 90's

From Wisconsin State Journal, 1990.

antiprostitution laws in 1973. The American Civil Liberties Union has begun to fight all laws that prohibit sexual activities between consenting adults, including prostitution. Also, former prostitute Margo St. James has established a union for prostitutes called COYOTE (Call Off Your Old Tired Ethics) not only to fight against antiprostitution laws but also to be an advocate for prostitutes.

There are two main alternatives to the antiprostitution laws currently in effect. Prostitution could be either legalized or decriminalized. If prostitution were legalized, the government would in effect be condoning it. Under such circumstances the government could regulate prostitution. The government could require that prostitutes be registered and follow various licensing procedures such as having periodic checks for sexually transmitted disease. Then prostitutes would also have to pay taxes on their income. In many European countries today prostitutes are registered and licensed in this way.

The alternative to legalization is decriminalization. With decriminalization, the criminal penalties for prostitution would be removed but prostitutes would be neither registered nor licensed. With decriminalization prostitution would not be condoned by the government. Some individuals prefer decriminalization to legalization because prostitutes would not be totally regulated by the government but would have some control over their own work. Others prefer decriminalization because they do not want the government to condone prostitution.

Children in Prostitution

Because prostitutes and their clients both consent to sexual relations, prostitution is often called a victimless crime. While that notion in itself may seem inaccurate considering the prostitutes' plight, it is especially inaccurate when considering teenage prostitution. As many as 2.4 million teenagers in the United States are prostitutes (U.S. General Accounting Office, 1982). Teenagers who have run away from home often become prostitutes because they have no other means of earning money. As one teenage prostitute explained:

> There's no doors opened to us. . . . How are you going to be able to hold down a job if you have no high school diploma, if you're not able to take a shower every day, if you don't have clean clothes to wear to work. And let's say you came out here because of "certain circumstances" at home. You're scared out here.
>
> Hersch, 1988, p. 35

The majority of teenage prostitutes come from dysfunctional families. Hersch (1988) reported that approximately 70% of runaways who go to emergency shelters are victims of physical and sexual abuse. Teenage male prostitutes also are likely to come from unstructured and unsupervised homes and to have felt rejected by peers at school (Price, Scanlon, and Janus, 1984).

In addition to trying to obtain a means of survival, teenage prostitutes are often seeking adult affection and attention and believe at first that prostitution promises a life of glamour and adventure. In reality, children involved in prostitution often suffer emotional distress and have a poor adjustment to life. Many have difficulty finding other employment because of the stigma of their prostitution and their dissatisfaction with the lower pay of a regular job (Burgess et al., 1984).

PORNOGRAPHY

The definitions of *pornography* and the related term *obscenity* have often been debated. The term **pornography** comes from a Greek word that means "writing of prostitutes." It generally refers to written, visual, or spoken material that is sexually arousing. It can range from what is often called "soft-core" pornography to "hard-core" pornography. Soft-core pornography is often defined as material that is suggestive but not explicit in portraying sexual acts. Hard-core pornography, on the other hand, explicitly portrays either the genitals or sexual acts. A picture of a naked woman in *Playboy* might be considered soft-core pornography, while a picture showing sexual violence against a woman would be considered hard-core pornography. **Obscenity** comes from a Latin word that means filthy, dirty, disgusting, or offensive. Obscene materials are considered offensive to morality and virtue and therefore to society. Thus, although a great deal of overlap exists between the two concepts, they have somewhat different meanings. What is sexually arousing is not necessarily considered disgusting and offensive, and what is disgusting and offensive is not necessarily sexually arousing. Unlike pornography, however, obscenity is a term with legal meaning. Pornographic material that is considered obscene is prohibited by the law. Clearly more hard-core than soft-core pornography falls into the category of obscene material.

The first obscenity case in the United States was tried in Pennsylvania in 1815. In *Commonwealth v. Sharpless* several men were charged with exhibiting a painting of a nude man and woman. After 1815 government prosecution of people for selling or exhibiting sexual material increased. Contraceptives were banned as well as scientific writings about contraceptives, abortion, and sterilization. Anthony Comstock founded and led the Society for the Suppression of Vice, a group whose purpose was to suppress the spread of any sexually oriented material. In 1873 Comstock persuaded Congress to pass a law banning all sexually related materials from the mail. The Comstock laws led to the prosecution of Margaret Sanger, an early advocate of birth control and women's rights.

Margaret Sanger and her fight for women's right to birth control are discussed in Chapter 1.

One problem with the laws on obscenity is the difficulty of defining the term. In the 1800s obscenity meant almost any sexually oriented material, including sexual information and contraceptive information. As a result of such laws, many books such as Henry Havelock Ellis' *Studies in the Psychology of Sex*, James Joyce's *Ulysses*, D.H. Lawrence's *Lady Chatterley's Lover*, and Henry Miller's *Tropic of Cancer* were banned. A breakthrough occurred in 1933 when *Ulysses* was declared acceptable for importation by a New York District Federal Court in *United States v. "Ulysses."* The reason given was that it had literary merit and was not written only for pornographic purposes. This decision suggested that books must be judged on their overall purpose and effect rather than banned solely because they have some erotic content. In 1957 the U.S. Supreme Court, in *Ross v. United States*, defined obscenity as sexually explicit material that offended contemporary community standards and whose dominant intent was purely erotic (Moretti, 1984). In 1966 the U.S. Supreme Court decided, in *Memoirs v. Massachusetts*, which centered on the erotic classic *Fanny Hill*, that obscene material was erotic material without redeeming social value. Thus three criteria emerged by which to determine whether material was obscene. First, the dominant theme of the work as a whole had to appeal to a purely erotic interest in sex. Second, it had to be offensive to contemporary community standards. Third, it had to be without serious literary, artistic, political, or scientific value.

As soon as the three criteria were established, difficulties arose in applying them. Since values differ from community to community, it was not clear what community values would be employed. Furthermore, the meaning of "contemporary" was not evident. In addition, the author's or artist's motives were not easy to determine.

In 1973 the U.S. Supreme Court decided in *Miller v. California* that the three-part definition of obscenity no longer applied. The court ruled that local communities should judge for themselves what they consider to be obscene and should be free to prosecute the producers and distributors of material they find obscene even if those individuals live in and produce their materials in another community. Thus if one community judges a particular movie to be obscene, the community can prosecute the people involved in making the movie (even though the movie was not produced in that community). Furthermore, books that are banned in one community may be sold legally in other communities. The lack of a generally accepted definition of obscenity continues today. This standard presents problems because it is impossible to predict what any given community will judge to be obscene at any particular time.

Effects of Pornography

The public tends to be concerned about the effects of pornography. In a recent poll (Pornography: a poll, 1986) nearly two thirds of the respondents reported being "very" or "fairly" concerned about the pervasiveness of pornography in the United States. When respondents were asked about the effects of sexually explicit movies, magazines, and books, 65% reported believing that such materials cause people to be more sexually promiscuous, 61% said that such materials encourage people to consider women as sex objects, 56% said that such materials lead people to commit rape, and 54% said that such materials lead people to commit acts of sexual violence. The legislation on pornography and obscenity has been based on the assumption that pornographic and obscene materials will have negative effects either on individual people or on the society as a whole.

In 1970 a commission on obscenity and pornography, composed of clergy, teachers, health care professionals, researchers, and legal authorities, concluded that "there is no warrant for continued governmental interference with the full freedom of adults to read, obtain, or view whatever such material they wish" (The Report of the Commission on Obscenity and Pornography, 1970). They went on to say that they had found "no evidence to date that exposure to explicit sexual material plays a significant role in the causation of delinquent or criminal behavior among youth or adults." Some of the evidence that was used to arrive at this conclusion is reviewed here.

Some data indicate that pornographic materials are not commonly used by individuals who commit crimes of any sort. For example, according to a national survey (Abelson et al., 1971), the typical user of pornography is male, college educated, married, 30 to 40 years old, and above average in socioeconomic status. These individuals are not generally considered to have low moral standards or to be prone to antisocial sexual acts.

In some studies sex offenders have been compared with other types of offenders to see whether they have had different experiences with pornography or whether they respond differently to pornography. In one study the sexual histories of sex offenders, other types of offenders, and nonoffenders were compared. Surprisingly few differences in experience with pornography were found among the three groups of people (Gebhard et al., 1965).

Goldstein and associates (1971) compared the experiences of rapists, pedophiles, homosexuals, transsexuals, and control subjects with pornographic materials. The individuals in the two sexual offender groups (rapists and pedophiles) apparently had less exposure to pornography during adolescence than the control individuals. The same results were found when the sex offenders were asked about their recent experiences with pornography; rapists and pedophiles reported significantly less use of pornography than the control individuals. In summary, early comparisons of sex offenders with persons who are not sex offenders did not provide any evidence that pornography increases the likelihood of antisocial sexual behavior.

Further evidence for the lack of a relationship between pornography and crime came from the change in pornography restrictions in Denmark. In 1969 the Danish Parliament removed restrictions against the dissemination of pornographic materials to individuals over 16 years of age. The number of pornographic materials produced and the number of Danish people who purchased pornography initially increased. After a few years, however, the sale of pornographic materials to Danish people decreased. Apparently the Danish people became satiated with pornography. The Danish pornographic industry now serves mainly tourists and export markets.

The legalization and increased availability of pornography in Denmark paralleled a decrease in the incidence of reported sex crimes (Kutchinsky, 1973). The rate of reported child molestation cases, for example, dropped by about 80% after the legalization of pornography. *The Report of the Commission on Obscenity and Pornography* suggested that this decrease was probably attributable to the greater availability of pornographic materials because no other changes, such as in law enforcement practices, police reporting, or data-collecting procedures, occurred at the same time.

In 1985 a second commission was appointed to examine the effects of pornography on society. The Attorney General's Commission on Pornography was composed of 11 members, including judges, lawyers, politicians, and mental health professionals. Their final report was issued in 1986. The conclusions from this second report differed from those of the 1970 commission. In the 1986 report the commission concluded that "available evidence strongly supports the hypothesis that substantial exposure to sexually violent materials . . . bears a causal relationship to antisocial acts of sexual violence and, for some subgroups, possibly to unlawful acts of sexual violence." This conclusion was based in part on research evidence that was obtained after the 1970 commission completed its work.

Research conducted after the 1970 commission report indicates that pornography involving aggression against women may, in fact, increase the tendency of males to behave more aggressively toward women and to be more accepting of violence toward women (Donnerstein, Linz, and Penrod, 1987; Russell, 1988; Zillmann and Bryant, 1989). A number of studies have demonstrated that even a brief exposure to sexually aggressive pornography can affect attitudes. For example, Check and Malamuth (1985) exposed some college students to a depiction of a woman portrayed as sexually aroused by sexual violence. Others were exposed to a control condition. All of the students were then exposed to a depiction of a rape. The subjects who had seen the woman portrayed as enjoying sexual violence were significantly more likely than the control subjects to perceive the second rape victim as suffering less trauma, to believe that she enjoyed the rape, and to believe that women in general enjoy sexual violence. Others have also reported that exposure to sexually violent pornography affects men's attitudes toward women and sexual violence (Linz, Donnerstein, and Penrod, 1984; Demare, Briere, and Lips, 1988; Linz, Donnerstein, and Adams, 1989).

Other studies have demonstrated that brief exposures to violent pornography involving aggression can affect behavior as well as attitudes. For example, Donnerstein and Berkowitz (1981) conducted a study in which male college students were angered by either a male or a female confederate. The males were then shown a neutral film; an erotic, nonaggressive film; an erotic, aggressive film in which the female victim responded positively; or an erotic, aggressive film in which the female victim responded negatively. After viewing the films, the male subjects were allowed to administer shocks to the confederate when he or she made mistakes on a learning task. They found that the aggressive films had no effect on the shock levels administered to the male confederate but that both of the erotic, aggressive films increased aggression against women. Similar results have been obtained in other studies (Donnerstein, 1980).

The Attorney General's Commission on Pornography defined nonviolent pornography as two types: material that is "degrading" and material that is not. Degrading sexual material was defined as that depicting degradation, domination, subordination, or humiliation. The commission concluded that substantial exposure to degrading but nonviolent sexually explicit material may increase the acceptance of certain negative attitudes toward women. For ex-

Pornographic movies.

ample, the commission suggested that such material may contribute to the view that rape is not serious, that rape victims are somehow responsible for being raped, that women like to be forced to engage in sexual activities, and that women who say no really mean yes. The commission further concluded that "substantial exposure to materials of this type bears some causal relationship to the level of sexual violence, sexual coercion, or unwanted sexual aggression in the population so exposed." Research tends to support this conclusion.

Several investigators have examined the effects of nonviolent but degrading pornography. For the most part brief exposures to nonviolent pornography have not been demonstrated to increase aggressive behavior specifically toward women, although in some cases it has caused a general increase in aggression (Donnerstein, Linz, and Penrod, 1987). However, Check (1985; Check and Guloien, 1989) and Zillman and Bryant (1982, 1984) have studied the effects of massive exposure to degrading but nonviolent pornography. Their research indicates that longer term exposure causes males to become more callous and domineering in their attitudes toward women. Zillman and Bryant (1982, 1984) found that 6 weeks of exposure to nonviolent but degrading sexual material resulted in increased acceptance of rape myths and sexual callousness. Check and Guloien (1989) found that viewing three nonviolent but degrading videotapes over a 1- to 2-week period increased men's self-reported likelihood of committing a rape.

The research presented has demonstrated that brief exposures to violent pornography can negatively affect both attitudes and behavior toward women and that long-term exposure to degrading but nonviolent pornography can also negatively affect attitudes toward women. However, this research indicates only that sexually violent and degrading pornography results in attitude or behavior change toward women; the research does not indicate that viewing nonviolent, nondegrading, sexually explicit material can increase violence against women. In fact, Check and Guloien (1989) found that nonviolent, nondegrading sexual material did not have any of the negative attitudinal and behavioral effects associated with both violent and degrading pornographic materials.

The Attorney General's Commission could not reach a consensus about nonviolent, nondegrading sexual material. Some of the members thought that such material may be harmful in some instances and beneficial in others (e.g., in the context of sex education). Others thought that it was "appropriate to identify the class as harmful as a whole." More research will be needed before definitive conclusions can be drawn.

Clearly, the conclusions of the 1970 study and the 1986 Meese Commission Report vary remarkably. Osanka and Johann (1989) argue that the 1970 U.S. study was simply biased in favor of the pornography industry. They further argue that the 1970 study dealt with a type of pornography that was much milder than the pornographic materials available today.

Others have criticized the conclusion of the 1986 study. Nobile and Nadler (1986) argue that the panel's determination was a foregone conclusion even before the commission members were appointed. Indeed, the orders from President Reagan calling for a "new look" at pornography and the commission's subsequent composition suggest from the start the verdict that pornography is harmful. Nobile and Nadler contend that to secure the appropriate conclusion, the commission was packed with priests, child abuse experts, and criminologists but included no men and women who stress sexual freedom and civil liberties.

Another criticism has arisen from the Meese Commission's reliance on the "totality of the evidence" to support their conclusion. Baron and Straus, two researchers who presented evidence to the commission, point out that the "totality of the evidence" approach allowed the commission to give as much weight to the testimony of antipornography zealots and religious authorities as to conscientiously conducted social research (Nobile and Nadler, 1986). Baron and Straus argue that the totality of the scientific evidence does not support a causal relationship between pornography and rape. They note that even Donnerstein's research suggests a reduction in aggression after exposure to violent pornography. Baron and Straus maintain that the commission ignored or distorted the scientific evidence because it was more interested in censoring pornography than in eliminating the violence the commission "found" pornography to cause. Nobile and Nadler argue that Reagan's attack on pornography was designed to blame pornographers for the plight of battered wives in order to excuse his administration's closing shelters for women. Unfortunately, as Pally, a member of the Feminist Anti-Censorship Taskforce, argued, "If we go after pornography when rape, battery and discrimination thrived for so long without it, we'll still be left with rape, battery, and discrimination" (Nobile and Nadler, 1986).

Feminist Views on Pornography

Many feminists are also concerned about the effects of certain types of pornography (Assiter, 1989). They tend to draw a distinction between eroticism and pornography (see accompanying box). They define eroticism as the portrayal of sexuality in ways that do not encourage exploitation or violence and

Gloria Steinem's View of Erotica and Pornography

Erotica is rooted in *eros* or passionate love, and thus in the idea of positive choice, free will, the yearning for a particular person. (Interestingly, the definition of erotica leaves open the question of gender.) "Pornography" begins with a root meaning "prostitution" or "female captives," thus letting us know that the subject is not mutual love, or love at all, but domination and violence against women.

The first is erotic: a mutually pleasurable, sexual expression between people who have enough power to be there by positive choice. It may or may not strike a sense-memory in the viewer, or be creative enough to make the unknown seem real; but it doesn't require us to identify with a conqueror or a victim. It is truly sensuous, and may give us a contagion of pleasure.

The second is pornographic: its message is violence, dominance, and conquest. It is sex being used to reinforce some inequality, or to create one, or to tell us the lie that pain and humiliation (ours or someone else's) are really the same as pleasure. If we are to feel anything, we must identify with conqueror or victim. That means we can only experience pleasure through the adoption of some degree of sadism or masochism. It also means that we may feel diminished by the role of conquerer, or enraged, humiliated, and vengeful by sharing identity with the victim.

From Steinem, 1978.

Many feminists are concerned about the harmful effects of the exploitation of women in some pornography.

contend that erotic material is not objectionable. They define pornography as "propaganda against women" because, they say, it fosters the view that violence against women is a normal and acceptable part of sexual expression. Thus it is the violence rather than the sexual content that concerns them. Feminists are against pornography when it portrays women as sex objects and victims and encourages a view of sexuality that equates pleasure with power. They believe that seeing women as passive sexual objects who enjoy being dominated will cause both men and women to think that men should dominate and women should be subjugated. Therefore individuals may think of sexuality in terms of aggression and dominance rather than in terms of love and tenderness.

While almost all feminists are troubled by pornography, they are divided on what should be done about it to best promote women's rights (Leo, 1986; Osanka and Johann, 1989). Law professor Catharine MacKinnon hailed the Meese Commission Report and for years has been pushing for antipornography legislation to more adequately protect the civil rights of women. Other feminists argue that women should fight for liberation, not special protection from the state. They fear that protectionist attitudes from the state may actually hurt women. For example, some feminists oppose censorship of pornography for fear that material concerning feminist issues such as abortion, contraception, and control of one's own body might be censored as well.

Child Pornography

Whether degrading or nondegrading, violent or nonviolent, obscene or not, child pornography generates greater wrath from the legal system than pornography involving adults. Largely because of the harmful effects on children involved in pornography and the states' compelling need to protect children, laws regarding child pornography are much stricter and more vigorously enforced than those involving other pornography. State and federal statutes allow prosecution of both producers and distributors of child pornography, and statutes in 13 states also make it illegal to possess child pornography. Thus, through strict enforcement of statutes such as the Protection of Children Against Sexual Exploitation Act of 1977, commercially produced child pornography has declined (Cohn, 1988).

In 1982 the U.S. Supreme Court held in *New York v. Ferber* that it is constitutional to ban distribution of material "depicting children engaged in sexual conduct" without requiring that the material be considered legally obscene. A lower court had decided that the statute involved violated the first amendment and that the statute was overly broad because it could be used to prohibit realistic educational materials dealing with adolescent sex. However, the Supreme Court concluded that states are permitted greater license in regulating child pornography because of the states' compelling interest in protecting the physical and psychological well-being of children. The Supreme Court further stated that whether or not a sexually explicit depiction is obscene bears no relation to the primary concern of whether a child has been psychologically or physically harmed in the production of that work. Because children under a certain age cannot legally consent to sexual activity, the production of child pornography often entails the criminal sexual abuse of children who are made to perform sexual acts. Thus child pornography is in many cases evidence of sexual abuse.

The defendant in *New York v. Ferber* argued that it is the producer who harms the children, not the distributor; however, the court agreed with the state that the circulation of the photographs exacerbates the psychological harm to the child by haunting him or her throughout life. Furthermore, only by prosecuting distributors can sexual exploitation of children be effectively stopped, especially because most production is clandestine while the distribution is more visible.

In addition to suffering the torment of knowing that pornographic materials of them are circulating, children involved in pornography often bear other psychological scars and have poor adjustment to life. Many view themselves as objects to be sold. They feel dirty and unwanted and become bitter toward adults. Some wind up as drug addicts and prostitutes. Many suffer from anxiety, depression, guilt, and self-destructive and antisocial behavior (Burgess et al., 1984).

Evidence suggests that child pornography is harmful not only to the children depicted, but to other children as well. While a direct causal link between child pornography and child molestation has not been scientifically established, investigators of child pornography cases say that child molestation evidence turns up in about 30% of pornography arrests (Gest, 1989). Law enforcement officials have cited cases in which child molesters used pornography, including child pornography, to seduce children (Osanka and Johann, 1989).

Pornographers induce children to pose for pornographic photographs, videotapes, or movies in exchange for money or friendship, by fraud (the child may not know photographs will be used as pornography), or by threats. As with prostitution, some children become involved in pornography to survive after running away from home. Others are lured into it by other children, neighbors, or relatives.

RAPE

For a discussion of the nonlegal aspects of rape see Chapter 21.

Rape was addressed in Chapter 21; only the legal aspects of rape are considered here. As discussed in the previous chapter, in its most narrow sense rape occurs when a woman chooses not to have sexual intercourse with a particular man and that man nevertheless chooses to proceed without her consent. Many states have broadened the definition of rape to encompass any sexual activity without an individual's consent. A lack of consent occurs both when an individual has sex against his or her will (without consent) and when the individual is legally unable to consent to sexual relations because of age, mental retardation, mental illness, or incapacitated state from alcohol or drugs. Thus, even if the victim appeared to consent, the law in many cases treats sexual relations with an individual having particular characteristics as lacking consent because the individual was legally unable to give consent. Rape is treated as one of the most serious crimes, after murder and kidnapping. All 50 states prescribe harsh punishment for rape (Mueller, 1980).

Despite the seriousness with which rape is treated, it is one of the most underreported crimes. Only 10% to 50% of rapes are reported to the police (Williams, 1984). Rape is underreported for several reasons, which are more thoroughly discussed in Chapter 21. Two significant factors reducing the likelihood that a victim will report a rape are the victim's lack of confidence that the criminal justice system will punish the rapist and the victim's subsequent reluctance to undertake the often time-consuming and potentially humiliating procedures necessary to prosecute and only possibly convict the rapist. To convict a rapist, the victim must be prepared to report the experience in detail to the police and then to the court. The victim must be prepared to be cross-examined in a way that will suggest that she provoked the attack. Furthermore, in many states the victim may be asked to describe her previous sexual experiences.

These influences may help explain the findings of Williams (1984) that a woman is more likely to report her rape if it resembles the classic rape situation: a sexual assault by a stranger or acquaintance in a nonsocial situation with a threat or use of force for which the victim received medical treatment. Williams suggests that the classic rape furnishes the victim with evidence she needs to convince herself and others, including the police and court, that she was a rape victim. Thus many rapes and rapists that do not fit the classic rape presentation have gone and may continue to go unreported and unprosecuted. Perhaps this tendency will decline with the increasing awareness of acquaintance rape (see the accompanying box).

For a complete discussion of acquaintance rape, see Chapter 21.

Few rapists are convicted. Our legal system gives the benefit of the doubt to the accused, believing that it is better to free a guilty person than to imprison an innocent one. This concern with the unjust punishment of an innocent person has contributed to the failure to convict many rapists. When a woman reports a rape to the police, the police decide whether the charge seems valid before they search for and arrest the accused man. The police are most likely to believe a report of rape if the rapist and victim are strangers, if the rapist used physical violence, if the victim has evidence that proves that she tried to resist, and if the victim has a good reputation and is considered to be a respectable citizen. The police are much less likely to investigate a rape if the woman is an acquaintance of the rapist (see box), if she has no evidence that

Acquaintance Rape

Russell (1984) interviewed a random sample of 930 women from the San Francisco area. Forty-four percent of the women reported having experienced at least one incident of either rape or attempted rape. Only 16% of the incidents involved a rapist or attempted rapist who was a total stranger to the woman. The remainder of the rapes and attempted rapes were perpetrated by a man whom the woman knew. Twenty-three percent of the men were described as acquaintances, 16% as dates, and 10% as husbands or ex-husbands. Also included were lovers and ex-lovers, boyfriends, friends, friends of the family, authority figures, and other relatives.

Why is the prevalence of rape so high among individuals who know each other? In part, there is some tendency in our culture to believe that it is acceptable for a man to rape a woman in some circumstances. This is illustrated by a study conducted by Giarusso and associates (reported in Bart and O'Brien, 1985). They interviewed 432 high school students and found that between 36% and 45% of the males thought that it was "O.K." for a man to "force sex" on a woman if (1) he had spent a lot of money on the woman; (2) he was so "turned on he couldn't stop"; (3) he knew the woman had had sexual intercourse with other guys; (4) the woman was drunk or stoned; (5) the woman let him touch her above the waist; or (6) he had been dating the woman for a long time. Fifty-one percent of the males agreed that it was acceptable to "force sex" if the woman was "getting the man sexually excited." This study indicates that it is common for individuals to believe that rape (forced sex) is acceptable under certain conditions. It is hoped that the recent publicity given to acquaintance rape and date rape will make people more aware of the fact that rape is rape regardless of the circumstances in which it occurs.

---

the rapist used violence or that she resisted, or if she is not considered a respectable community member. A woman gets even less cooperation from the police if she accuses her husband of rape or if she accuses a person with whom she has had previous sexual relations.

If the police are not convinced that a rape occurred, they will not try to find and arrest the accused rapist. Thus, the police do not follow up many reported rapes. If the police are convinced that a rape did occur, they often urge the victim to press charges. Many victims are reluctant to do this; as a result of this reluctance, even fewer rapes are prosecuted. Even if the victim does not want to press charges, the police can. However, knowing that a rapist will not be convicted unless the victim testifies against him, the police seldom bring charges against the rapist when the victim is unwilling to do so. One study (Holmstrom and Burgess, 1978) found that about half of the reported rapes in Boston were not followed up either because the victim could not identify the rapist or because she did not want to press charges.

In court the defense attorney who represents the rapist traditionally uses the strategy of blaming the woman and suggesting that she was responsible for causing the rape. The defense attorney often asks needling and probing questions about her personal life and sexual history. If the defense attorney can establish that the woman knew the rapist, had sex with him in the past, frequented bars, was poor, wore sensual clothing, or was calm during the attack rather than resistant, the rapist will be unlikely to be convicted. This strategy is extremely effective in protecting the rapist. This defense further increases the number of rapists who are not convicted. A study by the Battelle Institute (Schram, 1978) found that although 1 of 4 rape complaints results in arrest, only 1 of 60 results in conviction.

Some states are changing their laws so that convicting rapists will be less difficult. Some states have adopted "rape shield laws" that prevent defense attorneys from questioning rape victims about their sexual histories unless these histories involve previous sex with the accused rapist. In many states, proving that the victim resisted strongly is no longer necessary because experts believe that if the woman struggles she may increase the likelihood of violence. The number of rape convictions increased substantially in Michigan after the rape law was reformed (Marsh, Geist, and Caplan, 1982).

Many of the rape convictions that are obtained are for statutory rape, which is sexual intercourse with someone below the legal age of consent regardless of whether she has given her consent. Statutory rape laws protect females who are judged too young to make reasonable decisions about their own sexual behavior. The legal age of consent varies from state to state. In some it is as low as 13 years old, and in others it is as high as 21 years old.

Although rape has traditionally been defined as a man forcing himself sexually on an unconsenting female, rape laws in some states now include male sexual assaults against other men (Marsh, Geist, and Caplan, 1982). In states in which the legal definition of rape involves only sexual intercourse with a female, sexual attacks by men against other men have been prosecuted as "sexual assault." Such assaults are most likely to occur in prison populations or homosexual communities. Prison officials tend to ignore sexual attacks; there are virtually no convictions for rape or sexual assault among inmates. Occasionally, however, men are convicted of rape against other men outside prisons. Men who are sexually assaulted are less likely than women to report the incident. Thus rapes or sexual assaults committed by a man against another man are even less likely to lead to conviction than are rapes committed by a man against a woman.

Another category of rape that has a low likelihood of conviction is the rape committed by a husband against his wife (Russell, 1982). The old common law rule still upheld in most states suggests that marriage is a token consent to sexual relations. Even wives whose husbands violently force them to have intercourse have not tended to think of that aggressive act as rape, and neither have the courts. Oregon is one of the few states in which a man can be prosecuted for forcing his wife to have sexual intercourse, and it is the first state in which a case of marital rape was prosecuted. In 1978 Greta Rideout made national headlines by accusing her husband of raping her. Some witnesses reported that violent breakups and passionate reconciliations were a pattern in the Rideout marriage. This fact made it difficult for the jury to know whether the husband was totally at fault or whether the wife in some way encouraged the husband's aggressive behavior. Thus Mr. Rideout was not convicted of rape. In fact, only 2 weeks after the end of the court case, Mr. and Mrs. Rideout were reconciled once again. However, the marriage did not last; the Rideouts were later divorced.

Although marital rape is not against the law in most states, a woman can bring charges against her spouse if she was either legally separated or divorced from him at the time the rape occurred. In 1979, for example, a court in Salem,

Massachusetts, convicted James Chretian of raping his wife (Russell, 1982). He was sentenced to 3 to 5 years in prison in addition to 3 years of probation. James Chretian and his wife were separated when he forcibly entered her apartment and raped her. He threatened that if she was not quiet, he would kill her. Although the Chretians were in the process of obtaining a divorce, it was not final at the time of the rape.

In summary, most states have strict rape laws. However, few rapes actually result in the conviction of the rapist. There is a trend now toward decreasing the penalties for rape to increase the number of rape convictions. There is also a trend toward defining rape more broadly to include sexual assaults by men on men and by husbands on wives.

SEXUAL HARASSMENT

Sexual harassment has only recently become a legal issue in the United States. In 1980 the Equal Employment Opportunity Commission (EEOC) Guidelines on Sexual Harassment were approved as an amendment to the Civil Rights Act of 1964, which bars discrimination on the basis of race, religion, or gender. The EEOC guidelines are as follows:

> Unwelcome sexual advances, requests for sexual favors, and other verbal or physical conduct of a sexual nature constitute sexual harassment when (1) submission to such conduct is made either explicitly or implicitly a term or condition of an individual's employment, (2) submission to or rejection of such conduct by an individual is used as the basis for employment decisions affecting such individual, or (3) such conduct has the purpose or effect of unreasonably interfering with an individual's work performance or creating an intimidating, hostile, or offensive working environment.
>
> Code of Federal Regulations: Labor, 1986, p. 137

Sexual harassment can involve either physical or verbal behaviors of a sexual nature. Verbally harassing behaviors may include sexual jokes and comments, as well as sexual proposals. Physically harassing behaviors may include touching, hugging, grabbing, pinching, kissing, or even more extreme behaviors such as rape or attempted rape. Women are subjected to such behavior in all types of settings. However, when it occurs in the workplace, women are particularly vulnerable. The harasser may say or imply that refusal will lead to reprisals. Many women are therefore put in a position of either tolerating unwelcome sexual advances or putting their jobs in jeopardy. An example of sexual harassment is presented on pp. 648 and 649.

A number of recent surveys of sexual harassment indicate that it is a widespread and serious problem. The surveys show that women are much more likely than men to be victims of sexual harassment. A survey of over 17,000 federal employees found that 15% of the men and 42% of the women had experienced sexual harassment (Tangri, Burt, and Johnson, 1982). The Working Women United Institute conducted a survey of 155 working women in upstate New York; 70% of the women reported that they had experienced sexual harassment personally, and 92% reported that they thought it to be a serious problem.

The negative effects of harassment on the victim are both financial and emotional. Many women have quit or been fired from their jobs as a result of

A Personal Glimpse

An Example of Sexual Harassment

This is the case of Ms. Carol Lindsay, a thirty-five-year-old woman who formerly worked as a clerical worker at a small advertising agency. Ms. Lindsay has two children, a thirteen-year-old son and a nine-year-old daughter. She is happily married to a man who was her childhood sweetheart, whom she has known most of her life. As she says, "Ken is not only my husband but my very best friend." Before she held this job, Ms. Lindsay had been out of the work force for nine years raising her two children.

When she decided to return to the work force, it took her five months of an intensive search to secure a position. Four months after being hired she was fired for failing to comply with her boss's sexual demands.

MS. LINDSAY: I was so excited the first day of my new job. Although I was nervous about being back at work after so long at home, I liked the place and the people, and I planned to work hard and make a success out of the job.

It all began two weeks after I started. My boss, who was the vice-president of the company and the son-in-law of the owner, was a man in his late forties. He was married, with five children.

He was not particularly well liked, because he was very authoritarian and humiliated his employees publicly, although I must admit he was very intelligent and really ran the company. I would have to say I respected him for that.

My job involved working directly with him, meeting with him five to six times a day in his office. From the very first day I found Mr. Lodge intimidating. He was always yelling, trying to wear down people's nerves. I was very unsure of myself as a new person, so I kept quiet and would just sit there waiting for his instructions. I was trying hard to concentrate and learn the ropes, so I tried to ignore his remarks.

INTERVIEWER: Could you describe what happened next?

MS. LINDSAY: Mr. Lodge had this really beautiful office. It was expensively decorated, very classy and elegant. In one corner there was a plush purple velvet loveseat. When I was called into his office to confer with him, he would be sitting on the loveseat and he would say, tapping the loveseat, "Come over and sit beside me." I thought this was odd, but decided it was okay because we both had to go over the same set of figures. He talked very softly, so that I had to sit close to hear what he was saying. I became very embarrassed and found myself scrunching over on my side of the seat.

The next time he called me in, I wanted to avoid the loveseat, so I immediately sat down in the chair opposite his desk. His reaction was to close his door and pull his chair from behind the desk around close to mine and to touch my knees. I was very surprised but decided I was overreacting. I felt that the best way to stop it was to ignore it.

But the situation became worse. The office had a conference room in it with a bar, which was often used to entertain customers. Mr. Lodge had a habit of calling me into the conference room and closing the door. On many occasions he would ask me to make him a drink and often asked me if I wanted one myself. I quite firmly said "no." His response was to ask if I was afraid I wouldn't be able to control myself. I was somewhat shocked, blushed, but let it go. At that point I didn't discuss it with anyone and felt I owed it to myself to handle it on my own.

The situation deteriorated to the point where he began to suggest that we find a quiet hotel room. Over the weekend I psyched myself up to fight back, because I realized the situation was getting out of hand.

INTERVIEWER: What did you do?

MS. LINDSAY: The next time he shut the door and asked me if I was in the mood, I replied, looking him straight in the eye, "I've got the best at home. I don't need to settle for second best." He ignored my comment completely and came up and whispered in my ear, "Next time you come in my office, I won't let you out." Frightened, I fled from his office.

From Backhouse and Cohen, 1981.

INTERVIEWER: How did he treat you after that?

MS. LINDSAY: I guess he realized he wasn't going to get anywhere with me. He became very cold and refused to speak to me except to yell about my work. He started to criticize everything I did, making my life unbearable. I realized I was in trouble, so I thought if I worked harder and showed him what a good employee I was, it might help. I began to take work home at night and stayed up late memorizing office procedures.

INTERVIEWER: How did you come to be fired?

MS. LINDSAY: I still hoped that the whole thing would blow over, and I was working doubly hard. However, for several weeks I noticed that the office manager, a woman in her fifties who was a grandmotherly type, seemed uneasy. Finally, she called me into her office and told me she would have to let me go. My boss had complained that I wasn't working fast enough. He told her I was doing a lousy job. The office manager was sympathetic. She said it was unfortunate, but that when Mr. Lodge took a dislike to someone, it didn't matter how hard they worked. She confided that many other women had been fired for the same reason.

INTERVIEWER: Did you tell the office manager about your sexual harassment?

MS. LINDSAY: Although the office manager could not get me my job back, she promised to give me a good job recommendation on the sly, saying that I was laid off due to cutbacks in staff. But I wasn't prepared to leave it at that. I was too angry. I was still smarting because I hadn't fought back immediately. I shouldn't have put up with it, but I thought it would pass. Who knows how many women Mr. Lodge had harassed? I wanted to stop it.

INTERVIEWER: How did you proceed from there?

MS. LINDSAY: My last few days at work I spoke to every woman in the office. Each and every one of them had had a lewd sexual pass made at them by Mr. Lodge. They said I was lucky. The woman before me, Shirley Green, had been publicly humiliated in front of the whole office. But these women, who did not work directly for Mr. Lodge, felt they had to go along with him. Most of them were single or divorced and desperately needed their jobs. They made it clear to me that they could not afford to support any action I took. The men in the office all knew what was going on. Their response was to smile and chuckle and to speculate whether or not Frank had "scored" this time around.

I managed to track down Shirley Green, who had been able to find another job. She told me Mr. Lodge had also sexually harassed her, to such an extent that she had totally lost her self-confidence. She had wanted to speak up at the time she was fired but was afraid it would jeopardize her next job. But she informed me that she would support any action I took and that she would testify for me if necessary.

[At the time this interview was first published, Ms. Lindsay had hired a lawyer and was going to sue.]

harassment. In addition, women report feeling embarrassed, demeaned, intimidated, angry, and upset as a result of harassment they have experienced (Lebrato, 1986). Such an experience, Lebrato argues, diminishes the victim's motivation and self-confidence, which in turn reduces the chance for career advancement.

Crull (1982) studied women who had experienced sexual harassment and found that many experienced negative consequences as a result of the harassment. She found that 25% had been either fired or laid off. In addition, 75% reported that the experience interfered with their work performance, 90% reported that it had a negative effect on their psychological health, and 63% reported a negative effect on their physical health. Gutek (1985) also surveyed victims of sexual harassment and found that 38% reported that it had affected their feelings about their jobs and 28% reported that it had negatively affected their relationships with their co-workers.

Despite the larger percentage of individuals reporting sexual harassment in surveys, sexual harassment more often than not goes unreported at the workplace. In a survey of 156 companies across the nation conducted by the Bureau of National Affairs (Personnel Policies Forum, 1987), only 37% reported having received any formal complaints in 1986. Of the 57 firms at which complaints were lodged, 55 (96%) indicated that one or more complaints were filed by women against men. Three firms reported cases of a female employee alleging harassment by another woman, five had at least one case of a male worker accusing another man, and one firm reported a case of a male employee complaining of sexual harassment by a woman.

In the survey by the Working Women United Institute, of those who were harassed, 75% ignored the harassment, and only 18% reported the harassment through the appropriate channels. Those who did not complain said that they felt that nothing would be done, that they would be blamed, or that there would be negative repercussions.

---

2 in 3 Military Women Report Harassment

In the first major study of sexual harassment in the military, the Pentagon has said that more than a third of the women surveyed experienced some form of direct harassment, including touching, pressure for sexual favors and rape.

In all, about two out of every three women surveyed, or 64 percent, said they had been sexually harassed, directly, or in more subtle ways, such as by catcalls, dirty looks and teasing. . . .

NEWS of the 90's

The Pentagon report . . . appears to challenge the military's contention that women have integrated smoothly into the services, and raises doubts about the success of new policies to change the ways of the tradition-bound military.

The findings come at a time when women make up 11 percent of the 2 million people on active duty in the military. . . .

Although many women in the service say conditions have improved in the past several years, some signs suggest otherwise.

The U.S. Naval Academy, for example, is the target of at least six inquiries into allegations of sexual harassment of female midshipmen. . . .

The Pentagon report, which collected responses from more than 20,000 men and women on active duty and took two years to complete, described a pervasive and often subtle denigration of women in an environment where policies aimed at preventing abuses are in place but not enforced frequently.

Researchers said the survey was the largest attempt to measure sexual harassment in the workplace, public or private, and marked only the second time a federal agency had conducted such a poll to guide its policy-makers.

In another finding, 17 percent of the men surveyed said they had been sexually harassed by male or female colleagues.

The study did not give a breakdown of the sex of the harassers. . . .

From Schmitt, 1990.

Indeed, when a woman is subjected to sexual harassment, she is confronted with a difficult dilemma. When the sexual advances are subtle, as they sometimes are in the beginning, the woman is often ridiculed (e.g., "Don't flatter yourself") if she complains. However, if the woman ignores the subtle advances, the incidents often escalate. When a woman tolerates early subtle advances, she is often accused of "asking for it" when less subtle demands are made.

Ironically, while indirect responses such as ignoring the sexually harassing behavior, avoiding the perpetrator, making jokes, giggling, or crying are most common, direct assertive responses such as telling the harasser to stop or reporting the behavior to a supervisor or other officials are most effective (Lebrato, 1986). Lebrato warns, however, that while a direct response appears to work well for the majority of women, for some it may worsen the situation (Lebrato citing Merit Systems Protection Board, Survey of Sexual Harassment in the Federal Workforce, 1980).

There is no one solution when dealing with sexual harassment. Lebrato suggests that if you are a victim of sexual harassment, you should take several factors into account when deciding what to do about it. First, personal considerations must be carefully weighed before taking any action. For example, you should consider the time and energy you have available to resolve the problem; if it is at work, whether you can afford to risk losing your job; and the resources you have available in pursuing a resolution (e.g., attorneys, unions, or support groups).

Second, you should consider the result you want. Some remedies are avail-

A Setback for Pinups at Work

In Florida a federal judge rules that pictures of nude women can be considered a form of sexual harassment.

At factories, construction sites and shipyards across the U.S., girly pinups . . . are the workingman's constant companion. Although women hold 8.6% of skilled blue-collar jobs, their presence has done little to diminish the existence of these graphic images. For their part, courts have been reluctant to rule that pornographic pictures constitute a form of sexual harassment in the workplace, mainly because such photos are ubiquitous.

Now a ground-breaking decision by the federal district court in Jacksonville has changed all that. The court ruled that pictures of naked and scantily clad women displayed at the Jacksonville Shipyards qualify as harassment under Title VII of the 1964 Civil Rights Act. Such a "boys' club" atmosphere, wrote Judge Howell Melton in his 98-page opinion, is "no less destructive to workplace equality than a sign declaring 'Men Only.'" The Florida branch of the American Civil Liberties Union promptly denounced the decision as a possible violation of free speech, but many women were jubilant. Exulted University of Michigan law professor Catherine MacKinnon: "This is a stunning victory."

NEWS of the 90's

The landmark case was brought by shipyard welder Lois Robinson, who accused her employer of ignoring the display of pornographic images and condoning the routine verbal abuse of the six females among the 846 skilled-crafts employees. Robinson and two other women testified that they endured a barrage of comments from their male peers, perhaps the mildest of which was "I'd like to get in bed with that." The offending photos, many of which came from calendars provided by tool-supply companies, included a nude woman bending over with her buttocks and genitals exposed, a nude female torso with USDA CHOICE written on it and a dart board that displayed a drawing of a woman's breast, with her nipple as the bull's eye.

At the trial, the shipyard presented an expert witness who asserted that such depictions would not offend the "average woman." Judge Melton was not persuaded. Among other things, he said, females in a "sexually hostile" workplace are a captive audience for pornography and are usually reluctant to challenge superiors and colleagues over the issue. "Nobody's stopping the men at Jacksonville Shipyards from reading pornography," says Alison Wetherfield, an attorney with the women's advocacy group that represented Robinson. "They're just saying, 'You can't do it here, boys.'"

. . . Under the federal-court decision, the company must institute an anti-harassment policy and take down the photos. But it will doubtless be a long time before similar displays are removed from work sites around the U.S. Technically, the decision applies only to Judge Melton's jurisdiction and is unlikely to spur a surge of harassment suits elsewhere. Besides, says Boston University law professor Kathryn Abrams, "pornography is considered in the tradition of good old, all-male fun, so it's going to be very hard to change." Hard, but no longer impossible.

From Tifft, 1991.

able only through certain routes. For example, back pay cannot be obtained through informal complaints or from criminal actions but may be obtained through a complaint to a federal or state agency or through a civil lawsuit or settlement. Whatever remedy you want, for example, back pay or a personal apology (which is in many cases more difficult to obtain), it must be appropriate for the harm suffered.

The final step is deciding which strategy or combination of strategies is best suited to getting what you want. Lebrato warns that no perfect strategies exist. Carefully analyzing personal considerations, deciding what you want, and forming strategies will increase your chances of obtaining an acceptable resolution. (A more elaborate delineation of action you can take if you, as a student, are the victim of sexual harassment on campus is given in the box below.)

In 1980 *Redbook* and the *Harvard Business Review* conducted a joint survey on the issue of sexual harassment in the workplace (Collins and Blodgett, 1981). They found that men and women agree on what harassment is but disagree strongly on how frequently it occurs. Furthermore, they found that women "despair of having traditionally male-dominated management understand how much harassment humiliates and frustrates them, and they despair of having management's support in resisting it." The following quotation from a 38-year-old plant manager suggests these women may be right. When asked about sexual harassment this man said, "This entire subject is a perfect example of a minor special interest group's ability to blow up any 'issue' to a level of importance which in no way relates to the reality of the world in which we live and work" (Collins and Blodgett, 1981).

What You Can Do If You Are Sexually Harassed

If you are sexually harassed:

1. Investigate the university's policy and grievance procedure for sexual harassment cases. Know the university's past record before you act.

2. Document what's happened. Keep a diary; save any notes, correspondence, pictures from the harasser—don't throw them away in anger. Write down specific dates, times, places, kinds of incidents, your responses, his answers, any witnesses.

3. Generate support for yourself before you take action: break the silence, talk with others at your school and outside, ask for help in working out a response. They may feel responsible for backing you up if your response to the harasser fails.

4. You may discover others who have been harassed who can act with you. Collective action and joint complaints strengthen your position. Some who have not been harassed may join in collec-

tive action. Consider organizing parents and alumni to complain.

5. Let the harasser know as clearly, directly, and explicitly as possible that you are not interested in his attentions. If you do this in writing, make a copy of your letter.

6. Evaluate your options. What do you want to get out of any action you take? What are your primary concerns and goals? What courses of action are available to you? What are the possible outcomes, including the risks, of each course of action?

From Field, 1981.

Sexual Harassment on Campus

The following examples illustrate how sexual harassment might occur on a college campus:

Anne B. is a junior, on the dean's list, whose English professor repeatedly asked her to go out with him throughout the semester. She refused. Now she finds that her papers in his class are getting very low marks and she is in danger of getting a D for the semester. She is sure that it is retaliation for her refusal.

Every time Margaret R. sees her advisor in his office, he closes the door, sits close to her, and seems to pat her knee a lot in the course of their discussion. Margaret is uncomfortable with this behavior and tries to move away so he can't touch her. He only moves closer to her and continues the behavior. Margaret doesn't know what to do about it.

Katherine B. is a work-study student who needs her job to stay in school. One day while she is working alone with her boss he puts his arms around her and invites her to come home with him that night. She refuses and leaves immediately. In the days following, her boss continues to suggest she come home with him and finally she can't face going back to work again. Now she worries about not having a job and how she is going to make her tuition payment next semester.

Judith M., a single mother who has returned to school to complete her degree after a ten-year absence, asks her professor how she might improve her grade. He suggests they spend more time together, perhaps have dinner, so he could get to know her better and figure out how to give her extra help.

Maria V. is a sophomore and depressed over the break-up of her relationship with Bill. She had spent all her free time with him and was emotionally dependent on him. She goes to the school counselor who is sympathetic and kind and always available to talk. This interest boosts her self-esteem and convinces her that she is an attractive person. One afternoon he suggests that she have drinks with him at a new bar so that they can get closer.

From In case of sexual harassment: a guide for women students, 1986.

Backhouse and Cohen (1981) suggest that sexual harassment is not an expression of sexual desire but rather an assertion of power: "It is the ultimate reminder to women that their fundamental status in society is that of sex object and that they hold their positions in the workforce only on male sufferance." They go on to suggest that virtually any kind of woman can be the victim and virtually any type of man can be the perpetrator.

There are three legal routes a woman who feels she has been sexually harassed can take: a criminal proceeding, a complaint to a human rights organization, and civil litigation in the courts. Cases of rape, assault, threats, and intimidation can be prosecuted as criminal cases. In such a situation the woman may want to contact the police. Women may also contact the Equal Employment Opportunity Commission, a government agency set up to mediate civil rights violations. When the EEOC receives a complaint, it will investigate, and if it finds reasonable cause to believe that a violation has occurred, it will try to negotiate a settlement informally. If the attempt to reach a settlement is unsuccessful, the woman may file a civil suit on her own. It is difficult to say how the courts are interpreting the sexual harassment amendment to the Civil Rights Act. Decisions vary from one court to the next; the reasons given for decisions vary widely as well. Furthermore, courts of appeal are constantly overturning the decisions of lower courts. In some cases women have won sexual harassment suits, and in others they have not won even in cases in which the sexual harassment was blatant. It will take time and many more court decisions before a uniform legal policy on sexual harassment develops.

SUMMARY

1 For the most part the law in the United States has restricted legal sexual relations to people who are related by marriage, to private places, and to genital-genital heterosexual contact.

2 The two legal categories for nonmarital sexual intercourse are fornication and adultery. Fornication occurs when unmarried adults have intercourse. Adultery occurs when a married person has sexual intercourse with someone other than his or her spouse.

3 Many states have laws against homosexual behavior, transvestism, voyeurism, exhibitionism, indecent exposure, oral-genital intercourse, and anal-genital intercourse.

4 Although prostitution is legal in many countries, it is illegal in all states in the United States except Nevada.

5 Pornography generally refers to material that is sexually arousing, and obscenity refers to material that is filthy, dirty, disgusting, or offensive. The laws against pornography and obscenity are based on the assumption that pornographic and obscene materials have negative effects either on individual people or on the society as a whole.

6 Although the 1970 Commission on Obscenity and Pornography, after studying the effects of pornography, concluded that exposure to explicit sexual material does not play a significant role in causing criminal behavior among youths or adults, the 1986 Attorney General's Commission on Pornography concluded that both violent pornography and degrading pornography bear a causal relationship to sexual violence and aggression toward women.

7 Recent experimental studies indicate that pornography involving aggression against women may, in fact, increase the tendency of males to behave more aggressively toward women and be more accepting of violence toward women. Even nonviolent pornography that is degrading to women tends to increase negative attitudes toward women. However, sexually explicit material that is neither violent or degrading does not appear to have a negative effect on either attitudes or behavior.

8 Many feminists are opposed to pornography if it portrays women and children as sex objects and victims because they believe such material encourages violence and hostility toward women and children.

9 Rape is one of the most underreported of all crimes. Many women are reluctant to undertake the often humiliating procedures necessary to convict a rapist. Some states have adopted "rape shield laws" that prevent defense attorneys from questioning rape victims about their sexual history unless it involves previous sex with the accused rapist.

10 Although rape has traditionally been defined as a male forcing himself sexually on an unconsenting female, some states are beginning to include male sexual assault against other men in their rape laws. Such assaults are most likely to occur in prison populations or homosexual communities.

11 Sexual harassment has recently become a legal issue in the United States. Surveys indicate that sexual harassment is a widespread and serious problem in the workplace today.

FACT
OR
FICTION

ANSWERS

1. For the most part, the law in the United States has restricted legal sexual relations to people who are married, to private places, and to genital-genital heterosexual contact. Thus many of the sexual behaviors of consenting adults are illegal.

2. In most states in the United States a woman is not able to charge her husband with rape unless she is legally separated or divorced from him.

3. Recent surveys of the incidence of sexual harassment indicate that about three fourths of all working women report that they have experienced sexual harassment.

QUESTIONS FOR THOUGHT

1. Do you believe that two consenting adults ought to be able to do whatever they want in their own bedroom or do you believe we should have laws to regulate sexual behavior?

2. Do you believe prostitution is a victimless crime?

3. Do you believe there should be laws regulating pornography or do you believe people ought to have free access to pornographic materials?

4. Do you think the rape laws ought to apply to husbands who force their wives to have sexual intercourse?

5. Do you think it should be against the law for men to put up posters of scantily clad women in their place of work?

SUGGESTED READINGS

Assiter, A.: Pornography, feminism and the individual, London, 1989, Pluto Press.
  A book about feminist perspectives on pornography.

Donnerstein, E., Linz, D., and Penrod, S.: The question of pornography: research findings and policy implications, New York, 1987, The Free Press.
  A book that covers research on the effects of pornographic materials on behavior.

Dziech, B.W., and Weiner, L.: The lecherous professor: sexual harassment on campus, Boston, 1984, Beacon Press.
  A book that thoroughly discusses the problem of sexual harassment on campus.

Ennew, J.: The sexual exploitation of children, New York, 1986, St. Martin's Press, Inc.
  A book about various types of sexual exploitation of children including their use in pornography and prostitution.

Hobson, B.: Uneasy virtue, New York, 1987, Basic Books, Inc.
  A historical analysis of legislative attempts to control prostitution and a search for an alternative regarding prostitution.

Lebrato, M.: Help yourself: a manual for dealing with sexual harassment, Sexual Harassment in Employment Project of the California Commission on the Status of Women, 1986.
  A manual that candidly provides informal and formal means for dealing effectively with sexual harassment.

Mueller, G.O.W.: Sexual conduct and the law, Dobbs Ferry, N.Y., 1980, Oceana Publications.
  An easy-to-read short discussion of the law as it relates to such topics as rape, prostitution, homosexuality, pornography, and adultery.

Symanski, R.: The immoral landscape, Toronto, 1981, Butterworth & Co.
  A thorough and interesting discussion of all aspects of prostitution, including the legal aspects.

Zillmann, D., and Bryant, J.: Pornography: research advances and policy considerations, Hillsdale, N.J., 1989, Lawrence Erlbaum Associates.
  A collection of readings on various aspects of pornography, including the uses of pornography, the effects of pornography, legal issues related to pornography, and educational issues.

23

Sex Education

FACT
OR
FICTION

1
As a result of the "sexual revolution," both parents and teachers are much more open with children about sexual issues today than they were in the past. Children now get most of their sexual information from their parents and teachers.

2
Teenagers who have had sex education courses in school are more likely to be sexually active than teenagers who have not had such courses.

What a curious thing is man, who has to be taught the most basic behavior patterns: how to drink, how to eat, how to talk—and even how to copulate. Spider and beetle, salmon and crab, sparrow and chipmunk all know what to do sexually when the time comes, without ever having been taught, or even, in the case of the lower orders, without having seen it done. But not us: Lacking built-in instinctual guidance, we must be taught the words and looks of courtship, the touches and caresses of sexual wooing, the signs and signals of readiness, the very positions and movement of coitus. Without training we are no better equipped to copulate than we are to drive a car or sail a boat.

MORTON HUNT
Sexual Behavior in the 1970's, p. 120

lthough human beings have to learn about sexuality, the United States has not had any commonly accepted system for providing sex education. The young in this country have often had to learn about sexuality through gossip, jokes, and reading. In 1948 Kinsey, Pomeroy, and Martin reported that the men they interviewed learned most of what they knew about sex as children from other children. In 1953 Kinsey and associates reported that no more than 5% of the women interviewed had received more than incidental information from their parents; again, they said that most of their sexual information had come from peers.

HOW DO WE TEACH ABOUT SEXUALITY?

We might assume that given our culture's increasingly liberal views about sexuality, parents today would be much more likely to talk to their children about sexual issues than they were in the 1940s and 1950s. However, the research indicates that there may not have been much of a change since the time of the early Kinsey studies. In the late 1960s Libby and Nass (1971) found that 87% of the parents they interviewed refused to discuss sexual issues with their children when the children asked relevant questions. These parents felt that their children did not need sex information (see box, p. 661). Their attitudes are exemplified by the following comments:

> I try to keep them from knowing too much.

> My parents did not tell me about it. I don't discuss it either.

> I think sex education corrupts the minds of 15- to 16-year-olds.

> Kids know too much already.

> I just tell them to behave and keep their eyes open.

Hunt (1974) obtained similar results. He asked individuals what their main source of knowledge about sexual matters had been while they were growing up. Both males and females said that friends were the major source of information. Parents were listed as only the third most important source of information. As can be seen from Table 23-1, the importance of the parents was not even close to the importance of friends and reading. Hunt reported that the figures for young adults were almost the same as for older adults. On the

TABLE 23-1 Main Source of Sexual Information★

	Males (%)	Females (%)
Friends	59	46
Reading	20	22
Mother	3	16
Father	6	1
School program	3	5
Adults outside home	6	4
Brothers, sisters	4	6
Other, and no answer	7	7

Reprinted with permission from Playboy Enterprises, Inc., from "Sexual Behavior in the 1970's" by Morton Hunt. Copyright © 1974 by Morton Hunt.
★Percents total more than 100 because some respondents checked more than one answer.

basis of these results, he concluded that "it would appear that American sex education, at least as far as sexual behavior is concerned (as distinguished from biological information), has undergone no fundamental change since Kinsey's time; it is still up to the young to find out for themselves as best they can what to expect of the sex act and how to do it."

Hunt reported that two thirds of the males and four fifths of the females said that their fathers had never talked to them about sexual matters and that three fourths of the males and nearly half of the females said that their mothers had never talked to them about sexual matters. Hunt noted that only 9% of the males said that they had learned anything new and important from talks with their fathers and even fewer learned anything new from their mothers. Although only 8% of the females learned anything new and important from their fathers, 28% learned something new and important from their mothers.

Hunt (1974) concluded that the "traditional taboo on sexual communication between parent and child, and the native American reluctance to teach the young about sexual behavior, remain powerful bars to sex education within the home, even at the upper social level and even after a generation of sexual liberation." Hunt presented the following examples to illustrate the similarities between socioeconomic classes. This quotation represents a typical blue-collar, middle-aged man speaking of his parents' treatment of sex education:

> When I was sixteen I started to go out with the daughter of friends of the family, and my dad said to me, "You lay a hand on that girl and I'll kill you," and later, when I was dating different girls, he handed me a rubber one day and again he said, not even looking at me, "If you ever get any girl in trouble, I'll kill you" and that was my sex education as far as he was concerned.
>
> Hunt, 1974, p. 124

A similar example comes from a well-educated woman in her thirties whose mother was a trained nurse:

> She was so shy that she never told me a thing; she just gave me little hints now and then. When I was 11 or 12, a friend's mother lent me a book about how babies are conceived and born and told me not to read it but first to ask my mother if I could, and my mother studied it and heaved a great sigh of relief because now she

didn't have to tell me anything. . . . One time I found her diaphragm in a little box and asked her what it was and she went into a real flap and told me it was none of my business and never to go near it again.

Hunt, 1974, pp. 124-125

Hunt found that those few individuals who reported that their parents had helped them with their sex education by buying them books, answering their questions, or initiating talks seemed to appreciate their parents' help.

Hunt also discovered that school sex education programs were mentioned even less frequently than parents as the main source of sex information for the individuals he interviewed. Hunt reported that half of all individuals interviewed who were under 35 years of age received some sex education in school, but few individuals mentioned school programs as their main source of information. He suggested that the explanation for this somewhat unusual finding may be that most of the school programs deal primarily with biology rather than what the students feel is more important—information about how various sex acts are performed.

The fact that a majority of individuals get most of their sex information from friends means that their information may not be completely accurate. This is illustrated by two of the responses Hunt obtained. The first came from a 48-year-old man:

I was 10 when I first went to camp, and one kid in the bunk was a big-city wise guy and said he knew how a baby was made. None of the rest of us did so he told us—he said the man stuck his thing in a hole in the woman's body and squirted some seeds in there. We were all disbelieving and sort of shocked but he said his older brother had told him. So, then, we asked him what hole, and he didn't know—not one of us knew—and after a lot of talk, we decided it was probably the behind, because where else? I didn't get it straightened out until three years later.

Hunt, 1974, p. 126

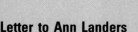

A Personal Glimpse

Letter to Ann Landers

Dear Ann: Twenty-plus years ago when I reached puberty my mother couldn't talk to me about sex and I grew up completely ignorant about pregnancy.

When I was 13, my sister and I moved from the double bed in the small bedroom to twin beds in a larger room. Not long after that I got up one night to go to the bathroom and wandered back into our old bedroom. I woke up to discover I had been "sleeping with" my brother. I lived in terror for 3 weeks—sure I was pregnant because I had slept with a man. The relief when my menstrual cycle came around was indescribable. I still re-member those terrifying weeks, and it has taught me the importance of explaining sex properly and early to my children.

I was almost 20 before I learned what it was all about and I shall never get over my anger at being so ignorant for so many years.—**No Joke In Austin**

Dear N.J.: Parents today are more open than they were 30 years ago, but still the ignorance among teenagers who are supposed to be savvy is appalling—and society is paying a big price for it. Wake up out there!

From Ann Landers, News America Syndicate.

And a 28-year-old woman reported the following:

> When I was 12 or 13, my three best friends and I used to talk about it all the time and try to figure it out, but we couldn't imagine why any girl would want a boy to urinate inside her. Then, later, another girl explained what the emission was—but she also said that a girl had emission, too, just like a man.
>
> Hunt, 1974, p. 126

Evidence from the authors' human sexuality courses indicates that in 1981 college students still reported learning most of their information about sex from their peers. The percentages for all sources of information on sex are given in Table 23-2. These percentages suggest that not much changed between the time of Hunt's study in 1974 and the later study in 1981. This finding has been confirmed in other studies (Thornburg, 1981; Davis and Harris, 1982; Handelsman, Cabral, and Weisfeld, 1987).

What is the effect of the lack of sex education in our homes and schools? One result is that children have a great deal of incorrect information (see the accompanying box). Many of us tend to think that the children of today "know everything about sex" at very early ages; however, children have many misconceptions. In one study Gordon (1982) asked 300 pregnant teenagers why they had not used some form of birth control. Most of the teenagers responded by saying that they had. When asked what method they had used, they gave answers such as the following:

> I used one of my mother's birth control pills.
>
> I didn't think I could get pregnant standing up.
>
> He said he'd pull out in time.
>
> I used foam [as a douche *after* intercourse].

The lack of adequate sex education in our homes and schools has had disastrous effects on our teenagers. Wallace and Vienonen (1989) reported that the pregnancy rate in the United States was 62 per 1,000 among 15- to 17-year-olds and 144 per 1,000 among 18- to 19-year-olds. This is almost double the rate of most other Western countries. Furthermore, the incidence of sexually transmitted diseases has increased sharply in recent years. In addition to the increases in the incidence of genital herpes and acquired immunodeficiency

TABLE 23-2 Sources of Sex Education for Students in Authors' Human Sexuality Courses, 1981*

Main source of information	Students (%)
Peers and friends	48
Books and magazines	18
Parents	17
School sex education programs	15
Siblings	<1
Doctors	<1

*The answers were gathered from 128 students in response to the questions, "How did you receive your sex education?" and "Where did you learn most of the facts from?"

HUMAN SEXUALITY

syndrome (AIDS), the rate of gonorrhea increased by more than four times between 1960 and 1990 (VD Statistical Letter, 1978; STD Statistical Letter, 1990). The number of individuals who seek psychological help in clinics for sexual problems has also increased (LoPiccolo and Miller, 1975). These facts clearly indicate the need for better sex education. However, many parents are afraid of the effects of sex education programs.

EFFECTS OF SEX EDUCATION

Many people oppose sex education because they feel that the less children and adolescents know about sex, the less likely they are to become sexually involved. However, research does not support this assumption. Rather, research indicates that being exposed to sex education has no effect on the age of onset or frequency of heterosexual intercourse (Zelnik and Kim, 1982) or may actually delay the onset (Zabin et al., 1986).

Evidence suggests that receiving sex education from parents or teachers may actually decrease the incidence of some sexual problems. For example, initiating sex education programs in schools reportedly reduced the incidence of gonorrhea by as much as 50% in the year following the institution of the program (Levine, 1970). Young women who have had sex education in school are less likely to become pregnant before marriage than are young women who have not had sex education (Zelnik and Kim, 1982; Zabin et al., 1986; Vincent, Clearier, and Schluchter, 1987). Furthermore, it has been demonstrated that sex education can increase contraceptive knowledge and use (Kirby, 1985; Zabin et al., 1986). Research also indicates that adolescents whose parents play a major role in their sex education are less likely to engage in early sexual activity than less informed adolescents (Lewis, 1973). In addition, research shows that providing individuals with sex information has a positive effect on their psychological and sexual adjustment (McCary and Flake, 1971). Thus, in contrast to what many believe, informing children about sexual matters is more likely to decrease than increase premature and irresponsible sexual behavior.

SEX EDUCATION IN THE HOME

Parents do much to determine their children's view of sexuality whether they intend to or not. The child's views begin to form at an early age. Parents provide children with a basic orientation to sexual matters by the way in which they treat their own sexual and affectionate behavior, nudity, masturbation, and sex play (Ehrenberg and Ehrenberg, 1988).

Most parents keep their affectionate behavior hidden from their children. They tend not to hug, kiss, or talk about their affection in front of their children. Thus most children see their parents as asexual beings. The majority of children have a difficult time imagining that their parents share a sexual relationship. Children obtain a much more positive view of sexuality if they are able to observe their parents showing both verbal and physical affection.

By dealing with sexual matters openly, parents can provide their children with a positive view of sexuality.

If children see their parents being openly loving and affectionate with each other, they develop an acceptance of their own sexuality rather than feel that their sexuality is something that should be hidden (Ehrenberg and Ehrenberg, 1988).

The way that parents handle nudity in the home also affects their children's view of sexuality. If the family is open and accepting of one anothers' bodies, the children will not grow up to feel ashamed of their bodies and their sexuality. They will not need to feel embarrassed or inhibited about their sexuality. If, however, the parents are intolerant of nudity in the home, the children will not learn about adult male and female bodies. Furthermore, they will come to view their own bodies as something about which they should be embarrassed. In addition, of course, they will learn that the most embarrassing and "disgusting" parts of their bodies—the parts that most need to be covered up—are the sexual parts. This perception will result in the feeling that sex is somehow dirty and disgusting.

The way parents treat masturbation has an impact on their children's view of sexuality. Parents need to remember that masturbation is normal for young children. They should accept such activities, although they need to teach their children when and where the activities are acceptable. They must teach their children, for example, that it is inappropriate to masturbate in public. It is best that parents not inhibit or try to prevent such activities in private. When parents act as if masturbation is shocking and disgusting, they give their children the impression that the children's sexual feelings and behaviors are somehow shocking, dirty, and disgusting. These kinds of views interfere with enjoyable, healthy sexuality during adulthood. Some individuals never recover from the guilt and anxiety instilled by such parental treatment of sexuality. Others are able to overcome such attitudes but only with great difficulty.

How parents treat sex play is a more difficult issue. Sex play among children is normal behavior. It is important that parents treat it as if it were natural and not shocking and disgusting; yet at the same time many parents will want to set limits on such behavior. If parents believe that their children's sex play with other children could for any reason have damaging effects, they can tell their children that they want the behavior to stop without making the children feel that they have done something terribly wrong. For example, the parents could say something similar to: "When we have visitors over to our house, we don't take our clothes off. When we have company, we leave our clothes on. So, we want you to do just like Mommy and Daddy do; we want you to leave your clothes on when your friends come over." Or the parents could say, "Daddy and Mommy don't feel that children should touch the sexual parts of anyone else." These messages can be conveyed matter of factly without giving the children the feeling that sex play is shocking or disgusting.

In addition to influencing the child's view of sexuality through these indirect sources, the way parents deal with more direct sexual information has a profound effect on their children's attitudes. Parents are the ideal individuals to teach children about sexuality. If children learn about sex from their parents, they are more likely to receive accurate information than if they learn about sexuality from their peers. Furthermore, since children probably feel closer to their parents than to other adults such as teachers, they should feel freer to ask the questions that really concern them.

Learning about sex from peers often results in misinformation.

Parents who are interested in teaching their children about sex often wonder when and how to begin. Some experts suggest waiting until the children ask questions. Then the parents can give them the type of information for which they seem to be asking. Young children typically ask their parents about every aspect of life. Unless they feel inhibited about sexuality, some of their questions should deal with sex. The parents should answer sex-related questions in the same matter-of-fact and relaxed fashion in which they answer all other questions.

Some children do not ask questions about sex. If parents believe that the child is old enough to know certain things about sex but the child has not yet asked, the parents might bring up the topic themselves. Again, they should do this in a matter-of-fact and relaxed way. Sometimes it is easiest to provide the children with sexual information when the topic arises naturally. For example, if the parent and child are watching a television program in which someone mentions the pill, the parent might take that opportunity to explain to the child what the pill refers to. Likewise, if there is a discussion about homosexuality on television or in a movie or a book, the parents might use that opening to explain homosexuality to the child. Many sexual concepts can be explained in this way. Even if children do not ask questions, it is important for the parents to try to talk to their children about sexuality before the age at which the children will learn from peers. If the children learn about sexuality from their parents, they receive a much more positive view of sexuality. If they learn about it from their peers, they may learn that sex is "dirty" and something to be ashamed of.

The majority of adolescents report that they would prefer to get their primary information about sex from their parents (Handelsman, Cabral, and Weisfeld, 1987). However, in several studies adolescents who reported receiving the majority of their sex education from their parents were no better informed than those who received the majority of their sex education from their peers. This is probably because many parents are not well informed about sexual matters. It suggests that an effort to provide better information about sexual matters to adults might be beneficial. Such information could be disseminated by government brochures, through newspapers, or on television.

While adolescents who receive most of their information about sex from their parents are no better informed than adolescents who receive information from their peers, adolescents who report good communication with their parents about sexual matters are more likely to use contraception than adolescents who report poor communication with their parents (Handelsman, Cabral, and Weisfeld, 1987). Thus, even though they may not be more knowledgeable about sex, adolescents who receive sex education from their parents are more likely to behave in ways consistent with their knowledge. This is advantageous because a number of researchers have reported that increases in knowledge about sexual matters do not necessarily result in changes in sexual behavior (Fan and Shaffer, 1990).

A Personal Glimpse

When Sex Education Fails

Kim loves babies. She's always wanted to have a big family.

But when she found out she was three months pregnant, she said, "I was crying every day."

After all . . . she was just 16. . . . Kim is a soft-spoken, attractive, articulate teenager. She could be anyone's daughter or sister.

"Everybody always used to call me [Kim] sweet. . . . I thought I had learned to say 'no.' I kept telling myself I don't believe in sex before marriage. I'm not going to do that. Then I just found myself in a situation where I couldn't stop."

And Kim said, "I didn't know anything about sex at all. We didn't really have any kind of sex education in school. When Mom told me about abortions, we opted for the only other choice, giving birth. There were some tough times ahead though."

"Dad cried and said he was sorry, and Mom got mad when they found out."

The remaining six months of the pregnancy weren't easy either.

"I kept worrying what people thought. I kept wondering what I was going to do. I felt like a loose person. I felt lowdown. I worried about my figure. By the fifth month I wanted it to be all over. I was afraid it [giving birth] was going to hurt. . . ."

Besides those anxieties, there were some monumental decisions that had to be faced.

"I knew I couldn't get married. . . . Things would have been worse. We were too young. We were both still in school and didn't have jobs. There was just no way it could have worked, I don't think. You shouldn't bring up a baby in that kind of atmosphere. I didn't want to disrupt the life of a child."

Another choice had to be made. After giving birth, Kim, in tears, held the baby for just five minutes. During those few minutes she signed the release papers and the baby was taken from her for adoption.

"I love babies," she said. "I wanted to keep her so bad, but I decided giving her up was the unselfish thing to do. I think it would have been selfish not to give the baby a chance to have a mother and a father. . . . I just sat there thinking should I keep her, should I give her up. I kept thinking how pretty she was. But something just told me to give her up."

Two years later, Kim's eyes filled with tears again as she talked about the life she had given. The baby's birthday is only a few days away. "So this is kind of a hard time for me," she explained.

Still, she added, "I don't regret it at all. I'm happy I gave a family a new life and I feel good about it."

From Lawrence (Kan.) Journal-World, 1981.

SEX EDUCATION IN SCHOOL

Most sex education programs in the United States in the past dealt with information on only the physical changes at puberty, menstruation, reproduction, and sexually transmitted disease. Over the years some of the programs were dropped as a result of parental objection. Thus the emphasis on sex education in the schools has varied since the early programs. For example, in the early 1960s the emphasis on sex education in the schools was strong as a result of concern over increases in both teenage pregnancy and sexually transmitted disease. In the late 1960s, however, a decrease in sex education programs occurred because many people feared that such programs were promoting permissive sexual attitudes and behaviors.

More recently the prevalence of sex education programs has begun to increase. Surveys indicate that in recent years the vast majority of adults in the United States have supported having sex education in the public schools (Leo, 1986). In fact, when parents are given the opportunity to withdraw their children from sex education programs, few actually do. In Illinois less than 1% of the children were excused from sex education courses, while in California less than 2% were excused.

The increase in public support for sex education in the schools has been accompanied by an increase in sex education courses in the schools. In a survey of 179 urban school districts, Sonenstein and Pittman (1984) found that 75% offered some form of sex education in junior and senior high school and 66% offered sex education in elementary school. Rather than offer sex education courses, however, most districts integrate the material into biology, physical education, or health courses and offer no more than 10 hours of instruction on sexuality. Thus, although the majority of school districts offer sex education, the amount of time spent on the topic is minimal. Kirby (1985) concluded that less than 10% of all public school students are given comprehensive sex education courses.

Sex education in the classroom.

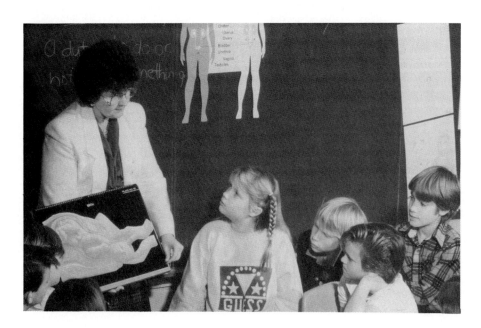

How Sex Education Has Changed over the Years

The following is a hypothetical example of how a high school graduate in 1900 might have described his sex education in school:

I had one teacher who talked to a group of us boys about sexual matters. He was very concerned that we understood that sex was given to man in order that he could reproduce. Sex is for marriage. He told us that in our relationship with girls we should think of all girls in the way we think of our sisters or our mothers. We should never do or say anything to a girl that we would not want another boy to do or say to our sisters or mothers.

Our teacher also talked a little about what he called sex hygiene. He warned us that to touch certain parts of our body unnecessarily would cause harm to us. We might not grow and develop as we should. He scared us a little by telling us that we could get horrible diseases if we had illicit sex relationships. Apparently nearly everyone who has unwholesome sex relationships will "get caught" and pay for it with an infection.

The last thing he talked about he called eugenics. Times being like they

are it is most important for us to be thinking of improving the race through our choice of a desirable wife who will produce good children. Having children out of wedlock and by degenerate women would not only show lack of self control and restraint but also lack of concern for mankind. He said that above all we should strive for the virtues of self control and restraint.

After he finished talking he asked us if we had any questions, but when we asked, he explained that some of our questions did not concern us now. They were important only to married men.

A hypothetical high school graduate of 1940 might describe his sex education in the following way:

We had what you might call sex education in biology, in science, on physiology and hygiene, and in physical education, I guess. I think the girls learned about babies and families and that sort of thing in their home economics classes.

We learned all about reproduction in plants, in animals, and in humans, and

about development of the embryo. We learned the scientific names for things relating to the physiology of reproduction. We spent a lot of time talking about heredity and the ways in which children are like their parents.

Our physical education teacher tried to discuss with us "moral training," telling us that we should be considerate and respectful of girls and that we should plan for the future and see sex as a part of marriage and family. We should be strong enough to do what we know is right even if our friends encourage us to do otherwise. As adolescents we should enjoy sports and activities and spend our time in worthwhile pursuits. We talked about boy-girl relationships, how to get along with girls and with our families now and in the future. We talked about what husbands and wives and children should do to make families happy. We even talked a little about deciding who to marry. We had several films about venereal disease. Our teacher emphasized that we must think not only about what would happen to ourselves if we got one of these diseases but what would happen to our wives and children. The venereal diseases are so common and so dangerous, our teacher said, that some states now require people to be tested for them before they can get married.

From Penland, L.R.: Sex education in 1900, 1940 and 1980: an historical sketch, J. Sch. Health 51(4):305-309, 1981. Copyright, 1981. American School Health Association, Kent, OH 44240.

The topics most often covered in sex education programs in the schools are sexual physiology, sexually transmitted diseases, pregnancy, and childbirth. Intermediate in coverage are such topics as sexual relationships, communication, dating, and contraception. The topics least likely to be covered are sexual techniques and more controversial subjects such as masturbation, abortion, and homosexuality (Orr, 1982; Sonenstein and Pittman, 1984).

The teenage pregnancy rate in the United States has declined somewhat in the last couple of decades (Furstenberg and Brooks-Gunn, 1989). The increase in sex education in the schools over the same period may be at least partly responsible for the decline in the number of teenage pregnancies. However, the teenage pregnancy rate in the United States is still the highest of any in the Western world (Jones et al., 1985). Teenagers in the United States are no

A Comparison of Teenage Pregnancy Rates in the United States and Sweden

The teenage pregnancy rate is much higher in the United States than in most other developed countries in northern and western Europe (Wallace and Vienonen, 1989). The following are the number of pregnancies per year for 1,000 women:

| Country | Teenage pregnancy rates | |
	Age 15-17	Age 18-19
United States	62	144
England and Wales	27	75
France	19	79
Canada	28	68
Sweden	20	59
Netherlands	7	25

The teenage pregnancy rate in one of those countries, Sweden, has decreased significantly over the last four decades (Bernhardt, 1987):

Years	Teen pregnancy rate in Sweden
1951-1955	37.8
1956-1960	36.7
1961-1965	42.8
1966-1970	41.9
1971-1975	32.1
1976-1980	19.8
1981-1985	12.2

The decrease in the teenage pregnancy rate is probably attributable to the number of national programs. Sex education, which has been required in the schools since 1964, begins in the first few years of school. The Swedish Board of Education publishes a sex education manual that details educational topics and goals. It covers not only the biological aspects of sex and reproduction, but also instruction concerning values and interpersonal relations. In addition, sex education teachers are given specific training in sex education. Finally, Sweden has a system of family planning clinics whose services are free. These clinics provide pregnancy testing, counseling, contraception, Papanicolaou (Pap) smears, prenatal testing, and gynecological examinations. Women are also provided with birth control pills at a low cost and with intrauterine devices at no cost. Special family planning clinics are available for teenagers, and parental consent is not required for any of their services.

Given the relatively low rate of teenage pregnancies in Sweden compared with the United States, sex educators in the United States might do well to investigate the Swedish sex education programs for ways to improve current programs or establish more effective programs in this country.

more sexually active than adolescents from other Western countries, but they are much more likely to become pregnant. These pregnancies occur because of a lack of adequate knowledge about sexuality and contraception. Our schools could do a much better job of providing teenagers with an adequate sex education.

The scope of many sex education programs is too limited. The focus is often restricted to biological functioning, and the importance of interpersonal relationships and responsibilities is often omitted. The information conveyed in such programs is frequently aimed at preventing unwanted pregnancies and avoiding sexually transmitted diseases and seldom focused on how sex might be used as a means of personal enjoyment and a way of enriching intimate relationships. Furthermore, since most sex education is integrated into other types of courses rather than being presented in a separate course, most instructors are not well prepared to teach such information. Like past instructors (see box, p. 669), many of today's instructors feel uncomfortable talking about sex and convey this attitude to the students, thereby reinforcing the view that sex is a dirty subject that should not be discussed openly.

So far no standard curriculum is available for sex educators. However, Bruess and Greenberg (1981) suggest that the following concepts be taught at each of the following developmental levels:

Preschool
1. A recognition of the roles of family members
2. A recognition of the authority and concern of parents and others responsible for the care of preschool children
3. Emphasis on the development of a positive self-image
4. Opportunities to make friends with children of both sexes
5. Ways to cooperate with family members and others in work and play
6. An understanding that living things grow, may reproduce, and die
7. Consideration of the behavior of babies

Early Elementary Grades
1. The basics of plant and animal (including human) reproduction
2. The similarities and differences in males and females
3. Growth and development (physical changes and emotional feelings)
4. Family roles and responsibilities
5. Discussions of individual feelings about oneself and other people

Upper Elementary Grades
1. Biological information in greater depth
   a. The endocrine system
   b. Menstruation
   c. Birth and pregnancy
   d. Nocturnal emissions
   e. Masturbation
   f. Body size differences (temporary and permanent)
   g. Intercourse
   h. Response to sexual stimulation (contact, pictures, and reading)
   i. Birth control and abortion
   j. Physical abnormalities
2. Interpersonal relations
   a. Heterosexual feelings
   b. Homosexual feelings
   c. How emotions affect body functions
   d. Changing family responsibilities and privileges
   e. The need to use different approaches with different people
   f. Different male and female feelings
   g. Why brothers and sisters (mothers and fathers) fight
3. Self-concept
   a. How do people react to me?
   b. What kind of a person am I?
   c. How do I feel about myself?
   d. Why do people like me sometimes and not other times?
   e. Why do I hate people sometimes?

Lower Secondary Grades
1. Overview of biological material
2. More detail on birth control

    a. How various methods work

    b. Research in contraception

3. More on intimate sexual behavior

    a. How far to go

    b. Why individuals feel the way they do

    c. Why people behave sexually the way they do

4. Dating and interpersonal relationships

    a. What to expect from a date (both the person and the experience)

    b. Why people date; why some do not date

5. Variations in sexual behavior

    a. Homosexuality

    b. Voyeurism

    c. Transvestism

    d Transsexualism

    e. Exhibitionism

Upper Secondary Grades

1. Birth control research and details

    a. Population dynamics

    b. Abortion

2. Dating decisions

    a. Dating standards and regulations

    b. Premarital sexual behavior

    c. Communication

3. Contemporary marriage patterns

    a. Companionship and patriarchal structures

    b. Communes and group marriages

    c. Three-way marriages

    d. Living together

    e Contract marriages

4. Sexual myths

5. Moral decisions

6. Control of sex drives

7. Parenthood

    a. Childbirth

    b. Childrearing

    c. Sex education of children

8. Masculinity and femininity

9. Research in sexuality

    a. Human sexual response

    b. Sexual dysfunction

    c. Sterility

    d. Pornography

10. Sexuality and legality

    a. Personal behavior

    b. Treatment and information

    c. Sex education

11. Historical and social factors affecting sexuality

    a. Selected historical accounts related to sexuality

    b. Cultural aspects of sexuality

12. Sexuality and advertising

Bruess and Greenberg, 1981, pp. 226-228

CURRENT CONTROVERSIES

The issue of providing sex education in schools has always been controversial in the United States. To avoid controversial topics, many sex education programs have dealt only with biological facts. As a result, they have provided insufficient information. Recently, however, there have been calls for stronger and more comprehensive sex education programs.

In response to the epidemic rates of teenage pregnancies and abortions, the National Academy of Sciences recommended an increased emphasis on sex education (The National Academy of Sciences Urges Establishment of School-Based Clinics, 1986). After 2 years of research a panel of 15 physicians, social scientists, and public health experts concluded that efforts to dissuade teenagers from engaging in sexual intercourse have been ineffective. As a result, the panel urged that governments and schools give pregnancy prevention the "highest priority." In addition, the panel recommended that teenagers be given assertiveness and decision-making training aimed at helping them delay the onset of sexual activity.

The advent of AIDS has also caused many to believe that comprehensive sex education is a must. Proponents of sex education attest that with the threat of AIDS, lack of accurate information on human sexuality has become potentially fatal. One powerful adherent of this belief is the former surgeon general C. Everett Koop (Koop, 1986). In the autumn of 1986 Koop issued a 36-page report on AIDS filled with the most recent scientific evidence and diagrams showing how the virus can be transmitted through anal sex and drug use. Koop stated that since no cure or reliable vaccine has been found, education is the most important step that can be taken to limit the spread of AIDS. Koop proposed teaching students about AIDS as part of a continuing sex education program beginning as early as third grade.

Although Koop's report supports the importance of sex education in schools, it created new controversies over what should be included in sex education programs. Many critics reacted angrily to the prospect of explicit teaching of homosexuality and anal sex (Leo, 1986). However, the surgeon general's belief that AIDS education should start in third grade created the greatest controversy (Kantrowitz, 1986). In a survey taken after Koop's report was released, only 23% of those polled agreed with the suggestion; most professional educators opposed it (Leo, 1986). Those against the suggestion feared that young children would be unable to understand topics dealing with AIDS and might only become frightened of both sex and death by receiving such information.

However, some experts support Koop's proposal. They say that children as young as 7 or 8 have heard about AIDS on television or elsewhere but often have difficulty getting answers to their questions (Kantrowitz, 1986). Their incomplete knowledge and fears of real or imagined hazards might create anxiety about AIDS in young children (Klein, 1987). Some experts suggest that to prevent such anxiety, people explaining AIDS to young children should be careful to use simple explanations and to avoid alarming language (Kantrowitz, 1986).

Other experts believe that early adolescence is the appropriate time to teach the details of AIDS. A number of cities have begun using different approaches

When should students be informed about the precautions to take against AIDS?

to warn teenagers of the threat of AIDS (Kantrowitz, 1986). In San Francisco a series of classes on AIDS that discusses the disease and how to take precautions against it, first taught to high school students, has been extended to include sixth- and eight-grade classes. In Greater Miami schools, AIDS information has become part of the sex education program: AIDS is mentioned briefly to seventh graders as one of many sexually transmitted diseases, and a more thorough presentation on AIDS is given to tenth graders.

Unfortunately, the most controversial problem cannot be resolved as easily: the question of values. The most common argument against sex education programs is that they undermine the family and cause children to experiment sexually because they do not teach moral standards (Leo, 1986). However, many sex education programs described as "value free" are actually based on the ethics of caring and respect for others (Scales, 1981). As was pointed out by Peter Scales, a sex educator and avid proponent of sex education, "It is true most public school sex education programs do not adopt rigid moral stances urging young people to refrain from sexual activity; neither do they urge students to have sexual experiences" (1984). Rather than try to decide what values should be taught, a number of sex education programs include exercises to help students recognize and understand their own sexual values. Such contemporary approaches also emphasize assertiveness training and the mechanics of decision making (Leo, 1986).

Because American society lacks a consensus on the moral issue of human sexuality, the acceptance of or resistance to sex education programs seems to rest largely on each program's match to the individual community. Those communities with the strongest sex education programs share some general characteristics: a high degree of parental involvement, administrative efforts to promote teacher training, a cooperative relationship between the school and a family planning agency, and strong school board support (Scales, 1984).

Although opposition to sex education in schools might seem pervasive because of some highly publicized protests, for years surveys have shown that about 80% of Americans favor comprehensive sex education in public schools. In fact, after the surgeon general's report concerning AIDS, support reached a high of 86% (Leo, 1986). It seems that most parents welcome sex education in schools even if they have reservations about it (Scales, 1984). Many parents, embarrassed and reluctant to talk to their children about sex, realize they do not provide adequate sex education for their children. Therefore the school provides the only sex education many children ever receive. Perhaps because of this realization, when parents are given the opportunity to refuse permission for their child to participate in a sex education course, only 1% to 3% do so.

As the debate over sex education has been coming closer to a consensus for comprehensive sex education programs, school districts across the nation are facing another heated controversy: school clinics. School clinics are health facilities in or near public schools that are funded by public and private money. In 1986, 72 such clinics were open around the nation and more than 100 others were planned (Leo, 1986). Although all school clinics offer across-the-board medical care, their association with contraceptives has led to an emotional debate. In 1986 only 28% of the school clinics actually dispensed contraceptives, 52% prescribed them, and the rest made referrals to family planning agencies (Leo, 1986).

Criticism of school clinics has come from many directions. Church officials have accused school systems with such clinics of usurping the parent's role and of promoting promiscuity by making contraception available (Katz, 1986). Opponents also fear that such clinics would refer pregnant girls to abortion clinics; school officials have sworn this would not be the case.

School clinics have also attracted strong support. In addition to supporting more comprehensive sex education, as mentioned earlier, the National Academy of Science has expressed strong favor for school clinics in high-risk pop-

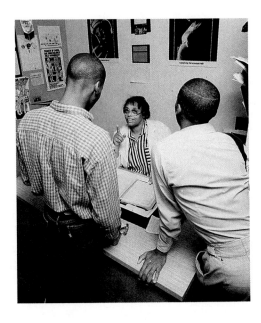

School clinics like this one are highly controversial.

ulations as a means of decreasing the rate of teen pregnancy and abortions (The National Academy of Sciences Urges Establishment of School-Based Clinics, 1986). They have attested that making contraceptive methods available and accessible and urging those who are sexually active to use these methods is the most effective strategy for pregnancy prevention. Proponents of school clinics believe these facilities will also combat the spread of AIDS and other sexually transmitted diseases (Leo, 1986). Finally, those in support of school clinics feel that students who are afraid to talk to their parents about sex might be more willing to talk with clinic physicians (Katz, 1986).

Although few studies on the effects of school clinics have been completed, those that have seem to show that such facilities are effective. Zabin and associates (1986) found that school-based clinics tend to increase contraceptive use and decrease the pregnancy rate among adolescents. When the clinics dispensed contraceptives, there was a corresponding decrease in the age of onset of heterosexual intercourse. In addition to the decrease in pregnancy rate, schools with clinics have reported a virtual nonexistence of repeat pregnancies (Leo, 1986).

In summary, the high teenage pregnancy rate and the fear of AIDS have led to calls for more comprehensive and effective sex education programs. However, the view that more thorough sex education is needed has been controversial. Some people believe that sex education will result in more sexual experimentation. Some believe that our current sex education programs are not good because they do not teach moral values. Others are against the establishment of school clinics because they believe such clinics will dispense contraceptives and encourage abortions. Although the opponents of sex education have received a great deal of attention, most Americans support sex education in the schools.

SUMMARY

1 There has not traditionally been any commonly accepted system by which individuals in the United States have been provided with sex education. In 1948 Kinsey reported that the men he interviewed had received most of their sex information as children from other children. In 1953 he reported that no more than 5% of the women he interviewed had received more than incidental information from their parents; again, most of their sexual information came from peers. Given our culture's increasingly liberal views about sexuality, one might assume that parents are more likely to talk to their children about sexual issues now than they were in the 1940s and 1950s. However, in the 1960s, 87% of the parents interviewed by Libby and Nass refused to discuss sexual issues with their children when the children asked relevant questions. And in 1974 Hunt reported that both males and females still listed friends as their major source of sex information as they were growing up.

2 Hunt found that school sex education programs were mentioned even less frequently than parents as the main source of sex education for the individuals he interviewed.

3 Since most individuals get their sex education from friends rather than parents or teachers, much of their information may be inaccurate.

4 Many parents are opposed to sex education because the parents feel that the less adolescents know about sex, the less likely they are to be involved sexually. However, research does not support this assumption. Receiving one's sex education from parents and teachers may actually decrease the incidence of problems such as sexually transmitted diseases, unwanted pregnancies, exploitive relationships, and nonfulfilling sexual experiences. Research also indicates that adolescents whose parents play a major role in their sex education are less likely to engage in early sexual activity than less well-informed adolescents.

5 Parents do much to determine their children's view of sexuality whether they intend to or not. The child's views begin to form at an early age. Parents provide children with a basic orientation to sexual matters by their own sexual and affectionate behavior and attitudes. If the parents hide their verbally and physically affectionate behavior from their children, prohibit nudity in the home, and treat masturbation and sex play as if they were shocking, dirty, and disgusting, they transmit to their children the feeling that sexuality is dirty and disgusting. Such views interfere with enjoyable, healthy sexuality during adulthood.

6 In addition to influencing the child's view of sexuality through indirect sources, parents profoundly affect their children's sexual attitudes by the way they provide direct sexual information. If children learn about sex from their parents, they are more likely to get accurate information than if they learn about sexuality from their peers. Peers are more likely to give the impression that sex is "dirty" and shameful.

7 Most schools in the United States provide some type of sex education. However, many of these programs are much too limited in both the amount of time devoted to sex education and the topics discussed. Most early sex education programs dealt only with the physical changes of puberty, menstruation, reproduction, and sexually transmitted diseases. Information regarding interpersonal relationships and responsibilities still is often omitted.

8 The high teenage pregnancy rate and the fear of AIDS have renewed calls for more comprehensive sex education programs. However, not everyone agrees that we need more thorough sex education. Opponents of sex education believe that it will increase sexual experimentation, will not convey appropriate moral values, and will increase contraceptive use and abortions. Nevertheless, the majority of Americans support sex education in the schools.

FACT
OR
FICTION

ANSWERS

1 Research indicates that children still obtain most of their information about sex from their peers rather than from adults.
2 Studies have shown that no relationship exists between having had sex education courses in school and engaging in sexual activity.

QUESTIONS FOR THOUGHT ?

1 From whom, as a child, did you learn most about sex?
2 Do you wish your parents had told you more about sex?
3 What type of sex education did you get in school? What do you think the schools could do to improve sex education?
4 Do you think children should be taught about AIDS in elementary school as former surgeon general Koop has suggested?
5 Do you think high schools should have family planning clinics?
6 Do you think high school clinics should distribute condoms?

SUGGESTED READINGS

Calderone, M., and Ramey, J.: Talking with your child about sex, New York, 1982, Random House, Inc.
  A book to help parents talk with their children about sex.
Carrera, M.: Sex: the facts, the acts, and your feelings, New York, 1981, Crown Publishers, Inc.
  A comprehensive and easy-to-read book about sexuality and relationships.
Ehrenberg, M., and Ehrenberg, O.: The intimate circle, New York, 1988, Simon & Schuster, Inc.
  A book written for parents about how they can be involved in their children's sex education.
Lewis, H.R., and Lewis, M.E.: The parent's guide to teenage sex and pregnancy, New York, 1980, St. Martin's Press, Inc.
  A book to help parents deal with their teenager's sexuality.

Religious and Ethical Views of Sexuality

Some churches have very strong pro-life views.

For man, precisely because he has the power to reason, can, in his actions, not only clearly distinguish pleasure from its opposite, but can also isolate it, so to speak, and treat it as a distinct aim of his activity. His actions are then shaped only with a view to the pleasure he wishes to obtain, or the pain he wishes to avoid. If actions involving a person of the opposite sex are shaped exclusively or primarily with this in view, then that person will become only the means to an end. . . . This variant . . . does not arise in the sexual life of animals, which is conducted exclusively at the natural and instinctive level, and is therefore directed solely to the purpose which the sexual urge serves—i.e. procreation, the maintenance of the species. At this level sexual pleasure—purely animal sexual pleasure, of course—cannot constitute an end in itself. It is different with man. Here it is easy to see how the fact of being a person, and rational, begets morality. This morality is personalistic both in relation to its subject and in relation to its object—objectively because it is concerned with the proper treatment of a person in the context of sexual pleasure.

KAROL WOJTYLA (POPE JOHN PAUL II)
Love and Responsibility, pp. 33-34

This final chapter discusses sexual ethics, or our standards of conduct and values regarding sexual issues. The chapter begins with a discussion of religion and sexuality. A consideration of religion is important because religious views have been instrumental in determining the sexual attitudes and values of people throughout history. The discussion is limited to the three religions that have had the greatest impact on Western culture. The consideration of religious influences is followed by a description of other factors that influence our sexual morals and conduct. The chapter ends with a discussion of some major controversies in our culture regarding sexual ethics: abortion, contraception, premarital sex, extramarital sex, and homosexuality. Ethical issues raised by recent technological advances are also addressed. These issues include artificial insemination, in vitro fertilization, and prenatal screening.

RELIGIOUS VIEWS OF SEXUALITY

The three major religions that have had a substantial impact on Western culture are Judaism, Catholicism, and Protestantism. The sexual ethics prescribed by each of these major religious traditions will be presented. However, it is important to remember that not all proponents of a particular religion adhere to the same attitudes and values regarding sexual issues. Rather, great diversity exists in the sexual values and behaviors among members of these three major religions.

Judaism

There are three major subtypes of Judaism in the United States today: Orthodox, Conservative, and Reform. The Orthodox Jews are the most conservative in both sexual and nonsexual matters. Although all subtypes of Jews tend to follow Old Testament proscriptions regarding sexual issues, Orthodox Jews follow those proscriptions most closely.

In the Jewish faith, sex in marriage is considered a natural bodily function to be enjoyed equally between partners.

Judaism accepts sexuality as a normal, natural body function that should be enjoyed. In this sense Judaism differs from some other religious traditions in which sex is not considered to be good, clean, and natural, but sinful. Unlike the Catholic religion, Judaism rejects sexual abstinence: "Not only is celibacy not valued as a virtue, but it is considered a sin for layman and priest alike" (Rosenheim, 1977). Sex is considered to have two beneficial functions. First, it has a procreative function ("Be fruitful and multiply," Genesis 1:28). Second, it facilitates bonds between people ("It is not good that man should be alone," Genesis 2:18). Marriage is considered important for the well-being of every individual, and therefore all Jews are expected to marry. They are also expected to stay married. Although divorce is permitted, it is considered a tragedy (Rosenheim, 1977). Jews in the United States are more likely to get married (Waxman, 1983) and less likely to get divorced (Cohen, 1983; Waxman, 1983) than the non-Jewish population.

It is the husband's duty to have intercourse with his wife, although the prescribed frequency varies with the man's physical capacity and occupation (Rosenheim, 1977). Laborers are expected to have intercourse at least twice weekly, and scholars are expected to have sexual relations at least once each week. The woman is not viewed as someone whose purpose is to gratify her husband's sexual needs but rather as someone who should share in mutual gratification. The man is encouraged to arouse his wife and make sure she is ready for intercourse because mutual willingness is considered necessary for sexual relations. Intercourse is thought to be inappropriate if the husband and wife no longer love each other (Schwartz, Jewelewicz, and Wiele, 1980).

Although sex is considered to be positive and pleasurable, sexual behavior is highly regulated in Judaism. Sex in marriage is thought of as a gift from God. However, intercourse during the woman's menstrual period and the week following has traditionally been forbidden. The woman is considered unclean during the menstrual period, and the week following her period is a time of purification. At the end of this week the woman takes a ritual bath in a pool called a *mikvah* for purification. Thus the couple is expected to abstain from sexual intercourse for the first 12 to 14 days of the woman's menstrual cycle. Although the original reasons for these restrictions are not known, it is interesting that these restrictions allow the couple to resume intercourse at the time the woman would tend to ovulate (about midcycle). As a result, this practice may increase the likelihood of a woman being impregnated.

In addition to regulations regarding when sexual behavior should occur in a marital relationship, there are regulations regarding what types of sexual behaviors are appropriate. Since reproduction is the main goal of sex, masturbation, coitus interruptus, anal intercourse, and other practices that result in ejaculation outside the vagina are prohibited (Schwartz, Jewelewicz, and Wiele, 1980). If a man engages in any of these activities and thereby wastes his sperm, he is considered to be depriving unborn children of life, which is akin to killing them. For the same reason, contraception is typically not permitted, although it may be approved for medical reasons. Elective abortion is also forbidden unless birth of a child would put the mother at risk.

All sexual activity outside marriage is prohibited. Premarital sexual relations are strongly discouraged. Adultery is considered a severe violation of approved sexual behavior, and homosexuality is also forbidden.

In summary, the Orthodox Jewish views of sexuality tend to be accepting of sexuality within marriage but conservative with respect to issues such as contraception, abortion, and masturbation (if it leads to ejaculation). Reform Jews take a much more liberal view of all of these matters. They are generally not opposed to contraception and abortion. They do not forbid masturbation or premarital sex. They do not prohibit sexual intercourse during the first 12 to 14 days of the menstrual cycle. Furthermore, the Union of Hebrew Congregations, the national agency of the Reform synagogues, has recently accepted homosexual congregations into its ranks (Waxman, 1983). Conservative Jews tend to fall somewhere between Orthodox and Reform Jews on most sexual issues.

Catholicism

Whereas the Jewish views on sexuality are taken from the Old Testament, Roman Catholic positions are based on the teachings of the Old Testament, the New Testament, and the popes. According to the Roman Catholic view, the only approved sexuality is that which occurs within marriage and for the purpose of procreation. Marriage (between two baptized Christians) is considered a sacrament. Once a couple is married, second marriages are prohibited except in special circumstances such as when the previous spouse has died or the previous marriage has been annulled.

All forms of sexuality outside of the marriage bond are prohibited. Masturbation is considered sinful. Premarital sex is not approved even if the couple is engaged to be married. Extramarital sex is always forbidden.

Although the official Catholic position has always been to condemn homosexuality, some of the more liberal dioceses in the United States, particularly in California, have recently taken more accepting attitudes toward homosexuality. For example, a commission on social justice of the San Francisco diocese appointed a task force on gay-lesbian issues. The task force report, which was accepted by the commission as an unofficial report, advocates a policy of forgiveness toward homosexuals and states that the traditional (official) church views are "practically meaningless and pastorally useless" (At bay in San Francisco, 1982). This was the first report issued by a panel in any U.S. diocese that had actually accepted homosexual behavior. Of course, many of the more conservative members of the diocese were not pleased with the report. Likewise, the diocese of San Jose, California, has recently issued guidelines for the pastoral ministry of homosexuals. The guidelines state that all baptized persons have an equal claim to the church's ministry regardless of their sexual orientation or social attitudes (Ministry to homosexuals, 1986). Although some Catholics in the United States are pushing for more liberal views, the Catholic Church still holds that homosexuality is a sin.

The Catholic Church is opposed not only to sex that occurs outside of marriage, such as premarital, extramarital, and homosexual sex, but also to sex that is not used for its natural, biological purpose—procreation. The Catholic stance is that sexual interaction has two purposes: to unify and to procreate. If these two purposes are separated, human sexuality is downgraded (Use of the "morning-after" pill in cases of rape, 1986). If a husband and wife give themselves completely to each other, they should not refuse to be open to the new life that naturally follows from such a union. Although the official Catholic position forbids the use of artificial contraception, a large number of Catholics in the United States oppose the official Catholic view on contraception (Pastors and people: viewpoints on church policies and positions, 1986).

Just as the Catholic Church opposes contraception, it also opposes abortion. "Life must be protected with the utmost care from the moment of conception: Abortion and infanticide are abominable crimes" (Flannery, 1975). Even in cases of threat to the mother's life, rape, and incest, abortion is forbidden:

> In a very small number of cases, conception may in fact occur [with an] individuality, distinct from each of its parents and from any of their cells. . . . From that time, the requirements of the moral law, transcending even the most understandable emotional reactions, are clear: The newly conceived child cannot rightly be made to suffer the penalty of death for a man's violation of the woman.
>
> Use of the "morning-after" pill in cases of rape, 1986, p. 636

While there is widespread opposition among Catholics to the official condemnation of the use of artificial contraception, there is also some opposition to the official Catholic position on abortion, although it is much less widespread. During the 1984 presidential campaign an advertisement titled "Catholic Statement on Pluralism and Abortion" appeared in the *New York Times* (New York Times, Oct. 7, 1984). The advertisement was signed by 97 Catholic scholars and religious and social leaders. Because many of the signers later were censured by the Catholic Church and other Catholics, a second advertisement appeared in the *New York Times* in 1986, this one signed by approximately 1,000 people, to show solidarity with those who signed the first advertisement. In the second advertisement the signers affirmed that "we believe that Catholics who, in good conscience, take positions on the difficult questions of legal abortion and other controversial issues that differ from the official hierarchical positions act within their rights and responsibilities as Catholics and citizens" (New York Times, March 2, 1986).

As a result of the advertisements in the *New York Times,* the National Conference of Catholic Bishops was asked if a Catholic can legitimately dissent from the church's teaching on abortion. The response was as follows: "In view of the consistency and universality of this Catholic teaching, there is no such thing as legitimate dissent by a Catholic from the proposition that to seek or perform a direct abortion is, objectively considered, a grave moral evil" (Pluralism, dissent and abortion, 1986).

In spite of the position taken by the National Conference of Catholic Bishops, only one fourth of Catholics in general and three fourths of their pastors believe that abortion is never acceptable (Pastors and people: viewpoints on church policies and positions, 1986). The majority of Catholics believe that abortion is acceptable in extreme circumstances such as threat to the mother's life, rape, and incest. Most Catholics do not believe that abortion should be available on demand.

In summary, the official Roman Catholic position is fairly conservative on most issues relating to human sexuality, including contraception, abortion, masturbation, premarital sex, extramarital sex, and homosexuality. However, not all Catholics adhere to the official beliefs. In the United States a sizable proportion of Catholics hold more liberal views on many of these issues. Thus, although there is one official Catholic position on many sexual issues, a diversity of opinion exists among Catholics.

Protestantism

In the sixteenth century Martin Luther led the Protestant Reformation, in which the Protestants broke away from the Roman Catholic Church. One issue on which the early Protestants differed from the Catholics was the celibacy of priests and the importance of marriage. Catholics believed that their priests should be celibate and that marriage was a necessary evil for laypersons (Tannahill, 1980). To Martin Luther and his followers, however, sex and marriage were a normal and good part of life and there was no reason for the clergy to remain celibate.

Just as the Protestants were more accepting of sex and more positive about marriage than the Catholics, they were also more accepting of marital separation, divorce, and remarriage. Whereas the Catholic Church believed marriage to be a sacrament and considered it to be a lifetime contract, the early Protestants did not view marriage as a sacrament.

With the exception of their views about marriage, divorce, and celibacy for the clergy, the early Protestants' attitudes about sexual issues did not differ much from the Catholics' views. Both used the Old and New Testaments for sexual guidance. Both Protestants and Catholics disapproved of premarital, extramarital, and homosexual sex.

As a result of Martin Luther's emphasis on the importance of the common people and deemphasis of the clergy and church hierarchy, among Protestants the individual became more important and the church authorities became less powerful. Decreased church authority led to more tolerance of individual differences in opinion on various religious and sexual issues. As a result, today it is impossible to make a statement about a unified Protestant view on any religious or sexual topic. Different Protestant denominations have different views, and diverse attitudes exist within any one denomination. However, some general statements about conservative, moderate, and liberal Protestants can be made.

fundamentalist
One who adheres to a strict and literal interpretation of the Bible.

The most conservative Protestants are called **fundamentalists.** Fundamentalists believe in a strict and literal interpretation of the Bible. They are conservative on sexual issues. For the most part they strongly oppose premarital and extramarital sex (Maret and Maret, 1982), homosexuality (Maret, 1984), abortion, and divorce. These attitudes are similar to the positions of the Catholic Church. In addition, the fundamentalists consider themselves to be "pro-family." Many of them oppose the changes that have resulted from the women's movement. Many fundamentalists believe that a woman's place is in the home taking care of her husband and children. They believe that the man should be the breadwinner and leader and the woman should be subservient to the man.

Drawing conclusions about the views of moderate Protestants is more difficult because they hold such diverse opinions. However, moderate Protestants tend to accept abortion, be unwilling to condemn premarital sex, believe that divorce is an acceptable solution to an unhappy marriage, and believe that remarriage after divorce is acceptable in all cases. Moderate Protestants are at least somewhat tolerant of homosexuality. However, most think that extramarital sex is wrong.

Liberal Protestants tend to believe that some of the sexual prohibitions of early Christianity were a result of the cultural conditions of the time rather than absolute moral principles that should apply in any historical time. Many liberal Protestants feel that because cultural conditions have changed since biblical times, people's moral and ethical values should change as well. They tend to believe that views about what is right and wrong with respect to sexual issues should be based on current cultural conditions rather than on what is written in the Bible. For example, many liberal Protestants believe that the need for strong prohibitions against premarital and extramarital sex has diminished because new contraceptive techniques can eliminate the possibility of conceiving children outside of marriage. They argue that restricting sexual relationships to marriage is no longer necessary. In addition to being tolerant of both premarital and extramarital sex, liberal Protestants tend to accept almost any other type of sexual activity as long as it is not harmful to anyone. They believe that sexual decisions should be left to the discretion of each individual.

This discussion illustrates that Protestants have no unified position on sexual issues. Protestant thinking ranges from very conservative to extremely liberal on all sexual issues. Even within denominations and within specific churches, members typically hold a wide array of opinions on any sexual issue.

OTHER DETERMINANTS OF SEXUAL ETHICS

Although our religious traditions have had an important impact on our views about sexual ethics, the various religious traditions are not the sole determinant of these views. A variety of other factors are also influential. Most of these factors have been discussed in other chapters, but some of the most important influences will be discussed briefly here.

The law has an important influence on our views of what is right and wrong. We may generally think of our laws as reflecting the values held by individuals in our culture, but changes in the law tend to influence our attitudes and values as well. For example, changes in the law such as those that made abortion legal and sex discrimination illegal have made many of us more accepting of abortion and less accepting of sex discrimination. The legal issues involved in some of the current ethical controversies are discussed in the following section.

Cultural change has a definite impact on our views of ethical sexual behavior. With time the sexual values portrayed in our movies, television programs, magazines, and music have changed substantially. These cultural changes influence individuals' values. When a culture becomes more liberal with respect to sexual behavior, as ours did in the 1960s and 1970s, the attitudes and values of many individuals in that culture change correspondingly.

Probably the most important factor in determining our sexual ethics is the family, whether or not they intend to teach specific attitudes. In addition, both peers and the schools can affect sexual ethics. Sex education programs influence the sexual behavior of adolescents, and this effect may last well into adulthood. However, the values the family conveys to the child are the most important single influence on that individual's sexual ethics.

CURRENT CONTROVERSIES IN SEXUAL ETHICS
Abortion

The sexual issue that is receiving the most public debate today is abortion. On the one hand, the pro-life individuals believe that abortion should be prohibited in any circumstances. The pro-life group is composed of Catholics, Orthodox

See Chapters 1, 10, 12, 22, and 23 for additional discussion of factors that affect sexual ethics.

A much more detailed discussion of the legal issues that relate to sexuality is presented in Chapter 22.

The importance of culture in determining views about sexual ethics is covered in Chapter 1.

As discussed in Chapter 23, the family has an important impact on the individual's sexual ethics.

The impact of sex education programs and peer influence on sexual ethics is discussed in Chapter 23.

Abortion is discussed in greater detail in Chapter 8.

Pro-life demonstration.

Pro-choice demonstration.

Jews, conservative Protestants, and others. These individuals believe that the embryo is a human being from the moment of conception and, as a result, should have a right to life. They believe that abortion is murder regardless of when in the pregnancy it occurs.

At the other end of the continuum are the pro-choice individuals. The pro-choice group believes that a woman has a right to decide what happens to her body and that she should have the right to terminate a pregnancy for any reason. This position is also called the abortion-on-demand position. These individuals usually believe that human life does not begin at conception but later in the pregnancy. Therefore they do not view early abortion as murder (see accompanying box).

Many individuals take an intermediate position that abortions should not be performed on demand but only in special circumstances. Such circumstances might include a situation in which the health of the mother is threatened by the continuation of a pregnancy, a pregnancy that resulted from a rape, or a pregnancy in a young girl as a result of an incestuous relationship. Such abortions are often called **therapeutic abortions.**

therapeutic abortions
Abortions administered because of special circumstances, such as a pregnancy that is a threat to the mother's health or the result of a rape or incestuous relationship.

The legal right to abortion has been assured since the 1973 decision of the U.S. Supreme Court in *Roe v. Wade.* In that decision the court struck down the laws that prohibited abortion in both Texas and Georgia. The court ruled that (1) a state cannot bar any woman from obtaining an abortion from a licensed physician during the first 3 months of pregnancy; (2) in the second trimester the state can regulate abortions only when the regulation is related to the preservation of the mother's health; and (3) in the last trimester the state

Ethics of Abortion: The Case of the Famous Violinist

The U.S. Supreme Court in *Roe v. Wade* (1973) declared that abortion is legal and acceptable. Is the court morally correct? Nearly 20 years after this landmark decision the debate over whether abortion is right or wrong continues. An analysis of the ethics involved in abortion is complex and intricate. Thomson (1971) illustrates some of these ethical issues in a clever analogy of pregnancy as a result of rape:

Imagine you wake up one day to find yourself in a hospital bed back to back with an unconscious man. This man is a famous violinist who has been found to have a serious kidney disease. He needs the use of another person's kidneys to survive. The Society of Music Lovers had you knocked out and kidnapped because you were the only person with the needed blood type. While you were unconscious the violinist's circulatory system was connected to yours and now your kidneys are filtering poisons from his blood as well as from your own. The director of the hospital informs you that if you are disconnected, the violinist will certainly die. For the violinist to be cured you need to remain attached to his kidneys for 9 months.

Thomson's analogy presents us with an interesting moral dilemma. Are you obligated to remain attached to the violinist? He is a human, and he has a right to life. What if it were necessary to stay attached to him for the rest of your life? What if you ran the risk of damage to your kidneys and eventual death because of this connection? Even in these circumstances is it true that if you disconnect your kidneys from his you are violating his right to life? Does a person's right to life outweigh your right to decide what happens to your body?

Thomson argues that although the violinist has a right to life, he does not have the right to demand the use of another's body to continue his life. She suggests that although it would be very nice of you to remain attached to the violinist, therefore saving his life, and although it is probably something you "should" do, it is not something you *must* do. She points out that you have never made a commitment to help the violinist. The Society of Music Lovers forced you to give him the use of your body, and therefore you are not responsible for maintaining his life. In the case of a threat to your own life both you and the violinist have a right to life, but you both also have the right to control your own bodies; therefore the violinist cannot expect you to remain attached to him.

Meilaender (1979) does not agree that the situation of the violinist is a good analogy. He points out that your connection to the violinist was not the cause of his origin, but a fetus is created through its attachment in the womb. This natural development, he contends, gives the fetus special human rights that the violinist, who is not genetically related, does not possess. This genetic relationship, according to Meilaender, makes the mother responsible for remaining attached to the fetus.

The above discussion exemplifies some of the complex ethical problems involved in the abortion issue. There may never be an enduring "right" or "wrong" verdict on the morality of the legalization of abortion. Morals are subjective and change with time and culture. The complicated, intense debate on the morality of abortion will probably continue for some time.

can regulate or even prohibit abortions except those necessary "in appropriate medical judgment to protect the woman's life and health" (Frohock, 1983). The court's decision was reaffirmed in 1986 when the court struck down a Pennsylvania law that would have made abortions more difficult to obtain. Again the court decided that states do not have the right to interfere with a woman's right to end a pregnancy. Justice Blackmun, who wrote the 1986 decision for the court, concluded, "States are not free, under the guise of protecting maternal health or potential life, to intimidate women into continuing pregnancies" (Carelli, 1986). Thus the Supreme Court took a pro-choice stance.

In more recent years the Supreme Court has made decisions that have limited women's access to abortion. In 1989, in *Webster v. Reproductive Health Services,* the court upheld a Missouri statute that forbids the use of state funds for abortion. In 1990 the court upheld a Minnesota law that requires unwed teenagers to notify both parents before having an abortion *(Hodgson v. Minnesota)* and an Ohio law that requires a physician to notify one parent before performing an abortion on a teenager *(Ohio v. Akron Center for Reproductive Health).* Both laws provide an alternative to parental consent: a judge can give permission for an abortion.

Abortion's Hardest Cases

Afterward, when their daughter was buried and their hearts broken, the Bells could see everything clearly. Until then, they had not thought about their teenager's getting pregnant or what they would do if she did. They did not know that there was any such thing as a parental-consent law.

NEWS of the 90's

But there is such a law in Indiana, where the Bells live and where their daughter Becky, 17, died after an illegal abortion. In 1984 the state legislature voted to require a minor to get a parent's permission for an abortion or else to convince a judge that she is mature enough to make the decision on her own.

Becky, whose room in Indianapolis is still filled with stuffed animals and riding gear, felt she could do neither. She had gone to Planned Parenthood for a pregnancy test, the Bells learned as they tried to retrace the steps she took during those final days, and there she was told of the Indiana law. No one knows what happened between that moment and her death two months later. When the Bells went through Becky's purse after she died, they found telephone numbers of abortion clinics in Kentucky, which did not require parental consent. "Becky just happened to live in the wrong state," says her father.

Should a teenage girl have the right—and the burden—of deciding about abortion on her own? Isn't abortion at least as serious a medical procedure as a tonsillectomy or a tooth extraction, both of which require parental involvement in most states? Shouldn't the law force a parent and a child to communicate, especially if the child is in trouble?

From Time, July 9, 1990.

A 1991 U.S. Supreme Court decision may make it more difficult for pregnant women to gain information about abortion. In the case of *Rust v. Sullivan* the Supreme Court ruled that federal regulations can prohibit clinics that receive federal funds for family planning services from supplying information about abortion to their patients. *Rust v. Sullivan* does not forbid women from seeking an abortion or abortion counseling. It does, however, uphold regulations barring health professionals practicing in government-funded clinics from providing a pregnant woman with information about her full range of options, options that include legal abortion—even if a pregnant woman were to ask for such information and even if her health were at risk. Thus family planning clinics must now decide whether to comply with this ruling so they will keep receiving federal funding or to continue to provide information about abortion and thereby forgo government subsidies that allow clinics to provide affordable reproductive health services to low-income women and teens. Some fear that this decision will lead to a more pronounced two-tiered health care system: one that offers affluent women a complete range of options but offers poor women either incomplete information or a range of services severely constrained by funding limitations (Smolowe, 1991). Pro-choice advocates hope that Congress will adopt legislation to reverse the court's decision.

How does the general public feel about abortion? An ABC-Harris poll indicated that 60% of U.S. citizens approved of the *Roe v. Wade* decision. That poll showed that 80% of the public approve of abortion in cases of rape and incest and when the mother's life is endangered but that only 40% approve in other circumstances (Frohock, 1983). A recent Gallup Poll (Gallup and Newport, 1990) indicated that 53% of people believe that abortion should be legal under certain circumstances and 31% believe that it should be legal in all cases. Only 12% thought it should be illegal in all cases and 4% had no opinion. Thus it appears that the majority of Americans believe that abortion is acceptable in special circumstances and that only a minority of Americans support the extreme pro-life position.

Contraception

Contraception is related to abortion in that both are methods that have been developed to interfere with conception or birth. However, contraception is not nearly as controversial as abortion. Few adults in the United States believe that using contraceptives is unethical or immoral. However, as recently as 1965 there were laws against the dissemination of contraceptive information and contraceptive devices. In 1965 the U.S. Supreme Court ruled these laws unconstitutional in *Griswold v. Connecticut*. The court stated that such laws were an invasion of one's right to privacy.

What concern exists about contraception comes primarily from the religious teachings of Roman Catholics and Orthodox Jews who oppose the use of artificial means of contraception. Conservative and Reform Jews and most Protestants favor the use of contraceptive techniques and are often supportive of family planning measures. However, even though the official Catholic and Orthodox Jewish positions oppose artificial methods of birth control, not all proponents of these faiths endorse these views. For example, more than 70%

Battle over the Abortion Pill: Pressure Is Mounting to Introduce the Drug RU 486 in the U.S.

If maintaining a woman's right to have an abortion tops the agenda of pro-choice forces, then introducing RU 486, the so-called abortion pill, into the U.S. ranks second. So far the foes of abortion have managed to keep the French-made drug out of the country. But last week a delegation of American feminists and scientists met in Paris with executives of Roussel Uclaf, the French company that manufactures the drug, and in Frankfurt with officials from Hoechst AG, Roussel's parent company. The Americans presented a petition signed by 115,000 people urging the distribution of RU 486 in the U.S. American support for the drug has also been growing rapidly among physicians. In June the American Medical Association passed a resolution supporting the "legal availability of RU 486 for appropriate research and, if indicated, clinical practice."

NEWS of the 90's

Judged simply on efficacy and safety, RU 486 marks a major advancement over other pregnancy-ending techniques. The drug, which is most effective if used within seven weeks of conception, prevents the hormone progesterone from being absorbed by the lining of the uterus. Without that nourishment the uterus cannot support the growth of the embedded fertilized egg, and the woman miscarries. Taken with prostaglandin, a naturally occurring substance that causes mild uterine contractions, the drug is 95% effective. Developed in 1982 by Dr. Etienne-Emile Baulieu, RU 486 has so far been used by an estimated 55,000 women in 15 countries.

France and China in 1988 formally approved use of the drug, and Roussel will shortly apply to market it in Britain. The company has refused to export it to any country unless several conditions are met, including the legality of abortion and its acceptance by public, political and medical opinion. According to Ariel Mouttet, head of international marketing for RU 486 at Roussel, the sticking point in the U.S. is the political climate. Says she: "We don't want to enter into a social debate in the U.S."

American advocates of RU 486 contend that the company is overestimating the opposition. A Louis Harris survey released last week found that 73% of American adults support abortion rights. Supporters believe that acceptance of RU 486 in other countries will lead women to push harder to bring it to the U.S. Doctors also warn that if the drug is not made officially available in the U.S., a black market for it will develop.

Determined pro-choicers say RU 486 could enter the U.S. through the back door. The drug has potential as a therapy for endometriosis and breast cancer. If RU 486 were approved to treat these conditions, doctors could also prescribe it for abortions. Roussel opposes any deception. Says Dr. Baulieu: "RU 486 has to be sold as the abortion pill that it is."

From Time, Aug. 6, 1990.

of churchgoing Catholic women of childbearing age use artificial contraceptives, and less than 30% of Catholic priests in the United States consider the use of artificial contraceptives to be a sin (Murphy, 1981). Thus even among the individuals most likely to oppose contraception, the opposition is not very strong. Most other people readily accept the use of contraceptives.

Premarital Sex

Not long ago most adults in the United States believed that having sexual relations with someone before marriage was immoral. These beliefs were reinforced by the religious teachings of Roman Catholics, conservative Protestants, and Orthodox Jews, among others. However, in recent decades these views have changed drastically. Since 1970 more than half of the states in the United States have rescinded laws that prohibited sex outside marriage, and there is evidence that many religious leaders no longer consider premarital sex to be a sin. In one study, for example, questionnaires were sent to 469 Jewish and Christian religious leaders and pastors. Only 40% of the respondents reported that they believed premarital sex to be immoral (Meer, 1985).

There have also been changes in the way the general public views premarital sex. According to a *U.S. News and World Report* survey, the majority of adults in the United States believe that premarital sex is not wrong (Heller, 1985). This is a substantial change from only a few years ago. In 1969 only 32% of adults approved of premarital sex (Heller, 1985).

Not only do a substantial number of adults believe that premarital sex is not immoral, but also many individuals engage in sexual relations before marriage. Over half of all 18-year-olds report having experienced sexual intercourse,

Laws and religious teachings concerning premarital sex have changed over the years.

and by the time they are 20 about 80% of both males and females report having had intercourse (Moore, Nord, and Peterson, 1989).

Approval of premarital sex often depends on the degree of affection and commitment shared by the couple. Hass (1979) found that among high school students 41% of the males and 68% of the females approved of sexual contact only when the sex occurred in a romantic relationship. As reported in Chapter 11, in the 1970s the majority of adults believed that premarital sex was acceptable if the couple had a strong emotional involvement (Hunt, 1974).

Extramarital Sex

Extramarital sex is also discussed in Chapter 15.

Although the majority of adults have become much more accepting of premarital sex over the last couple of decades, no corresponding increase has occurred in the acceptance of extramarital sex. As mentioned in Chapter 14, in one survey only 2.5% of those questioned did not believe that extramarital relationships are wrong and 75% thought extramarital relationships are wrong in all cases (Singh, Walton, and Williams, 1976).

The view that extramarital relationships are immoral is consistent with the religious doctrines of Protestants, Catholics, and Jews. Only the most liberal Protestants and Jews have a more accepting attitude toward extramarital relations. Until recently extramarital sex was against the law. However, since 1970 more than half of the states in the United States have eliminated their laws against sex outside marriage (Meer, 1985).

Although the overwhelming majority of adults believe that extramarital sex is unacceptable, these expressed attitudes do not appear to predict actual behavior. There appears to be little relationship between one's reported attitude toward extramarital sex and one's behavior (Thompson, 1983). Individuals who report that they approve of extramarital sex do not necessarily become involved in such relationships, and individuals who report that they disapprove do not necessarily avoid such relationships.

In spite of their reported disapproval, a sizable proportion of adults engage in extramarital relationships at one time or another. At least half of all married men and somewhere between one fourth and one half of all married women report having had at least one extramarital affair. Although the number of men involved in extramarital relationships has remained fairly stable over the last couple of decades, the number of women who report such involvements has increased. This increase may result from a number of factors. Because of the women's movement and consequent decline of the double standard for sexual behavior, women have become more willing to experiment sexually and to report their sexual experiences accurately. Furthermore, since women are spending less time in the home and more in the workplace, they have more opportunity to meet and become involved with men other than their husbands than they did a few decades ago.

Although the number of adults who report having extramarital relationships is fairly high, probably an even greater number of adults actually have such relationships. Given that the majority of adults consider extramarital sex to be wrong, it is likely that a number of adults who have had such relationships will not admit it.

Homosexuality

Homosexuality has long been considered unnatural and immoral in the Jewish, Catholic, and Protestant traditions. Until as late as 1961 homosexual acts were against the law in all 50 states. However, in the last several decades the so-called sexual revolution, the civil rights movement, and the gay liberation movement have produced debate and discussion about the morality of homosexual behavior and the civil rights of homosexuals. As a result of these societal changes, many people have become more tolerant of homosexuality. Since 1961, 26 states have repealed laws criminalizing homosexual acts. However, in spite of these recent changes, in July 1986 the U.S. Supreme Court ruled that individual states may outlaw sodomy (oral or anal sex) among homosexuals (see accompanying box).

A wide range of attitudes toward homosexuality can be found among the religions. Some of the more conservative religions believe that homosexuals are sinners and that all homosexual behavior is immoral. The people who hold these views often contend that homosexuals should be denied basic civil rights.

Knocking on the Bedroom Door

The opinions were occasionally sarcastic as well as blunt. But then, the issue was one that arouses intense emotion among legions of Americans. The basic questions: May a state define some types of activity widely practiced by homosexuals as a crime? Or do the antisodomy laws of 24 states violate the constitutionally protected right to privacy that the court has been expanding in decisions stretching back more than 60 years?

To the dismay of gay-rights activists and many civil libertarians—and to the delight of religious Fundamentalists and other antigays—the Supreme Court ruled 5 to 4 . . . that a state may indeed outlaw sodomy among homosexuals, even if it is practiced by consenting adults in the privacy of a home. The ruling has implications far be-

yond the legal result. By deferring to the state as moral arbiter in this case, the Court raises essential questions about its role as the guardian of individual freedoms against the will of the majority.

The case began in 1982 when Michael Hardwick was late paying a fine for drinking on the streets of Atlanta. A police officer with a warrant entered Hardwick's bedroom and found him engaged in oral sex with another man. The officer arrested both for violating a Georgia statute that prohibits "any sexual act involving the sex organs of one person and the mouth or anus of another" (punishment: 1 to 20 years in prison). Fulton County District Attorney Lewis Slaton declined to prosecute, but Hardwick filed suit anyway, asking for a declaratory

judgment that the law is unconstitutional.

Though the Georgia statute was deliberately framed to apply to everyone, Justice Byron White's majority opinion (joined by Chief Justice Warren Burger, William Rehnquist, Sandra Day O'Connor and Lewis Powell) was careful to "express no opinion" about sodomy among heterosexuals. . . .

Essentially, the decision leaves it up to each state whether to tolerate or forbid homosexual sodomy. Though all 50 states had antisodomy laws as late as 1961, those statutes have since been repealed or struck down by courts in 26 states; the Supreme Court's ruling will have little immediate effect there. Even the laws still on the books in 24 states—19 states and the District of Columbia criminalize all sodomy; five have laws that apply only to homosexual conduct—are rarely enforced. Generally, authorities expect no sudden wave of prosecutions. . . .

From Time, July 14, 1986.

For example, they may believe that homosexuals should not be allowed to hold public office, to be teachers, or to assume other positions of responsibility. Many fundamentalist Protestants fall into this category.

Other religions hold the view that it is not a sin to be a homosexual but that homosexual acts are sins. This tends to be the position of the Catholic Church, as well as many other religious denominations. It is often assumed that homosexuality is not a matter of choice and that homosexuals should therefore not be held responsible for their sexual orientation. However, according to this view, the only morally acceptable course of action for the homosexual is to remain celibate. The people who hold this position tend to support homosexuals' civil rights; they believe that homosexuals should be able to hold public office, teach, and do anything else any heterosexual can do. They are generally not concerned that homosexuals will corrupt young children and others with whom they come in contact.

More liberal religious denominations tend not to view homosexuals as sinners or homosexual behavior as immoral. The more liberal religious groups strongly support the civil rights of homosexuals; they believe that homosexuals should be entitled to all the rights to which anyone else is entitled.

A survey of 469 religious leaders in the United States (Meer, 1985) illustrates the diversity of opinion among religious leaders. The religious leaders were asked to fill out a questionnaire anonymously. Only half of those individuals who responded reported that they believed that homosexual behavior is wrong. The same diversity of opinion can be found among the general population. A *Los Angeles Times* 1983 survey of 1,653 adults in the United States found that 52% disapprove of homosexual behavior (Schneider and Lewis, 1984). Thus only about half of the adults in the United States—religious leaders and general public—still believe that homosexual behavior is always wrong.

A gay religious congregation.

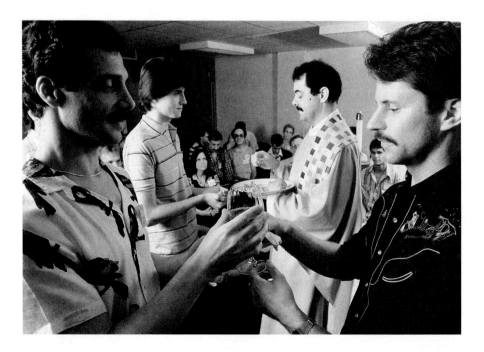

Technological Issues

As a result of recent technological advances that relate to conception, pregnancy, and childbirth, a number of new ethical issues have been raised. Some of these technological advances and the related ethical issues are discussed in the remainder of this chapter.

Artificial insemination   In artificial insemination a man's sperm are obtained (usually through masturbation) and are artificially injected into a woman's cervix or uterus around the time of ovulation. The most common reason for using artificial insemination is the husband's infertility. In such cases a physician finds a sperm donor who is willing to contribute his sperm for an agreed-on amount of money. The donor is assured of confidentiality; in fact, in most cases all information related to the donor's identity is destroyed. Although most of the women who are artificially inseminated are married women with infertile husbands, single women and lesbian couples have used artificial insemination to have children. Physicians began using artificial insemination techniques about 40 years ago. Since the procedure was first used, a number of women have given birth to children conceived in this manner. Curie-Cohen, Luttrell, and Shapiro (1979) estimate that approximately 6,000 to 10,000 women each year give birth to children conceived through artificial insemination.

> Artificial insemination is also discussed in Chapter 6.

The use of artificial insemination has raised a number of ethical questions (Annas, 1981). The Catholic Church, for example, has condemned the use of artificial insemination primarily on the grounds that it is not natural and that it separates sexual intercourse from procreation. The Catholic Church tends to oppose (1) methods that allow couples to have sexual intercourse without the possibility of conception (using contraceptives) and (2) the reverse—methods that allow couples to conceive by means other than sexual intercourse. Furthermore, the sperm for artificial insemination are obtained through masturbation, which the Catholic Church considers a sin. In addition to religious considerations, other ethical issues have been voiced in recent years. For example, Annas (1981) has questioned the method by which donors are currently chosen. Today it is almost always the physician who chooses the donor, and he or she almost always chooses a medical student or a medical resident. Annas wonders whether physicians should be the only ones making such decisions.

Another ethical question is whether the donor's identity should be kept confidential, even to the point of destroying records of the donor's identity. One study found that only 30% of the physicians kept permanent records of the donors (Curie-Cohen, Luttrell, and Shapiro, 1979). There is a fear that if the donor's identity could be determined, the children that result from the artificial insemination might have financial claim on the donor for child support or inheritance. If anonymity were not ensured, presumably the pool of donors would be much smaller. Although this policy may be in the donor's best interest, it may not always be in the best interests of the child (Annas, 1981). If records were kept, physicians could observe the results of the artificial insemination pregnancies to see if any of the resulting children were defective in any way that could be attributed to genes. Then the individuals who had contributed the sperm in those cases could be discontinued as donors. Since

A Personal Glimpse

Sperm Bank Deposit Pays Off

SEATTLE—When John Travaglini made a deposit at the sperm bank, he never dreamed he'd have to wait 14 years for a dividend.

But come February he and his wife, Kris, are due to become the proud parents of a bouncing baby.

The baby was conceived with the aid of test tubes, Federal Express, post-menopausal Italian nuns and plenty of love.

John is a doctor, and Kris is a nurse. The couple have been married 2½ years and live in Seattle, but the story of their future child's conception begins in New York, a long, long time before the two ever met.

It was 1976. John was just entering his senior year at the University of Vermont when he learned he had Hodgkins disease, which affects the lymph nodes. He would be receiving radiation and chemotherapy—treatment that can render a man infertile, as it did in his case.

John's sister urged him to go to a sperm bank in New York before receiving treatment. She realized he might want to be a father one day.

"I felt horribly embarrassed," John recalled. "Here I was foot-loose and fancy-free, angry that I had this terrible disease in the first place, but I went in and made my deposit."

John recovered from the disease and went on to medical school. He led an aspiring doctor's hectic life—no time for women—with impending fatherhood seeming about as likely as winning the lottery.

There was a $50 annual maintenance fee to keep his sperm frozen in a liquid nitrogen tank. John faithfully paid up, but he had some doubts.

"I wondered if I was throwing away $50 a year on a pipe dream," he said.

John became a radiation therapist and worked temporarily at Swedish Hospital in Seattle. But he remained so preoccupied with work that he didn't notice the pretty nurse in radiation oncology trying to catch his eye.

"She could have run me over with a Mack truck, and I barely would have noticed," he said.

"But I noticed," Kris said. Finally, she called him up and asked him for a date.

He said yes, and the two were engaged within a year.

In March 1989, about a year after they'd been married, the Travaglinis decided to become parents, and John sent away to New York for his sperm. It was shipped Federal Express in a metal Thermos to the Seattle sperm bank at Swedish Hospital.

The sperm was then moved to the University Hospital, where doctors tried four times through simple insemination to impregnate Kris with her husband's sperm. It didn't work.

Then it was time for the big step—in-vitro fertilization, a $6,000 procedure in which eggs are removed from the woman, mixed with the sperm and reinserted inside the woman's uterus.

Enter those post-menopausal nuns. Kris took a fertility drug called Pergonal, which is common for in-vitro procedures.

The drug is derived from the urine of nuns at various Italian convents for reasons having to do with hormones found in older women and the American distaste for human excrement in medical processing.

Dr. Mary Forster, with the reproductive genetics department at Swedish Hospital, says it's rare for 14-year-old sperm to take, not because of the age of the substance but because of the likelihood for things to go wrong in storage.

In other words, the banks did a good job protecting John's investment. And how many banks can you say that about these days?

From Seattle Times, 1990.

at least in some cases donors are used more than once, such record keeping could prevent unnecessary problems in artificially inseminated children. One study (Curie-Cohen, Luttrell, and Shapiro, 1979) reported that one donor was used 50 times! Furthermore, if the donor's identity is kept secret, the child and parents will never be able to respond accurately in cases in which the family genetic history is important for some medical problem. Finally, if the donor's identity is kept confidential, the child will never be able to find out who his or her genetic father is. Given the reaction of adopted children to a similar circumstance, it is possible that the children who find out that they were conceived as a result of artificial insemination might also want to find out who their genetic father is. Should they be able to?

A related ethical question is whether the parents should tell the child that he or she was conceived via artificial insemination. The current practice tends to be not to tell the children because they are unlikely to find out on their own. With adopted children, on the other hand, parents are advised to tell their children that they were adopted because they might find out from someone else and then be upset that the parents had not told them the truth. Since women who are artificially inseminated appear to the world to have had a completely normal pregnancy, no one would suspect that the conception did not occur in the traditional fashion. As a result, it is much less likely that the children will find out from someone else. Are the children who are conceived through artificial insemination entitled to just as much parental honesty as adopted children?

This section has raised a number of ethical and moral questions about the use of artificial insemination and about some of the common practices in its use. We do not have answers to these questions. The fact that we asked the questions should not be interpreted as suggesting that we believe that any particular answer is correct. We raised the questions only because we believe that they need to be given serious consideration by our society.

Surrogate parenthood   Surrogate parenthood has also raised a number of ethical questions. Surrogate parenthood refers to the situation in which a woman is artificially inseminated with sperm from a man whose wife is sterile or unable to carry a pregnancy to term. The surrogate mother carries the baby to term and then gives the baby to the man who donated the sperm and his wife. The fee that couples have to pay for this procedure ranges from about $20,000 to over $50,000. The surrogate mother receives a portion of the money, and the rest covers medical, legal, and business expenses.

Some believe that surrogate parenthood is a good alternative to adoption, since the pool of adoptable babies is decreasing. Others, however, are concerned about the legal and ethical issues involved. What would happen, for example, if the baby carried by a surrogate mother were born handicapped and the sperm donor and his wife decided they did not want the child? What if the sperm donor and his wife decided after the surrogate mother was artificially inseminated that they did not want a child? What if the sperm donor and his wife died before the birth of the child? What if the surrogate mother decided to keep her child? This last possibility did, in fact, occur in the case of Baby M (see the box on p. 700).

The Case of Baby M

Mary Beth Whitehead, a New Jersey housewife, volunteered her services as a surrogate mother because she wanted to help a childless couple. She agreed to be artificially inseminated by William Stern, whose wife, for medical reasons, believed that she should not carry a child herself. In return, the Sterns agreed to pay $10,000 to Ms. Whitehead, $10,000 to the Infertility Center of New York, and $5,000 in other expenses.

After the baby was born, however, Ms. Whitehead began to have misgivings. She said she had developed a strong maternal bond with the baby and felt that a mother ought to have a right to her own

baby. As a result, Ms. Whitehead refused to take the $10,000 that Mr. Stern agreed to pay her and refused to return the baby to the Sterns. When the police arrived at her house to retrieve the baby, Ms. Whitehead handed the infant out the back window of her house to her husband, who took the child to Florida. After a 3-month search by police, the FBI, and private detectives, the Whiteheads were located and the baby was returned to the Sterns.

The New Jersey Superior Court was then asked to determine whether custody of the child (dubbed "Baby M") should be awarded to the child's biological

mother or to her biological father. The judge ruled that the contract Ms. Whitehead signed with Mr. Stern was legal. He concluded that just as men have a constitutional right to sell their sperm, women have a right to decide what to do with their wombs. He argued that surrogate parenting does not constitute baby selling, since the sperm donor is already the father; he stated that the father "cannot purchase something that is already his."

The judge awarded custody to Mr. Stern and stripped Ms. Whitehead of all parental rights. He then allowed Ms. Stern to adopt the child. However, the New Jersey Supreme Court ruled that surrogacy contracts cannot be enforced and thereby invalidated the adoption by Ms. Stern and ruled that Ms. Whitehead should be given visitation rights.

FIRST ROW: BABY X. SECOND ROW: SURROGATE MOTHER, FOSTER FATHER, ADOPTIVE MOTHER, BIOLOGICAL FATHER, FOSTER MOTHER, GUARDIAN. THIRD ROW: ATTORNEYS.

A Personal Glimpse

Birth Mother Wants to Keep Baby Secret

Dear Ann Landers: A few days ago, a woman phoned and announced she was the daughter I had put up for adoption many years ago. She tried to be non-threatening and sounded like a nice person, but I was absolutely stunned. Old heartaches and fear overwhelmed me. She asked if I wanted to see her. When I said, "No," she politely rang off. I sat by the phone shaking for 30 minutes.

I made a mistake when I was young, and I suffered for it. I never told a soul about the child I had. It was my intention to take the secret to my grave.

Can you imagine the pain of telling a thing like that to your husband, children, grandchildren, nieces, nephews and friends? I don't think I could have lived through it.

Please advise people who assist in such searches to find another hobby. Inform those wrongheaded do-gooders who reveal confidential information that it is highly unethical and probably illegal, and it can do incalculable damage.

I can appreciate people's curiosity about their biological parents, but I beg them to consider our right to keep this part of our lives secret. Although the woman who phoned seemed perfectly content to leave me alone, I have no assurance that she will. I now live in fear that she might appear at my door.

That telephone call has forever changed my life and robbed me of my peace of mind. No one has the right to visit this kind of hell on another person. Please say so, Ann.—**Petrified in Iowa**

Dear Iowa: I have said so in my column repeatedly, but thanks for the opportunity to say it again.

Adopted children should have access to the health histories of their biological parents, especially if there are abnormalities that may be genetic. But it should end there. No one has the right to disrupt lives and cause the kind of anguish you described.

As is clear from the case of Baby M, a number of legal and ethical decisions need to be made regarding surrogate parenthood. It is not yet clear whether a dispute between the surrogate mother and the biological father over the baby will be treated as a normal custody case, in which custody is awarded to the better parent, or as a contract case, in which the individual who is named as parent in the contract is always given custody. These and other legal and ethical decisions will need to be made in the near future, since similar disputes will almost certainly arise with other surrogate parenthood arrangements.

In vitro fertilization The recent use of in vitro fertilization has also raised a number of ethical questions. In this technique one or more eggs (ova) are extracted from the woman and are fertilized in a petri dish with sperm, often from the woman's husband. The conceptus is incubated until there is evidence of cell division and then placed in the woman's uterus. This procedure has been used much less frequently than artificial insemination and has been made available mainly to stable married couples in which the woman is otherwise unable to conceive, often because of blocked fallopian tubes. The success rate with this procedure is not high; only about 20% of all attempts result in pregnancy (Holden, 1984). Furthermore, the procedure is expensive, often costing $6,000 or more for each attempt.

In vitro fertilization is also discussed in Chapter 6.

Two Fertilized Eggs Stir Global Furor

The case of the frozen zygotes in Australia has recently triggered a public debate covering issues raised by artificial insemination and surrogate mothering as well as in vitro fertilization, according to some observers.

The story, in brief, concerns a couple from Los Angeles, Mario and Elsa Rios, who flew to Melbourne in 1981 to seek the services of the Queen Victoria Medical Clinic's fertility program. There doctors extracted and fertilized three of the woman's ova and implanted one, which resulted in a miscarriage. The couple departed, leaving the remaining two fertilized eggs, which were frozen in liquid nitrogen. In 1983 the Rioses were killed in a plane crash. The story suddenly gained international prominence after London newspapers reported that the couple had left no will and a substantial fortune was at stake.

The zygotes are probably no longer viable because methods of preservation were considerably more primitive in 1981 than they are today, experts say. But feverish debates have arisen over the disposition of the two microscopic blastulae—whether they should be implanted in someone, and what inheritance rights they may possess. The center has been deluged by women who want to be impregnated. The premier of Victoria meanwhile has established a committee to ascertain the legal rights of the frozen embryos. The Rioses' lawyer, Laura Horwitch, has announced that she will ask the Los Angeles Superior Court to determine their legal status. That issue has been further complicated by her assertion that the sperm used in the procedure was not the husband's.

According to a leading center for in vitro fertilization in this country, such a preposterous situation could not arise in the United States because of universally accepted guidelines governing the disposition of unused fertilized eggs. Also, very few places freeze the eggs, which otherwise survive only a few hours. Howard Jones, director of the Institute for Reproductive Medicine at Eastern Virginia Medical School, says guidelines promulgated by the American Fertility Society specify that cryopreservation should not be sustained beyond the reproductive life of the mother. Furthermore, if fertilized eggs are frozen, their disposition, if unused, has to be decided prior to the procedure. They can either be thrown out, used for research up to the age of 14 days, or offered for adoption, in which case anonymity is required. Any subsequent claim to the progeny by the biological parents would be waived.

Although these principles would seem to cover the ground, the problem, according to Alexander Capron, former head of the President's ethics commission, is that they have not been sanctioned either by law or by society. Nor do they address future procedures that science will be making available.

Capron says the Rios case may turn out to be a "beacon"—like the Karen Quinlan case—signaling that "we have a lot of problems to deal with here" in the whole area of fertility manipulation. One issue relates to the rights of children who want to know the identity of their biological or (in the case of surrogate mothering) gestational parents. Clinics generally try to make identification of donors impossible by mixing sperm from more than one and by destroying records. This issue will also be arising where donated sperm has been used for in vitro fertilization.

As for the legal and moral status of zygotes, Capron notes that contracts are "naive" because they "only work if society legitimates them." He is sharply critical of the Department of Health and Human Services for shying away from the subject of in vitro fertilization, despite the fact that an ethics advisory board over 5 years ago recommended such research and called the procedure "ethically defensible."

But what is really needed, he says, is a new presidential commission and hearings to arrive at a public consensus on parentage and the disposition of the results of conception, which would supply the basis for much needed legal guidance.

In vitro fertilization is now being practiced in about 200 clinics around the world. The Victoria group does around 400 a year. Successful pregnancies result in approximately 20 percent of the cases. So far, at least 450 babies have been produced, one of them from a frozen zygote.

From Holden, 1984.

Some religious groups object to in vitro fertilization. The Catholic Church opposes it on grounds similar to those on which it opposes artificial insemination. In vitro fertilization also separates sexual intercourse from procreation and is "unnatural" (McDowell, 1983). The majority of Protestants, on the other hand, do not believe that conception needs to occur as a result of a specific instance of sexual intercourse but rather believe that procreation should occur within a loving relationship (McDowell, 1983).

In addition to religious concerns, a number of other ethical issues have been raised about in vitro fertilization and the procedures that are used or could be used. Some people are concerned that some of the fertilized ova that result from in vitro fertilization will either be destroyed or be subjected to experimentation. These concerns are expressed mainly by those who believe that a fertilized ovum is a human life and deserves to be treated as such. These individuals believe that the destruction of or experimentation with the fertilized

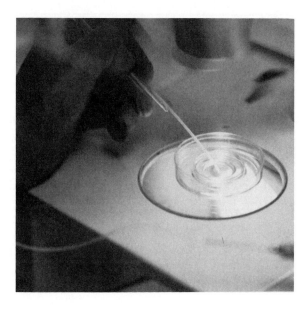

In vitro fertilization.

Court Splits Custody of Embryos

The Tennessee Court of Appeals . . . granted joint custody of seven frozen embryos to a divorced couple, overturning a landmark ruling that had granted custody to the ex-wife. . . .

The intermediate-level appeals court ruled in the divorce case of Junior Lewis Davis, 31, of Maryville, and his 29-year-old former wife, Mary Sue Davis Stowe, now of Titusville, Fla.

"It would be repugnant and offensive to constitutional principles to order Mary Sue to implant these fertilized ova against her will," Judge Herschel Franks wrote for the three-member court.

"It would be equally repugnant to order Junior to bear the psychological, if not the legal, consequences of paternity against his will."

The court ruled that both Stowe and Davis should "share an interest in the seven fertilized ova."

The case was remanded to Blount County Circuit Judge W. Dale Young to enter a judgement giving Stowe and Davis "joint control of the fertilized ova (and) equal voice over their disposition." . . .

The embryos were created in vitro at a Knoxville fertility clinic in December 1988 by mixing Davis' sperm with eggs removed from his wife.

There originally were nine embryos. Two were implanted at the time but did not develop. The remaining seven were frozen for later use after developing to between four and eight cells each.

In February 1989, Davis sued his wife for divorce, asking the court to prevent any use of the embryos without his consent. Davis argued that he should not be forced to become a parent against his wishes.

From Wisconsin State Journal, 1990.

ovum is similar to abortion. Of course, such destruction or experimentation is not a necessary component of in vitro fertilization and thus could be prohibited if judged to be unethical.

The ability to perform in vitro fertilization paved the way for other developments that also present moral dilemmas, such as ova and embryo banking and embryo transfer. Embryo banking and transfer allow women who are unable to become pregnant or to maintain a pregnancy to have their own genetic children. In embryo transfer an embryo that results from the in vitro fertilization of a woman's egg with her husband's sperm is implanted in a surrogate mother. After the child is born, the child is given back to the genetic parents. This procedure is often referred to as gestational surrogacy. Worldwide, over 80 gestational surrogate mothers have given birth so far. At least one of the gestational surrogate mothers has decided to try to keep the baby she carried. Chris and Mark Calvert of Orange County, California, paid Anna Johnson $10,000 to carry their baby because Chris Calvert had a hysterectomy and was unable to carry a baby. However, before the end of the pregnancy Anna Johnson changed her mind and decided to sue for the right to keep her baby. The *Johnson v. Calvert* case differs from the Baby M case in that Anna Johnson was not genetically related to the baby she was carrying. Mary Beth Whitehead was given parental rights because she was Baby M's biological parent—she was genetically related to Baby M as well as being the woman who carried Baby M during pregnancy. In *Johnson v. Calvert* the surrogate mother was not genetically related but was related only by the fact that she carried the fetus during pregnancy. It will be interesting to see how this case is decided.

Prenatal screening A variety of methods have recently been developed to screen for various birth defects before a child is born. For example, amniocentesis is used to diagnose genetic disorders for persons who are considered to be at high risk, that is, for men and women with a family history of genetic problems or women over 35 years of age. Disorders such as Down's syndrome, Tay-Sachs disease, and sickle cell anemia can be discovered before birth by amniocentesis.

As discussed in Chapter 6, amniocentesis is a procedure in which a needle is inserted through the pregnant woman's abdomen and into the amniotic sac. Fluid containing cells is then removed, and chromosomal analyses are performed to detect disease or defect. **Fetoscopy** is a related technique in which a fiber-optic lens is pushed down through the needle so the fetus can actually be seen. **Sonography,** an indirect method of viewing the fetus by way of ultrasound, is also used to detect fetal abnormalities.

The ability to detect various defects prenatally has presented new moral and ethical questions. If parents learn before the birth of their child that he or she has a serious disease or defect, should those parents abort their child? How severe should the abnormality be before parents make a decision to abort? If the parents tell their physician that they do not want to know about any defects in which prenatal treatment would not help but that are discovered during prenatal screening, should the physician tell them anyway if a serious defect is discovered? If the physician does not tell them about such a serious defect, could the parents bring and win a "wrongful life" suit against the physician? A "wrongful life" suit is a suit placed on behalf of a child that contends that the child should have never been born. Parents have brought and won such cases in the past (Shapiro, 1983). Certainly physicians do not want to increase the likelihood of such suits by withholding information from their patients.

As these few examples illustrate, many of the medical advances in recent years have presented moral and ethical issues that need to be given a great deal of consideration. The decisions we make on many of these issues will determine the future of our species.

Prenatal screening and genetic problems are also covered in Chapters 6 and 7.

fetoscopy
(fee TOS kuh pee) Method used for detection of fetal abnormalities in which the fetus can actually be seen; a fiber-optic lens is pushed through a needle that is inserted through the pregnant woman's abdomen and into the amniotic sac.

sonography
(suhn OG ruh fee) Indirect way of viewing the fetus by means of ultrasound to detect fetal abnormalities.

SUMMARY

1 According to the U.S. Supreme Court, a state cannot prohibit any woman from obtaining an abortion from a licensed physician during the first 3 months of a pregnancy.

2 A recent Gallup Poll indicated that 53% of the people believe that abortion should be legal under certain circumstances, while 31% believe that it should be legal in all cases. Only 12% think it should be illegal in all cases, and 4% reported having no opinion. Thus it appears that the vast majority of Americans believe that abortion is acceptable in special circumstances

and that only a minority of Americans support the extreme pro-life position.

3 Although the majority of adults have become much more accepting of premarital sex in the last couple of decades, there has not been a corresponding increase in the acceptance of extramarital sex. In one survey only 2.5% of those questioned reported that they do not see anything wrong with having an extramarital relationship.

4 In general, Judaism does not view sex as sinful but as a "gift from God" to be enjoyed by both husband and wife only within a loving marriage. Sex should be engaged in only to satisfy two main functions: procreation and unification.

5 Traditional Catholicism asserts that the only approved sexuality is that which occurs within marriage and for the purpose of procreation and unification. Any method that results in conception outside the act of intercourse is considered unnatural and wrong.

6 Protestants hold a variety of viewpoints on sex, so it is difficult to present the "Protestant position."

7 Pro-life advocates believe that a human is created at the moment of conception and thus has a right to life. This view regards abortion as impermissible under any circumstances.

8 Pro-choice advocates believe that a human life is not created until later in a pregnancy and that a woman has a right to decide what happens to her body and therefore discontinue her pregnancy for any reason.

9 Most Americans believe that abortion is justified in some circumstances.

10 Most Americans consider contraceptive use morally acceptable.

11 U.S. religious leaders and the general public find premarital sex increasingly acceptable.

12 Over the last few decades adults have not become increasingly accepting of extramarital sex. Only 2.5% of people questioned see nothing wrong with adultery. Seventy-five percent think adultery is wrong in all cases.

13 There is little relationship between one's reported attitude toward extramarital sex and one's actual behavior. At least half of all married men and somewhere between one fourth and one half of all married women have engaged in at least one extramarital affair.

14 The sexual revolution, civil rights movements, and gay liberation movement have caused society to become more accepting of homosexuality. Only about half of all Americans believe homosexuality is always wrong.

15 The use of artificial insemination raises some ethical questions. Should only the doctor be allowed to choose the donors? Should the donor's identity remain confidential?

16 Surrogate mothering also presents some difficult issues. What if the sperm donor and his wife decide they do not want the baby after the surrogate mother is inseminated? What if the surrogate mother decides she does not want to give up the baby after it is born?

17 In vitro fertilization raises additional moral dilemmas. If one destroys or experiments with the resulting zygote, is this considered a violation of human life? Would ova and embryo banking and embryo transfer result in the depersonalization of procreation?

18 Amniocentesis is used during pregnancy to diagnose genetic disorders in the fetus. Fetoscopy and sonography are also used to detect fetal defects.

The use of these prenatal screening procedures has also given rise to ethical questions. Should abortion be allowed if the fetus is defective? Should the physician be required to tell the parents about a defect even if the parents requested not to be told?

QUESTIONS FOR THOUGHT   ?

1 How has your religious background (or lack thereof) affected your sexual attitudes and behavior?
2 Under what circumstances (if any) do you approve of abortion? Why?

3 What do you think should happen if a surrogate mother decides, when the baby is born, that she wants to keep it rather than turn it over to the couple who paid her to carry the child?

ANSWERS

FACT
OR
FICTION

1 According to the U.S. Supreme Court, a state cannot prohibit any woman from obtaining an abortion from a licensed physician during the first 3 months of a pregnancy.
2 Although the majority of adults have become much more accepting of premarital sex in the last couple of decades, there has not been a corresponding increase in the acceptance of extramarital sex. In one survey only 2.5% of those questioned reported that they do not think there is anything wrong with having an extramarital relationship.

SUGGESTED READINGS

Baird, R.M., and Rosenbaum, S.E.: The ethics of abortion, Buffalo, N.Y., 1989, Prometheus Books.
    This book includes a number of essays from a variety of perspectives about the ethics of abortion.
Corea, G.: The mother machine, New York, 1985, Harper & Row, Publishers, Inc.
    A feminist viewpoint of the social implications of the use of artificial reproductive methods; examines artificial insemination, embryo transfer, in vitro fertilization, and surrogate mothering.
Frohock, F.M.: Abortion, Westport, Conn., 1983, Greenwood Press.
    A comprehensive examination of the legal, philosophical, moral, and political issues involved in both the pro-life and pro-choice positions on abortion.
Nugent, R., editor: A challenge to love: gay and lesbian Catholics in the church, New York, 1983, Crossroad Publishing Co.
    A collection of essays offering insight into the religious, emotional, and moral needs of gay males and lesbians.
Parrinder, G.: Sex in the world's religions, London, 1980, Sheldon Press.
    A review of various religious perspectives on human sexuality from around the world; includes a discussion of the views of sexuality found in India, China, Japan, Africa, the Middle East, Israel, and the West.
Stream, H.S.: Extramarital affair, New York, 1980, The Free Press.
    Presents many case studies of extramarital affairs, each with a psychoanalytical explanation of why it occurred.
Whiteford, L.M., and Poland, M.L.: New approaches to human reproduction, Boulder, Colo., 1989, Westview Press.
    A collection of readings about various ethical issues related to human reproduction. Topics include care during pregnancy, treatment of newborns, and surrogate parenthood.
Wojtyla, K. (Pope John Paul II): Love and responsibility, New York, 1981, Farrar, Straus, & Giroux, Inc.
    Pope John Paul II expresses his views on the moral issues involved in sex, marriage, and love.

GLOSSARY

abortion termination of pregnancy before embryo or fetus is viable. Abortions are classified as spontaneous (natural causes) or induced (brought on by deliberate intervention).

acquired immunodeficiency syndrome sexually transmitted disease in which the immune system fails to protect the individual from other diseases.

activation series of biochemical changes in sperm cell that affect its swimming motion and membrane to allow it to fuse with egg.

adolescence the period from puberty to the attainment of adult growth and maturity.

adrenogenital syndrome (uh dree noh JEN i tuhl) clinical condition caused by excess secretion of male hormones by adrenal glands.

adultery sexual intercourse between a married person and someone other than his or her spouse.

afterbirth the placenta and amniotic sac that are expelled after the infant is delivered.

allantois membrane (uh LAN toh is) tissues that contribute to development of placenta.

Pronunciation Guide: \a\ bat \air\ bear \ar\ are \aw\ bawdy \e\ bet \ee\beet \er\ bird \i\ bit \ing\ bingo \y\ byte \o\ bottle \or\ boar \oh\ boat \ou\ bounty \uh\ but \uhngk\ punk \oo\ boot \yoo\ beautiful \ch\ child \sh\ bash \th\ bath \zh\ vision

alveoli (al VEE uh lee′) small sacs within mammary glands that contain milk-producing cells.

amebiasis (am′ uh BY uh sis) infection of the large intestine caused by the protozoan *Entamoeba histolytica;* can be transmitted by both sexual and nonsexual routes.

amenorrhea (ay men′ uh REE uh) abnormal absence or suppression of menstruation in woman of reproductive age.

amniocentesis (am′ nee oh sen TEE suhs) procedure to detect fetal defects in which the amniotic sac is punctured with needle and syringe and amniotic fluid is obtained for analysis.

amnion (AM nee uhn, -on′) inner membrane that holds fetus suspended in amniotic fluid.

amniotic fluid watery fluid that surrounds a developing embryo and fetus in the uterus.

amniotic sac sac containing the amniotic fluid and the developing embryo and fetus in the uterus.

ampulla (am POOL uh, -PUL uh) widened portion of vas deferens that acts as prime storage area for sperm cells.

anal stage in Freudian theory, the second stage of psychosexual development, which occurs in the second and third years of life.

androgens (an DROJ uhnz) male sex hormones secreted by the testes.

androgynous having both masculine and feminine characteristics.

anemia (uh NEE mee uh) reduced number of circulating red blood cells.

anilingus (ay' nuh LING guhs) erotic stimulation of the anus with the tongue.

anorexia nervosa (an uh REK see uh ner voh suh) an abnormal psychological condition in which a person loses his or her appetite, eats very little, and loses weight.

anovulatory (an OV yuh luh tor' ee) when no eggs are released from the ovaries during a menstrual cycle.

anterior pituitary gland (pi TOO i ter ee) portion of the pituitary gland that develops from nonnervous tissue and is connected to the brain by blood vessels.

arthritis disease in which there is an inflammation of the joints with pain and loss of function.

asexual person who does not have sexual desires.

autoeroticism (au toh i ROT i siz' uhm) sexual self-pleasuring.

autonomic hyperreflexia (HY per ree FLEK see uh) exaggerated response by the autonomic nervous system in response to the birth process.

Bartholin's glands (BAR tl inz) two small mucus-producing glands located on each side of vaginal orifice.

basal body temperature method (BAY zuhl) fertility awareness method that involves charting body temperature on a daily basis until a rise in temperature, associated with ovulation, is noted.

bestiality (bes' chee AL i tee, bees'-) sexual activity between a human being and an animal.

birth canal passage through which the fetus travels during childbirth.

birthing rooms Rooms for childbirth that are made to be as much like home and as little like a hospital as possible.

bisexual a person who is sexually attracted to members of both sexes.

blastocyst (BLAS tuh sist) mass of cells that results from repeated divisions of zygote.

brothel house where prostitutes meet customers for sexual activity.

bulbs of the vestibule (ves tuh byool') masses of erectile tissue located on either side of vaginal orifice.

bundling courting custom that was formerly used in New England in which a courting couple would sleep in the same bed with all their clothes on. The couple was typically separated by some barrier.

calendar method method of fertility awareness, also called the rhythm method, that involves calculation of the woman's fertile period based on history of menstrual cycles.

capacitation process of biochemical changes in the sperm cell that allows sperm to penetrate egg.

carcinogen (kar SIN uh jen, KAR suh nuh jen) cancer-producing substance.

celibacy abstention from sexual behavior.

cerebral palsy disease state resulting from damage to the brain before or at the time of birth.

cervical cap (suhr vi kuhl) tight-fitting cap, made of rubber or plastic, that fits over the cervix so sperm cannot reach the egg in the fallopian tubes.

cervical intraepithelial neoplasia (in truh ep' uh THEE lee uhl NEE uh play' zhuh) early cancerous or precancerous changes of the cervical epithelial cells.

cervical mucus method method in which the fertile period is calculated by examining changes in types of cervical mucus produced, which are correlated with fertile and nonfertile portions of cycle.

cervix the lower part of the uterus that extends into the vagina.

cesarean section (si ZAIR ee uhn) surgical delivery of an infant through an incision in the abdomen and uterus.

chancre (SHANG kuhr) an infectious lesion, usually caused by primary syphilis, which develops on the genitalia or mouth.

chancroid (shang' kroid) disease of the genitals by the bacterium *Haemophilus ducreyi*.

child sexual abuse sexual act or acts performed by an adult with a minor under 18 years of age.

Chlamydia trachomatis (kluh MID ee uh truh KOH muh tis) a species of microorganism that lives and reproduces within the cells of the host.

chorion (KOR ee on') outer membrane that forms outer wall of blastocyst.

chorionic villi (kor ee ON ik VIL ee') fetal part of placenta; branching extensions that carry fetal blood vessels close to maternal blood vessels.

chorionic villi sampling (KOR ee on ic VIL ee') procedure to detect fetal abnormalities in which the chorionic villi are examined.

chromosome (KROH muh sohm') a structure in the nucleus of a cell containing genetic information.

cilia (SIL ee uh) hairlike processes found in various parts of the body.

circumcision (sur kuhm sizh uhn) removal of prepuce.

clitoridectomy surgical removal of the clitoris.

clitoris (KLIT uhr is, KLEE tuh-) small erectile structure located beneath prepuce that is very sensitive to sexual stimulation.

closet homosexual homosexual who is not open about his or her homosexuality.

cohabitation relationship in which two members of the opposite gender are sexually intimate and live together without being married.

cohort membership (KOH hort') factors besides age that a sample of individuals have in common; include values and mores of particular social periods.

colostrum (kuh LOS truhm) thin yellowish fluid secreted from the nipples at the end of pregnancy and during the first few days after birth.

coming out "coming out of the closet"; becoming open about one's homosexuality.

conception union of male sperm and egg of female; also called fertilization.

concubine (KONG kyuh byn') woman who lives with a man without being married to him.

condom rubber or natural skin sheath that fits over the penis and catches sperm in its end at ejaculation.

congenital present at birth.

consensual extramarital sex extramarital sex to which the nonparticipating spouse consents.

consensual sexual behaviors sexual behaviors that occur between adults who agree to participate.

contraceptive a device used to prevent conception, such as a diaphragm or condom.

contraceptive sponge small, spermicide-impregnated sponge that is inserted into vagina before intercourse.

copulation (KOP yuh lay shuhn) sexual intercourse.

corona (kuh ROH nuh) ridge of tissue separating glans penis from shaft.

corpora cavernosa clitoridis (KOR puhr uh KAV uhr NOH suh kli' toh ri DIS) two columns of erectile tissue within clitoris.

corpora cavernosa penis (KOR puhr uh KAV uhr NOH suh) two side-by-side columns of erectile tissue in penis.

corpus luteum (KOR puhs LOO tee uhm) small structure that develops within ruptured ovarian follicle and secretes progesterone.

corpus spongiosum penis (KOR puhs spun jee OH suhm) erectile tissue surrounding urethra.

Cowper's glands (KOU puhrz) pea-shaped glands that secrete mucus into urethra before ejaculation.

cross-sectional data data collected from the subjects at only one point in time.

cruising looking for a sexual partner.

cunnilingus (kun' uh LING guhs) sexual stimulation of the female genitals using the mouth and tongue.

cystitis (si STY tis) inflammation or infection of the bladder.

date rape forced sexual intercourse by an acquaintance while on a date with the victim.

diabetes mellitus (dy uh BEE tis, -teez muh LEE tuhs, MEL i-) disorder of carbohydrate utilization characterized by a high blood glucose level and the presence of glucose in the urine.

diaphragm (DY uh fram') dome-shaped rubber cup that blocks cervix so sperm cannot reach egg in fallopian tubes (oviducts). Must be used with spermicide to be effective.

dilatation and curettage (DY lay tay shuhn / kyoor' i TAZH) widely used gynecological procedure in which the contents of uterus are scraped out after cervix is dilated.

dilatation and evacuation (DY lay tay shuhn / i vak' yoo AY shuhn) Gynecological procedure that combines dilatation and curettage and vacuum curettage.

dildo (DIL doh) penis-shaped object that is used for sexual stimulation.

douching (DOOSH ing) flushing of vagina with liquid.

Down's syndrome congenital condition of various degrees of mental retardation and abnormal development caused by extra chromosome, usually number 21 or 22

(i.e., there are three instead of two chromosomes).

duct (duhkt) a tube for the passage of secretions.

dysmenorrhea (dis men' uh REE uh) painful or difficult menstruation.

dyspareunia (dis' puh ROO nee uh) painful or difficult sexual intercourse.

eclampsia (i KLAMP see uh) coma and convulsive seizures during second half of pregnancy in a woman with preeclampsia.

ectoderm (EK tuh duhrm') outer layer of cells in embryo that will develop into skin structures and nervous system.

ectopic pregnancy (ek TOP ik) result of implantation of fertilized egg outside uterus.

edema (i DEE muh) accumulation of fluid within tissues of body.

ejaculation (i JAK yuh lay shuhn) expulsion of semen from penis caused by muscular reaction.

ejaculatory ducts (i JAK yuh luh tuh ree duhkts) narrowed portions of male reproductive tract where vasa deferentia join ducts of seminal vesicles.

Electra complex in Freudian theory, the attraction of a young girl in the phallic stage to her father.

electronic fetal monitoring observation of fetal heart rate and maternal uterine contractions through an internal or external monitoring device.

endocrinology (en doh kri NOL uh jee) study of endocrine glands of body and the hormones they produce.

endoderm (EN duh duhrm') innermost layer of cells in embryo that will develop into digestive tract.

endometriosis (en doh mee tree oh sis) presence of endometrial tissue in locations other than the uterus.

endometrium (en doh MEE tree uhm) lining of the uterus that varies in thickness depending on phase of cycle and is shed during menstrual flow.

epididymis (ep' i DID uh mis) comma-shaped structure that receives sperm cells from testes.

episiotomy (i pee' zee OT uh mee) incision in the mother's perineum that provides more room for the infant during delivery and helps prevent tearing of the vaginal tissues.

erectile dysfunction (i REK tuhl) inability to have or maintain an erection sufficient for sexual intercourse.

erectile tissue (i REK tuhl) vascular tissue that, when filled with blood, becomes erect or rigid.

erection (i REK shuhn) vascular phenomenon that produces enlargement and hardening of penis.

erogenous (i ROJ uh nuhs) sexually sensitive areas that produce sexual arousal when touched.

erotic (i ROT ik) causing sexual feelings or desires.

erotophilia (i ro' tuh PHIL ee uh) set of attitudes and behaviors that characterize a sexually liberal individual.

erotophobia (i ro' tuh FOH bee uh) set of attitudes and behaviors that characterize a sexually conservative individual.

erythroblastosis (i rith' roh bla STOH sis) disease of newborn caused by transmission of maternal antibody that involves maternal and fetal blood group incompatibility.

estrogen (ES truh juhn) female sex hormones.

excitement phase first phase of human sexual response cycle, which results from physical and/or psychological sexual stimulation. Vasocongestion and myotonia begin at this time.

exhibitionism sexual arousal from exposing the genitals to unsuspecting strangers.

fallopian tubes (fuh LOH pee uhn) short tubes, also called oviducts, that connect the ovaries with the uterus.

fellatio (fuh LAY shee oh) sexual stimulation of the male genitals using the mouth and tongue.

fertility the ability to sexually reproduce.

fetishism sexual arousal by nongenital body parts or inanimate objects.

fertilization (fir tuhl uh ZAY shuhn) union of egg and sperm cell, which usually takes place in fallopian tubes.

fetoscopy (fee TOS kuh pee) method used for the detection of fetal abnormalities in which the fetus can actually be seen; a fiberoptic lens is pushed through a needle that is inserted through the pregnant woman's abdomen and into the amniotic sac.

fimbriae (FIM bree ee') fingerlike projections that form fringe around entrance to fallopian tubes.

flaccid (FLAS sid) relaxed or flabby.

flapper an emancipated young woman of the 1920s.

foreskin loose fold of skin that covers the end of the penis; also referred to as the *prepuce*.

fornication sexual intercourse between people who are not married to each other.

fornices (FOR ni seez) structures with vaultlike or arched shape.

frenulum (FREN yuh luhm) small fold of skin that unites foreskin with glans penis.

frottage (froh TAZH) sexual arousal caused by pressing or rubbing against someone in a crowd.

fundamentalist one who adheres to a strict and literal interpretation of the Bible.

gay homosexual; usually refers to male homosexual.

gender dysphoria situation in which an individual is not content with his or her biological sex, desires to possess the body of the opposite sex, and desires to be regarded by others as a member of the opposite sex.

gender identity feeling or belief that one is either male or female.

gender role socialization process by which one learns the cultural expectations for the two genders.

gender roles societal expectations about how males and females should behave.

genital herpes (JEN i tuhl HUR peez) sexually transmitted disease caused by a virus that results in painful blisters on the genitals.

genital stage in Freudian theory, the fifth and final stage of psychosexual development, which begins with puberty.

genital warts or venereal warts growths of the internal and external reproductive structures caused by a virus; can be transmitted by both sexual and nonsexual routes.

genitalia (JEN uh TAY lee uh, -TAYL yuh) external and internal reproductive structures.

gigolo man who sells his sexual services to women.

glans penis (glanz PEE nis) bulbous tip of penis.

gonadotropins (goh nad' uh TROH pinz) hormones, produced by the anterior pituitary gland, that stimulate gonads.

gonads sex glands; testes in the male, ovaries in the female.

gonococcus bacteria (gon' uh KOK uhs) bacteria that cause gonorrhea.

gonorrhea (gon uh REE uh) a disease of the reproductive structures and mucous membranes of the throat and rectum caused by the bacterium *Neisseria gonorrhoeae*.

Gräfenberg area (G spot) (GRAF in buhrg) an area located on the anterior wall of the vagina, which some claim is highly sensitive to stimulation.

hepatitis B (hep' uh TY tis) disease of the liver caused by the hepatitis B virus; can be transmitted by both sexual and nonsexual routes.

hermaphroditism (huhr MAF ruh dy tiz' uhm) literally means presence of both male and female gonadal tissues in same individual. Very rare occurrence and not the case in progesterone-induced hermaphroditism syndrome.

herpes (HUHR peez) common sexually transmitted disease that causes blisters to appear on the penis or vaginal area.

heterosexual person who is sexually attracted to members of the opposite sex.

HIV (human immunodeficiency virus) virus that causes AIDS.

homologous structures (hoh MOL uh guhs) structures that are similar in developmental origin.

homophobia (hoh' muh FOH bee uh) persistent and irrational fear of homosexuals; negative attitude and hostility toward homosexuals.

homosexual (hoh' moh SEK shoo uhl) person who is sexually attracted to members of the same sex.

hood of clitoris or prepuce fold of labia minora that covers clitoris.

hormones (HOHR mohnz) chemical substances produced in specialized structure. Chemicals are carried via blood to influence specific tissues within the body.

hot flash sudden sensation of warmth and blushing that commonly occurs in menopausal women.

human immunodeficiency virus (HIV) the virus that causes AIDS.

human placental lactogen (HYOO muhn pluh SEN tuhl LAK tuh jen) hormone that stimulates breast growth during pregnancy.

hustler man who provides sexual services to other men in exchange for money.

hymen or maidenhead (HY muhn) membrane that can cover vaginal orifice to various degrees.

hyperemia (hy' puh REE mee uh) increased amount of blood that expands or distends blood vessels.

hypothalamus (hy puh THAL uh muhs, HIP uh-) portion of brain that is in direct contact with pituitary gland. Secretions from hypothalamus control pituitary gland.

immunosuppression (i MYOO noh suh PRESH uhn) condition in which the body's immune system, which protects us from disease, is suppressed.

impotence (IM puh tuhns) inability to get or maintain an erection.

in vitro fertilization (IVF) (in VEE troh fuhr tl i ZAY shuhn) fertilization of an egg with sperm in a laboratory dish.

incest (IN sest') sexual activity between close relatives.

infatuation an attraction to another person that is based on little real knowledge of the person.

infertility diminished ability to produce offspring.

infibulation (in fib yoo LAY shuhn) process of closing or fastening.

inhibin (in HIB in) chemical secreted by the testes that inhibits FSH output by the anterior pituitary gland.

intimacy sharing one's innermost thoughts, feelings, and experiences with another person.

intrauterine device (in' truh YOO tuhr in) small object placed in uterus to prevent implantation of fertilized egg.

Kegel exercises (KEG uhl) exercises that contract and strengthen the pubococcygeal muscles.

labia majora (LAY bee uh muh JOR uh) two folds of tissue lying on either side of vaginal orifice to form outermost borders of vulva.

labia minora (LAY bee uh muh NOR uh) two thin folds of tissue that lie within boundaries of labia majora and enclose vestibule of vagina.

labor series of processes involved in giving birth.

lactation production of milk in the female breasts.

Lamaze method (luh MAZ) method of childbirth that emphasizes relaxation, controlled breathing, and knowledge of the birth process.

laparoscopic surgery (LAP uhr uh skop' ik) surgical procedure in which an endoscope, a small tube-like instrument that contains a light and optical system, is inserted through incision in abdomen and allows physician to view the oviducts and other structures.

latency stage (LAYT n see) in Freudian theory, the fourth stage of psychosexual development that begins at about 6 and ends with puberty.

Leboyer method (luh BOI uhr) method of childbirth that attempts to lessen the shock of birth to the newborn by minimizing the differences between the uterine environment and the external environment.

lesbian (LEZ bee uhn) female homosexual.

lesion (LEE zhuhn) injury or wound.

Leydig cells (LY dig) hormone-producing cells of testes.

libido (li BEE doh) in Freudian theory, sexual energy or motivation.

longitudinal data data collected from the same subjects at several points in time.

lymph nodes (limf nohdz) small "knobs" or "knots," incorrectly called glands, that are important to the functioning of the lymph system. The lymph system protects us from disease.

lymphogranuloma venereum (lim' fuh gran' yuh LOH muh vuh NEE ree uhm) disease of the lymphatic system caused by a member of the *Chlamydia* genus of organisms.

mammary glands (MAM uh ree) glands in the breasts that produce milk.

mammography (muh MOG ruh fee) X-ray of the female breast.

masochism (MAS uh kiz uhm) sexual arousal from being physically or psychologically dominated by another.

masturbation (mas tuhr BAY shuhn) stimulation of one's own genitals to produce sexual pleasure.

menarche (muh NAR kee) onset of menstruation.

menopause time that marks permanent cessation of menstrual activity.

menses (MEN seez) monthly blood flow from uterus.

menstrual cycle (MEN stroo uhl) cyclical recurrent series of changes occurring in the female reproductive tract associated with menstruation.

menstrual synchrony (MEN stroo uhl SING kruh nee) similar menstrual cycle sometimes followed by women who live together.

menstruation (men stroo AY shuhn) cyclical uterine bleeding.

mesoderm (MEZ uh duhrm') middle layer of cells in embryo between ectoderm and endoderm that will give rise to muscular, skeletal, circulatory, and urogenital (structures common to urinary and genital) systems.

metastasis (muh TAS tuh sis) movement of cells from one part of the body to another.

midwives individuals other than a physician who have been trained to assist a woman during childbirth.

miscarriage or spontaneous abortion abortion that occurs without cause or is medically unaided.

mittelschmerz (mit TIL shmertz) abdominal pain occurring at time of ovulation.

monogamy (muh NOG uh mee) marriage of one man to one woman.

mons pubis (monz pyoo bis) pad of fatty tissue in pubic region.

mucopurulent cervicitis (myoo kuh PYOOR yuh luhnt) infection of the cervix that produces a discharge.

multiple orgasms (OR gaz uhmz) series of two or more orgasms that occur within a matter of minutes.

multiple sclerosis (skluh ROH sis) chronic progressive disease of the brain and spinal cord.

mutagen (myoo tuh juhnz) agent that causes permanent changes in the genetic information of cells.

myocardial infarction (my' oh KAR dee uhl in fark shuhn) development of an infarct (area of tissue that dies because of loss of blood supply) in the heart muscle.

myometrium (my' uh MEE tree uhm) muscular layer of uterus.

myotonia (my' uh TOH nee uh) involuntary muscle tension.

natural childbirth childbirth in which minimal medication is used and the mother is educated about the birth process and taught breathing techniques to reduce fear and increase relaxation.

necrophilia (nek' roh FIL ee uh) sexual arousal through sexual contact with corpses.

negative feedback system a feedback system in which stability is maintained by opposing change.

neuroendocrine reflex (noo' roh EN doh krin) a reflex involving input to the nervous system and output by an endocrine gland.

neuroendocrinology (noo' roh en' doh kri NOL uh jee) study of how central nervous system and endocrine system interact to promote normal body functioning.

neurohormones (noo' roh HOR mohnz) hormones produced in hypothalamus.

neuropathy (noo ROP uh thee) improper functioning of the nervous system as the result of disease.

nonconsensual extramarital sex extramarital sex in which the non-participating spouse does not consent to and probably does not know about the affair.

nongonococcal or nonspecific urethritis (non gon' uh KOHK uhl/ yoor' uh THRY tis) urethritis (inflammation or infection of the urethra) caused by bacteria other than *Neisseria gonorrhoeae*, usually *Chlamydia*.

nonrandom sample sampling in which not all members in a population have an equal chance of being selected for the study.

obscene telephone calling sexual excitation from use of obscene language while speaking to a stranger on the telephone.

obscenity (ob SEN i tee) pictures, written material, or speech that is disgusting to the senses and offensive to morality or virtue.

Oedipal complex (ED uh puhl) in Freudian theory, the attraction of a young boy in the phallic stage to his mother.

oral contraceptive commonly called "the pill," this drug preparation, taken by mouth, suppresses ovulation and makes cervical mucus "hostile" to sperm cells so that sperm cannot penetrate mucus.

oral stage in Freudian theory, the first stage of psychosexual development, which occurs in the first year of life.

orgasm (OR gaz uhm) release of sexual tensions. This phase of human sexual response cycle is reached when maximum sexual (physical or psychological or both) stimulation occurs.

orgasmic dysfunction (or GAZ mik) inability to experience orgasm.

osteoporosis (OS′ tee oh poh ROH sis) condition in which the bones become thin and brittle as a result of mineral loss.

ovarian follicles (oh VAR ee uhn FOL i kuhlz) structures in the ovaries that produce female gametes—eggs.

ovaries (OH vuh reez) paired structures located in pelvis that produce eggs and female hormones.

ovulation (OV yuh lay shuhn) release of an egg from the ovary.

ovum (OH vuhm) egg; female reproductive cell that is released from the ovary at ovulation.

oxytocin (ok si TOH sin) posterior pituitary hormone involved in "milk-letdown" in lactating women.

paraphilia (par′ uh FIL ee uh) sexual behavior considered to be socially undesirable.

parasympathetic nervous system that part of the autonomic nervous system that tends to stimulate or excite the various organ systems in the individual as in preparation for an emergency (e.g., increase heart rate).

pedophilia (pee′ duh FIL ee uh) sexual gratification from sexual contacts with children.

pelvic inflammatory disease infection of the cervix, uterus, and ovaries, including some infections within the pelvis.

penile prosthesis (pee′ nyl pros THEE sis) replacement of portions of penis with artificial materials.

penis (PEE nis) male organ for copulation.

perimetrium (per′ uh MEE tree uhm) outer covering of uterus.

perineum (per′ uh NEE uhm) area between the anus and the genitals.

petting sexual activity that involves touching the breasts or genitals of one's partner.

phallic stage (FAL ik) in Freudian theory, the third stage of psychosexual development, which occurs

during the fourth and fifth years of life.

phallus (FAL uhs) penis; or representation of the penis.

phenylketonuria (fen′ uhl keet n OOR ee uh) recessive hereditary disease caused by body's inability to convert phenylalanine (an amino acid) to tyrosine because of defective enzyme.

phimosis (fy MOH sis) tightness of the foreskin so that it cannot be drawn back over the glans.

pituitary (pi TOO i ter′ ee) small gland located at the base of the brain, which secretes several hormones related to sexual and reproductive functioning.

placenta (pluh SEN tuh) structure through which fetus derives its nourishment and rids itself of waste products.

plateau phase (pla TOH) second phase of human sexual response cycle. Sexual tensions reach fairly steady level.

polyandry (POL ee an′ dree) marriage of one woman to two or more men.

polygyny (puh LIJ uh nee) marriage of one man to two or more women.

pornography (por NOG ruh fee) sexually arousing written, visual, or spoken material.

posterior pituitary gland (pi TOO uh ter′ ee) portion of pituitary gland that develops from nervous tissue and is connected to brain by nerves. Storage area for neurohormones produced in hypothalamus.

postpartum depression (pohst PAR tuhm) mild to moderate depression that occurs in some mothers following the birth of their infants.

postpartum period (pohst PAR tuhm) the time period following birth.

preeclampsia (pree′ i KLAMP see uh) condition of high blood pressure, protein in urine, water retention, and swelling of legs during second half of pregnancy.

premature ejaculation (i jak yuh LAY shuhn) ejaculation before or just on penetration of the vagina.

prepared childbirth childbirth with little or no medical intervention.

prepuce (PREE pyoos) foreskin or fold of skin over glans penis.

prepuce or hood of clitoris (PREE pyoos/KLIT uhr is) fold of labia minora that covers clitoris.

probability sampling method of obtaining a sample population in which all members of the population have a known probability of being recruited into the study.

procreation (proh′ kree AY shuhn) production of offspring.

progesterone (proh JES tuh rohn′) female sex hormone produced by the corpus luteum in the ovary.

progestin-induced hermaphroditism (proh JES tin/her MAF ruh dy tiz′ uhm) clinical condition that formerly occurred when females were exposed prenatally to progesterone and the females showed virilized external genitalia.

prolactin (proh LAK tin) hormone, secreted by the anterior pituitary gland, that is involved in lactation.

prostaglandins (pros′ tuh GLAN dinz) group of chemical compounds produced by many tissues of the body. These compounds mimic actions of hormones; they can act at a distance from where they are produced.

prostate gland (PROS tayt) gland that surrounds outlet of bladder and secretes thin fluid into urethra at ejaculation.

prostatitis (pros′ tuh TY tis) inflammation or infection of the prostate gland.

prostitution exchange of sexual services for money.

puberty (PYOO buhr tee) the beginning of the sexual maturation process.

pubic lice and scabies (PYOO bik lys/SKAY beez) parasites found in the pubic region that cause intense itching; can be transmitted by both sexual and nonsexual routes.

pubococcygeal muscle (pyoo boh kok SIJ ee uhl) muscle that acts to constrict vaginal orifice, urethral orifice, and anus.

random sampling type of probability sampling in which each subject in a population has an equal chance of being recruited into the study.

rape oral, anal, or vaginal penetration that a man forces on an unconsenting or unwilling victim.

rape trauma syndrome psychological adjustments that occur in the rape victim after the rape.

reflexogenic (ri FLEK soh jen' ik) reflex action caused by physical stimulation.

refractory period (ri FRAK tuhr ee) time period immediately after orgasm when a man cannot be sexually restimulated.

reliability process of using multiple or different measures to probe the same item (for example, subjects would be asked in several different ways about types of sexual behaviors they practice).

religious rites religious ceremonies.

resolution phase (rez' uh LOO shuhn) last phase of human sexual response cycle when man or woman returns to unexcited state.

retarded ejaculation (i jak yuh LAY shuhn) inability to ejaculate or inhibition of ejaculation.

retrograde ejaculation (RET ruh grayd i JAK yuh lay shuhn) abnormal condition in which semen is emptied into urinary bladder because outlet of bladder does not close before ejaculation.

rhythm method method of birth control that involves abstaining from sexual intercourse during the fertile period of the woman's menstrual cycle.

rooming-in program program in which the mother is allowed to keep her newborn in her hospital room most of the day rather than in a hospital nursery.

sadism (SAY diz' uhm) sexual arousal from inflicting pain or humiliation on others.

scrotum (SKROH tuhm) pouch consisting of muscles and skin that contains testes.

semen (SEE muhn) mucous secretion containing sperm that is discharged from urethra of a male at the time of ejaculation.

seminal vesicles (SEM uh nuhl ves uh kuhlz) saclike structures connected to vasa deferentia at ejaculatory ducts. Produce thick fluid that forms part of semen.

seminiferous tubules (sem' uh NIF uhr uhs TOO byoolz) specialized tubular structures that produce sperm cells.

sensate focus (SEN sayt') touching exercises to reduce anxiety and teach nonverbal communication.

sequential orgasms series of two or more orgasms that occur within an hour or two but are separated by more than just a few minutes.

seropositive (sir' oh POZ uh tiv) showing antibodies to HIV.

sex flush red rash resembling blush caused by dilation of blood vessels just below skin in region of face, neck, and chest.

sexual attraction attraction to another person in which sexual satisfaction is the main goal and concern for the other person is not necessarily present.

sexual disorders clinical conditions of the reproductive structures that are usually of biological origin.

sexual dysfunctions clinical conditions of the reproductive structures that are usually of psychological origin.

sexual intercourse coitus; the insertion of the penis into the vagina.

sexual orientation sexual preferences—whether one is attracted to members of the same sex, opposite sex, or both sexes.

sexual response cycle series of events that occurs as a man or woman becomes sexually aroused.

sexual systems anatomical structures involved in procreation, as well as mammary glands that some women use to nourish the newborn.

sexually transmitted disease infection spread mainly by sexual contact.

smegma (SMEG muh) secretions produced by sebaceous glands (produce sebum) located beneath prepuce.

socialization process by which one learns to behave according to the expectations of one's culture.

sodomy (SOD uh mee) sometimes refers to sex with animals, sometimes to oral and anal sex, and sometimes to sex between same-sex individuals.

somatotropic hormone (soh' muh toh TROH pik) growth hormone that causes the growth spurt that occurs during puberty.

sonography (suhn OG ruh fee) indirect way of viewing the fetus by means of ultrasound to detect fetal abnormalities.

squeeze technique method used to reduce the tendency for rapid or premature ejaculation.

sterility inability to produce offspring.

sterilization process by which the male or female reproductive tract is altered so the individual cannot produce offspring.

stroke condition in which a portion of the brain is deprived of oxygen.

supine position (soo PYN) lying on one's back.

surrogate mother (SUR uh git) a woman who is impregnated with a man's sperm in order to conceive and deliver a child for the man and his partner.

sympathetic nervous system that part of the autonomic nervous system that tends to relax the various organ systems in the individual as when a person is at rest or after a large meal (e.g., decrease heart rate).

syphilis (SIF uh lis) a sexually transmitted disease caused by a spirochete.

T4 helper/inducer lymphocytes (LIM fuh sytes) specialized type of white blood cell that organizes the body's defenses against invading microorganisms, including HIV.

teratogen (TER uh tuh juhnz) causing fetal defects and malformations.

testes (TES teez) paired structures located in scrotum that produce sperm and male hormones.

testosterone (tes TOS tuh rohn) potent male hormone belonging to androgen class of hormones.

therapeutic abortions abortions administered because of special circumstances, such as a pregnancy that is a threat to the mother's health or the result of a rape or incestual relationship.

toxemia of pregnancy (tok see mee uh) condition of preeclampsia and eclampsia.

transsexualism (tran SEK shoo uhl izm) condition in which individuals feel uncomfortable with their anatomical sex and want to change their sexual anatomy and live as a member of the opposite sex.

transvestism (trans VES tizm) sexual gratification from dressing in opposite-sex clothing.

Treponema pallidum (trep′ uh NEE muh PAL id uhm) spirochete that causes syphilis.

trichomoniasis (trik′ uh muh NY uh sis) vaginitis caused by the single-celled organism *Trichomonas vaginalis;* can be transmitted by both sexual and nonsexual routes.

trophic hormones (TROF ik HOHR mohnz) hormones that stimulate the secretion of other hormones.

troubadours poets and poet-musicians who lived in Europe in the eleventh, twelfth, and thirteenth centuries and wrote about love and chivalry.

tubal ligation (TOO buhl ly GAY shuhn) female sterilization procedure that involves blocking or cutting the fallopian tubes.

tumescence (too MES uhns) condition of being swollen with blood. This condition causes erection of the penis.

ulcers sores that are open to the skin surface or in a cavity such as the digestive tract.

umbilical cord (uhm BIL i kuhl) tubelike structure that connects the embryo and fetus with the placenta through which nutrients and wastes are passed.

urethra (yoo REE thruh) canal for discharge of urine that extends from bladder to outside body. In male, urethra also carries ejaculate out of body.

urethral orifice (yoo REE thruhl OR uh fis) outlet of urethra located in vestibule of vagina.

uterus (yoo tuhr uhs) hollow, muscular, pear-shaped structure that is organ for containing and nourishing developing embryo and fetus.

vacuum curettage (kyoor′ i TAZH) method of abortion employing a scraping instrument (curette) and vacuum or suction apparatus.

vagina (vuh JY nuh) muscular membranous tube that connects cervix of uterus with vulva.

vaginal orifice (VAJ uh nl OR uh fis) entrance to vagina located in vestibule of vagina.

vaginal photoplethysmograph (VAJ uh nl foh′ toh pluh THIZ moh graf) small device shaped like a tampon that is inserted into the vagina. It measures vaginal vasocongestion, an indication of sexual arousal.

vaginal spermicide (SPER muh syd′) chemical preparation that is placed in vagina and has sperm-killing properties.

vaginal yeast infections vaginitis caused by the yeast fungus *Candida albicans;* rare in men.

vaginismus (vaj′ uh NIZ muhs) painful involuntary muscular spasms of the vagina when intercourse is attempted.

validation process of measuring the accuracy of reported behaviors.

validity process of determining that you are measuring what you claim to be measuring.

varicoceles (VAR i koh seelz′) twisting and enlargement of veins that drain the testes.

vas deferens (VAS DEF uh renz′) long tubular structure that receives sperm cells from epididymis and conveys sperm cells to urethra.

vasectomy (va SEK tuh mee) male sterilization procedure that involves cutting and/or blocking the vas deferens.

vasocongestion (vas′ oh kuhn JES chuhn) increased amount of blood concentrated in body tissues.

vernix caseosa (VUHR niks KAY see oh suh) covering produced by fetus to protect its skin.

vestibule of the vagina (ves tuh byool/vuh JY nuh) structure located between labia minora that houses urethral orifice and vaginal orifice.

vitelline membrane (vi TEL in) membrane forming surface layer of egg.

voyeurism (vwa YER izm) sexual from secretly watching people undress or engage in sexual activities.

vulva (VUHL vuh) external genitalia of female.

withdrawal known as coitus interruptus, this involves withdrawing the penis from the vagina just before the male ejaculates.

zona pellucida (ZOH nuh puh LOO sid uh) thick, jellylike membrane envelope surrounding egg.

zoophilia or bestiality (zoh FIL ee uh) sexual excitation through sexual contact with animals.

zygote (ZY goht′) fertilized ovum before cell division.

REFERENCES

CHAPTER 1

Bronowski, J.: The ascent of man, Boston, 1973, Little, Brown & Co., Inc.

Bullough, V.L.: Sexual variance in society and history, New York, 1976, John Wiley & Sons, Inc.

Bush, G. (with Gold, V.): Looking forward, New York, 1987, Doubleday & Co.

Centers for Disease Control: AIDS due to HIV-2 infection—New Jersey, MMWR 37:33-35, 1988.

D'Emilio, J., and Freedman, E.B.: Intimate matters: a history of sexuality in America, New York, 1988, Harper & Row, Publishers, Inc.

Fineberg, H.B.: Education to prevent AIDS: prospects and obstacles, Science 239:592-596, 1988.

Gregersen, E.: Sexual practices: the story of human sexuality, New York, 1983, Franklin Watts, Inc.

Haller, J.S., and Haller, R.M.: The physician and sexuality in Victorian America, New York, 1974, W.W. Norton & Co., Inc.

Juran, S.: Sexual behavior changes as a result of a concern about AIDS: gays, straights, females and males, J. Psychol. Hum. Sexual. 2(2):61-77, 1989.

Larkin, M.: Not the end of sex, Health 12:48, 1985.

Masters, W.H., Johnson, V.E., and Kolodny, R.C.: Sex in the age of AIDS, Newsweek, Mar. 14, 1988, pp. 45-50.

Murstein, B.I.: Love, sex, and marriage through the ages, New York, 1974, Springer Publishing Co., Inc.

Perlez, J.: Old rites bring new hopes to Zambian marriage, New York Times, May 30, 1990, Section 1.

Shostak, M.: Nisa: the life and words of a !Kung woman, New York, 1983, Vintage Books.

Sussman, N.: Sex and sexuality in history. In Sadock, B.J., Kaplan, H.I., and Freedman, A.M., editors: The sexual experience, Baltimore, 1976, Williams & Wilkins.

Tannahill, R.: Sex in history, New York, 1980, Stein & Day Publishers.

Wead, D.: George Bush: man of integrity, Eugene, Ore., 1988, Harvest House Publishers, Inc.

CHAPTER 2

Alzate, H., and Londono, M.: Vaginal erotic sensitivity, J. Sex Marital Ther. 10:49-56, 1984.

Alzate, H., and Londono, M.: Subjects' reactions to a sexual experimental situation, J. Sex. Res. 23:362-367, 1987.

Bartell, G.: Group sex among the mid-Americans, J. Sex. Res. 6:113-130, 1970.

Bell, A., and Weinberg, M.: Homosexualities: a study of diversity among men and women, New York, 1978, Simon & Schuster, Inc.

Blumstein, P., and Schwartz, P.: American couples: money, work and sex, New York, 1983, William Morrow & Co., Inc.

De Buono, B., et al.: Sexual behavior of college women in 1975, 1986 and 1989, N. Engl. J. Med. 322:821-825, 1990.

Denney, N.W., Field, J.K., and Quadagno, D.: Sex differences in sexual needs and desires, Arch. Sex. Behav. 13:233-245, 1984.

Farkas, G.M., Sine, L.F., and Evans, I.M.: Personality, sexuality, and demographic differences between volunteers and nonvolunteers for a laboratory study of male sexual behavior, Arch. Sex. Behav. 7:513-519, 1978.

Gerrard, M.: Sex, sex guilt, and contraceptive use, J. Pers. Soc. Psychol. 42:153-158, 1982.

Gerrard, M., McCann, L., and Geis, B.: The antecedents and prevention of unwanted pregnancy. In Rickel, A., Gerrard, M., and Iseve, I., editors: Social and psychological problems of women: prevention and crisis interventions, New York, 1984, Hemisphere Publishing Corp.

Hite, S.: The Hite Report: a nationwide study of female sexuality, New York, 1976, Dell Publishing Co., Inc.

Hite, S.: The Hite Report on male sexuality, New York, 1981, Alfred A. Knopf, Inc.

Humphreys, L.: Tearoom trade: impersonal sex in public restrooms, Hawthorne, N.Y., 1970, Aldine Publishing Co.

Hunt, M.: Sexual behavior in the 1970s, Chicago, 1974, Playboy Press.

Johnston, B.L., and Fletcher, G.F.: Dynamic EEG recording during sexual activity in recent post-myocardial infarction and revascularization patients, Am. Heart J. 98:736-741, 1979.

Julien, E., and Over, R.: Male sexual arousal with repeated exposure to erotic stimuli, Arch. Sex. Behav. 13:211-222, 1984.

Kinsey, A., Pomeroy, W., and Martin, C.: Sexual behavior in the human male, Philadelphia, 1948, W.B. Saunders Co.

Kinsey, A., et al.: Sexual behavior in the human female, Philadelphia, 1953, W.B. Saunders Co.

Lafferty, F., and Helmuth, D.: Postmenopausal estrogen replacement: the prevention of osteoporosis and systemic effects, Maturitas 7:147-159, 1985.

Masters, W.: Summary and future considerations. In Masters, W., Johnson, V., and Kolodny, R., editors: Ethical issues in sex therapy and research, Boston, 1977, Little, Brown & Co., Inc., pp. 206-219.

Masters, W.H., and Johnson, V.E.: Human sexual response, Boston, 1966, Little, Brown & Co., Inc.

Mohl, P.C., et al.: Prepuce restoration seekers: psychiatric aspects, Arch. Sex. Behav. 10:383-393, 1981.

Sorenson, R.: Adolescent sexuality in contemporary America, New York, 1973, World Books.

Suddman, S., and Bradburn, N.: Asking questions, San Francisco, 1985, Jossey-Bass Inc., Publishers.

Tavris, C., and Sadd, S.: The Redbook report on female sexuality, New York, 1977, Delacorte Press.

Wolchik, S., Braver, S., and Jensen, B.: Volunteer bias in erotica research: effects of intrusiveness of measure and sexual background, Arch. Sex. Behav. 14:93-108, 1985.

Wolchik, S., Spencer, S., and Lisi, I.: Volunteer bias in research employing vaginal measures of sexual arousal, Arch. Sex. Behav. 12:399-408, 1983.

Zelnick, M., and Kantner, J.: Sexual and contraceptive experiences of young unmarried women in the United States, 1976 and 1971, Fam. Plann. Perspect. 9:55-71, 1977.

Zelnick, M., and Kantner, J.: Sexual activity, contraceptive use and pregnancy among metropolitan-area teenagers, 1971-1979, Fam. Plann. Perspect. 12:230-237, 1980.

Zelnick, M., and Shah, F.: First intercourse among young Americans, Fam. Plann. Perspect. 15:64-70, 1983.

Zuckerman, M., Tushup, R., and Finner, S.: Sexual attitudes and experience: attitude and personality correlates and changes produced by a course in sexuality, J. Consult. Clin. Psychol. 44:7-19, 1976.

CHAPTER 3

Addiego, F., et al.: Female ejaculation: a case study, J. Sex. Res. 17:13-21, 1981.

Alzate, H., and Londono, M.: Vaginal erotic sensitivity, J. Sex Marital Ther. 10:49-56, 1984.

American Academy of Pediatrics: Report of the task force on circumcision, Pediatrics 84:388-391, 1989.

Barbach, L.G.: For yourself: the fulfillment of female sexuality, New York, 1975, Doubleday Co., Inc.

Chambless, D.L., et al.: The pubococcygens and female orgasm: a correlational study with normal subjects, Arch. Sex. Behav. 11:479-490, 1982.

Dittmann, R., Kappes, M., and Kappes, M.: Sexual behavior in adolescent and adult females with congenital adrenal hyperplasia, Psychoneuroendocrinology. In press.

Edwardes, A., and Masters, R.E.: The cradle of erotica, New York, 1963, The Julian Press, Inc.

Fink, A.: Circumcision and heterosexual transmission of HIV infection in men, N. Engl. J. Med. 316:1545-1547, 1987.

Gebhard, P.H., and Johnson, A.B.: The Kinsey data: marginal tabulations of the 1938-1963 interviews conducted by the Institute for Sex Research, Philadelphia, 1979, W.B. Saunders Co.

Goldberg, D.C., et al.: The Grafenberg spot and female ejaculation: a review of initial hypotheses, J. Sex. Marital Ther. 9:27-37, 1983.

Hafez, E.S.E.: Human semen and fertility regulation in men, St. Louis, 1976, Mosby–Year Book, Inc.

Hafez, E.S.E.: Human reproduction: conception and contraception, ed. 2, New York, 1980, Harper & Row Publishers, Inc.

Kaplan, H.S.: The new sex therapy, New York, 1974, Brunner/Mazel, Inc.

Kegel, A.H.: Sexual functions of the pubococcygeus muscle, West. J. Surg. Obstet. Gynecol. 60:521-524, 1952.

Ladas, A., Whipple, B., and Perry, J.: The G spot and other recent discoveries about human sexuality, New York, 1982, Dell Publishing Co., Inc.

Ladjali, M., and Toubia, N.: Female circumcision: desperately seeking a space for women, Int. Planned Parenthood Federation Med. Bull. 24:1-2, 1990.

Lightfoot-Klein, H.: Rites of purification and their effects: some psychological aspects of female genital circumcision and infibulation (Pharaonic circumcision) in an Afro-Arab Islamic society (Sudan), J. Psychol. Hum. Sex. 2:61-78, 1989.

Mahran, M.: Proceedings of the Third International Congress of Medical Sexology, Littleton, Mass., 1978, PSG Publishing Co., Inc.

Mahran, M.: Medical dangers of female circumcision, Int. Planned Parenthood Federation Med. Bull. 2:1-2, 1981.

Marx, J.: Circumcision may protect against the AIDS virus, Science 245:470-471, 1989.

Masters, W.H., and Johnson, V.E.: Human sexual response, Boston, 1966, Little, Brown & Co., Inc.

Messe, M.R., and Geer, J.: Voluntary vaginal musculature contractions as an enhancer of sexual arousal, Arch. Sex. Behav. 14:13-28, 1985.

Money, J., and Ehrhardt, A.A.: Man and woman, boy and girl: differentiation and dimorphism of gender identity from conception to maturity, Baltimore, 1973, Johns Hopkins University Press.

Nalbandov, A.V.: Reproductive physiology of mammals and birds, San Francisco, 1976, W.H. Freeman & Co. Publishers.

Oppenheimer, S., and LeFevre, G.: Introduction to embryonic development, Boston, 1984, Allyn & Bacon, Inc.

O'Rahilly, R.: Basic human anatomy, Philadelphia, 1983, W.B. Saunders Co.

Page, E., Villee, C., and Villee, D.: Human reproduction: essentials of reproductive and perinatal medicine, Philadelphia, 1981, W.B. Saunders Co.

Parker, S., et al.: Circumcision and sexually transmissible diseases, Med. J. Aust. 2:288-290, 1983.

Perry, J., and Whipple, B.: Pelvic strength of female ejaculations: evidence in support of a new theory of orgasm, J. Sex. Res. 17:22-39, 1981.

Quadagno, D.M., Briscoe, R., and Quadagno, J.B.: Effect of perinatal gonadal hormones on selected nonsexual behavior patterns: a critical assessment of the nonhuman and human literature, Psychol. Bull. 84:62-80, 1977.

Romberg, R.: Circumcision: the painful dilemma, South Hadley, Mass., 1985, Bergin & Garvey Publishers, Inc.

Wallenstein, E.: Circumcision: an American health fallacy, New York, 1980, Springer Publishing Co., Inc.

Wentz, A.C.: Assessment of estrogen and progestin therapy in gynecology and obstetrics, Clin. Obstet. Gynecol. 20:461-482, 1977.

Wiswell, T.: Routine neonatal circumcision: a reappraisal, Am. Fam. Pract. 41:859-863, 1990.

Wiswell, T., Smith, F., and Bass, J.: Decreased incidence of urinary tract infections in circumcised male infants, Pediatrics 75:901-903, 1985.

Zaviacic, M., et al.: Female urethral expulsions evoked by local digital stimulation of the G-spot: differences in the response patterns, J. Sex. Res. 24:311-318, 1988a.

Zaviacic, M., et al.: Concentrations of fructose in female ejaculate and urine: a comparative biochemical study, J. Sex. Res. 24:319-325, 1988b.

CHAPTER 4

Abplanalp, M., et al.: Cortisol and growth hormone responses to psychological stress during the menstrual cycle, Psychosom. Med. 39:158-176, 1977.

Abraham, G., and Rumley, R.: Role of nutrition in managing the premenstrual tension syndromes, J. Reprod. Med. 32:405-416, 1987.

Adams, D.B.: Rise in female sexual activity at ovulation: married vs. college women (abstract), Eastern Conference on Reproductive Behavior, 1980.

Adams, D.B., Gold, A.R., and Burt, A.D.: Rise in female-initiated sexual activity at ovulation and its suppression by oral contraceptives, N. Engl. J. Med. 299:1145-1150, 1978.

American Psychiatric Association: Diagnostic and statistical manual of mental disorders, ed. 3 revised, Washington, D.C., 1987, The Association.

Bancroft, J.: Hormones and human sexual behavior, J. Sex Marital Ther. 10:3-21, 1984.

Benkert, O., et al.: Sexual impotence: a double-blind study of LHRH nasal spray versus placebo, Neuropsychobiology 1:203-210, 1975.

Berne, R., and Levy, M.: Physiology, ed. 3,

St. Louis, 1992, Mosby–Year Book, Inc.

Bernstein, B.E.: Effect of menstruation on academic performance among college women, Arch. Sex. Behav. 6:289-296, 1977.

Bremner, W., et al.: Reproductive neuroendocrinology of the aging male. In Norman, R.L., editor: Neuroendocrine aspects of reproduction, New York, 1983, Academic Press, Inc.

Brown, W., Monti, P., and Coniveau, D.: Serum testosterone and sexual activity and interest in men, Arch. Sex. Behav. 7:97-103, 1978.

Carey, P., Howard, S., and Vance, M.: Transdermal testosterone treatment of hypogonadal men, J. Urol. 140:76-79, 1988.

Casper, R., and Yen, S.: Neuroendocrine changes during menopausal flushes. In Norman, R.L., editor: Neuroendocrine aspects of reproduction, New York, 1983, Academic Press, Inc.

Christiansen, K., and Knussman, R.: Androgen levels and components of aggressive behavior in men, Horm. Behav. 21:170-180, 1987.

Chuong, C., and Gibbons, W.: Premenstrual syndrome: update on therapy, Med. Aspects Hum. Sex. 24:58-66, 1990.

Connaughton, J.F., et al.: Induction of ovulation with cisclomiphene and a placebo, Obstet. Gynecol. 43:697-701, 1974.

Cooper, A., et al.: Antiandrogen (cyproterone acetate) therapy in deviant hypersexuality, Br. J. Psychiatry 120:59-63, 1972.

Cumming, D., et al.: Reproductive hormone responses to resistance exercise, Med. Sci. Sports Exercise 19:234-238, 1987.

Dale, E., et al.: Physical fitness profiles and reproductive physiology of the female distance runner, Physician Sports Med. 7:83-95, 1979.

Dalton, K.: Menstruation and acute psychiatric illnesses, Br. Med. J. 1:148-149, 1959.

Dalton, K.: Menstruation and accidents, Br. Med. J. 2:1425-1426, 1960.

Dalton, K.: Menstruation and crime, Br. Med. J. 2:1752-1753, 1961.

Davidson, J.: Response to "Hormones and human sexual behavior," J. Sex Marital Ther. 10:23-27, 1984.

Davidson, J., et al.: Maintenance of sexual function in a castrated man treated with ovarian steroids, Arch. Sex. Behav. 12:263-274, 1983.

Doering, C.H., et al.: Negative affect and plasma testosterone: longitudinal human study, Psychosom. Med. 37:484-491, 1975.

Elias, M.: Serum cortisol, testosterone and

testosterone-binding globulin responses to competitive fighting in human males, Aggressive Behav. 7:215-224, 1981.

Ewing, L., Davis, J.C., and Zirkin, B.R.: Regulation of testicular function: a spatial and temporal view. In Greep, R.D., editor: Reproductive physiology III, Baltimore, 1980, University Park Press.

Feder, H.H.: Hormones and sexual behavior, Annu. Rev. Psychol. 35:165-200, 1984.

Ford, C.S., and Beach, F.A.: Patterns of sexual behavior, New York, 1951, Harper & Row, Publishers, Inc.

Frisch, R., and McArthur, J.: Menstrual cycles: fatness as a determinant of minimum weight for height necessary for their maintenance or onset, Science 185:949-951, 1974.

Frisch, R.E., Wyshak, G., and Vincent, L.: Delayed menarche and amenorrhea in ballet dancers, N. Engl. J. Med. 303:17-19, 1980.

Gallant, S., et al.: Daily moods and symptoms: effects of awareness of study focus, gender, menstrual cycle phase and day of the week, Health Psychol. In press.

Gladue, B., Boechler, M., and McCaul, K.: Hormonal response to competition in human males, Aggressive Behav. 15:409-422, 1989.

Gottschalk, L., et al.: Variations in magnitude of emotion: a method applied to anxiety and hostility during phases of the menstrual cycle, Psychosom. Med. 24:300-311, 1962.

Heim, N.: Sexual behavior of castrated sex offenders, Arch. Sex. Behav. 10:11-19, 1981.

Kendall, D., and Schnurr, P.: The effects of vitamin B_6 supplementation on premenstrual symptoms, Obstet. Gynecol. 70:145-151, 1987.

Kraemer, H.C., et al.: Orgasmic frequency and plasma testosterone levels in normal human males, Arch. Sex. Behav. 5:125-132, 1976.

Kwan, M., et al.: The nature of androgen action on male sexuality: a combined laboratory-self report study on hypogonadal men, J. Clin. Endocrinol. Metab. 57:557-562, 1983.

Lahmeyer, H., Miller, M., and DeLeon-Jones, F.: Anxiety and mood fluctuation during the normal menstrual cycle, Psychosom. Med. 44:183-194, 1982.

Lark, S.: The PMS prevention diet, New Woman, February 1985, pp. 18-25.

Laws, S.: The sexual politics of premenstrual tension, Women's Studies Int. Forum 6:19-31, 1983.

Lee, P.A., Jaffe, R., and Midgley, A.R.: Lack of alteration of serum gonadotropins in men and women following sexual intercourse, Am. J. Obstet. Gynecol. 120:985-987, 1974.

Lein, A.: The cycling female: her menstrual rhythm, San Francisco, 1979, W.H. Freeman & Co. Publishers.

London, R., Murphy, L., and Kittowski, K.: Efficacy of alpha-tocopherol in the treatment of the premenstrual syndrome, J. Reprod. Med. 32:400-411, 1987.

Mandell, A., and Mandell, M.: Suicide and the menstrual cycle, JAMA 200:792-793, 1967.

Masters, W.H., and Johnson, V.E.: Human sexual response, Boston, 1966, Little, Brown & Co., Inc.

Mazur, A., and Lamb, T.: Testosterone, status, and mood in human males, Horm. Behav. 14:236-246, 1980.

McClintock, M.: Menstrual synchrony and suppression, Nature 229:244-245, 1971.

Mira, M., Stewart, P., and Abraham, S.: Vitamin and trace element status in premenstrual syndrome, Am. J. Clin. Nutr. 47:636-641, 1988.

Moos, R.H.: The development of a menstrual distress questionnaire, Psychosom. Med. 30:853-867, 1968.

Morris, N., et al.: Marital sex frequency and mid-cycle female testosterone, Arch. Sex. Behav. 16:27-37, 1987.

Norris, R.V.: PMS: premenstrual syndrome, New York, 1983, Berkley Publishing Group.

Page, E.W., Villee, C.A., and Villee, D.B.: Human reproduction: essentials of reproductive and perinatal medicine, Philadelphia, 1981, W.B. Saunders Co.

Paige, K.E.: Effects of oral contraceptives on affective fluctuations associated with the menstrual cycle, Psychosom. Med. 33:515-537, 1971.

Paige, K.E.: Women learn to sing the menstrual blues, Psychol. Today 4:41-48, 1973.

Paige, K.E.: Sexual pollution: reproductive sex taboos in American society, J. Soc. Issues 33:144-152, 1977.

Parlee, M.: Changes in mood and activation levels during the menstrual cycle in experimentally naive subjects, Psychol. Women Q. 12:119-131, 1982.

Peyser, M.R., et al.: Stress induced delay of ovulation, Obstet. Gynecol. 42:667-671, 1973.

Preti, G., et al.: Human axillary secretions influence women's menstrual cycles: the role of donor extract of females, Horm. Behav. 20:474-482, 1986.

Quadagno, D.M.: Pheromones and human sexuality, Med. Aspects Hum. Sex. 12:149-154, 1987.

Quadagno, D.M., et al.: A study of males, exercise and all female living conditions on the menstrual cycle, Psychoneuroendocrinology 6:239-244, 1981.

Quadagno, D.M., et al.: The menstrual cycle: does it affect athletic performance? Physician Sports Med. 19:121-124, 1991.

Ramasharma, K., et al.: Isolation, structure, and synthesis of a human seminal plasma peptide with inhibin-like activity, Science 223:1199-1201, 1984.

Reinberg, A., and Lagoguey, M.: Circadian and circannual rhythms in sexual activity and plasma hormones of five human males, Arch. Sex. Behav. 7:13-30, 1978.

Ribeiro, A.: Menstruation and crime, Br. Med. J. 1:640, 1962.

Rolker-Dolinsky, B.: The premenstrual syndrome. In Kelley, K., editor: Females, males and sexuality, Albany, 1987, State University of New York Press, pp. 101-126.

Rossi, A.S., and Rossi, P.E.: Body time and social time: mood patterns by menstrual cycle phase and day of week, Soc. Sci. Res. 6:273-308, 1977.

Sanborn, C.: Etiology of athletic amenorrhea. In Puhl, J., and Brown, C., editors: The menstrual cycle and physical activity, Champaign, Ill., 1986, Human Kinetics Publishing, Inc.

Sanders, D., and Bancroft, J.: Hormones and the sexuality of women—the menstrual cycle, Clin. Endocrinol. Metab. 11:639-659, 1982.

Shangold, M.: Menstruation. In Shangold, M., and Mirkin, G., editors: Women and exercise: physiology and sports medicine, Philadelphia, 1988, F.A. Davis Co.

Sommer, B.: The effect of menstruation on cognitive and perceptual motor behavior: a review, Psychosom. Med. 35:515-534, 1973.

Sturgis, S.: Psychophysiologic disorders and ovulatory failure. In Greenblatt, R.R., editor: Ovulation: stimulation, suppression, detection, Philadelphia, 1966, J.B. Lippincott Co.

Svare, B., and Kinsley, C.: Hormones and sex-related behavior: a comparative analysis. In Kelley, K., editor: Females, males and sexuality: theories and research, Albany, 1987, State University of New York Press.

Thornton, J.: Sexual activity and athletic performance: is there a relationship? Physician Sports Med. 18:148-154, 1990.

Timonen, S., and Procope, B.: Premenstrual syndrome and physical exercise, Acta Obstet. Gynecol. Scand. 50:331-337, 1971.

Whalen, R.E.: Cyclic changes in hormones and behavior, Arch. Sex. Behav. 4:313-314, 1975.

Wickham, M.: The effects of the menstrual cycle on test performance, Br. J. Psychol. 49:34-41, 1958.

CHAPTER 5

Bohlen, J., et al.: The female orgasm: pelvic contractions, Arch. Sex. Behav. 11:367-386, 1982.

Dunn, M., and Trost, J.: Male multiple orgasms: a descriptive study, Arch. Sex. Behav. 18:377-388, 1989.

Kaplan, H.S.: Disorders of sexual desire, New York, 1979, Brunner/Mazel, Inc.

Kelley, K., and Byrne, D.: Assessment of sexual responding: arousal, affect, and behavior. In Cacioppo, J., and Petty, R., editors: Social psychophysiology, New York, 1983, The Guilford Press.

Masters, W.H., and Johnson, V.E.: Human sexual response, Boston, 1966, Little, Brown & Co., Inc.

Masters, W.H., and Johnson, V.E.: Homosexuality in perspective, Boston, 1979, Little, Brown & Co., Inc.

Masters, W., Johnson, V., and Kolodny, R.: Masters and Johnson on sex and human loving, Boston, 1986, Little, Brown & Co., Inc.

Perry, J., and Whipple, B.: Pelvic strength of female ejaculations: evidence in support of a new theory of orgasm, J. Sex. Res. 17:22-39, 1981.

Robbins, M., and Jensen, G.D.: Multiple orgasm in males, J. Sex. Res. 14:21-26, 1978.

Rosen, R., and Leiblum, S.: Current approaches to the evaluation of sexual desire disorders, J. Sex. Res. 23:141-162, 1987.

Singer, J., and Singer, I.: Types of female orgasms. In LoPiccolo, J., and LoPiccolo, L., editors: Handbook of sex therapy, New York, 1978, Plenum Publishing Corp.

Vance, E.B., and Wagner, N.N.: Written descriptions of orgasm: a study of sex differences, Arch. Sex. Behav. 5:87-98, 1976.

Weiss, H.: Mechanism of erection, Med. Aspects Hum. Sex. 7:28-40, 1973.

Zilbergeld, B., and Ellison, C.R.: Desire discrepancies and arousal problems in sex therapy. In Leiblum, S.R., and Pervin, L.A., editors: Principles and practice of sex therapy, New York, 1980, The Guilford Press.

CHAPTER 6

Andrews, L.: New conceptions, New York, 1987, Ballantine Books.

Berkow, R.: The Merck manual, Rahway, N.J., 1988, Merck and Co., Inc.

Berne, R., and Levy, M.: Physiology, ed. 2, St. Louis, 1988, Mosby–Year Book, Inc.

Bracken, M., et al.: Association of cocaine use with sperm concentration, motility and morphology, Fertil. Steril. 53:315-322, 1990.

Bracker, M., et al.: Letter to editor, N.Engl. J. Med. 306:1548-1549, 1982.

Brambati, B.: Chorionic villus sampling: a safe and reliable alternative in fetal diagnosis, Res. Reprod. 19:1-2, 1987.

Cefalo, R, and Moos, M.: Preconceptional health promotion: a practical guide, Rockville, Md., 1988, Aspen Publishing Co.

Centers for Disease Control: Fetal alcohol syndrome, MMWR 33:1-2, 1984.

Domar, A., Seibel, M., and Benson, H.: The mind/body program for infertility: a new behavioral treatment approach for females with infertility, Fertil. Steril. 53:246-260, 1990.

Edwards, R.: The current situation of in vitro fertilization, Int. Planned Parenthood Federation Med. Bull. 18(5):1-2, 1984.

Edwards, R., and Steptoe, P.: Current status of in vitro fertilization and implantation of human embryos, Hum. Reprod. Pilot Issue: 6-10, 1985.

Feldman, P.: Smoking and healthy pregnancy: now is the time to quit, Md. State Med. J., Oct., 1985, pp. 982-986.

Gavalas, N.: Personal communication to the authors, 1990.

Greil, A., Porter, K., and Leitko, T.: Sex and intimacy among infertile couples, J. Psychol. Hum. Sex. 2:117-138, 1989.

Guerrero, R.: Type and time of insemination within the menstrual cycle and the human sex ratio at birth, Stud. Fam. Plann. 6:367-371, 1975.

Guyton, A.: Textbook of medical physiology, Philadelphia, 1986, W.B. Saunders Co.

Harlap, S.: Gender of infants conceived on different days of the menstrual cycle, N. Engl. J. Med. 300:1445-1448, 1979.

Harlap, S., and Shiono, P.: Alcohol, smoking and incidence of spontaneous abortions in the first and second trimester, Lancet 2:173-176, 1980.

Hatcher, R., et al.: Contraceptive technology, New York, 1990, Irvington Publishers, Inc.

Hotchner, T.: Pregnancy and childbirth, New York, 1979, Avon Books.

Institute of Medicine: Preventing low birthweight, Washington, D.C., 1985, National Academy Press.

IVF, GIFT and intraperitoneal and intrauterine insemination for human infertility, Res. Reprod. 19(1):1, 1987.

Johnson, M., and Everitt, B.E.: Essential reproduction, Boston, 1980, Blackwell Scientific Publications, Inc.

Jones, R.E.: Human reproduction and sexual behavior, Englewood Cliffs, N.J., 1984, Prentice-Hall, Inc.

Kline, J., et al.: Environmental influences on early reproductive loss in current New York study. In Porter, H., and Hook, E., editors: Human embryonic and fetal death, New York, 1980, Academic Press, Inc., pp. 225-240.

Kruppa, K., et al.: Coffee consumption during pregnancy and selected congenital malformations: a nationwide control study, Am. J. Pub. Health 73:1397-1399, 1983.

Langman, L.: Medical embryology, Baltimore, 1981, Williams & Wilkins.

Lenard, L.: Hi-tech babies, Sci. Dig. 8:86-116, 1981.

Lincoln, R.: Smoking and reproduction, Fam. Plann. Perspect. 18:79-84, 1986.

Linn, S., et al.: No association between coffee consumption and adverse outcomes of pregnancy, N. Engl. J. Med 306:141-145, 1982.

Longo, L.: Some health consequences of maternal smoking: issues without answers. Birth Defects: Original Article Series. March of Dimes Birth Defects Foundation, 18:13-31, 1982.

Luke, B.: Letter to editor, N. Engl. J. Med. 306:1549, 1982.

Martin, T., and Bracken, M.: Association of low birth weight with passive smoke exposure in pregnancy, Am. J. Epidemiol. 124:633-642, 1986.

Marzollo, J.: 9 months, 1 day, 1 year, New York, 1976, Harper & Row, Publishers, Inc.

Masters, W.H., and Johnson, V.E.: Human sexual response, Boston, 1966, Little, Brown & Co., Inc.

Miller, R.K.: Drugs during pregnancy: a therapeutic dilemma, Drug Ther. 15:1-9, 1981.

Mills, J.L., Harlay, S., and Harley, E.E.: Should coitus late in pregnancy be discouraged, Lancet (8238)2:136-138, 1981.

Naeye, R.L.: Coitus and associated amniotic-fluid infections, N. Engl. J. Med. 301:1198-1200, 1979.

Odell, W.D., and Moyer, D.L.: Physiology of reproduction, St. Louis, 1971, Mosby–Year Book, Inc.

Page, E.W., Villee, C.A., and Villee, D.B.: Human reproduction: essentials of reproductive and perinatal medicine, Philadelphia, 1981, W.B. Saunders Co.

Rosenberg, L., et al.: Selected birth defects in relation to caffeine containing beverages, JAMA 247:1429-1432, 1982.

Rosett, H.L.: Clinical pharmacology of the fetal alcohol syndrome. In Majchrowicz, E., and Noble, E.P., editors: Biochemistry and pharmacology of ethanol, vol. 2, New York, 1979, Plenum Publishing Corp.

Rubenstein, B.B., et al.: Sperm survival in women: motile sperm in the fundus and tubes of surgical cases, Fertil. Steril. 2:15-22, 1951.

Rugh, R., and Shettles, L.B.: From conception to birth: the drama of life's beginning, New York, 1971, Harper & Row, Publishers, Inc.

Schwan, K.: The infertility maze, New York, 1988, Contemporary Books.

Seibel, M.: A new era in reproductive technology, N. Engl. J. Med. 317:828-834, 1988.

Shettles, L., and Rorvik, D.: Your baby's sex: now you can choose, New York, 1970, Dodd Mead.

Steinmann, W.C.: Letter to editor, N. Engl. J. Med. 306:1549, 1982.

Wagner, N., and Solberg, D.: Pregnancy and sexuality, Med. Aspects Hum. Sex. 8:44-79, 1974.

White, S., and Reamy, K.: Sexuality and pregnancy: a review, Arch. Sex. Behav. 11:429-444, 1982.

Wilson, J., et al.: Obstetrics and gynecology, St. Louis, 1991, Mosby–Year Book, Inc.

CHAPTER 7

Arms, S.: Immaculate deception: a new look at women and childbirth in America, Boston, 1975, Houghton Mifflin Co.

Bongaarts, J.: Infertility after age 30: a false alarm, Fam. Plann. Perspect. 14:75-78, 1982.

Brackbill, Y.: Obstetrical medication and infant behavior. In Osofsky, J.D., editor: Handbook of infant development, New York, 1979, John Wiley & Sons, Inc.

Brackbill, Y., McManus, K., and Woodward, L.: Medication in maternity: infant exposure and maternal information, Ann Arbor, 1985, University of Michigan Press.

Brody, J.E.: Research casts doubt on need

for many caesarean births as their rate soars, New York Times, July 27, 1989.

Buehler, J.W., et al.: Maternal mortality in women aged 35 years and older: United States, JAMA 255:53-57, 1986.

Calhoun, C.A., and Espenshade, T.J.: The opportunity cost of rearing children: final report, Washington, D.C., 1985, Urban Institute Publications.

Chess, S., and Thomas, A.: Infant bonding: mystique and reality, Am. J. Orthopsychiatry 52:213-222, 1982.

Clarke-Stewart, A.: Daycare, Cambridge, Mass., 1982, Harvard University Press.

Cowan, P.A., and Cowan, A.P.: Changes in marriage during the transition to parenthood: must we blame the baby? In Michaels, G.Y., and Goldberg, W.A., editors: The transition to parenthood, New York, 1988, Cambridge University Press.

DeParle, J.: The case against kids, The Washington Monthly, July/August 1988, pp. 36-43.

Dick-Read, G.: Childbirth without fear, New York, 1932, Harper & Row, Publishers, Inc.

Elkins, S.: Personal communication to the authors, 1982.

Entwisle, D.R., and Doering, S.G.: The first birth, Baltimore, 1981, The Johns Hopkins University Press.

Fabe, M., and Wikler, N.: Up against the clock, New York, 1979, Random House, Inc.

Glenn, N.D., and McLanahan, S.: Children and marital happiness, J. Marriage Fam. 44:63-72, 1982.

Goetting, A.: Parental satisfaction, J. Fam. Issues 7:83-109, 1986.

Graham, D.: The obstetric and neonatal consequences of adolescent pregnancy. In McAnarney, E.R., and Stickle, G., editors: Pregnancy and childbearing during adolescence: research priorities for the 1980s, New York, 1981, Alan R. Liss.

Greenberg, M., Rosenberg, I., and Lind, J.: First mothers rooming-in with their newborns: its impact upon the mother, Am. J. Orthopsychiatry 43:783-788, 1973.

Grossman, L.K., et al.: Breastfeeding among low-income, high-risk women, Clin. Pediatr. 28(1):38-42, 1989.

Hamburg, D.A., Moos, R.H., and Yalom, I.D.: Studies of distress in the menstrual cycle and the postpartum period. In Michael, R.P., editor: Endocrinology and human behavior, New York, 1968, Oxford University Press.

Hamilton, J.A.: Postpartum psychiatric syndromes, Psychiatr. Clin. North Am. 12(1):89-103, 1989.

Kazandjian, V.A., Dans, P.E., and Scherlis, L.: What physicians should know about small area variation analysis, Md. Med. J. 38:477-481, 1989.

Kazandjian, V.A., and Summer, S.J.: Evaluating the appropriateness of care: a study of cesarean section rates, Qual. Res. Bull. 15:206-214, 1989.

Kendell, R.E.: Emotional and physical factors in the genesis of puerperal mental disorders, J. Psychosom. Res. 29:3-11, 1985.

Klaus, M.H., and Kennell, J.H.: Maternal-infant bonding, St. Louis, 1976, Mosby-Year Book, Inc.

Kolata, G.B.: NIH panel urges fewer cesarean births, Science 210:176-177, 1980.

Kuchner, J.F., and Porcino, J.: Delayed motherhood. In Birns, B., and Hay, D.F., editors: The different faces of motherhood, New York, 1988, Plenum Press.

Lamanna, M.: The value of children to natural and adoptive parents, doctoral dissertation, South Bend, Ind., 1977, University of Notre Dame.

Lamanna, M., and Riedmann, A.: Marriages and families, Belmont, Calif., 1981, Wadsworth, Inc.

Lamb, M.E.: Early contact and maternal-infant bonding: one decade later, Pediatrics 70:763-768, 1982.

LaRossa, R.: The transition of parenthood and the social reality of time, J. Marriage Fam. 45:579-589, 1983.

Lawrence, R.A.: Breastfeeding, St. Louis, 1989, Mosby-Year Book, Inc.

Leboyer, F.: Birth without violence, New York, 1975, Alfred A. Knopf, Inc.

Leifer, M.: Psychological changes accompanying pregnancy and motherhood, Genet. Psychol. Monogr. 95:55-96, 1977.

Lester, B.M., Als, H., and Brazelton, T.B.: Regional obstetric anesthesia and newborn behavior: a reanalysis toward synergistic effects, Child Dev. 53:687-692, 1982.

Liu, Y.C.: The effects of the upright position during childbirth, Image 21(1):14-18, 1988.

Livingston, M.: Choice in childbirth: power and the impact of the modern childbirth reform movement, Women Ther. 6(1-2):1235-1248, 1987.

Manion, J.: A study of fathers and infant caretaking, Birth Fam. J. 4:174-179, 1977.

Martinez, G.A., and Krieger, F.W.: Milk-feeding patterns in the United States, Pediatrics 76(6):1004-1008, 1985.

May, K.A., and Perrin, S.P.: Prelude: pregnancy and birth. In Hanson, S.M.H., and Bozett, F.W., editors: Dimensions of fa-

therhood, Beverly Hills, Calif., 1985, Sage Publications, Inc.

McCauley, C.S.: Pregnancy after 35, New York, 1976, Pocket Books.

Monkus, E., and Bancalari, E.: Neonatal outcome. In Scott, K.G., Field, T., and Robertson, E.G., editors: Teenage parents and their offspring, New York, 1981, Grune & Stratton, Inc.

Nelson, N.M., et al.: A randomized clinical trial of the Leboyer approach to childbirth, N. Engl. J. Med. 302:655-660, 1980.

Norton, F.C., Placek, P.J., and Taffel, S.M.: Comparisons of national cesarean-section rates, N. Engl. J. Med. 316:386-389, 1987.

Phillips, C., and Anzalone, J.: Fathering participation in labor and birth, ed. 2, St. Louis, 1982, Mosby-Year Book, Inc.

Powledge, T.M.: Windows on the womb, Psychology Today 17:37-42, 1983.

Pritchard, J.A., and MacDonald, P.C.: Williams' obstetrics, ed. 16, New York, 1980, Appleton-Century-Crofts.

Quadagno, D.M., et al.: Postpartum moods in men and women, Am. J. Obstet. Gynecol. 154:1018-1023, 1986.

Reamy, K., and White, S.: Sexuality in the puerperium: a review, Arch. Sex. Behav. 16:165-186, 1987.

Resnik, R.: Age-related changes in gestation and pregnancy. In Mastroianni, L., Jr., and Paulson, C.A., editors: Aging, reproduction and the climacteric, New York, 1986, Plenum Press.

Rich, A.: Of woman born, New York, 1977, Bantam Books, Inc.

Romito, P.: Unhappiness after childbirth. In Chalmers, I., Enkin, M., and Keirse, M., editors: Effective care in pregnancy and childbirth, Oxford, Eng., 1989, Oxford University Press.

Rubenstein, E.: Birth dearth confirmed, National Review, May 5, 1989, p. 13.

Russell, C.S.: Transition to parenthood: problems and gratifications, J. Marriage Fam. 36:294-302, 1974.

Sepkowski, C.: Maternal obstetric medication and newborn behavior. In Scanlon, J.W., editor: Prenatal anesthesia, London, 1985, Blackwell Scientific Publications, Inc.

Spanier, G.B., and Lewis, R.A.: Marital quality: a review of the seventies, J. Marriage Fam. 42:825-839, 1980.

Statistical bulletin: infant mortality, 1986; national and international differences, Met. Life Q. 69(2):2-8, 1988.

Taffel, S.: Midwife and out-of-hospital deliveries, United States: an analysis of the demographic characteristics and pregnancy history of mothers and birthweight of babies delivered in non-hospital setting or by a midwife in a hospital, Vital and Health Statistics, series 21(40), Hyattsville, Md., 1984, Dept. of Health and Human Services.

Torres, A., and Reich, M.R.: The shift from home to institutional childbirth: a comparative study of the United Kingdom and the Netherlands, Int. J. Health Serv. 19:405-414, 1989.

Ventura, J.: The stresses of parenthood reexamined, Fam. Relations 36:26-69, 1987.

Veroff, J., Douvan, E., and Kulka, R.A.: The inner American: a self portrait from 1957 to 1976, New York, 1981, Basic Books.

Viorst, J.: Nice baby. In It's hard to be hip over thirty and other tragedies of married life, New York, 1970, The New American Library, Inc.

Walker, K., and Woods, M.: Time use: a measure of household production of family goods and services, Washington, D.C., 1976, American Home Economics Association.

Wegman, M.E.: Annual summary of vital statistics—1986, Pediatrics 80:817-827, 1987.

Wideman, M.V., and Singer, J.E.: The role of psychological mechanisms in preparation for childbirth, Am. Psychol. 39:1357-1371, 1984.

Worthington, E., and Buston, B.: The marriage relationship during the transition to parenthood, J. Fam. Issues 7:443-473, 1986.

CHAPTER 8

Bachrach, C., and Mosher, W.: Use of contraceptives in the United States, Advancedata 102:18, 1984.

Billings, E., Billings, J., and Catarinch, M.: Atlas of the ovulation method, Collegeville, Minn., 1974, The Liturgical Press.

Bruce, J., and Schearer, S.B.: Contraceptives and common sense: conventional methods reconsidered, New York, 1979, The Population Council, Inc.

Byrne, D.: A pregnant pause in the sexual revolution, Human sexuality 80/81, Guilford, Conn., 1980, Dushkin Publishing Group, Inc.

Byrne, D.: Sex without contraception. In Byrne, D., and Fisher, W.A., editors: Adolescents, sex and contraception, Hillsdale, N.J., 1983, Lawrence Erlbaum Associates, Inc.

Cancer and Steroid Hormone Study Group: The reduction in risk of ovarian cancer

associated with oral-contraceptive use, N. Engl. J. Med. 316:650-655, 1987.

Centers for Disease Control: Abortion surveillance, United States, 1984-1985, MMWR 38:11-45, 1988.

Cramer, D., et al.: Tubal infertility and the intrauterine device, N. Engl. J. Med. 312:941-947, 1985.

Daling, J., et al.: Primary tubal infertility in relation to the use of an intrauterine device, N. Engl. J. Med. 312:937-941, 1985.

Djerassi, C.: The politics of contraception, San Francisco, 1981, W.H. Freeman & Co. Publishers.

Fisher, W., et al.: Erotophobia-erotophilia as a dimension of personality, J. Sex. Res. 25:123-151, 1988.

Fliegelman, E.: Contraception, Med. Aspects Hum. Sex. 20:104-117, 1986.

Forrest, J., and Fordyce, R.: U.S. women's contraceptive attitudes and practices: have they changed in the 1980s? Fam. Plann. Perspect. 20:112-118, 1988.

Gerrard, M.: Sex, sex guilt and contraceptive use, J. Pers. Soc. Psychol. 42:153-158, 1982.

Gossypol, a new contraceptive for men, Int. Planned Parenthood Med. Bull. 11:2, 1979.

Grieco, A.: Cutting the risks for STDs, Med. Aspects Hum. Sex. 21:70-84, 1987.

Hatcher, R.A., et al.: Contraceptive technology, ed. 13, New York, 1986, Irvington Publishers, Inc.

Hatcher, R., et al.: Contraceptive technology, International Edition, Atlanta, 1990a, Printed Matter, Inc.

Hatcher, R., et al.: Contraceptive technology, ed. 15, New York, 1990b, Irvington Publishers, Inc.

Hilgers, T.W., Prebil, A.M., and Daly, K.D.: The effectiveness of the ovulation method as a means of achieving and avoiding pregnancy, Paper presented at Education Phase III, the meeting of Continuing Education Conference for Natural Family Planning Practitioners, Omaha, Neb., July 24, 1980.

Hogue, C., Cates, W., and Tietze, C.: Effects of induced abortion on subsequent reproduction, Epidemiol. Rev. 4:66-94, 1982.

Howe, L.: Moments of Maple Avenue, New York, 1984, Macmillan Publishing Co.

Jick, H., et al.: Vaginal spermicides and congenital disorders, JAMA 245:1329-1332, 1981.

Johnson, V., and Masters, W.: Intravaginal contraceptive study: phase I. Anatomy, West. J. Surg. Obstet. Gynecol. 70:202-207, 1962.

Kaufman, D., et al.: Decreased risk of endometrial cancer among oral contraceptives users, N. Engl. J. Med. 303:1045-1050, 1980.

Kenny, M.: Abortion: the whole story, New York, 1986, Quartet Books.

King, T.M., and Zabin, L.S.: Sterilization: efficacy, safety, regret and reversal, The Female Patient 1(suppl.):3-9, 1981.

Kleinman, R.: Barrier methods of contraception, London, 1985, International Planned Parenthood Federation.

Kowal, D.: OCs do not raise breast, endometrium, ovary cancer risks, Contraceptive Technol. Update 3:69-73, 1982.

Louik, C., et al.: Maternal exposure to spermicides in relation to certain birth defects, N. Engl. J. Med. 317:474-477, 1987.

Milan, R., and Kilmann, P.: Interpersonal factors in premarital contraception, J. Sex. Res. 23:289-291, 1987.

Mishell, D.R.: Clinical and legal implications of contraception in the 80s, The Female Patient 1(suppl.):2, 1981.

Natural family planning in today's world, Res. Reprod. 22:1-2, 1990.

North, B., and Vorhauer, B.: Use of the Today contraceptive sponge in the United States, Int. J. Fertil. 30:81-84, 1985.

Progestagen-releasing vaginal rings—an update, Int. Planned Parenthood Med. Bull. 19:1-2, 1985.

Protzman, F.: Germanys facing abortion battle, New York Times, Aug. 26, 1990, p. 6.

Report of the Royal College of General Practitioners: Oral contraception and health, London, 1974, Pitman Medical.

Rosenberg, M., et al.: Effect of contraceptive sponge on chlamydial infection, gonorrhea and candidiasis, JAMA 257:2308-2312, 1987.

Scholl, T., et al.: Effects of vaginal spermicides on pregnancy outcome, Fam. Plann. Perspect. 15:244-250, 1983.

Schostak, A., and McLouth, G.: Men and abortion: lessons, losses and love, New York, 1984, Praeger Publishers.

Shapiro, S., et al.: Birth defects and vaginal spermicides, JAMA 247:2381-2384, 1982.

Sivin, I.: IUDs are contraceptives, not abortifacients: a comment on research and belief, Stud. Fam. Plann. 20:355-359, 1989.

Statement on steroidal oral contraception, Int. Planned Parenthood Med. Bull. 21:1-4, 1987.

Tietze, C.: New estimates on mortality associated with fertility control, Fam. Plann. Perspect. 9:74-76, 1977.

Tonzetich, J., Preti, G., and Huggins, G.R.:

Changes in concentration of volatile sulphur compounds of mouth air during the menstrual cycle, J. Intern. Med. Res. 6:245-254, 1978.

The vaginal contraceptive sponge, Int. Planned Parenthood Med. Bull. 18:1-2, 1984.

Walker, A.M., et al.: Hospitalization rates in vasectomized men, JAMA 245:2315-2317, 1981.

Warburton, D., et al.: Lack of association between spermicide use and trisomy, N. Engl. J. Med. 317:478-481, 1987.

Zimmerman, M.: Passage through abortion: the personal and social reality of women's experiences, New York, 1977, Praeger Publishers.

CHAPTER 9

Arndt, W., Foehl, J., and Good, E.: Specific sexual fantasy themes: a multidimensional study, J. Pers. Soc. Psychol. 48:472-480, 1985.

Beach, F.: Human sexuality in four perspectives, Baltimore, 1978, The Johns Hopkins University Press.

Blumstein, P., and Schwartz, P.: American couples, New York, 1983, William Morrow & Co., Inc.

Comfort, A.: The joy of sex, New York, 1972, Crown Publishers, Inc.

Davenport, W.: Sex in cross cultural perspective. In Beach, F., editor: Human sexuality in four perspectives, Baltimore, 1978, The Johns Hopkins University Press.

Dickson, A.: The mirror within: a new look at sexuality, New York, 1989, Quartet Books.

Ford, C., and Beach, F.: Patterns of sexual behavior, New York, 1951, Harper & Row, Publishers, Inc.

Halpern, J., and Sherman, M.: Afterplay: a key to intimacy, New York, 1981, Simon & Schuster, Inc.

Hearst, N., and Hulley, S.: Preventing the heterosexual spread of AIDS, JAMA 259:2428-2432, 1988.

Hite, S.: The Hite Report: a nationwide study of female sexuality, New York, 1976, Dell Books.

Hunt, M.: Sexual behavior in the 1970s, Chicago, 1974, Playboy Press.

Kinsey, A., Pomeroy, W., and Martin, C.: Sexual behavior in the human male, Philadelphia, 1948, W.B. Saunders Co.

Kinsey, A., et al.: Sexual behavior in the human female, Philadelphia, 1953, W.B. Saunders Co.

Klinger, E.: Daydreaming: using waking fantasies and imagery for self-knowledge and creativity, New York, 1990, Jeremy Tarcher, Inc.

Masters, W., and Johnson, V.: Human sexual response, Boston, 1966, Little, Brown & Co., Inc.

Masters, W., and Johnson, V.: The pleasure bond, New York, 1980, Bantam Books, Inc.

Masters, W.H., Johnson, V.E., and Kolodny, R.C.: Masters and Johnson on sex and human loving, Boston, 1986, Little, Brown & Co., Inc.

Sadock, B., and Sadock, V.: Techniques of coitus. In Sadock, B., Kaplan, H., and Freedman, A., editors: The sexual experience, Baltimore, 1976, Williams & Wilkins.

Steinhart, J.E.: Sexology today, p. 50.

CHAPTER 10

Athanasiou, R., Shaver, P., and Tavris, C.: Sex, Psychology Today 4(2):39-52, 1970.

Atkin, C.: Changing male and female roles. In Schwartz, M., editor: TV & teens: experts look at the issues, Reading, Mass., 1982, Addison-Wesley Publishing Co.

Bardwick, J.M.: The psychology of women: a study of biocultural conflicts, New York, 1971, Harper & Row, Publishers, Inc.

Bell, A.P., and Weinberg, M.S.: Homosexualities: a study of diversity among men and women, New York, 1978, Simon & Schuster, Inc.

Bem, S.L.: Sex role adaptability: one consequence of psychological androgyny, J. Pers. Soc. Psychol. 31:634-643, 1975.

Bem, S.L.: Gender schema theory: a cognitive account of sex typing, Psychol. Rev. 88:354-364, 1981.

Blanchard, R., Clemmensen, L., and Steiner, B.: Heterosexual and homosexual dysphoria, Arch. Sex. Behav. 16:139-152, 1987.

Blanchard, R., Legault, S., and Lindsay, W.R.N.: Vaginoplasty outcome in male-to-female transsexual, J. Sex Marital Ther. 13(4):265-275, 1987.

Block, J.H.: Differential premises arising from differential socialization of the sexes: some conjectures, Child Dev. 54:1335-1354, 1983.

Blumenfeld, W., and Raymond, D.: Looking at gay and lesbian life, New York, 1988, Philosophical Library.

Bretl, D.J., and Cantor, J.: The portrayal of men and women in U.S. television commercials: a recent content analysis and trends over 15 years, Sex Roles 18:595-609, 1988.

Brown, M., and Auerback, A.: Communication patterns in initiation of marital sex, Med. Aspects Hum. Sex. 15:107-117, 1981.

Carroll, J., Volk, K., and Hyde, J.: Differences between males and females in motives for engaging in sexual intercourse, Arch. Sex. Behav. 14:131-139, 1985.

Centers for Disease Control: Number of sex partners and potential risk of sexual exposure to human immunodeficiency virus, MMWR, Sept. 23, 1988, pp. 565-568.

Davie, C.E., et al.: The young child at home, Windsor, Conn., 1984, NFER-Nelson.

DeLamater, J.: Gender differences in sexual scenarios. In Kelley, K., editor: Females, males, and sexuality: theories and research, Albany, 1987, State University of New York Press, pp. 127-139.

de Monteflores, C., and Schultz, S.: Coming out: similarities and differences for lesbians and gay men, J. Soc. Issues 34:59-72, 1978.

Denney, N.W., Field, J.K., and Quadagno, D.: Sex differences in sexual needs and desires, Arch. Sex. Behav. 13:233-245, 1984.

Ehrhardt, A., et al.: Sexual orientation after prenatal exposure to exogenous estrogen, Arch. Sex. Behav. 14:57-75, 1985.

Fagot, B.I.: The influence of sex of child on parental reactions to toddler children, Child Dev. 49:459-465, 1978.

Feder, H.H.: Hormones and sexual behavior, Annu. Rev. Psychol. 35:165-200, 1984.

Fisher, H.E.: The sex contract: the evolution of human behavior, New York, 1982, William Morrow & Co., Inc.

Frisch, H.L.: Sex stereotypes in adult-infant play, Child Dev. 48:1671-1675, 1977.

Giddings, M., and Halverson, C.F.: Young children's use of toys in home environments, Fam. Rel. 30:69-74, 1981.

Green, R.: Adults who want to change sex; adolescents who cross-dress; and children called "sissy" and "tomboy." In Green, R., editor: Human sexuality: a health practitioner's text, Baltimore, 1975, Williams & Wilkins.

Halpern, J., and Sherman, M.A.: Afterplay: a key to intimacy, New York, 1979, Pocket Books.

Hatfield, E., Sprecher, S., and Traupmann, J.: Men's and women's reactions to sexually explicit films: a serendipitous finding, Arch. Sex. Behav. 7:583-592, 1978.

Hatfield, E., et al.: Gender differences in what is desired in the sexual relationship, J. Psychol. Hum. Sex. 1(2):39-52, 1988.

Heiman, J.R.: A psychophysiological exploration of sexual arousal patterns in females and males, Psychophysiology 14:266-274, 1977.

Hite, S.: The Hite Report: a nationwide study of female sexuality, New York, 1976, Macmillan Publishing Co.

Hite, S.: The Hite Report on male sexuality, New York, 1981, Alfred A. Knopf, Inc.

Howells, K.: Sex roles and sexual behavior. In Hargreaves, D.J., and Colley, A.M., editors: The psychology of sex roles, London, 1986, Harper & Row, Publishers, Inc.

Hunt, M.: Sexual behavior in the 1970s, Chicago, 1974, Playboy Press.

Kalisch, P.A., and Kalisch, B.J.: Sex-role stereotyping of nurses and physicians on prime-time television: a dichotomy of occupational portrayals, Sex Roles 10:533-553, 1984.

Kelly, J.A., O'Brien, G.G., and Hosford, R.: Sex roles and social skills: considerations for interpersonal adjustment, Psychol. Women Q. 5:758-766, 1981.

Kimball, M.: Television and sex-role attitudes. In Williams, T.M., editor: The impact of television, London, 1986, Academic Press.

Kimlicka, T., Cross, H., and Tarnai, J.: A comparison of androgynous, feminine, masculine and undifferentiated women on self-esteem, body satisfaction, and sexual satisfaction, Psychol. Women Q. 1:291-294, 1983.

Kinsey, A.C., Pomeroy, W.B., and Martin, C.E.: Sexual behavior in the human male, Philadelphia, 1948, W.B. Saunders Co.

Kinsey, A., et al.: Sexual behavior in the human female, Philadelphia, 1953, W.B. Saunders Co.

Lamb, M.E., Easterbrooks, M.A., and Holden, G.W.: Reinforcement and punishment among preschoolers: characteristics, effects, and correlates, Child Dev. 51:1230-1236, 1980.

Langlois, J.H., and Downs, A.C.: Mothers, fathers, and peers as socialization agents of sex-typed play behaviors in young children, Child Dev. 51:1237-1247, 1980.

Leigh, B.C.: Reasons for having and avoiding sex: gender, sexual orientation, and relationship to sexual behavior, J. Sex. Res. 26(2):199-209, 1989.

Liebert, R.M., and Sprafkin, J.: The early window: effects of television on children and youth, New York, 1988, Pergamon Press.

Mamay, P.D., and Simpson, R.L.: Three female roles in television commercials, Sex Roles 7:1223-1232, 1981.

Mancini, J., and Orthner, D.: Recreational sexuality preferences among middle-class

husbands and wives, J. Sex. Res. 14:96-104, 1978.

Martin, J., et al.: The impact of AIDS on a gay community: changes in sexual behavior, substance use, and mental health, Am. J. Commun. Psychol. 17:269-293, 1989.

Masters, W.H., and Johnson, V.E.: Orgasm, anatomy of the female. In Ellis, A., and Abarbanel, A., editors: Encyclopedia of sexual behavior, vol. 2, New York, 1961, Hawthorn Books.

Masters, W.H., and Johnson, V.E.: Human sexual response, Boston, 1966, Little, Brown & Co., Inc.

McArthur, L.Z.: Television and sex role stereotyping: are children being programmed? Brandeis Q. 2:12-13, 1982.

Mead, M.: Sex and temperament in three primitive societies, New York, 1963, William Morrow & Co., Inc.

Meyer, W., et al.: Physical and hormonal evaluation of transsexual patients: a longitudinal study, Arch. Sex. Behav. 15:121-138, 1986.

Monzon, O.T., and Capellan, J.M.: Female-to-female transmission of HIV, Lancet 2:40-41, 1987.

Morgan, M.: Television and adolescents' sex role stereotypes: a longitudinal study, J. Pers. Soc. Psychol. 43:947-955, 1982.

Phillips, S., King, S., and DuBois, L.: Spontaneous activities of female versus male newborns, Child Dev. 49:590-597, 1978.

Quadagno, D., Briscoe, R., and Quadagno, J.: Effect of perinatal gonadal hormones on selected nonsexual behavior patterns: a critical assessment of the nonhuman and human literature, Psychol. Bull. 84:62-80, 1977.

Radlove, S.: Sexual response and gender roles. In Allgeier, E.R., and McCormick, N.B., editors: Changing boundaries: gender roles and sexual behavior, Palo Alto, Calif., Mayfield Publishing Co.

Reinisch, J.M.: Prenatal exposure to synthetic progestins increases potential for aggression in humans, Science 211:1171-1173, 1981.

Riddle, D.I., and Morin, S.F.: Removing the stigma: data from individuals, APA Monitor 8(11):16, 28, 1977.

Roberto, L.: Issues in diagnosis and treatment of transsexualism, Arch. Sex. Behav. 12:445-473, 1983.

Rubin, J.Z., Provenzano, F.J., and Luria, Z.: The eye of the beholder: parents' views on sex of newborns. In Williams, J.H., editor: Psychology of women: selected readings, New York, 1985, W.W. Norton & Co., Inc.

Rubinsky, H., et al.: Early-phase physiological response patterns to psychosocial stimuli: comparison of male and female patterns, Arch. Sex. Behav. 16:45-56, 1987.

Sadker, M., and Sadker, D.: Sexism in the school room of the 80s, Psychology Today 19:54-57, 1985.

Sedney, M.: Development of androgyny: parental influences, 1987, Psychol. Women Q. 11:311-326, 1987.

Serbin, L.A., et al.: A comparison of teacher response to the pre-academic and problem behavior of boys and girls, Child Dev. 33:796-804, 1973.

Shore, E.: The former transsexual: a case study, Arch. Sex. Behav. 13:277-289, 1984.

Siegel, K., and Glassman, M.: Individual and aggregate level change in sexual behavior among gay men at risk for AIDS, Arch. Sex. Behav. 18:335-348, 1989.

Smith, C., and Lloyd, B.: Maternal behavior and perceived sex of infant: revisited, Child Dev. 49:1263-1265, 1978.

Sprague, J., and Quadagno, D.: Gender and sexual motivation: an exploration of two assumptions, J. Psychol. Hum. Sex. 2:57-76, 1989.

Tavris, C., and Wade, C.: The longest war: sex differences in perspective, New York, 1984, Harcourt Brace Jovanovich, Inc.

Taylor, M.C., and Hall, J.A.: Psychological androgyny: theories, methods and conclusions, Psychol. Bull. 92:347-366, 1982.

U.S. women find Saudi customs perplexing, Wisconsin State Journal, 1990.

Walfish, S., and Myerson, M.: Sex role identity and attitudes toward sexuality, Arch. Sex. Behav. 9:199-204, 1980.

CHAPTER 11

Bancroft, J.: Hormones and human sexual behavior, Br. Med. Bull. 37:153-158, 1981.

Bell, A.P.: Sexual preference: a postscript, SIECUS Rep. 11:1-3, 1982.

Bell, A.P., and Weinberg, M.S.: Homosexualities, New York, 1978, Simon & Schuster, Inc.

Bell, A.P., Weinberg, M.S., and Hammersmith, S.K.: Sexual preference: its development in men and women, Bloomington, 1981, Indiana University Press.

Bieber, I., et al.: Homosexuality: a psychoanalytic study of male homosexuals, New York, 1962, Basic Books, Inc., Publishers.

Blumstein, P.W., and Schwartz, P.: Bisexuality in women, Arch. Sex. Behav. 5:171-181, 1976.

Blumstein, P., and Schwartz, P.: Bisexuality: some social psychological issues, J. Soc. Issues 33:30-45, 1977.

Blumstein, P., and Schwartz, P.: American couples, New York, 1983, William Morrow & Co., Inc.

Bowers v. Hardwick, 106 S. Ct. 2841 (1986).

Buchanan, P.: New York Post, May 24, 1983.

Caldwell, M.A., and Peplau, L.A.: The balance of power in lesbian relationships, Sex Roles 10:587-599, 1984.

Coleman, E.M., Hoon, P.W., and Hoon, E.F.: Arousability and sexual satisfaction in lesbian and heterosexual women, J. Sex. Res. 19:58-73, 1983.

Davis, J.A., and Smith, T.: General social surveys, 1972-1987: cumulative data, Storrs, 1987, University of Connecticut, Roper Center for Public Opinion Research.

Doerr, P., et al.: Plasma testosterone, estradiol, and semen analysis in male homosexuals, Arch. Gen. Psychiatry 29:829-833, 1973.

Dorner, G.: Hormones and brain differentiation, Amsterdam, 1976, Elsevier Scientific Publishing Co.

Ehrhardt, A.A., et al.: Sexual orientation after prenatal exposure to exogenous estrogen, Arch. Sex. Behav. 14:57-72, 1985.

Ellis, L., and Ames, M.A.: Prenatal neurohormonal functioning and sexual orientation: a theory of homosexuality-heterosexuality, Psychol. Bull. 101:233-258, 1987.

Feldman, D.A.: AIDS health promotion and clinically applied anthropology. In Feldman, D.A., and Johnson, T.M., editors: The social dimensions of AIDS: method and theory, New York, 1986, Praeger Publishers.

Friedman, R., and Stern, L.: Juvenile aggressivity and sissiness in homosexual and heterosexual males, J. Am. Acad. Psychoanalysis 8:427-440, 1980.

Gadpaille, W.J.: Homosexuality. In Simons, R.C., and Pardes, H., editors: Understanding human behavior in health and illness, Baltimore, 1981, Williams & Wilkins.

Gallup, G.: Gallup poll, April 12, 1987.

Gay bashing reported prevalent, Wisconsin State Journal, June 8, 1990.

Green, R.: The "sissy boy syndrome" and the development of homosexuality, New Haven, Conn., 1987, Yale University Press.

Greer, W.R.: Violence against homosexuals rising, groups seeking wider protection

say, New York Times, Nov. 23, 1986, p. 36.

Herek, G.M.: Religious orientation and prejudice: a comparison of racial and sexual attitudes, Pers. Soc. Psychol. Bull. 13(1):34-44, 1987.

Herek, G.M.: Heterosexuals' attitudes toward lesbians and gay men: correlates and gender differences, J. Sex. Res. 25(4):451-477, 1988.

Herek, G.M., and Glunt, E.K.: An epidemic of stigma: public reactions to AIDS, Am. Psychol. 43(1):886-891, 1988.

Hite, S.: The Hite Report: a nationwide study on female sexuality, New York, 1976, Macmillan Publishing Company.

Hite, S.: The Hite Report on male sexuality, New York, 1981, Alfred A. Knopf, Inc.

Jones, C.C., et al.: Persistence in high risk sexual activity among homosexual men in an area of low incidence of acquired immunodeficiency syndrome, Sex. Transm. Dis. 14:79-82, 1987.

Kallman, F.J.: Comparative twin study on the genetic aspects of male homosexuality, J. Nerv. Ment. Dis. 115:283-298, 1952.

Kinsey, A.C., et al.: Sexual behavior in the human female, Philadelphia, 1953, W.B. Saunders Co.

Kirk, M., and Madsen, H.: After the ball: how America will conquer its fear and hatred of gays in the '90's, New York, 1989, Doubleday & Co.

Klein, F.: The bisexual option: a concept of one hundred percent intimacy, New York, 1978, Arbor House Publishing Co.

Kurdek, L.A., and Schmitt, J.P.: Relationship quality of partners in heterosexual married, heterosexual cohabiting, and gay and lesbian relationships, J. Pers. Soc. Psychol. 51(4):711-720, 1986.

LeVay, S.: A difference in hypothalamic structure between heterosexual and homosexual men, Science 253:1034-1037, 1991.

Loraine, J.A., et al.: Endocrine function in male and female homosexuals, Br. Med. J. 4:406-408, 1970.

Loraine, J.A., et al.: Patterns of hormone excretion in male and female homosexuals, Nature 234:552-554, 1971.

Lynch, J.M., and Reilly, M.E.: Role relationships: lesbian perspectives, J. Homosexuality 12(2):53-69, 1985-1986.

Martin, D., and Lyon, P.: Lesbian/woman, San Francisco, 1972, Glide Publications.

Martin, J.L., et al.: The impact of AIDS on a gay community: changes in sexual behavior, substance use, and mental health, Am. J. Commun. Psychol. 17(3):269-293, 1989.

Masters, W.H., and Johnson, V.E.: Homosexuality in perspective, Boston, 1979, Little, Brown & Co., Inc.

McKusick, L., Horstman, W., and Coates, T.J.: AIDS and sexual behavior reported by gay men in San Francisco, Am. J. Pub. Health 75:493-496, 1985.

McWhirter, D., and Mattison, A.: The male couple: how relationships develop, Englewood Cliffs, N.J., 1984, Prentice-Hall, Inc.

Mendola, M.: The Mendola Report: a new look at gay couples, New York, 1980, Crown Publishers, Inc.

Meyer-Bahlburg, H.F.L.: Homosexual orientation in women and men: a hormonal basis? In Parsons, J.E., editor: The psychobiology of sex differences and sex roles, New York, 1980, McGraw-Hill, Inc.

Money, J.: Genetic and chromosomal aspects of homosexual etiology. In Marmor, J., editor: Homosexual behavior, New York, 1980, Basic Books, Inc., Publishers.

Money, J., and Schwartz, M.: Dating, romantic and nonromantic friendships, and sexuality in 17 early-treated andrenogenital females, aged 16-25. In Lee, P.A., et al., editors: Congenital andrenal hyperplasia, Baltimore, 1977, University Park Press.

Moral Majority report, July, 1983. In Bayer, R.: AIDS and the gay community: between the specter and the promise of medicine, Soc. Res. 52(3):581-606, 1985.

Moses, A.E., and Hawkins, R.O.: Counseling lesbian women and gay men: a life-issues approach, St. Louis, 1982, Mosby–Year Book, Inc.

Peplau, L.A.: What homosexuals want in relationships, Psychology Today 15:28-38, 1981.

Peplau, L.A., and Amaro, H.: Understanding lesbian relationships. In Paul, W., et al., editors: Homosexuality: social, psychological, and biological issues, Beverly Hills, Calif., 1982, Sage Publications, Inc.

Peplau, L.A., Padesky, C., and Hamilton, M.: Satisfaction in lesbian relationships, J. Homosexuality 8(2):23-35, 1982.

Peplau, L.A., et al.: Loving women: attachment and autonomy in lesbian relationships, J. Soc. Issues 34:7-27, 1978.

Risman, B., and Schwartz, P.: Sociological research on male and female homosexuality, Am. Rev. Sociol. 14:125-147, 1988.

Ruse, M.: Homosexuality: a philosophical inquiry, Oxford, Eng., 1988, Basil Blackwell, Ltd.

Sage, W.: The homosexuality hang-up, Hum. Behav. 1:56-61, 1972.

Schafer, S.: Sociosexual behavior in male and female homosexuals: a study in sex differences, Arch. Sex. Behav. 6:335-364, 1977.

Scheider, W.: Homosexuals: is AIDS changing attitudes? Public Opinion 10:6-7, 1987.

Siegel, K., et al.: Patterns of change in sexual behavior among gay men in New York City, Arch. Sex. Behav. 17(6):481-497, 1988.

Silverstein, C.: Man to man: gay couples in America, New York, 1981, William Morrow & Co., Inc.

Stevenson, M.R.: Promoting tolerance for homosexuality: an evaluation of intervention strategies, J. Sex. Res. 25(4):500-511, 1988.

Storms, M.: A theory of erotic orientation development, Psychol. Rev. 88:340-353, 1981.

Tourney, G.: Hormones and homosexuality. In Marmor, J., editor: Homosexual behavior, New York, 1980, Basic Books, Inc., Publishers.

Troiden, R.R., and Goode, E.: Variables related to the acquisition of a gay identity, J. Homosexuality 5:383-392, 1980.

Weinberg, M.S., and Williams, C.: Male homosexuals: their problems and adaptations, New York, 1974, Oxford University Press, Inc.

Whitam, F.L.: The homosexual role: a reconsideration, J. Sex. Res. 13:1-11, 1977.

Whitley, B.E.: The relationship of sex-role orientation to heterosexuals' attitudes toward homosexuals, Sex Roles 17(1/2):103-113, 1987.

Whitman, W.: Leaves of grass, Garden City, N.Y., 1920, Doubleday, Page, & Co.

Wolf, D.G.: The lesbian community, Los Angeles, 1979, University of California Press.

Wolff, C.: Love between women, New York, 1971, Harper & Row, Publishers, Inc.

Zuger, B.: Homosexuality in families of boys with early effeminate behavior: an epidemiological study, Arch. Sex. Behav. 18:155-166, 1989.

CHAPTER 12

Alan Guttmacher Institute: Teenage pregnancy: the problem that hasn't gone away, New York, 1982, The Institute.

Bell, R.R.: Premarital sex in a changing society, Englewood Cliffs, N.J., 1966, Prentice-Hall, Inc.

Beyene, Y.: From menarche to menopause: reproductive lives of peasant women in two cultures, Albany, 1989, State University of New York Press.

Calderone, M.S.: Fetal erection and its message to us, SIECUS Report XI, 1983, pp. 9-10.

Calderone, M.S., and Ramey, J.: Talking with your child about sex, New York, 1982, St. Martin's Press, Inc., p. 5.

Elster, A.B., and Panzarine, S.: Adolescent fathers. In McAnarney, E.R., editor: Premature adolescent pregnancy and parenthood, New York, 1983, Grune & Stratton, Inc., pp. 231-252.

Finkelhor, D.: Sex play between siblings: sex play, incest and aggression. In Constantine, L.L., and Martinson, F.M., editors: Children and sex, Boston, 1981, Little, Brown & Co., Inc.

Ford, C.S., and Beach, F.A.: Patterns of sexual behavior, New York, 1951, Harper & Row, Publishers, Inc.

Furstenberg, F.F., Brooks-Gunn, J., and Chase-Lansdale, L.: Teenaged pregnancy and childbearing, Am. Psychol. 44(2):313-320, 1989.

Furstenberg, F.F., Brooks-Gunn, J., and Morgan, S.P.: Adolescent mothers in later life, New York, 1988, Cambridge University Press.

Goldman, R.J., and Goldman, J.D.: Show me yours: understanding children's sexuality, Ringwood, Aust., 1988, Penguin Books.

Hafez, E.S.E.: Human reproduction: conception and contraception, Hagerstown, Md., 1980, Harper & Row, Publishers, Inc.

Hass, A.: Teenage sexuality, New York, 1979, Macmillan Publishing Co.

Hayes, C.D., editor: Risking the future, vol. 1, Washington, D.C., 1987, National Academy Press.

Hunt, M.: Sexual behavior in the 1970s, Chicago, 1974, Playboy Press.

Kinsey, A.C., Pomeroy, W.B., and Martin, C.E.: Sexual behavior in the human male, Philadelphia, 1948, W.B. Saunders Co.

Kinsey, A.C., et al.: Sexual behavior in the human female, Philadelphia, 1953, W.B. Saunders Co.

Koenig, M.A., and Zelnik, M.: The risk of premarital first pregnancy among metropolitan-area teenagers: 1976 and 1979, Fam. Plann. Perspect. 14:239-247, 1982.

Langfeldt, T.: Childhood masturbation: individual and social organization. In Constantine, L.L., and Martinson, F.M., editors: Children and sex, Boston, 1981a, Little, Brown & Co., Inc.

Langfeldt, T.: Sexual development in children. In Cook M., and Howells, K., editors: Adult sexual interest in children, London, 1981b, Academic Press.

Leitenberg, H., Greenwald, E., and Tarran, M.J.: The relation between sexual activity among children during preadolescence and/or early adolescence and sexual behavior and sexual adjustment in young adulthood, Arch. Sex. Behav. 18(4):299-313, 1989.

Makinson, C.: The health consequences of teenage fertility, Fam. Plann. Perspect. 17:132-139, 1985.

Marsiglio, W.: Teenage fatherhood: high school accreditation and educational attainment. In Elster, A.B., and Lamb, M.E., editors: Adolescent fatherhood, Hillsdale, N.J., 1986, Lawrence Erlbaum Associates, Inc.

Martinson, F.M.: Childhood sexuality. In Wolman, B.B., and Money, J., editors: Handbook of human sexuality, Englewood Cliffs, N.J., 1980, Prentice-Hall, Inc.

Martinson, F.M.: Eroticism in infancy and childhood. In Constantine, L.L., and Martinson, F.M., editors: Children and sex, Boston, 1981, Little, Brown & Co., Inc.

Meyer-Bahlburg, H.F.L.: Sexuality in early adolescence. In Wolman, B.B., and Money, J., editors: Handbook of human sexuality, Englewood Cliffs, N.J., 1980, Prentice-Hall, Inc.

Moore, K.A., and Wertheimer, R.F.: Teenage childbearing and welfare: preventive and ameliorative strategies, Fam. Plann. Perspect. 16:285-289, 1984.

Morgan, S.P., and Rindfuss, R.R.: Marital disruption: structural and temporal dimensions, Am. J. Sociol. 90:1055-1077, 1985.

Morrison, E.S., et al.: Growing up sexual, New York, 1980, Van Nostrand Reinhold Co., Inc.

Murstein, B.L., et al.: Sexual behavior, drugs, and relationship patterns on a college campus over thirteen years, Adolescence 24(93):125-139, 1989.

National Center for Health Statistics: Advanced report of final natality statistics, 1981, Monthly Vital Statistics Report, 32(9), Hyattsville, Md., 1983, Public Health Service.

Newton, N., and Newton, M.: Psychological aspects of lactation, N.Engl. J. Med. 277:1179-1188, 1967.

O'Connell, M., and Rogers, C.C.: Out-of-wedlock births, premarital pregnancies and their effect on family formation and dissolution, Fam. Plann. Perspect. 16:157-162, 1984.

Redmond, M.A.: Attitudes of adolescent

males toward adolescent pregnancy and fatherhood, Fam. Relations 34:337-342, 1985.

Reiss, I.L.: Premarital sexual standards in America, New York, 1960, Holt, Rinehart & Winston.

Reiss, I.L.: The social context of premarital sexual permissiveness, New York, 1967, Holt, Rinehart & Winston General Book.

Rivara, F.P., Sweeney, P.J., and Henderson, B.F.: Black teenage fathers, Pediatrics 78:151-158, 1986.

Robinson, B.E.: Teenage fathers, Lexington, Mass., 1988a, Lexington Books.

Robinson, B.E.: Teenage pregnancy from the father's perspective, Am. J. Orthopsychiatry 58(1):46-51, 1988b.

Robinson, B.E., and Barret, R.L.: The developing father: emerging roles in contemporary society, New York, 1986, The Guilford Press.

Robinson, I.E., and Jedlicka, D.: Change in sexual attitudes and behavior of college students from 1965-1980: a research note, J. Marriage Fam. 44:237-241, 1982.

Roche, J.P.: Premarital sex: attitudes and behavior by dating stage, Adolescence 21(81):108-121, 1986.

Smith, P.B., and Mumford, D.M., editors: Adolescent pregnancy: new perspectives for the health professional, Boston, 1980, G.K. Hall & Co.

Sonenstein, F.L.: Risking paternity: sex and contraception among adolescent males. In Elster, A.B., and Lamb, M.E., editors: Adolescent fatherhood, Hillsdale, N.J., 1986, Lawrence Erlbaum Associates, Inc., pp. 31-54.

Sorenson, R.C.: Adolescent sexuality in contemporary America: personal values and sexual behavior, ages 13-19, New York, 1973, World Publishing Co.

Spitz, R.A.: Autoeroticism: some empirical findings and hypotheses on three of its manifestations in the first year of life, The psychoanalytic study of the child vol. 3/4, New York, 1949, International Universities Press, Inc.

The story of a teenage pregnancy, Lawrence (Kan.) Journal-World, 1981.

Vaz, R., Smolen, P., and Miller, C.: Adolescent pregnancy: involvement of the male partner, J. Adolesc. Health Care 4:246-250, 1983.

Westney, O.E., Cole, O.J., and Munford, T.L.: Adolescent unwed prospective fathers: readiness for fatherhood and behaviors toward the mother and the expected infant, Adolescence 21:901-911, 1986.

Westoff, C.F., Calot, G., and Foster, A.D.: Teenage fertility in developed nations: 1971-1980, Fam. Plann. Perspect. 15:105, 1983.

Zellman, G.: Public school programs for adolescent pregnancy and parenthood: an assessment, Fam. Plann. Perspect. 14:15-21, 1982.

Zelnik, M., Kantner, J.F., and Ford, K.: Sex and pregnancy in adolescence, Beverly Hills, Calif., 1981, Sage Publications, Inc.

Zelnik, M., and Shah, F.K.: First intercourse among young Americans, Fam. Plann. Perspect. 15:64-70, 1983.

CHAPTER 13

Adams, C.G., and Turner, B.F.: Reported change in sexuality from young adulthood to old age, J. Sex. Res. 21:126-141, 1985.

Archer, D.F.: Biochemical findings and medical management of the menopause. In Voda, A.M., Dinnerstein, M., and O'Donnell, S.R., editors: Changing perspectives on menopause, Austin, 1982, University of Texas Press.

Bancroft, J.: Hormones and human sexual behavior, J. Sex Marital Ther. 10:3-21, 1984.

Bates, G.W.: On the nature of the hot flash, Clin. Obstet. Gynecol. 24:231-241, 1981.

Bergkvist, L., et al.: The risk of breast cancer after estrogen and estrogen-progestin replacement, N. Engl. J. Med. 321(5):293-297, 1989.

Beyene, Y.: From menarche to menopause, Albany, 1989, State University of New York Press.

Blumstein, P., and Schwartz, P.: American couples, New York, 1983, William Morrow & Co., Inc.

Bowles, C.: Measure of attitude toward menopause using the semantic differential model, Nurs. Res. 35(2):81-85, 1986.

Brecher, E.M.: Love, sex, and aging: a Consumers Union report, Boston, 1984, Little, Brown & Co., Inc.

Broderick, C.B.: Adult sexual development. In Wolman, B.B., and Stricker, G., editors: Handbook of developmental psychology, Englewood Cliffs, N.J., 1982, Prentice-Hall, Inc.

Butler, R.N., and Lewis, M.I.: Love and sex after 40, New York, 1986, Harper & Row, Publishers, Inc.

Carney, A., Bancroft, J., and Mathews, A.: Combination of hormonal and psychological treatment for female sexual unresponsiveness: a comparative study, Br. J. Psychiatry 133:339-346, 1978.

Corby, N., and Zarit, J.M.: Old and alone: the unmarried in later life. In Weg, R.B., editor: Sexuality in the later years: roles and behavior, New York, 1983, Academic Press, Inc.

Daugherty, L.R., and Burger, J.M.: The influences of parents, church, and peers on the sexual attitudes and behaviors of college students, Arch. Sex. Behav. 13:351-359, 1984.

Davidson, J.M.: Sexuality and aging. In Andres, R., Bierman, E.L., and Hazzard, W.R., editors: Principles of geriatric medicine, New York, 1984, McGraw-Hill, Inc.

deVries, H.A.: Physiology of exercise and aging. In Woodruff, D.S., and Birren, J.E., editors: Aging: scientific perspectives and social issues, ed. 2, Monterey, Calif., 1983, Brooks/Cole Publishing Co.

Dewhurst, C.J.: Frequency and severity of menopausal symptoms. In Campbell, S., editor: The management of the menopause and post-menopausal years, Baltimore, Md., 1976, University Park Press.

Diczfalusy, E.: Menopause, developing countries, and the 21st century. In Mishell, D.R., editor: Menopause: physiology and pharmacology, St. Louis, 1987, Mosby–Year Book, Inc.

Gambrell, R.D.: The menopause: benefits and risks of estrogen-progestogen replacement therapy, Fertil. Steril. 37:457-474, 1982.

Greenblatt, R.B.: The use of androgens in the menopause and other gynecic disorders, Obstet. Gynecol. Clin. North Am. 14(1):251-268, 1987.

Hafez, E.S.E.: Reproductive senescence. In Hafez, E.S.E., editor: Human reproduction: conception and contraception, New York, 1980, Harper & Row, Publishers, Inc.

Hunt, M.: Sexual behavior in the 1970s, Chicago, 1974, Playboy Press.

Kannel, W.B., and Gordon, T.: Cardiovascular effects of the menopause. In Mishell, D.R., editor: Menopause: physiology and pharmacology, St. Louis, 1987, Mosby–Year Book, Inc.

Kaplan, H.S.: Sex, intimacy, and the aging process, J. Am. Acad. Psychoanalysis 18:185-205, 1990.

Kinsey, A.C., Pomeroy, W.B., and Martin, C.E.: Sexual behavior in the human male, Philadelphia, 1948, W.B. Saunders Co.

Kinsey, A.C., et al.: Sexual behavior in the human female, Philadelphia, 1953, W.B. Saunders Co.

Kletzky, O.A., and Borenstein, R.: Vasomotor instability of the menopause. In Mishell, D.R., editor: Menopause: physiology and pharmacology, St. Louis, 1987, Mosby–Year Book, Inc.

Lindsay, R., and Tohme, J.F.: Alterations in skeletal homeostasis with age and menopause. In Mishell, D.R., editor: Menopause: physiology and pharmacology, St. Louis, 1987, Mosby–Year Book, Inc.

Mahoney, E.R.: Religiosity and sexual behavior among heterosexual college students, J. Sex. Res. 16:97-113, 1980.

Masters, W.H., and Johnson, V.E.: Human sexual response, Boston, 1966, Little, Brown & Co., Inc.

Masters, W.H., and Johnson, V.E.: Human sexual inadequacy, Boston, 1970, Little, Brown & Co., Inc.

Matthews, K.A., et al.: Influences of natural menopause on psychological characteristics and symptoms of middle-aged healthy women, J. Consult. Clin. Psychol. 58(3):345-351, 1990.

McCartney, J.R., et al.: Sexuality and the institutionalized elderly, J. Am. Geriatr. Soc. 35:331-333, 1987.

Meldrum, D.R.: Treatment of hot flushes. In Mishell, D.R., editor: Menopause: physiology and pharmacology, St. Louis, 1987, Mosby–Year Book, Inc.

Money, J., and Erhardt, A.A.: Man and woman, boy and girl: the differentiation and dimorphism of gender identity from conception to maturity, Baltimore, Md., 1972, Johns Hopkins University Press.

Persky, H., et al.: Plasma testosterone level and sexual behavior of couples, Arch. Sex. Behav. 7:157-173, 1978.

Raphael, S.M., and Robinson, M.K.: The older lesbian: love relationships and friendship patterns, Alternative Lifestyles 3:207-229, 1980.

Rienzo, B.A.: The impact of aging on human sexuality, J. Sch. Health 55:66-68, 1985.

Saghir, M.T., and Robins, E.: Male and female homosexuality—a comprehensive investigation, Baltimore, Md., 1973, Williams & Wilkins.

Schiavi, R.C., et al.: Pituitary-gonadal function during sleep in men with hypoactive sexual desire and in normal controls, Psychosom. Med. 50:304-318, 1988.

Schiavi, R.C., et al.: Healthy aging and male sexual functioning, Am. J. Psychiatry 147:766-771, 1990.

Semmens, J.P., and Wagner, G.: Estrogen deprivation and vaginal function in postmenopausal women, JAMA 248:445-448, 1982.

Sherwin, B.B., and Gelfand, M.M.: The role of androgen in the maintenance of sexual functioning in oophorectomized women, Psychosom. Med. 49:397-409, 1987.

Sherwin, B.B., Gelfand, M.M., and Brender, W.: Androgen enhances sexual mo-tivation in females: a prospective, crossover study of sex steroid administration in the surgical menopause, Psychosom. Med. 47:339-351, 1985.

Solnick, R.E., and Corby, N.: Human sexuality and aging. In Woodruff, D.S., and Birren, J.E., editors: Aging: scientific perspectives and social issues, ed. 2, Monterey, Calif., 1983, Brooks/Cole Publishing Co.

Sontag, S.: The double standard of aging, Saturday Review, September, 1972.

Spence, A.P.: Biology of human aging, Englewood Cliffs, N.J., 1989, Prentice-Hall, Inc.

Steege, J.F.: Sexual function in the aging woman, Clin. Obstet. Gynecol. 29(2):462-469, 1986.

Walling, M., Andersen, B.L., and Johnson, S.R.: Hormonal replacement therapy for postmenopausal women: a review of sexual outcomes and related gynecologic effects, Arch. Sex. Behav. 19(2):119-137, 1990.

Watts, N.B., et al.: Intermittent cyclical etidronate treatment of postmenopausal osteoporosis, N. Engl. J. Med. 323(2):73-79, 1990.

Wax, J.: Sex and the single grandparent, New Times, September, 1975.

Weg, R.B.: The physiological perspective. In Weg, R.B., editor: Sexuality in the later years: roles and behavior, New York, 1983, Academic Press, Inc.

Weg, R.: Sexuality in the menopause. In Mishell, D.R., editor: Menopause: physiology and pharmacology, St. Louis, 1987, Mosby–Year Book, Inc.

Weinberg, M.S., and Williams, C.J.: Male homosexuals—their problems and adaptations, New York, 1974, Oxford University Press.

White, S.E., and Reamy, K.: Sexuality and pregnancy: a review, Arch. Sex. Behav. 11:429-444, 1982.

Woodruff-Pak, D.: Psychology and aging, Englewood Cliffs, N.J., 1988, Prentice-Hall, Inc.

CHAPTER 14

Adams, G.R.: The physical attractiveness stereotype. In Miller, A.G., editor: In the eye of the beholder: contemporary issues in stereotyping, New York, 1982, Praeger Publishers.

Backman, C.W., and Secord, P.F.: The effect of perceived liking on interpersonal attraction, Hum. Rel. 12:379-384, 1959.

Berg, J.H., and McQuinn, R.D.: Attraction and exchange in continuing and noncon-tinuing dating relationships, J. Pers. Soc. Psychol. 50:942-952, 1986.

Berscheid, E.: Interpersonal attraction. In Lindzey, G., and Alronson, E., editors: Handbook of social psychology, ed. 3, New York, 1985, Random House, Inc.

Berscheid, E., and Walster, E.: A little bit about love. In Huston, T.L., editor: Foundations of interpersonal attraction, New York, 1974, Academic Press, Inc.

Blumstein, P., and Schwartz, P.: American couples, New York, 1983, William Morrow & Co., Inc.

Brehm, S.S.: Intimate relationships, New York, 1985, Random House, Inc.

Buss, D.M.: Human mate selection, Am. Sci. 73:47-51, 1985.

Buss, D.M.: Sex differences in human mate preferences: evolutionary hypotheses tested in 37 cultures, Behav. Brain Sci. 12:1-49, 1989.

Buss, D.M., and Barnes, M.: Preferences in human mate selection, J. Pers. Soc. Psychol. 50(3):559-570, 1986.

Buunk, B., and Bringle, R.G.: Jealousy in love relationships. In Perlman, D., and Duck, S., editors: Intimate relationships: development, dynamics and deterioration, Newbury Park, Calif., 1987, Sage Publications, Inc.

Buunk, B., and Hupka, R.B.: Cross-cultural differences in the elicitation of sexual jealousy, J. Sex Res. 23:12-22, 1987.

Byrne, D., Ervin, C., and Lamberth, J.: Continuity between the experimental study of attraction and real-life computer dating, J. Pers. Soc. Psychol. 16:157-165, 1970.

Campbell, R.N.: The new science: self-esteem psychology, Lanham, Md., 1984, University Press of America, Inc.

Chelune, G.J., Robison, J.T., and Kommor, M.J.: A cognitive interactional model of intimate relationships. In Delerga, V.J., editor: Communication, intimacy and close relationships, Orlando, Fla., 1984, Academic Press, Inc.

Clark, M.S.: Record keeping in two types of relationships, J. Pers. Soc. Psychol. 52:749-758, 1984.

Clark, M.S., and Reis, H.T.: Interpersonal processes in close relationships, Annu. Rev. Psychol. 39:609-672, 1988.

Clark, M.S., and Waddell, B.: Perceptions of exploitation in communal and exchange relationships, J. Soc. Pers. Relat. 2:403-418, 1985.

Duck, S.: Human relationships, Beverly Hills, Calif., 1986, Sage Publications, Inc.

Dutton, D.G., and Aron, A.P.: Some evidence for heightened sexual attraction under conditions of high anxiety, J. Pers. Soc. Psychol. 30(4):510-517, 1974.

Fisher, J.L., and Narus, L.R.: Sex roles and intimacy in same-sex and othersex relationships, Psychol. Women Q. 5:444-455, 1981.

Frankel, B.: Intimacy and conjoint marital therapy. In Fisher, M., and Stricker, G., editors: Intimacy, New York, 1982, Plenum Publishing Corp.

Fromm, E.: The art of loving, New York, 1956, Harper & Row, Publishers, Inc.

Garrity, J.: Total loving, New York, 1977, Simon & Schuster, Inc.

Gonzales, M.H., et al.: Interactional approach to interpersonal attraction, J. Pers. Soc. Psychol. 44:1192-1197, 1983.

Hacker, H.M.: Blabbermouths and clams: sex differences in self-disclosure in same-sex and cross-sex friendship dyads, Psychol. Women Q. 5:385-401, 1981.

Hagen, R., and Kahn, A.: Discrimination against competent women, Paper presented at the Mid-western Psychological Association Meeting, Chicago, 1975.

Hatfield, E.: The dangers of intimacy. In Derlega, V.J., editor: Communication, intimacy and close relationships, Orlando, Fla., 1984, Academic Press, Inc.

Hatfield, E., and Traupmann, J.: Intimate relationships: a perspective from equity theory. In Duck, S., and Gilmour, R., editors: Personal relationships. 1. Studying personal relationships, Orlando, Fla., 1981, Academic Press, Inc.

Hatfield, E., et al.: Equity and intimate relations: recent research. In Ickes, W., editor: Compatible and incompatible relationships, New York, 1985, Springer-Verlag New York, Inc.

Hays, R.B.: A longitudinal study of friendship development, J. Pers. Soc. Psychol. 48:909-924, 1985.

Hill, C.T., Rubin, Z., and Peplau, L.A.: Breakups before marriage: the end of 103 affairs, J. Soc. Issues 32:147-168, 1976.

Hobart, C.W.: The incidence of romanticism during courtship, Soc. Forces 36:364, 1958.

Jones, E.E.: Ingratiation: a social psychological analysis, New York, 1964, Irvington Publishers, Inc.

Jourard, S.M.: The transparent self, New York, 1971, D. Van Nostrand Co., Inc.

Kanin, E.J., Davidson, K.D., and Scheck, S.R.: A research note on male-female differentials in the experience of heterosexual love, J. Sex. Res. 6:64-72, 1970.

Kelley, H.H., and Thibaut, J.W.: Interpersonal relations: a theory of interdependence, New York, 1978, Wiley-Interscience.

Larzelere, R.E., and Huston, T.L.: The dyadic Trust Scale: toward understanding interpersonal trust in close relationships, J. Marriage Fam. 42:595-604, 1980.

Lasswell, M., and Lobsenz, N.M.: Styles of loving, New York, 1980, Ballantine/Del Rey/Fawcett Books.

Levinger, G., Rands, M., and Talaber, R.: The assessment of involvement and rewardingness in close and causal pair relationships: National Science Foundation Technical Report DK, Amherst, 1977, University of Massachusetts Press.

Liebowitz, M.R.: The chemistry of love, Boston, 1983, Little, Brown & Co., Inc.

Masters, W.H., Johnson, V.E., and Kolodny, R.C.: Masters and Johnson on sex and human loving, Boston, 1986, Little, Brown & Co., Inc.

McGill, M.E.: The McGill report on male intimacy, New York, 1985, Holt, Rinehart & Winston General Book.

Meyer, J.P., and Pepper, S.: Need compatibility and marital adjustment in young married couples, J. Pers. Soc. Psychol. 35:331-342, 1977.

Michaels, J.W., Edwards, J.N., and Acock, A.C.: Satisfaction in intimate relationships as a function of inequality, inequity, and outcomes, Soc. Psychol. Q. 47:347-357, 1984.

Murstein, B.I.: Paths to marriage, Beverly Hills, Calif., 1986, Sage Pubications, Inc.

Perlman, D., and Fehr, B.: The development of intimate relationships. In Perlman, D., and Duck, S., editors: Intimate relationships: development, dynamics and deterioration, Beverly Hills, Calif., 1987, Sage Publications, Inc., pp. 13-42.

Proxmire, W.: The fleecing of America, Boston, 1980, Houghton Mifflin Co.

Przybyla, D.P.J., and Byrne, D.: Sexual relationships. In Duck, S., and Gilmour, R., editors: Personal relationships. 1. Studying personal relationships, Orlando, Fla., 1981, Academic Press, Inc.

Reis, H.T., Senchak, M., and Solomon, B.: Sex differences in the intimacy of social interaction, J. Pers. Soc. Psychol. 48:1204-1217, 1985.

Rubin, Z.: Measurement of romantic love, J. Pers. Soc. Psychol. 16:265-273, 1970.

Rubin, Z., et al.: Self-disclosure in dating couples: sex roles and the ethic of openness, J. Marriage Fam. 42:305-318, 1980.

Rusbult, C.E.: Satisfaction and commitment in relationships, Rep. Res. Soc. Psychol. 11:96-105, 1980.

Sabatelli, R.M., and Cecil-Pigo, E.F.: Relational interdependence and commitment in marriage, J. Marriage Fam. 47:513-527, 1985.

Salovey, P., and Rodin, J.: The heart of jealousy, Psychology Today 19:22-25, 28-29, 1985.

Schachter, S.: The interaction of cognitive and physiological determinants of emotional state. In Berkowitz, L., editor: Advances in experimental social psychology, vol. I, New York, 1964, Academic Press, Inc.

Spence, J.T., and Helmreich, R.: Who likes competent women? Competence, sex-role congruence of interests, and subjects' attitudes toward women as determinants of interpersonal attraction, J. Appl. Soc. Psychol. 3:197-213, 1972.

Sprecher, S.: The relation between inequity and emotions in close relationships, Soc. Psychol. Q. 49:309-321, 1986.

Sternberg, R.J.: Triangulating love. In Sternberg, R.J., and Barnes, M.L., editors: The psychology of love, New Haven, Conn., 1988, Yale University Press.

Sternberg, R.J., and Grajek, S.: The nature of love, J. Pers. Soc. Psychol. 47:312-313, 1984.

Townsend, J.M., and Levy, G.D.: Effects of potential partners' physical attractiveness and socioeconomic status on sexuality and partner selection, Arch. Sex. Behav. 19(2):149-164, 1990.

Viorst, J.: It's hard to be hip over thirty and other tragedies of married life, Cleveland, 1968, The New American Library, Inc.

Viorst, J.: What is this thing called love? Reprint from Redbook, February, 1975, p. 12.

White, G.L.: A model of romantic jealousy, Motivation Emotion 5:295-310, 1981.

White, G.L., Fishbein, S., and Rutsein, J.: Passionate love and the misattribution of arousal, J. Pers. Soc. Psychol. 41(1):56-62, 1981.

Whyte, M.K.: Dating, mating, and marriage, New York, 1990, Aldine de Gruyter, Inc.

Zajonc, R.B.: Attitudinal effects of mere exposure, J. Pers. Soc. Psychol. Monograph Suppl. 9(2):2-27, 1968.

CHAPTER 15

Angier, N.: Marriage is a life saver for men over 45, New York Times, Oct. 16, 1990, p. 88N.

Arafat, I., and Yorburg, B.: On living together without marriage, J. Sex. Res. 9:21-29, 1973.

Atwater, L.: The extramarital connection, New York, 1982, Irvington Publishers, Inc.

Banmen, J., and Vogel, N.A.: The relationship between marital quality and interpersonal sexual communication, Fam. Ther. 12:45-58, 1985.

Bell, A.P., and Weinberg, M.S.: Homosexualities: a study of diversity among men and women, New York, 1978, Simon & Schuster, Inc.

Bennett, N.G., Blanc, A.K., and Bloom, D.E.: Commitment and the modern union: assessing the link between premarital cohabitation and subsequent marital stability, Am. Sociol. Rev. 53:127-138, 1988.

Benson-von der Ohe, E.: First and second marriages, New York, 1987, Praeger Publishers.

Berman, E.M., and Goldberg, M.: Therapy with unmarried couples. In Jacobson, N., and Gurman, A., editors: Clinical handbook of marital therapy, New York, 1986, The Guilford Press.

Bernard, J.: The future of marriage, New York, 1972, Bantam Books, Inc.

Blumstein, P., and Schwartz, P.: American couples, New York, 1983, William Morrow & Co., Inc.

Booth, A., and Johnson, D.: Premarital cohabitation and marital success, J. Fam. Issues 9:255-272, 1988.

Broderick, C.B.: Adult sexual development. In Wolman, B.B., and Stricker, G., editors: Handbook of developmental psychology, Englewood Cliffs, N.J., 1982, Prentice-Hall, Inc.

Brozan, N.: Woman's hospital visit marks gay rights fight, New York Times, Feb. 8, 1989, p. 25.

Campbell, A.A.: The American way of mating: marriage, si; children, maybe, Psychology Today 8:37-43, 1975.

Cargan, L., and Melko, M.: Singles: myths and realities, Beverly Hills, Calif., 1982, Sage Publications, Inc.

Carter, H., and Glick, P.C.: Marriage and divorce, Cambridge, Mass., 1970, Harvard University Press.

Clayton, R.R., and Voss, H.L.: Shacking up: cohabitation in the 1970's, J. Marriage Fam. 39:273-283, 1977.

Clunis, D.M., and Green, G.D.: Lesbian couples, Seattle, 1988, Seal Press.

DeMaris, A.: Predicting premarital cohabitation: employing individuals versus couples as the units of analysis, Alternative Lifestyles 6:270-283, 1984.

DeMaris, A., and Leslie, G.: Cohabitation with the future spouse: its influence on marital satisfaction and communication, J. Marriage Fam. 46:77-84, 1984.

Divorce data stir doubt on trial marriage, New York Times, June 9, 1989.

Doherty, W.J., and Jacobson, N.S.: Marriage and the family. In Wolman, B.B., and Stricker, G., editors: Handbook of developmental psychology, Englewood Cliffs, N.J., 1982, Prentice-Hall, Inc.

Ewing, L., Davis, J.C., and Zirkin, B.R.: Regulation of testicular function: a spatial and temporal view. In Greep, R.D., editor: Reproductive physiology III, Baltimore, Md., 1980, University Park Press.

Furstenberg, F.F.: Conjugal succession: reentering marriage after divorce. In Baltes, P.B., and Brim, O.G., Jr., editors: Life-span development and behavior, vol. 4, New York, 1982, Academic Press, Inc.

Gebhard, P.H.: Factors in marital orgasm, J. Soc. Issues 22(4):88-95, 1966.

Gebhard, P.H.: Postmarital coitus among widows and divorcees. In Bohannan, P., editor: Divorce and after, Garden City, N.Y., 1968, Doubleday Publishing Co.

Gutis, P.: Small steps toward acceptance renew debate on gay marriage, New York Times, Nov. 5, 1989, Sect. IV, p. 24.

Hanna, S.L., and Knaub, P.K.: Cohabitation before remarriage: its relationship to family strengths, Alternative Lifestyles 4:507-521, 1981.

Harry, J.: Gay couples, New York, 1984, Praeger Publishers.

Harry, J.: Some problems of gay/lesbian families. In Chilman, C.S., Nunnally, E.W., and Cox, F.M., editors: Variant family forms, Newbury Park, Calif., 1988, Sage Publications, Inc.

Hunt, M.: Sexual behavior in the seventies, Chicago, 1974, Playboy Press.

Jackson, P.G.: On living together unmarried: awareness contexts and social interaction, J. Soc. Issues 4:35-39, 1983.

Jorgenson, S.R., and Gaudy, J.: Self-disclosure and satisfaction in marriage: the relationship examined, Fam. Coordinator 29:281-287, 1980.

Kelly, J.B.: Divorce: the adult perspective. In Wolman, B.B., and Stricker, G., editors: Handbook of developmental psychology, Englewood Cliffs, N.J., 1982, Prentice-Hall, Inc.

Kiernan, K.E.: Who remains celibate? J. Biosoc. Sci. 20:253-263, 1988.

Kinsey, A.C., Pomeroy W.B., and Martin, C.E.: Sexual behavior in the human male, Philadelphia, 1948, W.B. Saunders Co.

Kinsey, A., et al.: Sexual behavior in the human female, Philadelphia, 1953, W.B. Saunders Co.

Knox, D.: Trends in marriage and the family—the 1980s, Fam. Rel. 39:145-150, 1980.

Kotkin, M.: To marry or to live together? Lifestyles: A Journal of Changing Patterns 7:156-170, 1985.

Kurdek, L.: Relationship quality in gay and lesbian cohabiting couples: a 1-year follow-up study, J. Soc. Pers. Rel. 6:39-59, 1989.

Lamanna, M., and Riedmann, A.: Marriages and families, Belmont, Calif., 1981, Wadsworth Publishing Co.

Levitan, S.A., Belous, R.S., and Gallo, F.: What's happening to the American family? Baltimore, 1988, The Johns Hopkins University Press.

Macklin, E.D.: Heterosexual cohabitation among unmarried students, Fam. Coordinator 21:463-472, 1972.

Macklin, E.D.: Cohabitation in college: going very steady, Psychology Today 7:53-59, 1974.

Macklin, E.D.: Nonmarital sexual cohabitation: an overview. In Macklin, E.D., and Rubin, R.H., editors: Contemporary families and alternative lifestyles, Beverly Hills, Calif., 1983, Sage Publications, Inc.

Macklin, E.D.: Nonmarital heterosexual cohabitation: an overview. In Macklin, E.M., and Rubin, R.H., editors: Contemporary families and alternative lifestyles: handbook on research and theory, ed. 2, Beverly Hills, Calif., 1985, Sage Publications, Inc.

Macklin, E.D.: Heterosexual couples who cohabit nonmaritally: some common problems and issues. In Chilman, C.S., Nunnally, E.W., and Cox, F.M., editors: Variant family forms, Newbury Park, Calif., 1988, Sage Publications, Inc.

Marecek, J., Finn, S.E., and Cardell, M.: Gender roles in the relationships of lesbians and gay men, J. Homosexuality 8:45-49, 1982.

Masters, W.H., and Johnson, V.E.: Human sexual response, Boston, Mass., 1966, Little, Brown & Co., Inc.

Masters, W.H., and Johnson, V.E.: The pleasure bond, Boston, Mass., 1970, Little, Brown & Co., Inc.

Murstein, B.I.: Paths to marriage, Beverly Hills, Calif., 1986, Sage Publications, Inc.

Newcomb, M.D.: Heterosexual cohabitation relationships. In Duck, S., and Gilmour, R., editors: Personal relationships. 1. Studying personal relationships, New

York, 1981, Academic Press, Inc., pp. 131-164.

Newcomb, M.D.: Sexual behavior of cohabitors: a comparison of three independent samples, J. Sex. Res. 22:492-513, 1986.

Newcomb, M.D., and Bentler, P.M.: Assessment of personality and demographic aspects of cohabitation and marital success, J. Pers. Assess. 44:11-24, 1980.

Noller, P.: Nonverbal communication in marriage. In Perlman, D., and Duck, S., editors: Intimate relationships: development, dynamics and deterioration, Beverly Hills, Calif., 1987, Sage Publications, Inc., pp. 149-175.

Orthner, D.K.: Intimate relationships: an introduction to marriage and the family, Reading, Mass., 1981, Addison-Wesley Publishing Co., Inc.

Peplau, L.A., Padesky, C., and Hamilton, M.: Satisfaction in lesbian relationships, J. Homosexuality 8:23-35, 1982.

Przybyla, D.P.J., and Bryne, D.: Sexual relationships. In Duck, S., and Gilmour, R., editors: Personal relationships. 1. Studying personal relationships, New York, 1981, Academic Press, Inc.

Riche, M.: Postmarital society, Am. Demogr. 60:23-26, 1988.

Rubenstein, C.: The modern art of courtly love, Psychology Today 17:40-41, 44-49, 1983.

Saxton, L.: The individual marriage, and the family, Belmont, Calif., 1977, Wadsworth Publishing Co.

Schenk, J., Pfrang, H., and Rausche, A.: Personality traits versus the quality of the marital relationship as the determinant of marital sexuality, Arch. Sex. Behav. 12:31-42, 1983.

Stein, P.J.: Understanding single adulthood. In Stein, P.J., editor: Single life: unmarried adults in social context, New York, 1981, St. Martin's Press.

Tanfer, K.: Patterns of premarital cohabitation among never-married women in the United States, J. Marriage Fam. 49:483-497, 1987.

Thompson, A.P.: Extramarital sex: a review of the research literature, J. Sex. Res. 19:1-22, 1983.

U.S. Bureau of the Census: Marital status, Tables 4, 5, and 6, Washington, D.C., 1960, U.S. Government Printing Office.

U.S. Bureau of the Census: Statistical abstract of the United States, Washington, D.C., 1982, U.S. Government Printing Office.

U.S. Bureau of the Census: Statistical abstract of the United States, 1985, Washington, D.C., 1985, U.S. Government Printing Office.

U.S. Bureau of the Census: Households, families, marital status and living arrangements: March 1986, Current Population Reports, Ser. P-20, No. 412, Washington, D.C., 1986, U.S. Government Printing Office.

U.S. Bureau of the Census: Marital status and living arrangements: March, 1989, Current Population Reports, Ser. P-20, No. 445, Washington, D.C., 1989, U.S. Government Printing Office.

Viorst, J.: It's hard to be hip over thirty and other tragedies of married life, Cleveland, 1968, The New American Library, Inc.

Walster, E., Traupman, J., and Walster, G.W.: Equity and extramarital sexuality, Arch. Sex. Behav. 7:127-142, 1978.

Watson, R.E.L.: Premarital cohabitation vs. traditional courtship: their effects on subsequent marital adjustment, Fam. Rel. 32:139-147, 1983.

Watson, R.E.L., and DeMeo, P.: Premarital cohabitation vs. traditional courtship and subsequent marital adjustment: a replication and follow-up, Fam. Rel. 36:193-197, 1987.

Weed, J.A.: National estimates of marriage dissolution and survivorship: United States, Vital and health statistics, Ser. 3, Analytical Studies; No. 19, U.S. Public Health Service Pub. No. 81-1403, Hyattsville, MD, 1980, National Center for Health Statistics; Office of Health Research, Statistics and Technology; Public Health Service; U.S. Department of Health and Human Services.

White, L.K., and Booth, A.: The quality and stability of remarriages: the role of stepchildren, Am. Sociol. Rev. 50:689-698, 1985.

Whyte, M.K.: Dating, mating and marriage, New York, 1990, Walter De Gruyter, Inc.

Wood, W., Rhodes, N., and Whelan, M.: Sex difference in positive well-being: a consideration of emotional style and marital status, Psychol. Bull. 106:249-264, 1989.

Zola, M.: All the good ones are married, New York, 1982, Berkley Publishing Group.

CHAPTER 16

Allen, D.F., and Allen, V.S.: Ethical issues in mental retardation, Nashville, Tenn., 1979, Abingdon Press.

Baugh, R.J.: Sexuality education for the visually and hearing impaired child in the regular classroom, J. Sch. Health 54:407-409, 1984.

Berkow, R.: The Merck manual, Rahway, N.J., 1987, Merck & Co., Inc.

Bors, E., and Coman, A.E.: Neurological disturbances of sexual function with special reference to 529 patients with spinal cord injury, Urol. Surv. 10:191-222, 1960.

Cole, T.M., and Cole, S.S.: The handicapped and sexual health. In Comfort, A., editor: Sexual consequences of disability, Philadelphia, 1978, G.F. Stickley Co.

Derogatis, L.R., and King, K.M.: The coital coronary: a reassessment of the concept, Arch. Sex. Behav. 10:325-335, 1981.

Ellenberg, M.: Sexual aspects of the female diabetic, Mt. Sinai J. Med. 44:495-499, 1977.

Fitting, M.D., et al.: Self concept and sexuality of spinal cord injured women, Arch. Sex. Behav. 7:143-156, 1978.

FitzGerald, D., and FitzGerald, M.: The potential effects of deafness upon sexuality, Sex. Disabil. 3:177-181, 1980.

Garden, F.: Sex after stroke, Med. Aspects Hum. Sex. 24:27-30, 1990.

Glass, D.D.: Sexuality and the spinal cord injured patient. In Oaks, W.W., Melchiode, G.A., and Ficher, I., editors: Sex and the life cycle, New York, 1977, Grune & Stratton, Inc.

Hall, J.E.: Sexuality and the mentally retarded person. In Green, R.E., editor: Human sexuality: a health practitioner's text, Baltimore, 1979, Williams & Wilkins.

Haring, M., and Meyerson, L.: Attitudes of college students toward sexual behavior of disabled persons, Arch. Phys. Med. Rehabil. 60:257-260, 1979.

Hellerstein, H.K., and Friedman, E.H.: Sexual activity and the post-coronary patient, Arch. Intern. Med. 125:987-999, 1970.

Higgins, G.E.: Sexual response in spinal cord injured adults: a review of the literature, Arch. Sex. Behav. 8:173-196, 1979.

Jensen, S.B.: Diabetic sexual dysfunction: a comparative study of 160 insulin treated diabetic men and women and an age-matched control group, Arch. Sex. Behav. 10:493-504, 1981.

Johnston, B.L., and Fletcher, G.F.: Dynamic electrocardiographic recording during sexual activity in recent post-myocardial infarction and revascularization patients, Am. Heart J. 98:736-741, 1979.

Joy of sex needn't stop with heart attack, American Health, July/Aug. 1985, p. 30.

Kentsmith, D.K., and Eaton, M.T.: Treating sexual problems in medical practice, New York, 1979, Arco Publishing Inc.

Kolodny, R.C., Masters, W.H., and Johnson, V.E.: Textbook of sexual medicine, Boston, 1979, Little, Brown & Co., Inc.

Masters, W.H., and Johnson, V.E.: Human sexual response, Boston, 1966, Little, Brown & Co., Inc.

Papadopoulos, C.: A survey of sexual activity after myocardial infarction, Cardiovasc. Med. 3:821-827, 1978.

Papadopoulos, C.: Sexuality of women after myocardial infarction, Med. Aspects Hum. Sex. 19:221-223, 1985.

Papadopoulos, C., et al.: Sexual concerns and needs of the postcoronary patient's wife, Arch. Intern. Med. 140:38-47, 1980.

Papadopoulos, C., et al.: Myocardial infarction and sexual activity of the female patient, Arch. Intern. Med. 143:1528-1535, 1983.

Pietropinto, A., and Arora, A.: Sexual functioning in diabetics, Med. Aspects Hum. Sex. 23:72-76, 1989.

Schiavi, R.C.: Sexuality and medical illness: specific reference to diabetes mellitus. In Green, R.E., editor: Human sexuality: a health practitioner's text, Baltimore, 1979, Williams & Wilkins.

Van Buren, A.: Dear Abby: whole truth will mend parents' broken hearts, The Kansas City Star, Apr. 30, 1981.

Wagner, N.N., and Sivarajan, E.S.: Sexual activity and the cardiac patient. In Green, R.E., editor: Human sexuality: a health practitioner's text, Baltimore, 1979, Williams & Wilkins.

Walbroehl, G.: Effects of medical problems on sexuality in the elderly, Med. Aspects Hum. Sex. 22:56-66, 1988.

Wise, T.: Sexual dysfunction in the medically ill, Psychosomatics 24:787-805, 1983.

Young, B.K., Katz, M., and Klein, S.: Pregnancy after spinal cord injury: altered maternal and fetal responses to labor, Obstet. Gynecol. 62:59-63, 1983.

CHAPTER 17

Albert, H., et al.: Sexual therapy for patients without partners, Am. J. Psychother. 34:228-239, 1980.

American Cancer Society: Facts on testicular cancer, 1988, The Society.

Berkow, R.: The Merck manual, Rahway, N.J., 1987, Merck & Co., Inc.

Catania, J., et al.: Help-seeking behaviors of people with sexual problems, Arch. Sex. Behav. 19:235-250, 1990.

Fisher, B., et al.: Five-year results of a randomized clinical trial comparing total mastectomy and segmental mastectomy with or without radiation in the treatment of breast cancer, N. Engl. J. Med. 312:665-673, 1985a.

Fisher, B., et al.: Ten-year results of a randomized clinical trial comparing radical mastectomy and total mastectomy with or without radiation, N. Engl. J. Med. 312:674-681, 1985b.

Grosskopf, D.: Sex and the married woman, New York, 1983, Wallaby Books.

Hatcher, R., et al.: Contraceptive technology, ed. 15, New York, 1990, Irvington Publishers, Inc.

Jacobs, L.I.: Chief complaint: sexual inadequacy, Med. Aspects Hum. Sex. 20:44-50, 1986.

Kaplan, H.S.: The new sex therapy, New York, 1974, Brunner/Mazel Inc.

Kaplan, H.S.: Disorders of sexual desire, New York, 1979, Simon & Schuster.

Kravis, D., and Molitch, M.: Endocrine causes of impotence, Med. Aspects Hum. Sex. 24:62-67, 1990.

Lizza, E., and Cricco-Lizza, R.: Impotence—finding the cause, Med. Aspects Hum. Sex. 24:30-40, 1990.

LoPiccolo, J., and Lobitz, W.C.: The role of masturbation in the treatment of orgasmic dysfunction, Arch. Sex. Behav. 2:163-171, 1972.

Mahoney, L., and Csima, A.: Clinical screening for breast cancer, N. Engl. J. Med. 306:546, 1982.

Malloy, T., and Wein, A.: Erectile dysfunction: effects of pharmacotherapy, Med. Aspects Hum. Sex. 22:42-48, 1988.

Masters, W.H., and Johnson, V.E.: Human sexual response, Boston, 1966, Little, Brown & Co., Inc.

Masters, W.H., and Johnson, V.E.: Human sexual inadequacy, Boston, 1970, Little, Brown & Co., Inc.

Masters, W.H., and Johnson, V.E.: Homosexuality in perspective, Boston, 1979, Little, Brown & Co., Inc.

Milan, R., Kilmann, P., and Borland J.: Treatment outcome of secondary orgasmic dysfunction: a two to six year follow-up, Arch. Sex. Behav. 17:463-480, 1988.

Moore, C., and Kotrla, K.: When female behavior contributes to premature ejaculation, Med. Aspects Hum. Sex. 23:42-48, 1989.

Physician's desk reference, Oradell, N.J., 1990, Medical Economics Co., Inc.

Price, S.C., et al.: Group treatment of erectile dysfunction for men without partners: a controlled evaluation, Arch. Sex. Behav. 10:253-268, 1981.

Rosen, R., Kostis, J., and Jekelis, A.: Beta-blocker effects on sexual function in normal males, Arch. Sex. Behav. 17:241-255, 1988.

Semans, J.H.: Premature ejaculation: a new approach, South. Med. J. 49:353-357, 1956.

Smith, D., Wesson, D., and Apter-Marsh, M.: Cocaine and alcohol-induced sexual dysfunctions in patients with addictive disease, J. Psychoactive Drugs 16:359-361, 1984.

Smith, D., et al.: A clinical guide to the diagnosis and treatment of heroin-related sexual dysfunction, J. Psychoactive Drugs 14:91-99, 1982.

Somers, W.: Preventing postprostatectomy sexual dysfunction, Med. Aspects Hum. Sex. 23:16-20, 1989.

Spector, I., and Carey, M.: Incidence and prevalence of the sexual dysfunctions: a critical review of the empirical literature, Arch. Sex. Behav. 19:389-408, 1990.

Strassberg, D., et al.: The role of anxiety in premature ejaculation: a psychophysiological model, Arch. Sex. Behav. 19:251-257, 1990.

Stuntz, R.C.: Physical obstructions to coitus in women, Med. Aspects Hum. Sex. 20:117-134, 1986.

Tullman, G.M., et al.: The pre- and post-therapy measurement of communication skills of couples undergoing sex therapy at the Masters and Johnson Institute, Arch. Sex. Behav. 10:95-110, 1981.

Veronesi, V., Saccozzi, R., and Vecchio, D.: Comparing radical mastectomy with quadrantectomy, axillary dissection and radiotherapy in patients with small cancers of the breast, N. Engl. J. Med. 305:6-11, 1981.

Vikram, B., and Vikram, R.: Prevention of impotence in patients with prostate cancer, Med. Aspects Hum. Sex. 22:29-33, 1988.

Wilson, B., and Niaura, R.: Alcohol and the disinhibition of sexual responsiveness, J. Studies Alcohol 45:219-224, 1984.

Zilbergeld, B., and Evans, M.: The inadequacy of Masters and Johnson, Psychology Today 14:28-43, 1980.

CHAPTER 18

Aral, S.O., Cates, W., and Jenkins, W.: Genital herpes: does knowledge lead to action? Am. J. Pub. Health 75:69-71, 1985.

Babin, V., and Ojanlatva, A.: The impact of *Chlamydia* infections on teen mothers and their children, J. Sch. Health 56:17-19, 1986.

Beeson, P.B., and McDermott, W.: Textbook of medicine, vols. 1 and 2, Philadelphia, 1975, W.B. Saunders Co.

Brock, C., et al.: Frequency of asymptomatic shedding of herpes simplex virus in women with genital herpes, JAMA 263:418-422, 1990.

Brown, Z.: Herpes in pregnancy, STD Bull. 8(4):3-15, 1988.

Buck, H.: Genital human papillomavirus (HPV) disease, Rockville, Md., 1989, American College Health Association, Task Force on HPV Disease.

Centers for Disease Control: Publications from public information office, Atlanta, 1987.

Centers for Disease Control: Sexually transmitted diseases: treatment guidelines, MMWR 38:1-36, 1989.

Corey, L., and Holmes, K.: Genital herpes simplex virus infections: current concepts in diagnosis, therapy, and prevention, Ann. Intern. Med. 98:973-983, 1983.

Ferris, D.: Diagnosing *Chlamydia* in minutes in your office, Med. Aspects Hum. Sex. 24:41-43, 1990.

Glover, E.D.: Herpes: removing fact from fiction, Health Ed. Aug./Sept. 1984, pp. 6-10.

Hatcher, R.A., et al.: Contraceptive technology, New York, 1990, Irvington Publishers, Inc.

Herpes relief, Time, p. 79, Feb. 11, 1985.

Judson, F.: Condoms and spermicides for the prevention of sexually transmitted diseases, STD Bull. 9(1):3-11, 1989.

Kingsley, H., et al.: Sexual transmission efficiency of hepatitis B virus and human immunodeficiency virus among homosexual men, JAMA 264:23-36, 1990.

Kolodny, R., Masters, W.H., and Johnson, V.E.: Textbook of sexual medicine, Boston, 1979, Little, Brown & Co., Inc.

McGregor, J.: Trichomoniasis: a common challenge in STD treatment, STD Bull. 8(6):3-11, 1989.

Mundy, P., Thomas, B., and Taylor-Robinson, D.: The microtrak test for rapid detection of *Chlamydia* in diagnosing and managing women with abdominal pain, Genitourinary Med. 62:15-19, 1986.

Pelvic inflammatory disease, Int. Planned Parenthood Med. Bull. 19:1-3, 1985.

Rooney, J., et al.: Acquisition of genital herpes from an asymptomatic sexual partner, N. Engl. J. Med. 314:1561-1564, 1986.

Schofield, C.B.: Sexually transmitted diseases, London, 1975, Churchill Livingstone.

Washington, A.: The hidden threat: *Chlamydia trachomatis* infections, STD Bull. 8(3):3-15, 1988.

Watts, H.: Sexually transmitted diseases in pregnancy, STD Bull. 9(6):3-10, 1990.

Witters, W.L., and Jones-Witters, P.: Human sexuality: a biological perspective, New York, 1980, Van Nostrand Reinhold Co., Inc.

Wolner-Hanssen, P.: Acute pelvic inflammatory disease, STD Bull. 10(1):3-9, 1990.

Yarber, W.L.: Preventing venereal disease. In Barbour, J.R., editor: Human sexuality 80/81 annual editions, Guilford, Conn., 1980, The Dushkin Publishing Group, Inc.

CHAPTER 19

Allard, R.: Beliefs about AIDS as determinants of preventive practices and of support for coercive measures, Am. J. Pub. Health 79:448-452, 1989.

AMA may push lawmakers to allow testing without consent, AIDS Alert 5:201-208, 1990.

Anderson, J., et al.: HIV/AIDS knowledge and sexual behavior among high school students, Fam. Plann. Perspect. 22:252-255, 1990.

Bacchetti, P., and Moss, A.: Incubation period of AIDS in San Francisco, Nature 338:251-253, 1989.

Baldwin, J., and Baldwin, D.: Factors affecting AIDS related sexual risk taking behavior among college students, J. Sex. Res. 25:181-196, 1988.

Becker, M., and Joseph, J.: AIDS and behavioral change to reduce risk: a review, Am. J. Pub. Health 78:394-410, 1988.

Brooks-Gunn, J., Boyer, C., and Hein, K.: Preventing HIV infection and AIDS in children and adolescents, Am. Psychol. 43:958-964, 1988.

Calabrese, L., et al.: Persistence of high risk sexual behavior among homosexual men in a area of low incidence for AIDS, AIDS Res. 2:357-361, 1986.

Centers for Disease Control: Classification system for human T-lymphotropic virus type III/lymphadenopathy-associated virus infections, MMWR 35:334-339, 1986.

Centers for Disease Control: Guidelines for prevention of transmission of HIV and hepatitis B to health care workers, MMWR 38:1-37, 1989.

Centers for Disease Control: HIV prevalance estimates and AIDS case projections for the United States: report based upon a workshop, MMWR 39:1-31, 1990a.

Centers for Disease Control: Update: acquired immunodeficiency syndrome—United States, 1989, MMWR 39:1-14, 1990b.

Centers for Disease Control: HIV/AIDS Surveillance Report, Dec. 1991a, pp. 1-18.

Centers for Disease Control: Update: transmission of HIV infection during invasive dental procedures—Florida, MMWR 40:377-381, 1991b.

Chervin, D., and Martinez, A.: Survey on the health of Stanford students, Report to the Board of Trustees of Stanford University, 1987.

Clayton, R., and Bokemeier, J.: Premarital sex in the seventies, J. Marriage Fam. 42:34-50, 1980.

Cox, F.: The AIDS booklet, Dubuque, Ia., 1990, Wm. C. Brown Group.

Crawford, I., and Robinson, W.: Adolescents and AIDS: knowledge and attitudes of African-American, Latino, and Caucasian midwestern U.S. high school seniors, AIDS Educ. Prevent. 3:25-33, 1990.

Denning, P.: Computer models of AIDS epidemiology, Am. Sci. 75:347-351, 1987.

DiClemente, R., Boyer, C., and Morales, E.: Minorities and AIDS: knowledge attitudes and misconceptions among Black and Latino adolescents, Am. J. Pub. Health 78:55-57, 1988.

DiClemente, R., et al.: College students' knowledge and attitudes and AIDS and changes in HIV-preventative behaviors, AIDS Educ. Prevent. 2:201-212, 1990.

Edgar, T., et al.: Communicating the AIDS risk to college students: the problem of motivating change, Health Educ. Res. 3:59-65, 1988.

Friedland, G., and Klein, R.: Transmission of the HIV, N. Engl. J. Med. 317:1125-1135, 1987.

Friedland, G., et al.: Additional evidence for lack of transmission of HIV infection by close interpersonal (casual) contact, AIDS 4:539-541, 1990.

Gallo, R., and Montagnier, L.: The AIDS epidemic. In The science of AIDS, San Francisco, 1989, W.H. Freeman & Co., pp. 1-12.

Gayle, H., et al.: Prevalence of the human immunodeficiency virus among university students, N. Engl. J. Med. 323:1538-1541, 1990.

Guinan, M., and Hardy, A.: Epidemiology of AIDS in women in the United States, 1981-1986, JAMA 257:2039-2042, 1987.

Harrison, D., et al.: AIDS knowledge and risk behaviors among culturally diverse women. AIDS Educ. Prevent. In press.

Hein, K.: AIDS in adolescents: a rationale for concern, N.Y. State J. Med. 87:290-295, 1987.

Hurst, N., and Hulley, S.: Preventing the

heterosexual spread of AIDS, JAMA 259:2429-2435, 1988.

Johnston, L., et al.: Drug use among American high school students, college and other young adults: national trends through 1986, Rockville, Md., 1987, National Institute of Drug Abuse.

Kegeles, S., et al.: Sexually active adolescents and condoms: changes over one year in knowledge, attitudes and use, Am. J. Pub. Health 78:460-461, 1988.

Koop, C.E.: Understanding AIDS, Atlanta, 1988, Centers for Disease Control.

Kramer, L.: A personal appeal, New York Native, Aug. 24-Sept. 6, 1981, p. 7.

Manning, O., et al.: College students' knowledge and health beliefs about AIDS: implications for education and prevention, College Health 37:254-259, 1989.

McKusick, L., Horstman, W., and Coates, T.: AIDS and sexual behavior reported by gay men in San Francisco, Am. J. Pub. Health 75:493-496, 1985.

Platt, J.: The future of AIDS, Futurist 21:10-16, 1987.

Price, J., et al.: High school students' perceptions and misperceptions of AIDS, J. Sch. Health 55:107-109, 1985.

Quadagno, D., et al.: Women at risk for HIV, J. Psychol. Hum. Sex. In press.

Rogers, M., and Williams, W.: AIDS in blacks and Hispanics: implications for prevention, Issues Sci. Technol. 20:89-94, 1987.

Rothstein, M.: Screening workers for AIDS. In Dalton, H., and Burris, S., editors: AIDS and the law, New Haven, Conn., 1988, Yale University Press, pp. 126-141.

St. Louis, M., et al.: Seroprevalence rates of human immunodeficiency virus infection at sentinel hospitals in the United States, N. Engl. J. Med. 323:213-218, 1990.

Schinke, S., et al.: African-American and Hispanic American adolescents HIV infection and preventive intervention, AIDS Educ. Prevent. 2:305-312, 1990.

Schuster, C., et al.: AIDS in children and adolescents: learning to cope with a harsh reality, School Nurse 17:14-25, 1986.

Strunin, L., and Hingson, R.: AIDS and adolescents: knowledge, beliefs, attitudes and behaviors, Pediatrics 79:825-828, 1987.

Waitley, C., et al.: HIV/AIDS knowledge, attitudes and behaviors of college aged individuals at a mid-western university, unpublished data, 1991.

Weber, J., and Weiss, R.: HIV infection: the cellular picture. In The science of AIDS, San Francisco, 1989, W.H. Freeman & Co., pp. 75-84.

Wofsy, C.: Human immunodeficiency virus infection in women, JAMA 257:2074-2076, 1987.

CHAPTER 20

American Psychiatric Association: Diagnostic and statistical manual of mental disorders, ed. 3 (DSM-III), Washington, D.C., 1986, The Association.

Baumeister, R.: Masochism and the self, Hillsdale, N.J., 1989, Lawrence Erlbaum Associates, Inc.

Beach, F.A., editor: Human sexuality in four perspectives, Baltimore, 1977, The Johns Hopkins University Press.

Becker, J., Skinner, L., and Abel, G.: Level of postassault sexual functioning in rape and incest victims, Arch. Sex. Behav. 15:37-47, 1986.

Boston Women's Health Book Collective: Our bodies, ourselves, New York, 1984, Simon & Schuster, Inc.

Brown, G., and Collier, L.: Transvestites' women revisited: a nonpatient sample, Arch. Sex. Behav. 18:73-83, 1989.

Carnes, P.: Out of the shadows: understanding sexual addiction, Minneapolis, 1983, CompCare Publishers.

Crewsdon, J.: By silence betrayed: sexual abuse of children in America, Boston, 1988, Little, Brown & Co., Inc.

Crooks, R., and Baur, K.: Our sexuality, ed. 4, Menlo Park, Calif., 1990, The Benjamin-Cummings Publishing Co.

Croughan, J., et al.: A comparison of treated and untreated male cross-dressers, Arch. Sex. Behav. 10:515-528, 1981.

Ellis, H.: Studies in the psychology of sex, New York, 1906, Random House, Inc.

Erickson, W., Walbek, N., and Seely, R.: Behavior patterns of child molesters, Arch. Sex. Behav. 17:77-86, 1988.

Finkelhor, D.: Child sexual abuse: new theory and research, New York, 1984, The Free Press.

Finkelhor, D., and Araji, S.: Explanations of pedophilia: a four factor model, J. Sex. Res. 22:145-161, 1986.

Francoeur, R.: Can sex be an addiction? In Francoeur, R., editor: Taking sides: clashing views of controversial issues in human sexuality, ed. 3, Guilford, Conn., 1991, Dushkin Publishing Group, Inc., pp. 32-33.

Gosselin, C., and Wilson, G.: Sexual variations, New York, 1980, Simon & Schuster Inc.

Greene, G., and Greene, C.: S-M: the last taboo, New York, 1974, Grove Press Inc.

Groth, A.N., and Birnbaum, H.J.: Adult sexual orientation and attraction to underage persons, Arch. Sex. Behav. 7:175-181, 1978.

Haslam, M.T.: Psychosexual disorders: a review, Springfield, Ill., 1979, Charles C Thomas, Publisher.

Hawton, K.: Behavioral approaches to the management of sexual deviations, Br. J. Psychiatry 143:248-255, 1985.

Hunt, M.: Sexual behavior in the 1970's, New York, 1974, Dell Books.

Innala, S., and Ernulf, K.: Asphyxiophilia in Scandinavia, Arch. Sex. Behav. 18:181-189, 1989.

Kinsey, A.C., Pomeroy, W.B., and Martin, C.E.: Sexual behavior in the human male, Philadelphia, 1948, W.B. Saunders Co.

Kinsey, A., et al.: Sexual behavior in the human female, Philadelphia, 1953, W.B. Saunders Co.

Klein, M.: Why there's no such thing as sexual addiction—and why it really matters. In Francoeur, R., editor: Taking sides: clashing views of controversial issues in human sexuality, ed. 3, Guilford, Conn., 1991, Dushkin Publishing Group, Inc., pp. 24-31.

Langevin, R., and Lang, R.: The courtship disorders. In Wilson, G., editor: Variant sexuality: research and theory, London, 1987, Croom Helm, pp. 202-228.

Lester, D.: Unusual sexual behavior, Springfield, Ill., 1975, Charles C Thomas, Publisher.

Levine, M., and Troiden, R.: The myth of sexual compulsivity, J. Sex. Res. 25:347-363, 1988.

McConaghy, N., et al.: Resistance to treatment of adolescent sex offenders, Arch. Sex. Behav. 18:97-107, 1989.

Mohr, J.W., Turner, R.E., and Terry, M.B.: Pedophilia and exhibitionism, Toronto, 1964, University of Toronto Press.

Money, J.: Love and love sickness: the science of sex, gender difference, and pairbonding, Baltimore, 1981, The Johns Hopkins University Press.

Prince, V., and Butler, P.M.: Survey of 504 cases of transvestism, Psychol. Rep. 31:903-917, 1972.

Reinisch, J.: The Kinsey Institute: new report on sex, New York, 1990, St. Martin's Press.

Rimza, M., and Niggeman, E.: Medical evaluation of sexually abused children: a review of 311 cases, Pediatrics 69:8-14, 1982.

Rooth, F.G., and Marks, I.M.: Persistent exhibitionism: short-term response to aversion, self-regulation, and relaxation treatments, Arch. Sex. Behav. 3:227-248, 1974.

Rubin, L.: Erotic wars, New York, 1990, Farrar, Straus & Giroux Inc.

Rush, F.: The best kept secret: sexual abuse of children, Englewood Cliffs, N.J., 1980, Prentice-Hall, Inc.

Russell, D.: The incidence and prevalence of intrafamilial and extrafamilial sexual abuse of female children, Child Abuse Neglect 7:133-146, 1982.

Scott, G.: Erotic power: an exploration of dominance and submission, Secaucus, N.J., 1983, Citadel Press.

Smith, R.S.: Voyeurism: a review of literature, Arch. Sex. Behav. 5:585-608, 1976.

Stoller, R.J.: Perversion: the erotic form of hatred, New York, 1975, Dell Books.

Stoller, R.J.: Sexual deviations. In Beach, F.A., editor: Human sexuality in four perspectives, Baltimore, 1977, The Johns Hopkins University Press.

Stoller, R.: Transvestism in women, Arch. Sex. Behav. 11:99-115, 1982.

Weissberg, J., and Levoy, A.: Compulsive sexual behavior, Med. Aspects Hum. Sex. 20:129-132, 1986.

Whitam, F.: A cross-cultural perspective on homosexuality, transvestism and transsexualism. In Wilson, G., editor: Variant sexuality: research and theory, London, 1987, Croom Helm, pp. 176-201.

Wincze, J., Bansal, S., and Malamud, M.: Effects of medroxyprogesterone acetate on subjective arousal, arousal to erotic stimulation, and nocturnal penile tumescence in male sex offenders, Arch. Sex. Behav. 15:293-306, 1986.

CHAPTER 21

Abarbanel, G.: The sexual assault patient. In Green, R., editor: Human sexuality: a health practitioner's text, Baltimore, 1979, Williams & Wilkins.

American Psychiatric Association: Diagnostic and statistical manual of mental disorders, Washington, D.C., 1987, The Association.

Amick, A., and Calhoun, K.: Resistance to sexual aggression: personality, attitudinal and situational factors, Arch. Sex. Behav. 16:153-163, 1987.

Amir, M.: Patterns in forcible rape, Chicago, 1971, University of Chicago Press.

Atkeson, B., Calhoun, K., and Morris, K.: Victim resistance to rape: the relationship of previous victimization, demographics and situational factors, Arch. Sex. Behav. 18:497-507, 1989.

Barnard, C.: Alcoholism and incest: improving diagnostic comprehensiveness, Int. J. Sex Res. 5:136-144, 1983.

Bart, P., and O'Brien, P.: Stopping rape: successful strategies, New York, 1985, Pergamon Press.

Beal, G., and Muelenhard, C.: Getting sexual aggressive men to stop their advances: information for rape prevention programs, Paper presented at a meeting of the Association for Advancement of Behavior Therapy, Boston, 1987.

Beyers, E., and Lewis, K.: Dating couples' disagreements over the desired level of sexual intimacy, J. Sex. Res. 24:15-29, 1988.

Bixler, R.: The multiple meanings of "incest," J. Sex. Res. 46:197-200, 1983.

Block, A.: Rape trauma syndrome as scientific expert testimony, Arch. Sex. Behav. 19:309-323, 1990.

Blumberg, M.: Sexual abuse of children—causes, diagnosis and management, Pediatr. Ann. 13:753-758, 1984.

Blythe, M., and Orr, D.: Childhood sexual abuse: guidelines for evaluation, Ind. Med 1:11-18, 1985.

Boston Women's Health Book Collective: Our bodies, ourselves, New York, 1984, Simon & Schuster, Inc.

Brant, R., and Tisza, V.: The sexually misused child, Am. J. Orthopsychiatry 47:80-87, 1977.

Bronson, C.: Growing through the pain: the incest survivor's companion, New York, 1989, Prentice-Hall, Inc.

Brownmiller, S.: Against our will: men, women, and rape, New York, 1975, Simon & Schuster, Inc.

Burgess, A.W., and Holmstrom, L.L.: Rape trauma syndrome, Am. J. Psychiatry 131:981-986, 1974a.

Burgess, A.W., and Holmstrom, L.L.: Rape: victims of crisis, Bowie, Md., 1974b, Robert J. Brady.

Burnett, R., Templer, D., and Baker, P.: Personality variables and circumstances of sexual assault predictive of a woman's resistance, Arch. Sex. Behav. 14:183-188, 1985.

Clark, L., and Lewis, D.: Rape: the price of coercive sexuality, Toronto, 1988, The Woman's Press.

Craig, E., Kalichman, S., and Follingstad, D.: Verbal coercive sexual behavior among college students, Arch. Sex. Behav. 18:421-434, 1989.

De Francis, V.: Protecting the child victim of sex crimes committed by adults, Denver, 1969, American Human Association.

Donohue, P.: The human animal, New York, 1985, Fireside Press.

Ellis, E.: A review of empirical rape research: victim reactions and response to treatment, Clin. Psychol. Rev. 3:473-490, 1983.

Finkelhor, D.: Sexually victimized children, New York, 1979, The Free Press.

Finkelhor, D.: Sex among siblings: a survey on prevalence, variety and effects, Arch. Sex. Behav. 9:171-194, 1980.

Fischer, G.: Presentation at a meeting of the Society for the Scientific Study of Sex, San Diego, Calif., Sept. 1985.

Fischer, G.: College student attitudes toward forcible date rape. I. Cognitive predictors, Arch. Sex. Behav. 15:457-466, 1986.

Ford, C., and Beach, F.A.: Patterns of sexual behavior, New York, 1951, Harper & Row, Publishers, Inc.

Gebhard, P.H., et al.: Sex offenders: an analysis of types. New York, 1965, Harper & Row, Publishers, Inc.

Giarrusso, R., et al.: Adolescents' cues and signals: sex and assault. In Johnson, P., chair: Acquaintance rape and adolescent sexuality. Symposium conducted at a meeting of the Western Psychological Association, San Diego, Calif., 1979.

Grant, L.: Assessment of child sexual abuse: eighteen months experience at the Child Protection Center, Am. J. Obstet. Gynecol. 148:617-620, 1984.

Groff, M.: Characteristics of incest offenders' wives, J. Sex. Res. 23:91-96, 1987.

Groth, A.N., and Burgess, A.W.: Male rape: offenders and victims, Am. J. Psychiatry 137:806-810, 1980.

Groth, A.N., Burgess, A.W., and Holmstrom, L.L.: Rape: power, anger and sexuality, Am. J. Psychiatry 134:1239-1243, 1977.

Herman, J.L.: Father-daughter incest, Cambridge, Mass., 1981, Harvard University Press.

Herman, J.L., and Hirschman, L.: Families at risk for father-daughter incest, Am. J. Psychiatry 138:967-970, 1981.

Holmstrom, L.L., and Burgess, A.W.: Sexual behavior of assailants during reported rapes, Arch. Sex. Behav. 9:427-439, 1980.

Jackson, J., et al.: Young adult women who report childhood intrafamilial sexual abuse: subsequent adjustment, Arch. Sex. Behav. 19:211-221, 1990.

Kanin, E.: Selected dyadic aspects of male sex aggression, J. Sex. Res. 5:12-28, 1969.

Katz, S., and Mazur, M.: Understanding the rape victim: a synthesis of research findings, New York, 1979, John Wiley & Sons, Inc.

Koss, M., Gidycsz, C., and Wisniewski, N.: The scope of rape: incidence and prevalence in a national sample of higher education students, J. Consult. Clin. Psychol. 55:162-170, 1988.

Landis, J.: Experiences of 500 children with adult sexual deviants, Psychiatr. Q. 30(suppl.):91-109, 1956.

LaPlante, M., McCormick, N., and Brannigan, G.: Living the sexual script: college students' views of influence in sexual encounters, J. Sex. Res. 6:338-355, 1980.

Levin, S., and Stava, L.: Personality characteristics of sex offenders: a review, Arch. Sex. Behav. 16:57-79, 1987.

MacDonald, J.: Rape offenders and their victims, Springfield, Ill., 1971, Charles C Thomas, Publishers.

McCahill, T., Meyer, L., and Gishman, A.: The aftermath of rape, Lexington, Mass., 1979, Lexington Books.

McDermott, M.: Rape victimization in 26 American cities, Washington, D.C., 1979, U.S. Government Printing Office.

Mega, L.T.: Incest-treatment dynamics: workshop presented at Fairleigh Dickinson University, Rutherford, N.J., 1981.

Mega, L.T., and Cuenca, R.: Incest and physician responsibility, South. Med. J. 77:1109-1114, 1984.

Mosher, D., and Anderson, R.: Macho personality, sexual aggression, and reactions to guided imagery of realistic rape, J. Res. Pers. 20:77-94, 1986.

Muehlenhard, C., and Andrews, S.: Open communication about sex: will it reduce risk factors related to date rape, Paper presented at a meeting of the Association for Advancement of Behavior Therapy, Houston, 1985.

Muehlenhard, C., and Cook, S.: Men's self-reports of unwanted sexual activity, J. Sex. Res. 24:58-72, 1988.

Muehlenhard, C., and Falcon, P.: Heterosocial skills and attitudes of nonincarcerated forceful rapists, Paper presented at a meeting of the Society for the Scientific Study of Sex, Atlanta, 1987.

Muehlenhard, C., and Felts, A.: An analysis of causal factors for men's attitudes about the justifiability of date rape, unpublished data, 1987.

Muehlenhard, C., and Hollabaugh, L.: Do women sometimes say no when they mean yes? The prevalence and correlates of women's token resistance to sex, J. Pers. Soc. Psychol. 54:872-879, 1988.

Muehlenhard, C., and Linton, M.: Date rape and sexual aggression in dating situations: incidence and risk factors, J. Counsel. Psychol. 34:186-196, 1987.

National Commission on the Causes and Prevention of Violence: Crimes of violence, vol. 2, Washington, D.C., 1969, U.S. Government Printing Office.

National Institute of Law Enforcement and Criminal Justice: Forcible rape: final project report, Washington, D.C., 1978, U.S. Government Printing Office.

Parrot, A.: Presentation at a meeting of the Society for the Scientific Study of Sex, San Diego, Calif., Sept. 1985.

Peters, J.: Children who are victims of sexual assault and the psychology of offenders, Am. J. Psychother. 30:398-409, 1976.

Queen's Bench Foundation: Rape: prevention and resistance, San Francisco, 1976, The Foundation.

Rapaport, K., and Burkhart, B.: Personality and attitudinal characteristics of sexually coercive college males, J. Abnorm. Psychol. 93:216-221, 1984.

Russell, D.: The incidence and prevalence of intrafamilial and extrafamilial sexual abuse of female children, Child Abuse Neglect 7:133-146, 1983.

Russell, D.: The prevalence and seriousness of incestuous abuse: stepfathers versus biological fathers, Child Abuse Neglect 8:15-22, 1984.

Russell, D.: The secret trauma: incest in the lives of girls and women, New York, 1986, Basic Books Inc., Publishers.

Russell, M.: Rape victims and police reporting, Canada's Mental Health 28:14-16, 1980.

Sandy, P.: The socio-cultural context of rape: a cross-cultural study, J. Soc. Issues 37:5-27, 1981.

Sanford, L.: The silent child, Garden City, N.Y., 1980, Doubleday & Co., Inc.

Sarles, R.: Incest, Pediatr. Rev. 2:51-54, 1980.

Sarrel, P., and Masters, W.: Sexual molestation of men by women, Arch. Sex. Behav. 11:117-132, 1982.

Schwendinger, J., and Schwendinger, H.: Rape and inequality, Beverly Hills, Calif., 1983, Sage Publications, Inc.

Scully, D., and Marolla, J.: Convicted rapists' vocabulary of motive: excuses and justification, Soc. Problems 31:530-544, 1984.

Sedney, M., and Brooks, B.: Factors associated with a history of childhood sexual experience in a nonclinical female population, J. Am. Acad. Child Psychiatry 23:215-218, 1984.

State v. Marks, Kansas, 647 P.2d 1292, 1982.

State v. Saldana, Minnesota, 234 N. W, 2ed 227, 1982.

Struckman-Johnson, C.: Forced sex on dates: it happens to men too, J. Sex. Res. 24:234-240, 1988.

Taubman, S.: Incest in context, Social Work 29:35-40, 1984.

Tsai, M., and Wagner, N.: Therapy groups for women sexually molested as children, Arch. Sex. Behav. 7:417-427, 1978.

Uniform Crime Reports for the United States—1982, Washington D.C., 1983, Federal Bureau of Investigation, U.S. Department of Justice.

Uniform Crime Reports for the United States—1987, Washington, D.C., 1988, Federal Bureau of Investigation, U.S. Department of Justice.

Veltkamp, L., et al.: Sexual child abuse: economic, psychosocial, ethical, preventative and medical aspects, South. Med. J. 77:879-885, 1984.

Weis, K., and Borges, S.: Victimology and rape: the case of the legitimate victim, Issues in Criminology 8:71-115, 1973.

Wilk, P.: Expert testimony on rape trauma syndrome: admissibility and effective use in criminal rape prosecution, American University Law Rev. 33:417-435, 1984.

Williams, L.: The classic rape: when do victims report? Soc. Problems 31:459-467, 1984.

Wilson, W., and Durrenberger, R.: Comparison of rape and attempted rape victims, Psychol. Rep. 50:198-205, 1982.

Zuelzer, M., and Reposa, R.: Mothers in incestuous families, Int. J. Fam. Theory 5:98-110, 1983.

CHAPTER 22

Abelson, H., et al.: Public attitudes toward and experience with erotic materials. Technical reports of the Commission on Obscenity and Pornography, vol. 6, Washington, D.C., 1971, U.S. Government Printing Office.

Appeals court rules: prostitution charges violated women's rights, Wisconsin State Journal, 1990.

Assiter, A. Pornography, feminism and the individual, London, 1989, Pluto Press.

Attorney General's Commission on Pornography: Washington, D.C., 1986, U.S. Department of Justice.

Backhouse, C., and Cohen, L.: Sexual harassment on the job, Englewood Cliffs, N.J., 1981, Prentice-Hall, Inc.

Bart, P.B., and O'Brien, P.H.: Stopping rape, New York, 1985, Pergamon Press.

Burgess, A., et al.: Response patterns in children in adolescents exploited through sex rings and pornography, Am. J. Psychiatry 141:656-662, 1984.

Check, J.V.P.: The effects of violent and nonviolent pornography (Department of Supply and Services Contract No. 05SV

19200-3-0899), Ottawa, Ontario, 1985, Canadian Department of Justice.

Check, J.V.P., and Guloien, T.H.: Reported proclivity for coercive sex following repeated exposure to sexually violent pornography, nonviolent dehumanizing pornography and erotica. In Zillmann, D., and Bryant, J., editors: Pornography: research advances and policy considerations, Hillsdale, N.J., 1989, Lawrence Erlbaum Associates, Inc.

Check, J.V.P., and Malamuth, N.: An empirical assessment of some feminist hypotheses about rape, Int. J. Women Studies 8:414-423, 1985.

Code of Federal Regulations: Labor, revised July, 1986, Washington, D.C., 1986, Office of the Federal Register National Archives and Records Administration.

Cohn, B.: A fresh assault on an ugly crime, Newsweek, Mar. 14, 1988, pp. 64-65.

Collins, E.G.C., and Blodgett, T.B.: Some see it . . . some won't, Harvard Business Review, March-April 1981, pp. 77-94.

Crull, P.: Stress effects of sexual harassment on the job: implications for counseling, J. Orthopsychiatry 52:539-544, 1982.

Demare, D., Briere, J., and Lips, H.M.: Violent pornography and self-reported likelihood of sexual aggression, J. Res. Pers. 22:140-153, 1988.

Dolgin, J., and Dolgin, B.: Sex and the law. In Wolman, B., and Money, J., editors: Handbook of human sexuality, Englewood Cliffs, N.J., 1980, Prentice-Hall, Inc.

Donnerstein, E.: Aggressive erotica and violence against women, J. Pers. Soc. Psychol. 39:269-277, 1980.

Donnerstein, E., and Berkowitz, L.: Victim reactions in aggressive erotic films as a factor in violence against women, J. Pers. Soc. Psychol. 41:710-723, 1981.

Donnerstein, E., Linz, D., and Penrod, S.: The question of pornography, New York, 1987, The Free Press.

Gebhard, P.H., et al.: Sex offenders: an analysis of types, New York, 1965, Harper & Row, Publishers, Inc.

Gest, T.: The drive to make America porn-free, U.S. News and World Report, Feb. 6, 1989, pp. 26-27.

Goldstein, M., et al.: Experience with pornography: rapists, pedophiles, homosexuals, transsexuals, and controls, Arch. Sex. Behav. 1:1-15, 1971.

Gutek, B.A.: Sex and the workplace, San Francisco, 1985, Jossey-Bass, Inc.

Hersch, P.: Coming of age on city streets, Psychology Today, Jan. 1988, pp. 28-37.

Hobson, B.: Uneasy virtue, New York, 1987, Basic Books, Inc.

Holmstrom, L., and Burgess, A.: The victim of rape, New York, 1978, John Wiley & Sons, Inc.

Hughes, J.O., and Sandler, B.R.: In case of sexual harassment: a guide for women students, Washington, D.C., 1986, Association of American Colleges.

Kutchinsky, B.: The effect of easy availability of pornography on the incidence of sex crimes: the Danish experience, J. Soc. Issues 29:163-182, 1973.

Lebrato, M.: Help yourself: a manual for dealing with sexual harassment, Sexual Harassment in Employment Project of the California Commission on the Status of Women, 1986.

Leo, J.: Pornography: the feminist dilemma, Time, July 21, 1986, p. 18.

Linz, D., Donnerstein, E., and Adams, S.M.: Physiological desensitization and judgements about female victims of violence, Hum. Commun. Res. 15:509-522, 1989.

Linz, D., Donnerstein, E., and Penrod, S.: The effects of multiple exposures to filmed violence against women, J. Commun. 34:130-147, 1984.

Lynch, T., and Neckes, M.: The cost-effectiveness of enforcing prostitution laws, San Francisco, 1978, Unitarian Universalist Service Committee.

Marsh, J.C., Geist, A., and Caplan, N.: Rape policy: the limits of law reform, Boston, 1982, Auburn House Publishing Co.

Masters, W.H., Johnson, V.E., and Kolodny, R.C.: Masters and Johnson on sex and human loving, Boston, 1986, Little, Brown & Co.

Moretti, S.S.: Obscenity and pornography, New York, 1984, Oceana Publications.

Mueller, G.O.W.: Sexual conduct and the law, Dobbs Ferry, N.Y., 1980, Oceana Publications.

Nobile, P., and Nadler, E.: United States of America vs. sex: how the Meese Commission lied about pornography, New York, 1986, Minotaur Press.

Osanka, F.M., and Johann, S.L.: Sourcebook on pornography, Lexington, Mass., 1989, Lexington Books.

Personnel Policies Forum: Sexual harassment: employer policies and problems, PPF Survey No. 144, June 1987, The Bureau of National Affairs, Inc.

Pornography: a poll, Time, July 21, 1986, p. 22.

Price, V., Scanlon, B., and Janus, M.-D.: Social characteristics of adolescent male

prostitution, Victimology 9:211-221, 1984.

Prus, R., and Irini, S.: Hookers, rounders, and desk clerks, Toronto, 1980, Gage Publishing.

The report of the Commission on Obscenity and Pornography, New York, 1970, Bantam Books.

Richards, D.A.J.: Sex, drugs, death, and the law, Totowa, N.J., 1982, Rowman & Littlefield.

Russell, D.E.H.: Rape in marriage, New York, 1982, Macmillan Publishing Co., Inc.

Russell, D.E.H.: Sexual exploitation, Beverly Hills, Calif., 1984, Sage Publications.

Russell, D.E.H.: Pornography and rape: a causal model, Political Psychol. 9:41-73, 1988.

Schram, D.: Forcible rape: final project report, Washington, D.C., March 1978, National Institute of Law Enforcement and Criminal Justice, Law Enforcement Assistance Administration, U.S. Department of Justice.

Steinem, G.: Erotica and pornography; a clear and present difference, Ms. 11:53-55, 1978.

Schmitt, E.: 2 in 3 military woman report harassment, New York Times, 1990.

Tangri, S., Burt, M., and Johnson, L.: Sexual harassment at work: three explanatory models, J. Soc. Issues 38(4):33-54, 1982.

Taylor, R.: Sex in history, New York, 1970, Harper & Row, Publishers, Inc.

Tifft, S.: A setback for pinups at work, Time, Feb. 4, 1991, p. 61.

U.S. General Accounting Office: Sexual exploitation of children—a problem of unknown magnitude, Gaithersburg, Md., 1982.

Williams, L.: The classic rape: when do victims report? Soc. Problems 31:459-467, 1984.

Wing, K.R.: Constitutional protection of sexual privacy in the 1980s: what is Big Brother doing in the bedroom? Am. J. Pub. Health 76:201-204, 1986.

Zillman, D., and Bryant, J.: Pornography, sexual callousness, and the trivialization of rape, J. Commun. 32:10-21, 1982.

Zillman, D., and Bryant, J.: Effects of massive exposure to pornography. In Malamuth, N., and Donnerstein, E., editors: Pornography and sexual aggression, New York, 1984, Academic Press, Inc.

Zillman, D., and Bryant, J.: Pornography: research advances and policy considerations, Hillsdale, N.J., 1989, Lawrence Erlbaum Associates, Inc.

CHAPTER 23

Bernhardt, E.: National Board of Health and Welfare, Stockholm, 1987.

Bruess, C.E., and Greenberg, J.S.: Sex education: theory and practice, Belmont, Calif., 1981, Wadsworth Publishing Co.

Davis, S.M., and Harris, B.: Sexual knowledge, sexual interests, and sources of sexual information of rural and urban adolescents from three cultures, Adolescence 17:471-492, 1982.

Ehrenberg, M., and Ehrenberg, O.: The intimate circle, New York, 1988, Simon & Schuster, Inc.

Fan, D.P., and Shaffer, C.L.: Use of open-ended essays and computer content analysis to survey college students' knowledge of AIDS, J. Am. Coll. Health 38:221-243, 1990.

Furstenberg, F.F., Jr., and Brooks-Gunn, J.: Causes and consequences of teenage pregnancy and childbearing. In Ozawa, M.N., editor: Women's life cycle and economic insecurity, New York, 1989, Greenwood Press.

Gordon, S.: Putting sex education back in the home. In Pocs, O., editor: Annual editions: human sexuality, Guilford, Conn., 1982, Dushkin Publishing Co.

Handelsman, C.D., Cabral, R.J., and Weisfeld, G.E.: Sources of information and adolescent sexual knowledge and behavior, J. Adolesc. Res. 2:455-463, 1987.

Hunt, M.: Sexual behavior in the 1970's, New York, 1974, Dell Books.

Jones, E.R., et al.: Teenage pregnancy in developed countries: determinants and policy implications, Fam. Plann. Perspect. 17:53-63, 1985.

Kantrowitz, B.: The grim ABC's of AIDS, Newsweek 108:66-67, 1986.

Katz, G.: Sex clinics for teens ignite uproar, USA Today, Nov. 11, 1986.

Kinsey, A.C., Pomeroy, W.B., and Martin, C.E.: Sexual behavior in the human male, Philadelphia, 1948, W.B. Saunders Co.

Kinsey, A.C., et al.: Sexual behavior in the human female, Philadelphia, 1953, W.B. Saunders Co.

Kirby, D.: School-based health clinics: an emerging approach to improving adolescent health and addressing teenage pregnancy, Washington, D.C., 1985, Center for Population Options.

Klein, J.: Scared sexless, Am. Health 7:83-91, 1987.

Koop, C.E.: Surgeon General's report on acquired immune deficiency syndrome, Washington, D.C., 1986, U.S. Department of Health and Human Services.

Leo, J.: Sex and schools, Time 128:54-60, 63, 1986.

Levine, M.: Sex education in the public elementary and high school curriculum. In Taylor, D., editor: Human sexual development, Philadelphia, 1970, F.A. Davis Co.

Lewis, R.: Parents and peers: socialization agents in the coital behavior of young adults, J. Sex. Res. 9:156-162, 1973.

Libby, R.W., and Nass, G.D.: Parental views on teenage sexual behavior, J. Sex. Res. 7:226-236, 1971.

LoPiccolo, J., and Miller, V.H.: A program for enhancing the sexual relationship of normal couples, Counseling Psychol. 5:41-45, 1975.

McCary, J., and Flake, M.: The role of bibliotherapy and sex education in counseling for sexual problems, Professional Psychol. 2:353-357, 1971.

Morrison, E.S., et al.: Growing up sexual, New York, 1980, Van Nostrand Reinhold Co., Inc.

The National Academy of Sciences urges establishment of school-based clinics to provide contraceptive to teens, Sexuality Today 10:1, 1986.

Orr, M.T.: Sex education and contraceptive education in U.S. public high schools, Fam. Plann. Perspect. 14:304-313, 1982.

Penland, L.R.: Sex education in 1900, 1940 and 1980: an historical sketch, J. Sch. Health 51(4):305-309, 1981.

Scales, P.: Arguments against sex education, Children Today 10:22-25, 1981.

Scales, P.: The front lines of sexuality education, Santa Cruz, Calif., 1984, Network Publications.

Sonenstein, F.L., and Pittman, K.J.: The availability of sex education in large city school districts, Fam. Plann. Perspect. 16:19-24, 1984.

STD Statistical Letter 38:887, 1990.

Thornburg, H.D.: Adolescent sources of information on sex, J. Sch. Health 51:272-277, 1981.

VD Statistical Letter, vol. 127, May 1978.

Vincent, M.L., Clearie, A.F., and Schluchter, M.D.: Reducing adolescent pregnancy through school and community-based education, JAMA 257:3382-3386, 1987.

Wallace, H.M., and Vienonen, M.: Teenage pregnancy in Sweden and Finland: implications for the United States, J. Adolesc. Health Care 10:231-236, 1989.

When sex education fails, Lawrence (Kan.) Journal-World, 1981.

Zabin, L., et al.: Evaluation of a pregnancy program for urban teenagers, Fam. Plann. Perspect. 14:117-126, 1986.

Zelnick, M., and Kim, Y.J.: Sex education and its association with teenage sexual activity, pregnancy and contraceptive use, Fam. Plann. Perspect. 14:117-126, 1982.

CHAPTER 24

Abortion's hardest cases, Time, July 9, 1990.

Annas, G.J.: Fathers anonymous: beyond the best interests of the sperm donor, Child Welfare 60:161-174, 1982.

At bay in San Francisco, Time 120:67, Oct. 11, 1982.

Carelli, R.: High court reaffirms pro-choice abortion stance, The Capital Times, p. 6, June 11, 1986.

Cohen, S.M.: Singlehood, childlessness, divorce, and intermarriage: the meaning of recent family trends for Jewish identification. In Cohen, S.M., editor: American modernity and Jewish identity, New York, 1983, Tavistock Publications.

Curie-Cohen, M., Luttrell, L., and Shapiro, S.: Current practice of artificial insemination by donor in the United States, N. Engl. J. Med. 300:585-590, 1979.

Flannery, A.P., editor: Pastoral constitution on the Church in the modern world (51): documents of Vatican II, Grand Rapids, Mich., 1975, William B. Eerdmans Publishing Co.

Frohock, F.M.: Abortion, Westport, Conn., 1983, Greenwood Press.

Gallup, G., Jr., and Newport, F.: Americans shift toward pro-choice position, Gallup Poll Monthly, April 1990, pp. 2-4.

Hass, A.: Teenage sexuality, New York, 1979, Macmillan Publishing Co., Inc.

Heller, K.: Modern morals: fibs and sex, USA Today, Dec. 2, 1985.

Holden, C.: Two fertilized eggs stir global furor, Science 225:35, 1984.

Hunt, M.: Sexual behavior in the 1970s, Chicago, 1974, Playboy Press.

Knocking on the bedroom door, Time, July 14, 1986.

Mansfield, D.: Court splits custody of embryos, Wisconsin State Journal, 1990.

Maret, S.M.: Attitudes of fundamentalists toward homosexuality, Psychol. Rep. 55:205-206, 1984.

Maret, S.M., and Maret, L.D.: Attitudes of fundamentalists toward nonmarital sex, Psychol. Rep. 52:921-922, 1982.

McDowell, J.D.: Ethical implications of in vitro fertilization, Christian Century 100:936-938, 1983.

Meer, J.: Sex and the Church, Psychology Today 19:67, 1985.

Meilaender, G.: The fetus as parasite and mushroom: Judith Jarvis Thomson's defense of abortion, Linacre Q. 46(2):126-135, 1979.

Ministry to homosexuals, Origins 15(40): 650-651, 1986.

Moore, K.A., Nord, C.W., and Peterson, J.L.: Nonvoluntary sexual activity among adolescents, Fam. Plann. Perspect. 21:110-114, 1989.

Murphy, F.X.: Of sex and the Catholic church, Atlantic Monthly 247(2):44-57, 1981.

Pastors and people: viewpoints on church policies and positions, Origins 15(45):738-744, 1986.

Pluralism, dissent and abortion, Origins 15(40):652-654, 1986.

Rosenheim, E.: Sexual attitudes and regulations in Judaism. In Handbook of sexuality, Holland, 1977, Elsevier/North-Holland Biomedical Press.

Scatarello, C.: Sperm bank deposit pays off, Wisconsin State Journal, 1990.

Schneider, W., and Lewis, I.A.: The straight story on homosexual and gay rights, Pub. Opinion 7:16-20, 59, 60, 1984.

Schwartz, M., Jewelewicz, R., and Wiele, R.L.V.: Application of orthodox Jewish law to reproductive medicine, Fertil. Steril. 33(5):474-475, 1980.

Shapiro, M.H.: Genetics and morality, Center Magazine 16:9-15, 1983.

Singh, R.K., Walton, B.L., and Williams, L.S.: Extramarital sexual permissiveness: conditions and contingencies, J. Marriage Fam. 38:701-712, 1976.

Smolowe, J.: Gagging the clinics, Time, June 3, 1991, pp. 16-17.

Tannahill, R.: Sex in history, New York, 1980, Stein & Day Publishers.

Thompson, A.P.: Extramarital sex: a review of the research literature, J. Sex. Res. 19:1-22, 1983.

Thomson, J.J.: A defense of abortion, Philosophy and Public Affairs 1(1):47-66, 1971.

Toufexis, A.: Battle over the abortion pill: pressure is mounting to introduce the drug RU 486 in the U.S., Time, 1990.

Use of the "morning-after pill" in cases of rape, Origins 15(39):633-638, 1986.

Waxman, C.I.: The contemporary American Jewish family. In Waxman, C.I., editor: American Jews in transition, Philadelphia, 1983, Temple University Press.

Wojtyla, K. (Pope John Paul II): Love and responsibility, New York, 1981, Farrar, Straus & Giroux, Inc.

INDEX

C

Humphreys study, 38
Hunt Report, 30-31
Hunt study, 659-662
Hustlers, 632
Hymen, 53, 54
  sexual dysfunction and, 490
Hyperemia, 86
Hyperphilia, 585
Hyperreflexia, autonomic, 465, 466
Hypersexuality, 585, 586
Hypertonic saline, 249-250
Hyperventilation, 110
Hypogonadism, 90
Hypothalamus, 75
  gonads and, 76, 77
Hysterosalpingography, 173

I

Ibuprofen, 159
Identical twins, 137
Identity, gender, 289
Illegal drugs, 484-485
Immunological approaches to contraception, 246
Immunosuppression, 545
Impotence, 386
  sexual dysfunction and, 484
In vitro fertilization, 173-174, 177
  religious and ethical views of, 701-705
Incest, 3, 618-623
  defined, 593
  father-daughter, 619-622
  personal account of, 620-621
  sibling, 619
Inderal; see Propranolol
Indomethacin, 159
Infancy, 350-352
Infatuation, 405-406
Infection
  external parasitic, 532
  pregnancy and, 159
  urinary tract, 465
Infertility, 169-178
  approaches to, 177-178
  causes of, 170
  female, 172-177
    sexual disorder and, 505
  intimacy and, 176
  male, 170-172
  sexual satisfaction and, 176
Inhibin, 80
Injectable progesterone, 217
Intellectual defense against erotic feelings, 494
Intercourse; see Sexual intercourse
Interdependence, 421
Intimacy, 420-427
  barriers to, 423-427

Intimacy—cont'd
  gender differences in, 425
  infertility and, 176
Intrauterine device, 230-232
  costs of, 239
  death and, 240
  failure rates of, 217, 239
  gonorrhea and, 529
  for mentally retarded, 479
  use of, 214
Intravenous drug use
  acquired immunodeficiency syndrome and, 551
  human immunodeficiency virus infection and, 562
Iodine, 153
Iron, 153
Irradiation, 158, 159
Ismelin; see Guanethidine
Isocarboxazid, 485
IUD; see Intrauterine device

J

Jealousy, 424
Jewish tradition, 4
Job discrimination, 323-324
Judaism, 681-683
Judeo-Christian ethic, 627, 628

K

Kama Sutra, 273
Kaplan, Helen Singer
  orgasmic dysfunction and, 501
  premature ejaculation and, 500
  sexual dysfunction and, 492-495
  sexual response cycle and, 124
Kaposi's sarcoma, 546-547
Kegel exercises, 55
Kinsey, Alfred C., 16, 29-30
Kinsey reports, 29-30
Kinsey studies, 315-316
Kissing, 265-266
Klismaphilia, 585

L

Labia majora, 53
  in sexual response cycle, 112
Labia minora, 53
  in sexual response cycle, 112
Labioscrotal swelling, 67
Labor, stages of, 181-185
Laboratory studies, 34-38
Lactation, 199
Lactogen, human placental, 199
  pregnancy and, 138-139
Lamaze method of childbirth, 191-193
Laparoscopic surgery, 243
  female infertility and, 173

Laparoscopy, 173
Laser surgery, 506
Latency stage, 349
Latent syphilis, 524
Law; see Legal aspects
Lead, 160
Learning theory, 341-342
Leboyer method of childbirth, 193-194
Legal aspects, 626-657
  of consensual sexual behaviors, 628-629
  of pornography, 636-643
  of prostitution, 629-735
  of rape, 644-647
  of sexual harassment, 647-655
Lesbian, 315; see also Homosexuality
Lesion in spinal cord injury, 462
Leukoplakia, oral, 546
Lewdness, 627
Leydig cells, 48, 80
LH; see Luteinizing hormone
Libido, 349
  dysfunction of, 490
Librium, 160
Life span, 444
Longitudinal data, 26
Love, 402-429
  biological theory of, 419
  defined, 403-406
  development of, 420-423
  gender differences in, 408, 412-413
  intimacy and, 423-427
  of others, 422
  scientific study of, 406-412
  sex and, 427
  theories of, 413-419
LSD; see Lysergic acid diethylamide
Luteinizing hormone, 74, 76-78
  amenorrhea and, 89
  testosterone and, 80
Lymph nodes, swollen, 520-526
Lymphatic drainage of mammary glands, 63
Lymphocytes, T4, 548
Lymphogranuloma venereum, 525
  causes, symptoms, and treatment of, 517
Lysergic acid diethylamide, 160

M

Maidenhead, 53, 54
Male
  infertility in, 170-172
Male-to-female transsexual, 296
Mammary glands, 62-63
  disorders of, 506-511
  menstrual cycle and, 86
Mammography, 510

Preeclampsia, 164
Preejaculation, 52
Pregnancy, 138-179
  alcohol and, 156
  caffeine and, 157
  chemicals and, 157-158
  chlamydial infections and, 538-539
  cigarette smoking and, 154-155
  versus contraception, 238-240
  death and, 240
  diagnosis of, 140
  ectopic, 162-163
  exercise and, 158
  first trimester of, 141-142, 148-149
  hormonal changes during, 138-139
  infertility and, 169-178
  irradiation and, 158
  medications and, 157-158
  mother and father and, 148-152
  nutrition in, 152-154
  problems during, 162-169
  rape and, 685
  second trimester of, 142-143
  sex education and, 662-663
  sexual intercourse and, 161-162
  sexually transmitted diseases in, 537-539
  in spinal cord injuries, 465-466
  teenage, 370-376
    sex education and, 667, 669-670
  third trimester of, 143-148
  toxemia of, 164-165
Premarital sex
  adolescent attitudes toward, 366-370
  Catholic church and, 684
  Judaism and, 683
  religious and ethical views of, 693-694
Premature ejaculation, 486-487
Premature labor and birth, 164
  in spinal cord injured, 466
Premenstrual syndrome, 86, 100-105
Premenstrual tension, 96-105
Prenatal development of reproductive system, 63-67
Prenatal hormones, 67-69
Prenatal screening, 705
Prepuce
  in female, 53
  in male, 44
Presentation, 196
Primary syphilis, 523
Prison rape, 611-612
Privacy rights, 629
Pro-choice, 246-247, 688
Pro-life, 687-688
Probability sampling, 27
Procreation, 4
Prodrome phase of herpesvirus, 521

Progestational phase of menstrual cycle, 83, 85
Progesterone, 74
  injectable, 217
  pregnancy and, 138-139
Progesterone-only pills, injections, and implants, 235-236
  noncontraceptive benefits of, 215
Progestin-induced hermaphroditism, 68-69
Progestins, 160
Prolactin, 74
  in postpartum period, 200
  pregnancy and, 139
Propranolol, 485
Prostaglandins
  labor and, 183
  menstrual cycle and, 86-87
  to terminate pregnancy, 249
Prostate gland, 49, 51
  cancer of, 504
  inflammation or infection of, 503
  sexual dysfunction and, 490
  in sexual response cycle, 114
Prostatitis, 503-504
Prosthesis, penile, 495-497
Prostitution
  defined, 629
  female, 630
  legal aspects of, 627, 629-635
  male, 631-632
  in middle ages, 9
  teenagers in, 635
  as victims, 630
Protection of Children Against Sexual Exploitation Act of 1977, 643
Protein, 153
Protestantism, 685-687
Proximity, 411-412
Psychiatric disorders, 485
Psychoanalyst, 491
Psychogenic erection, 464
Psychological explanations for homosexuality, 340-344
Psychological signs of child sexual abuse, 615
Psychosexual development, 349-350
Puberty, 357
  female, 359
  homosexuality and, 343
  male, 361
  rituals of, 360
Pubic lice, 532
  causes, symptoms, and treatment of, 517
Public lewdness, 627
Pubococcygeal muscle, 53, 55
Puritan tradition, 9-10

Q
Quintuplets, 137

R
Radiation
  breast cancer and, 510-511
  pregnancy and, 159
Radical mastectomy, 510-511
Random digit dialing, 27
Random sample, 27
Rape, 593-613
  act of, 595-597
  aftermath of, 606
  court system in, 607
  date, 599-605
  defined, 593, 646
  historical aspects of, 594-595
  homosexual, 611-612
  legal aspects of, 644-647
  legal definition of, 593
  males raping other males in, 611-612
  marital, 605-606, 646-647
  motivations for, 596
  myths about, 610
  pregnancy and, 685
  prevention of, 609
  prison system and, 612
  rapist and, 608-610
  reporting of, 597-599
  sexual assault by women and, 612-613
  stereotypes of, 595
  victim of, 610-611
Rape trauma syndrome, 606, 607
Rapist, 608-610
RDD; *see* Random digit dialing
Rear-entry position, 276
Reciprocal liking, 410
Recommended daily allowances, 153
Rectum, 110
Redbook surveys, 31
Reflexogenic erection, 464
Refractory period, 121-124
Refusal, problem of, 27
Reinforcement theory, 414-415
Rejection, fear of, 493
Releasing in homosexuality, 331
Reliability, 26
Religious and ethical views, 680-707
  of abortion, 687-691
  of abortion pill, 692
  of adoption, 701
  of artificial insemination, 698
  Catholicism and, 683-685
  of contraception, 691-693
  controversies in, 687-705
  determinants of, 687
  of extramarital sex, 694
  of homosexuality, 695-696

CREDITS

CHAPTER 6

pp. 130, 133, from A Child is Born, copyright © 1990 by Lennart Nilsson Photography AB, In Vitro AB, and Bonnier Fakta, AB. Published by Delacorte Press/Seymour Lawrence; **p. 135 (top),** Richard Hutchings/ Photo Researchers; **p.140,** courtesy of Whitehall Laboratories; **p. 143,** Medical and Scientific Illustration, Crozet, Virginia; **pp. 144-147,** from A Child is Born, copyright © 1990 by Lennart Nilsson Photography AB, In Vitro AB, and Bonnier Fakta, AB. Published by Delacorte Press/Seymour Lawrence; **p. 150,** Vincent Merritt/Photo Edit; **p. 151,** from Berne, R.M., and Levy, M.N.: Physiology, ed. 2, 1988, St. Louis, The C.V. Mosby Co.; **p. 152,** Joel Gordon Photography; **p. 153,** reprinted from Preconceptional health promotion: a practical guide by R. Cefalo and M.K. Moss, pp. 277-278, with permission of Aspen Publishers, Inc. © 1988; **p. 154,** Zefa U.K./H. Armstrong Roberts; **p. 155,** Joel Gordon Photography; **p. 156,** from Streissguth, A., et al.: Science 109:353, 1980. Copyright © 1980 American Association for the Advancement of Science; **p. 158,** Superstock/Four-by-Five; **p. 162,** Lisa Cheuk; **pp. 163, 166,** Medical and Scientific Illustration, Crozet, Virginia; **p. 167,** J. Pavlovsky/Sygma; **p. 168,** Medical and Scientific Illustration, Crozet, Virginia; **p. 174,** cartoon by Mike Keefe, © United Feature Syndicate; **p. 175,** Cleo Photography.

CHAPTER 7

p. 180, Joel Gordon Photography; **p. 181,** from Viorst, Judith: Nice baby, Cleveland, 1968, The New American Library, Inc. Copyright © 1968. Reprinted by permission of The New American Library, Inc.; **p. 183,** Jeffrey Reed/Medichrome; **p. 186,** Century Manufacturing Company; **p. 187,** Photo Researchers; **p. 189,** Jim Olive Photography; **p. 190,** from Elkins, S.: Recollections of a birth in a birthing center, personal communication to authors, May, 1982; **p. 192,** from Phillips, C., and Anzalone, J.: Fathering participation in labor and birth, ed. 2, St. Louis, 1982, The C.V. Mosby Co.; **p. 194,** Joel Gordon Photography; **p. 195,** from Herron, D.: Recollections of a birth, personal communication to the authors, May, 1982; **p. 199,** Lisa Cheuk; **p. 200,** Joel Gordon Photography; **pp. 203, 204,** Cathy Lander-Goldberg/Lander Photographics; **p. 205,** Doonesbury copyright © 1987 G.G. Trudeau, Reprinted with permission of Universal Press

Syndicate. All rights reserved; **p. 206,** Superstock/Four-by-Five.

CHAPTER 8

p. 212, Joel Gordon Photography; **p. 214,** from Forrest, J., and Fordyce, R.: United States women's contraceptive attitudes and practices: have they changed in the 1980's, Family Planning Perspectives 20:112-118, 1988, Alan Guttmacher Institute. Copyright © 1988. Reprinted with permission of Alan Guttmacher Institute; **pp. 217, 218,** from Hatcher, R.A., et al.: Contraceptive technology, ed. 15, New York, 1990, Irving Publishers, Inc.; **p. 220,** Courtesy of Whitehall Laboratories; **pp. 222, 223 (right),** 224, 226, 227, 228, 230, 233, Joel Gordon Photography; **pp. 237, 238,** Wide World Photos; **p. 240,** modified from Teitze, C.: New estimates on mortality associated with fertility control, Family Planning Perspectives 9:74-76, 1977; **p. 241,** Joel Gordon Photography; **p. 243,** Medical and Scientific Illustration, Crozet, Virginia; **p. 244,** from Raven, P.H., and Johnson, G.B.: Biology, St. Louis, 1986, Times Mirror/Mosby College Publishing; **p. 247,** Joel Gordon Photography; **p. 251,** Centers for Disease Control.

CHAPTER 9

p. 256, Kimberly Hatcher; **p. 258,** box courtesy of Ruth Westheimer; **pp. 261, 262,** Lisa Cheuk; **p. 263,** Joel Gordon Photography; **p. 266,** Joel Gordon Photography; **p. 267,** Frank Siteman/Stock Boston; **pp. 272, 273, 274, 275, 276,** Lisa Cheuk; **p. 278,** Image Bank.

CHAPTER 10

p. 282, Cathy Lander-Goldberg/Lander Photographics; **p. 283,** "General Review of the Sex Situation" from The Portable Dorothy Parker. Copyright 1926, renewed © 1954 by Dorothy Parker. Reprinted by permission of Viking Penguin, Inc.; **p. 284,** Kimberly Hatcher; **p. 285,** Copyright © 1990. Reprinted by permission of Wisconsin State Journal; **p. 285,** Sygma; **p. 286,** Image Bank; **p. 287,** "Hi & Lois," © 1980 King Features Syndicate; **p. 290,** Wide World Photos; **p. 292,** Joel Gordon Photography; **p. 296 (left)** from Grabb, W.C., and Smith, J.W., editors: Plastic surgery, ed. 3, Boston, 1979, Little, Brown & Co.; **(right)** from Noe, J.M., Birdsell, D., and Laub, D.R.: The surgical construction of the male genitalia for the female-to-male transsexual, Plastic Reconstructive Surgery 53:511-516, 1979; **p.**

297, Superstock/Four-by-Five; **p. 298,** Copyright © 1970 by Sam Levenson and Whitney Darrow; **p. 301,** Karen Fenton; **p. 303,** from Hite, Shere: The Hite report, New York, 1976, Macmillan Publishing Company. Copyright © 1976. Reprinted by permission of Macmillan Publishing Company; **p. 304,** from Hite, Shere: The Hite report, New York, 1976, Macmillan Publishing Company. Copyright © 1976. Reprinted by permission of Macmillan Publishing Company.

CHAPTER 11

p. 314, Joel Gordon Photography; **p. 315,** "We Two Boys Together Clinging" from the book Leaves of Grass by Walt Whitman. Published by Doubleday & Co.; **p. 316,** from Kinsey, A.C., et al.: Sexual behavior in the human female, Philadelphia, 1953, W.B. Saunders Co. Reprinted with permission of the Kinsey Institute for Research in Sex, Gender, and Reproduction, Inc.; **pp. 318, 321,** from Silverstein, C.: Man to man: gay couples in America, New York, 1981, William Morrow & Co. Copyright © 1981 by Charles Silverstein. By permission of William Morrow & Co.; **pp. 320, 322, 324, 326, 329,** Joel Gordon Photography; **p. 328,** from Mendola, M.: The Mendola report: a new look at gay couples, New York, 1980, Crown Publishers, Inc. Copyright © 1980 by Mary Mendola. Used by permission of Crown Publishers, Inc.; **p. 333,** Rob Nelson/Picture Group; **p. 334,** Owen Frankel/Stock Boston; **p. 335,** John P. Kelly; **p. 336,** from Mendola, M.: The Mendola report: a new look at gay couples, New York, 1980, Crown Publishers, Inc. Copyright © 1980 by Mary Mendola. Used by permission of Crown Publishers, Inc.; **p. 337,** excerpt from Hite, S: The Hite report on male sexuality, New York, 1981, Alfred A. Knopf, Inc. Copyright © 1981; **pp. 338, 342,** Joel Gordon Photography.

CHAPTER 12

p. 348, Cathy Lander-Goldberg/Lander Photographics; **p. 349,** excerpt from Calderone, M., and Ramey, J.W.: Talking with your child about sex, New York, 1982, Random House, Inc. Copyright © 1982; **pp. 351, 356,** Jeffrey Reed/Stock Shop; **pp. 354, 355,** from Morrison, E.S., et al.: Growing up sexual, New York, 1980, Van Nostrand Reinhold Co., Inc. Copyright © 1980. Reprinted by permission of Wadsworth, Inc.; **p. 357,** Superstock/Four-by-Five; **p. 358,** excerpts from Beyene, Y.:

From menarche to menopause: reproductive lives of peasant women in two cultures, New York, 1989, State University of New York Press. Copyright © 1989. Reprinted by permission of State University of New York Press; **pp. 359, 361,** Lisa Cheuk; **pp. 364-365,** excerpts from Hunt, M.: Sexual behavior in the seventies, Chicago, 1974, Playboy Press. Copyright © 1974. Reprinted by permission of Playboy Press; **p. 365,** Superstock; **pp. 366, 367,** from Murstein, B.L., et al.: Sexual behavior, drugs, and relationship patterns on a college campus thirteen years, Adolescence 24(93):125-139, 1989; **p. 369,** from Roche, J.P.:Premarital sex: attitudes and behavior by dating stage, Adolescence 21(81):108-121, 1986; **p. 370,** modified from Westloff, C.F., Calot, G., and Foster, A.D.: Table 1. Selected measures of teenage and overall fertility in 1971 and in 1979 or 1980, 1983, Family Planning and Perspectives 15(3). Copyright © 1983. Reprinted by permission of Family Planning Perspectives; **p. 371,** from The story of a teenage pregnancy, Lawrence (Kan.) Journal-World, November 29, 1981; **p. 373,** Joel Gordon Photography; **p. 375,** Cathy Lander-Goldberg/Lander Photographics.

CHAPTER 13

p. 380, Joel Gordon Photography; **p. 382,** Susan Lapides/Design Conceptions; **p. 383,** Doonesbury copyright © 1976 G.B. Trudeau. Reprinted with permission of Universal Press Syndicate. All rights reserved; **p. 387,** from Beyene, Y.: From menarche to menopause: reproductive lives of peasant women in two cultures, New York, 1989, State University of New York Press. Copyright © 1989. Reprinted by permission of State University of New York Press; **p. 388,** Image Bank; **p. 392,** from Brecher, E.M.: Love, sex and aging. Copyright © 1984 by Consumers Union of the United States, Inc. By permission of Little, Brown and Company; **p. 393,** from Wax, J.: Sex and the single grandparent, New Times, September, 1975; **p. 394,** Joel Gordon Photography; **p. 394,** excerpt from Rienzo, B.A.: The impact of aging on human sexuality, Journal of School Health, 1985. American School Health Association, Kent, OH 44240; **p. 395,** from Sontag, S.: The double standard of aging, Saturday Review, September, 1972; **p. 396,** Susan Lapides/Design Conceptions; **p. 397,** Superstock/Four-by-Five; **p. 398,** Herb Snitzer/Stock Shop.

CHAPTER 14

pp. 402, 404, Joel Gordon Photography; **p. 403,** from Viorst, Judith: True love, Cleveland, 1968, The New American Library, Inc., Copyright © 1968. Reprinted by permission of The New American Library, Inc.; **p. 406,** "Cathy", copyright © Cathy Guisewite. Reprinted with permission of Universal Press Syndicate; **p. 407,** Peanuts, © 1975 United Features Syndicate, Inc.; **p. 411,** from Garrity, Joan: Total loving, New York, 1977, Simon & Schuster. Copyright © 1977. Reprinted by permission of Simon & Schuster; **p. 415,** Miss Peach by Mell Lazarus, Courtesy of Mell Lazarus and New America Syndicate; **p. 417,** excerpts from Sternberg, R.J., and Barnes, M.L., eds.: The psychology of love, 1988, Yale University Press. Copyright © 1988. Reprinted by permission of Yale University Press; **p. 420,** Copyright © 1974 Ziggy and Friends, Inc./Distributed by Universal Press Syndicate; **p. 421,** Photo Edit; **p. 422,** Stockphotos; **p. 425,** "Cathy" copyright © 1981 Cathy Guisewite. Reprinted by permission of Universal Press Syndicate; **p. 426,** Joel Gordon Photography.

CHAPTER 15

p. 430, Cathy Lander-Goldberg/Lander Photographics; **p. 431,** from Viorst, Judith: Sex is not so sexy anymore, Cleveland, 1968, The New American Library, Inc., Copyright © 1968. Reprinted by permission of The New American Library, Inc.; **p. 432,** Superstock; **p. 433,** Drawing by Saxon, © 1970, The New Yorker Magazine, Inc.; **pp. 435, 437,** Joel Gordon Photography; **pp. 436, 439,** from Zola, M.: All the good ones are married, New York, 1982, Berkeley Publishing Group; **p. 438,** Superstock; **p. 442,** Superstock; **p. 443,** Dagmar Fabricius/Visions; **p. 444,** Wedlock may hold key to longer life, by Natalie Angier. Copyright © 1990, New York Times; **p. 446,** Ellis Herwig/Stock Boston; **p. 448,** Drawing by Stan Hunt, © 1980, The New Yorker Magazine, Inc.; **p. 451,** Divorce data stir doubt on trial marriage. Copyright © 1989, New York Times; **p. 452,** Joel Gordon Photography; **p. 457,** Woman's hospital visit marks gay rights fight, by Nadine Brozan. Copyright © 1989, New York Times.

CHAPTER 16

p. 460, Joel Gordon Photography; **p. 461,** excerpt from Glass, D.D.: Sexuality and the spinal cord injured patient. In Oaks,

W.W., Melchiode, G.A., and Ficher, R., editors: Sex and the life cycle, New York, 1977, Grune & Stratton, Inc. Reprinted by permission; **p. 462,** modified from Haring, M., and Meyerson, L.: Attitudes of college students toward sexual behavior of disabled persons, Archives of Physical Medicine and Rehabilitation 60:257-260, 1979; **p. 463,** Lisa Cheuk; **p. 464,** Cathy Lander-Goldberg/Lander Photographics; **p. 466,** Jeroboam; **p. 467,** Kathryn Dudek/Photo News Photography; **p. 469,** Magnum Photos; **p. 473,** The Bettmann Archive; **p. 477,** Ellis Herwig/Picture Cube; **p. 478,** Joel Gordon Photography.

CHAPTER 17

p. 482, Cathy Lander-Goldberg/Lander Photographics; **p. 489,** Medical and Scientific Illustration, Crozet, Virginia; **p. 492,** Picture Cube; **p. 498,** Lisa Cheuk; **pp. 508-509,** photos by Joel Gordon Photography, drawings by Lisa Cheuk; **p. 510,** West Stock.

CHAPTER 18

p. 514, Cathy Lander-Goldberg/Lander Photographics; **p. 521 (top),** from Habif, T.P.: Clinical dermatology, St. Louis, 1985, The C.V. Mosby Co.; **p. 522,** Photo Researchers; **p. 523,** Centers for Disease Control; **p. 525,** The Bettmann Archive; **p. 526,** Reproduced with permission of Burroughs Wellcome Co.; **p. 528,** Centers for Disease Control; **p. 531,** Reproduced with permission of Burroughs Wellcome Co.; **p. 534,** Cathy Lander-Goldberg/Lander Photographics; **p. 536,** Centers for Disease Control; **p. 537,** Image Bank; **p. 539,** © 1987, Washington Writers Post Writers Group, Reprinted with permission.

CHAPTER 19

pp. 544, 547, Joel Gordon Photography; **p. 548,** Medical and Scientific Illustration, Crozet, Virginia; **pp. 550, 551, 556, 563, 566,** Joel Gordon Photography; **p. 559,** Doonesbury Copyright © 1987, G.B. Trudeau. Reprinted by permission of Universal Press Syndicate. All rights reserved; **p. 561,** Anita Bartsch/Design Conceptions; **p. 567,** Cartoon by Don Addis, courtesy of the St. Petersburg Times.

CHAPTER 20

p. 570, Cathy Lander-Goldberg/Lander Photographics; **p. 573,** Joel Gordon Photography; **p. 577,** Photo Researchers; **p. 580,** Joel Gordon Photography; **p. 581,** Karen Fenton; **p. 582,** from Erotic power:

an exploration of dominance and submission, by Gini Graham Scott. Copyright © 1983 by Gini Graham Scott. Published by arrangement with Carol Publishing Group; **p. 583,** Joel Gordon Photography.

CHAPTER 21

p. 592, Joel Gordon Photography; **p. 594,** The Bettmann Archive; **p. 597,** Cathy Lander-Goldberg/Lander Photographics; **p. 604,** John Sunderland/Photostaff; **p. 609,** H. Armstrong Roberts, box modified from Boston Women's Health Book Collective: Our bodies, ourselves, New York, 1984, Simon & Schuster, Inc.

CHAPTER 22

p. 626, Cathy Lander-Goldberg/Lander Photographics; **p. 627,** excerpt from Richards, D.A.J.: Sex, drugs, death, and the law: an essay on human rights and overcriminalization, Totowa, N.J., 1982, Rowan & Littlefield, Publishers, p. 51; **p. 632,** Superstock; **p. 634,** Copyright © 1990. Reprinted by permission of Wisconsin State Journal; **p. 641,** from Steinem, G.: Erotica and pornography; a clear and present difference, Ms. 11:53-55, 1978; **p. 642,** Joel Gordon Photography; **pp. 648-649,** from the book Sexual harassment on the job, by Constance Backhouse and Leah Cohen. Copyright © 1981. Used by permission of the publisher, Prentice-Hall, Inc., Englewood Cliffs, N.J.; **p. 650,** 2 in 3 military

women report harassment, by Eric Schmitt. Copyright © 1990, New York Times; **p. 652,** Copyright © 1991 The Time Inc. Magazine Company. Reprinted by permission; **p. 653,** from Field, A.: Harassment on campus: sex in a tenured position, Ms. 9:73, 1981; **p. 654,** from Hughes, Jean O., and Sandler, Bernice R.: In case of sexual harassment: a guide for women students. Project on the Status and Education of Women, Association of American Colleges, 1986. Copies are available for $2.00, prepaid, from AAC/PSEW, 1818 R Street, N.W., Washington, DC 20009.

CHAPTER 23

p. 658, Elizabeth Crews/Stock Boston; **pp. 660, 661, 662,** excerpts from Hunt, Morton: Sexual behavior in the seventies, Chicago, 1974, Playboy Press. Copyright © 1974. Reprinted by permission of Playboy Press; **p. 661,** permission granted by Ann Landers and Creators Syndicate; **p. 663,** from Morrison, E.S., et al.: Growing up sexual, New York, 1980, Van Nostrand Reinhold Co., Inc., Copyright © 1980. Reprinted by permission of Wadsworth, Inc.; **p. 664,** Photophile; **p. 666,** Michael Carpenter Photography; **p. 667,** from When sex education fails, Lawrence (Kan.) Journal-World, November 20, 1981; **p. 668,** John Sunderland/Photostaff; **p. 669,** From Penland, L.R.: Sex education in 1900,

1940 and 1980: an historical sketch, J. Sch. Health 51(4):305-309, 1981; **p. 674,** D. Menuez/Picture Group; **p. 675,** David Walberg.

CHAPTER 24

p. 680, Cathy Lander-Goldberg/Lander Photographics; **p. 681,** excerpt from Love and responsibility from Karol Wojtyla (Pope John Paul II). Copyright © 1981 by Farrar, Straus, & Giroux, Inc., New York. Reprinted by permission of Farrar, Straus, & Giroux, Inc.; **p. 682,** Joel Gordon Photography; **p. 687,** A. Stevenson/Picture Group; **p. 688,** Joel Gordon Photography; **pp. 690, 692,** Copyright © 1990 The Time Inc. Magazine Company. Reprinted by permission; **p. 693,** Susan Lapides/Design Conceptions; **p. 695,** from Knocking on the bedroom door, Time, July 14, 1986. Copyright © 1986, Time Warner, Inc., All rights reserved. Reprinted by permission from Time; **p. 696,** Janice Rubin; **pp. 698, 700,** Copyright © 1990. Reprinted by permission of Wisconsin State Journal; **p. 700,** cartoon by Mike Keefe, The Denver Post; **p. 701,** Permission granted by Ann Landers and Creators Syndicate; **p. 702,** from Holden, C: Two fertilized eggs stir global furor, Science 225:35, 1984, Copyright © 1984 by the AAAS; **p. 701,** Jim Olive; **p. 704,** Copyright © 1990. Reprinted by permission of Wisconsin State Journal.

National Center for Missing and Exploited Children
1835 K Street, N.W., Suite 600
Washington, D.C. 20006
(800) 843-5678
(202) 634-9821

National Center for the Prevention and Control of Rape
500 Fishers Lane
Room 6C-12
Rockville, MD 20857

National Center of Child Abuse and Neglect
U.S. Department of Health and Human Services
P.O. Box 1182
Washington, D.C. 20013

National Clearinghouse for Family Planning Information
P.O. Box 10716
Rockville, MD 20850
(301) 558-4990

National Clearinghouse on Marital and Date Rape
2325 Oak Street
Berkeley, CA 94708
(415) 548-1770

National Coalition Against Sexual Assault
430 Metro Building
Minneapolis, MN 55105

National Committee on the Prevention of Child Abuse
332 S. Michigan Avenue
Chicago, IL 60604

National Family Planning and Reproductive Health Association
122 C Street N.W., Suite 380
Washington, D.C. 20001-2109
(202) 628-3535

National Gay and Lesbian Crisisline
(800) 221-7044
(212) 529-1604 (New York)

National Gay Task Force
80 Fifth Avenue
New York, NY 10011
(212) 741-5800

North American Council on Adoptable Children
2001 S Street, N.W., Suite 540
Washington, D.C. 20009

National Pregnancy Hotline
(800) 852-5683
(800) 493-6425 (Oklahoma)

National Runaway Switchboard
(800) 621-4000
(312) 880-9860

Parents Anonymous
(for abusive parents)
(800) 421-0353
(800) 352-0386 (California)
(213) 410-9732

Parents of Prematures
c/o Houston Organization for Parent Education, Inc.
2990 Richmond, Suite 240
Houston, TX 77098
(713) 524-3089

Parents Without Partners, Inc.
International Headquarters
8807 Colesville Road
Silver Spring, MD 20910
(301) 588-9354

Planned Parenthood Federation of America
810 7th Avenue
New York, NY 10019
(800) 829-7732
(212) 541-7800

Pregnancy Crisis Center
(800) 368-3336
(804) 847-6828 (Virginia)

Prevent Child Abuse
P.O. Box 2866
Chicago, IL 60690

Runaway Hotline
(800) 231-6946
(800) 392-3352 (Texas)

Sexaholics Anonymous
P.O. Box 300
Simi Valley, CA 93060